The Complete

BIBLICAL

LIBRARY

The Complete

BIBLICAL
LIBRARY

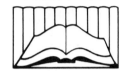

THE NEW TESTAMENT
STUDY BIBLE

ROMANS–
CORINTHIANS

The Complete
BIBLICAL
LIBRARY

The Complete Biblical Library, part 1, a 16-volume study series on the New Testament. Volume 7: STUDY BIBLE, ROMANS—CORINTHIANS. World copyright ©1986, 1991 by Thoralf Gilbrant and Tor Inge Gilbrant. © Published 1989, 1991 by THE COMPLETE BIBLICAL LIBRARY, Springfield, Missouri 65802, U.S.A.

Printed in the United States of America 1991 by R.R. Donnelley and Sons Company, Chicago, Illinois 60606. Library of Congress Catalog Card Number 88-63956 International Standard Book Number 0-88243-367-9.

THE NEW TESTAMENT
Study Bible, Greek-English Dictionary, Harmony of the Gospels

THE OLD TESTAMENT
Study Bible, Hebrew-English Dictionary

THE BIBLE ENCYCLOPEDIA

INTERNATIONAL EDITOR
THORALF GILBRANT

Executive Editor: Ralph W. Harris, M.A.
Computer Systems: Tor Inge Gilbrant

NATIONAL EDITORS

U.S.A.
Stanley M. Horton, Th.D.

NORWAY
Erling Utnem, Bishop
Arthur Berg, B.D.

DENMARK
Jorgen Glenthoj, Th.M.

SWEDEN
Hugo Odeberg, Ph.D., D.D.
Bertil E. Gartner, D.D.
Thorsten Kjall, M.A.
Stig Wikstrom, D.Th.M.

FINLAND
Aapelii Saarisalo, Ph.D.
Valter Luoto, Pastor
Matti Liljequist, B.D.

HOLLAND
Herman ter Welle, Pastor
Henk Courtz, Drs.

Project Coordinator: William G. Eastlake

INTERNATIONAL AND
INTERDENOMINATIONAL
BIBLE STUDY SYSTEM

THE NEW TESTAMENT STUDY BIBLE ROMANS–CORINTHIANS

Executive Editor: Ralph W. Harris, M.A.

Editor: Stanley M. Horton, Th.D.

Managing Editor: Gayle Garrity Seaver, J.D.

WORLD LIBRARY PRESS, INC.
Springfield, Missouri, U.S.A.

Table of Contents

VERSE-BY-VERSE COMMENTARY
G. RAYMOND CARLSON, D.D. **Romans**
PAUL A. HAMAR, D.Min. **1 Corinthians**
RUSSELL WISEHART, M.Div. **2 Corinthians 1:1–3:14**
CHARLES HARRIS, Ed.D. **2 Corinthians 3:15–13:14**

VARIOUS VERSIONS
GERARD J. FLOKSTRA, JR., D.Min.

BOARD OF REVIEW

Zenas Bicket, Ph.D.   Charles Harris, Ed.D.
Jesse Moon, D.Min.   Opal Reddin, D.Min.

STAFF

Production Coordinator: Cynthia Riemenschneider

Research Editor: Denis Vinyard, M.Div.

Senior Editors: Gary Leggett, M.A.; Dorothy B. Morris

Editorial Team: Patrick Alexander, M.A.; Lloyd Anderson; Ken Barney; Betty Bates; Faye Faucett; Charlotte Gribben; Wesley Smith, M.Div.

Art Director: Terry Van Someren, B.F.A.

Word Processing and Secretarial: Sonja Jensen; Don Williams, B.A.; Rachel Wisehart

Introduction

This volume of the *Study Bible* is part of a 16-volume set titled *The Complete Biblical Library*. It is an ambitious plan to provide all the information one needs for a basic understanding of the New Testament—useful for scholars but also for students and lay people.

In addition to the Harmony, *The Complete Biblical Library* provides a 9-volume *Study Bible* and a 6-volume *Greek-English Dictionary*. They are closely linked. You will find information about the *Study Bible*'s features later in the Introduction. The *Greek-English Dictionary* lists all the Greek words of the New Testament in their alphabetic order, provides a concordance showing each place the words appear in the New Testament, and includes an article explaining the background, significance, and meaning of the words.

FEATURES OF THE STUDY BIBLE

The *Study Bible* is a unique combination of study materials which will help both the scholar and the layman achieve a better understanding of the New Testament and the language in which it was written. All of these helps are available in various forms but bringing them together in combination will save many hours of research. Most scholars do not have in their personal libraries all the volumes necessary to provide the information so readily available here.

The editors of *The Complete Biblical Library* are attempting an unusual task: to help scholars in their research but also to make available to laymen the tools by which to acquire knowledge which up to this time has been available only to scholars.

Following are the major divisions of the *Study Bible*:

Overview

Each volume contains an encyclopedic survey of the New Testament book. It provides a general outline, discusses matters about which there may be a difference of opinion, and provides background information regarding the history, culture, literature, and philosophy of the era covered by the book.

Interlinear

Following the overall principle of providing help for both the scholar and the layman, we supply a unique *Interlinear*. Most interlinears, if not all, give merely the Greek text and the meanings of the words. Our *Interlinear* contains *five* parts:

1. *Greek Text.* Our Greek text is a comparative text which includes both the traditional text type and the text which is common in modern textual editions.

2. *Grammatical Forms.* These are shown above each Greek word, alongside its assigned number. This information is repeated, along with the Greek word, in the *Greek-English Dictionary* where more details may be found.

3. *Transliteration.* No other interlinears provide this. Its purpose is to familiarize laymen with the proper pronunciation of Greek words so they will feel comfortable when using them in teaching situations. Complete information on pronunciation is found on the page showing the Greek and Hebrew alphabets.

4. *Translation.* The basic meaning of each Greek word is found beneath it. Rather than merely accepting the work of past interlinears, we have assigned scholars to upgrade words to a more modern description. See a later section for the principles we have followed in translation of the Greek words in our *Interlinear*.

5. *Assigned Numbers.* The unique numbering system of *The Complete Biblical Library* makes cross-reference study between the *Study Bible* and the *Greek-English Dictionary* the ultimate in simplicity. Each Greek word has been assigned a number. *Alpha* is the first word in alphabetic order as well as the first letter of the Greek alphabet, so the number *1* has been assigned to it. The rest of the almost 5,000 words follow in numerical and alphabetic sequence.

The *Greek-English Dictionary* follows the same plan with each word listed in alphabetic sequence. If a student desires further study on a certain word, he can find its number above it and locate it in the dictionary. In moments he has access to all the valuable information he needs for a basic understanding of that word.

Textual Apparatus

As said above, our Greek text is a comparative text. A text based only upon the *Textus Receptus* is not adequate for today's needs. Also, an eclectic text—using the "best" from various text types—will not be satisfactory, because such an approach may be quite subjective, with decisions influenced by the personal viewpoint of the scholar. Our text is a combination of both the main types of the Greek New Testament text. We have the *Textus Receptus*, a Stephanus text, based on the Byzantine text type. When there are important variants which differ from the *Textus Receptus*, they are included within brackets in the text. In the narrow column to the left of the *Interlinear*, the sources of the variants are listed. This will provide a fascinating study for a scholar and student, and will save him innumerable hours of research.

Verse-by-Verse Commentary

Many Bible-loving scholars have combined their knowledge, study, and skills to provide this. It is not an exhaustive treatment (many other commentaries are available for that), but again it provides a basic understanding of every verse in the New Testament. It does not usually deal with textual criticism (that can be dealt with in another arena), but it opens up the nuances of the Greek New Testament as written by the inspired writers.

Various Versions

This offers a greatly amplified New Testament. Each verse is broken down into its phrases; the King James Version is shown in boldface type; then from more than 60 other versions we show various ways the Greek of that phrase may be translated. The Greek of the First Century was such a rich language that to obtain the full meaning of words, several synonyms may be needed.

TRANSLATION OF GREEK WORDS

No word-for-word translation can be fully "literal" in the sense of expressing all the nuances of the original language. Rather, our purpose is to help the student find the English word which most correctly expresses the original Greek word in that particular context. The Greek language is so rich in meaning that the same word may have a slightly different meaning in another context.

In any language idioms offer a special translation problem. According to the dictionary, this is an expression which has "a meaning which cannot be derived from the conjoined meanings of its elements." The Greek language abounds in such phrases which cannot be translated literally.

We have come to what we consider a splendid solution to the problem, whether the translation should be strictly literal or abound in a plethora of idiomatic expressions. From more than 60 translations, the *Various Versions* column presents the various ways phrases have been translated. Here the student will find the translations of the idioms. This enables us to make our English line in the *Interlinear* strictly literal. The student will have available both types of translation—and will have a fresh appreciation for the struggles through which translators go.

HOW THE NEW TESTAMENT CAME TO US

Volume 1 of *The Complete Biblical Library*, the *Harmony of the Gospels*, contains information on how the four Gospels came into being. The preponderance of proof points to the fact that the rest of the New Testament was written before A.D. 100. Like the Gospels, it was written in Greek, the universal language of that era. It was qualified in a special way for this purpose. Probably no other language is so expressive and able to provide such fine nuances of meaning.

Yet the New Testament Greek is not the perfectly structured form of the language from the old classical period. It is the more simple Koine Greek from the later Hellenistic age. This had become the lingua franca of the Hellenistic and Roman world. The Egyptian papyri have shown that the language which the New Testament writers used was the common language of the people. It seems as though God accommodated himself to a form of communication which would make His Word most readily accepted and easily understood.

At the same time we should recognize that the language of the Greek New Testament also is a *religious language*, with a tradition going back a couple of centuries to the Septuagint, the Greek translation of the Old Testament.

The Manuscripts

None of the original manuscripts (handwritten documents) still exist. Even in the First Century they must have often been copied so as to share their treasured truths with numerous congregations of believers. The original documents then soon became worn out through use. Evidently, only copies of the New Testament still exist.

Over 5,000 manuscripts of the New Testament have been discovered up to the present time. Most of them are small fragments of verses or chapters, a few books of the New Testament, some copies of the Gospels. Very few contain all or nearly all of the New Testament.

The manuscripts have come to us in various forms: (1) Egyptian papyri, (2) majuscules, (3) minuscules, (4) writings of the Early Church fathers, (5) lectionaries, and (6) early versions.

The Egyptian Papyri

These are the oldest copies of parts of the Greek New Testament. The earliest are dated about A.D. 200, a few even earlier, and the youngest are from the Seventh Century. Most of them date back to the Third, Fourth and Fifth Centuries of the Christian Era.

They were found in the late 1800s in Egypt. The dry climatic conditions of that country enabled them to be preserved. The largest fragments contain only a few dozen pages, while the smallest are the size of a postage stamp.

The papyri are listed in the back of this volume under the heading "Manuscripts."

The Majuscules

These are the second oldest kind of copies of New Testament manuscripts. They received this description because they were written in majuscules; that is, large letters (the uncials are a form of majuscules). Three major majuscules are the following:

1. Codex Aleph, also called Codex Sinaiticus, because it was discovered in the mid-1840s by the great scholar Tischendorf at St. Catharine's Monastery, located at the foot of Mount Sinai. Numbered 01, it contains all the New Testament and is dated in the Fourth Century.

2. Codex A, numbered 02, is named Alexandrinus, because it came from Alexandria in Egypt. In the Gospels, this manuscript is the foremost witness to the Byzantine text type.

3. Codex B, 03, is called Codex Vaticanus, because it is in the Vatican library. Along with the Sinaiticus, it is the main witness for the Egyptian text type. However, it is important to realize there are more than 3,000 differences between these 2 manuscripts in the Gospels alone (Hoskier).

See the list of majuscules in the back of this volume, under "Manuscripts."

The Minuscules

This is a kind of manuscript written in small letters. They are only a few hundred years old, beginning with the Ninth Century. Most come from the 12th to the 14th Century A.D. They form, by far, the greatest group of the New Testament manuscripts, numbering almost 2,800.

The minuscules represent the unbroken text tradition in the Greek Orthodox Church, and about 90 percent of them belong to the Byzantine text group. They are numbered 1, 2, 3, etc.

Lectionaries and Church Fathers

Lectionaries include manuscripts which were not Scripture themselves but contain Scripture quotations, used for the scheduled worship services of the annual church calendar. These are numbered consecutively and are identified by *lect.*

Practically all the New Testament could be retrieved from the writings of early Christian leaders, called church fathers. These lists are located in the back of this volume.

Early Versions

Translations of the New Testament from Greek are also of value. They are listed under "Manuscripts" in the back of this volume. The best known is the Latin Vulgate by Jerome.

Major Greek Texts

From the manuscripts which have just been described, various types of Greek texts have been formed:

The Western text can possibly be traced back to the Second Century. It was used mostly in Western Europe and North Africa. It tends to add to the text and makes long paraphrases of it. Today some scholars do not recognize it as a special text type.

The Caesarean text may have originated in Egypt and was brought, it is believed, to the city of Caesarea in Palestine. Later, it was carried to Jerusalem, then by Armenian missionaries into a province in the kingdom of Georgia, now a republic of the U.S.S.R. Some scholars consider it a mixture of other text types.

The two most prominent text types, however, are the Egyptian (also called the Alexandrian) and the Byzantine. These are the major ones considered in our *Interlinear* and *Textual Apparatus*. Except for the papyrus texts which are highly varied, these are the only text families which have any degree of support. References to numerous text groups which were so common a few decades ago must now probably be considered out of date. At any rate, out of practical considerations, we have kept the Byzantine and Egyptian (Alexandrian) as fixed text groups in our *Textual Apparatus*. Following is historical information about them.

The Byzantine Text

Many titles have been applied to this text type. It has been called the *K* (Koine), Syrian, Antiochian, and Traditional. It is generally believed to have been produced at Antioch in Syria, then taken to Byzantium, later known as Constantinople. For about 1,000 years, while the Byzantine Empire ruled the Middle East, this was the text used by the Greek Orthodox Church. It also influenced Europe.

Because of this background it became the basis for the first printed text editions, among others the famous *Textus Receptus*, called "the acknowledged text."

The Byzantine text form is also called the Majority text, since 80 to 90 percent of all existing manuscripts are represented in this text, though most of them are quite recent and evidently copies of earlier manuscripts. Like the Egyptian text, the Byzantine text can be traced back to the Fourth Century. It also contains some readings which seem to be the same as some papyri which can be traced back to a much earlier time. Among the oldest majuscules the Byzantine is, among others, represented by Codex Alexandrinus (02, A), 07, 08, 09, 010, 011, 012, 013, 015, and others.

The Egyptian Text

This text type originated in Egypt and is the one which gained the highest recognition and acceptance there in the Fourth Century. It was produced mainly by copyists in Alexandria, from which it received the name *Alexandrian*. This text form is represented mostly by two codices: Sinaiticus (01, Aleph) and Vaticanus (03, B) from the Fourth Century, also from Codex Ephraemi (04, C) from the Fifth Century. The use of this text type ceased about the year 450 but lived on in the Latin translation, the Vulgate version.

Printed Greek Texts

The invention of printing about 1450 opened the door for wider distribution of the Scriptures. In 1516 Erasmus, a Dutch scholar, produced the first *printed* Greek New Testament. It was based on the Byzantine text type, with most of the New Testament coming from manuscripts dated at about the 12th Century. He did his work very hurriedly, finishing his task in just a few months. His second edition, produced in 1519 with some of the mistakes corrected, became the basis for translations into German by Luther and into English by Tyndale.

A printed Greek New Testament was produced by a French printer, Stephanus, in 1550. His edition and those produced by Theodore Beza, of Geneva, between 1565 and 1604, based on the Byzantine text, have been entitled the *Textus Receptus*. That description, however, originated with the text produced by Elzevir. He described his second edition of 1633 by the Latin phrase *Textus Receptus*, or the "Received Text"; that is, the one accepted generally as the correct one.

A list of the printed editions of the Greek text is found in the section describing the relationship of the *Interlinear* and the *Textual Apparatus*.

Contribution of Westcott and Hort

Two British scholars, Westcott and Hort, have played a prominent role in deciding which text type should be used. They (especially Hort) called the Byzantine text "corrupt," because of the young age of its supporting manuscripts and proceeded to develop their own text (1881-86). It was really a restoration of the Egyptian text from the Fourth Century. It depended mainly on two codices, Sinaiticus and Vaticanus, but was also supported by numerous majuscules such as 02, 04, 019, 020, 025, 032, 033, 037, and 044.

Westcott and Hort opposed the *Textus Receptus* because it was based on the Byzantine text form. Most scholars agreed with their contention, and the *Textus Receptus* fell into disrepute. However, Westcott and Hort made their assumptions before the Greek papyri were discovered, and in recent years some scholars have come to the defense of the Byzantine text and the *Textus Receptus*. They have learned that some of the readings in the Byzantine text are the same as those found in the earliest papyri, dated about A.D. 200 and even earlier (p45, p46, p64 and p66, for example). This seems to take the Byzantine text back at least as far as the Egyptian.

Two important statements must be made: (1) We should always remember there are good men and scholars on both sides of the controversy, and their major concern is to obtain as pure a text as possible, to reassure Bible students that the New Testament we now possess conforms to that written in the First Century. (2) Since it was the original writings which were inspired by the Holy Spirit, it is important for us to ascertain as closely as possible how well our present-day text agrees with the original writings. It should alleviate the fears some may have as to whether we have the true gospel enunciated in the First Century to know that most of the differences in the Greek text (about 1 percent of the total) are minor in nature and do not affect the great Christian doctrines we hold dear. Significant differences may be found in only a very few cases.

We have consciously avoided polemics in the area of textual criticism. There is legitimacy for such discussion, but *The Complete Biblical Library* is not the arena for such a conflict. (1) Often the opposing views are conjectural. (2) There is insufficient space to treat subjects adequately and to raise questions without answering them fully leads to confusion.

LITERARY AND BIBLICAL STANDARDS

Several hundred people, highly qualified scholars and specialists in particular fields have participated in producing *The Complete Biblical Library*. Great care has been taken to maintain high standards of scholarship and ethics. By involving scholars in Boards of Review for the *Study Bible* and the *Greek-English Dictionary*, we added an extra step to the editorial process. We have been particularly concerned about giving proper credit for citations from other works and have instructed our writers to show care in this regard. Any deviation from this principle has been inadvertent and not intentional.

Obviously, with writers coming from widely differing backgrounds, there are differences of opinion as to how to interpret certain passages.

We have tried to be just. When there are strong differences on the meaning of a particular passage, we have felt it best to present the contrasting viewpoints.

STUDY HELPS

As you come to the Scripture section of this volume, you will find correlated pages for your study. The facing pages are designed to complement each other, so you will have a better understanding of the Word of God than ever before. Each two-page spread will deal with a group of verses.

On the left-hand page is the *Interlinear* with its fivefold helps: (1) the Greek text in which the New Testament was written; (2) the transliteration, showing how to pronounce each word; (3) the basic meaning of each word; (4) next to Greek words an assigned number (you will need this number to learn more about the word in the *Greek-English Dictionary*, companion to the *Study Bible*); and (5) the grammatical forms of each Greek word. The left-hand page also contains a column called the *Textual Apparatus*. This column is explained later.

The right-hand page contains two features. The *Verse-by-Verse Commentary* refers to each verse, except when occasionally it deals with some closely related verses. The *Various Versions* column provides an expanded understanding of the various ways Greek words or phrases can be translated. The phrase from the King James Version appears first in boldface print, then other meaningful ways the Greek language has been translated. This feature will bring to you the riches of the language in which the New Testament first appeared.

General Abbreviations

In a work of this nature it is necessary to use some abbreviations in order to conserve space. In deference to the Scriptures it is our custom not to abbreviate the titles of the books of the Bible, but abbreviations are used elsewhere. Becoming familiar with them will enable you to pursue in-depth study more effectively.

The following are general abbreviations which you will find used throughout the book:

cf.	compared to or see
ibid.	in the same place
id.	the same
idem	the same
i.e.	that is
e.g.	for example
f. ff.	and following page or pages
sic	intended as written
MS(S)	manuscript(s)
ET	editor's translation

Greek and Hebrew Alphabets

Greek

A	α	alpha	a	(f<u>a</u>ther)
B	β	beta	b	
Γ	γ	gamma	g	(g<u>o</u>t)
Δ	δ	delta	d	
E	ε	epsilon	e	(g<u>e</u>t)
Z	ζ	zeta	z	dz (lea<u>ds</u>)
H	η	eta	ē	(<u>a</u>te)
Θ	θ	theta	th	(<u>th</u>in)
I	ι	iota	i	(s<u>i</u>n or mach<u>i</u>ne)
K	κ	kappa	k	
Λ	λ	lambda	l	
M	μ	mu	m	
N	ν	nu	n	
Ξ	ξ	xi	x	
O	ο	omicron	o	(l<u>o</u>t)
Π	π	pi	p	
P	ϱ	rho	r	
Σ	σ,ς[1]	sigma	s	
T	τ	tau	t	
Y	υ	upsilon	u	German ü
Φ	φ	phi	ph	(<u>ph</u>ilosophy)
X	χ	chi	ch	(<u>ch</u>aos)
Ψ	ψ	psi	ps	(li<u>ps</u>)
Ω	ω	omega	ō	(<u>o</u>cean)

Hebrew

א	aleph	ʼ [2]	
בּ, ב	beth	b, v	
גּ, ג	gimel	g, gh	
דּ, ד	daleth	d, dh	(<u>th</u>ey)[3]
ה	he	h	
ו	waw	w	
ז	zayin	z	
ח	heth	ch	(kh)
ט	teth	t	
י	yodh	y	
כּ, כ ך	kaph	k, kh	
ל	lamedh	l	
מ ם	mem	m	
נ ן	nun	n	
ס	samekh	s̱	
ע	ayin	ʿ	
פּ, פ ף	pe	p, ph	
צ ץ	sadhe	ts	
ק	qoph	q	
ר	resh	r	
שׂ	sin	s	
שׁ	shin	sh	
תּ, ת	taw	t, th	(<u>th</u>ing)[3]

Hebrew Vowels

ā	father		u	rule		ê	they
a	dam		ō	role	âh	ah
e	men		û	tune		ă	hat
ē	they		ô	hole		ě	met
i	pin		î	machine		e	average
o	roll		ê	they		ǒ	not

Greek Pronunciation Rules

Before another *g*, or before a *k* or a *ch*, *g* is pronounced and spelled with an *n*, in the transliteration of the Greek word.

In the Greek, *s* is written at the end of a word, elsewhere it appears as σ. The rough breathing mark (ʻ) indicates that an *h*-sound is to be pronounced before the initial vowel or diphthong. The smooth breathing mark (ʼ) indicates that no such *h*-sound is to be pronounced. There are three accents, the acute (—́), the circumflex (—̑) and the grave (—̀). These stand over a vowel and indicate that stress in pronunciation is to be placed on the syllable having any one of the accents.

Pronouncing Diphthongs

ai is pronounced like *ai* in aisle
ei is pronounced like *ei* in eight
oi is pronounced like *oi* in oil
au is pronounced like *ow* in cow

eu is pronounced like *eu* in feud
ou is pronounced like *oo* in food
ui is pronounced like *ui* in suite (sweet)

1. Where two forms of a letter are given, the one at the right is used at the end of a word.
2. Not represented in transliteration when the initial letter.
3. Letters underscored represent pronunciation of the second form only.

Old and New Testament Books and Apocrypha

As a service to you, we have listed the books of the Bible in their order. The Apocrypha is a series of books which were included in the Vulgate version (the Latin translation of the Bible endorsed by the Roman Catholic Church). Though not considered part of the canon by either the Jews or Protestants, they give interesting insights, on occasion, concerning the times with which they deal. They are not on the same level as the 66 books of our canon. These lists are located in the back of the book.

Bibliographic Citations

The Complete Biblical Library has adopted a system of coordinated citations in the text and bibliography material which accommodates every type of reader. For the sake of simplicity and space, information given in the text to document a source is minimal, often including only the last name of the writer, or a shortened title and a page number.

Those who would like to research the subject more deeply can easily do so by looking in the Bibliography in the back of the book under the last name or shortened title. The Bibliography lists complete information necessary to locate the source in a library, supplemented by the page number given in the citation in the text.

RELATIONSHIP OF THE INTERLINEAR AND THE TEXTUAL APPARATUS

The Greek text of the *Study Bible* provides a means of collating the traditional texts with modern text editions; that is, comparing them critically to discover their degree of similarity or divergence. The *Textual Apparatus* column provides information as to which manuscripts or groups of manuscripts support certain readings. Some scholarly works use an eclectic text, selecting from various sources the text they consider to be the best. In our view, our comparative text provides a better system for considering the relative merits of the major texts.

The *Textual Apparatus* refers to many different manuscripts but to just two text groups, the Byzantine and the Egyptian, also known as Alexandrian. Except for the papyri texts, which are highly varied, these two text families are the only ones which have a significant degree

of support. Reference to many different text groups is now becoming passé. Using only the byz (Byzantine) and eg (Egyptian) text groups makes the work of the researcher less complicated and provides an adequate system of reference.

The *Interlinear* uses the Stephanus text as its basis but is not confined to it. Actually, most of the Greek text is the same in all the text types. For easy comparison variants are inserted in the text and are then considered in the *Textual Apparatus* column, which provides their background in the major and minor manuscripts.

Abbreviations and Signs Used in the Textual Apparatus

Using the information which follows you will be able to identify the variants and their sources and to compare them with the basic text and other variants.

Txt	The Greek text used, the TR
byz	Byzantine text form
eg	Egyptian text form
p 1, etc.	Papyrus manuscripts
01, etc.	Majuscule manuscripts
1, etc.	Minuscule manuscripts
lect	Lectionaries
org	Reading of original copier
corr 1, etc.	Change by another person
( )	Supports in principle
sa	Sahidic
bo	Bohairic

Printed Editions of the Greek Text (with abbreviations)

Steph	Stephanus, 1550
Beza	Beza, 1564-1604
Elzev	Elzevir, 1624
Gries	Griesbach, 1805
Lach	Lachmann, 1842-50
Treg	Tregelles, 1857-72
Alf	Alford, 1862-71
Tisc	Tischendorf, 1865-95
Word	Wordsworth, 1870
We/Ho	Westcott and Hort, 1881-86
Wey	Weymouth, 1885
Weis	Weiss, 1894-1900
Sod	von Soden, 1902-10
H/Far	Hodges and Farstad (Majority text)
★	various modern text editions
UBS	United Bible Society

Understanding the Codes in the Greek Text and the Textual Apparatus

Definitions:

TR. The *Textus Receptus*, the basic text of this *Interlinear*.

Reading. A word or phrase from a Greek text.

Variant. A reading which differs from the TR.

The *Textual Apparatus* contains two divisions for analyzing the text when variants occur: *Txt*, meaning the TR (*Textus Receptus*); and *Var*, meaning variants, readings which differ from the TR. Under these two headings are listed the manuscripts which support either the TR or the variant.

Illustrations:

The following examples from Luke 10:19-21 show how to understand the relationship between the Greek text and the *Textual Apparatus*.

The half-parenthesis indicates that the next word begins a TR reading for which a variant is shown. See example A.

The variant itself is enclosed in brackets (note the example of this at the beginning of verse 19). The text (TR) reads, "I give . . . , " but the variant reads, "I have given . . . ." See example B.

The small *a* at the beginning of the bracket refers back to the *Textual Apparatus* column, showing it is the first variant in that particular verse. See example C. Only those variants identified by *a, b, c,* etc., are considered in the *Textual Apparatus*.

The star following the *a* means that the variant is used in some modern text editions, such as the UBS text. See example D.

Note that in variant *b* of verse 19 the star appears before the TR word. This means that in this case UBS and/or others do not follow the variant but read the same as the TR. See example E.

In verse 20, variant *a* appears between two half-parentheses, showing *mallon* ("rather") is not included in some texts. The TR reads, "Rejoice but rather that . . . ," while the variant (without *mallon*) reads, "Rejoice but that . . . ." See example F.

It is important to recognize that the star in the *Textual Apparatus* for verse 20 means that UBS and other modern texts support the variant reading. If the UBS supported the TR, the star would have appeared under the *Txt* heading. See example G.

Sometimes there is more than one variant reading, as in variant *b* of verse 20. In such cases they are numbered in order (see the *2* before the star in the second reading). This shows the difference and also provides an easy reference in the *Textual Apparatus*. See example H.

In verse 21, variant *a* presents a case where the word *en* ("in") is not a part of the TR but appears in other texts. The + sign indicates this. See example I.

Understanding
the Codes in the
Greek Text
and the
Textual Apparatus

Example A.
⌐

Example B.
[ ]

Example C.
abc

Example D.
☆

Example E.

Example F.
( )

Example G.

Example H.
123

Example I.
+

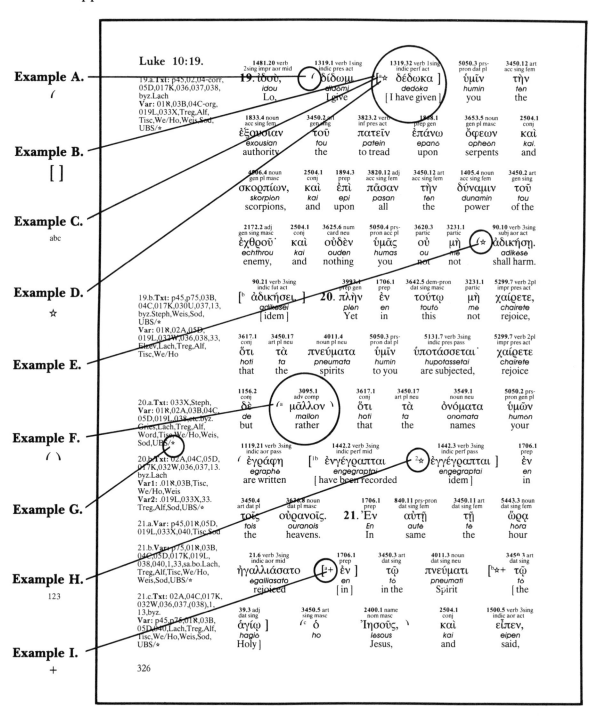

THE EPISTLE OF PAUL TO THE
ROMANS

Expanded Interlinear

Textual Critical Apparatus

Verse-by-Verse Commentary

Various Versions

3834.2 name gen masc	1976.1 noun nom sing fem	4242.1 prep	4371.6 name- adj acc pl masc
Παύλου	ἐπιστολὴ	πρὸς	Ῥωμαίους.
Paulou	epistolē	pros	Rhōmaious
Paul's	letter	to	Romans.

Textual Apparatus

3834.1 name nom masc	1395.1 noun nom sing masc	2400.2 name masc	5382.2 name gen masc	5382.2 name gen masc
1:1. Παῦλος	δοῦλος	ʹ Ἰησοῦ	Χριστοῦ,	[☆ Χριστοῦ
Paulos	doulos	Iēsou	Christou	Christou
Paul,	servant	of Jesus	Christ,	[of Christ

2400.2 name masc	2795.1 adj nom sing masc	646.1 noun nom sing masc	866.10 verb nom sing masc part perf pass	1519.1 prep
Ἰησοῦ,]	κλητὸς	ἀπόστολος,	ἀφωρισμένος	εἰς
Iēsou	klētos	apostolos	aphōrismenos	eis
Jesus]	a called	apostle,	having been separated	for

2077.1 noun sing neu	2296.2 noun gen sing masc	3614.16 rel- pron gen neu	4139.1 verb 3sing indic aor mid	1217.2 prep
εὐαγγέλιον	θεοῦ,	2. ὃ	προεπηγγείλατο	διὰ
euangelion	theou	ho	proepēngeilato	dia
good news	of God,	which	he before promised	through

3450.1 art gen pl	4254.5 noun gen pl masc	840.3 prs- pron gen sing	1706.1 prep	1118.7 noun dat pl fem	39.15 adj dat pl fem
τῶν	προφητῶν	αὐτοῦ	ἐν	γραφαῖς	ἁγίαις,
tōn	prophētōn	autou	en	graphais	hagiais
the	prophets	his	in	writings	holy,

3875.1 prep	3450.2 art gen sing	5048.2 noun gen sing masc	840.3 prs- pron gen sing	3450.2 art gen sing	1090.50 verb gen sing part aor mid
3. περὶ	τοῦ	υἱοῦ	αὐτοῦ,	τοῦ	γενομένου
peri	tou	huiou	autou	tou	genomenou
concerning	the	Son	his,	the	having come

1523.2 prep gen	4543.2 noun gen sing neu	1132.1 name masc	2567.3 prep	4418.4 noun acc sing fem	3450.2 art gen sing
ἐκ	σπέρματος	Δαβὶδ	κατὰ	σάρκα,	4. τοῦ
ek	spermatos	Dabid	kata	sarka	tou
of	seed	of David	according to	flesh,	the

3587.5 verb gen sing masc part aor pass	5048.2 noun gen sing masc	2296.2 noun gen sing masc	1706.1 prep	1405.3 noun dat sing fem
ὁρισθέντος	υἱοῦ	θεοῦ	ἐν	δυνάμει,
horisthentos	huiou	theou	en	dunamei
having been marked out	Son	of God	in	power,

2567.3 prep	4011.1 noun sing neu	41.1 noun gen sing fem	1523.1 prep gen	384.2 noun gen sing fem
κατὰ	πνεῦμα	ἁγιωσύνης,	ἐξ	ἀναστάσεως
kata	pneuma	hagiōsunēs	ex	anastaseōs
according to	Spirit	of holiness,	by	resurrection

3361.2 adj gen pl	2400.2 name masc	5382.2 name gen masc	3450.2 art gen sing	2935.2 noun gen sing masc	2231.1 prs- pron gen 1pl
νεκρῶν,	Ἰησοῦ	Χριστοῦ	τοῦ	κυρίου	ἡμῶν,
nekrōn	Iēsou	Christou	tou	kuriou	hēmōn
of dead	Jesus	Christ	the	Lord	our;

THE EPISTLE OF PAUL TO THE
ROMANS

1:1. Paul related himself to the Lord he served, to his apostolic office, and to the ministry God had given to him. He was the *doulos* ("slave") of Jesus Christ. His will was totally submitted to the will of his Lord.

Paul's vocation was a *klētos apostolos*, a chosen messenger. There are many servants, but not all are apostles.

Paul's entire life was "separated unto the gospel of God." The verse emphasizes that Paul was merely God's instrument. The proclamation of the gospel was his only pursuit.

Four words describe Paul and his mission. Two relate to character and two relate to service. He called himself "a servant" and "an apostle." Two words picture his career of service, "called . . . separated." Life to Paul was commitment (a servant), commission (an apostle), and consecration (called, separated).

1:2. *Ho proepēngeilato,* "*which he had promised afore* by his prophets in the holy Scriptures" indicates that Christ is the good news that fulfills God's promises.

Hagion ("in the *holy* Scriptures") is that which belongs to God. *Graphais hagiais* is the Old Testament, containing God's promises written by inspired men *dia tōn prophētōn autou,* "through his prophets."

1:3. The good news focuses on the Son of God who became the Son of Man. *Tou genomenou* means "came" or "born" (Galatians 4:4); *ek spermatos,* "of the seed of David." By His physical birth Jesus became a descendant of Israel's great king.

1:4. Jesus was "declared" *with power* to be the Son of God through the Resurrection which identifies Him as deity.

The birth and the resurrection of Christ are linked together. Divinely born, He was divinely raised. Here is the crowning proof of His deity, "according to the Spirit of holiness." This refers to the spiritual nature of the One who is human and divine. (Some commentators see this phrase as a Greek representation of the Hebrew idiom for "the Holy Spirit".)

Various Versions

1. Paul, a servant of Jesus Christ: My name is Paul, *Norlie* . . . a slave, *HistNT* . . . a bond-servant, *Weymouth* . . . a bondsman, *Conybeare.*

called [to be] an apostle: . . . especially selected for, *SEB* . . . appointed a special apostle, *Fenton* . . . an ambassador by divine summons, *Wuest.*

separated unto the gospel of God: . . . permanently separated to God's good news, *Wuest* . . . put apart to preache, *Geneva.*

2. (Which he had promised afore: . . . in advance, *Berkeley.*
by his prophets in the holy scriptures,): . . . holy Bible, *Beck.*

3. Concerning his Son Jesus Christ our Lord:
which was made of the seed of David according to the flesh: . . . as regards His human descent, belonged to the posterity of David, *Weymouth* . . . born of David's offspring, *HistNT* . . . as to His human nature, *Berkeley.*

4. And declared [to be] the Son of God with power: . . . vvas predestinate the sonne of God, *Rheims* . . . installed as Son of God, *HistNT* . . . was marked out, *Conybeare* . . . openly designated, *Berkeley* . . . miraculously proved to be the Son of God, *Adams* . . . powerfully defined a Son of God, *Fenton* . . . declared mightely to be, *Geneva.*
according to the spirit of holiness: . . . bi the spirit of halowynge, *Wyclif* . . . the spirit of sanctification, *Rheims* . . . on the holy spiritual side, *Williams.*
by the resurrection from the dead: . . . of the agenrisynge of deed men, *Wyclif* . . . rose agayne from deeth, *Tyndale.*

19

5. δι' / οὗ / ἐλάβομεν / χάριν / καὶ / ἀποστολὴν
1217.1 prep / 3614.2 rel-pron gen sing / 2956.15 verb 1pl indic aor act / 5322.4 noun acc sing fem / 2504.1 conj / 645.2 noun acc sing fem
di' / hou / elabomen / charin / kai / apostolēn
by / whom / we received / grace / and / apostleship

εἰς / ὑπακοὴν / πίστεως / ἐν / πᾶσιν / τοῖς / ἔθνεσιν,
1519.1 prep / 5056.4 noun acc sing fem / 3963.2 noun gen sing fem / 1706.1 prep / 3820.5 adj dat pl / 3450.4 art dat pl / 1477.6 noun dat pl neu
eis / hupakoēn / pisteōs / en / pasin / tois / ethnesin,
unto / obedience / of faith / among / all / the / nations,

ὑπὲρ / τοῦ / ὀνόματος / αὐτοῦ, / **6.** ἐν / οἷς
5065.1 prep / 3450.2 art gen sing / 3549.3 noun gen sing neu / 840.3 prs-pron gen sing / 1706.1 prep / 3614.4 rel-pron dat pl
huper / tou / onomatos / autou, / en / hois
in behalf of / the / name / his, / among / whom

ἐστε / καὶ / ὑμεῖς, / κλητοὶ / Ἰησοῦ / Χριστοῦ·
1498.6 verb 2pl indic pres act / 2504.1 conj / 5050.1 prs-pron nom 2pl / 2795.2 adj nom pl masc / 2400.2 name masc / 5382.2 name gen masc
este / kai / humeis, / klētoi / Iēsou / Christou·
are / also / you, / called / of Jesus / Christ:

7. πᾶσιν / τοῖς / οὖσιν / ἐν / Ῥώμῃ / ἀγαπητοῖς
3820.5 adj dat pl / 3450.4 art dat pl / 1498.24 verb dat pl masc part pres act / 1706.1 prep / 4373.2 name dat fem / 27.7 adj dat pl masc
pasin / tois / ousin / en / Rhōmē / agapētois
to all / the / being / in / Rome / beloved

θεοῦ, / κλητοῖς / ἁγίοις· / χάρις / ὑμῖν / καὶ
2296.2 noun gen sing masc / 2795.3 adj dat pl masc / 39.8 adj dat pl masc / 5322.1 noun nom sing fem / 5050.3 prs-pron dat 2pl / 2504.1 conj
theou, / klētois / hagiois· / charis / humin / kai
of God, / called / saints: / grace / to you / and

εἰρήνη / ἀπὸ / θεοῦ / πατρὸς / ἡμῶν / καὶ / κυρίου
1503.1 noun nom sing fem / 570.3 prep gen / 2296.2 noun gen sing masc / 3824.2 noun gen sing masc / 2231.2 prs-pron gen 1pl / 2504.1 conj / 2935.2 noun gen sing masc
eirēnē / apo / theou / patros / hēmōn / kai / kuriou
peace / from / God / Father / our / and / Lord

Ἰησοῦ / Χριστοῦ. / **8.** Πρῶτον / μὲν / εὐχαριστῶ / τῷ
2400.2 name masc / 5382.2 name gen masc / 4270.1 adv / 3173.1 conj / 2149.1 verb 1sing indic pres act / 3450.3 art dat sing
Iēsou / Christou. / Prōton / men / eucharistō / tō
Jesus / Christ. / First, / men / I thank / to

θεῷ / μου / διὰ / Ἰησοῦ / Χριστοῦ / ὑπὲρ
2296.3 noun dat sing masc / 1466.2 prs-pron gen 1sing / 1217.2 prep / 2400.2 name masc / 5382.2 name gen masc / 5065.1 prep
theō / mou / dia / Iēsou / Christou / huper
God / my / through / Jesus / Christ / for

[a☆ περὶ] / πάντων / ὑμῶν, / ὅτι / ἡ / πίστις
3875.1 prep / 3820.4 adj gen pl / 5050.2 prs-pron gen 2pl / 3617.1 conj / 3450.9 art nom sing fem / 3963.1 noun nom sing fem
peri / pantōn / humōn, / hoti / hē / pistis
[concerning] / all / you, / that / the / faith

ὑμῶν / καταγγέλλεται / ἐν / ὅλῳ / τῷ / κόσμῳ·
5050.2 prs-pron gen 2pl / 2576.9 verb 3sing indic pres pass / 1706.1 prep / 3513.3 adj dat sing / 3450.3 art dat sing / 2862.3 noun dat sing masc
humōn / katangelletai / en / holō / tō / kosmō·
your / is being announced / in / whole / the / world;

8.a.**Txt:** 06D-corr,020L 025P,byz.
Var: 01א,02A,03B,04C 06D-org,018K,Lach Treg,Alf,Word,Tisc We/Ho,Weis,Sod UBS/☆

1:5. Apostleship came to Paul through grace (unmerited favor). "Obedience to the faith" refers not to doctrine or belief, but belief itself. Grace comes before apostleship, salvation before service. Commitment to the truth comes before commitment to the task.

1:6. The previous verse concludes with "among all nations" which indicates Paul's special calling to be the apostle to the Gentiles. Paul now wrote to the Roman believers, "Among whom are ye also." They too were "the called of Jesus Christ."

1:7. God knows the whereabouts of those He has called. This verse speaks of a specific group, not all Romans. The called are "beloved of God"; literally "God's loved ones."

Believers are "called to be saints," meaning "holy ones." The emphasis is on being set apart to God. Christians are separated from the world in order to serve God with pure hearts.

Paul greeted these saints with the words "grace . . . and peace." Grace, the unmerited favor of God, always precedes peace. When one has grace from heaven, he has peace wherever he may go. Grace and peace are forever proceeding from God the Father and the Lord Jesus Christ.

Grace comes from *chaireim*, the typical greeting among the Greeks. Then as now the greeting used among Hebrews is *Shalom*, "peace." Possibly Paul used both of these words for he was writing to churches composed of both Jews and Gentiles. The Old Testament form of greeting was "Peace be to you." But in the New Testament grace is God's provision. By grace we are converted, by grace we live, by grace we draw from His bountiful provision. All the blessings of the gospel emanate from God's grace and peace. Peace with God, peace in one's conscience, peace in daily living, living in peace with others; all this is because of and through grace.

The first seven verses of this epistle, while given to greetings, develop a fundamental groundwork of Christian doctrine. Note the theology: the deity and humanity of Jesus, the place of believers as "saints," and the relationship of God the Father and God the Son. No word is wasted. Even the opening words of greeting present doctrine.

1:8. Following the salutation (verses 1-7), the epistle proper opens with thanksgiving for the faith of the Roman Christians which was widely known. Paul's thanksgiving was "through Jesus Christ." All our activities are pleasing to God only through Jesus Christ. God is well-pleased with His Son. The believer is accepted in the Son (Ephesians 1:6). Our praise to God is accepted in Christ, and our prayers are addressed to God in the name of Jesus Christ (John 14:13,14; 15:16; 16:23,24,26).

5. By whom we have received: Through him God gave me the privilege, *TEV*.

grace and apostleship: . . . the undeserved gift, *Berkeley* . . . and our apostolic mission, *JB* . . . a charge and commission to subdue all nations, *Fenton* . . . favour of my commission, *Moffatt* . . . even the apostolic office, *Campbell*.

for obedience to the faith among all nations, for his name: . . . to urge upon all the heathen obedience, *Williams* . . . to promote an obedience of faith, *Scarlett* . . . to secure for his Cause submission to the Faith, *TCNT* . . . to bring all maner hethen people vnto obedience of the fayth, *Tyndale* . . . in alle folkis, *Wyclif*.

6. Among whom are ye also the called of Jesus Christ: . . . of whose nombre you be, *Cranmer* . . . you also are divinely summoned ones, *Wuest* . . . you are also the Invited ones, *Wilson*.

7. To all that be in Rome, beloved of God, called [to be] saints: . . . to all God's loved ones in Rome, *Berkeley* . . . who are God's loved ones, *Williams* . . . God's beloved ones, *HistNT* . . . the holy chosen friends, *Fenton* . . . called to be His holy people, *Beck* . . . called to become Christ's People, *TCNT* . . . and Sainctes by callyng, *Geneva* . . . Constituted Holy ones, *Wilson*.

Grace to you and peace from God our Father, and the Lord Jesus Christ: May gracious love, *SEB* . . . spiritual blessing, *Williams*.

8. First, I thank my God: At the very outset, *HistNT* . . . I am constantly thanking, *Wuest*.

through Jesus Christ for you all:

that your faith is spoken of throughout the whole world: . . . the whole world is getting to know about your faith, *Norlie* . . . because the tidings of, *Conybeare* . . . your faith is proclaimed, *RSV* . . . your faith is publsshed throughout all, *Geneva* . . . your faith is renoumed in the vvhole vvorld, *Rheims* . . . is celebrated in, *Fenton*.

9.

3116.1 noun nom sing masc	1056.1 conj	1466.2 prs-pron gen 1sing	1498.4 verb 3sing indic pres act	3450.5 art sing masc	2296.1 noun nom sing masc
μάρτυς	γάρ	μού	ἐστιν	ὁ	θεός,
martus	gar	mou	estin	ho	theos
witness	for	my	is		God,

3614.3 rel-pron dat sing	2973.1 verb 1sing indic pres act	1706.1 prep	3450.3 art dat sing	4011.3 noun dat sing neu	1466.2 prs-pron gen 1sing
ᾧ	λατρεύω	ἐν	τῷ	πνεύματί	μου
hō	latreuō	en	tō	pneumati	mou
whom	I serve	in	the	spirit	my

1706.1 prep	3450.3 art dat sing	2077.3 noun dat sing neu	3450.2 art gen sing	5048.2 noun gen sing masc	840.3 prs-pron gen sing	5453.1 conj
ἐν	τῷ	εὐαγγελίῳ	τοῦ	υἱοῦ	αὐτοῦ,	ὡς
en	tō	euangeliō	tou	huiou	autou	hōs
in	the	good news	of the	Son	his,	how

88.1 adv	3281.2 noun acc sing fem	5050.2 prs-pron gen 2pl	4020.60 verb 1sing indic pres mid	3704.1 adv
ἀδιαλείπτως	μνείαν	ὑμῶν	ποιοῦμαι,	**10.** πάντοτε
adialeiptōs	mneian	humōn	poioumai	pantote
unceasingly	mention	of you	I make,	always

1894.3 prep	3450.1 art gen pl	4194.6 noun gen pl fem	1466.2 prs-pron gen 1sing	1183.3 verb nom sing masc part pres
ἐπὶ	τῶν	προσευχῶν	μου	δεόμενος,
epi	tōn	proseuchōn	mou	deomenos
at	the	prayers	my	beseeching,

1501.1 conj	1479.1 conj	4315.1 adv	2218.1 adv	4077.1 adv	2117.4 verb 1sing indic fut pass
⸂ εἴπως	[✶ εἴ	πως]	ἤδη	ποτὲ	εὐοδωθήσομαι
eipōs	ei	pōs	ēdē	pote	euodōthēsomai
if by any means	[if	how]	now	at last	I shall be prospered

1706.1 prep	3450.3 art dat sing	2284.3 noun dat sing neu	3450.2 art gen sing	2296.2 noun gen sing masc	2048.23 verb inf aor act	4242.1 prep
ἐν	τῷ	θελήματι	τοῦ	θεοῦ	ἐλθεῖν	πρὸς
en	tō	thelēmati	tou	theou	elthein	pros
by	the	will		of God	to come	to

5050.4 prs-pron acc 2pl	1955.1 verb 1sing indic pres act	1056.1 conj	1481.19 verb inf aor act	5050.4 prs-pron acc 2pl	2419.1 conj
ὑμᾶς·	**11.** ἐπιποθῶ	γὰρ	ἰδεῖν	ὑμᾶς,	ἵνα
humas	epipothō	gar	idein	humas	hina
you.	I long	for	to see	you,	that

4948.10 indef-pron sing neu	3200.3 verb 1sing subj aor act	5321.1 noun sing neu	5050.3 prs-pron dat 2pl	4012.8 adj sing neu
τι	μεταδῶ	χάρισμα	ὑμῖν	πνευματικὸν,
ti	metadō	charisma	humin	pneumatikon
some	I may impart	gift	to you	spiritual,

1519.1 prep	3450.16 art sing neu	4592.6 verb inf aor pass	5050.4 prs-pron acc 2pl	3642.17 dem-pron sing neu	1156.2 conj
εἰς	τὸ	στηριχθῆναι	ὑμᾶς,	**12.** τοῦτο	δέ
eis	to	stērichthēnai	humas	touto	de
to	the	to be established	you,	that	and

1498.4 verb 3sing indic pres act	4688.1 verb inf aor pass	1706.1 prep	5050.3 prs-pron dat 2pl	1217.2 prep
ἐστιν,	συμπαρακληθῆναι	ἐν	ὑμῖν	διὰ
estin	sumparaklēthēnai	en	humin	dia
is,	to be comforted together	among	you,	through

1:9. The phrase "with my *spirit*" is significant. Here Paul spoke of his spirit in worship (cf. John 4:24; 1 Corinthians 14:14). The terms "spirit" (*pneuma*) and "soul" (*psuchē*) are sometimes used interchangeably, but never in Paul's writings. The emphasis of Romans is spiritual life vs. natural life (cf. 1 Corinthians 2:14,15). Just as by the will of God Paul gave the clearest presentation of the gospel, so he also gave the clearest treatment of man's constitution (as in 1 Thessalonians 5:23). A study of these terms in the Epistles will cause one to agree with F.F. Bruce that " 'spirit' and 'soul' are not only distinguished in Paul, but set in contrast to each other" (*Tyndale New Testament Commentaries*, 6:47). First Thessalonians 5:17 urges us to "pray without ceasing." *Adialeiptōs*, "without ceasing," means "without letting up or leaving off." Paul practiced what he preached. Although he was not personally acquainted with many of the Roman Christians, he prayed for all of them.

1:10. Paul's desire to visit the Roman Christians was so strong that he said "if by any means." God honored this desire of Paul's heart, for he later went to Rome as a prisoner. He considered himself to be a prisoner of Christ and not of Nero (Philippians 1:12-14). How different his entrance into Rome was from the anticipated voluntary arrival. After a tempestuous voyage, he arrived as a prisoner. However he had the great privilege of testifying before "caesar's" household.

The apostle earnestly prayed for the privilege of visiting this assembly located in the capital of the Roman Empire. While all men of that time aspired to see the fabled capital city of the world of that day, Paul did not measure his longing on the basis of the outward magnificence of the great city; he longed to meet with his fellow believers. Some were his kinsmen, some had been fellow workers, some were prisoners, but all were his Christian brothers and sisters. The ties of Christian fellowship are very special, and particularly so during times of opposition and persecution. Love for Christ prevents narrowness of spirit. The richer our vertical relationship is to Christ, the greater will be our horizontal relationship with others.

The reason for Paul's desired visit was the mutual edification of himself and the assembly. He prayed that he would "have a prosperous journey." The Greek word is *euodoō* which comes from *eu*, "well" or "good," and *hodos* meaning "way." He expected to find that way "by the will of God." To find the will of God is the greatest discovery. To know the will of God is the greatest knowledge. To do the will of God is the greatest achievement.

Scorching suns, raging seas, weary miles, and bitter persecutions were to be a part of that journey. All was endured not for friends, fame or fortune, but for fruit.

1:11,12. Paul desired to "impart . . . some spiritual gift" (*ti charisma*). He would "impart"; they would be "established." Their mutual relationship would comfort preacher and people. The word

9. For God is my witness: . . . that what I say is true, *TEV*.

whom I serve with my spirit: I render holy service, *Montgomery* . . . my whole heart, *Norlie*.

in the gospel of his Son: . . . by telling the good news about, *Williams*.

that without ceasing I make mention of you always in my prayers: . . . vvithout intermission I make a memorie of you, *Rheims* . . . how incessantly, *Scarlett* . . . I regularly mention you, *Adams* . . . I make mynde of you euer in my preiers, *Wyclif*.

10. Making request: . . . always entreating, *Williams* . . . supplicating, *Noyes* . . . pleading, *Berkeley* . . . besechynge, *Cranmer* . . . continually inquiring, *Fenton*.

if by any means now at length: . . . that sometime, somehow, *Norlie* . . . that by some meane ...one tyme or other, *Cranmer* . . . if it be possible, *Noyes*.

I might have a prosperous journey by the will of God to come unto you: . . . succeed in coming to you, *Beck* . . . I may be sped upon my way, *HistNT* . . . myght fortune me, *Tyndale* . . . be favored with an opportunity of coming to you, *Noyes*.

11. For I long to see you: I do long to meet you, *Norlie* . . . I am yearning, *Berkeley*.

that I may impart unto you some spiritual gift: . . . may give you, *Adams* . . . myght bestowe, amonge you, *Geneva* . . . spiritual privilege, *HistNT* . . . spiritual help, *Weymouth* . . . spiritual grace, *Rheims, Confraternity*.

to the end ye may be established: . . . for your confirmation, *Berkeley, Noyes* . . . give you fresh strength, *TCNT* . . . make you strong, *TEV*, . . . for the establishment of your steadfastness, *Conybeare* . . . resulting in your being stabilized, *Wuest*.

12. That is, that I may be comforted together with you by the mutual faith both of you and me: . . . and I can obtain mutual comfort, *Norlie* . . . and I may find encouragement in, *TCNT* . . . receaue exhortation together with

Romans 1:13

3450.10 art gen sing fem	1706.1 prep	238.2 prs-pron dat pl	3963.2 noun gen sing fem	5050.2 prs-pron gen 2pl	4885.1 conj	2504.1 conj
τῆς	ἐν	ἀλλήλοις	πίστεως	ὑμῶν	τε	καὶ
tēs	en	allēlois	pisteōs	humōn	te	kai
the	in	one another	faith,	yours	both	and

1466.3 prs-pron gen 1sing	3620.3 partic	2286.1 verb 1sing pres act	1156.2 conj	5050.4 prs-pron acc 2pl	49.9 verb inf pres act
ἐμοῦ·	13. οὐ	θέλω	δὲ	ὑμᾶς	ἀγνοεῖν,
emou	ou	thelō	de	humas	agnoein
mine.	Not	I do want	but	you	to be ignorant,

79.6 noun pl masc	3617.1 conj	4038.1 adv	4246.1 verb 1sing indic aor mid	2048.23 verb inf aor act	4242.1 prep
ἀδελφοί,	ὅτι	πολλάκις	προεθέμην	ἐλθεῖν	πρὸς
adelphoi	hoti	pollakis	proethemēn	elthein	pros
brothers,	that	many times	I proposed	to come	to

5050.4 prs-pron acc 2pl	2504.1 conj	2940.12 verb 1sing indic aor pass	884.2 conj	3450.2 art gen sing	1198.1 adv	2419.1 conj
ὑμᾶς,	καὶ	ἐκωλύθην	ἄχρι	τοῦ	δεῦρο,	ἵνα
humas	kai	ekōluthēn	achri	tou	deuro	hina
you,	and	was hindered	until	the	present,	that

2561.3 noun acc sing masc	4948.5 indef-pron	4948.5 indef-pron	2561.3 noun acc sing masc	2174.33 verb 1sing subj aor act	2504.1 conj
ʽ καρπὸν	τινὰ	[☆ τινὰ	καρπὸν]	σχῶ	καὶ
karpon	tina	tina	karpon	schō	kai
fruit	some	[some	fruit]	I might have	also

1706.1 prep	5050.3 prs-pron dat 2pl	2503.1 conj	2504.1 conj	1706.1 prep	3450.4 art dat pl	3036.2 adj dat pl
ἐν	ὑμῖν,	καθὼς	καὶ	ἐν	τοῖς	λοιποῖς
en	humin	kathōs	kai	en	tois	loipois
among	you,	according as	also	among	the	other

1477.6 noun dat pl neu	1659.6 name dat pl masc	4885.1 conj	2504.1 conj	910.3 adj dat pl masc	4533.5 adj dat pl masc
ἔθνεσιν.	14. Ἕλλησίν	τε	καὶ	βαρβάροις,	σοφοῖς
ethnesin	Hellēsin	te	kai	barbarois	sophois
nations.	To Greeks	both	and	barbarians,	to wise

4885.1 conj	2504.1 conj	451.2 adj dat pl masc	3645.1 noun nom sing masc	1498.2 verb 1sing indic pres act	3643.1 adv
τε	καὶ	ἀνοήτοις,	ὀφειλέτης	εἰμί·	15. οὕτως
te	kai	anoētois	opheiletēs	eimi	houtōs
both	and	unintelligent,	a debtor	I am:	so

3450.16 art sing neu	2567.1 prep	1466.7 prs-pron acc 1sing	4148.1 adj nom sing neu	2504.1 conj	5050.3 prs-pron dat 2pl
τὸ	κατ'	ἐμὲ	πρόθυμον	καὶ	ὑμῖν
to	kat'	eme	prothumon	kai	humin
the	according to	me	readiness	also	to you

3450.4 art dat pl	1706.1 prep	4373.2 name dat fem	2076.25 verb inf aor mid	3620.3 partic
τοῖς	ἐν	Ῥώμῃ	εὐαγγελίσασθαι.	16. Οὐ
tois	en	Rhōmē	euangelisasthai	Ou
the	in	Rome	to announce the good news.	Not

16.a.**Txt**: 06D-corr,018K 020L,025P,byz.
Var: 01א,02A,03B,04C 06D-org,bo.Gries,Lach Treg,Alf,Word,Tisc We/Ho,Weis,Sod UBS/☆

1056.1 conj	1855.1 verb 1sing indic pres	3450.16 art sing neu	2077.1 noun sing neu	3450.2 art gen sing
γὰρ	ἐπαισχύνομαι	τὸ	εὐαγγέλιον	ʽª τοῦ
gar	epaischunomai	to	euangelion	tou
for	I am ashamed of	the	good news	of the

"comforted" (*sumparakaleō*) can also be translated "encouraged or strengthened together." Paul expressed with delicate courtesy and gracious humility that he needed them. Both Paul and the believers in Rome would benefit from his visit.

1:13. "I would not have you ignorant" is Paul's way of saying, "I want you to know." The phrase "oftentimes I purposed to come" explains that he had often tried to get to Rome but was hindered. The word "let" (King James Version) is a term which today is better translated "allow."

Verse 13 concludes with an expression of the driving force in his desire to come to the imperial city—"that I might have some fruit among you also, even as among other Gentiles." That was the passion of the great apostle to the Gentiles. Fruit (*karpas*) denotes the result of labor. He was ready to labor to see that fruit.

1:14. The word "debtor" (*opheiletēs*) means "one held by some obligation, bound to some duty." Paul felt this great obligation, and the only way he could repay was by loving service. The term "Barbarians" (*barbaros*) was applied to any foreigners who did not speak the Greek language. To the Greeks all non-Greeks were barbarians.

Paul had already given proof of his passion to share Christ with all men, whether a runaway slave like Onesimus or a proud king like Agrippa. The apostle's great desire was to preach to the wise and the unwise, the learned and the unlearned. His debt was to all men, whether divided by language or culture.

1:15. Wherever Paul went to preach he met opposition. Often the price was physical suffering even to the point of being left for dead. At Jerusalem, the religious center, he was mobbed. At Athens, the intellectual center, he was mocked. At Rome, the governmental center, he was martyred. But he was ready to preach at Rome. The only limit to that obligation was "as much as in me is."

1:16,17. Now comes the next assertion, one of the greatest: "For I am not ashamed of the gospel of Christ." The other assertions were positive; this one is also, but stated with a negative, "I am not ashamed." The word "for" relates to the assertion "I am ready." Paul felt it was a privilege to preach the gospel.

Verses 16 and 17 are the theme of the entire Book of Romans. When Paul boldly declared, "I am not ashamed," his statement was based on two premises: (1) the gospel is the power of God; (2) the gospel reveals the righteousness of God.

you through the commen faith, *Geneva* . . . that I might haue consolacion, *Cranmer.*

13. Now I would not have you ignorant, brethren: . . . wish you to ignore, *Fenton.*

that oftentimes I purposed to come unto you:

(but was let hitherto,): But, until now, I was stopped, *SEB* . . . so far I have always been hindered, *Norlie* . . . but thus far I have been prevented, *Berkeley.*

that I might have some fruit among you also: . . . that I might reap some harvest among you, *Berkeley* . . . enjoy some results of working among you, *Beck.*

even as among other Gentiles: . . . even as also in the rest of the Gentiles, *Alford* . . . as in other folkis, *Wyclif.*

14. I am debtor: I owe a duty, *Moffatt* . . . under obligations, *Weymouth* . . . I have a debt to discharge, *Montgomery.*

both to the Greeks, and to the Barbarians: . . . alike to Greek-speaking races, *Weymouth* . . . and non-Greeks, *Beck* . . . and to uncivilized nations, *TCNT* . . . to the civilized and to the savage, *TEV* . . . and to all the other nations, *Williams.*

both to the wise, and to the unwise: . . . to the educated, *Adams* . . . both to clever and to simpleminded people, *TCNT* . . . philosophers, and illiterates, *Fenton* . . . and the foolish, *Beck.*

15. So, as much as in me is: . . . hence my deep-felt eagerness, *Berkeley* . . . so, as far as it depends upon me, *Adams* . . . to the extent of my ability, *Williams.*

I am ready to preach the gospel: I am sincerely eager, *Norlie.*

to you that are at Rome also:

16. For I am not ashamed of: For I am proud of the Gospel, *Montgomery.*

the gospel of Christ: . . . the Glad-tidings, *Conybeare.*

for it is the power of God unto salvation to every one that believeth: . . . a Divine power, *Fenton* . . . for saving anyone who believes it, *SEB* . . . by which God

Romans 1:17

5382.2 name gen masc	1405.1 noun nom sing fem	1056.1 conj	2296.2 noun gen sing masc	1498.4 verb 3sing indic pres act	1519.1 prep
Χριστοῦ ⸀	δύναμις	γὰρ	θεοῦ	ἐστιν	εἰς
Christou	dunamis	gar	theou	estin	eis
Christ:	power	for	of God	it is	unto

4843.3 noun acc sing fem	3820.3 adj dat sing	3450.3 art dat sing	3961.11 verb dat sing masc part pres act	2428.1 name-adj dat sing masc
σωτηρίαν	παντὶ	τῷ	πιστεύοντι,	Ἰουδαίῳ
sōtērian	panti	tō	pisteuonti	Ioudaiō
salvation	to everyone	the	believing,	to Jew

16.b.Txt: 01א,02A,06D byz.
Var: 03B,012G

4885.1 conj	4270.1 adv	2504.1 conj	1659.3 name dat sing masc	1336.1 noun nom sing fem	1056.1 conj
τε	⸀ πρῶτον ⸀	καὶ	Ἕλληνι.	**17.** δικαιοσύνη	γὰρ
te	prōton	kai	Hellēni	dikaiosunē	gar
both	first	and	to Greek:	righteousness	for

2296.2 noun gen sing masc	1706.1 prep	840.4 prs- pron dat sing	596.5 verb 3sing indic pres pass	1523.2 prep gen	3963.2 noun gen sing fem
θεοῦ	ἐν	αὐτῷ	ἀποκαλύπτεται	ἐκ	πίστεως
theou	en	autō	apokaluptetai	ek	pisteōs
of God	in	it	is being revealed	from	faith

1519.1 prep	3963.4 noun acc sing fem	2503.1 conj	1119.22 verb 3sing indic perf pass	3450.5 art sing masc	1156.2 conj
εἰς	πίστιν,	καθὼς	γέγραπται,	Ὁ	δὲ
eis	pistin	kathōs	gegraptai	Ho	de
to	faith;	just as	it has been written,	The	but

1337.3 adj nom sing masc	1523.2 prep gen	3963.2 noun gen sing fem	2180.29 verb 3sing indic fut mid	596.5 verb 3sing indic pres pass
δίκαιος	ἐκ	πίστεως	ζήσεται.	**18.** Ἀποκαλύπτεται
dikaios	ek	pisteōs	zēsetai	Apokaluptetai
just	by	faith	shall live.	There is being revealed

1056.1 conj	3572.1 noun nom sing fem	2296.2 noun gen sing masc	570.2 prep gen	3636.2 noun gen sing masc	1894.3 prep	3820.12 adj acc sing fem
γὰρ	ὀργὴ	θεοῦ	ἀπ'	οὐρανοῦ	ἐπὶ	πᾶσαν
gar	orgē	theou	ap'	ouranou	epi	pasan
for	wrath	of God	from	heaven	upon	all

757.2 noun acc sing fem	2504.1 conj	92.4 noun acc sing fem	442.7 noun gen pl masc	3450.1 art gen pl
ἀσέβειαν	καὶ	ἀδικίαν	ἀνθρώπων	τῶν
asebeian	kai	adikian	anthrōpōn	tōn
ungodliness	and	unrighteousness	of men	the

3450.12 art acc sing fem	223.4 noun acc sing fem	1706.1 prep	92.3 noun dat sing fem	2692.6 verb gen pl masc part pres act
τὴν	ἀλήθειαν	ἐν	ἀδικίᾳ	κατεχόντων.
tēn	alētheian	en	adikia	katechontōn
the	truth	in	unrighteousness	holding.

1354.1 conj	3450.16 art sing neu	1104.4 adj nom sing neu	3450.2 art gen sing	2296.2 noun gen sing masc	5156.1 adj sing
19. διότι	τὸ	γνωστὸν	τοῦ	θεοῦ	φανερόν
dioti	to	gnōston	tou	theou	phaneron
Because	the	known		of God	manifest

1498.4 verb 3sing indic pres act	1706.1 prep	840.2 prs- pron dat pl	3450.5 art sing masc	1056.1 conj	2296.1 noun nom sing masc
ἐστιν	ἐν	αὐτοῖς,	ὁ	⸀ γὰρ	θεὸς
estin	en	autois	ho	gar	theos
is	among	them,		for	God

Verse 1 shows God as the source of the gospel. Verses 16 and 17 show further: (1) the dynamics of the gospel—"the power of God"; (2) the aim of the gospel—"salvation"; (3) the extent of the gospel—"to every one"; (4) the condition of the gospel—"that believeth"; and (5) the reason for the gospel—"the just shall live by faith."

Paul gloried in the gospel and felt it a great honor to proclaim it. The gospel is more than human might; it is actually the Holy Spirit's *dynamic* force, the inherent power of the Almighty employed for our salvation.

Salvation (*sōtēria* from *sōtēr*, "saviour") is the all-inclusive word in describing redemption. Righteousness is one of the key words. The *gospel* is God's *power* unto *salvation*, consisting of God's *righteousness*, which comes by *faith*. Salvation is from "faith to faith" meaning all of faith and not of works.

The gospel is God's righteousness revealed in a twofold manner: (1) how sinners can come to be "in the right" with God, and (2) how God vindicates His personal righteousness in the very act of declaring us righteous.

1:18. God's wrath (*orgē theou*) is revealed against all ungodliness (*asebia*) and unrighteousness (*adikia*). *Asebeia* means ungodlike. It connotes licentious living, but it also includes respected people who are ungodlike in heart and life. The basic idea is irreverence, disregard for God's law and disregard for God's person. *Adikia* refers to an absence of a right attitude inwardly and right conduct outwardly.

To "hold the truth in unrighteousness" implies to suppress, to hinder the truth. Although there may be verbal agreement given to doctrine, it is meaningless if there is unrighteous living.

God's wrath is the result of the clash of His righteousness with sin. He cannot love good unless He hates evil. God's wrath is revealed because of human ungodliness, human unrighteousness, and human unbelief. Attention is drawn to the righteousness of God in verse 17, the manifest wrath of God in verse 18, followed by the analysis of the sinful heart.

Sin established a process of degeneration, ending in judgment. The black background of gross sin and God's hatred of it is provided to bring into bright focus the blessing of God's provision for deliverance from sin's condemnation. We must see man "unrighteous and condemned" to get the full impact of man made "righteous and redeemed."

1:19,20. Now comes the proclamation of the tragic wickedness of man, leading from one stage of depravity to another.

The term "that which may be known of God" is not that which is knowable, but that knowledge of God as the Creator. Men see the attributes of God in His creation; they see His person only in His Son, the Lord Jesus Christ.

brings Salvation, *TCNT* . . . it is God's saving power for everyone who has faith, *Moffatt* . . . of everyone who trusts, *Williams*.

to the Jew first, and also to the Greek: . . . then non-Jews, *SEB*.

17. For therein is the righteousness of God revealed: God's plan to justify us, *Norlie* . . . the iustice of God, *Rheims* . . . is uncovered, *Williams*.

from faith to faith: It is by faith, first and last, *Norlie* . . . It begins and ends by faith, *SEB*.

as it is written:

The just shall live by faith: . . . will find Life as the result of faith, *TCNT* . . . by faith shall the upright live, *HistNT*.

18. For the wrath of God is revealed from heaven: God's indignation is revealed, *Berkeley* . . . Divine displeasure, *Fenton* . . . God in heaven shows He is angry, *Beck*.

against all ungodliness and unrighteousness of men: . . . upon every lack of reverence, *Williams* . . . against irreligion and wrong-doing in every form, *TCNT* . . . vpon al impietie and iniustice, *Rheims*.

who hold the truth in unrighteousness: . . . pervert the true into the false, *Fenton* . . . that deteine the veritie of God, *Rheims* . . . their wicked ways suppress the truth, *Norlie, Berkeley* . . . who smother the truth, *Montgomery* . . . through iniquity suppress the truth, *Weymouth* . . . whose evil ways prevent the truth from being known, *TEV* . . . who use sin to hide the truth, *SEB* . . . who keep truth imprisoned in their wickedness, *JB* . . . of those who hinder the Truth, *Moffatt* . . . who impede the truth, *HistNT*.

19. Because that which may be known of God: . . . what can be known about God is apparent to them, *Adams*.

is manifest in them: . . . is clear to them, *Beck* . . . is plain to their inmost consciousness, *Weymouth*.

for God hath showed [it] unto them: He himself gave it to them, *TCNT*.

Romans 1:20

[✶ **θεὸς** *theos* [God] **2296.1** noun nom sing masc]   **γὰρ]** *gar* [for] **1056.1** conj   **αὐτοῖς** *autois* to them **840.2** prs-pron dat pl   **ἐφανέρωσεν·** *ephanerōsen* manifested; **5157.3** verb 3sing indic aor act   **20.** **τὰ** *ta* the **3450.17** art pl neu   **γὰρ** *gar* for **1056.1** conj

ἀόρατα *aorata* invisible things **513.4** adj nom sing neu   **αὐτοῦ** *autou* his **840.3** prs-pron gen sing   **ἀπὸ** *apo* from **570.3** prep gen   **κτίσεως** *ktiseōs* creation **2909.2** noun gen sing fem   **κόσμου** *kosmou* of world **2862.2** noun gen sing masc   **τοῖς** *tois* by the **3450.4** art dat pl

ποιήμασιν *poiēmasin* things made **4021.2** noun dat pl neu   **νοούμενα** *nooumena* being understood **3401.8** verb nom pl neu part pres pass   **καθορᾶται,** *kathoratai* are being perceived, **2501.1** verb 3sing indic pres pass   **ἥ** *hē* which **3614.9** rel-pron nom sing fem

τε *te* both **4885.1** conj   **ἀΐδιος** *aidios* eternal **126.2** adj nom sing fem   **αὐτοῦ** *autou* his **840.3** prs-pron gen sing   **δύναμις** *dunamis* power **1405.1** noun nom sing fem   **καὶ** *kai* and **2504.1** conj   **θειότης,** *theiotēs* divinity; **2282.1** noun nom sing fem   **εἰς** *eis* for **1519.1** prep

τὸ *to* the **3450.16** art sing neu   **εἶναι** *einai* to be **1498.32** verb inf pres act   **αὐτοὺς** *autous* them **840.8** prs-pron acc pl masc   **ἀναπολογήτους.** *anapologētous* without excuse. **377.2** adj acc pl masc   **21.** **διότι** *dioti* Because **1354.1** conj

γνόντες *gnontes* having known **1091.28** verb nom pl masc part aor act   **τὸν** *ton* **3450.6** art acc sing masc   **θεὸν** *theon* God, **2296.4** noun acc sing masc   **οὐχ** *ouch* not **3620.1** partic   **ὡς** *hōs* as **5453.1** conj   **θεὸν** *theon* God **2296.4** noun acc sing masc

21.a.Txt: 03B,018K 020L,025P,byz.Weis Var: 01ℵ,02A,04C,06D Gries,Lach,Treg,Alf Tisc,We/Ho,Sod,UBS/✶

ἐδόξασαν *edoxasan* they glorified **1386.10** verb 3pl indic aor act   **ἢ** *ē* or **2211.1** conj   (**εὐχαρίστησαν,** *eucharistēsan* were thankful; **2149.10** verb 3pl indic aor act   [a✶ **ηὐχαρίστησαν,**] *ēucharistēsan* [idem] **2149.14** verb 3pl indic aor act

(✶ **ἀλλ'** *all'* but **233.1** conj   [**ἀλλὰ**] *alla* [idem] **233.2** conj   **ἐματαιώθησαν** *emataiōthēsan* became vain **3126.1** verb 3pl indic aor pass   **ἐν** *en* in **1706.1** prep   **τοῖς** *tois* the **3450.4** art dat pl

διαλογισμοῖς *dialogismois* reasonings **1255.6** noun dat pl masc   **αὐτῶν,** *autōn* their, **840.1** prs-pron gen pl   **καὶ** *kai* and **2504.1** conj   **ἐσκοτίσθη** *eskotisthē* was darkened **4509.1** verb 3sing indic aor pass   **ἡ** *hē* the **3450.9** art nom sing fem

ἀσύνετος *asunetos* without understanding **795.3** adj nom sing fem   **αὐτῶν** *autōn* their **840.1** prs-pron gen pl   **καρδία·** *kardia* heart: **2559.2** noun nom sing fem   **22.** **φάσκοντες** *phaskontes* professing **5173.1** verb nom pl masc part pres act

εἶναι *einai* to be **1498.32** verb inf pres act   **σοφοὶ** *sophoi* wise **4533.3** adj nom pl masc   **ἐμωράνθησαν,** *emōranthēsan* they became fools, **3333.2** verb 3pl indic aor pass   **23.** **καὶ** *kai* and **2504.1** conj   **ἤλλαξαν** *ēllaxan* changed **234.1** verb 3pl indic aor act

The witness of God is unmistakable (verse 19) and universal (verse 20). It is one of the most astounding facts of all Scripture that to *all* human beings of *all* time God has given a revelation of himself. As any person walks in the light he has, he will always be given more light from God. The Psalmist understood this truth when he wrote that the heavens and the firmament "declare the glory of God; . . . Day unto day . . . and night unto night" they give knowledge of God; "There is no speech nor language, where their voice is not heard" (Psalm 19:1-4). All created beings are accountable to their Creator for what has been "clearly seen." This witness from nature brings knowledge of the truth of His eternal power and the truth of Godhood (*theiotēs*). "Eternal power" emphasizes the eternity of God himself as well as of His power. *Theiotēs* emphasizes His deity—His being separate from and above His creation. A.W. Tozer speaks of the divine transcendence: "Forever God stands apart, in light unapproachable. He is as high above an archangel as above a caterpillar . . . they are alike created. They both belong in the category of that-which-is-not-God" (p.76). The greatness and detail of God's creation shows man His omnipotence and omniscience. Natural revelation shows that God exists and can be clearly seen by all mankind. The expression "without excuse" (*anapologētus*) means that men are defenseless on judgment day.

1:21. The universal willful rejection of God's salvation is seen in man's history. God revealed, but man rejected; he willfully chose not to receive the revelation of God. The downward path is tragic. Irreverence, "glorified him not as God," gives birth to ingratitude, "neither were thankful." This in turn begets rationalism, "became vain in their imaginations" (reasonings), followed by spiritual blindness, "their foolish heart was darkened." Filled with intellectual pride, "professing themselves to be wise," they became idolators.

All who are charged with unrighteousness are under God's wrath; neither their character nor conduct are acceptable. Unbelievers are guilty and inexcusable because they have seen God's eternal power and deity and yet have rejected it.

1:22. Claiming themselves to be wise, they became simpletons instead. The word for "wise" had the connotation among the Greeks of persons of culture and learning. The Greek word translated "fools" is *mōrainō*, the source of the English word *moron*. Moral denseness is implied.

Paul pointed out to the Athenians how foolish it was for them to claim to be the offspring of God and then call an idol of "gold, or silver, or stone" that God (Acts 17:28,29). The Areopagites prided themselves on their intellectual superiority; how ridiculous to worship something at best "unknown" and logically inferior to living human beings.

20. For the invisible things of him: His invisible qualities, *Berkeley* . . . His unseen attributes, *Fenton.*

from the creation of the world: are clearly seen, being understood by the things that are made: . . . brought within men's apprehension, *TCNT* . . . have been clearly perceptible, *Norlie* . . . they have seen the unseen things of God, *Beck* . . . have been rendered intelligible, *Weymouth* . . . being perceived, *Worrell* . . . and clearly visible, *Williams.*

[even] his eternal power and Godhead: . . . they can tell He has everlasting power, *Beck* . . . and divine character, *TCNT* . . . and divinity, *Confraternity* . . . and deity, *Sawyer.*

so that they are without excuse: Men have no excuse at all, *Norlie* . . . they are inexcusable, *Rheims.*

21. Because that, when they knew God: . . . though they knew God, *Alford.*

they glorified [him] not as God, neither were thankful: . . . they did not joyfully honour Him, *Fenton* . . . nor gave him thanks, *HistNT.*

but became vain in their imaginations: . . . but trifled in, *Fenton* . . . they busied themselves with silly speculations, *Norlie* . . . they indulged in their useless speculations, *Berkeley* . . . became vain in their reasonings, *Wesley, Confraternity* . . . their thoughts turned to worthless things, *Beck* . . . their thinking became nonsense, *SEB* . . . waxed ful of vanities in their imaginations, *Geneva* . . . are become vaine in their cogitations, *Rheims.*

and their foolish heart was darkened: . . . their insensible hearts have been shrouded, *Williams* . . . and their senseless minds, *Montgomery* . . . their inconsiderate heart, *Campbell* . . . their heart being without understanding, *Alford.*

22. Professing themselves to be wise, they became fools: Claiming to be smart, *Berkeley* . . . The more they called themselves philosophers, the more stupid they grew, *JB* . . . but became moronic, *Klingensmith.*

3450.12 art acc sing fem	1385.4 noun acc sing fem	3450.2 art gen sing	855.1 adj gen sing	2296.2 noun gen sing masc	1706.1 prep
τὴν tēn the	δόξαν doxan glory	τοῦ tou of the	ἀφθάρτου aphthartou incorruptible	θεοῦ theou God	ἐν en into

3530.1 noun dat sing neu	1494.2 noun gen sing fem	5186.2 adj gen sing masc	442.2 noun gen sing masc	2504.1 conj
ὁμοιώματι homoiōmati a likeness	εἰκόνος eikonos of an image	φθαρτοῦ phthartou of corruptible	ἀνθρώπου anthrōpou man	καὶ kai and

3932.2 adj gen pl neu	2504.1 conj	4922.2 adj gen pl neu	2504.1 conj	2046.2 noun gen pl neu
πετεινῶν peteinōn of birds	καὶ kai and	τετραπόδων tetrapodōn four-legged creatures	καὶ kai and	ἑρπετῶν. herpetōn creeping things.

24.a.Txt: 06D,018K 020L,025P,byz.
Var: 01א,02A,03B,04C Lach,Treg,Tisc,We/Ho Weis,Sod,UBS/✰

1346.1 conj	2504.1 conj	3722.10 verb 3sing indic aor act	840.8 prs-pron acc pl masc	3450.5 art sing masc
24. Διὸ Dio Wherefore	⸆ καὶ ⸆ kai also	παρέδωκεν paredōken gave up	αὐτοὺς autous them	ὁ ho

2296.1 noun nom sing masc	1706.1 prep	3450.14 art dat pl fem	1924.7 noun dat pl fem	3450.1 art gen pl	2559.6 noun gen pl fem
θεὸς theos God	ἐν en in	ταῖς tais the	ἐπιθυμίαις epithumiais desires	τῶν tōn of the	καρδιῶν kardiōn hearts

840.1 prs- pron gen pl	1519.1 prep	165.4 noun acc sing fem	3450.2 art gen sing	812.5 verb inf pres	3450.17 art pl neu
αὐτῶν autōn their	εἰς eis to	ἀκαθαρσίαν, akatharsian uncleanness,	τοῦ tou the	ἀτιμάζεσθαι atimazesthai to be dishonored	τὰ ta the

24.b.Txt: 06D-corr,018K 020L,025P,byz.
Var: 01א,02A,03B,04C 06D-org,Lach,Treg,Alf Tisc,We/Ho,Weis,Sod UBS/✰

4835.4 noun pl neu	840.1 prs- pron gen pl	1706.1 prep	1431.7 prs- pron dat pl masc	840.2 prs- pron dat pl
σώματα sōmata bodies	αὐτῶν autōn their	ἐν en between	⸂ ἑαυτοῖς· ⸃ heautois themselves:	[⸃✰ αὐτοῖς,] autois [them,]

3610.2 rel- pron nom pl masc	3207.1 verb 3pl indic aor act	3450.12 art acc sing fem	223.4 noun acc sing fem	3450.2 art gen sing
25. οἵτινες hoitines who	μετήλλαξαν metēllaxan changed	τὴν tēn the	ἀλήθειαν alētheian truth	τοῦ tou

2296.2 noun gen sing masc	1706.1 prep	3450.3 art dat sing	5414.3 noun dat sing neu	2504.1 conj	4428.1 verb 3pl indic aor pass
θεοῦ theou of God	ἐν en into	τῷ tō the	ψεύδει, pseudei lie,	καὶ kai and	ἐσεβάσθησαν esebasthēsan reverenced

2504.1 conj	2973.10 verb 3pl indic aor act	3450.11 art dat sing fem	2909.3 noun dat sing fem	3706.2 prep	3450.6 art acc sing masc
καὶ kai and	ἐλάτρευσαν elatreusan served	τῇ tē the	κτίσει ktisei created thing	παρὰ para beyond	τὸν ton the

2908.6 verb acc sing masc part aor act	3614.5 rel-pron nom sing masc	1498.4 verb 3sing indic pres act	2109.1 adj nom sing masc	1519.1 prep
κτίσαντα, ktisanta having created,	ὅς hos who	ἐστιν estin is	εὐλογητὸς eulogētos blessed	εἰς eis to

1:23. Four stages of idolatry are listed: worship of man, of birds, of beasts, and at the lowest level, snakes ("creeping things").

Man did not glorify God, but changed His glory by making images that looked like other men and even animals which were beneath him. By this process man sought to deify himself which resulted in degrading his concept of God. The vacuum of refusing the truth was filled with this exchange for idolatry. The glory of God was exchanged for humanism, the truth of God for a lie, and God-given relations of life for that which is unnatural.

Man is directly affected by the way he lives. His emotions, intellect, and body are affected by his rejection of God. By that rejection man has regressed to his own lusts, vile affections, and all unrighteousness.

The willful blindness of man became penal blindness. They would not see; therefore, they could not see. The next verses are not beautiful. Three times the expression "for this cause God gave them up" occurs. He gave them up to uncleanness, to vileness, and to a reprobate mind. The Greek word *paradidōmi* is the same in each instance and means "to give or hand over, to deliver to judgment or prison." Man's deliberate rejection of God brings judicial punishment.

1:24. God gave them over to lusts (*epithumias*), which means desire. In this instance the desire is evil. The picture is one of retrogression, not progression; downward, not upward, from illumination to futility to folly. Moral degradation went to the depths. The passionate desire (*epithumia*) was for forbidden pleasure, a desire that defied all reason. Those who are taken up with such evil, cease to be aware of God and give themselves to shameless cravings.

1:25. The word "changed" occurs in verses 23, 25, and 26. The word can also be translated "exchanged." Men exchanged the glory of the immortal God for images representing and resembling mortal man and birds, animals, and reptiles. They exchanged the truth of God for a lie, and God-ordained natural relations for unnatural functions.

Sin begets sin. When men give themselves to sin, they become slaves to sin. What at first appears to be freedom (e.g., drunkenness, immorality) becomes slavery. Free will eventually fades into oblivion. Man's only freedom is in total worship to God. Bondage is his only alternative: bondage to the lusts of the flesh and to Satan through worship of "the creature."

God has given people a free will. They have the privilege of choice. Choice is essential for a proper relationship between God and man. Without choice there would be neither love nor goodness. God has done everything possible to bring righteousness to men, but if they reject, He cannot make the choice for them. Coerced love is not true love; coerced goodness is not true goodness.

23. And changed the glory of the uncorruptible God: So they exchanged the glory, *Norlie, SEB* . . . and have transformed the splendor of the immortal God, *Williams* . . . transformed the majesty of the imperishable God, *Fenton* . . . of the undying God, *Klingensmith.*

into an image made like to corruptible man: . . . into an Image-likeness of Corruptible Man, *Wilson* . . . for idols graven in the likeness of, *Conybeare* . . . substituted images in the likeness, either of mortal man, *TCNT* . . . into a similitude, *Rheims* . . . for a worthless imitation, *JB* . . . of man, who dies, *Beck.*

and to birds, and fourfooted beasts, and creeping things: . . . reptiles, *Weymouth, Scarlett* . . . and of serpentes, *Tyndale.*

24. Wherefore God also gave them up to uncleanness through the lusts of their own hearts: They became sexually unclean, *SEB* . . . abandoned them in the lusts of their hearts to filthiness, *Fenton* . . . gave them up to live immorally, *Beck* . . . their own depraved cravings, *Weymouth* . . . in the evil trend of their heart's desires, *Williams* . . . in the passionate cravings, *Wuest.*

to dishonour their own bodies between themselves: . . . make a degrading use of their bodies, *TCNT* . . . to bestial profligacy, *Wuest* . . . their bodies be dishonored among them, *Panin* . . . to disgrace their bodies, *Sawyer* . . . to sexual vice, *Moffatt.*

25. Who changed the truth of God into a lie: . . . seeing they had bartered the truth, *Conybeare* . . . changed the veritie of God into lying, *Rheims* . . . they traded the true God for a lie, *Beck* . . . for a false religion, *Wilson.*

and worshipped and served the creature more than the Creator: . . . rendered religious service to the creation, *Wuest* . . . reverenced and worshipped the things made instead of the Maker, *Conybeare* . . . for they had bartered the reality, *Weymouth* . . . neglecting the Creator, *Geneva.*

who is blessed for ever. Amen: . . . who is to be eulogized forever, *Wuest.*

Romans 1:26

3450.8 art acc pl masc τοὺς *tous* the	**163.6** noun acc pl masc αἰῶνας. *aiōnas* ages.	**279.1** partic ἀμήν. *amēn* Amen.	**1217.2** prep **26.** διὰ *dia* Because of	**3642.17** dem- pron sing neu τοῦτο *touto* this	**3722.10** verb 3sing indic aor act παρέδωκεν *paredōken* gave up
840.8 prs-pron acc pl masc αὐτοὺς *autous* them	**3450.5** art sing masc ὁ *ho*	**2296.1** noun nom sing masc θεὸς *theos* God	**1519.1** prep εἰς *eis* to	**3669.3** noun acc pl neu πάθη *pathē* passions	**813.2** noun gen sing fem ἀτιμίας· *atimias* of dishonor,
3614.13 rel- pron nom pl fem αἵ *hai* which	**4885.1** conj τε *te* both	**1056.1** conj γὰρ *gar* for	**2315.2** adj nom pl fem θήλειαι *thēleiai* females	**840.1** prs- pron gen pl αὐτῶν *autōn* their	**3207.1** verb 3pl indic aor act μετήλλαξαν *metēllaxan* changed
3450.12 art acc sing fem τὴν *tēn* the	**5282.1** adj acc sing fem φυσικὴν *phusikēn* natural	**5375.1** noun acc sing fem χρῆσιν *chrēsin* use	**1519.1** prep εἰς *eis* into	**3450.12** art acc sing fem τὴν *tēn* the	**3706.2** prep παρὰ *para* contrary to
5285.4 noun acc sing fem φύσιν· *phusin* nature;	**3532.1** adv **27.** ὁμοίως *homoiōs* in like manner	**4885.1** conj τε *te* and	**2504.1** conj καὶ *kai* also	**3450.7** art pl masc οἱ *hoi* the	**724.2** adj nom pl masc (ἄρρενες *arrhenes* males
728.1 adj nom pl masc [✶ ἄρσενες] *arsenes* [idem]	**856.19** verb nom pl masc part aor act ἀφέντες *aphentes* having left	**3450.12** art acc sing fem τὴν *tēn* the	**5282.1** adj acc sing fem φυσικὴν *phusikēn* natural		**5375.1** noun acc sing fem χρῆσιν *chrēsin* use
3450.10 art gen sing fem τῆς *tēs* of the	**2315.1** adj gen sing fem θηλείας *thēleias* female,	**1559.1** verb 3pl indic aor pass ἐξεκαύθησαν *exekauthēsan* were inflamed	**1706.1** prep ἐν *en* in	**3450.11** art dat sing fem τῇ *tē* the	**3578.1** noun dat sing fem ὀρέξει *orexei* lust
840.1 prs- pron gen pl αὐτῶν *autōn* their	**1519.1** prep εἰς *eis* towards	**238.3** prs-pron acc pl masc ἀλλήλους, *allēlous* one another,	**728.1** adj nom pl masc ἄρσενες *arsenes* males	**1706.1** prep ἐν *en* with	**728.2** adj dat pl masc ἄρσεσιν *arsesin* males
3450.12 art acc sing fem τὴν *tēn* the	**802.1** noun acc sing fem ἀσχημοσύνην *aschēmosunēn* indecency	**2686.5** verb nom pl masc part pres κατεργαζόμενοι, *katergazomenoi* working out,		**2504.1** conj καὶ *kai* and	**3450.12** art acc sing fem τὴν *tēn* the
486.1 noun acc sing fem ἀντιμισθίαν *antimisthian* recompense	**3614.12** rel- pron acc sing fem ἣν *hēn* which	**1158.6** verb 3sing indic imperf act ἔδει *edei* was fit		**3450.10** art gen sing fem τῆς *tēs* of the	**3967.2** noun gen sing fem πλάνης *planēs* error
840.1 prs- pron gen pl αὐτῶν *autōn* their	**1706.1** prep ἐν *en* in	**1431.7** prs- pron dat pl masc ἑαυτοῖς *heautois* themselves	**612.2** verb nom pl masc part pres act ἀπολαμβάνοντες. *apolambanontes* receiving.		**2504.1** conj **28.** καὶ *kai* And

1:26. For the second time we read "God gave them up." This time it was to disgraceful passions. Sexual sins stand out first on the list. These include lesbianism and homosexuality. There are abuses of normal appetites, such as fornication and adultery, but this is a baser sin, for it is perversion. Paul mentions women first which accentuates the abomination of their sin.

The conjunction *te* may be translated "and" or "both" or "even." Here the meaning is best brought out, "for *even* their women . . . ." John Murray has written, "It is the delicacy which belongs to the woman that makes more apparent the degeneracy of homosexual indulgence in their case" (*New International Commentary on the New Testament*, 1:47). Women should be the bulwark of society. When they yield to sinful desires, the home and the nation are doomed. Lost men and women plunged deeper and deeper into the cesspool of shameful iniquity and did so unashamedly. The apostle here uses *thēleiai* for "women" rather than the usual *gunē* and *arsēn* for "men" rather than the usual *anēr*. A literal translation would be "females" and "males." This usage emphasizes the physical obsession with sex, de-emphasizing the emotional, intellectual, and spiritual aspects of a right relationship in marriage according to God's plan.

1:27. All sin is hideous, but the hideousness of sexual perversion brings an inevitable penalty. The threefold expression "God gave them up to uncleanness" describes a judicial abandonment.

The judgment of God on such sin was not arbitrary or capricious. Judgment came because of the refusal to recognize as God the One who revealed himself as deity through creation.

The *New English Bible* translates the latter part of verse 27, "and are paid in their own persons the fitting wages of such perversion." The penalty is to suffer "in their own bodies and personalities the inevitable consequences and penalty of their wrongdoing and going astray, which was (their) fitting retribution" (*The Amplified Bible*).

The transition into deifying man and turning loose animal passions ends in frightening immorality. Licentious practices frequently become entwined in religious practices. When men worship genius, passion, and the lower creation, there is no end to the extremes of sin in which they mire themselves. Sin has a tendency to lead to unnatural practices. Sin breeds sin. Wickedness fosters greater wickedness. Unrestrained licentiousness proceeds to outrageous lengths. The case in point is the homosexual. He leaves the *phusikēn chrēsin* ("natural use") of sex and moves into perversity and deviance. God created male and female sex organs to provide for union in marriage (Genesis 2:21-25). Anatomy clearly reveals the "natural use."

We read that men "burned in their lust one toward another." *Ekkaiō* ("burn") is found nowhere else in Scripture. The aorist passive may be translated "were set ablaze" or "were inflamed." The meaning is that men were "consumed" with the passion of lust for one another. Moral depravity accompanies rejection of God; total debauchery often springs from apostasy.

26. For this cause God gave them up unto vile affections: . . . shameful lusts, *Beck* . . . abandoned them to shameful passion, *Fenton* . . . to dishonorable passions, *RSV, Adams, Wuest, Klingensmith* . . . to degrading passions, *TCNT* . . . to immoral, unnatural drives, *SEB* . . . passions of ignominie, *Rheims.*

for even their women did change the natural use into that which is against nature: . . . exchanged their functions for practices contrary to nature, *Norlie* . . . perverted the natural use to one contrary to nature, *Fenton* . . . indulged in unnatural lust, *Noyes* . . . from natural intercourse, *JB* . . . natural sexual drives, *SEB.*

27. And likewise also the men, leaving the natural use of the woman: . . . disregarding that for which women were intended by nature, *TCNT* . . . leaving the natural enjoyment of the female, *Sawyer* . . . forsook their natural relationships, *Berkeley* . . . abandoning the, *HistNT* . . . neglecting that for which nature intends women, *Weymouth.*

burned in their lust one toward another: . . . were burnt up with their furious lust, *Wilson* . . . consumed by flaming passion, *Williams.*

men with men working that which is unseemly: . . . men perpetrating shameless acts with their own sex, *Moffatt* . . . males with males, *SEB* . . . working filthiness, *Wesley* . . . men perpetrating unseemliness, *HistNT* . . . practicing shameful vice, *Weymouth, Williams* . . . doing the shameful act with men, *Beck* . . . wroght filthines, *Geneva.*

and receiving in themselves that recompense of their error which was meet: . . . getting an appropriate reward for their perversion, *Beck* . . . on account of their wrong behavior, *Berkeley* . . . the inevitable punishment, *TCNT* . . . the full penalty that their error deserves, *Adams* . . . the rewarde of their erroure, *Tyndale* . . . the consequences for this error, *SEB* . . . because of their deviation, *Wuest* . . . for their own foul acts, *Klingensmith* . . . of their perversity, *Moffatt.*

Romans 1:29

2503.1 conj	3620.2 partic	1375.10 verb 3pl indic aor act	3450.6 art acc sing masc	2296.4 noun acc sing masc	2174.29 verb inf pres act
καθὼς	οὐκ	ἐδοκίμασαν	τὸν	θεὸν	ἔχειν
kathōs	ouk	edokimasan	ton	theon	echein
just as	not	they did approve		God	to have

1706.1 prep	1907.3 noun dat sing fem	3722.10 verb 3sing indic aor act	840.8 prs-pron acc pl masc	3450.5 art sing masc	2296.1 noun nom sing masc
ἐν	ἐπιγνώσει,	παρέδωκεν	αὐτοὺς	ὁ	θεὸς
en	epignōsei,	paredōken	autous	ho	theos
in	knowledge,	gave up	them		God

1519.1 prep	95.2 adj acc sing masc	3426.4 noun acc sing masc	4020.20 verb inf pres act	3450.17 art pl neu	3231.1 partic
εἰς	ἀδόκιμον	νοῦν,	ποιεῖν	τὰ	μὴ
eis	adokimon	noun,	poiein	ta	mē
to	a worthless	mind,	to do	the things	not

2492.2 verb acc pl neu part pres act	3997.31 verb acc pl masc part perf pass	3820.11 adj dat sing fem	92.3 noun dat sing fem
καθήκοντα,	29. πεπληρωμένους	πάσῃ	ἀδικίᾳ,
kathēkonta,	peplērōmenous	pasē	adikia,
fitting:	Having been filled	with all	unrighteousness,

29.a.Txt: 020L,044,byz. Var: 01אּ,02A,03B,04C 018K,33,sa.bo.Gries Lach,Treg,Alf,Word Tisc,We/Ho,Weis,Sod UBS/⋆

4061.3 noun dat sing fem	4049.2 noun dat sing fem	3984.3 noun dat sing fem	2520.3 noun dat sing fem	3194.3 adj acc pl masc
⌜a πορνείᾳ, ⌝	πονηρίᾳ,	πλεονεξίᾳ,	κακίᾳ·	μεστοὺς
porneia,	ponēria,	pleonexia,	kakia	mestous
fornication,	wickedness,	covetousness,	malice;	full

5192.2 noun gen sing masc	5245.1 noun gen sing masc	2038.2 noun gen sing fem	1382.2 noun gen sing masc	2521.1 noun gen sing fem
φθόνου,	φόνου,	ἔριδος,	δόλου,	κακοηθείας·
phthonou,	phonou,	eridos,	dolou,	kakoētheias
of envy,	murder,	strife,	guile,	evil dispositions;

5423.1 noun acc pl masc	2607.1 adj acc pl masc	2295.1 adj acc pl masc	5037.2 noun acc pl masc
ψιθυριστάς,	30. καταλάλους,	θεοστυγεῖς.	ὑβριστάς,
psithuristas	katalalous	theostugeis	hubristas,
whisperers,	slanderers,	hateful to God,	insolent,

5082.3 adj acc pl masc	211.2 noun acc pl masc	2164.1 noun acc pl masc	2527.1 adj gen pl
ὑπερηφάνους,	ἀλαζόνας,	ἐφευρετὰς	κακῶν,
huperēphanous	alazonas	epheuretas	kakōn,
proud,	boasting,	inventors	of evil things,

1112.3 noun dat pl masc	541.2 adj pl masc	795.2 adj acc pl masc	796.1 adj acc pl masc
γονεῦσιν	ἀπειθεῖς,	31. ἀσυνέτους,	ἀσυνθέτους,
goneusin	apeitheis,	asunetous	asunthetous
to parents	disobedient,	without understanding,	treacherous,

31.a.Txt: 04C,06D-corr 018K,020L,025P,byz. Var: 01אּ-org,02A,03B 06D-org,bo.Lach,Treg Alf,Word,Tisc,We/Ho Weis,Sod,UBS/⋆

788.2 adj acc pl masc	780.1 adj acc pl	413.1 adj acc pl masc
ἀστόργους,	⌜a ἀσπόνδους, ⌝	ἀνελεήμονας·
astorgous	aspondous	aneleēmonas
without natural affection,	irreconcilable,	unmerciful;

3610.2 rel-pron nom pl masc	3450.16 art sing neu	1339.1 noun sing neu	3450.2 art gen sing	2296.2 noun gen sing masc
32. οἵτινες	τὸ	δικαίωμα	τοῦ	θεοῦ
hoitines	to	dikaiōma	tou	theou
who	the	righteous judgment		of God

1:28. Moral perversion also brings mental perversion. As men did not see fit to acknowledge God, He gave them up to a "reprobate mind." The word "reprobate" (*adokimion*) means "rejected after testing." Since men rejected God, He rejected them. William's translation reads, "And so, as they did not approve of fully recognizing God any longer, God gave them up to minds that He did not approve."

God does not compel or entice men to evil. Responsibility rests with men. They give themselves to uncleanness and God gives them up to the judgment of their sin. The retributive act of God is a penal infliction of justice and punishment consistent with the holiness of God.

1:29-31. Paul writes of men who had God-rejected minds, unable to distinguish between right and wrong. Conybeare and Howson translate the preceding verse: "And as they thought fit to cast out the acknowledgement of God, God gave them over to an outcast mind, to do the things that are unseemly" (p.501).

These men were given over to think thoughts, do deeds, and live lives for which they were not created. Man was created in God's image and for God's glory. How he has fallen!

The last verses of this chapter list a catalog of sins which are the results of total depravity. The record presents a picture of the heathen world, but it is also a portrayal of the headlines of today's newspaper. God says man is filled with these sins—filled without limit—whether he belongs to a savage tribe or to high society.

Twenty-three frightful sins are listed. The first, "all unrighteousness," is a generic term. It is the genus that spawns all the other sins that follow. These are sins of thought, word, and deed. They are both against one's self and against one's neighbor. Some sins are inward, others are outward.

Some of the sins are wrong attitudes toward God, the beginning point of all evil. When men are destitute of a capacity for spiritual things, they become haters of God and constantly discover new evils. They are just plain wicked.

Sins of the spirit are also listed. They include greed, envy, pride, haughtiness, boastfulness. Evils in the area of human relationship are cataloged, including secret gossip and open slander. Deceitfulness, craftiness, faithlessness to one's word, sowing of discord, feelings of ill will, and holding of grudges are on the list. Abusiveness to others, lack of mercy, an unforgiving attitude, and a spirit of harming others are a part of the lurid picture.

Sins concerning the family include the absence of natural love and disobedience to parents. Character is defiled, conduct is defiled, conversation is defiled, companionship is defiled. The list of these sins is introduced by *peplērōnemous* from *plēroō* which means "fill to the full." All rules of conduct are broken, every kind of injustice is practiced, all kinds of new mischief are invented. Loyalty to parents, conscience, and fidelity to one's word are lacking. Natural affection and pity for others are totally absent.

28. And even as they did not like to retain God in [their] knowledge: . . . refused to see it was rational to acknowledge God, *Beck*.

God gave them over to a reprobate mind: . . . to a disapproved mind, *Adams* . . . vnto a lewde mynde, *Geneva*.

to do those things which are not convenient: . . . they do what is not fitting, *Confraternity* . . . they lived immorally, *Beck*.

29. Being filled with all unrighteousness: . . . crammed with, *Fenton* . . . all kinds of wrong, *SEB* . . . they overflow with every sort of evil-doing, *Williams*.
  fornication:
  wickedness: . . . maliciousness, *Wesley*.
  covetousness:
  maliciousness: . . . viciousness, *Moffatt*.
  full of envy: . . . crammed with, *Berkeley* . . . filled to the brim with, *Moffatt* . . . jealousy, *TEV*.
  murder:
  debate: . . . wrangling, *Wuest* . . . quarreling, *Beck*.
  deceit: . . . treachery, *Beck*.
  malignity: . . . spite, *TCNT*.
  whisperers: They gossip, *Beck*.

30. Backbiters: . . . open slanderers, *Williams*.
  haters of God: . . . loathed by God, *Moffatt*, *HistNT*.
  despiteful: . . . outrageous, *Conybeare* . . . insolent, *Wuest*.
  proud: . . . haughty, *Weymouth*.
  boasters: . . . braggarts, *HistNT* . . . swaggerers, *Wuest*.
  inventors of evil things: . . . devisers of evil, *HistNT* . . . new forms of sin, *Weymouth*.
  disobedient to parents:

31. Without understanding: . . . senseless, *Adams* . . . bereft of wisdom, *Conybeare*.
  covenantbreakers: They break their promises, *Beck* . . . untrue to their word, *HistNT*.
  without natural affection: . . . heartless, *Norlie*.
  implacable: . . . ruthless, *Norlie* . . . callous, *Moffatt*.
  unmerciful: . . . heartless, *SEB* . . . without human pity, *Weymouth*.

Romans 2:1

1906.10 verb nom pl masc part aor act	3617.1 conj	3450.7 art pl masc	3450.17 art pl neu	4955.14 dem-pron acc pl neu	4097.9 verb nom pl masc part pres act
ἐπιγνόντες,	ὅτι	οἱ	τὰ	τοιαῦτα	πράσσοντες
epignontes	hoti	hoi	ta	toiauta	prassontes
having known,	that	the	the	such things	doing

510.3 adj nom pl masc	2265.2 noun gen sing masc	1498.7 verb 3pl indic pres act	3620.3 partic	3303.1 adv	840.16 prs-pron pl neu
ἄξιοι	θανάτου	εἰσίν,	οὐ	μόνον	αὐτὰ
axioi	thanatou	eisin	ou	monon	auta
worthy	of death	are,	not	only	same things

4020.3 verb 3pl indic pres act	233.2 conj	2504.1 conj	4759.3 verb 3pl indic pres act	3450.4 art dat pl
ποιοῦσιν,	ἀλλὰ	καὶ	συνευδοκοῦσιν	τοῖς
poiousin	alla	kai	suneudokousin	tois
are practicing,	but	also	are consenting	to the

4097.10 verb dat pl masc part pres act	1346.1 conj	377.1 adj nom sing masc	1498.3 verb 2sing indic pres act
πράσσουσιν.	**2:1.** Διὸ	ἀναπολόγητος	εἶ,
prassousin	Dio	anapologētos	ei
doing.	Wherefore	inexcusable	you are,

5434.1 intrj	442.5 noun voc sing masc	3820.6 adj sing masc	3450.5 art sing masc	2892.8 verb sing masc part pres act	1706.1 prep
ὦ	ἄνθρωπε,	πᾶς	ὁ	κρίνων·	ἐν
ō	anthrōpe	pas	ho	krinōn	en
O	man,	everyone	the	judging,	in

3614.3 rel-pron dat sing	1056.1 conj	2892.4 verb 2sing indic pres act	3450.6 art acc sing masc	2066.1 adj sing	4427.4 prs-pron acc 2sing masc
ᾧ	γὰρ	κρίνεις	τὸν	ἕτερον,	σεαυτὸν
hō	gar	krineis	ton	heteron	seauton
which	for	you judge	the	other,	yourself

2602.2 verb 2sing indic pres act	3450.17 art pl neu	1056.1 conj	840.16 prs-pron pl neu	4097.2 verb 2sing indic pres act	3450.5 art sing masc
κατακρίνεις·	τὰ	γὰρ	αὐτὰ	πράσσεις	ὁ
katakrineis	ta	gar	auta	prasseis	ho
you condemn:	the	for	same things	you do	the

2892.8 verb sing masc part pres act	3471.5 verb 1pl indic perf act	1156.2 conj	3617.1 conj	3450.16 art sing neu	2890.1 noun sing neu
κρίνων.	**2.** οἴδαμεν	δὲ	ὅτι	τὸ	κρίμα
krinōn	oidamen	de	hoti	to	krima
judging.	We know	but	that	to	judgment

3450.2 art gen sing	2296.2 noun gen sing masc	1498.4 verb 3sing indic pres act	2567.3 prep	223.4 noun acc sing fem	1894.3 prep
τοῦ	θεοῦ	ἐστιν	κατὰ	ἀλήθειαν	ἐπὶ
tou	theou	estin	kata	alētheian	epi
of God	is	according to	truth	upon

3450.8 art acc pl masc	3450.17 art pl neu	4955.14 dem-pron acc pl neu	4097.11 verb acc pl masc part pres act	3023.3 verb 2sing indic pres
τοὺς	τὰ	τοιαῦτα	πράσσοντας.	**3.** λογίζῃ
tous	ta	toiauta	prassontas	logizē
the	the	such things	doing.	Reckon you

1156.2 conj	3642.17 dem-pron sing neu	5434.1 intrj	442.5 noun voc sing masc	3450.5 art sing masc	2892.8 verb sing masc part pres act
δὲ	τοῦτο,	ὦ	ἄνθρωπε,	ὁ	κρίνων
de	touto	ō	anthrōpe	ho	krinōn
and	this,	O	man,	the	judging

1:32. Here the climax is reached. This verse sums up all that has been written, beginning with verse 18. The most degraded persons are not destitute of the knowledge of God and of His righteous judgments. God's wrath has been revealed to man, and yet man ignores His judgment. Man goes all out in iniquity, revels in it, boasts about it, and has pleasure in others who do the same. This is the climax of sin. Man may deny the accusation and try to evade it, but man is guilty and without excuse. Degeneracy and disaster go hand in hand.

The rebellion of fallen men is epitomized in that they find pleasure in iniquity. Iniquity is most prevalent when it is not controlled by the disapproval of others, but rather it receives approbation and applause. One has only to observe the plots of popular entertainment to know that unregenerate men love sin as pigs love mud and dogs love their vomit.

Those who enjoy seeing others sin show that they hate their fellowman, because they know that such sin risks damnation. Rebellious human beings are not only bent on damning themselves but also stay busy seeing to it that others will also be damned. Thus, they judge themselves worthy of eternal death.

2:1-3. After charging the Gentiles with sin and guilt in chapter 1, Paul now speaks to the Jew. The Gentiles who rejected God's revelation of himself in nature were "without excuse," but the Jews who had God's revelation in the Law were also "inexcusable." While the Jews are not named earlier in the chapter, it is evident from verse 17 and on that the principles of divine judgment (2:1-16) are also applied to the Jew (2:17-24) and his covenant status (2:25-29).

The Jewish moralists were as guilty of *practicing* sin as were the Gentile heathen (1:18-32). The main differences were in the degree of knowledge possessed by each group and in the hypocrisy of the moralists. While the pagans openly approved of the sins of others, the moralists pronounced judgment and pretended to hate sins. Fallen man can no more stop sinning than he can stop breathing. All God asks is that he humbly accept the One who saves from sin. The common usage of "inexcusable" (*anapologētos*) came to mean "defenseless." The self-righteous man is defenseless. "Judgment" (*krina*) has the basic meaning of decision, and as used here indicates a judicial verdict with the sense of a sentence of condemnation.

The emphatic meaning of "thou" is "thou, of all men." This is an expansion of the revelation of the wrath of God to include another class of men, namely, "every man who passes judgment." The self-righteous moralist represented by the Jew is as guilty as the idolatrist Gentile. They practice or do (*prassō*) the same things that they condemn. The self-righteous moralist knows neither God's holiness nor man's sinfulness. The sin of judging and boasting is born of self-justification and indicates an unwillingness to recognize God's condemnation of all that we are as fallen men.

Man's judgment can only be partial, for he does not have all the facts. Paul describes in this chapter four simple principles upon

32. Who knowing the judgment of God: ... though knowing the judicial decision of God, *Scarlett* ... knowing the righteous sentence, *Clementson*.

that they which commit such things are worthy of death: ... deserve death, *Sawyer*.

not only do the same, but have pleasure in them that do them: ... and what is worse, *JB* ... even give their approval to those, *Berkeley* ... but they also that consent to them, *Douay* ... but heartily approve of those who practice them, *Adams* ... but also on terms of intimacy with those who indulge in them, *TCNT* ... but even encourage and applaud others, *Weymouth* ... but are even well pleased, *Scarlett* ... but also favour them, *Geneva* ... but delight in their fellowship with the sinners, *Conybeare*.

1. Therefore thou art inexcusable, O man, whosoever thou art that judgest: So no matter who you are, *JB* ... you have no excuse for condemning others, *Norlie* ... who set yourself up as a judge, *TCNT*.

for wherein thou judgest another, thou condemnest thyself: ... thou art passing sentence, *Scarlett* ... thou judgest thy neighbour, *Alford*.

for thou that judgest doest the same things: You, the judge, are habitually practising, *Montgomery* ... the same things that you are condemning! *SEB* ... since you behave no differently, *JB* ... indulge in the very same practices, *TCNT*.

2. But we are sure that the judgment of God is according to truth against them which commit such things: We know that the doom of God, *HistNT* ... God's judgement falls unerringly, *TCNT* ... God's judgment justly falls, *Williams* ... will be factual and impartial, *Norlie* ... against them who practise such things, *Wesley*.

3. And thinkest thou this, O man, that judgest them which do such things, and doest the same: But, mister, *SEB* ... who condemn those practicing, *Berkeley*.

3450.8 art acc pl masc	3450.17 art pl neu	4955.14 dem- pron acc pl neu	4097.11 verb acc pl masc part pres act	2504.1 conj	4020.15 verb sing masc part pres act
τοὺς	τὰ	τοιαῦτα	πράσσοντας	καὶ	ποιῶν
tous	ta	toiauta	prassontas	kai	poiōn
the	the	such things	doing,	and	practicing

840.16 prs- pron pl neu	3617.1 conj	4622.1 prs- pron nom 2sing	1614.5 verb 2sing indic fut mid	3450.16 art sing neu	2890.1 noun sing neu
αὐτά,	ὅτι	σὺ	ἐκφεύξῃ	τὸ	κρίμα
auta	hoti	su	ekpheuxē	to	krima
them,	that	you	shall escape	the	judgment

3450.2 art gen sing	2296.2 noun gen sing masc	2211.1 conj	3450.2 art gen sing	4009.2 noun gen sing masc	3450.10 art gen sing fem
τοῦ	θεοῦ;	**4.** ἢ	τοῦ	πλούτου	τῆς
tou	theou	ē	tou	ploutou	tēs
of	God?	or	the	riches	of the

5379.2 noun gen sing fem	840.3 prs- pron gen sing	2504.1 conj	3450.10 art gen sing fem	460.1 noun gen sing fem	2504.1 conj
χρηστότητος	αὐτοῦ	καὶ	τῆς	ἀνοχῆς	καὶ
chrēstotētos	autou	kai	tēs	anochēs	kai
kindness	his	and	the	forbearance	and

3450.10 art gen sing fem	3087.2 noun gen sing fem	2675.1 verb 2sing indic pres act	49.7 verb nom sing masc part pres act	3617.1 conj
τῆς	μακροθυμίας	καταφρονεῖς,	ἀγνοῶν	ὅτι
tēs	makrothumias	kataphroneis	agnoōn	hoti
the	long suffering	despise you,	not knowing	that

3450.16 art sing neu	5378.3 adj nom sing neu	3450.2 art gen sing	2296.2 noun gen sing masc	1519.1 prep	3211.2 noun acc sing fem	4622.4 prs- pron acc 2sing
τὸ	χρηστὸν	τοῦ	θεοῦ	εἰς	μετάνοιάν	σε
to	chrēston	tou	theou	eis	metanoian	se
the	kindness		of God	to	repentance	you

70.2 verb 3sing indic pres act	2567.3 prep	1156.2 conj	3450.12 art acc sing fem	4498.1 noun acc sing fem	4622.2 prs- pron gen 2sing
ἄγει;	**5.** κατὰ	δὲ	τὴν	σκληρότητά	σου
agei	kata	de	tēn	sklērotēta	sou
leads?	according to	but	the	hardness	your

2504.1 conj	277.1 adj acc sing fem	2559.4 noun acc sing fem	2320.1 verb 2sing indic pres act	4427.2 prs-pron dat 2sing masc
καὶ	ἀμετανόητον	καρδίαν	θησαυρίζεις	σεαυτῷ
kai	ametanoēton	kardian	thēsaurizeis	seautō
and	unrepentant	heart	treasure up	to yourself

3572.4 noun acc sing fem	1706.1 prep	2232.3 noun dat sing fem	3572.2 noun gen sing fem	2504.1 conj	597.2 noun gen sing fem
ὀργὴν	ἐν	ἡμέρᾳ	ὀργῆς	καὶ	ἀποκαλύψεως
orgēn	en	hēmera	orgēs	kai	apokalupseōs
wrath	in	a day	of wrath	and	revelation

1335.1 noun gen sing fem	3450.2 art gen sing	2296.2 noun gen sing masc	3614.5 rel-pron nom sing masc	586.17 verb 3sing indic fut act
δικαιοκρισίας	τοῦ	θεοῦ.	**6.** ὃς	ἀποδώσει
dikaiokrisias	tou	theou	hos	apodōsei
of righteous judgment	the	of God,	who	will render

1524.4 adj dat sing masc	2567.3 prep	3450.17 art pl neu	2024.4 noun pl neu	840.3 prs- pron gen sing	3450.4 art dat pl
ἑκάστῳ	κατὰ	τὰ	ἔργα	αὐτοῦ.	**7.** τοῖς
hekastō	kata	ta	erga	autou	tois
to each	according to	the	works	his:	the

which men are judged: "according to truth" (verse 2); "according to his deeds" (verse 6); "there is no respect of persons with God" (verse 11); "according to my gospel" (verse 16).

God's judgment is made "according to truth" (*kata alētheian*), according to the facts of the case, according to reality. It is made by God's standards. The hypocrite is indignant at other peoples' failure and indulgent of his own. The answer to the rhetorical question, "Do you think you will escape the judgment of God?" is an emphatic, "No."

2:4. The word "or" introduces the alternative. Is your estimate of God's goodness such that you have license to sin? Three words stand out for those who are trifling with the mercy of God.

The Greek term here for "goodness" is *chrēston* ("loving kindness") rather than the usual *agathos* ("rebuke, discipline").

"Forbearance" (*anochē*) is the word for a cessation of hostility, but with a limit, giving an opportunity for repentance.

"Long-suffering," or patience, (*makrothumia*) expresses patience with people. God's kindness is always active in the pursuit of repentance.

2:5. Verses 4 and 5 set forth sharp contrasts: repentance and impenitence, despising riches of goodness and treasuring up wrath. God's goodness is manifested to lead (present tense in the Greek) to repentance; it is a continuing activity.

As men continue to despise God's goodness, they amass an accumulation of divine wrath. Day by day a new deposit of wickedness is stored up for judgment in a coming day.

The phrase "*impenitent* heart" (*ametanoētos*) occurs in no other New Testament passage. It means "unrepentant." This is the apex of sin.

"Treasurest" (*thēsaurus*) had the meaning of a place of safekeeping, a treasury or a storehouse. As the word developed it came to mean the treasure which was stored. But the word here is the verb *thēsaurizō*. It has the basic meaning of laying up, keeping in store, of storing. And what is stored up? God's wrath. His wrath is the abhorrence of wrong. His holiness and character require that unrepented and unforgiven sin must come under the judgment of His wrath.

2:6,7. The second principle of judgment is "according to his deeds." This refers to the justice of the judgment, not to the divine provision of eternal life. The passage does not teach that salvation is earned by good deeds. Eternal life is not attained by patient continuing in well-doing. That would be a violation of the whole tenor of Scripture. Salvation is by faith, judgment is according to works.

that thou shalt escape the judgment of God?: ... that you will elude, *Montgomery* ... do you reckon upon escaping, *TCNT* ... schalt ascape the dome of god? *Wyclif*.

4. Or despisest thou the riches of his goodness and forbearance and longsuffering: Or perhaps you despise his great kindness, tolerance, *TEV, SEB* ... Or do you play fast and loose, *Klingensmith* ... mistake the wealth of His mercy and the gentleness of His forbearance, *Fenton* ... do you underestimate His wealth of kindness, *Berkeley* ... Or do you think lightly of, *TCNT* ... are you slighting all his forbearance, and patience? *Moffatt*.

not knowing that the goodness of God leadeth thee to repentance?: ... the kyndnes of God, *Geneva* ... to get you to feel sorry for your sins? *Beck* ... invites you to a reformation? *Campbell* ... leads you to a change of mind? *Sawyer* ... to a change of heart, *SEB*.

5. But after thy hardness and impenitent heart: Your stubborn refusal to repent, *JB* ... your perverse and unchanging heart, *Fenton* ... But according to your obstinate, *Wuest* ... you stubbornly refuse to turn from sin, *Beck* ... harde herte that cannot repent, *Tyndale*.

treasurest up unto thyself wrath: ... you are storing up, *RSV* ... heapest vnto thy selfe, *Cranmer* ... heapest the togedder the treasure of wrath, *Tyndale*.

against the day of wrath and revelation of the righteous judgment of God: ... against a day of fury, *Fenton* ... when God will reveal the justice of His judgments, *Norlie* ... the just doom of God is revealed, *Moffatt* ... of the just judgment, *Confraternity*.

6. Who will render to every man according to his deeds: God will pay back, *SEB* ... since He will pay every person exactly what his deeds deserve, *Adams* ... He will make an award corresponding to his actions, *Weymouth*

3173.1 conj	2567.2 prep	5119.4 noun acc sing fem	2024.2 noun gen sing neu	18.2 adj sing	1385.4 noun acc sing fem	2504.1 conj
μὲν	καθ'	ὑπομονὴν	ἔργου	ἀγαθοῦ,	δόξαν	καὶ
men	kath'	hupomonēn	ergou	agathou	doxan	kai
	with	endurance	in work	good,	glory	and

4940.4 noun acc sing fem	2504.1 conj	854.2 noun acc sing fem	2195.2 verb dat pl masc part pres act	2205.4 noun acc sing fem	164.1 adj sing
τιμὴν	καὶ	ἀφθαρσίαν	ζητοῦσιν,	ζωὴν	αἰώνιον.
timēn	kai	aphtharsian	zētousin	zōēn	aiōnion
honor	and	incorruptibility	seeking	life	eternal.

3450.4 art dat pl	1156.2 conj	1523.1 prep gen	2036.2 noun gen sing fem	2504.1 conj	540.1 verb dat pl masc part pres act
8. τοῖς	δὲ	ἐξ	ἐριθείας,	καὶ	ἀπειθοῦσιν
tois	de	ex	eritheias	kai	apeithousin
To the	but	of	self-seeking,	and	disobeying

8.a.Txt: 01א-corr,02A
06D-corr,018K,020L
025P,byz.Sod
Var: 01א-org,03B
06D-org,Lach,Treg,Tisc
We/Ho,Weis,UBS/✱

3173.1 conj	3450.11 art dat sing fem	223.3 noun dat sing fem	3844.23 verb dat pl masc part pres pass	1156.2 conj	3450.11 art dat sing fem
(ᵃ μὲν)	τῇ	ἀληθείᾳ,	πειθομένοις	δὲ	τῇ
men	tē	alētheia	peithomenois	de	tē
	the	truth,	obeying	but	the

92.3 noun dat sing fem	2349.1 noun nom sing masc	2504.1 conj	3572.1 noun nom sing fem	3572.1 noun nom sing fem	2504.1 conj
ἀδικίᾳ,	(θυμός	καὶ	ὀργὴ,	[✱ ὀργὴ	καὶ
adikia	thumos	kai	orgē	orgē	kai
unrighteousness	indignation	and	wrath,	wrath	and

2349.1 noun nom sing masc	2324.1 noun nom sing fem	2504.1 conj	4581.1 noun nom sing fem	1894.3 prep	3820.12 adj acc sing fem
θυμός,]	9. θλῖψις	καὶ	στενοχωρία,	ἐπὶ	πᾶσαν
thumos	thlipsis	kai	stenochōria	epi	pasan
indignation,]	tribulation	and	anguish,	on	every

5425.4 noun acc sing fem	442.2 noun gen sing masc	3450.2 art gen sing	2686.4 verb gen sing masc part pres	3450.16 art sing neu
ψυχὴν	ἀνθρώπου	τοῦ	κατεργαζομένου	τὸ
psuchēn	anthrōpou	tou	katergazomenou	to
soul	of man	the	working out	to the

2527.7 adj sing neu	2428.7 name-adj gen masc	4885.1 conj	4270.1 adv	2504.1 conj	1659.2 name gen sing masc
κακόν,	Ἰουδαίου	τε	πρῶτον	καὶ	Ἕλληνος
kakon	Ioudaiou	te	prōton	kai	Hellēnos
evil,	of Jew	both	first	and	of Greek;

1385.1 noun nom sing fem	1156.2 conj	2504.1 conj	4940.1 noun nom sing fem	2504.1 conj	1503.1 noun nom sing fem	3820.3 adj dat sing
10. δόξα	δὲ	καὶ	τιμὴ	καὶ	εἰρήνη	παντὶ
doxa	de	kai	timē	kai	eirēnē	panti
glory	but	and	honor	and	peace	to everyone

3450.3 art dat sing	2021.9 verb dat sing masc part pres	3450.16 art sing neu	18.3 adj sing	2428.1 name-adj dat sing masc	4885.1 conj
τῷ	ἐργαζομένῳ	τὸ	ἀγαθόν,	Ἰουδαίῳ	τε
tō	ergazomenō	to	agathon	Ioudaiō	te
the	working	the	good,	to Jew	both

4270.1 adv	2504.1 conj	1659.3 name dat sing masc	3620.3 partic	1056.1 conj	1498.4 verb 3sing indic pres act
πρῶτον	καὶ	Ἕλληνι·	11. οὐ	γὰρ	ἐστιν
prōton	kai	Hellēni	ou	gar	estin
first,	and	to Greek:	not	for	there is

Hupomonē is translated "patience" 28 times in the King James Version. In 2 Corinthians 1:6 it reads "enduring." It means "patient waiting" in 2 Thessalonians 1:4, and in Romans 2:7 it is "patient continuance." Other translations render the word "steadfastness," "endurance," "perseverance," "patiently enduring," and "enduring patiently." See *Various Versions. Makrothumia* refers to the long-suffering and patience of God. *Hupomonē* speaks of the patience of the believer. The steadfastness of patience is never passive. It is not mere endurance; it is perseverance in good work that is active and positive.

Aphtharsia, translated "immortality" in the King James Version, comes from the verb *phtheirō* which means "destroy, corrupt, spoil." The basic meaning is "incorruption."

2:8. The word translated "contentious" may also be rendered "strife," "self-seeking," "factious," "governed by selfish ambition." "Do not obey the truth" can be rendered "disloyal to the truth," "always resisting the right." Such persons are responsive only to what is wrong and yield to the wrong.

The last three words of the verse, *thumos kai orgē*, express God's abhorrence of sin and His hot anger, His fury that flows out in judgment.

2:9. *Thlipsis*, from the verb *thlibō*, is usually translated "tribulation," but on occasion it is "affliction." The verb means to "press," such as pressing out grapes in a winepress. Thus tribulation denotes the heavy pressures that make one almost despair of life. The tribulation referred to here is that of those who "do not obey the truth." The *New English Bible* states, "There will be grinding misery." Goodspeed's translation is "crushing distress."

Stenochōria, translated "anguish," is from *stenos* ("narrow") and *chōra* ("space"). One commentator defines it as "torturing confinement." How true the Scripture, "The way of transgressors is hard" (Proverbs 13:15). The apostle speaks of treasuring up "wrath against the day of wrath" (Romans 2:5) and "he that soweth to his flesh shall of the flesh reap corruption" (Galatians 6:8).

2:10. It may seem difficult to reconcile a judgment according to works with justification by faith. But as human society provides punishment for the evildoer and rewards for the one who does good, so it is in God's society. Grace through faith alone saves, but there is a reward in proportion to work. The fact is that no human being can "work good" in the absolute sense. Jesus asked, "Why callest thou me *good*? none is good, save one, that is, God" (Luke 18:19). *One* bad act spoils all "good" acts (James 2:10). Man's good works can come only by the life of Christ within.

... according to his works, *Confraternity* ... what his actions deserve, *TCNT*.

7. To them who by patient continuance in well doing seek for glory and honour and immortality, eternal life: ... by patiently doing good, *Moffatt* ... by perseverance in doing good...to attain, *Norlie* ... in good works, *PNT* ... of persistent right-doing, *Weymouth* ... seek rectification, *Fenton* ... enduring Life, *TCNT* ... the imperishable eternal life, *HistNT* ... and life with no end, *SEB* ... and incorruptibility, *Wuest* ... and incorruption, *ASV*.

8. But unto them that are contentious: ... for the unsubmissive, *JB* ... to those who are divisive, *Adams* ... to those who factiously disobey, *HistNT* ... vnto them that are rebelles, *Cranmer* ... Other people are selfish and reject, *TEV* ... to them who are obstinate, *PNT* ... that seek their own, *Alford*.
and do not obey the truth, but obey unrighteousness: ... and refuse to listen to the truth, *Beck* ... but assent to iniquity, *Confraternity*.
indignation and wrath:

9. Tribulation and anguish: Affliction and anxiety, *Berkeley* ... Distress and calamity, *HistNT* ... Affliction and Distress on every Soul, *Wilson* ... Affliction and anguish will come, *Adams* ... crushing suffering and awful anguish, *Williams*.
upon every soul of man that doeth evil: ... who deliberately does wrong, *Weymouth* ... that perpetrates evil, *HistNT* ... and yielding to the wrong, *Williams*.
of the Jew first, and also of the Gentile:

10. But glory, honour, and peace, to every man that worketh good: But distinction and honor, *Berkeley* ... shall come prayse, *Cranmer* ... shall be awarded, *Confraternity*.
to the Jew first, and also to the Gentile: ... also a non-Jew, *SEB*.

4240.1 noun nom sing fem ‛ προσωποληψία *prosōpolēpsia* respect of persons	**4240.3** noun nom sing fem [✶ προσωπολημψία] *prosōpolēmpsia* [idem]	**3706.2** prep παρὰ *para* with	**3450.3** art dat sing τῷ *tō*

2296.3 noun dat sing masc θεῷ. *theō* God.	**3607.2** rel- pron nom pl masc **12.** ὅσοι *hosoi* As many as	**1056.1** conj γὰρ *gar* for	**457.1** adv ἀνόμως *anomōs* without law	**262.11** verb indic aor act ἥμαρτον, *hēmarton* sinned,	**457.1** adv ἀνόμως *anomōs* without law

2504.1 conj καὶ *kai* also	**616.29** verb 3pl indic fut mid ἀπολοῦνται· *apolountai* shall perish;	**2504.1** conj καὶ *kai* and	**3607.2** rel- pron nom pl masc ὅσοι *hosoi* as many as	**1706.1** prep ἐν *en* in	**3414.3** noun dat sing masc νόμῳ *nomō* law

262.11 verb indic aor act ἥμαρτον, *hēmarton* sinned,	**1217.2** prep διὰ *dia* by	**3414.2** noun gen sing masc νόμου *nomou* law	**2892.41** verb 3pl indic fut pass κριθήσονται, *krithēsontai* shall be judged,	**3620.3** partic **13.** οὐ *ou* not	**1056.1** conj γὰρ *gar* for

3450.7 art pl masc οἱ *hoi* the	**200.2** noun nom pl masc ἀκροαταὶ *akroatai* hearers	**3450.2** art gen sing ‛ᵃ τοῦ ‛ *tou* of the	**3414.2** noun gen sing masc νόμου *nomou* law	**1337.6** adj nom pl masc δίκαιοι *dikaioi* just	**3706.2** prep παρὰ *para* with

3450.3 art dat sing ‛ᵇ τῷ ‛ *tō*	**2296.3** noun dat sing masc θεῷ, *theō* God,	**233.1** conj ἀλλ᾽ *all'* but	**3450.7** art pl masc οἱ *hoi* the	**4023.2** noun nom pl masc ποιηταὶ *poiētai* doers	**3450.2** art gen sing ‛ᶜ τοῦ ‛ *tou* of the

3414.2 noun gen sing masc νόμου *nomou* law	**1338.25** verb 3pl indic fut pass δικαιωθήσονται. *dikaiōthēsontai* shall be justified.	**3615.1** conj **14.** Ὅταν *Hotan* When	**1056.1** conj γὰρ *gar* for	**1477.4** noun pl neu ἔθνη *ethnē* nations

3450.17 art pl neu τὰ *ta* the	**3231.1** partic μὴ *mē* not	**3414.4** noun acc sing masc νόμον *nomon* law	**2174.15** verb part pres act ἔχοντα *echonta* having	**5285.3** noun dat sing fem φύσει *phusei* by nature	**3450.17** art pl neu τὰ *ta* the things

3450.2 art gen sing τοῦ *tou* of the	**3414.2** noun gen sing masc νόμου *nomou* law	**4020.8** verb 3sing subj pres act ‛ ποιῇ, *poiē* practice,	**4020.10** verb 3pl subj pres act [ᵃ✶ ποιῶσιν,] *poiōsin* [idem]	**3642.7** dem- pron nom pl masc οὗτοι *houtoi* these,

3414.4 noun acc sing masc νόμον *nomon* law	**3231.1** partic μὴ *mē* not	**2174.19** verb nom pl masc part pres act ἔχοντες, *echontes* having,	**1431.7** prs- pron dat pl masc ἑαυτοῖς *heautois* to themselves	**1498.7** verb 3pl indic pres act εἰσιν *eisin* are	**3414.1** noun nom sing masc νόμος· *nomos* a law;

3610.2 rel- pron nom pl masc **15.** οἵτινες *hoitines* who	**1715.1** verb 3pl indic pres mid ἐνδείκνυνται *endeiknuntai* show	**3450.16** art sing neu τὸ *to* the	**2024.1** noun sing neu ἔργον *ergon* work	**3450.2** art gen sing τοῦ *tou* of the

2:11. With the negating particle *ou* placed first in the sentence for the sake of emphasis, the phrase containing *prosōpolēpsia* ("partiality") is variously rendered "no human preferences," "no favoritism," "no attention to this world's distinctions." This verse states the third principle of God's righteous judgment. See also Matthew 4:45; Galatians 2:6; Colossians 3:25 for similar statements of this principle.

In Mayor's commentary, *The Epistle of St. James*, the author states, "In its strict sense the Greek would mean to accept the outside surface for the inner reality, the mask for the person" (p.78).

Whatever advantages certain races of mankind seem to have above others, all men stand on an equal footing at the bar of God's justice. Whether Jew or Gentile, none have a monopoly of divine favor with regard to salvation.

2:12,13. *Anomōs* is rendered "without law." The word "law" would seem to refer to the law of Moses. The *New English Bible* translates it, "Those who have sinned outside the pale of the law of Moses will perish outside its pale."

The judgment of God will be in accordance with the light men have. Those who "have sinned without law shall . . . perish without law." Those who "have sinned in the law shall be judged by the law." In both cases man has a responsibility to God. All will be dealt with fairly.

Those who have the Law have much more light than those without it. But light is light no matter how dim or bright it may be. Judgment and doom await all who reject the light, but those who have more light have less excuse and a greater measure of guilt. Knowing what is right is not enough. We must act accordingly.

In verse 13 we have the first occurrence of the term "justified." The verb *dikaiaō* ("justify") comes from the noun *dikē* ("law"). It is a forensic term meaning "to pronounce not guilty of breaking any law." Logically the one who "does the law" is justified. Of course, no human being can "do the law" perfectly. See comment on verse 7.

2:14,15. The law of the Gentiles to whom Paul was writing was not in code but in conscience. They did not have a specific set of rules, but they did have the basic moral concepts which are contained in the Law. The judgment of such people will be based on God's revelation through nature and the standard of right and wrong as revealed through conscience.

Anthropologists know by research what God has revealed in His Word. There is *no* societal group that is devoid of law in the sense of a standard of right vs. wrong. Also, all men know that they break their own laws and they suffer guilt. No one will be *saved* by the light he has; he will be *judged* by that light. Light will condemn. Christ alone can save.

11. For there is no respect of persons with God: For God is impartial and treats everyone alike, *Norlie* . . . God has no favorites, *JB* . . . God doesn't prefer one to another, *Beck* . . . God does not recognize human distinctions, *TCNT* . . . God pays no attention to this world's distinctions, *Weymouth* . . . For ther is no parcialyte with god, *Tyndale* . . . For God judges everyone by the same standard, *TEV* . . . there is no acceptance of faces, *Young* . . . there is no flattery with God, *Fenton*.

12. For as many as have sinned without law shall also perish without law: For whosoever have sinned, *Douay* . . . will be lost without reference, *Berkeley* . . . will be destroyed, *SEB* . . . without reference to the law, *Norlie* . . . are lost apart from the Law, *TEV*.

and as many as have sinned in the law shall be judged by the law: . . . whilst living under the Law, *Weymouth* . . . in the sphere of law, *Wuest*.

13. (For not the hearers of the law [are] just before God: For merely hearing the law read, *Williams* . . . are put right with God, *TEV*.

but the doers of the law shall be justified: . . . but those who practice, *Berkeley* . . . it is his obedience to the law, *Norlie* . . . who will be acquitted, *Moffatt* . . . shall be accounted righteous, *PNT*.

14. For when the Gentiles, which have not the law: . . . not possessing the law, *Fenton*.

do by nature the things contained in the law: . . . obey instinctively the Law's requirements, *Moffatt* . . . do habitually, *Wuest* . . . perform by natural disposition, *Scarlett* . . . what the Law prescribes, *Confraternity*.

these, having not the law: . . . may not actually "possess" the Law, *JB*.

are a law unto themselves: . . . they are their own law, *SEB*.

15. Which show the work of the law written in their hearts: They can point to the substance

Romans 2:16

3414.2 noun gen sing masc	1117.1 adj acc sing neu	1706.1 prep	3450.14 art dat pl fem	2559.7 noun dat pl fem	840.1 prs-pron gen pl
νόμου	γραπτὸν	ἐν	ταῖς	καρδίαις	αὐτῶν,
nomou	grapton	en	tais	kardiais	autōn
law	written	in	the	hearts	their,

4679.2 verb gen sing fem part pres act	840.1 prs-pron gen pl	3450.10 art gen sing fem	4743.2 noun gen sing fem	2504.1 conj
συμμαρτυρούσης	αὐτῶν	τῆς	συνειδήσεως,	καὶ
summarturousēs	autōn	tēs	suneidēseōs	kai
bearing witness with	their	the	conscience,	and

3212.1 adv	238.1 prs-pron gen pl	3450.1 art gen pl	3027.1 noun gen pl masc	2693.7 verb gen pl masc part pres act
μεταξὺ	ἀλλήλων	τῶν	λογισμῶν	κατηγορούντων
metaxu	allēlōn	tōn	logismōn	katēgorountōn
between	one another	the	reasonings	accusing

16.a.Var: 03B,We/Ho Weis,UBS/✶

2211.1 conj	2504.1 conj	620.4 verb gen pl masc part pres	1706.1 prep	3614.11 rel-pron dat sing fem	2232.3 noun dat sing fem
ἢ	καὶ	ἀπολογουμένων,	**16.** ἐν	[a✶+ ἦ]	ἡμέρα
ē	kai	apologoumenōn	en	hē	hēmera
or	also	defending;	in	[which]	a day

16.b.Txt: 01ℵ,06D,018K 020L,byz.Tisc,Sod
Var: 02A,03B,bo.Lach Alf,We/Ho,Weis,UBS/✶

3616.1 conj	2892.5 verb 3sing indic pres act	3450.5 art sing masc	2296.1 noun nom sing masc	3450.17 art pl neu	2899.4 adj pl neu
⌐b ὅτε ⌐	κρίνει	ὁ	θεὸς	τὰ	κρυπτὰ
hote	krinei	ho	theos	ta	krupta
when	shall judge	God	the	secrets

3450.1 art gen pl	442.7 noun gen pl masc	2567.3 prep	3450.16 art sing neu	2077.1 noun sing neu
τῶν	ἀνθρώπων,	κατὰ	τὸ	εὐαγγέλιόν
tōn	anthrōpōn	kata	to	euangelion
of the	men,	according to	to	good news

1466.2 prs-pron gen 1sing	1217.2 prep	2400.2 name masc	5382.2 name gen masc	5382.2 name gen masc	2400.2 name masc
μου,	διὰ	⌐✶ Ἰησοῦ	Χριστοῦ.	[Χριστοῦ	Ἰησοῦ.]
mou	dia	Iēsou	Christou	Christou	Iēsou
my,	by	Jesus	Christ.	[Christ	Jesus.]

17.a.Txt: 06D-corr,020L byz.
Var: 01ℵ,02A,03B 06D-org,018K,Gries Lach,Treg,Alf,Word Tisc,We/Ho,Weis,Sod UBS/✶

1481.14 verb 2sing impr aor act	1479.1 conj	1156.2 conj	4622.1 prs-pron nom 2sing	2428.6 name-adj nom masc
17. ⌐ Ἴδε	[a✶ Εἰ	δὲ]	σὺ	Ἰουδαῖος
Ide	Ei	de	su	Ioudaios
Lo,	[If	but]	you	a Jew

17.b.Txt: 06D-corr,018K 020L,byz.
Var: 01ℵ,02A,03B 06D-org,Lach,Treg,Alf Word,Tisc,We/Ho,Weis Sod,UBS/✶

2012.1 verb 2sing indic pres mid	2504.1 conj	1864.1 verb 2sing indic pres	3450.3 art dat sing	3414.3 noun dat sing masc	2504.1 conj
ἐπονομάζῃ,	καὶ	ἐπαναπαύῃ	⌐b τῷ ⌐	νόμῳ,	καὶ
eponomazē	kai	epanapauē	tō	nomō	kai
are being named,	and	rely on	the	law,	and

2714.2 verb 2sing indic pres	1706.1 prep	2296.3 noun dat sing masc	2504.1 conj	1091.2 verb 2sing indic pres act	3450.16 art sing neu
καυχᾶσαι	ἐν	θεῷ,	**18.** καὶ	γινώσκεις	τὸ
kauchasai	en	theō	kai	ginōskeis	to
boast	in	God,	and	know	the

2284.1 noun sing neu	2504.1 conj	1375.2 verb 2sing indic pres act	3450.17 art pl neu	1302.3 verb acc pl neu part pres act
θέλημα,	καὶ	δοκιμάζεις	τὰ	διαφέροντα,
thelēma	kai	dokimazeis	ta	diapheronta
will,	and	approve	the things	excelling more,

"Conscience" is a word often used by Paul. Scripture has a great deal to say about conscience. It speaks of a good conscience (1 Timothy 1:5,19), a convicting conscience (John 8:9), and a seared conscience (1 Timothy 4:2).

The conscience must be governed by the Word of God. Apart from the Word, conscience is an uncertain faculty. The Holy Spirit in His work of conviction takes hold of conscience and brings God's Word to bear upon it with great forcefulness.

Conscience can be said to be the mental faculty by which man judges his actions and passes judgment on those actions. The verdict of God on the Day of Judgment will be in line with what man has done at the heart of his existence with the measure of light and power that God's revelation has brought to his life. "Accusing or else excusing" suggests that as a rule the conscience condemns.

2:16. How devastating will be the judgment of God. All unbelievers live under the judgment of God, whether they are unrighteous or self-righteous. What we do with the light of the gospel determines our sentence. There will be no secrets on that day.

This verse states the fourth principle of God's judgment: "according to my gospel." Verse 12 connects with verse 16. The matter begins with "the law" (verse 12) and ends with the "gospel" (verse 16). All men will be brought face-to-face with Christ. What we have done with Christ now determines what He will do for us in eternity. Men will not be judged for keeping "the law" but for accepting or rejecting life through Jesus Christ.

2:17. *Ioudaios* is the Greek word for "Jew." Abraham was known as Hebrew. Most of those who returned from exile were from the tribe of Judah and became known as Jews.

This verse states the three reasons for which the Jews prided themselves. They were proud to be called Jews; they "rested," "felt secure" in the Law; and they "boasted," "bragged," "prided" themselves on a special favor or relationship with God.

2:18. The Jew was certain that God looked upon him with special favor, because of his national descent from Abraham and the badge of circumcision in his body. In these verses Paul shatters that confidence and continues to emphasize the truth again and again.

Katēchoumenos, from which we get the word *catechumen*, is the word used for one who is being instructed. From this we get our word *catechism*. The Jew had the advantage of being born a Jew. From childhood he was taught in the synagogue. He was indoctrinated in the Law, he kept the Sabbath, he was aware of the need of sacrifices and kept himself separate.

of the Law engraved on their hearts, *JB* . . . their conscience attesting, *Fenton* . . . Their actions show, *SEB* . . . they exhibit the effect of the Law, *Moffatt* . . . since they exhibit proof...is engraven on their hearts, *Weymouth*.

their conscience also bearing witness: . . . their conscience also testifies, *Adams* . . . testifying with it, *Worrell* . . . too, corroborate it, *TCNT* . . . giuing testimonie to them, *Rheims*.

and [their] thoughts the mean while accusing or else excusing one another;): . . . and their inner thoughts, *Williams* . . . arguing a case, either condemning or justifying it, *Norlie* . . . they argue either in self-accusation, or it may be, in self-defence, *TCNT* . . . even when conflicting thoughts accuse or defend them, *Confraternity*.

16. In the day when God shall judge the secrets of men by Jesus Christ according to my gospel:

17. Behold, thou art called a Jew: . . . be entitled a Jew, *Fenton* . . . since thou bearest the name of a Jew, *Clementson*.

and restest in the law: You depend on, *SEB* . . . rest comfortably in your Law, *Beck* . . . and trustest in the lawe, *Cranmer* . . . and have a blind and mechanical reliance, *Wuest* . . . and dost rely upon the Law, *Confraternity*.

and makest thy boast of God: You brag about being in God, *SEB* . . . and are proud of your God, *JB* . . . exulting in God, *HistNT* . . . and reioysist in God, *Tyndale* . . . and gloriest in God, *Panin*.

18. And knowest [his] will: . . . and understand His will, *Worrell*.

and approvest the things that are more excellent: . . . you can appreciate the more excellent way, *Norlie* . . . appreciate moral excellence, *TCNT* . . . and dost discern superior things, *Wilson* . . . and vote for the best, *Klingensmith* . . . and provest the things that differ, *PNT, Clementson* . . . and approvest the more profitable things, *Douay*.

Romans 2:19

2697.3 verb nom sing masc part pres pass	1523.2 prep gen	3450.2 art gen sing	3414.2 noun gen sing masc	3844.9 verb 2sing indic perf act	4885.1 conj
κατηχούμενος	ἐκ	τοῦ	νόμου·	19. πέποιθάς	τε
katēchoumenos	ek	tou	nomou	pepoithas	te
being instructed	out of	the	law;	are persuaded	and

4427.4 prs-pron acc 2sing masc	3458.2 noun acc sing masc	1498.32 verb inf pres act	5026.7 adj gen pl masc	5295.1 noun sing neu	3450.1 art gen pl
σεαυτὸν	ὁδηγὸν	εἶναι	τυφλῶν,	φῶς	τῶν
seauton	hodēgon	einai	tuphlōn	phōs	tōn
yourself	a guide	to be	of blind,	a light	of the

1706.1 prep	4510.4 noun dat sing neu		3673.1 noun acc sing masc	871.5 adj gen pl masc	1314.2 noun acc sing masc
ἐν	σκότει,	20. παιδευτὴν		ἀφρόνων,	διδάσκαλον
en	skotei	paideutēn		aphronōn	didaskalon
in	darkness,	a instructor		of foolish,	a teacher

3378.4 adj gen pl masc	2174.15 verb part pres act	3450.12 art acc sing fem	3309.1 noun acc sing fem	3450.10 art gen sing fem
νηπίων,	ἔχοντα	τὴν	μόρφωσιν	τῆς
nēpiōn	echonta	tēn	morphōsin	tēs
of infants,	having	the	form	of the

1102.2 noun gen sing fem	2504.1 conj	3450.10 art gen sing fem	223.2 noun gen sing fem	1706.1 prep	3450.3 art dat sing
γνώσεως	καὶ	τῆς	ἀληθείας	ἐν	τῷ
gnōseōs	kai	tēs	alētheias	en	tō
knowledge	and	of the	truth	in	the

3414.3 noun dat sing masc	3450.5 art sing masc	3631.1 conj	1315.6 verb sing masc part pres act	2066.1 adj sing	4427.4 prs-pron acc 2sing masc
νόμῳ·	21. ὁ	οὖν	διδάσκων	ἕτερον,	σεαυτὸν
nomō	ho	oun	didaskōn	heteron	seauton
law:	the	then	teaching	another,	yourself

3620.3 partic	1315.2 verb 2sing indic pres act	3450.5 art sing masc	2756.6 verb sing masc part pres act	3231.1 partic	2786.5 verb inf pres act
οὐ	διδάσκεις;	ὁ	κηρύσσων	μὴ	κλέπτειν
ou	didaskeis	ho	kērussōn	mē	kleptein
not	do you teach?	the	proclaiming	not	to steal,

2786.1 verb 2sing indic pres act	3450.5 art sing masc	2978.15 verb sing masc part pres act	3231.1 partic	3294.4 verb inf pres act
κλέπτεις;	22. ὁ	λέγων	μὴ	μοιχεύειν,
klepteis	ho	legōn	mē	moicheuein
do you steal?	the	saying	not	to commit adultery,

3294.1 verb 2sing indic pres act	3450.5 art sing masc	941.2 verb voc sing masc part pres	3450.17 art pl neu
μοιχεύεις;	ὁ	βδελυσσόμενος	τὰ
moicheueis	ho	bdelussomenos	ta
do you commit adultery?	the	abhorring	the

1487.5 noun acc pl neu	2391.1 verb 2sing indic pres act	3614.5 rel-pron nom sing masc	1706.1 prep	3414.3 noun dat sing masc
εἴδωλα,	ἱεροσυλεῖς;	23. ὃς	ἐν	νόμῳ
eidōla	hierosuleis	hos	en	nomō
idols,	do you commit sacrilege?	who	in	law

2714.2 verb 2sing indic pres	1217.2 prep	3450.10 art gen sing fem	3709.2 noun gen sing fem	3450.2 art gen sing	3414.2 noun gen sing masc
καυχᾶσαι,	διὰ	τῆς	παραβάσεως	τοῦ	νόμου
kauchasai	dia	tēs	parabaseōs	tou	nomou
boast,	through	the	transgression	of the	law

2:19,20. The Jew was confident that he was not only the possessor of truth, but that he was a teacher of others. He prided himself on his position to the extent that he looked with contemptuous scorn on those who did not have his good fortune.

Paul affirmed that it was a distinct privilege to be a Jew (3:1,2). But he charged the Jew that he thought too highly of himself and too poorly of others. This made his peril all the more real.

To have access to truth, to be born into a family where God and His Word are a central part of daily living, brings great responsibility to a person. To have such privileges and then to become a spiritual bigot exposes one to searing condemnation. Paul dwelt on the fact that the Jews preached too little to themselves.

2:21,22. These verses deal with spiritual insensitivity. Paul charged that the Jew preached high standards of holiness but was not concerned with the fact that he was living a lie. No man can expect to have God's blessing simply because the light of divine revelation shines brightly around him.

The word "therefore" placed here introduces an inference from the preceding words. If the Jew had such privileges, was it not reasonable to expect that he would live up to them?

From God's viewpoint all men are on the same level. Men may classify people by race, civilization, culture, wealth, education, and other human standards. God declares that "all have sinned." Human rationalization and judgment are inexcusable. The man who renders judgment upon another whom he considers below him by any natural standard is like a person in an airplane trying to determine the size of human beings on the earth beneath him.

Moral responsibility increases in direct ratio to knowledge and light. To excuse oneself from known duty on the basis of God's favoritism brings greater condemnation. Knowing never cancels doing; rather it calls for it.

2:23. The court scene continues. The self-righteous boaster is being stripped of his cloak of self-righteousness. The proud, self-sufficient Jew, the religious man of that day, with his claim to personal privilege, is shown for what he is—a hypocrite. Knowing the will of God only increases his condemnation. He claims privilege for both who he is and then for what he has done. Paul could well understand these claims, for no one had been more zealous as a Jew than he. The picture is that of being religious without being redeemed.

The Jew claimed profession, but God, in refuting his proud claim, demanded possession. He claimed precept; God demanded practice. He claimed religion; God demanded reality. Orthodoxy in religion does not make a person more acceptable with God. Neither are men impressed, for they too look for reality.

being instructed out of the law: . . . have an idea of the essentials, *Berkeley* . . . with a sense of what is vital in religion, *Moffatt.*

19. And art confident that thou thyself art a guide of the blind: . . . if you have convinced yourself, *Adams.*

a light of them which are in darkness: . . . be a beacon to the unlearned, *JB.*

20. An instructor of the foolish: . . . a trainer of the simple, *Berkeley* . . . a master over uneducated people, *SEB* . . . a corrector of the stupid, *HistNT* . . . a schoolmaster for the dull and ignorant, *Weymouth* . . . of them which lacke discretion, *Geneva.*

a teacher of babes: . . . a maister of yong children, *Wyclif* . . . of the immature, *Berkeley* . . . of the childish, *TCNT.*

which hast the form of knowledge and of the truth in the law: . . . you have the framework of knowledge, *Norlie* . . . possessing in the Law the perfect pattern of knowledge, *Conybeare* . . . thou hast the embodiment of knowledge, *HistNT.*

21. Thou therefore which teachest another, teachest thou not thyself?:

thou that preachest a man should not steal, dost thou steal?: You who proclaim, *Campbell.*

22. Thou that sayest a man should not commit adultery, dost thou commit adultery?: Do you forbid adultery, and yet commit it? *TCNT* . . . breakest thou wedlocke? *Geneva.*

thou that abhorrest idols, dost thou commit sacrilege?: You who detest idols, *Berkeley* . . . You are disgusted with idols, *Beck* . . . You loathing idols, *Fenton* . . . You who find idols an abomination, *Adams* . . . who shrink in horror from idols, *Williams* . . . and yet rob their temples? *TCNT* . . . and yet robbest God of his honoure, *Cranmer.*

23. Thou that makest thy boast of the law: You feel proud, *Beck.*

3450.6 art acc sing masc	2296.4 noun acc sing masc	812.1 verb 2sing indic pres act	3450.16 art sing neu	1056.1 conj	3549.2 noun sing neu
τὸν	θεὸν	ἀτιμάζεις;	**24.** Τὸ	γὰρ	ὄνομα
ton	*theon*	*atimazeis*	*To*	*gar*	*onoma*
	God	dishonor you?	The	for	name

3450.2 art gen sing	2296.2 noun gen sing masc	1217.1 prep	5050.4 prs-pron acc 2pl	980.17 verb 3sing indic pres pass	1706.1 prep
τοῦ	θεοῦ	δι'	ὑμᾶς	βλασφημεῖται	ἐν
tou	*theou*	*di'*	*humas*	*blasphēmeitai*	*en*
	of God	through	you	is being blasphemed	among

3450.4 art dat pl	1477.6 noun dat pl neu	2503.1 conj	1119.22 verb 3sing indic perf pass		3921.1 noun nom sing fem
τοῖς	ἔθνεσιν,	καθὼς	γέγραπται.		**25.** Περιτομὴ
tois	*ethnesin*	*kathōs*	*gegraptai*		*Peritomē*
the	nations,	just as	it has been written.		Circumcision

3173.1 conj	1056.1 conj	5456.1 verb 3sing indic pres act	1430.1 partic	3414.4 noun acc sing masc	4097.5 verb 2sing subj pres act
μὲν	γὰρ	ὠφελεῖ	ἐὰν	νόμον	πράσσῃς·
men	*gar*	*ōphelei*	*ean*	*nomon*	*prassēs*
indeed	for	profits	if	law	you do;

1430.1 partic	1156.2 conj	3710.1 noun nom sing masc	3414.2 noun gen sing masc	1498.9 verb 2sing subj pres act	3450.9 art nom sing fem
ἐὰν	δὲ	παραβάτης	νόμου	ᾖς,	ἡ
ean	*de*	*parabatēs*	*nomou*	*ēs*	*hē*
if	but	a transgressor	of law	you are,	the

3921.1 noun nom sing fem	4622.2 prs-pron gen 2sing	201.1 noun nom sing fem	1090.3 verb 3sing indic perf act		1430.1 partic
περιτομή	σου	ἀκροβυστία	γέγονεν.		**26.** ἐὰν
peritomē	*sou*	*akrobustia*	*gegonen*		*ean*
circumcision	your	uncircumcision	has become.		If

3631.1 conj	3450.9 art nom sing fem	201.1 noun nom sing fem	3450.17 art pl neu		1339.3 noun pl neu
οὖν	ἡ	ἀκροβυστία	τὰ		δικαιώματα
oun	*hē*	*akrobustia*	*ta*		*dikaiōmata*
therefore	the	uncircumcision	the		requirements

3450.2 art gen sing	3414.2 noun gen sing masc	5278.2 verb 3sing subj pres act	3644.1 adv	3620.1 partic	3450.9 art nom sing fem
τοῦ	νόμου	φυλάσσῃ,	☆ οὐχὶ	[οὐχ]	ἡ
tou	*nomou*	*phulassē*	*ouchi*	*ouch*	*hē*
of the	law	keep,	not	[idem]	the

201.1 noun nom sing fem	840.3 prs-pron gen sing	1519.1 prep	3921.4 noun acc sing fem		3023.18 verb 3sing indic fut pass
ἀκροβυστία	αὐτοῦ	εἰς	περιτομὴν		λογισθήσεται;
akrobustia	*autou*	*eis*	*peritomēn*		*logisthēsetai*
uncircumcision	his	for	circumcision		shall be reckoned?

2504.1 conj	2892.25 verb 3sing indic fut act	3450.9 art nom sing fem	1523.2 prep gen		5285.2 noun gen sing fem
27. καὶ	κρινεῖ	ἡ	ἐκ		φύσεως
kai	*krinei*	*hē*	*ek*		*phuseōs*
and	shall judge	the	by		nature

201.1 noun nom sing fem	3450.6 art acc sing masc	3414.4 noun acc sing masc	4903.3 verb nom sing fem part pres act		4622.4 prs-pron acc 2sing
ἀκροβυστία,	τὸν	νόμον	τελοῦσα,		σὲ
akrobustia	*ton*	*nomon*	*telousa*		*se*
uncircumcision,	the	law	fulfilling,		you

2:24. The thought expressed in the words "the name of God is blasphemed" is "to speak injuriously, to malign." In 3:8 and 14:16 the Greek is rendered "be slanderously reported" and "be evil spoken of." Paul wrote that the Jews were to a great extent responsible for causing the Gentiles to blaspheme (speak evil of) God.

"As it is written" refers to Isaiah 52:5. This was not a new revelation to the Jews but they needed to be reminded of it. They obviously fell into the same sort of thought patterns over and over just as all men do in all ages. All men need the Word of God every day of their lives "for doctrine, for reproof, for correction, for instruction in righteousness" (2 Timothy 3:16).

With this statement, Paul reaches the apex of his indictment of the hypocritical Jews. He reminds them that what the Gentiles know of the God of Abraham is what they see in Abraham's descendants. The Gentiles reason that a people are like their God; if the Jews can perpetrate such crimes, then their God must be wicked, and they can therefore desecrate His name with impunity.

The Jews who claimed to be leaders for the true worship of God became the instruments to provoke the nations to blasphemy. This solemn and searching charge should startle all who profess the name of *Christian*. Those who profess to be possessors of the truth should not parade lip service without exemplifying standards of holy living.

2:25. The Word now pursues the Jew into his last retreat of self-justification, his trust in circumcision. The apostle makes clear that circumcision itself is neutral. It *can* profit if it indeed is a sign of that which is of ultimate value; otherwise, it can be a liability. The word "circumcision" (*peritomē*) occurs 35 times in the New Testament, 15 times in Romans (6 times in this chapter) and 7 times in Galatians. Romans and Galatians give major attention to the means of salvation alike for both Jew and Gentile.

2:26,27. *Akrobustia*, "uncircumcision," occurs 19 times in the New Testament, 10 times in Romans and 3 times in Galatians. These two words are almost exclusive to Paul's epistles.

Paul's argument is that a rite or ritual has no meaning unless it is an outward expression of an inward experience. For circumcision to be of any value, the Jew must keep the Law. To keep the Law was humanly impossible. So, to break the Law was to make the rite null and void. The apostle proved that the ordinance of circumcision, which is a seal, was useless without personal righteousness. True circumcision is that of the heart.

The advantage of circumcision lapses unless the moral conditions to which the rite is joined are fulfilled. Wuest renders verse 25: "For indeed, circumcision is profitable if you are a practitioner of the law, but if on the other hand you are a transgressor of the law, your circumcision has become uncircumcision" (*Word Studies from*

through breaking the law dishonourest thou God?: . . . do you dishonor God by its violation? *Berkeley* . . . do you habitually dishonor, *Montgomery* . . . by trangressing its commandments? *Adams* . . . by your breaches of the Law? *Moffatt.*

24. For the name of God is blasphemed among the Gentiles through you: You make the non-Jews slander God's name, *Beck* . . . The very name of God is reviled among, *TCNT* . . . God's name is maligned, *HistNT* . . . is dishonored among the heathen, *Norlie* . . . is defamed among the heathen, *Fenton.*

as it is written:

25. For circumcision verily profiteth, if thou keep the law: . . . is really worthwhile, *Adams* . . . benefits only if you practice the Law, *Berkeley.*

but if thou be a breaker of the law: . . . but if you are a Law-breaker, *Weymouth* . . . a trespassour, *Wyclif* . . . a transgressor, *ASV, Confraternity.*

thy circumcision is made uncircumcision: . . . you have lost your circumcision, *Beck* . . . your circumcision becomes paganised, *Fenton* . . . has practically ceased to exist, *TCNT* . . . counts for nothing, *Weymouth.*

26. Therefore if the uncircumcision keep: . . . the physically uncircumcised, *Berkeley.*

the righteousness of the law: . . . meets the requirements of the law, *Norlie* . . . the ordinance of the law, *HistNT* . . . the precepts, *Confraternity.*

shall not his uncircumcision be counted for circumcision?: . . . would not his paganism be considered equivalent, *Fenton* . . . be regarded by God as if he were? *TCNT* . . . be reckoned equivalent to, *Moffatt.*

27. And shall not uncircumcision which is by nature, if it fulfil the law, judge thee: . . . those who are physically uncircumcised, *Adams* . . . and yet scrupulously obeys the Law, *TCNT.*

Romans 2:28

3450.6 art acc sing masc	1217.2 prep	1115.2 noun gen sing neu	2504.1 conj	3921.2 noun gen sing fem	3710.2 noun acc sing masc
τὸν	διὰ	γράμματος	καὶ	περιτομῆς	παραβάτην
ton	dia	grammatos	kai	peritomēs	parabatēn
the	with	letter	and	circumcision	a transgressor

3414.2 noun gen sing masc	3620.3 partic	1056.1 conj	3450.5 art sing masc	1706.1 prep	3450.3 art dat sing	5156.5 adj dat sing neu
νόμου.	**28.** οὐ	γὰρ	ὁ	ἐν	τῷ	φανερῷ
nomou	ou	gar	ho	en	tō	phanerō
of law?	Not	for	the	in	the	outwardly

2428.6 name- adj nom masc	1498.4 verb 3sing indic pres act	3624.1 adv	3450.9 art nom sing fem	1706.1 prep	3450.3 art dat sing
Ἰουδαῖός	ἐστιν,	οὐδὲ	ἡ	ἐν	τῷ
Ioudaios	estin,	oude	hē	en	tō
a Jew	is,	neither	the	in	the

5156.5 adj dat sing neu	1706.1 prep	4418.3 noun dat sing fem	3921.1 noun nom sing fem	233.1 conj	3450.5 art sing masc
φανερῷ	ἐν	σαρκὶ	περιτομή·	**29.** ἀλλ'	ὁ
phanerō	en	sarki	peritomē	all'	ho
outwardly	in	flesh	circumcision;	but	the

1706.1 prep	3450.3 art dat sing	2899.3 adj dat sing neu	2428.6 name- adj nom masc	2504.1 conj	3921.1 noun nom sing fem
ἐν	τῷ	κρυπτῷ	Ἰουδαῖος,	καὶ	περιτομή
en	tō	kruptō	Ioudaios,	kai	peritomē
in	the	hidden	a Jew;	and	circumcision

2559.1 noun fem	1706.1 prep	4011.3 noun dat sing neu	3620.3 partic	1115.3 noun dat sing neu	3614.2 rel- pron gen sing
καρδίας	ἐν	πνεύματι,	οὐ	γράμματι·	οὗ
kardias	en	pneumati,	ou	grammati	hou
of heart,	in	spirit,	not	in letter;	of whom

3450.5 art sing masc	1853.1 noun nom sing masc	3620.2 partic	1523.1 prep gen	442.7 noun gen pl masc	233.1 conj	1523.2 prep gen
ὁ	ἔπαινος	οὐκ	ἐξ	ἀνθρώπων,	ἀλλ'	ἐκ
ho	epainos	ouk	ex	anthrōpōn,	all'	ek
the	praise	not	of	men,	but	of

3450.2 art gen sing	2296.2 noun gen sing masc	4949.9 intr- pron sing neu	3631.1 conj	3450.16 art sing neu	3916.1 adj sing neu
τοῦ	θεοῦ.	**3:1.** Τί	οὖν	τὸ	περισσὸν
tou	theou	Ti	oun	to	perisson
	God.	What	then	the	superiority

3450.2 art gen sing	2428.7 name- adj gen masc	2211.1 conj	4949.3 intr- pron nom sing	3450.9 art nom sing fem	5455.1 noun nom sing fem
τοῦ	Ἰουδαίου,	ἤ	τίς	ἡ	ὠφέλεια
tou	Ioudaiou,	ē	tis	hē	ōpheleia
of the	Jew?	or	what	the	profit

3450.10 art gen sing fem	3921.2 noun gen sing fem	4044.16 adj sing neu	2567.3 prep	3820.1 adj	4999.3 noun acc sing masc
τῆς	περιτομῆς;	**2.** πολὺ	κατὰ	πάντα	τρόπον.
tēs	peritomēs	polu	kata	panta	tropon
of the	circumcision?	Much	by	every	way:

4270.1 adv	3173.1 conj	1056.1 conj	3617.1 conj	3961.59 verb 3pl indic aor pass	3450.17 art pl neu
πρῶτον	μὲν	(a γὰρ)	ὅτι	ἐπιστεύθησαν	τὰ
prōton	men	gar	hoti	episteuthēsan	ta
first	men	for	that	they were entrusted with	the

2.a.**Txt:** 01ℵ,02A
06D-corr3,byz.
Var: 03B,06D-org,012G
044,365,1506,2464

the Greek New Testament, Romans in the Greek New Testament, 1:49).

Romans 3:2

Paul makes three points: (1) The rite without reality is unrighteousness (verse 25); (2) The reality without the rite is righteousness (verses 26,27); (3) The reality is praised by God, the rite by men (verses 28,29). The uncircumcised Gentiles who kept the Law were more pleasing to God than the circumcised Jews who did not keep the Law.

2:28,29. *Phaneros*, "outwardly," carries the meaning of "apparent, manifest, evident, known." This speaks of that which can be observed on the outside. *Kruptos*, "inwardly," has the sense of "hidden, secret, concealed" and speaks of the soul-life of a man, his inner part.

The Jew who inwardly maintains his covenant relationship with God is truly a Jew in contrast to the one who is merely professional in his life-style. There must be concern to keep the heart right. It is not a matter of keeping "the letter of the law." The spiritual implications are far greater. Circumcision is reckoned as uncircumcision if not accompanied by heart devotion. Uncircumcision is reckoned as spiritual circumcision if obedience to God is practiced. Circumcision must be that of the heart. Circumcision relates to the organ that God ordained to transmit life. Without spiritual life there is no true spiritual circumcision.

"Whose praise is not of men, but of God." The Jews derived their name from their ancestor Judah whose name is associated with praise. His mother named him Judah at birth declaring, "Now will I praise the Lord." On his deathbed, his father stated, "Judah, thou art he whom thy brethren shall praise." But Paul states in verse 29 that the true Jew receives his praise from God and not from men.

3:1-3. Paul's preceding statements were disastrous blows to Jewish pride and ceremonies. His argument might at first reading appear to make invalid God's institutions for Israel in the Old Testament. His statement in 2:17, in particular, might be construed to imply that circumcision itself created a disadvantage. Therefore, two logical questions are posed in verse 1. The matter of Jewish superiority is dealt with briefly and then considered more fully in chapters 9, 10, and 11. Paul then shows that the Jew had an advantage, but it became his condemnation.

The answer to the first question is found in verse 2. It is "much." He says "chiefly" because, first of all, the Word of God was committed to the Jews. These oracles contain promises yet to be fulfilled. Note that Israel is set aside, not cast away.

Logia occurs four times in the New Testament and is translated "oracles." In every instance it means the words or utterances of God. At the time Paul was writing, these "oracles" comprised the Old Testament.

---

who by the letter and circumcision dost transgress the law?: ... for all your written code, *Moffatt* ... in spite of being circumcised, *JB* ... art a preuaricatour of the Lavv? *Rheims* ... who violate the Law in spite of instruction, *Fenton.*

28. For he is not a Jew, which is one outwardly: ... is not a real Jew, *TCNT* ... who is such in appearance, *Scarlett* ... who is so in an outward fashion, *Wuest* ... who just looks like one, *Klingensmith* ... is not one manifestly, *Panin.*

neither [is that] circumcision, which is outward in the flesh: ... nor is outward bodily circumcision real circumcision, *TCNT.*

29. But he [is] a Jew, which is one inwardly: ... who is a Jew in soul, *TCNT* ... that is in secrete, *Rheims* ... in the sphere of the inner man, *Wuest.*

and circumcision [is that] of the heart: ... of the herte is the true circumcisyon, *Cranmer.*

in the spirit, [and] not in the letter: ... not literal, *Weymouth* ... performed by the Spirit, not the written code, *SEB.*

whose praise [is] not of men, but of God: This man's praise originates, *Williams* ... the commendation of which is not of men, *Sawyer* ... wins praise from God, *TCNT.*

1. What advantage then hath the Jew?: What special privilege, then, *Williams* ... what is the Jew's superiority? *Moffatt.*

or what profit [is there] of circumcision?: ... what benefit does circumcision confer? *Williams* ... or what aduauntageth circumcisyon? *Cranmer.*

2. Much every way: Considerable in every respect, *Berkeley* ... from every point of view, *Weymouth.*

chiefly, because that unto them were committed: First indeed, *Douay* ... principally in that, *PNT* ... The most important advantage, *Beck* ... This at the outset...were intrusted to them, *HistNT.*

Romans 3:3

3025.2 noun acc pl neu	3450.2 art gen sing	2296.2 noun gen sing masc	4949.9 intr-pron sing neu	1056.1 conj	1479.1 conj	564.4 verb 3pl indic aor act
λόγια	τοῦ	θεοῦ.	3. τί	γὰρ	εἰ	ἠπίστησάν
logia	tou	theou	ti	gar	ei	ēpistēsan
oracles		of God.	What	for,	if	not believed

4948.7 indef-pron nom pl masc	3231.1 partic	3450.9 art nom sing fem	565.1 noun nom sing fem	840.1 prs-pron gen pl	3450.12 art acc sing fem	3963.4 noun acc sing fem
τινες;	μὴ	ἡ	ἀπιστία	αὐτῶν	τὴν	πίστιν
tines	mē	hē	apistia	autōn	tēn	pistin
some?	not	the	unbelief	their	the	faith

3450.2 art gen sing	2296.2 noun gen sing masc	2643.8 verb 3sing indic fut act	3231.1 partic	1090.44 verb 3sing opt aor mid
τοῦ	θεοῦ	καταργήσει;	4. μὴ	γένοιτο·
tou	theou	katargēsei	mē	genoito
	of God	shall make of no effect?	Not	may it be!

1090.18 verb 3sing impr pres	1156.2 conj	3450.5 art sing masc	2296.1 noun nom sing masc	225.2 adj nom sing	3820.6 adj sing masc
γινέσθω	δὲ	ὁ	θεὸς	ἀληθής,	πᾶς
ginesthō	de	ho	theos	alēthēs	pas
let be	but		God	true,	every

4.a.Txt: 02A,06D,018K 020L,etc.byz.Sod
Var: 01א,03B,Treg,Tisc We/Ho,Weis,UBS/☆

1156.2 conj	442.1 noun nom sing masc	5418.1 noun nom sing masc	2503.1 conj	2481.1 conj
δὲ	ἄνθρωπος	ψεύστης,	⟨☆ καθὼς	[a καθάπερ]
de	anthrōpos	pseustēs	kathōs	kathaper
and	man	a liar,	according as	[just as]

1119.22 verb 3sing indic perf pass	3567.1 conj	300.1 partic	1338.15 verb 2sing subj aor pass	1706.1 prep
γέγραπται,	Ὅπως	ἂν	δικαιωθῇς	ἐν
gegraptai	Hopōs	an	dikaiōthēs	en
it has been written,	That		you should be justified	in

4.b.Txt: 03B,018K,020L byz.Weis
Var: 01א,02A,06D,Tisc We/Ho,UBS/☆

3450.4 art dat pl	3030.7 noun dat pl masc	4622.2 prs-pron gen 2sing	2504.1 conj	3390.9 verb 2sing subj aor act	3390.17 verb 2sing indic fut act
τοῖς	λόγοις	σου,	καὶ	⟨ νικήσῃς	[b☆ νικήσεις]
tois	logois	sou	kai	nikēsēs	nikēseis
the	words	your,	and	overcome	[will overcome]

1706.1 prep	3450.3 art dat sing	2892.32 verb inf pres pass	4622.4 prs-pron acc 2sing	1479.1 conj	1156.2 conj
ἐν	τῷ	κρίνεσθαί	σε.	5. Εἰ	δὲ
en	tō	krinesthai	se	Ei	de
in	the	to be judged	your.	If	but

3450.9 art nom sing fem	92.1 noun nom sing fem	2231.2 prs-pron gen 1pl	2296.2 noun gen sing masc	1336.4 noun acc sing fem
ἡ	ἀδικία	ἡμῶν	θεοῦ	δικαιοσύνην
hē	adikia	hēmōn	theou	dikaiosunēn
the	unrighteousness	our	God's	righteousness

4771.2 verb 3sing indic pres act	4949.9 intr-pron sing neu	2029.12 verb 1pl indic fut act	3231.1 partic	93.1 adj nom sing masc
συνίστησιν,	τί	ἐροῦμεν;	μὴ	ἄδικος
sunistēsin	ti	eroumen	mē	adikos
commend,	what	shall we say?	not	unrighteous

3450.5 art sing masc	2296.1 noun nom sing masc	3450.5 art sing masc	2002.1 verb nom sing masc part pres act	3450.12 art acc sing fem	3572.4 noun acc sing fem
ὁ	θεὸς	ὁ	ἐπιφέρων	τὴν	ὀργήν;
ho	theos	ho	epipherōn	tēn	orgēn
	God	the	inflicting	the	wrath?

The second question is answered in 2:28,29.

A third question, posed in verse 3, is answered in verse 4. Though the advantage of the Jew did not serve God's intended purpose, their unfaithfulness did not cancel God's faithfulness.

"For what" is *ti gar*, "for how." "Did not believe" is the verb *pisteuō* meaning they were without faith. Several translations carry the thought of unfaithfulness. Commentators are divided on the rendering, but most agree that the "faith of God" refers to His faithfulness.

"Make . . . without effect" (*katargeō*) carries the thought of rendering it inoperative. Some prefer the rendering "to make ineffi-cient" rather than "to make without effect."

3:4. The question raised in the third verse is here answered with a firm "God forbid." Phillips renders it "of course not!"

Mē genoito literally means "let it not be" or "may it not come to pass." The expression occurs 15 times in the King James Version of the New Testament, 14 times by Paul, 10 of them in Romans.

Israel's unbelief does not nullify the faithfulness of God. What if some are unfaithful? Will their unfaithfulness make God un-faithful? The answer to the question is very simple. The faithfulness of God holds true even if men would be able to contend with Him in court. A guilty verdict will be returned against men even if it becomes necessary to declare all men are liars. God is true. His truth is due to the fact that He is a perfect Being, even though all men are proved to be liars.

"Let God be true." *Ginomai* is the verb and it means "become." The apparent meaning is that it becomes an apparent condition, that it "proves to be," "is seen to be."

Gegraptai, "as it is written," occurs 66 times in the New Testa-ment. Its clearest meaning is, "It has been written and still stands written."

3:5. The righteousness of God as used here is not a reference to His righteousness that is given in justification to men who believe. It is an attribute of righteousness which includes His faithfulness and truth, what has been called the "inherent equity of God."

The Jews' "unrighteousness" consisted of national disobedience to the Law given at Sinai, neglect of the Law (aptly illustrated in Josiah's time), pride because they were possessors of the Law, and ignorance of the spiritual meaning of the Old Testament Scrip-tures. They even killed the Righteous One (Acts 13:27).

Sunistēmi, "commend," can be rendered "demonstrate, show, prove, establish." "Taketh vengeance" is also translated "inflict an-ger, wrath." The answer to the question in this verse is given by another question: "God who inflicts wrath is not unjust, is He?" God's justice cannot be questioned.

When Paul said "I speak as a man," he was not speaking in his character as an apostle but rather in the character of men in general.

the oracles of God: . . . the vvordes of God, *Rheims* . . . God's revelatory words, *Adams* . . . God's utterances, *TCNT* . . . God's truth, *Weymouth*.

3. For what if some did not be-lieve?: . . . showed a want of faith, *TCNT*.

shall their unbelief make the faith of God without effect?: Will their unfaithfulness, *Beck* . . . lack of faith cancel God's loyalty? *SEB* . . . destroy God's trust? *Fenton* . . . make God break faith? *TCNT* . . . cancel God's fidelity? *JB* . . . make the promes of god with out effecte? *Tyndale* . . . make null and void God's faithfulness? *Wil-liams*.

4. God forbid: No, never! *Nor-lie* . . . That would be absurd, *JB* . . . By no means, *Scarlett*.
yea, let God be true, but every man a liar: . . . God must prove true, *TCNT* . . . though every man be a cheat, *Berkeley* . . . though all mankind prove false, *Montgomery*.
as it is written:
That thou mightest be justified in thy sayings: . . . be vindicated in, *Berkeley* . . . be declared righ-teous in thy words, *Clementson*.
and mightest overcome when thou art judged: . . . and will win the case when You are brought to trial, *Adams* . . . mayest be victo-rious, *Confraternity* . . . And mightest prevail, *ASV* . . . when you go into court, *Williams*.

5. But if our unrighteousness commend the righteousness of God: . . . if our wrongdoing brings out so strikingly, *Berkeley* . . . if our iniquitie, *Rheims* . . . But if our wickedness, *Confraternity* . . . simply serves to magnify God's righteousness? *Norlie* . . . dem-onstrates God's righteousness so clearly, *Adams*.
what shall we say?:
[Is] God unrighteous who tak-eth vengeance?: Is God wrong . . . when He's angry, *Beck* . . . be wrong to punish us, wouldn't He? *SEB* . . . that the angerbearing God is unjust? *Fenton* . . . wrong in inflicting punishment? *TCNT* . . . when inflicteth vengeance? *Scarlett*.

2567.3 prep κατὰ *kata* According to	**442.4** noun acc sing masc ἄνθρωπον *anthrōpon* man	**2978.1** verb 1sing pres act λέγω. *legō* I speak.	**3231.1** partic **6.** μὴ *mē* Not	**1090.44** verb 3sing opt aor mid γένοιτο· *genoito* may it be!	**1878.1** conj ἐπεὶ *epei* since
4316.1 adv πῶς *pōs* how	**2892.25** verb 3sing indic fut act κρινεῖ *krinei* shall judge	**3450.5** art sing masc ὁ *ho*	**2296.1** noun nom sing masc θεὸς *theos* God	**3450.6** art acc sing masc τὸν *ton* the	**2862.4** noun acc sing masc κόσμον; *kosmon* world?
1479.1 conj **7.** εἰ *ei* If	**1056.1** conj ʼ γὰρ *gar* for	**1156.2** conj [ᵃ δὲ] *de* [but]	**3450.9** art nom sing fem ἡ *hē* the	**223.1** noun nom sing fem ἀλήθεια *alētheia* truth	**3450.2** art gen sing τοῦ *tou*
2296.2 noun gen sing masc θεοῦ *theou* of God	**1706.1** prep ἐν *en* in	**3450.3** art dat sing τῷ *tō* the	**1684.2** adj dat 1sing ἐμῷ *emō* my	**5417.1** noun dat sing neu ψεύσματι *pseusmati* lie	**3915.13** verb 3sing indic aor act ἐπερίσσευσεν *eperisseusen* abounded
1519.1 prep εἰς *eis* to	**3450.12** art acc sing fem τὴν *tēn* the	**1385.4** noun acc sing fem δόξαν *doxan* glory	**840.3** prs- pron gen sing αὐτοῦ, *autou* his,	**4949.9** intr- pron sing neu τί *ti* why	**2068.1** adv ἔτι *eti* yet
					2476.3 conj κἀγὼ *kagō* also I
5453.1 conj ὡς *hōs* as	**266.1** adj nom sing ἁμαρτωλὸς *hamartōlos* a sinner	**2892.28** verb 1sing indic pres pass κρίνομαι; *krinomai* am being judged?	**2504.1** conj **8.** καὶ *kai* and	**3231.1** partic μὴ *mē* not,	**2503.1** conj καθὼς *kathōs* just as
980.18 verb 1pl indic pres pass βλασφημούμεθα, *blasphēmoumetha* we are being injuriously charged			**2504.1** conj καὶ *kai* and	**2503.1** conj καθώς *kathōs* just as	**5183.3** verb 3pl indic pres act φασίν *phasin* affirm
4948.7 indef- pron nom pl masc τινες *tines* some	**2231.4** prs- pron acc 1pl ἡμᾶς *hēmas* we	**2978.24** verb inf pres act λέγειν, *legein* to say,	**3617.1** conj Ὅτι *Hoti*	**4020.30** verb 1pl subj aor act ποιήσωμεν *poiēsōmen* Let us practice	**3450.17** art pl neu τὰ *ta* the
2527.9 adj pl neu κακὰ *kaka* evil things	**2419.1** conj ἵνα *hina* that	**2048.8** verb 3sing subj aor act ἔλθη *elthē* may come	**3450.17** art pl neu τὰ *ta* the	**18.14** adj pl neu ἀγαθά; *agatha* good things?	**3614.1** rel- pron gen pl ὧν *hōn* whose
3450.16 art sing neu τὸ *to* the	**2890.1** noun sing neu κρίμα *krima* judgment	**1722.1** adj sing ἔνδικόν *endikon* just	**1498.4** verb 3sing indic pres act ἐστιν. *estin* is.	**4949.9** intr- pron sing neu **9.** Τί *Ti* What	**3631.1** conj οὖν; *oun* then?
4143.1 verb 1pl indic pres προεχόμεθα; *proechometha* are we better?	**3620.3** partic οὐ *ou* not	**3705.1** adv πάντως· *pantōs* at all:	**4115.1** verb 1pl indic aor mid προῃτιασάμεθα *proētiasametha* we before charged		**1056.1** conj γὰρ *gar* for

7.a.Txt: 03B,06D,018K
020L,025P,044,33,byz.
sa.Weis,Sod
Var: 01א,02A,bo.Tisc
We/Ho,UBS/✶

He was voicing those questions that arise in flawed human reasoning, for the purpose of dealing with them and to express his horror at the very thought of any possibility of God's being unjust.

3:6. The foregoing questions again bring Paul's resounding answer, "God forbid!" God is just and righteous. God's righteousness is not determined by sin in itself, but by sin as God deals with it, whether punished by His wrath or pardoned by His grace. The sinner is under divine judgment. He can claim no merit if God turns his sin to His glory. "Shall not the Judge of all the earth do right?" (Genesis 18:25).

3:7. Commenting on the words "through (by) my lie," Vincent states, "The expression carries us back to verse 4, and is general for moral falsehood, unfaithfulness to the claims of conscience and of God, especially with reference to the proffer of salvation through Christ" (3:34). The two questions in verses 7 and 8 are as impertinent and out of place as those in verse 5. Paul knew that all men in general, and the Jews in particular, were always looking for a basis on which to rationalize away their accountability. By twisting what he was teaching, as in the first part of verse 5, they could "logically" progress to the total error of verse 8 (cf. 6:1).

3:8. Some had said that Paul was saying, "Let us do evil, that good may come." But Paul was not teaching the doctrine that sin magnifies the grace of God. This, they said, was accomplished by the contrast between man's failure and God's perfection. The absurd conclusion that sin enhances the glory of God and therefore excludes judgment, is not only incompatible with future judgment, but also ruinous to all morality. *Krima*, rendered "damnation" in the King James Version, is generally translated "condemnation."

3:9. The question of unrighteousness among Gentiles and Jews has been fully considered. Both are unrighteous. Now Paul charges that both are guilty. They are under the dominion of sin. The condemnation of God is upon them.

The Gentiles have been charged with sin and guilt in 1:18-32. The guilt of the Jews is declared in 2:8 to 3:8. The principles of divine judgment are outlined (2:1-16), with application being made to the Jews (2:17-24) and their covenant status (2:25-29). The answer to the counterclaims of the Jews is given in 3:1-8.

Proaitiaomai is a word not found elsewhere in the New Testament. While it is translated "proved" in the King James Version, most other translators render it "charged." Man is a sinner by nature, man is a sinner by deliberate choice, man is a sinner in God's sight. All men are under sin, and God will deal with them accordingly and without argument.

(I speak as a man): I am only speaking as men do, *TCNT* . . . I speak after a purely human manner, *Confraternity.*

6. God forbid: That be far from us, *Conybeare.*

for then how shall God judge the world?:

7. For if the truth of God hath more abounded through my lie unto his glory: . . . a falsehood of mine has made God's truthfulness more conspicuous, *Weymouth* . . . if my lie results in His glory by making God's truthfulness all the more obvious, *Adams.*

why yet am I also judged as a sinner?: . . . why am I still sentenced, *Scarlett* . . . why am I still tried as a sinner? *Montgomery* . . . as a wrong-doer? *Fenton.*

8. And not [rather], (as we be slanderously reported, and as some affirm that we say,) Let us do evil, that good may come?: Perhaps we should say, *SEB* . . . insulted me by accusing me, *TEV* . . . as people abusively say of us, *Williams* . . . Why not say...as some slanderously claim, *Adams* . . . Do evil as a means to good, *JB* . . . so that good may result! *Berkeley* . . . that good may come out of it? *Moffatt.*

whose damnation is just: The question justly deserves condemnation, *Norlie* . . . Deservedly are such talkers condemned, *Berkeley* . . . Such arguments are rightly condemned, *Moffatt* . . . The condemnation of those who would so argue is just, *Weymouth* . . . Such conduct is justly condemned, *HistNT* . . . They deserve to be condemned, *SEB* . . . Of such men the doom is just, *Conybeare.*

9. What then? are we better [than they]?: What defense then have we? *Sawyer* . . . Are the Jews better off? *SEB* . . . we are the superior? *Fenton* . . . Do we come out ahead? *Berkeley* . . . Do we excel them? *Douay* . . . in any better condition, *TEV.*

No, in no wise: No, not so, *Douay* . . . Not at all, *Worrell.*

2428.5 name-adj acc pl masc	4885.1 conj	2504.1 conj	1659.7 name acc pl masc	3820.8 adj acc pl masc	5097.1 prep
Ἰουδαίους	τε	καὶ	Ἕλληνας	πάντας	ὑφ'
Ioudaious	te	kai	Hellēnas	pantas	huph'
Jews	both	and	Greeks	all	under

264.4 noun acc sing fem	1498.32 verb inf pres act	2503.1 conj	1119.22 verb 3sing indic perf pass	3617.1 conj
ἁμαρτίαν	εἶναι,	**10.** καθὼς	γέγραπται	Ὅτι
hamartian	einai,	kathōs	gegraptai	Hoti
sin	to be:	just as	it has been written,	Hoti

3620.2 partic	1498.4 verb 3sing indic pres act	1337.3 adj nom sing masc	3624.1 adv	1518.3 num card nom masc	3620.2 partic
οὐκ	ἔστιν	δίκαιος	οὐδὲ	εἷς·	**11.** οὐκ
ouk	estin	dikaios	oude	heis	ouk
Not	there is	a righteous one,	not even	one:	not

1498.4 verb 3sing indic pres act	3450.5 art sing masc	4770.4 verb nom sing masc part pres act	3620.2 partic	1498.4 verb 3sing indic pres act	3450.5 art sing masc
ἔστιν	ὁ	συνίων,	οὐκ	ἔστιν	ὁ
estin	ho	suniōn,	ouk	estin	ho
there is	the	understanding,	not	there is	the

1554.1 verb nom sing masc part pres act	3450.6 art acc sing masc	2296.4 noun acc sing masc	3820.7 adj pl masc	1565.1 verb 3pl indic aor act
ἐκζητῶν	τὸν	θεόν.	**12.** πάντες	ἐξέκλιναν,
ekzētōn	ton	theon.	pantes	exeklinan,
seeking after	ton	God.	All	did go out of the way,

12.a.**Txt:** 03B-corr
06D-corr,018K,020L
025P,byz.Sod
Var: 01א,02A,03B-org
06D-org,Treg,Tisc
We/Ho,Weis,UBS/☆

12.b.**Var:** 01א,06D,Tisc
Weis,UBS/☆

12.c.**Txt:** 01א,02A,06D
012G,044,byz.
Var: 03B,6,1739

258.1 adv	882.1 verb 3pl indic aor pass	882.2 verb 3pl indic aor pass	3620.2 partic
ἅμα	ʼ ἠχρειώθησαν·	[a☆ ἠχρεώθησαν·]	οὐκ
hama	ēchreiōthēsan	ēchreōthēsan	ouk
together	they became unprofitable;	[idem]	not

1498.4 verb 3sing indic pres act	3450.5 art sing masc	4020.15 verb sing masc part pres act	5379.4 noun acc sing fem	3620.2 partic
ἔστιν	[b+ ὁ]	ποιῶν	χρηστότητα,	ʼc οὐκ
estin	ho	poiōn	chrēstotēta,	ouk
there is	[the]	practicing	kindness,	not

1498.4 verb 3sing indic pres act	2175.1 conj	1518.1 num card gen	4876.1 noun nom sing masc	453.25 verb nom sing masc part perf pass
ἔστιν ʼ	ἕως	ἑνός.	**13.** τάφος	ἀνεῳγμένος
estin	heōs	henos.	taphos	aneōgmenos
there is	so much as	one;	grave	having been opened

3450.5 art sing masc	2968.1 noun nom sing masc	840.1 prs-pron gen pl	3450.14 art dat pl fem	1094.7 noun dat pl fem	840.1 prs-pron gen pl
ὁ	λάρυγξ	αὐτῶν,	ταῖς	γλώσσαις	αὐτῶν
ho	larunx	autōn,	tais	glōssais	autōn
the	throat	their,	with the	tongues	their

1381.1 verb 3pl indic imperf act	2423.1 noun nom sing masc	779.1 noun gen pl fem	5097.3 prep	3450.17 art pl neu
ἐδολιοῦσαν·	ἰὸς	ἀσπίδων	ὑπὸ	τὰ
edoliousan	ios	aspidōn	hupo	ta
they were using deceit:	poison	of asps	under	the

5327.4 noun acc pl neu	840.1 prs-pron gen pl	3614.1 rel-pron gen pl	3450.16 art sing neu	4601.1 noun sing neu	142.16 verb nom sing masc part aor act
χείλη	αὐτῶν·	**14.** ὧν	τὸ	στόμα	ἀρᾶς
cheilē	autōn	hōn	to	stoma	aras
lips	their:	of whom	the	mouth	having cursed

The idea "that they are all under sin" is also expressed in Galatians 3:22, "The Scripture hath concluded all under sin." This seems to indicate that they are not only sinners, but are under an empire of sin.

3:10-12. Verse 10 begins an extended quotation from the Old Testament which runs through verse 18. The quotes are from six psalms and from Isaiah 59:7,8. God speaks as a judge (verses 10-12); as a physician (verses 13-15); and as a historian (verses 16-18).

The judge brings six sweeping charges of guilt: "There is none righteous . . . there is none that understandeth, there is none that seeketh after God. They are all gone out of the way, they are together become unprofitable; there is none that doeth good."

These are the evidences for the indictment. Two major emphases stand out. Sin is universal. All are under its power and condemnation. Not one person is excluded. The second emphasis is upon the depravity and intensity of sin. Every aspect of a man's life is affected, his thoughts, words, and deeds.

"None righteous." No mortal soul has ever been righteous. Even Adam was not righteous; he was innocent, that is, not knowing good from evil (Psalms 14:1; 53:1; Ecclesiastes 7:20). "Understandeth." Man by nature can understand nothing of God (1 Corinthians 1:21). "Gone out of the way" implies turning aside, backsliding. Apostasy is first described in 1:21. "Together" (*hama*) means "one and all," everyone individually.

3:13,14. God as physician diagnoses five deadly ailments: (1) Their throat is like an open sepulcher—death, decay, stench. (2) Their tongues use deceit—deceitful. (3) The venom of asps is under their lips—uncharitable. (4) Their mouth is full of cursing and bitterness—blasphemous. (5) Their feet are swift to shed blood—murderous. Four different bodily organs connected with speech and one connected with the feet are mentioned. This illustrates how man's sinfulness is exemplified in his words.

"Their throat is an open sepulchre," the grave has been opened and remains open. The stench is not due to the grave itself but to the rottenness within. Can you imagine a worse odor than that of a decaying carcass? That reeking smell depicts the corruption of so much of human speech. As the contents of the grave cause the stench, so the contents of the human heart and mind cause the unclean, unkind utterances.

The fangs of deadly serpents are to be feared. Their poisonous venom is easily fatal. Man is born with this venom under his tongue. Bitter, deceitful, poisonous words maim and kill. We will be held accountable for our words (Matthew 12:36). Words are like a bag of feathers in the wind. Once they are released they cannot be gathered again. Poisonous words do untold damage to God's work, to others, and to the speaker himself.

for we have before proved both Jews and Gentiles, that they are all under sin: . . . vve haue argued, *Rheims* . . . under sin's dominion, *JB* . . . being in thraldom to sin, *Weymouth* . . . in subjection to sin, *TCNT* . . . under the sway of sin, *Williams* . . . decided to serve sin, *Fenton*.

10. As it is written: There is none righteous, no, not one: . . . not one just man, *Confraternity* . . . who stands right with God, *TCNT* . . . single human creature is upright, *Williams*.

11. There is none that understandeth: there is none that seeketh after God: . . . diligently seeketh, *Noyes*.

12. They are all gone out of the way: All have swerved, *HistNT* . . . Al haue declined, *Rheims* . . . All have left the ranks, *Fenton* . . . Everyone has side stepped, *Klingensmith*.

they are together become unprofitable: . . . they have become utterly useless, *Berkeley* . . . one and all become worthless, *Beck* . . . one and all have become vile, *Adams* . . . become depraved, *TCNT* . . . gone wrong, *Moffatt* . . . have turned bad together, *HistNT* . . . become corrupt, *Weymouth*.

there is none that doeth good, no, not one: Not a single one practices kindness, *Norlie*.

13. Their throat [is] an open sepulchre: . . . are yawning graves, *JB, Fenton* . . . an open tomb, *PNT*.

with their tongues they have used deceit: They use their tongues to trick people, *SEB* . . . they are treacherous with their tongues, *Moffatt*.

the poison of asps [is] under their lips: Their lips hide the poison of snakes, *Beck* . . . cobras, *Adams* . . . the venym of snakis is vndir her lippis, *Wyclif*.

14. Whose mouth [is] full of cursing and bitterness: . . . full of imprecations, *Wuest*.

2504.1 conj	3949.2 noun gen sing fem	1066.1 verb 3sing indic pres act	3554.1 adj nom pl masc	3450.7 art pl masc	4087.4 noun nom pl masc
καὶ	πικρίας	γέμει·	**15.** ὀξεῖς	οἱ	πόδες
kai	*pikrias*	*gemei*	*oxeis*	*hoi*	*podes*
and	of bitternes	is full;	swift	the	feet

840.1 prs-pron gen pl	1618.4 verb inf aor act	129.1 noun sing neu	4790.1 noun nom sing neu	2504.1 conj	4855.1 noun nom sing fem
αὐτῶν	ἐκχέαι	αἷμα·	**16.** σύντριμμα	καὶ	ταλαιπωρία
autōn	*ekcheai*	*haima*	*suntrimma*	*kai*	*talaipōria*
their	to shed	blood;	ruin	and	misery

1706.1 prep	3450.14 art dat pl fem	3461.7 noun dat pl fem	840.1 prs-pron gen pl	2504.1 conj	3461.4 noun acc sing fem	1503.2 noun gen sing fem
ἐν	ταῖς	ὁδοῖς	αὐτῶν·	**17.** καὶ	ὁδὸν	εἰρήνης
en	*tais*	*hodois*	*autōn*	*kai*	*hodon*	*eirēnēs*
in	the	ways	their;	and	a way	of peace

3620.2 partic	1091.18 verb 3pl indic aor act	3620.2 partic	1498.4 verb 3sing indic pres act	5238.1 noun nom sing masc	2296.2 noun gen sing masc
οὐκ	ἔγνωσαν.	**18.** οὐκ	ἔστιν	φόβος	θεοῦ
ouk	*egnōsan*	*ouk*	*estin*	*phobos*	*theou*
not	they did know:	no	there is	fear	of God

558.1 prep gen	3450.1 art gen pl	3652.6 noun gen pl masc	840.1 prs-pron gen pl	3471.5 verb 1pl indic perf act
ἀπέναντι	τῶν	ὀφθαλμῶν	αὐτῶν.	**19.** Οἴδαμεν
apenanti	*tōn*	*ophthalmōn*	*autōn*	*Oidamen*
before	the	eyes	their.	We know

1156.2 conj	3617.1 conj	3607.8 rel-pron pl neu	3450.5 art sing masc	3414.1 noun nom sing masc	2978.5 verb 3sing indic pres act
δὲ	ὅτι	ὅσα	ὁ	νόμος	λέγει,
de	*hoti*	*hosa*	*ho*	*nomos*	*legei*
now	that	whatsoever	the	law	says,

3450.4 art dat pl	1706.1 prep	3450.3 art dat sing	3414.3 noun dat sing masc	2953.2 verb sing indic pres act	2419.1 conj	3820.17 adj sing neu
τοῖς	ἐν	τῷ	νόμῳ	λαλεῖ·	ἵνα	πᾶν
tois	*en*	*tō*	*nomō*	*lalei*	*hina*	*pan*
to the	in	the	law	it speaks,	that	every

4601.1 noun sing neu	5256.2 verb 3sing subj aor pass	2504.1 conj	5105.1 adj nom sing masc	1090.40 verb 3sing subj aor mid
στόμα	φραγῇ,	καὶ	ὑπόδικος	γένηται
stoma	*phragē*	*kai*	*hupodikos*	*genētai*
mouth	may be stopped,	and	under judgment	be

3820.6 adj sing masc	3450.5 art sing masc	2862.1 noun nom sing masc	3450.3 art dat sing	2296.3 noun dat sing masc	1354.1 conj
πᾶς	ὁ	κόσμος	τῷ	θεῷ·	**20.** διότι
pas	*ho*	*kosmos*	*tō*	*theō*	*dioti*
all	the	world	to	God.	Wherefore

1523.1 prep gen	2024.5 noun gen pl neu	3414.2 noun gen sing masc	3620.3 partic	1338.24 verb 3sing indic fut pass	3820.9 adj nom sing fem
ἐξ	ἔργων	νόμου	οὐ	δικαιωθήσεται	πᾶσα
ex	*ergōn*	*nomou*	*ou*	*dikaiōthēsetai*	*pasa*
by	works	of law	not	shall be justified	any

4418.1 noun nom sing fem	1783.1 prep gen	840.3 prs-pron gen sing	1217.2 prep	1056.1 conj	3414.2 noun gen sing masc
σὰρξ	ἐνώπιον	αὐτοῦ·	διὰ	γὰρ	νόμου
sarx	*enōpion*	*autou*	*dia*	*gar*	*nomou*
flesh	before	him;	through	for	law

3:15. The first recorded sin following the Fall was murder. The first sin separated man from God in Eden; the second sin separated man from man. In worship to God, Cain could not slay an animal, but in anger he could slay his brother.

3:16,17. Man's wicked ways bring nothing but "destruction and misery." This is true whether he is a Hitler, a well-known criminal, or an unknown sinner. Sin leaves a tragic trail.

"There is no peace, saith my God, to the wicked" (Isaiah 57:21). Isaiah 59 catalogs the way of sinners. They walk continually in paths of violence. Their crooked paths leave a trail of waste and destruction (Isaiah 59:8).

3:18,19. All man's sin seems to be summed up in Psalm 36:1 referred to here: "The transgression of the wicked saith within my heart, that there is no fear of God before his eyes." The wicked completely ignore God; they act as though He is nonexistent.

Hupodikos, found only here in the New Testament, means "under sentence of condemnation." The whole world is brought to trial before God, is found guilty, and is under a sentence of condemnation.

3:20. The words "deeds of the law" appear to go beyond the Mosaic law. "No flesh" can be "justified" in God's sight "by the law." The verb *dikaioō* indicates that only God can declare man righteous. Justification is the judicial act of God wherein He shows man free from guilt and acceptable to God (Ephesians 1:6).

At this point Calvinists and Arminians divide. It is imputation versus impartation. Calvinists state that in justification the righteousness of Christ is imputed to the sinner. The Arminians teach that God in one act of justification makes man righteous and then pronounces him righteous. Their reasoning is that God will not declare righteous what is not righteous.

The Law was given through Moses to give us the "knowledge of sin." God knew that the Law could never save us because of the weakness of our flesh. It could only give us the knowledge of sin's awful character.

Two expressions, "before God" (verse 19) and "in his sight" (verse 20), are significant. All the world is guilty "before God," and no flesh is justified "in his sight." The Law has done its work. It could not justify; it only condemned. The old covenant brought death, but the new covenant brings life.

The Law may be compared to a scale which tells us how much we weigh; it will not add to or subtract from our weight. The Law discovers the fact of sin, exposing its presence and revealing its nature in order that God might prescribe the remedy.

15. Their feet [are] swift to shed blood: They move quickly to kill someone, *SEB*.

16. Destruction and misery [are] in their ways: Ruin and misery mark their path, *Weymouth* . . . wherever they go there is havoc, *JB* . . . people are suffering and destroyed, *SEB* . . . break down and misery are in their road, *Klingensmith* . . . wretchednes, *Tyndale* . . . calamitie, *Geneva* . . . dog their steps, *TCNT*.

17. And the way of peace have they not known: And the path to peace, *TCNT*.

18. There is no fear of God before their eyes: No reverence of God is, *Berkeley* . . . God does not terrify them, *Beck*.

19. Now we know that what things soever the law saith: . . . whatever the Law enjoins, *Scarlett*.

it saith to them who are under the law: . . . it says to those under its control, *Berkeley* . . . who are under its authority, *Williams*.

that every mouth may be stopped: . . . in order to stop all human excuses, *TEV*.

and all the world may become guilty before God: . . . may become liable to divine retribution, *Berkeley* . . . made answerable to God, *Moffatt* . . . may be brought under the judgment of God, *Alford, Clementson* . . . that the whole world may be under the sentence, *Worrell*.

20. Therefore by the deeds of the law there shall no flesh be justified in his sight: . . . as the result of actions done in obedience to Law, *TCNT* . . . by the practice of a ritual, *Fenton* . . . into right standing with God, *Williams*.

for by the law [is] the knowledge of sin: . . . that one becomes fully aware of his sin, *Adams* . . . there comes a clear conception of sin, *TCNT* . . . a recognition of sin comes by means of, *Fenton* . . . comes the consciousness of sin, *Montgomery*.

Romans 3:21

1907.1 noun nom sing fem ἐπίγνωσις epignōsis knowledge	264.1 noun fem ἁμαρτίας. hamartias of sin.	3432.1 adv 21. Νυνὶ Nuni Now	1156.2 conj δὲ de but	5400.1 prep gen χωρὶς chōris apart from
3414.2 noun gen sing masc νόμου nomou law	1336.1 noun nom sing fem δικαιοσύνη dikaiosunē righteousness	2296.2 noun gen sing masc θεοῦ theou of God		5157.18 verb 3sing indic perf pass πεφανέρωται, pephanerōtai has been manifested,

3113.35 verb nom sing fem part pres pass μαρτυρουμένη marturoumenē being borne witness to	5097.3 prep ὑπὸ hupo by	3450.2 art gen sing τοῦ tou the	3414.2 noun gen sing masc νόμου nomou law	2504.1 conj καὶ kai and	3450.1 art gen pl τῶν tōn the
4254.5 noun gen pl masc προφητῶν· prophētōn prophets:	1336.1 noun nom sing fem 22. δικαιοσύνη dikaiosunē righteousness	1156.2 conj δὲ de even	2296.2 noun gen sing masc θεοῦ theou of God		1217.2 prep διὰ dia through
3963.2 noun gen sing fem πίστεως pisteōs faith	2400.2 name masc Ἰησοῦ Iēsou of Jesus	5382.2 name gen masc Χριστοῦ, Christou Christ,	1519.1 prep εἰς eis towards	3820.8 adj acc pl masc πάντας pantas all	⁽ᵃ 2504.1 conj καὶ kai and
1894.3 prep ἐπὶ epi upon	3820.8 adj acc pl masc πάντας ⑊ pantas all	3450.8 art acc pl masc τοὺς tous the	3961.15 verb acc pl masc part pres act πιστεύοντας· pisteuontas believing:	3620.3 partic οὐ ou no	1056.1 conj γάρ gar for

22.a.Txt: 01ℵ-corr,06D
018K,020L,33,byz.it.
Weis,Sod
Var: p40,01ℵ-org,02A
03B,04C,025P,sa.bo.
Lach,Treg,Tisc,We/Ho
UBS/⋆

1498.4 verb 3sing indic pres act ἐστιν estin there is	1287.1 noun nom sing fem διαστολή· diastolē difference:	3820.7 adj pl masc 23. πάντες pantes all	1056.1 conj γὰρ gar for	262.11 verb indic aor act ἥμαρτον hēmarton sinned
2504.1 conj καὶ kai and	5139.10 verb 3pl indic pres pass ὑστεροῦνται husterountai come short	3450.10 art gen sing fem τῆς tēs of the	1385.2 noun gen sing fem δόξης doxēs glory	3450.2 art gen sing τοῦ tou
2296.2 noun gen sing masc θεοῦ, theou of God:	1338.11 verb nom pl masc part pres pass 24. δικαιούμενοι dikaioumenoi being justified	1425.1 adv δωρεὰν dōrean freely	3450.11 art dat sing fem τῇ tē by the	840.3 prs- pron gen sing αὐτοῦ autou his
5322.3 noun dat sing fem χάριτι, chariti grace,	1217.2 prep διὰ dia through	3450.10 art gen sing fem τῆς tēs the	623.2 noun gen sing fem ἀπολυτρώσεως apolutrōseōs redemption	3450.10 art gen sing fem τῆς tēs the
1706.1 prep ἐν en in	5382.3 name dat masc Χριστῷ Christō Christ	2400.2 name masc Ἰησοῦ, Iēsou Jesus;	3614.6 rel-pron acc sing masc 25. ὃν hon whom	4246.2 verb 3sing indic aor mid προέθετο proetheto set forth	3450.5 art sing masc ὁ ho

3:21. For generations people had been sinning and learning that it was neither possible to put away or to conquer sin. "But now" God clearly and openly had revealed the way.

Since the Law cannot justify, man's only hope is for a "righteousness without the Law." It is not an unlawful righteousness or one that allows man to sin, but a change of position and condition produced apart from the Law. This does not mean that justification without the Law was now for the first time revealed and that earlier men had reason to believe that they could be justified by works of the Law. To prevent any such misunderstanding, Paul expressly stated that this righteousness of God was witnessed by the Law and the Prophets, the usual phrase signifying the entire Old Testament.

There is supernatural continuity between the two Testaments. What is emphasized here is the *manifestation* of God's righteousness. It can be stated unequivocally that Christ Jesus *is* God's righteousness. He who was promised in the Old Testament had now been manifested in the flesh, having been "delivered for our offenses, and was raised again for our justification" (4:25).

3:22. "The righteousness of God" is not a law-righteousness (verse 21) but a faith-righteousness (verse 22). It comes by faith in Jesus Christ and is imparted to all who believe.

"By faith of Jesus Christ" can be understood as faith *of* Him as well as faith *in* Him. It is impossible to have one without the other. In the Greek phraseology, we have the genitive form; this shows that it is faith possessed by Christ which He gives to those who are willing to receive. Of course, it operates as faith *in* Him. Faith as described in the Bible is God's gracious gift: "For by grace are ye saved through faith; *and that not of yourselves*" (Ephesians 2:8). To believe is to respond to God's gracious gift, exercising the faith He offers to all.

"No difference." The word *diastolē* is used in only two other places, Romans 10:12 and 1 Corinthians 4:7. Many translators render the word "distinction." There may be difference essentially between two things and yet no distinction is made, so "distinction" seems to be the better translation.

3:23. This is the most clear-cut statement about sin in all Scripture. All have fallen short. "There is none righteous, no, not one" (3:10). God has made no charges that He has not substantiated. The proof is clear and convincing. There is no appeal and no reversal of the verdict.

3:24. *Apolutrōsis*, "redemption," is the theme of this epistle. Christ paid the ransom and we are redeemed. We are justified (acquitted) and declared righteous "freely by his grace."

21. But now the righteousness of God without the law is manifested: . . . a Divine righteousness is exhibited, *Fenton* . . . the iustice of God, *Rheims* . . . has been revealed, *SEB* . . . has been disclosed apart from law, *HistNT*.

being witnessed by the law and the prophets: . . . testified to by the law, *Young* . . . point toward this truth, *SEB*.

22. Even the righteousness of God: . . . rightewesnes no dout which is good before God, *Tyndale*.

[which is] by faith of Jesus Christ unto all and upon all them that believe: . . . that is channeled through faith, *Adams*.

for there is no difference: For there is no distinction, *Berkeley* . . . It makes no difference who you are, *SEB*.

23. For all have sinned:
and come short of the glory of God: . . . and are destitute of, *Geneva* . . . and forfeited God's glory, *JB* . . . and are without God's glory, *Beck* . . . all fall short of God's glorious ideal, *TCNT* . . . and have need of the glory of God, *Confraternity* . . . and everybody continues to come short, *Williams* . . . and fall short of the majesty of, *HistNT* . . . and all consciously come short of, *Weymouth* . . . and fail of obtaining the glory which cometh from God, *Noyes* . . . are in need of rectification from God, *Fenton* . . . and lacke the prayse that is of valoure, *Tyndale*.

24. Being justified freely by his grace: . . . become righteous by a gift of His love, *Beck* . . . they are justified for nothing, *Moffatt* . . . gaining acquittal from guilt, *Weymouth* . . . being justified gratuitously by, *Wuest* . . . being declared righteous freely, *Young* . . . Iustified gratis by his grace, *Rheims*.

through the redemption that is in Christ Jesus: . . . through the ransom that Christ Jesus provided, *Berkeley* . . . which is paid in Christ Jesus, *Conybeare* . . . by His free unpurchased grace, *Weymouth* . . . paid to free them, *Beck*.

25.a.**Txt:** 03B,04C-corr
06D-corr,018K,020L
025P,33,byz.Weis,Sod
Var: 01א,04C-org
06D-org,Lach,Treg,Alf
Tisc,We/Ho,UBS/✶

2296.1 noun nom sing masc	2411.1 adj acc sing neu	1217.2 prep	3450.10 art gen sing fem	3963.2 noun gen sing fem	1706.1 prep
θεὸς	ἱλαστήριον	διὰ	[a τῆς]	πίστεως	ἐν
theos	hilastērion	dia	tēs	pisteōs	en
God	a mercy seat	through	the	faith	in

3450.3 art dat sing	840.3 prs-pron gen sing	129.3 noun dat sing neu	1519.1 prep	1716.2 noun acc sing fem	3450.10 art gen sing fem
τῷ	αὐτοῦ	αἵματι,	εἰς	ἔνδειξιν	τῆς
tō	autou	haimati	eis	endeixin	tēs
the	his	blood,	for	a demonstration	of the

1336.2 noun gen sing fem	840.3 prs-pron gen sing	1217.2 prep	3450.12 art acc sing fem	3791.1 noun acc sing fem
δικαιοσύνης	αὐτοῦ,	διὰ	τὴν	πάρεσιν
dikaiosunēs	autou	dia	tēn	paresin
righteousness	his,	because of	the	passing by

3450.1 art gen pl	4125.1 verb gen pl neu part perf act	263.3 noun gen pl neu	1706.1 prep
τῶν	προγεγονότων	ἁμαρτημάτων	26. ἐν
tōn	progegonotōn	hamartēmatōn	en
the	having before taken place	sins	in

26.a.**Var:** 01א,02A,03B
04C,06D-org,025P,Lach
Treg,Alf,Tisc,We/Ho
Weis,Sod,UBS/✶

3450.11 art dat sing fem	460.2 noun dat sing fem	3450.2 art gen sing	2296.2 noun gen sing masc	4242.1 prep	3450.12 art acc sing fem
τῇ	ἀνοχῇ	τοῦ	θεοῦ,	πρὸς	[a ✶+ τὴν]
tē	anochē	tou	theou	pros	tēn
the	tolerance		of God;	for	[the]

1716.2 noun acc sing fem	3450.10 art gen sing fem	1336.2 noun gen sing fem	840.3 prs-pron gen sing	1706.1 prep	3450.3 art dat sing
ἔνδειξιν	τῆς	δικαιοσύνης	αὐτοῦ	ἐν	τῷ
endeixin	tēs	dikaiosunēs	autou	en	tō
demonstration	of the	righteousness	his	in	the

3431.1 adv	2511.3 noun dat sing masc	1519.1 prep	3450.16 art sing neu	1498.32 verb inf pres act	840.6 prs-pron acc sing masc	1337.1 adj sing
νῦν	καιρῷ,	εἰς	τὸ	εἶναι	αὐτὸν	δίκαιον
nun	kairō	eis	to	einai	auton	dikaion
now	time,	for	the	to be	his	just

2504.1 conj	1338.3 verb acc sing masc part pres act	3450.6 art acc sing masc	1523.2 prep gen	3963.2 noun gen sing fem	2400.2 name masc
καὶ	δικαιοῦντα	τὸν	ἐκ	πίστεως	Ἰησοῦ.
kai	dikaiounta	ton	ek	pisteōs	Iēsou.
and	justifying	the	of	faith	of Jesus.

4085.1 adv	3631.1 conj	3450.9 art nom sing fem	2716.1 noun nom sing fem	1563.2 verb 3sing indic aor pass
27. Ποῦ	οὖν	ἡ	καύχησις;	ἐξεκλείσθη.
Pou	oun	hē	kauchēsis	exekleisthē
Where	then	the	boasting?	It was excluded.

1217.2 prep	4029.3 intr-pron gen sing masc	3414.2 noun gen sing masc	3450.1 art gen pl	2024.5 noun gen pl neu	3644.1 adv	233.2 conj
διὰ	ποίου	νόμου;	τῶν	ἔργων;	οὐχί,	ἀλλὰ
dia	poiou	nomou	tōn	ergōn	ouchi	alla
Through	what	law?	of the	works?	No,	but

1217.2 prep	3414.2 noun gen sing masc	3963.2 noun gen sing fem	3023.5 verb 1pl indic pres	3631.1 conj
διὰ	νόμου	πίστεως.	28. λογιζόμεθα	[οὖν]
dia	nomou	pisteōs	logizometha	oun
through	a law	of faith.	We reckon	therefore

3:25,26. The word *justify* as employed in the New Testament means more than to forgive sin and remove condemnation; it means also to place the offenders in the position of righteousness. God blots out the past with all its sin and then considers the sinner as if he had never sinned. The sinner is pronounced "justified." Justification has been purchased through the propitiatory sacrifice of Christ.

Propitiation means bringing together, making favorable, thus enabling someone to act with mercy and forgiveness. A propitiation is a sacrifice or gift which averts the wrath of God and enables Him to be merciful and favorable to the sinner.

In the Septuagint (Numbers 7:89) *hilastērion* translates the Hebrew term *kappōreth*, "mercy seat." This refers to the place on the ark of the covenant where the blood of the sacrifices was sprinkled on the Day of Atonement. (See Hebrews 9:5.) Access to God has been purchased at a great price, the blood of Christ.

En tō autou haimati. En is instrumental expressing means. *Haimati*, "blood," is the instrument. The reference is to the life blood of Jesus as the means of propitiation. Blood is regarded as the reservoir of life (Leviticus 17:11). Its application was the application of life, and the offering of the blood to God was an offering of life.

Autou ("his") emphasizes the identity of the sacrifices as that of the life of Jesus. The emphasis is on the voluntary offering of Jesus' life to God. His sacrificial death becomes in a twofold sense the means by which God does away with a person's sin. The sin is removed not only from the believer's life but also from the presence of God. The *hilastērion* which God provided in Christ not only removes the ungodliness and unrighteousness of men, but also averts the wrath and retribution which is its just due. Christ died in order to save us from God's wrath and to secure His favor for us.

The propitiation becomes effective *dia pisteōs*, "through faith" (Hebrews 10:19,20,22).

The effect of Christ's redemption was retroactive. Before Calvary God gave proof of His anger against sin by now and then inflicting punishment on sinners. But He did not inflict the full penalty, for if He had the race would have perished.

Paresin ("remission," literally "passed over") indicates a temporary passing by and not a permanent absolution of sin. Sins prior to Calvary were temporarily covered awaiting the perfect sacrifice: "for the remission of sins that are past, through the forbearance of God."

En tō nun kairō, "at the present time," is in contrast to the sins previously considered. Christ's blood was shed to cover and wash away sins that had been temporarily covered in the past and also to declare God's righteousness "at this time."

3:27,28. Man was not made righteous by the Law. Peter expressed the Jews' inability to keep the Law (Acts 15:10). The Law

25. Whom God hath set forth [to be] a propitiation through faith in his blood: . . . vvhom God hath proposed, *Rheims* . . . God once publicly offered Him in His death, *Williams* . . . as a reconciling sacrifice, *Berkeley* . . . by his sacrifice of himself, *TCNT* . . . as a Mercy-Seat, rendered efficacious through faith, *Weymouth* . . . to be the obtayner of mercy thorow fayth, *Cranmer* . . . to be a pacification, *Geneva* . . . as an offering of atonement, *Montgomery* . . . as an expiatory satisfaction, *Wuest.*

to declare his righteousness for the remission of sins that are past: . . . for the manifestation of His righteousness, *Worrell* . . . for a demonstration of his own justice, *Campbell* . . . that sins are taken away, *SEB* . . . because of the passing by of the errors committed previously, *Sawyer* . . . of the bygone sins, *Young.*

through the forbearance of God: . . . in His tolerance, *Adams.*

26. To declare, [I say], at this time his righteousness: . . . for the showing, I say, *Panin* . . . in our present period, *Berkeley.*

that he might be just, and the justifier of him which believeth in Jesus: . . . stand right with himself, *TCNT* . . . might justify the children of Faith, *Conybeare* . . . on the score of faith in Jesus, *Moffatt.*

27. Where [is] boasting then?: What then, becomes of our vain human pride? *Norlie* . . . Where is then the reioysyng? *Geneva* . . . where is the exulting? *HistNT.*

It is excluded: There is no room left for it, *TCNT* . . . outlawed, *Norlie* . . . It is ruled out absolutely, *Moffatt* . . . for ever shut out, *Weymouth* . . . banished, *Fenton* . . . It was once for all excluded, *Wuest.*

By what law? of works? Nay: but by the law of faith: On what principle? *Williams* . . . What sort of Law forbids it? A Law prescribing acts? No, a Law prescribing faith, *TCNT* . . . through the principle of faith, *SEB* . . . a law of deeds? *HistNT* . . . On the ground of merit? *Weymouth.*

Romans 3:29

28.a.Txt: 03B,04C
06D-corr,018K,020L
025P,33,byz.Weis,Sod
Var: 01ℵ,02A,06D-org
bo.Gries,Lach,Treg,Alf
Word,Tisc,We/Ho
UBS/✸

1056.1 conj	3963.3 noun dat sing fem	1338.12 verb inf pres pass	1338.12 verb inf pres pass
[ᵃ✸ γὰρ]	ʹ πίστει	δικαιοῦσθαι	[✸ δικαιοῦσθαι
gar	pistei	dikaiousthai	dikaiousthai
[for]	by faith	to be justified	[to be justified

3963.3 noun dat sing fem	442.4 noun acc sing masc	5400.1 prep gen	2024.5 noun gen pl neu	3414.2 noun gen sing masc
πίστει]	ἄνθρωπον,	χωρὶς	ἔργων	νόμου.
pistei	anthrōpon	chōris	ergōn	nomou
by faith]	a man	apart from	works	of law.

2211.1 conj	2428.3 name-adj gen pl masc	3450.5 art sing masc	2296.1 noun nom sing masc	3303.1 adv	3644.1 adv
29. ἤ	Ἰουδαίων	ὁ	θεὸς	μόνον;	οὐχὶ
ē	Ioudaiōn	ho	theos	monon	ouchi
Or	of Jews	the	God	only?	not

29.a.Txt: 020L,025P,byz.
Var: 01ℵ,02A,03B,04C
06D,018K,bo.Gries
Lach,Treg,Alf,Tisc
We/Ho,Weis,Sod
UBS/✸

1156.2 conj	2504.1 conj	1477.5 noun gen pl neu	3346.1 partic	2504.1 conj	1477.5 noun gen pl neu
ʳᵃ δὲ ʾ	καὶ	ἐθνῶν;	ναὶ	καὶ	ἐθνῶν·
de	kai	ethnōn	nai	kai	ethnōn
and	also	of Gentiles?	Yes,	also	of Gentiles:

30.a.Txt: 01ℵ-corr
06D-org,018K,020L
025P,byz.Weis
Var: 01ℵ-org,02A,03B
04C,06D-corr,Lach,Treg
Alf,Tisc,We/Ho,Sod
UBS/✸

1882.1 conj	1499.1 conj	1518.3 num card nom masc	3450.5 art sing masc	2296.1 noun nom sing masc
30. ʹ ἐπείπερ	[ᵃ✸ εἴπερ]	εἷς	ὁ	θεός
epeiper	eiper	heis	ho	theos
since indeed	[idem]	one	the	God

3614.5 rel-pron nom sing masc	1338.8 verb 3sing indic fut act	3921.4 noun acc sing fem	1523.2 prep gen	3963.2 noun gen sing fem	2504.1 conj
ὃς	δικαιώσει	περιτομὴν	ἐκ	πίστεως,	καὶ
hos	dikaiōsei	peritomēn	ek	pisteōs	kai
who	will justify	circumcision	by	faith,	and

201.4 noun acc sing fem	1217.2 prep	3450.10 art gen sing fem	3963.2 noun gen sing fem	3414.4 noun acc sing masc
ἀκροβυστίαν	διὰ	τῆς	πίστεως.	**31.** νόμον
akrobustian	dia	tēs	pisteōs	nomon
uncircumcision	through	the	faith.	Law

3631.1 conj	2643.2 verb 1pl indic pres act	1217.2 prep	3450.10 art gen sing fem	3963.2 noun gen sing fem	3231.1 partic
οὖν	καταργοῦμεν	διὰ	τῆς	πίστεως;	μὴ
oun	katargoumen	dia	tēs	pisteōs	mē
then	do we make of no effect	through	the	faith?	Not

31.a.Txt: 01ℵ-corr,018K
020L,025P,byz.
Var: 01ℵ-org,02A,03B
04C,06D,Lach,Treg,Alf
Tisc,We/Ho,Weis,Sod
UBS/✸

1090.44 verb 3sing opt aor mid	233.2 conj	3414.4 noun acc sing masc	2449.2 verb 1pl indic pres act	2449.50 verb 1pl indic pres act
γένοιτο·	ἀλλὰ	νόμον	ʹ ἱστῶμεν.	[ᵃ✸ ἱστάνομεν.]
genoito	alla	nomon	histōmen	histanomen
may it be!	but	law	we establish.	[idem]

4949.9 intr-pron sing neu	3631.1 conj	2029.12 verb 1pl indic fut act	11.1 name masc	3450.6 art acc sing masc	3824.4 noun acc sing masc
4:1. Τί	οὖν	ἐροῦμεν	ʹ Ἀβραὰμ	τὸν	πατέρα
Ti	oun	eroumen	Abraam	ton	patera
What	then	shall we say	Abraham	the	father

1.a.Txt: 018K,020L
025P,33,byz.
Var: 01ℵ,02A,04C-org
sa.Lach,Treg,Alf,Tisc
Weis,Sod,UBS/✸

2231.2 prs-pron gen 1pl	2128.24 verb inf perf act	2128.24 verb inf perf act	11.1 name masc	3450.6 art acc sing masc
ἡμῶν	εὑρηκέναι	[ᵃ✸ εὑρηκέναι	Ἀβραὰμ	τὸν
hēmōn	heurēkenai	heurēkenai	Abraam	ton
our	to have found	[to have found	Abraham	the

revealed he was not righteous. The law of *faith*, the gospel, completely excludes boasting. Righteousness is dependent upon merit. We receive it by accepting by faith the Christ who has merit.

3:29-31. God's plan of salvation casts all the provision on a God who cannot fail and brings all men to the same level of need and dependence on the grace of God. Pride is eliminated (3:27,28). There is no place for boasting. Prejudice is eliminated (3:29,30). There is no favored group and no special person. Presumption is eliminated. One dare not presume upon the grace of God.

If justification were possible by the Law, then God belonged only to the Jew, but since justification is by faith, He is God of both Jew and Gentile. There can be no boasting if man examines his record. It is black (1:18-32). There can be no boasting if man considers the Law, for the Law is a rigid, impartial measuring rod (2:17 to 3:8). There can be no boasting if man remembers the Cross, for there man's helplessness and God's love and mercy are revealed.

Three statements are made: (1) If the way of salvation is by faith alone, there is no place for human effort. (2) If the way of salvation is by faith alone, there is no difference between Jew and Gentile. "The Lord our God is one God" (Deuteronomy 6:4) is the basis of the Jewish creed and the opening words of every synagogue service. There is not one God for the Gentiles and another for the Jews.

(3) Though the way of salvation is by faith alone, it does not mean an end of the Law. Paul says in verse 31, "We establish the law." The doctrine of grace does not render the moral law void. In reality it confirms and establishes its validity. The Law required the death penalty for violation. Paul preached that Christ died for our sins. He tasted "death for every man" (Hebrews 2:9). Israel, under the Law, was redeemed from the curse of the Law through Christ who was made a curse at Calvary.

When Paul asked, "Do we then make void the law through faith?" he anticipated the questions dealt with in detail in chapter 6. He was well aware of the dangers of the antinomian inferences some wanted to draw from the doctrine of grace. He dealt that heresy a death blow summarily, saying that faith actually establishes the Law. Only Christ *can* establish (fulfill) the Law (8:2,3)!

Jew and Gentile alike are justified by faith. Righteousness comes by faith alone. No other claim will do. The law of faith does no violence to the law of Moses. That law is established through God's act in fulfilling it. All its benefits accrue to the believer through faith in the work of Christ. The believer, through Christ, attaches a new sacredness to the commands of the Law and finds a new power to fulfill its demands.

4:1-3. Romans often reads like a lawbook; many terms are law terms. Arguments often follow legal precedents and are in logical order. The indictment against sin and sinners has been argued and every plea known to legal practice has been exhausted. At Calvary

28. Therefore we conclude that a man is justified by faith without the deeds of the law: We are convinced, *Beck* . . . for our reasoned conclusion, *Wuest* . . . altogether apart from the deeds, *Montgomery* . . . independently of the works of the Law, *Confraternity.*

29. [Is he] the God of the Jews only? [is he] not also of the Gentiles?: . . . of the heathen? *TCNT.*
Yes, of the Gentiles also: Assuredly, of Gentiles also, *HistNT.*

30. Seeing [it is] one God, which shall justify the circumcision by faith, and uncircumcision through faith: Agreeing there is but one God, *Berkeley* . . . assuming that there is one God...through the intermediary instrumentality of faith, *Wuest* . . . For it is God only whych iustyfyeth, *Cranmer* . . . who will pronounce the circumcised to be acquitted, *Weymouth.*

31. Do we then make void the law through faith?: Do we then use faith to overthrow Law? *TCNT* . . . Do we then render law invalid, *Montgomery* . . . cancel the Law? *Beck* . . . do we nullify the law by this faith? *Adams* . . . destroy the Law? *Confraternity* . . . make the Lawe vnprofitable, *Geneva* . . . make law useless through the faith? *Campbell.*
God forbid: Let not such a thing be considered, *Wuest* . . . on the contrary, *Montgomery.*
yea, we establish the law: . . . we establish its authority, *TCNT* . . . rather it strengthens the law, *Norlie* . . . giving the Law its true value, *JB* . . . We uphold the Law, *Beck, RSV, HistNT* . . . we give the Law a firmer footing, *Weymouth* . . . we corroborate the Law, *Fenton* . . . we rather mayntayne the lawe, *Tyndale* . . . we make it stand, *Montgomery.*

1. What shall we say then that Abraham our father, as pertaining to the flesh, hath found?: . . . our human ancestor, *Berkeley* . . . the ancestor of our nation? *TCNT* . . . What did he gain from his human experience? *SEB*

65

Romans 4:2

4169.1 noun acc sing masc	**2231.2** prs-pron gen 1pl	**2567.3** prep	**4418.4** noun acc sing fem	**1479.1** conj	**1056.1** conj
προπάτορα	ἡμῶν]	κατὰ	σάρκα;	**2.** εἰ	γὰρ
propatora	hēmōn	kata	sarka	ei	gar
forefather	our]	according to	flesh?	If	for

11.1 name masc	**1523.1** prep gen	**2024.5** noun gen pl neu	**1338.13** verb 3sing indic aor pass	**2174.4** verb 3sing indic pres act
Ἀβραὰμ	ἐξ	ἔργων	ἐδικαιώθη,	ἔχει
Abraam	ex	ergōn	edikaiōthē	echei
Abraham	by	works	was justified,	he has

2.a.**Txt:** 06D-corr,018K 020L,025P,byz. **Var:** 01א,02A,03B,04C 06D-org,Lach,Treg,Alf Word,Tisc,We/Ho,Weis Sod,UBS/✶

2715.1 noun sing neu	**233.1** conj	**3620.3** partic	**4242.1** prep	**3450.6** art acc sing masc	**2296.4** noun acc sing masc
καύχημα,	ἀλλ'	οὐ	πρὸς	⌈a τὸν ⌉	θεόν.
kauchēma	all'	ou	pros	ton	theon
ground of boasting,	but	not	towards		God.

4949.9 intr-pron sing neu	**1056.1** conj	**3450.9** art nom sing fem	**1118.1** noun nom sing fem	**2978.5** verb 3sing indic pres act	**3961.20** verb 3sing indic aor act
3. τί	γὰρ	ἡ	γραφὴ	λέγει;	Ἐπίστευσεν
ti	gar	hē	graphē	legei	Episteusen
What	for	the	scripture	says?	Believed

1156.2 conj	**11.1** name masc	**3450.3** art dat sing	**2296.3** noun dat sing masc	**2504.1** conj	**3023.11** verb 3sing indic aor pass
δὲ	Ἀβραὰμ	τῷ	θεῷ,	καὶ	ἐλογίσθη
de	Abraam	tō	theō	kai	elogisthē
and	Abraham		God,	and	it was reckoned

840.4 prs-pron dat sing	**1519.1** prep	**1336.4** noun acc sing fem	**3450.3** art dat sing	**1156.2** conj	**2021.9** verb dat sing masc part pres
αὐτῷ	εἰς	δικαιοσύνην.	**4.** Τῷ	δὲ	ἐργαζομένῳ
autō	eis	dikaiosunēn	Tō	de	ergazomenō
to him	for	righteousness.	To the	now	working

3450.5 art sing masc	**3272.1** noun nom sing masc	**3620.3** partic	**3023.4** verb 3sing indic pres	**2567.3** prep	**5322.4** noun acc sing fem
ὁ	μισθὸς	οὐ	λογίζεται	κατὰ	χάριν,
ho	misthos	ou	logizetai	kata	charin
the	reward	not	is reckoning	according to	grace,

4.a.**Txt:** Steph **Var:** 01א,02A,03B,04C 06D,018K,020L,025P byz.Gries,Lach,Treg,Alf Word,Tisc,We/Ho,Weis Sod,UBS/✶

233.2 conj	**2567.3** prep	**3450.16** art sing neu	**3647.1** noun acc sing neu	**3450.3** art dat sing	**1156.2** conj
ἀλλὰ	κατὰ	⌈a τὸ ⌉	ὀφείλημα·	**5.** τῷ	δὲ
alla	kata	to	opheilēma	tō	de
but	according to	the	debt:	to the	but

3231.1 partic	**2021.9** verb dat sing masc part pres	**3961.11** verb dat sing masc part pres act	**1156.2** conj	**1894.3** prep	**3450.6** art acc sing masc
μὴ	ἐργαζομένῳ,	πιστεύοντι	δὲ	ἐπὶ	τὸν
mē	ergazomenō	pisteuonti	de	epi	ton
not	working,	believeing	but	on	the

1338.3 verb acc sing masc part pres act	**3450.6** art acc sing masc	**759.2** adj acc sing masc	**3023.4** verb 3sing indic pres	**3450.9** art nom sing fem	**3963.1** noun nom sing fem
δικαιοῦντα	τὸν	ἀσεβῆ,	λογίζεται	ἡ	πίστις
dikaiounta	ton	asebē	logizetai	hē	pistis
justifying	the	ungodly,	is reckoning	the	faith

840.3 prs-pron gen sing	**1519.1** prep	**1336.4** noun acc sing fem	**2481.1** conj	**2504.1** conj	**1132.1** name masc
αὐτοῦ	εἰς	δικαιοσύνην.	**6.** καθάπερ	καὶ	Δαβὶδ
autou	eis	dikaiosunēn	kathaper	kai	Dabid
his	for	righteousness.	Even as	also	David

are met together; righteousness and peace have kissed each other" (Psalm 85:10). But the Jews could not understand that righteousness could come apart from the Law. Note how skillfully Paul builds support for the doctrine of justification. He cites the example of Abraham.

Abraham, of all men, is an example of righteousness. He had many qualities, but the only basis for his justification was that he believed God (John 8:56). It was not on the merit of his faith, but faith in God. This is the second time Paul quoted Genesis 15:6; he also referred to it while writing to the Galatians when they were threatened by the Judaizing heresy (Galatians 3:6). Some teachers seem to place more emphasis on faith than on the God whom we believe. Note that the Word does not say that Abraham believed *in* God; he "believed God." To believe God removes all doubt once God has clearly spoken to an individual.

A fairly common teaching is that faith is a "leap in the dark." It is actually the opposite of that. It is a step in the light as God reveals the light. By faith Abraham "went out, not knowing whither he went" (Hebrews 11:8), but knowing full well that he was walking with God, who is Light. Faith is not a work; faith caused Abraham to leave Ur, but the faith was genuine and complete before he left.

4:4. "Worketh" is *ergazomai*, meaning "to do that from which something results." "Reward," *misthos*, means "dues paid for work, wages." "Reckoned," *logizomai*, means to "think, impute, count, account." "Grace," *charis*, speaks of "God's favor." "Debt," *opheilēma*, means "that which is justly or legally due, a debt."

Under works the sinner feels he can earn his salvation; under grace he understands he must rely totally on God. Under law God gives a fair trial; under grace He gives pardon. Work and wages are contrasted with faith and grace. Conybeare and Howson translate verse 4 as follows: "Now, if a man earn his pay by his work, it is not 'reckoned to him' as a favor, but it is paid him as a debt."

4:5. God's justification is given to a person as a sinner, not as a saint. Justification does not depend on growth in spiritual maturity. That is sanctification. The person who sees the futility of trying to obtain God's favor by works and casts himself wholly on God will be justified.

"Ungodly" is *asebēs*, meaning a person totally lacking in piety, destitute of reverential awe of God. But such are justified by faith. In the Old Testament the condemnation of the innocent and the acquittal of the sinner are alike censured as acts of unjust judges. God himself states, "I will not justify the wicked." How startling and paradoxical that under grace God justifies the sinner. But through the provision of Calvary God maintains His own character. Almost beyond human understanding, God solved this moral problem by His grace.

. . . found with reference to the flesh? *Wuest* . . . according to the flesh, *Confraternity*.

2. For if Abraham were justified by works: . . . made righteous by rituals, *Fenton* . . . by human effort, *SEB* . . . as the result of his actions, *TCNT* . . . on the score of what he did, *Moffatt* . . . on the ground of his actions, *Weymouth*.

he hath [whereof] to glory; but not before God: . . . he has something to brag about, *Berkeley* . . . he has something to exult about, *HistNT* . . . he hath ground of boasting, *Alford* . . . he has something to be proud of. But not to be proud of before God, *Moffatt* . . . But he couldn't feel proud before God, *Beck*.

3. For what saith the scripture?: . . . for what doth the writing say? *Young*.

Abraham believed God: . . . had faith in God, *Noyes*.

and it was counted unto him for righteousness: . . . and his faith was regarded by God, *TCNT* . . . so God declared him, *SEB* . . . placed to his credit, *Weymouth* . . . and it vvas reputed him to iustice, *Rheims* . . . and it was paid to him in righteousness, *Fenton* . . . and it was credited to him as right standing with God, *Williams*.

4. Now to him that worketh is the reward not reckoned of grace, but of debt: . . . is not imputed according to grace, *Rheims* . . . as a favor, *SEB* . . . pay is not reckoned a favour but a debt, *Weymouth* . . . the remuneration is not put down on his account...but as a legally contracted debt, *Wuest* . . . are not credited as a favor but as an obligation, *Berkeley* . . . a worker has his wage counted to him as a due, *Moffatt*.

5. But to him that worketh not: but believeth on him that justifieth the ungodly: . . . the impious, *Rheims* . . . who declares the guilty to be innocent, *TEV*.

his faith is counted for righteousness: . . . there is put to his account his faith, *Wuest*.

Romans 4:7

2978.5 verb 3sing indic pres act	3450.6 art acc sing masc	3080.2 noun acc sing masc	3450.2 art gen sing	442.2 noun gen sing masc
λέγει	τὸν	μακαρισμὸν	τοῦ	ἀνθρώπου
legei	*ton*	*makarismon*	*tou*	*anthrōpou*
declares	the	blessedness	of the	man

3614.3 rel-pron dat sing	3450.5 art sing masc	2296.1 noun nom sing masc	3023.4 verb 3sing indic pres	1336.4 noun acc sing fem
ᾧ	ὁ	θεὸς	λογίζεται	δικαιοσύνην
hō	*ho*	*theos*	*logizetai*	*dikaiosunēn*
to whom		God	reckons	righteousness

5400.1 prep gen	2024.5 noun gen pl neu	3079.4 adj nom pl masc	3614.1 rel-pron gen pl	856.27 verb 3pl indic aor pass
χωρὶς	ἔργων,	7. Μακάριοι	ὧν	ἀφέθησαν
chōris	*ergōn*	*Makarioi*	*hōn*	*aphethēsan*
apart from	works:	Blessed	of whom	were forgiven

3450.13 art pl fem	455.5 noun nom pl fem	2504.1 conj	3614.1 rel-pron gen pl	1928.1 verb 3pl indic aor pass	3450.13 art pl fem
αἱ	ἀνομίαι,	καὶ	ὧν	ἐπεκαλύφθησαν	αἱ
hai	*anomiai*	*kai*	*hōn*	*epekaluphthēsan*	*hai*
the	lawlessnesses,	and	of whom	were covered	the

8.a.Txt: 01**א**-corr,02A 04C,06D-corr,018K 020L,025P,byz.Sod **Var:** 01**א**-org,03B 06D-org,Treg,Tisc We/Ho,Weis,UBS/✱

264.5 noun nom pl fem	3079.2 adj nom sing masc	433.1 noun nom sing masc	3614.3 rel-pron dat sing	3614.2 rel-pron gen sing
ἁμαρτίαι.	8. μακάριος	ἀνὴρ	ᾧ	[ᵃ☆ οὗ]
hamartiai	*makarios*	*anēr*	*hō*	*hou*
sins:	blessed	man	to whom	[of whom]

3620.3 partic	3231.1 partic	3023.13 verb 3sing subj aor mid	2935.1 noun nom sing masc	264.4 noun acc sing fem	3450.5 art sing masc
οὐ	μὴ	λογίσηται	κύριος	ἁμαρτίαν.	9. Ὁ
ou	*mē*	*logisētai*	*kurios*	*hamartian*	*Ho*
not	not	will reckon	Lord	sin.	The

3080.1 noun nom sing masc	3631.1 conj	3642.4 dem-pron nom sing masc	1894.3 prep	3450.12 art acc sing fem	3921.4 noun acc sing fem
μακαρισμὸς	οὖν	οὗτος	ἐπὶ	τὴν	περιτομὴν,
makarismos	*oun*	*houtos*	*epi*	*tēn*	*peritomēn*
blessedness	then	this	on	the	circumcision,

2211.1 conj	2504.1 conj	1894.3 prep	3450.12 art acc sing fem	201.4 noun acc sing fem	2978.6 verb 1pl indic pres act	1056.1 conj
ἢ	καὶ	ἐπὶ	τὴν	ἀκροβυστίαν;	λέγομεν	γάρ,
ē	*kai*	*epi*	*tēn*	*akrobustian*	*legomen*	*gar*
or	also	on	the	uncircumcision?	We say	for

9.a.Txt: 02A,04C 06D-corr,018K,020L 025P,byz.Sod **Var:** 01**א**,03B,06D-org Treg,Tisc,We/Ho,Weis UBS/✱

3617.1 conj	3023.11 verb 3sing indic aor pass	3450.3 art dat sing	11.1 name masc	3450.9 art nom sing fem	3963.1 noun nom sing fem
[ᵃ Ὅτι]	Ἐλογίσθη	τῷ	Ἀβραὰμ	ἡ	πίστις
Hoti	*Elogisthē*	*tō*	*Abraam*	*hē*	*pistis*
that	was reckoned	to	Abraham	the	faith

1519.1 prep	1336.4 noun acc sing fem	4316.1 adv	3631.1 conj	3023.11 verb 3sing indic aor pass	1706.1 prep
εἰς	δικαιοσύνην.	10. πῶς	οὖν	ἐλογίσθη;	ἐν
eis	*dikaiosunēn*	*pōs*	*oun*	*elogisthē*	*en*
for	righteousness.	How	then	was it reckoned?	in

3921.3 noun dat sing fem	1498.22 verb dat sing masc part pres act	2211.1 conj	1706.1 prep	201.3 noun dat sing fem	3620.2 partic
περιτομῇ	ὄντι,	ἢ	ἐν	ἀκροβυστίᾳ;	οὐκ
peritomē	*onti*	*ē*	*en*	*akrobustia*	*ouk*
circumcision	being,	or	in	uncircumcision?	Not

4:6-8. The use of *kathaper* ("even as") introduces the revelation God gave to David also, regarding imputation of righteousness without works. It is clear that David understood by the Spirit exactly what Abraham knew and demonstrated, thus becoming the father of those of faith. The principle of God's acceptance of Abraham, the friend of God, by faith is the same as that used to accept the vile sinner. David was a man of God, yet his violation of three of the Ten Commandments—coveting, adultery, and murder—precludes the idea that he was justified by works.

In the case of Abraham, Paul dealt with the positive side of justification and shows how God reckons righteousness to the believer. In David's case Paul touched the negative side and showed how God does not impute (reckon, count, credit) sin to those whom He justifies.

Paul used the convincing illustration of David (Psalm 32; compare Psalm 51 and Proverbs 28:13). There was nothing that David could do to restore chastity to Bathsheba or life to Uriah. Into that hopeless case God by sovereign grace came and canceled his sin, counting him righteous. David was undeserving of pardon; he did not merit forgiveness. Forgiveness was freely bestowed and his sin was "covered," forever canceled. David rejoiced not only that sin was not imputed but also in the positive imputation of righteousness, the pronouncement of acquittal.

4:9. Abraham's example was the bulwark of the whole Jewish system of theology. After Paul introduced David as a demonstration of the faith of Abraham, he returned to discussing Abraham. He was ready to clinch the thesis that works can never produce faith nor procure righteousness. To do this he showed the absolute impossibility of Abraham's circumcision having any justifying merit. If that were the case with Abraham, then it applied also to Abraham's seed.

Peritomē ("circumcision") and *akrobustia* ("uncircumcision") occur six times each in verses 9 through 12. Paul is making the point that Abraham was justified by faith at least 14 years before he was circumcised. Circumcision is not essential to salvation. Man is always trying to claim credit for himself, but there is nothing he can do to earn salvation.

4:10,11. The Jewish disputant is still in Paul's mind. Paul has proved that Abraham and David were not justified by works. Some, however, will argue that this great provision is only for Jews—the "chosen" people of God. Even in the Old Testament, as in the New Testament, fellowship with God is based on grace through faith.

This passage emphasizes that faith, not works, was the real force behind God's declaration that Abraham was righteous. Genesis 15:6 says "he believed in the Lord; and he (God) counted it to him as righteousness." On the basis of this act of faith, then, God entered into a covenant with Abraham (15:18).

6. Even as David also describeth the blessedness of the man: Precisely as David mentions the blissfulness, *Berkeley* . . . also pronounceth blessing upon the man, *Panin* . . . describes the happiness, *Williams* . . . that man to be "happy,"*HistNT* . . . speaks of the spiritual prosperity of the man, *Wuest*.

unto whom God imputeth righteousness without works: . . . whom God ascribeth ryghtuousnes wythout dedes, *Geneva* . . . credits justice, *Confraternity* . . . irrespective of good deeds, *JB* . . . apart from rituals, *Fenton* . . . without human effort, *SEB*.

7. [Saying], Blessed [are] they whose iniquities are forgiven: Spiritually prosperous, *Wuest* . . . Happy are they, *Wesley* . . . whose breaches of the Law, *Moffatt* . . . whose lawless acts, *Adams, Young* . . . whose crimes are forgiven, *JB* . . . whose wrongdoings have been forgiven, *TCNT*.

and whose sins are covered: . . . whose sins are obliterated, *Fenton* . . . and over whose sins a veil has been drawn, *TCNT*.

8. Blessed [is] the man to whom the Lord will not impute sin: . . . will not record any sin, *Norlie* . . . whom the Lord considers less, *JB* . . . if the Lord doesn't count sins against you, *Beck* . . . will in no wise reckon sin, *Clementson*.

9. [Cometh] this blessedness then upon the circumcision [only], or upon the uncircumcision also?: Does this happiness, therefore, come, *Worrell* . . . does this ascription of bliss apply only, *Berkeley*.

for we say that faith was reckoned to Abraham for righteousness: . . . for we affirm, *Wilson* . . . was placed to his credit, *Weymouth*.

10. How was it then reckoned?: Under what circumstances, *Williams* . . . How then was it put to his account, *Wuest*.

when he was in circumcision, or in uncircumcision?:

Romans 4:11

1706.1 prep	3921.3 noun dat sing fem	233.1 conj	1706.1 prep	201.3 noun dat sing fem	2504.1 conj
ἐν	περιτομῇ,	ἀλλ'	ἐν	ἀκροβυστίᾳ·	11. καὶ
en	*peritomē*	*all'*	*en*	*akrobustia*	*kai*
in	circumcision,	but	in	uncircumcision.	And

4447.1 noun sing neu	2956.14 verb 3sing indic aor act	3921.2 noun gen sing fem	4825.2 noun acc sing fem	3450.10 art gen sing fem	
σημεῖον	ἔλαβεν	περιτομῆς,	σφραγῖδα	τῆς	
sēmeion	*elaben*	*peritomēs*	*sphragida*	*tēs*	
sign	he received	of circumcision,	seal	of the	

1336.2 noun gen sing fem	3450.10 art gen sing fem	3963.2 noun gen sing fem	3450.10 art gen sing fem	1706.1 prep	3450.11 art dat sing fem
δικαιοσύνης	τῆς	πίστεως	τῆς	ἐν	τῇ
dikaiosunēs	*tēs*	*pisteōs*	*tēs*	*en*	*tē*
righteousness	of the	faith	the	in	the

201.3 noun dat sing fem	1519.1 prep	3450.16 art sing neu	1498.32 verb inf pres act	840.6 prs-pron acc sing masc	3824.4 noun acc sing masc
ἀκροβυστίᾳ,	εἰς	τὸ	εἶναι	αὐτὸν	πατέρα
akrobustia	*eis*	*to*	*einai*	*auton*	*patera*
uncircumcision,	for	to	to be	him	father

3820.4 adj gen pl	3450.1 art gen pl	3961.14 verb gen pl masc part pres act		1217.1 prep	201.2 noun gen sing fem
πάντων	τῶν	πιστευόντων		δι'	ἀκροβυστίας,
pantōn	*tōn*	*pisteuontōn*		*di'*	*akrobustias*
of all	the	believing		through	uncircumcision,

11.a.Txt: 01ℵ-corr,04C 06D,018K,020L,025P byz.sa.Sod
Var: 01ℵ-org,02A,03B 044,bo.Treg,Tisc,We/Ho Weis,UBS/✶

11.b.Txt: 03B,04C-org 06D-corr3,010F,012G 044,byz.
Var: 01ℵ,06D-org 04C-corr2,6,365 424-corr3,1506,1739

1519.1 prep	3450.16 art sing neu	3023.16 verb inf aor pass	2504.1 conj	840.2 prs-pron dat pl	3450.12 art acc sing fem
εἰς	τὸ	λογισθῆναι	⌐a καὶ ⌐	αὐτοῖς	⌐b τὴν
eis	*to*	*logisthēnai*	*kai*	*autois*	*tēn*
for	the	to be reckoned	also	to them	the

1336.4 noun acc sing fem	2504.1 conj	3824.4 noun acc sing masc	3921.2 noun gen sing fem	3450.4 art dat pl	
δικαιοσύνην·	12. καὶ	πατέρα	περιτομῆς	τοῖς	
dikaiosunēn	*kai*	*patera*	*peritomēs*	*tois*	
righteousness;	and	father	of circumcision	to the	

3620.2 partic	1523.2 prep gen	3921.2 noun gen sing fem	3303.1 adv	233.2 conj	2504.1 conj	3450.4 art dat pl
οὐκ	ἐκ	περιτομῆς	μόνον,	ἀλλὰ	καὶ	τοῖς
ouk	*ek*	*peritomēs*	*monon*	*alla*	*kai*	*tois*
not	of	circumcision	only,	but	also	to the

12.a.Txt: 06D-corr,018K 020L,025P,byz.
Var: 01ℵ,02A,03B,04C 06D-org,Gries,Lach Treg,Alf,Word,Tisc We/Ho,Weis,Sod UBS/✶

4599.3 verb dat pl masc part pres act	3450.4 art dat pl	2460.1 noun dat pl neu	3450.10 art gen sing fem	1706.1 prep	3450.11 art dat sing fem
στοιχοῦσιν	τοῖς	ἴχνεσιν	τῆς	ἐν	⌐a τῇ
stoichousin	*tois*	*ichnesin*	*tēs*	*en*	*tē*
walking	in the	steps	of the	during	the

201.3 noun dat sing fem	3963.2 noun gen sing fem	3450.2 art gen sing	3824.2 noun gen sing masc	2231.2 prs-pron gen 1pl	11.1 name masc
ἀκροβυστίᾳ	πίστεως	τοῦ	πατρὸς	ἡμῶν	Ἀβραάμ.
akrobustia	*pisteōs*	*tou*	*patros*	*hēmōn*	*Abraam*
uncircumcision	faith	of the	father	our	Abraham.

3620.3 partic	1056.1 conj	1217.2 prep	3414.2 noun gen sing masc	3450.9 art nom sing fem	1845.2 noun nom sing fem	3450.3 art dat sing
13. Οὐ	γὰρ	διὰ	νόμου	ἡ	ἐπαγγελία	τῷ
Ou	*gar*	*dia*	*nomou*	*hē*	*epangelia*	*tō*
Not	for	by	law	the	promise	

Circumcision is spoken of as the "sign" and the "seal." Abraham had been justified before he was circumcised. Why, then, was circumcision ever practiced? The answer is twofold. First, circumcision was an outward sign given to Abraham as a seal of the righteousness he had received 14 years earlier. To seal means to validate. In other words, circumcision attested or bore witness to an existing righteousness. Circumcision was not the means of Abraham's justification. Of itself it did nothing for Abraham, other than giving the great assurance that the promise was certain.

Second, circumcision bore witness to the fact that Abraham "might be the father of all them that believe, though they be not circumcised." By this illustration God defines righteousness and establishes the basis on which a person is made righteous.

Abraham is not the father of those who have been circumcised; he is the father of all who exercise the same act of faith in God as he did. Every person in every age who takes the Word of God as Abraham did is a child of Abraham. The descendants of Abraham are those in every nation who belong to the family of God regardless of race, color, or national origin.

4:12. On the other hand, a man could be a Jew with no mixed blood line, and yet in a spiritual sense not be a descendant of Abraham. Abraham can only be his father as he acted in faith the way Abraham did. Circumcision provides neither God's saving grace nor immunity from punishment. The children of Abraham are those who have the faith of Abraham. The Jews failed to understand this essential truth, believing that the rite brought them rightness with God.

Was there no relation at all between Abraham's faith and circumcision? Was circumcision merely a secular rite to mark racial identity? Such is not the case. Circumcision in no way contributed to the exercise of his faith nor indeed to his justification; yet there was a relationship. Circumcision received its meaning from the fact that it was an act of faith; Abraham obeyed because he believed God. Thus it was both sign and seal.

The principle of faith is vital. We are saved and justified by faith alone. To illustrate this point Paul chose a term, *stoicheō*, that had military connotations in secular Greek literature. It differs from other Greek words for "walk" in that outside of its New Testament occurrences it means to follow a leader, to keep in rank, or to stay in step with those who went before. The implication is that Abraham is the "father" of those who keep in step with his example of faith or who walk in his footsteps.

The genuineness of New Testament Christian experience is that of circumcision of the heart—not a flesh mark, but a spirit mark. After faith has laid hold of the promise, then the ordinances are meaningful, and they bring blessing.

A great principle is established. The way to God is not through belonging to a given nation, nor through an ordinance which makes a mark on a person's body. Relationship to God is by faith, not through personal achievement.

Not in circumcision, but in uncircumcision: Not after, but before, *Berkeley.*

11. And he received the sign of circumcision: As a matter of fact, *Adams* . . . he received the Symbol, *Wilson* . . . it was a seal to prove that the faith he had, *SEB* . . . he received the attesting sign of circumcision, *Wuest.*

a seal of the righteousness of the faith which [he had yet] being uncircumcised: . . . as a mark to confirm the righteousness he got by believing, *Beck* . . . as a seal of the righteous character of the faith, *Wuest* . . . as a sign or seal of the righteousness, *Moffatt* . . . which belonged to the faith he had, *HistNT* . . . on condition of faith, *Williams* . . . while in uncircumcision, *Worrell.*

that he might be the father of all them that believe: . . . the father of all uncircumcised believers, *Berkeley.*

though they be not circumcised:

that righteousness might be imputed unto them also: . . . might be accredited, *Berkeley* . . . who are declared righteous, *SEB* . . . they also may be regarded by him as righteous, *TCNT.*

12. And the father of circumcision to them who are not of the circumcision only: . . . do not rely on that fact alone, *JB* . . . who are not merely circumcised, *Adams.*

but who also walk in the steps of that faith of our father Abraham, which [he had] being [yet] uncircumcised: . . . those also who tread in the footsteps of the faith, *Wilson* . . . to all arranging themselves in the path of the faith, *Fenton* . . . before the tyme of Circumcision, *Geneva* . . . while yet uncircumcised, *Confraternity.*

13. For the promise, that he should be the heir of the world, [was] not to Abraham, or to his seed, through the law: . . . that they should possess the earth, *Norlie* . . . would inherit the world, *SEB* . . . that the world should be theirs, *Beck* . . . that he should own the world, *Williams*

11.1 name masc	2211.1 conj	3450.3 art dat sing	4543.3 noun dat sing neu	840.3 prs-pron gen sing	3450.16 art sing neu
Ἀβραὰμ	ἢ	τῷ	σπέρματι	αὐτοῦ,	τὸ
Abraam	ē	tō	spermati	autou	to
to Abraham	or	to the	seed	his,	the

2791.2 noun acc sing masc	840.6 prs-pron acc sing masc	1498.32 verb inf pres act	3450.2 art gen sing	2862.2 noun gen sing masc	
κληρονόμον	αὐτὸν	εἶναι	[a τοῦ]	κόσμου,	
klēronomon	auton	einai	tou	kosmou	
heir	he	to be	of the	world,	

13.a.Txt: 018K,020L 025P,byz.
Var: 01א,02A,03B,04C 06D,Gries,Lach,Treg Alf,Word,Tisc,We/Ho Weis,Sod,UBS/✶

233.2 conj	1217.2 prep	1336.2 noun gen sing fem	3963.2 noun gen sing fem	1479.1 conj	1056.1 conj / 3450.7 art pl masc
ἀλλὰ	διὰ	δικαιοσύνης	πίστεως.	**14.** εἰ	γὰρ / οἱ
alla	dia	dikaiosunēs	pisteōs	ei	gar / hoi
but	by	righteousness	of faith.	If	for / the

1523.2 prep gen	3414.2 noun gen sing masc	2791.3 noun nom pl masc	2729.4 verb 3sing indic perf pass	3450.9 art nom sing fem
ἐκ	νόμου	κληρονόμοι,	κεκένωται	ἡ
ek	nomou	klēronomoi	kekenōtai	hē
of	law	heirs,	has been made void	the

3963.1 noun nom sing fem	2504.1 conj	2643.17 verb 3sing indic perf pass	3450.9 art nom sing fem	1845.2 noun nom sing fem
πίστις,	καὶ	κατήργηται	ἡ	ἐπαγγελία·
pistis	kai	katērgētai	hē	epangelia
faith,	and	has been destroyed	the	promise.

3450.5 art sing masc	1056.1 conj	3414.1 noun nom sing masc	3572.4 noun acc sing fem	2686.2 verb 3sing indic pres	3619.1 adv
15. ὁ	γὰρ	νόμος	ὀργὴν	κατεργάζεται·	οὖ
ho	gar	nomos	orgēn	katergazetai	hou
The	for	law	wrath	works out;	where

15.a.Txt: 01א-corr,06D 018K,020L,025P,byz. Sod
Var: 01א-org,02A,03B 04C,bo.Lach,Treg,Alf Word,Tisc,We/Ho,Weis UBS/✶

1056.1 conj	1156.2 conj	3620.2 partic	1498.4 verb 3sing indic pres act	3414.1 noun nom sing masc	3624.1 adv
(γὰρ	[a✶ δὲ]	οὐκ	ἔστιν	νόμος,	οὐδὲ
gar	de	ouk	estin	nomos	oude
for	[and]	not	is	law,	neither

3709.1 noun nom sing fem	1217.2 prep	3642.17 dem-pron sing neu	1523.2 prep gen	3963.2 noun gen sing fem	2419.1 conj
παράβασις.	**16.** διὰ	τοῦτο	ἐκ	πίστεως,	ἵνα
parabasis	dia	touto	ek	pisteōs	hina
transgression.	Because of	this	of	faith,	that

2567.3 prep	5322.4 noun acc sing fem	1519.1 prep	3450.16 art sing neu	1498.32 verb inf pres act	942.3 adj acc sing fem
κατὰ	χάριν,	εἰς	τὸ	εἶναι	βεβαίαν
kata	charin	eis	to	einai	bebaian
according to	grace,	for	the	to be	sure

3450.12 art acc sing fem	1845.4 noun acc sing fem	3820.3 adj dat sing	3450.3 art dat sing	4543.3 noun dat sing neu	3620.3 partic
τὴν	ἐπαγγελίαν	παντὶ	τῷ	σπέρματι,	οὐ
tēn	epangelian	panti	tō	spermati	ou
the	promise	to all	the	seed,	not

3450.3 art dat sing	1523.2 prep gen	3450.2 art gen sing	3414.2 noun gen sing masc	3303.1 adv	233.2 conj	2504.1 conj
τῷ	ἐκ	τοῦ	νόμου	μόνον,	ἀλλὰ	καὶ
tō	ek	tou	nomou	monon	alla	kai
to the	of	the	law	only,	but	also

4:13. God promised that Abraham would become a great nation and that in him all the families on the earth would be blessed (Genesis 12:2,3; 15:5; 22:17,18). This promise was given 430 years before the Law was given to Moses. The promise was not contingent on Abraham's obedience to the Law; it was unconditional.

The word *promise* may be translated from either of two Greek words, *huposchesis* and *epangelia*. The first word is made with a condition, the second is made unconditionally. The latter is the word used here. God's promise was not based on merit but strictly on grace. The Law dealt with the conduct of people who were already in a covenant relationship with God.

"The promise" was that Abraham should be "heir of the world." In geographic terms the inheritance touched land at the east of the Mediterranean. But Abraham's inheritance cannot be limited to such frontiers. He "looked for a city which hath foundations, whose builder and maker is God" (Hebrews 11:10).

Abraham had two seeds. One was of "the law" and the other "of faith." There are three words translated "seed" in the New Testament. *Spora* and *sporos* come from *speirō* ("sow"). These two are used regarding seed that is sown. The third which occurs in verses 13, 16, and 18 is *sperma*. In 38 of the 44 times where it appears it refers to descendants. The true interpretation comes through in Galatians 3:16, "And to thy seed, which is Christ." This gives understanding to Genesis 17:7,8. Heirship for the believer is through being in Christ (Ephesians 2:12,13; 3:5,6).

4:14. "Is made void" carries the meaning "has been voided and as a present result is in a state of invalidation." *Katargeō* means "made of none effect," "to render inoperative." If fulfillment depends on law-keeping, the inability of men to keep the Law makes certain that the promise will never be fulfilled.

4:15. God's promise is by grace through faith. In contrast, the Law cannot fulfill the promise. The Law can diagnose the malady but cannot effect a cure. It condemns but cannot save.

The phrase "no law . . . no transgression" brings out several principles. First, there must be law to have transgression of it. Second, there must be divine dispensations where the Law is not the principle of relationship with God. Third, man must be completely removed from under the principle of the Law if he is to come to a spiritual place where there will be no transgression. Fourth, the only place of freedom from the Law is the place of the inheritance.

4:16. *Ek pisteōs* ("of faith") indicates that it is "out of faith as a source." Salvation is by grace through faith and not of works. *Bebaian* ("sure") means "stable, valid, something realized." Abraham

. . . and to his posterity, *Confraternity* . . . did not reach him through the Law, *Moffatt* . . . conditioned by Law, *Weymouth.*

but through the righteousness of faith: . . . produced by faith, *Berkeley.*

14. For if they which are of the law [be] heirs: For if it is adherents of the Law, *Moffatt* . . . For if the subjects of the law, *Sawyer* . . . are to possess the world, *TCNT.*

faith is made void, and the promise made of none effect: . . . then is faith but vayne, *Geneva* . . . then faith is pointless, *JB* . . . faith is worthless, *Adams* . . . then faith is useless, *Weymouth* . . . is robbed of its value, *TCNT* . . . faith is empty of all meaning, *Moffatt* . . . faith would be nullified, and the promise abolished, *Fenton* . . . the promise is made void, *Confraternity* . . . has been rendered inoperative, *Wuest* . . . the promise abrogated, *Sawyer* . . . God's promise is worthless, *SEB* . . . and the promise is empty, *Klingensmith.*

15. Because the law worketh wrath: . . . the law abolished anger? *Fenton* . . . the law results in wrath alone, *Williams.*

for where no law is, [there is] no transgression: Where no law exists, there can be no sin, *SEB* . . . there is no breaking of the Law, *Beck* . . . no breach of it is possible, *TCNT* . . . there can be no violation of it, *Williams* . . . there can be no law-breaking, *Conybeare.*

16. Therefore [it is] of faith, that [it might be] by grace: For this cause, *Alford* . . . that it may be according to grace, *Young* . . . [it was] on the ground, *PNT.*

to the end the promise might be sure to all the seed: . . . that it might be secure for all the offspring, *Confraternity* . . . should hold for all descendants, *Beck* . . . may rest on a solid basis for all his descendants, *Adams* . . . should be guaranteed as God's free gift, *TEV.*

not to that only which is of the law:

3450.3 art dat sing	1523.2 prep gen	3963.2 noun gen sing fem	11.1 name masc	3614.5 rel-pron nom sing masc	1498.4 verb 3sing indic pres act
τῷ	ἐκ	πίστεως	Ἀβραάμ,	ὅς	ἐστιν
tō	ek	pisteōs	Abraam	hos	estin
to the	of	faith	of Abraham,	who	is

3824.1 noun nom sing masc	3820.4 adj gen pl	2231.2 prs-pron gen 1pl	2503.1 conj	1119.22 verb 3sing indic perf pass
πατὴρ	πάντων	ἡμῶν,	**17.** καθὼς	γέγραπται,
patēr	pantōn	hēmōn	kathōs	gegraptai
father	of all	us,	just as	it has been written,

3617.1 conj	3824.4 noun acc sing masc	4044.1 adj gen pl	1477.5 noun gen pl neu	4935.18 verb 1sing indic perf act	4622.4 prs-pron acc 2sing
Ὅτι	πατέρα	πολλῶν	ἐθνῶν	τέθεικά	σε,
Hoti	patera	pollōn	ethnōn	tetheika	se
A father	of many	nations	I have made	you,

2683.1 prep gen	3614.2 rel-pron gen sing	3961.20 verb 3sing indic aor act	2296.2 noun gen sing masc	3450.2 art gen sing
κατέναντι	οὗ	ἐπίστευσεν	θεοῦ,	τοῦ
katenanti	hou	episteusen	theou	tou
before	whom	he believed	God,	the

2210.2 verb gen sing masc part pres act	3450.8 art acc pl masc	3361.7 adj acc pl masc	2504.1 conj	2535.5 verb gen sing masc part pres act
ζῳοποιοῦντος	τοὺς	νεκρούς,	καὶ	καλοῦντος
zōopoiountos	tous	nekrous	kai	kalountos
making alive	the	dead,	and	calling

3450.17 art pl neu	3231.1 partic	1498.18 verb part pres act	5453.1 conj	1498.18 verb part pres act	3614.5 rel-pron nom sing masc
τὰ	μὴ	ὄντα	ὡς	ὄντα.	**18.** Ὅς
ta	mē	onta	hōs	onta	Hos
the things	not	being	as	being;	who

3706.1 prep	1667.4 noun acc sing fem	1894.2 prep	1667.3 noun dat sing fem	3961.20 verb 3sing indic aor act	1519.1 prep
παρ᾽	ἐλπίδα	ἐπ᾽	ἐλπίδι	ἐπίστευσεν,	εἰς
par'	elpida	ep'	elpidi	episteusen	eis
against	hope	in	hope	believed,	for

3450.16 art sing neu	1090.63 verb inf aor mid	840.6 prs-pron acc sing masc	3824.4 noun acc sing masc	4044.1 adj gen pl	1477.5 noun gen pl neu
τὸ	γενέσθαι	αὐτὸν	πατέρα	πολλῶν	ἐθνῶν,
to	genesthai	auton	patera	pollōn	ethnōn
the	to become	him	father	of many	nations,

2567.3 prep	3450.16 art sing neu	2029.16 verb sing neu part perf pass	3643.1 adv	1498.40 verb 3sing indic fut mid
κατὰ	τὸ	εἰρημένον,	Οὕτως	ἔσται
kata	to	eirēmenon	Houtōs	estai
according to	the	having been said,	So	shall be

3450.16 art sing neu	4543.1 noun sing neu	4622.2 prs-pron gen 2sing	2504.1 conj	3231.1 partic	764.14 verb nom sing masc part aor act
τὸ	σπέρμα	σου·	**19.** καὶ	μὴ	ἀσθενήσας
to	sperma	sou	kai	mē	asthenēsas
the	seed	your:	and	not	having weakened

19.a.Txt: 06D,018K 020L,025P,33,byz.it. We/Ho
Var: 01ℵ,02A,03B,04C sa.bo.Lach,Treg,Tisc Weis,Sod,UBS/⋆

3450.11 art dat sing fem	3963.3 noun dat sing fem	3620.3 partic	2627.4 verb 3sing indic aor act	3450.16 art sing neu	1431.4 prs-pron gen 3sing
τῇ	πίστει,	⟨a οὐ ⟩	κατενόησεν	τὸ	ἑαυτοῦ
tē	pistei	ou	katenoēsen	to	heautou
in the	faith,	not	he considered	the	of himself

was given a promise which, in the natural, could not be fulfilled. But he believed God!

4:17,18. In addition to their natural parents, believers have a threefold fatherhood relationship: (1) that of Abraham, the whole household of faith; (2) the person who was used of Christ to bring them to Christ ("I have begotten you through the gospel," 1 Corinthians 4:15); (3) God who begat us by the Holy Spirit through His Word. The first two fatherhoods are fatherhoods of relationship, but the last one is that and more; it is of life.

These verses and their context form a great and encouraging passage of Scripture. Faith is shown as bringing a person into right relations with God. The relationship will, in turn, encourage habits of submission and obedience to God. For Abraham to be the "father of many nations" was beyond human expectation and natural possibility. But Abraham exercised faith. His life became the great example of faith to us.

Abraham's faith was in God. It is most important to bear in mind that our faith is primarily not in a doctrine, not in a fact, even a fact such as Calvary, or a doctrine such as the Atonement. Faith must be in a Person who is what He is and does what He does by virtue of His death on the cross and all that is involved in the great doctrine of the Atonement.

Because Abraham believed in this Person, he could reckon "those things which be not as though they were." He believed in the God who calls the dead to life and who brings into being even things which were not in existence. Without faith there is no capacity for contact and communion with God. The things of God are spiritual and invisible—the natural eye cannot see them. Faith is the eye that sees. Faith is the taking hand of the soul. Without that hand man has no grasp of eternal things.

Abraham's faith was in the God "who quickeneth the dead" and in the God who actually creates new existences. "Against hope" Abraham "believed in hope." In hope he anticipated; by faith he appropriated. Humanly speaking, his case was hopeless.

Believing that God could bring the dead back to life, Abraham trusted in the omnipotence of God. When God told him, "Look now toward heaven, and tell (count) the stars . . . So shall thy seed be," Abraham immediately responded with faith. "And he believed in the Lord; and he counted it to him for righteousness" (Genesis 15:5,6).

4:19. The matter of a promised land had been considered. The matter of a promised seed is presented next. The promise of a son was given to Abraham when he was 75 years of age. His wife was 65. Obviously both were beyond the age of bearing children. But the patriarch believed. He believed in the One who made something out of nothing, as in creation (Hebrews 11:3), and in the One who could raise the dead as in the case of Isaac (Hebrews 11:19).

but to that also which is of the faith of Abraham: . . . but also to the adherents of, *Berkeley.*
who is the father of us all:

17. (As it is written, I have made thee a father of many nations,) before him whom he believed: . . . for I haue sette thee fadir of many folkis, *Wyclif* . . . I have constituted thee, *PNT* . . . I have appointed thee, *Confraternity* . . . I have established you permanently, *Wuest.*
[even] God: . . . bifor god, *Wyclif.*
who quickeneth the dead: . . . could make dead people come back to life, *SEB* . . . who gives life to the dead, *TCNT* . . . whych restored the deed vnto lyfe, *Cranmer.*
and calleth those things which be not as though they were: . . . calls into existence what has no being, *Berkeley* . . . and names the non-existent as if existent, *Fenton* . . . things which do not exist as existing, *Sawyer* . . . and calls the no being to being, *Klingensmith.*

18. Who against hope believed in hope: Under hopeless circumstances, *Weymouth* . . . Vvho contrarie to hope, *Rheims* . . . past hope, *Worrell* . . . contrary to what he could expect, *Beck* . . . calls into being what does not exist, *Moffatt* . . . in spite of hopeless circumstances, *Williams* . . . Though things looked hopeless...sustained by hope, put faith in God, *TCNT.*
that he might become the father of many nations, according to that which was spoken: . . . as many as the stars, *JB* . . . in agreement with the words, *Weymouth.*
So shall thy seed be: So numberless shall your descendants be, *Williams, Montgomery* . . . So shall thy offspring be, *Confraternity.*

19. And being not weak in faith: His faith never quailed, *Moffatt* . . . faith didn't weaken, *SEB* . . . there was no weakening, *Berkeley* . . . yet his faith did not fail him, *TCNT, Montgomery* . . . And without weakening in faith, *Confraternity.*

Romans 4:20

19.b.Txt: 01א,02A,04C
06D,018K,020L,025P
33,byz.Sod
Var: 03B,it.Tisc,We/Ho
Weis,UBS/✱

4835.1 noun sing neu		2218.1 adv	3362.3 verb acc sing neu part perf pass	1527.1 adj nom sing fem	4084.1 adv
σῶμα	⌐b ἤδη ⌐		νενεκρωμένον,	ἑκατονταετής	που
sōma	ēdē		nenekrōmenon	hekatontaetēs	pou
body	already		having become dead,	a hundred years old	about

5062.6 verb nom sing masc part pres act	2504.1 conj	3450.12 art acc sing fem	3363.1 noun acc sing fem	3450.10 art gen sing fem	3253.1 noun gen sing fem
ὑπάρχων,	καὶ	τὴν	νέκρωσιν	τῆς	μήτρας
huparchōn	kai	tēn	nekrōsin	tēs	mētras
being,	and	the	deadening	of the	womb

4421.2 name gen fem		1519.1 prep	1156.2 conj	3450.12 art acc sing fem	1845.4 noun acc sing fem	3450.2 art gen sing
Σάρρας·	20. εἰς	δὲ	τὴν	ἐπαγγελίαν	τοῦ
Sarrhas	eis	de	tēn	epangelian	tou
of Sarah,	at	and	the	promise	tou

2296.2 noun gen sing masc	3620.3 partic	1246.11 verb 3sing indic aor pass	3450.11 art dat sing fem	565.3 noun dat sing fem	233.1 conj
θεοῦ	οὐ	διεκρίθη	τῇ	ἀπιστίᾳ,	⌐✱ ἀλλ'
theou	ou	diekrithē	tē	apistia	all'
of God	not	was doubted	by the	unbelief;	but

233.2 conj	1727.6 verb 3sing indic aor pass	3450.11 art dat sing fem	3963.3 noun dat sing fem	1319.28 verb nom sing masc part aor act
[ἀλλὰ]	ἐνεδυναμώθη	τῇ	πίστει,	δοὺς
alla	enedunamōthē	tē	pistei	dous
[idem]	was strengthened	in the	faith,	having given

1385.4 noun acc sing fem	3450.3 art dat sing	2296.3 noun dat sing masc	2504.1 conj	3995.4 verb nom sing masc part aor pass
δόξαν	τῷ	θεῷ,	21. καὶ	πληροφορηθεὶς
doxan	tō	theō	kai	plērophorētheis
glory	tō	to God,	and	having been fully assured

3617.1 conj	3614.16 rel-pron sing neu	1846.7 verb 3sing indic perf	1409.1 adj nom sing masc	1498.4 verb 3sing indic pres act
ὅτι	ὃ	ἐπήγγελται,	δυνατός	ἐστιν
hoti	ho	epēngeltai	dunatos	estin
that	what	he has promised,	able	he is

22.a.Txt: 01א,02A,04C
06D,044,byz.
Var: 03B,010F,06D-org
012G

2504.1 conj	4020.41 verb inf aor act	1346.1 conj	2504.1 conj	3023.11 verb 3sing indic aor pass
καὶ	ποιῆσαι.	22. διὸ	⌐a καὶ ⌐	ἐλογίσθη
kai	poiēsai	dio	kai	elogisthē
also	to do;	wherefore	also	it was reckoned

840.4 prs-pron dat sing	1519.1 prep	1336.4 noun acc sing fem	3620.2 partic	1119.21 verb 3sing indic aor pass
αὐτῷ	εἰς	δικαιοσύνην.	23. Οὐκ	ἐγράφη
autō	eis	dikaiosunēn	Ouk	egraphē
to him	for	righteousness.	Not	it was written

1156.2 conj	1217.1 prep	840.6 prs-pron acc sing masc	3303.1 adv	3617.1 conj	3023.11 verb 3sing indic aor pass
δὲ	δι'	αὐτὸν	μόνον,	ὅτι	ἐλογίσθη
de	di'	auton	monon	hoti	elogisthē
but	on account of	him	only,	that	it was reckoned

840.4 prs-pron dat sing	233.2 conj	2504.1 conj	1217.1 prep	2231.4 prs-pron acc 1pl	3614.4 rel-pron dat pl
αὐτῷ·	24. ἀλλὰ	καὶ	δι'	ἡμᾶς,	οἷς
autō	alla	kai	di'	hēmas	hois
to him,	but	also	on account of	us,	to whom

Note the expressions regarding the patriarch's faith: "not weak in faith . . . considered not his own body . . . staggered not at the promise of God." The same power that brought forth Christ from the grave brought Isaac into the world. Isaac's birth is set forth as a resurrection from the dead in a sense (Hebrews 11:11,12). "Against hope" Abraham "believed in hope." Against a promise that in the normal course of events was unlikely to be fulfilled, Abraham's faith did not grow weak for he was fully assured, not just wishfully hoping. God had spoken, and with God nothing is impossible.

Katanoeō, "considered," means "to consider attentively, fix one's eyes or mind upon." Many manuscripts and translations omit the word "not" in "considered not." This gives greater impact to the expression. Abraham considered his own body being dead as far as its procreative functions were concerned, but he refused to accept the natural implications of his age, concluding that the certainty of the divine promise outweighed every natural improbability.

4:20. *Diakrinō*, "stagger," means "to be divided in one's mind, to hesitate, doubt." The word is translated "waver" twice in James 1:6. Abraham's confidence in God never wavered.

Endunamoō, "was strong," is "to make strong, endue with strength." A better translation seems to be "was made strong." *Tē pistei*, "in faith," translates "with respect to faith." There was no vacillation by Abraham between belief and unbelief.

Abraham gave "glory to God." Abraham weighed the human impossibility of becoming a father when both he and Sarah were far beyond childbearing age against the divine impossibility of God being able to break His word. If God be God, nothing is impossible. Look at the circumstances and one staggers; look to God and one is strong. Abraham did not stagger because he gave glory to God. Great men of faith bring glory to God.

4:21. This verse may be the best definition of faith to be found in the Word. Faith is described in Hebrew 11:1; here it is defined. Abraham received and believed God's promise. His secret was that he did not waver but gave glory to God.

In the study of righteousness, it is unnecessary to argue imputation versus impartation. The term *dikaiosunēn*, translated "righteousness" (verse 22), describes *what* God imparts. *Dikaiōsin*, translated "justification" (verse 25), names the *act* of God who does the imputing. Both are received when one receives Christ (1 Corinthians 1:30). Abraham was righteous; God declared him so, just as He did for Abel (Hebrews 11:4), Noah (Genesis 7:1), and other Old Testament saints.

4:22-24. Paul has given a great analysis of faith to show how justification comes by faith. The principle of justification, which

Romans 4:24

he considered not his own body now dead, when he was about an hundred years old: . . . when he thought about his almost dead body, *Klingensmith* . . . even when he noted the utter impotence of, *Moffatt* . . . then utterly worn out, *TCNT* . . . although he realized...he couldn't have children any more, *Beck*.

neither yet the deadness of Sarah's womb: . . . nether yet that Sara was past chyldeberinge, *Tyndale* . . . or the impotence of, *Moffatt* . . . was far too old to bear children, *Norlie*.

20. He staggered not at the promise of God through unbelief: There was no unbelief to make him doubt, *Beck* . . . no unbelief made him waver about, *Moffatt* . . . Nor did he doubtingly criticise the promise of God, *Fenton* . . . did not through unbelief question God's promise, *Norlie* . . . was not led by want of faith to doubt God's promise, *TCNT* . . . He was not shaken by unbelief, *Klingensmith*.

but was strong in faith: . . . but fortified by faith, *Adams* . . . his faith gave him strength, *TCNT*.

giving glory to God: . . . gave honour, *Tyndale* . . . gaue God the prayse, *Cranmer*.

21. And being fully persuaded that: He was absolutely certain, *Norlie* . . . most fully knovving, *Rheims* . . . since he was thoroughly convinced, *Adams* . . . in the firm conviction, *TCNT*.

what he had promised, he was able also to perform: . . . was able also to make it good, *Cranmer*.

22. And therefore it was imputed to him for righteousness: That is why he was counted righteous, *Beck*.

23. Now it was not written for his sake alone, that it was imputed to him: . . . that it was reckened to him, *Tyndale, Cranmer*.

24. But for us also, to whom it shall be imputed: . . . to whom it shalbe counted for, *Geneva*.

77

Romans 4:25

3165.3 verb 3sing indic pres act	**3023.10** verb inf pres pass	**3450.4** art dat pl	**3961.3** verb dat pl masc part pres act	**1894.3** prep
μέλλει	λογίζεσθαι,	τοῖς	πιστεύουσιν	ἐπὶ
mellei	*logizesthai*	*tois*	*pisteuousin*	*epi*
it is about	to be reckoned,	to the	believing	on

3450.6 art acc sing masc	**1446.9** verb acc sing masc part aor act	**2400.3** name acc masc	**3450.6** art acc sing masc	**2935.4** noun acc sing masc	**2231.2** prs-pron gen 1pl
τὸν	ἐγείραντα	Ἰησοῦν	τὸν	κύριον	ἡμῶν
ton	*egeiranta*	*Iēsoun*	*ton*	*kurion*	*hēmōn*
the	having raised	Jesus	the	Lord	our

1523.2 prep gen	**3361.2** adj gen pl	**3614.5** rel-pron nom sing masc	**3722.32** verb 3sing indic aor pass	**1217.2** prep	**3450.17** art pl neu
ἐκ	νεκρῶν,	**25.** ὃς	παρεδόθη	διὰ	τὰ
ek	*nekrōn*	*hos*	*paredothē*	*dia*	*ta*
from among	dead,	who	was delivered	for	the

3761.6 noun acc pl neu	**2231.2** prs-pron gen 1pl	**2504.1** conj	**1446.20** verb 3sing indic aor pass	**1217.2** prep	**3450.12** art acc sing fem
παραπτώματα	ἡμῶν,	καὶ	ἠγέρθη	διὰ	τὴν
paraptōmata	*hēmōn*	*kai*	*ēgerthē*	*dia*	*tēn*
offenses	our,	and	was raised	for	the

1340.1 noun acc sing fem	**2231.2** prs-pron gen 1pl	**1338.17** verb nom pl masc part aor pass		**3631.1** conj	**1523.2** prep gen
δικαίωσιν	ἡμῶν.	**5:1.** Δικαιωθέντες		οὖν	ἐκ
dikaiōsin	*hēmōn*	*Dikaiōthentes*		*oun*	*ek*
justification	our.	Having been justified		therefore	by

3963.2 noun gen sing fem	**1503.4** noun acc sing fem	**2174.5** verb 1pl indic pres act	**2174.8** verb 1pl subj pres act		**4242.1** prep
πίστεως,	εἰρήνην	☆ ἔχομεν	[a ἔχωμεν]		πρὸς
pisteōs	*eirēnēn*	*echomen*	*echōmen*		*pros*
faith,	peace	we have	[let us have]		toward

3450.6 art acc sing masc	**2296.4** noun acc sing masc	**1217.2** prep	**3450.2** art gen sing	**2935.2** noun gen sing masc	**2231.2** prs-pron gen 1pl
τὸν	θεὸν	διὰ	τοῦ	κυρίου	ἡμῶν
ton	*theon*	*dia*	*tou*	*kuriou*	*hēmōn*
	God	through	the	Lord	our

2400.2 name masc	**5382.2** name gen masc	**1217.1** prep	**3614.2** rel-pron gen sing	**2504.1** conj	**3450.12** art acc sing fem
Ἰησοῦ	Χριστοῦ,	**2.** δι’	οὗ	καὶ	τὴν
Iēsou	*Christou*	*di’*	*hou*	*kai*	*tēn*
Jesus	Christ,	through	whom	also	the

4176.1 noun acc sing fem	**2174.36** verb 1pl indic perf act	**3450.11** art dat sing fem	**3963.3** noun dat sing fem	**1519.1** prep	**3450.12** art acc sing fem
προσαγωγὴν	ἐσχήκαμεν	[a τῇ	πίστει]	εἰς	τὴν
prosagōgēn	*eschēkamen*	*tē*	*pistei*	*eis*	*tēn*
access	we have had	by the	faith	into	the

5322.4 noun acc sing fem	**3642.12** dem-pron acc sing fem	**1706.1** prep	**3614.11** rel-pron dat sing fem	**2449.19** verb 1pl indic perf act	**2504.1** conj
χάριν	ταύτην	ἐν	ἧ	ἑστήκαμεν·	καὶ
charin	*tautēn*	*en*	*hē*	*hestēkamen*	*kai*
grace	this	in	which	we stand,	and

2714.3 verb 1pl indic pres	**1894.2** prep	**1667.3** noun dat sing fem	**3450.10** art gen sing fem	**1385.2** noun gen sing fem	**3450.2** art gen sing
καυχώμεθα	ἐπ’	ἐλπίδι	τῆς	δόξης	τοῦ
kauchōmetha	*ep’*	*elpidi*	*tēs*	*doxēs*	*tou*
we boast	in	hope	of the	glory	

1.a.**Txt:** 01ℵ-corr1 03B-corr2,010F,012G 025P,044,0220,104,365 1241,etc.
Var: 01ℵ-org,02A 03B-org,04C,06D,018K 020L,33,81,630,1175,bo.

2.a.**Txt:** 01ℵ-org,04C 044,byz.
Var: 03B,06D,010F 012G,0220,sa.

Abraham experienced, is "for us also . . . if we believe on him that raised up Jesus our Lord from the dead."

if we believe on him that raised up Jesus our Lord from the dead:

4:25. Justification comes on the same principle, "(Christ) was delivered for our offenses, and was raised again for our justification." Abraham looked forward to the work of Christ (John 8:56); we look back to the finished work of Christ. The account of Abraham's faith and justification was written for the benefit of believers of all ages.

Notice how Paul turns to the personal touch in verses 24 and 25, "us also . . . we . . . our Lord . . . our offenses . . . our justification." We have been through the black scenes of the courtroom as all men were declared guilty. From there we came to the glorious light of God's provision of justification.

The Son of God "was delivered"—God spared not His own Son. Nothing less than the death of Jesus on the cursed tree would do. It was because of "our offenses." Calvary was essential because of a righteous God and His law. Nothing but the atoning death of Christ could meet the need of sinful man.

Our Lord was raised from the dead "for our justification." His resurrection was the validation of the sacrifice of His death and the proof of our acceptance. Our place of acceptance is in the risen Christ. The ungodly who believe on the Lord are declared righteous and are given a new standing in the risen Christ. All the promises center around the empty tomb. As Christ's resurrection was the proclamation of His acceptance as the propitiation, it is the demonstration of our acceptance in Him. By Him we are made righteous and acquitted of the Law's claims (1 Corinthians 15:17).

5:1. The chapter opens with the word "therefore," meaning "in view of the foregoing exposition." The statement of the benefits which follow shows the result of having been declared righteous. "Therefore" relates directly to chapter 4. Justification is not by works (4:1-8), not by ordinances (4:9-12), not by obedience to the Law (4:13-25). It is by faith. (See *Overview*, pp.665-667.)

Many scholars prefer the translation "let us have peace with God" rather than "we have." More than mere tranquility of mind, this peace is cessation of hostility. God has ceased righteous hostility toward us because we who were hostile toward Him have been reconciled to Him in Jesus.

5:2. We have "access by faith." We are not shut out because of our sins but are allowed an entrance through faith "into this grace." "Access" (literally, "introduction") brings another benefit: "wherein we stand." Our stand before God is the standing of Christ himself (2 Corinthians 5:21). A further benefit relates to the future: rejoicing "in hope of the glory of God." Exultation is in God, not in self.

25. Who was delivered for our offences: . . . who was surrendered to death, *Weymouth* . . . who was put to death for our sins, *JB* . . . who was handed over to die for our sins, *Beck* . . . delivered up for our trespasses, *Moffatt, ASV* . . . who was betrayed to death, *Montgomery.*

and was raised again for our justification: . . . because of the acquittal secured for us, *Weymouth* . . . and rose agayne for to iustifye vs, *Cranmer* . . . to make us right with God, *SEB.*

1. Therefore being justified by faith: Standing then acquitted as the result of faith, *Weymouth* . . . Having been declared righteous, *Young* . . . Since we stand justified as the result of faith, *Montgomery.*

we have peace with God through our Lord Jesus Christ: . . . let us continue enjoying peace, *Williams* . . . let us have peace, *Clementson.*

2. By whom also we have access by faith into this grace wherein we stand: . . . we have been introduced into this grace, *Sawyer* . . . by whom we have awaye in thorow fayth, *Tyndale* . . . by whom also it chaunsed vnto vs, *Cranmer* . . . we have obtained access to this grace in which we stand, *Norlie* . . . through whom we also have access, *Confraternity* . . . we have obtained our access, *HistNT* . . . we have obtained admission, *TCNT* . . . we have had admission by faith, *Scarlett* . . . who gave us the way to come to God's love, *Beck* . . . we have as a permanent possession, *Wuest* . . . entrance to this grace, *Berkeley* . . . in which we safely stand, *Williams.*

and rejoice in hope of the glory of God: And we feel proud as we hope for God's glory, *Beck* . . . and glorie, *Rheims* . . . and exult in the hope, *Confraternity* . . . and let us continue exulting in the hope, *Williams* . . . We feel good, because, *SEB* . . . So let us triumph in our hope of attaining God's glorious ideal, *TCNT.*

2296.2 noun gen sing masc	3620.3 partic	3303.1 adv	1156.2 conj	233.2 conj	2504.1 conj	2714.3 verb 1pl indic pres
θεοῦ.	3. οὐ	μόνον	δέ,	ἀλλὰ	καὶ	καυχώμεθα
theou	ou	monon	de	alla	kai	kauchōmetha
of God.	Not	only	and,	but	also	we boast

1706.1 prep	3450.14 art dat pl fem	2324.7 noun dat pl fem	3471.20 verb nom pl masc part perf act		3617.1 conj	3450.9 art nom sing fem
ἐν	ταῖς	θλίψεσιν,	εἰδότες		ὅτι	ἡ
en	tais	thlipsesin	eidotes		hoti	hē
in	the	tribulations,	knowing		that	the

2324.1 noun nom sing fem	5119.4 noun acc sing fem	2686.2 verb 3sing indic pres		3450.9 art nom sing fem	1156.2 conj
θλῖψις	ὑπομονὴν	κατεργάζεται,		4. ἡ	δὲ
thlipsis	hupomonēn	katergazetai		hē	de
tribulation	endurance	works out;		the	and

5119.1 noun nom sing fem	1376.4 noun acc sing fem	3450.9 art nom sing fem	1156.2 conj	1376.1 noun nom sing fem	1667.4 noun acc sing fem
ὑπομονὴ	δοκιμήν,	ἡ	δὲ	δοκιμὴ	ἐλπίδα,
hupomonē	dokimēn	hē	de	dokimē	elpida
endurance	proof;	the	and	proof	hope;

3450.9 art nom sing fem	1156.2 conj	1667.1 noun nom sing fem	3620.3 partic	2587.1 verb 3sing indic pres act	3617.1 conj
5. ἡ	δὲ	ἐλπὶς	οὐ	καταισχύνει	ὅτι
hē	de	elpis	ou	kataischunei	hoti
the	and	hope	not	does make ashamed,	because

3450.9 art nom sing fem	26.1 noun nom sing fem	3450.2 art gen sing	2296.2 noun gen sing masc	1619.4 verb 3sing indic perf pass
ἡ	ἀγάπη	τοῦ	θεοῦ	ἐκκέχυται
hē	agapē	tou	theou	ekkechutai
the	love		of God	has been poured out

1706.1 prep	3450.14 art dat pl fem	2559.7 noun dat pl fem	2231.2 prs-pron gen 1pl	1217.2 prep	4011.2 noun gen sing neu	39.2 adj gen sing
ἐν	ταῖς	καρδίαις	ἡμῶν	διὰ	πνεύματος	ἁγίου
en	tais	kardiais	hēmōn	dia	pneumatos	hagiou
in	the	hearts	our	by	the Spirit	Holy

3450.2 art gen sing	1319.52 verb gen sing neu part aor pass	2231.3 prs-pron dat 1pl		2068.1 adv	1056.1 conj	1479.1
τοῦ	δοθέντος	ἡμῖν.	6. '☆ Ἔτι	γὰρ	[ᵃ εἴ
tou	dothentos	hēmin	Eti	gar	ei
the	having been given	to us:	still	for	[if

6.a.Txt: 01א,02A,04C 06D-org,018K,025P,33 byz.Tisc,Sod **Var:** 03B,sa.Alf,We/Ho Weis,UBS/☆

1058.1 partic	5382.1 name nom masc	1498.20 verb gen pl part pres act	2231.2 prs-pron gen 1pl	766.5 adj gen pl masc
γε]	Χριστὸς	ὄντων	ἡμῶν	ἀσθενῶν
ge	Christos	ontōn	hēmōn	asthenōn
yet]	Christ	being	we	being without strength

6.b.**Var:** 01א,02A,03B 04C,06D-org,Gries,Lach Treg,Alf,Word,Tisc We/Ho,Weis,Sod UBS/☆

	2068.1 adv	2567.3 prep	2511.4 noun acc sing masc	5065.1 prep	759.4 adj gen pl masc
[ᵇ☆+	ἔτι]	κατὰ	καιρὸν	ὑπὲρ	ἀσεβῶν
	eti	kata	kairon	huper	asebōn
	[still]	according to	time	for	ungodly

594.10 verb 3sing indic aor act	3296.1 adv	1056.1 conj	5065.1 prep	1337.2 adj gen sing	4948.3 indef-pron nom sing
ἀπέθανεν.	7. μόλις	γὰρ	ὑπὲρ	δικαίου	τις
apethanen	molis	gar	huper	dikaiou	tis
died.	Hardly	for	for	a just	anyone

5:3. The implied meaning of this verse is that the justified person, enjoying his standing in God, is able to triumph not just in tribulation, but even because of it.

5:4,5. Jesus came into the world to atone for our sinful actions as well as to deal with our proneness to sin. Both the first Adam and the last Adam (Christ) were sinless before they were tempted of the devil. The first Adam fell. The last Adam did not fall. As we have our standing in Christ, we have the confidence that tribulation cannot destroy our hope. The believer glories in hope and in suffering, knowing that tribulation works patience (endurance); and endurance works experience; and experience, hope.

Dokimi, "experience," means "tested, accepted, approved." "Patience" can be rendered "endurance," "steadfastness." "Experience" relates to character, "strength of character," "ripeness of character," "tested character." Paul is saying that endurance produces character. "Experience" works hope. This hope will never make one ashamed (*kataischunō*), meaning it will never "dishonor, disgrace, or put to shame," or, as others translate it, will never "disappoint" or "prove illusory."

All these privileges assure us of this unashamed hope, for the "love of God is shed abroad in our hearts by the Holy Ghost." This is the first mention of the Holy Spirit in the Book of Romans. He, the Third Person of the Trinity, has brought us into all these blessings.

"Shed abroad" (*ekcheō*) is translated "pour out" 11 of 18 times in the King James Version and is so rendered in several other translations. The word *love* has probably been abused more than any other in the English language. Here it is "the love of God" that is being given to and through those who are justified. This love is defined in 1 Corinthians 13 and modeled perfectly in Jesus.

For a human being, even a redeemed one, to try to produce this love is an exercise in futility. When we are willing to receive, the Holy Spirit miraculously produces His fruit within us. With this kind of love, we never have to be ashamed before Him.

The very character of our present privilege, "peace," participates in our future perspective, "the glory of God." We rejoice in what is now ours and rejoice in what will then be fully ours. These two faith actions become fused as we appropriate in life the sanctification our justification provides.

5:6. The descending scale of man before God is described in verses 6, 8, and 10 as "without strength (weak) . . . sinners . . . enemies." *Asthenēs* translated "without strength" in the King James Version is rendered in various translations as "weak . . . feeble . . . helpless and hopeless apart from God's grace." Too weak to live a righteous life, man is a sinner disobeying God's law, and is in reality an enemy of God.

3. And not only [so], but we glory in tribulations also: . . . we also boast about afflictions, *Adams* . . . but we triumph even in our troubles, *Moffatt* . . . we exult also in our distresses, *HistNT* . . . but we also rejoice, *Worrell* . . . we also are exulting in our tribulations, *Wuest.*

knowing that tribulation worketh patience: . . . that suffering produces fortitude, *Weymouth* . . . that trouble produces endurance, *TCNT* . . . that suffering develops endurance, *SEB* . . . results in patient endurance, *HistNT* . . . works fortitude, *Montgomery* . . . stedfastness, *ASV.*

4. And patience, experience: . . . and patience approval, *Adams* . . . and patience, probation, *Rheims* . . . brings perseverance, *JB* . . . stability of character, *TCNT* . . . is the proof of soundness, *Conybeare* . . . tested character, *Williams.*

and experience, hope:

5. And hope maketh not ashamed: . . . this hope is not deceptive, *JB* . . . And we need not be ashamed of hope, *Adams* . . . In this hope we're not disappointed, *Beck.*

because the love of God is shed abroad in our hearts by the Holy Ghost which is given unto us: . . . has been diffused in our hearts, *Wilson* . . . is povvred forth in our hartes, *Rheims* . . . flooded our hearts, *Williams* . . . has overflowed, *Montgomery.*

6. For when we were yet without strength: We were entirely helpless, *Norlie* . . . when we were still strengthless, *Berkeley* . . . being yet helpless, *Wilson* . . . when we were yet weake, *Tyndale, Cranmer* . . . in our being still ailing, *Young.*

in due time Christ died for the ungodly: . . . in a strategic season, *Wuest* . . . at exactly the right time, *SEB* . . . precisely at that time when it was needed, *Adams* . . . Christ at the right moment, *Weymouth* . . . when Christ, in His appointed time, *Norlie* . . . died on behalf of the godless, *TCNT* . . . die for the impious? *Rheims.*

81

594.22 verb 3sing
indic fut mid
ἀποθανεῖται·
apothaneitai
will die;

5065.1
prep
ὑπὲρ
huper
on behalf of

1056.1
conj
γὰρ
gar
for

3450.2 art
gen sing
τοῦ
tou
the

18.2
adj sing
ἀγαθοῦ
agathou
good

4877.1
adv
τάχα
tacha
perhaps

4948.3 indef-
pron nom sing
τις
tis
someone

2504.1
conj
καὶ
kai
even

4958.1 verb
3sing pres act
τολμᾷ
tolma
might dare

594.20 verb
inf aor act
ἀποθανεῖν·
apothanein
to die;

4771.2 verb 3sing
indic pres act
8. συνίστησιν
sunistēsin
commends

1156.2
conj
δὲ
de
but

3450.12 art
acc sing fem
τὴν
tēn
the

1431.4 prs-
pron gen 3sing
ἑαυτοῦ
heautou
of himself

26.4 noun
acc sing fem
ἀγάπην
agapēn
love

1519.1
prep
εἰς
eis
to

2231.4 prs-
pron acc 1pl
ἡμᾶς
hēmas
us

3450.5 art
sing masc
ὁ
ho

2296.1 noun
nom sing masc
θεὸς,
theos
God,

3617.1
conj
ὅτι
hoti
that

2068.1
adv
ἔτι
eti
still

266.5 adj
gen pl masc
ἁμαρτωλῶν
hamartōlōn
sinners

1498.20 verb gen
pl part pres act
ὄντων
ontōn
being

2231.2 prs-
pron gen 1pl
ἡμῶν
hēmōn
we

5382.1 name
nom masc
Χριστὸς
Christos
Christ

5065.1
prep
ὑπὲρ
huper
for

2231.2 prs-
pron gen 1pl
ἡμῶν
hēmōn
us

594.10 verb 3sing
indic aor act
ἀπέθανεν.
apethanen
died.

4044.3 adj
dat sing
9. πολλῷ
pollō
Much

3631.1
conj
οὖν
oun
therefore

3095.1
adv comp
μᾶλλον,
mallon
more,

1338.17 verb nom pl
masc part aor pass
δικαιωθέντες
dikaiōthentes
having been justified

3431.1
adv
νῦν
nun
now

1706.1
prep
ἐν
en
by

3450.3 art
dat sing
τῷ
tō
the

129.3 noun
dat sing neu
αἵματι
haimati
blood

840.3 prs-
pron gen sing
αὐτοῦ,
autou
his,

4834.34 verb 1pl
indic fut pass
σωθησόμεθα
sōthēsometha
we shall be saved

1217.1
prep
δι'
di'
by

840.3 prs-
pron gen sing
αὐτοῦ
autou
him

570.3
prep gen
ἀπὸ
apo
from

3450.10 art
gen sing fem
τῆς
tēs
the

3572.2 noun
gen sing fem
ὀργῆς.
orgēs
wrath.

1479.1
conj
10. εἰ
ei
If

1056.1
conj
γὰρ
gar
for,

2172.5 adj
nom pl masc
ἐχθροὶ
echthroi
enemies

1498.23 verb nom pl
masc part pres act
ὄντες
ontes
being

2614.3 verb 1pl
indic aor pass
κατηλλάγημεν
katēllagēmen
we were reconciled

3450.3 art
dat sing
τῷ
tō

2296.3 noun
dat sing masc
θεῷ
theō
to God

1217.2
prep
διὰ
dia
through

3450.2 art
gen sing
τοῦ
tou
the

2265.2 noun
gen sing masc
θανάτου
thanatou
death

3450.2 art
gen sing
τοῦ
tou
of the

5048.2 noun
gen sing masc
υἱοῦ
huiou
Son

840.3 prs-
pron gen sing
αὐτοῦ,
autou
his,

4044.3 adj
dat sing
πολλῷ
pollō
much

3095.1
adv comp
μᾶλλον
mallon
more,

2614.6 verb nom pl
masc part aor pass
καταλλαγέντες
katallagentes
having been reconciled

4834.34 verb 1pl
indic fut pass
σωθησόμεθα
sōthēsometha
we shall be saved

1706.1
prep
ἐν
en
by

3450.11 art
dat sing fem
τῇ
tē
the

2205.3 noun
dat sing fem
ζωῇ
zōē
life

840.3 prs-
pron gen sing
αὐτοῦ·
autou
his.

3620.3
partic
11. οὐ
ou
Not

5:7. "Righteous . . . good." The meaning is simply "right or just" (*dikaios*), and *agathos* = "good," that is, "kind, generous, benevolent."

5:8. "Sinners" (*hamartōlōn*) includes everyone, for it means those who fall short of God's glory, i.e., all mankind. The proof of God's love is in the gift of His Son. Some might die for a friend or a kind and good person, but Christ died for sinners who were at enmity with Him. Such is the character of God's love that anchors our hope. Our Lord died in our place and took our penalty upon himself. His death was in our interest.

5:9,10. The expression "much more" occurs repeatedly in this chapter. Christ's work at Calvary did much more than restore what was lost in Adam. Because of the Cross and as the sons of God, we enjoy a richer relationship with God than did Adam. We are "justified by his blood" which denotes the laying down of His life and is synonymous with "by the death of his Son" (verse 10).

"Saved from wrath" means saved from anger, indignation, and divine reaction toward evil. Paul writes concerning the future wrath of God. If the believer has already been justified, Paul reasons, he will surely be spared the future judgments of God. If as an enemy he was reconciled to God, surely as a reconciled person he will be spared punishment on judgment day.

The expression "much more" occurs again. As offending sinners we are reconciled by the vicarious death of our Saviour. He provided for our restoration to a place of harmonious relationship.

"Justified by his blood," "saved from wrath through him," "reconciled to God by the death of his Son"—all great provisions. But there is more—"we shall be saved by his life." God's love reached us before when we were sinners, but now "much more" as we are linked to Him. We "shall be saved from wrath" and shall be kept "saved by his life." Christ's death was a sacrificial ministry for us, and His life is now an intercessory ministry for us.

Great mercies came as a result of His love. We have been saved from the guilt and penalty of sin; we are being saved from the power of sin in daily life: we shall be saved from the presence of sin in eternity. That is our threefold salvation.

Reconciliation is the work of God, whereby He effects in the believing sinner a thorough change from enmity and aversion to love and trust. This work is also through the death of Christ.

Reconciliation, the result of justification, is something *we* have, not God. It is something *we* needed, not God. Propitiation is the Godward side whereby He restores His favor manward. Reconciliation is the manward aspect of the death of Christ; our enmity Godward is removed (2 Corinthians 5:18,19). Our message is, "Be ye reconciled to God." Man must choose to lay down his arms and cease hostilities against God.

7. For scarcely for a righteous man will one die: It is rare to find anyone willing, *Norlie* . . . Why, it is scarcely conceivable, *Weymouth* . . . one wouldn't ordinarily die, *Adams.*

yet peradventure for a good man some would even dare to die: . . . though once in a while...for a generous friend, *Williams* . . . yet perhaps one might bring himself to die, *Confraternity* . . . for perhaps for a good man, *Rheims* . . . a benevolent person, *Berkeley* . . . someone really worthy, *JB* . . . for a kind person, *Beck* . . . though for a benefactor some might perhaps hazard death, *Fenton* . . . some one might actually have the courage to die, *TCNT* . . . for a good and lovable man, *Weymouth* . . . some one might even venture, *Wilson.*

8. But God commendeth his love toward us, in that, while we were yet sinners, Christ died for us: But God reassures us of His love, *SEB* . . . god comendith his charite in us, *Wyclif* . . . But God is constantly proving His own love, *Wuest* . . . But God setteth out his loue toward vs, *Cranmer* . . . established His love towards us, *Fenton* . . . But God recommends His own Love to us...died on our behalf, *Wilson* . . . but God gives proof of His own love, *Conybeare* . . . beyond doubt, *TCNT.*

9. Much more then, being now justified by his blood: Much rather therefore, *Panin* . . . we have now been pronounced free from guilt, *Weymouth.*

we shall be saved from wrath through him: . . . save us from God's anger, *Beck* . . . saved from God's punishment, *SEB* . . . from the madness of sin, *Fenton.*

10. For if, when we were enemies, we were reconciled to God by the death of his Son: . . . while we were His enemies we were made God's friends, *Beck* . . . we were led back to God, *Fenton.*

much more, being reconciled, we shall be saved by his life: . . . was used to make us God's friends, *SEB* . . . by sharing Christ's Life, *TCNT* . . . we shal be preservid by his lyfe, *Tyndale.*

3303.1 adv	1156.2 conj	233.2 conj	2504.1 conj	2714.8 verb nom pl masc part pres	1706.1 prep	3450.3 art dat sing
μόνον	δέ,	ἀλλὰ	καὶ	καυχώμενοι	ἐν	τῷ
monon	de	alla	kai	kauchōmenoi	en	tō
only	and,	but	also	boasting	in	to

2296.3 noun dat sing masc	1217.2 prep	3450.2 art gen sing	2935.2 noun gen sing masc	2231.2 prs-pron gen 1pl	2400.2 name masc
θεῷ	διὰ	τοῦ	κυρίου	ἡμῶν	Ἰησοῦ
theō	dia	tou	kuriou	hēmōn	Iēsou
God	through	the	Lord	our	Jesus

5382.2 name gen sing masc	1217.1 prep	3614.2 rel-pron gen sing	3431.1 adv	3450.12 art acc sing fem	2613.3 noun acc sing fem
Χριστοῦ,	δι᾽	οὗ	νῦν	τὴν	καταλλαγὴν
Christou	di'	hou	nun	tēn	katallagēn
Christ,	through	whom	now	the	reconciliation

2956.15 verb 1pl indic aor act	1217.2 prep	3642.17 dem-pron sing neu	5450.1 adv	1217.1 prep	1518.1 num card gen
ἐλάβομεν.	**12.** Διὰ	τοῦτο	ὥσπερ	δι᾽	ἑνὸς
elabomen	Dia	touto	hōsper	di'	henos
we received.	Because of	this,	as	by	one

442.2 noun gen sing masc	3450.9 art nom sing fem	264.2 noun nom sing fem	1519.1 prep	3450.6 art acc sing masc	2862.4 noun acc sing masc
ἀνθρώπου	ἡ	ἁμαρτία	εἰς	τὸν	κόσμον
anthrōpou	hē	hamartia	eis	ton	kosmon
man	the	sin	into	the	world

12.a.**Txt:** 01ℵ,02A,03B 04C,018K,025P,33,81 614,1739,byz. **Var:** 06D,010F,012G 2495

1511.3 verb 3sing indic aor act	2504.1 conj	1217.2 prep	3450.10 art gen sing fem	264.1 noun fem	3450.5 art sing masc
εἰσῆλθεν,	καὶ	διὰ	τῆς	ἁμαρτίας	⌐a ὁ
eisēlthen	kai	dia	tēs	hamartias	ho
entered,	and	by	the	sin	the

2265.1 noun nom sing masc	2504.1 conj	3643.1 adv	1519.1 prep	3820.8 adj acc pl masc	442.9 noun acc pl masc
θάνατος, ⌐	καὶ	οὕτως	εἰς	πάντας	ἀνθρώπους
thanatos	kai	houtōs	eis	pantas	anthrōpous
death,	and	thus	to	all	men

3450.5 art sing masc	2265.1 noun nom sing masc	1324.2 verb 3sing indic aor act	1894.1 prep	3614.3 rel-pron dat sing	3820.7 adj pl masc
ὁ	θάνατος	διῆλθεν,	ἐφ᾽	ᾧ	πάντες
ho	thanatos	diēlthen,	eph'	hō	pantes
the	death	passed,	for	that	all

262.11 verb indic aor act	884.2 conj	1056.1 conj	3414.2 noun gen sing masc	264.2 noun nom sing fem	1498.34 verb sing indic imperf act
ἥμαρτον	**13.** ἄχρι	γὰρ	νόμου	ἁμαρτία	ἦν
hēmarton	achri	gar	nomou	hamartia	ēn
sinned:	until	for	law	sin	was

1706.1 prep	2862.3 noun dat sing masc	264.2 noun nom sing fem	1156.2 conj	3620.2 partic	1664.2 verb 3sing indic pres pass	3231.1 partic
ἐν	κόσμῳ·	ἁμαρτία	δὲ	οὐκ	ἐλλογεῖται,	μὴ
en	kosmō	hamartia	de	ouk	ellogeitai,	mē
in	world;	sin	but	not	is put to account,	not

1498.19 verb gen sing part pres act	3414.2 noun gen sing masc	233.1 conj	233.2 conj	929.6 verb 3sing indic aor act
ὄντος	νόμου·	**14.** ⌐ ἀλλ᾽	[☆ ἀλλὰ]	ἐβασίλευσεν
ontos	nomou	all'	alla	ebasileusen
there being	law;	but	[idem]	reigned

5:11. "Atonement" is literally "reconciliation" and is so translated in verse 10. In reconciliation, Christ is always the Reconciler and man is the object of reconciliation. When Adam and Eve sinned there came an aversion to God. They hid from His presence. Those who accept reconciliation find "joy in God."

5:12. The section containing verses 12-21 is an analogy. It contrasts the disobedience of Adam, which brought universal death, and the obedience of Christ, which made eternal life possible for all human beings. The passage shows that just as the death of all rests on Adam, so the righteousness of all rests on Jesus Christ. "Death" in verse 12 refers specifically to physical death.

The meaning of the phrase *eph' hō pantes hēmarton* ("for that all have sinned") has been debated throughout the centuries. Many have concluded that the words *eph' hō* are best translated "because" (see 2 Corinthians 5:4; Philippians 3:12). However, others translate these words, *"in some way* all sinned." Adam's fall introduced the virus of sin into the entire human race, and death is the result of sin. When Adam fell, the race fell. Three basic theological positions attempt to explain this verse.

Calvinism says that phrase should be translated *"because* all have sinned," meaning that every human was "in Adam" (or represented by him) and therefore sinned because he sinned. The implication is that each individual is guilty of Adam's sin. Another consequence of his sin is that all men are born "totally depraved"; that is, they cannot help but choose evil. God's grace moves only upon the elect and produces faith unto repentance.

Pelagianism teaches that Adam's sin affected only himself. Guilt is imputed upon the individual only after he commits sin. Adam serves only as a bad example and each person starts life just as free from effects of sin as Adam was prior to the Fall. Every person is "born innocent and able to obey God."

Arminianism says that when Adam sinned, the race sinned. No human baby has been born with the righteousness Adam had prior to the Fall. Each is born with a nature bent toward sin that results in acts of sin when he reaches the age of accountability. But by a universal grace given to all men, each person is enabled to choose between God and Satan.

5:13. "The law" referred to here is the Mosaic law, as verse 14 shows. There was law prior to Moses, else there could have been no sin (4:15). Cain was guilty of sin (Genesis 4:7-11). Abel was righteous by faith (Hebrews 11:4) which motivated his obedience.

Many commentators state that the phrase "when there is no law" describes the condition of infants and children prior to the age of accountability. Jesus made it clear that children are in the Kingdom (Matthew 18:3; 19:14). Paul said, "I was alive without the law once: but when the commandment came, sin revived, and I died" (7:9). This describes the experience of every person who lives to the age of accountability. David knew he was born with a sinful nature (Psalm 51:5); he also knew that his infant son who died was with God (2 Samuel 12:23).

11. And not only [so], but we also joy in God through our Lord Jesus Christ: But that is not all, *NEB* . . . And this is not merely a future hope, *Barclay* . . . we are filled with joyful trust, *JB*.

by whom we have now received the atonement: . . . to whom we owe our reconciliation, *Norlie* . . . through whom we have now received reconciliation, *Confraternity* . . . who has now given us this friendship, *Beck* . . . we have been made friends with God, *Barclay* . . . by whom we haue now obtayned, *Cranmer*.

12. Wherefore, as by one man sin entered into the world: This comparison, *Weymouth* . . . For this cause, *Alford* . . . It is therefore as follows, *Berkeley* . . . as through one man, *Worrell* . . . gained an entry, *Barclay*.

and death by sin: . . . and through sin came death, *TCNT* . . . death came into the world through sin, *SEB* . . . by the meanes of synne, *Geneva*.

and so death passed upon all men: In this way death spread to all men, *SEB* . . . thus death pervaded the whole human race, *NEB* . . . to all mankind in turn, *Weymouth*.

for that all have sinned: . . . inasmuch as all men sinned, *Moffatt* . . . because everyone has sinned, *JB* . . . supposing indeed that all sin, *Fenton* . . . because all committed sin, *Conybeare*.

13. (For until the law sin was in the world: For prior to the Law, *Weymouth* . . . earlier than the Law, *Berkeley* . . . There was sin in the world, *Beck* . . . sin actually existed in the world, *Montgomery*.

but sin is not imputed when there is no law: . . . as long as there is no law, *Geneva* . . . in the absence of law, sin is not charged, *HistNT* . . . in the absence of law no reckoning is kept of sin, *NEB* . . . sin is not charged up, *Berkeley* . . . sin is not debited to anyone's account, *Barclay* . . . the sin of "law-breaking," *JB* . . . sin is not put to account, *Panin* . . . sin was not thought of as sin, *SEB* . . . cannot be charged, *TCNT* . . . no account is kept of sins, *TEV* . . . if a law did not exist, *Fenton*.

Romans 5:15

3450.5 art sing masc	2265.1 noun nom sing masc	570.3 prep gen	75.1 name masc	3230.1 prep gen	3337.2 name gen masc
ὁ	θάνατος	ἀπὸ	Ἀδὰμ	μέχρι	Μωσέως
ho	thanatos	apo	Adam	mechri	Mōseōs
the	death	from	Adam	until	Moses

	3338.2 name gen masc	2504.1 conj	1894.3 prep	3450.8 art acc pl masc	3231.1 partic	262.20 verb acc pl masc part aor act
	[✶ Μωϋσέως]	καὶ	ἐπὶ	τοὺς	μὴ	ἁμαρτήσαντας
	Mōuseōs	kai	epi	tous	mē	hamartēsantas
	[idem]	even	upon	the	not	having sinned

1894.3 prep	3450.3 art dat sing	3530.1 noun dat sing neu	3450.10 art gen sing fem	3709.2 noun gen sing fem	75.1 name masc
ἐπὶ	τῷ	ὁμοιώματι	τῆς	παραβάσεως	Ἀδάμ,
epi	tō	homoiōmati	tēs	parabaseōs	Adam
in	the	likeness	of the	transgression	of Adam,

3614.5 rel-pron nom sing masc	1498.4 verb 3sing indic pres act	5020.1 noun nom sing masc	3450.2 art gen sing	3165.9 verb gen sing masc part pres act
ὅς	ἐστιν	τύπος	τοῦ	μέλλοντος.
hos	estin	tupos	tou	mellontos
who	is	a figure	of the	coming.

233.1 conj	3620.1 partic	5453.1 conj	3450.16 art sing neu	3761.1 noun nom sing neu	3643.1 adv
15. Ἀλλ'	οὐχ	ὡς	τὸ	παράπτωμα,	οὕτως
All'	ouch	hōs	to	paraptōma	houtōs
But	not	as	the	offense,	so

2504.1 conj	3450.16 art sing neu	5321.1 noun sing neu	1479.1 conj	1056.1 conj	3450.3 art dat sing	3450.2 art gen sing
καὶ	τὸ	χάρισμα.	εἰ	γὰρ	τῷ	τοῦ
kai	to	charisma	ei	gar	tō	tou
also	the	free gift?	If	for	by the	of the

1518.1 num card gen	3761.3 noun dat sing neu	3450.7 art pl masc	4044.7 adj nom pl masc	594.9 verb indic aor act
ἑνὸς	παραπτώματι	οἱ	πολλοὶ	ἀπέθανον,
henos	paraptōmati	hoi	polloi	apethanon
one	offense	the	many	died,

4044.3 adj dat sing	3095.1 adv comp	3450.9 art nom sing fem	5322.1 noun nom sing fem	3450.2 art gen sing	2296.2 noun gen sing masc
πολλῷ	μᾶλλον	ἡ	χάρις	τοῦ	θεοῦ
pollō	mallon	hē	charis	tou	theou
much	more	the	grace		of God,

2504.1 conj	3450.9 art nom sing fem	1424.1 noun nom sing fem	1706.1 prep	5322.3 noun dat sing fem	3450.11 art dat sing fem
καὶ	ἡ	δωρεὰ	ἐν	χάριτι	τῇ
kai	hē	dōrea	en	chariti	tē
and	the	gift	in	grace,	by the

3450.2 art gen sing	1518.1 num card gen	442.2 noun gen sing masc	2400.2 name masc	5382.2 name gen masc	1519.1 prep
τοῦ	ἑνὸς	ἀνθρώπου	Ἰησοῦ	Χριστοῦ	εἰς
tou	henos	anthrōpou	Iēsou	Christou	eis
of the	one	man	Jesus	Christ,	to

3450.8 art acc pl masc	4044.8 adj acc pl masc	3915.13 verb 3sing indic aor act	2504.1 conj	3620.1 partic	5453.1 conj
τοὺς	πολλοὺς	ἐπερίσσευσεν.	**16.** καὶ	οὐχ	ὡς
tous	pollous	eperisseusen	kai	ouch	hōs
the	many	did abound.	And	not	as

86

5:14. For Adam's sin God pronounced the sentence of death on him and all his descendants. Adam is an antithetical type ("figure") of Christ who is "the last Adam" (1 Corinthians 15:45). The period from Adam to Moses served to illustrate that it was not the Mosaic law that determined the reign of death or the reality of sin.

As stated earlier (see verse 12), the death spoken of here is physical death. It is true that there is a relationship between the sin of Adam and spiritual death. This passage does not say, however, that Adam's sin caused the spiritual death of all. If that were true, the section 1:18 to 3:19 would be completely unnecessary. That section has already proved that all (assuming the age of accountability) are guilty (3:19) because they have knowingly rejected God's revelation of himself (1:18-32); they have knowingly broken the law they had (2:1-16); and all like sheep have gone astray, knowingly transgressing God's law as they understood it (2:17 to 3:19).

The sinful nature will inevitably manifest itself in actual sins as the person reaches the age of accountability. Many believe that God's grace prevents the spiritual death of a child, for sin is not imputed where there is no law (verse 13). Because sin is defined as the transgression of the law, they believe children are not charged with sin until they are old enough to commit a willful transgression. Others baptize infants to cleanse away the "original" sin and guilt inherited from Adam.

This passage marks a transition from the question of *sins* to that of *sin*. The matter of justification has been the apostle's burden, now he begins to lead up to sanctification.

5:15. In bringing the justification section to an end, Paul clearly establishes the grounds of it all. The sinner is not only justified by faith and reconciled to God by Christ, but his redemption is by grace alone. The words "gift" and "grace" are used repeatedly in this chapter.

"Through the offense of one many be dead," and "by one man's offense death reigned by one" (verse 17). If the person is not born again on reaching the age of accountability, he dies spiritually; spiritual death includes eternal death in hell. The fall of Adam caused untold evil, but the work of the last Adam "by grace" shall do "much more" good. He gave much more than was lost in the first Adam. The act of grace far outbalances Adam's act of sin.

Though the experiences of sin and death are universal through the first Adam, the experience of salvation is not universal through the last Adam. The former is a matter of sentence; the latter is a matter of choice (or election, depending on one's theology). Obviously God knows how we will choose, yet He still allows us the choice (Joshua 24:14,15). Some define this divine foreknowledge as predestination. Eternal life is the reward for choosing the gift of God's grace; eternal death is the penalty of unforgiven sin, of not accepting God's gift by grace.

Our sins are imputed to Christ; He bore the penalty of our guilt. Because His sacrifice was acceptable to the Father, His righteousness is imputed to us so that we are pronounced righteous (and are righteous) in God's sight (1 Peter 2:24).

14. Nevertheless death reigned from Adam to Moses: But death held sway, *NEB*.

even over them that had not sinned after the similitude of Adam's transgression: . . . in which Adam broke the command, *Barclay* . . . in a way that was exactly like, *Adams* . . . didn't break the law as Adam did, *Beck* . . . by disobeying a direct command, *NEB*.

who is the figure of him that was to come: Adam foreshadowed One who was to come, *Norlie* . . . who is a Type of that being about to come, *Wilson* . . . a type of the future, *Fenton* . . . Him whose coming was still future, *Weymouth* . . . Adam was a picture of what was going to happen, *SEB*.

15. But not as the offence, so also [is] the free gift: . . . but not as the fall, *Sawyer* . . . not as the trespass, *Worrell* . . . But there is no comparison between, *Barclay* . . . there is a great contrast between Adam's offence and God's gift of mercy, *TCNT* . . . thus also is the gratuitous favor, *Wuest* . . . free gift immeasurably outweighs the transgression, *Weymouth* . . . considerably outweighed the fall, *JB* . . . in proportion to Adam's transgression? *Norlie*.

For if through the offence of one many be dead: . . . through the lapsing of one person, *Berkeley* . . . if the wrongdoing of that one man brought death upon so many, *NEB* . . . the mass of mankind have died, *Weymouth* . . . the whole race of men have died, *Williams*.

much more the grace of God, and the gift by grace, [which is] by one man, Jesus Christ, hath abounded unto many: . . . to a much greater degree, *Williams* . . . infinitely greater is the generosity...have been bestowed on the mass of mankind, *Weymouth* . . . his mercy which found expression...were lavished upon the whole race, *TCNT* . . . has the freeness of God's bounty overflowed, *Conybeare* . . . overflowed far more richly upon the rest of men, *Moffatt* . . . have been richly poured out on all people, *Beck* . . . came to many in great surplus, *Klingensmith*.

1217.1 prep	1518.1 num card gen	262.17 verb gen sing masc part aor act	3450.16 art sing neu	1427.1 noun nom sing neu	3450.16 art sing neu
δι'	ἑνὸς	ἁμαρτήσαντος	τὸ	δώρημα·	τὸ
di'	henos	hamartēsantos	to	dōrēma	to
by	one	having sinned	the	gift?	The

3173.1 conj	1056.1 conj	2890.1 noun sing neu	1523.1 prep gen	1518.1 num card gen	1519.1 prep	2601.1 noun sing neu
μὲν	γὰρ	κρίμα	ἐξ	ἑνὸς	εἰς	κατάκριμα,
men	gar	krima	ex	henos	eis	katakrima
indeed	for	judgment	of	one	to	condemnation,

3450.16 art sing neu	1156.2 conj	5321.1 noun sing neu	1523.2 prep gen	4044.1 adj gen pl	3761.4 noun gen pl neu
τὸ	δὲ	χάρισμα	ἐκ	πολλῶν	παραπτωμάτων
to	de	charisma	ek	pollōn	paraptōmatōn
the	but	free gift	of	many	offenses

1519.1 prep	1339.1 noun sing neu		1479.1 conj	1056.1 conj	3450.3 art dat sing	3450.2 art gen sing
εἰς	δικαίωμα.	**17.**	εἰ	γὰρ	τῷ	τοῦ
eis	dikaiōma		ei	gar	tō	tou
to	justification.		If	for	by the	of the

1518.1 num card gen	3761.3 noun dat sing neu	3450.5 art sing masc	2265.1 noun nom sing masc	929.6 verb 3sing indic aor act
ἑνὸς	παραπτώματι	ὁ	θάνατος	ἐβασίλευσεν
henos	paraptōmati	ho	thanatos	ebasileusen
one	offense	the	death	reigned

1217.2 prep	3450.2 art gen sing	1518.1 num card gen	4044.3 adj dat sing	3095.1 adv comp	3450.7 art pl masc	3450.12 art acc sing fem
διὰ	τοῦ	ἑνός,	πολλῷ	μᾶλλον	οἱ	τὴν
dia	tou	henos	pollō	mallon	hoi	tēn
by	the	one,	much	more	the	the

3913.2 noun acc sing fem	3450.10 art gen sing fem	5322.2 noun gen sing fem	2504.1 conj	3450.10 art gen sing fem	1424.2 noun gen sing fem
περισσείαν	τῆς	χάριτος	καὶ	τῆς	δωρεᾶς
perisseian	tēs	charitos	kai	tēs	dōreas
abundance	of the	grace,	and	of the	gift

3450.10 art gen sing fem	1336.2 noun gen sing fem	2956.9 verb nom pl masc part pres act	1706.1 prep	2205.3 noun dat sing fem
τῆς	δικαιοσύνης	λαμβάνοντες,	ἐν	ζωῇ
tēs	dikaiosunēs	lambanontes	en	zōē
of the	righteousness	receiving,	in	life

929.13 verb 3pl indic fut act	1217.2 prep	3450.2 art gen sing	1518.1 num card gen	2400.2 name masc	5382.2 name gen masc
βασιλεύσουσιν	διὰ	τοῦ	ἑνὸς	Ἰησοῦ	Χριστοῦ.
basileusousin	dia	tou	henos	Iēsou	Christou
shall reign	by	the	one	Jesus	Christ:

	679.1 partic	3631.1 conj	5453.1 conj	1217.1 prep	1518.1 num card gen	3761.2 noun gen sing neu	1519.1 prep
18.	Ἄρα	οὖν	ὡς	δι'	ἑνὸς	παραπτώματος	εἰς
	Ara	oun	hōs	di'	henos	paraptōmatos	eis
	so	then	as	by	one	offense	toward

3820.8 adj acc pl masc	442.9 noun acc pl masc	1519.1 prep	2601.1 noun sing neu	3643.1 adv	2504.1 conj
πάντας	ἀνθρώπους	εἰς	κατάκριμα,	οὕτως	καὶ
pantas	anthrōpous	eis	katakrima	houtōs	kai
all	men	to	condemnation,	so	also

5:16. Here we have a contrast of the catastrophic result of the one offense of one man, Adam, and the gift by grace which is by one man, Jesus Christ. The gift by grace is much more than the consequence of the offense. Adam's offense brought physical death, but it could not doom all men to eternal death. Men go to hell for their own sins, not Adam's. Jesus was able to bring to all who are in Him eternal life.

Man was involved in circumstances in which there was no hope. Sin and death had man in their power and there was no escape. Into this setting Christ came. He conquered sin and death. By His death and resurrection He broke the stranglehold of sin. Man can escape but only by an act of his will, his free choice. Our relationship with the first Adam is automatic; our relationship with the last Adam is voluntary.

This verse tells us that out of Adam's one trespass came judgment but that out of many trespasses that were laid upon Christ came not judgment but a righteous act (*dikaiōma*).

Three Greek words translated "gift" appear in verses 15 and 16: *charisma*, *dōrea*, and *dōrēma*. *Charisma* is translated in the American Standard and the King James versions as "free gift." This suggests that there is a distinction between *charisma* and the other two words and that *charisma* carries a special sense.

5:17. God's grace abounds. "They which receive" is based on the principle of "the one for the many," but this does not include all men because some reject. The believer may receive the "abundance of grace." "Abound" and "abundance" are used many times to express the gracious kindness of the loving heart of God towards sinners. The believer may also receive the "gift of righteousness." This is apart from works, the Law, ordinances, and worthiness.

When speaking of God's grace, here as elsewhere, Paul seems compelled by the very nature of that grace to place extreme emphasis on its abundance. The point of this entire passage is to stress how "much more" effective God's grace is than any effects of sin. The Greek verb translated "to abound" carries with it the sense of being plentiful to the point of excess. The noun "abundance" may well be translated "superabundance."

Christ's atoning death, designed in the counsels of eternity and carried out on Golgotha's cross, is God's marvelous way of combining in one great and glorious act His holiness, righteousness, and justice together with His love, mercy, grace, and forgiveness. He bridged the great gulf which no man could span. The eternal Son of God, the perfect Son of Man, became the one Person who could take on himself the guilt, the penalty, and the effects of sin for time and eternity, thereby making it possible for the believer to become righteous in God's sight.

5:18. A key word in 5:12-21 is "one," occurring 12 times. One man brings the curse of sin and death. Without choice, all men are

16. And not as [it was] by one that sinned, [so is] the gift: Nor is the gift like the effect of the sin, *Adams* . . . as it was in the case of one man's sin, *Confraternity* . . . like the effect of the one man's sin, *Moffatt* . . . exceeds the fruit of Adam's sin, *Conybeare*.

for the judgment [was] by one to condemnation, but the free gift [is] of many offences unto justification: . . . that the judgment following the sin was a death sentence, *Norlie* . . . ensuing on a single sin resulted in doom, the free gift...issues in acquittal, *Moffatt* . . . The sentence...condemns us, but the gift, *Beck* . . . followed many sins and made people right with God, *SEB* . . . but divine grace led to, *Berkeley* . . . the free gift had to be great enough to result in, *Adams* . . . after a multitude of transgressions results in acquittal, *Weymouth* . . . led to our standing right with him, *TCNT* . . . the undeserved gift of "Not guilty!" *TEV* . . . to a declaration of 'Righteous,' *Young* . . . came rectification from many transgressions, *Fenton* . . . to a righteous ordinance, *Sawyer*.

17. For if by one man's offence death reigned by one: . . . if the reign of death was established...through the sin of him alone, *Conybeare* . . . death is king, *Berkeley* . . . to seize the sovereignty, *Weymouth*.

much more they which receive abundance of grace and of the gift of righteousness shall reign in life by one, Jesus Christ.): . . . it is far more certain that those who obtain in rich abundance God's mercy, *TCNT* . . . much more will God's abundant mercy and His gift of sanctification reign, *Norlie* . . . who receives the free gift that he does not deserve, *JB*.

18. Therefore as by the offence of one [judgment came] upon all men to condemnation: It follows then, *Montgomery* . . . just as a single offence resulted, *TCNT* . . . by one offence the sentence of death came upon, *Wesley* . . . as by one sin all people were condemned, *Beck* . . . is a condemnation which extends to the whole race, *Weymouth* . . . sentence passed upon all men, *Scarlett*.

1217.1 prep	1518.1 num card gen	1339.2 noun gen sing neu		1519.1 prep	3820.8 adj acc pl masc
δι'	ἑνὸς	δικαιώματος		εἰς	πάντας
di'	henos	dikaiōmatos		eis	pantas
by	one	accomplished righteousness		towards	all

442.9 noun acc pl masc	1519.1 prep	1340.1 noun acc sing fem	2205.2 noun gen sing fem	5450.1 adv	1056.1 conj
ἀνθρώπους	εἰς	δικαίωσιν	ζωῆς.	**19.** ὥσπερ	γὰρ
anthrōpous	eis	dikaiōsin	zōēs	hōsper	gar
men	to	justification	of life.	As	for

1217.2 prep	3450.10 art gen sing fem	3737.2 noun gen sing fem	3450.2 art gen sing	1518.1 num card gen	442.2 noun gen sing masc
διὰ	τῆς	παρακοῆς	τοῦ	ἑνὸς	ἀνθρώπου
dia	tēs	parakoēs	tou	henos	anthrōpou
by	the	disobedience	of the	one	man

266.4 adj pl masc	2497.10 verb 3pl indic aor pass	3450.7 art pl masc	4044.7 adj nom pl masc	3643.1 adv	2504.1 conj
ἁμαρτωλοὶ	κατεστάθησαν	οἱ	πολλοί,	οὕτως	καὶ
hamartōloi	katestathēsan	hoi	polloi	houtōs	kai
sinners	were constituted	the	many,	so	also

1217.2 prep	3450.10 art gen sing fem	5056.2 noun gen sing fem	3450.2 art gen sing	1518.1 num card gen	442.2 noun gen sing masc
διὰ	τῆς	ὑπακοῆς	τοῦ	ἑνὸς	[a+ ἀνθρώπου]
dia	tēs	hupakoēs	tou	henos	anthrōpou
by	the	obedience	of the	one	[man]

19.a.**Txt:** 06D-org,010F 012G
Var: p46,01ℵ,02A,03B 04C,We/Ho,UBS/✶

1337.6 adj nom pl masc	2497.11 verb 3pl indic fut pass	3450.7 art pl masc	4044.7 adj nom pl masc	3414.1 noun nom sing masc
δίκαιοι	κατασταθήσονται	οἱ	πολλοί.	**20.** Νόμος
dikaioi	katastathēsontai	hoi	polloi	Nomos
righteous	shall be constituted	the	many.	Law

1156.2 conj	3784.1 verb 3sing indic aor act	2419.1 conj	3981.4 verb 3sing subj aor act	3450.16 art sing neu
δὲ	παρεισῆλθεν,	ἵνα	πλεονάσῃ	τὸ
de	pareisēlthen	hina	pleonasē	to
but	slipped in,	that	might increase	the

3761.1 noun nom sing neu	3619.1 adv	1156.2 conj	3981.3 verb 3sing indic aor act	3450.9 art nom sing fem
παράπτωμα.	οὗ	δὲ	ἐπλεόνασεν	ἡ
paraptōma	hou	de	epleonasen	hē
offense;	where	but	increased	the

264.2 noun nom sing fem	5086.1 verb 3sing indic aor act	3450.9 art nom sing fem	5322.1 noun nom sing fem	2419.1 conj
ἁμαρτία,	ὑπερεπερίσσευσεν	ἡ	χάρις·	**21.** ἵνα
hamartia	hupereperisseusen	hē	charis	hina
sin,	superabounded	the	grace,	that

5450.1 adv	929.6 verb 3sing indic aor act	3450.9 art nom sing fem	264.2 noun nom sing fem	1706.1 prep	3450.3 art dat sing
ὥσπερ	ἐβασίλευσεν	ἡ	ἁμαρτία	ἐν	τῷ
hōsper	ebasileusen	hē	hamartia	en	tō
as	reigned	the	sin	in	the

2265.3 noun dat sing masc	3643.1 adv	2504.1 conj	3450.9 art nom sing fem	5322.1 noun nom sing fem	929.9 verb 3sing subj aor act
θανάτῳ,	οὕτως	καὶ	ἡ	χάρις	βασιλεύσῃ
thanatō	houtōs	kai	hē	charis	basileusē
death,	so	also	the	grace	might reign

"in Adam." His offense (Genesis 3:6,17-19) brought the judgment of God in a universal way. It brought physical death on every one in Adam's race, and it caused a sinful nature to be imparted to every human being. This sinful nature leads to condemnation because it will manifest itself in actual sin in everyone when he attains accountability to God.

Likewise, Jesus, by His death and resurrection (4:25), made the justification of life available to every person in Adam's race. If we take the words of verse 18 literally without interpreting in the light of all Scripture, we could assume a teaching of universal salvation of all men. This is totally unscriptural, as any true Bible student knows. Christ's atonement is efficacious for all men *potentially*, for no man *unconditionally*, and for all believers *efficiently*. In 1 Corinthians 15:22, Paul wrote: "As in Adam all die, even so in Christ shall all be made alive." Only those who are in Christ, by faith which includes voluntary obedience, receive the free gift.

One Man, the last Adam, brings all men who believe into a supernatural generation. We died with Him, we rose with Him, and we sit in "heavenly places" with Him. Offsetting "sin" and "death" is His bestowment of "grace," "righteousness," and "eternal life," which are ours "by Jesus Christ our Lord" (verse 21). As the guilt of Adam was reckoned to our account for condemnation, so the righteousness of Jesus Christ has been reckoned to us for our justification. When Christ died, He paid the penalty of sin in our stead. He took our place. He was our Representative, our Substitute.

5:19. The apostle continues his series of contrasts. Disobedience is contrasted with obedience. Sinners are contrasted with the righteous. This verse contrasts the vast difference between condemnation and justification, with the background indicating the prospect of judgment for the unbeliever as opposed to the assurance of acquittal for the believer.

The just rewards for the deeds of the ungodly are shown over against the rewards of those who accept God's free gift of righteousness.

Death is contrasted with life. In Jesus Christ we have righteousness and life, not as gifts apart from Him, but as life in Him. This life "in Christ" will be unfolded in the next three chapters of the epistle. Compare Colossians 3:3,4.

5:20,21. The final contrast is between the Law and grace. The Law entered (*pareiserchomai*). Other renderings are "came in beside," "intruded into this process," "slipped in." According to Galatians 3:19, the Law was given "to make wrongdoing a legal offense" (NEB).

The Law caused man to see the great wickedness of sin. By the Law the knowledge of sin increased. But as the guiltiness of sin

even so by the righteousness of one [the free gift came] upon all men unto justification of life: ... so also one Person's righteous act, *Adams* ... so, too, a single decree, *TCNT* ... to all men there resulted a righteous standing, *Wuest* ... so likewise the fruit of one acquittal shall reach to all, *Conybeare* ... leads to acquittal and life for all men, *RSV* ... spryngeth good vpon all men, *Cranmer.*

19. For as by one man's disobedience: For as bi inobedience of, *Wyclif.*
many were made sinners: ... many were constituted sinners, *HistNT, Wuest.*
so by the obedience of one: ... through one righteous act, *Worrell.*
shall many be made righteous: ... the whole race will be set right with God, *TCNT* ... be constituted upright, *HistNT* ... will be constituted righteous, *Wuest.*

20. Moreover the law entered, that the offence might abound: Now law was brought in, *Montgomery* ... But a law intervened, *Fenton* ... the result was that trespasses were on the increase, *Norlie* ... in to make the trespass more serious, *Berkeley* ... Law slipped in to aggravate the trespass, *Moffatt* ... came to multiply sin, *Beck* ... that gilte schulde be plenteuous, *Wyclif* ... that synne shuld encreace, *Tyndale, Cranmer.*
But where sin abounded, grace did much more abound: But where the sin was augmented, *Wuest* ... where the sin exceeded, the gift went far beyond it, *Fenton* ... grace surpassed far more, *Panin* ... grace overflows the more, *Berkeley* ... but however great the number of sins committed, grace was even greater, *JB* ... God's gift of love was so much greater, *Beck* ... the wider was God's mercy, *TCNT* ... there was more plenteousnes of grace, *Tyndale* ... grace was superabundant, *Sawyer.*

21. That as sin hath reigned unto death: Sin used death to rule, *SEB* ... in its deadly way, *Beck.*

1217.2 prep	1336.2 noun gen sing fem	1519.1 prep	2205.4 noun acc sing fem	164.1 adj sing	1217.2 prep
διὰ	δικαιοσύνης	εἰς	ζωὴν	αἰώνιον,	διὰ
dia	dikaiosunēs	eis	zōēn	aiōnion	dia
through	righteousness	to	life	eternal,	through

2400.2 name masc	5382.2 name gen masc	3450.2 art gen sing	2935.2 noun gen sing masc	2231.2 prs-pron gen 1pl	4949.9 intr-pron sing neu
Ἰησοῦ	Χριστοῦ	τοῦ	κυρίου	ἡμῶν.	6:1. Τί
Iēsou	Christou	tou	kuriou	hēmōn	Ti
Jesus	Christ	the	Lord	our.	What

1.a.Txt: Steph
Var: 02A,03B,04C,06D
Gries,Lach,Treg,Alf
Word,Tisc,We/Ho,Weis
Sod,UBS/☆

3631.1 conj	2029.12 verb 1pl indic fut act	1946.11 verb 1pl indic fut act	1946.15 verb 1pl subj pres act
οὖν	ἐροῦμεν;	ʿ ἐπιμενοῦμεν	[ᵃ☆ ἐπιμένωμεν]
oun	eroumen	epimenoumen	epimenōmen
then	shall we say?	Shall we continue	[may we continue]

3450.11 art dat sing fem	264.3 noun dat sing fem	2419.1 conj	3450.9 art nom sing fem	5322.1 noun nom sing fem	3981.4 verb 3sing subj aor act
τῇ	ἁμαρτίᾳ,	ἵνα	ἡ	χάρις	πλεονάσῃ;
tē	hamartia	hina	hē	charis	pleonasē
in the	sin	that	the	grace	may abound?

3231.1 partic	1090.44 verb 3sing opt aor mid	3610.2 rel-pron nom pl masc	594.11 verb 1pl indic aor act	3450.11 art dat sing fem
2. μὴ	γένοιτο.	οἵτινες	ἀπεθάνομεν	τῇ
mē	genoito	hoitines	apethanomen	tē
Not	may it be!	Who	we died	to the

264.3 noun dat sing fem	4316.1 adv	2068.1 adv	2180.26 verb 1pl indic fut act	1706.1 prep	840.11 prs-pron dat sing fem	2211.1 conj
ἁμαρτίᾳ,	πῶς	ἔτι	ζήσομεν	ἐν	αὐτῇ;	3. ἢ
hamartia	pōs	eti	zēsomen	en	autē	ē
sin,	how	still	shall we live	in	it?	Or

49.3 verb 2pl indic pres act	3617.1 conj	3607.2 rel-pron nom pl masc	901.15 verb 1pl indic aor pass	1519.1 prep
ἀγνοεῖτε	ὅτι	ὅσοι	ἐβαπτίσθημεν	εἰς
agnoeite	hoti	hosoi	ebaptisthēmen	eis
are you ignorant	that	as many as	we were baptized	unto

5382.4 name acc masc	2400.3 name acc masc	1519.1 prep	3450.6 art acc sing masc	2265.4 noun acc sing masc	840.3 prs-pron gen sing
Χριστὸν	Ἰησοῦν,	εἰς	τὸν	θάνατον	αὐτοῦ
Christon	Iēsoun	eis	ton	thanaton	autou
Christ	Jesus,	unto	the	death	his

901.15 verb 1pl indic aor pass	4766.1 verb 1pl indic aor pass	3631.1 conj	840.4 prs-pron dat sing	1217.2 prep
ἐβαπτίσθημεν;	4. συνετάφημεν	οὖν	αὐτῷ	διὰ
ebaptisthēmen	sunetaphēmen	oun	autō	dia
we were baptized?	We were buried	therefore	with him	by

3450.2 art gen sing	902.2 noun gen sing neu	1519.1 prep	3450.6 art acc sing masc	2265.4 noun acc sing masc	2419.1 conj
τοῦ	βαπτίσματος	εἰς	τὸν	θάνατον·	ἵνα
tou	baptismatos	eis	ton	thanaton	hina
the	baptism	unto	the	death,	that

5450.1 adv	1446.20 verb 3sing indic aor pass	5382.1 name nom masc	1523.2 prep gen	3361.2 adj gen pl	1217.2 prep
ὥσπερ	ἠγέρθη	Χριστὸς	ἐκ	νεκρῶν	διὰ
hōsper	ēgerthē	Christos	ek	nekrōn	dia
as	was raised up	Christ	from among	dead	by

became apparent, God manifested His grace, His unmerited favor, to guilty sinners. Grace did "much more" superabound.

To accept the affirmation of God's abundant grace is to free one once and for all from anxiety and concern about one's salvation. The message of divine grace can properly be received only with thanksgiving and joy. It is truth to be celebrated, truth that is more liberating, exhilarating, and gladdening than one could imagine.

6:1. The great theme of Romans, God's method of making sinners righteous, continues. Earlier the epistle showed how God changes a man's position, now we learn how God provides for a change in a man's condition. The former section dealt with the *sins* questions; now we consider the *sin* question. The former dealt with the pardon of sin's guilt; now we learn of deliverance from sin's power.

One of the last verses in chapter 5 states, "Where sin abounded, grace did much more abound." Some have wanted to use this and other verses to prove that justification encourages sin. They say if the guilty sinner is declared righteous, solely by faith and not by works, then, "Let us do evil, that good may come." If the more heinous the sins, the more abundant the grace to pardon, then may we not go on in sin that the grace of God may be the more magnified?

Such was the slanderous accusation that the Jews made of Paul's teaching (3:7,8). He defended the doctrine of justification against the charge that it encourages increasing sin in order to display grace more abundantly. This defense is the doctrine of sanctification.

This truth is set forth perhaps more completely in Romans 6 than anywhere else in Scripture. There are two divisions in the chapter, and both are introduced by a question which Paul answers with the firm statement, "God forbid."

6:2. To show how unreasonable the proposition of verse 1 is, Paul answers the question with another. "How shall we, that are dead to sin, live any longer therein?"

There are three kinds of death: (1) physical death, the separation of the personality from the physical body; (2) spiritual death, the separation of the person from the life of God; (3) death to sin, the separation of the believer from the power of the sinful nature.

6:3,4. The believer's experience involves a transformation so great as to be described as a resurrection to life. Water baptism pictures the experience. The believer's immersion testifies to the fact that because of his union with the crucified Saviour he has died to sin. Being raised from the watery "grave" testifies to the fact of his union with the risen Saviour and that he now walks "in newness of life." Christ died *for* sin that we might die *to* sin.

even so might grace reign through righteousness unto eternal life by Jesus Christ our Lord: . . . and result in enduring Life, *TCNT* . . . which issues in eternal life, *Montgomery* . . . unto life everlasting, *Douay.*

1. What shall we say then?: What inference, *TCNT.*
Shall we continue in sin, that grace may abound?: . . . continue living in sin, *SEB* . . . shall we persist in sin that the gift of grace may be more abundant? *Conybeare* . . . so as to give more room for grace? *Norlie* . . . to let grace become more plentiful? *Berkeley* . . . to let grace have greater scope? *JB* . . . that the grace extended to us may be the greater? *Weymouth* . . . that favor may abound? *Scarlett* . . . that grace may be multiplied? *Alford.*

2. God forbid: Surely not! *Norlie* . . . Certainly not, *TCNT* . . . No, indeed, *Weymouth* . . . May such a thing never occur, *Wuest* . . . It could not be! *Worrell.*
How shall we, that are dead to sin, live any longer therein?: . . . how can we endure living in it? *Norlie* . . . who have been separated once for all from the sinful nature, any longer to live in its grip? *Wuest* . . . we have ended our relation to sin, *Williams* . . . We died to it! *SEB.*

3. Know ye not, that so many of us as were baptized into Jesus Christ were baptized into his death?: Do you not know, *Confraternity* . . . Are you ignorant that, *Rheims* . . . all of us were immersed into Christ Jesus, *SEB* . . . in union with Christ Jesus, *Berkeley* . . . made us share his burial, *Moffatt.*

4. Therefore we are buried with him by baptism into death: Consequently, *TCNT* . . . we are jointly interred, *Berkeley* . . . and joined him in death, *JB* . . . We have therefore been entombed with him, *Wilson* . . . by means of Baptism, *Confraternity.*
that like as Christ was raised up from the dead:

3450.10 art gen sing fem	1385.2 noun gen sing fem	3450.2 art gen sing	3824.2 noun gen sing masc	3643.1 adv	2504.1 conj	2231.1 prs- pron nom 1pl
τῆς	δόξης	τοῦ	πατρός,	οὕτως	καὶ	ἡμεῖς
tēs	*doxēs*	*tou*	*patros*	*houtōs*	*kai*	*hēmeis*
the	glory	of the	Father,	so	also	we

1706.1 prep	2509.1 noun dat sing fem	2205.2 noun gen sing fem	3906.21 verb 1pl subj aor act	1479.1 conj	1056.1 conj
ἐν	καινότητι	ζωῆς	περιπατήσωμεν.	**5.** Εἰ	γὰρ
en	*kainotēti*	*zōēs*	*peripatēsōmen*	*Ei*	*gar*
in	newness	of life	should walk.	If	for

4705.1 adj nom pl masc	1090.4 verb 1pl indic perf act	3450.3 art dat sing	3530.1 noun dat sing neu	3450.2 art gen sing
σύμφυτοι	γεγόναμεν	τῷ	ὁμοιώματι	τοῦ
sumphutoi	*gegonamen*	*tō*	*homoiōmati*	*tou*
united	we have become	in the	likeness	of the

2265.2 noun gen sing masc	840.3 prs- pron gen sing	233.2 conj	2504.1 conj	3450.10 art gen sing fem	384.2 noun gen sing fem
θανάτου	αὐτοῦ,	ἀλλὰ	καὶ	τῆς	ἀναστάσεως
thanatou	*autou*	*alla*	*kai*	*tēs*	*anastaseōs*
death	his,	so	also	of the	resurrection

1498.41 verb 1pl indic fut mid	3642.17 dem- pron sing neu	1091.12 verb nom pl masc part pres act	3617.1 conj	3450.5 art sing masc	3683.2 adj nom sing masc
ἐσόμεθα·	**6.** τοῦτο	γινώσκοντες,	ὅτι	ὁ	παλαιὸς
esometha	*touto*	*ginōskontes*	*hoti*	*ho*	*palaios*
we shall be;	this	knowing,	that	the	old

2231.2 prs- pron gen 1pl	442.1 noun nom sing masc	4809.1 verb 3sing indic aor pass	2419.1 conj	2643.16 verb 3sing subj aor pass
ἡμῶν	ἄνθρωπος	συνεσταυρώθη,	ἵνα	καταργηθῇ
hēmōn	*anthrōpos*	*sunestaurōthē*	*hina*	*katargēthē*
our	man	was crucified with,	that	might be nullified

3450.16 art sing neu	4835.1 noun sing neu	3450.10 art gen sing fem	264.1 noun fem	3450.2 art gen sing	3239.1 adv
τὸ	σῶμα	τῆς	ἁμαρτίας,	τοῦ	μηκέτι
to	*sōma*	*tēs*	*hamartias*	*tou*	*mēketi*
the	body	of the	sin,	the	no longer

1392.8 verb inf pres act	2231.4 prs- pron acc 1pl	3450.11 art dat sing fem	264.3 noun dat sing fem	3450.5 art sing masc	1056.1 conj
δουλεύειν	ἡμᾶς	τῇ	ἁμαρτίᾳ.	**7.** ὁ	γὰρ
douleuein	*hēmas*	*tē*	*hamartia*	*ho*	*gar*
to be subservient	we	to the	sin.	The	for

594.15 verb nom sing masc part aor act	1338.21 verb 3sing indic perf pass	570.3 prep gen	3450.10 art gen sing fem	264.1 noun fem
ἀποθανὼν	δεδικαίωται	ἀπὸ	τῆς	ἁμαρτίας.
apothanōn	*dedikaiōtai*	*apo*	*tēs*	*hamartias*
having died	has been justified	from	the	sin.

1479.1 conj	1156.2 conj	594.11 verb 1pl indic aor act	4713.1 prep dat	5382.3 name dat masc	3961.7 verb 1pl indic pres act
8. Εἰ	δὲ	ἀπεθάνομεν	σὺν	Χριστῷ,	πιστεύομεν
Ei	*de*	*apethanomen*	*sun*	*Christō*	*pisteuomen*
Since	now	we died	with	Christ,	we believe

8.a.**Txt:** p46,01א,02A
03B,06D-corr3,08E
018K,019L,025P,We/Ho
Var: 06D-org,010F
012G

3617.1 conj	2504.1 conj	4651.2 verb 1pl indic fut act	840.4 prs- pron dat sing	4948.6 indef- pron dat sing masc
ὅτι	καὶ	συζήσομεν	῾ αὐτῷ,	[ᵃ τῷ
hoti	*kai*	*suzēsomen*	*autō*	*tō*
that	also	we shall live with	him,	[the

There is also a deeper significance to the phrase "baptized into Jesus Christ." Water baptism can be a mere ritual, a "work," apart from faith. According to Galatians 3:27, to be "baptized into Christ" means to have "put on Christ." "For by one Spirit are we all baptized into one body" (1 Corinthians 12:13). Water baptism is the outward symbol of what the Holy Spirit has done inwardly. The believer is separated from the evil nature, no longer compelled to follow its dictates. He receives a new nature (2 Peter 1:4), causing him to hate sin and love righteousness.

6:5. "Planted together" is literally "united together." We share the life of Christ just as a branch that is grafted into a tree shares the life of the tree (John 15:5). The believer becomes grafted into Christ.

Christ's death was our death, His burial was our burial, His resurrection was our resurrection. As a result of our union with Him, the power of sin is broken. God placed us in Christ when He died so we might share His death and receive the benefits of that identification with Him, specifically, to be separated from the evil nature as part of our salvation. We were also placed by the Holy Spirit in Christ in order to share a new environment, the sharing of newness of life through His resurrection power.

6:6,7. "Old man" refers to our former self, the unregenerate son of Adam. We were put to death with Christ. The emphasis is on the conclusion or results of an action. We have been buried, we have become united. The person we once were is now dead. While the "old man" is ourselves in union with the first Adam, the "new man" is ourselves in union with the last Adam. God says that my old life was destroyed, put to death, at Calvary. God's Word is the basis of fact. Our first step is "knowing."

The term "destroyed" does not mean annihilated but rendered "powerless." Sin is not destroyed, but is robbed of its power. The one who is born again is commanded to take his stand on this verse for "he that is dead is freed from sin." Death breaks all ties and cancels all obligations. By his union with Christ the Christian dies to the old self and is free from it, even as the Law has no jurisdiction over a dead man, regardless of his crime. The only power that can cause the believer to sin now is his own power of choice. He *can* sin, but he does not *have* to do so.

6:8,9. With great triumph Paul declares that the Resurrection forever ended the reign of death over the body of Christ. Jesus died "once for all." He arose from the grave immortal, never to be subject to death again. Death is an end. Once it is over for the Christian, it is forever ended. Life is a process. It will continue forever for the believer.

by the glory of the Father: . . . through the Father's glorious power, *Berkeley* . . . by a display of the Father's power, *TCNT*.

even so we also should walk in newness of life: . . . so we too shall conduct ourselves in a new way of living, *Berkeley* . . . ought to conduct ourselves in a renewed life, *Fenton*.

5. For if we have been planted together in the likeness of his death: . . . if we have become like-natured with him, *Panin* . . . if we have been united with him, *Confraternity* . . . by sharing His death, *Norlie* . . . by an experience resembling his death, *TCNT*.

we shall be also [in the likeness] of [his] resurrection: . . . we shall much more be, *Sawyer* . . . by a resurrection like his, *Moffatt*.

6. Knowing this, that our old man is crucified with [him]: . . . our old sinful self, *Norlie* . . . was nailed with Him, *Beck*.

that the body of sin might be destroyed: . . . so that the sin-controlled body might be devitalized, *Berkeley* . . . might be made ineffective, *Adams* . . . may cease to be under the tyranny of Sin, *TCNT* . . . might be deprived of its power, *Weymouth* . . . that is liable to sin inactive, *Williams* . . . might be rendered null, *PNT* . . . may be made useless, *Young* . . . might be brought to nought, *Worrell*.

that henceforth we should not serve sin: . . . and free us from any further slavery to sin, *Moffatt* . . . that we should no more be in bondage to sin, *Worrell* . . . that we should no longer be subservient to sin, *PNT* . . . rendering a slave's habitual obedience, *Wuest*.

7. For he that is dead is freed from sin: For a corpse is considered guiltless of sin, *Berkeley* . . . he who has paid the penalty of death stands absolved from his sin, *Weymouth* . . . is acquitted of sin, *Confraternity* . . . is absolved from sin, *HistNT*.

8. Now if we be dead with Christ, we believe that we shall also live with him:

5382.3 name dat masc	3471.20 verb nom pl masc part perf act	3617.1 conj	5382.1 name nom masc	1446.25 verb nom sing masc part aor pass
Χριστῷ,]	**9.** εἰδότες	ὅτι	Χριστὸς	ἐγερθεὶς
Christō	eidotes	hoti	Christos	egertheis
Christ,]	knowing	that	Christ	having been raised up

1523.2 prep gen	3361.2 adj gen pl	3629.1 adv	594.2 verb 3sing indic pres act	2265.1 noun nom sing masc
ἐκ	νεκρῶν,	οὐκέτι	ἀποθνῄσκει,	θάνατος
ek	nekrōn	ouketi	apothnēskei	thanatos
from among	dead,	no more	dies:	death

840.3 prs-pron gen sing	3629.1 adv	2934.1 verb 3sing indic pres act	3614.16 rel-pron sing neu	1056.1 conj	594.10 verb 3sing indic aor act
αὐτοῦ	οὐκέτι	κυριεύει.	**10.** ὃ	γὰρ	ἀπέθανεν,
autou	ouketi	kurieuei	ho	gar	apethanen
him	no more	rules over.	That	for	he died,

3450.11 art dat sing fem	264.3 noun dat sing fem	594.10 verb 3sing indic aor act	2160.1 adv	3614.16 rel-pron sing neu	1156.2 conj
τῇ	ἁμαρτίᾳ	ἀπέθανεν	ἐφάπαξ·	ὃ	δὲ
tē	hamartia	apethanen	ephapax	ho	de
to the	sin	he died	once for all;	that	but

2180.1 verb sing indic pres	2180.1 verb sing indic pres	3450.3 art dat sing	2296.3 noun dat sing masc	3643.1 adv	2504.1 conj
ζῇ,	ζῇ	τῷ	θεῷ.	**11.** οὕτως	καὶ
zē	zē	tō	theō	houtōs	kai
he lives,	he lives	to the	to God.	So	also

11.a.Var: 01א-org,03B
04C,Treg,Tisc,We/Ho
Weis,Sod,UBS/☆

5050.1 prs-pron nom 2pl	3023.1 verb 2pl pres	1431.8 prs-pron acc pl masc	1498.32 verb inf pres act	3361.7 adj acc pl masc
ὑμεῖς	λογίζεσθε	ἑαυτοὺς	[a☆+ εἶναι]	νεκροὺς
humeis	logizesthe	heautous	einai	nekrous
you	reckon	yourselves	[to be]	dead

11.b.Txt: 01א-corr,018K
020L,025P,byz.
Var: 01א-org,02A,03B
04C,06D,bo.Gries,Lach
Treg,Alf,Word,Tisc
We/Ho,Weis,Sod
UBS/☆

3173.1 conj	1498.32 verb inf pres act	3450.11 art dat sing fem	264.3 noun dat sing fem	2180.15 verb acc pl masc part pres act	1156.2 conj
μὲν	(b εἶναι)	τῇ	ἁμαρτίᾳ,	ζῶντας	δὲ
men	einai	tē	hamartia	zōntas	de
indeed	to be	to the	sin,	living	but

11.c.Txt: 01א,04C,018K
020L,025P,byz.bo.Sod
Var: p46,02A,03B,06D
044,it.sa.Gries,Lach
Treg,Alf,Word,Tisc
We/Ho,Weis,UBS/☆

3450.3 art dat sing	2296.3 noun dat sing masc	1706.1 prep	5382.3 name dat masc	2400.2 name masc	3450.3 art dat sing
τῷ	θεῷ,	ἐν	Χριστῷ	Ἰησοῦ	(c τῷ
tō	theō	en	Christō	Iēsou	tō
	to God,	in	Christ	Jesus	the

2935.3 noun dat sing masc	2231.2 prs-pron gen 1pl	3231.1 partic	3631.1 conj	929.2 verb 3sing impr pres act	3450.9 art nom sing fem
κυρίῳ	ἡμῶν.)	**12.** Μὴ	οὖν	βασιλευέτω	ἡ
kuriō	hēmōn	Mē	oun	basileuetō	hē
Lord	our.	Not	therefore	let reign	the

264.2 noun nom sing fem	1706.1 prep	3450.3 art dat sing	2326.3 adj dat sing neu	5050.2 prs-pron gen 2pl	4835.3 noun dat sing neu	1519.1 prep
ἁμαρτία	ἐν	τῷ	θνητῷ	ὑμῶν	σώματι,	εἰς
hamartia	en	tō	thnētō	humōn	sōmati	eis
sin	in	the	mortal	your	body,	for

12.a.Txt: 04C-corr,018K
020L,025P,044,byz.
Var: 01א,02A,03B
04C-org,Gries,Lach
Treg,Alf,Word,Tisc
We/Ho,Weis,Sod
UBS/☆

3450.16 art sing neu	5057.4 verb inf pres act	840.11 prs-pron dat sing fem	1706.1 prep	3450.14 art dat pl fem	1924.7 noun dat pl fem
τὸ	ὑπακούειν	(a αὐτῇ	ἐν)	ταῖς	ἐπιθυμίαις
to	hupakouein	autē	en	tais	epithumiais
the	to obey	it	in	the	desires

The significance of the Resurrection is that as we were identified with Christ in His death, we are also identified with Him in His resurrection. Since death has no more dominion over Christ, sin has no more dominion over us.

Because of the believer's union with the crucified and resurrected Christ, sin has been robbed of its power over the Christian, or, as someone stated, it has been put "out of commission." This truth is realized by faith in the fact of the Word and by the word we "know." Faith concludes about us what God has declared about us. When we believe what God says, something real and powerful happens.

6:10. Christ's death ended the earthly state in which He had contact with sin. His life is now one of unbroken communion with God. He is no longer on the cross or in the tomb. He is alive and holds the keys of hell and of death. Death has dominion over Him no more.

In the first 10 verses of this chapter, 2 main facts are laid before us. First, a Christian has a permanent relationship of freedom from his sinful nature. He need not submit to it or obey it. Second, by the miracle of the new birth he receives a new nature; he becomes a new creature. He is given the desire and the power to do God's will.

6:11,12. Verses 6 and 9 brought us the facts. We "know" our position of death to self and new life in Christ. But we must act on knowledge. It is one thing to "know," it is something else to "reckon." Verses 11-13 set forth the means for living that life of victory. It is a matter of appropriation.

We have now come to man's responsibility. We are to "reckon" two things: (1) that the "old man" has died, and the sinful nature has been rendered powerless; (2) that we are "alive unto God," new life has been imparted to us.

The term "reckon" is a mathematical term. It means "to count, compute, to take into account." The believer is to take into account the fact that he is dead to sin, that he is set free from the old evil nature, that he has been brought into new life, and that being a new creation (2 Corinthians 5:17), he can live above the desire to sin. When a sinner believes in Christ, he receives a new heart and becomes a new creature. He is under new management.

When we reckon ourselves dead to sin, we are free from it. Death breaks sin's dominion. The presence of sin is not removed; that will take place when salvation is complete on Resurrection Day. But while sin is still present, it is powerless, except by a deliberate act of the person's will.

But it is more than death; it is life (Galatians 2:20; Philippians 1:21). The divinely given self-control (verse 12) is as normal to a Christian as sin is to a sinner. But it must be appropriated and continually acted on. Faith concludes about ourselves what God has declared about us.

9. Knowing that Christ being raised from the dead dieth no more: He will never die again, *Norlie* . . . never dies after his resurrection, *Moffatt*.

death hath no more dominion over him: . . . death holds lordship over Him no longer, *Berkeley* . . . death no longer holds lordship, *Adams* . . . Death over Him no longer exercises lordship, *Wuest* . . . Death is no longer his boss, *Klingensmith* . . . can no more dominate Him, *Fenton* . . . no longer lords it over him, *Wilson*.

10. For in that he died, he died unto sin once: The death He died was because of sin, *Norlie* . . . and once only, unto sin, *Conybeare* . . . He once for all ended His relation to sin, *Williams*.

but in that he liveth, he liveth unto God: He lives in unbroken relation to God, *Williams*.

11. Likewise reckon ye also yourselves to be dead indeed unto sin, but alive unto God: Even so count yourselves, *Montgomery* . . . Thus do you consider yourselves, *Confraternity* . . . regard yourselves as dead to sin, *TCNT* . . . but you have been restored to life again, *Norlie*.

through Jesus Christ our Lord: . . . in the Anointed Jesus, *Wilson*.

12. Let not sin therefore reign: . . . rule as king, *Montgomery*.

in your mortal body: . . . over your dying bodies, *SEB* . . . in your dying bodies, *Beck*.

that ye should obey it in the lusts thereof: . . . compelling you to obey its lusts, *Montgomery* . . . with a view to obeying it...in its passionate cravings, *Wuest* . . . your obedience to bodily passions, *JB* . . . to make you obey their passions, *RSV, Moffatt* . . . with the result that you, *Adams* . . . and compel you to obey its cravings, *TCNT* . . . causing you to be in subjection to their cravings, *Weymouth* . . . obey it in its licentious desires, *Scarlett* . . . obey the concupiscences thereof, *Rheims* . . . to obey its whims, *Klingensmith* . . . to obey it in its evil propensities, *PNT*.

840.3 prs- pron gen sing	3234.1 adv	3798.1 verb 2pl pres act	3450.17 art pl neu	3166.2 noun pl neu
αὐτοῦ·	13. μηδὲ	παριστάνετε	τὰ	μέλη
autou	mēde	paristanete	ta	melē
its.	Neither	be yielding	the	members

5050.2 prs- pron gen 2pl	3559.1 noun pl neu	92.2 noun gen sing fem	3450.11 art dat sing fem	264.3 noun dat sing fem
ὑμῶν	ὅπλα	ἀδικίας	τῇ	ἁμαρτίᾳ·
humōn	hopla	adikias	tē	hamartia
your	instruments	of unrighteousness	to the	sin,

233.2 conj	3798.10 verb 2pl impr aor act	1431.8 prs- pron acc pl masc	3450.3 art dat sing	2296.3 noun dat sing masc	5453.1 conj
ἀλλὰ	παραστήσατε	ἑαυτοὺς	τῷ	θεῷ	(ὡς
alla	parastēsate	heautous	tō	theō	hōs
but	yield	yourselves	to the	to God	as

5448.1 adv	1523.2 prep gen	3361.2 adj gen pl	2180.15 verb acc pl masc part pres act	2504.1 conj	3450.17 art pl neu
[☆ ὡσεὶ]	ἐκ	νεκρῶν	ζῶντας,	καὶ	τὰ
hōsei	ek	nekrōn	zōntas	kai	ta
[idem]	from among	dead	living,	and	the

3166.2 noun pl neu	5050.2 prs- pron gen 2pl	3559.1 noun pl neu	1336.2 noun gen sing fem	3450.3 art dat sing	2296.3 noun dat sing masc
μέλη	ὑμῶν	ὅπλα	δικαιοσύνης	τῷ	θεῷ·
melē	humōn	hopla	dikaiosunēs	tō	theō
members	your	instruments	of righteousness	to the	to God.

264.2 noun nom sing fem	1056.1 conj	5050.2 prs- pron gen 2pl	3620.3 partic	2934.6 verb 3sing indic fut act	3620.3 partic	1056.1 conj
14. ἁμαρτία	γὰρ	ὑμῶν	οὐ	κυριεύσει·	οὐ	γὰρ
hamartia	gar	humōn	ou	kurieusei	ou	gar
Sin	for	you	not	shall rule over,	not	for

1498.6 verb 2pl indic pres act	5097.3 prep	3414.4 noun acc sing masc	233.1 conj	233.2 conj	5097.3 prep	5322.4 noun acc sing fem
ἐστε	ὑπὸ	νόμον,	(ἀλλ'	[☆ ἀλλὰ]	ὑπὸ	χάριν.
este	hupo	nomon	all'	alla	hupo	charin
are you	under	law,	but	[idem]	under	grace.

15.a.**Txt**: Steph
Var: 01א,02A,03B,04C
06D,018K,020L,025P
Lach,Treg,Alf,Word
Tisc,We/Ho,Weis,Sod
UBS/☆

4949.9 intr- pron sing neu	3631.1 conj	262.23 verb 1pl indic fut act	262.24 verb 1pl subj aor act
15. Τί	οὖν;	(ἁμαρτήσομεν	[a☆ ἁμαρτήσωμεν]
Ti	oun	hamartēsomen	hamartēsōmen
What	then?	shall we sin	[should we sin]

3617.1 conj	3620.2 partic	1498.5 verb 1pl indic pres act	5097.3 prep	3414.4 noun acc sing masc	233.1 conj	233.2 conj
ὅτι	οὐκ	ἐσμὲν	ὑπὸ	νόμον,	(ἀλλ'	[☆ ἀλλὰ]
hoti	ouk	esmen	hupo	nomon	all'	alla
because	not	we are	under	law	but	[idem]

5097.3 prep	5322.4 noun acc sing fem	3231.1 partic	1090.44 verb 3sing opt aor mid	3620.2 partic	3471.6 verb 2pl indic perf act
ὑπὸ	χάριν;	μὴ	γένοιτο.	16. οὐκ	οἴδατε
hupo	charin	mē	genoito	ouk	oidate
under	grace?	Not	may it be!	Not	know you

3617.1 conj	3614.3 rel- pron dat sing	3798.1 verb 2pl pres act	1431.8 prs- pron acc pl masc	1395.9 noun acc pl masc	1519.1 prep
ὅτι	ᾧ	παριστάνετε	ἑαυτοὺς	δούλους	εἰς
hoti	hō	paristanete	heautous	doulous	eis
that	to whom	you yield	yourselves	slaves	for

6:13. Paul goes on to show how we can put this matter of reckoning into actual practice. It is doing something that is a work of faith. The positive is prefaced by the command: "neither yield . . . but yield." This involves the matter of making right choices. Constantly we must choose between right and wrong, good and evil. The will is the steering gear of the soul, and we choose the right or the wrong road.

The passage exhorts believers to present their "members," i.e., the physical body, as an instrument or tool that God may use to bring forth righteousness. In fact, the entire self is to be given over to God since He gave us life.

6:14. Man is so made that he must be mastered. He was created a free moral agent, but he was not made to be his own sovereign; he was created to be mastered by God. When man fell, he came under the mastery of sin. Christ came to deliver us from sin. He provided grace to conquer sin. The work has been done for us, but we must yield ourselves to the divine will for it to be operative within us.

When the believer obeys the instructions of this passage relative to adjustment to the evil nature and the divine nature, this verse promises, "Sin need never again be your master, for now you are no longer tied to the law where sin enslaves you, but you are free under God's favor and mercy" (*Living Bible*).

6:15. It is totally false to believe that it is of no consequence whether or not Christians sin. Such doctrine is propounded by "no-Law people" otherwise known as antinomians. True, the Law was uncompromising, but grace while forgiving is never lenient. To be free from the Law does not mean one can sin with freedom from punishment. Being under grace must not be taken as liberty or license to sin. The grace of God is not in the heart of a man who looks upon grace as a loophole to sin. Those who continue in sin are the servants of sin (John 8:34).

6:16. Although the King James Version shows the word "servants," in this context perhaps the word *doulous* is better translated "slaves." During the New Testament era there were two kinds of slaves: those captured in war and those born in slavery. Here the word likely refers to those born slaves. By nature we were born slaves to sin and Satan. The believer, a former slave to the desires of the flesh and of Satan, is delivered by the power of God. Through being identified with Christ he becomes bound to Him—Jesus is his new Master.

Obedience and yielding are key words. We choose to whom we yield and whom we obey. The choice is between "sin unto death" or "obedience unto righteousness." This conflict is presented by Jesus in the gospels. He states that "no man can serve two masters" (Matthew 6:24), though Jesus is referring to a specific lust of the flesh.

13. Neither yield ye your members [as] instruments of unrighteousness unto sin: . . . stop putting your members at the disposal of, *Wuest* . . . Do not give up any part of your body to Sin, to be used in doing wrong, *TCNT* . . . But neither doe ye exhibite your members as instruments of iniquitie, *Rheims* . . . as evil tools for sin, *SEB* . . . no longer lend your faculties as unrighteous weapons for Sin to use, *Weymouth* . . . turn into an unholy weapon, *JB* . . . for the service of vice, *Moffatt* . . . as implements for vice, *HistNT* . . . as instruments for wrongdoing, *Williams*.

but yield yourselves unto God, as those that are alive from the dead: . . . surrender your whole being to him, *TEV* . . . as living persons who rose from, *Berkeley* . . . as people who have come back from the dead and live, *Beck*.

and your members [as] instruments of righteousness unto God: . . . and give up to him the various parts of your bodies to be used in doing right, *TCNT*.

14. For sin shall not have dominion over you: Sin must not be your lord and master, *Adams* . . . Let not sinne haue power ouer you, *Geneva* . . . must not any longer exert its mastery, *Williams* . . . must not govern you, *Fenton*.

for ye are not under the law, but under grace: . . . for you are not governed by Law, *Berkeley* . . . you are under God's gracious love! *SEB* . . . You are living under the reign, not of Law, but of Mercy, *TCNT* . . . but as subjects to God's favor, *Williams* . . . but under a gift, *Fenton*.

15. What then? shall we sin, because we are not under the law, but under grace?: What are we to conclude? *Williams* . . . Shall we sin occasionally, *Wuest* . . . Shall we commit an act of sin, *Montgomery*.

God forbid: Away with the thought, *Wuest* . . . Be it not so, *Panin* . . . let it not be! *Young*.

16. Know ye not, that to whom ye yield yourselves servants to obey: . . . whomever ye choose to obey as a master, *Noyes*.

5056.4 noun acc sing fem	1395.6 noun pl masc	1498.6 verb 2pl indic pres act	3614.3 rel-pron dat sing	5057.1 verb 2pl pres act
ὑπακοήν,	δοῦλοί	ἐστε	ᾧ	ὑπακούετε,
hupakoēn	*douloi*	*este*	*hō*	*hupakouete*
obedience,	slaves	you are	to whom	you obey,

2251.1 conj	264.1 noun fem	1519.1 prep	2265.4 noun acc sing masc	2211.1 conj	5056.2 noun gen sing fem
ἤτοι	ἁμαρτίας	ʳᵃ εἰς	θάνατον, ˋ	ἢ	ὑπακοῆς
ētoi	*hamartias*	*eis*	*thanaton*	*ē*	*hupakoēs*
whether	of sin	to	death,	or	of obedience

1519.1 prep	1336.4 noun acc sing fem		5322.1 noun nom sing fem	1156.2 conj	3450.3 art dat sing	2296.3 noun dat sing masc
εἰς	δικαιοσύνην;	**17.**	χάρις	δὲ	τῷ	θεῷ,
eis	*dikaiosunēn*		*charis*	*de*	*tō*	*theō*
to	righteousness?	Thanks	but	tō	to God,

3617.1 conj	1498.1 verb 2pl act	1395.6 noun pl masc	3450.10 art gen sing fem	264.1 noun fem	5057.6 verb 2pl indic aor act
ὅτι	ἦτε	δοῦλοι	τῆς	ἁμαρτίας	ὑπηκούσατε
hoti	*ēte*	*douloi*	*tēs*	*hamartias*	*hupēkousate*
that	you were	slaves	of the	sin,	you obeyed

1156.2 conj	1523.2 prep gen	2559.1 noun fem	1519.1 prep	3614.6 rel-pron acc sing masc	3722.33 verb 2pl indic aor pass
δὲ	ἐκ	καρδίας	εἰς	ὃν	παρεδόθητε
de	*ek*	*kardias*	*eis*	*hon*	*paredothēte*
but	from	heart	to	which	you were delivered

5020.2 noun acc sing masc	1316.2 noun gen sing fem		1646.4 verb nom pl masc part aor pass	1156.2 conj	570.3 prep gen
τύπον	διδαχῆς.	**18.**	ἐλευθερωθέντες	δὲ	ἀπὸ
tupon	*didachēs*		*eleutherōthentes*	*de*	*apo*
a form	of teaching.	Having been set free	and	from

3450.10 art gen sing fem	264.1 noun fem		1396.3 verb 2pl indic aor pass	3450.11 art dat sing fem
τῆς	ἁμαρτίας,		ἐδουλώθητε	τῇ
tēs	*hamartias*		*edoulōthēte*	*tē*
the	sin,		you became servants	to the

1336.3 noun dat sing fem		440.4 adj acc sing neu	2978.1 verb 1sing pres act	1217.2 prep
δικαιοσύνῃ.	**19.**	Ἀνθρώπινον	λέγω	διὰ
dikaiosunē		*Anthrōpinon*	*legō*	*dia*
righteousness.		Humanly	I speak	on account of

3450.12 art acc sing fem	763.4 noun acc sing fem	3450.10 art gen sing fem	4418.2 noun gen sing fem	5050.2 prs-pron gen 2pl	5450.1 adv
τὴν	ἀσθένειαν	τῆς	σαρκὸς	ὑμῶν.	ὥσπερ
tēn	*astheneian*	*tēs*	*sarkos*	*humōn*	*hōsper*
the	weakness	of the	flesh	your.	As

1056.1 conj	3798.5 verb 2pl indic aor act	3450.17 art pl neu	3166.2 noun pl neu	5050.2 prs-pron gen 2pl	1394.1 adj acc pl neu
γὰρ	παρεστήσατε	τὰ	μέλη	ὑμῶν	δοῦλα
gar	*parestēsate*	*ta*	*melē*	*humōn*	*doula*
for	you yielded	the	members	your	in slavery

3450.11 art dat sing fem	165.3 noun dat sing fem	2504.1 conj	3450.11 art dat sing fem	455.3 noun dat sing fem	1519.1 prep
τῇ	ἀκαθαρσίᾳ	καὶ	τῇ	ἀνομίᾳ	εἰς
tē	*akatharsia*	*kai*	*tē*	*anomia*	*eis*
to the	uncleanness	and	to the	lawlessness	unto

16.a.**Txt:** 01‭א‬,02A,03B
04C,012G,018K,025P
044,33,81,330,614
UBS/⋆
Var: 06D,1739,sa.

The apostle is dealing with the great truth of sanctification, of holy living. Sanctification is not eradication (1 John 1:8). Sin is not dead, but the believer can be dead to sin. Neither is sanctification suppression. It is not boiling over inside with anger and suppressing our feelings so no one knows about it.

Sanctification is the operation of the law of life over the law of sin and death. It is not natural law, not legal law, but spiritual law. The believer is able to live above the selfish demands of self and live in triumph in a new life.

6:17. The phrase "that form of doctrine" means the pattern of Christian teachings referred to as "the traditions" in 1 Corinthians 11:2. The Greek implies they were "delivered into" that form of doctrine. "Form" *tupos* may refer to a mold into which molten metal is poured to be fashioned into the desired shape. The believer is the molten material and the gospel is the mold. The gospel delivers from sin and fashions character. Emphasis is placed on the tense of the verb: "you *were* the servants of sin."

6:18. The idea of slavery carries over into the balance of the chapter. Slavery was common in Paul's day. The Roman Christians no doubt clearly understood Paul's language. Possibly some of them had been in servitude.

"Being . . . made free" is *eleutheroō*, "to liberate, set free from bondage, to set at liberty." Believers are set free from the bondage of sin and Satan. But they are freed to a new slavery, to become slaves of righteousness. In verses 18 and 20 the expression "became . . . servants" is a form of the verb *douloō*. As used in these verses it means to "become a slave to someone." Freed from the slavery of sin, the believer has a glorious freedom enjoying a higher slavery, a slave to God.

In essence Paul is saying that at one time you gave yourself to sin as its slave, and when you did that righteousness had no claim over you. Now that you have given yourself to God as a slave to righteousness, sin has no claim on you.

Doulos ("slave") carries the thought of one who serves another to the disregard of his own interests. However, the sinner is in bondage to the flesh; he is self-serving. The lusts of the flesh dominate him, and he is a slave to that which he believes reflects personal liberty and free choice.

6:19,20. The apostle explained his reason for using the analogy of slavery. He says, "I am using this human illustration so your human minds can understand." The Roman believers did not yet have the spiritual insight to grasp the significance of their position as identified with Christ.

This passage is part of an argument that concludes in the next three verses. Paul is leading up to a description of inevitable consequences facing those involved in the two distinct lifestyles contrasted in the preceding discussion. Verse 20 begins the chain of events: slaves of sin are free from the demands of righteousness.

One way or another every person is a slave to someone. But every person must choose to whom he will be a slave. Either one is a slave

his servants ye are to whom ye obey: . . . as obedient servants, *Berkeley* . . . as obedient slaves, *HistNT* . . . when you submit to someone as master, *Norlie* . . . that one whom you are in the habit of obeying, *Williams* . . . his bondmen ye are, *Noyes*.

whether of sin unto death, or of obedience unto righteousness?: . . . with death as the result, *Weymouth* . . . obedience to His standard of teaching, *Norlie*.

17. But God be thanked, that ye were the servants of sin:

but ye have obeyed from the heart: . . . now you heartily obey, *Fenton* . . . you have rendered whole-hearted obedience, *Moffatt*.

that form of doctrine which was delivered you: . . . the rules of discipline under which you enlisted, *Fenton* . . . the standard of teaching, *RSV* . . . the pattern of teaching, *SEB* . . . that model of doctrine into which ye have been moulded, *Scarlett* . . . in which you were instructed, *Sawyer*.

18. Being then made free from sin, ye became the servants of righteousness: . . . from the tyranny of Sin, *Weymouth* . . . having been emancipated from sin, you became subservient to righteousness, *Wilson* . . . ye became bondservants of righteousness, *Clementson*.

19. I speak after the manner of men because of the infirmity of your flesh: I am using human illustrations, *Adams* . . . I am using an illustration drawn from human affairs, *Wuest* . . . I am speaking in familiar human terms because of the frailty of your nature, *Williams* . . . because you are naturally weak, *Beck* . . . Because of your human weakness, *SEB* . . . because of your natural limitations, *RSV*.

for as ye have yielded your members servants to uncleanness and to iniquity unto iniquity: . . . the various parts of your bodies to the service of impurity, *TCNT* . . . to moral impurity, *SEB* . . . to impurity and to wickedness in wickedness, *Sawyer* . . . always getting worse and worse, *Norlie*

3450.12 art acc sing fem τὴν tēn the	455.4 noun acc sing fem ἀνομίαν, anomian lawlessness,	3643.1 adv οὕτως houtōs so	3431.1 adv νῦν nun now	3798.10 verb 2pl impr aor act παραστήσατε parastēsate yield	3450.17 art pl neu τὰ ta the
3166.2 noun pl neu μέλη melē members	5050.2 prs- pron gen 2pl ὑμῶν humōn your	1394.1 adj acc pl neu δοῦλα doula in slavery	3450.11 art dat sing fem τῇ tē to the	1336.3 noun dat sing fem δικαιοσύνῃ dikaiosunē righteousness	1519.1 prep εἰς eis unto

38.3 noun acc sing masc ἁγιασμόν. hagiasmon holiness.	3616.1 conj **20.** ὅτε hote When	3056.1 conj γὰρ gar for	1395.6 noun pl masc δοῦλοι douloi slaves	1498.1 verb 2pl act ἦτε ēte you were	3450.10 art gen sing fem τῆς tēs of the
264.1 noun fem ἁμαρτίας, hamartias sin,	1645.2 adj nom pl masc ἐλεύθεροι eleutheroi free	1498.1 verb 2pl act ἦτε ēte you were	3450.11 art dat sing fem τῇ tē to the	1336.3 noun dat sing fem δικαιοσύνῃ. dikaiosunē righteousness.	

4949.1 intr-pron **21.** τίνα tina What	3631.1 conj οὖν oun therefore	2561.3 noun acc sing masc καρπὸν karpon fruit	2174.47 verb 2pl indic imperf act εἴχετε eichete had you	4966.1 adv τότε tote then,	1894.1 prep ἐφ᾽ eph' over
3614.4 rel- pron dat pl οἷς hois which	3431.1 adv νῦν nun now	1855.3 verb 2pl indic pres ἐπαισχύνεσθε; epaischunesthe you are ashamed?	3450.16 art sing neu τὸ to the	1056.1 conj γὰρ gar for	4904.1 noun sing neu τέλος telos end

1552.1 dem- pron gen pl ἐκείνων ekeinōn of those things	2265.1 noun nom sing masc θάνατος. thanatos death.	3432.1 adv **22.** νυνὶ nuni Now	1156.2 conj δέ, de but	1646.4 verb nom pl masc part aor pass ἐλευθερωθέντες eleutherōthentes having been set free	
570.3 prep gen ἀπὸ apo from	3450.10 art gen sing fem τῆς tēs the	264.1 noun fem ἁμαρτίας, hamartias sin,	1396.4 verb nom pl masc part aor pass δουλωθέντες doulōthentes having become servants	1156.2 conj δὲ de and	3450.3 art dat sing τῷ tō to

2296.3 noun dat sing masc θεῷ, theō to God,	2174.2 verb 2pl pres act ἔχετε echete were you having	3450.6 art acc sing masc τὸν ton the	2561.3 noun acc sing masc καρπὸν karpon fruit	5050.2 prs- pron gen 2pl ὑμῶν humōn your	1519.1 prep εἰς eis unto
38.3 noun acc sing masc ἁγιασμόν, hagiasmon holiness,	3450.16 art sing neu τὸ to the	1156.2 conj δὲ de and	4904.1 noun sing neu τέλος telos end	2205.4 noun acc sing fem ζωὴν zōēn life	164.1 adj sing αἰώνιον. aiōnion eternal.

3450.17 art pl neu **23.** τὰ ta The	1056.1 conj γὰρ gar for	3664.2 noun nom pl neu ὀψώνια opsōnia wages	3450.10 art gen sing fem τῆς tēs of the	264.1 noun fem ἁμαρτίας hamartias sin	2265.1 noun nom sing masc θάνατος· thanatos death;

to the tyranny of uncleanness and iniquity, or a slave to "righteousness unto holiness." If slaves to sin there is no righteousness.

Paul was reminding them that in their former state of slavery to sin they were in no way bound by righteousness. Righteousness had no mastery or authority over them. They could sin all they wanted to, with no respect to the demands of righteousness.

He was using this fact, which they all could understand, to show them that likewise they now were free from the mastery of sin. His thought could be paraphrased: "Consider how that you once were carefree where righteousness was concerned. No one could say to you, 'You must be holy,' for you made no claim to holiness. One slavery always brings freedom from the other. Slavery to sin is coexistent with freedom from righteousness; slavery to righteousness is coexistent with freedom from sin."

These verses show clearly that the believer still is faced with the decision of whether to yield his members to sin and uncleanness or to yield his members to righteousness unto holiness. Paul had already warned them of the possibility of losing their life in Christ if they chose to yield themselves to sin (verse 16).

6:21. The apostle calls attention to the shameful fruit of the life of sin. The old life was characterized by uncleanness and lawlessness. Evil desires reigned and, as is always true, sin begat sin. Sin becomes less repulsive as it is repeated. When indulged in, it eventually becomes effortless to sin. The road to sin leads down more and more. It leaves one with shame, remorse, and regret.

Believers are ashamed of their past sins; this leads to a horror of any new occurrence of sin. "Death," which is the end of such sins, includes the second death (Revelation 20:14).

6:22. The new life is different. The birth and resultant end of sin is that "when it is finished, (it) bringeth forth death" (James 1:14,15). In sharp contrast slaves to God have "fruit unto holiness, and the end everlasting life." The believer, justified and sanctified, enjoys daily fruit, revealed in holiness and climaxing in eternal life.

Here Paul was showing the "double" aspect of holiness. We are sanctified by Christ (1 Corinthians 1:30). Then we are commanded to "cleanse ourselves from all filthiness of the flesh and spirit, perfecting holiness in the fear of God" (2 Corinthians 7:1).

Believe and behave! The first brings us into fellowship with God; the latter gives evidence that we have fellowship with God. When we believe, we enter the "strait gate"; when we behave, we walk in the "narrow way."

6:23. Thayer states that the definition of "wages" (*opsōnion*) is "whatever is bought to be eaten with bread, as fish, flesh, and the like. And as corn, meat, fruits, salt, were given to the soldiers instead of pay, *opsōnion* began to signify that part of a soldier's

...to greater and greater iniquity, *RSV* ...and unrestrained lawlessness, *Fenton* ...from one iniquitye to another, *Cranmer*.

even so now yield your members servants to righteousness unto holiness: ...now you must surrender your faculties, *Montgomery* ...as slaves of justice unto sanctification, *Confraternity* ...which leads on to holiness, *TCNT* ...that means consecration, *Moffatt* ...that ye maye be sanctifyed, *Cranmer* ...in order to become holy, *Noyes*.

20. For when ye were the servants of sin:

ye were free from righteousness: ...you are freemen, *Fenton* ...you weren't free to serve righteousness, *Beck*.

21. What fruit had ye then in those things whereof ye are now ashamed?: ...that now make you blush, *JB*.

for the end of those things [is] death: Death is their consequence, *Berkeley* ...actions whose outcome is death, *HistNT* ...for the reward of these things is death, *Campbell*.

22. But now being made free from sin, and become servants to God:

ye have your fruit unto holiness, and the end everlasting life: ...your fruite vnto sanctification, *Rheims* ...you have the fruit of your consecration, *Fenton* ...you are being made holy, *TCNT* ...You get something good for being holy, *SEB* ...you have your reward in being made holy...the Life of the ages as the final result, *Weymouth* ...your fruit is growth in holiness, *Conybeare* ...the final destiny is eternal life, *Williams* ...and the end eonian life, *Clementson*.

23. For the wages of sin [is] death: Sin pays off with death, *Beck* ...For the stipends of sin, *Rheims* ...For the subsistence pay which the sinful nature, *Wuest* ...The pay you get for sinning is death, *SEB* ...the poor wages, *Montgomery* ...For death is the wages of sin, *Wesley*.

3450.16 art sing neu	1156.2 conj	5321.1 noun sing neu	3450.2 art gen sing	2296.2 noun gen sing masc	2205.1 noun nom sing fem
τὸ	δὲ	χάρισμα	τοῦ	θεοῦ	ζωὴ
to	*de*	*charisma*	*tou*	*theou*	*zōē*
the	but	free gift		of God	life

164.3 adj nom sing	1706.1 prep	5382.3 name dat masc	2400.2 name masc	3450.3 art dat sing	2935.3 noun dat sing masc	2231.2 prs-pron gen 1 pl
αἰώνιος	ἐν	Χριστῷ	Ἰησοῦ	τῷ	κυρίῳ	ἡμῶν.
aiōnios	*en*	*Christō*	*Iēsou*	*tō*	*kuriō*	*hēmōn*
eternal	in	Christ	Jesus	the	Lord	our.

2211.1 conj	49.3 verb 2pl indic pres act	79.6 noun pl masc	1091.13 verb dat pl masc part pres act	1056.1 conj
7:1. Ἤ	ἀγνοεῖτε,	ἀδελφοί,	γινώσκουσιν	γὰρ
E	*agnoeite*	*adelphoi*	*ginōskousin*	*gar*
Or	are you ignorant,	brothers,	to knowing	for

3414.4 noun acc sing masc	2953.1 verb 1sing pres act	3617.1 conj	3450.5 art sing masc	3414.1 noun nom sing masc	2934.1 verb 3sing indic pres act
νόμον	λαλῶ,	ὅτι	ὁ	νόμος	κυριεύει
nomon	*lalō*	*hoti*	*ho*	*nomos*	*kurieuei*
law	I speak,	that	the	law	rules over

3450.2 art gen sing	442.2 noun gen sing masc	1894.1 prep	3607.1 rel-pron sing	5385.4 noun acc sing masc	2180.1 verb sing indic pres
τοῦ	ἀνθρώπου	ἐφ'	ὅσον	χρόνον	ζῇ;
tou	*anthrōpou*	*eph'*	*hoson*	*chronon*	*zē*
the	man	over	as long as	time	he may live?

3450.9 art nom sing fem	1056.1 conj	5058.1 adj nom sing fem	1129.1 noun nom sing fem	3450.3 art dat sing	2180.12 verb dat sing masc part pres act
2. ἡ	γὰρ	ὕπανδρος	γυνὴ	τῷ	ζῶντι
hē	*gar*	*hupandros*	*gunē*	*tō*	*zōnti*
The	for	married	woman	to the	living

433.3 noun dat sing masc	1204.15 verb 3sing indic perf pass	3414.3 noun dat sing masc	1430.1 partic	1156.2 conj	594.13 verb 3sing subj aor act
ἀνδρὶ	δέδεται	νόμῳ·	ἐὰν	δὲ	ἀποθάνῃ
andri	*dedetai*	*nomō*	*ean*	*de*	*apothanē*
husband	is bound	by law;	if	but	should die

3450.5 art sing masc	433.1 noun nom sing masc	2643.17 verb 3sing indic perf pass	570.3 prep gen	3450.2 art gen sing	3414.2 noun gen sing masc
ὁ	ἀνήρ	κατήργηται	ἀπὸ	τοῦ	νόμου
ho	*anēr*	*katērgētai*	*apo*	*tou*	*nomou*
the	husband,	she is cleared	from	the	law

3450.2 art gen sing	433.2 noun gen sing masc	679.1 partic	3631.1 conj	2180.11 verb gen sing part pres act	3450.2 art gen sing
τοῦ	ἀνδρός.	**3.** ἄρα	οὖν	ζῶντος	τοῦ
tou	*andros*	*ara*	*oun*	*zōntos*	*tou*
of the	husband:	so	then,	living	the

433.2 noun gen sing masc	3291.1 adj nom sing fem	5372.3 verb 3sing indic fut act	1430.1 partic	1090.40 verb 3sing subj aor mid
ἀνδρὸς	μοιχαλὶς	χρηματίσει,	ἐὰν	γένηται
andros	*moichalis*	*chrēmatisei*	*ean*	*genētai*
husband,	an adulteress	she shall be called,	if	she be

433.3 noun dat sing masc	2066.2 adj dat sing	1430.1 partic	1156.2 conj	594.13 verb 3sing subj aor act	3450.5 art sing masc	433.1 noun nom sing masc
ἀνδρὶ	ἑτέρῳ·	ἐὰν	δὲ	ἀποθάνῃ	ὁ	ἀνήρ,
andri	*heterō*	*ean*	*de*	*apothanē*	*ho*	*anēr*
to man	another;	if	but	should die	the	husband,

support given him in place of pay (i.e., rations) and the money in which he is paid" (Thayer, "opsōnion"). This was the pay which the soldier earned with the sweat of his brow and the risk of his body. It was due him and could not be taken from him.

On special occasions an emperor handed out a free gift of money to his soldiers. This was not earned and came through the emperor's kindness and grace. This was *charisma*.

Sin pays wages and the pay is death. In contrast to the horrible wages of sin, there is the gift of "eternal life through Jesus Christ our Lord." Men merit hell not eternal life. Christ alone procured that kind of life and gives it freely to all who believe.

7:1-3. Denny's comment on this chapter, which is complicated and difficult, is helpful. "The subject of chapter 6 is continued. The apostle shows how by death the Christian is freed from the law, which, good as it is in itself and in the divine intention, nevertheless, owing to the corruption of man's nature, instead of helping to make him good, perpetually stimulates sin. Verses 1-6 describe the liberation from the law; verses 7-13, the actual working of the law; in verses 14-25 we are shown that this working of the law is not due to anything in itself, but to the power of sin in the flesh" (*The Expositor's Greek Testament*, 2:637).

Sanctification, introduced in chapter 6, is the theme of chapters 7 and 8. All three chapters deal with the believer's deliverance from the power of sin and his growth in holiness. In chapter 6 we see that victory over sin is achieved by the attitude and work of faith. Another ally, the Holy Spirit, is introduced in chapter 8. Chapter 7 describes a man who earnestly desires to be holy by his own efforts—by the Law—apart from grace. The chapter presents the hopeless conflict of the better side of a man with his sinful nature.

Chapter 6 makes clear what was meant by "ye are . . . under grace" (6:14). Chapter 7 shows that the Law has no claim on the believer. Christ terminated the Law at Calvary for He met its demand of death when He died on the cross. The believer who dies with Him is also dead to the Law.

Verse 1 lays down the general principle that death frees a man from the dominion of the marriage vow. The wife is bound to her husband as long as he lives. Both husband and wife are free from the other when either one dies.

Paul then compares the Law to a husband and shows that we cannot be married to Christ and enjoy the blessings of grace until the Law is dead to us, or we to the Law. To do otherwise is to be "fallen from grace" (Galatians 5:4).

Believers are dead to the Law as the wife is dead in respect to the marriage vow when her husband dies. Paul makes the application: when the Christian died in Christ to sin, he became dead to the Law. The bondage imposed by the law of sin was completely severed.

Some will ask the question, who or what dies? Is it the Law? Christ? or we? True, Christ died, but more than that, we died with Him. The Law did not die, but we did, and when we died we were

but the gift of God [is] eternal life through Jesus Christ our Lord: . . . but the free gift, *Montgomery* . . . is the Life of the ages bestowed upon us, *Weymouth* . . . is aionian Life, by the Anointed Jesus, our Lord, *Wilson* . . . through union with, *TCNT, Williams* . . . our Lord and Master, *Conybeare.*

1. Know ye not, brethren, (for I speak to them that know the law,): Are you ignorant brethren, *Rheims* . . . to those who have an experiential knowledge of law, *Wuest* . . . them that are skilful in the Lawe, *Geneva.*

how that the law hath dominion over a man as long as he liveth?: . . . that the law rules a man's actions only during his lifetime? *Norlie* . . . the lawe hath lordship in man, *Wyclif* . . . That the Law controls a man, *Wilson* . . . the law governs man, *Fenton.*

2. For the woman which hath an husband: . . . for the married woman, *Young.*

is bound by the law to [her] husband so long as he liveth: . . . the woman which is in subiection to a man, *Geneva* . . . is by law secured to the husband, *Berkeley* . . . binds a married woman, *Beck* . . . has legal obligations, *JB* . . . to the living Husband, *Wilson* . . . during his lifetime, *Montgomery.*

but if the husband be dead: . . . should die, *Scarlett.*

she is loosed from the law of [her] husband: . . . she is released from the law of marriage, *SEB* . . . she is discharged, *RSV, Scarlett, Panin.*

3. So then if, while [her] husband liveth, she be married to another man: . . . during her husband's lifetime, *TCNT, Montgomery* . . . she couple her selfe, *Geneva* . . . she connect herself with another man, *Noyes* . . . if she lives with another man, *Klingensmith.*

she shall be called an adulteress: . . . she shall be styled "adulteress," *HistNT* . . . she will be stigmatized as an adulteress, *Weymouth* . . . shalbe counted a wedlocke breaker, *Cranmer.*

1645.5 adj nom sing fem	1498.4 verb 3sing indic pres act	570.3 prep gen	3450.2 art gen sing	3414.2 noun gen sing masc	3450.2 art gen sing	3231.1 partic
ἐλευθέρα	ἐστὶν	ἀπὸ	τοῦ	νόμου,	τοῦ	μὴ
eleuthera	estin	apo	tou	nomou	tou	mē
free	she is	from	the	law,	the	not

1498.32 verb inf pres act	840.12 prs-pron acc sing fem	3291.4 adj acc sing fem	1090.58 verb acc sing fem part aor mid	433.3 noun dat sing masc
εἶναι	αὐτὴν	μοιχαλίδα,	γενομένην	ἀνδρὶ
einai	autēn	moichalida	genomenēn	andri
to be	for her	an adulteress	having become	to man

2066.2 adj dat sing	5452.1 conj	79.6 noun pl masc	1466.2 prs- pron gen 1sing	2504.1 conj	5050.1 prs- pron nom 2pl
ἑτέρῳ.	4. ὥστε,	ἀδελφοί	μου,	καὶ	ὑμεῖς
heterō	hōste	adelphoi	mou	kai	humeis
another.	So that,	brothers	my,	also	you

2266.7 verb 2pl indic aor pass	3450.3 art dat sing	3414.3 noun dat sing masc	1217.2 prep	3450.2 art gen sing	4835.2 noun gen sing neu
ἐθανατώθητε	τῷ	νόμῳ	διὰ	τοῦ	σώματος
ethanatōthēte	tō	nomō	dia	tou	sōmatos
were made dead	to the	law	by	the	body

3450.2 art gen sing	5382.2 name gen masc	1519.1 prep	3450.16 art sing neu	1090.63 verb inf aor mid	5050.4 prs- pron acc 2pl
τοῦ	Χριστοῦ,	εἰς	τὸ	γενέσθαι	ὑμᾶς
tou	Christou	eis	to	genesthai	humas
of the	Christ,	for	the	to be	you

2066.2 adj dat sing	3450.3 art dat sing	1523.2 prep gen	3361.2 adj gen pl	1446.26 verb dat sing masc part aor pass
ἑτέρῳ,	τῷ	ἐκ	νεκρῶν	ἐγερθέντι,
heterō	tō	ek	nekrōn	egerthenti
to another,	to the	from among	dead	having been raised,

2419.1 conj	2563.4 verb 1pl subj aor act	3450.3 art dat sing	2296.3 noun dat sing masc	3616.1 conj
ἵνα	καρποφορήσωμεν	τῷ	θεῷ.	5. ὅτε
hina	karpophorēsōmen	tō	theō	hote
that	we should bring forth fruit	to	to God.	When

1056.1 conj	1498.36 verb 1pl indic imperf act	1706.1 prep	3450.11 art dat sing fem	4418.3 noun dat sing fem	3450.17 art pl neu
γὰρ	ἦμεν	ἐν	τῇ	σαρκί,	τὰ
gar	ēmen	en	tē	sarki	ta
for	we were	in	the	flesh,	the

3667.2 noun pl neu	3450.1 art gen pl	264.6 noun gen pl fem	3450.17 art pl neu	1217.2 prep	3450.2 art gen sing
παθήματα	τῶν	ἁμαρτιῶν	τὰ	διὰ	τοῦ
pathēmata	tōn	hamartiōn	ta	dia	tou
passions	of the	sins,	the	through	the

3414.2 noun gen sing masc	1738.12 verb 3sing indic imperf mid	1706.1 prep	3450.4 art dat pl	3166.4 noun dat pl neu	2231.2 prs- pron gen 1pl	1519.1 prep
νόμου	ἐνηργεῖτο	ἐν	τοῖς	μέλεσιν	ἡμῶν	εἰς
nomou	enērgeito	en	tois	melesin	hēmōn	eis
law,	worked	in	the	members	our	to

3450.16 art sing neu	2563.5 verb inf aor act	3450.3 art dat sing	2265.3 noun dat sing masc	3432.1 adv	1156.2 conj
τὸ	καρποφορῆσαι	τῷ	θανάτῳ·	6. νυνὶ	δὲ
to	karpophorēsai	tō	thanatō	nuni	de
the	to bring forth fruit	to the	death;	now	but

separated from the former husband of sin and united with Christ by faith. All the virtues of Christ's death, in meeting the claims of the Law, became ours, and we were set free from the power of sin to which the Law had committed us.

7:4. The word "body" in the phrase "dead to the law by the body of Christ" means sacrifice, not the Church.

It is important to remember that freedom from the former union is not an end in itself. This severance is for a positive purpose—to be "married to another." And He is none other than the One "who is raised from the dead." By the spiritual union with Jesus, the representative of the sinner on the cross, we have had the payment of the death penalty imputed to us by faith. Death in Christ leads to resurrection in Him. We are united with Him and come under His authority.

The purpose of this new union with Jesus is "that we should bring forth fruit unto God." In our natural condition we "walked according to the course of this world . . . children of disobedience . . . lusts of our flesh . . . children of wrath . . . " (Ephesians 2:2,3). The issue from that union, the offspring of that relationship, made us ashamed. It worked "in our members to bring forth fruit unto death" (7:5). It worked actively in our faculties, both mental and physical, resulting in death.

In chapter 5 we read that we are brought to peace with God through our Lord Jesus Christ, having been justified in Him. In chapter 6 we see that we are serving a new master, Christ. In chapter 7 we are viewed as united to a new husband, Christ. The old marriage to the Law brought unbearable bondage (Acts 15:10) and continuous frustration because we could never fully please the old husband (James 2:10). That marriage has been ended not by divorce, but by death to the Law so that we might be married to Christ Jesus (cf. Ephesians 5:32; Revelation 19:7).

7:5. "In the flesh" refers to the unrenewed and legal state, under the Law and not under Christ, under control of the evil nature. *Pathēmata*, rendered "motions" in the King James Version, is more often rendered "passions" in other translations. Very possibly the King James translators chose "motions" since in earlier English the word was sometimes used in the sense of "emotion." "Which were by the law" may also be rendered "occasioned or aroused by the law." "Did work in our members" implies working both physically and mentally. And it brought "forth fruit unto death." How the Law can arouse sinful passions is defined in verses 7-13. The "fruit unto death" comprises those evil works whose end is death, according to verse 21.

7:6. "Now . . . delivered" could be translated "now released." The Jewish believer was put under the Law at Sinai. Now he is released

but if her husband be dead, she is free from that law: . . . she is legally free, *Berkeley* . . . no longer under the old prohibition, *Weymouth* . . . from that marriage bond, *Williams* . . . she is delivered from the law, *Douay*.

so that she is no adulteress, though she be married to another man: . . . she is legally a free woman, *TEV* . . . even though she marries again, *Weymouth* . . . to a different man later, *SEB*.

4. Wherefore, my brethren, ye also are become dead to the law by the body of Christ: . . . are put to death, *Scarlett* . . . The crucified body of Christ, *Moffatt* . . . the incarnation of Christ, *Weymouth*.

that ye should be married to another, [even] to him who is raised from the dead: You can marry someone else—the one who was raised from death, *SEB* . . . that ye might be joined to another, *Worrell* . . . to marry Another—Him who rose from the dead, *Beck*.

that we should bring forth fruit unto God: . . . that we might yield God a harvest, *Berkeley* . . . that we should bear fruit, *Sawyer*.

5. For when we were in the flesh: Before our conversion, *JB* . . . we were in our sensuality, *Fenton* . . . whilst we were under the thraldom of our earthly natures, *Weymouth* . . . while we were unspiritual, *Montgomery* . . . with our lower nature, *Williams*.

the motions of sins: . . . sinful passions, *Norlie, Berkeley, JB, TCNT, ASV, Confraternity* . . . the passions of sinnes, *Rheims, Douay, Worrell* . . . the stirrings of sins, *Alford* . . . the sinful cravings, *Moffatt* . . . the lustes of synne, *Cranmer*.

which were by the law: . . . quite unsubdued by the Law, *JB* . . . aroused by the Law, *TCNT* . . . whych were stered vp by the lawe, *Cranmer* . . . excited by the Law, *Moffatt*.

did work in our members to bring forth fruit unto death: . . . wrought effectually in our members, *Campbell* . . . were active in every part, *TCNT* . . . to bring a harvest of death, *Norlie*.

Romans 7:7

6.a.Txt: 01ℵ,02A,03B
04C,018K,025P,044,33
81,614,1739,co.
Var: 06D,010F,012G

2643.14 verb 1pl indic aor pass	570.3 prep gen	3450.2 art gen sing	3414.2 noun gen sing masc	594.18 verb nom pl masc part aor act
κατηργήθημεν	ἀπὸ	τοῦ	νόμου,	ʿ☆ ἀποθανόντες
katērgēthēmen	apo	tou	nomou	apothanontes
we were cleared	from	the	law,	having died

3450.2 art gen sing	2265.2 noun gen sing masc	1706.1 prep	3614.3 rel-pron dat sing	2692.12 verb 1pl indic imperf pass
[ᵃ+ τοῦ	θανάτου]	ἐν	ᾧ	κατειχόμεθα,
tou	thanatou	en	hō	kateichometha
[of the	death]	in	which	we were being held,

5452.1 conj	1392.8 verb inf pres act	2231.4 prs-pron acc 1pl	1706.1 prep	2509.1 noun dat sing fem	4011.2 noun gen sing neu
ὥστε	δουλεύειν	ἡμᾶς	ἐν	καινότητι	πνεύματος,
hōste	douleuein	hēmas	en	kainotēti	pneumatos
so that	to serve	we	in	newness	of spirit,

2504.1 conj	3620.3 partic	3684.1 noun dat sing fem	1115.2 noun gen sing neu	4949.9 intr-pron neu	3631.1 conj
καὶ	οὐ	παλαιότητι	γράμματος.	7. Τί	οὖν
kai	ou	palaiotēti	grammatos	Ti	oun
and	not	in oldness	of letter.	What	then

2029.12 verb 1pl indic fut act	3450.5 art sing masc	3414.1 noun nom sing masc	264.2 noun nom sing fem	3231.1 partic
ἐροῦμεν;	ὁ	νόμος	ἁμαρτία;	μὴ
eroumen	ho	nomos	hamartia	mē
shall we say?	The	law	sin?	Not

1090.44 verb 3sing opt aor mid	233.2 conj	3450.12 art acc sing fem	264.4 noun acc sing fem	3620.2 partic	1091.15 verb 1sing indic aor act
γένοιτο·	ἀλλὰ	τὴν	ἁμαρτίαν	οὐκ	ἔγνων
genoito	alla	tēn	hamartian	ouk	egnōn
may it be!	But	the	sin	not	I knew

1479.1 conj	3231.1 partic	1217.2 prep	3414.2 noun gen sing masc	3450.12 art acc sing fem	4885.1 conj	1056.1 conj
εἰ	μὴ	διὰ	νόμου·	τήν	τε	γὰρ
ei	mē	dia	nomou	tēn	te	gar
if	not	by	law:	the	also	for

1924.4 noun acc sing fem	3620.2 partic	3471.9 verb 1sing indic plperf act	1479.1 conj	3231.1 partic	3450.5 art sing masc
ἐπιθυμίαν	οὐκ	ᾔδειν	εἰ	μὴ	ὁ
epithumian	ouk	ēdein	ei	mē	ho
lust	not	I had been conscious of	if	not	the

3414.1 noun nom sing masc	2978.26 verb 3sing indic imperf act	3620.2 partic	1922.9 verb 2sing indic fut act	867.1 noun acc sing fem
νόμος	ἔλεγεν,	Οὐκ	ἐπιθυμήσεις.	8. ἀφορμὴν
nomos	elegen	Ouk	epithumēseis	aphormēn
law	was saying,	Not	you shall lust;	an occasion

1156.2 conj	2956.29 verb nom sing fem part aor act	3450.9 art nom sing fem	264.2 noun nom sing fem	1217.2 prep	3450.10 art gen sing fem
δὲ	λαβοῦσα	ἡ	ἁμαρτία	διὰ	τῆς
de	labousa	hē	hamartia	dia	tēs
but	having taken	the	sin	by	the

1769.2 noun gen sing fem	2686.9 verb 3sing indic aor mid	1706.1 prep	1466.5 prs-pron dat 1sing	3820.12 adj acc sing fem
ἐντολῆς	κατειργάσατο	ἐν	ἐμοὶ	πᾶσαν
entolēs	kateirgasato	en	emoi	pasan
commandment	worked out	in	me	every

from the Law. If so, the Gentile has also been released from the Law. "That being dead" is better translated "having died" (*apothanontes*); it is we who died to that which held us in bondage. The bondage was marriage to the Law. That was a union that could only produce death. The Law could not deliver from sin; that was not God's purpose in giving it. It was given to inform men that death is the inevitable result of sin. God had a better plan, provided through the death of His Son. "Wherein we were held" really means "in which we were constantly held down." We were dead in sins while under the Law and held helpless to free ourselves from its bondage and death.

Deliverance brings us freedom to "serve in newness of spirit, and not in the oldness of the letter." "Letter" is *gramma* which was used of a "bond, a document, a letter one writes." The word "oldness" used here is *palaiotēs* meaning that which is obsolete. Newness means that which is new as to quality in contrast to that which is worn out. Spirit refers to the Holy Spirit.

The believer is not bound to the minute particulars of legal observances according to the traditions of the fathers. His life does not consist in mere conformity to a list of rules and regulations. He serves in a new spiritual state in Christ and not in the old bondage of the Law. He is free from the slavish fear of the Law.

Note the word "serve." Even though married to a new husband, we must still serve. But this is a service of freedom in contrast to the drudgery of the old life. Service is not determined by the old externals but by new spiritual principles (2 Corinthians 5:14,15).

7:7,8. This section begins in the logical sequence by asking a question, which is a pattern in Romans. No doubt the question, like others which Paul raised, was being asked by the legalists who were constantly attempting to bring the Church back into bondage. They taught that the believer, even though justified by faith, was after justification put under Law as a rule of faith. Is the Law sinful? Is the Law the cause of sin? Is there something wrong with the Law?

Paul answers clearly. He does not reflect dishonorably on the Law. The Law is like the Lawgiver. It is holy, just, and good, commanding holiness and outlining those things which are right and just. But the Law is powerless to save and sanctify, not because it is not good, but because of the sinful bias in human nature.

There was a time when sin was dead; without the Law sin was dead. Before God gave Adam the law regarding the tree of the knowledge of good and evil, sin was dead in that man was separated from it. The Garden was all holy until man rebelled against God's law. Adam and Eve were free from sin in a way that none of their progeny can be. However, Paul knew by revelation and by experience that he was alive without the Law once, when as a child he was "without the law" in that he was not then personally accountable to God for his sinful nature. The child has selfish desires but is not aware of lust or coveting per se.

6. But now we are delivered from the law: ...now we have been loosed, *Alford* ...set free, *Confraternity* ...fully discharged, *Worrell.*

that being dead wherein we were held: We died to what bound us, *SEB* ...held us captive, *RSV* ...kept us under restraint, *TCNT* ...vvherin vve vvere deteined, *Rheims.*

that we should serve in newness of spirit, and not [in] the oldness of the letter: ...under new and spiritual conditions, *TCNT* ...but in the new service of the spirit, *Conybeare* ...not under the written code as of old, *Moffatt* ...in the old age of a writing, *Sawyer* ...not by following a strict code, *SEB.*

7. What shall we say then?: ...do we conclude? *Berkeley.*

[is] the law sin?: That the Law is equivalent to sin? *Moffatt.*

God forbid: Far be it from our thoughts, *Berkeley.*

Nay, I had not known sin, but by the law: I should not have comprehended the sin, *Fenton* ...Yet, if it had not been for the law, *Williams* ...it was the law that made clear my knowledge of sin, *Norlie* ...I should have known nothing of sin as sin, *Weymouth* ...an experiential knowledge of sin except through the instrumentality of law, *Wuest.*

for I had not known lust, except the law had said, Thou shalt not covet: I had not known even inordinate desire, *Campbell* ...strong desire, *Wilson* ...except the Law had repeatedly said, *Montgomery* ...Don't lust, *Beck.*

8. But sin, taking occasion by the commandment, wrought in me all manner of concupiscence: ...when sin had gained a vantage-ground, *Montgomery* ...Sin found its rallying point, *Williams* ...Taking the commandment as a challenge, sin worked in me every kind of wrong desire, *Beck* ...to make me want all kinds of things which didn't belong to me, *SEB* ...made that command a fulcrum that effected in me all sorts of covetousness, *Berkeley* ...to arouse in me every form of covetousness, *TCNT.*

Romans 7:9

1924.4 noun acc sing fem	5400.1 prep gen	1056.1 conj	3414.2 noun gen sing masc	264.2 noun nom sing fem	3361.8 adj nom sing fem
ἐπιθυμίαν.	χωρὶς	γὰρ	νόμου	ἁμαρτία	νεκρά·
epithumian	chōris	gar	nomou	hamartia	nekra
lust;	apart from	for	law	sin	dead.

1466.1 prs-pron nom 1sing	1156.2 conj	2180.27 verb 1sing indic imperf act	5400.1 prep gen	3414.2 noun gen sing masc	4077.1 adv
9. ἐγὼ	δὲ	ἔζων	χωρὶς	νόμου	ποτέ·
egō	de	ezōn	chōris	nomou	pote
I	but	was living	apart from	law	then;

2048.20 verb gen sing fem part aor act	1156.2 conj	3450.10 art gen sing fem	1769.2 noun gen sing fem	3450.9 art nom sing fem	
ἐλθούσης	δὲ	τῆς	ἐντολῆς,	ἡ	
elthousēs	de	tēs	entolēs	hē	
having come	but	the	commandment,	the	

264.2 noun nom sing fem	324.1 verb 3sing indic aor act	1466.1 prs-pron nom 1sing	1156.2 conj	594.9 verb indic aor act	2504.1 conj
ἁμαρτία	ἀνέζησεν,	ἐγὼ	δὲ	ἀπέθανον·	10. καὶ
hamartia	anezēsen	egō	de	apethanon	kai
sin	revived,	I	but	died.	And

2128.32 verb 3sing indic aor pass	1466.4 prs-pron dat 1sing	3450.9 art nom sing fem	1769.1 noun nom sing fem	3450.9 art nom sing fem	
εὑρέθη	μοι	ἡ	ἐντολὴ	ἡ	
heurethē	moi	hē	entolē	hē	
was found	to me	the	commandment	the	

1519.1 prep	2205.4 noun acc sing fem	3642.9 dem-pron nom sing fem	1519.1 prep	2265.4 noun acc sing masc	3450.9 art nom sing fem
εἰς	ζωὴν,	αὕτη	εἰς	θάνατον.	11. ἡ
eis	zōēn	hautē	eis	thanaton	hē
to	life,	this	to	death:	the

1056.1 conj	264.2 noun nom sing fem	867.1 noun acc sing fem	2956.29 verb nom sing fem part aor act	1217.2 prep	3450.10 art gen sing fem
γὰρ	ἁμαρτία	ἀφορμὴν	λαβοῦσα	διὰ	τῆς
gar	hamartia	aphormēn	labousa	dia	tēs
for	sin	an occasion	having taken	by	the

1769.2 noun gen sing fem	1802.3 verb 3sing indic aor act	1466.6 prs-pron acc 1sing	2504.1 conj	1217.1 prep	840.10 prs-pron gen sing fem
ἐντολῆς	ἐξηπάτησέν	με,	καὶ	δι'	αὐτῆς
entolēs	exēpatēsen	me	kai	di'	autēs
commandment,	deceived	me,	and	by	it

609.5 verb 3sing indic aor act	5452.1 conj	3450.5 art sing masc	3173.1 conj	3414.1 noun nom sing masc	39.5 adj sing masc
ἀπέκτεινεν.	12. ὥστε	ὁ	μὲν	νόμος	ἅγιος,
apekteinen	hōste	ho	men	nomos	hagios
slew.	So that	the	indeed	law	holy,

2504.1 conj	3450.9 art nom sing fem	1769.1 noun nom sing fem	39.10 adj nom sing fem	2504.1 conj	1337.10 adj nom sing fem	2504.1 conj
καὶ	ἡ	ἐντολὴ	ἁγία	καὶ	δικαία	καὶ
kai	hē	entolē	hagia	kai	dikaia	kai
and	the	commandment	holy	and	just	and

18.9 adj nom sing fem	3450.16 art sing neu	3631.1 conj	18.3 adj sing	1466.5 prs-pron dat 1sing	1090.3 verb 3sing indic perf act
ἀγαθή.	13. Τὸ	οὖν	ἀγαθὸν	ἐμοὶ	ʼ γέγονεν
agathē	To	oun	agathon	emoi	gegonen
good.	The	then	good,	to me	has it become

7:9. Paul was speaking both by revelation and by his experience when he wrote, "I was alive without the law once." Some believe this is the time in Paul's life prior to the age of accountability. Others say it also may point to his *bar mitzvah*, when at age 13 he became a "son of the commandment." In either case sin was dead (verse 8) because he was not aware of what was sin. At some point—by the revelation of God in (1) creation (1:18-20), (2) the written Word (verse 7), and (3) his conscience as pricked by the Holy Spirit (2:15)—sin came to life. He then knew what it was to sin against God. Bent toward sin by his sinful nature he died spiritually; he was separated from God until he was born again.

7:10,11. The Law reveals the sinful nature of man and the vile nature of sin. Sin is shown in its seriousness (verses 10,11) and its sinfulness (verses 12,13). The Law revealed the fact (verse 7), the occasion (verse 8), the power (verse 9), the deceitfulness (verse 11), the effect (verses 10,11), and the sinfulness of sin (verses 12,13). The Law made Paul discover his sin. It served as a mirror to reveal his need of washing. The Law, reflecting the holy will of God, defined evil. Sin has no existence apart from the Law, for sin is the transgression of the Law.

The Law was a schoolmaster to bring us to Christ (Galatians 3:24,25). The Roman schoolmaster was a pedagogue who did not teach but was the slave whose duty it was to take the child to school. Paul tells the Galatians that the person who is justified by faith is no longer under the schoolmaster.

"Ordained to life" has the meaning of "tending to life." The aim was to life, for it set forth nothing but that which was right and perfect; to keep it perfectly insured life eternal. "Found to be" means proved to be death to me because I could not keep it.

The word "deceived" is *exapataō* which literally means "completely make one lose one's way." Sin leads one to confusion and lostness, to completely lose the way. Sin, like the tempter before Eve, took the commandment for a starting point and deceived him.

7:12,13. There is no defect in the Law, "the law is holy." It is holy because it was given by God and expresses part of His will. The Law being "holy," "just," and "good," heartily approves righteousness but without reservation condemns evil. Other than Jesus, the Law never saw a man righteous through obedience.

Paul again poses a question. If the Law is holy, just, and good, how then is it the cause of death? Again comes the firm response, "God forbid." Paul points out that it was not the Law that killed him but sin that would not let him obey the Law. This made sin appear for what it really is—a decision, a deadly enemy, a killer.

Earlier the question was posed, "Is the law sin?" (verse 7). The Law is good for it is "the commandment . . . ordained to life" (verse 10). It is "holy" as God's revelation of himself, "just" in its prerequisites, and "good" because of its end.

For without the law sin [was] dead: In the absence of Law sin shows no sign of life, *TCNT* . . . disconnected from law, sin is non-existent, *Fenton* . . . for apart from law sin is dead, *Panin* . . . sin is lifeless, *Norlie, HistNT, Williams*.

9. For I was alive without the law once: but when the commandment came:

sin revived, and I died: . . . sin sprang into life, *Weymouth* . . . synne lyued agen, *Wyclif* . . . sin lived again, *Wilson* . . . sin came to life, *Alford*.

10. And the commandment, which [was ordained] to life: . . . that was aimed to give life, *Berkeley* . . . which was intended for life, *Wesley* . . . whose design was life, *Noyes* . . . which should have meant life, *Montgomery*.
I found [to be] unto death: . . . actually proved to be a sentence of death to me, *Norlie* . . . brought death instead! *SEB* . . . I found to result in Death! *TCNT* . . . proved in my experience death, *HistNT* . . . this I found unto death, *Wesley* . . . me tending to death, *Scarlett* . . . vnto me an occasion of deeth, *Tyndale* . . . I found to issue in death, *Noyes*.

11. For sin, taking occasion by the commandment, deceived me, and by it slew [me]: Taking the commandment as a challenge, sin seduced me, *Beck* . . . beguiled me and, *Wuest, Panin* . . . to take hold of me, *SEB* . . . gave sin a chance, and sin deceived me, *Norlie* . . . by taking its incentive from the command, cheated me, *Berkeley* . . . beguiled me through the commandment, *HistNT* . . . seized the advantage, *Weymouth* . . . to mislead me, *JB* . . . and slew me by the sentence of the Law, *Conybeare*.

12. Wherefore the law [is] holy, and the commandment holy: The conclusion, then, is, *TCNT* . . . and its specific commands are, *Williams* . . . holy, fair and good, *SEB*.

and just, and good:

Romans 7:14

13.a.Txt: 018K,020L,byz.
Var: 01א,02A,03B,04C
06D,025P,Lach,Treg
Alf,Word,Tisc,We/Ho
Weis,Sod,UBS/✶

1090.33 verb 3sing
indic aor mid
[ᵃ✶ ἐγένετο]
egeneto
[became]

2265.1 noun
nom sing masc
θάνατος;
thanatos
death?

3231.1
partic
μὴ
mē
Not

1090.44 verb
3sing opt aor mid
γένοιτο·
genoito
may it be!

233.2
conj
ἀλλὰ
alla
But

3450.9 art
nom sing fem
ἡ
hē
the

264.2 noun
nom sing fem
ἁμαρτία,
hamartia
sin,

2419.1
conj
ἵνα
hina
that

5154.1 verb
3sing subj aor
φανῇ
phanē
it might appear

264.2 noun
nom sing fem
ἁμαρτία,
hamartia
sin,

1217.2
prep
διὰ
dia
by

3450.2 art
gen sing
τοῦ
tou
the

18.2
adj sing
ἀγαθοῦ
agathou
good

1466.4 prs-
pron dat 1sing
μοι
moi
to me

2686.6 verb nom
sing fem part pres
κατεργαζομένη
katergazomenē
working out

2265.4 noun
acc sing masc
θάνατον,
thanaton
death;

2419.1
conj
ἵνα
hina
that

1090.40 verb
3sing subj aor mid
γένηται
genētai
might become

2567.2
prep
καθ'
kath'
according to

5073.3 noun
acc sing fem
ὑπερβολὴν
huperbolēn
excess

266.1 adj
nom sing
ἁμαρτωλὸς
hamartōlos
sinful

3450.9 art
nom sing fem
ἡ
hē
the

264.2 noun
nom sing fem
ἁμαρτία
hamartia
sin

1217.2
prep
διὰ
dia
by

3450.10 art
gen sing fem
τῆς
tēs
the

1769.2 noun
gen sing fem
ἐντολῆς.
entolēs
commandment.

3471.5 verb 1pl
indic perf act
14. Οἴδαμεν
Oidamen
We know

1056.1
conj
γὰρ
gar
for

3617.1
conj
ὅτι
hoti
that

3450.5 art
sing masc
ὁ
ho
the

3414.1 noun
nom sing masc
νόμος
nomos
law

4012.2 adj
nom sing masc
πνευματικός
pneumatikos
spiritual

1498.4 verb 3sing
indic pres act
ἐστιν·
estin
is;

14.a.Txt: 01א-corr,018K
020L,025P,byz.
Var: 01א-org,02A,03B
04C,06D,Gries,Lach
Treg,Alf,Word,Tisc
We/Ho,Weis,Sod
UBS/✶

1466.1 prs-
pron nom 1sing
ἐγὼ
egō
I

1156.2
conj
δὲ
de
but

4416.2 adj
nom sing masc
⸀σάρκικός
sarkikos
fleshly

4417.3 adj
nom sing masc
[ᵃ✶ σάρκινός]
sarkinos
[idem]

1498.2 verb 1sing
indic pres act
εἰμι,
eimi
am,

3958.7 verb nom sing
masc part perf pass
πεπραμένος
pepramenos
having been sold

5097.3
prep
ὑπὸ
hupo
under

3450.12 art
acc sing fem
τὴν
tēn
the

264.4 noun
acc sing fem
ἁμαρτίαν.
hamartian
sin.

3614.16 rel-
pron sing neu
15. ὃ
ho
What

1056.1
conj
γὰρ
gar
for

2686.1 verb
1sing indic pres
κατεργάζομαι,
katergazomai
I work out,

3620.3
partic
οὐ
ou
not

1091.1 verb 1sing
indic pres act
γινώσκω·
ginōskō
I do know:

3620.3
partic
οὐ
ou
not

1056.1
conj
γὰρ
gar
for

3614.16 rel-
pron sing neu
ὃ
ho
what

2286.1 verb
1sing pres act
θέλω,
thelō
I will,

3642.17 dem-
pron sing neu
τοῦτο
touto
this

4097.1 verb 1sing
indic pres act
πράσσω·
prassō
I do;

233.1
conj
ἀλλ'
all'
but

3614.16 rel-
pron sing neu
ὃ
ho
what

3268.1 verb 1sing
indic pres act
μισῶ,
misō
I hate,

3642.17 dem-
pron sing neu
τοῦτο
touto
this

4020.1 verb
1sing pres act
ποιῶ.
poiō
I practice.

1479.1
conj
16. εἰ
ei
If

1156.2
conj
δὲ
de
but

3614.16 rel-
pron sing neu
ὃ
ho
what

3620.3
partic
οὐ
ou
not

2286.1 verb
1sing pres act
θέλω,
thelō
I do will,

Sin is basically disobedience, and there must be a law to disobey before one is conscious of sin. Dormant sinful nature springs into life, sin revived when the Law came. It was not the Law that brought the state of death. The Law was good, but the villain was sin. Sin seized the opportunity when the Law revealed what was right and what was wrong. The Law was powerless to help a person do the right and unable to avoid the wrong. Sin works in men, against their better judgment, causing them to do what the Law showed them to be wrong, thus bringing condemnation and death.

7:14-18. Three words are used by Paul to describe man. *Pneumatikos* is the spiritual man who "walks after the Spirit." *Psuchikos* is the unsaved or natural man. *Sarkikos* is the carnal Christian who does not have victory in his life. The spiritual man is delivered from the Law. The natural man is doomed by the Law. The carnal man is defeated by the Law.

Paul, who seems to be describing his own past experience, says that the Law which he desired so much to obey stirred sinful impulses within him. He was hindered from doing the good that he wanted to do and was driven to do the thing that he hated. This civil war raged between his mind and his flesh. The passage presents the picture of a man under law who has come to grips with the searching spirituality of the Law, but in his attempt to keep the Law finds himself stymied by indwelling sin.

When Paul wrote "I am carnal," he was not necessarily speaking of his life prior to conversion. In 1 Corinthians 3:1-3 Paul described as carnal those who were immature believers who should have developed beyond the stage of being "babes in Christ." They were carnal because they were choosing to give way to envy, strife, and divisions. They were regenerate; they were "brethren" and they were "in Christ," even if only "babes." They were behaving, however, like unregenerate men.

When the believer tries to be spiritual by keeping the Law, any law, he becomes very aware of his carnality. His sinful human nature is aroused by law because the Christian is to live from Christ's life within rather than by trying to do good works of law. The Law was spiritual, a written expression of the character of God and could only be kept by one who was perfect spiritually. Paul, and every man, was "sold under sin" by Adam who made it impossible for anyone except Jesus Christ to be perfect spiritually in himself.

This particular passage has been the battleground of theological difference. Able Bible students are divided in interpreting this experience as being that of the regenerate or unregenerate. (1) Some say it is the struggle of one who is endeavoring to overcome sin by his own strength. (2) Others say that this is the experience of all true Christians in their disappointing conflict with inward sin and no deliverance is to be expected until they reach heaven. (3) Others hold that it is the struggle that can only be won by a second definite work of grace in becoming "wholly sanctified." (4) Still others hold that these verses describe the struggle and defeat of

13. Was then that which is good made death unto me? God forbid:
But sin, that it might appear sin, working death in me by that which is good: . . . that it might be manifest as sin, *Confraternity* . . . clearly used this good thing to kill me, *Beck* . . . producing death to me, *Sawyer* . . . that it might be shown to be sin, *Worrell*.

that sin by the commandment might become exceeding sinful: . . . that the unutterable malignity of sin, *Montgomery* . . . might be beyond doubt excessively sinful, *Fenton* . . . how intensely sinful sin is, *TCNT* . . . the unspeakable sinfulness of sin might be plainly shown, *Weymouth* . . . myght be out of measure synfull, *Cranmer* . . . sin might appear surpassingly sinful, *Williams* . . . might become immeasurably sinful, *Confraternity*.

14. For we know that the law is spiritual:
but I am carnal, sold under sin: It is I who am sensual, *Norlie* . . . but I am unspiritual, *JB, Weymouth* . . . but I am earthly, *TCNT* . . . I am made of flesh that is frail, *Williams* . . . and I am fleshly, *Young* . . . bought and sold under the dominion of sin, *Montgomery*.

15. For that which I do I allow not: For what I work I know not, *Panin* . . . what I perform, *Alford* . . . what I accomplish, *Worrell* . . . I do not understand my own actions, *RSV* . . . I do not practise what I would, *Wesley* . . . what I work out, I do not approve, *Wilson* . . . I don't always do what I really want to do, *SEB*.

for what I would, that do I not; but what I hate, that do I: What I want to do I don't practice, but instead what I hate is exactly what I do, *Adams* . . . I do not act according to my will, *HistNT* . . . I do what I detest, *Moffatt* . . . doing what I actually hate, *SEB* . . . but what I am averse to is what I do, *Weymouth* . . . that I habitually do, *Montgomery*.

16. If then I do that which I would not: In view of the fact then, *Wuest*.

3642.17 dem-pron sing neu	4020.1 verb 1sing pres act	4703.1 verb 1sing indic pres act	3450.3 art dat sing	3414.3 noun dat sing masc	3617.1 conj
τοῦτο	ποιῶ,	σύμφημι	τῷ	νόμῳ	ὅτι
touto	poiō	sumphēmi	tō	nomō	hoti
this	I practice,	I consent	to the	law	that

2541.3 adj nom sing masc	3432.1 adv	1156.2 conj	3629.1 adv	1466.1 prs-pron nom 1sing	2686.1 verb 1sing indic pres
καλός.	**17.** νυνὶ	δὲ	οὐκέτι	ἐγὼ	κατεργάζομαι
kalos	nuni	de	ouketi	egō	katergazomai
right.	Then	now	no longer	I	am working out

840.15 prs-pron sing neu	233.1 conj	233.2 conj	3450.9 art nom sing fem	3474.3 verb nom sing fem part pres act
αὐτὸ,	⸀ ἀλλ'	[☆ ἀλλὰ]	ἡ	⸀☆ οἰκοῦσα
auto	all'	alla	hē	oikousa
it;	but	[idem]	the	dwelling

17.a.Txt: 02A,04C,06D 018K,020L,025P,byz. Var: 01ℵ,03B,Tisc We/Ho,Weis,Sod UBS/☆

1758.6 verb nom sing fem part pres act	1706.1 prep	1466.5 prs-pron dat 1sing	264.2 noun nom sing fem	3471.2 verb 1sing indic perf act
[a ἐνοικοῦσα]	ἐν	ἐμοὶ	ἁμαρτία.	**18.** Οἶδα
enoikousa	en	emoi	hamartia	Oida
[idem]	in	me	sin.	I know

1056.1 conj	3617.1 conj	3620.2 partic	3474.1 verb 3sing indic pres act	1706.1 prep	1466.5 prs-pron dat 1sing	4969.1 verb
γὰρ	ὅτι	οὐκ	οἰκεῖ	ἐν	ἐμοί,	⸀ τουτέστιν
gar	hoti	ouk	oikei	en	emoi	toutestin
for	that	not	there dwells	in	me,	that is

3642.16 dem-pron sing neu	1498.4 verb 3sing indic pres act	1706.1 prep	3450.11 art dat sing fem	4418.3 noun dat sing fem	1466.2 prs-pron gen 1sing
[☆ τοῦτ'	ἔστιν]	ἐν	τῇ	σαρκί	μου,
tout'	estin	en	tē	sarki	mou
[that	is]	in	the	flesh	my,

18.3 adj sing	3450.16 art sing neu	1056.1 conj	2286.19 verb inf pres act	3734.1 verb 3sing indic pres	1466.4 prs-pron dat 1sing
ἀγαθόν·	τὸ	γὰρ	θέλειν	παράκειταί	μοι,
agathon	to	gar	thelein	parakeitai	moi
good:	the	for	to will	is present with	me,

3450.16 art sing neu	1156.2 conj	2686.7 verb inf pres	3450.16 art sing neu	2541.1 adj sing	3620.1 partic
τὸ	δὲ	κατεργάζεσθαι	τὸ	καλὸν	⸀ οὐχ
to	de	katergazesthai	to	kalon	ouch
the	but	to work out	the	right	not

2128.2 verb 1sing indic pres act	3620.3 partic	3620.3 partic	1056.1 conj	3614.16 rel-pron sing neu	2286.1 verb 1sing pres act
εὑρίσκω.	[a☆ οὔ]	**19.** οὐ	γὰρ	ὃ	θέλω
heuriskō	ou	ou	gar	ho	thelō
I find.	[not.]	Not	for	what	I will

18.a.Txt: 06D,018K 020L,025P,044,33,byz.it. Var: 01ℵ,02A,03B,04C sa.bo.Lach,Treg,Alf,Tisc We/Ho,Weis,Sod UBS/☆

4020.1 verb 1sing pres act	18.3 adj sing	233.1 conj	233.2 conj	3614.16 rel-pron sing neu	3620.3 partic
ποιῶ	ἀγαθόν·	⸀ ἀλλ'	[☆ ἀλλὰ]	ὃ	οὐ
poiō	agathon	all'	alla	ho	ou
do I practice	good;	but	[idem]	what	not

2286.1 verb 1sing pres act	2527.7 adj sing neu	3642.17 dem-pron sing neu	4097.1 verb 1sing indic pres act	1479.1 conj	1156.2 conj
θέλω	κακὸν,	τοῦτο	πράσσω.	**20.** εἰ	δὲ
thelō	kakon	touto	prassō	ei	de
I do will	evil,	this	I do.	If	but

devout Jews in their attempt to keep the Law which they reverenced so highly. (See *Overview*, pp.669-671.)

Very possibly there is a measure of truth in some if not all of the various interpretations; however, most evangelicals are inclined to agree with the first statement. It is certain that application can be made in every instance. The fact remains that this experience describes a man who struggles to be holy and good in his own strength but fails miserably because of sin's power.

The contrast between chapters 7 and 8 is most significant. In chapter 7 the pronoun "I" occurs 31 times (KJV) without one mention of the Holy Spirit, unless verse 6 refers to the newness *He* brings. Obviously "I" am struggling to do and completely failing for it is an attempt in my own strength. In chapter 8 the Holy Spirit is mentioned at least 20 times. In chapter 8 law is scarcely mentioned while there are 20 references to law in chapter 7.

The carnal Christian finds it impossible to behave the way God expects him to because he is in bondage to the flesh. The unbeliever has only one nature, the Adamic or human nature with which he was born. When he reaches the age of accountability he either immediately chooses to obey God by receiving Christ as Saviour, or he chooses to live according to that nature and becomes a literal sinner, a slave of Satan. If he rejects God's revelation to him he is then under the wrath of God (John 3:36). The only thing that keeps him out of hell at any moment is the mercy of God who is long-suffering, "not willing that any should perish" (2 Peter 3:9).

The believer has two natures. He has the nature with which he was born, the Adamic nature, which is unable to obey God's law. This nature is also called the "flesh" (verse 18), "carnal" (verse 14), the "I" that does what the new nature hates (verse 15), "the body of this death" (verse 24), the "old man" (6:6). This nature is to be reckoned dead; but it is not nonexistent, as any truthful believer can attest. In the Bible *death* never means annihilation, but always separation. When we died with Jesus (6:3-7), we were indeed separated from this nature, but it is a separation that depends on constant reckoning (6:11) and conscious yielding to the new nature (6:12-19). Just as in the case of the Law (verse 4), we died to the old nature, but the old nature itself did not die.

The believer has been made partaker of the "divine nature" (2 Peter 1:4), the "new man" (Colossians 3:10), the "I" that delights in the law of God (Romans 7:22) because of being crucified with Christ (Galatians 2:20).

Chapters 6 to 8 all deal with the believer's sanctification. Chapter 6 gives the machinery, chapter 7 describes the malfunction when the believer tries to "do it" himself, and chapter 8 shows the victory that comes by being led of the Spirit, trusting Him for actualization.

7:19,20. Paul had just stated that he had a will to do right. The predicament that he was describing could be that of a Jewish legalist trying to become holy by doing works of self-righteousness. It can also be that of any Christian who is trying by his own willpower

I consent unto the law that [it is] good: I agree that the Law is right, *Beck* . . . I admit that the Law is good, *Concordant* . . . that it is noble, *Fenton* . . . I concur in the excellence of the law, *HistNT*.

17. Now then it is no more I that do it: . . . it is no longer I who perform the action, *NEB*.

but sin that dwelleth in me: . . . sin which has its home within me, *Weymouth* . . . that lodges in me, *NEB*.

18. For I know that in me (that is, in my flesh,) dwelleth no good thing: I am well aware that, as far as my lower nature goes, *Barclay* . . . that is, in my human nature, *TEV* . . . in my unspiritual nature, *NEB* . . . in my sensuality, *Fenton* . . . does not live in me, *SEB*.

for to will is present with me; but [how] to perform that which is good I find not: I can will what is right, but I cannot do it, *RSV* . . . for though the will to do good is there, the deed is not, *NEB* . . . To will I find is attainable, *HistNT* . . . but I am not producing fine things, *Adams* . . . but not the power of doing what is right, *Moffatt* . . . the power to carry it out is not, *Weymouth* . . . but I fynde no meanes to performe that, *Tyndale, Geneva* . . . but I do not find the strength to accomplish what is good, *Confraternity* . . . but to accomplish that vvhich is good, *Rheims* . . . to avail myself of its benefit? *Fenton* . . . but to do it, I find difficult, *Campbell* . . . but to work the good, *Panin* . . . the power to do it I do not possess, *Barclay* . . . but to work out what is excellent I find not, *Wilson*.

19. For the good that I would I do not: I desire, *Alford* . . . I intend to do, *Montgomery* . . . I fail to do, *NEB*.

but the evil which I would not, that I do: I practice the bad I do not want to practice, *Berkeley* . . . that I habitually do, *TCNT* . . . I do wrong against my wishes, *Moffatt* . . . is what I constantly do, *Weymouth* . . . that I am ever practising, *Montgomery* . . . that I perform, *Confraternity*.

Romans 7:21

3614.16 rel-pron sing neu	3620.3 partic	2286.1 verb 1sing pres act	1466.1 prs-pron nom 1sing	3642.17 dem-pron sing neu	4020.1 verb 1sing pres act
ὅ	οὐ	θέλω	ἐγὼ,	τοῦτο	ποιῶ,
ho	ou	thelō	egō	touto	poiō
what	not	do will	I,	this	I practice,

20.a.Txt: 01ℵ,02A,044 bo.byz.
Var: 03B,04C,06D,010F 012G,104,1241,1506 2464

3629.1 adv	1466.1 prs-pron nom 1sing	2686.1 verb 1sing indic pres	840.15 prs-pron sing neu	233.1 conj
οὐκέτι	(a ἐγὼ)	κατεργάζομαι	αὐτὸ,	(ἀλλ'
ouketi	egō	katergazomai	auto	all'
no longer	I	work out	it,	but

233.2 conj	3450.9 art nom sing fem	3474.3 verb nom sing fem part pres act	1706.1 prep	1466.5 prs-pron dat 1sing
[✶ ἀλλὰ]	ἡ	οἰκοῦσα	ἐν	ἐμοὶ
alla	hē	oikousa	en	emoi
[idem]	the	dwelling	in	me

264.2 noun nom sing fem	2128.2 verb 1sing indic pres act	679.1 partic	3450.6 art acc sing masc	3414.4 noun acc sing masc
ἁμαρτία.	21. Εὑρίσκω	ἄρα	τὸν	νόμον
hamartia	Heuriskō	ara	ton	nomon
sin.	I find	then	the	law

3450.3 art dat sing	2286.14 verb dat sing masc part pres act	1466.5 prs-pron dat 1sing	4020.20 verb inf pres act	3450.16 art sing neu
τῷ	θέλοντι	ἐμοὶ	ποιεῖν	τὸ
tō	thelonti	emoi	poiein	to
the	desiring	to me	to practice	the

2541.1 adj sing	3617.1 conj	1466.5 prs-pron dat 1sing	3450.16 art sing neu	2527.7 adj sing neu	3734.1 verb 3sing indic pres
καλὸν,	ὅτι	ἐμοὶ	τὸ	κακὸν	παράκειται·
kalon	hoti	emoi	to	kakon	parakeitai
right,	that	me	the	evil	is present with.

4763.1 verb 1sing indic pres	1056.1 conj	3450.3 art dat sing	3414.3 noun dat sing masc	3450.2 art gen sing	2296.2 noun gen sing masc
22. συνήδομαι	γὰρ	τῷ	νόμῳ	τοῦ	θεοῦ
sunēdomai	gar	tō	nomō	tou	theou
I delight	for	in the	law		of God

2567.3 prep	3450.6 art acc sing masc	2059.1 prep gen	442.4 noun acc sing masc	984.2 verb 1sing indic pres act
κατὰ	τὸν	ἔσω	ἄνθρωπον·	23. βλέπω
kata	ton	esō	anthrōpon	blepō
according to	the	inward	man:	I see

1156.2 conj	2066.1 adj sing	3414.4 noun acc sing masc	1706.1 prep	3450.4 art dat pl	3166.4 noun dat pl neu	1466.2 prs-pron gen 1sing
δὲ	ἕτερον	νόμον	ἐν	τοῖς	μέλεσίν	μου
de	heteron	nomon	en	tois	melesin	mou
but	another	law	in	the	members	my

494.1 verb acc sing masc part pres mid	3450.3 art dat sing	3414.3 noun dat sing masc	3450.2 art gen sing	3426.2 noun gen sing masc
ἀντιστρατευόμενον	τῷ	νόμῳ	τοῦ	νοός
antistrateuomenon	tō	nomō	tou	noos
warring against	the	law	of the	mind

23.a.Var: 01ℵ,03B,06D 018K,025P,33,sa.bo. Treg,Alf,Tisc,We/Ho Weis,Sod,UBS/✶

1466.2 prs-pron gen 1sing	2504.1 conj	161.1 verb acc sing masc part pres act	1466.6 prs-pron acc 1sing	1706.1 prep
μου,	καὶ	αἰχμαλωτίζοντά	με	[a✶+ ἐν]
mou	kai	aichmalōtizonta	me	en
my,	and	leading captive	me	[in]

to be holy. The clue to the problem is in the emphasis on "I." The flesh thrives on what "I" can do and on what "I" do not do. No believer has to settle for fleshly efforts, bringing the wretched state of doing what he does not want to do. His deliverance is as near as Calvary.

If to know to do right was to do it, how easy life would be. Knowing what is right behavior does not necessarily make us perform correctly. Human resolution is inadequate. The human will, apart from the strength of the Holy Spirit, is destined to fail under pressure. In human nature there is a weakness in the will. And yet the will is an obstacle of God's own creation. He never violates that will; He never crosses the threshold of the door to man's will unless invited to do so.

The carnal believer finds himself at cross purposes, desiring two different patterns of life at the same time. He is trying to do the impossible—to serve two masters at the same time. He is allowing sin to dwell in him when he has actually been set free (6:16). It seems that he is unaware of the freedom that is his, just as some slaves lived on in slavery after the close of the Civil War because they did not know they were free.

7:21. We must keep this portion of Scripture in context if we are to interpret it correctly. The Holy Spirit desired to portray the flesh in all its hideousness and viciousness. Paul by inspiration of the Spirit was describing the misery of one who has not yet yielded to the deliverance provided and described in verses following (7:25; 8:1-4). He was not delineating what should be the normal experience of the believer. Chapter 6 had already made that clear.

The military motif of verse 13 is continued in verse 23. Paul stated that if he tried to overcome the "law in my members" with "the law of my mind," he could not have victory. Rather, the law of sin brought him into captivity; he was pitting his own strength against the flesh. In 8:2,3, he described the "law" that can give victory, "the law of the Spirit of life in Christ Jesus."

7:22,23. The apostle goes on to speak of the various laws which bring conflicting purposes and principles to bear upon him. They are four in number.

There is the "law of God" in which his better nature, his inner nature delights or takes "sympathetic pleasure." This is the moral law, written or unwritten.

There is the "law of sin" which is also called the "law of sin and death" (8:2). The entire human race came under the dominion of this law through the Fall in Eden. This law operates in the moral realm as the law of gravity acts in the physical realm. Unless its power is revoked by the "law of the Spirit" (8:2), it can only bring one down on a relentless march to hell.

There is the "law of my mind." "Mind" is variously rendered "will," "reason," "conscience." This is the moral sense in man.

20. Now if I do that I would not:

it is no more I that do it: . . . it is no longer I who am responsible for the results, *TCNT*.

but sin that dwelleth in me: . . . but sin living in me, *Beck* . . . that makes itself at home in me, *Berkeley*.

21. I find then a law: Consequently, *Worrell* . . . this seems to be the rule, *JB* . . . I discover this law, *Confraternity*.

that, when I would do good, evil is present with me: . . . when I intend to, *Montgomery* . . . when I have a will, *Douay* . . . that every single time I want to, *JB* . . . when I desire to do that which is good, *Alford* . . . it is easier for me to do wrong! *TCNT* . . . but wrong is all I can manage, *Moffatt* . . . is lying in ambush for me, *Weymouth* . . . is always in my way, *Williams* . . . evil is controlling me, *SEB* . . . lies near me, *Wilson* . . . close at hand, *PNT*.

22. For I delight in the law of God after the inward man: In my inmost self I dearly love God's Law, *JB* . . . for I consent gladly to the law of God, *Conybeare* . . . I gladly approve God's law, *HistNT* . . . all my sympathy is with the Law, *Weymouth* . . . in accordance with my better inner nature, *Williams*.

23. But I see another law in my members: . . . but I perceive a foreign law, *Fenton* . . . but I find a different law in my bodily faculties, *Montgomery* . . . and I behold another law, *Young* . . . but I see another power operating, *Williams* . . . I see a different law, *ASV, Panin*.

warring against the law of my mind: . . . battling against the principles which my reason dictates, *Berkeley* . . . rebelling against, *Geneva* . . . fighting against, *Douay* . . . operated by, *Williams*.

and bringing me into captivity: . . . and holding me captive, *Adams* . . . It is making me a prisoner to the sinful law, *SEB* . . . making me a prisoner of war, *Wuest* . . . and captivating me, *Scarlett, Wesley*.

3450.3 art dat sing	3414.3 noun dat sing masc	3450.10 art gen sing fem	264.1 noun fem	3450.3 art dat sing	1498.22 verb dat sing masc part pres act
τῷ	νόμῳ	τῆς	ἁμαρτίας	τῷ	ὄντι
tō	nomō	tēs	hamartias	tō	onti
to the	law	of the	sin	the	being

1706.1 prep	3450.4 art dat pl	3166.4 noun dat pl neu	1466.2 prs- pron gen 1sing	4856.1 adj nom sing masc	1466.1 prs- pron nom 1sing
ἐν	τοῖς	μέλεσίν	μου.	24. ταλαίπωρος	ἐγὼ
en	tois	melesin	mou.	talaipōros	egō
in	the	members	my.	Wretched	I

442.1 noun nom sing masc	4949.3 intr- pron nom sing	1466.6 prs- pron acc 1sing	4363.12 verb 3sing indic fut mid	1523.2 prep gen	3450.2 art gen sing
ἄνθρωπος·	τίς	με	ῥύσεται	ἐκ	τοῦ
anthrōpos	tis	me	rhusetai	ek	tou
man!	who	me	shall deliver	out of	the

4835.2 noun gen sing neu	3450.2 art gen sing	2265.2 noun gen sing masc	3642.1 dem- pron gen sing	2149.1 verb 1sing indic pres act
σώματος	τοῦ	θανάτου	τούτου;	25. ʿ εὐχαριστῶ
sōmatos	tou	thanatou	toutou;	eucharistō
body	of the	death	this?	I thank

25.a.Txt: 01א-org,02A
018K,020L,025P,byz.
Sod
Var: (01א-corr),03B
(04C-corr),(06D),(33),sa.
Lach,Treg,Alf,Tisc
We/Ho,Weis,UBS/⋆

5322.1 noun nom sing fem	1156.2 conj	3450.3 art dat sing	2296.3 noun dat sing masc	1217.2 prep	2400.2 name masc
[a⋆ χάρις	δὲ]	τῷ	θεῷ	διὰ	Ἰησοῦ
charis	de	tō	theō	dia	Iēsou
[thanks	and]	to	to God	through	Jesus

5382.2 name gen masc	3450.2 art gen sing	2935.2 noun gen sing masc	2231.2 prs- pron gen 1pl	679.1 partic	3631.1 conj	840.5 prs-pron nom sing masc
Χριστοῦ	τοῦ	κυρίου	ἡμῶν.	ἄρα	οὖν	αὐτὸς
Christou	tou	kuriou	hēmōn.	ara	oun	autos
Christ	the	Lord	our.	So	then	myself

1466.1 prs- pron nom 1sing	3450.3 art dat sing	3173.1 conj	3426.3 noun dat sing masc	1392.2 verb 1sing indic pres act	3414.3 noun dat sing masc
ἐγὼ	τῷ	μὲν	νοῒ	δουλεύω	νόμῳ
egō	tō	men	noi	douleuō	nomō
I	with the	indeed	mind	serve	law

2296.2 noun gen sing masc	3450.11 art dat sing fem	1156.2 conj	4418.3 noun dat sing fem	3414.3 noun dat sing masc	264.1 noun fem
θεοῦ·	τῇ	δὲ	σαρκὶ	νόμῳ	ἁμαρτίας.
theou	tē	de	sarki	nomō	hamartias.
God's;	with the	but	flesh	law	of sin.

3625.6 num card neu	679.1 partic	3431.1 adv	2601.1 noun sing neu	3450.4 art dat pl	1706.1 prep	5382.3 name dat masc
8:1. Οὐδὲν	ἄρα	νῦν	κατάκριμα	τοῖς	ἐν	Χριστῷ
Ouden	ara	nun	katakrima	tois	en	Christō
No	then	now	condemnation	to the	in	Christ

1.a.Txt: 01א-corr
06D-corr,018K,020L
025P,33,byz.
Var: 01א-org,03B
04C-corr,06D-org,sa.bo.
Gries,Lach,Treg,Alf
Word,Tisc,We/Ho,Weis
Sod,UBS/⋆

2400.2 name masc	3231.1 partic	2567.3 prep	4418.4 noun acc sing fem	3906.2 verb dat pl masc part pres act
Ἰησοῦ,	ʿa μὴ	κατὰ	σάρκα	περιπατοῦσιν,
Iēsou	mē	kata	sarka	peripatousin
Jesus,	not	according to	flesh	walking,

233.2 conj	2567.3 prep	4011.1 noun sing neu	3450.5 art sing masc	1056.1 conj	3414.1 noun nom sing masc
ἀλλὰ	κατὰ	πνεῦμα. ˋ	2. ὁ	γὰρ	νόμος
alla	kata	pneuma.	ho	gar	nomos
but	according to	Spirit.	The	for	law

There is the "law in my members." It wars against the law of the mind and brings man's faculties into captivity as a prisoner of "the law of sin." By this means "the law of sin" asserts itself. Mentally there is the desire to do right. Intellectual assent is given to the law of God. But the law of the members (bodily faculties, lower nature, or self) asserts itself. The eyes look with lust, the untamed tongue builds fires of evil through gossip, boasting, and evil speech (James 3), and the ears listen to that which is unedifying.

7:24. The gulf between the demands of the Law and the ability of the flesh to fulfill them is like a vast chasm which seems impossible to bridge. It results in a wail of anguish and a cry for help. "Wretched" is translated from *talaipōros* which carries the thought of being "wretched through the exhaustion of hard labor."

The words "the body of this death" seem to be an allusion to an ancient custom from days of horrible tyranny. At times a convicted criminal was bound face-to-face, hand to hand, to the corpse of his victim and forced to carry it, until he died of contagion from the putrid, decaying body. That is the result of the conflict described in the previous verses. From that wretched condition comes the cry of despair: "Who can rescue me," "who can save me," "who can set me free?"

7:25. Paul's answer is clear. Deliverance must come through Christ and, in turn, through yielding to the Holy Spirit, whose work is to produce the Christ life in those who receive Him. The chasm has been completely spanned. There is deliverance from the penalty of sin in the past as we believe and from the power of sin in the present as we walk by the law of the Spirit. Sin and Satan are conquered foes and the self-nature can also be brought into subjection.

The mind is willing, the flesh is weak, but the defeat described in chapter 7 yields to the victory of chapter 8, if we allow the law of the Spirit to reign.

8:1. This chapter puts the capstone on the doctrinal portion of the book. Vividly setting forth the life of triumph, the chapter begins with "no condemnation," ends with "no separation," and in between there is "no defeat." The work of the Holy Spirit is introduced. The Holy Spirit is referred to 19 times in Romans 8. The dominant theme is the victorious message of deliverance from sin by the power of the Holy Spirit.

The word *katakrima* ("condemnation") is often misunderstood; many take it to mean no more conviction for sin for believers. F.F. Bruce has well defined it as "punishment following sentence—in other words, penal servitude. There is no reason for those who are in Christ Jesus to serve sin as if they had never been pardoned and never been liberated from the prison-house of sin" (*Tyndale New Testament Commentaries*, 6:159).

to the law of sin which is in my members: . . . and subduynge me vnto the law of synne, *Cranmer* . . . that controls my bodily organs, *Berkeley* . . . which is in my bodily faculties, *Montgomery*.

24. O wretched man that I am!: What a miserable man I am! *Norlie* . . . Man of toils and troubles that I am, *Berkeley* . . . Vnhappie man that I am, *Rheims*.
who shall deliver me from the body of this death?: Who will rescue me, *Moffatt, Scarlett, Wilson* . . . from this slave of death? *Montgomery* . . . help me escape, *SEB* . . . from this death-burdened body? *Weymouth* . . . from this body which turns life into death, *Barclay* . . . from my own sinful body? *Norlie* . . . from this deadly carcase? *Fenton* . . . this body doomed to death? *Berkeley* . . . from this deadly lower nature? *Williams* . . . which is dragging me down to Death? *TCNT*.

25. I thank God through Jesus Christ our Lord: He does it through, *Beck* . . . God alone, through Jesus Christ, *NEB*.
So then with the mind I myself serve the law of God: This, then, is my condition, *TEV* . . . I myself, subject to God's law as a rational being, *NEB* . . . with the spiritual part of my nature, *Barclay*.
but with the flesh the law of sin: . . . but by my sensuality, *Fenton* . . . yet in my animal nature, *Montgomery* . . . yet, in my unspiritual nature, a slave to the law of sin, *NEB* . . . but my human nature is under sin's control, *Berkeley*.

1. [There is] therefore now no condemnation to them which are in Christ Jesus: Consequently, there is now, *Worrell* . . . For this very reason, *Berkeley* . . . there is no doom, *Moffatt* . . . no death sentence hanging over those, *Norlie* . . . not even one bit of, *Wuest* . . . no damnacion...who are in union, *TCNT*.
who walk not after the flesh, but after the Spirit: . . . and behave in no flesh-governed way, *Berkeley* . . . whiche wandren not aftir the fleisch, *Wyclif*.

Romans 8:3

2.a.**Txt:** 02A,04C-corr
06D,018K,020L,025P
byz.sa.Sod
Var: 01א,03B,Tisc
We/Ho,Weis

3450.2 art gen sing	4011.2 noun gen sing neu	3450.10 art gen sing fem	2205.2 noun gen sing fem	1706.1 prep	5382.3 name dat masc
τοῦ	πνεύματος	τῆς	ζωῆς	ἐν	Χριστῷ
tou	pneumatos	tēs	zōēs	en	Christō
of the	Spirit	of the	life	in	Christ

2400.2 name masc	1646.1 verb 3sing indic aor act	1466.6 prs-pron acc 1sing	4622.4 prs-pron acc 2sing	570.3 prep gen	3450.2 art gen sing
Ἰησοῦ	ἠλευθέρωσέν	[☆ με	[a σε]	ἀπὸ	τοῦ
Iēsou	ēleutherōsen	me	se	apo	tou
Jesus	set free	me	[you]	from	the

3414.2 noun gen sing masc	3450.10 art gen sing fem	264.1 noun fem	2504.1 conj	3450.2 art gen sing	2265.2 noun gen sing masc
νόμου	τῆς	ἁμαρτίας	καὶ	τοῦ	θανάτου.
nomou	tēs	hamartias	kai	tou	thanatou
law	of the	sin	and	of the	death.

3450.16 art neu	1056.1 conj	101.3 adj sing neu	3450.2 art gen sing	3414.2 noun gen sing masc	1706.1 prep
3. Τὸ	γὰρ	ἀδύνατον	τοῦ	νόμου,	ἐν
To	gar	adunaton	tou	nomou	en
The	for	powerless	the	law,	in

3614.3 rel-pron dat sing	764.16 verb 3sing indic imperf act	1217.2 prep	3450.10 art gen sing fem	4418.2 noun gen sing fem	3450.5 art sing masc
ᾧ	ἠσθένει	διὰ	τῆς	σαρκός,	ὁ
hō	ēsthenei	dia	tēs	sarkos	ho
that	it was weak	through	the	flesh,	

2296.1 noun nom sing masc	3450.6 art acc sing masc	1431.4 prs-pron gen 3sing	5048.4 noun acc sing masc	3854.11 verb nom sing masc part aor act
θεὸς	τὸν	ἑαυτοῦ	υἱὸν	πέμψας
theos	ton	heautou	huion	pempsas
God,	the	of himself	Son	having sent,

1706.1 prep	3530.1 noun dat sing neu	4418.2 noun gen sing fem	264.1 noun fem	2504.1 conj	3875.1 prep
ἐν	ὁμοιώματι	σαρκὸς	ἁμαρτίας	καὶ	περὶ
en	homoiōmati	sarkos	hamartias	kai	peri
in	likeness	of flesh	of sin,	and	for

264.1 noun fem	2602.4 verb 3sing indic aor act	3450.12 art acc sing fem	264.4 noun acc sing fem	1706.1 prep	3450.11 art dat sing fem
ἁμαρτίας	κατέκρινεν	τὴν	ἁμαρτίαν	ἐν	τῇ
hamartias	katekrinen	tēn	hamartian	en	tē
sin,	condemned	the	sin	in	the

4418.3 noun dat sing fem	2419.1 conj	3450.16 art sing neu	1339.1 noun sing neu	3450.2 art gen sing	3414.2 noun gen sing masc
σαρκί,	4. ἵνα	τὸ	δικαίωμα	τοῦ	νόμου
sarki	hina	to	dikaiōma	tou	nomou
flesh,	that	the	requirement	of the	law

3997.22 verb 3sing subj aor pass	1706.1 prep	2231.3 prs-pron dat 1pl	3450.4 art dat pl	3231.1 partic	2567.3 prep
πληρωθῇ	ἐν	ἡμῖν,	τοῖς	μὴ	κατὰ
plērōthē	en	hēmin,	tois	mē	kata
should be fulfilled	in	us,	the	not	according to

4418.4 noun acc sing fem	3906.2 verb dat pl masc part pres act	233.2 conj	2567.3 prep	4011.1 noun sing neu
σάρκα	περιπατοῦσιν,	ἀλλὰ	κατὰ	πνεῦμα.
sarka	peripatousin,	alla	kata	pneuma
flesh	walking,	but	according to	Spirit.

8:2. The deliverance from condemnation and the bondage of legalism is achieved through the operation of a new law, "the law of the Spirit of life in Christ Jesus," which is more powerful than the law of sin and death. Those who are "in Christ" have escaped the realm of the Law's condemnation and have a vantage point from which they can subdue the flesh.

The believer is positionally "in Christ Jesus" as a result of his union with Christ in death, burial, and resurrection (6:1-13). Notice three ways in which believers are "in Christ": (1) by birth as we were in Adam, we are born again in Christ (1 Corinthians 15:22; Romans 5:12-21); (2) vitally, as the branch is in the vine (John 15:1-7), or as all members are in the body (1 Corinthians 12:27; Ephesians 1:23); (3) by faith (Ephesians 3:17; Galatians 3:26,27).

8:3. Two words keep appearing again and again in this chapter: "flesh" (*sarx*) and "spirit" (*pneuma*). Paul often uses these words in his epistles. *Sarx* is used in three different ways. He speaks of literal flesh, such as physical circumcision, "in the flesh" (2:28). Then he speaks of *kata sarka*, or "according to the flesh," which means from the human point of view, such as the Jews were Jesus' *kata sarka*, or kinsmen (1:3). Such usage refers to human relationships (1:3; 9:3). The word is again used in a way peculiar to Paul, such as *en sark* (7:5; 8:4-6,8,9,12). In these instances he is not referring to our bodies, flesh and blood, but rather to human nature, dominated by the desires of the sinful, lower side of man's nature (Galatians 5:19-21).

The words "what the law could not do" could be rendered "the impossible (thing) of the Law." The Law was "weak through the flesh" in that it could do nothing with flesh except stir it up (7:7-14). It could condemn the sinner (3:19), but it could not stop his sinning. Christ Jesus could and did solve both problems.

He came "in flesh" (Romans 1:3; John 1:14), but not in *sinful* flesh. He "knew no sin" (2 Corinthians 5:21), even though He was fully human. He came in the *likeness* of sinful flesh; His flesh was not sinful flesh for there was no sin in Him (Hebrews 4:15).

Christ's mission was "for sin." He came and condemned sin through the Atonement. Jesus became the perfect sin offering when He took our nature, lived a sinless life that condemned sin in our lives, and then, nailed to the cross, took God's condemnation of sin. By this act, conceived in the counsels of eternity, sin's doom was pronounced, and God rejected its claim upon us.

8:4. "Righteousness" (*diakaiōma*) is used here in its most usual meaning as "righteous requirement." It is fulfilled in us by the One who lives within: "Christ in you, the hope of glory" (Colossians 1:27). The Law could not become flesh and live within us. Jesus became flesh, fulfilled the Law, and now lives in us. As we walk after the Spirit, we are "dead indeed unto sin" (6:11) and to self (8:8-10), and alive to God through Christ Jesus (6:11).

2. For the law of the Spirit of life in Christ Jesus: The rule, *Beck* ... the life-giving Spirit, *TCNT*.

hath made me free: ... hath delyuerid me fro, *Wyclif* ... liberated me, *Wilson*.

from the law of sin and death: ... from the rule of sin that kills, *Beck* ... that deals only with sin and death, *Weymouth*.

3. For what the law could not do, in that it was weak through the flesh: What the Law, weakened by the flesh, *Beck* ... because of the inability of the Law, *Fenton* ... For the law being powerless, *PNT* ... that which is an impossibility for the law, *Wuest* ... because of our unspiritual nature, *JB* ... as our earthly nature weakened its action, *TCNT* ... because it was made helpless, *Williams*.

God sending his own Son in the likeness of sinful flesh, and for sin: For God effected, *HistNT* ... in the guise of sinful flesh, *Moffatt* ... with a nature like man's sinful human nature, *SEB* ... in the similitude of, *Rheims* ... in a body like that of sinful human nature, *Weymouth* ... to atone for sin, *TCNT* ... as a sin-offering, *HistNT* ... who on account of sin, *Noyes* ... and, respecting sin, *Worrell*.

condemned sin in the flesh: He pronounced sentence upon sin in human nature, *Weymouth* ... overcame sin, *Conybeare*.

4. That the righteousness of the law: ... that the requirement of the law, *Worrell* ... in order to secure the fulfilment, *Moffatt* ... as righteous as the Law demands, *Beck* ... the Law's just demands, *JB* ... that the righteous ordinance of the law, *Sawyer*.

might be fulfilled in us: ... be satisfied, *JB* ... may be performed by us, *Sawyer*.

who walk not after the flesh, but after the Spirit: ... who do not live by the standard, *Williams* ... for our lives are regulated, *Weymouth* ... not in harmony with sensuality, *Fenton* ... not in a fleshly but in a spiritual way, *Berkeley* ... not as dominated by the sinful nature, *Wuest*.

Romans 8:5

3450.7 art pl masc	1056.1 conj	2567.3 prep	4418.4 noun acc sing fem	1498.23 verb nom pl masc part pres act	3450.17 art pl neu
5. Οἱ	γὰρ	κατὰ	σάρκα	ὄντες,	τὰ
Hoi	gar	kata	sarka	ontes	ta
The	for	according to	flesh	being,	the things

3450.10 art gen sing fem	4418.2 noun gen sing fem	5262.4 verb 3pl indic pres act	3450.7 art pl masc	1156.2 conj	2567.3 prep
τῆς	σαρκὸς	φρονοῦσιν·	οἱ	δὲ	κατὰ
tēs	sarkos	phronousin	hoi	de	kata
of the	flesh	mind;	the	and	according to

4011.1 noun sing neu	3450.17 art pl neu	3450.2 art gen sing	4011.2 noun gen sing neu	3450.16 art sing neu	1056.1 conj
πνεῦμα	τὰ	τοῦ	πνεύματος.	6. τὸ	γὰρ
pneuma	ta	tou	pneumatos	to	gar
Spirit,	the things	of the	Spirit.	The	for

5263.1 noun nom sing neu	3450.10 art gen sing fem	4418.2 noun gen sing fem	2265.1 noun nom sing masc	3450.16 art sing neu	1156.2 conj
φρόνημα	τῆς	σαρκὸς	θάνατος·	τὸ	δὲ
phronēma	tēs	sarkos	thanatos	to	de
mind	of the	flesh	death;	the	but

5263.1 noun nom sing neu	3450.2 art gen sing	4011.2 noun gen sing neu	2205.1 noun nom sing fem	2504.1 conj	1503.1 noun nom sing fem
φρόνημα	τοῦ	πνεύματος,	ζωὴ	καὶ	εἰρήνη.
phronēma	tou	pneumatos	zōē	kai	eirēnē
mind	of the	Spirit,	life	and	peace.

1354.1 conj	3450.16 art sing neu	5263.1 noun nom sing neu	3450.10 art gen sing fem	4418.2 noun gen sing fem	2171.1 noun nom sing fem
7. Διότι	τὸ	φρόνημα	τῆς	σαρκὸς	ἔχθρα
Dioti	to	phronēma	tēs	sarkos	echthra
Because	the	mind	of the	flesh	enmity

1519.1 prep	2296.4 noun acc sing masc	3450.3 art dat sing	1056.1 conj	3414.3 noun dat sing masc	3450.2 art gen sing	2296.2 noun gen sing masc
εἰς	θεόν·	τῷ	γὰρ	νόμῳ	τοῦ	θεοῦ
eis	theon	tō	gar	nomō	tou	theou
towards	God:	to the	for	law		of God

3620.1 partic	5131.7 verb 3sing indic pres pass	3624.1 adv	1056.1 conj	1404.4 verb 3sing indic pres	3450.7 art pl masc
οὐχ	ὑποτάσσεται,	οὐδὲ	γὰρ	δύναται·	8. οἱ
ouch	hupotassetai	oude	gar	dunatai	hoi
not	it is being subject;	neither	for	can it;	the

1156.2 conj	1706.1 prep	4418.3 noun dat sing fem	1498.23 verb nom pl masc part pres act	2296.3 noun dat sing masc	694.9 verb inf aor act
δὲ	ἐν	σαρκὶ	ὄντες,	θεῷ	ἀρέσαι
de	en	sarki	ontes	theō	aresai
and	in	flesh	being,	God	to please

3620.3 partic	1404.7 verb 3pl indic pres	5050.1 prs-pron nom 2pl	1156.2 conj	3620.2 partic	1498.6 verb 2pl indic pres act	1706.1 prep
οὐ	δύνανται.	9. Ὑμεῖς	δὲ	οὐκ	ἐστὲ	ἐν
ou	dunantai	Humeis	de	ouk	este	en
not	can.	You	but	not	are	in

4418.3 noun dat sing fem	233.1 conj	233.2 conj	1706.1 prep	4011.3 noun dat sing neu	1499.1 conj
σαρκὶ,	ʼ ἀλλʼ	[☆ ἀλλὰ]	ἐν	πνεύματι,	εἴπερ
sarki	all'	alla	en	pneumati	eiper
flesh,	but	[idem]	in	Spirit,	if indeed

122

8:5. This verse sets forth two classes of men. Those who live to the flesh and those who live to the Spirit are set in contrast. The believer does not have to walk after the flesh, but he can still allow the flesh to dominate his life.

Note the significance of the mind. We can know to what extent the old nature is influencing us by what our minds like to dwell on.

8:6. "Mind" (*phroneō*) occurs in verses 5 and 6. It means to have understanding, to feel or think, to direct the mind, to seek or strive for. The human mind is indeed difficult to define fully. Words are at times frail vehicles by which to convey the concepts of deep reality. The mind uses the brain, but it cannot be completely identified with the brain. The brain per se is not what is being discussed here; it is physical and is not necessarily changed by the new birth.

It could be said that the mind is the way the spirit of man uses the brain. Without the brain the mind cannot manifest itself. It is closely related to the basic attitude or stance in the heart (Romans 10:10; Proverbs 4:23; 23:7; Philippians 4:7; 1 Peter 3:4) or spirit of man (1 Corinthians 2:11; Hebrews 4:12).

"To be carnally minded" is literally the mind of the flesh. The noun *phronēma* is found only in Romans 8 (verses 6,7,27) and means the pattern of thought and motive, the interests and aims. The carnal mind is the mind dominated by the flesh.

"To be spiritually minded" is to have "the mind of Christ" (1 Corinthians 2:16). A renewed spirit will result in a renewed mind as we walk after the Spirit.

8:7-9. The carnal mind is an enemy to God and is in rebellion against the law of God. Therefore carnality will always bring God's displeasure and rob the believer of peace.

The law of sin and death is in operation in human nature, but that law is counteracted by the law of the Spirit of life. The presence of Christ within is a higher law than any other; it can permeate our motives and innermost desires.

The Law could not meet our need. In itself the Law was good, but man, being carnal, was without power to obey it. Someone has said that the anchor of the Law was strong in itself, but it could not hold firm in the soft earth of the heart. God did not change the principles of righteousness, but He made provision for changing human nature by sending forth a new spiritual power which was released through the atoning work of Jesus Christ. The Holy Spirit is able to produce a righteous life in us by Christ's work at Calvary.

We have died to the first Adam to be united to the last Adam. We have died to sin, the old master, to be raised with Christ, our new Master. We have died to the old husband, the Law, to "be married to another," our heavenly Bridegroom (7:4). "There is therefore now no condemnation."

5. For they that are after the flesh do mind the things of the flesh: . . . meditate about the gratification of their sensuality, *Fenton* . . . give their attention to the things, *Montgomery.*

but they that are after the Spirit the things of the Spirit: . . . have their interests in the Spirit, *Moffatt* . . . usually thinking the things suggested by the Spirit, *Williams* . . . are gostly mynded, *Tyndale.*

6. For to be carnally minded [is] death: For the inclination of the flesh, *Confraternity* . . . For the wisdom of the flesh, *Douay* . . . The way human nature thinks, *SEB* . . . to have the mind dominated, *Wuest* . . . to limit oneself to what is unspiritual, *JB.*

but to be spiritually minded [is] life and peace: . . . but the minding of the Spirit, *Sawyer.*

7. Because the carnal mind [is] enmity against God: . . . the mind of the flesh, *Panin* . . . which is interested only in carnal things, *Norlie* . . . worldly-mindedness is hostile to God, *Berkeley* . . . is an enemy against, *Klingensmith.*

for it is not subject to the law of God: . . . such a limitation never could and never does submit to God's law, *JB* . . . It refuses to obey God's Law, *Beck* . . . is not subordinate, *Scarlett.*

neither indeed can be: . . . for neither is it able, *Young.*

8. So then they that are in the flesh: So, those controlled by the flesh, *Berkeley* . . . they who are carnal, *Confraternity* . . . they who are earthly minded, *Montgomery* . . . they whose hearts are absorbed in, *Weymouth* . . . on the plane of the lower nature, *Williams* . . . controlled by human nature, *SEB* . . . who are in a Sensual state, *Wilson.*

cannot please God: . . . do not have the power, *Klingensmith* . . . are unable to please God, *Berkeley.*

9. But ye are not in the flesh, but in the Spirit: But you are not earthly, *Montgomery* . . . are not devoted to earthly, *Weymouth* . . . you are not Sensual, *Wilson.*

Romans 8:10

4011.1 noun sing neu	2296.2 noun gen sing masc	3474.1 verb 3sing indic pres act	1706.1 prep	5050.3 prs- pron dat 2pl	1479.1 conj	1156.2 conj
πνεῦμα	θεοῦ	οἰκεῖ	ἐν	ὑμῖν.	εἰ	δέ
pneuma	theou	oikei	en	humin	ei	de
Spirit	of God	dwells	in	you;	if	but

4948.3 indef- pron nom sing	4011.1 noun sing neu	5382.2 name gen masc	3620.2 partic	2174.4 verb 3sing indic pres act	3642.4 dem-pron nom sing masc
τις	πνεῦμα	Χριστοῦ	οὐκ	ἔχει,	οὗτος
tis	pneuma	Christou	ouk	echei	houtos
anyone	Spirit	of Christ	not	has,	this

3620.2 partic	1498.4 verb 3sing indic pres act	840.3 prs- pron gen sing	1479.1 conj	1156.2 conj	5382.1 name nom masc	1706.1 prep
οὐκ	ἔστιν	αὐτοῦ.	**10.** εἰ	δὲ	Χριστὸς	ἐν
ouk	estin	autou	ei	de	Christos	en
not	is	his:	if	but	Christ	in

5050.3 prs- pron dat 2pl	3450.16 art sing neu	3173.1 conj	4835.1 noun sing neu	3361.1 adj sing	1217.1 prep
ὑμῖν,	τὸ	μὲν	σῶμα	νεκρὸν	ʹ δι'
humin	to	men	sōma	nekron	di'
you,	the	indeed	body	dead	on account of

1217.2 prep	264.4 noun acc sing fem	3450.16 art sing neu	1156.2 conj	4011.1 noun sing neu	2205.1 noun nom sing fem
[✭ διὰ]	ἁμαρτίαν,	τὸ	δὲ	πνεῦμα	ζωὴ
dia	hamartian	to	de	pneuma	zōē
[idem]	sin,	the	but	Spirit	life

1217.2 prep	1336.4 noun acc sing fem	1479.1 conj	1156.2 conj	3450.16 art sing neu
διὰ	δικαιοσύνην.	**11.** εἰ	δὲ	τὸ
dia	dikaiosunēn	ei	de	to
on account of	righteousness.	If	but	the

11.a.Var: 01א,02A,03B Treg,Alf,Tisc,We/Ho Weis,Sod,UBS/✭

4011.1 noun sing neu	3450.2 art gen sing	1446.8 verb gen sing masc part aor act	3450.6 art acc sing masc	2400.3 name acc masc
πνεῦμα	τοῦ	ἐγείραντος	[a✭+ τὸν]	Ἰησοῦν
pneuma	tou	egeirantos	ton	Iēsoun
Spirit	the	having raised up		Jesus

1523.2 prep gen	3361.2 adj gen pl	3474.1 verb 3sing indic pres act	1706.1 prep	5050.3 prs- pron dat 2pl	3450.5 art sing masc
ἐκ	νεκρῶν	οἰκεῖ	ἐν	ὑμῖν,	ὁ
ek	nekrōn	oikei	en	humin	ho
from among	dead	dwells	in	you,	the

1446.7 verb nom sing masc part aor act	3450.6 art acc sing masc	5382.4 name acc masc	1523.2 prep gen	3361.2 adj gen pl
ἐγείρας	ʹ✭ τὸν	Χριστὸν	ἐκ	νεκρῶν
egeiras	ton	Christon	ek	nekrōn
having raised up	the	Christ	from among	dead

11.b.Txt: 01א-corr,018K 020L,025P,33,byz. Var: 01א-org,02A,Tisc We/Ho,UBS/✭

1523.2 prep gen	3361.2 adj gen pl	5382.4 name acc masc	2400.3 name acc masc	2210.5 verb 3sing indic fut act
[b ἐκ	νεκρῶν	Χριστὸν	Ἰησοῦν]	ζωοποιήσει
ek	nekrōn	Christon	Iēsoun	zōopoiēsei
[from among	dead	Christ	Jesus]	will quicken

2504.1 conj	3450.17 art pl neu	2326.4 adj acc pl neu	4835.4 noun pl neu	5050.2 prs- pron gen 2pl	1217.2 prep	3450.2 art gen sing
καὶ	τὰ	θνητὰ	σώματα	ὑμῶν	διὰ	ʹ τοῦ
kai	ta	thnēta	sōmata	humōn	dia	tou
also	the	mortal	bodies	your	through	the

Through union with the risen and glorified Saviour, a new power—the Holy Spirit—enters human nature to subdue sin. Through the Spirit the righteousness which the Law required is fulfilled in us (not *by* us), because we walk in yieldedness to the Spirit.

When our life is in Christ, He inspires new desires and new affections. A holy life gives evidence that our life is in Christ. Though a saved person can and at times may yield to the flesh, he is not "in the flesh," the domain of sin. He will not practice a walk in the flesh. The word "flesh" refers to the old, unrenewed sinful nature by which the unregenerate man lives. The life in the flesh can be lived by the cultured, educated, and refined, as well as the murderers, thieves, and harlots. Every Christian has the Spirit of Christ. At the moment of our new birth we were placed in Christ and He in us. This is the instant aspect of sanctification. This experience does not make it *impossible* for us to have fleshly attitudes or deeds, but it does make it possible for us *not* to have them.

The process by which we are being conformed to the image of Christ (verse 29) is the practical, continuing aspect of sanctification. The Holy Spirit is doing in us what He has done for us. We do not grow *into* sanctification, but we grow *in* sanctification.

All human activities that center around self are in the flesh. As the hub of our life changes from self to God we begin walking in the Spirit instead of in the flesh. The walk in the flesh brings death or separation from God. The carnal (fleshly) mind resents the will of God. It opposes God and loves to have self pampered and praised. No matter how good a person might be, no matter how benevolent one's work might be, if self has the center, such a person "cannot please God." But if the Spirit of God is in us, we are enabled to live above the desires of the flesh; if we do not have the Spirit of Christ we do not belong to God.

8:10,11. In verse 10 having "Christ in you" represents the same truth worded two different ways in the previous verse. Evidently, if the Spirit of God or the Spirit of Christ dwells within (verse 9), Christ himself resides in the believer. These verses, along with Acts 5:3,4 and Ephesians 3:16,17, are often cited as support for the doctrine of the trinity.

When Christ is in us we have "life"—even though our bodies are sentenced to die—because of the active principle of righteousness. The implanted righteousness of the Spirit possesses the human spirit, but physical death prevails over the body. Verse 23 shows that redemption of the body is a future hope. It is the culminating hope of every adopted child of God.

Each human being dies physically because of Adam's sin (Romans 5:12). However, verse 11 makes it clear that a greater power than that which brings death is resident in the believer, that is, the Holy Spirit. The bodily resurrection of believers is contingent upon Christ's own resurrection. Jesus was raised by the same Spirit that will one day redeem Christians. Meanwhile, He serves as the earnest or guarantee of our future redemption and inheritance.

if so be that the Spirit of God dwell in you: . . . is at home in you, *Berkeley* . . . has made his home in you, *JB* . . . is in residence in you, *Wuest.*

Now if any man have not the Spirit of Christ: But, assuming that a person does not have, *Wuest* . . . No one who does not possess the Spirit, *Barclay* . . . if one doth not profess, *Scarlett.*

he is none of his: . . . he does not belong to Him, *Berkeley* . . . he does not belong to Christ, *TCNT, SEB* . . . such a one does not belong to Him, *Weymouth* . . . he is not of him, *Wilson.*

10. And if Christ [be] in you: . . . if Christ lives in you, *Williams.*

the body [is] dead because of sin: . . . even though your body is dying (because of sin), *SEB* . . . though the body is a dead thing owing to Adam's sin, *Moffatt* . . . even though your bodies are going to die, *TEV* . . . the physical part of you may be doomed to death because of, *Barclay* . . . your body must die because of sin, *Norlie* . . . indeed, is dead, with respect to sin, *Campbell* . . . as a consequence of sin, *TCNT* . . . by reason of sin, *Alford, Confraternity* . . . because you were sinful, *Beck.*

but the Spirit [is] life because of righteousness: . . . your spirits are now enjoying life because of right standing, *Williams* . . . is destined for life because of the right relationship with God, *Barclay* . . . full of life because of righteousness, *Montgomery.*

11. But if the Spirit of him that raised up Jesus from the dead dwell in you: . . . is in residence in you, *Wuest.*

he that raised up Christ from the dead shall also quicken your mortal bodies: . . . will animate even, *Scarlett* . . . will make your dead bodies live, *SEB* . . . will revive your deadened bodies by His indwelling Spirit, *Fenton* . . . shall give life also, *ASV* . . . shall endow with life also your dying bodies, *Conybeare* . . . shall make alive also, *Panin* . . . also your dying bodies, *Young* . . . also make your dying bodily self live, *Montgomery.*

Romans 8:12

11.c.**Txt:** 03B,06D,018K
020L,025P-org,33,byz.it.
Steph,Weis
Var: 01א,02A,04C
025P-corr,sa.bo.Elzev
Tisc,We/Ho,Sod,UBS/⋆

1758.3 verb acc sing neu part pres act	840.3 prs-pron gen sing	4011.1 noun sing neu	3450.2 art gen sing	1758.2 verb gen sing neu part pres act
ἐνοικοῦν	αὐτοῦ	πνεῦμα	[ᶜ⋆ τοῦ	ἐνοικοῦντος
enoikoun	autou	pneuma	tou	enoikountos
indwelling	his	Spirit	[the	indwelling

840.3 prs-pron gen sing	4011.2 noun gen sing neu	1706.1 prep	5050.3 prs-pron dat 2pl		679.1 partic	3631.1 conj
αὐτοῦ	πνεύματος]	ἐν	ὑμῖν.	**12.**	Ἄρα	οὖν,
autou	pneumatos	en	humin		Ara	oun
his	Spirit]	in	you.		So	then,

79.6 noun pl masc	3645.2 noun nom pl masc	1498.5 verb 1pl indic pres act	3620.3 partic	3450.11 art dat sing fem	4418.3 noun dat sing fem
ἀδελφοί,	ὀφειλέται	ἐσμέν	οὐ	τῇ	σαρκὶ,
adelphoi	opheiletai	esmen	ou	tē	sarki
brothers,	debtors	we are,	not	to the	flesh,

3450.2 art gen sing	2567.3 prep	4418.4 noun acc sing fem	2180.19 verb inf pres act		1479.1 conj	1056.1 conj
τοῦ	κατὰ	σάρκα	ζῆν·	**13.**	εἰ	γὰρ
tou	kata	sarka	zēn		ei	gar
the	according to	flesh	to live;		if	for

2567.3 prep	4418.4 noun acc sing fem	2180.7 verb 2pl indic pres act	3165.5 verb 2pl indic pres act	594.8 verb inf pres act
κατὰ	σάρκα	ζῆτε,	μέλλετε	ἀποθνήσκειν·
kata	sarka	zēte	mellete	apothnēskein
according to	flesh	you live,	you are about	to die;

1479.1 conj	1156.2 conj	4011.3 noun dat sing neu	3450.15 art acc pl fem	4093.4 noun acc pl fem	3450.2 art gen sing	4835.2 noun gen sing neu
εἰ	δὲ	πνεύματι	τὰς	πράξεις	τοῦ	σώματος
ei	de	pneumati	tas	praxeis	tou	sōmatos
if	but	by Spirit	the	deeds	of the	body

2266.1 verb 2pl indic pres act	2180.31 verb 2pl indic fut mid		3607.2 rel-pron nom pl masc	1056.1 conj	4011.3 noun dat sing neu
θανατοῦτε,	ζήσεσθε.	**14.**	Ὅσοι	γὰρ	πνεύματι
thanatoute	zēsesthe		Hosoi	gar	pneumati
you put to death,	you will live:		as many as	for	by Spirit

2296.2 noun gen sing masc	70.20 verb 3pl indic pres pass	3642.7 dem-pron nom pl masc	1498.7 verb 3pl indic pres act	5048.6 noun pl masc
θεοῦ	ἄγονται,	οὗτοι	‘ εἰσιν	υἱοὶ
theou	agontai	houtoi	eisin	huioi
of God	are being led,	these	are	sons

2296.2 noun gen sing masc	5048.6 noun pl masc	2296.2 noun gen sing masc	1498.7 verb 3pl indic pres act	3620.3 partic	1056.1 conj
θεοῦ.	[⋆ υἱοὶ	θεοῦ	εἰσιν.]	**15.** οὐ	γὰρ
theou	huioi	theou	eisin	ou	gar
of God.	[sons	of God	are.]	Not	for

2956.16 verb 2pl indic aor act	4011.1 noun sing neu	1391.1 noun gen sing fem	3687.1 adv	1519.1 prep	5238.4 noun acc sing masc
ἐλάβετε	πνεῦμα	δουλείας	πάλιν	εἰς	φόβον,
elabete	pneuma	douleias	palin	eis	phobon
you received	a spirit	of bondage	again	unto	fear,

233.1 conj	233.2 conj	2956.16 verb 2pl indic aor act	4011.1 noun sing neu	5047.2 noun gen sing fem
‘ ἀλλ’	[⋆ ἀλλὰ]	ἐλάβετε	πνεῦμα	υἱοθεσίας,
all'	alla	elabete	pneuma	huiothesias
but	[idem]	you received	a Spirit	of adoption,

Verses 10 and 11, contrast the human body and the spirit. The body dies physically because of Adam's sin, but the spirit indwelt by the Holy Spirit becomes a living power. The indwelling Spirit is a guarantee of a future bodily resurrection. Not only are we delivered from the law of sin (verses 3-8), we shall be delivered from the law of death.

8:12. With the gracious privilege of having Christ in our lives, there come certain obligations—"we are debtors." There is danger if we live according to the flesh after what God has done for us. It is to court disaster.

8:13. To allow the things of the world to completely dominate one's life is spiritual suicide. This verse is perhaps the clearest, most concise statement of the way a person once in grace can lose his salvation. John Murray is basically Calvinistic in his theology, but in commenting on 8:13 he states: "Paul is speaking here to believers and to them he says, 'If ye live after the flesh, ye shall die.' The death referred to must be understood in its broadest scope and does not stop short of death in its ultimate manifestation, eternal separation from God" (*New International Commentary on the New Testament*, 1:293).

The believer finds his victory in Christ by the power of the Holy Spirit. Nothing is owed to the flesh. It is to have no more control. He is to mortify the deeds of the body. *Thanatoō* means to "put to death, destroy, render extinct."

8:14,15. To be led of the Spirit is to live a normal Christian life. By following the Spirit's leading we realize and prove our sonship. It is God's purpose that all New Testament saints are to be the "sons of God." But some turn "again to the weak and beggarly elements, whereunto . . . (they) desire again to be in bondage" (Galatians 4:9).

Servants obey because they are subject to rules; sons of God obey because they are led by the Spirit into a clear realization that the Father's will is the best possible way. Like their Elder Brother they delight to do God's will.

Jesus did not come to give us a system by which we could live; He came to be our life. The Holy Spirit bears unmistakable witness to our spirit that we are children of God. The new birth (John 3:3-6) gives spiritual life; the adoption as sons guarantees privileges of sonship.

If we are to live a victorious life, there must be a definite assurance of our standing in grace and of our relationship to God. Unbelievers may call on God in times of calamity, but only a son can truly pray, "Our Father."

by his Spirit that dwelleth in you: . . . by his Spirit that keeps house in you, *Klingensmith.*

12. Therefore, brethren, we are debtors, not to the flesh, to live after the flesh: Accordingly, then, *Worrell* . . . bound not to the Flesh, *Conybeare* . . . we don't owe it, *Beck* . . . we are under no obligation to our earthly nature, that we should live in obedience to it, *TCNT* . . . bound to follow the standards set by our fleshly natures, *Norlie.*

13. For if ye live after the flesh: . . . if you go on living according to the flesh, *Montgomery.*

ye shall die: . . . you are on the road to death, *Moffatt* . . . death awaits you, *HistNT* . . . you are doomed to die, *Conybeare.*

but if ye through the Spirit do mortify the deeds of the body: . . . by the helpe of the sprite, *Tyndale* . . . you deaden the practices of the body, *Berkeley* . . . kill the evil deeds, *SEB* . . . you put an end to the misdeeds, *JB* . . . you kill the activities of, *Beck* . . . you destroy the practices of sensuality, *Fenton* . . . through being under the sway of the spirit, you are putting your old bodily habits to death, *Weymouth.*

ye shall live: . . . you will attain to life, *Conybeare.*

14. For as many as are led by the Spirit of God, they are the sons of God: All who are moved by God's Spirit, *Beck* . . . All who are guided by, *TCNT, Williams.*

15. For ye have not received the spirit of bondage again to fear: . . . you do not have a sense of servitude to fill you with dread again, *Williams* . . . that would re-enslave you to fear, *Berkeley* . . . received no slavish spirit that would make you relapse into fear, *Moffatt* . . . to fall back into fear, *RSV* . . . to fill you once more, *TCNT* . . . with terror, *Weymouth* . . . leading back unto fear, *Alford.*

but ye have received the Spirit of adoption: Who adopts you, *Adams* . . . who places you as adult sons, *Wuest.*

1706.1 prep	3614.3 rel-pron dat sing	2869.2 verb 1pl indic pres act	5.2 noun voc sing masc	3450.5 art sing masc	3824.1 noun nom sing masc
ἐν	ᾧ	κράζομεν,	Ἀββα,	ὁ	πατήρ.
en	*hō*	*krazomen*	*Abba*	*ho*	*patēr*
by	which	we cry,	Abba,		Father.

840.15 prs-pron sing neu	3450.16 art sing neu	4011.1 noun sing neu	4679.1 verb 3sing indic pres act	3450.3 art dat sing
16. Αὐτὸ	τὸ	πνεῦμα	συμμαρτυρεῖ	τῷ
Auto	*to*	*pneuma*	*summarturei*	*tō*
Itself	the	Spirit	bears witness with	the

4011.3 noun dat sing neu	2231.2 prs-pron gen 1pl	3617.1 conj	1498.5 verb 1pl indic pres act	4891.4 noun pl neu	2296.2 noun gen sing masc
πνεύματι	ἡμῶν,	ὅτι	ἐσμὲν	τέκνα	θεοῦ.
pneumati	*hēmōn*	*hoti*	*esmen*	*tekna*	*theou*
spirit	our,	that	we are	children	of God.

1479.1 conj	1156.2 conj	4891.4 noun pl neu	2504.1 conj	2791.3 noun nom pl masc	2791.3 noun nom pl masc
17. εἰ	δὲ	τέκνα,	καὶ	κληρονόμοι·	κληρονόμοι
ei	*de*	*tekna*	*kai*	*klēronomoi*	*klēronomoi*
If	and	children,	also	heirs:	heirs

3173.1 conj	2296.2 noun gen sing masc	4640.1 adj nom pl masc	1156.2 conj	5382.2 name gen masc	1499.1 conj
μὲν	θεοῦ,	συγκληρονόμοι	δὲ	Χριστοῦ,	εἴπερ
men	*theou*	*sunklēronomoi*	*de*	*Christou*	*eiper*
indeed	of God,	joint heirs	and	of Christ;	if indeed

4692.2 verb 1pl indic pres act	2419.1 conj	2504.1 conj	4738.1 verb 1pl subj aor pass
συμπάσχομεν,	ἵνα	καὶ	συνδοξασθῶμεν.
sumpaschomen	*hina*	*kai*	*sundoxasthōmen*
we suffer together,	that	also	we may be glorified together.

3023.2 verb 1sing indic pres	1056.1 conj	3617.1 conj	3620.2 partic	510.6 adj pl neu	3450.17 art pl neu	3667.2 noun pl neu
18. Λογίζομαι	γὰρ	ὅτι	οὐκ	ἄξια	τὰ	παθήματα
Logizomai	*gar*	*hoti*	*ouk*	*axia*	*ta*	*pathēmata*
I reckon	for	that	not	worthy	the	sufferings

3450.2 art gen sing	3431.1 adv	2511.2 noun gen sing masc	4242.1 prep	3450.12 art acc sing fem	3165.16 verb acc sing fem part pres act
τοῦ	νῦν	καιροῦ	πρὸς	τὴν	μέλλουσαν
tou	*nun*	*kairou*	*pros*	*tēn*	*mellousan*
of the	now	time	with	the	being about

1385.4 noun acc sing fem	596.10 verb inf aor pass	1519.1 prep	2231.4 prs-pron acc 1pl	3450.9 art nom sing fem	1056.1 conj
δόξαν	ἀποκαλυφθῆναι	εἰς	ἡμᾶς.	**19.** Ἡ	γὰρ
doxan	*apokaluphthēnai*	*eis*	*hēmas*	*Hē*	*gar*
glory	to be revealed	to	us.	The	for

598.1 noun nom sing fem	3450.10 art gen sing fem	2909.2 noun gen sing fem	3450.12 art acc sing fem	597.4 noun acc sing fem
ἀποκαραδοκία	τῆς	κτίσεως	τὴν	ἀποκάλυψιν
apokaradokia	*tēs*	*ktiseōs*	*tēn*	*apokalupsin*
earnest expectation	of the	creation	the	revelation

3450.1 art gen pl	5048.7 noun gen pl masc	3450.2 art gen sing	2296.2 noun gen sing masc	549.1 verb 3sing indic pres	3450.11 art dat sing fem
τῶν	υἱῶν	τοῦ	θεοῦ	ἀπεκδέχεται.	**20.** τῇ
tōn	*huiōn*	*tou*	*theou*	*apekdechetai*	*tē*
of the	sons		of God	awaits;	to the

8:16. Not all men are children of God. The liberals' teaching of the brotherhood of man and the fatherhood of God is a doctrine that is foreign to Scripture (John 8:44; 1 John 3:10). On the contrary, how wonderful is sonship. By and through Christ is the only way to be brought into the family of God.

The knowledge of sonship comes through the witness of the Holy Spirit. It is not necessary for us to tell people they are saved; that is the Spirit's prerogative. The Spirit makes our position as sons (literally, "adult sons") real to us as believers.

The word *tekna* is used here, while *huioi* appears in verse 14. *Tekna* refers to children; *huioi* to sons. The words are used interchangeably.

The King James translation, "the Spirit itself," is better rendered "the Spirit himself," for He is a person.

8:17. The apostle points out another great privilege. Because believers are children of God, they are "heirs of God, and joint-heirs with Christ." The saints are called "joint-heirs with Christ" because God "hath in these last days spoken unto us by his Son, whom he hath appointed heir of all things" (Hebrews 1:2). The words *inheritance, inherit, heir,* and *joint heir* are all from the same root in the Greek. The believers' joint-heirship with Christ begins at once and includes suffering with Him in this present time, as well as glory with Him at His return. If we are to enter into our "adoption," or rights and privileges, we must accept the whole inheritance, suffering as well as glory (John 15:19,20). All that belongs to Christ as the Firstborn belongs to His brethren as well, and this includes both a dark and a bright side. It was necessary for Him to suffer to enter into His glory (Luke 24:26; Acts 17:3). We are joint heirs, "if so be that we suffer with him." To wear the crown, we must share the Cross.

8:18. The trials of those who are the sons of God are not inconsistent with the ultimate glory of those who are "in Christ Jesus," and that theme is dominant in the entire chapter. The trials are limited to the "present time." It is noteworthy that this passage which begins with glory and ends with glory, in between deals with suffering. The believer in his suffering is hemmed by glory. The suffering is so minor in comparison with the greatness of the glory, that there is no real comparison. Think of Hebrews 11:35-38 in that light.

8:19,20. When God's sons are unveiled, the whole creation, now groaning under the bondage of sin, will be redeemed. Dominion over a renewed creation, lost in Adam, will be restored to the redeemed race.

whereby we cry, Abba, Father: . . . by which we shout, *Klingensmith.*

16. The Spirit itself beareth witness with our spirit: . . . the Spirit him self, giueth testimonie to our spirit, *Rheims* . . . This Spirit assures, *Beck* . . . The same sprete certifyeth, *Cranmer* . . . bears witness jointly with our spirits, *Berkeley* . . . is a co-witness, *Sawyer.*

that we are the children of God:

17. And if children, then heirs; heirs of God, and joint-heirs with Christ: And if sonnes...co-heires of Christ, *Rheims* . . . in fact, God's heirs, *Berkeley* . . . who share Christ's inheritance with Him, *Beck.*

if so be that we suffer with [him], that we may be also glorified together: . . . we have a share in His sufferings, *Norlie* . . . so that we may also enjoy glory jointly, *Berkeley.*

18. For I reckon that the sufferings of this present time: I confirme, that the afflictions, *Geneva* . . . I have come to a reasoned conclusion, *Wuest* . . . what we suffer now isn't important, *Beck* . . . this temporal suffering is of no account, *Berkeley.*

[are] not worthy [to be compared] with the glory which shall be revealed in us: . . . is a mere nothing, *Moffatt* . . . are of no weight, *Wuest* . . . are of no account in comparison, *Alford, Worrell* . . . which will soon be unveiled to us, *Montgomery.*

19. For the earnest expectation of the creature waiteth for the manifestation of the sons of God: For in eager anticipation, *HistNT* . . . For all nature is expectantly waiting for the unveiling, *Williams* . . . the feruent desire, *Geneva* . . . the eager longing of creation, *Confraternity* . . . gazing eagerly as if with outstretched neck, *Weymouth* . . . is waiting for the revelation of, *Worrell* . . . is waiting on tiptoe to see the unveiling of God's family, *Beck* . . . the making plain, *Klingensmith.*

Romans 8:21

1056.1 conj	3125.2 noun dat sing fem	3450.9 art nom sing fem	2909.1 noun nom sing fem	5131.16 verb 3sing indic aor pass	3620.1 partic
γὰρ	ματαιότητι	ἡ	κτίσις	ὑπετάγη,	οὐχ
gar	*mataiotēti*	*hē*	*ktisis*	*hupetagē*	*ouch*
for	vanity	the	creation	was subjected,	not

1622.2 adj nom sing fem	233.2 conj	1217.2 prep	3450.6 art acc sing masc	5131.5 verb acc sing masc part aor act
ἑκοῦσα	ἀλλὰ	διὰ	τὸν	ὑποτάξαντα,
hekousa	*alla*	*dia*	*ton*	*hupotaxanta*
willingly,	but	by reason of	the	having subjected,

21.a.Txt: p46,02A,03B 04C,06D-corr,018K 020L,025P,33,etc.byz. Lach,We/Ho,Sod
Var: 01ℵ,06D-org,Tisc Weis,UBS/☆

1894.2 prep	1894.1 prep	1667.5 noun dat sing fem	3617.1 conj	1354.1 conj	2504.1 conj
ʽ ἐπ'	[☆ ἐφ']	ἐλπίδι	**21.** ʽ☆ ὅτι	[a διότι]	καὶ
ep'	*eph'*	*helpidi*	*hoti*	*dioti*	*kai*
in	[idem]	hope	that	[because]	also

840.9 prs-pron nom sing fem	3450.9 art nom sing fem	2909.1 noun nom sing fem	1646.5 verb 3sing indic fut pass	570.3 prep gen
αὐτὴ	ἡ	κτίσις	ἐλευθερωθήσεται	ἀπὸ
autē	*hē*	*ktisis*	*eleutherōthēsetai*	*apo*
itself	the	creation	shall be freed	from

3450.10 art gen sing fem	1391.1 noun gen sing fem	3450.10 art gen sing fem	5193.2 noun gen sing fem	1519.1 prep	3450.12 art acc sing fem
τῆς	δουλείας	τῆς	φθορᾶς	εἰς	τὴν
tēs	*douleias*	*tēs*	*phthoras*	*eis*	*tēn*
the	bondage	of the	corruption	into	the

1644.4 noun acc sing fem	3450.10 art gen sing fem	1385.2 noun gen sing fem	3450.1 art gen pl	4891.5 noun gen pl neu	3450.2 art gen sing
ἐλευθερίαν	τῆς	δόξης	τῶν	τέκνων	τοῦ
eleutherian	*tēs*	*doxēs*	*tōn*	*teknōn*	*tou*
freedom	of the	glory	of the	children	

2296.2 noun gen sing masc	3471.5 verb 1pl indic perf act	1056.1 conj	3617.1 conj	3820.9 adj nom sing fem	3450.9 art nom sing fem
θεοῦ.	**22.** οἴδαμεν	γὰρ	ὅτι	πᾶσα	ἡ
theou	*oidamen*	*gar*	*hoti*	*pasa*	*hē*
of God.	We know	for	that	all	the

2909.1 noun nom sing fem	4811.1 verb 3sing indic pres act	2504.1 conj	4796.1 verb 3sing indic pres act	884.2 conj	3450.2 art gen sing
κτίσις	συστενάζει	καὶ	συνωδίνει	ἄχρι	τοῦ
ktisis	*sustenazei*	*kai*	*sunōdinei*	*achri*	*tou*
creation	groans together	and	travails together	until	the

3431.1 adv	3620.3 partic	3303.1 adv	1156.2 conj	233.2 conj	2504.1 conj	840.7 prs-pron nom pl masc
νῦν·	**23.** οὐ	μόνον	δέ,	ἀλλὰ	καὶ	αὐτοὶ
nun	*ou*	*monon*	*de*	*alla*	*kai*	*autoi*
now.	Not	only	and,	but	even	ourselves

3450.12 art acc sing fem	532.2 noun acc sing fem	3450.2 art gen sing	4011.2 noun gen sing neu	2174.19 verb nom pl masc part pres act	2504.1 conj
τὴν	ἀπαρχὴν	τοῦ	πνεύματος	ἔχοντες,	ʽ καὶ
tēn	*aparchēn*	*tou*	*pneumatos*	*echontes*	*kai*
the	first fruit	of the	Spirit	having,	also

23.a.Txt: 018K,020L 025P,byz.
Var: 01ℵ,02A,04C,Lach Treg,Alf,Tisc,We/Ho Sod,UBS/☆

2231.1 prs-pron nom 1pl	2231.1 prs-pron nom 1pl	2504.1 conj	840.7 prs-pron nom pl masc	1706.1 prep	1431.7 prs-pron dat pl masc
ἡμεῖς	[a☆ ἡμεῖς	καὶ]	αὐτοὶ	ἐν	ἑαυτοῖς
hēmeis	*hēmeis*	*kai*	*autoi*	*en*	*heautois*
we	[we	also]	ourselves	in	ourselves

The vegetable kingdom involved in the curse, since the temptation in Eden related to a tree, will be delivered. The animal kingdom involved, since the Fall was introduced by a serpent, will be set free. All of the earth came under the curse because man relinquished his God-given dominion to Satan. The creation was thus made subject to pain and futility "not willingly." Animals and vegetables did not sin, but God "subjected" them "in hope" that man will learn that all sin exacts too great a price. The entire human family awaits the lifting of the curse. When that comes all creation will be delivered. The whole creation is now on "tiptoe" awaiting the completion of redemption.

8:21. "Delivered" and "liberty" are from the same root in the Greek. The whole creation will gain the glorious freedom of God's children when His children are glorified. Creation will be rescued from the tyranny of change and decay. James 1:18 expresses the thought: "Of his own will begat he us with the word of truth, that we should be a kind of firstfruits of his creatures." Creation will be delivered from corruption, decay, and ruin.

8:22. Two compound verbs are found only here in the New Testament: *sustenazō* means "groan together"; *sunōdinō* means "travail together." "Together" refers to all the elements of creation having a common longing, a common groaning. The following passages present the thought of nature's cry: Psalm 98:7; Isaiah 35:1; Hosea 2:21. The transformation that will take place at the time of that deliverance is revealed in Psalms 96:11-13; 98:7-9; Isaiah 11:6-9; 65:20. The whole world of nature sighs for release from the agony of the ages, convulsing in birth pangs and awaiting deliverance. As a woman in travail has the hope of bearing her child, creation groans in hope. The groaning is not that of death throes, but of birth. That gives meaning to the cry of travail which nature now endures.

8:23. The pains of birth are not only the experience of "dumb" creation, but Christians groan awaiting the redemption of the body. The obstetric metaphor used by Paul in one other passage (Galatians 4:19) illustrates how God's children and all creation are in the hour of labor, but the anguish will all be forgotten in the day of glory (John 16:21).

Present distress will give way to future glory when the curse is lifted. God's people are His sons. They have the Spirit. Sonship and Spirit are inseparably entwined in this chapter (verses 9,14). Sons of God have the Holy Spirit. That possession is a promise of the harvest yet to come as stated concerning those who await the resurrection: "Christ the firstfruits; afterward they that are Christ's at his coming" (1 Corinthians 15:23).

20. For the creature was made subject to vanity: Nature must waste away, *Beck* ... had to submit to imperfection, *TCNT* ... was tied to worthlessness, *SEB* ... was subjected to failure, *Norlie* ... under the bondage of transitoriness, *Berkeley* ... to a perishable condition, *Sawyer* ... to frailty, *Wilson*.

not willingly, but by reason of him who hath subjected [the same] in hope: It was not for any fault on the part of creation, *JB* ... not from choice, *Berkeley* ... not voluntarily, *PNT*.

21. Because the creature itself also:

shall be delivered from: ... shall be liberated from the enslavement, *Berkeley* ... will be set free from, *Adams* ... will be emancipated from, *Wilson*.

the bondage of corruption: ... from the seruitude, *Rheims* ... from its enslavement to corruption, *TCNT* ... from the slavery of decay, *SEB* ... from the bondage of a perishing state, *Campbell* ... from the thraldom of decay, *Montgomery*.

into the glorious liberty of the children of God:

22. For we know that the whole creation groaneth and travaileth in pain together until now: We are conscious, somehow, *Norlie* ... euery creature, *Rheims* ... the entire creation sighs and throbs with pain, *Moffatt* ... creation is to this day sighing and in throes in unison, *Berkeley* ... and laboureth in pain, *Scarlett* ... travailing together until this hour, *Montgomery* ... up to this very hour, *TCNT* ... up to this moment, *Wuest*.

23. And not only [they], but ourselves also:

which have the firstfruits of the Spirit: ... the Spirit whom we have is our first taste of heaven, *Beck* ... who enjoy the Spirit as a foretaste of the future, *Williams* ... pledge of the glorious future, *Weymouth*.

even we ourselves groan within ourselves: ... also groan inwardly, *Adams* ... groan with pain also, *SEB*.

23.b.**Var:** p46-vid,06D
010F,012G,614

4578.1 verb 1pl
indic pres act
στενάζομεν,
stenazomen
groan,

5047.3 noun
acc sing fem
⟨ᵇ υἱοθεσίαν ⟩
huiothesian
adoption

549.3 verb nom
pl masc part pres
ἀπεκδεχόμενοι,
apekdechomenoi
awaiting

3450.12 art
acc sing fem
τὴν
tēn
the

623.3 noun
acc sing fem
ἀπολύτρωσιν
apolutrōsin
redemption

3450.2 art
gen sing
τοῦ
tou
of the

4835.2 noun
gen sing neu
σώματος
sōmatos
body

2231.2 prs-
pron gen 1pl
ἡμῶν.
hēmōn
our.

24. **3450.11** art
dat sing fem
τῇ
tē
In the

1056.1 conj
γὰρ
gar
for

1667.3 noun
dat sing fem
ἐλπίδι
elpidi
hope

4834.23 verb 1pl
indic aor pass
ἐσώθημεν·
esōthēmen
we were saved;

1667.1 noun
nom sing fem
ἐλπὶς
elpis
hope

1156.2 conj
δὲ
de
but

984.24 verb nom sing
fem part pres pass
βλεπομένη
blepomenē
being seen

3620.2 partic
οὐκ
ouk
not

1498.4 verb 3sing
indic pres act
ἔστιν
estin
is

1667.1 noun
nom sing fem
ἐλπίς·
elpis
hope;

3614.16 rel-
pron sing neu
ὃ
ho
what

1056.1 conj
γὰρ
gar
for

984.4 verb 3sing
indic pres act
βλέπει
blepei
sees

4948.3 indef-
pron nom sing
τις
tis
anyone

24.a.**Txt:** 01ℵ-corr2,02A
04C,044,sa.byz.
Var: p46-vid,03B-org
1739,bo.

24.b.**Txt:** p46,02A,03B
06D,012G,044,33,81
614,1739-org
Var: 01ℵ-org,1739-mg

4949.9 intr-
pron sing neu
⟨ᵃ τί
ti
why

2504.1 conj
καὶ ⟩
kai
also

1666.2 verb 3sing
indic pres act
⟨✶ ἐλπίζει;
elpizei
does he hope for?

5116.3 verb 3sing
indic pres act
[ᵇ ὑπομένει;]
hupomenei
[is awaiting?]

25. **1479.1** conj
εἰ
ei
If

1156.2 conj
δὲ
de
but

3614.16 rel-
pron sing neu
ὃ
ho
what

3620.3 partic
οὐ
ou
not

984.5 verb 1pl
indic pres act
βλέπομεν
blepomen
we see

1666.3 verb 1pl
indic pres act
ἐλπίζομεν,
elpizomen
we hope for,

1217.1 prep
δι'
di'
in

5119.2 noun
gen sing fem
ὑπομονῆς
hupomonēs
endurance

549.2 verb
1pl indic pres
ἀπεκδεχόμεθα.
apekdechometha
we await.

26. **5447.1** adv
Ὡσαύτως
Hōsautōs
In like manner

1156.2 conj
δὲ
de
and

2504.1 conj
καὶ
kai
also

3450.16 art
sing neu
τὸ
to
the

4011.1 noun
sing neu
πνεῦμα
pneuma
Spirit

4729.1 verb
3sing indic pres
συναντιλαμβάνεται
sunantilambanetai
jointly helps

3450.14 art
dat pl fem
⟨ ταῖς
tais
the

763.6 noun
dat pl fem
ἀσθενείαις
astheneiais
weaknesses

26.a.**Txt:** 018K,020L
025P,byz.bo.
Var: 01ℵ,02A,03B,04C
06D,Lach,Treg,Alf
Word,Tisc,We/Ho,Weis
Sod,UBS/✶

3450.11 art
dat sing fem
[ᵃ✶ τῇ
tē
[the

763.3 noun
dat sing fem
ἀσθενείᾳ]
astheneia
weakness]

2231.2 prs-
pron gen 1pl
ἡμῶν·
hēmōn
our;

3450.16 art
sing neu
τὸ
to
the

1056.1 conj
γὰρ
gar
for

4949.9 intr-
pron sing neu
τί
ti
which

4195.21 verb
1pl subj aor mid
προσευξώμεθα
proseuxōmetha
we should pray for

2498.1 conj
καθὸ
katho
according as

1158.1 verb 3sing
indic pres act
δεῖ,
dei
is necessary,

3620.2 partic
οὐκ
ouk
not

3471.5 verb 1pl
indic perf act
οἴδαμεν,
oidamen
we know,

233.1 conj
⟨ ἀλλ'
all'
but

233.2 conj
[✶ ἀλλὰ]
alla
[idem]

840.15 prs-
pron sing neu
αὐτὸ
auto
itself

3450.16 art
sing neu
τὸ
to
the

4011.1 noun
sing neu
πνεῦμα
pneuma
Spirit

5079.1 verb 3sing
indic pres act
ὑπερεντυγχάνει
huperentunchanei
makes intercession

All creation groans with a common cry, awaiting deliverance from the tensions and yearnings. Christians long for release from the final traces of sin and death. They are heirs of God and joint heirs with Christ, but they still tabernacle in mortal bodies subject to pain and death, with the vestment of a fallen nature to overcome (2 Corinthians 5:2; Romans 7:24).

8:24,25. Full and final redemption, the culmination of our "adoption," will see the transformation of our bodies into a glorified state. That is our hope, a hope rooted in God himself.

Take note of the development of the theme: "the glory which shall be revealed in us" (verse 18); "the manifestation of the sons of God" (verse 19); "the glorious liberty of the children of God" (verse 21); "the adoption, to wit, the redemption of our body" (verse 23). We are brought to our anchor of hope. Our salvation is partial now; it will be complete with the redemption of our body.

"Saved by hope" is not in conflict with being saved by faith. The salvation spoken of here relates to the redemption of the body.

Complete deliverance through redemption will be accomplished only when "this corruptible shall have put on incorruption, and this mortal shall have put on immortality" (1 Corinthians 15:54). That is the "hope which is laid up" (Colossians 1:5) and "the hope set before us" (Hebrews 6:18). It is the "blessed hope" (Titus 2:13). Further, it is "Christ in you, the hope of glory" (Colossians 1:27). Hope inspires joy in the believing heart. Those saved by faith find themselves rejoicing in hope.

8:26,27. Chapter 8, solving the defeat of chapter 7, brings into focus the provision of victory: (1) a new law, "the law of the Spirit of life in Christ Jesus" (8:2), and (2) a new power to replace the weakness of the flesh.

This new power, the Holy Spirit, fulfills the righteousness of the Law (verse 4), provides power to please God (verse 8), power to live (verse 13), and power in prayer (verse 26). Verse 37 tells us that God also empowers us in suffering.

The *Amplified New Testament* gives this rendering: "So too the (Holy) Spirit comes to our aid and bears us up in our weakness." He takes the burden on himself and in our place, to share the load and make our part easier.

The Holy Spirit "maketh intercession." The ministry of prayer is spiritual ministry, and that is why we need the help of the Holy Spirit. He is able to express what we cannot put into words. Also, He knows the mind of God, so whatever the Spirit prays through us will be in perfect harmony with the will of God. Intercessory prayer reaches its greatest impact when it passes beyond the realm of our words and finds expression in the words of the Spirit and "with groanings which cannot be uttered." One of the most valuable ministries of the Spirit is that of helping us in prayer. The Spirit

waiting for the adoption, [to wit], the redemption of our body: ... as we await that right of sonship that involves our bodily redemption, *Berkeley* ... for our privileges as sons, *TCNT* ... waiting to become true sons, *SEB* ... for open recognition as sons, *Weymouth* ... for the delivraunce of oure bodyes, *Tyndale* ... the redemption from our sensuality, *Fenton*.

24. For we are saved by hope: but hope that is seen is not hope: ... is attained, *Campbell*.
for what a man seeth, why doth he yet hope for?: ... for who hopeth for that which he beholdeth? *Clementson*.

25. But if we hope for that we see not:
[then] do we with patience wait for [it]: ... we eagerly anticipate it, *Adams* ... we steadfastly endure the present, *Conybeare* ... we wait for it with endurance, *Klingensmith*.

26. Likewise: And in like manner, *PNT, Panin*.
the Spirit also helpeth our infirmities: ... also supports us, *TCNT* ... also takes hold with us in our weakness, *Montgomery* ... assists us in our weakness, *Moffatt*.
for we know not what we should pray for as we ought: ... we do not know how to pray aright, *Moffatt*.
but the Spirit itself maketh intercession for us with groanings which cannot be uttered: He personally talks to God for us with feelings which our language cannot express, *SEB* ... requesteth for vs, *Rheims* ... comes to our rescue, *Wuest* ... strongly intercedeth for us, with unutterable groans, *Scarlett* ... the like spirit axeth for us with sorwynge, *Wyclif* ... pleads for us with unutterable groanings, *Confraternity* ... pleads for us with unspeakable yearnings, *Williams* ... pleads for us with sighs that are beyond words, *Moffatt* ... that words cannot express, *TEV* ... with yearnings that can't find any words, *Beck*.

Romans 8:27

26.b.Txt: 01ℵ-corr,04C
018K,020L,025P,33,byz.
it.sa.bo.
Var: p27,01ℵ-org,02A
03B,06D,Lach,Treg,Alf
Word,Tisc,We/Ho,Weis
Sod,UBS/✶

5065.1 prep	2231.2 prs-pron gen 1pl	4577.2 noun dat pl masc	213.1 adj dat pl masc	3450.5 art sing masc
⸂ᵇ ὑπὲρ	ἡμῶν ⸃	στεναγμοῖς	ἀλαλήτοις·	27. ὁ
huper	hēmōn	stenagmois	alalētois	ho
for	us	with groanings	inexpressible.	The

1156.2 conj	2028.3 verb nom sing masc part pres act	3450.15 art acc pl fem	2559.1 noun fem	3471.4 verb 3sing indic perf act	4949.9 intr-pron sing neu
δὲ	ἐρευνῶν	τὰς	καρδίας	οἶδεν	τί
de	ereunōn	tas	kardias	oiden	ti
but	searching	the	hearts	knows	what

3450.16 art sing neu	5263.1 noun nom sing neu	3450.2 art gen sing	4011.2 noun gen sing neu	3617.1 conj	2567.3 prep
τὸ	φρόνημα	τοῦ	πνεύματος,	ὅτι	κατὰ
to	phronēma	tou	pneumatos	hoti	kata
the	mind	of the	Spirit,	because	according to

2296.4 noun acc sing masc	1777.1 verb 3sing indic pres act	5065.1 prep	39.4 adj gen pl	3471.5 verb 1pl indic perf act	1156.2 conj
θεὸν	ἐντυγχάνει	ὑπὲρ	ἁγίων.	28. Οἴδαμεν	δὲ
theon	entunchanei	huper	hagiōn	Oidamen	de
God	he intercedes	for	saints.	We know	but

3617.1 conj	3450.4 art dat pl	25.4 verb dat pl part pres act	3450.6 art acc sing masc	2296.4 noun acc sing masc	3820.1 adj
ὅτι	τοῖς	ἀγαπῶσιν	τὸν	θεὸν	πάντα
hoti	tois	agapōsin	ton	theon	panta
that	the	loving		God	all things

28.a.Var: p46,02A,03B
sa.Lach,We/Ho,Weis
UBS/✶

4753.1 verb 3sing indic pres act	3450.5 art sing masc	2296.1 noun nom sing masc	1519.1 prep	18.3 adj sing	3450.4 art dat pl
συνεργεῖ	[ᵃ+ ὁ	θεὸς]	εἰς	ἀγαθόν,	τοῖς
sunergei	ho	theos	eis	agathon	tois
work together		[God]	for	good,	to the

2567.3 prep	4145.4 noun acc sing fem	2795.3 adj dat pl masc	1498.24 verb dat pl masc part pres act	3617.1 conj
κατὰ	πρόθεσιν	κλητοῖς	οὖσιν.	29. ὅτι
kata	prothesin	klētois	ousin	hoti
according to	purpose	called	being.	Because

3614.8 rel-pron acc pl masc	4126.2 verb 3sing indic aor act	2504.1 conj	4168.1 verb 3sing indic aor act	4683.1 adj acc pl masc
οὓς	προέγνω,	καὶ	προώρισεν	συμμόρφους
hous	proegnō	kai	proōrisen	summorphous
whom	he foreknew,	also	he predestined	conformed to

3450.10 art gen sing fem	1494.2 noun gen sing fem	3450.2 art gen sing	5048.2 noun gen sing masc	840.3 prs-pron gen sing	1519.1 prep
τῆς	εἰκόνος	τοῦ	υἱοῦ	αὐτοῦ,	εἰς
tēs	eikonos	tou	huiou	autou	eis
the	image	of the	Son	his,	for

3450.16 art sing neu	1498.32 verb inf pres act	840.6 prs-pron acc sing masc	4274.2 adj acc sing masc	1706.1 prep	4044.4 adj dat pl
τὸ	εἶναι	αὐτὸν	πρωτότοκον	ἐν	πολλοῖς
to	einai	auton	prōtotokon	en	pollois
the	to be	him	firstborn	among	many

79.8 noun dat pl masc	3614.8 rel-pron acc pl masc	1156.2 conj	4168.1 verb 3sing indic aor act	3642.8 dem-pron acc pl masc
ἀδελφοῖς·	30. οὓς	δὲ	προώρισεν,	τούτους
adelphois	hous	de	proōrisen	toutous
brothers.	Whom	but	he predestined,	these

possessing all knowledge joins in intercession. Since He knows the will of God, we have assurance that since the intercession is according to God's will, we have the guarantee it will be answered (1 John 5:14,15).

We have two intercessors: (1) the Lord Jesus Christ at the right hand of God prays for us; (2) the Holy Spirit here on earth prays in and through us.

8:28. Though we do not always know what we should pray for as we ought, we do know that God causes all things to continually work together for our good. This does not mean Paul is teaching fatalism, the resignation to the inevitable. The assurance is conditional. Subjectively, it is to all who "love God." Objectively, it is to those "who are the called according to his purpose."

Our interests are never absent from the heart of God; our destinies are never adrift from His loving and guiding hand.

8:29,30. Foreknowledge and predestination have been understood in various ways. Some (Arminius, Wesley) say that predestination is founded upon God's foreknowledge of how individuals will respond to God's offer of salvation. Verse 29, then, indicates that God's foreknowledge precedes His predestination.

This group believes that to "foreknow" does not imply prompting or the extraordinary working of God's selective will. He foreknows by the ordinary process of His prescience (knowledge of events before they take place). Predestination, then, refers to those whom God foreknew would be in Christ (Romans 8:29,30; Ephesians 1:5,11). This predestination is not to heaven per se, but "to be conformed to the image of his Son." That God knows what will take place does not mean He is responsible for all that happens. For example, God foresaw that sin and death would enter the world; this does not mean that He is the author or creator of evil.

Clearly, God foresees who will have faith to believe in Christ; however, some ask, "Where does such faith come from?" Scripture says that saving faith is a gift from God. Therefore, they conclude that God foresees those He will give faith to, and so predetermines who shall be among the elect.

In addressing the difficulties of these theological issues, some maintain that the way is predestined, not the individual. He predestined Christ as the way, and He predestined all who are "in Christ" to be conformed to the image of Christ. If that were not so, we would be saved by decree, not by faith.

Others have no problem accepting that a sovereign God may in all fairness have mercy on whom He will have mercy (cf. 9:15). In this view to foreknow is to choose. Partial support for this position is drawn from a study of the words "know" and "foreknow," which often include the idea of to "know intimately or lovingly." In both the Old and New Testament, these words can denote God's advanced knowledge about and His actual choosing of individuals (see Genesis 18:19; Amos 3:2; Hosea 13:5; 1 Thessalonians 5:12;

27. And he that searcheth the hearts: Yet he who fathoms the depths of our hearts, *TCNT*.

knoweth what [is] the mind of the Spirit: . . . knows what the Spirit thinks, *Williams* . . . what is the meanynge of the spryte, *Cranmer* . . . knovveth vvhat the Spirit desireth, *Rheims*.

because he maketh intercession for the saints according to [the will of] God: . . . he pleads for the saints, *Confraternity* . . . talks to God in behalf of holy people, *SEB* . . . for holi men, *Wyclif* . . . in agreement with God's will, *TCNT* . . . according to the pleasure of god, *Tyndale*.

28. And we know that all things work together for good to them that love God: . . . worcke for the best, *Geneva* . . . co-operate for good, *Scarlett*.

to them who are the called according to [his] purpose: . . . to those being invited, *Wilson* . . . to those who are set apart, *Fenton*.

29. For whom he did foreknow: . . . whom God knew about long ago, *SEB* . . . those on whom He set His heart beforehand, *Williams*.

he also did predestinate: He also appointed long ago, *Beck* . . . he also marked out, *TCNT* . . . he predetermined, *Scarlett* . . . he also ordeyned before, *Geneva*.

[to be] conformed to the image of his Son: . . . to become just like His Son, *SEB* . . . to be made like to the pattern, *Conybeare* . . . to share the likeness of His Son, *Berkeley* . . . that they shulde be lyke fassyoned vnto the shape, *Cranmer*.

that he might be:

the firstborn among many brethren: . . . so that he might be the eldest of a great brotherhood, *Montgomery* . . . be the fyrst begotten, *Geneva* . . . in a vast family of, *Weymouth*.

30. Moreover whom he did predestinate: . . . those whom he before approved, *Scarlett* . . . whom he appoynted before, *Cranmer*.

Romans 8:31

2504.1 conj	2535.9 verb 3sing indic aor act	2504.1 conj	3614.8 rel-pron acc pl masc	2535.9 verb 3sing indic aor act	3642.8 dem-pron acc pl masc
καὶ	ἐκάλεσεν·	καὶ	οὓς	ἐκάλεσεν,	τούτους
kai	ekalesen	kai	hous	ekalesen	toutous
also	he called;	and	whom	he called,	these

2504.1 conj	1338.6 verb 3sing indic aor act		3614.8 rel-pron acc pl masc	1156.2 conj	1338.6 verb 3sing indic aor act
καὶ	ἐδικαίωσεν·		οὓς	δὲ	ἐδικαίωσεν,
kai	edikaiōsen		hous	de	edikaiōsen
also	he justified;		whom	but	he justified,

3642.8 dem-pron acc pl masc	2504.1 conj	1386.9 verb 3sing indic aor act	4949.9 intr-pron sing neu	3631.1 conj	2029.12 verb 1pl indic fut act
τούτους	καὶ	ἐδόξασεν.	**31.** Τί	οὖν	ἐροῦμεν
toutous	kai	edoxasen	Ti	oun	eroumen
these	also	he glorified.	What	then	shall we say

4242.1 prep	3642.18 dem-pron pl neu	1479.1 conj	3450.5 art sing masc	2296.1 noun nom sing masc	5065.1 prep	2231.2 prs-pron gen 1pl
πρὸς	ταῦτα;	εἰ	ὁ	θεὸς	ὑπὲρ	ἡμῶν,
pros	tauta	ei	ho	theos	huper	hēmōn
to	these things?	If	the	God	for	us,

4949.3 intr-pron nom sing	2567.2 prep	2231.2 prs-pron gen 1pl	3614.5 rel-pron nom sing masc	1058.1 partic	3450.2 art gen sing
τίς	καθ᾽	ἡμῶν;	**32.** ὅς	γε	τοῦ
tis	kath'	hēmōn	hos	ge	tou
who	against	us?	Who	indeed	the

2375.2 adj gen sing	5048.2 noun gen sing masc	3620.2 partic	5177.4 verb 3sing indic aor mid	233.1 conj	233.2 conj
ἰδίου	υἱοῦ	οὐκ	ἐφείσατο,	ʼ ἀλλ᾽	[✶ ἀλλὰ]
idiou	huiou	ouk	epheisato	all'	alla
his own	Son	not	spared,	but	[idem]

5065.1 prep	2231.2 prs-pron gen 1pl	3820.4 adj gen pl	3722.10 verb 3sing indic aor act	840.6 prs-pron acc sing masc	4316.1 adv
ὑπὲρ	ἡμῶν	πάντων	παρέδωκεν	αὐτόν,	πῶς
huper	hēmōn	pantōn	paredōken	auton	pōs
for	us	all	gave up	him,	how

3644.1 adv	2504.1 conj	4713.1 prep dat	840.4 prs-pron dat sing	3450.17 art pl neu	3820.1 adj	2231.3 prs-pron dat 1pl
οὐχὶ	καὶ	σὺν	αὐτῷ	τὰ	πάντα	ἡμῖν
ouchi	kai	sun	autō	ta	panta	hēmin
not	also	with	him	the	all things	us

5319.14 verb 3sing indic fut mid	4949.3 intr-pron nom sing	1451.2 verb 3sing indic fut act	2567.3 prep
χαρίσεται;	**33.** τίς	ἐγκαλέσει	κατὰ
charisetai	tis	enkalesei	kata
will he grant?	Who	shall bring an accusation	against

1575.4 adj gen pl masc	2296.2 noun gen sing masc	2296.1 noun nom sing masc	3450.5 art sing masc	1338.2 verb nom sing masc part pres act	4949.3 intr-pron nom sing
ἐκλεκτῶν	θεοῦ;	θεὸς	ὁ	δικαιῶν·	**34.** τίς
eklektōn	theou	theos	ho	dikaiōn	tis
elect	of God?	God	the	justifying:	who

34.a.Var: 01ℵ,02A,04C 020L,bo.Lach,Tisc We/Ho,Weis,Sod UBS/✶

3450.5 art sing masc	2602.3 verb nom sing masc part pres act	5382.1 name nom masc	2400.1 name nom masc	3450.5 art sing masc
ὁ	κατακρινῶν;	Χριστὸς	[ᵃ✶+ Ἰησοῦς]	ὁ
ho	katakrinōn	Christos	Iēsous	ho
the	condemning?	Christ	[Jesus]	the

1 John 2:3). The consequence of such a view is to present fore-knowledge as the confirmation rather than the cause of predestination.

John Calvin defined predestination by saying, "God has once for all determined, both whom he would admit to salvation, and whom he would condemn to destruction" (*Institutes of the Christian Religion*, 3:21:181). He went on to state that their perdition depends on the predestination of God (ibid.). Clearly, great men of God have taken opposing views on the subject.

One thing that cannot be denied is that even Christ presented a choice to His hearers. Throughout Scripture, the call to repentance is universal (Isaiah 55:1; Acts 17:30f.; 1 Timothy 2:3f.; 2 Peter 3:9). Limiting this call to a predetermined elect seems to conflict with many important passages.

8:31,32. Here is the first of six questions. From this point on through the balance of the chapter we are given the grand climax, the mountaintop of Christian position and experience. The apostle's heart was filled with absolute confidence. God who gave the best (His Son) will in no wise withhold the rest. He lavished mercy and grace, and He has more than sufficient to bestow upon His redeemed children, providing all that is needed for their good.

It was the Father who handed His Son over to suffering and death. Since God did this, and since the Son is seated at His right hand in heaven, what will He not do for His children on earth? If He was not reluctant to make such a major provision, will He not respond to any smaller favor?

8:33. In triumphant tone Paul declares that no one dare lay a charge against the elect of God since God himself has justified them. There is no ground for bringing charges. Neither men nor Satan can resurrect the believer's past. No forgiven sin can ever be held against the forgiven since God has justified them. Satan, the "accuser of the brethren," may try to harass, but that which God has forgiven He will never remember against us anymore.

God alone is the Judge. When He justifies, no claim of past wrong will be held against us. Unconfessed sin is a different matter.

The word "justified" appears often in this epistle. It is used for the last time in this verse. And who shall accuse the man whom God declares righteous? No accusation will stand when God, the righteous Judge, has justified a person.

8:34. The next stroke of the hammer drives the nail with greater finality. There is no ground for condemnation. The Christ who died for us is at the Father's right hand interceding for us. Four great truths are our assurance and protection: (1) Christ died for our sins. He is our propitiation. (2) He is risen again for our justification (4:25). We are "saved by his life" (5:10). (3) "At the right

them he also called: and whom he called:

them he also justified: He has also declared free from guilt, *Weymouth* . . . he also accepted as righteous, *Noyes.*

and whom he justified: He declared righteous, *Young.*

them he also glorified: . . . he shared his glory, *JB* . . . also crowned with glory, *Weymouth* . . . and distinguished them, *Fenton.*

31. What shall we then say to these things?: . . . our response to these facts? *Adams.*

If God [be] for us, who [can be] against us?: If God be on our syde, *Geneva* . . . In view of the fact that God is on our behalf, *Wuest* . . . what does it matter who may be against us? *Norlie.*

32. He that spared not his own Son, but delivered him up for us all: . . . who did not protect, *Klingensmith* . . . but parted with Him for us all, *Fenton* . . . to benefit us all, *JB.*

how shall he not with him also freely give us all things?: Therefore, wouldn't God give us everything, *SEB* . . . how can he fail to grant us also all things with him? *Confraternity* . . . what is to hinder His favoring us with everything along with Him? *Berkeley* . . . also bestow on us all, *HistNT.*

33. Who shall lay any thing to the charge of God's elect?: Who shall impeach those, *Weymouth* . . . accuse against, *Rheims* . . . bring a charge against, *Panin* . . . accuse God's elect? *Montgomery* . . . make accusation against the elect, *Confraternity* . . . bring an accusation against God's elect? *Worrell* . . . bring an accusation against God's Chosen ones? *Wilson* . . . the approved people of God? *Scarlett.*

[It is] God that justifieth: Shall God that justifieth? *Alford* . . . God acquits them, *Montgomery.*

34. Who [is] he that condemneth?: . . . who is the condemner? *Berkeley* . . . What judge can doom us? *Conybeare.*

Romans 8:35

34.b.**Txt:** 06D,018K
020L,byz.
Var: 01ℵ,02A,03B,04C
bo.Lach,Treg,Tisc
We/Ho,Weis,Sod
UBS/✩

34.c.**Txt:** p27-vid,p46
01ℵ-corr3,03B,06D,08E
010F,012G,018K,020L
byz.
Var: 01ℵ-org,02A,04C
33,104,326,co.We/Ho

34.d.**Txt:** 01ℵ-corr,03B
06D,018K,020L,byz.
Weis,Sod
Var: 01ℵ-org,02A,04C
bo.Tisc,We/Ho,UBS/✩

594.15 verb nom sing masc part aor act	3095.1 adv comp	1156.2 conj	2504.1 conj	1446.25 verb nom sing masc part aor pass
ἀποθανών,	μᾶλλον	δὲ	(b καὶ)	(✩ ἐγερθείς,
apothanōn	mallon	de	kai	egertheis
having died,	rather	but	also	having been raised up;

1446.25 verb nom sing masc part aor pass	1523.2 prep gen	3361.2 adj gen pl	3614.5 rel-pron nom sing masc	2504.1 conj
[c ἐγερθείς	ἐκ	νεκρῶν,]	ὃς	(d καί)
egertheis	ek	nekrōn,	hos	kai
[having been raised up	from	dead;]	who	also

1498.4 verb 3sing indic pres act	1706.1 prep	1182.5 adj dat sing fem	3450.2 art gen sing	2296.2 noun gen sing masc	3614.5 rel-pron nom sing masc
ἐστιν	ἐν	δεξιᾷ	τοῦ	θεοῦ,	ὃς
estin	en	dexia	tou	theou	hos
is	at	right hand		of God;	who

2504.1 conj	1777.1 verb 3sing indic pres act	5065.1 prep	2231.2 prs-pron gen 1pl	4949.3 intr-pron nom sing	2231.4 prs-pron acc 1pl
καὶ	ἐντυγχάνει	ὑπὲρ	ἡμῶν.	35. τίς	ἡμᾶς
kai	entunchanei	huper	hēmōn.	tis	hēmas
also	intercedes	for	us:	who	us

5398.3 verb 3sing indic fut act	570.3 prep gen	3450.10 art gen sing fem	26.2 noun gen sing fem	3450.2 art gen sing	5382.2 name gen masc
χωρίσει	ἀπὸ	τῆς	ἀγάπης	τοῦ	Χριστοῦ;
chōrisei	apo	tēs	agapēs	tou	Christou
shall separate	from	the	love		of Christ?

2324.1 noun nom sing fem	2211.1 conj	4581.1 noun nom sing fem	2211.1 conj	1369.1 noun nom sing masc	2211.1 conj
θλῖψις,	ἢ	στενοχωρία,	ἢ	διωγμὸς,	ἢ
thlipsis	ē	stenochōria	ē	diōgmos	ē
tribulation,	or	distress,	or	persecution,	or

3016.1 noun nom sing masc	2211.1 conj	1126.1 noun nom sing fem	2211.1 conj	2766.1 noun nom sing masc	2211.1 conj
λιμὸς,	ἢ	γυμνότης,	ἢ	κίνδυνος,	ἢ
limos	ē	gumnotēs	ē	kindunos	ē
famine,	or	nakedness,	or	danger,	or

3134.1 noun nom sing fem	2503.1 conj	1119.22 verb 3sing indic perf pass	3617.1 conj	1736.3 prep
μάχαιρα;	36. καθὼς	γέγραπται,	Ὅτι	(ἕνεκά
machaira	kathōs	gegraptai,	Hoti	heneka
sword?	Just as	it has been written,		For sake

36.a.**Txt:** 04C,018K,byz.
Var: 01ℵ,02A,03B,06D
020L,Gries,Lach,Treg
Alf,Word,Tisc,We/Ho
Weis,Sod,UBS/✩

1736.2 prep	4622.2 prs-pron gen 2sing	2266.5 verb 1pl indic pres pass	3513.9 adj acc sing fem
[a✩ Ἕνεκεν]	σοῦ	θανατούμεθα	ὅλην
Heneken	sou	thanatoumetha	holēn
[idem]	your	we are being put to death	whole

3450.12 art acc sing fem	2232.4 noun acc sing fem	3023.12 verb 1pl indic aor pass	5453.1 conj	4122.3 noun pl neu	4819.1 noun gen sing fem
τὴν	ἡμέραν·	ἐλογίσθημεν	ὡς	πρόβατα	σφαγῆς.
tēn	hēmeran	elogisthēmen	hōs	probata	sphagēs
the	day;	we were reckoned	as	sheep	of slaughter.

233.1 conj	1706.1 prep	3642.3 dem-pron dat pl	3820.5 adj dat pl	5083.1 verb 1pl indic pres act
37. Ἀλλ'	ἐν	τούτοις	πᾶσιν	ὑπερνικῶμεν
All'	en	toutois	pasin	hupernikōmen
But	in	these things	all	we more than overcome

hand of God," He is our representative. (4) Making intercession, He is our Advocate pleading our case (1 John 2:1).

Our future in glory is assured by the perfect defeat of our adversary, and the perfect intercession of our Advocate. Christ died, He arose, He ascended, He intercedes—all for us!

[It is] Christ that died:
yea rather, that is risen again:
. . . more than that, He rose, *Beck.*
who is even at the right hand of God: . . . at God's right side, *SEB.*
who also maketh intercession for us: . . . is there to intercede for us...He pleads in our behalf, *Norlie* . . . who actually pleads for us! *Moffatt.*

8:35,36. With another masterful stroke of the hammer Paul drives home the truth of "no separation." No one can drive a wedge and create distance between Christ's love and us. No one can cause Him to cease loving us. No power outside us can cause us to cease loving Him.

The apostle was convinced beyond the shadow of a doubt that no opposing force can bring about separation between Christ and the Christian. He lists several forces which work to separate us from His love.

"Distress" speaks of being surrounded by difficult circumstances until one is literally in a tight squeeze. "Persecution" is associated with tribulation and affliction. "Famine" is absence of food. Of this, we in this land know little, but millions in other countries suffer and die because of this. "Nakedness" does not refer to immodest, immoral dress, but to the fact of not having sufficient clothing and no means of securing any. Paul spoke of being "in fastings often, in cold and nakedness" (2 Corinthians 11:27). "Peril" refers to danger and risk. "Sword" refers to the threat of martyrdom. This threat was in Paul's mind. He knew what it was to be left for dead after being stoned. Hebrews 11 records other heroes of faith who were victorious over all types of external difficulties, including death.

The perils mentioned by Paul may not be common to us where we live, but we are faced with numberless spiritual perils which threaten our relationship. The one thing that can separate us is spiritual death, described in verse 13. The believer can choose to leave Christ out of his life; then he is separated from salvation by his own will.

35. Who shall separate us from the love of Christ?: What can drive us from the love of Christ? *Fenton* . . . from the charitie of Christ? *Rheims.*

[shall] tribulation, or distress: Will sorrow, hardship, *Beck* . . . Will trouble, or difficulties, *TCNT* . . . Will trouble, pain, *SEB* . . . shall anguish, or calamity, *Montgomery* . . . or oppression? *Fenton.*

or persecution, or famine, or nakedness, or peril, or sword?: . . . or even attacked, *JB* . . . persecution, having no food, *SEB* . . . or want of clothing, *TCNT* . . . or danger? *Rheims.*

36. As it is written:
For thy sake we are killed all the day long: . . . on account of you! *Fenton* . . . we are being put to death the livelong day, *Williams* . . . we are being massacred daily, *JB* . . . we are in danger of death at all times, *TEV* . . . trying to kill us, *Weymouth.*

we are accounted as sheep for the slaughter: We are regarded, *Fenton* . . . as sheep destined for slaughter, *Weymouth, Wuest* . . . as shepe apoynted to be slayne, *Tyndale.*

8:37. *Hupernikōmen* is rendered "we are more than conquerors." The word comes from *huper* (Latin, "super") meaning "above," and *nikaō*, from *nikē*, meaning "victory." The literal meaning is "we are super victors." A whole phrase in English is needed to translate one strong, vivid Greek word.

Despite the seven enemies listed in verse 35, we are super victors. Through the centuries Christians have often been "accounted as sheep for the slaughter," but they lived triumphantly through it all.

The ability to be a super victor is not based on human ability or self-determination. The victory comes "through him that loved us." The Christ who conquered every foe because of His love for us imparts His grace and strength to make us "more than conquerors." *Hupernikōmen* is a very expressive term. *Nike* was the god of victory; in Christ we can be "hyper" victorious, *super*conquerors.

37. Nay, in all these things we are more than conquerors: Yet amidst all these trials we are more than victorious, *TCNT* . . . Yet amid all these things, *Weymouth* . . . helps us win an overwhelming victory, *Beck* . . . we overcome strongly, *Tyndale* . . . we have complete victory, *TEV* . . . we keep on gloriously conquering, *Williams* . . . we do more than overcome, *Wilson* . . . we more than come out ahead by him, *Klingensmith* . . . we overcome because of him, *Confraternity.*
through him that loved us:

1217.2 prep	3450.2 art gen sing	25.21 verb gen sing masc part aor act	2231.4 prs-pron acc 1pl	3844.28 verb 1sing indic perf pass
διὰ	τοῦ	ἀγαπήσαντος	ἡμᾶς.	38. πέπεισμαι
dia	tou	agapēsantos	hēmas	pepeismai
through	the	having loved	us.	I am persuaded

1056.1 conj	3617.1 conj	3641.1 conj	2265.1 noun nom sing masc	3641.1 conj	2205.1 noun nom sing fem	3641.1 conj
γὰρ	ὅτι	οὔτε	θάνατος,	οὔτε	ζωὴ,	οὔτε
gar	hoti	oute	thanatos	oute	zōē	oute
for	that	neither	death,	nor	life,	nor

38.a.**Txt:** 018K,020L,byz.
Var: 01ℵ,02A,03B,04C
06D,bo.Gries,Lach,Treg
Alf,Word,Tisc,We/Ho
Weis,Sod,UBS/✶

32.5 noun nom pl masc	3641.1 conj	741.5 noun nom pl fem	3641.1 conj	1405.5 noun pl fem
ἄγγελοι,	οὔτε	ἀρχαὶ,	[a οὔτε	δυνάμεις, ⟩
angeloi	oute	archai	oute	dunameis
angels,	nor	principalities,	nor	powers,

38.b.**Var:** 01ℵ,02A,03B
04C,06D,bo.Gries,Lach
Treg,Alf,Word,Tisc
We/Ho,Weis,Sod
UBS/✶

3641.1 conj	1748.5 verb nom pl neu part perf act	3641.1 conj	3165.8 verb part pres act	3641.1 conj
οὔτε	ἐνεστῶτα,	οὔτε	μέλλοντα,	[b✶+ οὔτε
oute	enestōta	oute	mellonta	oute
nor	things having come,	nor	things coming,	[nor

1405.5 noun pl fem	3641.1 conj	5151.1 noun sing neu	3641.1 conj	893.1 noun sing neu	3641.1 conj
δυνάμεις]	39. οὔτε	ὕψωμα,	οὔτε	βάθος,	οὔτε
dunameis	oute	hupsōma	oute	bathos	oute
powers]	nor	height,	nor	depth,	nor

4948.3 indef-pron nom sing	2909.1 noun nom sing fem	2066.9 adj	1404.30 verb 3sing indic fut mid	2231.4 prs-pron acc 1pl
τις	κτίσις	ἑτέρα	δυνήσεται	ἡμᾶς
tis	ktisis	hetera	dunēsetai	hēmas
any	created thing	other	will be able	us

5398.2 verb inf aor act	570.3 prep gen	3450.10 art gen sing fem	26.2 noun gen sing fem	3450.2 art gen sing	2296.2 noun gen sing masc
χωρίσαι	ἀπὸ	τῆς	ἀγάπης	τοῦ	θεοῦ,
chōrisai	apo	tēs	agapēs	tou	theou
to separate	from	the	love		of God,

3450.10 art gen sing fem	1706.1 prep	5382.3 name dat masc	2400.2 name masc	3450.3 art dat sing	2935.3 noun dat sing masc	2231.2 prs-pron gen 1pl
τῆς	ἐν	Χριστῷ	Ἰησοῦ	τῷ	κυρίῳ	ἡμῶν.
tēs	en	Christō	Iēsou	tō	kuriō	hēmōn
the	in	Christ	Jesus	the	Lord	our.

1.a.**Txt:** p46,01ℵ,02A
03B,04C,06D-corr3
018K,020L,We/Ho,byz.
Var: 06D-org,08E,010F
012G

223.4 noun acc sing fem	2978.1 verb 1sing pres act	1706.1 prep	5382.3 name dat masc	2400.2 name masc
9:1. Ἀλήθειαν	λέγω	ἐν	Χριστῷ,	[a+ Ἰησοῦ,]
Alētheian	legō	en	Christō	Iēsou
Truth	I say	in	Christ,	[Jesus,]

3620.3 partic	5409.1 verb 1sing indic pres	4679.2 verb gen sing fem part pres act	1466.4 prs-pron dat 1sing	3450.10 art gen sing fem
οὐ	ψεύδομαι,	συμμαρτυρούσης	μοι	τῆς
ou	pseudomai	summarturousēs	moi	tēs
not	I lie,	bearing witness with	me	the

4743.2 noun gen sing fem	1466.2 prs-pron gen 1sing	1706.1 prep	4011.3 noun dat sing neu	39.3 adj dat sing	3617.1 conj
συνειδήσεώς	μου	ἐν	πνεύματι	ἁγίῳ,	2. ὅτι
suneidēseōs	mou	en	pneumati	hagiō	hoti
conscience	my	in	Spirit	Holy,	that

8:38,39. "I am persuaded" can be translated "absolutely convinced," "certain," "stand convinced." There was no uncertainty in Paul's mind. Nothing need "separate us from the love of Christ" (verse 35). The one thing required of us, made possible by grace, is that we be willing to let His victory be made real in us moment by moment. This means that all self-interest will be subordinated to His lordship.

In triumphant confidence Paul wrote of the enemies which must be contended with and defeated. For the most part they are in couplets.

"Death" and "life." There is nothing to fear from the aloneness of one and the trials of the other. Physical death cannot alter the believer's spiritual union with Christ Jesus (1 Corinthians 6:17). It can only enhance the reality of His presence (2 Corinthians 5:6; Philippians 1:21).

"Angels" and "principalities." Invisible, mysterious forces aligned against God's people are conquered foes through Christ. "Powers" refers to hostility in the spirit world. In context these angels would be only evil angels who fell with Satan. God's angels are busy ministering to those who "shall be heirs of salvation" (Hebrews 1:14). The principalities are high-ranking fallen angels. Gabriel needed help from Michael to overcome the "prince of the kingdom of Persia" (Daniel 10:13); evil spirits are no match for Jesus!

"Things present" and "things to come" sum up the unlimited dimensions of time, as "height" and "depth" sum up the endless proportions of space. *Hupsōma* was worshiped as the god of high places, and *Bathos* as the god of the deep. No "god" can be high enough to surpass the love of God; nor can any be deep enough to undermine His love.

The secret is to remain "in Christ." Eternal security is provided, but it is only available as long as we remain "in Christ." By the decision of our will we came into the relationship of being "in Christ." By a decision of our will we can choose to terminate that relationship. If we do that we have lost our security. In summary, there is nothing in all creation that can separate us from the love of Christ outside of ourselves. The only thing that can effect that separation is human will.

9:1,2. The first eight chapters of the Book of Romans are doctrinal, setting forth great basic truths. Chapters 12 through 16 are practical exhortations. Chapters 9 to 11 have often been called parenthetical, and a casual reader might consider them unrelated to the rest of the book. Closer study, however, reveals they are an integral part of Romans. Understanding how the principles apply to Israel makes it possible to move properly from the theological portion to the practical section.

Chapter 9 opens with Paul's great burden for his Jewish brethren. He stated that he had a joint witness of his conscience and of the Holy Spirit regarding the sincerity of his expression of the "great heaviness and continual sorrow" he carried in his heart for them.

38. For I am persuaded: For I am sure, *Rheims* . . . I have full assurance, *Williams* . . . I am fully persuaded, *Montgomery*.

that neither death, nor life:

nor angels, nor principalities, nor powers: . . . neither the lower ranks of evil angels, *Weymouth* . . . among angels or spiritual powers, *Norlie* . . . no angels or their rulers, *Beck* . . . nor any force, *TCNT* . . . nether vertues...nether strengthe, *Wyclif* . . . nor all the Principalities and Powers of Angels, *Conybeare*.

nor things present, nor things to come: . . . nothing that exists, *JB* . . . neither present nor future affairs, *Berkeley* . . . nor the forces of nature, *Weymouth*.

39. Nor height, nor depth, nor any other creature: . . . nor evil forces above or beneath, *Williams* . . . nothing above or below, *Beck* . . . nor anything else in all creation, *RSV* . . . nor any other created thing, *Weymouth* . . . nor any power in the whole creation, *Conybeare*.

shall be able to separate us from the love of God: . . . will be able to part us, *Moffatt* . . . shalbe able to depart vs, *Geneva*.

which is in Christ Jesus our Lord: . . . which rests upon us, *Weymouth* . . . displayed in Christ Jesus, *TCNT* . . . made visible in, *JB* . . . shewed in Christ, *Tyndale*.

1. I say the truth in Christ, I lie not: I am not falsifying, *Berkeley* . . . I speak the verity in Christ, *Rheims* . . . I speak the truth in Christ, *Confraternity* . . . as a Christian man, *Williams* . . . as a Christian, *TCNT* . . . and do not misrepresent, *Murdock* . . . I do not speak falsely, *Campbell* . . . now is no pretence, *JB*.

my conscience also bearing me witness in the Holy Ghost: . . . because my conscience enlightened by the Holy Spirit, *Williams* . . . guided and enlightened by the Holy Ghost, *Locke* . . . and my own conscience, prompted by the Holy Spirit, *Way* . . . my conscience in union with the Holy Spirit assures me of it too, *JB* . . . fortified by the Holy Spirit, *Berkeley* . . . ruled by the Holy Spirit, *TEV* . . . bearing joint-testimony, *Wuest*.

Romans 9:3

3049.1 noun nom sing fem	1466.4 prs-pron dat 1sing	1498.4 verb 3sing indic pres act	3144.9 adj sing fem	2504.1 conj	87.1 adj nom sing fem
λύπη	μοί	ἐστιν	μεγάλη,	καὶ	ἀδιάλειπτος
lupē	moi	estin	megalē	kai	adialeiptos
grief	to me	is	great,	and	unceasing

3464.1 noun sing fem	3450.11 art dat sing fem	2559.3 noun dat sing fem	1466.2 prs-pron gen 1sing	2153.5 verb 1sing indic imperf	1056.1 conj
ὀδύνη	τῇ	καρδίᾳ	μου·	3. ηὐχόμην	γὰρ
odunē	tē	kardia	mou	euchomēn	gar
sorrow	in the	heart	my,	I was wishing	for

840.5 prs-pron nom sing masc	1466.1 prs-pron nom 1sing	329.1 noun nom sing neu	1498.32 verb inf pres act	329.1 noun nom sing neu
῾ αὐτὸς	ἐγὼ	ἀνάθεμα	εἶναι	[☆ ἀνάθεμα
autos	egō	anathema	einai	anathema
myself	I	a curse	to be	[a curse

1498.32 verb inf pres act	840.5 prs-pron nom sing masc	1466.1 prs-pron nom 1sing	570.3 prep gen	3450.2 art gen sing	5382.2 name gen masc
εἶναι	αὐτὸς	ἐγὼ]	ἀπὸ	τοῦ	Χριστοῦ
einai	autos	egō	apo	tou	Christou
to be	myself	I]	from	the	Christ

5065.1 prep	3450.1 art gen pl	79.7 noun gen pl masc	1466.2 prs-pron gen 1sing	3450.1 art gen pl	4624.4 adj gen pl masc
ὑπὲρ	τῶν	ἀδελφῶν	μου	τῶν	συγγενῶν
huper	tōn	adelphōn	mou	tōn	sungenōn
for	the	brothers	my,	the	relatives

1466.2 prs-pron gen 1sing	2567.3 prep	4418.4 noun acc sing fem	3610.2 rel-pron nom pl masc	1498.7 verb 3pl indic pres act
μου	κατὰ	σάρκα·	4. οἵτινές	εἰσιν
mou	kata	sarka	hoitines	eisin
my	according to	flesh;	who	are

2448.2 name pl masc	3614.1 rel-pron gen pl	3450.9 art nom sing fem	5047.1 noun nom sing fem	2504.1 conj	3450.9 art nom sing fem
Ἰσραηλῖται,	ὧν	ἡ	υἱοθεσία	καὶ	ἡ
Israēlitai	hōn	hē	huiothesia	kai	hē
Israelites,	whose	the	adoption	and	the

4.a.Var: p46,03B,06D,sa. Lach

1385.1 noun nom sing fem	2504.1 conj	3450.13 art pl fem	1236.5 noun nom pl fem	3450.9 art nom sing fem	1236.1 noun nom sing fem
δόξα,	καὶ	῾ αἱ	διαθῆκαι	[ᵃ ἡ	διαθήκη]
doxa	kai	hai	diathēkai	hē	diathēkē
glory,	and	the	covenants	[the	covenant]

2504.1 conj	3450.9 art nom sing fem	3411.1 noun nom sing fem	2504.1 conj	3450.9 art nom sing fem	2972.2 noun nom sing fem	2504.1 conj
καὶ	ἡ	νομοθεσία,	καὶ	ἡ	λατρεία	καὶ
kai	hē	nomothesia	kai	hē	latreia	kai
and	the	lawgiving,	and	the	service	and

3450.13 art pl fem	1845.5 noun nom pl fem	3614.1 rel-pron gen pl	3450.7 art pl masc	3824.6 noun pl masc	2504.1 conj	1523.1 prep gen
αἱ	ἐπαγγελίαι,	5. ὧν	οἱ	πατέρες,	καὶ	ἐξ
hai	epangeliai	hōn	hoi	pateres	kai	ex
the	promises;	whose	the	fathers;	and	of

3614.1 rel-pron gen pl	3450.5 art sing masc	5382.1 name nom masc	3450.16 art sing neu	2567.3 prep	4418.4 noun acc sing fem
ὧν	ὁ	Χριστὸς	τὸ	κατὰ	σάρκα,
hōn	ho	Christos	to	kata	sarka
whom	the	Christ	to	according to	flesh,

142

His concern bore witness to the fact that his beloved kinsmen were eternally lost apart from the saving grace of Christ. What a Christlike spirit Paul exhibited in his intense love for those who beat him, cast him into prison, cursed him, and reviled him.

9:3. Paul outlined God's dealings with His chosen people in the past, in the present, and in the future. He had been writing concerning the Church; now he discussed a nation and its destiny. In this division of Romans the objections and questions regarding the promised special privileges of Israel are clarified. God will keep His word to Israel, for Israel is only temporarily set aside because of unbelief. Chapter 9 deals with Israel's election, chapter 10 with Israel's rejection, and chapter 11 with Israel's restoration.

This division begins with the expression of Paul's pain, his "heaviness" and "sorrow." The Berkeley Version expresses it as "intense grief and unceasing distress." Paul was so burdened for his kinsmen in the flesh that he could wish himself accursed from Christ, were that possible, if that would bring about the salvation of Israel.

The tense used in the Greek is the imperfect of the verb *euchomai* and is well expressed by "I could wish." Paul knew that one person cannot take the place of another in the matter of his will. Each one must decide for or against God for himself. The intensity of his love prompted his strong statement.

There is only one source of love such as Paul experienced. It comes from the heart of God. It is the same kind of love that caused God to send the Son and that caused Jesus to be made a curse for us (2 Corinthians 5:21; Galatians 3:13). The only way we can be recipients of this love is for the Holy Spirit to pour it into our hearts (5:5).

His comment reminds one of the similar expression of Moses (Exodus 32:32f.). Moses was prepared to perish for his people; Paul was also prepared to perish for them.

9:4,5. The earnestness of Paul's pain, and of his deep desire for the salvation of his kin, is explained in part in these verses. Paul wrote of the greatness of his people, their special privileges, the magnificence of their inheritance and hopes, all of which they forfeited by their unbelief.

Eight special privileges are listed: (1) adopted, sonship in God's earthly family; (2) glory, the Shekinah presence of God; (3) covenants, made to "the fathers"; (4) the Law given at Sinai; (5) the service of God, worship as detailed in Leviticus; (6) the promises of the Messiah and others through Him; (7) the Fathers—Abraham, Isaac, and Jacob—God's chosen leaders for a special people; (8) the promised Messiah, who came in the Person of One virgin born, the Son of God.

Paul ascribed full deity to Christ here. The most natural translation of the Greek is "Christ who is God over all, forever praised!

2. That I have great heaviness and continual sorrow in my heart: I suffer endless anguish of heart, *Moffatt* . . . my heart is never free from sorrow, *TCNT* . . . intense grief and unceasing distress, *Berkeley* . . . I have a consuming grief, *Wuest* . . . I have great sadness, *Douay* . . . great grief and unceasing anguish, *Macknight* . . . a pain that never leaves me, *Beck* . . . and incessant anguish, *Scarlett* . . . and neverending pain, *Klingensmith.*

3. For I could wish that myself were accursed from Christ: For I was on the point of praying to be accursed, *Montgomery* . . . would I be myself the accursed scapegoat, *Way* . . . that I myself might be sentenced to separation, *Norlie* . . . and banished from Christ, *HistNT* . . . to be anathema, *Rheims* . . . cut off from Christ, *RSV.*

for my brethren, my kinsmen according to the flesh: . . . if so I might deliver my brothers, *Way* . . . my own blood relatives, *Norlie* . . . my kindred, *Young.*

4. Who are Israelites:

to whom [pertaineth] the adoption, and the glory, and the covenants: . . . the sonship, the glorious Presence, *Berkeley* . . . theirs the Glory of the Visible Presence...were His covenants made, *Way* . . . They were made God's family, *Beck* . . . whom God adopted as sons, *Noyes* . . . the Shekinah glory, *Montgomery* . . . and the testament, *Douay.*

and the giving of the law, and the service [of God], and the promises: . . . the divine legislation, *Moffatt* . . . To them was revealed the Temple-ritual, *Way* . . . and a form of divine worship, *Locke.*

5. Whose [are] the fathers: They trace their descent, *TCNT* . . . from the famous Hebrew ancestors, *TEV.*

and of whom as concerning the flesh Christ [came]: . . . in so far as He is human, theirs is the Messiah, *Way* . . . in human lineage sprang, *Berkeley* . . . according to His body came Christ, *Beck* . . . as a human being, *TEV.*

3450.5 art sing masc	1498.21 verb sing masc part pres act	1894.3 prep	3820.4 adj gen pl	2296.1 noun nom sing masc	2109.1 adj nom sing masc
ὁ	ὢν	ἐπὶ	πάντων	θεὸς	εὐλογητὸς
ho	ōn	epi	pantōn	theos	eulogētos
the	being	over	all	God	blessed

1519.1 prep	3450.8 art acc pl masc	163.6 noun acc pl masc	279.1 partic	3620.1 partic	3497.1 rel- pron sing	1156.2 conj	3617.1 conj
εἰς	τοὺς	αἰῶνας.	ἀμήν.	**6.** Οὐχ	οἷον	δὲ	ὅτι
eis	tous	aiōnas.	amēn.	Ouch	hoion	de	hoti
to	the	ages.	Amen	Not	however	but	that

1588.10 verb 3sing indic perf act	3450.5 art sing masc	3030.1 noun nom sing masc	3450.2 art gen sing	2296.2 noun gen sing masc	3620.3 partic	1056.1 conj
ἐκπέπτωκεν	ὁ	λόγος	τοῦ	θεοῦ.	οὐ	γὰρ
ekpeptōken	ho	logos	tou	theou.	ou	gar
has failed	the	word		of God;	not	for

3820.7 adj pl masc	3450.7 art pl masc	1523.1 prep gen	2447.1 name masc	3642.7 dem- pron nom pl masc	2447.1 name masc
πάντες	οἱ	ἐξ	Ἰσραήλ,	οὗτοι	Ἰσραήλ·
pantes	hoi	ex	Israēl,	houtoi	Israēl·
all	the	of	Israel	these	Israel:

3624.2 adv	3617.1 conj	1498.7 verb 3pl indic pres act	4543.1 noun sing neu	11.1 name masc	3820.7 adj pl masc
7. οὐδ'	ὅτι	εἰσὶν	σπέρμα	Ἀβραάμ,	πάντες
oud'	hoti	eisin	sperma	Abraam,	pantes
nor	because	they are	seed	of Abraham	all

4891.4 noun pl neu	233.1 conj	1706.1 prep	2439.1 name masc	2535.52 verb 3sing indic fut pass	4622.3 prs- pron dat 2sing
τέκνα,	ἀλλ',	Ἐν	Ἰσαὰκ	κληθήσεταί	σοι
tekna,	all',	En	Isaak	klēthēsetai	soi
children:	but,	In	Isaac	shall be called	to you

4543.1 noun sing neu	4969.1 verb	3642.16 dem- pron sing neu	1498.4 verb 3sing indic pres act	3620.3 partic
σπέρμα.	**8.** ʽ Τουτέστιν,	[✶ τοῦτ'	ἔστιν,]	οὐ
sperma.	Toutestin,	tout'	estin,	ou
a seed.	This is,	[this	is]	not

3450.17 art pl neu	4891.4 noun pl neu	3450.10 art gen sing fem	4418.2 noun gen sing fem	3642.18 dem- pron pl neu	4891.4 noun pl neu
τὰ	τέκνα	τῆς	σαρκὸς,	ταῦτα	τέκνα
ta	tekna	tēs	sarkos,	tauta	tekna
the	children	of the	flesh	these	children

3450.2 art gen sing	2296.2 noun gen sing masc	233.2 conj	3450.17 art pl neu	4891.4 noun pl neu	3450.10 art gen sing fem
τοῦ	θεοῦ·	ἀλλὰ	τὰ	τέκνα	τῆς
tou	theou·	alla	ta	tekna	tēs
	of God;	but	the	children	of the

1845.1 noun fem	3023.4 verb 3sing indic pres	1519.1 prep	4543.1 noun sing neu	1845.1 noun fem
ἐπαγγελίας	λογίζεται	εἰς	σπέρμα.	**9.** ἐπαγγελίας
epangelias	logizetai	eis	sperma.	epangelias
promise	are reckoning	for	seed.	Of promise

1056.1 conj	3450.5 art sing masc	3030.1 noun nom sing masc	3642.4 dem-pron nom sing masc	2567.3 prep	3450.6 art acc sing masc
γὰρ	ὁ	λόγος	οὗτος,	Κατὰ	τὸν
gar	ho	logos	houtos,	Kata	ton
for	the	word	this,	According to	the

Amen!" The same ascription of full Godhood to Jesus occurs in John 1:1, Philippians 2:6, and Hebrews 1:8. (See *Overview*, pp.677f.)

9:6,7. God had given great honor to Israel. His Son was born into the human family by a Jewish mother. He was raised in a Jewish home, attended a Jewish synagogue, and received a Jewish education.

Paul never denied that the Jews were God's chosen people. Not all Jews rejected Christ; nearly all His early followers were Jews. God always had a righteous remnant who were true to Him. The apostle in summary stated that Israel is the chosen people, but to be a member of Israel means more than racial descent.

God had not failed to keep His promise. It was limited to the remnant. Physical descent from Abraham does not make one a child of God (John 8:37-44; Galatians 3:7). Ishmael was the seed of the flesh. Isaac was the child of promise. Mere birth into the nation did not make a person a real Israelite. God-accepted Israelites were those of spiritual character.

The Israel distinguished from the Israel of natural descent is the true Israel. Jesus made a parallel distinction when He spoke of Nathanael as "an Israelite indeed" (John 1:47). Paul referred to the true Israel as Israel "according to the Spirit" (Galatians 4:29, NASB). The same distinction was stated earlier as related to the term "Jew" and to circumcision (2:29). Both believing Jews and believing Gentiles are included in "the Israel of God" (Galatians 6:16).

9:8-10. The "children of the promise" were those who, like Abraham, believed the promise of God and as a result were Abraham's spiritual offspring. Paul made it very plain that the Jews could not base their claims to "election" upon their fleshly relationship to Abraham. The fleshly children were not necessarily the children of God. This was contrary to the general viewpoint.

Israel "according to the flesh" was the avenue by which God chose to bring the Messiah, and as such Israel enjoyed certain privileges. God's promise to Abraham or his seed that he should be the heir of the world was not by the Law, but through righteousness by faith (4:13). That promise still continues even to this day. Abraham is the father in a spiritual sense of all those who believe, Jew or Gentile, who walk in the steps of that faith (4:12). Paul exploded the idea that being a physical descendant of Abraham automatically made one a child of God.

The emphasis here is on the premium God places on our standing on His promises. The "word of promise" of verse 9 is the same as "word of God" in verse 6. Children of God are the children of promise (verse 8).

God promised Abraham a son and kept His promise by performing a miracle. That son of promise was Isaac. In God's sovereign plan, Sarah's son, not Hagar's or Keturah's son, was the one selected.

who is over all, God blessed for ever. Amen: . . . is supreme over all things, *TCNT* . . . is exalted above all, *Weymouth* . . . to whom be praises and benediction, *Murdock* . . . unto the ages, *Clementson.*

6. Not as though the word of God hath taken none effect: Not as implying that God's message fell short, *Berkeley* . . . I am not implying that God's promise 'to Israel' has been stultified, *Way* . . . I am far from suggesting, *TCNT* . . . it is not that God's word has failed, *Williams* . . . not such as that the word of God has lapsed, *Confraternity* . . . has come to naught, *Hanson* . . . is frustrate, *Rheims* . . . had fallen to the ground, *Wesley* . . . has failed of being accomplished, *Sawyer* . . . hath miscarried, *Douay.*

For they [are] not all Israel, which are of Israel: Not all who are descended from Israel are the real Israel, *Beck* . . . that comprise the true Israel, *Way.*

7. Neither, because they are the seed of Abraham, [are they] all children: . . . who are the race, *Locke* . . . are for that reason his real children, *Beck* . . . nether are they all chyldren strayght waye, *Cranmer* . . . does not constitute them all his sons, *Way.*

but, In Isaac shall thy seed be called: . . . your posterity be reckoned, *Weymouth* . . . your descendants will be counted, *Williams.*

8. That is, They which are the children of the flesh: Which means: Not his physical descendants make up the children of God, *Berkeley* . . . children born in a natural way, *Beck* . . . by natural descent, *Weymouth.*

these [are] not the children of God:

but the children of the promise are counted for the seed: . . . to whom the promise applied, *Way* . . . will be spoken of as descendants, *Klingensmith* . . . reckoned as a posterity, *Confraternity.*

9. For this [is] the word of promise:

2511.4 noun acc sing masc	3642.6 dem-pron acc sing masc	2048.54 verb 1sing indic fut mid	2504.1 conj	1498.40 verb 3sing indic fut mid
καιρὸν	τοῦτον	ἐλεύσομαι,	καὶ	ἔσται
kairon	touton	eleusomai	kai	estai
time	this	I will come,	and	there shall be

3450.11 art dat sing fem	4421.3 name dat fem	5048.1 noun nom sing masc	3620.3 partic	3303.1 adv	1156.2 conj	233.2 conj
τῇ	Σάῤῥᾳ	υἱός.	10. Οὐ	μόνον	δέ,	ἀλλὰ
tē	Sarrha	huios	Ou	monon	de	alla
	to Sarah	a son.	Not	only	and,	but

2504.1 conj	4336.1 name nom fem	1523.1 prep gen	1518.1 num card gen	2818.2 noun acc sing fem	2174.22 verb nom sing fem part pres act
καὶ	Ῥεβέκκα	ἐξ	ἑνὸς	κοίτην	ἔχουσα,
kai	Rhebekka	ex	henos	koitēn	echousa
also	Rebecca	by	one	conception	having,

2439.1 name masc	3450.2 art gen sing masc	3824.2 noun gen sing masc	2231.2 prs-pron gen 1pl	3247.1 adv	1056.1 conj
Ἰσαὰκ	τοῦ	πατρὸς	ἡμῶν	11. μήπω	γὰρ
Isaak	tou	patros	hēmōn	mēpō	gar
Isaac	the	father	our,	not yet	for

1074.19 verb gen pl masc part aor pass	3234.1 adv	4097.21 verb gen pl masc part aor act	4948.10 indef-pron sing neu	18.3 adj sing
γεννηθέντων,	μηδὲ	πραξάντων	τι	ἀγαθὸν
gennēthentōn	mēde	praxantōn	ti	agathon
having been born,	nor	having done	anything	good

11.a.Txt: p46,06D,018K 020L,33,byz. **Var:** 01ℵ,02A,03B,Lach Treg,Alf,Tisc,We/Ho Weis,Sod,UBS/✶

2211.1 conj	2527.7 adj sing neu	5175.1 adj sing neu	2419.1 conj	3450.9 art nom sing fem	2567.1 prep
ἤ	' κακόν,	[a✷ φαῦλον,]	ἵνα	ἡ	κατ'
ē	kakon	phaulon	hina	hē	kat'
or	evil,	[idem]	that	the	according to

1576.3 noun acc sing fem	3450.2 art gen sing	2296.2 noun gen sing masc	4145.1 noun nom sing fem	4145.1 noun nom sing fem
ἐκλογὴν	' τοῦ	θεοῦ	πρόθεσις	[✷ πρόθεσις
eklogēn	tou	theou	prothesis	prothesis
election		of God	purpose	[purpose

3450.2 art gen sing	2296.2 noun gen sing masc	3176.7 verb 3sing subj pres act	3620.2 partic	1523.1 prep gen	2024.5 noun gen pl neu	233.1 conj
τοῦ	θεοῦ]	μένῃ,	οὐκ	ἐξ	ἔργων,	ἀλλ'
tou	theou	menē	ouk	ex	ergōn	all'
the	of God]	might abide,	not	of	works,	but

12.a.Txt: 03B-corr 06D-corr,020L,byz. **Var:** 01ℵ,02A,03B-org 06D-org,018K,025P Lach,Treg,Alf,Tisc We/Ho,Weis,Sod UBS/✶

1523.2 prep gen	3450.2 art gen sing	2535.5 verb gen sing masc part pres act	1500.22 verb 3sing indic aor pass	1500.23 verb 3sing indic aor pass
ἐκ	τοῦ	καλοῦντος	12. ' ἐῤῥήθη	[a✷ ἐῤῥέθη]
ek	tou	kalountos	errhēthē	errhethē
of	the	calling,	it was said	[idem]

840.11 prs-pron dat sing fem	3617.1 conj	3450.5 art sing masc	3157.2 adj comp nom sing	1392.13 verb 3sing indic fut act	3450.3 art dat sing
αὐτῇ,	Ὅτι	ὁ	μείζων	δουλεύσει	τῷ
autē	Hoti	ho	meizōn	douleusei	tō
to her,	Hoti	The	greater	shall serve	the

13.a.Txt: 01ℵ,02A,06D 018K,020L,etc.byz.Tisc Sod **Var:** 03B,We/Ho,Weis UBS/✶

1629.1 adj comp dat sing masc	2503.1 conj	2481.1 conj	1119.22 verb 3sing indic perf pass
ἐλάσσονι	13. '✷ καθὼς	[a καθάπερ]	γέγραπται,
elassoni	kathōs	kathaper	gegraptai
lesser:	just as	[idem]	it has been written,

The Jews understood the selection process among their fore-
bears. Ishmael was the son of Abraham, born into the patriarchal
family. But no Jew would acknowledge Ishmael's descendants, the
Arabs, as being the chosen people. Esau was as much a son of Isaac
as was Jacob, and yet no Jew would countenance Esau as their
leader. Abraham pleaded with God on behalf of Ishmael (Genesis
17:18), and Isaac tried to give the patriarchal blessing to Esau
(Genesis 27:1-4,30-33). But the promise came through Isaac.

By that line of argument Paul presented the fact that the seed
was not by human lineage but through the righteousness of faith.

9:11. Two expressions need explanation. First, "the purpose of
God" was to have a family who, through the righteousness provided
by His Son, would be like His Son (8:29). The second term needing
explanation is "election." Election is not based on the "flesh" (verse
8), nor on "works" (verse 11). The basis is "him that calleth."

The Jew cannot say, "I am elected because I descended from
Abraham." The self-righteous cannot say, "We are elected because
of our good works." The legalist cannot say, "I am chosen because
I have obeyed the Law." Election is not based on works, but on the
call of God. Those who answer the call are the elected. Some would
say that those who are elected will answer the call. The Jew, the
self-righteous, and the legalist, all could argue their case, but to no
avail. God will save whom He will.

Who is the saved one? The answer is, "Whosoever believeth in
him should not perish, but have everlasting life" (John 3:16). The
unrighteous Gentiles and the self-righteous Jews can be saved only
through faith. (See *Overview*, pp.676-679.)

9:12,13. Not all the descendants of Abraham, Isaac, and Jacob
were within the design of God to carry out His plan. There was
more than physical descent; there was specific selection. Paul noted
that there was electing within the family of Abraham's physical
descendants, a point the Jews understood and accepted.

A further point is that the election was not on the basis of deed
or merit; Jacob was chosen and Esau was rejected before they were
born. The only preference would normally be priority of birth,
and God disregarded that. No legal works, no Jewish birth, could
give a person a claim that God must honor. He acts according to
His sovereign will.

Esau never served Jacob; therefore, we know that God was speaking of the time when Esau's descendants, the Edomites, would serve
Israel. Paul quoted from the Septuagint (Malachi 1:1,4) in order
to show that God has always acted in accordance with the principle
of divine election. This discussion will eventually show that salvation
for both Jew and Gentiles is according to God's election and not
by human will or effort.

"Loved" and "hated" are contrasted. It is not a literal hatred, but
the same kind Jesus requires, as stated in Luke 14:26. A form of

**At this time will I come, and
Sarah shall have a son:** About this
time next year, *Berkeley.*

**10. And not only [this]; but
when Rebecca also had conceived by one, [even] by our father Isaac:** Even more to the
point, *JB* . . . Nor is that all. There
is also the case of Rebecca, *TCNT*
. . . when she had cohabited with
one [man], *Murdock* . . . She was
soon to bear two children, *Weymouth* . . . when Rebecca became
pregnant, *Moffatt* . . . who was
impregnated by our forefather
Isaac, *Williams* . . . when she was
to have twins, *Norlie* . . . had conceived two sons by the same husband, *Conybeare.*

**11. (For [the children] being not
yet born, neither having done any
good or evil:** . . . nor having practiced, *Wuest* . . . and had done
nothing, *HistNT.*

**that the purpose of God ac-
cording to election might stand:**
. . . to confirm the divine purpose
in election, *Moffatt* . . . dominated by an act of selecting out,
Wuest . . . in order that the purpose of God's choice might prevail, *Berkeley* . . . so that God's
purpose of choice might stay,
Klingensmith . . . may carry out
His purpose according to His
choice, *Beck* . . . according to
election might continue, *Sawyer*
. . . according to the predetermin-
ation of his own choice, *Locke*
. . . might not be frustrated, *Weymouth* . . . God's purpose...is unconditional, *Way.*

**not of works, but of him that
calleth;):** . . . not on human merit,
JB . . . independent of deeds, entirely a matter of his calling,
HistNT . . . yet God had made an
election, *Norlie* . . . conditioned
not on men's actions but on God's
calling them, *Williams.*

**12. It was said unto her:
The elder shall serve the
younger:** The superior shall be
subject to the inferior, *Wilson*
. . . The elder shall be subject to
the younger, *Way* . . . The greater
shall be slaving for the inferior,
Concordant . . . will be bondser-
vant, *Weymouth* . . . will be a slave
to the younger, *Williams.*

Romans 9:14

3450.6 art acc sing masc	2361.1 name masc	25.12 verb 1sing indic aor act	3450.6 art acc sing masc	1156.2 conj	2247.1 name masc
Τὸν	Ἰακὼβ	ἠγάπησα,	τὸν	δὲ	Ἠσαῦ
Ton	Iakōb	ēgapēsa	ton	de	Ēsau
	Jacob	I loved,		and	Esau

3268.11 verb 1sing indic aor act	4949.9 intr-pron sing neu	3631.1 conj	2029.12 verb 1pl indic fut act	3231.1 partic
ἐμίσησα.	**14.** Τί	οὖν	ἐροῦμεν;	μὴ
emisēsa	Ti	oun	eroumen	mē
I hated.	What	then	shall we say?	Not

92.1 noun nom sing fem	3706.2 prep	3450.3 art dat sing	2296.3 noun dat sing masc	3231.1 partic	1090.44 verb 3sing opt aor mid
ἀδικία	παρὰ	τῷ	θεῷ;	μὴ	γένοιτο·
adikia	para	tō	theō	mē	genoito
unrighteousness	with	to	God?	Not	may it be!

3450.3 art dat sing	1056.1 conj	3337.4 name dat masc	3338.3 name dat masc	1056.1 conj	2978.5 verb 3sing indic pres act
15. τῷ	῾ γὰρ	Μωσῇ	[✶ Μωϋσεῖ	γὰρ]	λέγει,
tō	gar	Mōsē	Mōusei	gar	legei
to	For	to Moses	[to Moses	for]	he says,

1640.11 verb 1sing indic fut act	3614.6 rel-pron acc sing masc	300.1 partic	1640.2 verb 1sing subj pres act	2504.1 conj
Ἐλεήσω	ὃν	ἂν	ἐλεῶ,	καὶ
Eleēsō	hon	an	eleō	kai
I will show mercy	to whomsoever		I show mercy,	and

3489.2 verb 1sing indic fut act	3489.4 verb 1sing indic fut act	3614.6 rel-pron acc sing masc	300.1 partic
῾ οἰκτειρήσω	[✶ οἰκτιρήσω]	ὃν	ἂν
oikteirēsō	oiktirēsō	hon	an
I will feel compassion on	[idem]	whomsoever	

3489.1 verb 1sing subj pres act	3489.3 verb 1sing subj pres act	679.1 partic	3631.1 conj	3620.3 partic	3450.2 art gen sing
῾ οἰκτείρω.	[✶ οἰκτίρω.]	**16.** Ἄρα	οὖν	οὐ	τοῦ
oikteirō	oiktirō	Ara	oun	ou	tou
I feel compassion.	[idem]	So	then	not	the

2286.13 verb gen sing masc part pres act	3624.1 adv	3450.2 art gen sing	4983.7 verb gen sing masc part pres act	233.2 conj	3450.2 art gen sing
θέλοντος,	οὐδὲ	τοῦ	τρέχοντος,	ἀλλὰ	τοῦ
thelontos	oude	tou	trechontos	alla	tou
willing,	nor	of the	runing,	but	the

1640.4 verb gen sing masc part pres act	1635.2 verb gen sing part	2296.2 noun gen sing masc	2978.5 verb 3sing indic pres act	1056.1 conj
῾ ἐλεοῦντος	[ᵃ✶ ἐλεῶντος]	θεοῦ.	**17.** λέγει	γὰρ
eleountos	eleōntos	theou	legei	gar
showing mercy	[idem]	of God.	Says	for

16.a.**Txt:** 03B-corr,018K byz.Sod
Var: 01א,02A,03B-org 06D,025P,Lach,Treg Alf,Tisc,We/Ho,Weis UBS/✶

3450.9 art nom sing fem	1118.1 noun nom sing fem	3450.3 art dat sing	5166.1 name masc	3617.1 conj	1519.1 prep	840.15 prs-pron sing neu
ἡ	γραφὴ	τῷ	Φαραὼ,	Ὅτι	εἰς	αὐτὸ
hē	graphē	tō	Pharaō	Hoti	eis	auto
the	scripture	to	to Pharaoh,	For		same

3642.17 dem-pron sing neu	1809.1 verb 1sing indic aor act	4622.4 prs-pron acc 2sing	3567.1 conj	1715.6 verb 1sing subj aor mid
τοῦτο	ἐξήγειρά	σε,	ὅπως	ἐνδείξωμαι
touto	exēgeira	se	hopōs	endeixōmai
this thing	I raised out	you,	so that	I might demonstrate

the Greek term *miseō* ("hate") is used here in verse 13 (*emisēsa*). It does not mean to detest or to reject. It means to place in much lower priority in one's concern.

It was not possible for both Esau and Jacob to receive the birthright and be in the line of Messiah. Therefore one must be chosen (elected) and the other not chosen (hated).

Our love for Jesus must be so much greater than our love for father, mother, and all else, that by comparison the lesser love could be called "hate." There will be times when we have to choose between Him and other loved ones. When choice is unavoidable, the "not chosen," whether Esau or our treasures, may be described as "hated."

The choice of Jacob rather than Esau had nothing to do with their eternal salvation. Esau still had the opportunity to serve God and put his faith in Him. The repentance he could not find was the recovery of the birthright he had forfeited; he did not seek to repent of his profane life-style and immorality (Hebrews 12:16,17).

The destiny of Israel has been shaped by their experience with two persons—Moses and Jacob. The Jews were separated from other peoples to be God's witness to the nations and to be custodians of His law. Their choice was not based upon (1) numerical strength—Deuteronomy 7:7; (2) power and wealth—Deuteronomy 8:18; or (3) righteousness—Deuteronomy 9:6.

This passage lays the foundation for the truth of God's sovereignty over Israel. Israel, God's chosen nation, came into existence by the supernatural act of God. The bodies of Abraham and Sarah were as good as dead, but God performed a miracle to beget Abraham's seed. If God had not acted, there would have been no nation.

9:14-17. In the pattern found so often in Romans, Paul opened this portion with a question, "Is there unrighteousness with God?" The answer is a resounding, "God forbid." Paul presented a discussion that contains one of the most profound mysteries of our world: Israel must leave God to His sovereignty. Like Jacob, Moses received the mercy of God and by obeying became the deliverer of Israel. Like Esau, Pharaoh rejected God's mercy and was hardened. Moses was the vessel of mercy; Pharaoh, the vessel of wrath.

God does not create human beings for the purpose of condemning them; nor is He responsible for the sinfulness of men. In Pharaoh's case God gave him chance after chance to repent. Pharaoh's heart was not hardened until after he had rejected the light which came from God. The Scripture recounts 10 times when it is said that Pharaoh hardened himself. Pharaoh did not want God; he hardened his heart first of his own volition; then God made him an example of His displeasure with sin and of those who spurn His love and grace.

God gave Pharaoh, as well as Moses, an outstanding revelation of His power and of His mercy. Moses was responsive, but Pharaoh was rebellious. The revelation melted and shaped Moses, while it hardened Pharaoh. The gospel does the same wherever it is

Romans 9:17

13. As it is written:
Jacob have I loved, but Esau have I hated: To Jacob I was drawn, but Esau I repudiated, *Berkeley.*

14. What shall we say then? [Is there] unrighteousness with God?: . . . what do we infer? That with God there is injustice? *Berkeley* . . . what shall we conclude? That God is unjust? *Norlie* . . . Do you dare insinuate that partiality—injustice, in fact—is an attribute of God? *Way* . . . Is there iniquitie vvith God? *Rheims.*
God forbid: Perish the thought! *Berkeley* . . . No indeed, *Montgomery* . . . Away with the thought! God's decision is beyond challenge, *Way.*

15. For he saith to Moses:
I will have mercy on whom I will have mercy: I will do kindness, *Young* . . . on whom I choose to have mercy, *Moffatt.*
and I will have compassion on whom I will have compassion: I will pity whom I want to pity, *Beck.*

16. So then [it is] not of him that willeth, nor of him that runneth: . . . it isn't a question of, *Adams* . . . is not on account of man's will or his readiness, *Norlie* . . . So it depends not upon man's will or exertion, *RSV* . . . nor of him who is racing, *Concordant* . . . it doesn't depend on anyone wanting it or trying hard, *Beck* . . . not on human wishes or human efforts, *TCNT.*
but of God that showeth mercy: . . . that exercises mercy, *Sawyer* . . . but of the pitying God, *Hanson* . . . but on His own fiat, *Way.*

17. For the scripture saith unto Pharaoh:
Even for this same purpose have I raised thee up, that I might show my power in thee: For this very thing, *Panin* . . . to high position...to show My power in dealing with you, *Norlie* . . . I set you up high, to present in you the evidence of My power, *Berkeley* . . . that I may exhibit my power, *Hanson* . . . to demonstrate My power, *Beck.*

149

1706.1 prep	4622.3 prs-pron dat 2sing	3450.12 art acc sing fem	1405.4 noun acc sing fem	1466.2 prs-pron gen 1sing	2504.1 conj	3567.1 conj
ἐν	σοὶ	τὴν	δύναμίν	μου,	καὶ	ὅπως
en	soi	tēn	dunamin	mou	kai	hopōs
in	you	the	power	my,	and	so that

1223.3 verb 3sing subj aor pass	3450.16 art sing neu	3549.2 noun sing neu	1466.2 prs-pron gen 1sing	1706.1 prep	3820.11 adj dat sing fem
διαγγελῇ	τὸ	ὄνομά	μου	ἐν	πάσῃ
diangelē	to	onoma	mou	en	pasē
should be declared	to	name	my	in	all

3450.11 art dat sing fem	1087.3 noun dat sing fem	679.1 partic	3631.1 conj	3614.6 rel-pron acc sing masc	2286.3 verb 3sing indic pres act
τῇ	γῇ.	**18.** Ἄρα	οὖν	ὃν	θέλει
tē	gē	Ara	oun	hon	thelei
the	earth.	So	then	to whom	he will

1640.1 verb 3sing indic pres act	3614.6 rel-pron acc sing masc	1156.2 conj	2286.3 verb 3sing indic pres act	4500.1 verb 3sing indic pres act
ἐλεεῖ·	ὃν	δὲ	θέλει	σκληρύνει.
eleei	hon	de	thelei	sklērunei
he shows mercy,	whom	and	he will	he hardens.

2029.10 verb 2sing indic fut act	3631.1 conj	1466.4 prs-pron dat 1sing	1466.4 prs-pron dat 1sing	3631.1 conj	4949.9 intr-pron sing neu
19. Ἐρεῖς	˹ οὖν	μοι,	[☆ μοι	οὖν,]	Τί
Ereis	oun	moi	moi	oun	Ti
You will say	then	to me,	[to me	then,]	Why

2068.1 adv	3171.1 verb 3sing indic pres	3450.3 art dat sing	1056.1 conj	1006.2 noun dat sing neu	840.3 prs-pron gen sing
ἔτι	μέμφεται;	τῷ	γὰρ	βουλήματι	αὐτοῦ
eti	memphetai	tō	gar	boulēmati	autou
yet	does he find fault?	the	for	purpose	his

4949.3 intr-pron nom sing	434.5 verb 3sing indic perf act	3174.1 partic	5434.1 intrj
τίς	ἀνθέστηκεν;	**20.** ˹ Μενοῦνγε,	ὦ
tis	anthestēken	Menounge	ō
who	has resisted?	On the contrary,	O

442.5 noun voc sing masc	5434.1 intrj	442.5 noun voc sing masc	3173.1 partic	1058.1 partic	4622.1 prs-pron nom 2sing
ἄνθρωπε,	[☆ ὦ	ἄνθρωπε,	μενοῦν	γε]	σὺ
anthrōpe	ō	anthrōpe	menoun	ge	su
man,	[O	man,	rather	yet]	you

4949.3 intr-pron nom sing	1498.3 verb 2sing indic pres act	3450.5 art sing masc	467.1 verb nom sing masc part pres	3450.3 art dat sing
τίς	εἶ	ὁ	ἀνταποκρινόμενος	τῷ
tis	ei	ho	antapokrinomenos	tō
who	are	the	answering against	

2296.3 noun dat sing masc	3231.1 partic	2029.11 verb 3sing indic fut act	3450.16 art sing neu	3971.1 noun nom sing neu	3450.3 art dat sing
θεῷ;	μὴ	ἐρεῖ	τὸ	πλάσμα	τῷ
theō	mē	erei	to	plasma	tō
God?	Not	shall say	to	thing formed	to the

3972.1 verb dat sing masc part aor act	4949.9 intr-pron sing neu	1466.6 prs-pron acc 1sing	4020.23 verb 2sing indic aor act	3643.1 adv
πλάσαντι,	Τί	με	ἐποίησας	οὕτως;
plasanti	Ti	me	epoiēsas	houtōs
having formed,	Why	me	made you	thus?

preached; some will yield, and others will reject (2 Corinthians 2:16-18).

Again quoting the Scriptures, Paul points out a truth undeniable to the Jew, undeniable because "the Scripture saith." The truth is this: that God, according to His sovereign design, raised up Pharaoh (Exodus 9:16). The most natural understanding of these words is that God caused Pharaoh to come upon the scene at that particular point in time for a very specific reason.

In Exodus 9:15 God says to Pharaoh, "Now I will stretch out my hand and smite thee . . . ." In verse 16, quoted here in Romans, He continues by stating, "And in very deed for this cause I have raised thee up." The implication is that God would demonstrate His power to the whole world through the plagues He sent against Pharaoh and Egypt. Though difficult to grasp, it appears that God chose him to be a vessel of wrath (cf. verse 22).

9:18,19. Verse 18 is one of the strongest statements in the New Testament about the sovereignty of God's will. Some point to it as proof that God is sovereign in predestinating some to salvation and some to perdition ("double predestination"). It must be kept in mind, however, that the context involves the salvation history of a nation. Furthermore, this passage must be balanced with the many universal invitations in the New Testament to believe and accept Christ.

From a New Testament perspective we know that God does not entice men to do evil, nor does He cause them to do so (James 1:13,14). When people do wrong, it comes from their depraved nature. Contextually, verses 19 through 33 attempt to explain principles overlooked by many Jews of the day.

Earlier in the chapter Paul stated that not all Israelites were "true Jews" in the spiritual sense (verses 6-8). The examples he gave to describe election no doubt would create questions. In verse 19 Paul anticipates objections the Jewish readers would raise. Confronted with God's sovereignty, first in choosing Jacob over Esau and then in hardening whom He will harden (Pharaoh), the logical objection is this: How can God find fault with a person if it is He himself who caused that person to be hardened?

In addition, Paul meets another objection offered by sincere Jewish believers. They could not understand how Israel, to whom belonged the honors listed in 9:4,5, could be set aside for the Gentiles, who were brought from their alienated and lost status to the place of blessing. The apostle proves that the Word of God cannot fail and that His character is beyond questioning.

The rabbis of Paul's day looked upon God's covenant with Israel as such that no matter how sinful Israel was, their place in God could never change. They held to the premise of absolute predestination; the Gentiles were to be destroyed, but nothing could dissolve God's covenant with the Jews.

9:20. It is incongruous for the creature to judge the Creator. Men are not lost because God has hardened them. They are hardened because they are lost; they are lost because they are sinners. God is not responsible for man's sin, but He offers mercy to all.

and that my name might be declared throughout all the earth: . . . so that My name may be famed, *Berkeley* . . . my name may be scattered abroad, *Klingensmith* . . . might be published abroad, *HistNT, Worrell* . . . might be renowned through, *Locke* . . . the entire earth, *Concordant* . . . in all the land, *Young*.

18. Therefore hath he mercy on whom he will [have mercy], and whom he will he hardeneth: He hardens the heart, *Weymouth, RSV* . . . and he makes anyone stubborn just as he pleases, *Moffatt* . . . He confirms in their stubbornness, *Way* . . . just as he chooses, *TCNT*.

19. Thou wilt say then unto me: . . . you will retort, *Moffatt*.
Why doth he yet find fault?: Why does He still complain, *Berkeley* . . . Why does He still blame people, *Adams* . . . He still persist in finding fault? *Wuest*.
For who hath resisted his will?: For who withstandeth his purpose? *Panin* . . . for His counsel who hath resisted, *Young* . . . since no one can oppose his will? *JB* . . . who can oppose his purpose? *HistNT* . . . who hath withstood His Will? *Clementson*.

20. Nay but, O man, who art thou that repliest against God?: I might rather ask...frail mortal, who are arguing with God? *TCNT* . . . who are you anyway, to talk back to God? *Berkeley* . . . mere human creature that you are, dare arraign God? *Way* . . . who art thou replying against God? *Wilson* . . . whych disputest with God? *Cranmer* . . . to cross-examine God? *JB* . . . to answer back to God? *RSV*.
Shall the thing formed say to him that formed [it]: Will anything shaped by a man say to him, *Beck* . . . Doth the vvorke say to him that vvrought it, *Rheims* . . . The moldable material shall not say, *Wuest* . . . say to him who moulded it, *Weymouth*.
Why hast thou made me thus?: Why did you make me this shape? *JB* . . . Why didst thou fashion me into this form? *Way*.

21. Ἤ οὐκ ἔχει ἐξουσίαν ὁ κεραμεὺς
E ouk echei exousian ho kerameus
Or not has authority the potter

τοῦ πηλοῦ, ἐκ τοῦ αὐτοῦ φυράματος
tou pēlou ek tou autou phuramatos
of the clay, out of the same lump

ποιῆσαι ὃ μὲν εἰς τιμὴν σκεῦος, ὃ
poiēsai ho men eis timēn skeuos ho
to make that to honor vessel, that

δὲ εἰς ἀτιμίαν; **22.** εἰ δὲ θέλων
de eis atimian ei de thelōn
and to dishonor? If and willing

ὁ θεὸς ἐνδείξασθαι τὴν ὀργὴν, καὶ
ho theos endeixasthai tēn orgēn kai
God to demonstrate the wrath, and

γνωρίσαι τὸ δυνατὸν αὐτοῦ, ἤνεγκεν ἐν
gnōrisai to dunaton autou ēnenken en
to make known the power his, bore in

πολλῇ μακροθυμίᾳ σκεύη ὀργῆς κατηρτισμένα
pollē makrothumia skeuē orgēs katērtismena
much longsuffering vessels of wrath having been fitted

εἰς ἀπώλειαν· **23.** καὶ ἵνα γνωρίσῃ τὸν
eis apōleian kai hina gnōrisē ton
for destruction; and that he might make known the

πλοῦτον τῆς δόξης αὐτοῦ ἐπὶ σκεύη ἐλέους,
plouton tēs doxēs autou epi skeuē eleous
riches of the glory his upon vessels of mercy,

ἃ προητοίμασεν εἰς δόξαν· **24.** οὓς καὶ
ha proētoimasen eis doxan hous kai
which he before prepared for glory, whom also

ἐκάλεσεν ἡμᾶς οὐ μόνον ἐξ Ἰουδαίων,
ekalesen hēmas ou monon ex Ioudaiōn
he called us not only from among Jews,

9:21,22. The apostle offers another illustration of God's sovereignty. As the potter has absolute sovereignty over the clay, so God has absolute sovereignty over men. God does not need to answer man because He is infinite and independent. Even though He is unanswerable for what He does, He can be trusted to act in consistency with His character. And though He is free to act according to His pleasure, He is patient and full of long-suffering. His sovereignty is exercised in mercy.

The potter may take a lump of clay. Twisting it in half, he places one part on the worktable and makes of it a beautiful, graceful, almost priceless piece of pottery. Out of the same lump of clay he will take the other half and make it into a common, ordinary vessel that could be bought for a few cents at some store. Both vessels are made from the same lump of clay, by the same master potter. First Corinthians 10:1-12 illustrates this point very well.

Isolated from other Bible truths, this passage seems to suggest partiality on God's part. It is possible to take it out of context and make it a basic doctrine. But if one attempts to divorce teaching on election from teaching on divine foreknowledge, the result may be a religious fatalism giving license for sin.

9:23. The omnipotent God may do with that which belongs to Him just as He wills. So even if an extreme teaching of election is maintained, and God assigns certain men to go to hell and certain men to go to heaven, God would still be just because He would be disposing of His property according to His will as the omnipotent God.

The language of verses 22 and 23 represents two distinct categories of individuals: "vessels" that are fitted or designed for destruction (the phrase further describes Pharaoh [see verse 17ff.], as well as apostate Jews being described in these chapters), and vessels on whom God chose to show mercy and prepare in advance for glory. It is hard to deny that the wording points to the sovereignty of God over the destiny of men. It seems that the believer must be content to live with the tension created by statements regarding free will and those which seemingly imply predestination.

God's patience is revealed again and again. The judgments of His wrath have always been preceded with much long-suffering. That was true of Cain, of Pharaoh, of Lot and Sodom. Warning after warning is given until the offender crosses an invisible line and there remains no more repentance but "a certain fearful looking for of judgment and fiery indignation" (Hebrews 10:27).

9:24. Not only has God been long-suffering in judgment, but the bestowal of His mercy has always been impartial and all of grace. There is no difference between Jew or Gentile (Romans 10:12; cf. Lamentations 3:22,23). The called were not found among the Jews only but also among the Gentiles. The promise of salvation was not based on nationality but is "of him that calleth" (verse 11).

21. Hath not the potter power over the clay: ... dominion, *Murdock* ... in dealing with clay, a perfect right, *TCNT* ... authority over, *Klingensmith* ... rightful power, *Weymouth* ... at his absolute disposal, *Way.*

of the same lump to make one vessel unto honour, and another unto dishonour?: ... to fashion of the same paste, *Way* ... out of the same mass, *Scarlett* ... out of the same Mixture, *Wilson* ... the one for distinguished service, *Norlie* ... one utensil for noble use, *Berkeley* ... one thing for a noble purpose and another for a lowly purpose? *Beck* ... one jar as a decorative item and another jar for everyday use? *Adams* ... another for degrading service? *Williams.*

22. [What] if God, willing to show [his] wrath: ... desiring to demonstrate His wrath, *Wuest* ... wishing to exhibit his displeasure, *Hanson* ... wishing to exhibit his indignation, *Wilson.*

and to make his power known: ... and to reveal all His irresponsible power, *Way.*

endured with much longsuffering: ... yet He endures long and patiently, *Norlie* ... has tolerated most patiently, *Moffatt* ... tolerated with much longsuffering, *HistNT* ... with great patience enduring the agents, *Berkeley* ... suffered wyth longe pacyence, *Cranmer* ... susteined in much patience, *Rheims.*

the vessels of wrath fitted to destruction: ... the vases of wrath, *Adams* ... the objects of his anger, ripe and ready to be destroyed? *Moffatt* ... made ready to damnation, *Geneva.*

23. And that he might make known the riches of his glory on the vessels of mercy: ... made his mercy flow forth, *Murdock* ... to the recipients of mercy, *Berkeley* ... which he had previously prepared for majesty, *HistNT* ... which He flooded with His mercy, *Way.*

which he had afore prepared unto glory:

24. Even us, whom he hath called:

153

233.2 conj	2504.1 conj	1523.1 prep gen	1477.5 noun gen pl neu		5453.1 conj	2504.1 conj	1706.1 prep
ἀλλὰ	καὶ	ἐξ	ἐθνῶν·	**25.**	ὡς	καὶ	ἐν
alla	kai	ex	ethnōn		hōs	kai	en
but	also	from among	Gentiles?		As	also	in

3450.3 art dat sing	5449.1 name masc	2978.5 verb 3sing indic pres act	2535.22 verb 1sing indic fut act	3450.6 art acc sing masc	3620.3 partic
τῷ	Ὡσηὲ	λέγει,	Καλέσω	τὸν	οὐ
tō	Ōsēe	legei	Kalesō	ton	ou
to	Hosea	he says,	I will call	the	not

2967.4 noun acc sing masc	1466.2 prs-pron gen 1sing	2967.4 noun acc sing masc	1466.2 prs-pron gen 1sing	2504.1 conj	3450.12 art acc sing fem	3620.2 partic
λαόν	μου,	λαόν	μου·	καὶ	τὴν	οὐκ
laon	mou	laon	mou	kai	tēn	ouk
people	my,	People	my;	and	the	not

25.31 verb acc sing fem part perf pass	25.31 verb acc sing fem part perf pass	2504.1 conj	1498.40 verb 3sing indic fut mid
ἠγαπημένην,	ἠγαπημένη.	**26.** Καὶ	ἔσται,
ēgapēmenēn	ēgapēmenē	Kai	estai
having been loved,	having been loved.	And	it shall be,

26.a.Txt: 03B-corr
06D-corr,020L,byz.
Var: 01א,02A,03B-org
06D-org,018K,025P
Lach,Treg,Alf,Tisc
We/Ho,Weis,Sod
UBS/☆

1706.1 prep	3450.3 art dat sing	4964.3 noun dat sing masc	3614.2 rel-pron gen sing	1500.22 verb 3sing indic aor pass	1500.23 verb 3sing indic aor pass
ἐν	τῷ	τόπῳ	οὗ	(ἐρρήθη	[a☆ ἐρρέθη]
en	tō	topō	hou	errhēthē	errhethē
in	the	place	that	it was said	[idem]

840.2 prs-pron dat pl	3620.3 partic	2967.1 noun sing masc	1466.2 prs-pron gen 1sing	5050.1 prs-pron nom 2pl	1550.1 adv
αὐτοῖς,	Οὐ	λαός	μου	ὑμεῖς,	ἐκεῖ
autois	Ou	laos	mou	humeis	ekei
to them,	Not	people	my	you,	there

2535.53 verb 3pl indic fut pass	5048.6 noun pl masc	2296.2 noun gen sing masc	2180.11 verb gen sing part pres act	2246.5 name nom masc
κληθήσονται	υἱοὶ	θεοῦ	ζῶντος.	**27.** Ἡσαΐας
klēthēsontai	huioi	theou	zōntos	Esaias
they shall be called	sons	of God	living.	Isaiah

1156.2 conj	2869.1 verb 3sing indic pres act	5065.1 prep	3450.2 art gen sing	2447.1 name masc	1430.1 partic
δὲ	κράζει	ὑπὲρ	τοῦ	Ἰσραήλ,	Ἐὰν
de	krazei	huper	tou	Israēl	Ean
but	cries	concerning	the	Israel,	If

1498.10 verb 3sing subj pres act	3450.5 art sing masc	700.1 noun nom sing masc	3450.1 art gen pl	5048.7 noun gen pl masc	2447.1 name masc
ᾖ	ὁ	ἀριθμὸς	τῶν	υἱῶν	Ἰσραὴλ
ē	ho	arithmos	tōn	huiōn	Israēl
should be	the	number	of the	sons	of Israel

5453.1 conj	3450.9 art nom sing fem	283.1 noun nom sing fem	3450.10 art gen sing fem	2258.2 noun gen sing fem	3450.16 art sing neu
ὡς	ἡ	ἄμμος	τῆς	θαλάσσης,	τὸ
hōs	hē	ammos	tēs	thalassēs	to
as	the	sand	of the	sea,	to the

27.a.Txt: 01א-corr,06D
018K,020L,025P,byz.
Sod
Var: 01א-org,02A,03B
Lach,Treg,Alf,Tisc
We/Ho,Weis,UBS/☆

2610.1 noun nom sing neu	5112.1 noun nom sing neu	4834.33 verb 3sing indic fut pass	3030.4 noun acc sing masc
(κατάλειμμα	[a☆ ὑπόλειμμα]	σωθήσεται·	**28.** λόγον
kataleimma	hupoleimma	sōthēsetai	logon
remnant	[idem]	shall be saved:	matter

9:25,26. Hosea, through his own tragic domestic life, saw a picture of the relationship between God and Israel. When he took Gomer as his wife, and she later gave birth to a son, he acknowledged the child as his. But he was convinced that the second and third children were not his. The names he gave them expressed his disappointment—Lo-ruhamah (meaning one for whom no natural affection is felt) and Lo-ammi (meaning no kin of mine). Their names pictured God's attitude toward His people Israel. But God will not allow that broken relationship to remain forever. He looks forward to the day when those who at present are estranged from Him will again be His people, and when those who now have no claim on His kindly feelings will again be objects of His mercy.

There is a principle of divine action at work in God's extension of His mercy. He is always desirous of restoring those who have departed from His favor. The Gentile rejection of God is described in a general way in 1:18-32. Just as God promised to restore Israel to His love and favor, He promised grace and mercy to Gentiles.

The revelation that Jews and Gentiles stood on equal ground before God was astounding to Jews. As the "minister of Jesus Christ to the Gentiles" (15:16), Paul placed great importance on that revelation. He called it "the mystery, which was kept secret since the world began" (16:25). Ephesians 3:1-9 explains this mystery, defined as "that the Gentiles should be fellow heirs" to Christ.

It was always God's will that all men be saved. Ruth is one example of the Gentiles who came to God through Jewish witness. When God chose Abraham it was with the intent that all the world be blessed. The Jews had lost the sense of their reason for being. When they failed to take the Word to all, both they and Gentiles suffered inestimable loss.

God's dealings with Israel were based on His wisdom, His sovereignty, and His Word. The prophecy of Hosea foretold a revival by which the blessing of God would ultimately reach Gentiles also. No Gentiles had ever been called the people of God, but now both Jews and Gentiles are brought into the Church, the great New Testament body (Ephesians 2:12-19).

9:27-29. The prophecies of Hosea and Isaiah are quoted to show that the call of the Gentiles had been foretold. The backslidings and waywardness of Israel would result in the acceptance of but a remnant of a people as numerous "as the sand of the sea."

Hosea had said that God would make His people a people who were not His people (Hosea 2:23), and that those people would be called the sons of God (Hosea 1:10). He also showed how Isaiah had been made aware that Israel would have been wiped out had not a remnant been left (Isaiah 10:22,23; 37:32). The apostle is saying that Israel would have known of her fate if she had listened to and understood the Word of the Lord to her.

The context of Isaiah's prophecy was the impending Assyrian invasion of Israel. Only a minority survived the captivity and exile (Isaiah 10:21). Isaiah's elder son was named Shear-jashub ("rem-

not of the Jews only, but also of the Gentiles?: . . . not only from among the Jews, *Barclay.*

25. As he saith also in Osee: That is exactly what God says in Hosea, *JB* . . . as was prophesied in Hosea, *ET.*

I will call them my people, which were not my people: I will give the title of, *Barclay* . . . that was not mine, *Way* . . . I will make them my people who were not my people, *ET.*

and her beloved, which was not beloved: I will call My loved ones, *Beck* . . . I will love her which I did not love, *ET* . . . an unbeloved, beloved, *Confraternity* . . . I never loved, *JB* . . . and the unloved nation, *NEB.*

26. And it shall come to pass, [that] in the place where it was said unto them, Ye [are] not my people: . . . and it will happen that, *ET* . . . in the very place where they were told, "you are no people of mine,"*NEB.*

there shall they be called the children of the living God: . . . of the ever-living God, *Weymouth* . . . they shall be numbered with God's people, *ET* . . . sons of the living God, *Barclay.*

27. Esaias also crieth concerning Israel: Isaiah shouted out about Israel, *Klingensmith* . . . Besides, Isaiah crieth, *Macknight* . . . Isaiah also prophesied over Israel, *ET* . . . cries in anguish concerning Israel, *Wuest* . . . exclaims concerning Israel, *TCNT* . . . how the cry of Isaiah peals over Israel, *Way.*

Though the number of the children of Israel be as the sand of the sea: . . . schal be as grauel of the see, *Wyclif* . . . are as numberless as the sands, *Williams* . . . are as uncountable as, *ET* . . . be countless as the sands, *NEB.*

a remnant shall be saved: . . . but it is only the remnant who will be saved, *Barclay* . . . the residue, *Concordant* . . . only a remnant, *RSV* . . . the leftovers shall be saved, *Berkeley* . . . the remaines shal be saued, *Rheims* . . . there will always be some leftovers, *ET* . . . of them will live, *Murdock.*

Romans 9:29

28.a.**Txt:** 01אּ-corr,06D
018K,020L,025P,044
33,byz.it.Weis
Var: p46,01אּ-org,02A
03B,sa.bo,Lach,Treg
Tisc,We/Ho,Sod,UBS/✶

1056.1 conj	4783.1 verb nom sing masc part pres act	2504.1 conj	4784.1 verb nom sing masc part pres act	1706.1 prep	1336.3 noun dat sing fem
γὰρ	συντελῶν	καὶ	συντέμνων	[a ἐν	δικαιοσύνῃ·
gar	suntelōn	kai	suntemnōn	en	dikaiosunē
for	concluding	and	cutting short	in	righteousness:

3617.1 conj	3030.4 noun acc sing masc	4784.2 verb acc sing masc part perf pass	4020.52 verb 3sing indic fut act	2935.1 noun nom sing masc
ὅτι	λόγον	συντετμημένον ⟩	ποιήσει	κύριος
hoti	logon	suntetmēmenon	poiēsei	kurios
because	a matter	having been cut short	will do	Lord

1894.3 prep	3450.10 art gen sing fem	1087.2 noun gen sing fem	2504.1 conj	2503.1 conj	4136.2 verb 3sing indic perf act
ἐπὶ	τῆς	γῆς.	**29.** καὶ	καθὼς	προείρηκεν
epi	tēs	gēs.	kai	kathōs	proeirēken
upon	the	earth.	And	just as	has said before

2246.1 name nom masc	1479.1 conj	3231.1 partic	2935.1 noun nom sing masc	4376.1 noun nom masc	1452.3 verb 3sing indic aor act
Ἡσαΐας,	Εἰ	μὴ	κύριος	Σαβαὼθ	ἐγκατέλιπεν
Hēsaias	Ei	mē	kurios	Sabaōth	enkatelipen
Isaiah,	If	not	Lord	of Hosts	had left

2231.3 prs-pron dat 1pl	4543.1 noun sing neu	5453.1 conj	4525.1 name neu	300.1 partic	1090.34 verb 1pl indic aor pass
ἡμῖν	σπέρμα,	ὡς	Σόδομα	ἂν	ἐγενήθημεν,
hēmin	sperma	hōs	Sodoma	an	egenēthēmen
us	a seed,	as	Sodom		we should have become,

2504.1 conj	5453.1 conj	1110.1 name nom	300.1 partic	3529.4 verb 1pl indic aor pass
καὶ	ὡς	Γόμορρα	ἂν	ὡμοιώθημεν.
kai	hōs	Gomorrha	an	hōmoiōthēmen
and	as	Gomorrah		we should have been made like.

4949.9 intr-pron sing neu	3631.1 conj	2029.12 verb 1pl indic fut act	3617.1 conj	1477.4 noun pl neu	3450.17 art pl neu	3231.1 partic
30. Τί	οὖν	ἐροῦμεν;	ὅτι	ἔθνη	τὰ	μὴ
Ti	oun	eroumen	hoti	ethnē	ta	mē
What	then	shall we say?	That	Gentiles	the	not

1371.11 verb nom pl neu part pres act	1336.4 noun acc sing fem	2608.1 verb 3sing indic aor act	1336.4 noun acc sing fem
διώκοντα	δικαιοσύνην,	κατέλαβεν	δικαιοσύνην,
diōkonta	dikaiosunēn	katelaben	dikaiosunēn
following after	righteousness,	attained	righteousness,

1336.4 noun acc sing fem	1156.2 conj	3450.12 art acc sing fem	1523.2 prep gen	3963.2 noun gen sing fem	2447.1 name masc
δικαιοσύνην	δὲ	τὴν	ἐκ	πίστεως·	**31.** Ἰσραὴλ
dikaiosunēn	de	tēn	ek	pisteōs	Israēl
righteousness	but	the	by	faith.	Israel

1156.2 conj	1371.7 verb nom sing masc part pres act	3414.4 noun acc sing fem	1336.2 noun gen sing fem	1519.1 prep
δὲ	διώκων	νόμον	δικαιοσύνης,	εἰς
de	diōkōn	nomon	dikaiosunēs	eis
but,	following after	a law	of righteousness,	to

31.a.**Txt:** 01אּ-corr,018K
020L,025P,byz.
Var: 01אּ-org,02A,03B
06D,Lach,Treg,Alf
Word,Tisc,We/Ho,Weis
Sod,UBS/✶

3414.4 noun acc sing masc	1336.2 noun gen sing fem	3620.2 partic	5185.1 verb 3sing indic aor act	1296.1 adv
νόμον	[a δικαιοσύνης ⟩	οὐκ	ἔφθασεν.	**32.** [διατί;
nomon	dikaiosunēs	ouk	ephthasen	diati
a law	of righteousness	not	did attain.	Why?

nant will return") as a sign to Judah. Only a remnant were true to God.

Israel did not fail of righteousness because of nonelection. Their failure was their own fault. They stumbled over Christ. He is either a steppingstone or "a stumblingstone and rock of offense" (9:33).

Israel's "stumblingstone" was the necessity of faith in Christ as the Messiah. They had prayed for, hoped for, and looked for the promised Messiah. But when He came as the crucified Christ they would not accept Him. The Cross was an "offense" to the Jew. Calvary did away with works, with legalism.

9:30. This verse shows the Gentiles have attained that for which they had no desire, and the Jews have failed in securing that to which they had devoted their lives. The condition of the Gentile world, apart from Christ, is pictured in Ephesians 2:12. We "followed not after righteousness." Romans 3:11 tells us there is "none that understandeth, . . . none that seeketh after God."

But now we, who were outside and had no aspirations spiritually or Godward, have through the infinite mercy and grace of God attained to that righteousness which the Jews desired, but were never able to attain.

9:31. Why could not Israel attain to the righteousness they desired? The key is in the preceding verse. The Gentiles had attained righteousness by faith. In a sense there are two kinds of righteousness. There is the righteousness which Paul describes, the righteousness which the Gentiles attained. Then there is the righteousness which the Jews sought after, what the Bible calls their own righteousness, which is "as filthy rags" (Isaiah 64:6).

All that we receive from God comes through faith. We are saved by faith (Ephesians 2:8,9). We are justified by faith, not by the works of the Law (Romans 5:1; Galatians 2:16). We have access to God's throne by faith (5:2). All that we have comes by faith and is entirely divorced from works and self-effort: "Not of works, lest any man should boast" (Ephesians 2:9). It is all based on faith.

Paul makes the point clearly. The Jews had no claim to salvation as a national right. The way was plain, but they refused to accept it. On the other hand, the Gentiles who were not seeking righteousness, gladly accepted salvation by faith when they heard the good news of the gospel. By the hundreds and thousands, they "turned to God from idols to serve the living and true God; and to wait for his Son from heaven" (1 Thessalonians 1:9,10).

Except for a believing remnant, the Jews turned in hatred on the Christians, driving them from their homes and scattering them abroad.

All Jews believed that possession of the law of Moses was all that was required, providing they lived by it. That goal was unattainable. When Messiah came, they rejected Him. They wanted a militant Lion; God sent a Lamb. They wanted a throne; God gave the Cross.

28. For he will finish the work, and cut [it] short in righteousness: . . . for "a conclusive and concise accounting," *Concordant* . . . the Lord fulfills his word speedily in justice, *Confraternity* . . . for he executes and performs his word, *Sawyer* . . . abbridging it in equitie, *Rheims*.

because a short work will the Lord make upon the earth: . . . for thoroughly and with dispatch, *Berkeley* . . . fully and without delay, *TCNT* . . . the Lord will carry out His orders, *Norlie* . . . will completely and decisively execute His sentence, *Beck*.

29. And as Esaias said before: . . . as Isaiah has before announced, *Hanson* . . . Even as in an earlier passage, *Montgomery*.

Except the Lord of Sabaoth had left us a seed: Unless the Lord of hosts, *Wesley* . . . If the Lord of armies hadn't left us some survivors, *Beck* . . . had left us a posterity, *Confraternity*.

we had been as Sodoma, and been made like unto Gomorrha: . . . our nation would have disappeared as utterly, *Way* . . . and had bene lykened to, *Cranmer* . . . and should have resembled Gomorrah, *Wilson* . . . and should have fared like, *Montgomery*.

30. What shall we say then?: . . . what is our inference? *Berkeley*.

That the Gentiles:
which followed not after righteousness: . . . who never ran in the race for righteousness, *Way* . . . who did not pursue righteousness, *Macknight*.

have attained to righteousness: . . . haue ouertaken rightuousnes? *Geneva* . . . haue apprehended, *Rheims*.

even the righteousness which is of faith: . . . a right standing conditioned on faith, *Williams*.

31. But Israel, which followed after the law of righteousness: Contrary wise, *Cranmer* . . . was in search of a Law, *TCNT* . . . for the securing of, *Berkeley*.

hath not attained to the law of righteousness: . . . did not arrive at that law, *Clementson*.

Romans 9:33

32.a.**Txt:** 01ℵ-corr,06D
018K,020L,025P,044
33,byz.We/Ho
Var: p46,01ℵ-org,02A
03B,it.sa.bo.Lach,Treg
Word,Tisc,Weis,Sod
UBS/✶

32.b.**Txt:** 01ℵ-corr
06D-corr,018K,020L
025P,byz.
Var: 01ℵ-org,02A,03B
06D-org,Lach,Treg,Alf
Tisc,We/Ho,Weis,Sod
UBS/✶

1217.2 prep	4949.9 intr-pron sing neu	3617.1 conj	3620.2 partic	1523.2 prep gen	3963.2 noun gen sing fem	233.1 conj
[✶ διὰ	τί;]	ὅτι	οὐκ	ἐκ	πίστεως,	ἀλλ᾽
dia	ti	hoti	ouk	ek	pisteōs	all'
[idem]		Because	not	by	faith,	but

5453.1 conj	1523.1 prep gen	2024.5 noun gen pl neu	3414.2 noun gen sing masc	4208.3 verb 3pl indic aor act	1056.1 conj
ὡς	ἐξ	ἔργων	ᵃ νόμου᾿	προσέκοψαν	ᵇ γὰρ᾿
hōs	ex	ergōn	nomou	prosekopsan	gar
as	by	works	of law.	They stumbled	for

3450.3 art dat sing	3012.3 noun dat sing masc	3450.2 art gen sing	4206.2 noun gen sing neu	2503.1 conj
τῷ	λίθῳ	τοῦ	προσκόμματος,	33. καθὼς
tō	lithō	tou	proskommatos	kathōs
at the	stone	of the	stumbling,	just as

1119.22 verb 3sing indic perf pass	1481.20 verb 2sing impr aor mid	4935.1 verb 1sing indic pres act	1706.1 prep	4477.1 name fem
γέγραπται,	Ἰδοὺ	τίθημι	ἐν	Σιὼν
gegraptai	Idou	tithēmi	en	Siōn
it has been written,	Behold	I place	in	Zion

3012.4 noun acc sing masc	4206.2 noun gen sing neu	2504.1 conj	3934.4 noun acc sing fem	4480.2 noun gen sing neu
λίθον	προσκόμματος	καὶ	πέτραν	σκανδάλου᾿
lithon	proskommatos	kai	petran	skandalou
a stone	of stumbling	and	rock	of offense:

33.a.**Txt:** 018K,020L
025P,33,1739,byz.
Var: 01ℵ,02A,03B,06D
sa.bo.Lach,Treg,Alf
Word,Tisc,We/Ho,Weis
Sod,UBS/✶

2504.1 conj	3820.6 adj sing masc	3450.5 art sing masc	3961.10 verb nom sing masc part pres act	1894.2 prep	840.4 prs-pron dat sing
καὶ	ᵃ πᾶς᾿	ὁ	πιστεύων	ἐπ᾽	αὐτῷ
kai	pas	ho	pisteuōn	ep'	autō
and	everyone	the	believing	on	him

3620.3 partic	2587.8 verb 3sing indic fut pass		79.6 noun pl masc	3450.9 art nom sing fem	3173.1 conj
οὐ	καταισχυνθήσεται.	10:1. Ἀδελφοί,		ἡ	μὲν
ou	kataischunthēsetai	Adelphoi		hē	men
not	shall be ashamed.	Brothers,		the	men

2086.1 noun nom sing fem	3450.10 art gen sing fem	1684.7 adj gen 1sing fem	2559.1 noun gen sing fem	2504.1 conj	3450.9 art nom sing fem
εὐδοκία	τῆς	ἐμῆς	καρδίας,	καὶ	ἡ
eudokia	tēs	emēs	kardias	kai	hē
good pleasure	of the	my own	heart,	and	the

1.a.**Txt:** 018K,020L,byz.
Var: 01ℵ,02A,03B,06D
025P,Lach,Treg,Alf
Word,Tisc,We/Ho,Weis
Sod,UBS/✶

1.b.**Txt:** 018K,020L
1241,byz.
Var: p46,01ℵ-org,02A
03B,06D,sa.bo.Gries
Lach,Treg,Alf,Word
Tisc,We/Ho,Weis,Sod
UBS/✶

1157.1 noun nom sing fem	3450.9 art nom sing fem	4242.1 prep	3450.6 art acc sing masc	2296.4 noun acc sing masc	5065.1 prep
δέησις	ᵃ ἡ᾿	πρὸς	τὸν	θεὸν	ὑπὲρ
deēsis	hē	pros	ton	theon	huper
petition	the	to	God	God	on behalf of

3450.2 art gen sing	2447.1 name masc	1498.4 verb 3sing indic pres act	840.1 prs-pron gen pl	1519.1 prep
ᵃ τοῦ	Ἰσραὴλ	ἐστιν	[ᵇ✶ αὐτῶν]	εἰς
tou	Israēl	estin	autōn	eis
	Israel	is	[their]	for

4843.3 noun acc sing fem	3113.1 verb 1sing pres act	1056.1 conj	840.2 prs-pron dat pl	3617.1 conj	2188.4 noun acc sing neu
σωτηρίαν.	2. μαρτυρῶ	γὰρ	αὐτοῖς	ὅτι	ζῆλον
sōtērian	marturō	gar	autois	hoti	zēlon
salvation.	I bear witness	for	to them	that	zeal

9:32. The puzzling, haunting question is: How could Israel have missed out on righteousness when it was ostensibly their number one concern? It was because they did not seek righteousness in the only way it can come—by faith. Their "works of the law" nullified faith and blinded them to God's righteousness (seen in Christ when He came). If God had intended that man could become righteous by his works, He would never have given His Son to die. The Jews, like Cain, decided to bring what they wanted to bring rather than what God had commanded to be brought (Jude 11).

9:33. The major reason for the Jews' failure to attain righteousness is that they stumbled over Christ Jesus. There is implicit imagery in verses 30 and 31 of a race, or an obstacle course, in the pursuit of righteousness. When Christ came across their path as the goal which they sought, the Jews instead stumbled and fell, missing the goal entirely.

God had forewarned Israel of the possibility of falling as a result of stumbling over the coming One. Isaiah prophesied that the "Lord of hosts" would be a stone of stumbling and a rock of offense (Isaiah 8:14) over which many would stumble and fall. Isaiah 28:16 foretold of "a tried stone, a precious corner stone, a sure foundation," promising that "he that believeth shall not make haste."

The Psalmist foresaw the Jews' rejection of Jesus as he wrote, "The stone which the builders refused is become the head stone of the corner" (Psalm 118:22). Jesus applied this prophecy to himself and warned His hearers that "whosoever shall fall on this stone shall be broken: but on whomsoever it shall fall, it will grind him to powder" (Matthew 21:42-44).

When Jesus asked the Jewish leaders to explain Psalm 118:22, they had no answer (Luke 20:17). When He applied it to himself, they understood His claim and tried to take Him for trial, but His time had not yet come (Mark 12:10-12).

The joyous aspect of the stumbling stone is that "whosoever believeth on him shall not be ashamed." Isaiah 28:16 stated that the believer would "not make haste." The two ideas are complementary.

The believer rests on the solid rock Christ Jesus; he does not have to rush about in anxiety but can move in deliberation and peace. Jesus will never allow him to be put to shame. In a world of mutability and uncertainty, Jesus never changes (Hebrews 13:8).

10:1. God has offered righteousness to Israel three times: (1) under the prophets (9:30-33); (2) under the Law (10:1-13); (3) under the gospel (10:14-21).

Paul did not discuss Israel's rejection with coldness and anger. He felt deeply about the matter (cf. 9:1-3). Paul's life was often endangered by the Jews; many a beating and stoning left marks upon his body. But despite this he was deeply grieved over their ways; he desired above all else that they might be saved. The burden of souls left no room in his heart for the condemnation of souls.

32. Wherefore?: For what reason? *Sawyer* . . . And why? *Confraternity.*

Because [they sought it] not by faith: . . . their principle was not faith, *Berkeley* . . . they did not pursue it, *RSV* . . . has relied not on faith, *Moffatt* . . . they did not try through faith, *Williams* . . . they shaped their course not by faith, *Way.*

but as it were by the works of the law: . . . but thought to gain it by works, *Montgomery* . . . they relied on good deeds, *JB* . . . on what they could do, *Moffatt* . . . from what they regarded as merit, *Weymouth* . . . but in reliance on meritorious deeds, *Way.*

For they stumbled at that stumblingstone: . . . they tripped over the, *Adams.*

33. As it is written:

Behold, I lay in Sion a stumblingstone and rock of offence: . . . people will trip over and a rock that will make them fall, *Adams* . . . even a rock to trip them up, *Moffatt* . . . and a rock of hindrance, *HistNT* . . . and a stoon of sclaundre, *Wyclif* . . . that men shallbe offended at, *Cranmer* . . . a rocke which shal make men fall, *Geneva* . . . and a rocke of scandal, *Rheims* . . . a rock from which they shall recoil, *Way.*

and whosoever believeth on him shall not be ashamed: . . . yet, he who rests his faith thereon, *Way* . . . yet no one relying on it shall be disappointed, *Wilson* . . . schal not be confoundid, *Wyclif.*

1. Brethren, my heart's desire and prayer to God for Israel is: . . . the kindly intent, *Berkeley* . . . the will of my heart, *Douay* . . . the pleasure indeed of my heart, *Young* . . . indeed and my supplication, *Clementson* . . . and my intercession, *Murdock* . . . the longing of my heart...for my countrymen, *Montgomery* . . . my entreaty to God, *Way.*

that they might be saved:

2. For I bear them record that they have a zeal of God: I can vouch for, *Moffatt* . . . I bear witness that they possess an enthusiasm for God, *Weymouth* . . . to

Romans 10:3

2296.2 noun gen sing masc θεοῦ *theou* for God	**2174.6** verb 3pl indic pres act ἔχουσιν, *echousin* they have,	**233.1** conj ἀλλ' *all'* but	**3620.3** partic οὐ *ou* not	**2567.1** prep κατ' *kat'* according to	**1907.4** noun acc sing fem ἐπίγνωσιν. *epignōsin* knowledge.

49.8 verb nom pl masc part pres act 3. ἀγνοοῦντες *agnoosuntes* Being ignorant of	**1056.1** conj γὰρ *gar* for	**3450.12** art acc sing fem τὴν *tēn* the	**3450.2** art gen sing τοῦ *tou*	**2296.2** noun gen sing masc θεοῦ *theou* of God

3.a.Txt: 01ℵ,018K,020L byz.Tisc
Var: 02A,03B,06D,025P Gries,Lach,Treg,Word We/Ho,Weis,Sod UBS/⋆

1336.4 noun acc sing fem δικαιοσύνην, *dikaiosunēn* righteousness,	**2504.1** conj καὶ *kai* and	**3450.12** art acc sing fem τὴν *tēn* the	**2375.11** adj acc sing fem ἰδίαν *idian* own	**1336.4** noun acc sing fem ⌐a δικαιοσύνην ⌐ *dikaiosunēn* righteousness

2195.10 verb nom pl masc part pres act ζητοῦντες *zētountes* seeking	**2449.15** verb inf aor act στῆσαι, *stēsai* to establish,	**3450.11** art dat sing fem τῇ *tē* to the	**1336.3** noun dat sing fem δικαιοσύνη *dikaiosunē* righteousness	**3450.2** art gen sing τοῦ *tou*

2296.2 noun gen sing masc θεοῦ *theou* of God	**3620.1** partic οὐχ *ouch* not	**5131.17** verb 3pl indic aor pass ὑπετάγησαν. *hupetagēsan* they submitted.	**4904.1** noun sing neu 4. τέλος *telos* End	**1056.1** conj γὰρ *gar* for	**3414.2** noun gen sing masc νόμου *nomou* of law

5382.1 name nom masc Χριστὸς *Christos* Christ	**1519.1** prep εἰς *eis* for	**1336.4** noun acc sing fem δικαιοσύνην *dikaiosunēn* righteousness	**3820.3** adj dat sing παντὶ *panti* to everyone	**3450.3** art dat sing τῷ *tō* the	**3961.11** verb dat sing masc part pres act πιστεύοντι. *pisteuonti* believing.

5.a.Var: 01ℵ-org,02A 06D-org,sa.bo.Tisc We/Ho,Sod,UBS/⋆

3337.1 name nom masc 5. ⌐ Μωσῆς *Mōsēs* Moses	**3338.1** name nom masc [⋆ Μωϋσῆς] *Mōusēs* [idem]	**1056.1** conj γὰρ *gar* for	**1119.2** verb 3sing indic pres act γράφει *graphei* writes	**3617.1** conj [a⋆+ ὅτι] *hoti*

5.b.Txt: p46,01ℵ-corr 03B,06D-corr,018K 020L,025P,byz.Sod
Var: 01ℵ-org,02A 06D-org,Treg,Alf,Tisc We/Ho,Weis,UBS/⋆

3450.12 art acc sing fem τὴν *tēn* the	**1336.4** noun acc sing fem δικαιοσύνην *dikaiosunēn* righteousness	**3450.12** art acc sing fem τὴν *tēn* the	**1523.2** prep gen ἐκ *ek* of	**3450.2** art gen sing ⌐b τοῦ ⌐ *tou* the	**3414.2** noun gen sing masc νόμου, *nomou* law,

5.c.Txt: p46,06D,018K 020L,025P,byz.Weis
Var: 01ℵ,03B,Tisc We/Ho,Sod,UBS/⋆

3617.1 conj ⌐c Ὅτι ⌐ *Hoti* That	**3450.5** art sing masc ὁ *ho* the	**4020.37** verb nom sing masc part aor act ποιήσας *poiēsas* having practiced	**840.16** prs- pron pl neu ⌐d αὐτὰ ⌐ *auta* them	**442.1** noun nom sing masc ἄνθρωπος *anthrōpos* man

5.d.Txt: p46,01ℵ-corr 03B,018K,020L,025P byz.Weis
Var: 01ℵ-org,02A,06D Tisc,We/Ho,Sod,UBS/⋆

2180.29 verb 3sing indic fut mid ζήσεται *zēsetai* shall live	**1706.1** prep ἐν *en* by	**840.2** prs- pron dat pl ⌐ αὐτοῖς. *autois* them.	**840.11** prs-pron dat sing fem [e⋆ αὐτῇ.] *autē* [it.]	**3450.9** art nom sing fem 6. Ἡ *Hē* The	**1156.2** conj δὲ *de* but

5.e.Txt: p46,01ℵ-corr 06D,018K,020L,025P byz.
Var: 01ℵ-org,02A,03B Lach,Treg,Alf,Tisc We/Ho,Weis,Sod UBS/⋆

1523.2 prep gen ἐκ *ek* of	**3963.2** noun gen sing fem πίστεως *pisteōs* faith	**1336.1** noun nom sing fem δικαιοσύνη *dikaiosunē* righteousness	**3643.1** adv οὕτως *houtōs* thus	**2978.5** verb 3sing indic pres act λέγει, *legei* speaks:	**3231.1** partic Μὴ *Mē* Not

10:2-4. The Jews failed to submit to the righteousness of God. They had great zeal, they knew the Law, they gave themselves to the Law, and they endeavored to convert Gentiles to the Law. But since their zeal was "not according to knowledge," it was not acceptable. It was misguided to a wrong cause.

The Jews had not properly interpreted the purpose of the Law. Ignoring the sinfulness of their hearts, they had come to trust in the keeping of the letter of the Law. When Jesus came, offering free pardon for sin, they felt they had no need of Him. "They answered him, We be Abraham's seed, and were never in bondage to any man: how sayest thou, Ye shall be made free?" (John 8:33). On more than one occasion they asked, "What shall we do?" Notice John 6:28,29 where we read they asked, "What shall we do, that we might work the works of God?" Jesus answered, "This is the work of God, that ye believe."

The human desire to merit God's favor by works is present among all men; it is not limited to the Jew with his alms, prayers, and traditions. The African brings offerings to his fetish; the Hindu bathes in the Ganges; those of the other world religions journey to shrines and perform various rites.

Christ came both to fulfill the Law and to remove the need for the Law. Myer Pearlman (pp.232,233) likened the Law to a train. In the days of train travel, we used a train as a means to an end. We had no intention of making the train our home. When we reached our destination, we left the train. But the self-satisfied Jews refused to move from the seats of the old-covenant train even though they were at the end of the line. Christ is the "end of the law" in that He fulfilled it (Matthew 5:17). He did not destroy it nor make it void; He is our righteousness and He fulfills the Law in us (Romans 3:21,31; 1 Corinthians 1:30). The Law can find no fault in Him.

10:5,6. Moses described "righteousness which is of the law" (cf. Leviticus 18:5). Paul reiterated that same principle in 2:7: God could not deny eternal life to the person who totally always kept His law.

Scripture is very clear, however, that no human being except our Lord Jesus ever met that qualification. Adam could have, but since the Fall there has been no human who could keep even the first commandment in totality (Romans 3:20,23; Acts 15:10; Galatians 3:10; James 2:10). Blood sacrifice was always necessary for atonement (Hebrews 9:22).

The Law declares that if a person wants to be right with God, then he must do right. Salvation by grace declares that if a person wants to do right, he must be right with God. Imputed righteousness consists of a Person rather than an effort. Through Christ we have a righteousness which is not dependent upon us or what we have done but upon Christ himself.

The Law was given to Israel as a temporary thing, a "ministration of death" (2 Corinthians 3:7) to reveal sin and the necessity of

their jealousy for God's honour, *Way* . . . that they haue a feruent mynde to Godwarde, *Geneva*.

but not according to knowledge: . . . their zeal is misguided, *JB* . . . their zeal is not guided by true knowledge, *Locke* . . . but they lack certain knowledge, *Norlie* . . . but it is an unenlightened enthusiasm, *Weymouth* . . . but they are not intelligently so, *Williams* . . . but not according to a full and accurate knowledge, *Wuest*.

3. For they being ignorant of God's righteousness: They are densely ignorant, *Norlie* . . . They steadily ignore, *Way* . . . they have not submitted, *Berkeley* . . . which is alowed before God, *Tyndale*.

and going about to establish their own righteousness: . . . and seeking to establish, *Panin, Hanson* . . . while they try to earn, *Norlie* . . . they try to set up a private standard of righteousness, *Way* . . . to make stidfast her owne, *Wyclif* . . . and were trying to set up one of their own, *Williams*.

have not submitted themselves unto: . . . haue not bene obedient vnto, *Geneva* . . . they haue not been subiect to, *Rheims* . . . they were not submissive, *Wilson, Hanson*.

the righteousness of God:

4. For Christ [is] the end of the law for righteousness to every one that believeth: For Messiah is the aim of the law, *Murdock* . . . is the fulfyllynge of the lawe, *Cranmer* . . . For the termination of the law, *Wuest* . . . is the consummation of the Law, *Confraternity*.

5. For Moses describeth: For Moses wryteth of, *Cranmer*.

the righteousness which is of the law:

That the man which doeth those things shall live by them: The man who fulfils its requirements (which no man ever did) shall find life in it, *Way*.

6. But the righteousness which is of faith: . . . based on faith, *RSV*.

speaketh on this wise:

Romans 10:7

1500.7 verb 2sing subj aor act	1706.1 prep	3450.11 art dat sing fem	2559.3 noun dat sing fem	4622.2 prs-pron gen 2sing	4949.3 intr-pron nom sing
εἴπῃς	ἐν	τῇ	καρδίᾳ	σου,	Τίς
eipēs	en	tē	kardia	sou	Tis
you may say	in	the	heart	your,	Who

303.25 verb 3sing indic fut mid	1519.1 prep	3450.6 art acc sing masc	3636.4 noun acc sing masc	3642.16 dem-pron sing neu	1498.4 verb 3sing indic pres act
ἀναβήσεται	εἰς	τὸν	οὐρανόν;	τοῦτ'	ἔστιν
anabēsetai	eis	ton	ouranon	tout'	estin
shall ascend	to	the	heaven?	that	is,

5382.4 name acc masc	2580.6 verb inf aor act	2211.1 conj	4949.3 intr-pron nom sing	2568.28 verb 3sing indic fut mid
Χριστὸν	καταγαγεῖν·	7. ἤ,	Τίς	καταβήσεται
Christon	katagagein	ē	Tis	katabēsetai
Christ	to bring down.	Or,	Who	shall descend

1519.1 prep	3450.12 art acc sing fem	12.2 noun acc sing fem	3642.16 dem-pron sing neu	1498.4 verb 3sing indic pres act	5382.4 name acc masc
εἰς	τὴν	ἄβυσσον;	τοῦτ'	ἔστιν	Χριστὸν
eis	tēn	abusson	tout'	estin	Christon
into	the	abyss?	that	is,	Christ

1523.2 prep gen	3361.2 adj gen pl	319.3 verb inf aor act	233.2 conj	4949.9 intr-pron sing neu
ἐκ	νεκρῶν	ἀναγαγεῖν.	8. ἀλλὰ	τί
ek	nekrōn	anagagein	alla	ti
from among	dead	to bring up.	But	what

2978.5 verb 3sing indic pres act	1445.1 adv	4622.2 prs-pron gen 2sing	3450.16 art sing neu	4343.1 noun sing neu	1498.4 verb 3sing indic pres act
λέγει;	Ἐγγύς	σου	τὸ	ῥῆμά	ἔστιν,
legei	Engus	sou	to	rhēma	estin
says it?	Near	you	the	word	is,

1706.1 prep	3450.3 art dat sing	4601.3 noun dat sing neu	4622.2 prs-pron gen 2sing	2504.1 conj	1706.1 prep	3450.11 art dat sing fem
ἐν	τῷ	στόματί	σου	καὶ	ἐν	τῇ
en	tō	stomati	sou	kai	en	tē
in	the	mouth	your	and	in	the

2559.3 noun dat sing fem	4622.2 prs-pron gen 2sing	3642.16 dem-pron sing neu	1498.4 verb 3sing indic pres act	3450.16 art sing neu	4343.1 noun sing neu
καρδίᾳ	σου.	τοῦτ'	ἔστιν	τὸ	ῥῆμα
kardia	sou	tout'	estin	to	rhēma
heart	your:	that	is	the	word

3450.10 art gen sing fem	3963.2 noun gen sing fem	3614.16 rel-pron sing neu	2756.3 verb 1pl indic pres act	3617.1 conj	1430.1 partic
τῆς	πίστεως	ὃ	κηρύσσομεν·	9. ὅτι	ἐὰν
tēs	pisteōs	ho	kērussomen	hoti	ean
of the	faith	which	we proclaim,	that	if

9.a.Txt: 01ℵ,06D,012G 018K,025P,044,33,88 104,181,etc.byz. Var: 03B,81,sa.

3533.9 verb 2sing subj aor act	3450.16 art sing neu	4343.1 noun sing neu	1706.1 prep	3450.3 art dat sing	4601.3 noun dat sing neu
ὁμολογήσῃς	[a+ τὸ	ῥῆμα]	ἐν	τῷ	στόματί
homologēsēs	to	rhēma	en	tō	stomati
you confess	[the	word]	with	the	mouth

4622.2 prs-pron gen 2sing	2935.4 noun acc sing masc	2400.3 name acc masc	2504.1 conj	3961.24 verb 2sing subj aor act	1706.1 prep
σου	κύριον	Ἰησοῦν,	καὶ	πιστεύσῃς	ἐν
sou	kurion	Iēsoun	kai	pisteusēs	en
your	Lord	Jesus,	and	believe	in

Calvary. The day of the Law is over, since Christ, having paid the penalty for sin, disannulled it (Hebrews 7:18).

10:7,8. Imputed righteousness provides an ever-present spiritual standard for believers. In other words, it is a righteousness that is centered in the Word of God. In writing of this, Paul asks questions that may have appeared foolish. In essence, he asks those who are searching for righteousness if they must go up to heaven and bring Christ down in order to have someone to keep them righteous. Or must they go down to the grave to bring Him up from the dead to have someone to keep them righteous.

Paul's use of Deuteronomy showed that he was not preaching a new concept; the only new part was the work Jesus had accomplished. Hebrews discusses the relationship of Jesus to the Levitical system, showing the "better" way of Jesus' finished work (John 19:30; Hebrews 10:9-14).

Verses 6-8 are taken from Moses' inspired teaching in Deuteronomy 30:12-14. When Jews were inclined to say that it was impossible to please God, Moses reminded them that "it is not hidden from thee, neither is it far off" (Deuteronomy 30:11). God through Moses was saying to Israel that He had made faith and life accessible to them. For every sin and transgression He had made a plan for forgiveness. Their faith was demonstrated by their obedience.

The Jews of Paul's day were liable to make the same error as those of Moses' day. To question how they could "ascend into heaven" in order to find a way of perfection was a denial of the incarnation of Christ. To question the need for bringing someone from "the deep" was a denial of Jesus' resurrection.

Paul's answer was that the Word was near them, seated at the right hand of the throne of God, and He (Jesus) is identified and inseparably connected with the written Word, which is "even in thy mouth." The righteousness by faith can be maintained by adhering to and abiding in the Word of God.

The message of salvation by faith conveys the good news that Christ, the Son of God, came down from heaven to become the Son of Man and to die for us, and that He has ascended again from the dead. The two greatest miracles of the Christian faith are the Incarnation which tells us that Christ came down from heaven, and the Resurrection which tells us He came up from the regions of the dead. These truths must be believed in the heart. The Scriptures, "the word of faith," are the means of relaying this to us.

10:9,10. God's great plan of righteousness is so wonderful and so complete that man's efforts are excluded. Salvation can only be received by faith. Faith does not earn a Saviour, faith accepts a Saviour. All that is required is the act of believing; proof is the act of confessing Him. Salvation is as close as the air we breathe. We only need to receive Him and confess Him. Salvation is for "whosoever shall call upon the name of the Lord" (verse 13).

Say not in thine heart, Who shall ascend into heaven?: Do not say to yourself, *ET.*

(that is, to bring Christ down [from above]:): This, in its implications, *Wuest* . . . euen to fetche Christ downe from aboue, *Geneva* . . . to drag the Messiah down from heaven, *ET.*

7. Or, Who shall descend into the deep?: . . . who schal go doun in to helle? *Wyclif* . . . who is able to descend into the grave, *ET* . . . down to the underworld? *JB* . . . into the depths? *Beck* . . . into the abyss? *HistNT* . . . to the abyss of the grave, *Murdock.*

(that is, to bring up Christ again from the dead.): . . . that is, to bring again Christ, *Macknight* . . . back from the dead, *Norlie* . . . to be leading Christ up, *Concordant* . . . restore Christ from among the dead, *ET.*

8. But what saith it?: But what does it say? *Montgomery* . . . what do the scriptures say? *ET.*

The word is nigh thee, [even] in thy mouth, and in thy heart: The matter is nigh thee, *Macknight* . . . it is the inspired word on your very tongue, *ET* . . . near you, on your lips, *RSV* . . . and in your mind, *Sawyer.*

that is, the word of faith, which we preach: That is the very word of faith, *Montgomery* . . . the word of the faith, *Panin* . . . that is, the saying of the faith, *Young* . . . or the doctrine of the Gospel, *Locke* . . . which we publish, *Hanson* . . . which we are heralding, *Concordant* . . . We proclaim the Word that brings faith, *ET.*

9. That if thou shalt confess with thy mouth the Lord Jesus: . . . that Iesus is the lorde, *Tyndale* . . . For yf thou knowledge wyth thy mouth, *Cranmer* . . . if you will openly confess, *Campbell* . . . if thou wilt openly confess, *Wilson* . . . openly own Jesus the Lord, *Locke* . . . that Jesus is the Lord, *Confraternity.*

and shalt believe in thine heart: . . . and have faith or trust in your inward being, *ET.*

3450.11 art dat sing fem	2559.3 noun dat sing fem	4622.2 prs-pron gen 2sing	3617.1 conj	3450.5 art sing masc	2296.1 noun nom sing masc
τῇ	καρδίᾳ	σου	ὅτι	ὁ	θεὸς
tē	kardia	sou	hoti	ho	theos
the	heart	your	that		God

840.6 prs-pron acc sing masc	1446.5 verb 3sing indic aor act	1523.2 prep gen	3361.2 adj gen pl	4834.32 verb 2sing indic fut pass
αὐτὸν	ἤγειρεν	ἐκ	νεκρῶν,	σωθήσῃ·
auton	ēgeiren	ek	nekrōn	sōthēsē
him	raised	from among	dead,	you shall be saved.

2559.3 noun dat sing fem	1056.1 conj	3961.56 verb 3sing indic pres pass	1519.1 prep	1336.4 noun acc sing fem
10. καρδίᾳ	γὰρ	πιστεύεται	εἰς	δικαιοσύνην.
kardia	gar	pisteuetai	eis	dikaiosunēn
With heart	for	is being believed	to	righteousness;

4601.3 noun dat sing neu	1156.2 conj	3533.15 verb 3sing indic pres pass	1519.1 prep	4843.3 noun acc sing fem
στόματι	δὲ	ὁμολογεῖται	εἰς	σωτηρίαν.
stomati	de	homologeitai	eis	sōtērian
with mouth	and	is being confessed	to	salvation.

2978.5 verb 3sing indic pres act	1056.1 conj	3450.9 art nom sing fem	1118.1 noun nom sing fem	3820.6 adj sing masc	3450.5 art sing masc
11. Λέγει	γὰρ	ἡ	γραφή,	Πᾶς	ὁ
Legei	gar	hē	graphē	Pas	ho
Says	for	the	scripture,	Everyone	the

3961.10 verb nom sing masc part pres act	1894.2 prep	840.4 prs-pron dat sing	3620.3 partic	2587.8 verb 3sing indic fut pass
πιστεύων	ἐπ'	αὐτῷ	οὐ	καταισχυνθήσεται.
pisteuōn	ep'	autō	ou	kataischunthēsetai
believing	on	him	not	shall be ashamed.

3620.3 partic	1056.1 conj	1498.4 verb 3sing indic pres act	1287.1 noun nom sing fem	2428.7 name-adj gen masc	4885.1 conj	2504.1 conj
12. Οὐ	γάρ	ἐστιν	διαστολὴ	Ἰουδαίου	τε	καὶ
Ou	gar	estin	diastolē	Ioudaiou	te	kai
Not	for	there is	a difference	of Jew	both	and

1659.2 name gen sing masc	3450.5 art sing masc	1056.1 conj	840.5 prs-pron nom sing masc	2935.1 noun nom sing masc	3820.4 adj gen pl
Ἕλληνος·	ὁ	γὰρ	αὐτὸς	κύριος	πάντων
Hellēnos	ho	gar	autos	kurios	pantōn
Greek;	the	for	same	Lord	of all

4007.1 verb nom sing masc part pres act	1519.1 prep	3820.8 adj acc pl masc	3450.8 art acc pl masc	1926.9 verb acc pl masc part pres mid
πλουτῶν	εἰς	πάντας	τοὺς	ἐπικαλουμένους
ploutōn	eis	pantas	tous	epikaloumenous
being rich	toward	all	the	calling upon

840.6 prs-pron acc sing masc	3820.6 adj sing masc	1056.1 conj	3614.5 rel-pron nom sing masc	300.1 partic	1926.12 verb 3sing subj aor mid
αὐτόν.	**13.** Πᾶς	γὰρ	ὃς	ἂν	ἐπικαλέσηται
auton	Pas	gar	hos	an	epikalesētai
him.	Everyone	for,	whoever		may call on

3450.16 art sing neu	3549.2 noun sing neu	2935.2 noun gen sing masc	4834.33 verb 3sing indic fut pass	4316.1 adv	3631.1 conj
τὸ	ὄνομα	κυρίου,	σωθήσεται.	**14.** Πῶς	οὖν
to	onoma	kuriou	sōthēsetai	Pōs	oun
the	name	of Lord,	shall be saved.	How	then

Most translations render "confess . . . the Lord Jesus" as "confess . . . Jesus as Lord." The emphasis is on the lordship of Christ.

At the very heart of the gospel is the Resurrection. Salvation is to confess with the mouth the lordship of Christ and to believe in the heart His resurrection. Believing comes before confession. Lack of confession indicates lack of faith. Confession is first of all Godward in the heart, then outward and manward. Heart trust and true confession cannot be separated.

Believing with the heart is different than intellectual belief. Faith, as used in Scripture, is not a natural attribute of fallen man. Faith is "not of yourselves; it is the gift of God" (Ephesians 2:8). Calvinists are scriptural when they say that man cannot believe apart from God's gracious help. Arminians agree that only by God's grace is the sinner drawn to Jesus. They go on to say that the Holy Spirit offers faith to all (verse 11), but man must will to exercise that faith by receiving Christ, committing himself to Jesus as his Lord.

Confession of mouth and belief of heart are the prime requisites of salvation, representing the believers' outward and inward responses. Inward conviction must find outward expression. Salvation comes by faith which inevitably will cause the believer to confess Christ both in word and deed.

10:11. This verse is a quotation from Isaiah 28:16. "He" in Isaiah is changed to "whosoever." Several translations render "ashamed" as "disappointed." There is nothing mentioned about law; it is all by faith. None of these renderings—ashamed, put to shame, disappointed—mean to be ashamed of the Lord. Rather, whosoever anchors his faith in Christ can be certain that the gospel works; it has power to save and deliver.

10:12. "Difference" is rendered "distinction" in several translations. There is no distinction between Jew and Greek (Gentile) in their sinfulness (3:22,23), and no distinction in the plan to deliver them from sin. God's mercy is rich unto all. The lordship of Christ is equally relevant to all in the matter of salvation.

10:13. Nothing can be simpler: "Whosoever"—one and all, anyone; "call"—call on the name of the only One who can help; "shall be saved." It is just that simple. Jew or Gentile, rich or poor, bond or free, black or white, educated or uneducated, refined or crude—anyone can simply call. The promise of salvation is here presented as a universal call to believe on the Lord Jesus Christ. The only prerequisite is faith, which is a gift from God.

The thrust of these verses is an appeal to the Jews to forsake the road of legalism and walk the way of grace. Paul appeals to them to see that their zeal is wrongly placed. Generations before the prophets had declared that faith is the way to God and that the door is open to all who believe.

that God hath raised him from the dead: . . . that God actually raised him, *Montgomery* . . . that God did really raise Him, *Way*.

thou shalt be saved: . . . thou shalt live, *Murdock* . . . you shall find salvation, *Way*.

10. For with the heart man believeth unto righteousness: For with the inmost heart, *Way* . . . faith is exercised, *Wuest* . . . in order to be justified, *Adams*.

and with the mouth confession is made unto salvation: . . . and to knowledge with the mouth maketh a man safe, *Tyndale* . . . profession of faith is made, *Confraternity* . . . they make open acknowledgement and so find Salvation, *TCNT* . . . they make confession and obtain salvation, *Weymouth* . . . is restored to life, *Murdock*.

11. For the scripture saith: . . . for the Writing saith, *Young*.

Whosoever believeth on him shall not be ashamed: Whoever depends on Him, *Adams* . . . shall not be put to shame, *Berkeley* . . . shall not be confounded, *Cranmer* . . . shall not be disgraced, *Concordant*.

12. For there is no difference between the Jew and the Greek: . . . are on precisely the same footing, *Weymouth* . . . it discriminateth neither, *Murdock* . . . there is no distinccioun, *Wyclif*.

for the same Lord over all is rich unto all that call upon him: . . . the same Person is Lord, *Adams* . . . His riches are for everyone who calls, *Klingensmith* . . . full of blessing for all who at any time call upon Him, *Way* . . . and He gives richly to all, *Conybeare* . . . and he is bountiful to all who invoke his aid, *TCNT* . . . is infinitely kind to all, *Weymouth* . . . constantly rich toward all, *Wuest* . . . for all who invoke him, *Moffatt*.

13. For whosoever shall call upon the name of the Lord shall be saved: Everyone who invokes the name, *Moffatt* . . . For everyone, without exception, *Weymouth*.

Romans 10:15

14.a.Txt: 018K,020L 025P,byz. **Var:** 01‭א‬,02A,03B,06D Lach,Treg,Alf,Word Tisc,We/Ho,Weis,Sod UBS/✶

1926.22 verb 3pl indic fut mid	**1926.24** verb 3pl subj aor mid	**1519.1** prep	**3614.6** rel-pron acc sing masc
ʽ ἐπικαλέσονται	[ᵃ✩ ἐπικαλέσωνται]	εἰς	ὃν
epikalesontai	*epikalesōntai*	*eis*	*hon*
shall they call	[may they call]	on	whom

3620.2 partic	**3961.23** verb 3pl indic aor act	**4316.1** adv	**1156.2** conj	**3961.27** verb 3pl subj aor act
οὐκ	ἐπίστευσαν;	πῶς	δὲ	ʽ πιστεύσωσιν
ouk	*episteusan*	*pōs*	*de*	*pisteusōsin*
not	they believed?	how	and	shall they believe on

14.b.Txt: byz. **Var:** 01‭א‬,03B,06D,025P Lach,Treg,Alf,Word Tisc,We/Ho,Weis,Sod UBS/✶

3961.27 verb 3pl subj aor act	**3614.2** rel-pron gen sing	**3620.2** partic	**189.24** verb 3pl indic aor act	**4316.1** adv	**1156.2** conj
[ᵇ✩ πιστεύσωσιν]	οὗ	οὐκ	ἤκουσαν;	πῶς	δὲ
[may they believe on]	*hou*	*ouk*	*ēkousan*	*pōs*	*de*
	of whom	not	they heard?	how	and

14.c.Txt: 020L,byz. **Var:** 01‭א‬-corr,02A-corr 03B,Lach,Treg,Alf Word,We/Ho,Weis,Sod UBS/✶

189.44 verb 3pl indic fut act	**189.27** verb 3pl subj aor act	**5400.1** prep gen	**2756.7** verb gen sing masc part pres act
ʽ ἀκούσουσιν	[ᶜ✩ ἀκούσωσιν]	χωρὶς	κηρύσσοντος;
akousousin	*akousōsin*	*chōris*	*kērussontos*
shall they hear	[may they hear]	apart from	preaching?

15.a.Txt: byz. **Var:** 01‭א‬,02A,03B,06D 018K,020L,025P,Lach Treg,Alf,Word,Tisc We/Ho,Weis,Sod UBS/✶

4316.1 adv	**1156.2** conj	**2756.19** verb 3pl indic fut act	**2756.29** verb 3pl subj aor act	**1430.1** partic
15. πῶς	δὲ	ʽ κηρύξουσιν,	[ᵃ✩ κηρύξωσιν,]	ἐὰν
pōs	*de*	*kēruxousin*	*kēruxōsin*	*ean*
how	and	shall they preach,	[may they preach,]	if

3231.1 partic	**643.26** verb 3pl subj aor pass	**2503.1** conj	**1119.22** verb 3sing indic perf pass	**5453.1** conj
μὴ	ἀποσταλῶσιν;	καθὼς	γέγραπται,	ʽΩς
mē	*apostalōsin*	*kathōs*	*gegraptai*	*Hōs*
not	they be sent?	just as	it has been written,	How

15.b.Txt: 01‭א‬-corr,06D 018K,020L,025P,33,byz. it.Weis **Var:** p46,01‭א‬-org,02A 03B,04C,sa.bo.Lach Treg,Tisc,We/Ho,Sod UBS/✶

5444.1 adj nom pl masc	**3450.7** art pl masc	**4087.4** noun nom pl masc	**3450.1** art gen pl	**2076.13** verb gen pl masc part pres mid
ὡραῖοι	οἱ	πόδες	τῶν	ʽᵇ εὐαγγελιζομένων
hōraioi	*hoi*	*podes*	*tōn*	*euangelizomenōn*
beautiful	the	feet	of the	announcing the good news of

15.c.Txt: 01‭א‬-org 06D-corr,018K,020L Tisc **Var:** 01‭א‬-corr,02A,03B 04C,06D-org,025P,Lach Treg,Alf,Word,We/Ho Weis,Sod,UBS/✶

1503.4 noun acc sing fem	**3450.1** art gen pl	**2076.13** verb gen pl masc part pres mid	**3450.17** art pl neu
εἰρήνην,	τῶν ʽ	εὐαγγελιζομένων	ʽᶜ τὰ ʽ
eirēnēn	*tōn*	*euangelizomenōn*	*ta*
peace,	of the	announcing the good news of	the

18.14 adj pl neu	**233.1** conj	**3620.3** partic	**3820.7** adj pl masc	**5057.7** verb 3pl indic aor act	**3450.3** art dat sing
ἀγαθά.	**16.** Ἀλλ'	οὐ	πάντες	ὑπήκουσαν	τῷ
agatha	*All'*	*ou*	*pantes*	*hupēkousan*	*tō*
good things!	But	not	all	obeyed	the

2077.3 noun dat sing neu	**2246.1** name nom masc	**1056.1** conj	**2978.5** verb 3sing indic pres act	**2935.5** noun voc sing masc	**4949.3** intr-pron nom sing
εὐαγγελίῳ·	Ἡσαΐας	γὰρ	λέγει,	Κύριε,	τίς
euangeliō	*Hēsaias*	*gar*	*legei*	*Kurie*	*tis*
good news.	Isaiah	for	says,	Lord,	who

3961.20 verb 3sing indic aor act	**3450.11** art dat sing fem	**187.3** noun dat sing fem	**2231.2** prs-pron gen 1pl	**679.1** partic	**3450.9** art nom sing fem
ἐπίστευσεν	τῇ	ἀκοῇ	ἡμῶν;	**17.** Ἄρα	ἡ
episteusen	*tē*	*akoē*	*hēmōn*	*Ara*	*hē*
believed	the	report	our?	So	the

10:14,15. At this point Paul turned emphatically to the responsibility of the Church to get the Word to everyone. He had already said that the Word is near (verse 8). He had already shown in chapters 1 and 2 that even pagan Gentiles who had not heard the written Word did have the unwritten revelation of God in creation (1:18-20) and in their conscience (2:6-16).

The only way, however, that the pagan can ever find salvation is to hear the Word in some way. Scripture indicates that the person who does not have the Bible but walks in all the light he has will be given more light. Examples are Abraham, Ruth, Rahab, the Ethiopian eunuch, and Cornelius. If we could see God's agenda in heaven, we would see that He has someone in mind to take the good news to every unreached person.

In the Great Commission, recorded five times (Matthew 28:19,20; Mark 16:15; Luke 24:47-49; John 20:21-23; Acts 1:8), Jesus made clear that the responsibility for taking the good news of salvation rests on His followers. The responsibility of each human being to God (1:18 to 3:20) in no way lessens the responsibility of every Christian to do his part in taking the gospel to every creature.

Nowhere in Romans is this set forth more plainly than in this Jewish section of the book. But faith or belief in this gospel depends on hearing it; and this requires preaching; and preaching requires pastors, evangelists, and missionaries carrying the good news to all parts of the world.

The oft-repeated "how" in these verses represents vital, searching, and challenging questions. These questions must be carefully considered today. Paul was talking about evangelizing the world, about getting the good news to all men. The Great Commission calls for living preachers to be living messengers of a living Saviour to a dying world.

The preacher must be sent. He must be God-called. God calls, but men do not hear. Jesus charged the Church to pray that God would send forth laborers (Matthew 9:37,38). How will people hear without a preacher? Preaching is God's plan (1 Corinthians 1:21). There are other means of declaring the message, but they must never replace preaching. Righteousness is proclaimed by preaching.

The feet of the preacher are beautiful to the one who is in the prison of sin, just as Isaiah described the beauty of the feet of the messenger coming with good news of deliverance for the Jews in Babylonian captivity (Isaiah 52:7).

10:16. In various passages the Scriptures teach that man has been confronted with a message he is free to choose or to reject. He then is responsible for the consequences of his choice. Free will and faith are involved in receiving God's saving grace. Man's will must respond to God's will, but God never crosses the threshold of human will unless He is invited. As a result some "have not . . . obeyed the gospel." If salvation comes to all who call on the Lord, then it is imperative that all shall hear so they can know on whom to call. Paul quotes Isaiah 53:1 to show that Israel historically rejected God's call to repent.

14. How then shall they call on him in whom they have not believed?:
and how shall they believe in him: Moreover, how is it possible, *Wuest* . . . can men believe in a Lord, *Way.*
of whom they have not heard?: . . . in one whose words they have not heard? *TCNT* . . . of whom they did not hear? *Clementson.*
and how shall they hear without a preacher?: . . . how shall they listen, *Berkeley* . . . if no one preaches? *Confraternity* . . . unless some one proclaims him? *TCNT* . . . apart from one heralding? *Concordant.*

15. And how shall they preach, except they be sent?: . . . unless they are sent as his messengers? *TCNT* . . . if ever they should not be commissioned? *Concordant.*
as it is written:
How beautiful are the feet of them that preach the gospel of peace, and bring glad tidings of good things!: How pleasant is the coming of men, *Moffatt* . . . hou faire ben the feet of hem, *Wyclif* . . . those who bring a glad gospel, *Montgomery* . . . that euangelize peace, of them that euangelize good things, *Rheims* . . . that proclaim glad-tidings of blessings! *Way* . . . are the heralds of peace, *Murdock* . . . who bring the good tidings of peace, *Wesley.*

16. But they have not all obeyed the gospel: . . . they have not all accepted the glad news, *Norlie* . . . But not all lent an obedient ear, *Wuest* . . . they did not all hearken to the glad tidings, *ASV, Clementson* . . . they have not all heeded, *RSV* . . . they all have not listened to the good news, *Hanson* . . . it is not to be expected that all should receive and obey it, *Locke.*
For Esaias saith:
Lord, who hath believed our report?: . . . what they heard from us? *Moffatt* . . . who hath beleued oure sayinges? *Cranmer* . . . who has put faith in what we told? *Williams* . . . Lord, who did give credence to, *Young* . . . our message? *Klingensmith* . . . our proclamation? *Murdock* . . . that which he heard from me? *Way.*

17.a.**Txt:** 01ℵ-corr,02A
06D-corr,018K,020L
025P,33,byz.
Var: p46,01ℵ-org,03B
04C,06D-org,it.sa.bo.
Lach,Treg,Alf,Tisc
We/Ho,Weis,Sod
UBS/⋆

3963.1 noun nom sing fem	1523.1 prep gen	187.2 noun gen sing fem	3450.9 art nom sing fem	1156.2 conj	187.1 noun nom sing fem	1217.2 prep
πίστις	ἐξ	ἀκοῆς,	ἡ	δὲ	ἀκοὴ	διὰ
pistis	ex	akoēs	hē	de	akoē	dia
faith	by	report,	the	but	report	by

4343.2 noun gen sing neu	2296.2 noun gen sing masc	5382.2 name gen masc	233.2 conj	2978.1 verb 1sing pres act
ῥήματος	ʹ Θεοῦ.	[ᵃ⋆ Χριστοῦ.]	18. ἀλλὰ	λέγω,
rhēmatos	Theou	Christou	alla	legō
word	of God.	[of Christ.]	But	I say,

3231.1 partic	3620.2 partic	189.24 verb 3pl indic aor act	3174.1 partic	3173.1 partic	1058.1 partic
Μὴ	οὐκ	ἤκουσαν;	ʹ⋆ μενοῦνγε	[μενοῦν	γε]
Mē	ouk	ēkousan	menounge	menoun	ge
Not	not	did they hear?	Yes rather,	[rather	yet]

1519.1 prep	3820.12 adj acc sing fem	3450.12 art acc sing fem	1087.4 noun acc sing fem	1814.3 verb 3sing indic aor act	3450.5 art sing masc
Εἰς	πᾶσαν	τὴν	γῆν	ἐξῆλθεν	ὁ
Eis	pasan	tēn	gēn	exēlthen	ho
Into	all	the	earth	went out	the

5190.1 noun nom sing masc	840.1 prs-pron gen pl	2504.1 conj	1519.1 prep	3450.17 art pl neu	3872.3 noun acc pl neu	3450.10 art gen sing fem
φθόγγος	αὐτῶν,	καὶ	εἰς	τὰ	πέρατα	τῆς
phthongos	autōn	kai	eis	ta	perata	tēs
voice	their,	and	to	the	ends	of the

3487.2 noun gen sing fem	3450.17 art pl neu	4343.4 noun pl neu	840.1 prs-pron gen pl	233.2 conj
οἰκουμένης	τὰ	ῥήματα	αὐτῶν.	19. ʼΑλλὰ
oikoumenēs	ta	rhēmata	autōn	Alla
habitable world	the	words	their.	But

2978.1 verb 1sing pres act	3231.1 partic	3620.2 partic	1091.17 verb 3sing indic aor act	2447.1 name masc	2447.1 name masc
λέγω,	Μὴ	ʹ οὐκ	ἔγνω	ʼΙσραήλ;	[⋆ ʼΙσραὴλ
legō	Mē	ouk	egnō	Israēl	Israēl
I say,	Not	not	did know	Israel?	[Israel

3620.2 partic	1091.17 verb 3sing indic aor act	4272.5 num ord nom sing masc	3337.1 name nom masc	3338.1 name nom masc
οὐκ	ἔγνω;]	πρῶτος	ʹ Μωσῆς	[⋆ Μωϋσῆς]
ouk	egnō	prōtos	Mōsēs	Mōusēs
not	knew?]	First,	Moses	[idem]

2978.5 verb 3sing indic pres act	1466.1 prs-pron nom 1sing	3725.2 verb 1sing act	5050.4 prs-pron acc 2pl	1894.2 prep	3620.2 partic
λέγει,	ʼΕγὼ	παραζηλώσω	ὑμᾶς	ἐπ'	οὐκ
legei	Egō	parazēlōsō	humas	ep'	ouk
says,	I	will make jealous	you	through	not

1477.3 noun dat sing neu	1894.3 prep	1894.2 prep	1477.3 noun dat sing neu	795.4 adj dat sing neu
ἔθνει,	ʹ ἐπὶ	[⋆ ἐπ']	ἔθνει	ἀσυνέτῳ
ethnei	epi	ep'	ethnei	asunetō
a nation,	through	[idem]	a nation	without understanding

3811.2 verb 1sing indic fut act	5050.4 prs-pron acc 2pl	2246.1 name nom masc	1156.2 conj	656.1 verb 3sing indic pres act	2504.1 conj
παροργιῶ	ὑμᾶς.	20. ʼΗσαΐας	δὲ	ἀποτολμᾷ	καὶ
parorgiō	humas	Hēsaias	de	apotolma	kai
I will anger	you.	Isaiah	but	is very bold	and

10:17. While emphasis is placed on preaching, let it never be forgotten that the preaching of the gospel is not the exclusive responsibility of the clergy (Acts 8:4). Nor is preaching the exclusive means by which men may be saved. The written word, for example, is often an effective evangelistic tool. But in this context Paul is emphasizing the report or message spoken by men of God.

With regard to the question of hearing (Romans 10:14), salvation does not occur apart from the Word of God (John 5:24; Acts 10:44; Ephesians 1:3). And with regard to believing, lost men cannot call without believing. Here is where faith enters in.

Why do the heathen bow to idols of wood and stone? It may be that no one ever told them of the living God and the loving Saviour. Or, why do Jewish friends continue to emphasize following the legalism of the Law? Could it be that they have not understood that Isaiah 53 pictures Jesus as their Messiah, the One who came to die for all? The "report" now going out is that if one repents and believes the word of God, sin will be cleansed away and fellowship with the Lord restored.

To receive this message of salvation requires faith. Much is being said and written about faith today. The simple truth is that faith comes from hearing the Word of God. The Word is the source of all true faith. The faith which the Word produces brings an awareness of God to the soul. By faith the believer hears God's voice. Faith enables the believer to walk through deep waters and suffer in the furnace of afflictions, for he sees God's hand in all things. Faith which the Word produces enables the believer to exercise confidence in God and to believe Him for impossible things.

The energizing power of the Word assures us that if we will attune our ears to hear, our faith will be quickened and God will work wondrous things on our behalf.

The responsibility of man comes clearly into focus. The Word must be preached. That requires a human channel. The Word must be heard. That requires the listener who really hears. The Word must be believed. That requires the listener to act in faith on the facts of the Word as presented.

10:18,19. In these verses Paul shifted the emphasis from the responsibility of the messenger to that of the hearer. Verse 18 deals with mankind in general; verse 19 focuses on Israel in particular. Paul indicated that Israel had no excuse. Even their prophets had declared salvation by faith.

When Paul referred to Psalm 19:4 in verse 18, he was showing that all human beings have heard the "sound" and the "words" of God. This is the same concept developed in 1:18-32. Some can say they never heard the gospel per se, but no one can say he never heard God speak.

In verse 19, quoting Deuteronomy 32:21, Paul reminded unbelieving Jews that their mental assent (they *knew* the truth) was not enough. There are two kinds of hearing, physical and spiritual. Hearing with a receptive heart produces faith; otherwise it hardens (Hebrews 4:2).

17. So then faith [cometh] by hearing: Consequently, *Worrell* . . . So belief, *ASV* . . . faith comes from the message, *HistNT* . . . must depend upon having heard the Message, *Way* . . . comes from a Report, *Wilson*.

and hearing by the word of God: . . . is through the message of Christ, *Berkeley* . . . comes by the preaching of Christ, *RSV*.

18. But I say, Have they not heard?:
Yes verily: No doubt, *Geneva*.
their sound went into all the earth: Fly Abroad, Thou Mighty Gospel, *Montgomery* . . . All over the earth their voices have gone, *Williams* . . . into the extremities of the inhabited earth, *Wuest*.
and their words unto the ends of the world: . . . to the very ends of the habitable world, *Norlie* . . . the ends of the inhabited earth, *Clementson*.

19. But I say: But I demaunde, *Tyndale, Cranmer*.
Did not Israel know?: . . . not understand? *RSV*.
First Moses saith:
I will provoke you to jealousy by [them that are] no people: I will fire you with jealousy, *Weymouth* . . . make you jealous, *Norlie* . . . will move you to jealousy, *Scarlett* . . . I will prouoke you to enuy, *Cranmer* . . . to rivalry, *Worrell* . . . with a nobody people, *Klingensmith*.
[and] by a foolish nation I will anger you: . . . against a Gentile nation without understanding will I make you wroth, *Conybeare* . . . with an irreligious people, *JB* . . . With a nation void of understanding, *Panin* . . . I will infuriate you, *Berkeley* . . . make you angry over a senseless nation, *Adams* . . . I vvil driue you into anger, *Rheims* . . . I will excite you to indignation, *Noyes* . . . By an unenlightened nation, *Hanson* . . . as yet untutored, *Way*.

20. But Esaias is very bold, and saith: Nay, Isaiah throws off all reserve, *Way* . . . said more clearly, *JB* . . . dares to say, *Confraternity* . . . quite boldly says, *Adams* . . . with strange boldness, exclaims, *Weymouth*.

169

Romans 10:21

20.a.Txt: 01א,02A,04C
06D-corr1,044,byz.
Var: p46,03B,06D-org
010F,012G

2978.5 verb 3sing indic pres act	2128.31 verb 1sing indic aor pass	1706.1 prep	3450.4 art dat pl	1466.7 prs-pron acc 1sing	3231.1 partic
λέγει,	Εὑρέθην	[ᵃ+ ἐν]	τοῖς	ἐμὲ	μὴ
legei	Heurethēn	en	tois	eme	mē
says,	I was found	[by]	by the	me	not

2195.2 verb dat pl masc part pres act	1701.1 adj nom sing masc	1090.30 verb 1sing indic aor mid	3450.4 art dat pl	1466.7 prs-pron acc 1sing	3231.1 partic
ζητοῦσιν,	ἐμφανὴς	ἐγενόμην	τοῖς	ἐμὲ	μὴ
zētousin	emphanēs	egenomēn	tois	eme	mē
seeking;	manifested	I became	to the	me	not

1890.1 verb dat pl part pres act	4242.1 prep	1156.2 conj	3450.6 art acc sing masc	2447.1 name masc
ἐπερωτῶσιν.	**21.** πρὸς	δὲ	τὸν	Ἰσραὴλ
eperōtōsin	pros	de	ton	Israēl
inquiring after.	To	but		Israel

2978.5 verb 3sing indic pres act	3513.9 adj acc sing fem	3450.12 art acc sing fem	2232.4 noun acc sing fem	1587.1 verb 1sing indic aor act
λέγει,	Ὅλην	τὴν	ἡμέραν	ἐξεπέτασα
legei	Holēn	tēn	hēmeran	exepetasa
he says,	Whole	the	day	I stretched out

3450.15 art acc pl fem	5331.8 noun acc pl fem	1466.2 prs-pron gen 1sing	4242.1 prep	2967.4 noun acc sing masc	540.3 verb acc sing masc part pres act
τὰς	χεῖράς	μου	πρὸς	λαὸν	ἀπειθοῦντα
tas	cheiras	mou	pros	laon	apeithounta
the	hands	my	to	a people	disobeying

2504.1 conj	480.2 verb acc sing masc part pres act	2978.1 verb 1sing indic pres act	3631.1 conj	3231.1 partic	676.2 verb 3sing indic aor mid
καὶ	ἀντιλέγοντα.	**11:1.** Λέγω	οὖν,	Μὴ.	ἀπώσατο
kai	antilegonta	Legō	oun	Mē	apōsato
and	contradicting.	I say	then,	Not	did thrust away

1.a.**Var:** p46,01א-corr
02A,06D-org,Lach

3450.5 art sing masc	2296.1 noun nom sing masc	3450.6 art acc sing masc	2967.4 noun acc sing masc	840.3 prs-pron gen sing	3614.6 rel-pron acc sing masc
ὁ	θεὸς	τὸν	λαὸν	αὐτοῦ;	[ᵃ+ ὃν
ho	theos	ton	laon	autou	hon
	God	the	people	his?	[whom

4126.2 verb 3sing indic aor act	3231.1 partic	1090.44 verb 3sing opt aor mid	2504.1 conj	1056.1 conj	1466.1 prs-pron nom 1sing
προέγνω;]	μὴ	γένοιτο·	καὶ	γὰρ	ἐγὼ
proegnō	mē	genoito	kai	gar	egō
he foreknew?]	May	it not be!	Also	for	I

2448.1 name nom sing masc	1498.2 verb 1sing indic pres act	1523.2 prep gen	4543.2 noun gen sing neu	11.1 name masc
Ἰσραηλίτης	εἰμί,	ἐκ	σπέρματος	Ἀβραάμ,
Israēlitēs	eimi	ek	spermatos	Abraam
an Israelite	am,	of	seed	of Abraham,

5279.1 noun gen sing fem	951.1 name masc	3620.2 partic	676.2 verb 3sing indic aor mid	3450.5 art sing masc	2296.1 noun nom sing masc
φυλῆς	Βενιαμίν.	**2.** οὐκ	ἀπώσατο	ὁ	θεὸς
phulēs	Beniamin	ouk	apōsato	ho	theos
of tribe	of Benjamin.	Not	did thrust away		God

3450.6 art acc sing masc	2967.4 noun acc sing masc	840.3 prs-pron gen sing	3614.6 rel-pron acc sing masc	4126.2 verb 3sing indic aor act	2211.1 conj
τὸν	λαὸν	αὐτοῦ,	ὃν	προέγνω.	ἢ
ton	laon	autou	hon	proegnō	ē
the	people	his,	whom	he foreknew.	Or

10:20,21. Throughout this section Paul had been driving home to the Jews their responsibility. They should have known better, they had every chance to know better, but they rejected God's appeal. Of all people, they should have understood. Even though Moses and Isaiah had foretold the salvation of the Gentiles, with Isaiah even foretelling Israel's opposition to that action, the Jews persisted in their rejection of salvation provided by faith through Christ.

The emphasis in these two verses is that the Gentiles who had much lesser revelation responded with greater faith. This contrast, described in Romans 9:30,31, was foretold by Isaiah (Isaiah 65:1,2).

God's outstretched arms are an indication of His great love and mercy. The fact that they were coldly rejected indicates how hard and cantankerous were the hearts of God's people. The Jews had been chosen to be God's primary messengers (3:2; 9:4). When as a nation they rejected their Messiah, they lost that place. The teaching that God sovereignly decreed that some men reject Him is shown to be utterly false. If He had predetermined that Israel reject Him, He surely would not have pleaded with them to return to Him. He would have let them go without the poignant pleading we read in the writings of prophets such as Hosea, Jeremiah, and Isaiah.

Paul maintained his profound feeling for perishing Israel. To coldhearted Christians the passionate love of Paul in 9:3 may seem like a mystery. God grant that our hearts may so feel for lost men today that with heartfelt prayer (10:1) and willing feet (10:15) we may with great faith and perseverance propagate the faith-inspiring Word of God (10:17) to men everywhere.

11:1,2. In enunciating the theme of Romans, Paul said, "To the Jew first" (1:16). Now he asks if God has forgotten His promise? Has "God cast away his people?" he says. Notice Paul's clear answer: "God forbid." God is concerned for His people. He will see to it that the glorious promises in which the prophets delighted will come to complete fulfillment. The chosen people are only temporarily set aside. When the gathering of all believers takes place at the end of this age of grace, God will turn again to Israel and make good His covenant promises.

The solemn promises made to Abraham and his seed regarding the Hebrew racial family, and those God gave to David and his seed regarding the Hebrew royal family, have not been canceled—only postponed. In this Church age, the Jewish nation is blinded, yet individual Jews are being saved.

The first answer to the important question, "Hath God cast away his people?" is the great apostle himself. The salvation of Paul proves there is still a remnant. His conversion is a striking preview to Israel's future conversion. The learned Pharisee in his campaign against the Church illustrated Israel's zeal for God was without knowledge. Even the manner of Paul's miraculous meeting with Jesus on the Damascus Road prefigures Christ's glorious appearing to the Jews as their Messiah.

I was found of them that sought me not: . . . who don't look for Me find Me, *Beck* . . . who were not seeking me, *Montgomery.*

I was made manifest unto them that asked not after me: I have shown myself, *RSV* . . . I have been made plain, *Klingensmith* . . . I appeared openly to those who made no inquiry of me, *Confraternity* . . . who did not consult me, *JB* . . . who were not consciously enquiring for me, *Way.*

21. But to Israel he saith: But in regard of Israel he saith, *Alford* . . . But in respect to Israel, *Worrell.*

All day long I have stretched forth my hands:

unto a disobedient and gainsaying people: . . . contradicting people, *Berkeley* . . . a people who disobey Me and oppose Me, *Beck* . . . that is disobedient and obstinate, *Williams* . . . antagonistic people, *Adams* . . . contrary people, *Moffatt, RSV* . . . but speaketh agaynst me, *Tyndale, Cranmer* . . . cantankerous people, *Wuest* . . . complaining people, *Klingensmith.*

1. I say then, Hath God cast away his people?: . . . must we think that, *Conybeare* . . . God repudiated his People, *TCNT, Moffatt* . . . Does not God thrust away, *Concordant* . . . has God rejected his people? *RSV* . . . push His people aside? *Adams.*

God forbid: By no means, *Campbell* . . . It never was, *Klingensmith.*

For I also am an Israelite:

of the seed of Abraham, [of] the tribe of Benjamin: . . . a member of the tribe of Benjamin, *Williams* . . . of the posterity, *Weymouth* . . . of the race, *Sawyer.*

2. God hath not cast away his people: . . . has not disowned His people, *Norlie, Williams* . . . hath not reiected, *Rheims.*

which he foreknew: . . . his predestined People! *Moffatt* . . . he chose specially long ago, *JB* . . . of whom he took note from the first, *TCNT* . . . whom formerly he acknowledged, *Campbell* . . . whom He marked out for His own so long ago, *Way.*

Romans 11:3

2.a.Txt: 01ℵ-org,020L
byz.
Var: 01ℵ-corr,02A,03B
04C,06D,025P,Gries
Lach,Treg,Alf,Word
Tisc,We/Ho,Weis,Sod
UBS/✶

3.a.Txt: 06D,020L,byz.
Var: 01ℵ-org,02A,03B
04C,025P,sa.bo.Lach
Treg,Alf,Word,Tisc
We/Ho,Weis,Sod
UBS/✶

3620.2 partic	3471.6 verb 2pl indic perf act	1706.1 prep	2226.3 name dat masc	4949.9 intr-pron sing neu	2978.5 verb 3sing indic pres act
οὐκ	οἴδατε	ἐν	Ἠλίᾳ	τί	λέγει
ouk	oidate	en	Hēlia	ti	legei
not	know you	in	Elijah	what	says

3450.9 art nom sing fem	1118.1 noun nom sing fem	5453.1 conj	1777.1 verb 3sing indic pres act	3450.3 art dat sing	2296.3 noun dat sing masc
ἡ	γραφή;	ὡς	ἐντυγχάνει	τῷ	θεῷ
hē	graphē	hōs	entunchanei	tō	theō
the	scripture?	how	he pleads		with God

2567.3 prep	3450.2 art gen sing	2447.1 name masc	2978.15 verb sing masc part pres act	2935.5 noun voc sing masc
κατὰ	τοῦ	Ἰσραήλ,	[a λέγων,]	3. Κύριε,
kata	tou	Israēl	legōn	Kurie
against		Israel,	saying,	Lord,

3450.8 art acc pl masc	4254.7 noun acc pl masc	4622.2 prs-pron gen 2sing	609.7 verb 3pl indic aor act	2504.1 conj
τοὺς	προφήτας	σου	ἀπέκτειναν,	[a καὶ]
tous	prophētas	sou	apekteinan	kai
the	prophets	your	they killed,	and

3450.17 art pl neu	2356.4 noun acc pl neu	4622.2 prs-pron gen 2sing	2649.1 verb 3pl indic aor act	2476.3 conj
τὰ	θυσιαστήριά	σου	κατέσκαψαν·	κἀγὼ
ta	thusiastēria	sou	kateskapsan	kagō
the	altars	your	they dug down;	and I

5113.1 verb 1sing indic aor pass	3304.2 adj nom sing masc	2504.1 conj	2195.2 verb 3pl indic pres act	3450.12 art acc sing fem	5425.4 noun acc sing fem
ὑπελείφθην	μόνος,	καὶ	ζητοῦσιν	τὴν	ψυχήν
hupeleiphthēn	monos	kai	zētousin	tēn	psuchēn
was left	alone,	and	they seek	the	life

1466.2 prs-pron gen 1sing	233.2 conj	4949.9 intr-pron sing neu	2978.5 verb 3sing indic pres act	840.4 prs-pron dat sing	3450.5 art sing masc
μου.	4. Ἀλλὰ	τί	λέγει	αὐτῷ	ὁ
mou	Alla	ti	legei	autō	ho
my.	But	what	says	to him	the

5373.1 noun nom sing masc	2611.2 verb indic aor act	1670.2 prs-pron dat 1sing masc	2018.1 num card acc masc
χρηματισμός;	Κατέλιπον	ἐμαυτῷ	ἑπτακισχιλίους
chrēmatismos	Katelipon	emautō	heptakischilious
divine answer?	I left	to myself	seven thousand

433.9 noun acc pl masc	3610.2 rel-pron nom pl masc	3620.2 partic	2549.2 verb 3pl indic aor act	1113.1 noun sing neu	3450.11 art dat sing fem
ἄνδρας	οἵτινες	οὐκ	ἔκαμψαν	γόνυ	τῇ
andras	hoitines	ouk	ekampsan	gonu	tē
men	who	not	bowed	a knee	

890.1 name masc	3643.1 adv	3631.1 conj	2504.1 conj	1706.1 prep	3450.3 art dat sing	3431.1 adv	2511.3 noun dat sing masc
Βάαλ.	5. Οὕτως	οὖν	καὶ	ἐν	τῷ	νῦν	καιρῷ
Baal	Houtōs	oun	kai	en	tō	nun	kairō
to Baal.	Thus	then	also	in	the	now	time

2979.1 noun nom sing neu	2567.1 prep	1576.3 noun acc sing fem	5322.2 noun gen sing fem	1090.3 verb 3sing indic perf act
λεῖμμα	κατ'	ἐκλογὴν	χάριτος	γέγονεν.
leimma	kat'	eklogēn	charitos	gegonen
a remnant	according to	election	of grace	there has been.

Though under chastisement and temporarily set aside, the Jews are still God's people, and they will be restored. Israel's future gave the prophets one of their most glorious themes. And Israel's future is still glorious. Even though God deals with Israel in a disapproving way at the present time, He is doing so with the prospect of Israel's restoration in mind.

There are many evidences that God is turning His attention toward the Jewish people and their land. The fulfillment of prophecy indicates that we are nearing the "fulness of the Gentiles" (11:25).

11:3-6. God has always had a faithful group. Elijah felt he was all alone, but God revealed 7,000 had not bowed their knees to Baal. As it was in the time of Elijah, so now the elect are a remnant. Although the Jewish leaders called for the death of Christ and asked that His blood be upon them—a much worse condition than Ahab's Baal worship in Elijah's day—there was a remnant that received Jesus and were put into His body, the Church. Every converted Jew abandoned his Jewish hopes and became a "partaker of the heavenly calling" (Hebrews 3:1). The Book of Acts gives us the record of thousands of Jews who became the early Christians, from the Day of Pentecost and on. All these came in by grace only and not by works. Not by the keeping of the Law but by the grace of God alone has there been a faithful remnant among the chosen people. Those who thus partake are no longer Jew or Gentile; they are called saints (Romans 1:6,7; 1 Corinthians 1:2; Ephesians 1:1). The Church is not Jewish, nor national, nor earthly; the Church is a "new body," a heavenly Body.

In this passage Paul presents the Jews in two classes—a minority who believed and accepted salvation by grace and a majority who rejected with blinded eyes and hardened hearts.

There has never been nor will there ever be a time when God does not have a corps of loyal followers. Before the Flood there was Noah and his family. The Scriptures are replete with the accounts of the lives of those who were true to God—an Abraham, a Moses, an Ezra, a Nehemiah, and many others.

On the other hand there never was a time that a whole nation was true to God. Again and again God had to send His prophets and leaders to call Israel to repentance. But always there was a faithful remnant. The prophets became aware of this loyal remnant. Micah envisioned the gathering of the remnant as did Zephaniah and Jeremiah (Micah 2:12; 5:3; Zephaniah 3:12,13; Jeremiah 23:3). Isaiah even named his son Shear-jashub which means "The Salvation of the Remnant." Over and over Isaiah writes of the faithful remnant who will be saved (Isaiah 7:3; 8:2,18; 9:12; 6:9-13). Amos presents the picture of God sifting people as corn in a sieve and saving only the good (Amos 9:9). He indicates the word from God as a promise that the house of Jacob will not be utterly destroyed. When writing of the remnant, Ezekiel clearly states that people are not saved because of either national or inherited righteousness (Ezekiel 14:14,18,20,22).

Wot ye not what the scripture saith of Elias?: . . . know you not? *ET.*

how he maketh intercession to God against Israel, saying: . . . hovv he requesteth God, *Rheims* . . . how he pleadeth with, *Panin* . . . how he complains to God, *Wilson.*

3. Lord, they have killed thy prophets: . . . they haue slaine thy Prophets, *Rheims* . . . they have massacred thy prophets, *Way.*
and digged down thine altars: . . . they tore down, *Adams* . . . they have demolished thine altars, *Moffatt* . . . they have razed thy altars, *Confraternity* . . . they have dug up the very foundations, *Way.*
and I am left alone: I alone am left over, *Berkeley* . . . I am the sole survivor, *Way.*
and they seek my life: They are thirsting for my blood, *Weymouth* . . . and they are trying to kill me, *Williams* . . . and they hunt for my life, *Klingensmith.*

4. But what saith the answer of God unto him?: But what says the divine oracle to him? *Wilson, Hanson* . . . what is God's reply, *RSV* . . . what doth the divine answer say, *Scarlett.*
I have reserved to myself seven thousand men, who have not bowed the knee to [the image of] Baal: I have yet left to myself a remnant, *Conybeare* . . . kept for myself, *RSV* . . . so loyal that they have never bowed a knee, *Way.*

5. Even so then at this present time also:
there is a remnant according to the election of grace: . . . a remnant God has chosen by His love, *Beck* . . . in agreement with His gracious choice, *Berkeley* . . . a remnant according to a choice of grace, *Wuest* . . . chosen by gift of grace, *Conybeare* . . . selected by grace, *Moffatt* . . . to a gratuitous election, *Scarlett* . . . in accordance with God's unmerited favor, *Williams* . . . to an Election of Favor, *Wilson* . . . chosen by favor, *Klingensmith* . . . by the election of grace, *Murdock.*

1479.1 conj	1156.2 conj	5322.3 noun dat sing fem	3629.1 adv	1523.1 prep gen	2024.5 noun gen pl neu	1878.1 conj
6. εἰ	δὲ	χάριτι,	οὐκέτι	ἐξ	ἔργων·	ἐπεὶ
ei	de	chariti	ouketi	ex	ergōn	epei
If	but	by grace,	no longer	of	works;	else

3450.9 art nom sing fem	5322.1 noun nom sing fem	3629.1 adv	1090.14 verb 3sing indic pres	5322.1 noun nom sing fem	1479.1 conj
ἡ	χάρις	οὐκέτι	γίνεται	χάρις.	⌐a εἰ
hē	charis	ouketi	ginetai	charis	ei
the	grace	no longer	becomes	grace;	if

6.a.Txt: 01ℵ-corr,(03B) 020L,byz.Weis,Sod **Var:** p46,01ℵ-org,02A 04C,06D,025P,sa.bo. Gries,Lach,Treg,Tisc We/Ho,UBS/✻

1156.2 conj	1523.1 prep gen	2024.5 noun gen pl neu	3629.1 adv	1498.4 verb 3sing indic pres act	5322.1 noun nom sing fem
δὲ	ἐξ	ἔργων,	οὐκέτι	ἐστὶν	χάρις·
de	ex	ergōn	ouketi	estin	charis
but	of	works,	no longer	is it	grace;

1878.1 conj	3450.16 art sing neu	2024.1 noun sing neu	3629.1 adv	1498.4 verb 3sing indic pres act	2024.1 noun sing neu
ἐπεὶ	τὸ	ἔργον	οὐκέτι	ἐστὶν	ἔργον. ⌐
epei	to	ergon	ouketi	estin	ergon
else	the	work	no longer	is	work.

4949.9 intr-pron sing neu	3631.1 conj	3614.16 rel-pron sing neu	1919.2 verb 3sing indic pres act	2447.1 name masc	3642.1 dem-pron gen sing
7. τί	οὖν;	ὃ	ἐπιζητεῖ	Ἰσραήλ,	⌐ τούτου
ti	oun	ho	epizētei	Israēl	toutou
What	then?	What	seeks for	Israel,	this

7.a.Txt: byz. **Var:** 01ℵ,02A,03B,04C 06D,020L,025P,Gries Lach,Treg,Alf,Word Tisc,We/Ho,Weis,Sod UBS/✻

3642.17 dem-pron sing neu	3620.2 partic	1997.1 verb 3sing indic aor act	3450.9 art nom sing fem	1156.2 conj	1576.1 noun nom sing fem
[a✻ τοῦτο]	οὐκ	ἐπέτυχεν,	ἡ	δὲ	ἐκλογὴ
touto	ouk	epetuchen	hē	de	eklogē
[idem]	not	it did obtain;	the	but	election

1997.1 verb 3sing indic aor act	3450.7 art pl masc	1156.2 conj	3036.3 adj nom pl masc	4313.3 verb 3pl indic aor pass	2503.1 conj
ἐπέτυχεν·	οἱ	δὲ	λοιποὶ	ἐπωρώθησαν,	**8.** ⌐✻ καθὼς
epetuchen	hoi	de	loipoi	epōrōthēsan	kathōs
obtained,	the	and	rest	were hardened,	just as

8.a.Txt: 02A,04C,06D 020L,025P,etc.byz.Lach Sod **Var:** 01ℵ,03B,Treg,Tisc We/Ho,Weis,UBS/✻

2481.1 conj	1119.22 verb 3sing indic perf pass	1319.14 verb 3sing indic aor act	840.2 prs-pron dat pl	3450.5 art sing masc
[a καθάπερ]	γέγραπται,	Ἔδωκεν	αὐτοῖς	ὁ
kathaper	gegraptai	Edōken	autois	ho
[idem]	it has been written,	Gave	them	the

2296.1 noun nom sing masc	4011.1 noun sing neu	2629.1 noun gen sing fem	3652.8 noun acc pl masc	3450.2 art gen sing
θεὸς	πνεῦμα	κατανύξεως,	ὀφθαλμοὺς	τοῦ
theos	pneuma	katanuxeōs	ophthalmous	tou
God	a spirit	of stupor,	eyes	the

3231.1 partic	984.17 verb inf pres act	2504.1 conj	3640.2 noun pl neu	3450.2 art gen sing	3231.1 partic	189.17 verb inf pres act
μὴ	βλέπειν,	καὶ	ὦτα	τοῦ	μὴ	ἀκούειν,
mē	blepein	kai	ōta	tou	mē	akouein
not	to see,	and	ears	the	not	to hear,

2175.1 conj	3450.10 art gen sing fem	4449.1 adv	2232.1 noun fem	2504.1 conj	1132.1 name masc
ἕως	τῆς	σήμερον	ἡμέρας.	**9.** καὶ	Δαβὶδ
heōs	tēs	sēmeron	hēmeras	kai	Dabid
unto	the	day	this.	And	David

In fact, the wording indicates that it was only by the grace of God that this remnant existed, both in the days of the prophets and in Paul's day. The remnant is described as being in accordance with His "election by grace" (verse 5). The term *eklogēn* can be translated "election," "choosing," or "choice." It is the same term used in the Gospels to tell of Jesus' choosing of the Twelve.

Verse 6 emphasizes that the remnant existed not because of any action on their part, but because God himself reserved or kept them. Not only did they gain access to God's family by grace, they remained in a position of loyalty by grace. This theme is further addressed by Paul in his letter to the Galatians. Human performance can neither cause one to be saved, nor can it maintain a vital relationship with God. Grace is always needed.

11:7,8. Election is of grace, not of works, so while the remnant obtained grace, the rest were "blinded." "Election" may be one of the most difficult biblical concepts to understand—along with predestination and foreordination. Some define predestination and foreordination exactly alike. Others say that predestination refers to the choice God makes concerning who will be saved and who will be lost, with foreordination signifying the broad term describing God's will over all matters. Election, then, is the process that defines those who will inherit eternal life.

The majority of individuals fell out of favor with God. This was foretold (Deuteronomy 29:4; Isaiah 6:9; 29:10; Jeremiah 5:21; Ezekiel 12:2). God's judgment has its ground in antecedent sin. Those Jews who loved God—such as Zacharias, Elizabeth, Mary, Joseph, Anna, Simeon, and others—were not blinded, but recognized Jesus as Saviour. The reason so many did not is that they had closed their eyes and ears to God's revelation for so long that they became spiritually blind and deaf.

In outlining this history, God said the Jews were to be scattered to all corners of the world because they were blinded and had forsaken God. Their apostasy and decline were clearly delineated.

The Greeks of Paul's day were consumed with a passion for knowledge. The Romans lusted for power, but the Jews searched for righteousness. They did not find the righteousness they desired because they rejected the only One who could make them righteous. This rebellion against God resulted in blindness. The word "blinded" bears the meaning of "hardened" or "calloused." The verb is *pōroō* and the noun is *pōrōsis*, a medical word meaning a callous. Callouses become hardened and more or less insensitive to feeling.

As a callous forms on the hand, a spiritual callous can grow on the heart. For a person to insist on going his own way despite the warning flags will eventuate in his becoming insensitive to the voice of God. That is what happened to Israel. Their hearts were insensitive and thus insensible to the gospel. Their eyes were sightless, and their ears were deaf. Paul had previously related God's dealings with Pharaoh as an example of judicial hardening. The more God demanded that Pharaoh let Israel go, the more stubborn and rebellious he became.

6. And if by grace, then [is it] no more of works: . . . else the grace is coming to be no longer grace, *Concordant* . . . His choice is not conditioned by works of theirs, the era for which is past, *Way* . . . it can no more be deemed the wage of works, *Conybeare*.

otherwise grace is no more grace: . . . would cease to be mercy, *TCNT* . . . is no longer a favour, *Scarlett* . . . would be a mere misnomer, *Way*.

But if [it be] of works, then is it no more grace: otherwise work is no more work: . . . for work claims wages, and not gifts, *Conybeare* . . . otherwise it wouldn't be His unearned love anymore, *Beck*.

7. What then?:
Israel hath not obtained that which he seeketh for: It was not Israel as a whole, *JB* . . . failed to obtain what it sought, *RSV* . . . enthusiastically sought, *Adams* . . . he has not attained, *Way*.

but the election hath obtained it: Only the chosen remnant got it, *Norlie* . . . yet the chosen encountered it, *Concordant*.

and the rest were blinded: . . . the rest grew callous, *TCNT* . . . the rest have been hardened, *HistNT* . . . The remnaunt are blynded, *Tyndale* . . . The rest have become insensible to it, *Williams* . . . the rest have been callously indifferent, *Way*.

8. (According as it is written:
God hath given them the spirit of slumber: . . . hath cast them into a trance of stupor, *Way* . . . them a sluggish spirit, *JB* . . . has given them a deadness of mind, *TCNT* . . . a spirit of stupidity, *Scarlett* . . . the sprete of vnquyetnes, *Tyndale, Cranmer* . . . given them over to an attitude of insensibility, *Williams* . . . a spirit of deep sleep, *Campbell, Young* . . . a spirit of sleepiness, *Klingensmith*.

eyes that they should not see, and ears that they should not hear;) unto this day: . . . eyes to see nothing, *Weymouth* . . . unseeing eyes and inattentive ears, *JB* . . . a condition that continues, *Adams* . . . ears for the purpose of not hearing, *Wuest* . . . down to this very day, *RSV*.

2978.5 verb 3sing indic pres act	1090.45 verb 3sing impr aor pass	3450.9 art nom sing fem	4971.1 noun nom sing fem	840.1 prs-pron gen pl	1519.1 prep
λέγει,	Γενηθήτω	ἡ	τράπεζα	αὐτῶν	εἰς
legei	Genēthētō	hē	trapeza	autōn	eis
says,	Let be	the	table	their	for

3666.3 noun acc sing fem	2504.1 conj	1519.1 prep	2316.1 noun acc sing fem	2504.1 conj	1519.1 prep	4480.1 noun sing neu
παγίδα,	καὶ	εἰς	θήραν,	καὶ	εἰς	σκάνδαλον,
pagida	kai	eis	thēran	kai	eis	skandalon
a snare,	and	for	a trap,	and	for	cause of offense,

2504.1 conj	1519.1 prep	465.1 noun sing neu	840.2 prs-pron dat pl		4509.3 verb 3pl impr aor pass
καὶ	εἰς	ἀνταπόδομα	αὐτοῖς·	**10.**	σκοτισθήτωσαν
kai	eis	antapodoma	autois		skotisthētōsan
and	for	a recompense	to them:		let be darkened

3450.7 art pl masc	3652.5 noun nom pl masc	840.1 prs-pron gen pl	3450.2 art gen sing	3231.1 partic	984.17 verb inf pres act	2504.1 conj
οἱ	ὀφθαλμοὶ	αὐτῶν	τοῦ	μὴ	βλέπειν,	καὶ
hoi	ophthalmoi	autōn	tou	mē	blepein	kai
the	eyes	their	the	not	to see,	and

3450.6 art acc sing masc	3439.1 noun acc sing masc	840.1 prs-pron gen pl	1269.1 adv	1217.2 prep	3820.2 adj gen sing
τὸν	νῶτον	αὐτῶν	῾ διαπαντὸς	[✶ διὰ	παντὸς]
ton	nōton	autōn	diapantos	dia	pantos
the	back	their	continually	[through	all]

4632.1 verb 2sing impr aor act		2978.1 verb 1sing pres act	3631.1 conj	3231.1 partic	4275.3 verb 3pl indic aor act	2419.1 conj
σύγκαμψον.	**11.**	Λέγω	οὖν,	μὴ	ἔπταισαν	ἵνα
sunkampson		Legō	oun	mē	eptaisan	hina
bow you down.		I say	then,	Not	did they stumble	that

3959.9 verb 3pl subj aor act	3231.1 partic	1090.44 verb 3sing opt aor mid	233.2 conj	3450.3 art dat sing	840.1 prs-pron gen pl
πέσωσιν;	μὴ	γένοιτο·	ἀλλὰ	τῷ	αὐτῶν
pesōsin	mē	genoito	alla	tō	autōn
they might fall?	Not	may it be!	but	by the	their

3761.3 noun dat sing neu	3450.9 art nom sing fem	4843.1 noun nom sing fem	3450.4 art dat pl	1477.6 noun dat pl neu
παραπτώματι	ἡ	σωτηρία	τοῖς	ἔθνεσιν,
paraptōmati	hē	sōtēria	tois	ethnesin
offense	the	salvation	to the	nations,

1519.1 prep	3450.16 art sing neu	3725.3 verb inf aor act	840.8 prs-pron acc pl masc		1479.1 conj	1156.2 conj
εἰς	τὸ	παραζηλῶσαι	αὐτούς.	**12.**	εἰ	δὲ
eis	to	parazēlōsai	autous		ei	de
for	the	to provoke to jealousy	them.		If	but

3450.16 art sing neu	3761.1 noun nom sing neu	840.1 prs-pron gen pl	4009.1 noun sing masc	2862.2 noun gen sing masc	2504.1 conj
τὸ	παράπτωμα	αὐτῶν	πλοῦτος	κόσμου,	καὶ
to	paraptōma	autōn	ploutos	kosmou	kai
the	offense	their	wealth	of world,	and

3450.16 art sing neu	2253.1 noun nom sing neu	840.1 prs-pron gen pl	4009.1 noun sing masc	1477.5 noun gen pl neu	4073.9 intr-pron dat sing neu
τὸ	ἥττημα	αὐτῶν	πλοῦτος	ἐθνῶν,	πόσῳ
to	hēttēma	autōn	ploutos	ethnōn	posō
the	default	their	wealth	of nations,	how much

11:9. The reference to the "table" is a quotation from Psalm 69:22,23. There was a table in the tabernacle of Israel which was not reserved for the priests alone. The people could bring their peace offerings to this table (Leviticus 6:16; 7:18,20). This high and holy privilege became a trap to the people, for they became more absorbed in the outward ceremonial than in the spiritual reality.

The word "table" also suggests feasting. The thought may well be that while they were lounging at the feast in presumptuous security, they were suddenly caught and destroyed.

11:10. The word for "bow down" is the compound *sunkamptō*, meaning "bend completely" or "bend together." The bowed back is a striking picture of servitude. The curse of anti-Semitism has driven the Jew from land to land. The torture and suffering has been almost unbelievable. The price has been bitter and will continue, for ahead lie the horrors of the Great Tribulation. But the final agony will end as they "shall look upon (Him) whom they have pierced" (Zechariah 12:10-12). Until that day the blinded majority of Israel will continue with unseeing eyes and bowed backs as the prophets warned.

11:11. The many promises made to Israel in the Old Testament have not been canceled. They relate to matters of national position and blessing.

This chapter shows that Israel's failure is neither complete (verses 1-11) nor permanent (verses 11-32). Israel's fall is not complete because the remnant, made up of Jews like Paul, have accepted Christ. Neither is Israel's fall permanent, because God will fulfill the national promises made to His people. True, Israel has stumbled—"we preach Christ crucified, unto the Jews a stumblingblock" (1 Corinthians 1:23)—but their failure is not permanent. God will not allow their fall to be the dismal climax to a marvelous history. God has a glorious future in store for them.

Rather, God has overruled and "through their fall salvation is come unto the Gentiles." The sons of Jacob persecuted their brother Joseph and finally sold him into slavery, but God overruled their wicked actions for the good of the Gentiles. The Jews were provoked to jealousy by observing the blessings being outpoured upon the "unworthy" Gentiles (Deuteronomy 32:21; Acts 13:45).

11:12. When the Jews rejected Christ, they were set aside as God's witnesses on a sidetrack. A new chosen people (the Church) was placed on the main line. But the setting aside is not permanent, and it has been used to bring salvation to the Gentiles. If their fall and diminishing brought riches to the Gentiles, how much more will their restoration to full privilege.

9. And David saith:

Let their table be made a snare, and a trap: . . . in stede of a snare, and a net, *Geneva*.

and a stumblingblock, and a recompense unto them: . . . a scandal and repayment, *Klingensmith* . . . an occasion to faule, and a rewarde vnto them, *Tyndale* . . . a pitfall, a retribution, *Way*.

10. Let their eyes be darkened that they may not see: . . . may their eyes be struck incurably blind, *JB* . . . Let their eyes be shrouded in gloom, *Way*.

and bow down their back alway: . . . make thou their back stoop beneath this burden for ever! *Way*.

11. I say then:

Have they stumbled that they should fall?: . . . have the Jews fallen for ever, *JB* . . . to be lost altogether? *Beck* . . . did they trip in order to fall? *Adams* . . . that they shuld vtterly fall, *Cranmer* . . . to fall in utter ruin, *Williams*.

God forbid:

but [rather] through their fall salvation [is come] unto the Gentiles: But through the instrumentality of their fall, *Wuest* . . . But by their offense, *Douay, Confraternity* . . . that by their lapse, *Moffatt* . . . through their misbehavior, *Berkeley* . . . By their error, *Beck* . . . through their false step, *TCNT* . . . it is by their slip, *HistNT* . . . But by their trespass, *Worrell* . . . has left the field clear for the salvation of the Gentiles, *Way*.

for to provoke them to jealousy: . . . to excite them to emulation, *Hanson* . . . to make the Jews jealous, *Beck* . . . that they may emulate them, *Rheims* . . . to provoke them to rivalry, *Worrell*.

12. Now if the fall of them [be] the riches of the world: . . . the world's enrichment, *Berkeley* . . . is the Wealth of the World, *Wilson*.

and the diminishing of them the riches of the Gentiles: . . . and their failure, *Hanson* . . . if their defection, *Moffatt* . . . if even their shortcoming gave such riches to, *Way*.

Romans 11:13

3095.1 adv comp	3450.16 art sing neu	3998.1 noun sing neu	840.1 prs-pron gen pl	5050.3 prs-pron dat 2pl	1056.1 conj
μᾶλλον	τὸ	πλήρωμα	αὐτῶν;	13. Ὑμῖν	' γὰρ
mallon	to	plērōma	autōn	Humin	gar
more	the	fulness	their?	To you	for

13.a.**Txt**: 06D,020L,byz. **Var**: 01ℵ,02A,03B,025P bo.Lach,Treg,Alf,Tisc We/Ho,Weis,Sod UBS/☆

13.b.**Var**: 01ℵ,02A,03B 04C,025P,bo.Lach,Treg Alf,Word,Tisc,We/Ho Weis,Sod,UBS/☆

1156.2 conj	2978.1 verb 1sing pres act	3450.4 art dat pl	1477.6 noun dat pl neu	1894.1 prep	3607.1 rel-pron sing
[a☆ δὲ]	λέγω	τοῖς	ἔθνεσιν·	ἐφ᾽	ὅσον
de	legō	tois	ethnesin	eph'	hoson
[but]	I speak,	the	Gentiles,	upon	as much as

3173.1 conj	3631.1 conj	1498.2 verb 1sing indic pres act	1466.1 prs-pron nom 1sing	1477.5 noun gen pl neu
μὲν	[b☆+ οὖν]	εἰμι	ἐγὼ	ἐθνῶν
men	oun	eimi	egō	ethnōn
	[therefore]	am	I	of Gentiles

646.1 noun nom sing masc	3450.12 art acc sing fem	1242.4 noun acc sing fem	1466.2 prs-pron gen 1sing	1386.1 verb 1sing indic pres act
ἀπόστολος,	τὴν	διακονίαν	μου	δοξάζω,
apostolos	tēn	diakonian	mou	doxazō
apostle,	the	service	my	I glorify,

1479.1 conj	4315.1 adv	3725.2 verb 1sing act	1466.2 prs-pron gen 1sing	3450.12 art acc sing fem
14. εἴ	πως	παραζηλώσω	μου	τὴν
ei	pōs	parazēlōsō	mou	tēn
if	perhaps	I shall make jealous	my	the

4418.4 noun acc sing fem	2504.1 conj	4834.4 verb 1sing act	4948.9 indef-pron acc pl masc	1523.1 prep gen	840.1 prs-pron gen pl
σάρκα,	καὶ	σώσω	τινὰς	ἐξ	αὐτῶν.
sarka	kai	sōsō	tinas	ex	autōn
flesh,	and	shall save	some	from among	them.

1479.1 conj	1056.1 conj	3450.9 art nom sing fem	575.1 noun nom sing fem	840.1 prs-pron gen pl	2613.1 noun nom sing fem
15. εἰ	γὰρ	ἡ	ἀποβολὴ	αὐτῶν	καταλλαγὴ
ei	gar	hē	apobolē	autōn	katallagē
If	for	the	casting away	their	reconciliation

2862.2 noun gen sing masc	4949.3 intr-pron nom sing	3450.9 art nom sing fem	4214.1 noun nom sing fem	4214.2 noun nom sing fem
κόσμου,	τίς	ἡ	' πρόσληψις,	[☆ πρόσλημψις]
kosmou	tis	hē	proslēpsis	proslēmpsis
of world,	what	the	reception,	[idem]

1479.1 conj	3231.1 partic	2205.1 noun nom sing fem	1523.2 prep gen	3361.2 adj gen pl	1479.1 conj	1156.2 conj
εἰ	μὴ	ζωὴ	ἐκ	νεκρῶν;	16. εἰ	δὲ
ei	mē	zōē	ek	nekrōn	ei	de
if	not	life	from among	dead?	If	now

3450.9 art nom sing fem	532.1 noun nom sing fem	39.10 adj nom sing fem	2504.1 conj	3450.16 art sing neu	5281.1 noun sing neu	2504.1 conj
ἡ	ἀπαρχὴ	ἁγία,	καὶ	τὸ	φύραμα·	καὶ
hē	aparchē	hagia	kai	to	phurama	kai
the	first fruit	holy,	also	the	lump;	and

1479.1 conj	3450.9 art nom sing fem	4347.1 noun nom sing fem	39.10 adj nom sing fem	2504.1 conj	3450.7 art pl masc	2771.2 noun nom pl masc
εἰ	ἡ	ῥίζα	ἁγία,	καὶ	οἱ	κλάδοι.
ei	hē	rhiza	hagia	kai	hoi	kladoi
if	the	root	holy,	also	the	branches.

11:13,14. Paul stated he was the apostle to the Gentiles. He magnified his office, that is, his ministry (*diakonia*) to the Gentiles, before the Jews. The Jews did not want the gospel, but they did not want the Gentiles to have it either. Paul was showing, before his kinsmen in the flesh, the blessing of his ministry to the Gentiles, for God was saving them and filling them with His Spirit.

In effect he was saying that he was interested in the Jews for the sake of the Gentiles. According to the prophets, the restoration of Israel will be the starting point for the coming of God's kingdom on earth. Knowing the blessing to the world that will be brought by their restoration, Paul wanted to do all he could to further that goal. He wanted to provoke the Jews to emulation, "jealousy," that they might accept the Messiah and be saved.

11:15. Up to this point Paul had spoken mainly of Israel's disobedience and futile attempts at self-righteousness. Here he began to reveal God's acts of judgment. Jesus had warned the Jews of this (Matthew 21:43). Scripture clearly indicates that after Christ came unto His own and His own rejected Him, He was preached to the Gentiles. The failure of Israel brought salvation to the Gentiles. Their fall was the wealth of the world; their loss the wealth of the Gentiles, and their casting away the reconciliation of the world. How much greater will be the blessing to the world when Israel is received (in restoration) back again. It will be "life from the dead." (See Isaiah 11:9; 40:1-5.) The nation will be saved by the sovereign grace of God out from a spiritually dead state and from those who remain spiritually dead.

Paul thrilled with thoughts of the future. If the tragedy of rejection has had such wonderful results, what will the glorious ending be, when the tragedy of rejection has changed to the glory of reception. It will be like life from the dead.

11:16. Paul used two pictures to show that the Jews can never be finally rejected. The Law provided (Numbers 15:19,20) that all food before it was eaten was to be offered to God. When the dough was being prepared, the first part was to be offered to God. That firstfruit of the bread, the first cake, was set aside for the priests. When that was done, the entire lump of dough became sacred. The offering of the first part sanctified the whole. When a sapling was planted, it was dedicated to God and from then on every branch that came from it was sacred to God.

A key word is "holy." The meaning is that the call and destiny of Israel sets them apart unto God. The "firstfruit" can refer to the first Jews blessed in the gospel and the "lump" to the whole nation that will be blessed and become holy in the end. Or, in connection with Israel, the "firstfruit" would be Abraham, Isaac, and Jacob. The "lump" would be the whole line of descent from the patriarchs. The "root" would be Abraham and the "branches" the descendants of Israel.

how much more their fulness?: . . . their perfectnesse? *Cranmer* . . . when the full quota of Jews comes in, *Williams* . . . will their full inclusion mean! *RSV* . . . when their whole nation shall be restored? *Locke* . . . shall their full reinstatement bring! *Way.*

13. For I speak to you Gentiles: I turn now to you, the Gentiles, *Way.*

inasmuch as I am the apostle of the Gentiles, I magnify mine office: I attach great importance, *Norlie* . . . I insist upon the grandeur of my function, *Way* . . . I magnify my ministry, *RSV* . . . I take pride in my service to them, *Adams* . . . I lay great stress on my office, *Moffatt* . . . I vvil honour my ministerie, *Rheims.*

14. If by any means I may provoke to emulation [them which are] my flesh: . . . awaken my own people to interest, *Norlie* . . . make my own people envious of you, *JB* . . . I shall arouse to jealousy, *Young.*
and might save some of them:

15. For if the casting away of them [be] the reconciling of the world: For if the losse of them, *Rheims* . . . For if their rejection, *Hanson* . . . if their exclusion means, *Moffatt.*
what [shall] the receiving [of them be], but life from the dead?: . . . what will their restoration be, *Montgomery* . . . so what will their final acceptance mean, *Norlie.*

16. For if the firstfruit [be] holy, the lump [is] also [holy]: If the first part of the dough, *Norlie* . . . if the first portion of the dough is holy, *Noyes* . . . of the dough are holy, *Weymouth* . . . If the first handful of dough is consecrated, *Williams* . . . for if a litil part of that that is taastid be holi, *Wyclif* . . . the whole produce of the year, *Locke* . . . the mass is also, *Hanson* . . . the whole mass of dough...shares in the consecration, *Way* . . . so is the loaf, *Klingensmith* . . . is given to God, *TEV.*
and if the root [be] holy, so [are] the branches: . . . the boughs are also, *Concordant.*

Romans 11:17

1479.1 conj	1156.2 conj	4948.7 indef-pron nom pl masc	3450.1 art gen pl	2771.3 noun gen pl masc	1562.1 verb 3pl indic aor pass
17. Εἰ	δέ	τινες	τῶν	κλάδων	ἐξεκλάσθησαν,
Ei	*de*	*tines*	*tōn*	*kladōn*	*exeklasthēsan,*
If	but	some	of the	branches	were broken off,

4622.1 prs-pron nom 2sing	1156.2 conj	64.1 noun nom sing fem	1498.21 verb sing masc part pres act	1454.2 verb 2sing indic aor pass
σὺ	δὲ	ἀγριέλαιος	ὢν	ἐνεκεντρίσθης
su	*de*	*agrielaios*	*ōn*	*enekentristhēs*
you	and,	a wild olive tree	being,	was grafted in

1706.1 prep	840.2 prs-pron dat pl	2504.1 conj	4642.1 noun nom sing masc	3450.10 art gen sing fem	4347.2 noun gen sing fem
ἐν	αὐτοῖς,	καὶ	συγκοινωνὸς	τῆς	ῥίζης
en	*autois,*	*kai*	*sunkoinōnos*	*tēs*	*rhizēs*
among	them,	and	a fellow partaker	of the	root

17.a.Txt: 01ℵ-corr,02A 06D-corr,020L,025P,33 byz.Sod
Var: 01ℵ-org,03B,04C bo.Alf,Tisc,We/Ho,Weis UBS/✶

2504.1 conj	3450.10 art gen sing fem	3957.1 noun gen sing fem	3450.10 art gen sing fem	1623.1 noun fem
(a καὶ)	τῆς	πιότητος	τῆς	ἐλαίας
kai	*tēs*	*piotētos*	*tēs*	*elaias*
and	of the	richness	of the	olive tree

1090.31 verb 2sing indic aor mid	3231.1 partic	2590.3 verb 2sing impr pres	3450.1 art gen pl	2771.3 noun gen pl masc	1479.1 conj
ἐγένου,	18. μὴ	κατακαυχῶ	τῶν	κλάδων·	εἰ
egenou,	*mē*	*katakauchō*	*tōn*	*kladōn*	*ei*
became,	not	boast against	the	branches;	if

1156.2 conj	2590.1 verb 2sing indic pres	3620.3 partic	4622.1 prs-pron nom 2sing	3450.12 art acc sing fem	4347.3 noun acc sing fem
δὲ	κατακαυχᾶσαι,	οὐ	σὺ	τὴν	ῥίζαν
de	*katakauchasai,*	*ou*	*su*	*tēn*	*rhizan*
but	you boast against,	not	you	the	root

934.2 verb 2sing indic pres act	233.1 conj	233.2 conj	3450.9 art nom sing fem	4347.1 noun nom sing fem
βαστάζεις,	(ἀλλ᾽	[✶ ἀλλὰ]	ἡ	ῥίζα
bastazeis,	*all'*	*alla*	*hē*	*rhiza*
bear,	but	[idem]	the	root

19.a.Txt: 06D-org,byz.
Var: 01ℵ,02A,03B,04C 06D-corr,020L,025P Gries,Lach,Treg,Alf Word,Tisc,We/Ho,Weis Sod,UBS/✶

4622.4 prs-pron acc 2sing	2029.10 verb 2sing indic fut act	3631.1 conj	1562.1 verb 3pl indic aor pass	3450.7 art pl masc
σέ.	19. Ἐρεῖς	οὖν,	Ἐξεκλάσθησαν	(a οἱ)
se.	*Ereis*	*oun,*	*Exeklasthēsan*	*hoi*
you.	You will say	then,	Were broken off	the

2771.2 noun nom pl masc	2419.1 conj	1466.1 prs-pron nom 1sing	1454.3 verb 1sing subj aor pass	2544.1 adv
κλάδοι,	ἵνα	ἐγὼ	ἐγκεντρισθῶ.	20. Καλῶς·
kladoi,	*hina*	*egō*	*enkentristhō.*	*Kalōs*
branches,	that	I	might be grafted in.	Well,

3450.11 art dat sing fem	565.3 noun dat sing fem	1562.1 verb 3pl indic aor pass	4622.1 prs-pron nom 2sing	1156.2 conj
τῇ	ἀπιστίᾳ	ἐξεκλάσθησαν,	σὺ	δὲ
tē	*apistia*	*exeklasthēsan*	*su*	*de*
by the	unbelief	they were broken off,	you	and

3450.11 art dat sing fem	3963.3 noun dat sing fem	2449.17 verb 2sing indic perf act	3231.1 partic	5147.1 verb 2sing impr pres act
τῇ	πίστει	ἕστηκας.	μὴ	(ὑψηλοφρόνει,
tē	*pistei*	*hestēkas.*	*mē*	*hupsēlophronei,*
by the	faith	have stood.	Not	be high minded,

11:17-19. The natural branches are the Jews and the ingrafted branches are the Gentiles. The Gentile does not become a Jew nor does he become "of Israel." He comes directly into the promise of blessing given by God to the Gentiles through Abraham (Genesis 12:3).

There are three figures of botanical speech relating to Israel. The "fig tree" speaks of Israel's national privilege (Matthew 24:32-34). The "vine" symbolizes Israel's spiritual privilege (Isaiah 5:1-7; Matthew 21:33,34). The "olive tree" symbolizes Israel's religious privilege (Romans 11:16,17; Judges 9:9; Zechariah 4:3).

As a result of unbelief the Jews were broken off. Not all were broken off; it was an individual matter. The ones who were broken off were formerly in vital connection with the root. In other words, they were at one time in the election of grace. By their own rejection of God they lost their elect position and perished.

We see the same principle in John 15:1-6. Jesus, speaking to believers, told them that He was the Vine. They were in vital union with Him. He warned them of the necessity of their abiding in Him, showing that the branches do not have an unconditional union with the vine. The branches must abide of their own volition, or they will be cut off, rejected, and cast into the fire. Throughout the Bible, there is evidence that man's volitional attitude toward God determines his destiny.

The Gentiles in turn were grafted in as wild olive branches. They were given the privilege of sharing the root and riches of the olive. They share the benefits of the covenant made to Abraham.

Just as not all Jewish branches were broken off, so not all Gentiles are grafted in. Only some branches of the wild olive tree were grafted in and made to draw life from the root. Gentiles must always remember that they owe much to the faithful Jews; they have been grafted in among them and live by the same root.

11:20,21. Unbelief is what brought about the breaking off of the Jews. But the Gentiles "stand by faith." It is not superiority in which the Gentiles stand; it is only by faith.

The Gentiles must not allow a spirit of contempt to possess them. The Jews of that day were hated, and it would have been easy for Gentile Christians to have wrong attitudes toward the Christ-rejecting Jews. We must remember that there never would have been such a thing as Christianity unless there had been Judaism first. Christians must never forget the roots from which they sprang.

Israel chosen, blessed, favored above all others, was not spared. The Gentiles are the wild branches grafted into their place. The Gentiles are enjoying the privileges and blessings of the olive tree. The olive tree is named as king of the trees. The only evergreen in the Parable of the Trees (Judges 9:8-15), the olive tree speaks of Israel's covenant blessings and privileges. Its enduring green illustrates the enduring covenant which God made with Abraham. The tree is characterized by fatness (privileges). Surely no other nation has ever been so blessed of the Lord. And yet, with all of

17. And if some of the branches be broken off: . . . have been pruned away, *Berkeley.*

and thou, being a wild olive tree, wert grafted in among them: . . . a wild olive shoot, *Berkeley, RSV* . . . art grafted in their place, *Confraternity.*

and with them partakest of the root and fatness of the olive tree: . . . to share the rich growth of the olive-stem, *Moffatt* . . . and there partakest of the blessings promised, *Locke* . . . and a fellow-partaker of the root, *Young* . . . in the fertility of the olive, *Way* . . . and art become a joint partaker, *Macknight* . . . the strong spiritual life of the Jews, *TEV* . . . nourishes you too, *Beck.*

18. Boast not against the branches: . . . beware of assuming airs of superiority over those branches, *Way* . . . glorie not, *Rheims* . . . do not boast over the branches, *RSV* . . . glory not over the branches, *Clementson* . . . don't brag of being more than the other branches, *Beck* . . . you must not exult over the other branches, *TCNT.*

But if thou boast, thou bearest not the root, but the root thee: If you must brag remember, *Adams* . . . If you are inclined to look down on them, let this reflection sober you, *Way* . . . thou sustainest not the root, *Murdock* . . . it is not thou that supportest the stem, *Confraternity* . . . you are not sustaining the root, *Wuest* . . . instead, the root supports you, *Berkeley* . . . the root upholds you, *Weymouth.*

19. Thou wilt say then:
The branches were broken off, that I might be grafted in: . . . branches have been snapped off, *Way* . . . have been lopped off, *Weymouth.*

20. Well; because of unbelief they were broken off: True, *Montgomery* . . . right! *Young* . . . for infidelity, *Scarlett* . . . because of incredulitie, *Rheims.*

and thou standest by faith: . . . yet you stand in faith, *Concordant* . . . you owe your position to your faith, *Moffatt* . . . but you stand by believing, *Beck.*

Romans 11:21

20.a.Txt: 04C,06D,020L
025P,etc.byz.Sod
Var: 01‭א‬,02A,03B,Treg
Tisc,We/Ho,Weis
UBS/✶

5146.4 adj acc pl neu	5262.14 verb 2sing impr pres act	233.2 conj	5236.5 verb 2sing impr pres		1479.1 conj	1056.1 conj
[ª✶ ὑψηλὰ	φρόνει,]	ἀλλὰ	φοβοῦ·	**21.**	εἰ	γὰρ
hupsēla	phronei	alla	phobou		ei	gar
[high things	were minding,]	but	fear:		if	for

3450.5 art sing masc	2296.1 noun nom sing masc	3450.1 art gen pl	2567.3 prep	5285.4 noun acc sing fem	2771.3 noun gen pl masc	3620.2 partic
ὁ	θεὸς	τῶν	κατὰ	φύσιν	κλάδων	οὐκ
ho	theos	tōn	kata	phusin	kladōn	ouk
	God	the	according to	nature	branches	not

21.a.Txt: p46,06D,020L
33,byz.it.Weis,Sod
Var: 01‭א‬,02A,03B,04C
025P,sa.bo.Lach,Treg
Tisc,We/Ho,UBS/✶

5177.4 verb 3sing indic aor mid	3248.1 conj	3624.1 adv	4622.2 prs-pron gen 2sing	5177.5 verb 3sing subj aor mid
ἐφείσατο,	⌐ª μήπως ⌐	οὐδὲ	σοῦ	⌐ φείσηται.
epheisato	mēpōs	oude	sou	pheisētai
spared	perhaps not	neither	you	he should spare.

21.b.Txt: Steph
Var: 01‭א‬,02A,03B,04C
06D,020L,025P,Gries
Lach,Treg,Alf,Word
Tisc,We/Ho,Weis,Sod
UBS/✶

5177.7 verb 3sing indic fut mid	1481.14 verb 2sing impr aor act	3631.1 conj	5379.4 noun acc sing fem	2504.1 conj
[ᵇ✶ φείσεται.]	**22.** Ἴδε	οὖν	χρηστότητα	καὶ
pheisetai	Ide	oun	chrēstotēta	kai
[he will spare.]	Behold	then	kindness	and

657.1 noun acc sing fem	2296.2 noun gen sing masc	1894.3 prep	3173.1 conj	3450.8 art acc pl masc	3959.14 verb acc pl masc part aor act
ἀποτομίαν	θεοῦ·	ἐπὶ	μὲν	τοὺς	πεσόντας,
apotomian	theou	epi	men	tous	pesontas
severity	of God:	upon	men	the	having fallen

22.a.Txt: 01‭א‬-corr,06D
020L,byz.
Var: 01‭א‬-org,02A,03B
04C,Lach,Treg,Alf,Tisc
We/Ho,Weis,Sod
UBS/✶

657.1 noun acc sing fem	657.2 noun nom sing fem	1894.3 prep	1156.2 conj	4622.4 prs-pron acc 2sing
⌐ ἀποτομίαν·	[ª✶ ἀποτομία,]	ἐπὶ	δὲ	σὲ,
apotomian	apotomia	epi	de	se
severity;	[idem]	upon	and	you,

22.b.Txt: 06D-corr,020L
byz.
Var: 02A,03B,04C
06D-org,bo.Lach,Treg
Alf,Tisc,We/Ho,Weis
Sod,UBS/✶

5379.4 noun acc sing fem	5379.1 noun nom sing fem	2296.2 noun gen sing masc	1430.1 partic	1946.7 verb 2sing subj aor act
⌐ χρηστότητα,	[ᵇ✶ χρηστότης	θεοῦ,]	ἐὰν	⌐ ἐπιμείνῃς
chrēstotēta	chrēstotēs	theou	ean	epimeinēs
kindness,	[kindness	of God,]	if	you continue

22.c.Txt: 02A,04C
06D-corr,020L,byz.Sod
Var: 01‭א‬,03B,06D-org
Treg,Tisc,We/Ho,Weis
UBS/✶

1946.14 verb 2sing subj pres act	3450.11 art dat sing fem	5379.3 noun dat sing fem	1878.1 conj	2504.1 conj	4622.1 prs-pron nom 2sing
[ᶜ✶ ἐπιμένῃς]	τῇ	χρηστότητι·	ἐπεὶ	καὶ	σὺ
epimenēs	tē	chrēstotēti	epei	kai	su
[idem]	in the	kindness,	else	also	you

1568.7 verb 2sing indic fut pass	2504.1 conj	1552.6 dem-pron nom pl masc	2519.4 conj	1156.2 conj
ἐκκοπήσῃ.	**23.** ⌐ καὶ	ἐκεῖνοι	[✶ κἀκεῖνοι]	δέ,
ekkopēsē	kai	ekeinoi	kakeinoi	de
will be cut off.	Also	those	[and those]	and,

23.a.Txt: 01‭א‬-corr,02A
04C,06D-corr,020L,byz.
Sod
Var: 01‭א‬-org,03B
06D-org,Treg,Tisc
We/Ho,Weis,UBS/✶

1430.1 partic	3231.1 partic	1946.8 verb 3pl subj aor act	1946.16 verb 3pl subj pres act	3450.11 art dat sing fem
ἐὰν	μὴ	⌐ ἐπιμείνωσιν	[ª✶ ἐπιμένωσιν]	τῇ
ean	mē	epimeinōsin	epimenōsin	tē
if	not	they continue	[idem]	in the

565.3 noun dat sing fem	1454.4 verb 3pl indic fut pass	1409.1 adj nom sing masc	1056.1 conj	1498.4 verb 3sing indic pres act
ἀπιστίᾳ,	ἐγκεντρισθήσονται·	δυνατὸς	γάρ	ἐστιν
apistia	enkentristhēsontai	dunatos	gar	estin
unbelief,	shall be grafted in;	able	for	is

their privileges, some of the branches were cut off.

Israel's greatest privilege was the gift of God's Word and God's Son. Think of it—Gentiles believing on God's Son as Saviour and preaching God's Word—blessings through Israel.

If God did not spare unbelieving Israel, He will not spare faithless Gentiles. The Jews had been more securely rooted in the Kingdom as natural branches. How much more then must the wild branch (the Gentiles) be careful to maintain the relationship which is by faith alone.

11:22. Israel fell in unbelief. That brought God's severity. Rejecting the righteousness which God provided in Christ, they followed self-righteousness and pride. They did not submit to God's provision but went about to establish their own righteousness (10:3).

While God's severity fell on Israel, His goodness and kindness came to the Gentiles. They were given the place of privilege even though they had not merited the place of blessing. This came about entirely by grace; it was by the "goodness" of God. Goodness as used here is "kindness," "benignity."

Epimenō rendered "continue" bears the thought of "to remain, to abide." The message is clear. If one is to avoid the severity of God—avoid being cut off—be he Jew or Gentile, he must remain and abide in God's grace. *Epimenō* speaks of relationship to and position in. The word is used to express friendship and companionship and often expressed the idea of abiding in a home as a guest.

The phrase "if thou continue" (see also in Colossians 1:23) indicates that our security in Christ is based on our willingness to continue abiding. Christ is always willing to abide if we will welcome and acknowledge Him as Lord. (Compare John 15:1-6.)

Some theologians say that no individual can lose his place in Christ. The age-old debate over eternal security, as well as predestination and election, cannot be settled here. Evidence for a variety of viewpoints may be extracted from the Bible. Each believer must settle for a balanced tension, in this case on the subject of the believer's security. This balance is stated by Bruce: "The perseverance of the saints is a doctrine firmly grounded in the New Testament (and not least in Pauline) teaching; but the corollary to it is that it is the saints who persevere" (*Tyndale New Testament Commentaries*, 6:219).

Neither the position of security nor the position of being cut off is unconditional. Both are conditional on the attitude and will of the individual; God has sovereignly made it so.

11:23. If Israel will not persist in their unbelief, God is able to graft them in. Israel's blindness will be taken away (2 Corinthians 3:13-16). The Jews do not have to abide in unbelief just as they did not have to abide in faith. A broken, dried branch cannot in the natural be grafted back in, but God brings life from the dead (verse 15).

Be not highminded, but fear: So you must not be proud; you ought rather to be fearful, *Norlie* ... Stop having a superiority complex, *Wuest* ... Do not be puffed up, *Montgomery* ... be not to highly vvise, *Rheims* ... There is no ground for arrogance here, but rather for dread, *Way* ... Be not haughty, but feel awe, *Berkeley* ... Do not cherish lofty thoughts, *Worrell* ... Stop your haughty thinking; instead be concerned, *Adams* ... do not become proud, but stand in awe, *RSV* ... You should feel awed instead of being uplifted, *Moffatt* ... Be not exalted, *Murdock* ... but take warning, *TCNT* ... tremble rather, *Weymouth* ... continue to be reverent, *Williams*.

21. For if God spared not the natural branches: ... own natural branches, *Norlie*.

[take heed] lest he also spare not thee: ... perhaps, neither will he spare you, *Campbell*.

22. Behold therefore the goodness and severity of God: Consider carefully, *Norlie* ... Fix your gaze, *Montgomery* ... Now see how kind and how severe God can be, *Beck* ... and rigorousnes of God, *Geneva*.

on them which fell, severity; but toward thee, goodness, if thou continue in [his] goodness: ... them surely that are fallen, *Rheims* ... if you cling to His kindness, *Beck* ... if thou abidest in his goodness, *Confraternity* ... on the one hand, strictness toward those, *Adams*.

otherwise thou also shalt be cut off: ... will be pruned away, *Williams* ... else, you also shall be hewn away, *Way*.

23. And they also:
if they abide not still in unbelief: ... if they give up their unbelief, *JB*.
shall be grafted in:
for God is able to graft them in again: ... is able to graft them back, *Confraternity* ... is amply able to graft them in, *Williams*.

3450.5 art sing masc	2296.1 noun nom sing masc	3687.1 adv	1454.1 verb inf aor act	840.8 prs-pron acc pl masc	1479.1 conj
ὁ	θεὸς	πάλιν	ἐγκεντρίσαι	αὐτούς.	**24.** εἰ
ho	theos	palin	enkentrisai	autous	ei
	God	again	to graft in	them.	If

1056.1 conj	4622.1 prs- pron nom 2sing	1523.2 prep gen	3450.10 art gen sing fem	2567.3 prep	5285.4 noun acc sing fem	1568.6 verb 2sing indic aor pass
γὰρ	σὺ	ἐκ	τῆς	κατὰ	φύσιν	ἐξεκόπης
gar	su	ek	tēs	kata	phusin	exekopēs
for	you	out of	the	according to	nature	was cut off

64.2 noun gen sing fem	2504.1 conj	3706.2 prep	5285.4 noun acc sing fem	1454.2 verb 2sing indic aor pass	1519.1 prep
ἀγριελαίου,	καὶ	παρὰ	φύσιν	ἐνεκεντρίσθης	εἰς
agrielaiou	kai	para	phusin	enekentristhēs	eis
wild olive tree,	and,	contrary to	nature,	was grafted in	to

2536.1 noun acc sing fem	4073.9 intr- pron dat sing neu	3095.1 adv comp	3642.7 dem- pron nom pl masc	3450.7 art pl masc
καλλιέλαιον,	πόσῳ	μᾶλλον	οὗτοι	οἱ
kallielaion	posō	mallon	houtoi	hoi
a good olive tree,	how much	more	these	the

2567.3 prep	5285.4 noun acc sing fem	1454.4 verb 3pl indic fut pass	3450.11 art dat sing fem	2375.10 adj dat sing fem
κατὰ	φύσιν,	ἐγκεντρισθήσονται	τῇ	ἰδίᾳ
kata	phusin	enkentristhēsontai	tē	idia
according to	nature,	shall be grafted into	the	own

1623.2 noun dat sing fem	3620.3 partic	1056.1 conj	2286.1 verb 1sing pres act	5050.4 prs- pron acc 2pl	49.9 verb inf pres act
ἐλαίᾳ˙	**25.** Οὐ	γὰρ	θέλω	ὑμᾶς	ἀγνοεῖν,
elaia	Ou	gar	thelō	humas	agnoein
olive tree?	Not	for	do I wish	you	to be ignorant,

79.6 noun pl masc	3450.16 art sing neu	3328.1 noun sing neu	3642.17 dem- pron sing neu	2419.1 conj	3231.1 partic
ἀδελφοί,	τὸ	μυστήριον	τοῦτο,	ἵνα	μὴ
adelphoi	to	mustērion	touto	hina	mē
brothers,	of the	mystery	this,	that	not

25.a.**Txt:** 01א,04C,06D
020L,byz.Tisc,Sod
Var: 02A,03B,Treg,Alf
We/Ho,Weis,UBS/✱

1498.1 verb 2pl act	3706.1 prep	1706.1 prep	1431.7 prs- pron dat pl masc	5265.1 adj nom pl	3617.1 conj
ἦτε	ʼ παρʼ	[ᵃ✱ ἐν]	ἑαυτοῖς	φρόνιμοι,	ὅτι
ēte	par'	en	heautois	phronimoi	hoti
you may be	in	[idem]	yourselves	wise,	that

4314.1 noun nom sing fem	570.3 prep gen	3183.2 noun gen sing neu	3450.3 art dat sing	2447.1 name masc	1090.3 verb 3sing indic perf act
πώρωσις	ἀπὸ	μέρους	τῷ	Ἰσραὴλ	γέγονεν,
pōrōsis	apo	merous	tō	Israēl	gegonen
hardness	in	part		to Israel	has happened,

884.1 conj	3614.2 rel- pron gen sing	3450.16 art sing neu	3998.1 noun sing neu	3450.1 art gen pl	1477.5 noun gen pl neu
ἄχρις	οὗ	τὸ	πλήρωμα	τῶν	ἐθνῶν
achris	hou	to	plērōma	tōn	ethnōn
until	which	to	the fulness	of the	nations

1511.7 verb 3sing subj aor act	2504.1 conj	3643.1 adv	3820.6 adj sing masc	2447.1 name masc	4834.33 verb 3sing indic fut pass
εἰσέλθῃ˙	**26.** καὶ	οὕτως	πᾶς	Ἰσραὴλ	σωθήσεται,
eiselthē	kai	houtōs	pas	Israēl	sōthēsetai
be come in;	and	so	all	Israel	shall be saved,

11:24. Paul speaks of being grafted contrary to nature. Normally the good branch or graft is grafted into a poor stock. The good shoot receives the needed sap for growth from the inferior tree or stock. The graft retains the characteristics and qualities of its own heritage though it receives the sap of the inferior stock and is thus enabled to produce good fruit.

If God grafted the wild olive (Gentiles) into good stock (Israel), He is able to graft the natural branches, which were broken off, back into the good stock. God will bring all of this about. He will bring Israel to a place of repentance and faith and lead them to the Messiah.

Even then, each individual will have to choose, just as now in the time of the Gentiles each has to choose. Not every Jew will be saved, just as in the "fulness of the Gentiles" not every Gentile will be saved. God foreknows all things, but His prescience is not necessarily causative.

Prior to Calvary, Gentile salvation was accompanied by becoming a part of Jewish religious life, a type of the coming grafting described here. The restoration of Israel is very important and should be understood. What will it be when the natural branches come back into their own!

11:25. In his characteristic way, Paul drew attention to this important truth as he used the words "ignorant," "mystery," "blindness," and "fulness."

On six occasions Paul declared, "I would not have you ignorant" (Romans 1:13; 11:25; 1 Corinthians 10:1; 12:1; 2 Corinthians 1:8; 1 Thessalonians 4:13). In this verse Paul refers to ignorance concerning a mystery.

The word "mystery" refers to a truth, once hidden, now revealed, the understanding of which requires spiritual perception. What is that mystery? That Israel's blindness and rejection will continue "until the fulness of the Gentiles be come in." This connects with the statement of James at the Council in Jerusalem (Acts 15:14).

The blindness of Israel refers specifically to their refusal to see God's plan in Jesus (verse 7). In a general sense it describes the spiritual condition of any individual who rejects light. Because he refuses to acknowledge God's truth, God gives eyes that cannot see and ears that cannot hear (verse 8).

In this age God is dealing particularly with the Gentiles, and He who knows all things and controls the times and seasons will one day bring this period of time to an end and begin dealing with the Jews in a special way.

The "fulness of the Gentiles" should be distinguished from the "times of the Gentiles." The latter was ushered in with the destruction of Jerusalem by Nebuchadnezzar and will continue through the Great Tribulation to the return of Christ to establish His kingdom on earth. The "fulness of the Gentiles" began with the calling out of the Church (on the Day of Pentecost) and will continue until the rapture of the Church.

Romans 11:26

24. For if thou wert cut out of the olive tree which is wild by nature: ... from your natural stock, *TCNT.*

and wert grafted contrary to nature into a good olive tree: ... in violation of Nature, *Wilson* ... by a process which is the very opposite of the natural one, *Way* ... a cultivated olive tree, *Adams* ... into a garden olive, *HistNT.*

how much more: ... is it not much more reasonable, *Way.*

shall these, which be the natural [branches]:

be grafted into their own olive tree?: ... be regrafted into, *Montgomery* ... on to their parent-tree? *Way* ... into the fruitful stock, *Conybeare* ... into their parent olive tree, *Norlie* ... on their own original tree! *Berkeley.*

25. For I would not, brethren, that ye should be ignorant of: ... be hyd from you, *Geneva.*

this mystery: There is a hidden reason for all this, *JB* ... I want you to know this secret truth, *Beck* ... you should learn this Secret of the Initiated, *Way.*

lest ye should be wise in your own conceits: ... keep you from thinking too well of yourselves, *Beck* ... lest you may be passing for prudent among yourselves, *Concordant* ... that you might not be self-opinionated, *Berkeley* ... To save you from self-conceit, *TCNT* ... for fear you should attribute superior wisdom to yourselves, *Weymouth.*

that blindness in part is happened to Israel: Hardness in some Measure, *Wilson* ... a hardening in part hath befallen Israel, *Panin* ... only temporary insensibility, *Williams* ... that the partial obduracy, *Way* ... partial obtuseness, *Berkeley* ... that callousness, *TCNT.*

until the fulness of the Gentiles be come in: ... will last only until the full ingathering of the Gentiles has been secured, *Way* ... until the full number of the Gentiles should enter, *Confraternity* ... until all the rest of the world, *TCNT* ... until the great mass, *Weymouth* ... until the full quota of the heathen peoples, *Williams* ... until the completion of the pagans comes, *Klingensmith* ... until the complement of the nations, *Concordant.*

185

2503.1 conj	1119.22 verb 3sing indic perf pass	2223.7 verb 3sing indic fut act	1523.2 prep gen	4477.1 name fem
καθὼς	γέγραπται,	Ἥξει	ἐκ	Σιὼν
kathōs	*gegraptai*	*Hēxei*	*ek*	*Siōn*
just as	it has been written,	Shall come	out of	Zion

26.a.Txt: 06D-corr,020L byz.bo.
Var: 01**ℵ**,02A,03B,04C 06D-org,Lach,Treg,Alf Word,Tisc,We/Ho,Weis Sod,UBS/✶

3450.5 art sing masc	4363.2 verb nom sing masc part pres	2504.1 conj	648.4 verb 3sing indic fut act	757.1 noun fem
ὁ	ῥυόμενος,	⌜ᵃ καὶ ⌝	ἀποστρέψει	ἀσεβείας
ho	*rhuomenos*	*kai*	*apostrepsei*	*asebeias*
the	delivering,	and	he shall turn away	ungodliness

570.3 prep gen	2361.1 name masc	2504.1 conj	3642.9 dem-pron nom sing fem	840.2 prs-pron dat pl	3450.9 art nom sing fem
ἀπὸ	Ἰακώβ·	**27.** καὶ	αὕτη	αὐτοῖς	ἡ
apo	*Iakōb*	*kai*	*hautē*	*autois*	*hē*
from	Jacob.	And	this	to them	the

3706.1 prep	1466.3 prs-pron gen 1sing	1236.1 noun nom sing fem	3615.1 conj	844.7 verb 1sing subj aor mid
παρ᾽	ἐμοῦ	διαθήκη,	ὅταν	ἀφέλωμαι
par'	*emou*	*diathēkē*	*hotan*	*aphelōmai*
from	me	covenant,	when	I may have taken away

3450.15 art acc pl fem	264.1 noun fem	840.1 prs-pron gen pl	2567.3 prep	3173.1 conj	3450.16 art sing neu
τὰς	ἁμαρτίας	αὐτῶν.	**28.** Κατὰ	μὲν	τὸ
tas	*hamartias*	*autōn*	*Kata*	*men*	*to*
the	sins	their.	As regards	indeed	to

2077.1 noun sing neu	2172.5 adj nom pl masc	1217.1 prep	5050.4 prs-pron acc 2pl	2567.3 prep	1156.2 conj
εὐαγγέλιον,	ἐχθροὶ	δι᾽	ὑμᾶς·	κατὰ	δὲ
euangelion	*echthroi*	*di'*	*humas*	*kata*	*de*
good news,	enemies	because of	you;	as regards	but

3450.12 art acc sing fem	1576.3 noun acc sing fem	27.6 adj pl masc	1217.2 prep	3450.8 art acc pl masc	3824.9 noun acc pl masc
τὴν	ἐκλογὴν,	ἀγαπητοὶ	διὰ	τοὺς	πατέρας.
tēn	*eklogēn*	*agapētoi*	*dia*	*tous*	*pateras*
the	election,	beloved	on account of	the	fathers.

276.2 adj nom pl neu	1056.1 conj	3450.17 art pl neu	5321.3 noun pl neu	2504.1 conj	3450.9 art nom sing fem
29. ἀμεταμέλητα	γὰρ	τὰ	χαρίσματα	καὶ	ἡ
ametamelēta	*gar*	*ta*	*charismata*	*kai*	*hē*
Irrevocable	for	the	gifts	and	the

2794.1 noun nom sing fem	3450.2 art gen sing	2296.2 noun gen sing masc	5450.1	1056.1 conj	2504.1 conj
κλῆσις	τοῦ	θεοῦ.	**30.** ὥσπερ	γὰρ	⌜ᵃ καὶ ⌝
klēsis	*tou*	*theou*	*hōsper*	*gar*	*kai*
calling		of God.	As	for	also

30.a.Txt: 01**ℵ**-corr 06D-corr,020L,byz.
Var: 02A,03B,04C 06D-org,bo.Gries,Lach Treg,Alf,Word,Tisc We/Ho,Weis,Sod UBS/✶

5050.1 prs-pron nom 2pl	4077.1 adv	540.7 verb 2pl indic aor act	3450.3 art dat sing	2296.3 noun dat sing masc	3431.1 adv
ὑμεῖς	ποτέ	ἠπειθήσατε	τῷ	θεῷ,	νῦν
humeis	*pote*	*ēpeithēsate*	*tō*	*theō*	*nun*
you	once	were disobedient	to the	to God,	now

1156.2 conj	1640.14 verb 2pl indic aor pass	3450.11 art dat sing fem	3642.2 dem-pron gen pl	539.2 noun dat sing fem
δὲ	ἠλεήθητε	τῇ	τούτων	ἀπειθείᾳ·
de	*eleēthēte*	*tē*	*toutōn*	*apeitheia*
but	have been shown mercy	by the	these	disobedience;

11:26. Paul is nearing the end of his argument. As a Jew he has faced a heartbreaking situation. He has shown, however, that God has turned Israel's failure into salvation for the Gentiles. Now he looks ahead to a glorious prospect—"all Israel shall be saved." He was not saying that all individuals will be saved, but was speaking of national destiny. Putting it simply, Israel as a nation will be delivered from her enemies, both spiritually and earthly, and be restored to her ancient privileges as God's witness.

11:27. Jesus is the Deliverer who will rescue the Jews from their enemies (Zechariah 12:10). Best of all, He "shall turn away ungodliness" for this is His covenant. The reference to "taking away their sins" goes back to Isaiah 27:9. Their acceptance of the new covenant of grace, in contrast to the conditional covenant at Sinai, will find fulfillment (Jeremiah 31:31-34).

Israel's restoration is seen in the restored branches and the renewed fatness of the olive tree in that day when "all Israel shall be saved." God's Word also predicts a restoration of the fig tree which will put forth leaves and bear fruit again (Matthew 24:32,33; Luke 21:29-31). This is happening today. The fig tree is budding; there are great signs of life in the Holy Land. Read Psalm 80:14-19.

There will be a spiritual revival among the Jews. It will be the fulfillment of Ezekiel's vision of the valley of dry bones. At present the bones seem to have come together; there is again a nation of Israel. But there is no spiritual life. Fulfillment of this element of the vision is yet to occur.

11:28. The Jews are the enemies of the gospel, but beloved for the Father's sake. Note two things. The Jews in their relation to the gospel are regarded by God as enemies for the sake of the Gentiles. But in respect to election the Jews, having been God's choice (Deuteronomy 7:6), are beloved for the fathers' sake (Abraham, Isaac, and Jacob).

11:29. Paul was discussing the earthly destiny of Israel, not the heavenly destiny of the individual.

The gifts and calling are subject to no recall; they are irrevocable. God will not change His mind regarding His chosen people and their mission and destiny. His promises concerning them are unconditional.

11:30-32. Paul points to God's mercy four times in these verses. First, there is God's mercy to the Gentiles (verse 30). God's dealings with Israel have been the means of extending His grace and mercy to the Gentiles. Verse 31 relates God's mercy to the Jews. The

26. And so all Israel shall be saved: And when this has happened, *TCNT* ... And, in this way, all Israel will be saved, *Adams* ... shall be converted, *Locke.*

as it is written:
There shall come out of Sion the Deliverer: ... shall be the Rescuer, *Concordant.*

and shall turn away ungodliness from Jacob: ... rid Jacob of his ungodliness, *Norlie* ... He shall banish impieties, *HistNT.*

27. For this [is] my covenant unto them: And this will be my agreement with them, *Klingensmith* ... is the promise, *Sawyer.*

when I shall take away their sins: I should be eliminating their sins, *Concordant.*

28. As concerning the gospel: As touching, *Alford* ... As regards, *RSV* ... In view of, *Confraternity* ... In relation to the good news, *Hanson.*

[they are] enemies for your sakes: ... enemies on your account, *Young.*

but as touching the election, [they are] beloved for the fathers' sakes: ... in view of the divine choice, *Confraternity* ... from the point of view of God's irrevocable choice, *Way* ... for Abraham, Isaac, and Jacob's sake, *Locke.*

29. For the gifts and calling of God [are] without repentance: God never takes back his gifts or revokes his choice, *JB* ... for no change of purpose can annul God's gifts and call, *Conybeare* ... never changes His mind when He gives anything or calls anyone, *Beck* ... are with respect to a change of mind irrevocable, *Wuest* ... and the vocation of God, *Rheims* ... God never regrets, *TCNT* ... For unregretted are the graces, *Concordant* ... are unchangeable, *Norlie* ... are not recalled, *Adams.*

30. For as ye in times past have not believed God: ... as you once disobeyed, *Hanson.*

yet have now obtained mercy through their unbelief: ... through stepping into the place they vacated, *Way.*

31.a.**Var:** 01ℵ,03B
06D-org,bo.Lach,Tisc
We/Ho,Sod,UBS/∗

3643.1 adv	2504.1 conj	3642.7 dem-pron nom pl masc	3431.1 adv	540.8 verb 3pl indic aor act	3450.3 art dat sing
31. οὕτως	καὶ	οὗτοι	νῦν	ἠπείθησαν	τῷ
houtōs	kai	houtoi	nun	ēpeithēsan	tō
so	also	these	now	were disobedient	to the

5052.1 adj dat 2sing	1643.4 noun dat sing neu	2419.1 conj	2504.1 conj	840.7 prs-pron nom pl masc	3431.1 adv
ὑμετέρῳ	ἐλέει,	ἵνα	καὶ	αὐτοὶ	[a☆+ νῦν]
humeterō	eleei	hina	kai	autoi	nun
your	mercy,	that	also	they	[now]

1640.15 verb 3pl subj aor pass		4639.1 verb 3sing indic aor act	1056.1 conj	3450.5 art sing masc	2296.1 noun nom sing masc
ἐλεηθῶσιν.	**32.** συνέκλεισεν		γὰρ	ὁ	θεὸς
eleēthōsin	sunekleisen		gar	ho	theos
may have mercy shown.	Shut up together		for		God

3450.8 art acc pl masc	3820.8 adj acc pl masc	1519.1 prep	539.3 noun acc sing fem	2419.1 conj	3450.8 art acc pl masc	3820.8 adj acc pl masc
τοὺς	πάντας	εἰς	ἀπείθειαν,	ἵνα	τοὺς	πάντας
tous	pantas	eis	apeitheian	hina	tous	pantas
the	all	in	disobedience,	that	the	all

1640.8 verb 3sing subj aor act	5434.1 intrj	893.1 noun sing neu	4009.2 noun gen sing masc	2504.1 conj
ἐλεήσῃ.	**33.** Ὦ	βάθος	πλούτου	καὶ
eleēsē	Ō	bathos	ploutou	kai
he might show mercy to.	O	depth	of riches	both

4531.2 noun gen sing fem	2504.1 conj	1102.2 noun gen sing fem	2296.2 noun gen sing masc	5453.1 conj	417.1 adj nom pl neu
σοφίας	καὶ	γνώσεως	θεοῦ.	ὡς	ἀνεξερεύνητα
sophias	kai	gnōseōs	theou	hōs	anexereunēta
of wisdom	and	knowledge	of God!	How	unsearchable

3450.17 art pl neu	2890.4 noun pl neu	840.3 prs-pron gen sing	2504.1 conj	419.1 adj nom pl fem	3450.13 art pl fem
τὰ	κρίματα	αὐτοῦ,	καὶ	ἀνεξιχνίαστοι	αἱ
ta	krimata	autou	kai	anexichniastoi	hai
the	judgments	his,	and	untraceable	the

3461.5 noun nom pl fem	840.3 prs-pron gen sing	4949.3 intr-pron nom sing	1056.1 conj	1091.17 verb 3sing indic aor act
ὁδοὶ	αὐτοῦ.	**34.** Τίς	γὰρ	ἔγνω
hodoi	autou	Tis	gar	egnō
ways	his!	Who	for	did know

3426.4 noun acc sing masc	2935.2 noun gen sing masc	2211.1 conj	4949.3 intr-pron nom sing	4676.1 noun nom sing masc	840.3 prs-pron gen sing
νοῦν	κυρίου;	ἢ	τίς	σύμβουλος	αὐτοῦ
noun	kuriou	ē	tis	sumboulos	autou
mind	of Lord,	or	who	counselor	his

1090.33 verb 3sing indic aor mid	2211.1 conj	4949.3 intr-pron nom sing	4131.1 verb 3sing indic aor act	840.4 prs-pron dat sing	2504.1 conj
ἐγένετο;	**35.** ἢ	τίς	προέδωκεν	αὐτῷ,	καὶ
egeneto	ē	tis	proedōken	autō	kai
became?	Or	who	first gave	to him,	and

464.3 verb 3sing indic fut pass	840.4 prs-pron dat sing	3617.1 conj	1523.1 prep gen	840.3 prs-pron gen sing	2504.1 conj
ἀνταποδοθήσεται	αὐτῷ;	**36.** ὅτι	ἐξ	αὐτοῦ	καὶ
antapodothēsetai	autō	hoti	ex	autou	kai
it shall be recompensed	to him?	For	of	him	and

Gentiles had been the unbelievers but found mercy because of the disobedience of the Jews. Now by the mercy of the Gentiles the unbelieving Jews may find mercy. Finally God's mercy reaches to all the world (verse 32).

The word *sunekleisen*, translated "concluded," is more often rendered "imprisoned." It is used only here, in Galatians 3:22,23 and in Luke 5:6 where the thought is of the fish enclosed in the net.

The Law was God's net in which to enclose all men. This would include the pagan who is a law to himself (2:14). No human being can say that he has without fail kept his own law. All men thus are caught in the awareness of their sinfulness and their helplessness to escape, apart from Christ Jesus.

11:33-36. Just as the doctrinal portion of Romans (chapters 1 to 8) climaxes in a glorious and grand expression of worship to God (8:31-39), the dispensational portion (chapters 9 to 11) is brought to a sublime conclusion in these verses.

This section is praise, pure praise, and is not given to argument at all; yet it is the greatest argument of all. If we do not understand God's ways in His dealings with all men, Jew and Gentile, or even with the Church, it is because we are unable to comprehend the wisdom and knowledge and ways of God.

It has been said that the ways of God are beyond all human inferences (verses 33-35) and beyond all human interferences (verse 36). The mind of man constantly searches to know and to understand. God created him with this ability. But God's thoughts are not man's thoughts, nor are God's ways man's ways. God declares that His thoughts and ways are higher than those of men (Isaiah 55:8,9).

Human interferences will never stop the fulfillment of God's will. All things and events are of Him, through Him, and for Him. He makes "known unto us the mystery of his will, according to his good pleasure, which he hath purposed in himself" (Ephesians 1:9; cf. 1 Corinthians 2:7). We are ignorant of the mind and purposes of God unless He chooses to reveal them to us (cf. Job 38:4,36). When those ways are revealed to us, all we can do is bow and worship.

Anexereunetos, found only here in the New Testament, is rendered "unsearchable" in the King James Version. Several translations render it "unfathomable"; others use the word "inscrutable." Translations struggle to plumb the depths of the meaning of the Greek which is used to describe the profundity of the riches of the wisdom and knowledge of God. It is impossible for the human mind to grasp!

The apostle states God's ways are "past finding out." The translation comes from the adjective *anexichniastos*. The word comes from "to track out," so that literally it means "that cannot be traced out." Like the previous word it can be translated "inscrutable, incomprehensible, unfathomable." Expressed in simplest terms, Paul

31. Even so have these also now not believed: . . . they are temporarily disobedient, *Way*.

that through your mercy they also may obtain mercy: . . . that through the occasion of the mercy which is yours, *Wuest*.

32. For God hath concluded them all in unbelief: . . . has shut up all in unbelief, *Confraternity* . . . has locked up all in the prison of disobedience, *Montgomery* . . . has consigned all men to disobedience, *RSV, Moffatt* . . . For God had wrapped all nacyons in vnbeleue, *Cranmer*.

that he might have mercy upon all: . . . in order to be merciful to all, *Beck*.

33. O the depth of the riches both of the wisdom and knowledge of God!: What an inexhaustible mine, *TCNT* . . . O fathomless abyss of God's rich bounty, *Way* . . . hovv incomprehensible, *Rheims* . . . of the aboundaunt wysdome, *Tyndale*.

how unsearchable [are] his judgments, and his ways past finding out!: . . . how inscrutable, *Sawyer* . . . How incomprehensible, *Douay* . . . how impossible to penetrate his motives, *JB* . . . how untraceable His footsteps, *Berkeley* . . . how impossible it is to find out His decisions, *Beck* . . . How mysterious his methods! *Moffatt, Williams* . . . How impossible it is to search into His decrees, *Weymouth* . . . his ways past tracing out! *Scarlett* . . . past reaching the end his ways, *Klingensmith*.

34. For who hath known the mind of the Lord? or who hath been his counsellor?: Who can explore His decisions, *Way* . . . Who has ever comprehended, *TCNT* . . . Or who has begun to tell him what to do? *Klingensmith*.

35. Or who hath first given to him:

and it shall be recompensed unto him again?: . . . that He is indebted to return to him? *Adams* . . . so as to receive payment in return, *Montgomery* . . . and it shall be repaid him? *Sawyer*.

1217.1 prep	840.3 prs-pron gen sing	2504.1 conj	1519.1 prep	840.6 prs-pron acc sing masc	3450.17 art pl neu	3820.1 adj
δι᾽	αὐτοῦ	καὶ	εἰς	αὐτὸν	τὰ	πάντα·
di'	autou	kai	eis	auton	ta	panta
through	him	and	unto	him	the	all things:

840.4 prs-pron dat sing	3450.9 art nom sing fem	1385.1 noun nom sing fem	1519.1 prep	3450.8 art acc pl masc	163.6 noun acc pl masc
αὐτῷ	ἡ	δόξα	εἰς	τοὺς	αἰῶνας.
autō	hē	doxa	eis	tous	aiōnas
to him	the	glory	to	the	ages.

279.1 partic	3731.1 verb 1sing indic pres act	3631.1 conj	5050.4 prs-pron acc 2pl	79.6 noun pl masc
ἀμήν.	12:1. Παρακαλῶ	οὖν	ὑμᾶς,	ἀδελφοί,
amēn	Parakalō	oun	humas	adelphoi
Amen.	I exhort	therefore	you,	brothers,

1217.2 prep	3450.1 art gen pl	3490.2 noun gen pl masc	3450.2 art gen sing	2296.2 noun gen sing masc	3798.12 verb inf aor act
διὰ	τῶν	οἰκτιρμῶν	τοῦ	θεοῦ,	παραστῆσαι
dia	tōn	oiktirmōn	tou	theou	parastēsai
by	the	compassions	of God,		to present

3450.17 art pl neu	4835.4 noun pl neu	5050.2 prs-pron gen 2pl	2355.4 noun acc sing fem	2180.17 verb acc sing fem part pres act	39.13 adj acc sing fem
τὰ	σώματα	ὑμῶν	θυσίαν	ζῶσαν,	ἁγίαν,
ta	sōmata	humōn	thusian	zōsan	hagian
the	bodies	your	a sacrifice	living,	holy,

2080.4 adj sing	3450.3 art dat sing	2296.3 noun dat sing masc	3450.3 art dat sing	2296.3 noun dat sing masc
⟨☆ εὐάρεστον	τῷ	θεῷ,	[τῷ	θεῷ,
euareston	tō	theō	tō	theō
well pleasing		to God,		[to God

2080.4 adj sing	3450.12 art acc sing fem	3024.1 adj acc sing fem	2972.3 noun acc sing fem	5050.2 prs-pron gen 2pl
εὐάρεστον]	τὴν	λογικὴν	λατρείαν	ὑμῶν·
euareston	tēn	logikēn	latreian	humōn
well pleasing]	the	reasonable	service	your.

2.a.Txt: p46,03B-org
020L,025P,104,365
1241,1739
Var: 02A,03B-corr2
06D-org,010F,012G,044
81,630,1175,1506,2495

2504.1 conj	3231.1 partic	4816.1 verb 2pl impr pres	4816.3 verb inf pres mid
2. καὶ	μὴ	⟨☆ συσχηματίζεσθε	[ᵃ συσχηματίζεσθαι]
kai	mē	suschēmatizesthe	suschēmatizesthai
And	not	fashion yourselves	[to conform]

3450.3 art dat sing	163.2 noun dat sing masc	3642.5 dem-pron dat sing masc	233.2 conj	3209.2 verb 2pl impr pres pass
τῷ	αἰῶνι	τούτῳ,	ἀλλὰ	μεταμορφοῦσθε
tō	aiōni	toutō	alla	metamorphousthe
to the	age	this,	but	be transformed

2.b.Txt: 01א,06D-corr
020L,025P,byz.Sod
Var: 02A,03B,06D-org
bo.Lach,Treg,Alf,Word
Tisc,We/Ho,Weis
UBS/☆

3450.11 art dat sing fem	340.2 noun dat sing fem	3450.2 art gen sing	3426.2 noun gen sing masc	5050.2 prs-pron gen 2pl	1519.1 prep
τῇ	ἀνακαινώσει	τοῦ	νοός,	⟨ᵇ ὑμῶν, ⟩	εἰς
tē	anakainōsei	tou	noos	humōn	eis
by the	renewing	of the	mind	your,	for

3450.16 art sing neu	1375.8 verb inf pres act	5050.4 prs-pron acc 2pl	4949.9 intr-pron sing neu	3450.16 art sing neu	2284.1 noun sing neu
τὸ	δοκιμάζειν	ὑμᾶς	τί	τὸ	θέλημα
to	dokimazein	humas	ti	to	thelēma
the	to prove	you	what	the	will

is saying that this reservoir of divine wisdom and knowledge cannot be searched to the depths, nor traced to the end.

Three prepositions, *ek*, *dia*, and *eis*, in verse 36 show God is the source, the agency, and ultimate end. He is the Creator, Sustainer, and Goal of all life. All events are of Him, through Him, and for Him. One can only join the apostle in the outburst of praise to our great God whose greatness and glory are unsearchable, unfathomable, and beyond comprehension.

12:1. In chapters 1 to 8 the plan of salvation (doctrinal) is presented; the hope of Israel (dispensational) in chapters 9 to 11; and an exhortation to godliness (devotional) in chapters 12 to 16. Doctrine must be followed by duty, for privilege brings responsibility and precept must have practice.

12:2. From the pinnacle of glorious exultation over the greatness of God in the last verses of chapter 11, believers are brought to the valley of daily duty. The journey in the valley is not irksome, not tiring; it is realistic. The plane of service is made easy because of the glorious heights of Christian doctrine and experience.

The laws of Christian life are discussed in 12:1 to 13:7; the laws of Christian love are discussed in 13:8 to 16:24. Verses 1 and 2 of chapter 12 deal with the Christian attitude toward God. Verses 3-13 consider the Christian attitude toward fellowmen. Verses 14-21 discuss the Christian attitude toward enemies.

Service to God is vitally related to consecration and separation. Paul does not command, he entreats. The compassion of our Lord, not His stern command, is the basis of the appeal.

Believers consecrate themselves to God because of His "mercies." The glorious mercies listed in the previous chapters, including justification by faith, assurance, freedom from the penalty and power of sin, and the promise of ultimate glorification, are the bases for moving Christians toward God.

Believers' bodies are to be presented (offered) a "living sacrifice" in contrast to the dead sacrifices of the Levitical priesthood. Fallen creatures can be cleansed and become holy and acceptable. The body is physical, but the intent seems to include all members and faculties. That is reasonable (intelligent) service.

The call is for nonconformity to the world. This is not merely an outward act of self-renunciation. Anything that would displease God and dishonor His holy name is conformity to the world. The Christian is to have God's viewpoint in relation to the world. The word "world" refers to the spirit which moves humans contrary to the will of God—the spirit of selfishness, the pleasing of self, and submission to the devil. J.B. Phillips renders it: "Don't let the world around you squeeze you into its own mold."

The Christian is called upon to be transformed (transfigured, or changed) by the renewing of his mind. *Metamorphoō*, translated "transformed" here, occurs four times in the New Testament—

36. For of him, and through him, and to him, [are] all things: For the universe owes its origin to Him, *Weymouth* . . . For from Him is the beginning, and by Him the life, and in Him the end of all things, *Conybeare*.

to whom [be] glory for ever. Amen: . . . through the eternities! *Way*.

1. I beseech you therefore, brethren: I appeal to you, *RSV* . . . I intreat you, *Hanson* . . . I exhort you, *Confraternity*.

by the mercies of God: . . . because of God's compassion, *Norlie* . . . tender mercies, *Scarlett* . . . the pities of God, *Concordant*.

that ye present your bodies a living sacrifice: . . . to make a decisive dedication of your bodies, *Williams* . . . bring your lives, and set them by the altar, *Way* . . . all your faculties, *Weymouth*.

holy, acceptable unto God: . . . dedicated to his service, *TEV* . . . pleasing unto God, *Douay* . . . consecrated, *Moffatt*.

[which is] your reasonable service: . . . and so worship Him as thinking beings, *Beck* . . . your spiritual worship, *Noyes* . . . which is the reasonable way to serve Him in worship, *Adams* . . . your rational, sacred service, *Wuest*.

2. And be not conformed to this world: Do not live according to the fashions of the times, *Norlie* . . . Do not model yourselves on the behavior of the world, *JB* . . . Do not conform to the externalities, *Way* . . . and not to be configured, *Concordant* . . . stop assuming an outward expression, *Wuest* . . . do not follow the customs, *Weymouth* . . . Instead of being moulded to this world, *Moffatt* . . . do not be patterned, *Klingensmith* . . . to the way of our modern age, *Adams* . . . to the present world scheme, *Berkeley*.

but be ye transformed by the renewing of your mind: Be completely made over, *Klingensmith* . . . by your new attitude of mind, *TCNT* . . . by the renovation of your mind, *Wilson*.

that ye may prove what [is] that good, and acceptable, and perfect, will of God: . . . be able to determine, *Adams* . . . that ye may

3450.2 art gen sing
τοῦ
tou
of God

2296.2 noun gen sing masc
θεοῦ
theou
of God

3450.16 art sing neu
τὸ
to
the

18.3 adj sing
ἀγαθὸν
agathon
good

2504.1 conj
καὶ
kai
and

2080.4 adj sing
εὐάρεστον
euareston
well pleasing

2504.1 conj
καὶ
kai
and

4894.1 adj sing
τέλειον.
teleion
perfect.

2978.1 verb 1sing pres act
3. Λέγω
Legō
I say

1056.1 conj
γὰρ
gar
for

1217.2 prep
διὰ
dia
through

3450.10 art gen sing fem
τῆς
tēs
the

5322.2 noun gen sing fem
χάριτος
charitos
grace

3450.10 art gen sing fem
τῆς
tēs
the

1319.49 verb gen sing fem part aor pass
δοθείσης
dotheisēs
having been given

1466.4 prs-pron dat 1sing
μοι,
moi,
to me,

3820.3 adj dat sing
παντὶ
panti
to everyone

3450.3 art dat sing
τῷ
tō
the

1498.22 verb dat sing masc part pres act
ὄντι
onti
being

1706.1 prep
ἐν
en
among

5050.3 prs-pron dat 2pl
ὑμῖν,
humin,
you,

3231.1 partic
μὴ
mē
not

5090.1 verb inf pres act
ὑπερφρονεῖν
huperphronein
to be high minded

3706.1 prep
παρ'
par'
above

3614.16 rel-pron sing neu
ὃ
ho
what

1158.1 verb 3sing indic pres act
δεῖ
dei
it necessary

5262.9 verb inf pres act
φρονεῖν,
phronein,
to be minded;

233.2 conj
ἀλλὰ
alla
but

5262.9 verb inf pres act
φρονεῖν
phronein
to be minded

1519.1 prep
εἰς
eis
to

3450.16 art sing neu
τὸ
to
the

4845.3 verb inf pres act
σωφρονεῖν,
sōphronein,
to be sober minded

1524.4 adj dat sing masc
ἑκάστῳ
hekastō
to each

5453.1 conj
ὡς
hōs
as

3450.5 art sing masc
ὁ
ho

2296.1 noun nom sing masc
θεὸς
theos
God

3177.1 verb 3sing indic aor act
ἐμέρισεν
emerisen
divided

3228.3 noun acc sing neu
μέτρον
metron
a measure

3963.2 noun gen sing fem
πίστεως.
pisteōs
of faith.

2481.1 conj
4. Καθάπερ
Kathaper
Even as

1056.1 conj
γὰρ
gar
for

1706.1 prep
ἐν
en
in

1518.2 num card dat
ἑνὶ
heni
one

4835.3 noun dat sing neu
σώματι
sōmati
body

3166.2 noun pl neu
μέλη
melē
members

4044.17 adj pl neu
πολλὰ
polla
many

4044.17 adj pl neu
[★ πολλὰ
polla
[many

3166.2 noun pl neu
μέλη]
melē
members]

2174.5 verb 1pl indic pres act
ἔχομεν,
echomen,
we have,

3450.17 art pl neu
τὰ
ta
the

1156.2 conj
δὲ
de
but

3166.2 noun pl neu
μέλη
melē
members

3820.1 adj
πάντα
panta
all

3620.3 partic
οὐ
ou
not

3450.12 art acc sing fem
τὴν
tēn
the

840.12 prs-pron acc sing fem
αὐτὴν
autēn
same

2174.4 verb 3sing indic pres act
ἔχει
echei
have

4093.2 noun acc sing fem
πρᾶξιν·
praxin
function;

3643.1 adv
5. οὕτως
houtōs
thus

3450.7 art pl masc
οἱ
hoi
the

4044.7 adj nom pl masc
πολλοὶ
polloi
many

1518.9 num card neu
ἓν
hen
one

4835.1 noun sing neu
σῶμά
sōma
body

1498.5 verb 1pl indic pres act
ἐσμεν
esmen
we are

1706.1 prep
ἐν
en
in

5382.3 name dat masc
Χριστῷ,
Christō
Christ,

3450.5 art sing masc
ὁ
ho
the

twice in the account of the Transfiguration and in 2 Corinthians 3:18 where it is rendered "changed."

From these instances believers gain insight as to how to live the transfigured life. When Jesus was transfigured before Peter, James, and John, God's glory shone through Him, not upon Him. Even so, the indwelling Christ is to control the believer's entire being so he will reflect His glory. This is that which is willed by God; it is good, acceptable, and therefore perfect.

The term used here for "mind" (*noos*) can include the intellect, the will, and the emotions. As Paul made clear in 8:5-7, the mind is the battlefield where most of Satan's attacks come. The outcome of the battle depends on whether we yield our minds to the flesh or to the Spirit. James warned that the double-minded man is unstable in all his ways (James 1:8). The goal God has for His children is to have "the mind of Christ" (1 Corinthians 2:16).

The "renewing" indicates present continuous action on the mind. In the new birth, the believer receives a renewed spirit (John 3:1-8); this is regeneration. The continuous renewing of the mind is a major part of the process of sanctification. When one's mind is being renewed by the Word, prayer, and right choices, it becomes easy to know and to live in God's perfect will.

12:3,4. Christians are to render service in humility (verse 3) and in unity (verse 4) to fellow members in the body of Christ. As in the human body there should be no rivalry between members, only mutual respect and harmony.

Verse 3 deals with the believer's self-esteem. He is not to esteem himself more highly than he should; this would cause one to think he is better than others. If he thinks "soberly," he will know that others are not better either. He will be neither conceited nor the victim of an inferiority complex.

The statement that God has given to each one "the measure of faith" applies only to those who are in the body of Christ. In Scripture faith is much more than mental assent or trust because of experience. It is a gift of grace from God (1 Corinthians 12:9; Galatians 5:22; Ephesians 2:8).

12:5. Humility is a noteworthy characteristic of the new nature. Paul is saying believers should not overestimate their own importance. Whatever success may come their way is not due to their ability—rather, it is God who has blessed. The possession of spiritual talent should not make Christians feel superior to other members in the Body. Spiritual power is a gift of God (1 Corinthians 4:6,7). To avoid pride and maintain humility involves the recognition of one's dependence upon fellow Christians, appreciating the place and ministry each one fills and fulfills in the assembly.

Christians, collectively, are linked to a Body. Each member in the Body fulfills his own office (function). Each member is needed. The members have different functions, and these functions are

search out, *Scarlett* . . . that ye may discern, *Alford* . . . that by an unerring test, *Conybeare* . . . that you may approve the will of God, *Campbell* . . . how kind, how gladdening, how flawless it is, *Way* . . . and perfect pleasure of God, *Murdock.*

3. For I say, through the grace given unto me, to every man that is among you: I command every one, *Macknight* . . . I warn every individual among you, *Weymouth* . . . who is self-important, *Moffatt.*

not to think [of himself] more highly than he ought to think: . . . let no one rate himself more than he ought, *Confraternity* . . . no man stonde hye in hys owne conceate, *Cranmer* . . . not to value himself higher, *Berkeley* . . . not to exaggerate his real importance, *JB* . . . not to estimate himself above his real value, *Williams.*

but to think soberly: Let your thoughts tend to sober views, *Way* . . . but to make a sober rating of himself, *Williams* . . . with a view to a sensible appraisal of himself, *Wuest* . . . think modestly, *Campbell* . . . so as to think wisely, *Young.*

according as God hath dealt to every man the measure of faith: . . . each measuring himself by the faith which God has allotted to him, *TCNT* . . . as God has apportioned to each one the measure of faith, *Confraternity* . . . distributed to each of you, *Adams* . . . God has assigned to each, *HistNT* . . . which God hath imparted to each, *Noyes* . . . has allotted to each man, *Way.*

4. For as we have many members in one body: . . . we have a union of many parts, *TCNT* . . . as we have many limbs, *Conybeare* . . . compose collectively one body, *Way.*

and all members have not the same office: . . . all the same function, *Moffatt* . . . are not appointed to the same work, *Locke.*

5. So we, [being] many, are one body in Christ: . . . as individual members are mutually dependent, *Way.*

5.a.**Txt:** 06D-corr,020L
byz.
Var: 01א,02A,03B
06D-org,025P,Lach
Treg,Alf,Word,Tisc
We/Ho,Weis,Sod
UBS/✶

3450.16 art sing neu	1156.2 conj	2567.2 prep	1518.3 num card nom masc	238.1 prs-pron gen pl	3166.2 noun pl neu
[ᵃ✶ τὸ]	δὲ	καθ᾽	εἷς	ἀλλήλων	μέλη.
to	de	kath'	heis	allēlōn	melē
[idem]	and	by	one	of each other	members.

2174.19 verb nom pl masc part pres act	1156.2 conj	5321.3 noun pl neu	2567.3 prep	3450.12 art acc sing fem
6. ἔχοντες	δὲ	χαρίσματα	κατὰ	τὴν
echontes	de	charismata	kata	tēn
Having	but	gifts	according to	the

5322.4 noun acc sing fem	3450.12 art acc sing fem	1319.51 verb acc sing fem part aor pass	2231.3 prs-pron dat 1pl	1307.2 adj acc pl neu
χάριν	τὴν	δοθεῖσαν	ἡμῖν	διάφορα·
charin	tēn	dotheisan	hēmin	diaphora
grace	the	having been given	to us	different,

1521.1 conj	4252.4 noun acc sing fem	2567.3 prep	3450.12 art acc sing fem	354.1 noun acc sing fem
εἴτε	προφητείαν,	κατὰ	τὴν	ἀναλογίαν
eite	prophēteian	kata	tēn	analogian
whether	prophecy	according to	the	proportion

3450.10 art gen sing fem	3963.2 noun gen sing fem	1521.1 conj	1242.4 noun acc sing fem	1706.1 prep	3450.11 art dat sing fem
τῆς	πίστεως·	**7.** εἴτε	διακονίαν,	ἐν	τῇ
tēs	pisteōs	eite	diakonian	en	tē
of the	faith;	or	service	in	the

1242.3 noun dat sing fem	1521.1 conj	3450.5 art sing masc	1315.6 verb sing masc part pres act	1706.1 prep	3450.11 art dat sing fem
διακονίᾳ·	εἴτε	ὁ	διδάσκων,	ἐν	τῇ
diakonia	eite	ho	didaskōn	en	tē
service;	or	the	teaching	in	the

1313.3 noun dat sing fem	1521.1 conj	3450.5 art sing masc	3731.7 verb nom sing masc part pres act	1706.1 prep	3450.11 art dat sing fem
διδασκαλίᾳ·	**8.** εἴτε	ὁ	παρακαλῶν,	ἐν	τῇ
didaskalia	eite	ho	parakalōn	en	tē
teaching;	or	the	exhorting	in	the

3735.3 noun dat sing fem	3450.5 art sing masc	3200.1 verb nom sing masc part pres act	1706.1 prep	567.2 noun dat sing fem	3450.5 art sing masc
παρακλήσει·	ὁ	μεταδιδοὺς,	ἐν	ἁπλότητι·	ὁ
paraklēsei	ho	metadidous	en	haplotēti	ho
exhortation;	the	sharing	in	simplicity,	the

4150.3 verb nom sing masc part pres mid	1706.1 prep	4561.2 noun dat sing fem	3450.5 art sing masc	1640.3 verb nom sing masc part pres act	1706.1 prep
προϊστάμενος,	ἐν	σπουδῇ·	ὁ	ἐλεῶν,	ἐν
proistamenos	en	spoudē	ho	eleōn	en
taking the lead	with	diligence;	the	showing mercy	with

2408.1 noun dat sing fem	3450.9 art nom sing fem	26.1 noun nom sing fem	502.1 adj nom sing fem	649.1 verb nom pl masc part pres act
ἱλαρότητι.	**9.** Ἡ	ἀγάπη	ἀνυπόκριτος·	ἀποστυγοῦντες
hilarotēti	Hē	agapē	anupokritos	apostugountes
cheerfulness.	The	love	without pretense;	abhorring

3450.16 art sing neu	4050.1 adj sing	2827.2 verb nom pl masc part pres pass	3450.3 art dat sing	18.4 adj dat sing	3450.11 art dat sing fem
τὸ	πονηρόν,	κολλώμενοι	τῷ	ἀγαθῷ·	**10.** τῇ
to	ponēron	kollōmenoi	tō	agathō	tē
the	evil,	cleaving	to the	good;	in the

not interchangeable. The person who has given himself to God has a big reason for doing anything, be it ever so small, in a big way.

12:6-8. In the Church members have "gifts differing according to the grace that is given" them. Seven gifts are enumerated. The purpose of the variety is to enable the whole Body to function as a unit (1 Corinthians 12:12). The various gifts and ministries are as integral to the body of Christ as the parts of the natural body.

Three sections of Scripture in the New Testament describe Body ministry gifts: Romans 12:3-8; 1 Corinthians 12:4-31; and Ephesians 4:4-16. They have much in common, yet each has a different perspective. All are dealing with gifts of grace operative in the Body, and yet each has a distinctive. All are showing the unity of the Body comprised of the diversity of various members with various gifts.

Ephesians 4:11 lists the gifts of Christ to the Body. These are *persons* who have a lifelong calling to be apostles, prophets, evangelists, pastors, or teachers. First Corinthians 12:8-10 is a distinctive list of *manifestations*, rather than persons with a calling for life. They are never called gifts of Christ as in Ephesians 4:11; they are in a special sense gifts (or better, manifestations) of the Holy Spirit. The Holy Spirit is sovereign in bestowing these gifts; they are apportioned according to His will. They are resident in the Spirit and are available at any time as the need exists. They never really belong to the believer in the sense that he does not need to depend on Him in faith for every expression of them. Here in Romans 12 we have a composite list which covers a broad scope, naming gifts of grace which are not distinctive as to a specific Giver, or as to a calling for life, or a temporary manifestation.

The gifts mentioned here are only a partial list. They are: "Prophecy"—the gift of uttering God's will under the direct impulse of the Holy Spirit. The utterance will always be in accord with Scripture which is the criterion for creed and conduct. "Ministry"—this is one of the Greek words (*diakonia*) for a servant. This can include many kinds of service. "Teaching"—to instruct in the truths of Scripture. "Exhortation"—to encourage, to entreat, an appeal to the will in comparison to teaching which is an appeal to the mind. "Giveth"—sharing substance readily and liberally. "Ruleth"—referring to the office of elders and deacons. "Showeth mercy"—engaging in practical deeds of helpfulness and doing so cheerfully.

12:9. This verse begins a list of 20 commands regulating Christian brotherhood. Verse 9 must be interpreted in the light of those that follow. There must be love without "dissimulation" (without hypocrisy, genuine, sincere). This is a warning against being two-faced, pretending an affection which is not meant. See 1 John 3:18. Believers are to be glued to that which is good (Psalm 97:10). Those who love righteousness intensely will hate sin. They must regard evil with horror.

and every one members one of another: . . . and are all fellow-members one of another, *Locke.*

6. Having then gifts differing according to the grace that is given to us: . . . but possessed of varied talents, *Berkeley* . . . according to the respective favour that is bestowed upon us, *Locke.*
whether prophecy, [let us prophesy] according to the proportion of faith: . . . whose gift is inspired eloquence, *Way* . . . exercise it in accord with the analogy of the faith, *Concordant.*

7. Or ministry, [let us wait] on [our] ministering: . . . if it is the gift of administration, *Weymouth* . . . then faithfulness in that ministry is required, *Norlie.*
or he that teacheth, on teaching: . . . take hede to his doctrine, *Tyndale* . . . led him be occupied in teaching, *Geneva.*

8. Or he that exhorteth, on exhortation: . . . if he is a counselor, in counseling, *Adams* . . . the entreater, in entreaty, *Concordant.*
he that giveth, [let him do it] with simplicity: . . . who has wealth to distribute, *Way* . . . imparts, *Worrell* . . . who contributes, *HistNT* . . . without display, *Norlie* . . . in singleness of mind, *Conybeare.*
he that ruleth, with diligence: . . . presideth over others, *Noyes* . . . the office-holder must be faithful, *Norlie* . . . he who is leading, *Young* . . . do it with care, *Macknight.*
he that showeth mercy, with cheerfulness: . . . he that pities, *Hanson* . . . he that shows compassion, *PNT* . . . with a joyous abandon, *Wuest.*

9. [Let] love be without dissimulation: . . . perfectly sincere, *Berkeley* . . . genuine, *RSV* . . . without hypocrisy, *Adams* . . . without pretense, *Confraternity* . . . unfeigned, *Hanson.*
Abhor that which is evil: Regard with horror, *Weymouth* . . . Loathe all wickedness, *Way* . . . Detest the evil, *Wilson.*
cleave to that which is good: Stick fast, *Wuest.*

5197.3 noun dat sing fem
φιλαδελφίᾳ
philadelphia
brotherly love

1519.1 prep
εἰς
eis
towards

238.3 prs-pron acc pl masc
ἀλλήλους
allēlous
one another

5223.1 adj nom pl masc
φιλόστοργοι·
philostorgoi
kindly affectioned;

3450.11 art dat sing fem
τῇ
tē
in the

4940.3 noun dat sing fem
τιμῇ
timē
honor

238.3 prs-pron acc pl masc
ἀλλήλους
allēlous
one another

4144.1 verb nom pl masc part pres
προηγούμενοι·
proēgoumenoi
going before;

11. **3450.11** art dat sing fem
τῇ
tē
in the

4561.2 noun dat sing fem
σπουδῇ
spoudē
diligence,

3231.1 partic
μὴ
mē
not

3499.2 adj nom pl masc
ὀκνηροί,
oknēroi
slothful;

3450.3 art dat sing
τῷ
tō
in the

4011.3 noun dat sing neu
πνεύματι
pneumati
spirit,

2186.2 verb nom pl masc part pres act
ζέοντες,
zeontes
being fervent;

3450.3 art dat sing
⌐ τῷ
tō
in the

2511.3 noun dat sing masc
καιρῷ
kairō
season

3450.3 art dat sing
[a✶ τῷ
tō
[in the

2935.3 noun dat sing masc
κυρίῳ]
kuriō
Lord]

1392.7 verb nom pl masc part pres act
δουλεύοντες·
douleuontes
serving.

12. **3450.11** art dat sing fem
τῇ
tē
In the

1667.3 noun dat sing fem
ἐλπίδι
elpidi
hope,

5299.9 verb nom pl masc part pres act
χαίροντες,
chairontes
rejoicing;

3450.11 art dat sing fem
τῇ
tē
in the

2324.3 noun dat sing fem
θλίψει
thlipsei
tribulation,

5116.5 verb nom pl masc part pres act
ὑπομένοντες,
hupomenontes
enduring;

3450.11 art dat sing fem
τῇ
tē
in the

4194.3 noun dat sing fem
προσευχῇ
proseuchē
prayer,

4201.4 verb nom pl masc part pres act
προσκαρτεροῦντες·
proskarterountes
steadfastly continuing;

13. **3450.14** art dat pl fem
ταῖς
tais
to the

5367.4 noun dat pl fem
χρείαις
chreiais
needs

3450.1 art gen pl
τῶν
tōn
of the

39.4 adj gen pl
ἁγίων
hagiōn
saints

2814.5 verb nom pl masc part pres act
κοινωνοῦντες,
koinōnountes
communicating;

3450.12 art acc sing fem
τὴν
tēn
the

5218.2 noun acc sing fem
φιλοξενίαν
philoxenian
hospitality

1371.8 verb nom pl masc part pres act
διώκοντες·
diōkontes
pursuing.

14. **2108.2** verb 2pl impr pres act
εὐλογεῖτε
eulogeite
Bless

3450.8 art acc pl masc
τοὺς
tous
the

1371.10 verb acc pl masc part pres act
διώκοντας
diōkontas
persecuting

5050.4 prs-pron acc 2pl
⌐a ὑμᾶς· ⌐
humas
you;

2108.2 verb 2pl impr pres act
εὐλογεῖτε,
eulogeite
bless,

2504.1 conj
καὶ
kai
and

3231.1 partic
μὴ
mē
not

2642.2 verb 2pl impr pres
καταρᾶσθε.
katarasthe
curse.

15. **5299.11** verb inf pres act
χαίρειν
chairein
To rejoice

3196.3 prep
μετὰ
meta
with

5299.10 verb gen pl masc part pres act
χαιρόντων,
chairontōn
rejoicing,

2504.1 conj
⌐a καὶ ⌐
kai
and

2772.12 verb inf pres act
κλαίειν
klaiein
to weep

3196.3 prep
μετὰ
meta
with

2772.7 verb gen pl masc part pres act
κλαιόντων.
klaiontōn
weeping;

16. **3450.16** art sing neu
τὸ
to
the

840.15 prs-pron sing neu
αὐτὸ
auto
same thing

1519.1 prep
εἰς
eis
toward

238.3 prs-pron acc pl masc
ἀλλήλους
allēlous
one another

5262.8 verb nom pl masc part pres act
φρονοῦντες·
phronountes
thinking,

11.a.**Txt:** 06D-org,Steph **Var:** p46,01ℵ,02A,03B 06D-corr,020L,025P,33 byz.Elzev,Lach,Treg,Alf Word,Tisc,We/Ho,Weis Sod,UBS/✶

14.a.**Txt:** 01ℵ,02A,06D 020L,025P,etc.byz.it.sa. bo.Tisc,Sod **Var:** p46,03B,We/Ho Weis,UBS/✶

15.a.**Txt:** 02A,06D-corr 020L,025P,byz.bo.Weis Sod **Var:** 01ℵ,03B,06D-org Lach,Treg,Alf,Word Tisc,We/Ho,UBS/✶

12:10. The Church is a spiritual family, and warm affection should characterize the members of a family. The idea expressed here is that of the affection between a mother and her children. One of the evidences of Christianity in the Apostolic Church (and today it should be the same) was the testimony in word and deed of brotherly love, an evidence of real discipleship.

12:11. Christians are not to be lazy, slothful, or careless in zeal. They are to import God's love and grace, then export what they have received in praise to God and service for Him.

The word rendered "fervent" here occurs in only one other place (Acts 18:25) and carries the thought to "boil," to be ardent in boiling over with holy enthusiasm. To lack this is to result in what the Scripture calls a lukewarm or cold condition (Matthew 24:12; Revelation 2:4; 3:15).

12:12. The hope of the Christian is the imminent return of Christ. Believers are not without hope (1 Thessalonians 4:13). The hope of future glory should make them patient. Paul has already written on the subject of patience (5:3,4; 8:25) and says more in 15:4,5.

Hupomenontes ("patient," KJV) is given a stronger rendering by many translators by the use of "enduring" or "steadfast." The general sense is to stand one's ground, to hold out, to endure. Paul urges believers to continue "instant in prayer." In 1611 the word *instant* had a different meaning. "Insistent" seems to be more correct.

12:13. The word *saint* means "belonging to God." The amazing results are that God will supply the believer's necessities as he ministers to the ones "belonging to Him." The literal meaning of "hospitality" is "love to strangers." See 1 Timothy 3:2; Titus 1:8; Hebrews 13:2; 1 Peter 4:9.

12:14. In this verse Paul reiterates Jesus' teaching as found in Matthew 5:44 and Luke 6:27,28.

12:15. The believer should enter into both the joys and sorrows of other believers. The best example of this is our Lord who could enter into the joyfulness of the wedding in Cana of Galilee, yet weep at the tomb of Lazarus.

It is far easier to weep with the other person in his troubles, than to rejoice with the person whose successes are greater. To be able to rejoice with and for him is the test of true Christian character.

12:16. The literal Greek is "thinking the same thing toward another." Without agreeing on all things, Christians can have a mutual

10. [Be] kindly affectioned one to another with brotherly love: Louing the charitie of the brotherhod one toward an other, *Rheims* . . . in a brotherhood of mutual love, *Berkeley.*

in honour preferring one another: . . . in matters of worldly honour, *Weymouth* . . . put others before yourselves, *TCNT.*

11. Not slothful in business: . . . never let your zeal flag, *Moffatt.*

fervent in spirit: Be boiling hot, *Klingensmith* . . . be aglow with, *RSV* . . . always on fire, *Williams.*

serving the Lord: . . . slaving for the Lord, *Concordant.*

12. Rejoicing in hope: Let your hope be something exultant, *Way.*

patient in tribulation: . . . be steadfast in time of trouble, *Norlie* . . . in affliction, *Macknight* . . . in distress, *HistNT.*

continuing instant in prayer: . . . earnest and persistent in prayer, *Weymouth* . . . persevering in prayer, *Scarlett.*

13. Distributing to the necessity of saints: Help the saints, *Norlie* . . . Be liberal to the needs of the saints, *Conybeare* . . . Contributing to the wants of the saints, *Wilson.*

given to hospitality: Eagerly welcome strangers as guests, *Beck* . . . always practise hospitality, *Weymouth* . . . shewing hospitality to strangers, *Scarlett* . . . be readie to harboure, *Cranmer.*

14. Bless them which persecute you: bless, and curse not: Shower blessings on those who persecute you, *Way.*

15. Rejoice with them that do rejoice, and weep with them that weep: Share the joy of those who are glad, *Berkeley* . . . Be mery with them that are mery, *Tyndale* . . . lamenting with those lamenting, *Concordant.*

16. [Be] of the same mind one toward another: Live in harmony together, *Norlie.*

Romans 12:17

3231.1 partic	3450.17 art pl neu	5146.4 adj acc pl neu	5262.8 verb nom pl masc part pres act	233.2 conj	3450.4 art dat pl
μὴ	τὰ	ὑψηλὰ	φρονοῦντες,	ἀλλὰ	τοῖς
mē	ta	hupsēla	phronountes	alla	tois
not	the	high things	thinking,	but	with the

4862.1 adj dat pl	4730.1 verb nom pl masc part pres pass	3231.1 partic	1090.19 verb 2pl impr pres	5265.1 adj nom pl
ταπεινοῖς	συναπαγόμενοι.	μὴ	γίνεσθε	φρόνιμοι
tapeinois	sunapagomenoi	mē	ginesthe	phronimoi
humble	going along:	not	let	wise

3706.1 prep	1431.7 prs-pron dat pl masc	3235.2 num card dat	2527.7 adj sing neu	470.2 prep gen	2527.8 adj gen sing neu
παρ'	ἑαυτοῖς.	17. μηδενὶ	κακὸν	ἀντὶ	κακοῦ
par'	heautois	mēdeni	kakon	anti	kakou
in	yourselves:	to no one	evil	for	evil

586.4 verb nom pl masc part pres act	4165.2 verb nom pl masc part pres mid	2541.11 adj pl neu	1783.1 prep gen	3820.4 adj gen pl
ἀποδιδόντες·	προνοούμενοι	καλὰ	ἐνώπιον	πάντων
apodidontes	pronooumenoi	kala	enōpion	pantōn
rendering:	providing	right	before	all

442.7 noun gen pl masc	1479.1 conj	1409.3 adj sing neu	3450.16 art sing neu	1523.1 prep gen	5050.2 prs-pron gen 2pl
ἀνθρώπων·	18. εἰ	δυνατόν,	τὸ	ἐξ	ὑμῶν,
anthrōpōn	ei	dunaton	to	ex	humōn
men:	if	possible,	the	from	yourselves,

3196.3 prep	3820.4 adj gen pl	442.7 noun gen pl masc	1502.2 verb nom pl masc part pres act	3231.1 partic
μετὰ	πάντων	ἀνθρώπων	εἰρηνεύοντες.	19. μὴ
meta	pantōn	anthrōpōn	eirēneuontes	mē
with	all	men,	being at peace;	not

1431.8 prs-pron acc pl masc	1543.2 verb nom pl masc part pres act	27.6 adj pl masc	233.2 conj	1319.27 verb 2pl impr aor act
ἑαυτοὺς	ἐκδικοῦντες,	ἀγαπητοί,	ἀλλὰ	δότε
heautous	ekdikountes	agapētoi	alla	dote
yourselves	avenging,	beloved,	but	give

4964.4 noun acc sing masc	3450.11 art dat sing fem	3572.3 noun dat sing fem	1119.22 verb 3sing indic perf pass	1056.1 conj	1466.5 prs-pron dat 1sing
τόπον	τῇ	ὀργῇ·	γέγραπται	γάρ,	Ἐμοὶ
topon	tē	orgē	gegraptai	gar	Emoi
place	to the	wrath;	it has been written	for,	To me

1544.1 noun nom sing fem	1466.1 prs-pron nom 1sing	464.2 verb 1sing indic fut act	2978.5 verb 3sing indic pres act	2935.1 noun nom sing masc
ἐκδίκησις,	ἐγὼ	ἀνταποδώσω,	λέγει	κύριος.
ekdikēsis	egō	antapodōsō	legei	kurios
vengeance!	I	will recompense,	says	Lord.

20.a.Txt: 06D-corr,020L byz.
Var: 01א,02A,03B,025P bo.Lach,Treg,Alf,Tisc We/Ho,Weis,UBS/✸

1430.1 partic	3631.1 conj	233.2 conj	1430.1 partic	3845.1 verb 3sing pres act
20. ⸂Ἐὰν	οὖν	[ᵃ✰ ἀλλὰ	ἐὰν]	πεινᾷ
Ean	oun	alla	ean	peina
If	therefore	[but	if]	should hunger

3450.5 art sing masc	2172.1 adj nom sing masc	4622.2 prs-pron gen 2sing	5430.1 verb 2sing impr pres act	840.6 prs-pron acc sing masc	1430.1 partic
ὁ	ἐχθρός	σου,	ψώμιζε	αὐτόν·	ἐὰν
ho	echthros	sou	psōmize	auton	ean
the	enemy	your,	feed	him;	if

198

trust which makes for unity. Snobbishness is not Christian. Believers are not to think too highly of themselves.

12:17,18. The desire to get even has no place in the life of the believer. Christ gave the example; His followers are to forgive even as He forgave them (Colossians 3:13). There are those who will treat a Christian unkindly and often with purpose, and to retaliate is a natural response. But to turn the other cheek, to go the second mile, is Christlike.

The Christian will do his best to live at peace with all men and avoid giving offense to any. Rather than to avenge himself of unjust attacks, he is to return good for evil.

In all his social and business dealings the Christian must maintain a standard that is above reproach. His word must be his bond. There must be no policy other than honesty. The Christian's conduct must at all times commend the gospel witness. He declares by his actions the righteousness of God.

Pronoeō, translated "provide," means literally to take thought in advance, to foresee, to think beforehand. *Kala*, rendered "things honest," is one of several Greek words describing that which is good. *Kalos*, the root of the word used here, speaks of that which is fitting and useful. The Christian is to exercise care, to plan in advance so his way of life will properly represent his inward experience.

The believer who lives by Biblical principles will take thought for things honorable "not only in the sight of the Lord, but also in the sight of men" (2 Corinthians 8:21). Character is of supreme importance, but reputation is also of vital importance (Acts 6:3; 16:2).

Christians are to love peace and not be guilty in claiming their rights at the expense of others. The initiative in disturbing peaceful relations with those around them must never be theirs.

"If it be possible" indicates the time may come when courtesy needs to submit to principle. Easygoing tolerance is not always right. The Christian should not back off from a battle if principle is violated.

12:19,20. Any thought of taking revenge must be banished from the mind. Opposition, persecution, and hatred are to be repaid positively with good.

Scripture makes it very clear that vengeance belongs to God, not to the Christian. God's way of avenging is infinitely better for all conerned and brings glory to Him.

Christians need to realize that they live in a moral universe that is under the authority of God. They must not play God by seeking revenge for personal affronts. God has His way of dealing with offenders either through governmental authority (13:4) or in the final judgment.

Mind not high things, but condescend to men of low estate: Do not pay special attention to important persons, *Klingensmith* . . . Avoid being haughty; mingle with the lowly, *Norlie* . . . Don't be too ambitious, *Beck* . . . do not aspire to eminence, but willingly adjust yourselves to humble situations, *Berkeley* . . . Do not cherish a spirit of pride, *TCNT* . . . but make youre selues equall to them of the lower sorte, *Cranmer*.

Be not wise in your own conceits: Do not over-estimate your own discernment, *Way* . . . Don't think you are wise, *Beck* . . . Do not be self important, *Klingensmith* . . . in youre awne opinions, *Tyndale* . . . in your own estimation, *Hanson*.

17. Recompense to no man evil for evil: Never pay back injury with injury, *TCNT* . . . Repay no one, *RSV*.

Provide things honest in the sight of all men: Be concerned with things that everybody considers noble, *Beck* . . . Aim to do what is honorable, *Montgomery* . . . what all men will recognize as honourable, *TCNT*.

18. If it be possible, as much as lieth in you: . . . without sacrificing your principles, *Way*.

live peaceably with all men: . . . live on good terms, *TCNT*.

19. Dearly beloved, avenge not yourselves:
but [rather] give place unto wrath: . . . let God handle it, *Norlie* . . . leave room for divine retribution, *Berkeley* . . . for God's judgement, *TCNT* . . . leave a place for God's anger, *Williams*.
for it is written:
Vengeance [is] mine: Judgment is mine, *Sawyer* . . . To me belongs punishment, *Wuest* . . . Vengeance belongs to me, *Campbell* . . . is my prerogative, *Way*.

I will repay, saith the Lord: I will pay them back, the Lord says, *Berkeley*.

20. Therefore if thine enemy hunger, feed him: And if thy adversary, *Murdock*.

1366.3 verb 3sing subj pres act	4081.2 verb 2sing impr pres act	840.6 prs-pron acc sing masc	3642.17 dem-pron sing neu	1056.1 conj
διψᾷ,	πότιζε	αὐτόν·	τοῦτο	γὰρ
dipsa	*potize*	*auton*	*touto*	*gar*
he should thirst,	give drink	him;	this	for

4020.15 verb sing masc part pres act	438.1 noun acc pl masc	4300.2 noun gen sing neu	4839.1 verb 2sing indic fut act	1894.3 prep
ποιῶν,	ἄνθρακας	πυρὸς	σωρεύσεις	ἐπὶ
poiōn	*anthrakas*	*puros*	*sōreuseis*	*epi*
doing,	coals	of fire	you will heap	upon

3450.12 art acc sing fem	2747.4 noun acc sing fem	840.3 prs-pron gen sing	3231.1 partic	3390.16 verb 2sing impr pres pass	5097.3 prep
τὴν	κεφαλὴν	αὐτοῦ.	**21.** μὴ	νικῶ	ὑπὸ
tēn	*kephalēn*	*autou*	*mē*	*nikō*	*hupo*
the	head	his.	Not	be overcome	by

3450.2 art gen sing	2527.8 adj gen sing neu	233.2 conj	3390.2 verb 2sing impr pres act	1706.1 prep	3450.3 art dat sing	18.4 adj dat sing
τοῦ	κακοῦ,	ἀλλὰ	νίκα	ἐν	τῷ	ἀγαθῷ
tou	*kakou*	*alla*	*nika*	*en*	*tō*	*agathō*
the	evil,	but	overcome	with	the	good

3450.16 art sing neu	2527.7 adj sing neu	3820.9 adj nom sing fem	5425.1 noun sing fem	1833.7 noun dat pl fem
τὸ	κακόν.	**13:1.** Πᾶσα	ψυχὴ	ἐξουσίαις
to	*kakon*	*Pasa*	*psuchē*	*exousiais*
the	evil.	Every	soul	to authorities

5080.4 verb dat pl fem pres pres act	5131.9 verb 3sing impr pres pass	3620.3 partic	1056.1 conj	1498.4 verb 3sing indic pres act
ὑπερεχούσαις	ὑποτασσέσθω.	οὐ	γὰρ	ἔστιν
huperechousais	*hupotassesthō*	*ou*	*gar*	*estin*
being above	let be subject.	No	for	there is

1833.2 noun nom sing fem	1479.1 conj	3231.1 partic	570.3 prep gen	5097.3 prep	2296.2 noun gen sing masc
ἐξουσία	εἰ	μὴ	(ἀπὸ	[a✫ ὑπὸ]	θεοῦ·
exousia	*ei*	*mē*	*apo*	*hupo*	*theou*
authority	if	not	from	[by]	God;

3450.13 art pl fem	1156.2 conj	1498.30 verb nom pl fem part pres act	1833.5 noun nom pl fem	5097.3 prep	3450.2 art gen sing
αἱ	δὲ	οὖσαι	(b ἐξουσίαι)	ὑπὸ	(c τοῦ)
hai	*de*	*ousai*	*exousiai*	*hupo*	*tou*
the	and	being	authorities,	by	

2296.2 noun gen sing masc	4872.7 verb nom pl fem part perf pass	1498.7 verb 3pl indic pres act	5452.1 conj	3450.5 art sing masc
θεοῦ	τεταγμέναι	εἰσίν.	**2.** ὥστε	ὁ
theou	*tetagmenai*	*eisin*	*hōste*	*ho*
God	having been appointed	are.	So that	the

495.2 verb nom sing masc part pres mid	3450.11 art dat sing fem	1833.3 noun dat sing fem	3450.11 art dat sing fem	3450.2 art gen sing
ἀντιτασσόμενος	τῇ	ἐξουσίᾳ,	τῇ	τοῦ
antitassomenos	*tē*	*exousia*	*tē*	*tou*
setting himself against	the	authority,	the	

2296.2 noun gen sing masc	1290.1 noun dat sing fem	434.5 verb 3sing indic perf act	3450.7 art pl masc	1156.2 conj	434.6 verb nom pl masc part perf act
θεοῦ	διαταγῇ	ἀνθέστηκεν·	οἱ	δὲ	ἀνθεστηκότες,
theou	*diatagē*	*anthestēken*	*hoi*	*de*	*anthestēkotes*
of God	ordinance	has resisted;	the	and	having resisted,

When the Christian avoids avenging himself and returns good for evil, he gives God an opportunity to work. Further, he transforms enemies into friends. Kindness shown to one who has caused injury will make him ashamed of his meanness. Vengeance may break an enemy's spirit, but kindness will break his heart. Kindness can bring shame like burning coals of fire on the offender's head.

Those who take vengeance into their own hands are apt to find that at the last it produces bitter fruit. When God avenges wrong it is not done with a retaliation which is so representative of human scheming. God avenges wrong with perfect equity and justice.

12:21. Those who stoop to vengeance are themselves conquered by evil. To think to overcome evil with evil, hatred with hatred, anger with anger, is to expect that two wrongs make a right, and that is never so. To meet wrong with wrong is to only increase the wrong. There is power for overcoming evil in the simple might of goodness. If there is anything that will cause an enemy to change his mind, it will be the goodness he sees in the one he has wronged. The only real way to destroy an enemy is to make him a friend.

The risk Paul saw was that a Christian, by giving way to revengeful conduct, would be "overcome of evil," that the wrong in others would produce wrong in his own life. The believer must guard against this by taking the initiative of love and so "overcome evil with good."

13:1-3. In chapter 12 Paul exhorted the believer, as a member of the body of Christ, to perform duties related to his gifts and callings. Romans 13:1-7 deals with the Christian's responsibility as a citizen. His citizenship is in heaven (Philippians 3:20), but he lives in this present world and as a Christian citizen must walk circumspectly. The believer, united to Christ, must still obey the laws of the state. To violate these laws is to sin against God.

Both the Church and the state are institutions of God. Spiritual obligations concern the Christian's relationships to Christ and the Church. Other obligations which some choose to call divine obligations relate to institutions which came into existence before the Church.

Human government is a divine institution. The Christian is a member of a spiritual institution, the Church, and is under the law of God. He is also a member of a divine institution, the state, and is subject to the law of the state. The Church is a spiritual institution; the state is a secular institution. The saved and the unsaved are both under the laws of the state.

Believers must never reject governmental authority; they are never terrorists or anarchists. However, if government opposes God's laws then they must "obey God rather than men" (Acts 5:29). Unless governmental authority opposes God's commands, they are to submit to it, even though the men who administer the authority are ungodly and wicked.

if he thirst, give him drink: . . . in case he is thirsty, *Berkeley* . . . quench his thirst, *Weymouth*.

for in so doing thou shalt heap coals of fire on his head: . . . you will make him burn with shame, *TEV*.

21. Be not overcome of evil, but overcome evil with good: Stop being conquered by evil, *Williams* . . . Be not subdued by evil, *Wilson* . . . but master evil with good, *Berkeley* . . . conquer evil by kindness, *Way*.

1. Let every soul be subject unto: Let every person, *RSV* . . . submitte him selfe, *Geneva* . . . be in subjection, *Worrell* . . . be submissive, *Hanson*.

the higher powers: . . . governing authorities, *RSV* . . . supreme authorities, *Scarlett* . . . superior powers, *Sawyer* . . . authorities that are over him, *Worrell*.

For there is no power but of God: . . . there is no government, *Beck* . . . no one is a ruler except by God's permission, *Weymouth* . . . for there exists no authority except from God, *Confraternity*.

the powers that be are ordained of God: . . . the existing authorities are instituted by, *HistNT* . . . stand permanently ordained, *Wuest* . . . have been arranged under God, *Wilson* . . . those in charge are divinely constituted, *Berkeley* . . . have had their rank and power assigned to them by, *Weymouth* . . . are placed under God, *Macknight* . . . by God's sanction, *Way*.

2. Whosoever therefore resisteth the power: So that he which setteth himself against the authority, *Alford* . . . he who sets himself in opposition to, *Campbell*.

resisteth the ordinance of God: . . . he really sets himself against a plan that God has ordained, *Norlie* . . . stands against the command, *Klingensmith* . . . is opposing the divine order, *Moffatt* . . . is rebelling against God's decision, *JB* . . . resists what God has appointed, *RSV* . . . is resisting God's will, *Weymouth* . . . is a rebel against God's arrangement, *Way*.

and they that resist:

Romans 13:3

1431.7 prs-pron dat pl masc	2890.1 noun sing neu	2956.42 verb 3pl indic fut mid	2956.48 verb 3pl indic fut mid
ἑαυτοῖς	κρίμα	ʼ λήψονται.	[✶ λήμψονται.]
heautois	krima	lēpsontai	lēmpsontai
to themselves	judgment	shall receive.	[idem]

3450.7 art pl masc	1056.1 conj	752.5 noun pl masc	3620.2 partic	1498.7 verb 3pl indic pres act	5238.1 noun nom sing masc	3450.1 art gen pl
3. οἱ	γὰρ	ἄρχοντες	οὐκ	εἰσὶν	φόβος	ʼ τῶν
hoi	gar	archontes	ouk	eisin	phobos	tōn
The	for	rulers	not	are	a terror	of the

3.a.Txt: 06D-corr,020L byz.
Var: 01א,02A,03B 06D-org,025P,Lach Treg,Alf,Word,Tisc We/Ho,Weis,UBS/✶

18.1 adj gen	2024.5 noun gen pl neu	3450.3 art dat sing	18.4 adj dat sing	2024.3 noun dat sing neu	233.2 conj
ἀγαθῶν	ἔργων,	[a✶ τῷ	ἀγαθῷ	ἔργῳ]	ἀλλὰ
agathōn	ergōn	tō	agathō	ergō	alla
good	works,	[to the	good	work]	but

3.b.Txt: 06D-corr,020L byz.
Var: 01א,02A,03B 06D-org,025P,Lach Treg,Alf,Word,Tisc We/Ho,Weis,UBS/✶

3450.1 art gen pl	2527.1 adj gen pl	3450.3 art dat sing	2527.10 adj dat sing neu	2286.2 verb 2sing indic pres act	1156.2 conj
ʼ τῶν	κακῶν.	[b✶ τῷ	κακῷ.]	θέλεις	δὲ
tōn	kakōn	tō	kakō	theleis	de
of the	evils.	[to the	evil.]	Do you desire	and

3231.1 partic	5236.11 verb inf pres	3450.12 art acc sing fem	1833.4 noun acc sing fem	3450.16 art sing neu	18.3 adj sing
μὴ	φοβεῖσθαι	τὴν	ἐξουσίαν;	τὸ	ἀγαθὸν
mē	phobeisthai	tēn	exousian	to	agathon
not	to be afraid of	the	authority?	to	good

4020.11 verb 2sing impr pres act	2504.1 conj	2174.38 verb 2sing indic fut act	1853.2 noun acc sing masc	1523.1 prep gen	840.10 prs-pron gen sing fem
ποίει,	καὶ	ἕξεις	ἔπαινον	ἐξ	αὐτῆς·
poiei	kai	hexeis	epainon	ex	autēs
practice,	and	you shall have	praise	from	it;

2296.2 noun gen sing masc	1056.1 conj	1243.1 noun nom sing masc	1498.4 verb 3sing indic pres act	4622.3 prs-pron dat 2sing	1519.1 prep
4. θεοῦ	γὰρ	διάκονός	ἐστιν	σοὶ	εἰς
theou	gar	diakonos	estin	soi	eis
of God	for	a servant	it is	to you	for

3450.16 art sing neu	18.3 adj sing	1430.1 partic	1156.2 conj	3450.16 art sing neu	2527.7 adj sing neu	4020.7 verb 2sing subj pres act
τὸ	ἀγαθόν.	ἐὰν	δὲ	τὸ	κακὸν	ποιῇς,
to	agathon	ean	de	to	kakon	poiēs
to	good,	if	but	to	evil	you practice,

5236.5 verb 2sing impr pres	3620.3 partic	1056.1 conj	1488.1 adv	3450.12 art acc sing fem	3134.4 noun acc sing fem	5246.1 verb 3sing indic pres act
φοβοῦ·	οὐ	γὰρ	εἰκῇ	τὴν	μάχαιραν	φορεῖ
phobou	ou	gar	eikē	tēn	machairan	phorei
fear;	not	for	in vain	the	sword	it wears;

2296.2 noun gen sing masc	1056.1 conj	1243.1 noun nom sing masc	1498.4 verb 3sing indic pres act	1545.1 adj nom sing masc	1519.1 prep
θεοῦ	γὰρ	διάκονός	ἐστιν,	ἔκδικος	εἰς
theou	gar	diakonos	estin	ekdikos	eis
of God	for	a servant	it is,	an avenger	for

3572.4 noun acc sing fem	3450.3 art dat sing	3450.16 art sing neu	2527.7 adj sing neu	4097.8 verb dat sing masc part pres act	1346.1 conj
ὀργὴν	τῷ	τὸ	κακὸν	πράσσοντι.	5. διὸ
orgēn	tō	to	kakon	prassonti	dio
wrath	to the	to	evil	doing.	Wherefore

Christians have the duty of civil obedience. Disobedience to governmental authority is disobedience to God and will be judged. Since governments are appointed by God, they must be obeyed. The rule of law militates against the right of the person to decide which laws are right and which are wrong, or to assume the responsibility to obey or disobey as he may please.

While not all rulers are chosen by God, all rule is divinely ordained. The only ones who should live in fear of the representatives of the law are those who break the law. The man who does right has nothing to fear from the authorities, for government, a terror to crime, has no terrors for good behavior.

13:4,5. The scriptural point of view is that God commands respect for government, whether good or bad. Paul, with real significance, based his emphasis upon the God-appointed aspect of governmental authority. Five times in the first four verses of this chapter the phrase "of God" occurs. It indicates the origin of government; the origin is God's authority. All government goes back to God. In the covenant with Noah (Genesis 9), God gave the renewed earth into man's hand and instituted human government. God has never revoked that covenant. Therefore, it is the Christian's duty to be a good citizen. Not only is this the teaching of Paul in Romans, but Peter also gives the same counsel (1 Peter 2:12-17).

God has decreed governments but not what form they shall be. Among the nations, there has been every form of government from tribal rule to democracy, monarchy, and dictatorship.

The first clause of verse 4 gives the chief purpose of civil authority. The ruler is the minister "for good," so that "we may lead a quiet and peaceable life in all godliness and honesty" (1 Timothy 2:2). The second clause tells us that the evildoer should fear because the magistrate "beareth not the sword in vain." In most countries the current counterpart of the sword is a gun. The sword or gun is the sign of his authority to use the weapon when necessary.

The fact that an official carries an instrument of death makes clear the God-ordained right of the state to require the death penalty for some crimes. Genesis 9:6, given prior to the Law, has never been revoked. In the New Testament the sword is associated with death as the instrument of execution (Matthew 26:52; Luke 21:24; Acts 12:2; Hebrews 11:34,37; Revelation 13:10). As John Murray has observed, "To exclude its use for this purpose in this instance would be so arbitrary as to bear upon its face prejudice contrary to the evidence" (*New International Commentary*, 2:153). A sword is not used to rap knuckles; "in vain" would be to a wrong purpose.

Paul was here writing to the Christians in Rome, the capital of the great Roman Empire. Its government was an absolute dictatorship. The emperor had the power of life and death over the empire, and there was no appeal. At the time Nero was emperor. He was a man so sinful and bloodthirsty that his very name remains to this day a synonym for lust, cruelty, and corruption. Yet Paul wrote to the Christians of the Roman Empire that they were to be

shall receive to themselves damnation: ... bring on themselves condemnation, *Confraternity* ... shall be sentenced, *HistNT* ... will incur judgment, *RSV* ... shall procure punishment to themselves, *Macknight.*

3. For rulers are not a terror to good works, but to the evil: Magistrates are no terror, *Moffatt* ... only criminals have anything to fear, *JB* ... is not terrible to, *Conybeare* ... to good conduct, *HistNT* ... but by wrong-doers, *Weymouth* ... but to bad actions, *Way.*

Wilt thou then not be afraid of the power?: Would you like to be unafraid of, *TEV* ... Dost thou desire not to be afraid, *Alford.*

do that which is good, and thou shalt have praise of the same: Act uprightly, *Way* ... Do what is right, *Beck* ... and you will be commended for it, *Williams.*

4. For he is the minister of God to thee for good: It is God's servant to help you, *Beck* ... The magistrate should be, in your eyes, God's steward, *Way* ... for he is God's servant, *RSV* ... is God's minister appointed, *Montgomery* ... for thy wealth, *Geneva.*

But if thou do that which is evil: ... doest amiss, *Locke.*

be afraid: ... then be alarmed, *Berkeley.*

for he beareth not the sword in vain: ... for not in vain does it wear the sword, *HistNT* ... He does not carry the sword uselessly, *Klingensmith* ... just for show, *Norlie* ... without a purpose, *Beck* ... without cause, *Rheims* ... is not without meaning! *TCNT* ... his power to punish is real, *TEV* ... is invested with the power of life and death, *Way.*

for he is the minister of God, a revenger to [execute] wrath upon him that doeth evil: ... the exponent of God's wrath, *Way* ... to bring deserved punishment on the evildoer, *Berkeley* ... a revenger to inflict wrath on him, *Campbell* ... for the infliction of divine vengeance, *Moffatt* ... since he is God's avenging Servant, *Wilson* ... they carry out God's revenge by punishing wrongdoers, *JB* ... to him who practiseth evil, *Clementson.*

Romans 13:6

5.a.Txt: 01ℵ,02A,03B
044,048,byz.co.
Var: p46,06D,010F
012G

316.1 noun nom sing fem ἀνάγκη *anankē* necessary	**5131.15** verb inf pres pass ⟨✶ ὑποτάσσεσθαι, *hupotassesthai* to be subject,		**5131.10** verb 2pl impr pres pass [a ὑποτάσσεσθε,] *hupotassesthe* [be subjected,]		**3620.3** partic οὐ *ou* not

3303.1 adv μόνον *monon* only	**1217.2** prep διὰ *dia* on account of	**3450.12** art acc sing fem τὴν *tēn* the	**3572.4** noun acc sing fem ὀργὴν, *orgēn* wrath,	**233.2** conj ἀλλὰ *alla* but	**2504.1** conj καὶ *kai* also

1217.2 prep διὰ *dia* on account of	**3450.12** art acc sing fem τὴν *tēn* the	**4743.4** noun acc sing fem συνείδησιν. *suneidēsin* conscience.	**6.** **1217.2** prep διὰ *dia* Because of		**3642.17** dem- pron sing neu τοῦτο *touto* this

1056.1 conj γὰρ *gar* for	**2504.1** conj καὶ *kai* also	**5247.2** noun acc pl masc φόρους *phorous* tribute	**4903.2** verb 2pl indic pres act τελεῖτε· *teleite* pay you;	**2985.3** noun nom pl masc λειτουργοὶ *leitourgoi* ministers	**1056.1** conj γὰρ *gar* for	**2296.2** noun gen sing masc θεοῦ *theou* of God

1498.7 verb 3pl indic pres act εἰσιν, *eisin* they are,	**1519.1** prep εἰς *eis* on	**840.15** prs- pron sing neu αὐτὸ *auto* same thing	**3642.17** dem- pron sing neu τοῦτο *touto* this	**4201.4** verb nom pl masc part pres act προσκαρτεροῦντες. *proskarterountes* attending continually.

7.a.Txt: 01ℵ-corr
06D-corr,020L,025P,byz.
Var: 01ℵ-org,02A,03B
06D-org,sa.bo.Lach
Treg,Alf,Word,Tisc
We/Ho,Weis,Sod
UBS/✶

7. **586.12** verb 2pl impr aor act ἀπόδοτε *apodote* Render	**3631.1** conj ⟨a οὖν ⟩ *oun* therefore	**3820.5** adj dat pl πᾶσιν *pasin* to all	**3450.15** art acc pl fem τὰς *tas* the	**3646.2** noun acc pl fem ὀφειλάς, *opheilas* dues:	**3450.3** art dat sing τῷ *tō* to the

3450.6 art acc sing masc τὸν *ton* the	**5247.1** noun acc sing masc φόρον, *phoron* tribute,	**3450.6** art acc sing masc τὸν *ton* the	**5247.1** noun acc sing masc φόρον· *phoron* tribute;	**3450.3** art dat sing τῷ *tō* to the	**3450.16** art sing neu τὸ *to* the

4904.1 noun sing neu τέλος, *telos* custom,	**3450.16** art sing neu τὸ *to* the	**4904.1** noun sing neu τέλος, *telos* custom;	**3450.3** art dat sing τῷ *tō* to the	**3450.6** art acc sing masc τὸν *ton* the	**5238.4** noun acc sing masc φόβον, *phobon* fear,

3450.6 art acc sing masc τὸν *ton* the	**5238.4** noun acc sing masc φόβον· *phobon* fear;	**3450.3** art dat sing τῷ *tō* to the	**3450.12** art acc sing fem τὴν *tēn* the	**4940.4** noun acc sing fem τιμήν, *timēn* honor,	**3450.12** art acc sing fem τὴν *tēn* the

4940.4 noun acc sing fem τιμήν. *timēn* honor:	**8.** **3235.2** num card dat Μηδενὶ *Mēdeni* to no one	**3235.6** num card neu μηδὲν *mēden* nothing	**3648.1** verb 2pl pres act ὀφείλετε, *opheilete* owe you,	**1479.1** conj εἰ *ei* if	**3231.1** partic μὴ *mē* not

3450.16 art sing neu τὸ *to* the	**25.36** verb inf pres act ⟨ ἀγαπᾶν *agapan* to love	**238.3** prs-pron acc pl masc ἀλλήλους· *allēlous* one another:	**238.3** prs-pron acc pl masc [✶ ἀλλήλους *allēlous* [one another	**25.11** verb inf pres act ἀγαπᾶν·] *agapan* to love:]

"subject unto the higher powers" (verse 1).

Those in authority are placed in the position of rulership. They protect law-abiding citizens and they have power to restrain evil men from their wicked deeds. To disobey the law is to resist God's ordinance. Those who keep the law will have nothing to fear; if believers are good citizens those in authority will usually have a good word for them.

In these verses the ruler is twice called "the minister of God"—another testimony to the essentially divine character of civil authority. First Peter 3:13 states, "And who is he that will harm you, if ye be followers of that which is good?"

The Christian's submission should be motivated by more than that which is morally wrong. He obeys the law for a civil reason as well as a moral reason. He obeys in order to escape the wrath of rulers, but a higher law also motivates him. Paul was very concerned about keeping a good conscience before God and man (Acts 23:1; 24:16; 2 Corinthians 1:12; 4:2; 5:11; 1 Timothy 1:5; 3:9; 2 Timothy 1:3). We obey God's ministers because of our obligation to God himself.

The moral "conscience," however, limits obedience. If the civil power commands us to violate the law of God, we must obey God before man. Obtaining, by lawful means, the abrogation of unjust laws must be by legitimate protest and not disobedience.

God has ordained that government shall prescribe laws and then punish the offenders. Government is to protect the community and to punish the criminal.

13:6,7. Because government is of God, we are to pay taxes. Even if taxes seem exorbitant, tax collectors "are God's ministers, attending continually upon this very thing." The office, and not necessarily the man, is a ministry ordained by God. Christians are to pay taxes, show proper respect to officers, and courteous deference to all. Just as we owe money in payment of taxes and dues, so we owe a debt of "fear" and "honor" to those whom God has appointed to care for us.

13:8. Christians must live with a view to Christ's return, and verses 8-14 tell us how. In addition to obligations to the state the Christian has obligations to members of the state.

The Christian is to "owe no man any thing, but . . . love." No conscientious Christian will assume more financial obligations than he can care for. To go beyond his means in contracting a debt may be plain carelessness; to make no effort to settle the debt is plain dishonesty. Believers should never dishonor the name of Christ by dishonest treatment of the creditor. Every man's word should be absolutely dependable. Nothing will ruin a Christian's testimony faster than chronic indebtedness. The Apostolic Church was given a first requisite for the candidates for the office of deacons—that they should be "men of honest report" (Acts 6:3).

5. Wherefore [ye] must needs be subject: . . . there is a necessity for putting one's self in subjection, *Wuest* . . . you are absolutely bound to loyal submission, *Way*.

not only for wrath, but also for conscience sake: . . . not for feare of vengeance onely, *Geneva* . . . not only for the sake of escaping punishment, *Williams* . . . for conscientious reasons, *TCNT*.

6. For for this cause pay ye tribute also: For the same reason, *Norlie, RSV* . . . On the same principle, *Way* . . . therefore you are settling taxes, *Concordant* . . . tribute money, *Murdock*.

for they are God's ministers: . . . are God's official servants, *Williams* . . . they are God's public ministers, *Hanson*.

attending continually upon this very thing: . . . to this very business, *Campbell* . . . that constantly attend to this task, *Berkeley* . . . who must attend to this very matter, *Adams* . . . devoting themselves to this special work, *TCNT* . . . serving unto this purpose, *Douay*.

7. Render therefore to all their dues: Pay to all whatever you owe them, *Beck* . . . Pay promptly to all men what is due to them, *Weymouth* . . . Deliver to all the debts due them, *Wuest*.

tribute to whom tribute [is due]; custom to whom custom: . . . tariff to whom tariff is due, *Norlie* . . . rates where rates are due, *TCNT* . . . fees to the fees, *Klingensmith* . . . revenue to whom revenue is due, *RSV*.

fear to whom fear; honour to whom honour: . . . respect to those who should be respected, honor to those entitled to it, *Norlie* . . . reverence to whom reverence, *Hanson* . . . homage to whom homage is due, *Montgomery, Way* . . . to whom drede: drede, *Wyclif*.

8. Owe no man any thing, but to love one another: Avoid getting into debt, *JB* . . . Stop owing even one person even one thing, *Wuest* . . . Be under obligation to no one, *TEV* . . . except mutual love, *Weymouth* . . . save the debt of love alone, *Conybeare*.

Romans 13:9

3450.5 art sing masc
ὁ
ho
the

1056.1 conj
γὰρ
gar
for

25.8 verb nom sing masc part pres act
ἀγαπῶν
agapōn
loving

3450.6 art acc sing masc
τὸν
ton
the

2066.1 adj sing
ἕτερον,
heteron
other,

3414.4 noun acc sing masc
νόμον
nomon
law

3997.10 verb 3sing indic perf act
πεπλήρωκεν.
peplērōken
has fulfilled.

3450.16 art sing neu
9. τὸ
to
The

1056.1 conj
γὰρ,
gar
for,

3620.3 partic
Οὐ
Ou
Not

3294.7 verb 2sing indic fut act
μοιχεύσεις,
moicheuseis
you shall commit adultery,

3620.3 partic
Οὐ
Ou
Not

5244.6 verb 2sing indic fut act
φονεύσεις,
phoneuseis
you shall commit murder,

3620.3 partic
Οὐ
Ou
Not

2786.10 verb 2sing indic fut act
κλέψεις,
klepseis
you shall steal,

3620.3 partic
⌐a οὐ
ou
Not

5410.2 verb 2sing indic fut act
ψευδομαρτυρήσεις, ⌐
pseudomarturēseis
you shall bear false witness,

3620.2 partic
Οὐκ
Ouk
Not

1922.9 verb 2sing indic fut act
ἐπιθυμήσεις,
epithumēseis
you shall lust;

2504.1 conj
καὶ
kai
and

1479.1 conj
εἴ
ei
if

4948.3 indef-pron nom sing
τις
tis
any

2066.9 adj
ἑτέρα
hetera
other

1769.1 noun nom sing fem
ἐντολή,
entolē
commandment,

1706.1 prep
ἐν
en
in

3642.5 dem-pron dat sing masc
⌐ τούτῳ
toutō
this

3450.3 art dat sing
τῷ
tō
the

3030.3 noun dat sing masc
λόγῳ
logō
word

3450.3 art dat sing
[☆ τῷ
tō
[the

3030.3 noun dat sing masc
λόγῳ
logō
word

3642.5 dem-pron dat sing masc
τούτῳ]
toutō
this]

344.1 verb 3sing indic pres pass
ἀνακεφαλαιοῦται,
anakephalaioutai
it is being summed up,

1706.1 prep
⌐b ἐν
en
in

3450.3 art dat sing
τῷ ⌐
tō
the,

25.24 verb 2sing indic fut act
Ἀγαπήσεις
Agapēseis
You shall love

3450.6 art acc sing masc
τὸν
ton
the

3999.1 adv
πλησίον
plēsion
neighbor

4622.2 prs-pron gen 2sing
σου
sou
your

5453.1 conj
ὡς
hōs
as

1431.6 prs-pron acc 3sing masc
⌐ ἑαυτόν.
heauton
himself.

4427.4 prs-pron acc 2sing masc
[c☆ σεαυτόν.]
seauton
[yourself.]

3450.9 art nom sing fem
10. Ἡ
Hē
The

26.1 noun nom sing fem
ἀγάπη
agapē
love

3450.3 art dat sing
τῷ
tō
to the

3999.1 adv
πλησίον
plēsion
neighbor,

2527.7 adj sing neu
κακὸν
kakon
evil

3620.2 partic
οὐκ
ouk
not

2021.4 verb 3sing indic pres
ἐργάζεται·
ergazetai
does work:

3998.1 noun sing neu
πλήρωμα
plērōma
fulness

3631.1 conj
οὖν
oun
therefore

3414.2 noun gen sing masc
νόμου
nomou
of law

3450.9 art nom sing fem
ἡ
hē
the

26.1 noun nom sing fem
ἀγάπη.
agapē
love.

2504.1 conj
11. Καὶ
Kai
Also

3642.17 dem-pron sing neu
τοῦτο,
touto
this,

3471.20 verb nom pl masc part perf act
εἰδότες
eidotes
knowing

3450.6 art acc sing masc
τὸν
ton
the

2511.4 noun acc sing masc
καιρόν,
kairon
time,

3617.1 conj
ὅτι
hoti
that

5443.2 noun nom sing fem
ὥρα
hōra
hour

2231.4 prs-pron acc 1pl
⌐ ἡμᾶς
hēmas
we

Verse 8 brings a transition, broadening the scope from our relationship to the state to our relationship to all people. Not only are we to render to rulers their just dues, we also are to pay our debts to all. This is in the imperative mood; it is our Lord's command.

This does not necessarily mean that credit is always a sin. For example, a person buying a home with a plan for paying off a mortgage does not "owe a debt" as long as he makes payments on time. The collateral of the home itself covers the lender so that neither the buyer nor the creditor is at loss. This principle should be followed in all purchases involving any credit. A believer is wise to use credit very sparingly, if at all.

Financial obligations can be paid, but there is another obligation that can never be fully paid—the debt to love one another. If a Christian loves his neighbor as he loves himself, he will take as much care of his neighbor's interests, his property, his good name, as he would of his own. He will never do anything to harm him and will thus fulfill God's law and man's law.

To say that love fulfills the Law does not mean that love displaces law. Love is a higher motive than law, but it is law that love fulfills. Love, as defined by the Bible, will never cause a person to break any of God's laws nor to influence anyone else to do so. Jesus said that if we love Him we will keep His commandments (John 14:15).

The love described here is supernatural, given by the Holy Spirit (5:5). It is the love of God manifested in and through His children.

13:9,10. When a person becomes a child of God he comes under the influence of the law of love, and that law inspires the love of law. If a person tries to pay the debt of love, he will instinctively keep the commandments.

God gave Moses two tables of commandments. One concerns man's relationship to God, the other man's duty and attitude toward his fellowman. Paul stated that the last five are summed up in this law, "Thou shalt love thy neighbor as thyself."

A person who truly loves will not commit adultery. If two people allow physical passions to entice them to sin, it is not because they love each other too much, but because they love each other too little. In true love there is respect and restraint. One who truly loves will never murder, for love never seeks to destroy; it is always kind, even to an enemy. One who truly loves will never steal, for love is more concerned with giving than getting. One who truly loves will not covet, for to covet is to desire that which is forbidden. God's love removes all such unholy desires.

Love works no ill. If a person's heart and life is controlled by love, he will need no other law.

13:11. The imminence of the Lord's return was a message used by the apostles to urge people to live holy lives. Considering the nearness of eternity, Christians should fulfill every duty. Paul em-

for he that loveth another: ... that loveth his neighbour, *Douay.*

hath fulfilled the law: ... has perfectly satisfied, *Williams* ... has fully performed the law, *Sawyer* ... has already completed the law, *Klingensmith.*

9. For this: For, take the prohibitions, *Way.*

Thou shalt not commit adultery:

Thou shalt not kill: Thou shall not murder, *ET.*

Thou shalt not steal, Thou shalt not bear false witness:

Thou shalt not covet: ... don't be greedy, *Beck* ... thou shalt not lust, *Cranmer* ... do not desire what belongs to someone else, *TEV.*

and if [there be] any other commandment: ... any other precept, *Concordant.*

it is briefly comprehended in this saying, namely: ... it all heads up in one word, *Berkeley* ... are summed up in this one command, *Weymouth* ... are gathered up in this word, *HistNT* ... it in short is comprehended in this, *Locke* ... it is comprised in this word, *Rheims* ... in this one injunction, *Way.*

Thou shalt love thy neighbour as thyself: ... thy fellow man as much as thou lovest thyself, *Weymouth.*

10. Love worketh no ill to his neighbour: Love is the one thing that cannot hurt your neighbor, *JB* ... works no evil, *Campbell* ... can perpetrate no wrong, *Way* ... permits us to do no harm to our neighbour, *Locke.*

therefore love [is] the fulfilling of the law: ... so love meets all the Law's requirements, *Berkeley* ... and is therefore complete obedience to Law, *Weymouth* ... so love is the perfect satisfaction, *Williams.*

11. And that, knowing the time: What I have said is the more urgent, *TCNT* ... knowing the strategic season, *Wuest* ... the critical period at which we are living, *Weymouth* ... if you recognise the imminence of a great crisis, *Way.*

Romans 13:12

11.a.Txt: 01‭א‬-corr,06D
020L,byz.sa.
Var: 01‭א‬-org,02A,03B
04C,025P,bo.Alf,Tisc
We/Ho,Weis,Sod
UBS/✶

2218.1 adv	2218.1 adv	5050.4 prs-pron acc 2pl	1523.1 prep gen	5096.1 noun gen sing masc	1446.27 verb inf aor pass
ἤδη	[ᵃ✶ ἤδη	ὑμᾶς]	ἐξ	ὕπνου	ἐγερθῆναι·
ēdē	ēdē	humas	ex	hupnou	egerthēnai
already	[already	you]	out of	sleep	to be awoke;

3431.1 adv	1056.1 conj	1445.2 adv comp	2231.2 prs-pron gen 1pl	3450.9 art nom sing fem	4843.1 noun nom sing fem	2211.1 conj
νῦν	γὰρ	ἐγγύτερον	ἡμῶν	ἡ	σωτηρία,	ἢ
nun	gar	enguteron	hēmōn	hē	sōtēria	ē
now	for	nearer	our	the	salvation,	than

3616.1 conj	3961.21 verb 1pl indic aor act	3450.9 art nom sing fem	3433.1 noun nom sing fem	4157.1 verb 3sing indic aor act
ὅτε	ἐπιστεύσαμεν.	12. ἡ	νὺξ	προέκοψεν,
hote	episteusamen	hē	nux	proekopsen
when	we believed.	The	night	is advanced,

3450.9 art nom sing fem	1156.2 conj	2232.2 noun nom sing fem	1443.15 verb 3sing indic perf act	653.2 verb 1pl subj aor mid
ἡ	δὲ	ἡμέρα	ἤγγικεν.	ἀποθώμεθα
hē	de	hēmera	ēngiken	apothōmetha
the	and	day	has drawn near;	we should cast off

3631.1 conj	3450.17 art pl neu	2024.4 noun pl neu	3450.2 art gen sing	4510.3 noun gen sing neu	2504.1 conj
οὖν	τὰ	ἔργα	τοῦ	σκότους,	⸂ καὶ
oun	ta	erga	tou	skotous	kai
therefore	the	works	of the	darkness,	and

12.a.Txt: 01‭א‬-corr
04C-corr,06D-corr,020L
byz.
Var: 02A,03B,04C-org
06D-org,025P,bo.Lach
Treg,Alf,Word,Tisc
We/Ho,Weis,Sod
UBS/✶

1730.6 verb 1pl subj aor mid	1730.6 verb 1pl subj aor mid	1156.2 conj	3450.17 art pl neu	3559.1 noun pl neu
ἐνδυσώμεθα	[ᵃ✶ ἐνδυσώμεθα	δὲ]	τὰ	ὅπλα
endusōmetha	endusōmetha	de	ta	hopla
should put on	[should put on	and]	the	armor

3450.2 art gen sing	5295.2 noun gen sing neu	5453.1 conj	1706.1 prep	2232.3 noun dat sing fem	2137.1 adv
τοῦ	φωτός.	13. ὡς	ἐν	ἡμέρα,	εὐσχημόνως
tou	phōtos	hōs	en	hēmera	euschēmonōs
of the	light.	As	in	day,	becomingly

3906.21 verb 1pl subj aor act	3231.1 partic	2943.2 noun dat pl masc	2504.1 conj	3149.3 noun dat pl fem	3231.1 partic
περιπατήσωμεν,	μὴ	κώμοις	καὶ	μέθαις,	μὴ
peripatēsōmen	mē	kōmois	kai	methais	mē
we should walk;	not	in orgies	and	drunkenness,	not

2818.3 noun dat pl fem	2504.1 conj	760.4 noun dat pl fem	3231.1 partic	2038.3 noun dat sing fem	2504.1 conj
κοίταις	καὶ	ἀσελγείαις,	μὴ	ἔριδι	καὶ
koitais	kai	aselgeiais	mē	eridi	kai
sexual misconduct	and	wantonness,	not	in rivalry	and

2188.3 noun dat sing neu	233.1 conj	233.2 conj	1730.8 verb 2pl impr aor mid	3450.6 art acc sing masc
ζήλῳ·	14. ⸂ ἀλλ'	[✶ ἀλλὰ]	ἐνδύσασθε	τὸν
zēlō	all'	alla	endusasthe	ton
jealousy.	But	[idem]	put on	the

2935.4 noun acc sing masc	2400.3 name acc masc	5382.4 name acc masc	2504.1 conj	3450.10 art gen sing fem	4418.2 noun gen sing fem
κύριον	Ἰησοῦν	Χριστόν,	καὶ	τῆς	σαρκὸς
kurion	Iēsoun	Christon	kai	tēs	sarkos
Lord	Jesus	Christ,	and	of the	flesh

phasized the need for believers to do everything in the light of the uncertainty of life and the certainty of eternity. He underscored the tendency to slumber and sleep. To "sleep" indicates unconcern. Being "awake" implies spiritual readiness. The reference is to salvation as the consummation of God's final redemptive act.

13:12. The last four verses of this chapter list eight commands for Christians: (1) cast off the works of darkness; (2) put on the armor of light; (3) live honorably; (4) stop rioting and drinking; (5) shun all immoral living; (6) refrain from quarrels, contentions, jealousies; (7) clothe one's self with the character of Jesus Christ; (8) make no provision for lust. These verses are a call to holiness.

The "night" symbolizes a time of great spiritual darkness, a time when planet Earth is beset with the darkness of sin, evil, war, hunger, and suffering. The "day" pictures the coming of Christ as the "Sun of righteousness (who shall) arise with healing in his wings" (Malachi 4:2).

It is time to "cast off the works of darkness" as one would shed an unclean garment. All wicked ways and acts are to be thrown off. The antithesis between light and darkness is found repeatedly in Paul's epistles (2 Corinthians 6:14; Ephesians 5:8; Colossians 1:12, 13; 1 Thessalonians 5:4,5).

It is time to "put on the armor of light." "Armor" is *hopla*, meaning weapons. "Put on" is from *endunō* meaning to put on or clothe as with a garment. By prayer, self-discipline, reading and studying God's Word, we put on holy character, so that people can recognize us as belonging to Christ. The "armor of light" is listed in Ephesians 6:11-17.

13:13. *Peripateō* which means "walk" or literally "walk around" is also rendered "behave," "live," "conduct ourselves."

Euschēmonōs means "becomingly" or "decorously" and is so rendered in several translations. *Kōmos*, meaning "revelry," was a riotous procession at night of half-drunken carousers who made themselves a nuisance; *methē*, "drunkenness," was particularly disgraceful to the Greeks. *Koitē*, rendered "chambering," was sexual immorality. *Aselgeia*, "wantonness," described more than immorality. It was unbridled and shameless. *Eris*, contention, "strife," results from placing self first. *Zēlos*, "envy," means a contentious and jealous rivalry.

13:14. The believer is to "put on the Lord Jesus Christ." This is first done at regeneration and is to be a daily experience (Titus 3:5). This is a walk in the Spirit (8:2). There must be no provision for either gross appetites or refined carnal attitudes; all must be denied.

that now [it is] high time to awake out of sleep: ... because the hour has struck for us to wake up, *Berkeley* ... it is now the hour for us to rise, *Douay*.

for now [is] our salvation nearer than when we believed: Our Great Deliverance, *Way* ... we are now nearer being rescued, *Beck* ... than when you first entered into the profession of Christianity, *Locke*.

12. The night is far spent: The night is far gone, *Norlie* ... The night is passed, *Rheims, Douay*.

the day is at hand: ... and dawn is at hand, *Norlie* ... the day is drawing near, *Scarlett*.

let us therefore cast off the works of darkness: ... cast away the dedes of darkenes, *Geneva*.

and let us put on the armour of light: ... put on the weapons of light, *Adams*.

13. Let us walk honestly: Let us live nobly, *Beck* ... behave ourselves with propriety, *HistNT* ... walk decently, *Wesley* ... walk becomingly, *Sawyer, Confraternity* ... walk seemly, *Alford*.

as in the day: ... that is appropriate to the daytime, *Adams* ... in broad daylight, *Weymouth*.

not in rioting and drunkenness: Let us not carry on in carousing, *Norlie* ... not indulging in revelry, *Weymouth* ... not in glotonie, *Geneva* ... and drunken entertainments, *Wesley*.

not in chambering: ... not in prostitution, *Berkeley* ... nor in lust, *Weymouth* ... not in sexual orgies, *Adams* ... with no lewd or any sensual acts, *HistNT*.

and wantonness: ... or living wild, *Beck* ... debauchery, *Weymouth* ... a dissolute abandon, *Wuest* ... excesses, *Sawyer* ... licentiousness, *PNT*.

not in strife and envying: ... in quarreling, *RSV* ... in contention and emulation, *Rheims* ... strife and jealousy, *ASV*.

14. But put ye on the Lord Jesus Christ: But clothe yourselves, *Montgomery* ... be enveloped with, *Berkeley* ... put on the character of the Lord Jesus, *Moffatt*.

209

Romans 14:1

4166.2 noun acc sing fem	3231.1 partic	4020.63 verb 2pl impr pres mid	1519.1 prep	1924.1 noun fem	3450.6 art acc sing masc
πρόνοιαν	μὴ	ποιεῖσθε	εἰς	ἐπιθυμίας.	14:1. Τὸν
pronoian	mē	poieisthe	eis	epithumias	Ton
forethought	not	do take	for	desire.	The

1156.2 conj	764.7 verb acc sing masc part pres act	3450.11 art dat sing fem	3963.3 noun dat sing fem	4213.2 verb 2pl impr pres mid
δὲ	ἀσθενοῦντα	τῇ	πίστει	προσλαμβάνεσθε,
de	asthenounta	tē	pistei	proslambanesthe
but	being weak	in the	faith	receive

3231.1 partic	1519.1 prep	1247.2 noun pl fem	1255.5 noun gen pl masc	3614.5 rel-pron nom sing masc	3173.1 conj
μὴ	εἰς	διακρίσεις	διαλογισμῶν.	2. Ὃς	μὲν
mē	eis	diakriseis	dialogismōn	Hos	men
not	for	decisions	of reasonings.	Who	men

3961.6 verb 3sing indic pres act	2052.25 verb inf aor act	3820.1 adj	3450.5 art sing masc	1156.2 conj
πιστεύει	φαγεῖν	πάντα,	ὁ	δὲ
pisteuei	phagein	panta	ho	de
believes	to eat	all things;	the	but

764.6 verb nom sing masc part pres act	2974.3 noun acc pl neu	2052.2 verb 3sing indic pres act	3450.5 art sing masc	2052.8 verb nom sing masc part pres act
ἀσθενῶν	λάχανα	ἐσθίει.	3. ὁ	ἐσθίων,
asthenōn	lachana	esthiei	ho	esthiōn
being weak	vegetables	eats.	The	eating,

3450.6 art acc sing masc	3231.1 partic	2052.10 verb acc sing masc part pres act	3231.1 partic	1832.2 verb 3sing impr pres act	2504.1 conj
τὸν	μὴ	ἐσθίοντα	μὴ	ἐξουθενείτω·	⸂ καὶ
ton	mē	esthionta	mē	exoutheneitō	kai
the	not	eating	not	let him despise;	and

3450.5 art sing masc	3450.5 art sing masc	1156.2 conj	3231.1 partic	2052.8 verb nom sing masc part pres act	3450.6 art acc sing masc
ὁ	[a✶ ὁ	δὲ]	μὴ	ἐσθίων,	τὸν
ho	[ho	de]	mē	esthiōn	ton
the	[the	and]	not	eating,	the

2052.10 verb acc sing masc part pres act	3231.1 partic	2892.7 verb 3sing impr pres act	3450.5 art sing masc	2296.1 noun nom sing masc	1056.1 conj
ἐσθίοντα	μὴ	κρινέτω·	ὁ	θεὸς	γὰρ
esthionta	mē	krinetō	ho	theos	gar
eating	not	let him judge:	the	God	for

840.6 prs-pron acc sing masc	4213.3 verb 3sing indic aor mid	4622.1 prs-pron nom 2sing	4949.3 intr-pron nom sing	1498.3 verb 2sing indic pres act
αὐτὸν	προσελάβετο.	4. σὺ	τίς	εἶ
auton	proselabeto	su	tis	ei
him	received.	You	who	are

3450.5 art sing masc	2892.8 verb sing masc part pres act	243.2 adj acc sing masc	3473.3 noun acc sing masc	3450.3 art dat sing	2375.3 adj dat sing
ὁ	κρίνων	ἀλλότριον	οἰκέτην;	τῷ	ἰδίῳ
ho	krinōn	allotrion	oiketēn	tō	idiō
the	judging	another's	servant?	the	his own

2935.3 noun dat sing masc	4590.2 verb 3sing indic pres act	2211.1 conj	3959.1 verb 3sing indic pres act	2449.47 verb 3sing indic fut pass
κυρίῳ	στήκει	ἢ	πίπτει.	σταθήσεται
kuriō	stēkei	ē	piptei	stathēsetai
master	he stands	or	falls.	He shall be made to stand

14:1. This chapter comes to grips with the problems related to balancing two spiritual laws. The law of liberty permits a Christian to do certain things which may be perfectly lawful but may raise a question in the minds of others. The law of love motivates the Christian to readily sacrifice his liberty rather than to cause the other brother to stumble.

Christians are free from sin and bondage, but not from spiritual obligations. We have liberty, but not license, for none of us are free to live as we please without regard to others.

The Spirit was instructing the church not to discriminate against those who had conscientious scruples regarding things considered nonessentials by the more mature believers.

It is difficult to know the exact meaning of "doubtful disputations" (*diakriseis dialogismōn*, literally "judgment of thoughts"). It seems that God, who alone sees the heart, was telling the stronger not to subject the convictions of the weaker to censorious scrutiny.

14:2-4. There are certain essentials upon which all followers of Christ must agree, such as the inspiration and infallibility of the Bible, the deity of Christ, the Virgin Birth, the necessity of the vicarious sacrifice, the new birth, and many others. There are, however, matters over which Christians may disagree but are not essential to salvation. These are not the great questions of doctrine, nor are they questions of spirituality or morality; they are the smaller details which arise from day to day. In chapter 13 Paul condemned those things which are immoral, but in chapter 14 he warned against the dangers of being too severe in questionable matters that are not contrary to scriptural principles.

Verse 4 shows the danger of judging a brother in the area of his conscience. This does not eliminate all judging. Speaking to Pharisees, Jesus said, "Judge not" (Matthew 7:1), but in the same sermon He said, "By their fruits ye shall know them" (Matthew 7:20).

Paul, no doubt, was writing on this matter because of a problem in the church at Rome. Some of the Christians, whom he called "weak" brethren, were in bondage to regulations concerning food and holy days. Some Gentile Christians, influenced by pagan customs, believed in abstaining from meats (1 Timothy 4:3). Another group influenced by Judaism, felt it was sinful to eat food forbidden by Mosaic law. One group, the vegetarians, felt the meat eaters were backslidden, while the other group even thought of excluding the vegetarians from fellowship.

Romans 14 and 1 Corinthians 8 are devoted to a burning question in the Apostolic Church. Large quantities of meat were brought to the heathen temples for idol worship. What the priest could not consume was sold to the public in the marketplace. Since it was almost impossible to know if the meat purchased at the market had come from an idol's temple, the weaker brethren found themselves unable to eat *any* meat for fear it might have been offered unto an idol (1 Corinthians 8:7). Therefore, to avoid defiling their conscience they confined their diet to vegetables.

and make not provision for the flesh, to [fulfil] the lusts [thereof]: ... and take no forethought, *Alford* ... don't make plans to satisfy, *Adams* ... never think how to gratify the cravings of the flesh, *Moffatt* ... to gratify the irregular desires of, *Scarlett* ... for the indulgence of appetites, *Murdock.*

1. Him that is weak in the faith receive ye: ... who is feeble ...reach forth the hand, *Murdock* ... receive into full Christian fellowship, *Williams* ... be giving a cordial welcome, *Wuest.*
[but] not to doubtful disputations: ... and not just to argue about different opinions, *Beck* ... about his personal opinions, *TEV* ... not for mutual judgings of opinions, *PNT* ... without regard to differences of opinions, *Campbell* ... yet not for decisions of scruples, *Worrell.*

2. For one believeth that he may eat all things: ... allows him to eat anything, *Weymouth* ... has confidence, *Wuest.*
another, who is weak, eateth herbs: ... yet the infirm one is eating greens, *Concordant* ... lives upon vegetables, *Scarlett.*

3. Let not him that eateth despise him that eateth not: ... despise the vegetarian, *Norlie* ... should not feel contempt for the abstainer, *Berkeley* ... belittle the one who does not eat, *Klingensmith.*
and let not him which eateth not:
judge him that eateth: ... must not criticize, *Moffatt* ... condemn him who eats, *Hanson* ... censure the eater, *Berkeley.*
for God hath received him: ... has fully accepted, *Williams.*

4. Who art thou that judgest another man's servant?: ... condemnest another's household servant? *Macknight.*
to his own master he standeth or falleth: ... own personal master, *Wuest* ... own lord, *Worrell.*
Yea, he shall be holden up: Yea, he shall be made to stand, *Panin.*

Romans 14:5

1156.2 conj	1409.1 adj nom sing masc	1056.1 conj	1498.4 verb 3sing indic pres act	3450.5 art sing masc	2296.1 noun nom sing masc
δέ·	ʹ δυνατὸς	γὰϱ	ἐστιν	ὁ	Θεὸς
de	dunatos	gar	estin	ho	Theos
and;	able	for	is		God

1408.1 verb 3sing indic pres act	1056.1 conj	3450.5 art sing masc	2935.1 noun nom sing masc	2449.15 verb inf aor act	840.6 prs-pron acc sing masc
[ᵃ☆ δυνατεῖ	γὰϱ	ὁ	κύϱιος]	στῆσαι	αὐτόν.
dunatei	gar	ho	kurios	stēsai	auton
[able	for	the	Lord]	to make stand	him.

4.a.Txt: 020L,byz.
Var: 01א,02A,03B,04C
06D-org,Lach,Treg,Alf
Tisc,We/Ho,Weis,Sod
UBS/☆

5.a.Var: 01א-org,02A
04C-corr,025P,it.bo.
Lach,Tisc,We/Ho,Sod
UBS/☆

3614.5 rel-pron nom sing masc	3173.1 conj	1056.1 conj	2892.5 verb 3sing indic pres act	2232.4 noun acc sing fem	3706.1 prep
5. Ὃς	μὲν	[ᵃ☆+ γὰϱ]	κϱίνει	ἡμέϱαν	παϱ'
Hos	men	gar	krinei	hēmeran	par'
Who	men	[for]	judges	a day	above

2232.4 noun acc sing fem	3614.5 rel-pron nom sing masc	1156.2 conj	2892.5 verb 3sing indic pres act	3820.12 adj acc sing fem	2232.4 noun acc sing fem
ἡμέϱαν,	ὃς	δὲ	κϱίνει	πᾶσαν	ἡμέϱαν.
hēmeran	hos	de	krinei	pasan	hēmeran
a day;	who	but	judges	every	day.

1524.3 adj nom sing masc	1706.1 prep	3450.3 art dat sing	2375.3 adj dat sing	3426.3 noun dat sing masc	3995.2 verb 3sing impr pres pass
ἕκαστος	ἐν	τῷ	ἰδίῳ	νοῖ	πληϱοφοϱείσθω.
hekastos	en	tō	idiō	noi	plērophoreisthō
Each	in	the	his own	mind	let be fully assured.

3450.5 art sing masc	5262.7 verb nom sing masc part pres act	3450.12 art acc sing fem	2232.4 noun acc sing fem	2935.3 noun dat sing masc
6. ὁ	φϱονῶν	τὴν	ἡμέϱαν,	κυϱίῳ
ho	phronōn	tēn	hēmeran	kuriō
The	regarding	the	day,	to Lord

6.a.Txt: 04C-corr,020L
025P,byz.Sod
Var: 01א,02A,03B
04C-org,06D,bo.Lach
Treg,Tisc,We/Ho,Weis
UBS/☆

6.b.Var: 01א,02A,03B
04C,06D,020L,025P,bo.
Gries,Lach,Treg,Alf
Word,Tisc,We/Ho,Weis
Sod,UBS/☆

5262.3 verb 3sing indic pres act	2504.1 conj	3450.5 art sing masc	3231.1 partic	5262.7 verb nom sing masc part pres act	3450.12 art acc sing fem
φϱονεῖ·	ʹᵃ καὶ	ὁ	μὴ	φϱονῶν	τὴν
phronei	kai	ho	mē	phronōn	tēn
regards;	and	the	not	regarding	the

2232.4 noun acc sing fem	2935.3 noun dat sing masc	3620.3 partic	5262.3 verb 3sing indic pres act	2504.1 conj
ἡμέϱαν,	κυϱίῳ	οὐ	φϱονεῖ. ʹ	[ᵇ☆+ καὶ]
hēmeran	kuriō	ou	phronei	kai
day,	to Lord	not	regards.	[and]

3450.5 art sing masc	2052.8 verb nom sing masc part pres act	2935.3 noun dat sing masc	2052.2 verb 3sing indic pres act	2149.3 verb 3sing indic pres act
ὁ	ἐσθίων,	κυϱίῳ	ἐσθίει,	εὐχαϱιστεῖ
ho	esthiōn	kuriō	esthiei	eucharistei
The	eating,	to Lord	eats,	he gives thanks

1056.1 conj	3450.3 art dat sing	2296.3 noun dat sing masc	2504.1 conj	3450.5 art sing masc	3231.1 partic	2052.8 verb nom sing masc part pres act
γὰϱ	τῷ	θεῷ·	καὶ	ὁ	μὴ	ἐσθίων,
gar	tō	theō	kai	ho	mē	esthiōn
for	to	to God;	and	the	not	eating,

2935.3 noun dat sing masc	3620.2 partic	2052.2 verb 3sing indic pres act	2504.1 conj	2149.3 verb 3sing indic pres act	3450.3 art dat sing
κυϱίῳ	οὐκ	ἐσθίει,	καὶ	εὐχαϱιστεῖ	τῷ
kuriō	ouk	esthiei	kai	eucharistei	tō
to Lord	not	he eats,	and	gives thanks	to

Notice how Paul dealt with the problem. He did not put the strong in bondage, nor did he remove the scruples of the weak. Instead, he laid down principles which made it possible for both to live in peace with each other. These same principles are applicable today in matters between God's saints. As long as fundamental matters are not involved, Christians should live with harmonious consideration of each other. Paul warned believers neither to despise nor to judge another "for God hath received him," and he will stand or fall before the Lord whose servant he is.

14:5. Another problem was that of the observance of days. The Christian's Sunday is not a Sabbath in the sense of the old covenant Sabbath. The first day of the week was set apart by the resurrection of our Lord Jesus. On that day He appeared to His disciples. The Christians broke bread on that day (Acts 20:7), and on that day they brought their offerings to the Lord (1 Corinthians 16:2). The first day of the week is the Lord's Day. We are not told exactly how to keep the day, but it is to be observed in worship as a special day.

Regarding things not specifically regulated, Paul stated, "Let every man be persuaded in his own mind."

This chapter is often entitled "Questionable Things." Another term that perhaps best describes food and days is *neutral*. A neutral thing is anything that in itself is neither good nor bad; it can be used for either good or for bad. Along with food and days we could mention many things, such as money and houses. The list could be very lengthy.

14:6. Frequently a great deal of unbrotherliness has been generated in the Christian community by assuming judgmental attitudes concerning those who differ with us on some of the implications of the Christian life. The end product is a feeling of hostility and a breach of fellowship which is sometimes far worse from a Christian standpoint than the conduct being condemned. There comes a point at which we must leave the judgment of someone else's behavior up to the Lord.

At times, when we are wearied with controversy, we wish it were possible for all persons to be in agreement. To think that is to assume an impossibility. There will always be the stimulus of conflicting opinions. But we must learn to disagree without being disagreeable. There must be no compromise on doctrine, no concessions concerning truth, but there will be some give-and-take in the area of opinions.

Church members of Jewish background among the Romans and Corinthians tended to cling to the seventh day of the week for worship purposes. This viewpoint was in conflict with the trend toward observing the first day of the week. Opponents of this viewpoint apparently said that those who really wanted to honor the Lord would honor Him every day. The same conflict existed regarding eating meat which may have been dedicated to an idol.

for God is able to make him stand: . . . for the Master is able to make him stand, *Klingensmith* . . . is able to set him up, *Conybeare* . . . He will succeed, *ET* . . . he will assuredly stand, *Murdock.*

5. One man esteemeth one day above another: . . . decides for the superior sacredness, *Way* . . . discriminateth between days, *Murdock* . . . as holier than others, *JB* . . . some make one day more sacred than another, *ET* . . . as better than another, *RSV.*

another esteemeth every day [alike]: . . . another man counteth all dayes, *Geneva* . . . rates all days alike, *Berkeley* . . . subjects every day to a scrutiny, *Wuest* . . . another makes every day holy, *ET.*

Let every man be fully persuaded in his own mind: Let every one be convinced, *Macknight* . . . should firmly make up his own mind, *TEV* . . . know what he believes, *ET* . . . be fully assured, *Wuest.*

6. He that regardeth the day: . . . who observes the day, *Hanson* . . . that observes the day, *Sawyer* . . . he who reverences a day, *ET* . . . obserueth one day, more than another, *Geneva.*

regardeth [it] unto the Lord: . . . reverences it to the Lord, *ET* . . . does so in the Lord's service, *Way* . . . should observe it in the Lord's honor, *Norlie* . . . observes it with the Lord in view, *Berkeley* . . . means to honor the Lord, *Beck* . . . to the Master's honour, *TCNT.*

and he that regardeth not the day, to the Lord he doth not regard [it]: He that is not concerned about a day, *ET.*

He that eateth, eateth to the Lord: So also the non-abstainer eats, *Way.*

for he giveth God thanks:

and he that eateth not, to the Lord he eateth not: . . . refrains for the Lord's sake, *Berkeley* . . . he who abstains, *Montgomery* . . . abstains to the Lord, *Moffatt* . . . is doing it as unto the Lord, *ET* . . . abstains for the Lord, *Confraternity.*

and giveth God thanks: . . . since he, too, gives God thanks, *Montgomery.*

213

Romans 14:7

2296.3 noun dat sing masc	3625.2 num card nom masc	1056.1 conj	2231.2 prs- pron gen 1pl	1431.5 prs-pron dat 3sing masc	2180.1 verb sing indic pres
θεῷ.	7. οὐδεὶς	γὰρ	ἡμῶν	ἑαυτῷ	ζῇ,
theō	oudeis	gar	hēmōn	heautō	zē
to God.	No one	for	of us	to himself	lives,

2504.1 conj	3625.2 num card nom masc	1431.5 prs-pron dat 3sing masc	594.2 verb 3sing indic pres act	1430.1 partic	4885.1 conj
καὶ	οὐδεὶς	ἑαυτῷ	ἀποθνήσκει.	8. ἐάν	τε
kai	oudeis	heautō	apothnēskei	ean	te
and	no one	to himself	dies.	If	both

1056.1 conj	2180.3 verb 1pl pres act	3450.3 art dat sing	2935.3 noun dat sing masc	2180.3 verb 1pl pres act	1430.1 partic
γὰρ	ζῶμεν,	τῷ	κυρίῳ	ζῶμεν·	ἐάν
gar	zōmen	tō	kuriō	zōmen	ean
for	we should live,	to the	Lord	we should live;	if

4885.1 conj	594.5 verb 1pl subj pres act	3450.3 art dat sing	2935.3 noun dat sing masc	594.3 verb 1pl indic pres act	
τε	ἀποθνήσκωμεν,	τῷ	κυρίῳ	ἀποθνήσκομεν.	
te	apothnēskōmen	tō	kuriō	apothnēskomen	
and	we should die,	to the	Lord	we die:	

1430.1 partic	4885.1 conj	3631.1 conj	2180.3 verb 1pl pres act	1430.1 partic	4885.1 conj	594.5 verb 1pl subj pres act
ἐάν	τε	οὖν	ζῶμεν,	ἐάν	τε	ἀποθνήσκωμεν,
ean	te	oun	zōmen	ean	te	apothnēskōmen
if	both	then	we should live,	if	and	we should die,

3450.2 art gen sing	2935.2 noun gen sing masc	1498.5 verb 1pl indic pres act	1519.1 prep	3642.17 dem- pron sing neu	1056.1 conj	5382.1 name nom masc
τοῦ	κυρίου	ἐσμέν.	9. εἰς	τοῦτο	γὰρ	Χριστὸς
tou	kuriou	esmen	eis	touto	gar	Christos
the	Lord's	we are.	For	this	for	Christ

2504.1 conj	594.10 verb 3sing indic aor act	2504.1 conj	448.2 verb 3sing indic aor act	2504.1 conj	324.1 verb 3sing indic aor act
⌐a καὶ ⌐	ἀπέθανεν	καὶ	⌐ ἀνέστη	καὶ	ἀνέζησεν,
kai	apethanen	kai	anestē	kai	anezēsen
both	died	and	rose	and	lived again,

2180.21 verb 3sing indic aor act	2419.1 conj	2504.1 conj	3361.2 adj gen pl	2504.1 conj	2180.14 verb gen pl masc part pres act
[b✶ ἔζησεν]	ἵνα	καὶ	νεκρῶν	καὶ	ζώντων
ezēsen	hina	kai	nekrōn	kai	zōntōn
[lived]	that	both	dead	and	living

2934.5 verb 3sing subj aor act	4622.1 prs- pron nom 2sing	1156.2 conj	4949.9 intr- pron sing neu	2892.4 verb 2sing indic pres act
κυριεύσῃ.	10. Σὺ	δὲ	τί	κρίνεις
kurieusē	Su	de	ti	krineis
he might rule over.	You	but	why	judge you

3450.6 art acc sing masc	79.4 noun acc sing masc	4622.2 prs- pron gen 2sing	2211.1 conj	2504.1 conj	4622.1 prs- pron nom 2sing
τὸν	ἀδελφόν	σου;	ἢ	καὶ	σὺ
ton	adelphon	sou	ē	kai	su
the	brother	your?	or	also	you

4949.9 intr- pron sing neu	1832.1 verb 2sing indic pres act	3450.6 art acc sing masc	79.4 noun acc sing masc	4622.2 prs- pron gen 2sing
τί	ἐξουθενεῖς	τὸν	ἀδελφόν	σου;
ti	exoutheneis	ton	adelphon	sou
why	do you despise	the	brother	your?

9.a.**Txt:** 01א-corr
06D-corr,020L,byz.
Var: 01א-org,02A,03B
04C,06D-org,025P,bo.
Lach,Treg,Alf,Word
Tisc,We/Ho,Weis,Sod
UBS/✶

9.b.**Txt:** (01א-corr)
(06D-corr),(020L),(025P)
33,byz.
Var: 01א-org,02A,03B
04C,sa.bo.Gries,Lach
Treg,Alf,Word,Tisc
We/Ho,Weis,UBS/✶

14:7,8. In verse 5 Paul stated, "Let every man be fully persuaded in his own mind." Over against that we have this verse which indicates that there is not one whose life or death concerns himself alone. It is impossible to live in isolation. One cannot disentangle himself either from his fellowmen or from God. For this reason, among others, no one can make his own practice the universal standard. It is well to remember that believers have a right to have their own convictions, but they also have the duty to allow others to have theirs without regarding them as sinners.

Personal conviction is important. Christian life-style should not be governed by convention or by semisuperstitious taboos, but by a prayerfully and carefully thought-out conviction as to what is right and what is wrong.

There must be room for toleration and liberty of conscience. Extremes infect a man's thoughts and actions. Differences of opinions must not divide brethren. Each should treat the other in love, and avoid condemning another, for the Lord has received all believers into His divine favor.

Note that the questionable things under consideration are in themselves totally neutral. Jesus made clear that it is not food that defiles a man but rather those things that proceed out of his mouth, from his heart (Matthew 15:17-20). Food can, however, be used in a sinful way; this was true under the Law, and it is true now.

To eat something one knows to be harmful to the body is wrong (1 Corinthians 6:19; 10:31). Gluttony is condemned in the same way alcoholism is (Proverbs 23:21; Galatians 5:21). Jesus was called by His enemies a glutton and winebibber because He ate with sinners, but that was a false charge like many others made against Him. He never did anything that was in any way sinful.

Any neutral thing can be used in a sinful way. The motive is what God judges (1 Corinthians 4:5). Money can be used for good (Luke 16:9) or for evil (1 Timothy 6:10). A musical instrument can also be used for God or for Satan. Lyrics of songs are not neutral; they communicate meaning which always says something either conducive to godly living or to sinful living. Many believe that the same is true of music itself; there can be no doubt that some music communicates an evil message.

14:9. The Lord's will and His glory are always to be in view, in life and in death. Jesus died to redeem us and rose from the grave to reign. As the dying Christ, He saved us; as the living Christ, He regulates our daily walk. Christians should live in the shadows of the Cross by the power of the Resurrection. Whether liberty is enjoyed or scruples are adhered to, the Christian lives with Calvary in view and his life conditioned by the living Christ.

14:10. Paul declared that we must all stand before the Judgment Seat (*bēma*). God is the Judge, not we. Therefore we should leave the judging to Him.

7. For none of us liveth to himself: No man's life concerns only himself, *Barclay* . . . none of us can live alone by himself, *Williams* . . . as if he were his own man, *Locke* . . . lives for himself alone, *ET*.
and no man dieth to himself:

8. For whether we live: If we live, *ET*.
we live unto the Lord: In life we live for the Lord, *Barclay* . . . we always live in relation to the Lord, *Williams* . . . our life is appropriated to the Lord, *Locke*.
and whether we die: . . . or if we die, *ET*.
we die unto the Lord:
whether we live therefore, or die, we are the Lord's: In life and in death we belong to the Lord, *Barclay* . . . we belong to our Lord, *Montgomery*.

9. For to this end Christ both died, and rose, and revived: For this purpose, *Montgomery* . . . For this very reason, *NIV* . . . for because of this, *Young* . . . The very reason why Christ died and came to life again, *Barclay* . . . and continues alive, *Scarlett*.
that he might be Lord both of the dead and living: . . . to establish his lordship over dead and living, *NEB* . . . be lorde both of deed and quicke, *Tyndale* . . . that He might exercise lordship, *Wuest, Sawyer* . . . that he might rule over both, *Macknight*.

10. But why dost thou judge thy brother?: Then why should you criticize, *Williams* . . . Why do you pass judgment, *RSV* . . . as some of you have done, *JB* . . .
or why dost thou set at nought thy brother?: Why do you put down, *ET* . . . why do you look down on your brother? *Berkeley* . . . why do you look on your brother with contempt? *Adams* . . . why do you regard your brother with contempt? *Barclay* . . . why do you look down upon, *Weymouth* . . . why doest thou despyse thy brother? *Tyndale*.
for we shall all stand before the judgment seat of Christ: Surely, we shall all stand before God, *Williams* . . . seat of God, *Al-*

Romans 14:11

3820.7 adj pl masc	1056.1 conj	3798.22 verb 1pl indic fut mid	3450.3 art dat sing	961.2 noun dat sing neu
πάντες	γὰρ	παραστησόμεθα	τῷ	βήματι
pantes	gar	parastēsometha	tō	bēmati
All	for	we shall stand before	the	judgment seat

3450.2 art gen sing	5382.2 name gen masc	3450.2 art gen sing	2296.2 noun gen sing masc	1119.22 verb 3sing indic perf pass
ʼ τοῦ	Χριστοῦ·	[ᵃ☆ τοῦ	θεοῦ·]	11. γέγραπται
tou	Christou	tou	theou	gegraptai
of the	Christ.		[of God.]	It has been written

1056.1 conj	2180.5 verb 1sing indic pres act	1466.1 prs- pron nom 1sing	2978.5 verb 3sing indic pres act	2935.1 noun nom sing masc	3617.1 conj
γάρ,	Ζῶ	ἐγώ,	λέγει	κύριος·	ὅτι
gar	Zō	egō	legei	kurios	hoti
for,	Live	I,	says	Lord,	that

1466.5 prs- pron dat 1sing	2549.4 verb 3sing indic fut act	3820.17 adj sing neu	1113.1 noun sing neu	2504.1 conj	3820.9 adj nom sing fem
ἐμοὶ	κάμψει	πᾶν	γόνυ,	καὶ	πᾶσα
emoi	kampsei	pan	gonu	kai	pasa
to me	shall bow	every	knee,	and	every

1094.1 noun nom sing fem	1827.7 verb 3sing indic fut mid	3450.3 art dat sing	2296.3 noun dat sing masc	679.1 partic
γλῶσσα	ἐξομολογήσεται	τῷ	θεῷ.	12. Ἄρα
glōssa	exomologēsetai	tō	theō	Ara
tongue	shall confess		to God.	So

3631.1 conj	1524.3 adj nom sing masc	2231.2 prs- pron gen 1pl	3875.1 prep	1431.4 prs- pron gen 3sing	3030.4 noun acc sing masc
οὖν	ἕκαστος	ἡμῶν	περὶ	ἑαυτοῦ	λόγον
oun	hekastos	hēmōn	peri	heautou	logon
then	each	of us	concerning	himself	account

1319.38 verb 3sing indic fut act	3450.3 art dat sing	2296.3 noun dat sing masc	3239.1 adv	3631.1 conj
δώσει	ʼᵃ τῷ	θεῷ. ʼ	13. Μηκέτι	οὖν
dōsei	tō	theō	Mēketi	oun
shall give		to God.	No longer	therefore

238.3 prs-pron acc pl masc	2892.6 verb 1pl subj pres act	233.2 conj	3642.17 dem- pron sing neu	2892.16 verb 2pl impr aor act
ἀλλήλους	κρίνωμεν·	ἀλλὰ	τοῦτο	κρίνατε
allēlous	krinōmen	alla	touto	krinate
one another	should we judge;	but	this	judge you

3095.1 adv comp	3450.16 art sing neu	3231.1 partic	4935.7 verb inf pres act	4206.1 noun sing neu
μᾶλλον,	τὸ	μὴ	τιθέναι	πρόσκομμα
mallon	to	mē	tithenai	proskomma
rather,	the	not	to put	an occasion of stumbling

3450.3 art dat sing	79.3 noun dat sing masc	2211.1 conj	4480.1 noun sing neu	3471.2 verb 1sing indic perf act	2504.1 conj
τῷ	ἀδελφῷ	ἢ	σκάνδαλον.	14. οἶδα	καὶ
tō	adelphō	ē	skandalon	oida	kai
to the	brother	or	a cause of offense.	I know	and

3844.28 verb 1sing indic perf pass	1706.1 prep	2935.3 noun dat sing masc	2400.2 name masc	3617.1 conj	3625.6 num card neu
πέπεισμαι	ἐν	κυρίῳ	Ἰησοῦ,	ὅτι	οὐδὲν
pepeismai	en	kuriō	Iēsou	hoti	ouden
am persuaded	in	Lord	Jesus,	that	nothing

10.a.Txt: 01ℵ-corr
04C-corr,020L,025P
044,048,byz.
Var: 01ℵ-org,02A,03B
04C-org,06D,it.sa.bo.
Lach,Treg,Alf,Word
Tisc,We/Ho,Weis,Sod
UBS/☆

12.a.Txt: 01ℵ,02A,04C
06D,044,0209,byz.co.
Var: 03B,010F,012G,6
630,1739,1881

In the New Testament the word *bēma* refers to the judgment of believers for their works, in contrast to the Great White Throne Judgment where sinners will be judged. One can see the word today carved on the wall where Gallio sat on the judgment seat at Corinth (Acts 18:12,16,17). It is used of Pilate's judgment seat (Matthew 27:19), and also that of Festus (Acts 25:6,17). Here these governors passed judgment on offenders and exonerated the innocent. Paul lived his life with an awareness that he and all of us must stand before the great Judge of all. Little wonder that he sought always to have "a conscience void of offense toward God, and toward men" (Acts 24:16).

Only believers will be present; therefore the issue is not whether one is saved or not. It is rather that "every one may receive the things done in his body, . . . whether it be good or bad" (2 Corinthians 5:10).

God is very concerned about our stewardship with the gifts and opportunities He has given us. Jesus said He would come quickly to reward every believer according to his works. Works motivated by faith and love (Galatians 5:6) will prove to be gold, silver, and precious stones (1 Corinthians 3:12-15). Works done without *agapē* love as the motive will be burned, bringing loss of reward.

14:11,12. Every individual believer will answer; an individual inquiry will require individual responsibility. Let us not judge others, but rather let us keep our own house in order. Our personal liberty is to be enjoyed in the light of the presence of the Master of our lives and the certainty that each of us "shall give account of himself to God."

14:13,14. It has been said that those who are weak in faith live by conscience, those who are strong in faith by knowledge, but the more mature by love. The apostle chided those with a weak conscience, but in the fellowship of the Church, he put the burden for maintaining right relationship on the strong. If concessions had to be made, they must make them in a spirit of love. The weaker brethren were their solemn responsibility, and they must do nothing to offend their conscience or jeopardize their standing.

Paul's conclusion is emphatic. Even though he was stronger in faith, even though eating meat offered to idols did not bother him, he refrained voluntarily for the sake of his weaker brother. His cardinal concern was his brother's welfare.

The right use of liberty is important. Under the gospel the Christian is perfectly free from the externals of the law of Moses and from the bondage that some might be in, having not realized their liberty in Christ. But the gospel that grants liberty may also require the believer to sacrifice that liberty to help the weak. One is not truly free until he recognizes this. Otherwise he is a slave to liberty.

Liberty gives way to a brother's weaker conscience. He will do nothing to bring his brother spiritual harm. Christians are warned

ford . . . at the tribunal of God, *Sawyer* . . . the tribunal of Christ, *Scarlett, Wilson* . . . that we shall all have to present ourselves, *Way*.

11. For it is written:
[As] I live, saith the Lord, every knee shall bow to me: . . . everyone will kneel to Me, *Beck*.
and every tongue shall confess to God: . . . and every tongue shall make confession to God, *Norlie* . . . shall render acknowledgment to God, *Berkeley* . . . shall give praise to God, *Hanson* . . . shall be acclaiming God! *Concordant*.

12. So then every one of us shall give account of himself to God: . . . shal render account, *Rheims* . . . will give his own report to, *Klingensmith* . . . each of us concerning himself, *Young* . . . is to be answerable for his own actions, *Way*.

13. Let us not therefore judge one another any more: . . . let us no longer pass judgment, *Montgomery* . . . let us never again find fault, *Klingensmith* . . . stop criticizing one another, *Norlie, Moffatt*.
but judge this rather: . . . but let us rather decide this, *Berkeley* . . . let this be your resolution, *TCNT* . . . but rather determine this, *Scarlett* . . . But rather let us make up our minds, *Klingensmith*.
that no man put a stumblingblock or an occasion to fall in [his] brother's way: . . . that it is wrong to set in your brother's path anything, *Way* . . . decide not to lay any stumbling block or trap, *Beck* . . . not to put any hindrance, *HistNT* . . . a cause of offence, *PNT* . . . nor anything to trip him up, *Weymouth* . . . or a scandal before a brother, *Scarlett*.

14. I know, and am persuaded by the Lord Jesus: As one who lives in union, *Weymouth* . . . For I know with an absolute knowledge, *Wuest* . . . My union with the Lord Jesus, *TEV* . . . I know and am confident, *Confraternity* . . . and am full certified by, *Cranmer* . . . and am fully assured, *Locke*.

Romans 14:15

2812.1 adj sing	1217.1 prep	1431.4 prs-pron gen 3sing	1479.1 conj	3231.1 partic	3450.3 art dat sing	3023.8 verb dat sing masc part pres
κοινὸν	δι'	ἑαυτοῦ·	εἰ	μὴ	τῷ	λογιζομένῳ
koinon	di'	heautou	ei	mē	tō	logizomenō
unclean	of	itself;	if	not	to the	reckoning

4948.10 indef-pron sing neu	2812.1 adj sing	1498.32 verb inf pres act	1552.4 dem-pron dat sing masc	2812.1 adj sing	1479.1 conj
τι	κοινὸν	εἶναι,	ἐκείνῳ	κοινόν·	**15.** εἰ
ti	koinon	einai,	ekeinō	koinon	ei
anything	unclean	to be,	to that one	unclean.	If

1156.2 conj	1056.1 conj	1217.2 prep	1026.1 noun sing neu	3450.5 art sing masc	79.1 noun nom sing masc
δὲ	[a☆ γὰρ]	διὰ	βρῶμα	ὁ	ἀδελφός
de	gar	dia	brōma	ho	adelphos
but	[for]	on account of	food	the	brother

15.a.**Txt:** byz.
Var: 01‭א‬,02A,03B,04C 06D,025P,bo.Lach,Treg Alf,Word,Tisc,We/Ho Weis,Sod,UBS/☆

4622.2 prs-pron gen 2sing	3048.6 verb 3sing indic pres pass	3629.1 adv	2567.3 prep	26.4 noun acc sing fem
σου	λυπεῖται,	οὐκέτι	κατὰ	ἀγάπην
sou	lupeitai,	ouketi	kata	agapēn
your	is being grieved,	no longer	according to	love

3906.3 verb 2sing indic pres act	3231.1 partic	3450.3 art dat sing	1026.3 noun dat sing neu	4622.2 prs-pron gen 2sing	1552.5 dem-pron acc sing masc
περιπατεῖς.	μὴ	τῷ	βρώματί	σου	ἐκεῖνον
peripateis.	mē	tō	brōmati	sou	ekeinon
you walk.	Not	with the	food	your	that

616.1 verb 2sing impr pres act	5065.1 prep	3614.2 rel-pron gen sing	5382.1 name nom masc	594.10 verb 3sing indic aor act	3231.1 partic
ἀπόλλυε	ὑπὲρ	οὗ	Χριστὸς	ἀπέθανεν.	**16.** Μὴ
apollue	huper	hou	Christos	apethanen.	Mē
destroy	for	whom	Christ	died.	Not

980.20 verb 3sing impr pres pass	3631.1 conj	5050.2 prs-pron gen 2pl	3450.16 art sing neu	18.3 adj sing
βλασφημείσθω	οὖν	ὑμῶν	τὸ	ἀγαθόν·
blasphēmeisthō	oun	humōn	to	agathon
let be evil spoken of	therefore	your	the	good;

3620.3 partic	1056.1 conj	1498.4 verb 3sing indic pres act	3450.9 art nom sing fem	926.2 noun nom sing fem	3450.2 art gen sing
17. οὐ	γὰρ	ἐστιν	ἡ	βασιλεία	τοῦ
ou	gar	estin	hē	basileia	tou
not	for	is	the	kingdom	

2296.2 noun gen sing masc	1028.1 noun nom sing fem	2504.1 conj	4072.1 noun nom sing fem	233.2 conj	1336.1 noun nom sing fem
θεοῦ	βρῶσις	καὶ	πόσις,	ἀλλὰ	δικαιοσύνη
theou	brōsis	kai	posis,	alla	dikaiosunē
of God	eating	and	drinking;	but	righteousness

2504.1 conj	1503.1 noun nom sing fem	2504.1 conj	5315.1 noun sing fem	1706.1 prep	4011.3 noun dat sing neu	39.3 adj dat sing
καὶ	εἰρήνη	καὶ	χαρὰ	ἐν	πνεύματι	ἁγίῳ·
kai	eirēnē	kai	chara	en	pneumati	hagiō
and	peace	and	joy	in	Spirit	Holy.

18.a.**Txt:** 01‭א‬-corr 06D-corr,020L,byz.Sod **Var:** 01‭א‬-org,02A,03B 04C,06D-org,025P,sa.bo. Gries,Lach,Treg,Alf Word,Tisc,We/Ho,Weis UBS/☆

3450.5 art sing masc	1056.1 conj	1706.1 prep	3642.3 dem-pron dat pl	3642.5 dem-pron dat sing masc	1392.6 verb nom sing masc part pres act
18. ὁ	γὰρ	ἐν	τούτοις	[a☆ τούτῳ]	δουλεύων
ho	gar	en	toutois	toutō	douleuōn
The	for	in	these things	[this]	serving

against placing a stumbling block or hindrance in a brother's way. In other words, believers should not glory in their religious freedom in such a way as to cause a weaker, overscrupulous brother to stumble and fall. True love will put the interests of others first. Nothing is worth enjoying if it causes someone to lose his soul. The test by which we are to judge our life and action is not our own welfare but that of our brother.

14:15. The strong may be called upon to exercise great self-denial and sacrifice their liberty. Otherwise they would be slaves to liberty. They do this for three reasons: (1) for the good of the weaker brother (verse 13); (2) for Jesus' sake (verse 15); (3) for the good of the Church (verse 20).

If Jesus gave His life for these, should not the strong be willing to give up a small item of personal liberty for Jesus' sake?

Lupeō is translated "grieved" in the King James. Other translations use stronger words such as "pained, hurt, being injured." Possibly the latter is the best rendering.

Apollumi ("destroy", "destroy utterly") is used frequently in the New Testament of sinners perishing without salvation. This passage indicates that more is at stake than a weak brother having his life wasted or his reputation ruined. The "liberty" of another may actually precipitate his fall into a state of apostasy.

14:16. *Blasphēmeō*, translated "evil spoken of," is the Greek word from which comes our word *blaspheme*. It is not enough for the Christian to do what he feels is right. He must guard against doing anything that could cause his "good (to) be evil spoken of." He should be concerned about the impression he makes on others, as well as the relations of his own conscience to God.

14:17. The discussion of whether or not to eat certain foods became the occasion for Paul to make this profound statement of truth. The kingdom of God is not a matter of externals. God's kingdom is concerned with far greater matters than the mere question of eating and drinking. The apostle sweeps away the debris of rituals and traditions of men. Those externals are all too often the center of controversy and only hinder the growth of the Church.

The spiritual life of the believer receives experiences of: (1) righteousness—the state of being right and doing right in the sight of God; (2) peace—peace that passes understanding is the portion of all who are right with God and with men; (3) joy in the Holy Spirit—rightness with God brings the indwelling of the Holy Spirit.

14:18. When a person follows these principles he becomes a slave of Christ. Living for these, one serves Christ and has the approval

that [there is] nothing unclean of itself: . . . no food is impure, *Weymouth* . . . not even one thing is unhallowed, *Wuest* . . . nothing is common, *Panin* . . . nothing is contaminating, *Concordant*.

but to him that esteemeth any thing to be unclean, to him [it is] unclean: . . . only to him that accounteth anything unclean, *Alford* . . . to those who so regard it, *TCNT* . . . vnto him that iudgeth it to be vnclene, *Geneva* . . . to him it is defiled, *Sawyer*.

15. But if thy brother be grieved with [thy] meat: . . . is hurt by what you eat, *Klingensmith* . . . is continually pained because of your food, *Montgomery* . . . for a matter of mere food, *HistNT*.

now walkest thou not charitably: . . . you are not conducting yourself, *Montgomery* . . . your life has ceased to be ruled by love, *TCNT* . . . you are not living by the standard of love, *Williams*.

Destroy not him with thy meat, for whom Christ died: . . . you lead to ruin a man for whom, *Weymouth* . . . Do not persist in ruining him, *Way*.

16. Let not then your good be evil spoken of: . . . what is wholesome for you, *Berkeley* . . . Your rights must not get a bad name, *Moffatt* . . . become a subject of reproach, *Norlie* . . . be not oure good thing blasfemed, *Wyclif* . . . be spoken of in a reproachful and evil manner, *Wuest* . . . be injuriously spoken of, *Sawyer*.

17. For the kingdom of God is not meat and drink: For the Reign of God, *Campbell, Young* . . . since God's empire, *Adams* . . . do not consist in the enjoyment of greater variety of meats and drinks, *Locke*.

but righteousness, and peace, and joy in the Holy Ghost: . . . but justice, *Klingensmith* . . . but of right conduct, *Weymouth* . . . in the sphere of the Holy Spirit, *Wuest*.

18. For he that in these things serveth Christ [is] acceptable to God, and approved of men: . . . is well-pleasing to God, and cannot

3450.3 art dat sing	5382.3 name dat masc	2080.1 adj nom sing masc	3450.3 art dat sing	2296.3 noun dat sing masc	2504.1 conj
τῷ	Χριστῷ	εὐάρεστος	τῷ	θεῷ,	καὶ
tō	Christō	euarestos	tō	theō	kai
the	Christ	well pleasing		to God,	and

1378.1 adj nom sing masc	3450.4 art dat pl	442.8 noun dat pl masc		679.1 partic	3631.1 conj	3450.17 art pl neu
δόκιμος	τοῖς	ἀνθρώποις.	**19.** ἄρα		οὖν	τὰ
dokimos	tois	anthrōpois	ara	oun		ta
approved	by the	men.	So	then		the things

3450.10 art gen sing fem	1503.2 noun gen sing fem	1371.3 verb 1pl subj pres act	1371.27 verb 1pl indic pres act	2504.1 conj
τῆς	εἰρήνης	☆ διώκωμεν,	[a διώκομεν,]	καὶ
tēs	eirēnēs	diōkōmen	diōkomen	kai
of the	peace	we should pursue,	[we pursue,]	and

3450.17 art pl neu	3450.10 art gen sing fem	3482.2 noun gen sing fem	3450.10 art gen sing fem	1519.1 prep	238.3 prs-pron acc pl masc
τὰ	τῆς	οἰκοδομῆς	τῆς	εἰς	ἀλλήλους.
ta	tēs	oikodomēs	tēs	eis	allēlous
the things	of the	building up	the	to	one another.

	3231.1 partic	1736.2 prep	1026.2 noun gen sing neu	2617.1 verb 2sing impr pres act	3450.16 art sing neu
20. Μὴ		ἕνεκεν	βρώματος	κατάλυε	τὸ
Mē		heneken	brōmatos	katalue	to
Not		for the sake of	food	destroy	the

2024.1 noun sing neu	3450.2 art gen sing	2296.2 noun gen sing masc	3820.1 adj	3173.1 conj	2485.6 adj	233.2 conj
ἔργον	τοῦ	θεοῦ.	πάντα	μὲν	καθαρά,	ἀλλὰ
ergon	tou	theou	panta	men	kathara	alla
work		of God.	All things	indeed	pure;	but

2527.7 adj sing neu	3450.3 art dat sing	442.3 noun dat sing masc	3450.3 art dat sing	1217.2 prep	4206.2 noun gen sing neu
κακὸν	τῷ	ἀνθρώπῳ	τῷ	διὰ	προσκόμματος
kakon	tō	anthrōpō	tō	dia	proskommatos
evil	to the	man	the	through	stumbling

2052.9 verb dat sing masc part pres act		2541.1 adj sing	3450.16 art sing neu	3231.1 partic	2052.25 verb inf aor act	2880.1 noun acc pl neu
ἐσθίοντι.	**21.** καλὸν		τὸ	μὴ	φαγεῖν	κρέα,
esthionti	kalon		to	mē	phagein	krea
eating.	Right		the	not	to eat	flesh,

3234.1 adv	3956.23 verb inf aor act	3494.4 noun acc sing masc	3234.1 adv	1706.1 prep	3614.3 rel- pron dat sing	3450.5 art sing masc
μηδὲ	πιεῖν	οἶνον,	μηδὲ	ἐν	ᾧ	ὁ
mēde	piein	oinon	mēde	en	hō	ho
nor	to drink	wine,	nor	in	what	the

79.1 noun nom sing masc	4622.2 prs- pron gen 2sing	4208.1 verb 3sing indic pres act	2211.1 conj	4479.6 verb 3sing indic pres pass
ἀδελφός	σου	προσκόπτει	a ἢ	σκανδαλίζεται
adelphos	sou	proskoptei	ē	skandalizetai
brother	your	stumbles,	or	is being offended,

2211.1 conj	764.2 verb 3sing indic pres act		4622.1 prs- pron nom 2sing	3963.4 noun acc sing fem	2174.3 verb 2sing indic pres act
ἢ	ἀσθενεῖ.	**22.** Σὺ		πίστιν	ἔχεις·
ē	asthenei	Su		pistin	echeis
or	is weak.	You		faith	have?

19.a.Txt: 04C,06D,044
byz.
Var: 01ℵ,02A,03B,010F
012G,025P,048,0209,6
326,629

21.a.Txt: 01ℵ-corr,03B
06D,020L,025P,044,33
byz.it.sa.Weis,Sod
Var: 01ℵ-org,02A,04C
048,bo.Tisc,We/Ho
UBS/☆

of God and man. Christians should remember that their rights are far less important than their obligations. While they have Christian liberty, it is never to be used to cause pain and grief to a brother. The Church suffers if the members do not in love consider one another. There are people who need to be set right, but there is a right way to do it (Galatians 6:1-3).

The weak brother, in turn, is to avoid a critical spirit of fault-finding. A censorious person is usually a weak person.

14:19. How often the bickerings of believers have brought discredit to the work of God. Christians should never tear down the work of God in the hearing of a weak believer or in the eyes of the unconverted for the sake of their own gratification. The believer's self-denial does not involve asceticism—painful inflictions, torturous pilgrimages, living as a hermit—rather, it is lofty purpose within his own desire for the sake of others.

Diōkō, translated "follow after," means to "pursue." We are to keep on pursuing the things of peace.

The word "edify" as used here has the meaning of "building up." The message is, let us then pursue what makes for peace and for mutual upbuilding.

14:20. The unwise example of the strong may lead to the spiritual ruin of the weak. We are counseled not to break down, undo, and destroy the work of God for the sake of food. Even though everything may be ceremonially clean, we do wrong to bring damage to the conscience of others or to make them fall by what they eat.

The "all things" that are pure include only those things that are genuinely neutral. A television set, for example, is "pure," but the program will be either pure or impure according to the message communicated.

14:21. Conscious limitation for the sake of others is the Christian way. The believer must look at his life-style not only as to how it affects him personally but also how it affects others.

In Romans 14:21 and 1 Corinthians 8:13 Christians have a God-given code of conduct that is not determined by conscience or knowledge, but by love operating through truth.

The way a person uses his power is a good test of his character. Authority can become overbearing. The strong can look down on the weak, the prosperous can despise those of limited means, the educated can belittle the unlettered.

14:22,23. These verses point out two perils of liberty. First, the strong brother is not to parade his liberties and injure the feelings

be condemned by men, *Conybeare*... finds favor with God and is approved also by men, *Norlie* ... and esteemed by men, *Moffatt* ... and men highly commend him, *Weymouth*.

19. Let us therefore follow after the things which make for peace: So then let us eagerly pursue, *Montgomery* ... let us strive after peace, and mutual edification, *Campbell* ... that contributes to one another's peace, *Berkeley* ... after the things productive of peace, *Worrell*.

and things wherewith one may edify another: ... the upbuilding of each other, *Montgomery* ... and mutual upbuilding of character, *Weymouth* ... the upbuilding of the fabric of the church, *Way* ... the things that tend to mutual edification, *Worrell*.

20. For meat destroy not the work of God: Don't ruin God's work, *Beck* ... Overthrow not for meat's sake, *Panin* ... We must not undo God's work, *Adams* ... must not break down God's work for the mere sake, *Moffatt* ... for a meal of meat, *Conybeare* ... Do not demolish, *Hanson*.

All things indeed [are] pure: ... indeed are clean, *Douay*.

but [it is] evil for that man who eateth with offence: ... when it makes another stumble, *Williams*.

21. [It is] good neither to eat flesh, nor to drink wine, nor [any thing]: The right course is to go without meat, *TCNT* ... is to forego eating, *Weymouth* ... It is an excellent plan to abstain from flesh, *HistNT* ... It is better to forbear flesh, *Locke*.

whereby thy brother stumbleth, or is offended, or is made weak: ... that affords an occasion for your brother to stumble, *Adams* ... so as to be an occasion of sin, *Noyes* ... or is weakened, *Campbell*.

22. Hast thou faith? have [it] to thyself before God: Have it personally in the presence of God, *Berkeley* ... keep your own con-

Romans 14:23

22.a.**Txt:** 06D,020L
025P,byz.it.sa.bo.Weis
Var: 01א,02A,03B,04C
048,Lach,Treg,Alf,Tisc
We/Ho,Sod,UBS/⋆

22.b.**Txt:** Steph
Var: 01א,02A,03B,04C
06D,020L,025P,Gries
Lach,Treg,Alf,Word
Tisc,We/Ho,Weis,Sod
UBS/⋆

2567.3 prep	3614.12 rel-pron acc sing fem	2174.3 verb 2sing indic pres act	2567.3 prep	4427.3 prs-pron acc sing masc
κατὰ	[a☆ ἣν	ἔχεις	κατὰ]	ʿ σαυτὸν
kata	hēn	echeis	kata	sauton
To	[which	have	by]	yourself

4427.4 prs-pron acc 2sing masc	2174.13 verb 2sing impr pres act	1783.1 prep gen	3450.2 art gen sing	2296.2 noun gen sing masc
[b☆ σεαυτὸν]	ἔχε	ἐνώπιον	τοῦ	θεοῦ·
seauton	eche	enōpion	tou	theou
[idem]	have	before		God.

3079.2 adj nom sing masc	3450.5 art sing masc	3231.1 partic	2892.8 verb sing masc part pres act	1431.6 prs-pron acc 3sing masc	1706.1 prep
μακάριος	ὁ	μὴ	κρίνων	ἑαυτὸν	ἐν
makarios	ho	mē	krinōn	heauton	en
Blessed	the	not	judging	himself	in

3614.3 rel-pron dat sing	1375.3 verb 3sing indic pres act	3450.5 art sing masc	1156.2 conj	1246.8 verb nom sing masc part pres mid
ᾧ	δοκιμάζει·	**23.** ὁ	δὲ	διακρινόμενος,
hō	dokimazei	ho	de	diakrinomenos
what	he approves.	The	but	doubting,

1430.1 partic	2052.17 verb 3sing subj aor act	2602.11 verb 3sing indic perf pass	3617.1 conj	3620.2 partic	1523.2 prep gen
ἐὰν	φάγῃ,	κατακέκριται,	ὅτι	οὐκ	ἐκ
ean	phagē	katakekritai	hoti	ouk	ek
if	he eat,	has been condemned,	because	not	of

3963.2 noun gen sing fem	3820.17 adj sing neu	1156.2 conj	3614.16 rel-pron sing neu	3620.2 partic	1523.2 prep gen	3963.2 noun gen sing fem
πίστεως·	πᾶν	δὲ	ὃ	οὐκ	ἐκ	πίστεως,
pisteōs	pan	de	ho	ouk	ek	pisteōs
faith;	everything	and	which	not	of	faith,

264.2 noun nom sing fem	1498.4 verb 3sing indic pres act	3648.4 verb 1pl indic pres act	1156.2 conj	2231.1 prs-pron nom 1pl
ἁμαρτία	ἐστίν.	**15:1.** Ὀφείλομεν	δὲ	ἡμεῖς
hamartia	estin	Opheilomen	de	hēmeis
sin	is.	We ought	but,	we

3450.7 art pl masc	1409.2 adj nom pl masc	3450.17 art pl neu	765.1 noun acc pl neu	3450.1 art gen pl	101.2 adj gen pl masc
οἱ	δυνατοὶ	τὰ	ἀσθενήματα	τῶν	ἀδυνάτων
hoi	dunatoi	ta	asthenēmata	tōn	adunatōn
the	strong,	the	weaknesses	of the	weak

934.8 verb inf pres act	2504.1 conj	3231.1 partic	1431.7 prs-pron dat pl masc	694.5 verb inf pres act	1524.3 adj nom sing masc
βαστάζειν,	καὶ	μὴ	ἑαυτοῖς	ἀρέσκειν·	**2.** ἕκαστος
bastazein	kai	mē	heautois	areskein	hekastos
to bear,	and	not	ourselves	to please.	Each

2.a.**Txt:** Steph
Var: 01א,02A,03B,04C
06D,020L,025P,bo.Lach
Treg,Alf,Word,Tisc
We/Ho,Weis,Sod
UBS/⋆

1056.1 conj	2231.2 prs-pron gen 1pl	3450.3 art dat sing	3999.1 adv	694.2 verb 3sing impr pres act	1519.1 prep
ʿa γὰρ ˋ	ἡμῶν	τῷ	πλησίον	ἀρεσκέτω	εἰς
gar	hēmōn	tō	plēsion	aresketō	eis
for	of us	the	neighbor	let please	unto

3450.16 art sing neu	18.3 adj sing	4242.1 prep	3482.3 noun acc sing fem	2504.1 conj	1056.1 conj
τὸ	ἀγαθὸν	πρὸς	οἰκοδομήν.	**3.** καὶ	γὰρ
to	agathon	pros	oikodomēn	kai	gar
the	good	for	building up.	For	also

of others. If one is positive of his position, he need never make a display of it. The proper action for the strong brother is to choose, not on the basis of liberty, but for the sake of God and others. Quietly he makes his decision, and in refraining, he finds happiness beyond compare. The highest and holiest ambitions will call for abstinence instead of indulgence; for a walk on the narrow way instead of a broad-minded way.

Second, the weak brother has a peril too. If he, by the example of a stronger one, becomes bold enough to eat despite his conscience, he will be condemned. The term *katakekritai* ("has been condemned") is from the same root as *katakrima* ("condemnation") in 8:1. It is also translated "damned."

The problem for the "weaker" brother is this: he is persuaded that such an action on his part constitutes sin. When his conscience fully persuades him that a certain act is unlawful in the sight of God, he cannot wantonly engage in that behavior without being condemned in the eyes of God. Whether this condemnation is eternal constitutes an issue not clearly addressed in this passage.

The main point of the warning is this: the stronger can cause the weaker to stumble and fall (verse 13), thus destroying his brother (verse 15).

It is good to hesitate if one is not sure about indulgence, amusements, and recreation. Let conscience become clear on the basis of decisive Biblical principles.

15:1,2. With tenderness and patience Paul continues the matter of Christian example and liberty. Christians should help each other and consider the good of the weaker brother, while receiving one another in unity and fellowship to the glory of God before the Gentiles. The strong and enlightened must tolerate and bear with the weaker and less enlightened until they too become strong in faith and knowledge.

Spiritual unity in the Church is vital. To develop and maintain that unity requires that all parties, weak and strong, must be welcomed. The strong must relinquish certain things they are free to do, for the sake of those who are weaker.

When the stronger accepts the weaker he should not do so with the idea of arguing over scruples. He is not to criticize the weaker person's views. He should not even try to settle the doubtful points. Unfortunately, trouble usually begins when one side tries to argue the issue with the purpose of getting the other side to change. The essence of Christian fellowship does not require unanimity on doubtful points.

Churches sometimes divide because they attempt to require unanimity on debatable matters. That is a fruitless effort. It denies the nature of true Christian fellowship. Christian fellowship is built around the centrality of each person's relationship to Christ. Every believer is to be received warmly and openly, regardless of his views on nonessentials.

viction on the matter, *Moffatt* . . . keep it for thine own comfort before God, *Conybeare*.

Happy [is] he that condemneth not himself in that thing which he alloweth: . . . that is not self-condemned in the thing that he practises, *Locke* . . . who has no qualms of conscience in what he allows himself to do, *Berkeley* . . . if you never have to condemn yourself, *Beck*.

23. And he that doubteth is damned if he eat: But the person who entertains doubts, *Berkeley* . . . But he who has scruples, *PNT* . . . who discerns a difference, *Campbell* . . . he who feels any hesitation, *HistNT* . . . he who has misgivings, and yet eats meat, *Montgomery* . . . And he who doubts is condemned, *Worrell*.

because [he eateth] not of faith: . . . it was not an act of faith, *Norlie* . . . because he doesn't go by what he believes, *Beck* . . . his action is not based on faith, *Montgomery*.

for whatsoever [is] not of faith is sin: . . . and every act which is not from Conviction, *Wilson* . . . and any action that is not based on faith, *Moffatt* . . . for whatever is not from full persuasion is sin, *Scarlett* . . . whatever does not proceed from faith, *RSV* . . . and every faithless deed is sin, *Conybeare*.

1. We then that are strong ought to bear the infirmities of the weak: We then, who are able men, ought to bear the weaknesses of the unable, *Macknight* . . . we of the robust faith have a duty—to take up the burden of the tender scruples, *Way* . . . are indebted to carry, *Klingensmith* . . . must susteine, *Rheims* . . . with the failings, *RSV* . . . with the scruples of, *Norlie* . . . with the qualms of the weak, *JB*.

and not to please ourselves: . . . and not seek our own pleasure, *Weymouth*.

2. Let every one of us please [his] neighbour for [his] good to edification: . . . should please his neighbor...as conducive to edification, *Murdock* . . . unto his up-building, *Montgomery*.

Romans 15:4

3450.5 art sing masc	5382.1 name nom masc	3620.1 partic	1431.5 prs-pron dat 3sing masc	694.6 verb 3sing indic aor act	233.2 conj
ὁ	Χριστὸς	οὐχ	ἑαυτῷ	ἤρεσεν,	ἀλλὰ,
ho	Christos	ouch	heautō	ēresen	alla
the	Christ	not	himself	pleased;	but,

2503.1 conj	1119.22 verb 3sing indic perf pass	3450.7 art pl masc	3543.2 noun nom pl masc	3450.1 art gen pl
καθὼς	γέγραπται,	Οἱ	ὀνειδισμοὶ	τῶν
kathōs	gegraptai	Hoi	oneidismoi	tōn
just as	it has been written,	The	reproaches	of the

3.a.Txt: 020L,byz.
Var: 01א,02A,03B,04C 06D,025P,Lach,Treg Alf,Tisc,We/Ho,Weis Sod,UBS/✱

3542.2 verb gen pl masc part pres act	4622.4 prs-pron acc 2sing	1953.3 verb 3pl indic aor act	1953.7 verb 3pl indic aor act
ὀνειδιζόντων	σε	⌐ ἐπέπεσον	[a☆ ἐπέπεσαν]
oneidizontōn	se	epepeson	epepesan
reproaching	you	fell	[idem]

1894.2 prep	1466.7 prs-pron acc 1sing	3607.8 rel-pron pl neu	1056.1 conj	4129.2 verb 3sing indic aor pass
ἐπ'	ἐμέ.	4. Ὅσα	γὰρ	προεγράφη,
ep'	eme	Hosa	gar	proegraphē
on	me.	As many things as	for	were written before

1519.1 prep	3450.12 art acc sing fem	2233.6 adj acc 1sing fem	1313.4 noun acc sing fem	4129.2 verb 3sing indic aor pass
εἰς	τὴν	ἡμετέραν	διδασκαλίαν	⌐ προεγράφη,
eis	tēn	hēmeteran	didaskalian	proegraphē
for	the	our	instruction	were written before,

4.a.Txt: 01א-corr,02A 020L,025P,byz.
Var: 01א-org,03B,04C 06D,Lach,Treg,Alf Word,Tisc,We/Ho,Weis Sod,UBS/✱

1119.21 verb 3sing indic aor pass	2419.1 conj	1217.2 prep	3450.10 art gen sing fem	5119.2 noun gen sing fem	2504.1 conj
[a☆ ἐγράφη,]	ἵνα	διὰ	τῆς	ὑπομονῆς	καὶ
egraphē	hina	dia	tēs	hupomonēs	kai
[were written,]	that	through	the	endurance	and

4.b.Var: 01א,02A,03B 04C-org,020L,Gries Lach,Treg,Alf,Word Tisc,We/Ho,Weis,Sod UBS/✱

1217.2 prep	3450.10 art gen sing fem	3735.2 noun gen sing fem	3450.1 art gen pl	1118.6 noun gen pl fem
[b☆+ διὰ]	τῆς	παρακλήσεως	τῶν	γραφῶν
dia	tēs	paraklēseōs	tōn	graphōn
[through]	the	encouragement	of the	scriptures

3450.12 art acc sing fem	1667.4 noun acc sing fem	2174.8 verb 1pl subj pres act	3450.5 art sing masc	1156.2 conj	2296.1 noun nom sing masc
τὴν	ἐλπίδα	ἔχωμεν.	5. ὁ	δὲ	θεὸς
tēn	elpida	echōmen	ho	de	theos
the	hope	we might have.	The	now	God

3450.10 art gen sing fem	5119.2 noun gen sing fem	2504.1 conj	3450.10 art gen sing fem	3735.2 noun gen sing fem	1319.24 verb 3sing opt aor act
τῆς	ὑπομονῆς	καὶ	τῆς	παρακλήσεως	δῴη
tēs	hupomonēs	kai	tēs	paraklēseōs	dōē
of the	endurance	and	the	encouragement	give

5050.3 prs-pron dat 2pl	3450.16 art sing neu	840.15 prs-pron sing neu	5262.9 verb inf pres act	1706.1 prep	238.2 prs-pron dat pl
ὑμῖν	τὸ	αὐτὸ	φρονεῖν	ἐν	ἀλλήλοις
humin	to	auto	phronein	en	allēlois
you	to	same thing	to mind	with	one another

2567.3 prep	5382.4 name acc masc	2400.3 name acc masc	2419.1 conj	3524.1 adv	1706.1 prep
κατὰ	Χριστὸν	Ἰησοῦν·	6. ἵνα	ὁμοθυμαδὸν	ἐν
kata	Christon	Iēsoun	hina	homothumadon	en
according to	Christ	Jesus;	that	with one accord	with

15:3. The Lord Jesus is our example of self-sacrifice as the governing principle regarding our brother's conscience. His example teaches us to set aside personal prerogatives that may be all right in order to help those who are weak. He "pleased not himself."

In some decisions it is possible to please God, others, and oneself at the same time. Many times, however, one cannot please oneself and also please God. Even Jesus prayed "not my will, but thine, be done" (Luke 22:42).

The Scripture passage referred to here is Psalm 69:9 which speaks of the indescribable humiliation and suffering of Jesus in His passion. He could not please himself and also save the lost sinners He loved.

Paul's point was this: if Jesus could give His life to save a soul, it should be easy for a believer to sacrifice some meat—or any liberty—that might cause someone to stumble.

Jesus occupied His whole life with ministry to others. The multitudes thronged Him, taking His time, His strength, His ministry of teaching, healing, and blessing. He "came not to be ministered unto, but to minister" (Matthew 20:28).

As believers are identified with Jesus, their first concern will be to please Him and, in turn, their neighbor whenever it will promote the neighbor's good and Christian growth. The Lord Jesus received us when we were sinners, and He is very patient with us from day to day. He received the weaker brother. Can the "strong" refuse to be of the "same mind"? He is not only our Example; as our Redeemer and Sustainer, He will provide sufficient grace to enable us to imitate Him. He will help us not only by example but also by His presence through the Holy Spirit as we use the resources of the Word (verse 4) and prayer (verse 5).

15:4. The "for" at the beginning of this verse shows that Paul's appeal to Psalm 69:9 was an example of principles we learn from the Old Testament (1 Corinthians 10:6,10; 2 Timothy 3:16,17). The Christian fellowship should not only be stamped by consideration of its members one for anther; it should be known for its study of Scripture. The Bible is our great source of comfort and strength. By the Scriptures we learn that it is always better to be right with God and to suffer, than to be wrong to avoid trouble. The promises of God's Word comfort us in our sorrows and encourage us in our struggles.

15:5. This verse is a prayer of the apostle, the first of several wherein he petitioned for seven divine graces to be poured into the hearts of the Roman believers. He desired that they would find harmony which the disputes recorded in chapter 14 disturbed. The qualities which make for harmony in the local fellowship of believers are to be found in God. If each Christian would get to really know and follow the God of patience and comfort there would be no strife over nonessentials. The spirit of Christ would rule.

3. For even Christ pleased not himself: . . . never once consulted His own pleasure, *Way* . . . did not gratify himself, *Scarlett* . . . even the Messiah did not his own desires, *ET.*

but, as it is written: . . . as the Scripture says, *ET.*

The reproaches of them that reproached thee fell on me: The insults of those who insulted you, *Adams* . . . The insults which are hurled at you, *TEV* . . . The yackety yak of those who yaked at you, *Klingensmith* . . . who denounced...fell upon me, *HistNT.*

4. For whatsoever things were written aforetime were written for our learning: . . . whatever was written in former days, *RSV* . . . written of old has been written for our instruction, *Montgomery* . . . whatever the Prophets prophesied, *ET.*

that we through patience and comfort of the scriptures might have hope: . . . by means of the steadying and comforting power, *Berkeley* . . . we might continuously cherish our hope, *Williams* . . . through patient endurance and the encouragement to be gained from the Scriptures, *TCNT* . . . and consolation of, *Rheims* . . . and admonition, *Campbell.*

5. Now the God of patience and consolation: May the God of Dependableness and Encouragement, *Klingensmith* . . . Now the God who provides, *ET* . . . the God of the endurance, *Young* . . . who gives men patient endurance and encouragement, *Williams* . . . of steadfastness and encouragement, *Norlie* . . . and of comfort, *Clementson.*

grant you to be likeminded one toward another according to Christ Jesus: . . . help you all to be tolerant with each other, *JB* . . . grant you a Christ-like spirit of harmony, *TCNT* . . . give you that harmony, *Klingensmith* . . . may allow you to agree together, *ET* . . . be in full sympathy with one another, *Montgomery* . . . enable you to have the same point of view, *TEV* . . . and of comfort giue you to be of one minde, *Rheims* . . . after the ensample of, *Geneva.*

225

Romans 15:7

1518.2 num card dat	4601.3 noun dat sing neu	1386.2 verb 2pl subj pres act	3450.6 art acc sing masc	2296.4 noun acc sing masc	2504.1 conj
ἑνὶ	στόματι	δοξάζητε	τὸν	θεὸν	καὶ
heni	stomati	doxazēte	ton	theon	kai
one	mouth	you may glorify	the	God	and

3824.4 noun acc sing masc	3450.2 art gen sing	2935.2 noun gen sing masc	2231.2 prs- pron gen 1pl	2400.2 name masc	5382.2 name gen masc
πατέρα	τοῦ	κυρίου	ἡμῶν	Ἰησοῦ	Χριστοῦ.
patera	tou	kuriou	hēmōn	lēsou	Christou
Father	of the	Lord	our	Jesus	Christ.

1346.1 conj	4213.2 verb 2pl impr pres mid	238.3 prs-pron acc pl masc	2503.1 conj	2504.1 conj
7. Διὸ	προσλαμβάνεσθε	ἀλλήλους,	καθὼς	καὶ
Dio	proslambanesthe	allēlous	kathōs	kai
Wherefore	receive you	one another,	just as	also

3450.5 art sing masc	5382.1 name nom masc	4213.3 verb 3sing indic aor mid	5050.4 prs- pron acc 2pl	2231.4 prs- pron acc 1pl
ὁ	Χριστὸς	προσελάβετο	⟨✶ ὑμᾶς	[a ἡμᾶς]
ho	Christos	proselabeto	humas	hēmas
the	Christ	received	us	[you]

1519.1 prep	1385.4 noun acc sing fem	3450.2 art gen sing	2296.2 noun gen sing masc	2978.1 verb 1sing pres act	1156.2 conj
εἰς	δόξαν	[b ✶+ τοῦ]	θεοῦ.	**8.** Λέγω	⟨ δὲ,
eis	doxan	tou	theou	Legō	de
to	glory		of God.	I say	but,

1056.1 conj	2400.3 name acc masc	5382.4 name acc masc	1243.2 noun acc sing masc
[a ✶ γὰρ]	⟨b Ἰησοῦν ⟩	Χριστὸν	διάκονον
gar	lēsoun	Christon	diakonon
[for]	Jesus	Christ	a servant

1090.68 verb inf perf mid	3921.2 noun gen sing fem	5065.1 prep	223.2 noun gen sing fem	2296.2 noun gen sing masc
γεγενῆσθαι	περιτομῆς	ὑπὲρ	ἀληθείας	θεοῦ,
gegenēsthai	peritomēs	huper	alētheias	theou
to have become	of circumcision	for	truth	of God,

1519.1 prep	3450.16 art sing neu	943.3 verb inf aor act	3450.15 art acc pl fem	1845.1 noun fem	3450.1 art gen pl
εἰς	τὸ	βεβαιῶσαι	τὰς	ἐπαγγελίας	τῶν
eis	to	bebaiōsai	tas	epangelias	tōn
for	to	the	to confirm	the	promises	of the

3824.7 noun gen pl masc	3450.17 art pl neu	1156.2 conj	1477.4 noun pl neu	5065.1 prep	1643.3 noun gen sing neu	1386.15 verb inf aor act
πατέρων·	**9.** τὰ	δὲ	ἔθνη	ὑπὲρ	ἐλέους	δοξάσαι
paterōn	ta	de	ethnē	huper	eleous	doxasai
fathers;	the	and	nations	for	mercy	to glorify

3450.6 art acc sing masc	2296.4 noun acc sing masc	2503.1 conj	1119.22 verb 3sing indic perf pass	1217.2 prep
τὸν	θεόν,	καθὼς	γέγραπται,	Διὰ
ton	theon	kathōs	gegraptai	Dia
the	God;	just as	it has been written,	Because of

3642.17 dem- pron sing neu	1827.6 verb 1sing indic fut mid	4622.3 prs- pron dat 2sing	1706.1 prep	1477.6 noun dat pl neu
τοῦτο	ἐξομολογήσομαί	σοι	ἐν	ἔθνεσιν,
touto	exomologēsomai	soi	en	ethnesin
this	I will confess	to you	among	nations,

7.a.**Txt:** 01א,02A,04C 06D-corr2,010F,012G 044,byz.
Var: 03B,06D-org,048 104,614,629,1506

7.b.**Var:** 01א,02A,03B 04C,06D,025P,Lach Treg,Alf,Tisc,We/Ho Weis,Sod,UBS/✶

8.a.**Txt:** 020L,byz.
Var: 01א,02A,03B,04C 06D,025P,bo.Lach,Treg Alf,Word,Tisc,We/Ho Weis,Sod,UBS/✶

8.b.**Txt:** 06D,(020L) (025P),byz.Steph
Var: 01א,02A,03B,04C bo.Lach,Treg,Alf,Tisc We/Ho,Weis,Sod UBS/✶

15:6. Paul was asking a strange thing. He was suggesting that the strong and the weak, who disagreed concerning things, speak with "one mouth" and with "one mind" glorify God. He requested this after having made the point that there is room for differences of opinions concerning nonessential things and that every believer must be persuaded in his own mind. How can this be? Was he contradicting himself? What he was saying is that while believers may not be in total agreement concerning nonessentials, they can and should be in agreement that none should please himself but rather "his neighbor for his good to edification" (verse 2). With the "one mind" of self-denial, brethren can with "one mouth" glorify God.

15:7. The injunction to receive one another was possibly addressed to Jews and Gentiles. All through the epistle there are evidences of the possibility of differences between these two sections in the Church. Throughout his writing the apostle defended the Gentile against the self-satisfied national pride of the Jew, and the Jew against the probable contempt of the Gentile.

15:8. Note the change in the use of terms. Paul switched from the words "strong" and "weak" to terminology indicating two nationalities in the Church—Jews and Gentiles. Very possibly the "weak" were for the most part Jews and the "strong" were Gentiles.

As the "minister of the circumcision" Christ fulfilled the whole Mosaic requirement in His person and His work. He was the minister of the covenant that brought salvation to Israel and, in turn, to all people. He validated and carried out the promises made to Abraham, Isaac, and Jacob.

15:9. Christ came to the Jews because God had pledged himself by many promises to send the Redeemer to them. Jesus himself manifested concern for "the lost sheep of the house of Israel" (Matthew 10:6; 15:24). Paul in the opening of Romans declared that "the gospel . . . is the power of God unto salvation . . . to the Jew first" (1:16).

But while Christ honored the Jews by coming first to them, they by no means had exclusive possession of Him and His mercy. He came "that the Gentiles might glorify God for his mercy."

The quotation in the verse is from Psalm 18:49. Linking verses 8 and 9 to the quotation from Psalm 18 shows us that Christ's coming to the Jew was in the way of God's truth and to the Gentile it was in the way of mercy. The Jew can praise God for His faithfulness and the Gentile for His grace.

The underlying appeal of the apostle is that the Gentiles should not be contemptuous of the scruples of the Jewish saints and the Jews should not be censorious of the Gentile's liberty in the grace of God.

6. That ye may with one mind [and] one mouth glorify God, even the Father of our Lord Jesus Christ: . . . that unanimously as with one voice, *Berkeley* . . . That with one accord, *Alford, Young, Clementson* . . . grant to you to attain mutual unanimity, *Way* . . . That ye may unanimously with one mouth, *Scarlett* . . . that you may unite in a chorus of praise, *Moffatt* . . . that ye all agreynge [agreeing] together, *Tyndale* . . . with one mouth prayse God, *Cranmer* . . . with one heart and with one voice, *Montgomery* . . . in magnifying the God, *HistNT* . . . that you may be in perfect harmony, *ET*.

7. Wherefore receive ye one another: Welcome one another, *RSV* . . . Habitually therefore give one another a friendly reception, *Weymouth* . . . receive one another into the fellowship, *Conybeare*.

as Christ also received us to the glory of God: . . . even as the Messiah has welcomed us, *ET*.

8. Now I say that Jesus Christ was a minister of the circumcision: I maintain that Christ became a minister, *Norlie*.

for the truth of God: . . . in order to prove God's honesty, *Moffatt* . . . to prove God's truthfulness, *Williams* . . . in vindication of God's truth, *Montgomery*.

to confirm the promises [made] unto the fathers: . . . by fulfilling, *Moffatt* . . . in order to ratify the promise made to the patriarchs, *Scarlett* . . . to confirm the patriarchal promises, *Concordant* . . . to complete the covenant made, *ET*.

9. And that the Gentiles might glorify God for [his] mercy: . . . prayse God, *Geneva* . . . to honour God, *Rheims* . . . for His uncovenanted mercy to them, *Way*.

as it is written:

For this cause I will confess to thee among the Gentiles: Therefore I will offer praise, *Montgomery* . . . I will openly confess, *Wuest* . . . will I render thanks, *PNT* . . . will I give praise unto Thee, *Clementson*.

2504.1 conj	3450.3 art dat sing	3549.4 noun dat sing neu	4622.2 prs-pron gen 2sing	5402.3 verb 1sing indic fut act	2504.1 conj
καὶ	τῷ	ὀνοματί	σου	ψαλῶ.	10. Καὶ
kai	tō	onomati	sou	psalō	Kai
and	the	name	your	will I praise.	And

3687.1 adv	2978.5 verb 3sing indic pres act	2146.10 verb 2pl impr aor pass	1477.4 noun pl neu	3196.3 prep	3450.2 art gen sing
πάλιν	λέγει,	Εὐφράνθητε,	ἔθνη,	μετὰ	τοῦ
palin	legei	Euphranthēte	ethnē	meta	tou
again	it says,	Rejoice you,	nations,	with	the

2967.2 noun gen sing masc	840.3 prs-pron gen sing	2504.1 conj	3687.1 adv	134.1 verb 2pl impr pres act	3450.6 art acc sing masc
λαοῦ	αὐτοῦ.	11. Καὶ	πάλιν,	Αἰνεῖτε	῾ τὸν
laou	autou	Kai	palin	Aineite	ton
people	his.	And	again,	Praise	the

2935.4 noun acc sing masc	3820.1 adj	3450.17 art pl neu	1477.4 noun pl neu	3820.1 adj	3450.17 art pl neu
κύριον	πάντα	τὰ	ἔθνη,	[✰ πάντα	τὰ
kurion	panta	ta	ethnē	panta	ta
Lord,	all	the	nations,	[all	the

1477.4 noun pl neu	3450.6 art acc sing masc	2935.4 noun acc sing masc	2504.1 conj	1852.4 verb 2pl impr aor act
ἔθνη,	τὸν	κύριον,]	καὶ	῾ ἐπαινέσατε
ethnē	ton	kurion	kai	epainesate
Gentiles,	the	Lord,]	and	praise

1852.5 verb 3pl impr aor act	840.6 prs-pron acc sing masc	3820.7 adj pl masc	3450.7 art pl masc	2967.5 noun nom pl masc
[a✰ ἐπαινεσάτωσαν]	αὐτὸν	πάντες	οἱ	λαοί.
epainesatōsan	auton	pantes	hoi	laoi
[let praise]	him,	all	the	peoples.

11.a.**Txt:** 020L,025P,byz. **Var:** 01א,02A,03B,04C 06D,Lach,Treg,Alf,Tisc We/Ho,Weis,Sod UBS/✰

2504.1 conj	3687.1 adv	2246.1 name nom masc	2978.5 verb 3sing indic pres act	1498.40 verb 3sing indic fut mid	3450.9 art nom sing fem
12. Καὶ	πάλιν	῾Ησαΐας	λέγει,	Ἔσται	ἡ
Kai	palin	Hēsaias	legei	Estai	hē
And	again,	Isaiah	says,	There shall be	the

4347.1 noun nom sing fem	3450.2 art gen sing	2397.1 name masc	2504.1 conj	3450.5 art sing masc	448.18 verb nom sing masc part pres mid
ῥίζα	τοῦ	᾿Ιεσσαί,	καὶ	ὁ	ἀνιστάμενος
rhiza	tou	Iessai	kai	ho	anistamenos
root		of Jesse,	and	the	arising

751.1 verb inf pres act	1477.5 noun gen pl neu	1894.2 prep	840.4 prs-pron dat sing	1477.4 noun pl neu	1666.14 verb 3pl indic fut act
ἄρχειν	ἐθνῶν,	ἐπ᾿	αὐτῷ	ἔθνη	ἐλπιοῦσιν.
archein	ethnōn	ep'	autō	ethnē	elpiousin
to rule	nations:	in	him	nations	shall hope.

3450.5 art sing masc	1156.2 conj	2296.1 noun nom sing masc	3450.10 art gen sing fem	1667.2 noun gen sing fem	3997.6 verb 3sing opt aor act
13. ῾Ο	δὲ	θεὸς	τῆς	ἐλπίδος	πληρώσαι
Ho	de	theos	tēs	elpidos	plērōsai
The	now	God	of the	hope	may fill

5050.4 prs-pron acc 2pl	3820.10 adj gen sing fem	5315.2 noun gen sing fem	2504.1 conj	1503.2 noun gen sing fem	1706.1 prep	3450.3 art dat sing
ὑμᾶς	πάσης	χαρᾶς	καὶ	εἰρήνης	ἐν	τῷ
humas	pasēs	charas	kai	eirēnēs	en	tō
you	with all	joy	and	peace	in	the

15:10-12. Old Testament prophecy has much to say about the bringing of the Gentiles into the place of blessing. The apostle, in support of his argument, called attention to several passages. He quoted from Psalm 18:49 (verse 9), Deuteronomy 32:43 (verse 10), Psalm 117:1 (verse 11), and Isaiah 11:10 (verse 12).

In quoting Psalm 18:49, the Holy Spirit showed that David knew by revelation that God wanted His chosen people to proclaim Him to the Gentiles. He exhorted them to confess His name and sing praises to Him in their midst. When the Jews were in captivity in Babylon, Gentiles asked them to sing for them one of the songs of Zion (Psalm 137). What an opportunity to witness for God. They, however, were too engrossed in their sorrow to sing. They hung their harps on the willow trees and wept. Sometimes we become so self-centered and filled with self-pity because of temporal problems that we miss opportunities to win a soul for eternity.

Verse 10 uses a quotation from Deuteronomy 32:43. This is in the song of Moses shortly before his death. God was giving him prophetically a new understanding of God's judgments as well as His blessings. He was calling on Gentile nations to rejoice with Jews as they learned of God's power and glory.

Verse 12 draws the assurance from Isaiah 11:10 that Gentiles will surely respond to the good news. They will put their trust in the true and living God, as they hear of His mighty acts of grace.

The Old Testament lists many Gentiles who came to know God through the witness of Jews. Peoples of earth were divided into Jew/Gentile through the calling out of Abram from Gentile idolatry to become the ancestor of the Jewish race. One of the first Gentiles to come to know God was Hagar as she served in that home. The people of Nineveh were Gentiles won to God by a reluctant missionary, Jonah.

All three divisions of the Hebrew Bible—the Law, the Prophets, and the Psalms—were used to support the argument. The quote from Isaiah declares that the One who comes in the Davidic line will also rule over the Gentiles. Jew and Gentile alike will be united under Christ in a common hope. This is the hope which will be fulfilled at the Second Coming. Israel will come into its own, and the Gentiles will be blessed in Christ.

15:13. Paul had a beautiful way of concluding an argument with benediction. Here it is "the God of hope." There is nothing hopeless about the Christian experience. "The God of hope" is both the One who gives hope and the object of that hope. The joy is the joy of the Lord (John 15:11; Galatians 5:22; 1 John 1:4). The peace is not "as the world giveth" (John 14:27). It is Jesus' peace given by the Holy Spirit to those who hope in God (Galatians 5:22; Philippians 4:7). The Christian does not build on the experience of an hour or the happenings of a century; hope is in God, the One who sees the end from the beginning, planning and understanding it all. The result of joy and peace abounds "through the power of the Holy Spirit."

and sing unto thy name: And sing to honor Your name, *Beck* . . . shall I be playing music, *Concordant.*

10. And again he saith:
Rejoice, ye Gentiles, with his people: Be happy, *Norlie* . . . you heathen peoples, with His people! *Williams.*

11. And again, Praise the Lord, all ye Gentiles; and laud him, all ye people: . . . and once more, *Berkeley* . . . and magnify him, *Douay* . . . Be extolling, all you Gentiles, *Wuest* . . . Rejoice, pagans, with his people, *JB* . . . Extol the Lord, *HistNT* . . . And highly praise him, *PNT* . . . And let all the people extol him, *Montgomery* . . . and exceedingly praise him, *Macknight* . . . And sing his praises, all you peoples, *Confraternity* . . . Praise the Lord...and laud him, all ye nations, *Locke.*

12. And again, Esaias saith:
There shall be a root of Jesse: The noted Son of Jesse, *Williams* . . . shall be a sprout from, *Berkeley* . . . A descendant of Jesse, *TEV.*
and he that shall rise to reign over the Gentiles: . . . to rule, *RSV* . . . he who rises to govern the pagans, *Klingensmith* . . . to rule the heathen, *TCNT* . . . to be Chief of the nations, *Concordant.*
in him shall the Gentiles trust: . . . and hethen men, *Wyclif* . . . build their hopes, *Weymouth* . . . shall the Gentiles place their hope, *Campbell.*

13. Now the God of hope: May the hope-inspiring God, *Williams* . . . the fountain of hope, *Berkeley* . . . the source of hope, *TEV* . . . the God of expectation, *Concordant.*
fill you with all joy and peace in believing: . . . so fill you with perfect joy and peace through your continuing faith, *Williams* . . . replenish you, *Rheims* . . . fill you with perfect happiness, *Beck* . . . with every sort of joy, *Adams* . . . grant you perfect happiness, *TCNT* . . . fill you with continual joy, *Weymouth* . . . through the exercise of your faith, *Way.*

Romans 15:14

3961.16 verb inf pres act	1519.1 prep	3450.16 art sing neu	3915.12 verb inf pres act	5050.4 prs- pron acc 2pl	1706.1 prep
πιστεύειν,	εἰς	τὸ	περισσεύειν	ὑμᾶς	ἐν
pisteuein	eis	to	perisseuein	humas	en
to believe,	for	the	to prosper	you	in

3450.11 art dat sing fem	1667.3 noun dat sing fem	1706.1 prep	1405.3 noun dat sing fem	4011.2 noun gen sing neu	39.2 adj gen sing
τῇ	ἐλπίδι,	ἐν	δυνάμει	πνεύματος	ἁγίου.
tē	elpidi	en	dunamei	pneumatos	hagiou
the	hope,	in	power	of Spirit	Holy.

3844.28 verb 1sing indic perf pass	1156.2 conj	79.6 noun pl masc	1466.2 prs- pron gen 1sing	2504.1 conj	840.5 prs-pron nom sing masc
14. Πέπεισμαι	δέ,	ἀδελφοί	μου,	καὶ	αὐτὸς
Pepeismai	de	adelphoi	mou	kai	autos
Am persuaded	but,	brothers	my,	also	myself

1466.1 prs- pron nom 1sing	3875.1 prep	5050.2 prs- pron gen 2pl	3617.1 conj	2504.1 conj	840.7 prs-pron nom pl masc
ἐγὼ	περὶ	ὑμῶν,	ὅτι	καὶ	αὐτοὶ
egō	peri	humōn	hoti	kai	autoi
I	concerning	you,	that	also	yourselves

3194.2 adj nom pl masc	1498.6 verb 2pl indic pres act	19.2 noun gen sing fem	3997.30 verb nom pl masc part perf pass	3820.10 adj gen sing fem
μεστοί	ἐστε	ἀγαθωσύνης,	πεπληρωμένοι	πάσης
mestoi	este	agathōsunēs	peplērōmenoi	pasēs
full	are	of goodness,	having been filled	with all

	3450.10 art gen sing fem	1102.2 noun gen sing fem	1404.16 verb nom pl masc part pres	2504.1 conj	238.3 prs-pron acc pl masc
14.a.Var: 01א,03B,025P Alf,Tisc,We/Ho,Weis Sod,UBS/✶	[ᵃ✶+ τῆς]	γνώσεως,	δυνάμενοι	καὶ	ἀλλήλους
	tēs	gnōseōs	dunamenoi	kai	allēlous
	[the]	knowledge,	being able	also	one another

	3423.6 verb inf pres act	4959.1 adj comp acc sing neu	4959.1 adv comp	1156.2 conj
15.a.Txt: 01א,04C,06D 020L,025P,byz.Tisc,Sod Var: 02A,03B,Treg We/Ho,Weis,UBS/✶	νουθετεῖν.	15. ⸂ τολμηρότερον	[ᵃ τολμηροτέρως]	δὲ
	nouthetein	tolmēroteron	tolmēroterōs	de
	to admonish.	More boldly	[idem]	but

	1119.7 verb 1sing indic aor act	5050.3 prs- pron dat 2pl	79.6 noun pl masc	570.3 prep gen	3183.2 noun gen sing neu	5453.1 conj
15.b.Txt: 01א-corr,06D 020L,025P,byz.Sod Var: 01א-org,02A,03B 04C,bo.Lach,Treg,Tisc We/Ho,Weis,UBS/✶	ἔγραψα	ὑμῖν,	⸃ᵇ ἀδελφοί, ⸃	ἀπὸ	μέρους,	ὡς
	egrapsa	humin	adelphoi	apo	merous	hōs
	I did write	to you,	brothers,	in	part,	as

	1863.1 verb nom sing masc part pres act	5050.4 prs- pron acc 2pl	1217.2 prep	3450.12 art acc sing fem	5322.4 noun acc sing fem
	ἐπαναμιμνῄσκων	ὑμᾶς,	διὰ	τὴν	χάριν
	epanamimnēskōn	humas	dia	tēn	charin
	reminding	you,	because of	the	grace

	3450.12 art acc sing fem	1319.51 verb acc sing fem part aor pass	1466.4 prs- pron dat 1sing	5097.3 prep	570.3 prep gen	3450.2 art gen sing
15.c.Txt: 02A,04C,06D 020L,025P,byz.Sod Var: 01א,03B,Treg,Tisc We/Ho,Weis,UBS/✶	τὴν	δοθεῖσάν	μοι	⸂ ὑπὸ	[ᶜ ἀπὸ]	τοῦ
	tēn	dotheisan	moi	hupo	apo	tou
	the	having been given	to me	by	[from]	tou

2296.2 noun gen sing masc	1519.1 prep	3450.16 art sing neu	1498.32 verb inf pres act	1466.6 prs- pron acc 1sing	2985.2 noun acc sing masc
θεοῦ,	16. εἰς	τὸ	εἶναί	με	λειτουργὸν
theou	eis	to	einai	me	leitourgon
God,	for	the	to be	me	a minister

To summarize the argument, note these: (1) welcome the weaker brother (Romans 14:1,2); (2) do not despise one another (Romans 14:3); (3) don't pass judgment on your brother (Romans 14:4); (4) don't cause your fellow believer to sin (1 Corinthians 8:7-13); (5) accommodate the weaker brother in a spirit of love (Romans 14:14-23); (6) show the spirit of Christ (Romans 15:1-8).

15:14. In the concluding verses of this great Epistle to the Romans, Paul, the great example of Christian grace, speaks of his apostleship. He was writing not with a low estimate of the spirituality of the Roman Christians, but with the purpose of putting them in mind of what they already knew.

The concluding section, like the introductory section, is filled with personal allusion and revelation. While Paul carried the theme of the power of the gospel and Christian responsibility regarding its power throughout the epistle, the closing portion reveals the warmth of fellowship of all saints.

Few passages reveal Paul's character better that this. He was coming to the end of his letter and wanted to lay the groundwork for his forthcoming visit, the first ever for him. Ever gracious and tactful, he is a great pattern for all to emulate.

The gracious man is gentle. Strong men often have a special gentleness born of compassion and love through Christ. Paul recognized the goodness of the Romans. Goodness must keep pace with knowledge if a person is to be truly successful.

It may be that Paul referred to goodness and knowledge because of their special relevance to the subject dealt with in 14:1 to 15:13. Goodness will cause the stronger to refrain from what would damage the weaker. Right knowledge will correct the weakness of faith. The strong are in particular need of goodness; the weak are in particular need of knowledge.

Paul was careful to guard against any merely personal boastfulness, yet with unaffected modesty he did not hesitate to glory in the triumph of the gospel. The only glory he claimed was that he was the servant of Christ.

15:15. On the official basis of his God-appointed office Paul wrote them "the more boldly." Gentiles are accepted, apart from the Law, through Christ as preached by Paul. Paul was the apostle to the Gentiles. His ministry was astonishing, strong, and authoritative, for it was God-ordained. Therefore Paul wrote boldly.

His reason for writing was to "put them in mind" of what they already knew. He did not criticize to cause pain. He spoke with honesty and forthrightness, but always because he wished to enable people to be what they could be by the grace of God.

15:16. Paul made no apology, for he knew God had called him to minister to the Gentiles. God's chosen man is great in office; he

that ye may abound in hope: ... may be ryche, *Geneva* ... you may be overflowing with hope, *Montgomery* ... you may have abundant hope, *Weymouth* ... may have a surplus of hope, *Klingensmith* ... this hope of yours may be an overflowing fountain, *Way* ... you may bubble over, *Williams*.

through the power of the Holy Ghost: ... and in the vertue, *Rheims*.

14. And I myself also am persuaded of you, my brethren: ... also am confident regarding you, *Montgomery* ... And I am assured, *Hanson* ... I have reached a settled conviction, *Wuest*.

that ye also are full of goodness: ... that you are very good-hearted, *Norlie* ... that you also are ful of loue, *Rheims* ... you yourselves also are bulging with goodness, *Concordant* ... you are filled with perfect spiritual illumination, *Way*.

filled with all knowledge: ... replenished with, *Murdock* ... amply furnished with knowledge, *Berkeley* ... perfectly well instructed, *JB* ... fully equipped with every kind of knowledge, *TCNT*.

able also to admonish one another: ... and competent to counsel one another, *Adams* ... also competent to instruct one another, *Weymouth* ... and are able to exhorte, *Geneva*.

15. Nevertheless, brethren, I have written the more boldly unto you in some sort: I write you with somewhat greater boldness, *HistNT* ... written to you in some things pretty freely, *Locke* ... with more freedom, *Hanson* ... in some measure, *ASV* ... quite unreservedly, *Way*.

as putting you in mind: ... as it were to refresh your memory, *Confraternity*.

because of the grace that is given to me of God: ... has given me this special position, *JB* ... the foregoing principles, *Way*.

16. That I should be the minister of Jesus Christ to the Gentiles: ... the officiating priest of

2400.2 name masc	5382.2 name gen masc	5382.2 name gen masc	2400.2 name masc	1519.1 prep	3450.17 art pl neu
' Ἰησοῦ	Χριστοῦ	[✭ Χριστοῦ	Ἰησοῦ]	εἰς	τὰ
Iēsou	Christou	Christou	Iēsou	eis	ta
of Jesus	Christ	[of Christ	Jesus]	to	the

1477.4 noun pl neu	2394.1 verb acc sing masc part pres act		3450.16 art sing neu	2077.1 noun sing neu
ἔθνη,	ἱερουργοῦντα		τὸ	εὐαγγέλιον
ethnē	hierourgounta		to	euangelion
Gentiles,	administering in sacred service		the	good news

3450.2 art gen sing	2296.2 noun gen sing masc	2419.1 conj	1090.40 verb 3sing subj aor mid	3450.9 art nom sing fem	4234.1 noun nom sing fem
τοῦ	θεοῦ,	ἵνα	γένηται	ἡ	προσφορὰ
tou	theou	hina	genētai	hē	prosphora
of God,	that	might be	the	offering up

3450.1 art gen pl	1477.5 noun gen pl neu	2124.1 adj nom sing	37.19 verb nom sing fem part perf pass	1706.1 prep
τῶν	ἐθνῶν	εὐπρόσδεκτος,	ἡγιασμένη	ἐν
tōn	ethnōn	euprosdektos	hēgiasmenē	en
of the	Gentiles	acceptable,	having been sanctified	by

17.a.Var: 03B,04C,06D
Lach,Treg,Alf,Word
Tisc,We/Ho,Weis
UBS/✭

4011.3 noun dat sing neu	39.3 adj dat sing	2174.1 verb 1sing pres act	3631.1 conj	3450.12 art acc sing fem
πνεύματι	ἁγίῳ.	17. ἔχω	οὖν	[ᵃ✭+ τὴν]
pneumati	hagiō	echō	oun	tēn
Spirit	Holy.	I have	therefore	[the]

2716.3 noun acc sing fem	1706.1 prep	5382.3 name dat masc	2400.2 name masc	3450.17 art pl neu	4242.1 prep
καύχησιν	ἐν	Χριστῷ	Ἰησοῦ	τὰ	πρὸς
kauchēsin	en	Christō	Iēsou	ta	pros
boasting	in	Christ	Jesus	the things	pertaining to

17.b.Var: 01א,02A,03B
04C,06D,020L,025P
Gries,Lach,Treg,Alf
Word,Tisc,We/Ho,Weis
Sod,UBS/✭

3450.6 art acc sing masc	2296.4 noun acc sing masc	3620.3 partic	1056.1 conj	4958.8 verb 1sing indic fut act
[ᵇ✭+ τὸν]	θεόν·	18. οὐ	γὰρ	τολμήσω
ton	theon	ou	gar	tolmēsō
God.	Not	for	will I dare

2953.24 verb inf pres act	4948.10 indef-pron sing neu	4948.10 indef-pron sing neu	2953.24 verb inf pres act	3614.1 rel-pron gen pl	3620.3 partic
' λαλεῖν	τι	[✭ τι	λαλεῖν]	ὧν	οὐ
lalein	ti	ti	lalein	hōn	ou
to speak	anything	[anything	to speak]	of what	not

2686.9 verb 3sing indic aor mid	5382.1 name nom masc	1217.1 prep	1466.3 prs-pron gen 1sing	1519.1 prep	5056.4 noun acc sing fem
κατειργάσατο	Χριστὸς	δι'	ἐμοῦ,	εἰς	ὑπακοὴν
kateirgasato	Christos	di'	emou	eis	hupakoēn
worked out	Christ	by	me,	for	obedience

1477.5 noun gen pl neu	3030.3 noun dat sing masc	2504.1 conj	2024.3 noun dat sing neu	1706.1 prep	1405.3 noun dat sing fem
ἐθνῶν,	λόγῳ	καὶ	ἔργῳ,	19. ἐν	δυνάμει
ethnōn	logō	kai	ergō	en	dunamei
of Gentiles,	by word	and	work,	in	power

4447.3 noun gen pl neu	2504.1 conj	4907.2 noun gen pl neu	1706.1 prep	1405.3 noun dat sing fem	4011.2 noun gen sing neu
σημείων	καὶ	τεράτων,	ἐν	δυνάμει	πνεύματος
sēmeiōn	kai	teratōn	en	dunamei	pneumatos
of signs	and	wonders,	in	power	of Spirit

is the "minister of Jesus Christ." The true preacher's office is the greatest in the world. He does priestly work, offering up the gospel as his sacrifice as he stands between time and eternity. Many offer up people as a sacrifice on the altar of mammon. But Paul was a minister of the gospel acting as a priest of God's good news in order that the Gentiles when offered might be an acceptable sacrifice.

This offering of the Gentiles was consecrated and made holy by the Holy Spirit. No doubt some maintained that the Gentiles were "unclean" because they were not circumcised. To such Paul's reply was that they were "clean" because they were sanctified by the Holy Spirit.

15:17,18. Paul gloried in his labors because it was the preaching of the gospel message which had its basis in Christ. To the Galatians he wrote, "God forbid that I should glory, save in the cross of our Lord Jesus Christ" (Galatians 6:14).

The apostle was careful to give the credit to the One to whom it belongs. Note the expression "Christ . . . wrought by me." This is a commentary upon the proper position of the Christian worker. Christ is the actual worker, and the servant is the instrument through whom Christ accomplishes His purposes. Such a relationship leaves no room for personal pride, and yet therein is the place for great confidence and glorying in the Christ who does the work.

Paul saw himself as an instrument in the hands of Christ. He did not talk of what he had done, but of what Christ had done with him. He never said, "I did this, I did that"; it was always, "Christ used me to do this or that."

History is precept teaching by example; history is recorded experience, and this is all the more so when history is the biography of a person. The insights into the character of Paul afford tremendous examples which believers would do well to adopt for their lives and ministries.

15:19. As Paul worked to bring the Gentiles to obedience by word and work, God worked through him, confirming the Word with signs following. The God Paul proclaimed is the God who parted the waters, healed the sick, raised the dead, quieted the storm, delivered the faithful from prison, furnace, and lion's den. God confirmed His Word by working miracles. There are three Hebrew words which are translated by the English word *miracle* in the Old Testament: *mōpheth* ("sign," "wonder"); *'ōth* ("signs," "miracles," as pledges or attestations of divine presence and interposition); and *pala'* ("wonder acts"), (see Brown, Driver, and Briggs). Two Greek words occur in the New Testament: *dunamis* ("power, might, strength, force") and *sēmeion* ("sign" or distinguishing mark by which something is known) (see *BAGD*).

Everywhere Paul went he saw results. The Holy Spirit clothed him with divine authority. Mighty demonstrations of miracle-work-

the Glad-tidings of God, *Way.*

ministering the gospel of God: . . . exercising a sacred ministry, *Wuest* . . . doing priestly service, *Clementson* . . . sanctifying the Gospel, *Rheims* . . . in the sacred service of the gospel, *HistNT* . . . in which holy ministration I officiate, *Locke* . . . as a priest presents the offering, *Conybeare* . . . I serve like a priest in preaching, *TEV* . . . acting as priest in the good news of God, *Young* . . . of my divine commission as a priest of Christ, *Moffatt* . . . the glad tydinges of God, *Geneva.*

that the offering up of the Gentiles might be acceptable: . . . my charge being to make the sacrificial offering of the Gentiles, *Way* . . . an acceptable offering, *Moffatt* . . . that the oblation, *Rheims.*

being sanctified by the Holy Ghost: . . . hallowed by the working of, *Conybeare* . . . consecrated by, *Moffatt.*

17. I have therefore whereof I may glory through Jesus Christ in those things which pertain to God: . . . legitimate cause to exult in the presence of Jesus, *Way* . . . reason to be proud of the work, *TCNT* . . . In union with . . . in some affairs related to God, *Berkeley* . . . My exultation then is in, *HistNT* . . . the work for God in which I am engaged, *Weymouth.*

18. For I will not dare to speak of any of those things which Christ hath not wrought by me: For I will not presume, *Weymouth* . . . For I will venture to speak, *Worrell* . . . wrought by my means, *Scarlett* . . . has not performed by me, *Sawyer.*

to make the Gentiles obedient, by word and deed: . . . to win the allegiance of the pagans, *JB* . . . to make the nations obedient, *Beck* . . . both in profession and practice, *Locke.*

19. Through mighty signs and wonders, by the power of the Spirit of God: . . . has armed me with arguments, *Way* . . . by the force of miracles and marvels, *Moffatt* . . . through the energy of signs, *Scarlett* . . . in vertu of tokenes and greet wondris, *Wyclif.*

Romans 15:20

19.a.**Txt**: p46,01א
06D-corr,020L,025P
044,byz.Tisc,Sod
Var: 03B,Weis,UBS/☆

2296.2 noun gen sing masc	5452.1 conj	1466.6 prs-pron acc 1sing	570.3 prep gen	2395.1 name fem	2504.1 conj
[a Θεοῦ]	ὥστε	με	ἀπὸ	Ἱερουσαλὴμ	καὶ
Theou	*hōste*	*me*	*apo*	*Hierousalēm*	*kai*
of God:	so as for	me	from	Jerusalem,	and

2918.1 adv	3230.1 prep gen	3450.2 art gen sing	2413.1 name gen neu	3997.12 verb inf perf act
κύκλῳ	μέχρι	τοῦ	Ἰλλυρικοῦ	πεπληρωκέναι
kuklō	*mechri*	*tou*	*Illurikou*	*peplērōkenai*
in a circuit	unto		Illyricum,	to have fully preached

3450.16 art sing neu	2077.1 noun sing neu	3450.2 art gen sing	5382.2 name gen masc	3643.1 adv	1156.2 conj
τὸ	εὐαγγέλιον	τοῦ	Χριστοῦ·	**20.** οὕτως	δὲ
to	*euangelion*	*tou*	*Christou*	*houtōs*	*de*
the	good news	of the	Christ;	so	and

5226.2 verb acc sing masc part pres	2076.14 verb inf pres mid	3620.1 partic	3562.1 adv
φιλοτιμούμενον	εὐαγγελίζεσθαι,	οὐχ	ὅπου
philotimoumenon	*euangelizesthai*	*ouch*	*hopou*
being ambitious	to announce the good news,	not	where

3550.8 verb 3sing indic aor pass	5382.1 name nom masc	2419.1 conj	3231.1 partic	1894.2 prep	243.2 adj acc sing masc
ὠνομάσθη	Χριστός,	ἵνα	μὴ	ἐπ'	ἀλλότριον
ōnomasthē	*Christos*	*hina*	*mē*	*ep'*	*allotrion*
was named	Christ,	that	not	upon	another's

2287.4 noun acc sing masc	3481.1 verb 1sing pres act	233.2 conj	2503.1 conj	1119.22 verb 3sing indic perf pass
θεμέλιον	οἰκοδομῶ·	**21.** ἀλλὰ	καθὼς	γέγραπται,
themelion	*oikodomō*	*alla*	*kathōs*	*gegraptai*
foundation	I might build;	but	just as	it has been written,

21.a.**Var**: 03B,We/Ho Weis,UBS/☆

3571.40 verb 3pl indic fut mid	3614.4 rel-pron dat pl	3620.2 partic	310.10 verb 3sing indic aor pass	3875.1 prep
[a+ ὄψονται]	Οἷς	οὐκ	ἀνηγγέλη	περὶ
opsontai	*Hois*	*ouk*	*anēngelē*	*peri*
[they shall see]	To whom	not	it was announced	concerning

21.b.**Txt**: p46,01א,02A
04C,06D,020L,025P,byz.
Tisc,Sod
Var: 03B,We/Ho,Weis
UBS/☆

840.3 prs-pron gen sing	3571.34 verb 3pl indic fut mid	2504.1 conj	3614.7 rel-pron nom pl masc	3620.2 partic	189.40 verb 3pl indic perf act
αὐτοῦ,	[b ὄψονται]	καὶ	οἳ	οὐκ	ἀκηκόασιν,
autou	*opsontai*	*kai*	*hoi*	*ouk*	*akēkoasin*
him,	they shall see;	and	who	not	have heard,

4770.12 verb 3pl indic fut act	1346.1 conj	2504.1 conj	1458.3 verb 1sing indic imperf pass	3450.17 art pl neu
συνήσουσιν.	**22.** Διὸ	καὶ	ἐνεκοπτόμην	τὰ
sunēsousin	*Dio*	*kai*	*enekoptomēn*	*ta*
shall understand.	Wherefore	also	I was being hindered	the

4044.17 adj pl neu	3450.2 art gen sing	2048.23 verb inf aor act	4242.1 prep	5050.4 prs-pron acc 2pl	3432.1 adv	1156.2 conj
πολλὰ	τοῦ	ἐλθεῖν	πρὸς	ὑμᾶς.	**23.** νυνὶ	δὲ
polla	*tou*	*elthein*	*pros*	*humas*	*nuni*	*de*
many	the	to come	to	you.	Now	but,

3239.1 adv	4964.4 noun acc sing masc	2174.17 verb nom sing masc part pres act	1706.1 prep	3450.4 art dat pl	2797.1 noun dat pl neu
μηκέτι	τόπον	ἔχων	ἐν	τοῖς	κλίμασιν
mēketi	*topon*	*echōn*	*en*	*tois*	*klimasin*
no longer	place	having	in	the	regions

ing power wrought great changes not only in the lives of people but in the cities in which they lived. God truly confirmed the Word that was preached. Despite terrible obstacles and fierce persecution, God's servant pressed on and saw churches established from "Jerusalem . . . unto Illyricum."

15:20. Paul considered his work was to lay the foundation (1 Corinthians 3:10). Others were to follow and do the building. He proceeded upon the principle of preaching the gospel to those who had never heard the message. He was possessed of a holy ambition to preach in Christless regions. He went to those who needed the message the most.

15:21. This is the 19th and last Old Testament prophecy referred to in Romans. The quote from Isaiah 52:15 is translated in the *Amplified Bible,* "For that which has not been told them shall they see and that which they have not heard shall they consider and understand." Other translations are very similar. The reference is to the surprise of the nations and their leaders when they see the exaltation of the Suffering Servant, the One whom they had despised and rejected.

Paul was consumed with a burning ambition to fulfill this prophecy with respect to the spread of the gospel in heathen countries. Whenever God has work to do, He raises up men with a heart to do it.

15:22. The apostle mentioned in the beginning of his letter his long-cherished desire to come to Rome (1:9-13). He here repeated it. The cause which had frustrated fulfillment of this desire was the principle given in verses 20 and 21. City after city had been his challenge. He did not pretend that Rome was the sole object of his journey. Nor did he, for the sake of self-serving, make more of the Roman believers than the truth warranted. Hypocritical courtesy is wrong. It is better to say nothing if courtesy is stated at the expense of truth.

Paul had purposed to visit Rome but was hindered until he had finished the task at hand. He had been too busy in reaching the unreached to fit Rome into his immediate plans. Rome had been on the itinerary, but again and again the Holy Spirit had directed otherwise. Believers must never become slaves to plans. Plans must never be "set in concrete." God may have some better thing in mind.

15:23. Now his ministry had been accomplished "in these parts." Rome was to be the next stop. A review of the events surrounding Paul's trip to Rome as recorded in the Book of Acts is most inter-

so that from Jerusalem, and round about unto Illyricum: . . . complete circuit of all countries as far as Illyricum, *Way* . . . and the outlying districts, *Weymouth* . . . as far as the East of Europe, *TCNT.*

I have fully preached the gospel of Christ: I haue replenisyhed, *Rheims* . . . fulfylled myne office of preaching, *Geneva.*

20. Yea, so have I strived to preach the gospel, not where Christ was named: . . . also, that I was strongly desirous to declare, *Campbell* . . . thus making it my ambition, *RSV* . . . to announce the glad tidings, *Wuest* . . . So have I endorsed my selfe to preache, *Tyndale* . . . I have fully dispensed the Gospel, *Worrell* . . . not where Christ has [already] been announced, *PNT.*

lest I should build upon another man's foundation: . . . so as studiously to avoid the carrying of it to those places, *Locke* . . . leest I bilde [vpon] anotheris grounde, *Wyclif.*

21. But as it is written: . . . but to act on the principle embodied in these words of Scripture, *Way* . . . my chief concern has been to fulfill the text, *JB.*

To whom he was not spoken of, they shall see: . . . nothing was announced, *Worrell* . . . who have never been told of him, *RSV* . . . it hath not been preached of him, *Rheims* . . . no tidings of Him came, *Clementson.*

and they that have not heard shall understand:

22. For which cause also I have been much hindered from coming to you: I have been prevented, *Norlie* . . . All this press of work has again and again hindered me, *Way.*

23. But now having no more place in these parts: I can find no fresh field of labour in this country, *Way* . . . as there is no more unoccupied ground, *Weymouth* . . . there are no further openings, *TCNT* . . . But now having no more opportunity in these regions, *Noyes.*

Romans 15:24

3642.3 dem-pron dat pl	1958.1 noun acc sing fem	1156.2 conj	2174.17 verb nom sing masc part pres act	3450.2 art gen sing	2048.23 verb inf aor act
τούτοις,	ἐπιποθίαν	δὲ	ἔχων	τοῦ	ἐλθεῖν
toutois	epipothian	de	echōn	tou	elthein
these,	a longing	and	having	the	to come

23.a.Txt: p46,01ℵ,02A 06D,020L,044,33,etc. byz.Tisc
Var: 03B,04C,025P Treg,Alf,We/Ho,Weis Sod,UBS/✩

4242.1 prep	5050.4 prs-pron acc 2pl	570.3 prep gen	4044.1 adj gen pl	2401.1 adj gen pl	2073.4 noun gen pl neu
πρὸς	ὑμᾶς	ἀπὸ	(πολλῶν	[a ἱκανῶν]	ἐτῶν,
pros	humas	apo	pollōn	hikanōn	etōn
to	you	for	many	[several]	years,

24.a.Txt: 020L,byz.
Var: 01ℵ,02A,03B,04C 06D,025P,Lach,Treg Alf,Word,Tisc,We/Ho Weis,Sod,UBS/✩

	5453.1 conj	1430.1 partic	300.1 partic	4057.3 verb 1sing subj pres	1519.1 prep	3450.12 art acc sing fem
24.	ὡς	(ἐὰν	[a✩ ἂν]	πορεύωμαι	εἰς	τὴν
	hōs	ean	an	poreuōmai	eis	tēn
	whenever	ean	an	I may go	to	the

4534.1 name acc fem	2048.54 verb 1sing indic fut mid	4242.1 prep	5050.4 prs-pron acc 2pl	1666.1 verb 1sing indic pres act
Σπανίαν,	(b ἐλεύσομαι	πρὸς	ὑμᾶς·)	ἐλπίζω
Spanian	eleusomai	pros	humas	elpizō
Spain,	I will come	to	you;	I hope

24.b.Txt: 01ℵ-corr,020L byz.
Var: 01ℵ-org,02A,03B 04C,06D,025P,Gries Lach,Treg,Alf,Word Tisc,We/Ho,Weis,Sod UBS/✩

1056.1 conj	1273.1 verb nom sing masc part pres	2277.11 verb inf aor mid	5050.4 prs-pron acc 2pl	2504.1 conj	5097.1 prep
γὰρ	διαπορευόμενος	θεάσασθαι	ὑμᾶς,	καὶ	ὑφ'
gar	diaporeuomenos	theasasthai	humas	kai	huph'
for	going through	to see	you,	and	by

5050.2 prs-pron gen 2pl	4170.8 verb inf aor pass	1550.1 adv	1430.1 partic	5050.2 prs-pron gen 2pl	4270.1 adv
ὑμῶν	προπεμφθῆναι	ἐκεῖ,	ἐὰν	ὑμῶν	πρῶτον
humōn	propemphthēnai	ekei	ean	humōn	prōton
you	to be set forward	there	if	of you	first

570.3 prep gen	3183.2 noun gen sing neu	1689.4 verb 1sing subj aor pass		3432.1 adv	1156.2 conj	4057.1 verb 1sing indic pres
ἀπὸ	μέρους	ἐμπλησθῶ.	**25.** Νυνὶ		δὲ	πορεύομαι
apo	merous	emplēsthō	Nuni		de	poreuomai
in	part	I should be filled.	Now		but	I go

1519.1 prep	2395.1 name fem	1241.4 verb nom sing masc part pres act	3450.4 art dat pl	39.8 adj dat pl masc
εἰς	Ἰερουσαλὴμ,	διακονῶν	τοῖς	ἁγίοις.
eis	Hierousalēm	diakonōn	tois	hagiois
to	Jerusalem,	ministering	to the	saints;

	2085.9 verb 3pl indic aor act	2085.13 verb 3pl indic aor act	1056.1 conj	3081.1 name nom fem
26.	(εὐδόκησαν	[a✩ ηὐδόκησαν]	γὰρ	Μακεδονία
	eudokēsan	ēudokēsan	gar	Makedonia
	were pleased	[thought it good]	for	Macedonia

26.a.Txt: 02A,03B-corr 04C,06D,020L,025P,etc. byz.Weis,Sod
Var: 01ℵ,03B-org,Treg Tisc,We/Ho,UBS/✩

2504.1 conj	875.1 name nom fem	2815.4 noun acc sing fem	4948.5 indef-pron	4020.70 verb inf aor mid	1519.1 prep
καὶ	Ἀχαΐα	κοινωνίαν	τινὰ	ποιήσασθαι	εἰς
kai	Achaia	koinōnian	tina	poiēsasthai	eis
and	Achaia	a contribution	certain	to make	for

3450.8 art acc pl masc	4292.7 adj acc pl masc	3450.1 art gen pl	39.4 adj gen pl	3450.1 art gen pl	1706.1 prep
τοὺς	πτωχοὺς	τῶν	ἁγίων	τῶν	ἐν
tous	ptōchous	tōn	hagiōn	tōn	en
the	poor	of the	saints	the	in

236

esting. The great pioneer arrived in Rome, not as a free church planter but as a prisoner. God, however, was glorified, for Paul's chains gave him access to Caesar's household.

15:24. Having been delayed by his church planting efforts, he was now at last setting his face toward Rome. And yet Rome was not his final goal. His eyes were looking at the vast harvest field in the regions beyond. His intention was to reach Spain. His journey to Spain would afford him an opportunity to realize his long-cherished desire to see Rome and to meet the Christians in the capital of the world of that day. Above all, he looked forward to being refreshed by their fellowship.

Paul's aim was always to preach the gospel and establish local assemblies. He purposed to preach the gospel where it had not been preached before. Having completed his work in the east he set his face toward the west. He proposed to evangelize Spain and to visit Rome en route.

15:25-28. Paul had an immediate and a future plan. His future plan was to go to Spain. At the time Spain was, in a sense, the far end of the civilized world, and that alone was enough to motivate the apostle, for he wished to take the gospel where it had not been heard before.

It is possible that Paul did go to Spain. He may have been set free after his first imprisonment in Rome (Acts 28:30). He expected to be set free (Philemon 22). Some scholars believe the visit to Asia of 1 Timothy 1:3 was between imprisonments and that it was then he left the cloak at Troas (2 Timothy 4:13). J.B. Lightfoot states that Clement of Rome recorded Paul's ministry in the western part of Spain between the imprisonments (*The Apostolic Fathers*, 2:30). Of this we cannot be sure at this time.

But Paul had an immediate goal and that was to go to Jerusalem. He had been collecting the contributions of the Gentile saints to take to the poor in Jerusalem. This was a matter of great importance to him, a ministry very dear to his heart.

The desire to take this collection to the Jerusalem "saints" was born in the apostle's heart and met several obligations. No doubt it would bring about a better understanding between Gentiles and Jews (2 Corinthians 8 and 9). Cleavage between Jerusalem and the Gentile churches could only hinder the cause of Christ. This generous gesture of brotherly love could do nothing but forge the bonds of fellowship.

Not all the saints in Jerusalem were poor, but the poor saints (better translated "the poor of the saints") found themselves impoverished for several reasons. Possibly some were widows and family members whose husbands and fathers had been slain by Paul and his cohorts in the days of his persecution of the Church. Also much of the income of people in Jerusalem revolved around the religious activities in the temple and their worship. The Chris-

and having a great desire these many years to come unto you: ... a longing to come unto you, *Alford* ... to pay you a visit, *Weymouth*.

24. Whensoever I take my journey into Spain, I will come to you: I hope to see you in passing, *RSV* ... So now whenever I can go to Spain, *Klingensmith* ... as ever I extend my travels into Spain, *Weymouth*.

for I trust to see you in my journey: I do hope to see you with my own eyes, *Berkeley* ... as I proceed, *PNT* ... on my intended journey, *Way*.

and to be brought on my way thitherward by you: ... to have an escort from you on the way, *Berkeley* ... to be furnished with the necessities of travel, *Wuest*.

if first I be somewhat filled with your [company]: ... having enjoyed your fellowship for a while, *Berkeley* ... your society, *TCNT* ... after being somewhat satisfied with your companionship, *HistNT* ... after that I haue som what enioyed your acquayntaunce, *Cranmer* ... I shall have enjoyed you, *Douay* ... to some extent enjoyed your society, *Way*.

25. But now I go unto Jerusalem to minister unto the saints: Right now I am going, *Beck* ... Just now I am going to, *Montgomery* ... being employed in a ministration to the saints, *Conybeare* ... I am setting out for Jerusalem, *Locke* ... on an errand to the saints, *Moffatt* ... performing a service, *PNT* ... on a service of relief, *Noyes*.

26. For it hath pleased them of Macedonia and Achaia: For it has been the good pleasure, *Montgomery* ... For it delights, *Concordant* ... have freely decided, *TEV* ... have determined of their own accord, *TCNT*.

to make a certain contribution: ... to send a generous contribution, *JB* ... to make a certayne distribution vnto, *Geneva* ... to make a contribution, *Williams* ... jointly contributed for the poor, *Wuest*.

for the poor saints which are at Jerusalem:

27.a.Txt: 03B,04C,020L
025P,etc.byz.Weis,Sod
Var: 01א,02A,Treg,Tisc
We/Ho,UBS/☆

2395.1 name fem	2085.9 verb 3pl indic aor act	2085.13 verb 3pl indic aor act
Ἰερουσαλήμ·	27. εὐδόκησαν	[ᵃ☆ ηὐδόκησαν]
Hierousalēm	eudokēsan	ēudokēsan
Jerusalem.	They were pleased	[they thought it good]

1056.1 conj	2504.1 conj	3645.2 noun nom pl masc	840.1 prs-pron gen pl	1498.7 verb 3pl indic pres act	1498.7 verb 3pl indic pres act
γὰρ	καὶ	ὀφειλέται	ʳ αὐτῶν	εἰσὶν.	[☆ εἰσὶν
gar	kai	opheiletai	autōn	eisin	eisin
for	and	debtors	their	they are;	[they are

840.1 prs-pron gen pl	1479.1 conj	1056.1 conj	3450.4 art dat pl	4012.1 adj dat pl	840.1 prs-pron gen pl
αὐτῶν·]	εἰ	γὰρ	τοῖς	πνευματικοῖς	αὐτῶν
autōn	ei	gar	tois	pneumatikois	autōn
their;]	if	for	in the	spiritual things	their

2814.7 verb 3pl indic aor act	3450.17 art pl neu	1477.4 noun pl neu	3648.5 verb 3pl indic pres act	2504.1 conj	1706.1 prep
ἐκοινώνησαν	τὰ	ἔθνη,	ὀφείλουσιν	καὶ	ἐν
ekoinōnēsan	ta	ethnē	opheilousin	kai	en
participated	the	nations,	they ought	also	in

3450.4 art dat pl	4416.1 adj dat pl	2982.3 verb inf aor act	840.2 prs-pron dat pl	3642.17 dem-pron sing neu
τοῖς	σαρκικοῖς	λειτουργῆσαι	αὐτοῖς.	28. τοῦτο
tois	sarkikois	leitourgēsai	autois	touto
the	fleshly things	to minister	to them.	This

3631.1 conj	1989.6 verb nom sing masc part aor act	2504.1 conj	4824.7 verb nom sing masc part aor mid	840.2 prs-pron dat pl
οὖν	ἐπιτελέσας,	καὶ	σφραγισάμενος	αὐτοῖς
oun	epitelesas	kai	sphragisamenos	autois
therefore	having finished,	and	having sealed	to them

3450.6 art acc sing masc	2561.3 noun acc sing masc	3642.6 dem-pron acc sing masc	562.17 verb 1sing indic fut mid	1217.1 prep	5050.2 prs-pron gen 2pl
τὸν	καρπὸν	τοῦτον,	ἀπελεύσομαι	δι'	ὑμῶν
ton	karpon	touton	apeleusomai	di'	humōn
the	fruit	this,	I will set off	by	you

28.a.Txt: 01א-corr,04C
020L,byz.
Var: 01א-org,02A,03B
06D,025P,Lach,Treg
Alf,Tisc,We/Ho,Weis
Sod,UBS/☆

1519.1 prep	3450.12 art acc sing fem	4534.1 name acc fem	3471.2 verb 1sing indic perf act	1156.2 conj	3617.1 conj
εἰς	ʳᵃ τὴν ˋ	Σπανίαν.	29. οἶδα	δὲ	ὅτι
eis	tēn	Spanian	oida	de	hoti
into	the	Spain.	I know	and	that

2048.44 verb nom sing masc part pres	4242.1 prep	5050.4 prs-pron acc 2pl	1706.1 prep	3998.3 noun dat sing neu	2110.2 noun gen sing fem
ἐρχόμενος	πρὸς	ὑμᾶς,	ἐν	πληρώματι	εὐλογίας
erchomenos	pros	humas	en	plērōmati	eulogias
coming	to	you,	in	fulness	of blessing

29.a.Txt: 01א-corr,020L
044,33,byz.
Var: p46,01א-org,02A
03B,04C,06D,025P,it.sa.
bo.Gries,Lach,Treg,Alf
Word,Tisc,We/Ho,Weis
Sod,UBS/☆

3450.2 art gen sing	2077.2 noun gen sing	3450.2 art gen sing	5382.2 name gen sing masc	2048.54 verb 1sing indic fut mid
ʳᵃ τοῦ	εὐαγγελίου	τοῦ ˋ	Χριστοῦ	ἐλεύσομαι.
tou	euangeliou	tou	Christou	eleusomai
of the	good news	of the	Christ	I shall come.

30.a.Txt: 01א,04C,06D
010F,012G,044,byz.
Var: p46,03B

3731.1 verb 1sing indic pres act	1156.2 conj	5050.4 prs-pron acc 2pl	79.6 noun pl masc	1217.2 prep
30. Παρακαλῶ	δὲ	ὑμᾶς,	ʳᵃ ἀδελφοί, ˋ	διὰ
Parakalō	de	humas	adelphoi	dia
I exhort	but	you,	brothers,	by

tians, of course, could have no further employment in these activities; they were despised by the Jews.

For Paul this was payment of a debt. When the Jerusalem brethren agreed that Barnabas and Paul should go to the Gentiles, they requested one thing—that they should remember the poor in Jerusalem—a matter Paul was only too ready to do (Galatians 2:9,10). Duty now called Paul to take money to Jerusalem rather than the gospel to Rome.

This generous act was a beautiful gesture of practical action and demonstrated to one and all the essential unity of the Church—Jew and Gentile alike. The fellowship of the saints is not limited to one church but to the Church.

The Gentile Christians had become recipients of the blessings which had come to and through the Jews. Now they could fulfill a duty and minister to them with material things. The contribution was a voluntary gesture on the part of the Gentile section of the Church; yet it was the recognition of a moral debt. Paul left no stone unturned to do what he could to repay the debt.

The Gentile believers were debtors (*opheiletai*), just as Paul was a debtor (*opheiletēs*) to all, both Jews and Gentiles (1:14). They owed a debt, however, to Jewry, beyond the general sense in which Paul had earlier used the term.

They were, and are, in a sense indebted to Jews for their very hope of eternal life. They were partakers of spiritual blessings which emanated from God's chosen people, Israel.

Isaiah, among others, spoke of Israel as the source of blessings for all the earth (Isaiah 2:3; 11:1; 25:6; 42:1; 60:3). Jesus told the Samaritan woman, "Salvation is of the Jews" (John 4:22). Paul had already spoken to the Romans of the same fact (3:2; 4:16,17; 9:5; 11:17-24).

Paul mentioned the Christians in two provinces, Macedonia and Achaia, where he had been ministering for several months. But he had also organized a similar collection in the churches of Galatia (1 Corinthians 16:1-3). The party which would travel with Paul to Jerusalem was very representative—Sopater, Aristarchus, and Secundus from Macedonia; Gaius of Derbe and Timothy of Lystra, representatives of Galatia; and Tychicus and Trophimus of Asia Minor (Acts 20:4).

15:29. Paul was confident that when he came to Rome he would do so with a full measure of blessing from Christ. He did not know when he would come; he did not know that he would be in chains when he came; but he was certain of the condition of his soul. There is tremendous assurance when one knows he is in the will of God.

15:30. The request of Paul for the prayers of the Christians in Rome is very touching and beautiful. The request reveals that this

27. It hath pleased them verily; and they are their debtors: ... they certainly owe it to them, *Berkeley* ... and they really are under obligation to them, *Williams*.

For if the Gentiles have been made partakers of their spiritual things: For the converts from heathenism, *TCNT* ... Since the Jews shared their spiritual blessings, *TEV* ... spiritual possessions, *Berkeley* ... have been admitted into partnership with the Jews, *Weymouth* ... have participated in, *PNT* ... spiritual riches, *Montgomery*.

their duty is also to minister unto them in carnal things: ... they owe it in return, *Conybeare* ... they ought certainly, *Scarlett* ... they are bound also ...in fleshly things, *Hanson* ... a debt of aid in material blessings, *Moffatt* ... they are under moral obligation...of things needed for the sustenance of the body, *Wuest* ... bodily thynges, *Cranmer* ... physical things, *Clementson*.

28. When therefore I have performed this: So after discharging this duty, *Weymouth* ... I have despatched this business, *Locke* ... I have accomplished this, *ASV, Panin* ... I have settled this, *Montgomery* ... when I have completed this, *Confraternity* ... having finished this affair, *Campbell*.

and have sealed to them this fruit: ... and consigned to them this fruit, *Douay* ... the fruit of this collection, *Montgomery* ... and officially handed over, *JB* ... have delivered to them the proceeds, *Confraternity*.

I will come by you into Spain: I will return through you, to Spain, *Young* ... passing through Rome on my way there, *Weymouth*.

29. And I am sure that, when I come unto you: I shall come in the fulness of the blessing of the gospel of Christ: ... with abondance of, *Geneva* ... with Christ's abundant blessing on me, *Williams*.

30. Now I beseech you, brethren:

3450.2 art gen sing	2935.2 noun gen sing masc	2231.2 prs-pron gen 1pl	2400.2 name masc	5382.2 name gen masc	2504.1 conj	1217.2 prep
τοῦ	κυρίου	ἡμῶν	Ἰησοῦ	Χριστοῦ,	καὶ	διὰ
tou	kuriou	hēmōn	Iēsou	Christou	kai	dia
the	Lord	our	Jesus	Christ,	and	by

3450.10 art gen sing fem	26.2 noun gen sing fem	3450.2 art gen sing	4011.2 noun gen sing neu	4716.1 verb inf aor mid		
τῆς	ἀγάπης	τοῦ	πνεύματος,	συναγωνίσασθαί		
tēs	agapēs	tou	pneumatos	sunagōnisasthai		
the	love	of the	Spirit,	to strive together with		

1466.4 prs-pron dat 1sing	1706.1 prep	3450.14 art dat pl fem	4194.7 noun dat pl fem	5065.1 prep	1466.3 prs-pron gen 1sing
μοι	ἐν	ταῖς	προσευχαῖς	ὑπὲρ	ἐμοῦ
moi	en	tais	proseuchais	huper	emou
me	in	the	prayers	for	me

4242.1 prep	3450.6 art acc sing masc	2296.4 noun acc sing masc	2419.1 conj	4363.7 verb 1sing subj aor pass	570.3 prep gen
πρὸς	τὸν	θεόν·	**31.** ἵνα	ῥυσθῶ	ἀπὸ
pros	ton	theon	hina	rhusthō	apo
to		God,	that	I may be delivered	from

3450.1 art gen pl	540.5 verb gen pl masc part pres act	1706.1 prep	3450.11 art dat sing fem	2424.3 name dat fem	2504.1 conj
τῶν	ἀπειθούντων	ἐν	τῇ	Ἰουδαίᾳ,	καὶ
tōn	apeithountōn	en	tē	Ioudaia	kai
the	being disobedient	in	the	Judea;	and

31.a.**Txt:** 01ℵ-corr 06D-corr,020L,byz. **Var:** 01ℵ-org,02A,03B 04C,06D-org,025P,bo. Lach,Treg,Alf,Tisc We/Ho,Weis,Sod UBS/★

31.b.**Var:** 03B,06D-org Lach,Weis

2419.1 conj	3450.9 art nom sing fem	1242.1 noun nom sing fem	1428.1 noun nom sing fem	1466.2 prs-pron gen 1sing
⌐a ἵνα ⌐	ἡ	⌐ διακονία	[b δωροφορία]	μου
hina	hē	diakonia	dōrophoria	mou
that	the	service	[offering of gifts]	my

3450.9 art nom sing fem	1519.1 prep	2395.1 name fem	2124.1 adj nom sing	1090.40 verb 3sing subj aor mid
ἡ	εἰς	Ἱερουσαλὴμ	εὐπρόσδεκτος	⌐ γένηται
hē	eis	Hierousalēm	euprosdektos	genētai
the	for	Jerusalem	acceptable	may be

3450.4 art dat pl	39.8 adj dat pl masc	3450.4 art dat pl	39.8 adj dat pl masc	1090.40 verb 3sing subj aor mid	2419.1 conj
τοῖς	ἁγίοις·	[★ τοῖς	ἁγίοις	γένηται,]	**32.** ἵνα
tois	hagiois	tois	hagiois	genētai	hina
to the	saints;	[to the	saints	may be,]	that

32.a.**Txt:** p46,01ℵ-corr 03B,06D,020L,025P 044,byz.it.Weis **Var:** 01ℵ-org,02A,04C Tisc,We/Ho,Sod,UBS/★

32.b.**Var:** 03B,Lach Weis

1706.1 prep	5315.3 noun dat sing fem	2048.6 verb 1sing subj aor act	2048.13 verb nom sing masc part aor act	4242.1 prep	5050.4 prs-pron acc 2pl
ἐν	χαρᾷ	⌐ ἔλθω	[a★ ἐλθὼν]	πρὸς	ὑμᾶς
en	chara	elthō	elthōn	pros	humas
in	joy	I may come	[having come]	to	you

1217.2 prep	2284.2 noun gen sing neu	2296.2 noun gen sing masc	2935.2 noun gen sing masc	2400.2 name masc
διὰ	θελήματος	⌐ θεοῦ,	[b κυρίου	Ἰησοῦ]
dia	thelēmatos	theou	kuriou	Iēsou
by	will	of God,	[of Lord	Jesus]

32.c.**Txt:** 01ℵ-corr,06D 020L,025P,33,byz.Weis **Var:** 01ℵ-org,02A,04C bo.Tisc,We/Ho,Sod UBS/★

2504.1 conj	4726.1 verb 1sing subj aor mid	5050.3 prs-pron dat 2pl	3450.5 art sing masc	1156.2 conj
⌐c καὶ ⌐	συναναπαύσωμαι	ὑμῖν.	**33.** ὁ	δὲ
kai	sunanapausōmai	humin	ho	de
and	I may be refreshed with	you.	The	and

great warrior and pioneer who had undergone so much for the sake of the gospel (2 Corinthians 11:23-33) was very conscious of the perils which lay ahead. He was aware that people in Jerusalem were very suspicious of him, and he was evidently conscious that his coming could be an occasion for strife and persecution. He needed the assurance of the undergirding of prayer.

The apostle appealed to the believers at Rome to pray for him while they awaited his coming. Although he was absent from them, they were colaborers with him and could pray for him. The greatest gift we can give a fellow believer is that of prayer. "Pray one for another" (James 5:16). If you cannot help another to meet his need, whatever it may be, you can perform a beautiful ministry by praying with and for him.

15:31. Paul appealed to the Roman saints for prayer for the sake of the Lord Jesus Christ and for the love of the Spirit. It is noteworthy that Paul never felt he was so full of the fullness of God that he did not need the prayers of fellow believers.

"For the love of the Spirit" is parallel to "for the Lord Jesus Christ's sake." While this can mean the love that is the fruit of the Spirit (Romans 5:5; Galatians 5:22), it is more likely that Paul was speaking of the love the Holy Spirit, who is God, bore for the saints in Rome and indeed has for all saints. He is a Person who loves.

Paul gave the Roman believers specific prayer requests. He was definite in his request that he might be rescued from those in Judea who rejected the Faith. Even within the church there were those who were not willing to welcome Gentiles into the Body. The *New English Bible* rendering is, "Be my allies in the fight; pray to God for me." He apparently anticipated the trouble he was to face in Judea (Acts 21:27 to 26:32).

In addition, the Romans were asked to pray that the contribution he was taking from the churches would be received. Since the gift was basically from Gentile churches to a Jewish church, he foresaw the possibility of a racial issue due to the pride of Jewish prejudice. He did not want problems that would bring division to the body of Christ.

15:32. Finally he asked that they would pray that he might come to them "with joy by the will of God" and together with them find rest. The great pioneer desired a respite from the rigors of personal dangers and the ecclesiastical struggles which he constantly faced. Even coming to them in chains, as he later did, could not destroy this joy. God's will is always best, even in circumstances such as Paul faced.

Paul reached Rome and yet how different was his arrival from what he had originally expected. What did it matter, if it was in the will of God? That was the qualifying petition that was answered.

for the Lord Jesus Christ's sake: . . . in behalf of our Lord Jesus Christ, *ET.*

and for the love of the Spirit: . . . and by the charitie of the holy Ghost, *Rheims* . . . by the love that the Spirit inspires, *Williams.*

that ye strive together with me in [your] prayers to God for me: . . . to wrestle with me in prayers, *Williams* . . . struggle together with me in prayers, *Concordant* . . . to help me in my struggle, *Montgomery* . . . agonize together with me, *Klingensmith* . . . to help me through my dangers by praying, *JB* . . . rally round me by praying, *Moffatt* . . . to join with me in straining every nerve in prayer, *Barclay.*

31. That I may be delivered from them that do not believe in Judaea: . . . that I may escape the clutches of, *Barclay* . . . that I may be rescued from the disobedient, *HistNT* . . . that I may escape unhurt from, *Weymouth* . . . kept safe from unbelieving Jews, *ET* . . . rescued from the stubborn, *Concordant* . . . fro[m] the vnfeithful men, *Wyclif* . . . from the infidels, *Rheims* . . . who reject the Faith, *TCNT* . . . from them which are disobedient, *Geneva.*

and that my service which [I have] for Jerusalem may be accepted of the saints: . . . that my mission to Jerusalem may be favorably received, *Montgomery* . . . that my errand to Jerusalem may find acceptance with God's people, *NEB* . . . and the oblation, *Rheims* . . . and that my ministration, *ASV, Young* . . . and that that gift-bearing of mine may be acceptable, *Wilson* . . . that the offerings will be well received, *ET* . . . may welcome the help I bring to them, *Barclay.*

32. That I may come unto you with joy by the will of God: . . . that I may subsequently come to you, *Berkeley* . . . in a happy frame of mind, *NEB* . . . I want to come joyfully to you, *Barclay* . . . with a happy heart, *Williams.*

and may with you be refreshed: . . . be renewed, *ET* . . . and may with you find rest, *Alford* . . . with a light heart, *TCNT.*

Romans 16:1

2296.1 noun nom sing masc	3450.10 art gen sing fem	1503.2 noun gen sing fem	3196.3 prep	3820.4 adj gen pl	5050.2 prs- pron gen 2pl
θεὸς	τῆς	εἰρήνης	μετὰ	πάντων	ὑμῶν.
theos	tēs	eirēnēs	meta	pantōn	humōn
God	of the	peace	with	all	you.

279.1 partic	4771.1 verb 1sing indic pres act	1156.2 conj	5050.3 prs- pron dat 2pl	5239.1 name acc fem	3450.12 art acc sing fem
ἀμήν.	**16:1.** Συνίστημι	δὲ	ὑμῖν	Φοίβην	τὴν
amēn	Sunistēmi	de	humin	Phoibēn	tēn
Amen.	I commend	but	to you	Phoebe,	the

1.a.**Var:** 01א-corr,03B
04C,We/Ho,Weis,Sod
UBS/✪

78.4 noun acc sing fem	2231.2 prs- pron gen 1pl	1498.29 verb acc sing fem part pres act	2504.1 conj	1243.2 noun acc sing masc
ἀδελφὴν	ἡμῶν,	οὖσαν	[a✪+ καὶ]	διάκονον
adelphēn	hēmōn	ousan	kai	diakonon
sister,	our	being	[and]	servant

3450.10 art gen sing fem	1564.1 noun fem	3450.10 art gen sing fem	1706.1 prep	2717.1 name dat fem	2419.1 conj
τῆς	ἐκκλησίας	τῆς	ἐν	Κεγχρεαῖς·	**2.** ἵνα
tēs	ekklēsias	tēs	en	Kenchreais	hina
of the	assembly	the	in	Cenchreae;	that

840.12 prs-pron acc sing fem	4185.8 verb 2pl subj aor mid	1706.1 prep	2935.3 noun dat sing masc	512.1 adv	3450.1 art gen pl
αὐτὴν	προσδέξησθε	ἐν	κυρίῳ	ἀξίως	τῶν
autēn	prosdexēsthe	en	kuriō	axiōs	tōn
her	you may receive	in	Lord	worthily	of the

39.4 adj gen pl	2504.1 conj	3798.9 verb 2pl subj aor act	840.11 prs-pron dat sing fem	1706.1 prep	3614.3 rel- pron dat sing	300.1 partic
ἁγίων,	καὶ	παραστῆτε	αὐτῇ	ἐν	ᾧ	ἂν
hagiōn	kai	parastēte	autē	en	hō	an
saints,	and	you may assist	her	in	whatever	an

5050.2 prs- pron gen 2pl	5370.4 verb 3sing subj pres act	4088.3 noun dat sing neu	2504.1 conj	1056.1 conj	3642.9 dem-pron nom sing fem
ὑμῶν	χρῄζῃ	πράγματι·	καὶ	γὰρ	ʿ αὕτη
humōn	chrēzē	pragmati	kai	gar	hautē
of you	she may need	matter;	also	for	this

840.11 prs-pron dat sing fem	4226.1 noun nom sing fem	4044.1 adj gen pl	1090.32 verb 3sing indic aor pass	2504.1 conj
[✪ αὐτῇ]	προστάτις	πολλῶν	ἐγενήθη,	καὶ
autē	prostatis	pollōn	egenēthē	kai
[she]	a helper	of many	has been,	and

840.3 prs- pron gen sing	1466.3 prs- pron gen 1sing	1466.3 prs- pron gen 1sing	840.3 prs- pron gen sing	776.9 verb 2pl impr aor mid
ʿ αὐτοῦ	ἐμοῦ.	[✪ ἐμοῦ	αὐτοῦ.]	**3.** Ἀσπάσασθε
autou	emou	emou	autou	Aspasasthe
myself	of me.	[of me	myself.]	Greet

3.a.**Txt:** Steph
Var: 01א,02A,03B,04C
06D,020L,025P,byz.bo.
Gries,Lach,Treg,Alf
Word,Tisc,We/Ho,Weis
Sod,UBS/✪

4111.2 name acc fem	4110.1 name acc fem	2504.1 conj	205.2 name acc masc	3450.8 art acc pl masc
ʿ Πρίσκιλλαν	[a✪ Πρίσκαν]	καὶ	Ἀκύλαν	τοὺς
Priskillan	Priskan	kai	Akulan	tous
Priscilla	[Prisca]	and	Aquila	the

4754.6 adj acc pl masc	1466.2 prs- pron gen 1sing	1706.1 prep	5382.3 name dat masc	2400.2 name masc	3610.2 rel- pron nom pl masc
συνεργούς	μου	ἐν	Χριστῷ	Ἰησοῦ·	**4.** οἵτινες
sunergous	mou	en	Christō	Iēsou	hoitines
fellow workers	my	in	Christ	Jesus,	who

15:33. Paul closed the epistle proper with a benediction, breathing blessing on the church. Knowing danger and hatred lay ahead of him, he could face the journey to Jerusalem in peace because he knew "the God of peace." This was the benediction he gave to the saints at Rome.

16:1,2. Although Paul had never visited Rome at the time he wrote the epistle, he had many beloved friends there. Thirty-five names are listed, most of them mentioned in no other place. His mention of them illustrates this interest and love.

Phoebe was a *diakonos* in the assembly in Cenchreae, the seaport of Corinth. Her name indicates that she was a Gentile and she was probably a widow. According to Greek custom, she could not have traveled in the independent manner described if she had a husband or had never been married. She was given the honor of bearing to Rome the greatest theological document of the Christian Church.

Commentators have differed regarding her position in the church. In the Gospels, *diakonos* is sometimes used for "servant" as in John 2:9. In the Epistles, however, it is always used to indicate an official position of ministry in the church. *Diakonos* occurs 22 times in the Epistles. In the KJV it is translated "minister" 18 times, "deacon" 3 times (actually a transliteration), and "servant" only once—here in 16:1.

Diakonos is a title used of Paul, Timothy, Apollos, Tychicus, and Epaphras (1 Corinthians 3:5; 2 Corinthians 3:6; Ephesians 3:7; 6:21; Colossians 1:7; 4:7; 1 Thessalonians 3:2; 1 Timothy 4:6)—all of them recognized as full-fledged preachers, ministers. Phoebe's possible role of leadership is also shown by the term *prostatis* ("succorer") which, according to Liddell and Scott, means "one who is a leader or ruler; a front-rank person; one who exercises authority" (*LSJ*, "prostateia"). We have no parallel usage of this noun in the New Testament, but the verb form always calls for some aspect of leadership, ruling, commanding (Matthew 1:24; 8:4; 21:6; Luke 5:14; Acts 10:33,48; Romans 12:8; 1 Thessalonians 5:12; 1 Timothy 3:4,5,12). Because of these facts, some scholars believe Phoebe may have had some official position in the Cenchreae church.

16:3,4. Next on the list are Priscilla and Aquila. Here and in Acts 18:18 and 2 Timothy 4:19 the wife's name is first, indicating that she was the dominant one. Paul met this couple first at Corinth. They were tentmakers, the trade of Paul also (Acts 18:1-3). He made his home with them as he pioneered the Corinthian church. When Paul left Corinth they accompanied him to Ephesus and settled there. The brilliant scholar Apollos came to the city. He did not have a full grasp of the Christian faith, although he was mightily used of God. Aquila and Priscilla took him into their home, giving him fellowship and instruction (Acts 18:24 to 19:6). Their ministry, no doubt, did much to prepare the ground for the outpouring of the Holy Spirit when Paul returned to the city.

33. Now the God of peace [be] with you all. Amen:

1. I commend unto you Phebe our sister: I recommend to you, *Norlie, Macknight* . . . Now I introduce to you, *Williams* . . . I commend to your care, *TCNT.*

which is a servant of the church which is at Cenchrea: She is a worker, *Beck* . . . being a servant also of the ecclesia, *Concordant* . . . who is a ministering servant, *Conybeare* . . . being a ministrant, *Young* . . . a deaconess, *Scarlett* . . . who ministers to the Community, *HistNT* . . . a minister of the congregacion, *Tyndale* . . . who is a minister of the church, *Sawyer* . . . vvho is in the ministerie, *Rheims* . . . a Servant of the Congregation, *Wilson* . . . of the assembly, *Wuest.*

2. That ye receive her in the Lord, as becometh saints: Make her welcome in the Lord, *Norlie* . . . as befits the saints, *RSV* . . . give her a Christian welcome, *Montgomery* . . . as saints deserve, *Berkeley* . . . in a manner becoming God's people, *Williams* . . . in a way that is fitting for saints, *Adams* . . . as a fellow Christian...of God's people, *Weymouth* . . . as holy ones should, *Klingensmith* . . . worthily of the saints, *Worrell.*

and that ye assist her in whatsoever business she hath need of you: . . . give her any help she may require, *Moffatt.*

for she hath been a succourer of many, and of myself also: . . . she, indeed, has been a benefactor, *Adams* . . . For she herself has been made an overseer to many people, *Montgomery* . . . for she also became a leader of many, *Young* . . . she also has been a patroness of many and especially me, *Hanson* . . . she has looked after a great many people, *JB* . . . she has been an assistant to many, including myself, *Berkeley* . . . she has indeed been a kind friend to many, *Weymouth.*

3. Greet Priscilla and Aquila: Remember me to, *Williams* . . . Give my good wishes, *TCNT.*
my helpers in Christ Jesus: . . . my co-laborers, *Sawyer.*

Romans 16:5

5065.1 prep	3450.10 art gen sing fem	5425.2 noun gen sing fem	1466.2 prs-pron gen 1sing	3450.6 art acc sing masc	1431.2 prs-pron gen pl
ὑπὲρ	τῆς	ψυχῆς	μου	τὸν	ἑαυτῶν
huper	tēs	psuchēs	mou	ton	heautōn
for	the	life	my	the	of themselves

4976.1 noun acc sing masc	5132.1 verb 3pl indic aor act	3614.4 rel-pron dat pl	3620.2 partic	1466.1 prs-pron nom 1sing	3304.2 adj nom sing masc
τράχηλον	ὑπέθηκαν,	οἷς	οὐκ	ἐγὼ	μόνος
trachēlon	hupethēkan,	hois	ouk	egō	monos
neck	laid down:	whom	not	I	only

2149.1 verb 1sing indic pres act	233.2 conj	2504.1 conj	3820.13 adj nom pl fem	3450.13 art pl fem	1564.5 noun nom pl fem
εὐχαριστῶ,	ἀλλὰ	καὶ	πᾶσαι	αἱ	ἐκκλησίαι
eucharistō,	alla	kai	pasai	hai	ekklēsiai
thank,	but	also	all	the	assemblies

3450.1 art gen pl	1477.5 noun gen pl neu	2504.1 conj	3450.12 art acc sing fem	2567.1 prep	3486.4 noun acc sing masc	840.1 prs-pron gen pl
τῶν	ἐθνῶν·	5. καὶ	τὴν	κατ'	οἶκον	αὐτῶν
tōn	ethnōn	kai	tēn	kat'	oikon	autōn
of the	nations,	and	the	at	house	their

1564.4 noun acc sing fem	776.9 verb 2pl impr aor mid	1851.1 name acc masc	3450.6 art acc sing masc	27.1 adj sing
ἐκκλησίαν.	ἀσπάσασθε	Ἐπαίνετον	τὸν	ἀγαπητόν
ekklēsian	aspasasthe	Epaineton	ton	agapēton
assembly.	Greet	Epenetus	the	beloved

1466.2 prs-pron gen 1sing	3614.5 rel-pron nom sing masc	1498.4 verb 3sing indic pres act	532.1 noun nom sing fem	3450.10 art gen sing fem
μου,	ὅς	ἐστιν	ἀπαρχὴ	τῆς
mou,	hos	estin	aparchē	tēs
my,	who	is	a first fruit	the

5.a.Txt: 06D-corr,020L 025P,byz.
Var: 01א,02A,03B,04C 06D-org,bo.Gries,Lach Treg,Alf,Word,Tisc We/Ho,Weis,Sod UBS/☆

875.2 name gen fem	767.2 name gen fem	1519.1 prep	5382.4 name acc masc	776.9 verb 2pl impr aor mid
(Ἀχαΐας	[ᵃ☆ Ἀσίας]	εἰς	Χριστόν.	6. ἀσπάσασθε
Achaias	Asias	eis	Christon	aspasasthe
of Achaia	[of Asia]	for	Christ.	Greet

6.a.Txt: 01א,06D,020L byz.Tisc
Var: 02A,03B,04C,025P bo.Lach,Treg,Alf,We/Ho Weis,Sod,UBS/☆

3110.1 name fem	3109.4 name acc fem	3610.3 rel-pron nom sing fem	4044.17 adj pl neu	2844.11 verb 3sing indic aor act
(Μαριάμ,	[ᵃ☆ Μαριάν,]	ἥτις	πολλὰ	ἐκοπίασεν
Mariam,	Marian,	hētis	polla	ekopiasen
Mary,	[idem]	who	much	labored

6.b.Txt: 04C-corr,020L byz.
Var: 01א-org,02A,03B 04C-org,025P,bo.Lach Treg,Alf,Tisc,We/Ho Weis,Sod,UBS/☆

1519.1 prep	2231.4 prs-pron acc 1pl	5050.4 prs-pron acc 2pl	776.9 verb 2pl impr aor mid	406.1 name acc masc
εἰς	(ἡμᾶς.	[ᵇ☆ ὑμᾶς.]	7. ἀσπάσασθε	Ἀνδρόνικον
eis	hēmas.	humas.	aspasasthe	Andronikon
for	us.	[you.]	Greet	Andronicus

2504.1 conj	2433.1 name acc masc	3450.8 art acc pl masc	4624.3 adj pl masc	1466.2 prs-pron gen 1sing	2504.1 conj
καὶ	Ἰουνιᾶν	τοὺς	συγγενεῖς	μου	καὶ
kai	Iounian	tous	sungeneis	mou	kai
and	Junia	the	kinsmen	my	and

4720.2 noun acc pl masc	1466.2 prs-pron gen 1sing	3610.2 rel-pron nom pl masc	1498.7 verb 3pl indic pres act	1962.2 adj nom pl masc
συναιχμαλώτους	μου·	οἵτινές	εἰσιν	ἐπίσημοι
sunaichmalōtous	mou	hoitines	eisin	episēmoi
fellow prisoners	my,	who	are	outstanding

This fascinating couple risked their lives to save Paul's. We do not know how, nor when and where. It may have been during the riot in Corinth (Acts 18) or in Ephesus (Acts 19). This latter was so violent Paul compared it to fighting "with beasts" in the arena (1 Corinthians 15:32). It is quite certain that the reference is to beastly men and not to wild beasts.

16:5. Priscilla and Aquila had been driven from Rome along with all other Jews. We find them in Corinth, then Ephesus, back in Rome, and finally in Ephesus. Wherever they lived they were used of God. Their home became the place where the local assembly met. Our homes are our castles. We welcome the privacy they afford. At the sacrifice of comfort and privacy, they opened the doors of their household, and the home of Priscilla and Aquila became known as the church in Rome.

The next friend mentioned is the well-beloved Epenetus. Only two things are said of him. Paul called him, first of all, "well-beloved" and then spoke of him as his "firstfruits" of Achaia. It is possible that he was of the house of Stephanas, which is also called the firstfruits of Achaia (1 Corinthians 16:15).

Two-thirds of all the names are Greek. In all probability these are names of persons whom Paul had actually known in his work in Asia. All of those listed have an interrelationship as saints based upon their common relationship to Christ. Scattered throughout the record are phrases which indicate this common bond: "In the Lord . . . in Christ Jesus . . . unto Christ."

All the situations of life and service rest upon their relationship to Christ. Phoebe was to be received "in the Lord." Priscilla and Aquila were fellow workers "in Christ Jesus." Epenetus was the firstfruits of Achaia "unto Christ." His kinsmen, Andronicus and Junia, were "in Christ." The bond of service and the ties of fellowship knit by the impulse of love came about through union with Christ. Christ was their life. His love controlled their beings. The work they did was the activity of their Lord through them.

All these beloved people who are spoken of in this chapter became what they were through the life, the ministry, and the example of the apostle. In turn, Paul found comfort and encouragement in them. They provided him with assistance in the ministry.

16:6. Mary was known for her strenuous labor on behalf of God's servants. This is the only reference to this Mary, one of six women bearing the name in the New Testament.

16:7. The Bible only mentions Andronicus and Junia here. There is uncertainty as to whether or not Junia is male or female. Some versions use the masculine *Junias*.

All the early church fathers and commentators up to the 13th Century recognized Junia as a woman. For example, Chrysostom

4. Who have for my life laid down their own necks: . . . friends who have endangered their own lives for mine, *Weymouth* . . . who exposed their necks for my life, *Sawyer* . . . who risked death, *JB* . . . exposed their own to danger, *Locke* . . . who have risked their lives for me, *Moffatt* . . . for the sake of my soul, jeopardize their own necks, *Concordant.*

unto whom not only I give thanks: . . . to whom not I alone owe my thanks, *Scarlett* . . . feel grateful, *Berkeley* . . . to owe them a debt of gratitude, *JB.*

but also all the churches of the Gentiles: . . . also all the churches of the nations, *Panin* . . . among the non-Jews, *Beck.*

5. Likewise [greet] the church that is in their house: Also, greet the assembly which meets, *Wuest* . . . grete the congregacion that is in their house, *Cranmer* . . . their domestical Church, *Rheims* . . . that meets in their home, *Montgomery.*

Salute my wellbeloved Epaenetus: My greetings to, *Berkeley* . . . Greet my beloved, *Klingensmith.*

who is the firstfruits of Achaia unto Christ: . . . who was the earliest convert to Christ, *Weymouth* . . . the first man in Roman Asia to believe in Christ, *Montgomery* . . . to be reaped for Christ, *Moffatt.*

6. Greet Mary, who bestowed much labour on us: . . . who went through much trouble for you, *Berkeley* . . . who toiled terribly for you, *Montgomery* . . . who has laboured strenuously, *Weymouth* . . . who expended much labor for you, *Adams* . . . she laboured actively for you, *HistNT* . . . who toils much for you, *Concordant.*

7. Salute Andronicus and Junia:

my kinsmen, and my fellowprisoners: . . . my relatives, *Hanson* . . . my cosins and fellovv captiues, *Rheims* . . . who once shared my imprisonment, *Weymouth.*

who are of note among the apostles: . . . who are distinguished, *Confraternity* . . . who are of excellent reputation, *Wuest*

Romans 16:8

7.a.**Txt**: 04C,020L,025P
044,33,byz.Sod
Var: 01ℵ,02A,03B,Lach
Treg,Alf,Tisc,We/Ho
Weis,UBS/☆

8.a.**Txt**: 03B-corr,04C
06D,020L,025P,byz.Sod
Var: 01ℵ,02A,03B-org
bo.Treg,Alf,Tisc,We/Ho
Weis,UBS/☆

1706.1 prep	3450.4 art dat pl	646.6 noun dat pl masc	3614.7 rel-pron nom pl masc	2504.1 conj	4112.1 prep
ἐν	τοῖς	ἀποστόλοις,	οἳ	καὶ	πρὸ
en	tois	apostolois	hoi	kai	pro
among	the	apostles;	who	also	before

1466.3 prs-pron gen 1sing	1090.6 verb 3pl indic perf act	1090.73 verb 3pl indic perf act	1706.1 prep	5382.3 name dat masc
ἐμοῦ	(γέγονασιν	[ᵃ☆ γέγοναν]	ἐν	Χριστῷ.
emou	gegonasin	gegonan	en	Christō
me	have become	[idem]	in	Christ.

776.9 verb 2pl impr aor mid	289.1 name acc masc	289.1 name acc masc	3450.6 art acc sing masc
8. ἀσπάσασθε	(Ἀμπλίαν	[ᵃ☆ Ἀμπλιᾶτον]	τὸν
aspasasthe	Amplian	Ampliaton	ton
Greet	Amplias	[Ampliatus]	the

27.1 adj sing	1466.2 prs-pron gen 1sing	1706.1 prep	2935.3 noun dat sing masc	776.9 verb 2pl impr aor mid
ἀγαπητόν	μου	ἐν	κυρίῳ.	9. ἀσπάσασθε
agapēton	mou	en	kuriō	aspasasthe
beloved	my	in	Lord.	Greet

3637.1 name acc masc	3450.6 art acc sing masc	4754.3 adj acc sing masc	2231.2 prs-pron gen 1pl	1706.1 prep	5382.3 name dat masc
Οὐρβανὸν	τὸν	συνεργὸν	ἡμῶν	ἐν	Χριστῷ,
Ourbanon	ton	sunergon	hēmōn	en	Christō
Urbane	the	fellow worker	our	in	Christ,

2504.1 conj	4571.1 name acc masc	3450.6 art acc sing masc	27.1 adj sing	1466.2 prs-pron gen 1sing	776.9 verb 2pl impr aor mid
καὶ	Στάχυν	τὸν	ἀγαπητόν	μου.	10. ἀσπάσασθε
kai	Stachun	ton	agapēton	mou	aspasasthe
and	Stachys	the	beloved	my.	Greet

556.1 name acc masc	3450.6 art acc sing masc	1378.2 adj acc sing masc	1706.1 prep	5382.3 name dat masc	776.9 verb 2pl impr aor mid
Ἀπελλῆν	τὸν	δόκιμον	ἐν	Χριστῷ.	ἀσπάσασθε
Apellēn	ton	dokimon	en	Christō	aspasasthe
Apelles	the	approved	in	Christ.	Greet

3450.8 art acc pl masc	1523.2 prep gen	3450.1 art gen pl	705.1 name gen masc	776.9 verb 2pl impr aor mid
τοὺς	ἐκ	τῶν	Ἀριστοβούλου.	11. ἀσπάσασθε
tous	ek	tōn	Aristoboulou	aspasasthe
the	of	the	of Aristobulus.	Greet

2242.1 name acc masc	2242.2 name acc masc	3450.6 art acc sing masc	4624.2 adj acc sing masc	1466.2 prs-pron gen 1sing
(Ἡροδίωνα	[☆ Ἡρῳδίωνα]	τὸν	συγγενῆ	μου.
Hērodiōna	Hērōdiōna	ton	sungenē	mou
Herodion	[idem]	the	kinsman	my.

776.9 verb 2pl impr aor mid	3450.8 art acc pl masc	1523.2 prep gen	3450.1 art gen pl	3351.1 name gen masc	3450.8 art acc pl masc
ἀσπάσασθε	τοὺς	ἐκ	τῶν	Ναρκίσσου	τοὺς
aspasasthe	tous	ek	tōn	Narkissou	tous
Greet	the	of	the	of Narcissus,	the

1498.25 verb acc pl masc part pres act	1706.1 prep	2935.3 noun dat sing masc	776.9 verb 2pl impr aor mid	5011.1 name acc fem
ὄντας	ἐν	κυρίῳ.	12. ἀσπάσασθε	Τρύφαιναν
ontas	en	kuriō	aspasasthe	Truphainan
being	in	Lord.	Greet	Tryphaena

wrote, "Oh how great is the devotion of this woman that she should be even counted worthy of the appellation of apostle!" Whether this phrase means she was a notable apostle or was known by the apostles is still debated. In recent times some translators have used the masculine form, *Junias*. The name does not appear elsewhere.

Paul wrote of them as his kinsmen. This could mean they were blood relatives or else they were Jewish. They were early converts, having become Christians before Paul which must mean they had an early link with the Jerusalem church. It is evident that they were prominent for they were "of note among the apostles."

...who are well known by the apostles, *Adams*...vvho are noble, *Rheims*...among the legates, *Murdock*...They are well thought of among the missionaries, *Klingensmith*.

who also were in Christ before me: ...of longer standing than myself, *Weymouth*...who accepted the Messiah long before me, *ET*...they were Christians before I was, *Barclay*.

16:8. *Amplias* is an abbreviated form of *Ampliatus*. The name was found repeatedly among the members of the imperial family and in Roman inscriptions of that day. There is reason to believe that he was a slave but that he was of high standing in the church. During Paul's 20 years of labor in many lands he had won to Christ many who had afterward moved to the great city which was like the center of gravity of the world. He was not only commending them with sincere affection, he was preparing the church for his forthcoming visit. Paul was always thanking God for his friends and pouring love upon them.

8. Greet Amplias my beloved in the Lord: Give my good wishes to Ampliatus, my dear Christian friend, *Barclay*...my dear friend in the fellowship, *NEB*...my fellow toiler in Christ, *Montgomery*.

9. Salute Urbane, our helper in Christ, and Stachys my beloved: ...who shares with me in the work and in the fellowship of Christ, *Barclay*...our co-laborer, *Sawyer*...my comrade in Christ, *NEB*.

16:9. *Urbane* or *Urbanus* ("belonging to the city") was a name which by its very nature was quite common in Rome. On the other hand *Stachys* ("ear of grain") was not common. The name shows up once or twice in association with the imperial household. Urbane was Paul's "helper" and Stachys was his "beloved." While our information regarding these men is very limited, they were honored to be named in this great epistle by their friend and leader.

10. Salute Apelles approved in Christ: ...who has been tried and found trustworthy, *Conybeare* ...who has been tested and approved by, *Adams*...that sterling Christian, *Barclay*...well proved in Christ's service, *NEB* ...attested in Christ, *Concordant*...approved in Christ's service, *Norlie*...that tried Christian, *Moffatt*...that veteran believer, *Weymouth*...that most venerated Christian, *Williams*.
Salute them which are of Aristobulus' [household]:

16:10-12. There must have been many more names in the church at Rome, names possibly known to Paul in addition to those mentioned; but their names are not listed in this eternal scroll. It is very special to be among the bloodwashed, but how privileged to be listed as a worker with extra commendation. To leave behind a name which the world will not let fade into oblivion is significant; how much more to have a name that our Lord will mention with approval before the angels.

Such a person was Apelles. He was "approved," but most importantly, he was approved "in Christ." The word translated "approved" here is rendered "tried" in James 1:12. Origen says that Apelles was "approved by suffering and great tribulation."

Herodion may have belonged to the Herod family. The households of Aristobulus and Narcissus were very possibly slaves.

Tryphaena and Tryphosa which are slave names were near relatives, most likely sisters and possibly twins, to whom it was quite common to give names derived from the same root. Persis may

11. Salute Herodion my kinsman: ...to my fellow-countryman, *Barclay*...to my compatriot, *JB*.
Greet them that be of the [household] of Narcissus, which are in the Lord: ...the believing members, *Montgomery*...who have embraced the Gospel, *Locke* ...who are in the Lord's fellowship, *NEB*.

12. Salute Tryphena and Tryphosa, who labour in the Lord: ...to those strenuous Christian workers, *Berkeley*...to those Christian workers, *Weymouth*

2504.1 conj
καὶ
kai
and

5014.1 name acc fem
Τρυφῶσαν
Truphōsan
Tryphosa,

3450.15 art acc pl fem
τὰς
tas
the

2844.9 verb acc pl fem part pres act
κοπιώσας
kopiōsas
laboring

1706.1 prep
ἐν
en
in

2935.3 noun dat sing masc
κυρίῳ.
kuriō
Lord.

776.9 verb 2pl impr aor mid
ἀσπάσασθε
aspasasthe
Greet

3929.1 name acc fem
Περσίδα
Persida
Persis

3450.12 art acc sing fem
τὴν
tēn
the

27.9 adj acc sing fem
ἀγαπητήν,
agapētēn
beloved,

3610.3 rel-pron nom sing fem
ἥτις
hētis
who

4044.17 adj pl neu
πολλὰ
polla
much

2844.11 verb 3sing indic aor act
ἐκοπίασεν
ekopiasen
labored

1706.1 prep
ἐν
en
in

2935.3 noun dat sing masc
κυρίῳ.
kuriō
Lord.

776.9 verb 2pl impr aor mid
13. ἀσπάσασθε
aspasasthe
Greet

4361.2 name acc masc
Ῥοῦφον
Rhouphon
Rufus

3450.6 art acc sing masc
τὸν
ton
the

1575.1 adj sing
ἐκλεκτὸν
eklekton
chosen

1706.1 prep
ἐν
en
in

2935.3 noun dat sing masc
κυρίῳ,
kuriō
Lord,

2504.1 conj
καὶ
kai
and

3450.12 art acc sing fem
τὴν
tēn
the

3251.4 noun acc sing fem
μητέρα
mētera
mother

840.3 prs-pron gen sing
αὐτοῦ
autou
his

2504.1 conj
καὶ
kai
and

1466.3 prs-pron gen 1sing
ἐμοῦ.
emou
mine.

776.9 verb 2pl impr aor mid
14. ἀσπάσασθε
aspasasthe
Greet

793.1 name acc masc
Ἀσύγκριτον,
Asunkriton
Asyncritus,

5230.1 name acc masc
Φλέγοντα,
Phlegonta
Phlegon,

2041.1 name acc masc
Ἑρμᾶν,
Herman
Hermas,

2044.1 name acc masc
[☆ Ἑρμῆν,]
Hermēn
[Hermes,]

3831.1 name acc masc
Πατροβᾶν,
Patroban
Patrobas,

2044.1 name acc masc
Ἑρμῆν,
Hermēn
Hermes,

2041.1 name acc masc
[☆ Ἑρμᾶν,]
Herman
[Hermas,]

2504.1 conj
καὶ
kai
and

3450.8 art acc pl masc
τοὺς
tous
the

4713.1 prep dat
σὺν
sun
with

840.2 prs-pron dat pl
αὐτοῖς
autois
them

79.9 noun acc pl masc
ἀδελφούς.
adelphous
brothers,

776.9 verb 2pl impr aor mid
15. ἀσπάσασθε
aspasasthe
Greet

5215.1 name acc masc
Φιλόλογον
Philologon
Philologus

2504.1 conj
καὶ
kai
and

2431.1 name acc fem
Ἰουλίαν,
Ioulian
Julia,

3379.1 name acc masc
Νηρέα
Nērea
Nereus

2504.1 conj
καὶ
kai
and

3450.12 art acc sing fem
τὴν
tēn
the

78.4 noun acc sing fem
ἀδελφὴν
adelphēn
sister

840.3 prs-pron gen sing
αὐτοῦ,
autou
his,

2504.1 conj
καὶ
kai
and

3515.1 name acc masc
Ὀλυμπᾶν,
Olumpan
Olympas,

2504.1 conj
καὶ
kai
and

3450.8 art acc pl masc
τοὺς
tous
the

4713.1 prep dat
σὺν
sun
with

840.2 prs-pron dat pl
αὐτοῖς
autois
them

3820.8 adj acc pl masc
πάντας
pantas
all

39.9 adj acc pl masc
ἁγίους.
hagious
saints.

776.9 verb 2pl impr aor mid
16. Ἀσπάσασθε
Aspasasthe
Greet

238.3 prs-pron acc pl masc
ἀλλήλους
allēlous
one another

1706.1 prep
ἐν
en
with

5207.1 noun dat sing neu
φιλήματι
philēmati
a kiss

have been older for she "labored" as compared to the other two who "labor."

16:13. The name *Rufus* (meaning "red" or "red-haired") was so common among Italians that it would not be noted if it were not for two items. First, Rufus is mentioned in Mark 15:21 as one of the two sons of Simon of Cyrene, and second, the reference to the mother of Rufus as being a mother to Paul.

Mark addressed his Gospel to the Romans. Some 30 years after Simon bore Jesus' cross, Mark identified him to the Romans as the father of Alexander and Rufus. The fact that there was a well-known Rufus "chosen in the Lord" in Rome, may indicate that he was the one whose father was Simon of Cyrene. Simeon surnamed Niger ("the dark-skinned") was a colleague of Paul at Antioch (Acts 11:25,26; 13:1). Simeon has been identified with Simon of Cyrene.

All of those greeted show a relationship to Christ. Special attention was called to Phoebe, Priscilla and Aquila, Epenetus, Andronicus and Junia. Note how Amplias was "beloved in the Lord." Urbane was a "helper in Christ." Apelles was "approved in Christ." The greeting to those in the household of Narcissus was to those "in the Lord." Tryphaena and Tryphosa labored "in the Lord" and Persis "labored much in the Lord." Rufus was "chosen in the Lord."

16:14,15. The 10 persons mentioned in these verses are named only here. At least seven women are named in this chapter: Phoebe (verse 1), Priscilla (verse 3), Mary (verse 6), Tryphaena, Tryphosa, and Persis (verse 12), Julia (verse 15). In addition, there is Junia (verse 7), although some scholars believe that the person was a man named Junius. Mention is also made to an unnamed sister of Nereus (verse 15). All of them were Christian workers, deaconesses, and prophetesses who "labored . . . in the Lord" (verse 12). This would seem to indicate that some of them labored in the ministry of the Word. The Gospels name several women who proclaimed the good news (Matthew 28:1-10; Luke 24:9-11; John 4:28-30; 20:16-18). Bearing out the prophecy of Joel 2:28-31, Peter's sermon on the Day of Pentecost promised that this would be fulfilled in the last days (Acts 2:14-21). Philip the evangelist had four daughters who were prophetesses (Acts 21:9). See also Philippians 4:2,3.

Paul has at times been interpreted as being opposed to women in places of leadership in ministry. Stanley Horton has shown that Paul encouraged the public ministry of women (p.235). In spiritual gifts and ministries there are no racial, social, or sexual exclusions (Galatians 3:28). This does not impinge on the headship of the man in marriage and family structure (1 Corinthians 11:3). This basic distinction clarifies difficult Scripture passages.

16:16. The custom of combining a greeting and a kiss is still the custom in many parts of the world. There can be no doubt that

. . . who are such strenuous workers in the Lord's service, *Barclay* . . . vvho labour in our Lord, *Rheims* . . . who are ever toiling, *Montgomery.*

Salute the beloved Persis: . . . to my dear Persis, *Barclay.*

which laboured much in the Lord: . . . who has toiled in his service so long, *NEB* . . . who has toiled terribly in the Lord's service, *Montgomery* . . . a consistant hard worker, *ET* . . . who has worked hard, *RSV* . . . unwearied worker, *Berkeley.*

13. Salute Rufus chosen in the Lord: . . . eminent in the Lord, *RSV* . . . the choice one, *Young* . . . that choice Christian, *Moffatt, Barclay* . . . to that eminent Christian, *TCNT* . . . that choice character in Christ, *HistNT* . . . that outstanding worker, *TEV* . . . an outstanding follower of the Lord, *NEB* . . . the elect in our Lord, *Rheims* . . . who is noted in the Lord, *Klingensmith* . . . the special one, *ET* . . . selected to be a disciple, *Locke.*

and his mother and mine: . . . who has also been a mother to me, *Weymouth* . . . who has always treated me like a son, *TEV* . . . who is the mother both of him and of me, *Macknight* . . . whom I call mother too, *NEB.*

14. Salute Asyncritus, Phlegon, Hermas, Patrobas, Hermes: and the brethren which are with them: . . . and all friends in their company, *NEB* . . . and to all the members of their Christian community, *Barclay* . . . and the brothers who are associated with them, *Montgomery.*

15. Salute Philologus, and Julia, Nereus, and his sister, and Olympas: and all the saints which are with them: . . . and all God's people associated with them, *NEB* . . . all the saints associated with them, *Berkeley, Montgomery* . . . the brethren associated with them, *Weymouth.*

16. Salute one another with an holy kiss: Greet each other with the kiss of peace, *Barclay* . . . with

Romans 16:17

39.3 adj dat sing ἀγίῳ. hagiō holy.	**776.3** verb 3pl indic pres Ἀσπάζονται Aspazontai Greet	**5050.4** prs- pron acc 2pl ὑμᾶς humas you	**3450.13** art pl fem αἱ hai the	**1564.5** noun nom pl fem ἐκκλησίαι ekklēsiai assemblies

16.a.**Var:** 01א,02A,03B
04C,020L,025P,bo.
Gries,Lach,Treg,Alf
Word,Tisc,We/Ho,Weis
Sod,UBS/☆

3820.13 adj nom pl fem [ᵃ☆+ πᾶσαι] pasai [all]	**3450.2** art gen sing τοῦ tou	**5382.2** name gen masc Χριστοῦ. Christou of Christ.	**17.** verb 1sing **3731.1** indic pres act Παρακαλῶ Parakalō I exhort	**1156.2** conj δὲ de but
5050.4 prs- pron acc 2pl ὑμᾶς, humas you,	**79.6** noun pl masc ἀδελφοί, adelphoi brothers,	**4503.5** verb inf pres act σκοπεῖν skopein to consider	**3450.8** art acc pl masc τοὺς tous the	**3450.15** art acc pl fem τὰς tas the	**1364.2** noun acc pl fem διχοστασίας dichostasias division
2504.1 conj καὶ kai and	**3450.17** art pl neu τὰ ta the	**4480.4** noun acc pl neu σκάνδαλα, skandala causes of offense	**3706.2** prep παρὰ para contrary to	**3450.12** art acc sing fem τὴν tēn the	**1316.4** noun acc sing fem διδαχὴν didachēn teaching
3614.12 rel- pron acc sing fem ἣν hēn which	**5050.1** prs- pron nom 2pl ὑμεῖς humeis you	**3101.9** verb 2pl indic aor act ἐμάθετε, emathete learned,	**4020.18** verb acc pl masc part pres act ποιοῦντας· poiountas making,	**2504.1** conj καὶ kai and

17.a.**Txt:** 01א-corr,02A
06D,020L,025P,etc.byz.
Sod
Var: 01א-org,03B,04C
Treg,Tisc,We/Ho,Weis
UBS/☆

18.a.**Txt:** 020L,byz.bo.
Var: 01א,02A,03B,04C
06D,025P,Gries,Lach
Treg,Alf,Word,Tisc
We/Ho,Weis,Sod
UBS/☆

1565.3 verb 2pl act (ἐκκλίνατε ekklinate turn away	**1565.4** verb 2pl impr pres act [ᵃ☆ ἐκκλίνετε] ekklinete [idem]	**570.2** prep gen ἀπ' ap' from	**840.1** prs- pron gen pl αὐτῶν. autōn them.	**18.** art **3450.7** pl masc οἱ hoi The
1056.1 conj γὰρ gar for	**4955.7** dem- pron nom pl masc τοιοῦτοι toioutoi such	**3450.3** art dat sing τῷ tō the	**2935.3** noun dat sing masc κυρίῳ kuriō Lord	**2231.2** prs- pron gen 1pl ἡμῶν hēmōn our	**2400.2** name masc (ᵃ Ἰησοῦ) Iēsou Jesus
5382.3 name dat masc Χριστῷ Christō Christ	**3620.3** partic οὐ ou not	**1392.4** verb 3pl indic pres act δουλεύουσιν, douleuousin serve,	**233.2** conj ἀλλὰ alla but	**3450.11** art dat sing fem τῇ tē the
1431.2 prs- pron gen pl ἑαυτῶν heautōn of themselves	**2809.3** noun dat sing fem κοιλίᾳ· koilia belly,	**2504.1** conj καὶ kai and	**1217.2** prep διὰ dia by	**3450.10** art gen sing fem τῆς tēs the	**5377.1** noun gen sing fem χρηστολογίας chrēstologias kind speaking
2504.1 conj καὶ kai and	**2110.2** noun gen sing fem εὐλογίας eulogias praise	**1802.1** verb 3pl indic pres act ἐξαπατῶσιν exapatōsin deceive	**3450.15** art acc pl fem τὰς tas the	**2559.1** noun fem καρδίας kardias hearts	**3450.1** art gen pl τῶν tōn of the
170.2 adj gen pl masc ἀκάκων. akakōn innocent.	**19.** art **3450.9** nom sing fem ἡ hē The	**1056.1** conj γὰρ gar for	**5050.2** prs- pron gen 2pl ὑμῶν humōn your	**5056.1** noun nom sing fem ὑπακοὴ hupakoē obedience	**1519.1** prep εἰς eis to

the kiss was practiced as a token of Christian love. Jesus marked its absence in reprimanding Simon the Pharisee (Luke 7:45). Paul enjoined the practice elsewhere (1 Corinthians 16:20; 2 Corinthians 13:12; 1 Thessalonians 5:26). Peter gave the same admonition calling it a kiss of love (1 Peter 5:14). "Holy" distinguishes the greeting from the ordinary greeting of natural affection. The holy kiss is seldom practiced in churches in the West. Some leaders have thought that problems related to immorality among church members may have been aggravated by the practice; this applies especially to the heinous vice of homosexuality. It may also be that *agapē* love is less prevalent now than then.

16:17. "Mark them" and "avoid them" was Paul's solemn warning concerning those who caused "divisions" in the church. The consciousness of unity in Christ, evident in the greetings to the Roman believers, caused Paul to write this final and urgent caution. False teachers prowl stealthily to lead God's people into divisions and difficulties. Dissensions and discord cause the unwary to stumble and fall. Beware of those who come to divide and destroy.

16:18. There was the potential danger of the opponents of the gospel destroying the harmony and unity of the church. Throughout Paul's ministry opposition, especially by the Judaizers, came to disrupt. This was true almost everywhere he went, and he knew it would eventually get to Rome.

The believers were warned to avoid fellowship with these opponents of Christ. They are marked by deceitfulness, serving their own ends and purposes rather than the Lord's.

Some people apparently take pride in causing trouble and find satisfaction in sowing strife and dissension. Others mask their true motives behind a facade of piety. They lead people astray by subtle words and actions, avoiding a direct attack. They speak well but act with evil intent. False brethren cause divisions, occasion offenses, and pervert doctrines. Their motives are impure, their words deceptive, their victims the simple.

There is danger from without the Church, and there is danger from within. As the earth is assailed by two perils—storms from without and volcanic forces from within—the Church suffers from the same kind of dangers. The most dangerous is the volcanic force from within. Winds and waves may beat and cause exterior damage, but when internal fires and rumblings take place, the foundations quake, mighty rocks shiver and split, and the planet shakes.

The spirit of pride, discontent, jealousy, and all the other works of the flesh, along with false doctrine, are the greatest dangers as they attack the Church from within.

16:19. The "for" introduces a reason for the preceding admonition regarding erroneous doctrines. The church in Rome had

a Christian kiss, *ET* . . . with a sacred kiss, *TCNT* . . . with a consecrated kiss, *Williams.*

The churches of Christ salute you:

17. Now I beseech you, brethren: I implore you, *JB* . . . And I call upon you, *Young* . . . Now I am entreating you, *Concordant.*

mark them which cause divisions and offences: . . . watche diligently, *Geneva* . . . to take note, *RSV* . . . who cause splits and obstacles, *Berkeley* . . . who encourages trouble, *JB* . . . create difficulties, *TCNT* . . . who cause disagreements, *Beck* . . . who are making factions and stumblingblocks, *Hanson* . . . put hindrances in your way, *Moffatt* . . . geve occasions of evyll, *Tyndale.*

contrary to the doctrine which ye have learned: . . . in opposition to, *RSV* . . . quite out of harmony with the doctrine you have been taught, *Berkeley* . . . in defiance of the instruction which you have received, *Weymouth* . . . by disregarding the teaching that you have learned, *Adams.*

and avoid them: . . . to dissociate yourselves from them, *TCNT* . . . turn away from them, *Panin* . . . always avoid, *Williams.*

18. For they that are such serve not our Lord Jesus Christ: . . . for the master whom they serve is not, *Conybeare.*

but their own belly: . . . but are slaves of their own appetites, *Adams* . . . slaves of their own base desires, *Moffatt.*

and by good words and fair speeches deceive the hearts of the simple: By their honeyed words and flattery they deceive the hearts of the unsuspecting, *Norlie* . . . by smooth and complimentary speech, *Hanson* . . . with their plausible and pious talk they beguile, *Moffatt* . . . by svveete speaches and benedictions seduce, *Rheims* . . . with swete preachinges and flatteringe wordes...of the innocentes, *Tyndale* . . . of the harmless, *Young* . . . of ynnocent men, *Wyclif.*

19. For your obedience is come abroad unto all [men]: Your fi-

Romans 16:20

3820.8 adj acc pl masc	857.1 verb 3sing indic aor mid	5299.1 verb 1sing indic pres act	3631.1 conj	3450.16 art sing neu	1894.1 prep
πάντας	ἀφίκετο·	ʿ χαίρω	οὖν	τὸ	ἐφ'
pantas	*aphiketo*	*chairō*	*oun*	*to*	*eph'*
all	reached.	I rejoice	therefore	the	over

19.a.Txt: 01ℵ-corr 06D-corr,byz. **Var:** 01ℵ-org,02A,03B 04C,020L,025P,Lach Treg,Alf,Word,Tisc We/Ho,Weis,Sod UBS/✻

5050.3 prs- pron dat 2pl	1894.1 prep	5050.3 prs- pron dat 2pl	3631.1 conj	5299.1 verb 1sing indic pres act	2286.1 verb 1sing pres act
ὑμῖν.	[ᵃ✩ ἐφ'	ὑμῖν	οὖν	χαίρω,]	θέλω
humin	*eph'*	*humin*	*oun*	*chairō*	*thelō*
you;	[Over	you	therefore	I rejoice,]	I wish

19.b.Txt: 01ℵ,02A,04C 025P,byz.We/Ho,Sod **Var:** 03B,06D,020L,bo. Lach,Treg,Alf,Tisc Weis,UBS/✻

1156.2 conj	5050.4 prs- pron acc 2pl	4533.6 adj acc pl masc	3173.1 conj	1498.32 verb inf pres act	1519.1 prep	3450.16 art sing neu
δὲ	ὑμᾶς	σοφοὺς	ʿᵇ μὲν ˋ	εἶναι	εἰς	τὸ
de	*humas*	*sophous*	*men*	*einai*	*eis*	*to*
but	you	wise	men	to be	to	the

18.3 adj sing	183.2 adj acc pl masc	1156.2 conj	1519.1 prep	3450.16 art sing neu	2527.7 adj sing neu
ἀγαθόν,	ἀκεραίους	δὲ	εἰς	τὸ	κακόν.
agathon	*akeraious*	*de*	*eis*	*to*	*kakon*
good,	simple	and	to	the	evil.

3450.5 art sing masc	1156.2 conj	2296.1 noun nom sing masc	3450.10 art gen sing fem	1503.2 noun gen sing fem	4789.3 verb 3sing indic fut act
20. ὁ	δὲ	θεὸς	τῆς	εἰρήνης	συντρίψει
ho	*de*	*theos*	*tēs*	*eirēnēs*	*suntripsei*
The	but	God	of the	peace	will bruise

3450.6 art acc sing masc	4423.4 noun acc sing masc	5097.3 prep	3450.8 art acc pl masc	4087.7 noun acc pl masc	5050.2 prs- pron gen 2pl	1706.1 prep
τὸν	Σατανᾶν	ὑπὸ	τοὺς	πόδας	ὑμῶν	ἐν
ton	*Satanan*	*hupo*	*tous*	*podas*	*humōn*	*en*
ton	Satan	under	the	feet	your	in

4882.1 noun dat sing neu	3450.9 art nom sing fem	5322.1 noun nom sing fem	3450.2 art gen sing	2935.2 noun gen sing masc	2231.2 prs- pron gen 1pl
τάχει.	ἡ	χάρις	τοῦ	κυρίου	ἡμῶν
tachei	*hē*	*charis*	*tou*	*kuriou*	*hēmōn*
shortly.	The	grace	of the	Lord	our

20.a.Txt: 02A,04C,020L 025P,33,etc.byz.sa.bo. Sod **Var:** p46,01ℵ,03B,Tisc We/Ho,Weis,UBS/✻

2400.2 name masc	5382.2 name gen masc	3196.1 prep	5050.2 prs- pron gen 2pl	776.3 verb 3pl indic pres
Ἰησοῦ	ʿᵃ Χριστοῦ ˋ	μεθ'	ὑμῶν.	**21.** ʿ Ἀσπάζονται
Iēsou	*Christou*	*meth'*	*humōn*	*Aspazontai*
Jesus	Christ	with	you.	Greet

21.a.Txt: 06D-corr,020L byz. **Var:** 01ℵ,02A,03B,04C 06D-org,025P,bo.Lach Treg,Alf,Word,Tisc We/Ho,Weis,Sod UBS/✻

776.2 verb 3sing indic pres	5050.4 prs- pron acc 2pl	4943.1 name nom masc	3450.5 art sing masc	4754.1 adj nom sing masc
[ᵃ✩ Ἀσπάζεται]	ὑμᾶς	Τιμόθεος	ὁ	συνεργός
Aspazetai	*humas*	*Timotheos*	*ho*	*sunergos*
[Greets]	you	Timothy	the	fellow worker

1466.2 prs- pron gen 1sing	2504.1 conj	3038.1 name nom masc	2504.1 conj	2371.1 name nom masc	2504.1 conj	4841.1 name nom masc
μου	καὶ	Λούκιος	καὶ	Ἰάσων	καὶ	Σωσίπατρος
mou	*kai*	*Loukios*	*kai*	*Iasōn*	*kai*	*Sōsipatros*
my	and	Lucius	and	Jason	and	Sosipater

3450.7 art pl masc	4624.3 adj pl masc	1466.2 prs- pron gen 1sing	776.1 verb 1sing indic pres	5050.4 prs- pron acc 2pl
οἱ	συγγενεῖς	μου.	**22.** ἀσπάζομαι	ὑμᾶς
hoi	*sungeneis*	*mou*	*aspazomai*	*humas*
the	kinsmen	my.	Greet	you

been so well indoctrinated in truth that Paul could exhort them to judge any new teaching against what they had learned. He intensely desired that their doctrine be kept pure.

The reputation of the church at Rome for fidelity to the gospel was such that a brief warning against those who would sow discord was sufficient. Paul had confidence in them and yet he was constrained to warn them to "mark . . . and avoid" those who caused division. They were to be wise regarding good and simple concerning evil. *Akeraious* ("simple") is better translated "innocent." Paul hoped that they would be immune to any evil. Prior to disobedience, Adam and Eve were innocent, "simple" regarding the dichotomy of good and evil. His entreaty was to be "in malice . . . children" but "in understanding be men" (1 Corinthians 14:20).

16:20. All of the deceptions which plague the Church are from Satan, who in concert with corrupted human nature, cause untold damage within the Body of Christ. A massive struggle has gone on over the centuries between right and wrong, truth and error, God and Satan. But Satan shall soon be crushed to pieces. He will be finally defeated at the time of the Second Coming and chained for 1000 years before being cast into the lake of fire.

The God of peace shall crush Satan under our feet. The saints are going to share with Christ in His final absolute triumph over Satan. Heretics may plague the Church, Satan may scheme to defile and destroy it, but the God of peace shall conquer.

The apostle closed this section with a reminder of the channel through which ultimate victory is made possible—"The grace of our Lord Jesus Christ be with you."

16:21. The apostle had sent greetings to many at Rome, and now those laboring with him sent greetings as well. Timothy, of course, is well known. A native of Lystra, Timothy was Paul's convert and was chosen by him as an assistant and colleague in his apostolic ministry (Acts 16:1-5). The relationship was "as a son with the father" (Philippians 2:19-22). Paul's constant companion, Timothy became a special representative of the apostle from time to time. A great student of Scripture (2 Timothy 1:5; 2:15; 3:15), he was ordained the first bishop of the church at Ephesus. Timothy not only knew the rigors of travel with Paul, but he also knew the persecution for he too suffered imprisonment (Hebrews 13:23).

Lucius, Jason, and Sosipater are also mentioned elsewhere (Acts 13:1; 17:5; 20:4). Some feel that Lucius could be Luke the physician-turned-evangelist and the inspired writer of Luke and Acts.

16:22. Tertius acted as Paul's secretary, writing the epistle at Paul's dictation. Paul's gracious courtesy should be noted. He al-

delity to the truth, *Weymouth* . . . For your submission to the faith, *Confraternity* . . . The story of your Christian obedience is known to everyone, *Barclay* . . . The fame of your obedience has spread everywhere, *NEB* . . . is famous everywhere, *JB* . . . is published into euery place, *Rheims*.

I am glad therefore on your behalf: . . . so I am delighted about you, *Williams* . . . You make me very happy, *Barclay* . . . I rejoice therefore over you, *Alford*.

but yet I would have you wise unto that which is good: . . . be well versed when it comes to goodness, *Berkeley* . . . but I want you to be experts in goodness and, *Barclay* . . . experts in good, *Moffatt* . . . be wise with respect to, *Scarlett*.

and simple concerning evil: . . . and guileless, *Confraternity* . . . but simpletons in evil, *NEB* . . . and innocents in evil, *Moffatt* . . . and pure with respect to evil, *Macknight* . . . and harmless as to the evil, *Young* . . . and to be innocentes concerninge evyll, *Tyndale* . . . but unskilled about the evil, *Klingensmith*.

20. And the God of peace shall bruise Satan under your feet shortly: . . . our source of peace, *TEV* . . . shall treade Satan vnder youre fete, *Cranmer* . . . so crushes Satan that you will trample on him, *Barclay* . . . will soon rid you of these ministers of Satan, *Locke* . . . will soon bruise the adversary, *Hanson* . . . will soon crush Satan, *Adams* . . . vndir youre feet swiftli, *Wyclif* . . . will trample Satan under your feet, *Wuest* . . . under your feet quickly, *Clementson* . . . under your feet speedily, *Douay*.

The grace of our Lord Jesus Christ [be] with you. Amen:

21. Timotheus my workfellow, and Lucius, and Jason, and Sosipater, my kinsmen, salute you: . . . my compagnion, *Geneva* . . . my colleague, sends you his good wishes, *Barclay*.

22. I Tertius, who wrote [this] epistle, salute you in the Lord: . . . who recorded this letter, *Ad-*

1466.1 prs- pron nom 1sing	4908.1 name nom masc	3450.5 art sing masc	1119.13 verb nom sing masc part aor act	3450.12 art acc sing fem	1976.4 noun acc sing fem
ἐγὼ	Τέρτιος	ὁ	γράψας	τὴν	ἐπιστολὴν
egō	Tertios	ho	grapsas	tēn	epistolēn
I	Tertius	the	having written	the	epistle

1706.1 prep	2935.3 noun dat sing masc		776.2 verb 3sing indic pres	5050.4 prs- pron acc 2pl	1043.3 name masc	3450.5 art sing masc
ἐν	κυρίῳ.	**23.** ἀσπάζεται	ὑμᾶς	Γάϊος	ὁ
en	kuriō	aspazetai	humas	Gaios	ho
in	Lord.	Greets	you	Gaius,	the

3443.1 adj nom sing masc	1466.2 prs- pron gen 1sing	2504.1 conj	3450.10 art gen sing fem	1564.1 noun fem	3513.7 adj gen sing fem
ξένος	μου	καὶ	ʽ τῆς	ἐκκλησίας	ὅλης.
xenos	mou	kai	tēs	ekklēsias	holēs
host	my	and	of the	assembly	whole.

3513.7 adj gen sing fem	3450.10 art gen sing fem	1564.1 noun fem	776.2 verb 3sing indic pres	5050.4 prs- pron acc 2pl
[✶ ὅλης	τῆς	ἐκκλησίας.]	ἀσπάζεται	ὑμᾶς
holēs	tēs	ekklēsias	aspazetai	humas
[whole	of the	church.]	Greets	you

2020.1 name nom masc	3450.5 art sing masc	3485.1 noun nom sing masc	3450.10 art gen sing fem	4032.2 noun gen sing fem	2504.1 conj
Ἔραστος	ὁ	οἰκονόμος	τῆς	πόλεως	καὶ
Erastos	ho	oikonomos	tēs	poleōs	kai
Erastus	the	steward	of the	city,	and

24.a.**Txt:** 06D,020L,044
byz.it.
Var: p46,01ℵ,02A,03B
04C,sa.bo.Lach,Treg
Tisc,We/Ho,Weis,Sod
UBS/✶

2863.1 name nom masc	3450.5 art sing masc	79.1 noun nom sing masc	3450.9 art nom sing fem	5322.1 noun nom sing fem
Κούαρτος	ὁ	ἀδελφός.	**24.** ʽᵃ Ἡ	χάρις
Kouartos	ho	adelphos	Hē	charis
Quartus	the	brother.	The	grace

3450.2 art gen sing	2935.2 noun gen sing masc	2231.2 prs- pron gen 1pl	2400.2 name masc	5382.2 name gen masc	3196.3 prep
τοῦ	κυρίου	ἡμῶν	Ἰησοῦ	Χριστοῦ	μετὰ
tou	kuriou	hēmōn	Iēsou	Christou	meta
of the	Lord	our	Jesus	Christ	with

3820.4 adj gen pl	5050.2 prs- pron gen 2pl	279.1 partic	3450.3 art dat sing	1156.2 conj	1404.14 verb dat sing masc part pres
πάντων	ὑμῶν	ἀμήν. ʾ	**25.** Τῷ	δὲ	δυναμένῳ
pantōn	humōn	amēn	Tō	de	dunamenō
all	you.	Amen.	To the	now	being able

5050.4 prs- pron acc 2pl	4592.2 verb inf aor act	2567.3 prep	3450.16 art sing neu	2077.1 noun sing neu
ὑμᾶς	στηρίξαι	κατὰ	τὸ	εὐαγγέλιόν
humas	stērixai	kata	to	euangelion
you	to establish	according to	the	good news

1466.2 prs- pron gen 1sing	2504.1 conj	3450.16 art sing neu	2754.1 noun sing neu	2400.2 name masc	5382.2 name gen masc
μου	καὶ	τὸ	κήρυγμα	Ἰησοῦ	Χριστοῦ,
mou	kai	to	kērugma	Iēsou	Christou
my	and	the	proclamation	of Jesus	Christ,

2567.3 prep	597.4 noun acc sing fem	3328.2 noun gen sing neu	5385.6 noun dat pl masc	164.5 adj dat pl masc
κατὰ	ἀποκάλυψιν	μυστηρίου	χρόνοις	αἰωνίοις
kata	apokalupsin	mustēriou	chronois	aiōniois
according to	a revelation	of mystery	in times	of the ages

lowed Tertius to make his greeting personal instead of being treated as a dictating machine—"I Tertius . . . salute you in the Lord." The expression "in the Lord" establishes the fact that his greeting was on the basis of being a fellow Christian.

16:23. Gaius was one of the first converts at Corinth (1 Corinthians 1:14) and Paul's host at Corinth. There is a likelihood that he is the believer in whose home Paul ministered in Corinth earlier (Acts 18:7). Sir William Ramsey has so identified him, stating that he was a Roman citizen and giving his full name, consisting of praenomen, nomen gentile, and cognomen, as Gaius Titius Justus (p.205). This verse seems to indicate that he was also the host "of the whole church." This could mean that the Corinthian church met in his house or that he hosted all the visiting brothers and sisters who came to Corinth.

Erastus was the city treasurer, showing that people of prominence had accepted the gospel message.

In contrast there was Quartus. His name means "four." There is conjecture that he had been a slave, for many slaves had only numbers for a name. Whether he had been or was a slave, he had a beautiful tribute—he was "a brother." Since *Tertius* means "three," it may be that Tertius and Quartus were brothers, both freedmen.

16:24. This is Paul's familiar benediction (cf. 1 Corinthians 16:23; 2 Corinthians 13:14; Philippians 4:23; 1 Thessalonians 5:28; 2 Thessalonians 3:18).

16:25. Paul began the Epistle to the Romans with the prayer that he might "impart unto you some spiritual gift, to the end ye may be established" (1:11). He longed to visit them for that purpose, but although he had not been able to do so at the time of writing, he had through this letter been able to impart a rich treasure to them.

Paul concluded the epistle with an ascription of praise. All glory belongs to God—"to him." He alone has the power (is able) to keep the Christian in the right path and to keep him from falling (Ephesians 3:20; Jude 24). He is the One who will make the believer stable, strengthen and make him firm and able to stand (14:4). Saints are to be established in and by the gospel which Paul preached. Those doctrines which Paul preached and defended presented Christ as the answer. That communication long concealed had now been revealed.

When Paul said "my gospel," (cf. Romans 2:16; 1 Thessalonians 1:5; 2 Timothy 2:8), he was speaking of the gospel as it was revealed to him by Jesus. When Paul returned to Jerusalem (Acts 9), he had a clearer revelation of the gospel than any other apostle (Galatians 1:12-17).

ams . . . the one who is putting this letter in writing, *Wuest.*

23. Gaius mine host, and of the whole church, saluteth you: . . . who is entertaining me, *JB* . . . who extends his hospitality to, *TCNT* . . . and host of the whole assembly, *Wuest* . . . the hoste of all the congregacions, *Tyndale, Cranmer.*

Erastus the chamberlain of the city saluteth you: . . . tresorer of the citee, *Wyclif.*

and Quartus a brother:

24. The grace of our Lord Jesus Christ [be] with you all. Amen:

25. Now to him that is of power to stablish you: Now I commend you to Him who is able to keep you stedfast, *Montgomery* . . . who has power, *Klingensmith* . . . that is able to confirm you, *Rheims* . . . to make you strong, *Weymouth* . . . to establish you, *Concordant.*

according to my gospel: . . . in agreement with my Gospel, *Berkeley* . . . in an adherence, *Locke* . . . as promised in the Good News, *TCNT.*

and the preaching of Jesus Christ: . . . and the proclamation, *Worrell.*

according to the revelation of the mystery: . . . whereby is unveiled the secret truth, *Montgomery* . . . according to the revelation of the secret, *Adams* . . . according to the mandate of the eternal God, *Wuest* . . . which involves the revealing of the secret, *Berkeley* . . . by revealing the secret purpose, *Moffatt* . . . in vtteringe of the mistery, *Tyndale.*

which was kept secret since the world began: . . . that has been obscure for ages, *Norlie* . . . veiled in silence for long ages, *Beck* . . . after the silence of many centuries, *Berkeley* . . . that was kept quiet for ages, *Adams* . . . which has been kept silent, *HistNT* . . . which in the periods of past ages remained unuttered, *Weymouth* . . . which for eternal ages was unrevealed, *Noyes* . . . not revealed in ancient times, *Sawyer* . . . having been kept in silence, *Clementson* . . . kept secret in times of the ages, *Klingensmith*

4456.7 verb gen sing neu part perf pass	5157.14 verb gen sing masc part aor pass	1156.2 conj	3431.1 adv	1217.2 prep
σεσιγημένου,	26. φανερωθέντος	δὲ	νῦν,	διά
sesigēmenou	*phanerōthentos*	*de*	*nun*	*dia*
having been kept secret,	having been manifested	but	now,	by

4885.1 conj	1118.6 noun gen pl fem	4255.2 adj gen pl fem	2567.1 prep	1987.2 noun acc sing fem
τε	γραφῶν	προφητικῶν,	κατ'	ἐπιταγὴν
te	*graphōn*	*prophētikōn*	*kat'*	*epitagēn*
and	scriptures	prophetic,	according to	commandment

3450.2 art gen sing	164.2 adj gen sing	2296.2 noun gen sing masc	1519.1 prep	5056.4 noun acc sing fem	3963.2 noun gen sing fem	1519.1 prep
τοῦ	αἰωνίου	θεοῦ,	εἰς	ὑπακοὴν	πίστεως	εἰς
tou	*aiōniou*	*theou*	*eis*	*hupakoēn*	*pisteōs*	*eis*
of the	eternal	God,	for	obedience	of faith	to

3820.1 adj	3450.17 art pl neu	1477.4 noun pl neu	1101.16 verb gen sing neu part aor pass	3304.4 adj dat sing masc
πάντα	τὰ	ἔθνη	γνωρισθέντος,	27. μόνῳ
panta	*ta*	*ethnē*	*gnōristhentos*	*monō*
all	the	nations	having been made known	only

27.a.**Txt**: p46,01א,04C
06D,We/Ho,byz.
Var: 03B,33,72

4533.2 adj dat sing masc	2296.3 noun dat sing masc	1217.2 prep	2400.2 name masc	5382.2 name gen masc	3614.3 rel- pron dat sing
σοφῷ	θεῷ,	διὰ	Ἰησοῦ	Χριστοῦ,	⌈a ᾧ⌉
sophō	*theō*	*dia*	*Iēsou*	*Christou*	*hō*
wise	God,	through	Jesus	Christ,	to whom

27.b.**Var**: 01א,02A,06D
025P,it.bo.Lach,Tisc
Weis,Sod,UBS/✵

3450.9 art nom sing fem	1385.1 noun nom sing fem	1519.1 prep	3450.8 art acc pl masc	163.6 noun acc pl masc	3450.1 art gen pl
ἡ	δόξα	εἰς	τοὺς	αἰῶνας.	⌈b+ τῶν
hē	*doxa*	*eis*	*tous*	*aiōnas*	*tōn*
the	glory	to	the	ages.	[of the

27.c.**Txt**: Steph
Var: Gries,Lach,Word
Tisc,We/Ho,Weis,Sod
UBS/✵

163.4 noun gen pl masc	279.1 partic	4242.1 prep	4371.6 name- adj acc pl masc	1119.21 verb 3sing indic aor pass	570.3 prep gen
αἰώνων ⌉	ἀμήν.	⌈c Πρὸς	Ῥωμαίους	ἐγράφη	ἀπὸ
aiōnōn	*amēn*	*Pros*	*Rhōmaious*	*egraphē*	*apo*
ages]	Amen.	To	Romans	was written	from

2855.3 name gen sing masc	1217.2 prep	5239.2 name gen fem	3450.10 art gen sing fem	1243.6 noun gen sing fem	3450.10 art gen sing fem
Κορίνθου,	διὰ	Φοίβης	τῆς	διακόνου	τῆς
Korinthou	*dia*	*Phoibēs*	*tēs*	*diakonou*	*tēs*
Corinth,	by	Phoebe	the	servant	of the

1706.1 prep	2717.1 name dat fem	1564.1 noun fem
ἐν	Κεγχρεαῖς	ἐκκλησίας. ⌉
en	*Kenchreais*	*ekklēsias*
in	Cenchreae	assembly.

16:26. The "mystery" of verse 25 was the divine secret that Gentiles would be fellow heirs with Jews in the body of Christ (Ephesians 3). The gospel brought Gentiles to glory, and so glory came to God. This mystery is now being made known to all nations.

Paul constantly used the Old Testament Scriptures in his preaching. It was "according to the Scriptures" (1 Corinthians 15:3,4). His gospel, the mystery, was witnessed to by the Law and the Prophets but only became known as revealed by the one who had the key. Paul had that key, the knowledge of Christ which God had revealed to him. It was only in the light of the new revelation in Christ that Paul and the apostles were able to understand and expound the Scriptures (1 Peter 1:10-12).

This revelation was "according to the commandment of the everlasting God." He is the Eternal One and therefore unchanging. He had concealed this truth but He intended that it should be revealed. By His command the gospel has been known in and by His Son.

The expression "the obedience of faith" was also used in 1:5. The tendency of faith is to produce obedience. There is no true faith that does not produce obedience. This is a constant affirmation in the New Testament (Romans 15:18; 16:19; 2 Corinthians 7:15; James 2).

The original commission which Jesus gave His disciples was that the gospel was to be preached "among all nations" (Luke 24:27). It was the special commission which Paul received at his conversion (Acts 9:15). It is the privilege of all to receive and appropriate the message of the gospel; the duty of all who accept is to transmit the good news to others.

16:27. Paul resumed the doxology with a great expression of praise to God. The attribute of wisdom is brought into view, for it has surely been particularly on display in God's plan to save men as revealed in this great epistle. God's wisdom is shown in devising the plan and in bringing it about.

All men have been found guilty; the whole world was declared guilty before God. Justification by faith in Christ crucified is the only remedy for sin. It is by faith alone.

The remedy of the gospel for indwelling sin is sanctification. By union with Christ in His death and resurrection the dominion of sin is broken. "The law of the Spirit of life in Christ Jesus" (8:1,2) makes it possible for the believer to live victoriously with no condemnation and no separation.

God has turned His attention to the Gentiles, but the Jew is only temporarily set aside and will return to God.

Christian life and service calls for all believers to be considerate of others and to be motivated with an outflow of the love of Christ.

The long argument of the letter comes to a close with a great song of praise "to God only wise, be glory through Jesus Christ for ever. Amen."

. . . which was kept secret through immemorial ages, *Montgomery* . . . from eternal ages, *Confraternity* . . . from eternal times kept secrete, *Rheims* . . . through times eternal, *ASV* . . . for long ages, *RSV.*

26. But now is made manifest: But now is opened, and published, *Geneva* . . . But now disclosed, *Hanson* . . . with the uncovering of the secret, *Williams* . . . but is now disclosed, *RSV* . . . brought out into the open, *TEV.*

and by the scriptures of the prophets: . . . and through the prophetic Scriptures, *Adams* . . . by means of prophetic scriptures, *PNT* . . . on the basis of the prophetic scriptures, *Moffatt.*

according to the commandment of the everlasting God, made known to all nations: . . . according to the precept of the eternal God, *Confraternity* . . . to an appointment of the aeonian God, *Hanson* . . . of god withouten bigynnynge [and] endynge, *Wyclif* . . . according to the precept of the eternal God, *Rheims* . . . publisshed amonge all nacions, *Tyndale* . . . to the precept of the eternal God, *Douay.*

for the obedience of faith: . . . to bring about obedience to the faith, *RSV* . . . to secure submission to the Faith, *TCNT.*

27. To God only wise, [be] glory through Jesus Christ for ever. Amen: . . . into worldis of worldis, *Wyclif* . . . to the ages! *Scarlett* . . . for the eons of the eons, *Concordant.*

THE FIRST EPISTLE OF PAUL TO THE
CORINTHIANS

Expanded Interlinear

Textual Critical Apparatus

Verse-by-Verse Commentary

Various Versions

4242.1 prep	2854.3 name acc pl masc	1976.1 noun nom sing fem	4272.9 num ord nom sing fem
Πρὸς	Κορινθίους	ἐπιστολὴ	πρώτη.
Pros	Korinthious	epistolē	prōtē
To	Corinthians	letter	first.

Textual Apparatus

3834.1 name nom masc	2795.1 adj nom sing masc	646.1 noun nom sing masc	2400.2 name masc	5382.2 name gen masc
1:1. Παῦλος	κλητὸς	ἀπόστολος	ʽ Ἰησοῦ	Χριστοῦ,
Paulos	klētos	apostolos	Iēsou	Christou
Paul	a called	apostle	of Jesus	Christ,

5382.2 name gen masc	2400.2 name masc	1217.2 prep	2284.2 noun gen sing neu	2296.2 noun gen sing masc	2504.1 conj
[Χριστοῦ	Ἰησοῦ,]	διὰ	θελήματος	θεοῦ,	καὶ
Christou	Iēsou	dia	thelēmatos	theou	kai
[Christ	Jesus,]	by	will	of God,	and

4840.1 name nom masc	3450.5 art sing masc	79.1 noun nom sing masc	3450.11 art dat sing fem	1564.3 noun dat sing fem
Σωσθένης	ὁ	ἀδελφός,	**2.** τῇ	ἐκκλησίᾳ
Sōsthenēs	ho	adelphos	tē	ekklēsia
Sosthenes	the	brother,	to the	assembly

3450.2 art gen sing	2296.2 noun gen sing masc	3450.11 art dat sing fem	1498.28 verb dat sing fem part pres act	1706.1 prep	2855.1 name dat fem
τοῦ	θεοῦ	τῇ	οὔσῃ	ἐν	Κορίνθῳ,
tou	theou	tē	ousē	en	Korinthō
	of God	the	being	in	Corinth,

37.18 verb dat pl masc part perf pass	1706.1 prep	5382.3 name dat masc	2400.2 name masc	2795.3 adj dat pl masc
ἡγιασμένοις	ἐν	Χριστῷ	Ἰησοῦ,	κλητοῖς
hēgiasmenois	en	Christō	Iēsou	klētois
having been made holy	in	Christ	Jesus,	called

39.8 adj dat pl masc	4713.1 prep dat	3820.5 adj dat pl	3450.4 art dat pl	1926.8 verb dat pl masc part pres mid	3450.16 art sing neu
ἁγίοις,	σὺν	πᾶσιν	τοῖς	ἐπικαλουμένοις	τὸ
hagiois	sun	pasin	tois	epikaloumenois	to
saints,	with	all	the	calling on	the

3549.2 noun sing neu	3450.2 art gen sing	2935.2 noun gen sing masc	2231.2 prs-pron gen 1pl	2400.2 name masc	5382.2 name gen masc	1706.1 prep
ὄνομα	τοῦ	κυρίου	ἡμῶν	Ἰησοῦ	Χριστοῦ	ἐν
onoma	tou	kuriou	hēmōn	Iēsou	Christou	en
name	of the	Lord	our	Jesus	Christ	in

2.a.**Txt:** 01ℵ-corr
02A-corr,06D-corr,020L
025P,byz.
Var: 01ℵ-org,02A-org
03B,06D-org,bo.Lach
Treg,Tisc,We/Ho,Weis
Sod,UBS/★

3820.3 adj dat sing	4964.3 noun dat sing masc	840.1 prs-pron gen pl	4885.1 conj	2504.1 conj	2231.2 prs-pron gen 1pl	5322.1 noun nom sing fem
παντὶ	τόπῳ,	αὐτῶν	ʽᵃ τέ ʼ	καὶ	ἡμῶν·	**3.** χάρις
panti	topō	autōn	te	kai	hēmōn	charis
every	place,	theirs	both	and	ours:	grace

5050.3 prs-pron dat 2pl	2504.1 conj	1503.1 noun nom sing fem	570.3 prep gen	2296.2 noun gen sing masc	3824.2 noun gen sing masc	2231.2 prs-pron gen 1pl
ὑμῖν	καὶ	εἰρήνη	ἀπὸ	θεοῦ	πατρὸς	ἡμῶν
humin	kai	eirēnē	apo	theou	patros	hēmōn
to you	and	peace	from	God	Father	our

THE FIRST EPISTLE OF PAUL TO THE
CORINTHIANS

1:1. This letter opens in the usual first-century way, listing the writer(s), those addressed, and a prayer. That this letter was written by the apostle Paul is beyond doubt. This is the Paul who once called himself a "Hebrew of the Hebrews" (Philippians 3:5), saw the Lord on the Damascus Road, wrote nearly half the books of the New Testament, and has been designated "the Apostle of the Gentiles." In this verse, while suggesting his position and authority ("apostle"), he also noted its divine origin ("called") and its divine order ("will of God"). In the beginning, Paul wanted his readers to know that what he was writing to them was from the Lord.

The cowriter of this letter is not so easily identified. Apparently he was a fellow minister of more local rank. It could be he was a Corinthian. Some have suggested this is the Sosthenes mentioned in Acts 18:17. It is possible, but the name was common and it is difficult to be certain.

1:2. When we read further in this letter and see the problems plaguing the Corinthian Christians, we find it interesting that Paul called them saints. Yet it is the work of Christ that makes someone a saint, not the work of a body of men. Sainthood is caused by the internal purification and reformation of the soul, as here suggested by the word "sanctified."

We might conclude that this letter was intended at least for more than just the Corinthians. The phrase "with all that in every place" would suggest that.

In verse 10 Paul began to discuss the problem of division at Corinth. But even in this verse Paul made a veiled reference to that when he spoke of Christ as Lord of all. True sanctification will produce genuine fellowship with other believers in Christ.

1:3. The greeting of grace and peace from both God the Father and God the Son was to become the typical Christian greeting. Especially is that true of Paul's writings. (See, for example, Romans 1:7; 2 Corinthians 1:2; Galatians 1:3; Ephesians 1:2; Philippians 1:2; Colossians 1:2; 1 Thessalonians 1:1; 2 Thessalonians 1:2; 1 Timothy 1:2; 2 Timothy 1:2; Titus 1:4; Philemon 3.) The greeting spoke of God's gifts and blessings, and His attitude and desires toward those who love and serve Him.

Various Versions

1. Paul, called [to be] an apostle of Jesus Christ through the will of God: . . . by vocation an Apostle, *Geneva* . . . a Constituted Apostle, *Wilson* . . . chosen by divine will, *Fenton* . . . and sent by Jesus Messiah, *Murdock*.
and Sosthenes [our] brother:

2. Unto the church of God which is at Corinth: Unto the congregacyon, *Cranmer* . . . to the ecclesia, *Concordant* . . . to the Community of God, *HistNT* . . . to the assembly of God existing, *Fenton*.
to them that are sanctified in Christ Jesus: . . . hallowed, *Concordant, Conybeare* . . . to hem that ben halowid in crist, *Wyclif* . . . who are consecrated, *Moffatt*.
called [to be] saints: . . . the chosen saints, *Fenton* . . . sainctes by callynge, *Tyndale*.
with all that in every place call upon the name of Jesus Christ our Lord: . . . along with all, *HistNT* . . . to all them, *Murdock* . . . in conjunction with all, *Rotherham* . . . wherever they are, *Montgomery* . . . vvith al that inuocate the name, *Rheims* . . . invoke the name, *Moffatt* . . . all appealing to the Power of our, *Fenton*.
both theirs and ours: . . . which is their home—and our home also, *Conybeare*.

3. Grace [be] unto you, and peace: . . . favour unto you, *Rotherham* . . . be granted to you, *Weymouth*.
from God our Father, and [from] the Lord Jesus Christ:

261

1 Corinthians 1:4

2504.1 conj	2935.2 noun gen sing masc	2400.2 name masc	5382.2 name gen masc	2149.1 verb 1sing indic pres act	3450.3 art dat sing
καὶ	κυρίου	Ἰησοῦ	Χριστοῦ.	**4.** Εὐχαριστῶ	τῷ
kai	kuriou	Iēsou	Christou	Eucharistō	tō
and	Lord	Jesus	Christ.	I thank	

2296.3 noun dat sing masc	1466.2 prs-pron gen 1sing	3704.1 adv	3875.1 prep	5050.2 prs-pron gen 2pl	1894.3 prep
θεῷ	⌐a μου ⌐	πάντοτε	περὶ	ὑμῶν,	ἐπὶ
theō	mou	pantote	peri	humōn	epi
God	my	always	concerning	you,	for

3450.11 art dat sing fem	5322.3 noun dat sing fem	3450.2 art gen sing	2296.2 noun gen sing masc	3450.11 art dat sing fem	1319.50 verb dat sing fem part aor pass
τῇ	χάριτι	τοῦ	θεοῦ	τῇ	δοθείσῃ
tē	chariti	tou	theou	tē	dotheisē
the	grace		of God	the	having been given

5050.3 prs-pron dat 2pl	1706.1 prep	5382.3 name dat masc	2400.2 name masc	3617.1 conj	1706.1 prep	3820.3 adj dat sing
ὑμῖν	ἐν	Χριστῷ	Ἰησοῦ,	**5.** ὅτι	ἐν	παντὶ
humin	en	Christō	Iēsou	hoti	en	panti
to you	in	Christ	Jesus,	that	in	everything

4008.3 verb 2pl indic aor pass	1706.1 prep	840.4 prs-pron dat sing	1706.1 prep	3820.3 adj dat sing	3030.3 noun dat sing masc
ἐπλουτίσθητε	ἐν	αὐτῷ,	ἐν	παντὶ	λόγῳ
eploutisthēte	en	autō	en	panti	logō
you were enriched	in	him,	in	all	discourse

2504.1 conj	3820.11 adj dat sing fem	1102.3 noun dat sing fem	2503.1 conj	3450.16 art sing neu	3115.1 noun sing neu
καὶ	πάσῃ	γνώσει,	**6.** καθὼς	τὸ	μαρτύριον
kai	pasē	gnōsei	kathōs	to	marturion
and	all	knowledge,	just as	the	testimony

3450.2 art gen sing	5382.2 name gen masc	943.7 verb 3sing indic aor pass	1706.1 prep	5050.3 prs-pron dat 2pl	5452.1 conj
τοῦ	Χριστοῦ	ἐβεβαιώθη	ἐν	ὑμῖν	**7.** ὥστε
tou	Christou	ebebaiōthē	en	humin	hōste
of the	Christ	was confirmed	among	you,	so that

5050.4 prs-pron acc 2pl	3231.1 partic	5139.12 verb inf pres	1706.1 prep	3235.2 num card dat	5321.5 noun dat pl neu
ὑμᾶς	μὴ	ὑστερεῖσθαι	ἐν	μηδενὶ	χαρίσματι,
humas	mē	hustereisthai	en	mēdeni	charismati
you	not	to be lacking	in	not any	gift,

549.5 verb acc pl masc part pres	3450.12 art acc sing fem	597.4 noun acc sing fem	3450.2 art gen sing	2935.2 noun gen sing masc
ἀπεκδεχομένους	τὴν	ἀποκάλυψιν	τοῦ	κυρίου
apekdechomenous	tēn	apokalupsin	tou	kuriou
awaiting	the	revelation	of the	Lord

2231.2 prs-pron gen 1pl	2400.2 name masc	5382.2 name gen masc	3614.5 rel-pron nom sing masc	2504.1 conj	943.4 verb 3sing indic fut act
ἡμῶν	Ἰησοῦ	Χριστοῦ·	**8.** ὃς	καὶ	βεβαιώσει
hēmōn	Iēsou	Christou	hos	kai	bebaiōsei
our	Jesus	Christ;	who	also	will confirm

5050.4 prs-pron acc 2pl	2175.1 conj	4904.2 noun gen sing neu	408.4 adj acc pl masc	1706.1 prep	3450.11 art dat sing fem
ὑμᾶς	ἕως	τέλους,	ἀνεγκλήτους	ἐν	τῇ
humas	heōs	telous	anenklētous	en	tē
you	to	end,	above reproach	in	the

1:4. Paul said some difficult things before he concluded this letter. Yet despite the problems Paul encountered, he always found something for which to thank the Lord. This is the response of a man who spends more time dwelling on the goodness of the Lord than on his circumstances. Thanksgiving is essential to the Christian life, and Paul wanted the Corinthians to understand this. The grace of God has as its source Jesus Christ. He is its life-spring and the vessel through which it is imparted to the Church. Because of this, the grace of God is effective, even though the change may seem more apparent in some believers than others.

1:5. This grace is clearly of God; thus, the work done is of God also. He had enriched the Corinthian Christians in a large way. Surprisingly, Paul noted their enrichment in two particular ways: in utterance or telling of truth, and in knowledge or the grasp of truth. Later, it appears that he rebuked the readers for these very things. A careful reading, however, will lead us to understand that what Paul rebuked was the pride or the attitude in these things. With a proper, tender attitude, knowledge and utterance can be a very powerful combination.

1:6. This richness in Christ came as a result of clear and specific witness concerning Christ. We may conclude that there was certain testimony concerning Christ's death, burial, resurrection, ascension, and return, as well as specific teaching on the whole life of salvation and the work of the Holy Spirit.

This witness was confirmed in them. How was it confirmed? They heard the gospel, repented, believed on Christ, accepted the gospel, and the consequence was their fellowship and equality with other Christians.

1:7. Experientially, the Corinthians were not lacking in any "gift." This "gift" may refer to salvation, to good gifts in general, or to a special equipment of the Holy Spirit. Certainly it was intended to make them mature, effective Christians in life, deed, and thought. Whatever its precise reference, these so blessed were thus pointed to the second coming of Jesus Christ, when their use of these gifts would be tested or examined and they would see the culmination of the work of the Spirit.

1:8. Until that day Christ will continue what He has begun; i.e., the work of confirming, sanctifying, maturing, and making unreprovable or blameless. God's goal is to present us complete and accepted in Christ on that day when He shall return. As *The Ex-*

4. I thank my God always on your behalf: . . . I always thank, *HistNT* . . . continually on your behalf, *Weymouth, Conybeare.*
for the grace of God which is given you by Jesus Christ: . . . granted to you, *Fenton* . . . bestowed on you, *Moffatt.*

5. That in every thing ye are enriched by him: . . . ye are made riche in hym, *Geneva* . . . so richly blessed in Him, *Weymouth* . . . received a wealth of all blessing, *Moffatt.*
in all utterance, and [in] all knowledge: . . . with readiness of speech and fulness of knowledge, *Weymouth* . . . in all expression, *Concordant* . . . all the gifts of speech, *Conybeare* . . . with full reason and full knowledge, *Fenton* . . . in all discourse, *Rotherham* . . . and all extraordinary gifts, *Locke.*

6. Even as the testimony of Christ was confirmed in you: . . . by the which thynges the testimony of Iesus Christ, *Cranmer* . . . which verifies the testimony, *Moffatt.*

7. So that ye come behind in no gift: . . . you do not suffer want in any privilege, *HistNT* . . . may not be deficient in any spiritual gift, *Fenton* . . . lack no spiritual endowment, *Moffatt* . . . you lack no divine gift, *Montgomery* . . . in any one gift-of-favour, *Rotherham.*
waiting for the coming of our Lord Jesus Christ: . . . looking earnestly for the time, *Conybeare* . . . awaiting the unveiling, *Concordant* . . . expecting the reuelation, *Rheims* . . . waiting for the revelation, *Montgomery* . . . for the re-appearing, *Weymouth* . . . and wayte for the apperynge of oure lorde Iesus Christ, *Tyndale* . . . shall be revealed to sight, *Conybeare.*

8. Who shall also confirm you unto the end: . . . also support you until absolutely perfect, *Fenton* . . . keep you perfectly steadfast unto the end, *Montgomery* . . . until the consummation, *Concordant.*

1 Corinthians 1:9

8.a.Txt: 01ℵ,02A,04C
06D,010F,012G,044,byz.
Var: p46,03B

2232.3 noun dat sing fem	3450.2 art gen sing	2935.2 noun gen sing masc	2231.2 prs-pron gen 1pl	2400.2 name masc	5382.2 name gen masc
ἡμέρᾳ	τοῦ	κυρίου	ἡμῶν	Ἰησοῦ	[a Χριστοῦ. ˋ
hēmera	tou	kuriou	hēmōn	Iēsou	Christou
day	of the	Lord	our	Jesus	Christ.

3964.2 adj nom sing masc	3450.5 art sing masc	2296.1 noun nom sing masc	1217.1 prep	3614.2 rel-pron gen sing	2535.38 verb 2pl indic aor pass
9. πιστὸς	ὁ	θεὸς,	δι'	οὗ	ἐκλήθητε
pistos	ho	theos	di'	hou	eklēthēte
Faithful		God,	by	whom	you were called

1519.1 prep	2815.4 noun acc sing fem	3450.2 art gen sing	5048.2 noun gen sing masc	840.3 prs-pron gen sing	2400.2 name masc
εἰς	κοινωνίαν	τοῦ	υἱοῦ	αὐτοῦ	Ἰησοῦ
eis	koinōnian	tou	huiou	autou	Iēsou
into	fellowship	of the	Son	his	Jesus

5382.2 name gen masc	3450.2 art gen sing	2935.2 noun gen sing masc	2231.2 prs-pron gen 1pl		3731.1 verb 1sing indic pres act
Χριστοῦ	τοῦ	κυρίου	ἡμῶν.		10. Παρακαλῶ
Christou	tou	kuriou	hēmōn		Parakalō
Christ	of the	Lord	our.		I urge

1156.2 conj	5050.4 prs-pron acc 2pl	79.6 noun pl masc	1217.2 prep	3450.2 art gen sing	3549.3 noun gen sing neu
δὲ	ὑμᾶς,	ἀδελφοί,	διὰ	τοῦ	ὀνόματος
de	humas	adelphoi	dia	tou	onomatos
now	you,	brothers,	by	the	name

3450.2 art gen sing	2935.2 noun gen sing masc	2231.2 prs-pron gen 1pl	2400.2 name masc	5382.2 name gen masc	2419.1 conj
τοῦ	κυρίου	ἡμῶν	Ἰησοῦ	Χριστοῦ,	ἵνα
tou	kuriou	hēmōn	Iēsou	Christou	hina
of the	Lord	our	Jesus	Christ,	that

3450.16 art sing neu	840.15 prs-pron sing neu	2978.9 verb 2pl subj pres act	3820.7 adj pl masc	2504.1 conj	3231.1 partic
τὸ	αὐτὸ	λέγητε	πάντες,	καὶ	μὴ
to	auto	legēte	pantes	kai	mē
the	same thing	you say	all,	and	no

1498.10 verb 3sing subj pres act	1706.1 prep	5050.3 prs-pron dat 2pl	4830.2 noun pl neu	1498.1 verb 2pl act	1156.2 conj
ᾖ	ἐν	ὑμῖν	σχίσματα,	ἦτε	δὲ
ē	en	humin	schismata	ēte	de
there be	among	you	divisions;	you be	but

2645.7 verb nom pl masc part perf pass	1706.1 prep	3450.3 art dat sing	840.4 prs-pron dat sing	3426.3 noun dat sing masc	2504.1 conj
κατηρτισμένοι	ἐν	τῷ	αὐτῷ	νοῒ	καὶ
katērtismenoi	en	tō	autō	noi	kai
being knit together	in	the	same	mind	and

1706.1 prep	3450.11 art dat sing fem	840.11 prs-pron dat sing fem	1100.3 noun dat sing fem	1207.7 verb 3sing indic aor pass	1056.1 conj
ἐν	τῇ	αὐτῇ	γνώμῃ.	11. ἐδηλώθη	γὰρ
en	tē	autē	gnōmē	edēlōthē	gar
in	the	same	judgment.	It was made clear	for

1466.4 prs-pron dat 1sing	3875.1 prep	5050.2 prs-pron gen 2pl	79.6 noun pl masc	1466.2 prs-pron gen 1sing	5097.3 prep
μοι	περὶ	ὑμῶν,	ἀδελφοί	μου,	ὑπὸ
moi	peri	humōn	adelphoi	mou	hupo
to me	concerning	you,	brothers	my,	by

positor's Greek Testament suggests, He will confirm character as they have confirmed their testimony (Nicoll, 2:761).

1:9. We must be assured that this confirmation will continue because God is faithful; our security rests in the character of God. What He commits himself to will always be finished. Phillips' translation reads: "God is utterly dependable . . . ." It is this God who calls us to fellowship with His Son Jesus. This fellowship may be either subjective (with His Son) or objective (in His Son). The subjective sense would seem to be best because nowhere else is this noun used as the objective genitive of person, and the reference in context seems to be communion, of which Christ is the sum.

God will finish the beautiful work He has begun, if we remain in Christ. After all, Jesus Christ, under the direction of the Father, is the "author and finisher of our faith" (Hebrews 12:2).

1:10. After his very positive opening remarks, however, it did not take Paul long to begin to correct the difficulties at Corinth that had come to his attention. "Now" contrasts what follows with what has preceded. He appealed to them with great solemnity, yet great gentleness, to be united together under Christ. Some might argue that it was very difficult to be so united because of differences in background, personality, and approach. But when Paul urged them to "speak the same thing" and to be in unity, he was referring to unity in love, doctrine, and purpose which is both essential and mandatory. In fact, "speak the same thing" is a classical expression used of political communities that were free from factions, or of different states that entertained friendly relations with each other. Besides, the Spirit of Christ draws us together around a common theme and into a common bond.

Katērtismenoi is also used in Mark 1:19 of "mending" fishing nets. In the same way that torn fishing nets could be restored and mended, the factionalized people at Corinth were to be knit together. The word is also used by the Greek historian Herodotus for restoring peace after civil unrest and discord. The church at Corinth was acting more like a group of political rivals than the church of God. The knitting together that Paul desired for the church was a matter of both mind and judgment, that is, by true and correct doctrine.

Paul wished his readers to be restored to a rightful condition of love in Christ, and if there could not be a unity of choice, there could be a unity of feeling and affection. It is possible to hold someone in regard and love and treat him as a brother, without agreeing with him on everything. Without unity, the Church cannot present an effective witness to the world around it.

1:11. Lest the Corinthians deny the difficulties, Paul recorded his source of information. The reports had come from "the house

[that ye may be] blameless in the day of our Lord Jesus Christ: . . . there may be no charge against you, *Locke* . . . to be irreproachable, *HistNT* . . . you will be unreprovable in the Day, *Montgomery* . . . he will guarantee that you are vindicated on the day, *Moffatt* . . . unaccusable in the day, *Rotherham* . . . unimpeachable, *Concordant.*

9. God [is] faithful: . . . may be relied on, *Locke.*
by whom ye were called unto the fellowship of his Son Jesus Christ our Lord: . . . were chosen into a fellowship, *Fenton* . . . into the societie of his sonne, *Rheims.*

10. Now I beseech you, brethren: Now I appeal to you, *HistNT* . . . But I beg of you, *Fenton.*
by the name of our Lord Jesus Christ:
that ye all speak the same thing, and [that] there be no divisions among you: . . . that ye hold the same doctrines, *Locke* . . . you would all reason alike, *Fenton* . . . to be all in unison, *HistNT* . . . to shun disputes, *Conybeare* . . . that there be no dissencion amonge you, *Tyndale* . . . that there be no schisms among you, *Rheims* . . . must be no cliques, *Moffatt* . . . to speak in accord, *Montgomery* . . . to cultivate a spirit of harmony, *Weymouth.*
but [that] ye be perfectly joined together: . . . but be ye knyt togither, *Geneva* . . . but be at harmony together, *HistNT* . . . but you may be attuned, *Concordant* . . . may be trained in, *Fenton* . . . into one entire body, *Locke* . . . perfect in one sense, *Rheims.*
in the same mind and in the same judgment: . . . to be knit together in the same mind, *Conybeare* . . . to the same opinion, *Concordant* . . . in a common mind and temper, *Montgomery* . . . and in one knovvledge, *Rheims.*

11. For it hath been declared unto me of you, my brethren: For it was signified to me, *Rotherham* . . . For I have been distinctly informed, *Weymouth* . . . to me respecting you, *Fenton.*

1 Corinthians 1:12

3450.1 art gen pl	5350.1 name gen fem	3617.1 conj	2038.6 noun nom pl fem	1706.1 prep	5050.3 prs-pron dat 2pl
τῶν	Χλόης,	ὅτι	ἔριδες	ἐν	ὑμῖν
tōn	*Chloēs*	*hoti*	*erides*	*en*	*humin*
the	of Chloe,	that	rivalries	among	you

1498.7 verb 3pl indic pres act		2978.1 verb 1sing pres act	1156.2 conj	3642.17 dem-pron sing neu	3617.1 conj	1524.3 adj nom sing masc
εἰσιν·	**12.**	λέγω	δὲ	τοῦτο,	ὅτι	ἕκαστος
eisin		*legō*	*de*	*touto*	*hoti*	*hekastos*
there are.		I say	but	this,	that	each

5050.2 prs-pron gen 2pl	2978.5 verb 3sing indic pres act	1466.1 prs-pron nom 1sing	3173.1 conj	1498.2 verb 1sing indic pres act	3834.2 name gen masc
ὑμῶν	λέγει,	Ἐγὼ	μέν	εἰμι	Παύλου,
humōn	*legei*	*Egō*	*men*	*eimi*	*Paulou*
of you	says,	I	men	am	of Paul,

1466.1 prs-pron nom 1sing	1156.2 conj	619.2 name acc masc	1466.1 prs-pron nom 1sing	1156.2 conj	2758.2 name gen masc
Ἐγὼ	δὲ	Ἀπολλῶ,	Ἐγὼ	δὲ	Κηφᾶ,
Egō	*de*	*Apollō*	*Egō*	*de*	*Kēpha*
I	and	of Apollos,	I	and	of Cephas,

1466.1 prs-pron nom 1sing	1156.2 conj	5382.2 name gen masc	3177.6 verb 3sing indic perf pass	3450.5 art sing masc
Ἐγὼ	δὲ	Χριστοῦ.	**13.** Μεμέρισται	ὁ
Egō	*de*	*Christou*	*Memeristai*	*ho*
I	and	of Christ.	Has been divided	the

5382.1 name nom masc	3231.1 partic	3834.1 name nom masc	4568.12 verb 3sing indic aor pass	5065.1 prep	5050.2 prs-pron gen 2pl
Χριστός;	μὴ	Παῦλος	ἐσταυρώθη	ὑπὲρ	ὑμῶν,
Christos	*mē*	*Paulos*	*estaurōthē*	*huper*	*humōn*
Christ?	not	Paul	was crucified	for	you?

2211.1 conj	1519.1 prep	3450.16 art sing neu	3549.2 noun sing neu	3834.2 name gen masc	901.16 verb 2pl indic aor pass
ἢ	εἰς	τὸ	ὄνομα	Παύλου	ἐβαπτίσθητε;
ē	*eis*	*to*	*onoma*	*Paulou*	*ebaptisthēte*
or	to	the	name	of Paul	were you baptized?

14.a.Txt: 01א-corr2,02A 04C,06D,010F,012G 020L,025P,044,etc.byz. Lach,Sod
Var: 01א-org,03B,6,bo. Tisc,We/Ho,Weis UBS/✸

2149.1 verb 1sing indic pres act	3450.3 art dat sing	2296.3 noun dat sing masc	3617.1 conj	3625.3 num card acc masc	5050.2 prs-pron gen 2pl
14. εὐχαριστῶ	⌜ᵃ τῷ ⌝	θεῷ	ὅτι	οὐδένα	ὑμῶν
eucharistō	*tō*	*theō*	*hoti*	*oudena*	*humōn*
I thank		God	that	no one	of you

901.7 verb 1sing indic aor act	1479.1 conj	3231.1 partic	2894.2 name acc masc	2504.1 conj	1043.2 name acc masc	2419.1 conj
ἐβάπτισα,	εἰ	μὴ	Κρίσπον	καὶ	Γάϊον·	**15.** ἵνα
ebaptisa	*ei*	*mē*	*Krispon*	*kai*	*Gaion*	*hina*
I baptized,	if	not	Crispus	and	Gaius,	that

3231.1 partic	4948.3 indef-pron nom sing	1500.8 verb 3sing subj aor act	3617.1 conj	1519.1 prep	3450.16 art sing neu	1684.1 adj 1sing
μή	τις	εἴπῃ	ὅτι	εἰς	τὸ	ἐμὸν
mē	*tis*	*eipē*	*hoti*	*eis*	*to*	*emon*
not	anyone	should say	that	unto	the	my

15.a.Txt: 04C-corr3,06D 010F,012G,020L,025P 044,byz.
Var: 01א,02A,03B 04C-org,6,33,81,365 630,1175,1506,1739 p46,bo.Lach,Treg,Alf Word,Tisc,We/Ho,Weis Sod,UBS/✸

3549.2 noun sing neu	901.7 verb 1sing indic aor act	901.16 verb 2pl indic aor pass	901.7 verb 1sing indic aor act
ὄνομα	⌜ ἐβάπτισα.	[ᵃ✸ ἐβαπτίσθητε.]	**16.** ἐβάπτισα
onoma	*ebaptisa*	*ebaptisthēte*	*ebaptisa*
name	I baptized.	[you were baptized.]	I baptized

of Chloe." These were friends Paul respected and trusted. They had a deep and genuine concern for the church at Corinth. The reports were true beyond any reasonable doubt. Such problems need to be established as true before the minister of God proceeds with correction.

1:12. Paul told them precisely what they had been doing and saying. Unwilling to let the dishonor and sin continue, Paul confronted them directly and in love. It seems four major divisions had developed: One group followed Paul, with whom we are familiar already; one followed Apollos, who differed not in message but apparently in method, having a more rhetorical, eloquent style. His method of presentation was very popular with those of Greek background. One group followed Cephas or Peter, the "hero" of Pentecost and a true apostle (these were probably conservative Jewish-Christians). Another group said they followed Christ. These may have been ultraconservative followers, or individuals who were trying to satisfy their ego by convincing themselves that their religion was more pure and spiritual than anyone else's.

If he had been a lesser man, Paul might have been tempted to side with those who supported him. After all, he had begun this church and he had taught and trained them. Did that not make him right? But Paul did not yield to such temptation. This was Christ's church, not his, and such division had no place or value. They only make the Church weak, self-centered, and unprofitable.

1:13. Whatever the supports on which these groups rested, Paul quickly brought them to the real point with three short questions. These questions suggest the unity, work, and supremacy of Christ, and Paul intended a negative answer to each question. Christ is not divided; He died for all; He is Lord of all. Such division is the heart of folly. There is one Body and Paul made it clear, when he used those who followed him as examples, that it must remain one church under Jesus Christ.

1:14,15. Paul noted his thanks that he had not baptized many at Corinth in water, and especially that he had not baptized in his own name. "Name" implied ownership, fellowship, and allegiance. Paul did nothing to develop such a relationship with those he led to Christ.

Verse 15 begins with a *hina* clause (*hina mē tis*) which can be taken either as a purpose clause or a result clause. The KJV takes it as a purpose clause ("lest any should say . . . ") whereas a result clause would be rendered, "For this reason, none of you can say . . . ." The important thing to stress here is that Paul avoided anything in his ministry which could lead to division or factionalism, even where the sacraments were concerned.

by them [which are of the house] of Chloe:

that there are contentions among you: . . . to this effect, *HistNT* . . . that ther is strife among you, *Geneva* . . . that you are quarrelling, *Moffatt* . . . that party feeling exists among you, *TCNT* . . . there are strifes, *Confraternity* . . . disputes among you, *Adams* . . . there are wranglings among you, *Williams* . . . ye are fallen into parties, *Locke* . . . each of you is a partisan, *Weymouth*.

12. Now this I say, that every one of you saith: And I mention this, *Macknight* . . . I mean by this that one of you, *Montgomery* . . . that you each declare, *Fenton* . . . each one belongs to a faction, *Norlie*.

I am of Paul; and I of Apollos: Paul certainly is my leader, *Berkeley* . . . I follow Paul, *TCNT* . . . I holde of Paul, *Tyndale, Cranmer* . . . I belong to Apollos, *SEB*.

and I of Cephas; and I of Christ:

13. Is Christ divided?: Can you gamble upon Christ? *Fenton* . . . Is Christ dismembered? *Berkeley* . . . divided up into pieces? *SEB* . . . divided into parties, *Macknight* . . . You have torn the Christ to pieces! *TCNT* . . . Christ is parted! *Concordant* . . . Is the Christ in fragments? *Weymouth*.

was Paul crucified for you?: Paul was not nailed to the cross, *SEB* . . . on your behalf? *Weymouth*.

or were ye baptized in the name of Paul?: . . . were ye immersed? *Rotherham* . . . to be Paul's adherents? *Weymouth*.

14. I thank God that I baptized none of you, but Crispus and Gaius: . . . that I christened none of you, *Tyndale* . . . immersed on my authority, *SEB*.

15. Lest any should say that I had baptized in mine own name: Then nobody can say, *Beck* . . . so that no one might say, *TCNT* . . . may claim baptism in my name, *Berkeley* . . . to be my adherents, *Weymouth*.

1156.2 conj	2504.1 conj	3450.6 art acc sing masc	4585.1 name gen masc	3486.4 noun acc sing masc	3036.8 adj acc sing neu	3620.2 partic
δὲ	καὶ	τὸν	Στεφανᾶ	οἶκον·	λοιπὸν	οὐκ
de	kai	ton	Stephana	oikon	loipon	ouk
and	also	the	of Stephanas	house;	as to the rest	not

3471.2 verb 1sing indic perf act	1479.1 conj	4948.5 indef-pron	241.5 adj acc sing masc	901.7 verb 1sing indic aor act	3620.3 partic
οἶδα	εἴ	τινα	ἄλλον	ἐβάπτισα.	17. οὐ
oida	ei	tina	allon	ebaptisa	ou
I know	if	any	other	I baptized.	Not

1056.1 conj	643.8 verb 3sing indic aor act	1466.6 prs-pron acc 1sing	5382.1 name nom masc	901.6 verb inf pres act	233.1 conj
γὰρ	ἀπέστειλέν	με	Χριστὸς	βαπτίζειν,	᾽ ἀλλ᾽
gar	apesteilen	me	Christos	baptizein	all'
for	sent	me	Christ	to baptize,	but

233.2 conj	2076.14 verb inf pres mid	3620.2 partic	1706.1 prep	4531.3 noun dat sing fem
[ἀλλὰ]	εὐαγγελίζεσθαι·	οὐκ	ἐν	σοφίᾳ
alla	euangelizesthai	ouk	en	sophia
[idem]	to announce the good news;	not	in	wisdom

3030.2 noun gen sing masc	2419.1 conj	3231.1 partic	2729.3 verb 3sing subj aor pass	3450.5 art sing masc	4567.1 noun nom sing masc	3450.2 art gen sing
λόγου,	ἵνα	μὴ	κενωθῇ	ὁ	σταυρὸς	τοῦ
logou	hina	mē	kenōthē	ho	stauros	tou
of word,	that	not	be made void	the	cross	of the

5382.2 name gen masc	3450.5 art sing masc	3030.1 noun nom sing masc	1056.1 conj	3450.5 art sing masc	3450.2 art gen sing
Χριστοῦ.	18. Ὁ	λόγος	γὰρ	ὁ	τοῦ
Christou	Ho	logos	gar	ho	tou
Christ.	The	word	for	the	of the

4567.2 noun gen sing masc	3450.4 art dat pl	3173.1 conj	616.19 verb dat pl masc part pres	3334.1 noun nom sing fem	1498.4 verb 3sing indic pres act
σταυροῦ	τοῖς	μὲν	ἀπολλυμένοις	μωρία	ἐστίν,
staurou	tois	men	apollumenois	mōria	estin
cross	to the	men	perishing	foolishness	is,

3450.4 art dat pl	1156.2 conj	4834.19 verb dat pl masc part pres pass	2231.3 prs-pron dat 1pl	1405.1 noun nom sing fem	2296.2 noun gen sing masc
τοῖς	δὲ	σῳζομένοις	ἡμῖν	δύναμις	θεοῦ
tois	de	sōzomenois	hēmin	dunamis	theou
to the	but	being saved	to us	power	of God

1498.4 verb 3sing indic pres act	1119.22 verb 3sing indic perf pass	1056.1 conj	616.12 verb 1sing indic fut act	3450.12 art acc sing fem
ἐστιν.	19. γέγραπται	γάρ,	᾽Απολῶ	τὴν
estin	gegraptai	gar	Apolō	tēn
it is.	It has been written	for,	I will destroy	the

4531.4 noun acc sing fem	3450.1 art gen pl	4533.4 adj gen pl masc	2504.1 conj	3450.12 art acc sing fem	4757.3 noun acc sing fem
σοφίαν	τῶν	σοφῶν,	καὶ	τὴν	σύνεσιν
sophian	tōn	sophōn	kai	tēn	sunesin
wisdom	of the	wise,	and	the	understanding

3450.1 art gen pl	4758.2 adj gen pl masc	114.9 verb 1sing indic fut act	4085.1 adv	4533.1 adj nom sing masc
τῶν	συνετῶν	ἀθετήσω.	20. ποῦ	σοφός;
tōn	sunetōn	athetēsō	pou	sophos
of the	understanding ones	I will set aside.	Where	wise?

1:16,17. Paul's primary mission was to preach, not in his own wisdom or ability, but in the power of the Holy Spirit, the cross of Christ being the center of his message. To have ministered by his own eloquence or wit would have served only to detract from the message. It would have lifted up him instead of the Cross. Depending on the Holy Spirit instead of himself kept him where the Cross could be the center and source of Christian unity.

1:18. Paul wished to turn the minds of his readers to the source of our union and unity—the Cross. He did so by displaying it as the greatest expression of wisdom and power the world has ever seen. To some it does not appear that way; it appears foolish. How could a cross be of any value? Paul spoke in irony. The "preaching of the cross" seems foolish merely because the message is simple and the listeners are blind, proud, and mocking. Those who are perishing (who are being brought to nothing, who are being destroyed) stubbornly take their own way and consider the Cross foolish. But it is this choice and consideration that is causing them to perish. They mock their only hope. And the fact of their perishing proves the fallacy of their thinking.

But there is another group. To those who are being saved (who are being saved, rescued, and preserved from harm), the Cross is the very expression of God's power. Notice that Paul includes himself ("us") in those who are heirs of salvation. It is not glory in himself, but in the cross of Christ. He had experienced its power for himself and he wanted to share it. The range of God's power covers not only the material realm of controlling the universe, and not only the mental realm of changing men's opinions, particularly at salvation, but also the realm of the moral and spiritual. By the Cross we see the wonder of God's redemption; by the Cross we are united with Christ; by the Cross we are cleansed and purified, and by the Cross we are "kept" unto salvation.

1:19. Paul made an important comparison. While the Cross is exalted and shown in its true light, we are told of God's view of man's wisdom. Isaiah 29:14 is quoted in spirit, with slight alterations. God rendered useless the imagined wisdom of Jerusalem, and as it happened then so it will happen again. When God spoke to Jerusalem, she refused to hear Him, considering herself too high to respond to God. Exalted by God, she discovered what it was to be brought low by God.

Paul tells us that men of this world professed themselves to be wise, and in pride lifted themselves up. That very act was the beginning of their downfall (Romans 1:22). James tells us that true wisdom cannot be manufactured on this earth. It must come from above (James 3:17). Repeatedly Proverbs reminds us that real understanding and applicable knowledge is found in a proper attitude toward and fellowship with God.

16. And I baptized also the household of Stephanas:
besides, I know not whether I baptized any other: . . . beyond this I do not recollect, *Fenton* . . . I did not think, *Montgomery* . . . for the rest, I do not remember, *HistNT* . . . I am not aware, *Concordant.*

17. For Christ sent me not to baptize, but to preach the gospel: . . . does not commission me, *Concordant* . . . but to euangelize, *Rheims* . . . but to be declaring the joyful message, *Rotherham* . . . but to publish the Gladtidings, *Conybeare* . . . but to proclaim the Good News, *Weymouth.*

not with wisdom of words: . . . with no fine rhetoric, *Moffatt* . . . not with philosophical argument, *Fenton* . . . not in mere learned language, *Weymouth.*

lest the cross of Christ should be made of none effect: . . . might not be fruitless, *Fenton* . . . should be rendered void, *HistNT* . . . be made an empty thing, *Montgomery* . . . be deprived of its power, *Weymouth.*

18. For the preaching of the cross is to them that perish foolishness: For the discourse, *Rotherham* . . . the word of the cross to those in the way perdition is folly, *Conybeare* . . . is stupidity, *Concordant* . . . folly to the reprobate, *Fenton* . . . those on their way to destruction, *Montgomery.*

but unto us which are saved it is the power of God:

19. For it is written, I will destroy the wisdom of the wise: I will ruin, *HistNT* . . . exhibit the nothingness, *Weymouth* . . . the philosophy of the philosophers, *Fenton* . . . of the sages, *Moffatt.*

and will bring to nothing the understanding of the prudent: And the cleverness of the clever I will frustrate, *HistNT* . . . confound the insight, *Moffatt* . . . and upset the cleverness of the clever, *Fenton* . . . the discernment of the discerning ones will I set aside, *Rotherham* . . . will I confound, *Montgomery* . . . shall I be repudiating, *Concordant* . . . I vvil reiecte, *Rheims.*

1 Corinthians 1:21

4085.1 adv	1116.1 noun nom sing masc	4085.1 adv	4655.1 noun nom sing masc	3450.2 art gen sing	163.1 noun gen sing masc
ποῦ	γραμματεύς;	ποῦ	συζητητὴς	τοῦ	αἰῶνος
pou	grammateus	pou	suzētētēs	tou	aiōnos
where	scribe?	where	disputer	of the	age

3642.1 dem-pron gen sing	3644.1 adv	3333.1 verb 3sing indic aor act	3450.5 art sing masc	2296.1 noun nom sing masc	3450.12 art acc sing fem
τούτου;	οὐχὶ	ἐμώρανεν	ὁ	θεὸς	τὴν
toutou	ouchi	emōranen	ho	theos	tēn
this?	not	did make foolish		God	the

20.a.**Txt:** 01א-corr 04C-corr,06D-corr,020L byz.bo. **Var:** 01א-org,02A,03B 04C-org,06D-org,025P Lach,Treg,Alf,Word Tisc,We/Ho,Weis,Sod UBS/✶

4531.4 noun acc sing fem	3450.2 art gen sing	2862.2 noun gen sing masc	3642.1 dem-pron gen sing		1879.1 conj
σοφίαν	τοῦ	κόσμου	⌈ª τούτου; ⌉		**21.** Ἐπειδὴ
sophian	tou	kosmou	toutou		Epeidē
wisdom	of the	world	this?		Since

1056.1 conj	1706.1 prep	3450.11 art dat sing fem	4531.3 noun dat sing fem	3450.2 art gen sing	2296.2 noun gen sing masc	3620.2 partic
γὰρ	ἐν	τῇ	σοφίᾳ	τοῦ	θεοῦ	οὐκ
gar	en	tē	sophia	tou	theou	ouk
for,	in	the	wisdom		of God,	not

1091.17 verb 3sing indic aor act	3450.5 art sing masc	2862.1 noun nom sing masc	1217.2 prep	3450.10 art gen sing fem	4531.2 noun gen sing fem
ἔγνω	ὁ	κόσμος	διὰ	τῆς	σοφίας
egnō	ho	kosmos	dia	tēs	sophias
knew	the	world	by	the	wisdom

3450.6 art acc sing masc	2296.4 noun acc sing masc	2085.7 verb 3sing indic aor act	3450.5 art sing masc	2296.1 noun nom sing masc	1217.2 prep
τὸν	θεόν,	εὐδόκησεν	ὁ	θεὸς	διὰ
ton	theon,	eudokēsen	ho	theos	dia
	God,	was pleased	the	God	by

3450.10 art gen sing fem	3334.2 noun gen sing fem	3450.2 art gen sing	2754.2 noun gen sing neu	4834.10 verb inf aor act	3450.8 art acc pl masc
τῆς	μωρίας	τοῦ	κηρύγματος	σῶσαι	τοὺς
tēs	mōrias	tou	kērugmatos	sōsai	tous
the	foolishness	of the	proclamation	to save	the

3961.15 verb acc pl masc part pres act	1879.1 conj	2504.1 conj	2428.2 name-adj pl masc	4447.1 noun sing neu
πιστεύοντας·	**22.** ἐπειδὴ	καὶ	Ἰουδαῖοι	⌈ σημεῖον
pisteuontas	epeidē	kai	Ioudaioi	sēmeion
believing.	Since	both	Jews	a sign

22.a.**Txt:** 020L,byz.Weis **Var:** 01א,02A,03B,04C 06D,025P,Gries,Lach Treg,Alf,Word,Tisc We/Ho,Sod,UBS/✶

4447.2 noun pl neu	153.3 verb 3pl indic pres act	2504.1 conj	1659.4 name nom pl masc	4531.4 noun acc sing fem
[ª✶ σημεῖα]	αἰτοῦσιν,	καὶ	Ἕλληνες	σοφίαν
sēmeia	aitousin	kai	Hellēnes	sophian
[signs]	ask for,	and	Greeks	wisdom

2195.2 verb 3pl indic pres act	2231.1 prs-pron nom 1pl	1156.2 conj	2756.3 verb 1pl indic pres act	5382.4 name acc masc
ζητοῦσιν.	**23.** ἡμεῖς	δὲ	κηρύσσομεν	Χριστὸν
zētousin.	hēmeis	de	kērussomen	Christon
seek;	we	but	proclaim	Christ

4568.18 verb acc sing masc part perf pass	2428.4 name-adj dat pl masc	3173.1 conj	4480.1 noun sing neu
ἐσταυρωμένον,	Ἰουδαίοις	μὲν	σκάνδαλον,
estaurōmenon	Ioudaiois	men	skandalon
having been crucified,	to Jews	indeed	a cause of offense,

1:20. Paul established his point with four questions. "Where is the wise?" establishes that where the Cross is preached human wisdom cannot stand. How can it? What religion is there on the face of the earth that has brought salvation and peace to the hearts of men? Only the gospel of Jesus Christ and the message of the Cross has been able to do that. Paul did not say that there are no worldly-wise men left, only that they fade to nothing beside the Cross.

Paul used the word *sophian* ("wisdom") extensively throughout 1 Corinthians in a variety of ways, both negatively and positively. Paul used the word in at least two negative ways: the first as a manner or style of preaching which emphasizes eloquence based on logic and rhetoric apart from Christ (as at 1:17); also negatively as the very essence of salvation, that it equaled salvation. Paul was thus attacking a Gnostic view of wisdom which equated knowledge with the way of salvation rather than seeing Jesus as the way to salvation (cf. John 14:6).

In question two, the scribe is mentioned because wisdom in the human sphere may use Holy Writ by referring to some truth in Scripture. But a knowledge of the Word without submission to it only creates helplessness and a chaotic state. "Where is the scribe?" By the message of the Cross, he is silenced.

Again, in question three, "Where is the disputer of this world?" there is an indication of one who understands his own "times," who perceives something of the motivations of men; but that is not enough.

Question four is not so much an addition as it is a summation and answer to the other three questions.

1:21. God deliberately chose a way that would confound man's wisdom and reason. Man in his wisdom could not discover what God is like. He has never discovered his duty to God without revelation, and that is part of God's wise providence. God deliberately chose the "foolishness of preaching." It is possible that Paul was referring to content, the foolishness of the thing preached (the Cross).

1:22,23. These verses point to actual demonstrations of man's foolishness. One example is the Jews. They sought God in tradition, in the letter of the Law. They demanded evidence and visible positive affirmation and were interested in the practical. Yet they framed God in and offered Jesus only one pattern to fit. They stumbled over the fact of a crucified Messiah because it was not a "good sign." This ruined their selfish expectations.

The other example is the Greeks. They were absorbed in speculative philosophy, as Acts 17:21 points out. They were intellectual beings and proud of their reasoning which did not allow true faith; consequently, they considered the Cross ridiculous. To both Jew and Greek the Cross came simply and free, but that was too much

20. Where [is] the wise? where [is] the scribe?: Sage, rabbi, skeptic of this present age, *Montgomery* . . . the professor of human arts and sciences? *Locke* . . . your man of letters? *Williams* . . . your expounder of the Law? *Weymouth.*

where [is] the disputer of this world?: . . . the reasoner, *Conybeare* . . . your logician of this age? *Williams* . . . the discusser of this eon, *Concordant* . . . the debater of this age? *HistNT* . . . your investigator of the questions of this present age? *Weymouth.*

hath not God made foolish the wisdom of this world?: . . . to be utter foolishness? *Weymouth* . . . utter folly, *Norlie* . . . useless for the discovery of the truths of the Gospel? *Locke.*

21. For after that in the wisdom of God the world by wisdom knew not God: For since in accordance, *Williams* . . . by its philosophy, *Montgomery* . . . with all its wisdom failed to know God, *Moffatt, HistNT.*

it pleased God by the foolishness of preaching to save them that believe: God took delight, *Rotherham* . . . God delights, through the stupidity of the heralding, *Concordant* . . . by the apparent foolishness of the Message...to save those who accepted it, *Weymouth* . . . to quicken them who believe, *Murdock.*

22. For the Jews require a sign: Jews demand miracles, *Moffatt* . . . are always asking for proofs, *SEB* . . . demand extraordinary signs, *Locke* . . . demanding spectacular signs, *Williams* . . . continue to ask for miracles, *Montgomery.*

and the Greeks seek after wisdom: . . . are ever wanting philosophy, *Montgomery* . . . demand wisdom, *Murdock* . . . require wisdom, *HistNT.*

23. But we preach Christ crucified: . . . we are heralding Christ crucified, *Concordant* . . . a crucified Messiah, *Montgomery.*

unto the Jews a stumblingblock: . . . a certain offence, *Fenton* . . . a snare, *Concordant* . . . a

1 Corinthians 1:24

23.a.Txt: 04C-corr
06D-corr,byz.
Var: 01ℵ,02A,03B
04C-org,06D-org,020L
025P,bo.Gries,Lach
Treg,Alf,Word,Tisc
We/Ho,Weis,Sod
UBS/✶

1659.6 name dat pl masc	1477.6 noun dat pl neu	1156.2 conj	3334.3 noun acc sing fem	840.2 prs-pron dat pl
῞Ελλησιν	[ᵃ✶ ἔθνεσιν]	δὲ	μωρίαν·	24. αὐτοῖς
Hellēsin	ethnesin	de	mōrian	autois
to Greeks	[to Gentiles]	but	foolishness;	to them

1156.2 conj	3450.4 art dat pl	2795.3 adj dat pl masc	2428.4 name-adj dat pl masc	4885.1 conj	2504.1 conj	1659.6 name dat pl masc
δὲ	τοῖς	κλητοῖς,	᾿Ιουδαίοις	τε	καὶ	῞Ελλησιν,
de	tois	klētois	Ioudaiois	te	kai	Hellēsin
but	the	called,	Jews	both	and	Greeks,

5382.4 name acc masc	2296.2 noun gen sing masc	1405.4 noun acc sing fem	2504.1 conj	2296.2 noun gen sing masc	4531.4 noun acc sing fem	3617.1 conj
Χριστὸν	θεοῦ	δύναμιν	καὶ	θεοῦ	σοφίαν.	25. ὅτι
Christon	theou	dunamin	kai	theou	sophian	hoti
Christ	God's	power	and	God's	wisdom.	Because

3450.16 art sing neu	3336.7 adj nom sing neu	3450.2 art gen sing	2296.2 noun gen sing masc	4533.7 adj comp nom sing neu	3450.1 art gen pl
τὸ	μωρὸν	τοῦ	θεοῦ	σοφώτερον	τῶν
to	mōron	tou	theou	sophōteron	tōn
to	foolishness	tou	of God	wiser	of the

442.7 noun gen pl masc	1498.4 verb 3sing indic pres act	2504.1 conj	3450.16 art sing neu	766.7 adj sing neu	3450.2 art gen sing
ἀνθρώπων	ἐστίν·	καὶ	τὸ	ἀσθενὲς	τοῦ
anthrōpōn	estin	kai	to	asthenes	tou
men	is,	and	to	weakness	tou

2296.2 noun gen sing masc	2451.12 adj comp nom sing neu	3450.1 art gen pl	442.7 noun gen pl masc	1498.4 verb 3sing indic pres act
θεοῦ	ἰσχυρότερον	τῶν	ἀνθρώπων	[ᵃ ἐστίν.]
theou	ischuroteron	tōn	anthrōpōn	estin
of God	stronger	of the	men	is.

25.a.Txt: 01ℵ-corr,02A
04C,020L,025P,etc.byz.
Var: 01ℵ-org,03B,Treg
Tisc,We/Ho,Weis,Sod
UBS/✶

984.1 verb 2pl pres act	1056.1 conj	3450.12 art acc sing fem	2794.4 noun acc sing fem	5050.2 prs-pron gen 2pl	79.6 noun pl masc
26. Βλέπετε	γὰρ	τὴν	κλῆσιν	ὑμῶν,	ἀδελφοί,
Blepete	gar	tēn	klēsin	humōn	adelphoi
You see	for	the	calling	your,	brothers,

3617.1 conj	3620.3 partic	4044.7 adj nom pl masc	4533.3 adj nom pl masc	2567.3 prep	4418.4 noun acc sing fem	3620.3 partic
ὅτι	οὐ	πολλοὶ	σοφοὶ	κατὰ	σάρκα,	οὐ
hoti	ou	polloi	sophoi	kata	sarka	ou
that	not	many	wise	according to	flesh,	not

4044.7 adj nom pl masc	1409.2 adj nom pl masc	3620.3 partic	4044.7 adj nom pl masc	2083.2 adj nom pl masc	233.2 conj
πολλοὶ	δυνατοί,	οὐ	πολλοὶ	εὐγενεῖς·	27. ἀλλὰ
polloi	dunatoi	ou	polloi	eugeneis	alla
many	powerful,	not	many	noble born.	But

3450.17 art pl neu	3336.8 adj acc pl neu	3450.2 art gen sing	2862.2 noun gen sing masc	1573.3 verb 3sing indic aor mid	3450.5 art sing masc
τὰ	μωρὰ	τοῦ	κόσμου	ἐξελέξατο	ὁ
ta	mōra	tou	kosmou	exelexato	ho
the	foolish things	of the	world	chose	ho

2296.1 noun nom sing masc	2419.1 conj	3450.8 art acc pl masc	4533.6 adj acc pl masc	2587.3 verb 3sing subj pres act
θεός,	ἵνα	τοὺς	σοφούς	καταισχύνῃ·
theos	hina	tous	sophous	kataischunē
God,	that	the	wise	he might put to shame;

for those who should have understood so much. They could not accept a God who was that gracious.

1:24. The preaching of the cross of Christ has great effect. It changes people, calls them to faith, and unites and crosses all man-made boundaries, for it is the direct revelation and plan of God. Man, with his highest achievements, cannot touch God; he cannot find Him; he cannot exhaust Him; he cannot understand Him. The gospel, which speaks so eloquently of Jesus Christ, reveals God and demonstrates His power to every generation. To those who accept, it is power and wisdom.

1:25. The reason the Cross is so powerful to those who accept is because of the nature of God in comparison with man. It is difficult, even impossible, to believe God could do anything foolish or weak. That is not the point. The point is twofold. If God ever did anything foolish or weak, it would still far exceed man's capabilities. Yet even that falls somewhat short of Paul's point. Man often views something that God does as foolish or weak because he is too frail to understand God, too weak to see the power of His purposes. Thus, even though God appears foolish and weak in the eyes of men, it is because God's work is so much higher and better than men can grasp with their limited perception. So, in pride and weakness, they reject the program of God.

1:26. Because the Cross was considered foolish by many, God's call was readily heard by the weak and foolish, by those who needed Him. This has always been true. The poor, the hungry, the hurt, the needy were the ones that heard Jesus most eagerly. Within the context, Paul reminded the Corinthians of their own calling and experience. Paul explained the term "wise men after the flesh" with what immediately follows. Not many "mighty" men or men of influence, men of rank and government, are chosen. Not many noble men, or men of high birth (Roman nobles?) were called. There were some, but not many.

An examination of Acts 18:18, Romans 16:23, and several passages in First Corinthians reveals that in the church at Corinth (among people who might be considered well-to-do) were Crispus, the former synagogue ruler; Erastus, the city chamberlain; and Gaius, the director of the city public works. Overwhelmingly, however, the church at Corinth consisted of the poor, uneducated, and slaves. There was thus no excuse for any vanity or pride on their part. Simple faith is difficult for men of such position. The gospel was addressed to those the world considered fools and weaklings.

1:27,28. But God does nothing because of capriciousness or because He can get nothing better. He had a purpose in His calling.

hindrance, *HistNT* . . . an occasion of fallinge, *Tyndale* . . . a doctrine offensive to the hopes, *Locke.*

and unto the Greeks foolishness: . . . and folly to the heathen, *Fenton* . . . foolish to the acute men of learning, *Locke.*

24. But unto them which are called, both Jews and Greeks: . . . to those who have received the Call, *Weymouth.*

Christ the power of God, and the wisdom of God: . . . a Divine power, and a Divine philosophy, *Fenton.*

25. Because the foolishness of God is wiser than men: . . . the feble thing of god, *Wyclif.*

and the weakness of God is stronger than men: . . . that vvhich is the infirme of God, *Rheims* . . . the feebleness of God, *Murdock* . . . is mightier than men's might, *Weymouth* . . . surpasses the power of men, *Locke* . . . than human strength, *Fenton.*

26. For ye see your calling, brethren: For consider your own calling, *Montgomery* . . . behold your invitation, *Wilson* . . . contemplate your vocation, *Fenton.*

how that not many wise men after the flesh: . . . many eminent philosophers, *Fenton* . . . are wise with merely human wisdom, *Weymouth.*

not many mighty, not many noble, [are called]: . . . how few are powerful, *Conybeare* . . . not many principal men, not many of high birth, *HistNT* . . . not many of hye degre, *Tyndale, Cranmer* . . . not many of position and influence, *Weymouth* . . . many high-born, *Fenton* . . . many leading men, *Moffatt.*

27. But God hath chosen the foolish things of the world to confound the wise: He might shame the philosophic, *Fenton* . . . put its wise men to shame, *Weymouth* . . . to confound its philosophy, *Montgomery* . . . to confound its wisdom, *Conybeare* . . . to shame the wise, *Moffatt.*

1 Corinthians 1:28

2419.1 conj	2587.3 verb 3sing subj pres act	3450.8 art acc pl masc	4533.6 adj acc pl masc	2504.1 conj	3450.17 art pl neu
[☆ ἵνα	καταισχύνῃ	τοὺς	σοφούς,]	καὶ	τὰ
hina	kataischunē	tous	sophous,	kai	ta
[that	he might shame	the	wise;]	and	the

766.2 adj	3450.2 art gen sing	2862.2 noun gen sing masc	1573.3 verb 3sing indic aor mid	3450.5 art sing masc	2296.1 noun nom sing masc
ἀσθενῆ	τοῦ	κόσμου	ἐξελέξατο	ὁ	θεὸς,
asthenē	tou	kosmou	exelexato	ho	theos,
weak things	of the	world	chose		God,

2419.1 conj	2587.3 verb 3sing subj pres act	3450.17 art pl neu	2451.6 adj	2504.1 conj	3450.17 art pl neu
ἵνα	καταισχύνῃ	τὰ	ἰσχυρά·	**28.** καὶ	τὰ
hina	kataischunē	ta	ischura·	kai	ta
that	he might put to shame	the	strong things;	and	the

36.1 adj acc pl neu	3450.2 art gen sing	2862.2 noun gen sing masc	2504.1 conj	3450.17 art pl neu	1832.11 verb acc pl neu part perf pass
ἀγενῆ	τοῦ	κόσμου	καὶ	τὰ	ἐξουθενημένα
agenē	tou	kosmou	kai	ta	exouthenēmena
low born	of the	world,	and	the	having been despised

1573.3 verb 3sing indic aor mid	3450.5 art sing masc	2296.1 noun nom sing masc	2504.1 conj	3450.17 art pl neu	3231.1 partic
ἐξελέξατο	ὁ	θεός,	(a καὶ)	τὰ	μὴ
exelexato	ho	theos,	kai	ta	mē
chose	ho	God,	and	the things	not

28.a.**Txt:** 01**ℵ**-corr,03B 04C-corr,06D-corr,020L 025P,044,byz.sa.bo. We/Ho,Sod
Var: p46,01**ℵ**-org,02A 04C-org,06D-org,Lach Treg,Alf,Tisc,Weis UBS/☆

1498.18 verb part pres act	2419.1 conj	3450.17 art pl neu	1498.18 verb part pres act	2643.3 verb 3sing subj aor act	3567.1 conj
ὄντα,	ἵνα	τὰ	ὄντα	καταργήσῃ·	**29.** ὅπως
onta,	hina	ta	onta	katargēsē	hopōs
being,	that	the things	being	he may annul;	so that

3231.1 partic	2714.12 verb 3sing subj aor mid	3820.9 adj nom sing fem	4418.1 noun nom sing fem	1783.1 prep gen	840.3 prs-pron gen sing
μὴ	καυχήσηται	πᾶσα	σὰρξ	ἐνώπιον	(αὐτοῦ.
mē	kauchēsētai	pasa	sarx	enōpion	autou
not	might boast	all	flesh	before	him.

29.a.**Txt:** 04C-org,byz. **Var:** 01**ℵ**,02A,03B 04C-corr,06D,020L 025P,bo.Gries,Lach Treg,Alf,Word,Tisc We/Ho,Weis,Sod UBS/☆

3450.2 art gen sing	2296.2 noun gen sing masc	1523.1 prep gen	840.3 prs-pron gen sing	1156.2 conj	5050.1 prs-pron nom 2pl
[a☆ τοῦ	θεοῦ.]	**30.** ἐξ	αὐτοῦ	δὲ	ὑμεῖς
tou	theou.	ex	autou	de	humeis
[of God.]		Of	him	but	you

1498.6 verb 2pl indic pres act	1706.1 prep	5382.3 name dat masc	2400.2 name masc	3614.5 rel-pron nom sing masc	1090.32 verb 3sing indic aor pass
ἐστε	ἐν	Χριστῷ	Ἰησοῦ,	ὃς	ἐγενήθη
este	en	Christō	Iēsou,	hos	egenēthē
are	in	Christ	Jesus,	who	was made

2231.3 prs-pron dat 1pl	4531.1 noun nom sing fem	4531.1 noun nom sing fem	2231.3 prs-pron dat 1pl	570.3 prep gen	2296.2 noun gen sing masc
(ἡμῖν	σοφία	[☆ σοφία	ἡμῖν]	ἀπὸ	θεοῦ
hēmin	sophia	sophia	hēmin	apo	theou
to us	wisdom	[wisdom	to us]	from	God

1336.1 noun nom sing fem	4885.1 conj	2504.1 conj	38.1 noun nom sing masc	2504.1 conj	623.1 noun nom sing fem
δικαιοσύνη	τε	καὶ	ἁγιασμὸς	καὶ	ἀπολύτρωσις·
dikaiosunē	te	kai	hagiasmos	kai	apolutrōsis
righteousness	and	and	holiness	and	redemption;

God chose the weak and lowly. The world may laugh, but it is God himself who does the choosing. It must be added that not only does the world consider these weak and foolish; they really are. What a blow to pride! What a blow to those who have been seeking the world's approval, when they should be seeking only God's good pleasure. Yet Paul went further. He called them "despised," which Knox translated "contemptible." In "things" the neuter concentrates on the quality of foolishness possessed rather than on the individuals themselves (Morris, *Tyndale New Testament Commentaries*, 7:48).

1:29. God chose these apparently insignificant ones to shame and confuse the strong; to reduce to insignificance the great of the world. In so doing, He expressed His love, in that He would willingly choose and lift the lowly and ugly.

The words "that no flesh should glory in his presence" reminded the Corinthians of Paul's precise reason for writing. Paul was not especially concerned about the world's glorying and false boasting, but he did write to counter the false pride in the church at Corinth. The thought expressed in 1:5 made clear to the Corinthians that they were rich in utterance and knowledge, not because of human rhetoric and wisdom, but "by him" (God). Because they had wrongly evaluated their gifts and believed wisdom to be from man, they gloried in men (3:21) instead of realizing that they were believers because they had been called according to the purposes of Christ, not according to human wisdom.

God has done this so "no flesh," including all of mankind, could boast before Him. God has refuted the so-called wisdom of this world, and the Church is nothing without the Lord. There is nothing that a man can take hold of in the program of redemption and say, "This is what I did to help God and the Church along. Therefore I deserve some praise for this." We have a part, but it is God's work, from beginning to end.

1:30,31. The opposite side of the argument is that we are nevertheless blessed and rich because of the work of Jesus Christ. The debased are now exalted. But now the exaltation is real and is based on the right foundation. We are blessed because we are "in Christ." It is to be noted that Paul presented the work of Christ as also the work of the Father. Christ is made to all believers "wisdom," which stands alone and may be explained by the last three words of verse 31, "in the Lord."

God turned the world's wisdom to foolishness for our salvation. Christ is our "righteousness," which refers specifically to the doctrine of justification by faith and speaks of a law court where the verdict is "Not guilty." He is our "sanctification," which refers to the continuous process of holiness and perfection as we remain in Christ. He is our "redemption," which refers to deliverance by ransom, as when slaves are liberated with a purchase price. Our

and God hath chosen the weak things of the world to confound the things which are mighty: . . . the low-born things, *HistNT* . . . to confound its strength, *Montgomery* . . . to make strong people humble, *SEB* . . . to put the strong to shame, *Williams* . . . shame the strong, *Fenton*.

28. And base things of the world, and things which are despised, hath God chosen: . . . chosen the low-born, *Fenton* . . . beneath regard, *TCNT* . . . of low degree, *Williams* . . . the ignoble of the world, *Campbell* . . . the ignoble ones, *Macknight* . . . And byle thynges, *Cranmer* . . . and the contemptible, *Rheims* . . . the worthless, the trash, *Klingensmith* . . . which the world thinks are not important, *SEB* . . . which it sets utterly at nought, *Weymouth*.

[yea], and things which are not: . . . those that are nothing, *Campbell* . . . and thinges of no reputacion, *Tyndale*.

to bring to nought things that are: . . . to put down things that are, *Moffatt* . . . to annihilate what amounts to something, *Berkeley* . . . them who are something, *Murdock* . . . things that do exist, *Weymouth*.

29. That no flesh should glory in his presence: . . . to prevent any mortal man, *Weymouth* . . . that no person, *Moffatt* . . . Natural human abilities, *Locke* . . . to keep anybody from bragging, *Beck* . . . should exult before God, *HistNT* . . . can boast, *Fenton* . . . can brag in front of God, *SEB* . . . should pride itself before him, *Confraternity*.

30. But of him are ye in Christ Jesus: And vnto him partayne ye, *Tyndale* . . . you have your existence, *Berkeley*.

who of God is made unto us wisdom:

and righteousness, and sanctification, and redemption: . . . our means of right standing, *Williams* . . . being holy and free, *SEB* . . . justification, *Campbell* . . . holiness and deliverance, *Concordant* . . . our salvation, *Norlie* . . . ransom from sin, *Beck*.

1 Corinthians 1:31

31. ἵνα, καθὼς γέγραπται, Ὁ καυχώμενος,
hina *kathōs* *gegraptai* *Ho* *kauchōmenos*
2419.1 conj | 2503.1 conj | 1119.22 verb 3sing indic perf pass | 3450.5 art sing masc | 2714.7 verb nom sing masc part pres
that, | just as | it has been written, | The | boasting,

ἐν κυρίῳ καυχάσθω. **2:1.** Κἀγὼ ἐλθὼν πρὸς
en *kuriō* *kauchasthō* *Kagō* *elthōn* *pros*
1706.1 prep | 2935.3 noun dat sing masc | 2714.6 verb 3sing impr pres | 2476.3 conj | 2048.13 verb nom sing masc part aor act | 4242.1 prep
in | Lord | let him boast. | And I | having come | to

ὑμᾶς, ἀδελφοί, ἦλθον οὐ καθ' ὑπεροχὴν
humas *adelphoi* *ēlthon* *ou* *kath'* *huperochēn*
5050.4 prs-pron acc 2pl | 79.6 noun pl masc | 2048.1 verb indic aor act | 3620.3 partic | 2567.2 prep | 5085.2 noun acc sing fem
you, | brothers, | came | not | according to | excellency

λόγου ἢ σοφίας καταγγέλλων ὑμῖν τὸ
logou *ē* *sophias* *katangellōn* *humin* *to*
3030.2 noun gen sing masc | 2211.1 conj | 4531.2 noun gen sing fem | 2576.5 verb nom sing masc part pres act | 5050.3 prs-pron dat 2pl | 3450.16 art sing neu
of word | or | wisdom, | announcing | to you | the

1.a.Txt: 01ℵ-corr2,03B 06D,010F,012G,044,byz. **Var:** p46-vid,01ℵ-org 02A,04C,bo.

ʹ μαρτύριον [ᵃ☆ μυστήριον] τοῦ θεοῦ. **2.** οὐ
marturion *mustērion* *tou* *theou* *ou*
3115.1 noun sing neu | 3328.1 noun sing neu | 3450.2 art gen sing | 2296.2 noun gen sing masc | 3620.3 partic
testimony | [mystery] | | of God. | Not

2.a.Txt: 06D-corr,020L byz. **Var:** 01ℵ,02A,03B,04C 06D-org,025P,Gries Lach,Treg,Alf,Word Tisc,We/Ho,Weis,Sod UBS/☆

γὰρ ἔκρινά ʹᵃ τοῦ ʹ ʹ εἰδέναι τι [☆ τι
gar *ekrina* *tou* *eidenai* *ti* *ti*
1056.1 conj | 2892.13 verb 1sing indic aor act | 3450.2 art gen sing | 3471.25 verb inf perf act | 4948.10 indef-pron sing neu | 4948.10 indef-pron sing neu
for | I decided | the | to know | anything | [anything

εἰδέναι] ἐν ὑμῖν, εἰ μὴ Ἰησοῦν Χριστὸν,
eidenai *en* *humin* *ei* *mē* *Iēsoun* *Christon*
3471.25 verb inf perf act | 1706.1 prep | 5050.3 prs-pron dat 2pl | 1479.1 conj | 3231.1 partic | 2400.3 name acc masc | 5382.4 name acc masc
to know] | among | you, | if | not | Jesus | Christ,

καὶ τοῦτον ἐσταυρωμένον. **3.** ʹ καὶ ἐγὼ
kai *touton* *estaurōmenon* *kai* *egō*
2504.1 conj | 3642.6 dem-pron acc sing masc | 4568.18 verb acc sing masc part perf pass | 2504.1 conj | 1466.1 prs-pron nom 1sing
and | this one | having been crucified. | And | I

3.a.Txt: 06D,020L,byz. **Var:** 01ℵ,02A,03B,04C 025P,Lach,Treg,Alf Tisc,We/Ho,Weis,Sod UBS/☆

[ᵃ☆ κἀγὼ] ἐν ἀσθενείᾳ καὶ ἐν φόβῳ καὶ
kagō *en* *astheneia* *kai* *en* *phobō* *kai*
2476.3 conj | 1706.1 prep | 763.3 noun dat sing fem | 2504.1 conj | 1706.1 prep | 5238.3 noun dat sing masc | 2504.1 conj
[and I] | in | weakness | and | in | fear | and

ἐν τρόμῳ πολλῷ ἐγενόμην πρὸς ὑμᾶς· **4.** καὶ
en *tromō* *pollō* *egenomēn* *pros* *humas* *kai*
1706.1 prep | 4997.3 noun dat sing masc | 4044.3 adj dat sing | 1090.30 verb 1sing indic aor mid | 4242.1 prep | 5050.4 prs-pron acc 2pl | 2504.1 conj
in | trembling | much | was | with | you; | and

ὁ λόγος μου καὶ τὸ κήρυγμά
ho *logos* *mou* *kai* *to* *kērugma*
3450.5 art sing masc | 3030.1 noun nom sing masc | 1466.2 prs-pron gen 1sing | 2504.1 conj | 3450.16 art sing neu | 2754.1 noun sing neu
the | word | my | and | the | preaching

life in God is grounded in Jesus Christ, and that life "in Christ" will produce union and fellowship with others who are "in Christ."

When we discover the merits of Christ, we will glorify Him for this great revelation of wisdom and power. No other name can be placed alongside the name of Jesus. Paul transferred the idea of Jeremiah 9:23,24 where the reference is to Jehovah, to Christ, placing Him above all other names (except God the Father) and personalities. Jesus Christ is Lord.

2:1,2. "And I" begins to illustrate the truth of chapter 1. When Paul came to Corinth, from Athens with its idolatrous emphasis on philosophy, he came not as the usual itinerant professor of wisdom with which the Corinthians were so familiar. He was not witty, brilliant, or vain. Rather, his preaching was determined by the will of God and made effective by the power of God.

There is some debate as to whether Paul wrote that he came declaring the testimony (*marturion*) or mystery (*mustērion*) of God, but the evidence favors "testimony." One important reason is that "*testimony* is more suitable to the initial proclamation of the Gospel, whereas *mystery* suggests the wisdom Paul was able to speak among mature Christians" (Barrett, *Harper's New Testament Commentaries*, pp.62,63).

To enlarge and emphasize the thought, Paul reminded his readers of how he did not preach. Despite the comments of some modern expositors, it is entirely possible that Paul did have some oratorical ability. But if he did possess such, he made it a point not to depend on it at Corinth. Nor did he try to make the message sound humanly brilliant or intellectually intriguing. His presentation and the content of his message were rather plain and simple.

It is not necessary to distinguish the individual parts of his presentation. The dominant consideration that governed every part of his work among the Corinthians was to present nothing except the glory and power of Christ and the Cross. This is typical of Paul. In all the work he did and in each of the problems he discussed in his many letters, he always brings us back to the same point. How should this be considered in the light of the work of Christ? What does He teach us is the proper mode of action and response? Therefore, it is not surprising that Paul emphasized that here. The difficulties at Athens may have affected Paul's perspective, but they did not change, they only reinforced, Paul's fundamental attitude. Christ must be preeminent.

2:3,4. Paul came to the Corinthians in "weakness." This may refer to physical illness, but more probably it is a description of Paul's feeling of inadequacy in himself. Paul came in "fear," which is an inward emotion expressing fear of failure. Paul came with "trembling." This is used to describe the anxiety of one who distrusts his ability completely to meet all requirements, but does his utmost to fulfill his duty. (See Thayer, "astheneia," "phobos," and "tromos.")

31. That, according as it is written:
He that glorieth, let him glory in the Lord: Let the triumphant triumph with the Lord, *Fenton* . . . Let him who takes pride, *Confraternity* . . . boast of the Lord, *Moffatt*.

1. And I, brethren, when I came to you: And as for myself, *Weymouth*.
came not with excellency of speech or of wisdom: I did not endeavour to set it off with any ornaments of rhetoric, *Locke* . . . not in the highness of word, *Wyclif* . . . in magnificent speech, *Murdock* . . . with pretentious speech, *Sawyer* . . . with grand reasoning or philosophies, *Fenton* . . . with any elaborate words or wisdom, *Moffatt* . . . with superiority of word, *Concordant* . . . with no transcendent eloquence, *Way* . . . no distinction of eloquence, *Berkeley* . . . in gloriousnes of wordes or of wysdome, *Tyndale* . . . not in loftinesse of speache, *Rheims* . . . not with surpassing power of eloquence, *Weymouth*.
declaring unto you the testimony of God: . . . come proclaiming the testimony, *HistNT* . . . that I came announcing, *Weymouth*.

2. For I determined not to know any thing among you: I did not govern myself among you, as if I knew anything, *Murdock* . . . decided not to know, *HistNT* . . . to be utterly ignorant, *Weymouth*.
save Jesus Christ, and him crucified: . . . and him a crucified Christ, *Montgomery*.

3. And I was with you in weakness: I in sikenesse, *Wyclif* . . . in bodily weakness, *Way* . . . in conscious feebleness, *Weymouth*.
and in fear, and in much trembling: . . . and great timidity, *Fenton* . . . timid and greatly agitated, *TCNT* . . . and drede, *Wyclif* . . . and in deep anxiety, *Weymouth*.

4. And my speech and my preaching: And my thoughts and my language, *Fenton* . . . my proclamation, *Rotherham*.

4.a.Txt: 01ℵ-corr,02A 04C,020L,025P,044,byz. bo.
Var: 01ℵ-org,03B,06D Gries,Lach,Treg,Alf Word,Tisc,We/Ho,Weis Sod,UBS/✶

1466.2 prs-pron gen 1sing
μου
mou
my

3620.2 partic
οὐκ
ouk
not

1706.1 prep
ἐν
en
in

3843.1 adj dat pl masc
πειθοῖς
peithois
persuasive

440.2 adj gen sing fem
⌐a ἀνθρωπίνης ⌐
anthrōpinēs
human

4531.2 noun gen sing fem
σοφίας
sophias
of wisdom

3030.7 noun dat pl masc
λόγοις,
logois
words,

233.1 conj
ἀλλ'
all'
but

1706.1 prep
ἐν
en
in

580.1 noun dat sing fem
ἀποδείξει
apodeixei
demonstration

4011.2 noun gen sing neu
πνεύματος
pneumatos
of Spirit

2504.1 conj
καὶ
kai
and

1405.2 noun gen sing fem
δυνάμεως·
dunameōs
of power;

2419.1 conj
5. ἵνα
hina
that

3450.9 art nom sing fem
ἡ
hē
the

3963.1 noun nom sing fem
πίστις
pistis
faith

5050.2 prs-pron gen 2pl
ὑμῶν
humōn
your

3231.1 partic
μὴ
mē
not

1498.10 verb 3sing subj pres act
ᾖ
ē
might be

1706.1 prep
ἐν
en
in

4531.3 noun dat sing fem
σοφίᾳ
sophia
wisdom

442.7 noun gen pl masc
ἀνθρώπων,
anthrōpōn
of men,

233.1 conj
ἀλλ'
all'
but

1706.1 prep
ἐν
en
in

1405.3 noun dat sing fem
δυνάμει
dunamei
power

2296.2 noun gen sing masc
θεοῦ.
theou
of God.

4531.4 noun acc sing fem
6. Σοφίαν
Sophian
Wisdom

1156.2 conj
δὲ
de
but

2953.4 verb 1pl indic pres act
λαλοῦμεν
laloumen
we speak

1706.1 prep
ἐν
en
among

3450.4 art dat pl
τοῖς
tois
the

4894.5 adj dat pl masc
τελείοις·
teleiois
mature;

4531.4 noun acc sing fem
σοφίαν
sophian
wisdom

1156.2 conj
δὲ
de
but,

3620.3 partic
οὐ
ou
not

3450.2 art gen sing
τοῦ
tou
of the

163.1 noun gen sing masc
αἰῶνος
aiōnos
age

3642.1 dem-pron gen sing
τούτου,
toutou
this,

3624.1 adv
οὐδὲ
oude
nor

3450.1 art gen pl
τῶν
tōn
of the

752.6 noun gen pl masc
ἀρχόντων
archontōn
rulers

3450.2 art gen sing
τοῦ
tou
of the

163.1 noun gen sing masc
αἰῶνος
aiōnos
age

3642.1 dem-pron gen sing
τούτου,
toutou
this,

3450.1 art gen pl
τῶν
tōn
the

2643.10 verb gen pl masc part pres pass
καταργουμένων·
katargoumenōn
coming to nought.

233.2 conj
7. ἀλλὰ
alla
But

2953.4 verb 1pl indic pres act
λαλοῦμεν
laloumen
we speak

4531.4 noun acc sing fem
⌐ σοφίαν
sophian
wisdom

2296.2 noun gen sing masc
θεοῦ
theou
of God

2296.2 noun gen sing masc
[✶ θεοῦ
theou
[of God

4531.4 noun acc sing fem
σοφίαν]
sophian
wisdom]

1706.1 prep
ἐν
en
in

3328.3 noun dat sing neu
μυστηρίῳ,
mustēriō
a mystery,

3450.12 art acc sing fem
τὴν
tēn
the

607.3 verb acc sing fem part perf pass
ἀποκεκρυμμένην
apokekrummenēn
having been hidden

3614.12 rel-pron acc sing fem
ἣν
hēn
which

4168.1 verb 3sing indic aor act
προώρισεν
proōrisen
predetermined

3450.5 art sing masc
ὁ
ho

2296.1 noun nom sing masc
θεὸς
theos
God

4112.1 prep
πρὸ
pro
before

3450.1 art gen pl
τῶν
tōn
the

163.4 noun gen pl masc
αἰώνων
aiōnōn
ages

What preacher of the gospel is there anywhere who has not often known exactly what Paul is describing?

Yet the results were excellent. Paul preached with power, and God confirmed the Word with signs following. Paul understood his own deficiencies to present such a glorious gospel. He had to depend wholly on the Holy Spirit. The support was there in time of need. The premise on which he stood was true; the promises he declared were true; the power with which he spoke was true. Established on truth, presented in power, spoken in love, the results came. The only logical result was the persuasion of men concerning Christ and the enlargement of His kingdom.

In order to give fuller force to Paul's statement translated "in demonstration of the Spirit and of power," the dative preposition *en* is a dative of instrumentality and could thus be translated, "enforced by a demonstration of Spirit and power." The words "Spirit" and "power" are a hendiadys, that is, they are two words used to express the same thought. To preach in the Spirit is the same as preaching with power.

There is no substitute for God-ordained, Holy Spirit-anointed preaching of the Word of God. It may seem foolish to some, but it will produce results.

2:5. Paul's writing in this vein is clearly applied in this verse. If these believers stood on what someone said through his wisdom only, in time the foundation would crumble. This world's wisdom will fail, and so will those who rely upon it. But if these believers trusted in God they would not fall or fail. Faith in God's wisdom as displayed in Christ will produce maturity and also miracles.

2:6,7. Paul continued to demolish step-by-step the foundation of natural wisdom on which the Corinthians were tempted to build. In thus comparing spiritual wisdom with natural wisdom, Paul noted that among "perfect" or "full-grown" believers the gospel is recognized as wisdom. These mature thinkers have freed themselves from the world and its values and so can acknowledge and pursue truth. God's wisdom is not dependent on the world, for it is permanent, and the world is on its way to a foolish, nonsensical end. True wisdom is not governed by leaders who set the patterns of this world in general. Yet while noting that this simple gospel is free from human additives, we must also recognize that in another sense it is the most brilliant "philosophy" to ever appear.

Because it does not come from men it appears as a mystery, a secret which man by himself could never unfold. But when Paul used it in his epistles he used it in the sense of something long hidden, but now revealed. Indeed, when Christ came the mystery of the gospel was unfolded by God himself. Thus, Paul told the Corinthians that while they had been toying with the idea of abandoning this simple wisdom, in reality they were possessors of great benefits and the only true wisdom in all the world.

[was] not with enticing words of man's wisdom: . . . not adorned with persuasive words of earthly wisdom, *Weymouth* . . . not clothed in captivating philosophical phraseology, *Fenton* . . . not rest on the plausible arguments of 'wisdom,' *Moffatt* . . . on the persuasive language of philosophy, *Montgomery*.

but in demonstration of the Spirit and of power: . . . but in shewinge of the sprete, *Tyndale* . . . but in playne euidence of spiritual power, *Geneva* . . . on the proof supplied by the Spirit and its power, *Moffatt* . . . which the Spirit taught and mightily carried home, *Weymouth*.

5. That your faith should not stand in the wisdom of men: . . . that your trust, *Weymouth*.
but in the power of God: . . . but in the vertu of god, *Wyclif*.

6. Howbeit we speak wisdom among them that are perfect: . . . we can speak philosophy, *Fenton* . . . among the full-grown, *Rotherham* . . . those who are mature, *Montgomery*.

yet not the wisdom of this world, nor of the princes of this world: . . . which belongs to this age, *HistNT* . . . nor of the useless leaders of this time, *Fenton* . . . nether of the chiefest of this world, *Geneva*.

that come to nought: . . . who are being discarded, *Concordant* . . . who are to be set aside, *Rotherham* . . . who are soon to pass away, *Weymouth*.

7. But we speak the wisdom of God in a mystery, [even] the hidden [wisdom]: . . . the hidden mystery, *Fenton* . . . which is in secrete and lieth hyd, *Tyndale* . . . which has been concealed, *Concordant*.
which God ordained before the world unto our glory: . . . foreappointed before the ages, *HistNT* . . . vvhich God did predestinate, *Rheims* . . . which God marked out beforehand, before the ages, *Rotherham* . . . decreed from all eternity, *Moffatt* . . . for our rectification, *Fenton* . . . that it should result in glory to us, *Weymouth*.

1 Corinthians 2:8

1519.1 prep	1385.4 noun acc sing fem	2231.2 prs-pron gen 1pl	3614.12 rel-pron acc sing fem	3625.2 num card nom masc	3450.1 art gen pl
εἰς	δόξαν	ἡμῶν,	**8.** ἣν	οὐδεὶς	τῶν
eis	doxan	hēmōn	hēn	oudeis	tōn
for	glory	our,	which	no one	of the

752.6 noun gen pl masc	3450.2 art gen sing	163.1 noun gen sing masc	3642.1 dem-pron gen sing	1091.32 verb 3sing indic perf act	1479.1 conj
ἀρχόντων	τοῦ	αἰῶνος	τούτου	ἔγνωκεν·	εἰ
archontōn	tou	aiōnos	toutou	egnōken	ei
rulers	of the	age	this	has known,	if

1056.1 conj	1091.18 verb 3pl indic aor act	3620.2 partic	300.1 partic	3450.6 art acc sing masc	2935.4 noun acc sing masc
γὰρ	ἔγνωσαν,	οὐκ	ἂν	τὸν	κύριον
gar	egnōsan	ouk	an	ton	kurion
for	they had known,	not		the	Lord

3450.10 art gen sing fem	1385.2 noun gen sing fem	4568.3 verb 3pl indic aor act		233.2 conj	2503.1 conj
τῆς	δόξης	ἐσταύρωσαν·	**9.** ἀλλὰ		καθὼς
tēs	doxēs	estaurōsan	alla		kathōs
of the	glory	they would have crucified,	but		just as

1119.22 verb 3sing indic perf pass	3614.17 rel-pron pl neu	3652.1 noun nom sing masc	3620.2 partic	1481.3 verb 3sing indic aor act
γέγραπται,	Ἃ	ὀφθαλμὸς	οὐκ	εἶδεν,
gegraptai	Ha	ophthalmos	ouk	eiden
it has been written,	The things	eye	not	saw,

2504.1 conj	3640.1 noun sing neu	3620.2 partic	189.21 verb 3sing indic aor act	2504.1 conj	1894.3 prep	2559.4 noun acc sing fem
καὶ	οὖς	οὐκ	ἤκουσεν,	καὶ	ἐπὶ	καρδίαν
kai	ous	ouk	ēkousen	kai	epi	kardian
and	ear	not	heard,	and	into	heart

9.a.**Txt:** 01א,06D,020L 025P,byz.Tisc,Sod **Var:** 02A,03B,04C,Lach Treg,Alf,We/Ho,Weis UBS/✶

442.2 noun gen sing masc	3620.2 partic	303.13 verb 3sing indic aor act	3614.17 rel-pron pl neu	3607.8 rel-pron pl neu
ἀνθρώπου	οὐκ	ἀνέβη,	ᵃ ἃ	[ᵃ ὅσα]
anthrōpou	ouk	anebē	ha	hosa
of man	not	came,	which	[whatsoever]

2069.4 verb 3sing indic aor act	3450.5 art sing masc	2296.1 noun nom sing masc	3450.4 art dat pl	25.4 verb dat pl part pres act	840.6 prs-pron acc sing masc
ἡτοίμασεν	ὁ	θεὸς	τοῖς	ἀγαπῶσιν	αὐτόν·
hētoimasen	ho	theos	tois	agapōsin	auton
prepared		God	for the	loving	him,

10.a.**Txt:** 01א,02A,04C 06D,020L,025P,etc.byz. it.Tisc,Sod **Var:** p46,03B,1739,sa. We/Ho,Weis,UBS/✶

2231.3 prs-pron dat 1pl	1156.2 conj	1056.1 conj	3450.5 art sing masc	2296.1 noun nom sing masc	596.2 verb 3sing indic aor act
10. ἡμῖν	ᵃ δὲ	[ᵃ γὰρ]	ᵃ ὁ	θεὸς	ἀπεκάλυψεν
hēmin	de	gar	ho	theos	apekalupsen
to us	but	[for]		God	revealed

596.2 verb 3sing indic aor act	3450.5 art sing masc	2296.1 noun nom sing masc	1217.2 prep	3450.2 art gen sing	4011.2 noun gen sing neu
[✶ ἀπεκάλυψεν	ὁ	θεὸς]	διὰ	τοῦ	πνεύματος
apekalupsen	ho	theos	dia	tou	pneumatos
[revealed		God]	by	the	Spirit

10.b.**Txt:** 01א-corr,06D 020L,byz.sa. **Var:** 01א-org,02A,03B 04C,bo.Lach,Treg,Tisc We/Ho,Weis,Sod UBS/✶

840.3 prs-pron gen sing	3450.16 art sing neu	1056.1 conj	4011.1 noun sing neu	3820.1 adj	2028.1 verb 3sing indic pres act
ᵇ αὐτοῦ ᵇ	τὸ	γὰρ	πνεῦμα	πάντα	ἐρευνᾷ,
autou	to	gar	pneuma	panta	ereuna
his;	the	for	Spirit	all things	searches,

2:8. The "princes of this world" (including the Jews) did not fully comprehend God's plans or revelation. They did not really understand God's plan for salvation. Otherwise, they would have never crucified Christ. "Known" carries the idea of acknowledgment and so involves man's will. The implication is that God in His foreknowledge knew man would crucify Christ and worked it to man's hope or shame depending on personal choice. In any case, Christ, "the Lord of glory," of great position and title, would not have been crucified by wise men. In passing, our position is also noted by this term "Lord of glory," a position by association.

Some scholars prefer to take "princes of this world" as a reference to Satan because he is referred to as the *archōn tou kosmou* ("ruler of the world") in John 12:31; 14:30; and 16:11. There are, however, several reasons for not accepting this interpretation and for holding to the view that "princes of this world" refers to earthly princes. First of all, there is no evidence until the Second and Third Centuries that *archōn* was used in reference to devils, although in the singular it could sometimes be used of Satan. More importantly, however, is that *archōn* much more frequently explicitly refers to earthly rulers as it most certainly does in Romans 13:3. Finally, it was both Roman and Jewish leaders who caused Jesus' crucifixion.

2:9. That the plan of God would be a mystery was foretold by Scripture. Paul quoted from Isaiah 64:4 and 65:17. He referred to wonder beyond the senses, perception, or imagination of men. Here "heart" does not refer to the emotions, but to the understanding of natural man. "Mind" would be a better translation. Among the Greeks the seat of the emotions was the intestines. This revelation was beyond the ability of man to discover. We needed the help of the Holy Spirit. God had to tell us plainly of His wonderful plans for us.

2:10. It took a specific revelation by the Holy Spirit for us to understand the wisdom of God. The Holy Spirit has been a part of all God's work in this world; when the Church came into existence, His work took on a new feature. This verse does not refer to future glories still to be unfolded, but to wonders already shown to us. In other words, verse 9 has already begun to be fulfilled. Christ comes from God and so does the recognition of Him. The Holy Spirit must show those living in spiritual darkness that Christ is the wisdom of God.

This the Holy Spirit can do because He "searches" the things of God. This is basic. The word "searches" does not suggest incompleteness, but rather the opposite—fullness of knowledge, action, and penetration. The work He does can be done because He is God and understands all divine things. He searches the deep things of God. Salvation belongs here, but much more than just initial salvation is meant. Included is wisdom, knowledge, and judgment—the work of the Holy Spirit himself.

8. Which none of the princes of this world knew: None of the leaders of this age, *HistNT* . . . not one of the chief men, *Concordant* . . . none of the heades of this world, *Geneva* . . . of the Powers, *Moffatt* . . . of this age recognised, *Fenton* . . . world's leaders understands it, *Williams* . . . of this world comprehended, *Noyes.*

for had they known [it], they would not have crucified the Lord of glory: . . . for if they had possessed it, *Weymouth* . . . for had they understood, *Berkeley* . . . would not have nailed the lord of glory to the cross, *SEB* . . . the Lord of majesty, *HistNT* . . . our glorious master, *TCNT.*

9. But as it is written, Eye hath not seen: . . . according as it is written, *Rotherham* . . . What no one ever saw, *TEV.*

nor ear heard, neither have entered into the heart of man: . . . never have occurred to human hearts, *Williams* . . . what no one ever thought could happen, *TEV* . . . no human heart ever conceived, *Norlie* . . . No human being has ever imagined this, *SEB* . . . neither has it come up in the human heart, *Berkeley.*

the things which God hath prepared for them that love him: . . . all that God has in readiness for, *Weymouth.*

10. But God hath revealed [them] unto us by his Spirit: God used the Spirit to show this secret to you, *SEB* . . . God made known his secret, *TEV* . . . hath opened them vnto vs, *Tyndale* . . . has unveiled them, *Montgomery* . . . which are not discoverable by man's natural faculties and powers, *Locke* . . . has drawn aside the veil through the teaching of the Spirit, *Weymouth* . . . through the Spirit, *HistNT.*

for the Spirit searcheth all things: Spirit fathoms everything, *Moffatt, Montgomery, TCNT* . . . finds out everything, *Beck* . . . examines everything, *Berkeley* . . . exploreth all things, *Murdock* . . . can explore all things, *Way* . . . investigates all, *Fenton.*

2504.1 conj	3450.17 art pl neu	893.3 noun acc pl neu	3450.2 art gen sing	2296.2 noun gen sing masc	4949.3 intr-pron nom sing	1056.1 conj
καὶ	τὰ	βάθη	τοῦ	θεοῦ.	**11.** τίς	γὰρ
kai	ta	bathē	tou	theou	tis	gar
even	the	depths		of God.	Who	for

3471.4 verb 3sing indic perf act	442.7 noun gen pl masc	3450.17 art pl neu	3450.2 art gen sing	442.2 noun gen sing masc
οἶδεν	ἀνθρώπων	τὰ	τοῦ	ἀνθρώπου,
oiden	anthrōpōn	ta	tou	anthrōpou
knows	of man	the things	of the	man,

1479.1 conj	3231.1 partic	3450.16 art sing neu	4011.1 noun sing neu	3450.2 art gen sing	442.2 noun gen sing masc	3450.16 art sing neu
εἰ	μὴ	τὸ	πνεῦμα	τοῦ	ἀνθρώπου	τὸ
ei	mē	to	pneuma	tou	anthrōpou	to
if	not	the	spirit	of the	man	the

1706.1 prep	840.4 prs-pron dat sing	3643.1 adv	2504.1 conj	3450.17 art pl neu	3450.2 art gen sing	2296.2 noun gen sing masc
ἐν	αὐτῷ;	οὕτως	καὶ	τὰ	τοῦ	θεοῦ
en	autō	houtōs	kai	ta	tou	theou
in	him?	so	also	the things		of God

3625.2 num card nom masc	3471.4 verb 3sing indic perf act	1091.32 verb 3sing indic perf act	1479.1 conj	3231.1 partic	3450.16 art sing neu
οὐδεὶς	⸂ οἶδεν,	[ᵃ✶ ἔγνωκεν]	εἰ	μὴ	τὸ
oudeis	oiden	egnōken	ei	mē	to
no one	knows,	[had known]	if	not	the

4011.1 noun sing neu	3450.2 art gen sing	2296.2 noun gen sing masc	2231.1 prs-pron 1pl	1156.2 conj	3620.3 partic
πνεῦμα	τοῦ	θεοῦ.	**12.** ἡμεῖς	δὲ	οὐ
pneuma	tou	theou	hēmeis	de	ou
Spirit		of God.	We	but	not

3450.16 art sing neu	4011.1 noun sing neu	3450.2 art gen sing	2862.2 noun gen sing masc	2956.15 verb 1pl indic aor act	233.2 conj
τὸ	πνεῦμα	τοῦ	κόσμου	ἐλάβομεν,	ἀλλὰ
to	pneuma	tou	kosmou	elabomen	alla
the	spirit	of the	world	received,	but

3450.16 art sing neu	4011.1 noun sing neu	3450.16 art sing neu	1523.2 prep gen	3450.2 art gen sing	2296.2 noun gen sing masc
τὸ	πνεῦμα	τὸ	ἐκ	τοῦ	θεοῦ,
to	pneuma	to	ek	tou	theou
the	Spirit	the	from		God,

2419.1 conj	3471.16 verb 1pl subj perf act	3450.17 art pl neu	5097.3 prep	3450.2 art gen sing	2296.2 noun gen sing masc
ἵνα	εἰδῶμεν	τὰ	ὑπὸ	τοῦ	θεοῦ
hina	eidōmen	ta	hupo	tou	theou
that	we might know	the things	by		God

5319.8 verb acc pl neu part aor pass	2231.3 prs-pron dat 1pl	3614.17 rel-pron pl neu	2504.1 conj	2953.4 verb 1pl indic pres act	3620.2 partic
χαρισθέντα	ἡμῖν.	**13.** Ἃ	καὶ	λαλοῦμεν,	οὐκ
charisthenta	hēmin	Ha	kai	laloumen	ouk
having been granted	to us:	which	also	we speak,	not

1706.1 prep	1312.2 adj dat pl masc	440.2 adj gen sing fem	4531.2 noun gen sing fem	3030.7 noun dat pl masc	233.1 conj
ἐν	διδακτοῖς	ἀνθρωπίνης	σοφίας	λόγοις,	ἀλλ'
en	didaktois	anthrōpinēs	sophias	logois	all'
in	taught	of human	wisdom	words,	but

11.a.**Txt:** 020L,byz.
Var: 01א,02A,03B,04C 06D,025P,Lach,Treg Alf,Word,Tisc,We/Ho Weis,Sod,UBS/✶

2:11. Paul magnified his discussion with an illustration. From a human viewpoint, only the spirit of a man knows and understands the inner thoughts of a man. In other words, there are secrets kept from others. The comparison is made with the Spirit of God, but a point of clarification must be offered. "Spirit of man" refers to ego or self-consciousness. The "Spirit of God" could not be God's self-consciousness because this would take away the Spirit's personality and individuality. The point of comparison is that He can know that which no one except God could know. Only the Holy Spirit can recognize, understand, and reveal the heart and mind of God.

2:12. Now man may know the "things . . . of God" because, and only because, he has received the Spirit of God. What is meant by "the spirit of the world"? It refers to the attitudes and motivation which controls a world that is not in subjection to God. It is a part of fallen human nature. In contrast, when we become "partakers of the divine nature" (2 Peter 1:4), the Spirit of God comes to indwell us. Believers must battle against the spirit of the world and yield to the Spirit of God. Almost every chapter of 1 Corinthians abounds with examples of the way the Corinthians were in bondage to the spirit of this world—the spirit of worldliness. In chapters 1 to 4 the spirit of this world created petty divisions within the church; in chapter 5 the spirit of the world led to sexual immorality; in chapter 6 it led to legal suits; in chapters 8 and 10 it led to idolatry. Finally in chapters 11 to 14 this same spirit of the world led to a failure of love even in a worship service. That we have not received the "spirit of the world" may also refer to something human, an attitude, a disposition. If so, it is a reference that may allude to Pentecost and the historic coming of the Holy Spirit. Paul tells us "we have received . . . the Spirit which is of God."

The Holy Spirit was sent that we might understand, discern, and possess the gifts of the Spirit. He was sent that the fruit of the Spirit might be growing and maturing in our lives in a practical fashion. He was sent that we might discern what is spiritual and what is fleshly or satanic. Grace, which sums up all the work of God in our lives, can only be understood through the eyes of the Spirit. The Spirit desires that we know more than just the powerful displays of God. Israel saw God's actions. The Spirit desires that we understand the motives and character of God. Moses was shown the ways of God. The Spirit urges these deeper matters upon us.

Once more, notice the emphasis on God's free decision to allow us to know these deeper things of God. To know true wisdom and the gifts of God, the presence of the Spirit is mandatory.

2:13. Closely connected with knowledge is speaking. Spiritual things will come from the spiritual man. This verse points to what Christians endowed with the Spirit are always doing, for the verbs are in the present tense. These "spiritual" words have a definite

yea, the deep things of God: . . . ye the bottome of Goddes secretes, *Tyndale* . . . even the high purposes, *Fenton* . . . the abysmal depths, *Montgomery* . . . the profoundest secrets, *TCNT* . . . yea the profoundities of God, *Rheims* . . . including the depths of the divine nature, *Weymouth.*

11. For what man knoweth the things of a man: . . . what comprehends the human faculties, *Fenton* . . . can understand his own inner thoughts, *Williams* . . . the depths of man, *Montgomery* . . . man is inscrutable to his fellow-man, *Way.*

save the spirit of man which is in him?: . . . except the spirit of humanity, *Concordant* . . . except the man's own spirit, *Weymouth.*

even so the things of God knoweth no man, but the Spirit of God: In the same way, *SEB* . . . the thoughts of God no man knows, *Campbell* . . . no one comprehends the inner life of God, *TCNT* . . . is acquainted with God's inner thoughts, *Weymouth* . . . knows the deeps profound of God, *Montgomery* . . . knows all about God, *SEB.*

12. Now we have received, not the spirit of the world: Now we obtained, *Concordant.*

but the spirit which is of God: . . . but the Spirit proceeding from, *Fenton* . . . which comes forth from God, *Weymouth.*

that we might know the things that are freely given to us of God: . . . that we may understand, *SEB* . . . we can distinguish the gifts, *Fenton* . . . we may realize the graces, *Berkeley* . . . we may appreciate the gifts lavished on us, *Way* . . . we may realize the blessings freely given us, *Montgomery* . . . things which are gifted to us, *Campbell.*

13. Which things also we speak, not in the words which man's wisdom teacheth: We are not using human ideas, *SEB* . . . not in the connynge wordes, *Tyndale* . . . not in the rhetoric of the schools, *Way* . . . not in the learned words, *Douay* . . . vvordes of humane vvisedom, *Rheims.*

1 Corinthians 2:14

13.a.**Txt:** 06D-corr,020L
025P,byz.
Var: 01א,02A,03B,04C
06D-org,Gries,Lach
Treg,Alf,Word,Tisc
We/Ho,Weis,Sod
UBS/∗

1706.1 prep	1312.2 adj dat pl masc	4011.2 noun gen sing neu	39.2 adj gen sing	4012.1 adj dat pl
ἐν	διδακτοῖς	πνεύματος,	⸉ᵃ ἁγίου, ⸊	πνευματικοῖς
en	didaktois	pneumatos	hagiou	pneumatikois
in	taught	of Spirit	Holy,	by spiritual

4012.10 adj acc pl neu	4644.1 verb nom pl masc part pres act	5426.1 adj nom sing masc	1156.2 conj
πνευματικὰ	συγκρίνοντες.	**14.** ψυχικὸς	δὲ
pneumatika	sunkrinontes	psuchikos	de
spiritual things	communicating.	Natural	but

442.1 noun nom sing masc	3620.3 partic	1203.1 verb 3sing indic pres	3450.17 art pl neu	3450.2 art gen sing	4011.2 noun gen sing neu
ἄνθρωπος	οὐ	δέχεται	τὰ	τοῦ	πνεύματος
anthrōpos	ou	dechetai	ta	tou	pneumatos
man	not	receives	the things	of the	Spirit

14.a.**Txt:** p46,01א,02A
03B,04C,06D,012G
025P,044,33,81,88,104
etc.byz.
Var: 2,216-org,255,330
440,451,823,1827

3450.2 art gen sing	2296.2 noun gen sing masc	3334.1 noun nom sing fem	1056.1 conj	840.4 prs-pron dat sing	1498.4 verb 3sing indic pres act
⸉ᵃ τοῦ	θεοῦ ⸊	μωρία	γὰρ	αὐτῷ	ἐστιν,
tou	theou	mōria	gar	autō	estin
of God,		foolishness	for	to him	they are;

2504.1 conj	3620.3 partic	1404.4 verb 3sing indic pres	1091.29 verb inf aor act	3617.1 conj	4013.1 adv
καὶ	οὐ	δύναται	γνῶναι,	ὅτι	πνευματικῶς
kai	ou	dunatai	gnōnai	hoti	pneumatikōs
and	not	he can	to know,	because	spiritually

348.8 verb 3sing indic pres pass	3450.5 art sing masc	1156.2 conj	4012.2 adj nom sing masc	348.2 verb 3sing indic pres act
ἀνακρίνεται.	**15.** ὁ	δὲ	πνευματικὸς	ἀνακρίνει
anakrinetai	ho	de	pneumatikos	anakrinei
they are being discerned;	the	but	spiritual	discerns

15.a.**Txt:** 01א-corr1,03B
06D-corr2,044,104,181
326,330,436,etc.byz.
Var: p46,02A,04C
06D-org

3173.1 conj	3450.17 art pl neu	3820.1 adj	840.5 prs-pron nom sing masc	1156.2 conj	5097.2 prep	3625.1 num card gen
μὲν	[ᵃ+ τὰ]	πάντα,	αὐτὸς	δὲ	ὑπ'	οὐδενὸς
men	ta	panta	autos	de	hup'	oudenos
	[the]	all things,	he	but	by	no one

348.8 verb 3sing indic pres pass	4949.3 intr-pron nom sing	1056.1 conj	1091.17 verb 3sing indic aor act	3426.4 noun acc sing masc
ἀνακρίνεται.	**16.** τίς	γὰρ	ἔγνω	νοῦν
anakrinetai	tis	gar	egnō	noun
is being discerned.	Who	for	did know	mind

2935.2 noun gen sing masc	3614.5 rel-pron nom sing masc	4673.3 verb 3sing indic fut act	840.6 prs-pron acc sing masc	2231.1 prs-pron nom 1pl	1156.2 conj
κυρίου,	ὃς	συμβιβάσει	αὐτόν;	ἡμεῖς	δὲ
kuriou	hos	sumbibasei	auton	hēmeis	de
of Lord?	who	shall instruct	him?	We	but

16.a.**Txt:** p46,01א,02A
04C,06D-corr3,08E
020L,025P,byz.UBS/∗
Var: 03B,06D-org,010F
012G,We/Ho

3426.4 noun acc sing masc	5382.2 name gen masc	2935.2 noun gen sing masc	2174.5 verb 1pl indic pres act	2504.1 conj
νοῦν	⸉✰ Χριστοῦ	[ᵃ κυρίου]	ἔχομεν.	**3:1.** ⸉ Καὶ
noun	Christou	kuriou	echomen	Kai
mind	of Christ	[Lord]	have.	And

1.a.**Txt:** 020L,byz.
Var: 01א,02A,03B,04C
06D,025P,Gries,Lach
Treg,Alf,Word,Tisc
We/Ho,Weis,Sod
UBS/∗

1466.1 prs-pron nom 1sing	2476.3 conj	79.6 noun pl masc	3620.2 partic	1404.23 verb 1sing indic aor pass
ἐγώ,	[ᵃ✰ Κἀγώ,]	ἀδελφοί,	οὐκ	ἠδυνήθην
egō	Kagō	adelphoi	ouk	ēdunēthēn
I,	[And I,]	brothers,	not	was able

color and lead in a definite direction. Thus, Christians do speak what the world does not often understand. There is a comparison of "spiritual things" (a neuter referring to thoughts, opinions, and precepts attributable to the Holy Spirit working in us) with spiritual. These matters are formed into a correlated system.

2:14. Again, lest there be uncertainty in the minds of his readers, Paul compared the natural man and the spiritual man. The distinction is both absolute and general. It would seem that Paul suggests a total ignorance and rejection of *all* spiritual things. Unregenerate man calls the gospel nonsense because he has not received the Spirit to enlighten him, and he cannot by reasoning discover these things; they must be revealed. A deaf man cannot accurately "judge" music; a blind man cannot accurately "judge" the landscape; a natural man cannot receive or discern or "judge" spiritual things.

2:15. But the spiritual man is able to "judge" or compare and examine all things because his source of wisdom is completely accurate. The basis for this is found in verse 10. This is not to say, however, that the Christian believer could express knowledge and understanding on every subject. Since the believer is part of the world, however, his judgment involves secular as well as sacred matters. In judging the world's direction, philosophy, and attitude, some men are led to despair and even suicide. But as the Christian compares, examines, and in this specific sense "judges" but does not condemn, he is led to see the hope and victory for the man in Christ Jesus. At the same time, it is impossible for the natural man to make a similar judgment on the Christian, for he has no accurate source of knowledge. This is not pride, for the source of Christian confidence is not in oneself, but in the Holy Spirit.

2:16. In this verse Paul gives proof for the previous verse. By his question (to which he expects a particular answer), he tells us no man has ever given the Lord instruction, counsel, or advice, and no natural man is able to ascend to God or find out anything about Him apart from divine revelation. The quotation is from Isaiah 40:13. Rather, a gift from God by His Spirit must come. That gift is the mind of Christ, to know and understand. It must be implanted and exercised by the presence of the Holy Spirit. What we have presented, then, is a mystical union, difficult to fully comprehend yet miraculously true, a marvelous work of controlling grace. This discussion leads to understanding a deeper dimension of the Spirit's control and work. God has come to be in us.

3:1. Sad to say, these brethren at Corinth, with whom Paul had such a personal and loving relationship, were not mature, spiritual

but which the Holy Ghost teacheth: . . . but in the doctryne of spirit, *Wyclif* . . . but in the Spirit's school, *Way* . . . but by spiritual teachings, *Fenton.*

comparing spiritual things with spiritual: We interpret what is spiritual in spiritual language, *Moffatt* . . . Interpreting spiritual things, *HistNT* . . . matching that which is spiritual, *Concordant* . . . connecting what is spiritual, *Noyes.*

14. But the natural man receiveth not the things of the Spirit of God: But the sensual man, *Rheims* . . . the soulish man, *Concordant* . . . brutish man does not entertain, *Fenton* . . . perceaveth not, *Tyndale* . . . cannot grasp the revelations of the Spirit, *Way* . . . rejects the teachings, *Montgomery.*

for they are foolishness unto him: neither can he know [them]: They are for him meaningless, *Way* . . . for it is foli to hym, *Wyclif* . . . they are 'sheer folly,' he cannot understand them, *Moffatt* . . . and he cannot ascertain [them], *Rotherham* . . . and cannot attain to the knowledge of them, *Weymouth.*

because they are spiritually discerned: . . . for they are estimated spiritually, *HistNT* . . . spiritually investigated, *Fenton* . . . they are spretually examined, *Cranmer, Concordant.*

15. But he that is spiritual judgeth all things: . . . discerns everything, *Montgomery* . . . discusseth all thinges, *Tyndale.*

yet he himself is judged of no man: . . . be criticised by no one, *Fenton.*

16. For who hath known the mind of the Lord, that he may instruct him?: . . . who ever understood the thoughts, *Moffatt* . . . who has penetrated the mind, *Weymouth* . . . the sense of our Lord, *Rheims* . . . and who knewe the witte of the lord? *Wyclif* . . . have taught Him, *Fenton.*

But we have the mind of Christ: . . . we possess, *Fenton* . . . But we vnderstande the mynde of Christ, *Cranmer* . . . our thoughts are Christ's, *Moffatt.*

1 Corinthians 3:2

2953.37 verb inf aor act	5050.3 prs- pron dat 2pl	5453.1 conj	4012.1 adj dat pl	233.1 conj	5453.1 conj
λαλῆσαι	ὑμῖν	ὡς	πνευματικοῖς,	ἀλλ'	ὡς
lalēsai	humin	hōs	pneumatikois	all'	hōs
to speak	to you	as	to spiritual,	but	as

1.b.Txt: 06D-corr,020L
025P,byz.
Var: 01א,02A,03B
04C-org,06D-org,Gries
Lach,Treg,Alf,Word
Tisc,We/Ho,Weis,Sod
UBS/✩

4416.1 adj dat pl	4417.2 adj dat pl	5453.1 conj	3378.5 adj dat pl masc	1706.1 prep
⸂ σαρκίκοις,	[b✩ σαρκίνοις,]	ὡς	νηπίοις	ἐν
sarkikois	sarkinois	hōs	nēpiois	en
to fleshly;	[idem]	as	to babes	in

2.a.Txt: 06D,020L,byz.
Var: 01א,02A,03B,04C
025P,Gries,Lach,Treg
Alf,Word,Tisc,We/Ho
Weis,Sod,UBS/✩

5382.3 name dat masc	1044.2 noun acc sing neu	5050.4 prs- pron acc 2pl	4081.4 verb 1sing indic aor act	2504.1 conj	3620.3 partic
Χριστῷ.	**2.** γάλα	ὑμᾶς	ἐπότισα,	⸂a καὶ ⸃	οὐ
Christō	gala	humas	epotisa	kai	ou
Christ.	Milk	you	I gave to drink;	and	not

2.b.Txt: 06D,020L,byz.
Var: 01א,02A,03B,04C
025P,Gries,Lach,Treg
Alf,Word,Tisc,We/Ho
Weis,Sod,UBS/✩

1026.1 noun sing neu	3632.1 adv	1056.1 conj	1404.41 verb 2pl indic imperf mid	1404.39 verb 2pl indic imperf
βρῶμα·	οὔπω	γὰρ	⸂ ἠδύνασθε.	[b✩ ἐδύνασθε.]
brōma	oupō	gar	ēdunasthe	edunasthe
solid food	not yet	for	were you able,	[idem]

2.c.Txt: 020L,byz.
Var: 01א,02A,03B,04C
06D,025P,Gries,Lach
Treg,Alf,Word,Tisc
We/Ho,Weis,Sod
UBS/✩

233.1 conj	3641.1 conj	3624.1 adv	2068.1 adv	3431.1 adv	1404.6 verb 2pl indic pres
ἀλλ'	⸂ οὔτε	[c✩ οὐδὲ]	ἔτι	νῦν	δύνασθε·
all'	oute	oude	eti	nun	dunasthe
but	neither	[and not]	yet	now	are you able;

2068.1 adv	1056.1 conj	4416.3 adj nom pl masc	1498.6 verb 2pl indic pres act	3562.1 adv	1056.1 conj	1706.1 prep
3. ἔτι	γὰρ	σαρκικοί	ἐστε.	ὅπου	γὰρ	ἐν
eti	gar	sarkikoi	este	hopou	gar	en
yet	for	fleshly	you are.	Where	for	among

3.a.Txt: p46,06D,020L
33,byz.
Var: p11,01א,02A,03B
04C,025P,044,sa.bo.
Lach,Treg,Alf,Tisc
We/Ho,Weis,Sod
UBS/✩

5050.3 prs- pron dat 2pl	2188.1 noun sing neu	2504.1 conj	2038.1 noun nom sing fem	2504.1 conj	1364.1 noun nom pl fem
ὑμῖν	ζῆλος	καὶ	ἔρις	⸂a καὶ	διχοστασίαι, ⸃
humin	zēlos	kai	eris	kai	dichostasiai
you	jealousy	and	rivaly	and	divisions,

3644.1 adv	4416.3 adj nom pl masc	1498.6 verb 2pl indic pres act	2504.1 conj	2567.3 prep	442.4 noun acc sing masc
οὐχὶ	σαρκικοί	ἐστε.	καὶ	κατὰ	ἄνθρωπον
ouchi	sarkikoi	este	kai	kata	anthrōpon
not	fleshly	are you,	and	according to	man

3906.1 verb 2pl pres act	3615.1 conj	1056.1 conj	2978.7 verb 3sing subj pres act	4948.3 indef- pron nom sing	1466.1 prs- pron nom 1sing
περιπατεῖτε;	**4.** ὅταν	γὰρ	λέγῃ	τις,	Ἐγὼ
peripateite	hotan	gar	legē	tis	Egō
walk?	When	for	may say	one,	I

3173.1 conj	1498.2 verb 1sing indic pres act	3834.2 name gen masc	2066.5 adj nom sing masc	1156.2 conj	1466.1 prs- pron nom 1sing
μέν	εἰμι	Παύλου,	ἕτερος	δέ,	Ἐγὼ
men	eimi	Paulou	heteros	de	Egō
am	am	of Paul,	another	and,	I

4.a.Txt: (01א-corr),020L
025P,byz.
Var: 01א-org,02A,03B
04C,Lach,Treg,Alf,Tisc
We/Ho,Weis,Sod
UBS/✩

619.2 name acc masc	3644.1 adv	4416.3 adj nom pl masc	3620.2 partic	442.6 noun nom pl masc
Ἀπολλῶ,	⸂ οὐχὶ	σαρκικοί	[a✩ οὐκ	ἄνθρωποί]
Apollō	ouchi	sarkikoi	ouk	anthrōpoi
of Apollos,	not	fleshly	[not	men]

286

men. Up to this point in his discussion on wisdom Paul had been more general. Now he became specific and pointed. In chapter 2 Paul made clear that the wisdom of this world and the wisdom of this age are to be shunned, for they are contrary to the message of the Cross. There is, however, a proper way to view wisdom, and that is to see Jesus Christ as the wisdom of God (2:7). In chapter 3 Paul went on to say that although there is a spiritual wisdom, the Corinthians were not mature enough for it. When Paul first came to Corinth, these men had been converted and became spiritual "babes." They were young and weak. There is nothing wrong with that. Every Christian begins without experience, with little understanding; the need is for growth. But as we will shortly see, this entire section teaches the incapacity of the natural man for spiritual things. These believers were "carnal" Christians. They had not grown spiritually. They still showed traits of the old life.

3:2. Paul began his ministry by feeding them "milk." Paul was not saying he fed them on anything but the principles of Christ, but there is a realm in God that young Christians do not know and for which they are not yet ready. This soft diet was necessary because as spiritual babes they were not ready for the deeper truths of the gospel.

At this point Paul leveled a terrible charge. They had remained babes; they had not grown spiritually. They remained on the same plateau as when they first began and so proved themselves to be "carnal Christians." This was a strong rebuke to the Corinthians' pride and sense of accomplishment.

3:3. This verse explains what is meant by the previous two verses. The meaning of the word "carnal" in verse 1 is different from the word "carnal" in this verse. The first word means "fleshy" or fleshly and one *cannot* help it. The second means "fleshly" and one *will* not help it. They should have been bearing the fruit of the Spirit; instead they were producing the works of the flesh. This was particularly true as it applied to divisions in the Corinthian church. The divisions were not only bad; they proved these believers were immature. Their wrong attitudes, words, and actions proved their inclination toward natural, worldly living.

3:4. With strong words Paul attacked this specific arm of the problem. He denounced those in particular who followed him and Apollos. He might have done this to prove his own unworthiness; and he might have used Apollos because he was a close friend at Ephesus with him. Or these could have been the two strongest or the most quarrelsome parties. The question was intended to gain a positive answer.

1. And I, brethren, could not speak unto you as unto spiritual: As for me, brothers, *Montgomery.*

but as unto carnal: . . . address you as worldlings, *Moffatt* . . . as to animal, *Fenton* . . . but as to fleischli men, *Wyclif* . . . to be as to worldlings, *Weymouth* . . . as creatures of flesh, *HistNT, Montgomery* . . . in whom the fleshly nature predominated, *Way.*

[even] as unto babes in Christ: As it vvere to litle ones, *Rheims* . . . as to minors, *Concordant* . . . as to litil children in crist, *Wyclif* . . . mere infants in the New Life, *Way.*

2. I have fed you with milk, and not with meat: . . . not with solid food, *Moffatt.*

for hitherto ye were not able [to bear it]: . . . you were not yet strong enough, *Weymouth* . . . you could not have assimilated, *Way* . . . were not stronge, *Tyndale* . . . were not yet ready for it, *Confraternity.*

neither yet now are ye able:

3. For ye are yet carnal: . . . you are still worldly, *Moffatt* . . . still in the flesh, *Murdock.*

for whereas [there is] among you envying, and strife, and divisions: . . . where [there are] among you jealousy, *Rotherham* . . . is among you rivalry, *Noyes* . . . is rage and strife, *Fenton* . . . and quarrels, *Moffatt* . . . and factious parties, *Conybeare* . . . and sectes, *Cranmer.*

are ye not carnal, and walk as men?: . . . is it not evident that you are carnal, *Conybeare* . . . you are unspiritual, *Weymouth* . . . conducting yourselves like men? *Fenton* . . . walking after the manner of men? *HistNT* . . . behaving like worldlings, *Montgomery* . . . like ordinary men? *Moffatt.*

4. For while one saith, I am of Paul; and another, I [am] of Apollos:

are ye not carnal?: . . . can you deny, *Conybeare* . . . are you not mere men, *Confraternity* . . . you not merely man-followers? *Fenton* . . . is not this the way men of the world speak? *Weymouth.*

1 Corinthians 3:5

1498.6 verb 2pl indic pres act	4949.3 intr-pron nom sing	4949.9 intr-pron sing neu	3631.1 conj	1498.4 verb 3sing indic pres act
ἐστε;	5. ͑ Τίς	[ᵃ☆ τί]	οὖν	ἐστιν
este	Tis	ti	oun	estin
are you?	Who	[what]	then	is

3834.1 name nom masc	619.1 name nom masc	4949.3 intr-pron nom sing	4949.9 intr-pron sing neu	1156.2 conj
͑ Παῦλος,	[ᵇ☆ Ἀπολλῶς;]	͑ τίς	[ᶜ☆ τί]	δέ
Paulos	Apollōs	tis	ti	de
Paul,	[Apollos?]	who	[what]	and

1498.4 verb 3sing indic pres act	619.1 name nom masc	3834.1 name nom masc	233.1 conj
[ᵈ☆+ ἐστιν]	͑ Ἀπολλῶς,	[ᵉ☆ Παῦλος;]	͑ᶠ ἀλλ'
estin	Apollōs	Paulos	all'
[is]	Apollos?	[Paul?]	but

2211.1 conj	1243.3 noun nom pl masc	1217.1 prep	3614.1 rel-pron gen pl	3961.22 verb 2pl indic aor act	2504.1 conj
ἢ ͵	διάκονοι	δι'	ὧν	ἐπιστεύσατε,	καὶ
ē	diakonoi	di'	hōn	episteusate	kai
or	servants	through	whom	you believed,	and

1524.4 adj dat sing masc	5453.1 conj	3450.5 art sing masc	2935.1 noun nom sing masc	1319.14 verb 3sing indic aor act	1466.1 prs-pron nom 1sing
ἑκάστῳ	ὡς	ὁ	κύριος	ἔδωκεν;	6. ἐγὼ
hekastō	hōs	ho	kurios	edōken	egō
to each	as	the	Lord	gave?	I

5288.3 verb 1sing indic aor act	619.1 name nom masc	4081.5 verb 3sing indic aor act	233.1 conj	233.2 conj
ἐφύτευσα,	Ἀπολλῶς	ἐπότισεν,	͑ ἀλλ'	[☆ ἀλλὰ]
ephuteusa	Apollōs	epotisen	all'	alla
planted,	Apollos	watered;	but	[but]

3450.5 art sing masc	2296.1 noun nom sing masc	831.10 verb 3sing indic imperf act	5452.1 conj	3641.1 conj
ὁ	θεὸς	ηὔξανεν·	7. ὥστε	οὔτε
ho	theos	ēuxanen	hōste	oute
the	God	was giving growth.	So that	neither

3450.5 art sing masc	5288.2 verb nom sing masc part pres act	1498.4 verb 3sing indic pres act	4948.10 indef-pron sing neu	3641.1 conj	3450.5 art sing masc
ὁ	φυτεύων	ἐστίν	τι,	οὔτε	ὁ
ho	phuteuōn	estin	ti	oute	ho
the	planting	is	anything,	nor	the

4081.3 verb nom sing masc part pres act	233.1 conj	3450.5 art sing masc	831.4 verb nom sing masc part pres act	2296.1 noun nom sing masc	3450.5 art sing masc
ποτίζων,	ἀλλ'	ὁ	αὐξάνων	θεός.	8. ὁ
potizōn	all'	ho	auxanōn	theos	ho
watering;	but	the	giving growth	God.	The

5288.2 verb nom sing masc part pres act	1156.2 conj	2504.1 conj	3450.5 art sing masc	4081.3 verb nom sing masc part pres act	1518.9 num card neu
φυτεύων	δὲ	καὶ	ὁ	ποτίζων	ἕν
phuteuōn	de	kai	ho	potizōn	hen
planting	but	and	the	watering	one

1498.7 verb 3pl indic pres act	1524.3 adj nom sing masc	1156.2 conj	3450.6 art acc sing masc	2375.4 adj acc sing	3272.3 noun acc sing masc
εἰσιν·	ἕκαστος	δὲ	τὸν	ἴδιον	μισθὸν
eisin	hekastos	de	ton	idion	misthon
are;	each	but	the	his own	reward

3:5. The mature laborer for Christ does not involve himself in party dissension. The men whom God uses for work in His kingdom are really servants called to bring men to belief in Christ. God had given each minister a particular work, ability, and ministry which He used with the Word to bring the Corinthians to salvation. The emphasis is on God. As John wrote in his Gospel concerning John the Baptist: "There was a man sent from God, whose name was John" (John 1:6).

Paul here asked the question, "Who then is Paul, and who is Apollos . . . ?" Although a response of "nothing" might be expected because they were merely human instruments of God, Paul did not say that. Indeed, Paul and Apollos were *diakonoi* ("servants" or "ministers"). Paul said in 2 Corinthians 4:5 that they were "your servants for Jesus' sake." Paul also used the word "steward" (*oikonomous*) to describe his ministry (4:1).

Here in 1 Corinthians the word *diakonos* is used only in the general sense of servant (and probably not an exalted servant at that, since the word was also used of waiters!). By the time Paul had written the Pastoral Epistles, however, the word *diakonos* was a technical term denoting a specific function and office in the local church (cf. especially 1 Timothy 3:8-13).

Grammatically, the expression "and to each (*kai hekastō hōs* as the Lord gave" could refer back to the verb "believed" (*episteusate*), meaning the Lord gave faith to each, but it is better to interpret the clause in terms of verse 7 suggesting that the Lord gave specific tasks to each servant to perform (such as planting, watering, etc.).

3:6. Paul supported his point by way of illustration. He called attention to the illustration of a farmer or gardener. Paul had initiated the work; Apollos had strengthened and nurtured it. But these men had cooperated together under the direction of God, for it was God alone who gave the increase or harvest. The first two verbs of this verse are aorist and point to work already done. But God's activity is in the imperfect tense and indicates work continuing after a specific beginning.

3:7. Divisions such as were occurring at Corinth should not be allowed because leaders and laborers are merely instruments. God accomplishes through them what He will. The Christian worker must maintain the humility, submission, and unity that come from understanding that all men work in the place to which God calls them, and all are important under God. God does not have "big" preachers or "small" preachers, just faithful preachers.

3:8. All ministers and laborers then are on an equal plane. The job does not make one person more important than another. All share a common goal. Therefore, the reward given to these co-workers will depend on their personal labor. The emphasis seems

5. Who then is Paul, and who [is] Apollos:

but ministers by whom ye believed: Servants are they, *Concordant* . . . just God's servants, *Weymouth* . . . They are simply used by God to give you faith, *Moffatt* . . . We are simply God's servants, *TEV* . . . Ministers through whom you believed, *HistNT* . . . through whose agency you came to accept, *TCNT*.

even as the Lord gave to every man?: The Lord gave each of us a job to do, *SEB* . . . gave each his task, *Berkeley* . . . gave each of us his task, *Williams* . . . granted power to each, *Weymouth* . . . each endowed as the Lord decided, *Fenton* . . . only as the Lord appointed, *Adams*.

6. I have planted, Apollos watered; but God gave the increase: . . . apollo moistide, *Wyclif* . . . Apollos irrigates, *Concordant* . . . watered the plant, *TEV* . . . but God prospered it, *Fenton* . . . God caused to grow, *Rotherham* . . . made the growth, *HistNT* . . . produced the growth, *Murdock* . . . made the seed grow, *Moffatt, Montgomery, Conybeare* . . . gave the crop, *Klingensmith*.

7. So then neither is he that planteth any thing: Consequently, the planter, *Fenton* . . . nor the waterer counts for much, *Williams* . . . is of any importance, *Weymouth* . . . is not important, *SEB*.

neither he that watereth: . . . the man who waters, *TEV*.

but God that giveth the increase: . . . the only One who counts is God, *Adams*.

8. Now he that planteth and he that watereth are one: . . . so far from being rivals, *Way* . . . are for one thing, *Concordant* . . . are one in aim, *Williams* . . . are nether better then the other, *Tyndale* . . . are equal, *Fenton* . . . are on the same level, *Moffatt* . . . are on a par, *Murdock* . . . are together, *Beck* . . . work together, *SEB*.

and every man shall receive his own reward according to his own labour: . . . and eche schal take his owne mede, *Wyclif* . . . each will

1 Corinthians 3:9

2956.39 verb 3sing indic fut mid	2956.45 verb 3sing indic fut mid	2567.3 prep	3450.6 art acc sing masc	2375.4 adj acc sing
΄ λήψεται	[✶ λήμψεται]	κατὰ	τὸν	ἴδιον
lēpsetai	lēmpsetai	kata	ton	idion
shall receive	[idem]	according to	the	his own

2845.4 noun acc sing masc	2296.2 noun gen sing masc	1056.1 conj	1498.5 verb 1pl indic pres act	4754.4 adj nom pl masc	2296.2 noun gen sing masc
κόπον.	9. θεοῦ	γάρ	ἐσμεν	συνεργοί·	θεοῦ
kopon	theou	gar	esmen	sunergoi	theou
labor.	God's	for	we are	fellow workers;	God's

1085.1 noun nom sing neu	2296.2 noun gen sing masc	3482.1 noun nom sing fem	1498.6 verb 2pl indic pres act	2567.3 prep
γεώργιον,	θεοῦ	οἰκοδομή	ἐστε.	10. Κατὰ
geōrgion	theou	oikodomē	este	Kata
field,	God's	building	you are.	According to

10.a.Txt: 01ℵ,02A,03B
04C,06D,025P,044,33
614,1739,byz.
Var: p46,0142,81,1962
2495

3450.12 art acc sing fem	5322.4 noun acc sing fem	3450.2 art gen sing	2296.2 noun gen sing masc	3450.12 art acc sing fem	1319.51 verb acc sing fem part aor pass
τὴν	χάριν	΄ᵃ τοῦ	θεοῦ ΅	τὴν	δοθεῖσάν
tēn	charin	tou	theou	tēn	dotheisan
the	grace		of God	the	having been given

1466.4 prs-pron dat 1sing	5453.1 conj	4533.1 adj nom sing masc	748.1 noun nom sing masc	2287.4 noun acc sing masc	4935.18 verb 1sing indic perf act
μοι,	ὡς	σοφὸς	ἀρχιτέκτων	θεμέλιον	΄ τέθεικα,
moi	hōs	sophos	architektōn	themelion	tetheika
to me,	as	a wise	architect	foundation	I have laid,

10.b.Txt: 01ℵ-corr
04C-corr,06D,020L
025P,byz.
Var: 01ℵ-org,02A,03B
04C-org,33,Lach,Treg
Alf,Tisc,We/Ho,Weis
Sod,UBS/✶

4935.8 verb 1sing indic aor act	241.4 adj nom sing masc	1156.2 conj	2010.1 verb 3sing indic pres act	1524.3 adj nom sing masc
[ᵇ✶ ἔθηκα,]	ἄλλος	δὲ	ἐποικοδομεῖ.	ἕκαστος
etheka	allos	de	epoikodomei	hekastos
[I laid,]	another	and	builds up.	Each

1156.2 conj	984.11 verb 3sing impr pres act	4316.1 adv	2010.1 verb 3sing indic pres act	2287.4 noun acc sing masc	1056.1 conj
δὲ	βλεπέτω	πῶς	ἐποικοδομεῖ·	11. θεμέλιον	γὰρ
de	blepetō	pōs	epoikodomei	themelion	gar
but	let take heed	how	he builds up.	Foundation	for

241.5 adj acc sing masc	3625.2 num card nom masc	1404.4 verb 3sing indic pres	4935.17 verb inf aor act	3706.2 prep	3450.6 art acc sing masc
ἄλλον	οὐδεὶς	δύναται	θεῖναι	παρὰ	τὸν
allon	oudeis	dunatai	theinai	para	ton
other	no one	is able	to lay	besides	the

11.a.Txt: byz.
Var: 01ℵ,02A,03B,020L
025P,Gries,Treg,Alf
Word,Tisc,We/Ho,Weis
Sod,UBS/✶

2719.4 verb acc sing part pres	3614.5 rel-pron nom sing masc	1498.4 verb 3sing indic pres act	2400.1 name nom masc	3450.5 art sing masc
κείμενον,	ὅς	ἐστιν	Ἰησοῦς	΄ᵃ ὁ ΅
keimenon	hos	estin	Iēsous	ho
laying,	which	is	Jesus	the

5382.1 name nom masc	1479.1 conj	1156.2 conj	4948.3 indef-pron nom sing	2010.1 verb 3sing indic pres act	1894.3 prep
Χριστός.	12. εἰ	δέ	τις	ἐποικοδομεῖ	ἐπὶ
Christos	ei	de	tis	epoikodomei	epi
Christ.	If	now	anyone	build up	on

12.a.Txt: 01ℵ-corr
04C-corr,06D,020L
025P,byz.Sod
Var: p46,01ℵ-org,02A
03B,04C-org,sa.Lach
Treg,Tisc,We/Ho,Weis
UBS/✶

3450.6 art acc sing masc	2287.4 noun acc sing masc	3642.6 dem-pron acc sing masc	5392.4 noun acc sing masc	690.4 noun acc sing masc
τὸν	θεμέλιον	΄ᵃ τοῦτον ΅	΄ χρυσόν,	ἄργυρον,
ton	themelion	touton	chruson	arguron
the	foundation	this	gold,	silver,

to be on the labor, not the success; on the faithfulness of the servant involved. If man does his part in the work of the gospel, God will certainly do His part.

3:9. "We are laborers together with God"; that is, we are fellow workers who belong to God, and we are working with one another. The emphasis is on God. He is mentioned emphatically three times in this verse. We are, in keeping with the figures already suggested, God's "husbandry" and God's "building." "Husbandry" conveys the idea of cultivation, and "building" suggests the process of construction. God is cultivating and building the Church. God's possession then is in close view. If these Corinthians came to see God's proper place here then they would also come to see His minister's proper place. Without exception, the problems in the Church seem to be caused when we have a faulty view of God and His work. The problems would be resolved if we grasped His motive for doing something. To summarize, three things would be accomplished: The Corinthians (and we also) would come to a true view of human teachers, and would listen to them but not idolize them; we would not mistreat God's workers because they belong to God; and we would not mistreat ourselves because we belong to God.

3:10. So then man as a colaborer with God builds for Him. Paul as a master builder, architect, and superintendent, had skillfully laid a foundation. Paul guards against usurping divine glory, for he indicates that his wise building was due to the grace of God and not his own abilities. In his comment on this verse Matthew Henry says, "It is no crime in a Christian, but much to his commendation, to take notice of the good that is in him, to the praise of divine grace" (6:3:10).

3:11. But those who follow must be careful as to what they build on top of this wise foundation. In this chapter Paul introduced three classes of builders: (1) Those who are truly wise; (2) those who are unwise and introduce wrong material but do not leave the foundation; and (3) those who are fools and try to destroy God's temple. Paul acknowledged other builders besides himself, but he acknowledged no foundation other than Jesus Christ. Everything must be built on the person and doctrine of Christ. In an absolute sense, there can be no other foundation.

3:12. In building, men use different materials. Paul listed at least two categories of materials—good and bad. But he also set the stage for his next figure, fire, by listing three incombustible and three combustible types of material. These materials have been said to

receive his own special reward, *Weymouth* . . . his own pay, *Fenton* . . . his own wage, *Moffatt* . . . his individual reward, *HistNT* . . . will be paid according to his work, *Klingensmith* . . . his proper reward, according to his proper labor, *Campbell* . . . according to his own service, *Montgomery*.

9. For we are labourers together with God: . . . for we ben the helpers of god, *Wyclif* . . . joint laborers, *Campbell* . . . fellow-laborers, *Conybeare* . . . we are but labourers employed by God, *Locke* . . . in God's service, *Moffatt*.
ye are God's husbandry, [ye are] God's building: You are God's farm, *Fenton* . . . you are God's field, *Weymouth* . . . God's tillage, *Hanson* . . . and God's edifice, *Murdock*.

10. According to the grace of God which is given unto me, as a wise masterbuilder: In discharge of the task...God graciously entrusted to me, *Weymouth* . . . In virtue of my commission, *Moffatt* . . . By virtue of God's grace granted me, *HistNT* . . . having been imparted to me, *Wilson* . . . as a wise maister carpenter, *Wyclif* . . . as a wise foreman, *Concordant* . . . as a wyse bylder, *Tyndale* . . . as a skilful master builder, *Geneva* . . . like a skilful architect, *Fenton*.
I have laid the foundation, and another buildeth thereon: . . . and another bildith aboue, *Wyclif* . . . another is now carrying on the structure, *Way*.
But let every man take heed how he buildeth thereupon: . . . let him be careful how, *Moffatt* . . . take care how, *Fenton*.

11. For other foundation can no man lay than that is laid: The foundation is already laid, *Montgomery*.
which is Jesus Christ:

12. Now if any man build upon this foundation: . . . is erecting on that foundation, *Weymouth*.

1 Corinthians 3:13

12.b.Txt: 02A,06D,020L
025P,byz.Lach,Sod
Var: 01א,03B,Treg,Tisc
We/Ho,Weis,UBS/☆

5388.1 noun sing neu	688.1 noun sing neu	3012.8 noun acc pl masc	4941.5 adj acc pl masc	3448.5 noun acc pl neu
[ᵇ χρυσίον,	ἀργύριον,]	λίθους	τιμίους,	ξύλα,
chrusion	argurion	lithous	timious	xula
[gold,	silver,]	stones	precious,	wood,

5363.4 noun acc sing masc	2533.1 noun acc sing fem		1524.2 adj gen sing	3450.16 art sing neu	2024.1 noun sing neu	5156.1 adj sing
χόρτον,	καλάμην,	**13.** ἑκάστου		τὸ	ἔργον	φανερὸν
chorton	kalamēn	hekastou		to	ergon	phaneron
grass,	straw,	of each		the	work	manifest

1090.69 verb 3sing indic fut mid	3450.9 art nom sing fem	1056.1 conj	2232.2 noun nom sing fem	1207.5 verb 3sing indic fut act	3617.1 conj
γενήσεται·	ἡ	γὰρ	ἡμέρα	δηλώσει·	ὅτι
genēsetai	hē	gar	hēmera	dēlōsei	hoti
will become;	the	for	day	will make clear,	because

1706.1 prep	4300.3 noun dat sing neu	596.5 verb 3sing indic pres pass	2504.1 conj	1524.2 adj gen sing	3450.16 art sing neu
ἐν	πυρὶ	ἀποκαλύπτεται·	καὶ	ἑκάστου	τὸ
en	puri	apokaluptetai	kai	hekastou	to
in	fire	it is being revealed;	and	of each	the

13.a.Var: 02A,03B,04C
025P,33,Lach,Treg,Alf
Word,Tisc,We/Ho,Weis
Sod,UBS/☆

2024.1 noun sing neu	3560.3 intr-pron acc sing fem	1498.4 verb 3sing indic pres act	3450.16 art sing neu	4300.1 noun sing neu	840.15 prs-pron sing neu
ἔργον	ὁποῖόν	ἐστιν,	τὸ	πῦρ	[ᵃ☆+ αὐτὸ]
ergon	hopoion	estin	to	pur	auto
work	what sort	it is,	the	fire	[it]

1375.13 verb 3sing indic fut act	1479.1 conj	4948.1 indef-pron gen sing	3450.16 art sing neu	2024.1 noun sing neu	3176.32 verb 3sing indic fut act
δοκιμάσει.	**14.** εἴ	τινος	τὸ	ἔργον	μενεῖ
dokimasei	ei	tinos	to	ergon	menei
will prove.	If	of anyone	the	work	abides

14.a.Txt: 03B-corr,04C
byz.
Var: 01א,02A,03B-org
06D,020L,025P,33,Treg
Alf,Tisc,We/Ho,Weis
Sod,UBS/☆

3614.16 rel-pron sing neu	2010.3 verb 3sing indic aor act	2010.7 verb 3sing indic aor act	3272.3 noun acc sing masc
ὃ	⸆ ἐπῳκοδόμησεν,	[ᵃ☆ ἐποικοδόμησεν,]	μισθὸν
ho	epōkodomēsen	epoikodomēsen	misthon
which	he built up,	[he built on,]	a reward

2956.39 verb 3sing indic fut mid	2956.45 verb 3sing indic fut mid	1479.1 conj	4948.1 indef-pron gen sing	3450.16 art sing neu
⸆ λήψεται·	[☆ λήμψεται·]	**15.** εἴ	τινος	τὸ
lēpsetai	lēmpsetai	ei	tinos	to
he shall receive.	[idem]	If	of anyone	the

2024.1 noun sing neu	2588.8 verb 3sing indic fut pass	2193.5 verb 3sing indic fut pass	840.5 prs-pron nom sing masc	1156.2 conj
ἔργον	κατακαήσεται,	ζημιωθήσεται·	αὐτὸς	δὲ
ergon	katakaēsetai	zēmiōthēsetai	autos	de
work	shall be consumed,	he shall suffer loss,	himself	but

4834.33 verb 3sing indic fut pass	3643.1 adv	1156.2 conj	5453.1 conj	1217.2 prep	4300.2 noun gen sing neu	3620.2 partic
σωθήσεται,	οὕτως	δὲ	ὡς	διὰ	πυρός.	**16.** Οὐκ
sōthēsetai	houtōs	de	hōs	dia	puros	Ouk
shall be saved,	so	but	as	through	fire.	Not

3471.6 verb 2pl indic perf act	3617.1 conj	3348.1 noun nom sing masc	2296.2 noun gen sing masc	1498.6 verb 2pl indic pres act	2504.1 conj	3450.16 art sing neu
οἴδατε	ὅτι	ναὸς	θεοῦ	ἐστε,	καὶ	τὸ
oidate	hoti	naos	theou	este	kai	to
know you	that	temple	God's	you are,	and	the

refer to one of three areas: (1) Different sorts of persons in the Church; (2) moral fruits; and (3) doctrines of the different teachers. It seems difficult and impractical to distinguish so finely among the three suggestions, since they have a relationship with one another. There is, however, some emphasis on speculative, curious doctrine versus solid doctrine. At this point one thing is certain, the emphasis is on *what* is done, not *how* it is done. In the process of building the work of Christ it is essential that the best materials be used because the work will be exposed and evaluated.

3:13. Whatever is built will be tested. God uses the process of accountability. This verse clearly teaches there will be a definite judgment of Christians' works. This does not refer to salvation but to rewards. Paul is referring to the Bema judgment and the judging of believers for their service to God. This is a purging fire. The intent of the fire is to prove the value and good of the item tested. Sadly, some of the work will not stand the test of God's examination; it will be shown to be useless and without value and will be destroyed.

3:14,15. On the basis of the test, the builder will receive his reward. If his service has stood the fire of judgment, he will receive his honest and just reward. But what is built must be of the strongest materials to withstand the fire. "By fire" is proverbial for a hairbreadth escape; a very close, perilous, narrow escape, not necessarily without injury. The figure is slightly different from that in verse 13.

Note that the reward is conditional. If a man builds with the wrong materials, he will lose his reward but still retain eternal life. Apparently some built with the wrong materials on the right foundation. The verb *zemiōthēsetai* is capable of several translations, but the best way to understand the word is that the servant who uses faulty materials "will miss the reward he might have had" (Barrett, *Harper's New Testament Commentaries*, p.89). It must be said, however, that there appears to be a very fine line between the foolish builder of verse 15 and the one destroyed of verse 17. It is certainly a solemn warning to all who labor for the Lord, to be very careful not to be enticed by fads and doctrines that are only half true.

3:16. The reason for the mason's care is that this "building" is God's temple, the habitation of God's Spirit. This carries a collective meaning. The thought regarding the individual is better indicated in 6:19,20. "Know ye not" suggests something the Corinthians should have remembered but had forgotten. The "temple" (the word used here suggests especially the structure containing the Holy Place and the Holy of Holies) was the noblest of buildings, for it was

gold, silver, precious stones, wood, hay, stubble: . . . costly stones...straw, *Fenton* . . . grass, *Concordant* . . . reeds, *Hanson* . . . tymber, *Tyndale.*

13. Every man's work shall be made manifest: . . . the true character of each individual's work, *Weymouth* . . . the nature of his work will come out, *Moffatt* . . . shall be disclosed, *HistNT* . . . become apparent, *Concordant.*

for the day shall declare it, because it shall be revealed by fire: . . . the day of the Lord will declare it, *Confraternity* . . . will disclose it, *Weymouth* . . . will make it plain, *HistNT* . . . will make it evident, *Concordant.*

and the fire shall try every man's work of what sort it is: . . . the fire itself will test, *Rotherham* . . . the fire will prove, *Fenton* . . . will test each man's sort of work, *HistNT* . . . will assay the quality of everyone's work, *Confraternity* . . . what kind it is, *Concordant.*

14. If any man's work abide which he hath built thereupon: If one man's work stands, *Fenton* . . . structure raised by any man survives, *Moffatt, HistNT* . . . stands the test, *Weymouth.*
he shall receive a reward:

15. If any man's work shall be burned, he shall suffer loss: . . . he shal suffer detriment, *Rheims* . . . he will forfeit it, *Concordant* . . . He shall be a loser, *HistNT.*

but he himself shall be saved: . . . yet he will himself be rescued, *Weymouth* . . . he will be snatched, *Moffatt.*
yet so as by fire: . . . but in this way—as through fire, *Rotherham* . . . by passing through the fire, *Weymouth* . . . from the very flames, *Moffatt.*

16. Know ye not that ye are the temple of God: Are ye not ware that, *Tyndale* . . . Are you not aware, *Concordant* . . . you are a Divine temple, *Fenton* . . . you are God's Sanctuary, *Weymouth.*

1 Corinthians 3:17

4011.1 noun sing neu	3450.2 art gen sing	2296.2 noun gen sing masc	3474.1 verb 3sing indic pres act	1706.1 prep	5050.3 prs- pron dat 2pl
πνεῦμα pneuma Spirit	τοῦ tou	θεοῦ theou of God	ʿ οἰκεῖ oikei dwells	ἐν en in	ὑμῖν; humin you?

1706.1 prep	5050.3 prs- pron dat 2pl	3474.1 verb 3sing indic pres act	1479.1 conj	4948.3 indef- pron nom sing	3450.6 art acc sing masc
[ἐν en [in	ὑμῖν humin you	οἰκεῖ;] oikei dwells?]	**17.** εἴ ei If	τις tis anyone	τὸν ton the

3348.4 noun acc sing masc	3450.2 art gen sing	2296.2 noun gen sing masc	5188.1 verb 3sing indic pres act	5188.4 verb 3sing indic fut act
ναὸν naon temple	τοῦ tou	θεοῦ theou of God	φθείρει, phtheirei corrupt,	φθερεῖ phtherei shall bring to corruption

17.a.**Txt:** p46,01א,03B
04C,020L,025P,sa.bo.
We/Ho,byz.UBS/✶
Var: 02A,06D,08E,010F
012G

3642.6 dem-pron acc sing masc	840.6 prs-pron acc sing masc	3450.5 art sing masc	2296.1 noun nom sing masc	3450.5 art sing masc	1056.1 conj
ʿ✶ τοῦτον touton this	[a αὐτὸν] auton [him]	ὁ ho	θεός· theos God;	ὁ ho the	γὰρ gar for

3348.1 noun nom sing masc	3450.2 art gen sing	2296.2 noun gen sing masc	39.5 adj sing masc	1498.4 verb 3sing indic pres act	3610.2 rel- pron nom pl masc
ναὸς naos temple	τοῦ tou	θεοῦ theou of God	ἅγιός hagios holy	ἐστιν, estin is,	οἵτινές hoitines which

1498.6 verb 2pl indic pres act	5050.1 prs- pron nom 2pl	3235.3 num card nom masc	1431.6 prs-pron acc 3sing masc	1802.2 verb 3sing impr pres act
ἐστε este are	ὑμεῖς. humeis you.	**18.** Μηδεὶς Mēdeis No one	ἑαυτὸν heauton himself	ἐξαπατάτω· exapatatō let deceive;

1479.1 conj	4948.3 indef- pron nom sing	1374.5 verb 3sing indic pres act	4533.1 adj nom sing masc	1498.32 verb inf pres act	1706.1 prep
εἴ ei if	τις tis anyone	δοκεῖ dokei thinks	σοφὸς sophos wise	εἶναι einai to be	ἐν en among

5050.3 prs- pron dat 2pl	1706.1 prep	3450.3 art dat sing	163.2 noun dat sing masc	3642.5 dem-pron dat sing masc	3336.1 adj nom sing masc
ὑμῖν humin you	ἐν en in	τῷ tō the	αἰῶνι aiōni age	τούτῳ, toutō this,	μωρὸς mōros foolish

1090.46 verb 3sing impr aor mid	2419.1 conj	1090.40 verb 3sing subj aor mid	4533.1 adj nom sing masc	3450.9 art nom sing fem	1056.1 conj
γενέσθω, genesthō let him become,	ἵνα hina that	γένηται genētai he may be	σοφός. sophos wise.	**19.** ἡ hē The	γὰρ gar for

4531.1 noun nom sing fem	3450.2 art gen sing	2862.2 noun gen sing masc	3642.1 dem- pron gen sing	3334.1 noun nom sing fem	3706.2 prep
σοφία sophia wisdom	τοῦ tou of the	κόσμου kosmou world	τούτου toutou this	μωρία mōria foolishness	παρὰ para with

3450.3 art dat sing	2296.3 noun dat sing masc	1498.4 verb 3sing indic pres act	1119.22 verb 3sing indic perf pass	1056.1 conj	3450.5 art sing masc
τῷ tō	θεῷ theō God	ἐστιν· estin is;	γέγραπται gegraptai it has been written	γὰρ, gar for,	Ὁ Ho The

consecrated to the highest purposes—seeking and worshiping Almighty God.

3:17. The man who would destroy this building, then, would reap the most terrible of punishments. Actions are joined together here. The reason this man would be destroyed is that he attempted to destroy "the temple of God." No man may touch the Church in this way without paying for it. God will not allow evil to taint His possession, for He is holy and His own must be holy. In spite of her failures and weaknesses, the Church is blessed with great glory. She is precious in the sight of her God and protector.

Some object to the translation of *phtheirei* as "destroy" since the word elsewhere can mean "corrupt" or "spoil." It is true, on the one hand, that even the gates of hell cannot overcome the Church (Matthew 16:18), yet Paul here is speaking of a local church which has been beset by bitter factions. Nothing can destroy a local church like divisiveness. It is precisely because the church at Corinth was in such danger that Paul wrote so emphatically. Furthermore, we read in Revelation that God himself will bring judgment to any church which does not repent or is lukewarm (Revelation 2:5; 3:16).

3:18. Since so much emphasis must be placed on God, then man must take his proper place. To believe oneself to be wise is really dangerous self-deception. The word "seemeth" is better translated "thinketh." This is an obvious reference to those who thought themselves wise, attaching themselves to a certain teacher. The source of such self-deceit is pride. The antidote to such pride is humility which fosters a dependence on a higher source. A man cannot be wise in both the "world" (verse 19) and the Church. The world thinks Christian thinking and wisdom is foolish, and there is much that the world considers acceptable which is not acceptable to the Church. At the heart of wisdom is the Cross. Either a man will despise it or cling to it. If he holds to it, he will gain much. If he despises it, he will lose everything.

As God looks at man's wisdom from the viewpoint of its inability to discover and obtain salvation, He considers it utter nonsense. It has no value. This world has a tendency to consider symptoms and build elaborate systems on them. God looks at root causes.

3:19. God considers the wisdom of the world to be "foolishness." More than that, God proves it is foolish. He intervenes and brings it to nothing. How is this proved? Look at the Scriptures. Paul quoted first from Job 5:13. It is more of a summary than an exact quotation. The words were spoken by Eliphaz, who applied them inaccurately. The apostle did not refer to the application, but used the words themselves, which concerning God are true. God catches

and [that] the Spirit of God dwelleth in you?: . . . wherein God's Spirit dwells, *Conybeare* . . . lives in you, *Fenton, Beck* . . . has His home within you? *Weymouth* . . . has His permanent home in you? *Williams.*

17. If any man defile the temple of God, him shall God destroy: If any one corrupts, *Fenton, Klingensmith* . . . If any man ruin, *Conybeare, Berkeley* . . . is marring, *Rotherham* . . . defaceth, *Noyes* . . . if anyone destroys God's temple, *TEV* . . . corrupt the sanctuary, *PNT, Panin* . . . violate the temple, *Douay* . . . him will God mar, *Weymouth* . . . will bring him to ruin, *Norlie* . . . will waste him away, *Fenton.*

for the temple of God is holy, which [temple] ye are: . . . for God's temple is hallowed, *Way* . . . for God's temple is sacred, *Moffatt, Williams* . . . and you yourselves are his temple, *TEV.*

18. Let no man deceive himself: Let no one fool himself, *Berkeley, SEB* . . . Make no mistake about it, *JB* . . . No one should fool himself, *TEV* . . . be deluding himself, *Concordant* . . . beguile himself, *HistNT.*

If any man among you seemeth to be wise in this world: . . . imagines he is wise, *Rotherham, Weymouth, Moffatt* . . . imagines that, in regard to the present, he ranks among you as a wise man, *TCNT* . . . is presuming, *Concordant* . . . to be wise in this age, *Klingensmith* . . . in the ordinary sense of the word, *JB* . . . wise by this world's standards, *SEB, TEV.*

let him become a fool, that he may be wise: . . . in order to be truly wise, *Norlie* . . . in order to be really wise, *TEV* . . . to become really wise, *Beck.*

19. For the wisdom of this world is foolishness with God: For God ranks this world's wisdom, *Moffatt* . . . this world's wisdom to be foolish, *Beck* . . . is folly compared to God, *Fenton* . . . is mere nonsense to God, *Williams* . . . in God's estimation, *Berkeley* . . . in God's sight, *Weymouth, Way.*

1399.1 verb nom sing masc part pres	3450.8 art acc pl masc	4533.6 adj acc pl masc	1706.1 prep	3450.11 art dat sing fem	3696.1 noun dat sing fem
δρασσόμενος	τοὺς	σοφοὺς	ἐν	τῇ	πανουργίᾳ
drassomenos	tous	sophous	en	tē	panourgia
taking	the	wise	in	the	craftiness

840.1 prs-pron gen pl	2504.1 conj	3687.1 adv	2935.1 noun nom sing masc	1091.3 verb 3sing indic pres act	3450.8 art acc pl masc
αὐτῶν.	**20.** καὶ	πάλιν,	Κύριος	γινώσκει	τοὺς
autōn	kai	palin	Kurios	ginōskei	tous
their.	And	again,	Lord	knows	the

1255.7 noun acc pl masc	3450.1 art gen pl	4533.4 adj gen pl masc	3617.1 conj	1498.7 verb 3pl indic pres act	3124.1 adj nom pl
διαλογισμοὺς	τῶν	σοφῶν,	ὅτι	εἰσὶν	μάταιοι.
dialogismous	tōn	sophōn	hoti	eisin	mataioi
reasonings	of the	wise,	that	they are	vain.

5452.1 conj	3235.3 num card nom masc	2714.6 verb 3sing impr pres	1706.1 prep	442.8 noun dat pl masc
21. Ὥστε	μηδεὶς	καυχάσθω	ἐν	ἀνθρώποις·
Hōste	mēdeis	kauchasthō	en	anthrōpois
So that	no one	let boast	in	men;

3820.1 adj	1056.1 conj	5050.2 prs-pron gen 2pl	1498.4 verb 3sing indic pres act	1521.1 conj	3834.1 name nom masc
πάντα	γὰρ	ὑμῶν	ἐστιν,	**22.** εἴτε	Παῦλος,
panta	gar	humōn	estin	eite	Paulos
all things	for	yours	are.	Whether	Paul,

1521.1 conj	619.1 name nom masc	1521.1 conj	2758.1 name nom masc	1521.1 conj	2862.1 noun nom sing masc	1521.1 conj
εἴτε	Ἀπολλῶς,	εἴτε	Κηφᾶς,	εἴτε	κόσμος,	εἴτε
eite	Apollōs	eite	Kēphas	eite	kosmos	eite
or	Apollos,	or	Cephas,	or	world,	or

2205.1 noun nom sing fem	1521.1 conj	2265.1 noun nom sing masc	1521.1 conj	1748.5 verb nom pl neu part perf act	1521.1 conj
ζωὴ,	εἴτε	θάνατος,	εἴτε	ἐνεστῶτα,	εἴτε
zōē	eite	thanatos	eite	enestōta	eite
life,	or	death,	or	having been present,	or

22.a.Txt: 06D-corr,020L byz.bo.
Var: 01**א**,02A,03B,04C 06D-org,025P,33,Lach Treg,Alf,Tisc,We/Ho Weis,Sod,UBS/☆

3165.8 verb part pres act	3820.1 adj	5050.2 prs-pron gen 2pl	1498.4 verb 3sing indic pres act	5050.1 prs-pron nom 2pl
μέλλοντα·	πάντα	ὑμῶν	⟨a ἐστιν· ⟩	**23.** ὑμεῖς
mellonta	panta	humōn	estin	humeis
coming things,	all	yours	are;	you

1156.2 conj	5382.2 name gen masc	5382.1 name nom masc	1156.2 conj	2296.2 noun gen sing masc	3643.1 adv
δὲ	Χριστοῦ·	Χριστὸς	δὲ	θεοῦ.	**4:1.** Οὕτως
de	Christou	Christos	de	theou	Houtōs
and	Christ's,	Christ	and	God's.	So

2231.4 prs-pron acc 1pl	3023.6 verb 3sing impr pres	442.1 noun nom sing masc	5453.1 conj	5095.6 noun acc pl masc	5382.2 name gen masc
ἡμᾶς	λογιζέσθω	ἄνθρωπος	ὡς	ὑπηρέτας	Χριστοῦ
hēmas	logizesthō	anthrōpos	hōs	hupēretas	Christou
us	let reckon	a man	as	attendants	of Christ

2504.1 conj	3485.5 noun acc pl masc	3328.4 noun gen pl neu	2296.2 noun gen sing masc	3614.16 rel-pron sing neu	1156.2 conj
καὶ	οἰκονόμους	μυστηρίων	θεοῦ.	**2.** ⟨ Ὃ	δὲ
kai	oikonomous	mustēriōn	theou	Ho	de
and	stewards	mysteries	of God's.	Which	de

the crafty and exposes them. They are brought face-to-face with the fact that His wisdom totally surpasses theirs. He can so expose the faulty roots of a person's thinking that it is seen to be deceit and trickery.

3:20. Paul also quoted from Psalm 94:11 with minor changes. But the thought is clear. The idea is of total knowledge. No thought, not even the most secret, is hidden from God. This is part of the reason the Lord can intervene in the plans of men. He knows their thoughts from the very beginning.

3:21. "Let no man glory in" or boast of other men or himself. The creation must not be elevated above the Creator. In reality, Paul was not so much arguing against the lifting up of men as he was presenting the idea that these Corinthians were limiting themselves. Why should they listen to only one teacher, when all the teachers in their different aspects were given to benefit the Church?

3:22,23. Paul did not stop here. He enlarged the circle to include things of special interest to this particular church. The first group consisted of Christian ministers and teachers. There was Paul with his logical, anointed, and singular ministry. There was Apollos with his brilliant rhetoric. There was Peter with his fond memories of personal acquaintance with Christ on earth. Why should the Corinthians not appreciate all that was given by God.

The second group consisted of the world, life, and death. "World" refers to the ordered universe, "life" to the spiritual life in Christ (Philippians 1:21), and "death" to that painful obstacle which has become a servant through Jesus Christ.

The last group, "things present" and "things to come," included not only present blessings, but an array of yet unknown blessings. At the end Paul placed the foundation. We are laid at the feet of Christ. We are the stewards of certain riches, and we are possessions of Jesus Christ. Paul returns the reader to the idea of Christ's mastery. Our subordination to Christ is given a supreme example in Christ's subordination to God. Paul was taking nothing away from the deity of Christ, but was speaking of His office and mission.

4:1. To us then, who are servants of Christ, comes the designation of stewardship. This is the practical outcome of unity, wisdom, and service. Paul was a "minister of Christ." While he might be too highly valued by some of the Corinthians, nevertheless, he was a minister and should not be considered too lightly. A balance is needed. Ministers are not lords, but their stewardship deserves respect.

For it is written, He taketh the wise in their own craftiness: He catcheth the wyse, *Geneva* . . . He seizes, *Moffatt* . . . He catches the philosophers in their own craft, *Fenton* . . . He snares the wise with their own cunning, *Weymouth* . . . in their subteltie, *Rheims*.

20. And again, The Lord knoweth the thoughts of the wise, that they are vain: . . . takes note of the speculations of the wise, *Rotherham* . . . the reasonings, *Concordant, Moffatt* . . . the cogitations of the vvise, *Rheims* . . . the designs of the wise are futile, *HistNT* . . . they are empty, *Fenton* . . . how useless they are, *Weymouth*.

21. Therefore let no man glory in men: . . . about his human teachers, *Weymouth*.
For all things are yours: Everything belongs to you, *SEB*.

22. Whether Paul, or Apollos, or Cephas: . . . or a ritual, *Fenton*.
or the world, or life, or death, or things present, or things to come: . . . or that which is impending, *Concordant*.
all are yours: . . . everything belongs to you, *Weymouth* . . . all belongs to you, *Moffatt*.

23. And ye are Christ's; and Christ [is] God's:

1. Let a man so account of us, as of the ministers of Christ: Let a man regard us, *Fenton* . . . let any one take this view of us—we are Christ's officers, *Weymouth* . . . esteeme vs, *Rheims* . . . as deputies of, *Concordant* . . . as officers of Christ, *Rotherham*.
and stewards of the mysteries of God: . . . and administrators, *Fenton* . . . and the dispensers, *Rheims* . . . and disposers of the secretes of God, *Tyndale* . . . of God's secret truths, *Moffatt*.

1 Corinthians 4:3

2.a.**Txt:** 06D-corr,020L
byz.
Var: 01ℵ,02A,03B,04C
06D-org,025P,33,bo.
Lach,Treg,Alf,Tisc
We/Ho,Weis,Sod
UBS/✩

5436.1 adv	3036.8 adj acc sing neu	2195.27 verb 3sing indic pres pass	1706.1 prep	3450.4 art dat pl
[ᵃ✩ ὧδε]	λοιπόν,	ζητεῖται	ἐν	τοῖς
hōde	loipon	zēteitai	en	tois
[Here]	as to the rest,	it is being required	in	the

3485.4 noun dat pl masc	2419.1 conj	3964.2 adj nom sing masc	4948.3 indef-pron nom sing	2128.36 verb 3sing subj aor pass	1466.5 prs-pron dat 1sing
οἰκονόμοις	ἵνα	πιστός	τις	εὑρεθῇ.	3. ἐμοὶ
oikonomois	hina	pistos	tis	heurethē	emoi
stewards	that	faithful	anyone	be found.	To me

1156.2 conj	1519.1 prep	1633.6 adj sup acc sing neu	1498.4 verb 3sing indic pres act	2419.1 conj	5097.1 prep
δὲ	εἰς	ἐλάχιστόν	ἐστιν	ἵνα	ὑφ'
de	eis	elachiston	estin	hina	huph'
but	to	the smallest matter	it is	that	by

5050.2 prs-pron gen 2pl	348.10 verb 1sing subj aor pass	2211.1 conj	5097.3 prep	440.2 adj gen sing fem	2232.1 noun fem
ὑμῶν	ἀνακριθῶ,	ἢ	ὑπὸ	ἀνθρωπίνης	ἡμέρας·
humōn	anakrithō	ē	hupo	anthrōpinēs	hēmeras
you	I be examined,	or	by	man's	day.

233.1 conj	3624.1 adv	1670.3 prs-pron acc 1sing masc	348.1 verb 1sing indic pres act	3625.6 num card neu	1056.1 conj
ἀλλ'	οὐδὲ	ἐμαυτὸν	ἀνακρίνω.	4. οὐδὲν	γὰρ
all'	oude	emauton	anakrinō	ouden	gar
But	neither	myself	do I examine.	Of nothing	for

1670.2 prs-pron dat 1sing masc	4774.1 verb 1sing indic perf act	233.1 conj	3620.2 partic	1706.1 prep
ἐμαυτῷ	σύνοιδα·	ἀλλ'	οὐκ	ἐν
emautō	sunoida	all'	ouk	en
in myself	I am conscious;	but	not	by

3642.5 dem-pron dat sing masc	1338.20 verb 1sing indic perf pass	3450.5 art sing masc	1156.2 conj	348.3 verb nom sing masc part pres act
τούτῳ	δεδικαίωμαι·	ὁ	δὲ	ἀνακρίνων
toutō	dedikaiōmai	ho	de	anakrinōn
this	have I been justified	the	but	examining

1466.6 prs-pron acc 1sing	2935.1 noun nom sing masc	1498.4 verb 3sing indic pres act	5452.1 conj	3231.1 partic	4112.1 prep
με	κύριός	ἐστιν.	5. ὥστε	μὴ	πρὸ
me	kurios	estin	hōste	mē	pro
me	Lord	is.	So that	not	before

2511.2 noun gen sing masc	4948.10 indef-pron sing neu	2892.3 verb 2pl pres act	2175.1 conj	300.1 partic	2048.8 verb 3sing subj aor act
καιροῦ	τι	κρίνετε,	ἕως	ἂν	ἔλθῃ
kairou	ti	krinete	heōs	an	elthē
time	anything	judge,	until		may have come

3450.5 art sing masc	2935.1 noun nom sing masc	3614.5 rel-pron nom sing masc	2504.1 conj	5297.6 verb 3sing indic fut act	3450.17 art pl neu
ὁ	κύριος,	ὃς	καὶ	φωτίσει	τὰ
ho	kurios	hos	kai	phōtisei	ta
the	Lord,	who	both	will bring to light	the

2899.4 adj pl neu	3450.2 art gen sing	4510.3 noun gen sing neu	2504.1 conj	5157.6 verb 3sing indic fut act
κρυπτὰ	τοῦ	σκότους,	καὶ	φανερώσει
krupta	tou	skotous	kai	phanerōsei
hidden things	of the	darkness,	and	will make manifest

4:2. It is required in the very nature of such a man that he be faithful to his work. As he had been doing, Paul reproved the pride and disunity of the Corinthians by indicating that ultimately the test of a steward is not his "ability" but his faithfulness. A steward is expected to act in the interest of his master, not in his own interest. Such is the requirement of all stewards, not just some, because sometime their faithfulness will be judged. A steward is not always closely supervised, but he is always expected to work diligently.

4:3. Lest the Corinthians get the idea from 3:22 that they could judge these stewards, Paul added that neither they nor any other steward could judge another man's fidelity. In fact, not even Paul's own conscience was the final judge. Paul was not rejecting the place of conscience. He was simply comparing inferior with superior. Nor was he rejecting the importance of other men's ideas and opinions. But men are often fickle and prejudiced in their examination, and a man may find it difficult to be objective and honest with himself.

4:4. The Scriptures advise heart searching, but there is such a thing as too much self-examination. As far as Paul knew he had done his best and therefore knew no reason for condemnation. But he freely admitted his knowledge was limited. He that judges is the Master, the Lord himself. Paul was justified on the basis of Christ's righteousness. As Titus 3:5-8 indicates, this was the basis of his whole stand before God.

Good conscience is fine, but it cannot be relied on apart from the verdict of the Lord. The appraisal at the end will come from Him who justified at the beginning. Therefore, for the present, Paul left to Christ the testing of his actions, which Christ is doing for every believer in preparation for the judgment described in 3:11-15. At this point in time the criticism and the praise must rest with the Master Paul served.

4:5. In 3:13 and 15 Paul made his readers aware that there would be a judging at the Bema, the judgment seat of Christ. Now in 4:5 Paul reinforced this by saying that all judging would be at the time (*kairou*) when the Lord comes. *Kairou* is one of two Greek words for time, and this word frequently indicates a critical, crucial moment of time when one's personal destiny is decided (cf. Luke 12:56). When we arrive at this natural conclusion, we must understand that Paul was not forbidding examination, but was objecting to the proud judgment of teachers and the usurping of Christ's position. Only Christ can judge correctly because only He can see the unknown, the secret, the hidden things. The apostle Paul put all human judgments into proper perspective by telling the Corinthians that the only judgment that matters to believers is Christ's

2. Moreover it is required in stewards, that a man be found faithful: . . . in this matter of stewardship, *HistNT* . . . to prove each one's fidelity to his trust, *Way* . . . that a man be founden trewe, *Wyclif* . . . fidelity is what is required, *Weymouth* . . . they must be trustworthy, *Moffatt*.

3. But with me it is a very small thing that I should be judged of you, or of man's judgment: . . . it is a light matter, *Murdock* . . . of perfect indifference to me, *Way* . . . of very little importance, *Wilson* . . . it is quite indifferent whether I am criticised by you, *Fenton* . . . undergoing your scrutiny, *Weymouth* . . . I should be cross-questioned by you or by any human court, *HistNT* . . . or by a human tribunal, *Noyes*.
yea, I judge not mine own self: I do not even scrutinize myself, *Weymouth* . . . I do not even cross-question myself, *Moffatt* . . . do I criticise my own self, *Fenton*.

4. For I know nothing by myself: I am conscious to myself of no fault, *Campbell* . . . though I am conscious of nothing against myself, *HistNT*.
yet am I not hereby justified: . . . not in this am I declared righteous, *Rotherham* . . . am I cleared of blame, *Noyes* . . . I am not acquitted on account of that, *Fenton* . . . that does not clear me, *HistNT* . . . not for that reason stand acquitted, *Weymouth*.
but he that judgeth me is the Lord: He Who is examining me, *Concordant*.

5. Therefore judge nothing before the time, until the Lord come: So make no hasty judgment, *Montgomery* . . . do not risk any premature judgment, *Way* . . . form no premature judgements, *Weymouth* . . . judge nothing hastily, until the coming of the Lord, *Conybeare*.
who both will bring to light the hidden things of darkness: . . . who will pour light upon, *Murdock* . . . also illuminate the hidden, *Concordant* . . . the secrets of darkness, *Wilson* . . . the concealments of darkness, *Fenton*.

1 Corinthians 4:6

3450.15 art acc pl fem	1005.5 noun acc pl fem	3450.1 art gen pl	2559.6 noun gen pl fem	2504.1 conj	4966.1 adv	3450.5 art sing masc
τὰς	βουλὰς	τῶν	καρδιῶν·	καὶ	τότε	ὁ
tas	boulas	tōn	kardiōn	kai	tote	ho
the	counsels	of the	hearts;	and	then	the

1853.1 noun nom sing masc	1090.69 verb 3sing indic fut mid	1524.4 adj dat sing masc	570.3 prep gen	3450.2 art gen sing	2296.2 noun gen sing masc
ἔπαινος	γενήσεται	ἑκάστῳ	ἀπὸ	τοῦ	θεοῦ.
epainos	genēsetai	hekastō	apo	tou	theou
praise	shall be	to each	from	the	God.

3642.18 dem- pron pl neu	1156.2 conj	79.6 noun pl masc	3215.1 verb 1sing indic aor act	1519.1 prep	1670.3 prs-pron acc 1sing masc
6. Ταῦτα	δέ,	ἀδελφοί,	μετεσχημάτισα	εἰς	ἐμαυτὸν
Tauta	de	adelphoi	meteschēmatisa	eis	emauton
These things	now,	brothers,	I transferred	to	myself

6.a.**Txt**: 01**ℵ**-corr,04C 06D,020L,025P,byz.Sod
Var: 01**ℵ**-org,02A 03B-org,Treg,Tisc We/Ho,Weis,UBS/★

2504.1 conj	619.2 name acc masc	619.3 name acc masc	1217.1 prep	5050.4 prs- pron acc 2pl
καὶ	(Ἀπολλὼ	[a★ Ἀπολλῶν]	δι'	ὑμᾶς,
kai	Apollō	Apollōn	di'	humas
and	Apollos	[idem]	on account of	you,

6.b.**Txt**: 06D,020L,byz.
Var: 01**ℵ**,02A,03B,04C 025P,33,bo.Lach,Treg Alf,Word,Tisc,We/Ho Weis,Sod,UBS/★

2419.1 conj	1706.1 prep	2231.3 prs- pron dat 1pl	3101.10 verb 2pl subj aor act	3450.16 art sing neu	3231.1 partic	5065.1 prep
ἵνα	ἐν	ἡμῖν	μάθητε	τὸ	μὴ	ὑπὲρ
hina	en	hēmin	mathēte	to	mē	huper
that	in	us	you may learn	the	not	above

3614.16 rel- pron sing neu	3614.17 rel- pron pl neu	1119.22 verb 3sing indic perf pass	5262.9 verb inf pres act	2419.1 conj	3231.1 partic
(ὃ	[b★ ἃ]	γέγραπται	(c φρονεῖν,)	ἵνα	μὴ
ho	ha	gegraptai	phronein	hina	mē
what	[idem]	has been written	to think,	that	not

6.c.**Txt**: 01**ℵ**-corr 06D-corr,020L,025P,byz.
Var: 01**ℵ**-org,02A,03B 06D-org,Lach,Treg,Alf Word,Tisc,We/Ho,Weis Sod

1518.3 num card nom masc	5065.1 prep	3450.2 art gen sing	1518.1 num card gen	5284.3 verb 2pl indic pres pass	2567.3 prep
εἷς	ὑπὲρ	τοῦ	ἑνὸς	φυσιοῦσθε	κατὰ
heis	huper	tou	henos	phusiousthe	kata
one	for	the	one	you be puffed up	against

3450.2 art gen sing	2066.6 adj gen sing masc	4949.3 intr- pron nom sing	1056.1 conj	4622.4 prs- pron acc 2sing	1246.1 verb 3sing indic pres act
τοῦ	ἑτέρου.	**7.** τίς	γὰρ	σε	διακρίνει;
tou	heterou	tis	gar	se	diakrinei
the	other.	Who	for	you	makes to differ?

4949.9 intr- pron sing neu	1156.2 conj	2174.3 verb 2sing indic pres act	3614.16 rel- pron sing neu	3620.2 partic	2956.13 verb 2sing indic aor act
τί	δὲ	ἔχεις	ὃ	οὐκ	ἔλαβες;
ti	de	echeis	ho	ouk	elabes
what	and	have you	which	not	you did receive?

1479.1 conj	1156.2 conj	2504.1 conj	2956.13 verb 2sing indic aor act	4949.9 intr- pron sing neu	2714.2 verb 2sing indic pres
εἰ	δὲ	καὶ	ἔλαβες,	τί	καυχᾶσαι
ei	de	kai	elabes	ti	kauchasai
if	but	also	you did receive,	why	boast you

5453.1 conj	3231.1 partic	2956.25 verb nom sing masc part aor act	2218.1 adv	2853.2 verb nom pl masc part perf pass
ὡς	μὴ	λαβών;	**8.** ἤδη	κεκορεσμένοι
hōs	mē	labōn	ēdē	kekoresmenoi
as	not	having received?	Already	having been satisfied

decisions at the Bema judgment. Frequently the Holy Spirit guided Paul to provide information concerning future judgment. In 6:3 he said that we would later judge the angels. Even the reference in 11:26 to drinking the cup of the Lord's Supper until He comes again is in the context of judgment, because the Corinthians were in danger of drinking damnation to themselves by not discerning the body of Christ (11:17-34, especially 11:29). The Lord will make manifest the counsels and purposes of the heart. "Counsels" is neuter, indicating good or evil. Each one shall then receive his due praise from God.

4:6. Paul used a literary figure to apply what he had just said to Apollos and himself. The example was intended to help the Corinthians quell their pride and teach them not to exalt men unduly. "That which is written" refers to Scripture. Paul made this general reference to Scripture so that through this example the Corinthians would learn the subordination of man. The Bible exalts God. The Corinthians were exalting man.

What was even more damaging, not only were they exalting man instead of God, they were apparently also exalting their own traditions as equal to or better than the Scriptures. Literally, the Greek reads that "you may learn not above what is written," meaning that no human tradition or view can be placed above Scripture.

Paul dealt with this issue from many angles, going ever deeper until he had considered all aspects and came to the heart of the matter.

In this spirit of pride the Corinthians had made judgments on their teachers, and in adhering to one had really denounced and rejected the others. For that reason they were unbalanced; they were lacking part of the wisdom and counsel of God. Pride is a deadly sin. For that reason Paul attacked it from every side until he had fully exposed and dealt with the sin.

4:7. With three rhetorical questions Paul attacked the problem. The first question dealt with the fact that some of the Corinthians considered themselves superior in some way. Paul asserted that this personal conceit was presumptuous. The question demanded an answer that cut away at pride. The second question really answered the first. The Corinthians had received all they had from God. He was their sole supply. They had no right to boast and think they had obtained their position by their own hand. The third question went a step further. They could not boast as if they had not been given what they had; in so doing, they were glorifying themselves. It was a terrible response to a gracious God.

4:8. Paul painted a darker picture with each stroke of his brush. "Full" and "rich" denote the sense of satisfaction and attainment

and will make manifest the counsels of the hearts: ... will openly disclose the motives, *Weymouth* ... lay open the counsels of, *Campbell* ... bring to the light the plans people have in their hearts, *Beck* ... the purposes of men's hearts, *Montgomery*.

and then shall every man have praise of God: ... then applause will be coming, *Concordant* ... then shall the due praise be awarded, *Way* ... then the commendation will come, *Fenton* ... experience his due approval from God, *Berkeley*.

6. And these things, brethren, I have in a figure transferred to myself and [to] Apollos for your sakes: In writing this much, *Weymouth* ... I haue figuratiuely described, *Geneva* ... I have figuratively applied to myself, *Campbell, Hanson* ... for an ensample described in myne awne person, *Cranmer*.

that ye might learn in us not to think [of men] above that which is written: ... so that from our case you might learn, *HistNT* ... learn from our example, *SEB* ... might learn the lesson, *Williams* ... learn not to assume a rivalry between us, *Way*.

that no one of you be puffed up for one against another: Don't be more proud of one person, *SEB* ... be puffed up with rivalry, *Moffatt* ... may not be arrogantly for one teacher against the other, *Berkeley* ... brag about one man at the expense of another, *Beck* ... in favor of one teacher against another, *Williams* ... exalt himself in comparison with his fellow, *Murdock*.

7. For who maketh thee to differ [from another]?: For who distinguisheth thee? *Douay* ... Who singles you out? *Moffatt, HistNT* ... who is discriminating between, *Concordant* ... who gives you your superiority, *Weymouth*.

and what hast thou that thou didst not receive?: ... been given you, *Moffatt*.

now if thou didst receive [it]: But if you got it from someone, *Williams*.

why dost thou glory, as if thou hadst not received [it]?: ... as if it hadn't been given to you? *Beck*.

1 Corinthians 4:9

1498.6 verb 2pl
indic pres act
ἐστέ,
este
you are;

2218.1 adv
ἤδη
ēdē
already

4007.4 verb 2pl
indic aor act
ἐπλουτήσατε·
eploutēsate
you were enriched;

5400.1 prep gen
χωρὶς
chōris
apart from

2231.2 prs-
pron gen 1pl
ἡμῶν
hēmōn
us

929.7 verb 2pl
indic aor act
ἐβασιλεύσατε·
ebasileusate
you reigned;

2504.1 conj
καὶ
kai
and

3649.1 partic
ὄφελόν
ophelon
I would

1058.1 partic
γε
ge
surely

929.7 verb 2pl
indic aor act
ἐβασιλεύσατε,
ebasileusate
you did reign,

2419.1 conj
ἵνα
hina
that

2504.1 conj
καὶ
kai
also

2231.1 prs-
pron nom 1pl
ἡμεῖς
hēmeis
we

5050.3 prs-
pron dat 2pl
ὑμῖν
humin
you

4672.1 verb 1pl
subj aor act
συμβασιλεύσωμεν.
sumbasileusōmen
might reign with.

9.a.Txt: 01ℵ-corr
06D-corr,020L,025P,byz.
bo.
Var: 01ℵ-org,02A,03B
04C,06D-org,Lach,Treg
Alf,Word,Tisc,We/Ho
Weis,Sod,UBS/☆

1374.3 verb 1sing
indic pres act
9. δοκῶ
dokō
I think

1056.1 conj
γάρ
gar
for

3617.1 conj
⌐ᵃ ὅτι ⌐
hoti
that

3450.5 art
sing masc
ὁ
ho
the

2296.1 noun
nom sing masc
θεὸς
theos
God

2231.4 prs-
pron acc 1pl
ἡμᾶς
hēmas
us

3450.8 art
acc pl masc
τοὺς
tous
the

646.7 noun
acc pl masc
ἀποστόλους
apostolous
apostles

2057.7 adj
acc pl masc
ἐσχάτους
eschatous
last

579.2 verb 3sing
indic aor act
ἀπέδειξεν
apedeixen
set forth

5453.1 conj
ὡς
hōs
as

1920.1 adj
acc pl masc
ἐπιθανατίους·
epithanatious
appointed to death.

3617.1 conj
ὅτι
hoti
For

2279.1 noun
acc sing neu
θέατρον
theatron
a spectacle

1090.34 verb 1pl
indic aor pass
ἐγενήθημεν
egenēthēmen
we became

3450.3 art
dat sing
τῷ
tō
to the

2862.3 noun
dat sing masc
κόσμῳ,
kosmō
world,

2504.1 conj
καὶ
kai
both

32.7 noun
dat pl masc
ἀγγέλοις
angelois
to angels

2504.1 conj
καὶ
kai
and

442.8 noun
dat pl masc
ἀνθρώποις.
anthrōpois
to men.

2231.1 prs-
pron nom 1pl
10. ἡμεῖς
hēmeis
We

3336.4 adj
pl masc
μωροὶ
mōroi
fools

1217.2 prep
διὰ
dia
on account of

5382.4 name
acc masc
Χριστόν,
Christon
Christ,

5050.1 prs-
pron nom 2pl
ὑμεῖς
humeis
you

1156.2 conj
δὲ
de
but

5265.1 adj nom pl
φρόνιμοι
phronimoi
sensible

1706.1 prep
ἐν
en
in

5382.3 name
dat masc
Χριστῷ·
Christō
Christ;

2231.1 prs-
pron nom 1pl
ἡμεῖς
hēmeis
we

766.4 adj
pl masc
ἀσθενεῖς,
astheneis
weak,

5050.1 prs-
pron nom 2pl
ὑμεῖς
humeis
you

1156.2 conj
δὲ
de
but

2451.5 adj
nom pl masc
ἰσχυροί·
ischuroi
strong;

5050.1 prs-
pron nom 2pl
ὑμεῖς
humeis
you

1725.2 adj
nom pl masc
ἔνδοξοι,
endoxoi
glorious,

2231.1 prs-
pron nom 1pl
ἡμεῖς
hēmeis
we

1156.2 conj
δὲ
de
but

814.2 adj
nom pl masc
ἄτιμοι.
atimoi
without honor.

884.2 conj
11. ἄχρι
achri
To

3450.10 art
gen sing fem
τῆς
tēs
the

732.1 adv
ἄρτι
arti
present

5443.1 noun fem
ὥρας
hōras
hour

2504.1 conj
καὶ
kai
both

3845.2 verb 1pl
indic pres act
πεινῶμεν
peinōmen
we hunger

2504.1 conj
καὶ
kai
and

the Corinthians felt. Thinking they had come to some ultimate plateau, to some superior spiritual level, they did not think they needed the apostles and believed them unnecessary. After all, their accomplishments had come from their own hands.

Luther commented: "Paul mocks them, for he means the opposite of what he says" (cited in Lenski, p.179).

The truth is they had not attained. They were really spiritually weak when they thought themselves strong. They were foolish when they thought themselves very wise. Paul wished they had attained, that they were mature.

4:9. Paul established the position of the apostles and himself quickly, and it was far from what the Corinthians imagined it to be. It seemed as though the apostles were last in line and like men "appointed to death." In Paul's time criminals condemned to death were exhibited to amuse the crowds in the amphitheater. They were then brought to the arena to fight wild beasts; they did not leave the arena alive. More than one Christian faced unfair martyrdom in the arena, hearing the insults, the ridicule, the mockery, the slander. As men in the arena were exhibited to the crowds, so the apostles were exhibited to "the world," "to angels," which in comparison to men are not specifically noted as good or bad, and "to men" which might include good and bad.

Unlike what the Corinthians thought, Christian responsibility is not a "joyride." It is not attaining worldly success and involving oneself in the drive for the top and then sitting back and enjoying the world's applause and approval. The world does not like the Christian. The world does not like those who lead the vanguard toward spiritual heights. The apostles, as do all true spiritual leaders, suffered for their stand; they knew the pain of responsibility and the burden of continuing on when men did not speak well of them.

4:10. Next Paul specifically compared the apostles and the Corinthians. The contrast of "we" and "ye" is important. The opinion of the world was that the apostles were fanatical and foolish. Meanwhile, the Corinthians were supposed to be wise. "In Christ" the Corinthians really were wise, but they were building on the wisdom of the world, which Paul had already refuted. "For Christ" and "in Christ" carry a shade of distinction and meaning which shows the depth of the apostles' work. The world may have given some honor to this church because it desired it and had gone after it, but the apostles preached only Christ and so received dishonor from the world.

4:11,12. The list of difficulties continues. The apostles were enduring trials for the gospel even to the moment of writing. Paul

8. Now ye are full, now ye are rich: ... you are wealthy, *Fenton* ... you are already enriched! *Wilson* ... have all your heart's desire, *Moffatt.*

ye have reigned as kings without us: ... have reigned like princes, *Locke* ... you have ascended your thrones! *Weymouth.*

and I would to God ye did reign, that we also might reign with you: I too might share your royalty! *Way* ... might have jointly become kings, *Rotherham.*

9. For I think that God hath set forth us the apostles last: For I fancy God has exposed us, *Fenton* ... hath appoynted vs, *Geneva* ... God demonstrates with us, *Concordant* ... has exhibited us as apostles, *HistNT, Rotherham* ... has exhibited us apostles last of all, *Weymouth* ... for the lowest of all, *Tyndale.*

as it were appointed to death: ... like the doomed gladiators in the arena! *Moffatt* ... like criminals condemned to die, *Conybeare* ... doomed to death, *HistNT.*

for we are made a spectacle unto the world, and to angels, and to men: ... became a theater, *Concordant* ... we are a gasyngestocke, *Tyndale* ... we may become an exhibition, *Fenton* ... to all creation, *Weymouth.*

10. We [are] fools for Christ's sake, but ye [are] wise in Christ: ... we are labelled as "foolish": you...are men of shrewd intelligence, *Weymouth* ... you in Christ are sensible, *Moffatt* ... but you are quite philosophic in Christ, *Montgomery* ... prudent in Christ, *Rotherham.*

we [are] weak, but ye [are] strong: ... we are feeble—but you mighty, *Fenton.*

ye [are] honourable, but we [are] despised: You are glorious, *Concordant* ... you are illustrious, we unhonoured, *HistNT* ... but we in contempt, *Fenton* ... we are in disrepute, *Moffatt* ... we are outcasts, *Weymouth.*

11. Even unto this present hour we both hunger, and thirst:

1 Corinthians 4:12

11.a.Txt: 020L,byz.Sod
Var: 01א,02A-corr
03B-corr,04C,06D,025P
Lach,Treg,Alf,Word
Tisc,We/Ho,Weis
UBS/✶

1366.2 verb 1pl indic pres act
διψῶμεν,
dipsōmen
thirst,

2504.1 conj
καὶ
kai
and

1124.1 verb 1pl indic pres act
(γυμνητεύομεν,
gumnēteuomen
are naked,

1124.1 verb 1pl indic pres act
[ᵃ✰ γυμνιτεύομεν]
gumniteuomen
[idem]

2504.1 conj
καὶ
kai
and

2826.4 verb 1pl indic pres pass
κολαφιζόμεθα,
kolaphizometha
are being knocked around,

2504.1 conj
καὶ
kai
and

784.1 verb 1pl indic pres act
ἀστατοῦμεν,
astatoumen
wander without a home,

12. **2504.1** conj
καὶ
kai
and

2844.3 verb 1pl indic pres act
κοπιῶμεν,
kopiōmen
labor,

2021.10 verb pl masc part pres
ἐργαζόμενοι
ergazomenoi
working

3450.14 art dat pl fem
ταῖς
tais
with the

2375.12 adj dat pl fem
ἰδίαις
idiais
our own

5331.7 noun dat pl fem
χερσίν·
chersin
hands.

3032.4 verb nom pl masc part pres pass
λοιδορούμενοι,
loidoroumenoi
being reviled,

2108.1 verb 1pl indic pres act
εὐλογοῦμεν·
eulogoumen
we bless;

1371.24 verb nom pl masc part pres pass
διωκόμενοι,
diōkomenoi
being persecuted,

13.a.Txt: 01א-corr,03B
06D,020L,byz.
Var: 01א-org,02A,04C
025P,33,Alf,Tisc,We/Ho
Weis,Sod,UBS/✶

428.2 verb 1pl indic pres mid
ἀνεχόμεθα·
anechometha
we endure;

13. **980.21** verb nom pl masc part pres mid
(βλασφημούμενοι,
blasphēmoumenoi
being evilly spoken to,

1418.1 verb nom pl masc part pres pass
[ᵃ✰ δυσφημούμενοι]
dusphēmoumenoi
[being defamed]

3731.2 verb 1pl indic pres act
παρακαλοῦμεν·
parakaloumen
we encourage:

5453.1 conj
ὡς
hōs
as

3890.1 noun nom pl neu
περικαθάρματα
perikatharmata
refuse

3450.2 art gen sing
τοῦ
tou
of the

2862.2 noun gen sing masc
κόσμου
kosmou
world

1090.34 verb 1pl indic aor pass
ἐγενήθημεν,
egenēthēmen
we became,

3820.4 adj gen pl
πάντων
pantōn
of all

3927.1 noun nom sing neu
περίψημα
peripsēma
scum

2175.1 conj
ἕως
heōs
until

732.1 adv
ἄρτι.
arti
now.

14. **3620.2** partic
Οὐκ
Ouk
Not

1772.1 verb nom sing masc part pres act
ἐντρέπων
entrepōn
shaming

5050.4 prs-pron acc 2pl
ὑμᾶς
humas
you

1119.1 verb 1sing indic pres act
γράφω
graphō
do I write

3642.18 dem-pron pl neu
ταῦτα,
tauta
these things,

233.1 conj
ἀλλ'
all'
but

5453.1 conj
ὡς
hōs
as

14.a.Txt: 03B,06D,020L
byz.Weis
Var: 01א,02A,04C,025P
33,Tisc,We/Ho,Sod
UBS/✶

4891.4 noun pl neu
τέκνα
tekna
children

1466.2 prs-pron gen 1sing
μου
mou
my

27.10 adj pl neu
ἀγαπητὰ
agapēta
beloved

3423.1 verb 1sing indic pres act
(νουθετῶ.
nouthetō
I admonish.

3423.3 verb nom sing masc part pres act
[ᵃ✰ νουθετῶν·]
noutheton
[admonishing.]

15. ἐὰν
1430.1 partic
ean
If

1056.1 conj
γὰρ
gar
for

3325.1 adj acc pl masc
μυρίους
murious
ten thousand

3670.3 noun acc pl masc
παιδαγωγοὺς
paidagōgous
tutors

2174.9 verb 2pl subj pres act
ἔχητε
echēte
you should have

1706.1 prep
ἐν
en
in

5382.3 name dat masc
Χριστῷ,
Christō
Christ,

233.1 conj
ἀλλ'
all'
yet

3620.3 partic
οὐ
ou
not

4044.8 adj acc pl masc
πολλοὺς
pollous
many

3824.9 noun acc pl masc
πατέρας·
pateras
fathers;

1706.1 prep
ἐν
en
in

may be reminded of what he was undergoing at Ephesus. They were enduring many privations.

There is here little of the philosophy that Christians will always receive the best of this world here and now. As far as this world was concerned, Paul had little or nothing, and he supported himself by work that was exhausting. Again, this was for Christ and His church. To the Greeks, manual labor was low and insulting and debasing to those who did it. To the Greeks, life was in philosophical speculation, not in the work that produced dirt under the fingernails. That was beneath them.

4:13. But the picture is not quite finished. They were regarded as "filth" and "offscouring." "Filth" refers to the rubbish heap or litter gathered when one cleans. "Offscouring" is what is removed by scouring a filthy object. Beyond this Paul did not or could not go. Again the present and continuous is indicated by "unto this day" (even until now).

All of this is in opposition to the self-assertive spirit of the world and the self-sufficient, self-possessed spirit of the Corinthians. Paul and other men had sacrificed everything for Jesus, that the plan of salvation might be made known to all men. There can hardly be a more significant comparison than the one just made by Paul. What is most obvious is not the difference in work or position, but the difference in spirit. The Corinthians were motivated by a selfish, get-all spirit; the apostles and messengers of the gospel were motivated by a selfless, give-all spirit.

4:14. It was not Paul's aim to shame or embarrass the Corinthians. Rather, he wished to bring them to reason, to give them counsel, to make them understand their true position in Christ and the world and how foolish their pride and bigotry were. That is a painful lesson. Paul showed his deep feelings for them by calling them his "beloved sons." Their wrong actions and attitudes touched Paul deeply.

4:15. Paul had been strongly aroused by the Corinthians' behavior, yet the rebuke of verse 14 was mild. This verse helps explain why. The Corinthian believers had had many "instructors" or "tutors," that is, nurses or governors. "Ten thousand" may well be a hyperbole, but it emphasized Paul's point. Paul laid claim to the right to especially admonish and to be especially heeded because, unlike these other instructors, he was their spiritual father. Why did he claim this? He was the one who first brought the gospel to Corinth. It was through him by Christ that the Corinthian church

and are naked, and are buffeted, and have no certain dwellingplace: . . . with scanty clothing, *Weymouth* . . . are ill-clad and knocked about, *Moffatt* . . . are stripped and flogged, and homeless, *Fenton* . . . and are boffeted with fistes, *Tyndale* . . . we are victims of mob-violence, *Way* . . . and we ben vnstable, *Wyclif* . . . and are wanderers, *Rotherham* . . . and have no fixed abode, *Confraternity.*

12. And labour, working with our own hands: . . . work hard for our living, *Moffatt* . . . and toil, *Rotherham* . . . at our own expense, *Fenton.*
being reviled, we bless:
being persecuted, we suffer it: . . . we bear it patiently, *Weymouth.*

13. Being defamed, we entreat: We are evyll spoken of, and we praye, *Tyndale* . . . vve are blasphemed, *Rheims* . . . we give consolation, *Fenton* . . . we try to conciliate, *Moffatt.*
we are made as the filth of the world, [and are] the offscouring of all things unto this day: . . . vve are made the refuse of, *Rheims* . . . as the mere dirt and filth...even to this hour, *Weymouth* . . . refused by all—even until now! *Fenton* . . . the scum of all things hitherto, *Concordant* . . . as the scum of the earth, the very refuse, *Moffatt.*

14. I write not these things to shame you: Not to confound you, *Rheims* . . . Not to be abashing you, *Concordant.*
but as my beloved sons I warn [you]: . . . but I am offering you advice as my dearly-loved children, *Weymouth* . . . as my moost dereworthe sones, *Wyclif* . . . I wish to correct you, *Fenton* . . . to instruct you, *Moffatt* . . . I admonish you, *Rheims.*

15. For though ye have ten thousand instructors in Christ: . . . though perchance myriads of tutors, *Rotherham* . . . escorts in Christ, *Concordant.*
yet [have ye] not many fathers:

1 Corinthians 4:16

1056.1 conj	5382.3 name dat masc	2400.2 name masc	1217.2 prep	3450.2 art gen sing	2077.2 noun gen sing neu
γὰρ	Χριστῷ	Ἰησοῦ	διὰ	τοῦ	εὐαγγελίου
gar	Christō	Iēsou	dia	tou	euangeliou
for	Christ	Jesus	through	the	good news

1466.1 prs-pron nom 1sing	5050.4 prs-pron acc 2pl	1074.3 verb 1sing indic aor act		3731.1 verb 1sing indic pres act	3631.1 conj
ἐγὼ	ὑμᾶς	ἐγέννησα.	**16.** παρακαλῶ		οὖν
egō	humas	egennēsa	parakalō		oun
I	you	did beget.	I exhort		therefore

5050.4 prs-pron acc 2pl	3266.1 noun nom pl masc	1466.2 prs-pron gen 1sing	1090.19 verb 2pl impr pres	1217.2 prep	3642.17 dem-pron sing neu
ὑμᾶς,	μιμηταί	μου	γίνεσθε.	**17.** Διὰ	τοῦτο
humas	mimētai	mou	ginesthe	Dia	touto
you,	imitators	of me	become.	On account of	this

17.a.**Var:** p11,01א-org 02A,025P,33,Tisc,Weis Sod,UBS/✩

840.15 prs-pron sing neu	3854.5 verb 1sing indic aor act	5050.3 prs-pron dat 2pl	4943.4 name acc masc	3614.5 rel-pron nom sing masc
[a+ αὐτὸ]	ἔπεμψα	ὑμῖν	Τιμόθεον,	ὃς
auto	epempsa	humin	Timotheon	hos
[it]	I sent	to you	Timothy,	who

1498.4 verb 3sing indic pres act	4891.1 noun sing neu	1466.2 prs-pron gen 1sing	1466.2 prs-pron gen 1sing	4891.1 noun sing neu
ἐστίν	‘ τέκνον	μου	[✩ μου	τέκνον]
estin	teknon	mou	mou	teknon
is	child	my	[my	child]

27.1 adj sing	2504.1 conj	3964.1 adj sing	1706.1 prep	2935.3 noun dat sing masc	3614.5 rel-pron nom sing masc
ἀγαπητὸν	καὶ	πιστὸν	ἐν	κυρίῳ,	Ὃς
agapēton	kai	piston	en	kuriō	hos
beloved	and	faithful	in	Lord,	who

5050.4 prs-pron acc 2pl	362.2 verb 3sing indic fut act	3450.15 art acc pl fem	3461.8 noun acc pl fem	1466.2 prs-pron gen 1sing	3450.15 art acc pl fem
ὑμᾶς	ἀναμνήσει	τὰς	ὁδούς	μου	τὰς
humas	anamnēsei	tas	hodous	mou	tas
you	will remind of	the	ways	my	the

17.b.**Var:** 01א,04C 06D-corr,33,Lach,Tisc We/Ho,Sod,UBS/✩

1706.1 prep	5382.3 name dat masc	2400.2 name masc	2503.1 conj	3699.1 adv	1706.1 prep
ἐν	Χριστῷ,	[b✩+ Ἰησοῦ,]	καθὼς	πανταχοῦ	ἐν
en	Christō	Iēsou	kathōs	pantachou	en
in	Christ,	[Jesus,]	just as	everywhere	in

3820.11 adj dat sing fem	1564.3 noun dat sing fem	1315.1 verb 1sing indic pres act		5453.1 conj	3231.1 partic	2048.45 verb gen sing masc part pres
πάσῃ	ἐκκλησίᾳ	διδάσκω.	**18.** ὡς		μὴ	ἐρχομένου
pasē	ekklēsia	didaskō	hōs		mē	erchomenou
every	assembly	I teach.	As to		not	coming

1156.2 conj	1466.2 prs-pron gen 1sing	4242.1 prep	5050.4 prs-pron acc 2pl	5284.5 verb 3pl indic aor pass	4948.7 indef-pron nom pl masc
δέ	μου	πρὸς	ὑμᾶς	ἐφυσιώθησάν	τινες·
de	mou	pros	humas	ephusiōthēsan	tines
now	my	to	you	were puffed up	some;

	2048.54 verb 1sing indic fut mid	1156.2 conj	4878.1 adv	4242.1 prep	5050.4 prs-pron acc 2pl	1430.1 partic	3450.5 art sing masc
19. ἐλεύσομαι		δὲ	ταχέως	πρὸς	ὑμᾶς,	ἐὰν	ὁ
eleusomai		de	tacheōs	pros	humas	ean	ho
I shall come		but	shortly	to	you,	if	the

was founded, and by his preaching many of the converts there first met Christ. Spiritual fatherhood carries with it a solemn obligation, and Paul was fulfilling that by correcting the Corinthians and by admonishing them to godly living.

4:16,17. Paul continued the father-child figure by urging that as a child follows a father so they should follow him. It is a mark of Paul's deeply spiritual life that he could ask the Corinthians to imitate his example. We must set limitations, though, and say that Paul meant his example in Christ Jesus. This would not stir up divisions again. It was one thing to say "I am of Paul," and quite another to follow in Paul's steps as he pointed to the Master.

Because he had so much concern for the welfare of the Corinthians, Paul had sent Timothy to admonish and encourage them in the Lord. When Paul said that he had sent Timothy, the aorist verb (*epempsa*) is not used in its usual past sense but is an "epistolary aorist" meaning that by the time they receive the letter Timothy will have been sent (thus removing any apparent inconsistency with 16:10). Timothy was on his way, traveling by land before Paul wrote his first epistle to the Corinthians, but the letter, traveling by sea, would arrive first. We have a small profile on Timothy here. He was like a son, greatly loved by Paul. It may be Paul had a part in bringing Timothy to Christ. Certainly he influenced his spiritual maturation, and Timothy was a faithful Christian, true to his calling.

Timothy's purpose was to remind the Corinthians of Paul's actions and teachings in Christ. It is difficult to say exactly how this was to happen, but perhaps it would be by Timothy's teaching and life. In doing this, Paul was being very fair, for his life and doctrine remained constant—they began in Christ and ended there. He did not teach a different message according to the crowd, but everywhere proclaimed the same things.

Paul was consistently building the Church. He did it by consistent teaching; he did it by consistent living; he did it by preparing others such as Timothy, training and adding to their responsibility, and then sending them out to carry on the work to which he had given so much.

4:18,19. Because Timothy had been sent and Paul had not come, some of the Corinthians had become proud and said Paul was afraid to face them. It may be they hoped he would not come, so they had convinced themselves that he would not. Paul set the record straight. He would come, provided the Lord so directed, which is all any servant can say. In coming, he would not be interested in their speeches but in their effectiveness, their power. Again we are reminded that the gospel is not mere theory, but practice, with power to make that practice effective. We are also reminded of the

for in Christ Jesus I have begotten you through the gospel: I fathered you in Christ, *SEB* . . . begotten you by preaching, *Murdock*.

16. Wherefore I beseech you, be ye followers of me: Then imitate me, I beg of you, *Moffatt* . . . I plead with you, *Norlie* . . . I advise you, *Fenton* . . . I urge you, *Beck* . . . I entreat you therefore to become like me, *Weymouth* . . . make it your habit to follow my example, *Williams* . . . to copy my example, *TCNT* . . . imitate my example, *Montgomery*.

17. For this cause have I sent unto you Timotheus: For this reason, *Weymouth*.

who is my beloved son, and faithful in the Lord: . . . vvho is my deerest sonne, *Rheims* . . . faithful child in the Lord, *Norlie* . . . in the Master's service, *TCNT*.

who shall bring you into remembrance of my ways which be in Christ: . . . might bring to your recollection, *Murdock* . . . remind you of my principles, *Berkeley* . . . remind you of my habits as a Christian, *Weymouth* . . . will call to your minds my methods in the work, *Williams*.

as I teach every where in every church: . . . in all Congregations, *Geneva* . . . in every Community, *HistNT* . . . in every assembly, *Fenton*.

18. Now some are puffed up, as though I would not come to you: Some, I hear, are elated, *TCNT* . . . are acting proud, *SEB* . . . have been filled with arrogance, *Conybeare* . . . have grown inflated with pride, *Berkeley* . . . may be elated at my failing to come to you, *Fenton* . . . insinuating that I dare not come to you, *Way* . . . I would not [dare] come to you, *Murdock*.

19. But I will come to you shortly, if the Lord will: I shall come to you without delay, *Weymouth* . . . to you swiftly, *Concordant* . . . to you before long, *Moffatt* . . . if the Lord wants me to, *Beck* . . . will permit, *Fenton*.

1 Corinthians 4:20

2935.1 noun nom sing masc	2286.27 verb 3sing subj aor act	2504.1 conj	1091.47 verb 1sing indic fut mid	3620.3 partic	3450.6 art acc sing masc
κύριος	θελήσῃ,	καὶ	γνώσομαι,	οὐ	τὸν
kurios	thelēsē	kai	gnōsomai	ou	ton
Lord	will,	and	I will know,	not	the

3030.4 noun acc sing masc	3450.1 art gen pl	5284.7 verb gen pl masc part perf pass	233.2 conj	3450.12 art acc sing fem
λόγον	τῶν	πεφυσιωμένων,	ἀλλὰ	τὴν
logon	tōn	pephusiōmenōn	alla	tēn
word	of the	having been puffed up,	but	the

1405.4 noun acc sing fem	3620.3 partic	1056.1 conj	1706.1 prep	3030.3 noun dat sing masc	3450.9 art nom sing fem	926.2 noun nom sing fem
δύναμιν.	**20.** οὐ	γὰρ	ἐν	λόγῳ	ἡ	βασιλεία
dunamin	ou	gar	en	logō	hē	basileia
power.	Not	for	in	word	the	kingdom

3450.2 art gen sing	2296.2 noun gen sing masc	233.1 conj	1706.1 prep	1405.3 noun dat sing fem	4949.9 intr-pron sing neu	2286.5 verb 2pl indic pres act
τοῦ	θεοῦ,	ἀλλ'	ἐν	δυνάμει.	**21.** τί	θέλετε;
tou	theou	all'	en	dunamei	ti	thelete
of God,	but	in	power.	What	will you?

1706.1 prep	4321.3 noun dat sing fem	2048.6 verb 1sing subj aor act	4242.1 prep	5050.4 prs-pron acc 2pl	2211.1 conj	1706.1 prep
ἐν	ῥάβδῳ	ἔλθω	πρὸς	ὑμᾶς,	ἢ	ἐν
en	rhabdō	elthō	pros	humas	ē	en
with	a rod	I should come	to	you,	or	in

21.a.Txt: 01א,06D,025P
byz.Sod
Var: 02A,03B,04C,33
Lach,Treg,Alf,Tisc
We/Ho,Weis,UBS/☆

26.3 noun dat sing fem	4011.3 noun dat sing neu	4885.1 conj	4095.2 noun gen sing fem	4099.1 noun gen sing fem
ἀγάπῃ	πνεύματί	τε	ʻ πραότητος;	[a☆ πραΰτητος;]
agapē	pneumati	te	praotētos	prautētos
love	a spirit	and	of meekness?	[idem]

3517.1 adv	189.47 verb 3sing indic pres pass	1706.1 prep	5050.3 prs-pron dat 2pl	4061.2 noun nom sing fem
5:1. Ὅλως	ἀκούεται	ἐν	ὑμῖν	πορνεία,
Holōs	akouetai	en	humin	porneia
Commonly	is being reported	among	you	fornication,

2504.1 conj	4955.9 dem-pron nom sing fem	4061.2 noun nom sing fem	3610.3 rel-pron nom sing fem	3624.1 adv	1706.1 prep	3450.4 art dat pl
καὶ	τοιαύτη	πορνεία	ἥτις	οὐδὲ	ἐν	τοῖς
kai	toiautē	porneia	hētis	oude	en	tois
and	such	fornication	which	not even	among	the

1.a.Txt: 01א-corr,020L
025P,byz.
Var: 01א-org,02A,03B
04C,06D,33,bo.Gries
Lach,Treg,Alf,Word
Tisc,We/Ho,Weis,Sod
UBS/☆

1477.6 noun dat pl neu	3550.4 verb 3sing indic pres pass	5452.1 conj	1129.4 noun acc sing fem	4948.5 indef-pron	3450.2 art gen sing
ἔθνεσιν	ʻa ὀνομάζεται, ʼ	ὥστε	γυναῖκά	τινα	τοῦ
ethnesin	onomazetai	hōste	gunaika	tina	tou
nations	is being named,	so as	wife	one	of the

3824.2 noun gen sing masc	2174.29 verb inf pres act	2504.1 conj	5050.1 prs-pron nom 2pl	5284.6 verb nom pl masc part perf pass
πατρὸς	ἔχειν.	**2.** καὶ	ὑμεῖς	πεφυσιωμένοι
patros	echein	kai	humeis	pephusiōmenoi
father	to have.	And	you	having been puffed up

1498.6 verb 2pl indic pres act	2504.1 conj	3644.1 adv	3095.1 adv comp	3858.4 verb 2pl indic aor act	2419.1 conj
ἐστέ,	καὶ	οὐχὶ	μᾶλλον	ἐπενθήσατε,	ἵνα
este	kai	ouchi	mallon	epenthēsate	hina
are,	and	not	rather	did mourn,	that

comparisons Paul made between words (1:17) and power (1:24), and between excellency of speech (2:1) and power (2:4).

4:20. This verse supplies the base for verse 19. The Corinthians must show God's power in their lives because the kingdom of God is not in word, but power and deed. Thus, Paul not only revealed the objective nature of the kingdom of God, but he also condemned pride. It is also interesting to note that in 2 Corinthians 13:1-10, Paul applied this same test to himself.

4:21. The decision was left to the Corinthians. Paul had been stirred by what he had already written and by what he was about to write. But how he would come to them would be determined by their future actions. He could come with sharpness and discipline, albeit in love, or he could come in love and gentleness, with a special manifestation of his care and regard for them.

5:1. Without preamble, Paul began the discussion of the next problem in the Corinthian church: indifference toward immorality. The case of incest was very serious, but Paul could not treat it until he had spoken to the problem of division (chapter 8). Church discipline could not be handled by a disunited church. Incest was an undoubted, talked-about fact. "Fornication" normally denotes participation with a harlot, but here Paul used it in the sense of general sexual misconduct. While incest was not entirely unknown among the Gentiles, Paul indicated that it was not common and definitely not condoned. Since it was so shameful, it was not even named or mentioned among them. Both Greek and Roman law stamped it with infamy, and Jewish law provided harsh penalties for this act.

The sin was between a man and his "father's wife." It has been suggested this refers to a stepmother, that the offender had seduced his stepmother, that she was divorced, or the father had died, leaving her a widow. Such specifics are not stated. We only know this disgraceful union had been established and, as "should have" tells us, it was a continued relationship. Its existence reflected a weak church needing restoration.

5:2. The reaction of the church had been sadly amiss. The Corinthians' pride had reached such a point that they considered themselves above the standard of God. Perhaps they considered themselves broad-minded. They were not sorrowful over their indifference and reproach; they were blinded to what should have been their response. Paul indicated that they should expel the sin-

and will know, not the speech of them which are puffed up, but the power: . . . how great is their supernatural power, *Way* . . . I shall learn the power of those who are puffed up, *Confraternity.*

20. For the kingdom of God [is] not in word, but in power: . . . the reign of God, *Campbell* . . . For apostolic authority is not a thing of words, *Weymouth* . . . is not in talk, *Fenton* . . . but in the miraculous operations of the Holy Ghost, *Locke* . . . For mighty deeds, not empty words, are the tokens of God's kingdom, *Conybeare.*

21. What will ye? shall I come unto you with a rod: What are ye wishing? *Rotherham* . . . What do you want? *Fenton* . . . What do you incline? *Campbell* . . . Which shall it be? *Weymouth* . . . with a rod of discipline? *Moffatt.*
or in love, and [in] the spirit of meekness?: . . . with a loving and gentle spirit? *Fenton* . . . in the sprete of softnesse? *Cranmer* . . . and the spirit of mildnes? *Rheims, Noyes* . . . and tender spirit? *Weymouth* . . . and gentleness, *Moffatt.*

1. It is reported commonly [that there is] fornication among you: There goeth a commen sayinge, *Tyndale* . . . it is absolutely notorious, *Way* . . . It is heard for a trueth, *Geneva* . . . It is absolutely heard, *Douay* . . . It is actually reported that there is immorality among you, *Moffatt* . . . commonly reported there is depravity, *Fenton* . . . that there is prostitution, *Concordant* . . . is incest among you, *Sawyer.*
and such fornication as is not so much as named among the Gentiles: . . . such depravity, *Fenton* . . . and of a kind unheard of, *Weymouth* . . . even among pagans, *Moffatt.*
that one should have his father's wife: . . . living in intercourse, *Way.*

2. And ye are puffed up: . . . you are self elated! *Fenton* . . . are filled with self-complacency, *Weymouth.*

1 Corinthians 5:3

2.a.**Txt:** 020L,byz.
Var: 01א,02A,03B,04C
06D,025P,Gries,Lach
Treg,Alf,Word,Tisc
We/Ho,Weis,Sod
UBS/✩

2.b.**Txt:** p46,03B,06D
020L,025P,044,byz.
Var: p11,01א,02A,04C
33,Tisc,We/Ho,Weis
Sod,UBS/✩

3.a.**Txt:** 06D-corr,020L
byz.
Var: 01א,02A,03B,04C
06D-org,025P,33,bo.
Lach,Treg,Alf,Word
Tisc,We/Ho,Weis,Sod
UBS/✩

1792.2 verb 3sing subj aor pass	142.30 verb 3sing subj aor pass	1523.2 prep gen	3189.4 adj gen sing neu	5050.2 prs-pron gen 2pl	3450.5 art sing masc
῾ ἐξαρθῇ	[a✩ ἀρθῇ]	ἐκ	μέσου	ὑμῶν	ὁ
exarthē	arthē	ek	mesou	humōn	ho
might be taken	[idem]	out of	midst	your	the

3450.16 art sing neu	2024.1 noun sing neu	3642.17 dem-pron sing neu	4020.37 verb nom sing masc part aor act	4097.28 verb nom sing masc part aor act
τὸ	ἔργον	τοῦτο	῾ ποιήσας;	[b πράξας;]
to	ergon	touto	poiēsas	praxas
the	deed	this	having done!	[idem]

1466.1 prs-pron nom 1sing	3173.1 conj	1056.1 conj	5453.1 conj	544.2 verb nom sing masc part pres act	3450.3 art dat sing
3. ἐγὼ	μὲν	γὰρ	῾a ὡς ῾	ἀπὼν	τῷ
egō	men	gar	hōs	apōn	tō
I		for	as	being absent	in the

4835.3 noun dat sing neu	3780.6 verb nom sing masc part pres act	1156.2 conj	3450.3 art dat sing	4011.3 noun dat sing neu	2218.1 adv
σώματι,	παρὼν	δὲ	τῷ	πνεύματι,	ἤδη
sōmati	parōn	de	tō	pneumati	ēdē
body,	being present	but	in the	spirit,	already

2892.21 verb 1sing indic perf act	5453.1 conj	3780.6 verb nom sing masc part pres act	3450.6 art acc sing masc	3643.1 adv
κέκρικα	ὡς	παρὼν,	τὸν	οὕτως
kekrika	hōs	parōn	ton	houtōs
have judged	as	being present,	the	so

3642.17 dem-pron sing neu	2686.11 verb acc sing masc part aor mid	1706.1 prep	3450.3 art dat sing	3549.4 noun dat sing neu
τοῦτο	κατεργασάμενον,	4. ἐν	τῷ	ὀνόματι
touto	katergasamenon	en	tō	onomati
this	having worked out,	in	the	name

4.a.**Txt:** p46,03B,06D
020L,025P,33,byz.it.sa.
bo.We/Ho,Sod
Var: 01א,02A,044,Tisc
Weis,UBS/✩

4.b.**Txt:** p46,01א
06D-corr,020L,025P,33
byz.it.sa.bo.Sod
Var: 02A,03B,06D-org
044,Lach,Treg,Alf,Tisc
We/Ho,Weis,UBS/✩

3450.2 art gen sing	2935.2 noun gen sing masc	2231.2 prs-pron gen 1pl	2400.2 name masc	5382.2 name gen masc
τοῦ	κυρίου	῾a ἡμῶν ῾	Ἰησοῦ	῾b Χριστοῦ, ῾
tou	kuriou	hēmōn	Iēsou	Christou
of the	Lord	our	Jesus	Christ,

4714.22 verb gen pl masc part aor pass	5050.2 prs-pron gen 2pl	2504.1 conj	3450.2 art gen sing	1466.3 prs-pron gen 1sing
συναχθέντων	ὑμῶν	καὶ	τοῦ	ἐμοῦ
sunachthentōn	humōn	kai	tou	emou
having been gathered together	you	and	the	my

4011.2 noun gen sing neu	4713.1 prep dat	3450.11 art dat sing fem	1405.3 noun dat sing fem	3450.2 art gen sing	2935.2 noun gen sing masc
πνεύματος,	σὺν	τῇ	δυνάμει	τοῦ	κυρίου
pneumatos	sun	tē	dunamei	tou	kuriou
spirit,	with	the	power	of the	Lord

4.c.**Txt:** p46,06D-corr2
010F,012G,byz.
Var: 02A,044,2495

4.d.**Txt:** 06D-corr,020L
byz.bo.
Var: 01א,02A,03B
06D-org,025P,Lach
Treg,Alf,Tisc,We/Ho
Weis,Sod,UBS/✩

2231.2 prs-pron gen 1pl	2400.2 name masc	5382.2 name gen masc	3722.19 verb inf aor act
῾c ἡμῶν ῾	Ἰησοῦ	῾d Χριστοῦ, ῾	5. παραδοῦναι
hēmōn	Iēsou	Christou	paradounai
our	Jesus	Christ,	to deliver

3450.6 art acc sing masc	4955.2 dem-pron acc sing	3450.3 art dat sing	4423.3 noun dat sing masc	1519.1 prep	3502.2 noun acc sing masc
τὸν	τοιοῦτον	τῷ	Σατανᾷ	εἰς	ὄλεθρον
ton	toiouton	tō	Satana	eis	olethron
the	such a one	to	Satan	for	destruction

ner. The honor of God and the holiness of the Corinthian church were at stake.

The attitude of the Corinthian believers concerning this gross sin shows they still had a long way to go to rise above the wicked environment in which they lived. The city had become so notorious for its wickedness that its very name had become a symbol for the worst kind of immorality. Some scholars have deduced from the grammatical structure of the sentence that it was stated in the form of a question, but the situation was so gross it probably demanded a strong imperative from the apostle.

5:3,4. Paul thought of himself as present "in spirit" and having characterized the man by his deed, Paul disciplined with authority. The verb is in the perfect, which adds an air of finality. By this Paul had in mind both the welfare of the sinner and the purity of the local church. "In the name of our Lord Jesus" is the opening for a solemn judicial sentence and tells us under what authority all proper church gatherings and administrations must operate.

"When ye are gathered together" is probably associated with "with the power of our Lord Jesus" and indicated this was not to be a minority meeting but the gathering of the whole church to perform a solemn act. Paul would be there "in spirit" heading the proceedings. If the Corinthians had called Paul's spirit and teachings to remembrance and followed them, this discussion would have been unnecessary. "With" suggests not only Christ's power and presence would be there, but also His cooperation. It must be noted that Paul did not try to make his presence and Christ's coequal. The proceedings must be in Christ's authority and for His glory. His presence was necessary with Paul's spirit and the congregation, to make the sentence valid.

5:5. The purpose of this judgment is discussed here. "Deliver . . . unto Satan" may mean excommunication, or it may mean some physical affliction and spiritual visitation on the guilty. Those who support the first sometimes suggest that Paul had in mind the idea of letting the flesh go as far as it could in Satan's realm, and then the sinner would remember God's goodness and return. Those who support the second view remind us that physical maladies and even death are sometimes ascribed to Satan in the New Testament (Luke 13:16; John 8:44; 2 Corinthians 12:7; Hebrews 2:14), and sickness is sometimes the result of being withdrawn from the secure realm of fellowship with God. Affliction is often made an instrument of spiritual benefit (1 Corinthians 11:30-32; 2 Corinthians 4:16-18; 12:7; 1 Peter 4). The apostles did on occasion pronounce penal sentences in the physical realm (Acts 5:1-10; 13:1-12).

But we do know the intent of the sentence: to bring the offender back to Christ, that on the "day of the Lord," when every man's position shall be finalized, he would stand with the company of the redeemed. One note should be added. In this account Satan was

and have not rather mourned, that he that hath done this deed might be taken away from among you: . . . instead of being crushed with grief, *Way* . . . rather be sorrowfully indignant, *Fenton* . . . sitten down in grief, *Murdock* . . . instead of mourning and removing from among you the man who has done this thing, *Montgomery* . . . Expel the perpetrator of such a crime, *Moffatt* . . . expelling from your membership, *Norlie* . . . the man who has behaved in this way, *SEB* . . . that wrought this work! *Rotherham* . . . should be removed, *Sawyer* . . . from your midst, *Concordant.*

3. For I verily, as absent in body, but present in spirit:
have judged already, as though I were present: . . . have decided already, *Fenton* . . . already passed sentence, *Montgomery* . . . judged the one effecting this, *Concordant* . . . judged him who has so acted, *Weymouth.*
[concerning] him that hath so done this deed: . . . him who thus perpetrated this thing, *Rotherham, Murdock* . . . who has consummated this crime, *Way.*

4. In the name of our Lord Jesus Christ: And my sentence is this, *Macknight.*
when ye are gathered together: . . . meet in solemn congregation, *Way* . . . that you convene an assembly, *Conybeare* . . . when you are all assembled, *Weymouth* . . . call a meeting in the name of our Lord Jesus Christ, *Norlie.*
and my spirit, with the power of our Lord Jesus Christ: . . . and yours agreeing together, *Fenton* . . . in conjunction with the power, *Rotherham.*

5. To deliver such an one unto Satan for the destruction of the flesh: I have consigned that individual, *Moffatt* . . . to the perischynge of fleisch, *Wyclif* . . . for the extermination, *Concordant* . . . for the destruction of his fleshly lusts, *Conybeare* . . . for the destruction of his body, *Weymouth* . . . to be physically disciplined, *Norlie* . . . that he may blast the sinner's body, *Way.*

1 Corinthians 5:6

3450.10 art gen sing fem	4418.2 noun gen sing fem	2419.1 conj	3450.16 art sing neu	4011.1 noun sing neu	4834.26 verb 3sing subj aor pass	1706.1 prep
τῆς	σαρκός,	ἵνα	τὸ	πνεῦμα	σωθῇ	ἐν
tēs	sarkos	hina	to	pneuma	sōthē	en
of the	flesh,	that	the	spirit	may be saved	in

3450.11 art dat sing fem	2232.3 noun dat sing fem	3450.2 art gen sing	2935.2 noun gen sing masc	2400.2 name masc	3620.3 partic
τῇ	ἡμέρα	τοῦ	κυρίου	⌐a Ἰησοῦ. ⌐	6. Οὐ
tē	hēmera	tou	kuriou	Iēsou	Ou
the	day	of the	Lord	Jesus.	Not

5.a.Txt: 01‭א‬,02A,020L 025P,044,byz.Tisc,Sod Var: p46,03B,1739,Alf We/Ho,Weis,UBS/✶

2541.1 adj sing	3450.16 art sing neu	2715.1 noun sing neu	5050.2 prs-pron gen 2pl	3620.2 partic	3471.6 verb 2pl indic perf act	3617.1 conj
καλὸν	τὸ	καύχημα	ὑμῶν.	οὐκ	οἴδατε	ὅτι
kalon	to	kauchēma	humōn	ouk	oidate	hoti
good	the	boasting	your.	Not	know you	that

3262.9 adj nom sing fem	2202.1 noun nom sing fem	3513.1 adj sing	3450.16 art sing neu	5281.1 noun sing neu	2203.1 verb 3sing indic pres act
μικρὰ	ζύμη	ὅλον	τὸ	φύραμα	ζυμοῖ;
mikra	zumē	holon	to	phurama	zumoi
a little	leaven	whole	the	lump	leavens?

7.a.Txt: 01‭א‬-corr,04C 020L,025P,byz.Sod Var: 01‭א‬-org,02A,03B 06D,bo.Gries,Lach,Treg Alf,Word,Tisc,We/Ho Weis,UBS/✶

1558.2 verb 2pl impr aor act	3631.1 conj	3450.12 art acc sing fem	3683.7 adj acc sing fem	2202.4 noun acc sing fem	2419.1 conj
7. ἐκκαθάρατε	⌐a οὖν ⌐	τὴν	παλαιὰν	ζύμην,	ἵνα
ekkatharate	oun	tēn	palaian	zumēn	hina
Purge out	therefore	the	old	leaven,	that

1498.1 verb 2pl act	3365.1 adj sing	5281.1 noun sing neu	2503.1 conj	1498.6 verb 2pl indic pres act	105.1 adj nom pl masc
ἦτε	νέον	φύραμα,	καθὼς	ἐστε	ἄζυμοι·
ēte	neon	phurama	kathōs	este	azumoi
you may be	a new	lump,	just as	you are	unleavened.

7.b.Txt: 01‭א‬-corr 04C-corr,020L,025P,byz. Var: 01‭א‬-org,02A,03B 04C-org,06D,33,Lach Treg,Alf,Word,Tisc We/Ho,Weis,Sod UBS/✶

2504.1 conj	1056.1 conj	3450.16 art sing neu	3818.1 noun sing neu	2231.2 prs-pron gen 1pl	5065.1 prep	2231.2 prs-pron gen 1pl
καὶ	γὰρ	τὸ	πάσχα	ἡμῶν	⌐b ὑπὲρ	ἡμῶν ⌐
kai	gar	to	pascha	hēmōn	huper	hēmōn
Also	for	the	passover	our	for	us

2357.10 verb 3sing indic aor pass	5382.1 name nom masc	5452.1 conj	1843.1 verb 1pl subj pres act
ἐτύθη	Χριστός.	8. ὥστε	ἑορτάζωμεν,
etuthē	Christos	hōste	heortazōmen
was sacrificed	Christ.	So that	we should celebrate the feast,

3231.1 partic	1706.1 prep	2202.3 noun dat sing fem	3683.6 adj dat sing fem	3234.1 adv	1706.1 prep	2202.3 noun dat sing fem	2520.2 noun gen sing fem
μὴ	ἐν	ζύμη	παλαιᾷ,	μηδὲ	ἐν	ζύμη	κακίας
mē	en	zumē	palaia	mēde	en	zumē	kakias
not	with	leaven	old,	nor	with	leaven	of malice

2504.1 conj	4049.1 noun gen sing fem	233.1 conj	1706.1 prep	105.4 adj dat pl neu	1495.1 noun gen sing fem	2504.1 conj
καὶ	πονηρίας,	ἀλλ'	ἐν	ἀζύμοις	εἰλικρινείας	καὶ
kai	ponērias	all'	en	azumois	eilikrineias	kai
and	wickedness,	but	with	unleavened	of sincerity	and

223.2 noun gen sing fem	1119.7 verb 1sing indic aor act	5050.3 prs-pron dat 2pl	1706.1 prep	3450.11 art dat sing fem	1976.3 noun dat sing fem
ἀληθείας.	9. Ἔγραψα	ὑμῖν	ἐν	τῇ	ἐπιστολῇ,
alētheias	Egrapsa	humin	en	tē	epistolē
of truth.	I wrote	to you	in	the	epistle,

pictured as subject to God, and it is clear that God will gain final glory in every situation. Satan's power is limited and must serve the purpose of God which is redemptive. Paul was faithful to keep his priorities straight in this matter in loving the sinful and preserving the Church.

5:6. Having given this situation attention, Paul returned to the root of the problem—pride. He plainly stated that the resultant boasting of the Corinthians was wrong. Strictly speaking, "glorying" suggests content, not action. What Paul was really upset about was what they were bragging about. Paul used the illustration of yeast. It takes only a little to cause bread to rise. The application was that both the church as a whole and the individual, in allowing evil, would in time corrupt the whole Christian community, collectively and individually.

5:7. The command was to clean out the evil, probably meaning the pride and boasting, but also the sin they had allowed to be practiced among them. With that Paul reminded them of another figure. Certain ceremonies preceded the eating of the Passover. For 7 days Israel ate unleavened bread, having removed the leaven from their homes on the first day. This was to remind them of the Exodus and the liberation from the bondage of Egypt. What the Israelites used on their journey was different from that used in Egypt. The application? Too much of the heathen life-style remained with the Corinthians. They should have been new, fresh, and free in Christ, and in order for that to happen they must remove the leaven.

The figure was expanded. Israel ate the unleavened bread after the Passover. Christ as the Paschal Lamb enables His people to remain unleavened. Believers are free from sins objectively and, subjectively, are called to walk in holiness, confessing and forsaking all known sin. Christ has made believers free from corruption, and Christians should not allow old "yeast" to reenter the "new lump."

5:8. Paul exhorted the Corinthians to "keep the feast," not literally, but symbolically; not with the "leaven of malice and wickedness; but with the unleavened bread of sincerity and truth." "Let us keep" is present continuous and indicates a continued operation. "Malice" refers to an evil habit of the mind, and "wickedness" refers to the results of that mindset. Contrasted with it is purity of motive and purity of action. Purity must be retained in the Church. Christ is our example in this.

5:9. This subject had apparently come up before. We do not have the epistle referred to, but it seems fornication was a problem with

that the spirit may be saved in the day of the Lord Jesus:

6. Your glorying [is] not good: It isn't good for you to feel proud, *Beck* . . . Your pride is not noble, *Fenton* . . . not right that you boast about this case, *Norlie* . . . in a leader who drew you into this scandalous indulgence, *Locke* . . . Your boasting is no credit to you, *Moffatt* . . . is not praiseworthy, *Murdock* . . . is discreditable, *HistNT*.
Know ye not that a little leaven leaveneth the whole lump?: . . . a morsel of dough, *Moffatt* . . . a lytle leven sowreth the whole lompe of dowe, *Tyndale* . . . a little ferment ferments the whole mass? *Fenton* . . . a little yeast corrupts the whole of the dough? *Weymouth* . . . the whole kneading? *Concordant*.

7. Purge out therefore the old leaven: Clean out, *Adams* . . . Cleanse out every trace of this old leaven, *Way* . . . Houseclean the old yeast, *Klingensmith*.
that ye may be a new lump, as ye are unleavened: . . . as ye are swete bread, *Geneva* . . . may be an untainted mass, *Conybeare* . . . you are free from corruption, *Weymouth* . . . may be a fresh lump, *Moffatt*.
For even Christ our passover is sacrificed for us: . . . for our passover also was slain, *Rotherham* . . . our paschal lamb, *Moffatt, Conybeare* . . . oure estherlambe is offered vp, *Tyndale*.

8. Therefore let us keep the feast, not with old leaven: . . . celebrate the festival, *Norlie* . . . keep the unending feast, *Montgomery*.
neither with the leaven of malice and wickedness; but with the unleavened [bread] of sincerity and truth: . . . leaven of wickedness and bitterness, *Murdock* . . . but with unfermented batches of purity, *Berkeley* . . . the bread of transparent, *Weymouth* . . . of innocence and integrity, *Moffatt*.

9. I wrote unto you in an epistle not to company with fornicators: I enjoined you, *Conybeare* . . . in my letter, *Fenton*

1 Corinthians 5:10

10.a.Txt: 01ℵ-corr
06D-corr,020L,025P,byz.
Var: 01ℵ-org,02A,03B
04C,06D-org,33,bo.Lach
Treg,Alf,Word,Tisc
We/Ho,Weis,Sod
UBS/✶

3231.1 partic	4725.1 verb inf pres	4064.3 noun dat pl masc	10.	2504.1 conj	3620.3 partic
μὴ	συναναμίγνυσθαι	πόρνοις·		⌈a καὶ ⌉	οὐ
mē	sunanamignusthai	pornois		kai	ou
not	to associate with	fornicators;		and	not

3705.1 adv	3450.4 art dat pl	4064.3 noun dat pl masc	3450.2 art gen sing	2862.2 noun gen sing masc	3642.1 dem-pron gen sing
πάντως	τοῖς	πόρνοις	τοῦ	κόσμου	τούτου,
pantōs	tois	pornois	tou	kosmou	toutou,
altogether	with the	fornicators	of the	world	this,

10.b.Txt: p46,01ℵ-corr
06D-corr,020L,044,byz.
sa.bo.
Var: 01ℵ-org,02A,03B
04C,06D-org,025P,33
Lach,Treg,Alf,Word
Tisc,We/Ho,Weis,Sod
UBS/✶

2211.1 conj	3450.4 art dat pl	3983.3 noun dat pl masc	2211.1 conj	2504.1 conj	721.3 adj dat pl masc	2211.1 conj
ἢ	τοῖς	πλεονέκταις	⌈ ἢ	[b✶ καὶ]	ἅρπαξιν,	ἢ
ē	tois	pleonektais	ē	kai	harpaxin	ē
or	with the	greedy,	or	[and]	swindlers,	or

10.c.Txt: 03B-corr,025P
byz.
Var: 01ℵ,02A,03B-org
04C,06D,020L,Lach
Treg,Alf,Tisc,We/Ho
Weis,Sod,UBS/✶

1486.3 noun dat pl masc	1878.1 conj	3648.1 verb 2pl pres act	3648.13 verb 2pl indic imperf act	679.1 partic
εἰδωλολάτραις,	ἐπεὶ	⌈ ὀφείλετε	[c✶ ὠφείλετε]	ἄρα
eidōlolatrais,	epei	opheilete	ōpheilete	ara
idolaters,	since	you ought	[you were owing]	then

11.a.Txt: 01ℵ-org,04C
06D-org,byz.Tisc.
Var: 01ℵ-corr,02A,03B
06D-corr,020L,025P
Lach,Treg,Alf,We/Ho
Weis,Sod,UBS/✶

1523.2 prep gen	3450.2 art gen sing	2862.2 noun gen sing masc	1814.20 verb inf aor act	11.	3432.1 adv	3431.1 adv
ἐκ	τοῦ	κόσμου	ἐξελθεῖν.		⌈ νυνὶ	[a✶ νῦν]
ek	tou	kosmou	exelthein.		nuni	nun
out of	the	world	to go.		Now	[idem]

1156.2 conj	1119.7 verb 1sing indic aor act	5050.3 prs-pron dat 2pl	3231.1 partic	4725.1 verb inf pres	1430.1 partic
δὲ	ἔγραψα	ὑμῖν	μὴ	συναναμίγνυσθαι	ἐάν
de	egrapsa	humin	mē	sunanamignusthai	ean
but,	I wrote	to you	not	to associate with,	if

11.b.Txt: 03B-corr,06D
Steph
Var: Elzev,Gries,Lach
Treg,Alf,Word,Tisc
We/Ho,Weis,Sod
UBS/✶,bo.

4948.3 indef-pron nom sing	79.1 noun nom sing masc	3550.6 verb nom sing masc part pres pass	2211.1 conj	1498.10 verb 3sing subj pres act
τις	ἀδελφὸς	ὀνομαζόμενος	⌈ ἢ	[b✶ ᾖ]
tis	adelphos	onomazomenos	ē	ē
anyone	brother	being named	either	[is]

4064.1 noun nom sing masc	2211.1 conj	3983.1 noun nom sing masc	2211.1 conj	1486.1 noun nom sing masc	2211.1 conj
πόρνος,	ἢ	πλεονέκτης,	ἢ	εἰδωλολάτρης,	ἢ
pornos,	ē	pleonektēs,	ē	eidōlolatrēs,	ē
a fornicator,	or	covetous,	or	idolater,	or

3034.1 noun nom sing masc	2211.1 conj	3154.1 noun nom sing masc	2211.1 conj	721.1 adj nom sing masc	3450.3 art dat sing
λοίδορος,	ἢ	μέθυσος	ἢ	ἅρπαξ·	τῷ
loidoros,	ē	methusos	ē	harpax	tō
reviler,	or	a drunkard,	or	swindler;	with the

4955.6 dem-pron dat sing masc	3234.1 adv	4756.2 verb inf pres act	12.	4949.9 intr-pron sing neu	1056.1 conj	1466.4 prs-pron dat 1sing
τοιούτῳ	μηδὲ	συνεσθίειν.	12. τί		γὰρ	μοι
toioutō	mēde	sunesthiein.	ti		gar	moi
such a one	not even	to eat.	What		for	to me

12.a.Txt: 06D,020L,byz.
Var: 01ℵ,02A,03B,04C
025P,33,bo.Lach,Treg
Alf,Tisc,We/Ho,Weis
Sod,UBS/✶

2504.1 conj	3450.8 art acc pl masc	1838.1 prep gen	2892.12 verb inf pres act	3644.1 adv	3450.8 art acc pl masc	2059.1 prep gen
⌈a καὶ ⌉	τοὺς	ἔξω	κρίνειν;	οὐχὶ	τοὺς	ἔσω
kai	tous	exō	krinein;	ouchi	tous	esō
also	the	outside	to judge,	not	the	within

which the Corinthian church had repeated difficulty. The command had been to forbid social intimacy with those who were guilty of this sin.

5:10. Now, Paul discovered, a problem had arisen in an opposite direction. A misunderstanding had developed over the force and purpose of Paul's command, and now the Corinthians claimed a separation in a way that was impossible. Paul did not mean they should avoid contact with sinners in a general way; such absence of contact was impossible. Yet, Paul contended that in many circumstances the Corinthian Christians should not participate in the activities of those who did not obey the Lord. He listed, along with fornicators, the "covetous," those who are possessed by greed, "extortioners," who take what is not theirs (robbers in any form), and "idolaters" who worship the wrong things. The relationship of the Church to the world must be carefully balanced.

5:11. Paul made clear his meaning of "separation." The Corinthians could choose those with whom they formed close friendships and whether or not evil pervaded their fellowship. "I have written" allows a stronger possibility for meaning the present letter, but this is unnecessary. The kingdom of God is not of this world and cannot be carried out by worldly associations. It is preserved by the power of God. If one who professes himself a Christian is really involved in evil living he cannot be an intimate friend of a true believer. And to the list in verse 10 Paul added the "railer" who abuses others, and the "drunkard," which speaks for itself.

"Not to eat," according to many, refers to ordinary meals and not to the Lord's Supper, although that too would be forbidden. The difficulty is that Jesus ate with sinners, and Paul, in 10:27, allows one to accept invitations to eat in heathen homes. The answer may be in comparison of "not to keep company" and "not to eat." The former may denote regular fellowship and the latter not so. Without numerous hotels, private hospitality was important. The main theme remains: There is to be no close fellowship with one who claims to be a Christian, but whose life belies that claim.

5:12,13. Paul claimed no authority to judge sinners or those outside the Christian community. But the Church must guard and watch those inside the Church. God will judge those outside the Church. "Within" and "without" denoted in synagogue usage members and nonmembers of the sacred community (Nicoll, *Expositor's Greek Testament*, 2:813). The Corinthians' indifference toward impurity must be resolved. Verse 12 points to their responsibility, and verse 13 limits that responsibility.

The injunction was to remove the unrepentant offender because he was within the fold; he must be left to God's judgment. The purpose of this was to warn sinners of judgment and point them

... you were not to associate, *Weymouth, Montgomery, Macknight* ... to have no association, *Hanson* ... not to mingle, *Panin* ... not to get mixed up with those who are sexually immoral, *Adams* ... not to be mixing yourselves up with fornicators, *Rotherham* ... be not medlid with leccherous, *Wyclif* ... to be commingling with paramours, *Concordant* ... with licentious men, *Way* ... with the immoral, *Moffatt.*

10. Yet not altogether with the fornicators of this world: ... you are to keep wholly aloof, *Weymouth* ... not altogether meaning, *Clementson* ... I was not referring to the licentious of the heathen world, *Way.*

or with the covetous, or extortioners, or with idolaters: ... nor of the avaricious, *Murdock* ... or with the debauched, *Fenton* ... or people who worship false gods, *SEB.*

for then must ye needs go out of the world: ... to leave the world altogether, *Moffatt, Montgomery.*

11. But now I have written unto you not to keep company: But my meaning was, *Conybeare* ... let me explain that, *Adams* ... I have set it down plainly at this time, *Way* ... not to be associated, *Hanson* ... not to be associating with, *Fenton.*

if any man that is called a brother be a fornicator: ... who calls himself a Christian, *Beck.*

or covetous, or an idolater, or a railer, or a drunkard, or an extortioner: ... or a wanton, *Conybeare* ... a slanderer, *Adams* ... avarice or idol-worship or abusive language, *Weymouth* ... or debauchee...or a blackguard...or rapacious, *Fenton* ... or a curser, *Wyclif.*

with such an one no not to eat: ... do not even sit at table, *Montgomery* ... do not even eat with him! *Moffatt.*

12. For what have I to do to judge them also that are without?: For what business have I, *Murdock* ... It is none of my business to judge, *SEB.*

1 Corinthians 5:13

5050.1 prs-pron nom 2pl	2892.3 verb 2pl pres act		3450.8 art acc pl masc	1156.2 conj	1838.1 prep gen	3450.5 art sing masc
ὑμεῖς	κρίνετε;	**13.**	τοὺς	δὲ	ἔξω	ὁ
humeis	krinete		tous	de	exō	ho
you	do you judge?		The	but	outside	

13.a.**Txt:** 06D-corr,020L byz.
Var: 01ℵ,02A,03B,04C 06D-org,025P,Gries Lach,Treg,Alf,Word Tisc,We/Ho,Weis,Sod UBS/✶

2296.1 noun nom sing masc	2892.5 verb 3sing indic pres act	2504.1 conj	1792.1 verb 2pl indic fut act	1792.3 verb 2pl impr aor act
θεὸς	κρίνει.	καὶ	ἐξαρεῖτε	[ᵃ✶ ἐξάρατε]
theos	krinei	kai	exareite	exarate
God	judges.	And	you shall put out	[remove]

3450.6 art acc sing masc	4050.1 adj sing	1523.1 prep gen	5050.2 prs-pron gen 2pl	840.1 prs-pron gen pl
τὸν	πονηρὸν	ἐξ	ὑμῶν	αὐτῶν.
ton	ponēron	ex	humōn	autōn
the	wicked person	from among	your	selves.

	4958.1 verb 3sing pres act	4948.3 indef-pron nom sing	5050.2 prs-pron gen 2pl	4088.1 noun sing neu	2174.17 verb nom sing masc part pres act
6:1.	Τολμᾷ	τις	ὑμῶν	πρᾶγμα	ἔχων
	Tolma	tis	humōn	pragma	echōn
	Dare	anyone	of you,	a matter	having

4242.1 prep	3450.6 art acc sing masc	2066.1 adj sing	2892.32 verb inf pres pass	1894.3 prep	3450.1 art gen pl
πρὸς	τὸν	ἕτερον,	κρίνεσθαι	ἐπὶ	τῶν
pros	ton	heteron	krinesthai	epi	tōn
against	the	other,	to be judged	before	the

2.a.**Var:** 01ℵ,02A,03B 04C,06D-org,025P Gries,Lach,Treg,Alf Word,Tisc,We/Ho,Weis Sod,UBS/✶

93.4 adj gen pl masc	2504.1 conj	3644.1 adv	1894.3 prep	3450.1 art gen pl	39.4 adj gen pl		2211.1 conj
ἀδίκων,	καὶ	οὐχὶ	ἐπὶ	τῶν	ἁγίων;	**2.**	[ᵃ✶+ ἢ]
adikōn	kai	ouchi	epi	tōn	hagiōn		ē
unrighteous,	and	not	before	the	saints?		[or]

3620.2 partic	3471.6 verb 2pl indic perf act	3617.1 conj	3450.7 art pl masc	39.7 adj pl masc	3450.6 art acc sing masc	2862.4 noun acc sing masc
οὐκ	οἴδατε	ὅτι	οἱ	ἅγιοι	τὸν	κόσμον
ouk	oidate	hoti	hoi	hagioi	ton	kosmon
Not	know you	that	the	saints	the	world

2892.27 verb 3pl indic fut act	2504.1 conj	1479.1 conj	1706.1 prep	5050.3 prs-pron dat 2pl	2892.29 verb 3sing indic pres pass	3450.5 art sing masc
κρινοῦσιν;	καὶ	εἰ	ἐν	ὑμῖν	κρίνεται	ὁ
krinousin	kai	ei	en	humin	krinetai	ho
will judge?	and	if	by	you	is being judged	the

2862.1 noun nom sing masc	369.1 adj nom pl masc	1498.6 verb 2pl indic pres act	2895.1 noun gen pl neu	1633.1 adj sup gen pl
κόσμος,	ἀνάξιοί	ἐστε	κριτηρίων	ἐλαχίστων;
kosmos	anaxioi	este	kritēriōn	elachistōn
world,	unworthy	are you	of judgments	the smallest?

	3620.2 partic	3471.6 verb 2pl indic perf act	3617.1 conj	32.8 noun acc pl masc	2892.26 verb 1pl indic fut act	3252.1 partic
3.	οὐκ	οἴδατε	ὅτι	ἀγγέλους	κρινοῦμεν·	μήτι
	ouk	oidate	hoti	angelous	krinoumen	mēti
	Not	know you	that	angels	we shall judge?	perhaps

1058.1 partic	975.2 adj acc pl neu		975.2 adj acc pl neu	3173.1 conj	3631.1 conj	2895.2 noun acc pl neu
γε	βιωτικά;	**4.**	βιωτικὰ	μὲν	οὖν	κριτήρια
ge	biōtika		biōtika	men	oun	kritēria
even	things of this life?		Things of this life	then		judgment

to the grace of God. But the injunction rises to the greater principle that the Church must continually examine itself and keep itself from all unrighteousness for Christ's sake, for the Church belongs to Him.

In verse 13 Paul summed up the two most important aspects of this section. First was the command to exclude the "wicked person" (the fornicator) from the church. This thought is true not only of fornicators, but of any who would defile the Church, because it is the body of Christ. Second, because the Church is the body of Christ, Paul changed the Old Testament quote (Deuteronomy 17:7) from the singular to the plural to emphasize that the entire church community was involved in this action.

6:1. The problem discussed in chapter 5 and that of lawsuits (6:1-8) are related because both result from a spirit of greed and a lack of church discipline. Paul opposed the taking of difficulties between Christians before pagan courts. To do so was a bad example and showed immaturity. Generally, as Romans 13 indicates, Paul's opinion of pagan magistrates was favorable. But here we are carried back to the arguments on wisdom and reminded that the Corinthians could not settle disputes because they did not heed the revelation of God to them.

"Not before the saints" indicates that it was not forbidden to seek justice. Law and order and an honest court are blessings from God. But the Corinthians were seeking the wrong advice and disputing petty matters. Paul never used the courts to accuse his opponents but in defense of his work.

6:2. Paul thought the Corinthians should know already that the saints will participate with Christ in judging the world. They will applaud His actions and just decisions. Paul intended to emphasize a dignity, privilege, and association beyond the idea even of Christian magistrates. It is a picture of Christ and His saints in session, with the world brought in before them for judgment. With this position awaiting, are you unable, Paul asked, to handle petty matters among yourselves? Can you not form a "court" to settle your own disputes? The Corinthian church had forgotten its glory and the honor of God. This was an insult to God's ability to impart wisdom and ability in Christ. "Matters" actually denotes the rules and means of judging and thus means the court itself.

6:3. The Holy Spirit inspired Paul to add an interesting fact, that the Church will judge angels. This is discussed elsewhere in such passages as 2 Peter 2:4, Jude 6, and Revelation 20:10, but details are not included there either. Therefore, a discussion of the details would only be conjecture. Paul's purpose was to pick something lofty and beyond this world. The Church would judge these. Why could it not, then, handle smaller, less exalted matters?

do not ye judge them that are within?: . . . judge people on the inside, *SEB*.

13. But them that are without God judgeth: . . . who are outside? *Weymouth*.
Therefore put away from among yourselves that wicked person: In conclusion, *Norlie* . . . Throw out the profligate, *Fenton* . . . that bad man, *Noyes* . . . Remove the wicked man from among you, *Weymouth* . . . Banish the wicked one from your midst, *HistNT* . . . Expel the wicked from your company, *Moffatt, Berkeley* . . . from your membership, *Williams*.

1. Dare any of you, having a matter against another: . . . has a grievance against an opponent, *Weymouth* . . . an action, *Fenton* . . . against his neighbor, *Moffatt*.
go to law before the unjust: . . . their private differences into the courts of law, *Conybeare* . . . before irreligious men, *Weymouth* . . . a sinful pagan court, *Moffatt*.
and not before the saints?:

2. Do ye not know that the saints shall judge the world?: . . . are you not aware, *Concordant* . . . the saints are to manage the world? *Moffatt*.
and if the world shall be judged by you: . . . the world is subjected to your judgment, *Conybeare*.
are ye unworthy to judge the smallest matters?: . . . are you unworthy of the least tribunals, *Concordant* . . . are you unfit to deal with these petty matters? *Weymouth* . . . are you incapable of the smallest arbitrations? *Fenton* . . . are you incompetent to adjudicate upon trifles, *Moffatt* . . . to iudge small trifles? *Cranmer*.

3. Know ye not that we shall judge angels?: . . . judge messengers, *Rotherham*.
how much more things that pertain to this life?: . . . let alone mundane issues, *Moffatt* . . . hovv much more secular things? *Rheims* . . . not to mention life's affairs? *Concordant* . . . then why not business matters? *Fenton*.

1 Corinthians 6:5

1430.1 partic	2174.9 verb 2pl subj pres act	3450.8 art acc pl masc	1832.10 verb acc pl masc part perf pass		1706.1 prep	3450.11 art dat sing fem
ἐὰν	ἔχητε,	τοὺς	ἐξουθενημένους		ἐν	τῇ
ean	echēte	tous	exouthenēmenous		en	tē
if	you have,	the	having been least esteemed		in	the

1564.3 noun dat sing fem	3642.8 dem-pron acc pl masc	2495.1 verb 2pl indic pres act	4242.1 prep	1775.1 noun acc sing fem
ἐκκλησίᾳ,	τούτους	καθίζετε;	5. πρὸς	ἐντροπὴν
ekklēsia	toutous	kathizete	pros	entropēn
assembly,	these	set you up.	For	shame

5050.3 prs-pron dat 2pl	2978.1 verb 1sing pres act	3643.1 adv	3620.2 partic	1498.4 verb 3sing indic pres act	1746.1 verb 3sing indic pres act
ὑμῖν	λέγω.	οὕτως	οὐκ	ἔστιν	[a⋆ ἔνι]
humin	legō	houtōs	ouk	estin	eni
to you	I speak.	Thus	not	is there	[there is in]

1706.1 prep	5050.3 prs-pron dat 2pl	4533.1 adj nom sing masc	3624.1 adv	3625.2 num card nom masc
ἐν	ὑμῖν	σοφὸς	οὐδὲ	[b⋆ οὐδεὶς
en	humin	sophos	oude	oudeis
among	you	a wise	not even	[no one

4533.1 adj nom sing masc	1519.1 prep	3614.5 rel-pron nom sing masc	1404.30 verb 3sing indic fut mid	1246.6 verb inf aor act
σοφὸς]	εἷς,	ὃς	δυνήσεται	διακρῖναι
sophos	eis	hos	dunēsetai	diakrinai
wise]	one,	who	shall be able	to decide

301.1 adv	3189.5 adj acc sing neu	3450.2 art gen sing	79.2 noun gen sing masc	840.3 prs-pron gen sing	233.2 conj
ἀνὰ	μέσον	τοῦ	ἀδελφοῦ	αὐτοῦ;	6. ἀλλὰ
ana	meson	tou	adelphou	autou	alla
among	the midst of	the	brother	his?	But

79.1 noun nom sing masc	3196.3 prep	79.2 noun gen sing masc	2892.29 verb 3sing indic pres pass	2504.1 conj	3642.17 dem-pron sing neu
ἀδελφὸς	μετὰ	ἀδελφοῦ	κρίνεται,	καὶ	τοῦτο
adelphos	meta	adelphou	krinetai	kai	touto
brother	with	brother	is being judged,	and	this

1894.3 prep	566.5 adj gen pl masc	2218.1 adv	3173.1 conj	3631.1 conj	3517.1 adv
ἐπὶ	ἀπίστων;	7. ἤδη	μὲν	(a οὖν)	ὅλως
epi	apistōn	ēdē	men	oun	holōs
before	unbelievers!	Already	indeed	therefore	altogether

2253.1 noun nom sing neu	1706.1 prep	5050.3 prs-pron dat 2pl	1498.4 verb 3sing indic pres act	3617.1 conj	2890.4 noun pl neu
ἥττημα	(b ἐν)	ὑμῖν	ἔστιν,	ὅτι	κρίματα
hēttēma	en	humin	estin	hoti	krimata
a failure	among	you	is,	that	lawsuits

2174.2 verb 2pl pres act	3196.1 prep	1431.2 prs-pron gen pl	1296.1 adv	1217.2 prep 4949.9 intr-pron sing neu	3644.1 adv
ἔχετε	μεθ'	ἑαυτῶν	(διατί	[⋆ διὰ τί]	οὐχὶ
echete	meth'	heautōn	diati	dia ti	ouchi
you have	among	yourselves.	Why	[idem]	not

3095.1 adv comp	90.16 verb 2pl indic pres pass	1296.1 adv	1217.2 prep 4949.9 intr-pron sing neu	3644.1 adv
μᾶλλον	ἀδικεῖσθε;	(διατί	[⋆ διὰ τί]	οὐχὶ
mallon	adikeisthe	diati	dia ti	ouchi
rather	suffer wrong?	why	[idem]	not

6:4. The crucial issue here is, who are the "least esteemed (or count for nothing) in the church." The NIV takes *kathizete* as an imperative ("appoint as judges") making people within the church those who are least esteemed. It is much better, however, to take *kathizete* as an indicative and a question ("do you appoint as judges . . . ?") which makes secular judges the object of "least esteemed in the church." Nobody within the church counts for nothing!

Church matters should not be decided by secular judges. That would be foolish. But that is exactly what the Corinthians were allowing. By placing their cases before pagan judges, these men, who were less than the least in the church from a spiritual standpoint, had become their judges. We want the most competent judge that we can find for ourselves. The Corinthians were using the least competent. How foolish indeed!

6:5. To the further shame of the church, they had not even considered the idea of finding a wise man in their own midst to settle judiciary disputes, one who could discern the will of God, who was instructed in the wisdom of God, who was sensitive to the moving of the Spirit of God. An arbiter was needed, one who knew how to settle disputes as God desired. There is a sting here because the Corinthians considered themselves wise, yet they had not considered doing the wise thing.

6:6. This verse answers the previous verse. Brothers fought; wisdom was lacking; evil ruled the day. It was absurd that brothers should dispute like this. Yet it was the natural result where pride was dominant, where self was lifted up, and where love was lacking. Faith was not being built. Paul pointed to a proper answer and attitude, for at the base of their problem was a motivating attitude that was wrong.

If the spirit of a Christian or a church is wrong, it will affect its witness before unbelievers. There will be a misrepresented, misunderstood, and ineffective witness before those the church is seeking to win to Christ.

6:7. This litigation was soundly denounced. "Fault" is properly "defeat" or loss. While lawsuits were not branded as sinful, the nature and boasting behind them proved the Corinthians were defeated Christians. The defeat was proved by the lawsuits. Paul offered a solution and established the proper attitude for a Christian. Christians must serve their brethren (Matthew 20:25-28; John 13:13-20,34,35). Paul's aim was to show that seeking justice, particularly on external things, is not the highest goal; the rule of love is. By this statement Paul revealed the Corinthians' lack of understanding and maturity in Christian principles.

4. If then ye have judgments of things pertaining to this life: . . . have iudgements of worldely matters, *Tyndale* . . . which need to be decided, *Weymouth.*

set them to judge who are least esteemed in the church: . . . let the parties contending choose arbitrators, *Locke* . . . who are of no account, *Hanson* . . . who have been denied authority in the assembly? *Fenton* . . . the most despised, *Douay* . . . the meanest member of your own church is good enough, *Way.*

5. I speak to your shame: Is it so, that there is not a wise man among you?: . . . there is not an intelligent man, *Fenton* . . . not a single wise man, *Moffatt.*

no, not one that shall be able to judge between his brethren?: . . . capable of deciding, *Montgomery* . . . to adjudicate amidst his, *Concordant* . . . competent to settle a case in his brother's matter? *Confraternity.*

6. But brother goeth to law with brother: . . . contendeth in iudgement, *Rheims* . . . but brother is suing, *Concordant* . . . is suing for judgment, *Rotherham.*

and that before the unbelievers: . . . before infidels? *Rheims.*

7. Now therefore there is utterly a fault among you, because ye go to law one with another: . . . there is plainly a fault, *Douay* . . . there is indeed altogether a shortcoming, *PNT* . . . it is total defeat for you, *Rotherham* . . . it is wholly a loss to you, *Worrell* . . . it is a deep degradation to you, *Fenton* . . . altogether a defect, *Montgomery* . . . Even to have lawsuits with one another, *Moffatt.*

Why do ye not rather take wrong?: Why not rather endure injustice? *Weymouth* . . . you not rather being injured? *Concordant* . . . Why not rather endure to be wronged? *Fenton.*

why do ye not rather [suffer yourselves to] be defrauded?: . . . not rather being cheated? *Concordant* . . . why rather susteine ye not harme? *Geneva* . . . Why not rather be swindled? *Fenton.*

1 Corinthians 6:8

3095.1 adv comp	644.3 verb 2pl indic pres pass	233.2 conj	5050.1 prs-pron nom 2pl	90.2 verb 2pl indic pres act	2504.1 conj
μᾶλλον	ἀποστερεῖσθε;	8. ἀλλὰ	ὑμεῖς	ἀδικεῖτε	καὶ
mallon	apostereisthe	alla	humeis	adikeite	kai
rather	be defrauded?	But	you	do wrong	and

	644.1 verb 2pl pres act	2504.1 conj	3642.18 dem-pron pl neu	3642.17 dem-pron sing neu	79.9 noun acc pl masc
	ἀποστερεῖτε,	καὶ	ταῦτα	[a☆ τοῦτο]	ἀδελφούς.
	apostereite	kai	tauta	touto	adelphous
	defraud,	and	these things	[this]	brothers.

8.a.Txt: 020L,byz.
Var: 01⅂,02A,03B,04C
06D,025P,33,Lach,Treg
Alf,Word,Tisc,We/Ho
Weis,Sod,UBS/☆

2211.1 conj	3620.2 partic	3471.6 verb 2pl indic perf act	3617.1 conj	93.3 adj nom pl masc	926.4 noun acc sing fem	2296.2 noun gen sing masc
9. ἢ	οὐκ	οἴδατε	ὅτι	ἄδικοι	βασιλείαν	θεοῦ
ē	ouk	oidate	hoti	adikoi	basileian	theou
Or	not	you know	that	unjust	kingdom	of God

2296.2 noun gen sing masc	926.4 noun acc sing fem	3620.3 partic	2789.11 verb 3pl indic fut act	3231.1 partic
[☆ θεοῦ	βασιλείαν]	οὐ	κληρονομήσουσιν;	Μὴ
theou	basileian	ou	klēronomēsousin	Mē
[of God	kingdom]	not	shall inherit?	Not

3966.11 verb 2pl pres pass	3641.1 conj	4064.2 noun nom pl masc	3641.1 conj	1486.2 noun nom pl masc
πλανᾶσθε·	οὔτε	πόρνοι,	οὔτε	εἰδωλολάτραι,
planasthe	oute	pornoi	oute	eidōlolatrai
be misled;	neither	fornicators,	nor	idolaters,

3641.1 conj	3295.1 noun nom pl masc	3641.1 conj	3092.1 adj nom pl masc	3641.1 conj	727.1 noun nom pl masc
οὔτε	μοιχοὶ,	οὔτε	μαλακοὶ,	οὔτε	ἀρσενοκοῖται,
oute	moichoi	oute	malakoi	oute	arsenokoitai
nor	adulterers,	nor	effeminate,	nor	homosexuals,

10.a.Txt: 03B,06D,020L
byz.
Var: 01⅂,02A,04C,025P
33,Alf,Tisc,We/Ho,Weis
Sod,UBS/☆

3641.1 conj	2785.2 noun nom pl masc	3641.1 conj	3983.2 noun nom pl masc	3641.1 conj	3620.3 partic
10. οὔτε	κλέπται,	οὔτε	πλεονέκται,	οὔτε	[a☆ οὐ]
oute	kleptai	oute	pleonektai	oute	ou
nor	thieves,	nor	covetous,	nor	[not]

3154.2 noun nom pl masc	3620.3 partic	3034.2 noun nom pl masc	3620.1 partic	721.2 adj nom pl masc	926.4 noun acc sing fem
μέθυσοι,	οὐ	λοίδοροι,	οὐχ	ἅρπαγες,	βασιλείαν
methusoi	ou	loidoroi	ouch	harpages	basileian
drunkards,	nor	revilers,	nor	ravenous,	kingdom

10.b.Txt: 020L,025P,byz.
Var: 01⅂,02A,03B,04C
06D,Lach,Treg,Alf,Tisc
We/Ho,Weis,Sod
UBS/☆

2296.2 noun gen sing masc	3620.3 partic	2789.11 verb 3pl indic fut act	2504.1 conj	3642.18 dem-pron pl neu
θεοῦ	b οὐ	κληρονομήσουσιν.	11. καὶ	ταῦτά
theou	ou	klēronomēsousin	kai	tauta
of God	not	shall inherit.	And	these things

4948.7 indef-pron nom pl masc	1498.1 verb 2pl act	233.2 conj	622.1 verb 2pl indic aor mid	233.2 conj
τινες	ἦτε·	ἀλλὰ	ἀπελούσασθε,	ἀλλὰ
tines	ēte	alla	apelousasthe	alla
some	you were;	but	you were washed,	but

37.14 verb 2pl indic aor pass	233.1 conj	233.2 conj	1338.14 verb 2pl indic aor pass	1706.1 prep
ἡγιάσθητε,	ἀλλ᾽	[☆ ἀλλὰ]	ἐδικαιώθητε,	ἐν
hēgiasthēte	all'	alla	edikaiōthēte	en
you were made holy,	but	[idem]	you were justified,	in

320

6:8. Paul pointed out the hatred, self-righteousness, and jealousy in their midst. They were doing wrong to others. They were defrauding their own brothers in Christ. They were not ready to suffer wrong; they were committing wrong. The duty and the fact were leagues apart.

6:9,10. Lumped with the misconduct of the Corinthians were other evidences of unrighteousness, all of which will keep a man from the kingdom of God. The Corinthians had committed sins typical of the unrighteous, reflecting the condition of their hearts. Paul did not suggest they had committed all the sins listed, but he did suggest that by their sin they had joined this unrighteous company. They thought themselves kings (4:8), but they ran the risk of being outside God's kingdom because their spirits reflected the attitude of this world instead of that of Christ.

The list included "fornicators," which involved all trespassers of the seventh commandment; the "effeminate" and "abusers of themselves with mankind" designated passive and active homosexuals respectively; "idolaters" violated the first commandment; "adulterers," a more specific term than "fornicators," violated the seventh commandment also, and in particular the marriage bed. "Thieves" was a general description for robbers or thieves; the "covetous" included those who always lusted after someone else's possessions, although they might not steal.

To this point Paul was attentive to the commandments laid down in Exodus 20. Now he expanded the list somewhat. "Drunkards" consumed alcoholic beverages to excess; "revilers" were those who abused others; and "extortioners" suggested taking by force, violently. There was an air of undisciplined, "me-first" motivation.

Those who do these things have no part in the kingdom of God; the Spirit of Christ is not in them, and the Corinthians were in danger of missing the Kingdom. The list seems to fall into the rough categories of sins against self or against the temple of God and sins against others.

Such implications and associations should have moved the Corinthians to reexamine their actions in the light of God's desires. If they were sensitive at all to the conviction of the Holy Spirit, such potential association should have caused them to reject their desires and seek the Master's will.

6:11. Before their conversion some of these Corinthians were members of this group. Their lives had been changed. "Washed" carries the force of "you go yourselves washed." This could not refer to water baptism, because water cannot cleanse from sin. Others suggest the washing of Revelation 1:5. The tense is past, the aorist referring to a decisive action. "Sanctified" is in the same tense. They were set apart. "Justified" is also an aorist and looked back to the time of their acceptance as righteous before God. "In" indicated both the sphere and ground of these actions. Note the

8. Nay, ye do wrong, and defraud, and that [your] brethren: But ye injure, *Macknight, Sawyer* . . . ye youselves commit wrong, *Murdock* . . . you impose injustice, *Berkeley* . . . and you cheat, and swindle even your brothers, *Fenton* . . . yourselves inflict injustice and fraud, *Weymouth* . . . you inflict wrong and practise frauds, *Moffatt.*

9. Know ye not that the unrighteous shall not inherit the kingdom of God?: . . . that wrongdoers, *Rotherham* . . . that dishonest people, *Berkeley* . . . the unjust will not possess the kingdom, *Confraternity, Douay.*
Be not deceived: neither fornicators, nor idolaters: Cherish no delusion here, *Weymouth* . . . Don't be misled, *Adams* . . . neither profligates, *Berkeley.*
nor adulterers, nor effeminate, nor abusers of themselves with mankind: . . . nether wantons, *Geneva* . . . nor voluptuaries, *HistNT* . . . nor sodomites, *Moffatt* . . . nor sensualists, *Way* . . . guilty of unnatural crime, *Weymouth* . . . nor male prostitutes, *Adams* . . . not liers with mankind, *Douay.*

10. Nor thieves, nor covetous, nor drunkards, nor revilers: . . . nor avaricious people . . . addicted to hard drinking, *Weymouth* . . . greedy person, *Adams* . . . nor misers, *Campbell* . . . nether cursed speakers, *Tyndale* . . . nor the evil-tongued, *Confraternity* . . . nor foulmouthed men, *Way, Montgomery.*
nor extortioners, shall inherit the kingdom of God: . . . nor plunderers, *Fenton* . . . nor robbers, *Adams* . . . will possess, *Confraternity.*

11. And such were some of you: And all this describes what some of you were, *Weymouth.*
but ye are washed: . . . had every stain washed, *Weymouth* . . . but you have washed away your stains, *Conybeare.*
but ye are sanctified: . . . been set apart, *Weymouth* . . . you have been consecrated, *Montgomery* . . . made holy, *Noyes.*

11.a.Txt: p46,01ℵ,02A
06D,08E,020L,byz.
UBS/☆
Var: 03B,04C-vid,025P
33,69,We/Ho

11.b.Var: p11,p46,01ℵ
03B,04C,06D,025P,33
bo.Lach,Treg,Tisc
We/Ho,Weis,Sod
UBS/☆

3450.3 art dat sing	3549.4 noun dat sing neu	3450.2 art gen sing	2935.2 noun gen sing masc	2231.2 prs-pron gen 1pl	2400.2 name masc
τῷ	ὀνόματι	τοῦ	κυρίου	[ᵃ+ ἡμῶν]	Ἰησοῦ,
tō	onomati	tou	kuriou	hēmōn	Iēsou,
the	name	of the	Lord	[our]	Jesus,

5382.2 name gen masc	2504.1 conj	1706.1 prep	3450.3 art dat sing	4011.3 noun dat sing neu	3450.2 art gen sing
[ᵇ☆+ Χριστοῦ]	καὶ	ἐν	τῷ	πνεύματι	τοῦ
Christou	kai	en	tō	pneumati	tou
[Christ]	and	by	the	Spirit	

2296.2 noun gen sing masc	2231.2 prs-pron gen 1pl	3820.1 adj	1466.4 prs-pron dat 1sing	1815.1 verb 3sing indic pres act	233.1 conj
θεοῦ	ἡμῶν.	**12.** Πάντα	μοι	ἔξεστιν,	ἀλλ᾽
theou	hēmōn.	Panta	moi	exestin	all'
of God	our.	All things	to me	are lawful,	but

3620.3 partic	3820.1 adj	4702.1 verb 3sing indic pres act	3820.1 adj	1466.4 prs-pron dat 1sing	1815.1 verb 3sing indic pres act
οὐ	πάντα	συμφέρει·	πάντα	μοι	ἔξεστιν,
ou	panta	sumpherei	panta	moi	exestin
not	all things	do profit;	all things	to me	are lawful,

233.1 conj	3620.2 partic	1466.1 prs-pron nom 1sing	1834.3 verb 1sing indic fut pass	5097.3 prep	4948.1 indef-pron gen sing
ἀλλ᾽	οὐκ	ἐγὼ	ἐξουσιασθήσομαι	ὑπό	τινος.
all'	ouk	egō	exousiasthēsomai	hupo	tinos
but	not	I	will be brought under power	of	any.

3450.17 art pl neu	1026.4 noun pl neu	3450.11 art dat sing fem	2809.3 noun dat sing fem	2504.1 conj	3450.9 art nom sing fem
13. Τὰ	βρώματα	τῇ	κοιλίᾳ,	καὶ	ἡ
Ta	brōmata	tē	koilia	kai	hē
The	foods	for the	stomach,	and	the

2809.1 noun nom sing fem	3450.4 art dat pl	1026.6 noun dat pl neu	3450.5 art sing masc	1156.2 conj	2296.1 noun nom sing masc
κοιλία	τοῖς	βρώμασιν·	ὁ	δὲ	θεὸς
koilia	tois	brōmasin	ho	de	theos
stomach	for the	foods;	ho	but	God

2504.1 conj	3642.12 dem-pron acc sing fem	2504.1 conj	3642.18 dem-pron pl neu	2643.8 verb 3sing indic fut act	3450.16 art sing neu
καὶ	ταύτην	καὶ	ταῦτα	καταργήσει.	τὸ
kai	tautēn	kai	tauta	katargēsei	to
both	this	and	these	will bring to nought:	the

1156.2 conj	4835.1 noun sing neu	3620.3 partic	3450.11 art dat sing fem	4061.3 noun dat sing fem	233.2 conj	3450.3 art dat sing
δὲ	σῶμα	οὐ	τῇ	πορνείᾳ,	ἀλλὰ	τῷ
de	sōma	ou	tē	porneia	alla	tō
but	body	not	for the	fornication,	but	for the

2935.3 noun dat sing masc	2504.1 conj	3450.5 art sing masc	2935.1 noun nom sing masc	3450.3 art dat sing	4835.3 noun dat sing masc	3450.5 art sing masc
κυρίῳ,	καὶ	ὁ	κύριος	τῷ	σώματι·	**14.** ὁ
kuriō	kai	ho	kurios	tō	sōmati	ho
Lord,	and	the	Lord	for the	body.	

1156.2 conj	2296.1 noun nom sing masc	2504.1 conj	3450.6 art acc sing masc	2935.4 noun acc sing masc	1446.5 verb 3sing indic aor act	2504.1 conj
δὲ	θεὸς	καὶ	τὸν	κύριον	ἤγειρεν,	καὶ
de	theos	kai	ton	kurion	ēgeiren	kai
And	God	both	the	Lord	raised up,	and

full names of the Deity which suggest Christ in all His relationships. "The Spirit of our God" points to the source of the keeping power in these relationships. A great deliverance had occurred in their lives.

6:12. Paul concluded his statement by reminding the Corinthians that the body belongs to Christ. "All things are lawful" must have been a common saying in this church. Certainly the Holy Spirit speaking through the apostle Paul did not intend to tell Christians that "anything goes." Rather the Holy Spirit countered that slogan with "but all things are not expedient." In this verse Paul gave a principle of Christian liberty. Although "all things are lawful," there are certain limitations. The truth of this statement is important because it deals with what is possible, but not necessarily best. "All things" cannot be taken in an absolute sense. Paul's intent was to lead the readers to admit the truth of this verse and then later to see their wrong. If the Christian is free to do all things, he is still not free to sin. Limitations to a Christian's liberty are set by consequences and what is right.

Also, the possibility of being brought under the wrong power would limit the sentiment expressed in this verse. The Corinthians thought they were free, but their actions had brought them under the power of sin. The Christian shares the authority of Christ, but that does not give freedom to do all things, even if the right to do them is there.

6:13. God has an express purpose for the body. It may well be the Corinthians had placed fornication on a morally indifferent level, arguing that the presence of bodily appetites was enough reason to gratify them. Perhaps they considered body and soul separate, and since the body was to be done away with, it made little difference what it did. Paul quickly demolishes this viewpoint.

Paul admitted the fact there are certain natural appetites, but relegated them to a particular sphere because they are passing. In due time God will render them inoperative. But the body is not to be so done away with. Nor is fornication, etc., transient. It has a permanent effect. Likewise, the connection is not between body and fornication (as between meats and belly), but between the body and the Lord. "God did not design the body for fornication as He did the belly for food" (Morris, *Tyndale New Testament Commentaries*, 7:100). The body, the physical part of man, belongs to God who created it. The value of the body is increased because of the new birth. It is to be treated with honor; it is for the Lord and needs His help to function properly.

6:14. The potential of the body must be seen. As the Father raised Christ, so shall He raise believers by His power. The em-

but ye are justified in the name of the Lord Jesus, and by the Spirit of our God: . . . you were pardoned in the name, *TCNT* . . . ye were declared righteous, *Rotherham* . . . you have been pronounced righteous, *Way* . . . pronounced free from guilt, *Weymouth.*

12. All things are lawful unto me: I am allowed to do anything, *Beck* . . . I may do anything I want to do, *SEB* . . . is permissible for me, *Williams* . . . I maye do all thynges, *Cranmer.*

but all things are not expedient: . . . are not profitable, *Geneva* . . . not all are good for me, *Moffatt* . . . not everything is good for me, *Norlie* . . . not everything is beneficial, *Berkeley* . . . everything does not benefit, *Fenton* . . . But not everything is useful, *Klingensmith.*

all things are lawful for me: . . . are allowable, *Rotherham.*

but I will not be brought under the power of any: I will not let myself be enslaved by anything, *Norlie* . . . not be deluded by any, *Fenton* . . . I will not be mastered by anything, *Berkeley* . . . not going to let anything master me, *Moffatt.*

13. Meats for the belly, and the belly for meats: Food exists for, *TCNT* . . . Meates are ordeyned for, *Geneva* . . . Foods for the bowels, *Concordant* . . . the stomach craves food, *Norlie* . . . The stomach is supposed to receive food, *SEB.*

but God shall destroy both it and them: God will put an end to both, *TCNT* . . . shall bring to an end, *Alford* . . . will bring to nought, *Clementson* . . . will finally put a stop to both of them, *Williams* . . . God will eventually cause both of them to cease their work, *Norlie.*

Now the body [is] not for fornication: Committing sexual sin is not the purpose, *SEB.*

but for the Lord; and the Lord for the body: . . . for the service of the Lord, *Williams.*

14. And God hath both raised up the Lord: . . . raised the Master to life, *Weymouth.*

1 Corinthians 6:15

14.a.**Txt**: p46-corr1,01ℵ
04C,044,byz.
Var1: p46-corr2,03B
67-corr2,1739
Var2: p11,p46-org,02A
06D,025P,69,88

2231.4 prs-pron acc 1pl	**1809.2** verb 3sing indic fut act	**1809.3** verb 3sing indic aor act	**1809.4** verb 3sing indic pres act		**1217.2** prep
ἡμᾶς	⸂✶ ἐξεγερεῖ	[¹ᵃ ἐξηγείρεν	² ἐξεγείρει]		διὰ
hēmas	exegerei	exēgeiren	exegeirei		dia
us	will raise	[raised	raises]		by

3450.10 art gen sing fem	**1405.2** noun gen sing fem	**840.3** prs-pron gen sing	**3620.2** partic	**3471.6** verb 2pl indic perf act	**3617.1** conj
τῆς	δυνάμεως	αὐτοῦ.	**15.** οὐκ	οἴδατε	ὅτι
tēs	dunameōs	autou.	ouk	oidate	hoti
the	power	his,	Not	know you	that

3450.17 art pl neu	**4835.4** noun pl neu	**5050.2** prs-pron gen 2pl	**3166.2** noun pl neu	**5382.2** name gen masc	**1498.4** verb 3sing indic pres act
τὰ	σώματα	ὑμῶν	μέλη	Χριστοῦ	ἐστιν;
ta	sōmata	humōn	melē	Christou	estin
the	bodies	your	members	of Christ	are?

142.16 verb nom sing masc part aor act	**3631.1** conj	**3450.17** art pl neu	**3166.2** noun pl neu	**3450.2** art gen sing	**5382.2** name gen masc
ἄρας	οὖν	τὰ	μέλη	τοῦ	Χριστοῦ,
aras	oun	ta	melē	tou	Christou,
Having taken	then	the	members	of the	Christ,

4020.21 verb 1sing act	**4063.2** noun gen sing fem	**3166.2** noun pl neu	**3231.1** partic	**1090.44** verb 3sing opt aor mid	**2211.1** conj
ποιήσω	πόρνης	μέλη;	μὴ	γένοιτο.	**16.** ἢ
poiēsō	pornēs	melē	mē	genoito.	ē
shall I make	of a harlot	members?	Not	may it be!	Or

3620.2 partic	**3471.6** verb 2pl indic perf act	**3617.1** conj	**3450.5** art sing masc	**2827.1** verb nom sing masc part pres pass	**3450.11** art dat sing fem	**4063.3** noun dat sing fem
οὐκ	οἴδατε	ὅτι	ὁ	κολλώμενος	τῇ	πόρνῃ,
ouk	oidate	hoti	ho	kollōmenos	tē	pornē,
not	know you	that	the	being joined	to the	harlot,

1518.9 num card neu	**4835.1** noun sing neu	**1498.4** verb 3sing indic pres act	**1498.43** verb 3pl indic fut mid	**1056.1** conj	**5183.2** verb 3sing indic pres act
ἓν	σῶμά	ἐστιν;	Ἔσονται	γάρ,	φησίν,
hen	sōma	estin	Esontai	gar,	phēsin,
one	body	is?	Shall be	for,	he says,

3450.7 art pl masc	**1411.3** num card	**1519.1** prep	**4418.4** noun acc sing fem	**1518.8** num card acc fem	**3450.5** art sing masc	**1156.2** conj
οἱ	δύο	εἰς	σάρκα	μίαν·	**17.** ὁ	δὲ
hoi	duo	eis	sarka	mian·	ho	de
the	two	for	flesh	one.	The	but

2827.1 verb nom sing masc part pres pass	**3450.3** art dat sing	**2935.3** noun dat sing masc	**1518.9** num card neu	**4011.1** noun sing neu	**1498.4** verb 3sing indic pres act
κολλώμενος	τῷ	κυρίῳ,	ἓν	πνεῦμά	ἐστιν.
kollōmenos	tō	kuriō,	hen	pneuma	estin.
being joined	to the	Lord,	one	spirit	is.

5180.3 verb 2pl impr pres act	**3450.12** art acc sing fem	**4061.4** noun acc sing fem	**3820.17** adj sing neu	**263.1** noun nom sing neu
18. Φεύγετε	τὴν	πορνείαν.	πᾶν	ἁμάρτημα
Pheugete	tēn	porneian.	pan	hamartēma
Flee	the	fornication.	Every	sin

3614.16 rel-pron sing neu	**1430.1** partic	**4020.29** verb 3sing subj aor act	**442.1** noun nom sing masc	**1609.1** prep gen	**3450.2** art gen sing
ὃ	ἐὰν	ποιήσῃ	ἄνθρωπος,	ἐκτὸς	τοῦ
ho	ean	poiēsē	anthrōpos,	ektos	tou
which	if	may practice	a man,	outside	the

phasis is on the importance of the body. The destiny of the "belly" and "meats" is destruction. The destiny of the body is the resurrection and eternal life in Christ.

6:15. Paul said the body is the Lord's and cannot function properly without Him, then he made the union more intimate by establishing union with Christ as prohibitive to impurity. Paul asked a question intended to receive a negative answer: Shall I take the members of Christ away and make them members of a prostitute or submit them to sin? Absolutely not! This would involve deliberate alienation and defilement. Moral and spiritual ruin would be caused by such actions.

Paul is emphasizing the intimate and binding relationship between Christ and believers. As the Church is the body of Christ, so the various persons in the Church are members of Christ (verse 20).

6:16. On the other hand, being joined to a prostitute is also a complex union, for it involves physical, mental, and spiritual aspects. One unit is formed. Paul reminded his readers of such passages as Genesis 2:24, Matthew 19:5, and Mark 10:8. The "harlot" is associated with evil, and by this illicit union the union with Christ is damaged or even broken.

6:17. However, a proper relationship with Christ forms a total relationship that affects every part of the individual. It is a proven fact that the mind affects the body and spirit and vice versa. This relationship is on a far higher plane than the first. A man "joined to a harlot" descends to her filthiness. A man "joined unto the Lord" becomes one "spirit" and ascends to heavenly places. The believer's thoughts, desires, and actions become one with His in a spiritual, wondrous union. "Joined" (as in verse 16) is used of close bonds of various kinds. Literally, it refers to the process of gluing. A very close tie is the result.

6:18. Paul's conclusion was based on what has preceded: "Flee fornication." Recall the story of Joseph in Potiphar's house. We have to stand up to and fight some sins, but the answer to this one is flight. The sexual drive is very strong, and we must guard against striking a spark in the passions that would lead to such sin. Other sins which may affect the body, do not wreak the devastation this one does, for this sin aims only at the satisfaction of lust. God's chosen possessions dare not be defiled by such sacrilege. This sin goes against the very nature and purpose of the body. It becomes a self-violation, as well as a sin against God. It demands the partic-

and will also raise up us by his own power: . . . and will also restore us, *Fenton* . . . will He resurrect us, *Berkeley* . . . by His mighty power, *Conybeare* . . . by the exercise of his power, *TCNT.*

15. Know ye not that your bodies are the members of Christ?: Surely you realize, *SEB.*

shall I then take the members of Christ:

and make [them] the members of an harlot?: . . . join them to a prostitute, *Norlie* . . . of a prostitute? *Weymouth.*

God forbid: It could not be, *Worrell* . . . Never! *Moffatt, RSV.*

16. What? know ye not that he which is joined to an harlot is one body?: . . . he who is connected, *Noyes* . . . he who is strongly attached, *Macknight* . . . when one is united with a prostitute, *Norlie* . . . he which coupleth him selfe with an harlot, *Tyndale* . . . who has sex with a whore is one body with her? *SEB* . . . is in union, *Weymouth* . . . that union, *Fenton* . . . is one with her in body, *Moffatt.*

for two, saith he, shall be one flesh: The two shall be physically one, *Williams* . . . They twain shall be one body, *Murdock* . . . shall be united into one flesh, *Locke.*

17. But he that is joined unto the Lord is one spirit: . . . who unites with, *Berkeley* . . . is stongly attached, *Macknight* . . . he that is ioyned vnto the Lord, is one spirite, *Geneva.*

18. Flee fornication: Keep on running from, *Williams* . . . Shrink away from, *Way* . . . Avoid fornication, *Sawyer* . . . Shun immorality! *Moffatt, Norlie* . . . Shun unchastity, *Berkeley* . . . Shun all such immorality, *TCNT* . . . Flee from sexual sin, *Beck.*

Every sin that a man doeth is without the body: Any other sin, *Weymouth* . . . Every crime, *Wilson* . . . The penalty of every sin, *Concordant* . . . The root of sin is not in the body, *Conybeare* . . . is outside the body, *Fenton* . . . is external to the body, *Hanson.*

1 Corinthians 6:19

4835.2 noun gen sing neu	1498.4 verb 3sing indic pres act	3450.5 art sing masc	1156.2 conj	4062.2 verb nom sing masc part pres act
σώματός	ἐστιν·	ὁ	δὲ	πορνεύων,
sōmatos	estin	ho	de	porneuōn
body	is,	the	but	committing fornication,

1519.1 prep	3450.16 art sing neu	2375.4 adj acc sing	4835.1 noun sing neu	262.2 verb 3sing indic pres act	2211.1 conj
εἰς	τὸ	ἴδιον	σῶμα	ἁμαρτάνει.	19. ἢ
eis	to	idion	sōma	hamartanei	ē
against	to	his own	body	sins.	Or

19.a.Txt: p46,01א,03B 04C,06D,010F,012G 018K,025P,630,1739 Var: 02A,020L,044,33 81,104,365,1175,1881 2464,2495

3620.2 partic	3471.6 verb 2pl indic perf act	3617.1 conj	3450.16 art sing neu	4835.1 noun sing neu	3450.17 art pl neu
οὐκ	οἴδατε	ὅτι	ʽ☆ τὸ	σῶμα	[ª τὰ
ouk	oidate	hoti	to	sōma	ta
not	know you	that	the	body	[the

4835.4 noun pl neu	5050.2 prs- pron gen 2pl	3348.1 noun nom sing masc	3450.2 art gen sing	1706.1 prep	5050.3 prs- pron dat 2pl
σώματα]	ὑμῶν	ναὸς	τοῦ	ἐν	ὑμῖν
sōmata	humōn	naos	tou	en	humin
bodies]	your	a temple	of the	in	you

39.2 adj gen sing	4011.2 noun gen sing neu	1498.4 verb 3sing indic pres act	3614.2 rel- pron gen sing	2174.2 verb 2pl pres act	570.3 prep gen
ἁγίου	πνεύματός	ἐστιν,	οὖ	ἔχετε	ἀπὸ
hagiou	pneumatos	estin	hou	echete	apo
Holy	Spirit	is,	which	you have	from

2296.2 noun gen sing masc	2504.1 conj	3620.2 partic	1498.6 verb 2pl indic pres act	1431.2 prs- pron gen 2pl	58.18 verb 2pl indic aor pass
θεοῦ,	καὶ	οὐκ	ἐστὲ	ἑαυτῶν;	20. ἠγοράσθητε
theou	kai	ouk	este	heautōn	ēgorasthēte
God;	and	not	are you	yourself?	you were bought

1056.1 conj	4940.2 noun gen sing fem	1386.14 verb 2pl impr aor act	1205.1 partic	3450.6 art acc sing masc	2296.4 noun acc sing masc
γὰρ	τιμῆς·	δοξάσατε	δὴ	τὸν	θεὸν
gar	timēs	doxasate	dē	ton	theon
for	with a price;	glorify	indeed		God

20.a.Txt: p46,01א,03B 04C,06D,010F,012G 018K,025P,630,1739 Var: 02A,020L,044,33 81,104,365,1175,1881 2464,2495

1706.1 prep	3450.3 art dat sing	4835.3 noun dat sing neu	5050.2 prs- pron gen 2pl	2504.1 conj	1706.1 prep	3450.3 art dat sing
ἐν	τῷ	σώματι	ὑμῶν,	ʽª καὶ	ἐν	τῷ
en	tō	sōmati	humōn	kai	en	tō
in	the	body	your,	and	in	the

4011.3 noun dat sing neu	5050.2 prs- pron gen 2pl	3610.6 rel- pron nom pl neu	1498.4 verb 3sing indic pres act	3450.2 art gen sing	2296.2 noun gen sing masc
πνεύματι	ὑμῶν,	ἅτινά	ἐστιν	τοῦ	Θεοῦ. ʼ
pneumati	humōn	hatina	estin	tou	Theou
spirit	your,	which	are		God's.

1.a.Txt: 02A,06D,018K 020L,025P,byz. Var: 01א,03B,04C,33 Alf,Tisc,We/Ho,Weis Sod,UBS/☆

3875.1 prep	1156.2 conj	3614.1 rel- pron gen pl	1119.9 verb 2pl indic aor act	1466.4 prs- pron dat 1sing	2541.1 adj sing
7:1. Περὶ	δὲ	ὧν	ἐγράψατε	ʽª μοι, ʼ	καλὸν
Peri	de	hōn	egrapsate	moi	kalon
Concerning	now	what things	you wrote	to me:	good

442.3 noun dat sing masc	1129.2 noun gen sing fem	3231.1 partic	674.8 verb inf pres mid	1217.2 prep	1156.2 conj
ἀνθρώπῳ	γυναικὸς	μὴ	ἅπτεσθαι·	2. διὰ	δὲ
anthrōpō	gunaikos	mē	haptesthai	dia	de
for a man	a woman	not	to touch;	on account of	but

ipation of the whole person, for it stems from the heart, the spring of being (Mark 7:18-23). Most of the pagan temples of this part of the world, including the temple of Aphrodite in Corinth, not only condoned it, they encouraged it because it brought profit to them. Though condoned there, it is not to be condoned in the temple of God.

6:19. For the third time in this section, Paul turned to a fact the Corinthian readers should have known: "Know ye not . . . ." The Christian's body is the temple of the Holy Spirit. Filth has no right to be there. Paul referred to the whole Christian Church in 3:16,17; here he was speaking to the individual member in the body of Christ. The Holy Spirit, sent from God, abides within the Christian and purifies the temple. But believers as priests have a part in it also. This temple was purchased by God through the blood of Jesus Christ and is now possessed by Him, with the result that this shrine is owned and possessed by the Holy Spirit. The temple does not draw dignity or purity from itself, but from the God who inhabits it.

6:20. Here we have the basis for the previous verse. "Bought" is an aorist and points to a single decisive action in time past. This view of God as the One purchasing our salvation is the "ransom" theory of atonement. It reminds us of a custom in Paul's day. A slave could save the price of his freedom, pay it into the temple treasury, and be purchased by the god. He then served that god. It should be the Christian's constant goal to glorify God because he has been bought with a great "price." That principle of life applies directly to the body, and it requires immediate obedience.

7:1. The matter introduced here has often been the subject of controversy, partly because some reject its teaching, and partly because some misunderstand what Paul said. An understanding of the context will clear up this misunderstanding. This section was written in response to questions from the Corinthians themselves. This seems to be suggested throughout the letter by the phrase "now concerning." It is important to observe the use of the word "good" here. It denotes a commendable rather than a commanded attitude and refers to sexual relationships within marriage, as we see from "touch a woman." The question was whether or not one should marry. Later in this chapter, Paul offered his major reason for celibacy (verse 32).

Paul wanted the virtues of marriage understood. He was aware of the low moral tide in Corinth and of the dangers of fornication, as chapter 6 discussed.

It must be admitted that some scholars hold to the view that Paul is referring to sexual activity outside of marriage. (See the word study on "haptō" in the *Greek-English Dictionary*.)

but he that committeth fornication sinneth against his own body: . . . when one indulges in sexual immorality, *Norlie* . . . sins against his own constitution, *Fenton* . . . the sinner thereby blasts his own body, *Way*.

19. What? know ye not that your body is the temple of the Holy Ghost: . . . that your members, *Douay* . . . are a sanctuary, *Weymouth*.

[which is] in you, which ye have of God: Holy Spirit is inside you, *SEB* . . . you have as a gift, *Williams* . . . you have received from God, *Moffatt*.

and ye are not your own?:

20. For ye are bought with a price: For ye are dearly bought, *Tyndale* . . . have been redeemed at infinite cost, *Weymouth* . . . bought at a great price, *Confraternity* . . . you cost something, *SEB* . . . and at what a price! *Norlie*.

therefore glorify God in your body: By all means, *Concordant*.

and in your spirit, which are God's: . . . since both are God's, *Conybeare* . . . both of which belong to God, *Norlie*.

1. Now concerning the things whereof ye wrote unto me: Now about the things you wrote, *Beck* . . . The chief business of the foregoing chapters, *Locke* . . . I now deal with the subjects mentioned in your letter, *Weymouth* . . . now to the subjects on which you wrote to me, *TCNT* . . . To come to the subjects of your correspondence, *Berkeley* . . . those questions about which you wrote, *Adams* . . . this is my answer, *Conybeare*.

[It is] good for a man not to touch a woman: . . . the ideal state is abstention from marital intercourse, *Way* . . . it is praiseworthy for a man not to approach, *Murdock* . . . an excellent thing for a man to have no intercourse, *Moffatt* . . . have no intercourse with a woman, *Montgomery* . . . not to be entangling himself, *Rotherham* . . . not to marry, *SEB* . . . to have sex relations, *Beck* . . . to be encumbered with a wife, *Fenton* . . . to abstain altogether from marriage, *Weymouth*.

1 Corinthians 7:3

3450.15 art acc pl fem	4061.1 noun fem	1524.3 adj nom sing masc	3450.12 art acc sing fem	1431.4 prs- pron gen 3sing	1129.4 noun acc sing fem
τὰς	πορνείας	ἕκαστος	τὴν	ἑαυτοῦ	γυναῖκα
tas	porneias	hekastos	tēn	heautou	gunaika
the	fornication	each	the	of himself	wife

2174.14 verb 3sing impr pres act	2504.1 conj	1524.6 adj nom sing fem	3450.6 art acc sing masc	2375.4 adj acc sing	433.4 noun acc sing masc
ἐχέτω,	καὶ	ἑκάστη	τὸν	ἴδιον	ἄνδρα
echetō	kai	hekastē	ton	idion	andra
let have,	and	each	the	her own	husband

2174.14 verb 3sing impr pres act	3450.11 art dat sing fem	1129.3 noun dat sing fem	3450.5 art sing masc	433.1 noun nom sing masc	3450.12 art acc sing fem
ἐχέτω.	3. τῇ	γυναικὶ	ὁ	ἀνὴρ	τὴν
echetō	tē	gunaiki	ho	anēr	tēn
let have.	To the	wife	the	husband	the

3.a.Txt: 018K,020L,byz.
Var: p11,p46,01א,02A
03B,04C,06D,025P,33
sa.bo.Gries,Lach,Treg
Alf,Word,Tisc,We/Ho
Weis,Sod,UBS/⋆

3648.11 verb acc sing fem part pres pass	3646.1 noun acc sing fem	2114.2 noun acc sing fem	586.3 verb 3sing impr pres act
(ὀφειλομένην	[ᵃ⋆ ὀφειλὴν]	εὔνοιαν	ἀποδιδότω·
opheilomenēn	opheilēn	eunoian	apodidotō
being owed	[debt]	benevolence	let render,

3532.1 adv	1156.2 conj	2504.1 conj	3450.9 art nom sing fem	1129.1 noun nom sing fem	3450.3 art dat sing	433.3 noun dat sing masc
ὁμοίως	δὲ	καὶ	ἡ	γυνὴ	τῷ	ἀνδρί.
homoiōs	de	kai	hē	gunē	tō	andri
likewise	and	also	the	wife	to the	husband.

3450.9 art nom sing fem	1129.1 noun nom sing fem	3450.2 art gen sing	2375.2 adj gen sing	4835.2 noun gen sing neu	3620.2 partic
4. ἡ	γυνὴ	τοῦ	ἰδίου	σώματος	οὐκ
hē	gunē	tou	idiou	sōmatos	ouk
The	wife	the	her own	body	not

1834.1 verb 3sing indic pres act	233.1 conj	233.2 conj	3450.5 art sing masc	433.1 noun nom sing masc
ἐξουσιάζει,	(ἀλλ'	[⋆ ἀλλὰ]	ὁ	ἀνήρ·
exousiazei	all'	alla	ho	anēr
has authority over,	but	[idem]	the	husband;

3532.1 adv	1156.2 conj	2504.1 conj	3450.5 art sing masc	433.1 noun nom sing masc	3450.2 art gen sing	2375.2 adj gen sing
ὁμοίως	δὲ	καὶ	ὁ	ἀνὴρ	τοῦ	ἰδίου
homoiōs	de	kai	ho	anēr	tou	idiou
likewise	and	also	the	husband	the	his own

4835.2 noun gen sing neu	3620.2 partic	1834.1 verb 3sing indic pres act	233.1 conj	233.2 conj
σώματος	οὐκ	ἐξουσιάζει,	(ἀλλ'	[⋆ ἀλλὰ]
sōmatos	ouk	exousiazei	all'	alla
body	not	has authority over,	but	[idem]

3450.9 art nom sing fem	1129.1 noun nom sing fem	3231.1 partic	644.1 verb 2pl pres act	238.3 prs-pron acc pl masc	1479.1 conj
ἡ	γυνή.	5. μὴ	ἀποστερεῖτε	ἀλλήλους,	εἰ
hē	gunē	mē	apostereite	allēlous	ei
the	wife.	Not	deprive	one another,	if

3231.1 partic	4948.10 indef- pron sing neu	3252.1 partic	300.1 partic	1523.2 prep gen	4710.1 adj gen sing neu
(μή	τι	[⋆ μήτι]	ἂν	ἐκ	συμφώνου
mē	ti	mēti	an	ek	sumphōnou
not	a certain	[perhaps]		by	consent

7:2. Marriage is an antidote to perversion and lust. A particularly strong type of marriage is meant: "Every man" suggests a monogamous marriage, which is a commandment. This was applied first to the man, then to the woman. There is to be one mate (of the opposite sex). This restricts verse 1 which is only a restriction, not a universal rule. Paul was not downgrading marriage; he was replying within the context of a historical setting and problem. The emphasis was on the avoidance of sin.

It must be remembered that the primary heresy Paul was rebutting in Corinth, which appeared in various guises, was a form of gnosticism. Gnosticism taught that the spirit is good but that anything material or physical is evil. This in turn led to two opposite errors. The first error is that because the body is evil, the body can do anything it wants to, since it is totally unrelated to the spirit and to spiritual things. This error is manifest in chapter 5 where believers in Corinth seem unperturbed by the sexual immorality exhibited by the man sleeping with his father's wife, possibly his stepmother. The other error that arose from this heresy was the view that since the body is evil, the body must be thoroughly subdued and denied. As a result, even good and proper things that God had ordained for people, such as intercourse between married people, were rejected.

This latter error is in view here in chapter 7 where married men, in an effort to be "spiritual," were denying the right of intercourse to their wives. This heresy, and the word *heresy* is to be stressed, is thoroughly condemned by the apostle Paul.

7:3. The marriage contract includes obligations. Both the husband and the wife have duties to each other. Each partner has certain rights that should be respected. This is a mark against the one-sidedness of the Jewish marriage, where the woman was considered so inferior. "Due" involves the idea of a debt or what is owed.

7:4. It is a fair deduction that some members of the Corinthian church advocated sexual abstinence in marriage. This is wrong because it involves needless temptation and can lead to dangerous sins. The husband and wife have some authority over each other. A mutual surrender is involved. The husband, for example, cannot do what he pleases with his body. The wife has rights and privileges and vice versa. In view of the widespread exaltation of celibacy in Corinth, Paul's statements on the indispensability of the sex act in marriage are noteworthy.

7:5. What was stated positively in verse 3 is now stated negatively: Do not "defraud" your mate, for he/she has certain rights over your body. Paul approved separation from sexual intercourse only under certain conditions. It must involve mutual consent; therefore

2. Nevertheless, [to avoid] fornication: . . . to avoyde fornicacion, *Tyndale* . . . to avoyde whordome, *Cranmer* . . . but for fear of unchastity, *Fenton*.
let every man have his own wife, and let every woman have her own husband:

3. Let the husband render unto the wife due benevolence: . . . render his dette to the vvife, *Rheims* . . . should do his duty to his wife, *Fenton* . . . the kindness, *Murdock* . . . must fulfill his obligation, *Adams* . . . the conjugal obligation, *Wilson* . . . her conjugal dues, *Moffatt*.
and likewise also the wife unto the husband:

4. The wife hath not power of her own body, but the husband: The wife has not undisputed control, *Way* . . . is not the sovereign, *Murdock* . . . is not mistress of her own person, *Montgomery* . . . has not the command of her own person, *Campbell* . . . the jurisdiction of her own body, *Concordant* . . . cannot do as she pleases with her body, *Moffatt* . . . controls not her own Body, *Wilson* . . . has not absolute disposal of her own body, *Fenton*.
and likewise also the husband hath not power of his own body, but the wife: . . . does not control, *Hanson* . . . has not dominion over his own body, *Conybeare* . . . is not master of his own person, *Montgomery* . . . the wife has her rights, *Way* . . . has certain rights, *Weymouth*.

5. Defraud ye not one the other: Withdrawe not youre selves one from another, *Tyndale* . . . Withhold not yourselves from one another, *Sawyer* . . . You should not separate from one another, *Fenton, Conybeare* . . . Do not refuse one another, *Weymouth, Clementson* . . . Deny not one another, *Hanson* . . . Do not deprive each other, *Wilson, Confraternity* . . . Do not withhold sexual intercourse from one another, *Moffatt*.
except [it be] with consent for a time: . . . except by agreement, *Adams* . . . by mutual consent for a season, *Clementson*.

5.a.**Txt:** 018K,020L,byz.
Var: 01א,02A,03B,04C 06D,025P,Gries,Lach Treg,Alf,Word,Tisc We/Ho,Weis,Sod UBS/☆

5.b.**Txt:** 01א-corr,018K 020L,byz.
Var: p11,p46,01א-org 02A,03B,04C,06D,025P 33,it.sa.bo.Gries,Lach Treg,Alf,Word,Tisc We/Ho,Weis,Sod UBS/☆

5.c.**Txt:** p46,018K,020L 025P,byz.
Var: 01א,02A,03B,04C 06D,33,Gries,Lach,Treg Alf,Word,Tisc,We/Ho Weis,Sod,UBS/☆

4242.1 prep	2511.4 noun acc sing masc	2419.1 conj	4832.1 verb 2pl subj pres act	4832.3 verb 2pl subj aor act
πρὸς	καιρὸν,	ἵνα	⸂ σχολάζητε	[ᵃ☆ σχολάσητε]
pros	kairon	hina	scholazēte	scholasēte
for	a season,	that	you may be unoccupied	[idem]

3450.11 art dat sing fem	3383.1 noun dat sing fem	2504.1 conj	3450.11 art dat sing fem	4194.3 noun dat sing fem	2504.1 conj	3687.1 adv
⸂ᵇ τῇ	νηστείᾳ	καὶ ⸃	τῇ	προσευχῇ,	καὶ	πάλιν
tē	nēsteia	kai	tē	proseuchē	kai	palin
for the	fasting	and	for the	prayer,	and	again

1894.3 prep	3450.16 art sing neu	840.15 prs-pron sing neu	4755.17 verb 2pl subj pres	1498.1 verb 2pl act	2419.1 conj
ἐπὶ	τὸ	αὐτὸ	⸂ συνέρχησθε,	[ᶜ☆ ἦτε,]	ἵνα
epi	to	auto	sunerchēsthe	ēte	hina
into	the	it	come together,	[may be,]	that

3231.1 partic	3847.3 verb 3sing subj pres act	5050.4 prs-pron acc 2pl	3450.5 art sing masc	4423.1 noun nom sing masc	1217.2 prep
μὴ	πειράζῃ	ὑμᾶς	ὁ	Σατανᾶς	διὰ
mē	peirazē	humas	ho	Satanas	dia
not	may tempt	you		Satan	because of

3450.12 art acc sing fem	190.2 noun acc sing fem	5050.2 prs-pron gen 2pl	3642.17 dem-pron sing neu	1156.2 conj	2978.1 verb 1sing pres act
τὴν	ἀκρασίαν	ὑμῶν.	6. τοῦτο	δὲ	λέγω
tēn	akrasian	humōn	touto	de	legō
the	incontinence	your.	This	but	I say

2567.3 prep	4625.1 noun acc sing fem	3620.3 partic	2567.1 prep	1987.2 noun acc sing fem	2286.1 verb 1sing pres act
κατὰ	συγγνώμην,	οὐ	κατ᾽	ἐπιταγήν.	7. θέλω
kata	sungnōmēn	ou	kat᾽	epitagēn	thelō
by way of	permission,	not	by way of	command.	I wish

7.a.**Txt:** 01א-corr,03B 06D-corr,018K,020L 025P,044,byz.sa.Weis
Var: p46,01א-org,02A 04C,06D-org,33,it.bo. Lach,Treg,Alf,Word Tisc,We/Ho,Sod,UBS/☆

1056.1 conj	1156.2 conj	3820.8 adj acc pl masc	442.9 noun acc pl masc	1498.32 verb inf pres act	5453.1 conj
⸂ γὰρ	[ᵃ☆ δὲ]	πάντας	ἀνθρώπους	εἶναι	ὡς
gar	de	pantas	anthrōpous	einai	hōs
for	[but]	all	men	to be	as

2504.1 conj	1670.3 prs-pron acc 1sing masc	233.1 conj	233.2 conj	1524.3 adj nom sing masc	2375.4 adj acc sing
καὶ	ἐμαυτόν·	⸂ ἀλλ᾽	[☆ ἀλλὰ]	ἕκαστος	ἴδιον
kai	emauton	all᾽	alla	hekastos	idion
even	myself:	but	[idem]	each	his own

7.b.**Txt:** 01א-corr,018K 020L,byz.
Var: 01א-org,02A,03B 04C,06D,025P,33,Lach Treg,Alf,Word,Tisc We/Ho,Weis,Sod UBS/☆

5321.1 noun sing neu	2174.4 verb 3sing indic pres act	2174.4 verb 3sing indic pres act	5321.1 noun sing neu	1523.2 prep gen
⸂ χάρισμα	ἔχει	[☆ ἔχει	χάρισμα]	ἐκ
charisma	echei	echei	charisma	ek
gift	has	[has	gift]	from

2296.2 noun gen sing masc	3614.5 rel-pron nom sing masc	3450.5 art sing masc	3173.1 conj	3643.1 adv	3614.5 rel-pron nom sing masc
θεοῦ,	⸂ ὃς	[ᵇ☆ ὁ]	μὲν	οὕτως,	⸂ ὃς
theou	hos	ho	men	houtōs	hos
God;	which	[the]	men	so,	which

7.c.**Txt:** 01א-corr,018K 020L,byz.
Var: 01א-org,02A,03B 04C,06D,025P,33,Lach Treg,Alf,Word,Tisc We/Ho,Weis,Sod UBS/☆

3450.5 art sing masc	1156.2 conj	3643.1 adv	2978.1 verb 1sing pres act	1156.2 conj	3450.4 art dat pl	22.2 noun dat pl
[ᶜ☆ ὁ]	δὲ	οὕτως.	8. Λέγω	δὲ	τοῖς	ἀγάμοις
ho	de	houtōs	Legō	de	tois	agamois
[the]	and	so.	I say	but	to the	unmarried

it is not really separation. It must be only for a limited time, a fixed, agreed-upon time. It must have a definite purpose: to give oneself to prayer. The Greek includes the article, indicating a specific prayer. Married life may place such demands on a person that such specific prayer cannot be maintained. This is not right. At such times, under the conditions noted above, abstinence would be more profitable (1 Corinthians 7:33-40; 1 Peter 3:7).

Paul added a more general admonition, which was the real reason for his writing. It involved Satan's temptation of the Christian. Satan seeks to trap every Christian. Man was created with a desire to express himself in a sexual manner. This expression is proper in marriage. But Satan tempts people by urging them to express themselves in an illicit manner, such as fornication or adultery. And the temptation to "incontinence" is stronger if such matters are not properly handled in the marriage.

7:6. Paul speaks "by permission." Commandment is the opposite of concession. The crucial issue here has to do with what Paul meant by "this" when he said, "I speak this by permission." Some argue that it refers to 7:2-5, which would mean that Paul was conceding that it is permissible to marry. A second option is that by "this" Paul was referring to the latter portion of verse 5, which would then mean that Paul was conceding the necessity of resuming intercourse, although he was not commanding them to resume it. The first option is perhaps possible, but our discussion thus far has shown the second option to be untenable. Paul did not command Christians to marry. But on the other hand, neither did he reluctantly admit the right to marry. Every Christian has the right to marry, but exercising this right is not compulsory. The best option is to take "this" to refer to all of verse 5 which therefore means that intercourse is a necessity for marriage, and only as a concession to a season of prayer is abstinence allowable.

7:7. The exception is found in a man like Paul himself. The Corinthians knew what and who he was. It seems that Paul was unmarried at this time. Whether he was ever married is a more difficult question, which has not a conclusive answer. This ability, nonetheless, to remain unmarried and refrain from fornication, was due to a special ability and gift from God. It aided in the spread of the gospel (Matthew 19:9-12).

Paul did not exalt himself above any other Christian. God gives as He chooses, in His will and wisdom. This principle will appear again in 1 Corinthians 12. Paul's intention was that the gospel should be preached with great power and that nothing should interfere with it whether one was married or single. Purity and power with God were his goals. Paul may have preferred the celibate state, but he recognized that both marriage and celibacy are acceptable to God. Each person should recognize God's gifts and will for him.

that ye may give yourselves to fasting and prayer: . . . in order to devote yourselves, *Moffatt* . . . you may have leisure for prayer, *HistNT* . . . to leave yourselves free for prayer, *JB*.

and come together again: . . . resume conjugal relations, *Way* . . . may then associate again, *Weymouth*.

that Satan tempt you not for your incontinency: . . . lest the Adversary...because of your deficiency in self-control, *Weymouth* . . . should begin to take advantage of your want, *TCNT* . . . in case Satan should take advantage of your weakness to tempt you, *JB* . . . when you are weak, *Norlie* . . . because you lack self-control, *Confraternity* . . . through your fleshly passions, *Conybeare* . . . through not having enough self-control, *SEB* . . . for your want-of-self-control, *Rotherham* . . . may not tempt you through passion, *Fenton* . . . because of the concupiscence of your body, *Murdock*.

6. But I speak this by permission, [and] not of commandment: From my own knowledge, *SEB* . . . I saye of fauoure, *Cranmer* . . . I am giving this advice, *Norlie* . . . I say this by indulgence, *Rheims, Douay* . . . by way of advice, *Locke* . . . by suggestion, *Sawyer* . . . by way of concession, not by way of injunction, *Rotherham,* . . . not as an injunction, *Concordant, Wilson* . . . not command, *Moffatt* . . . not as a regulation, *Berkeley* . . . not of positive precept, *Murdock* . . . not by a special command, *Fenton*.

7. For I would that all men were even as I myself: . . . that all had my own powers of self-control, *Way* . . . had my own attitude, *Berkeley*.

But every man hath his proper gift of God: . . . has a personal gift, *Rotherham* . . . has his own, *Montgomery* . . . own special gift, *Weymouth, Williams* . . . is endowed with his gift, *Murdock*.

one after this manner, and another after that: . . . one this wise, *Panin* . . . one of this sort, *Adams* . . . one in one direction, *Weymouth, Berkeley* . . . and another with a gift for the opposite, *JB*.

1 Corinthians 7:9

8.a.Txt: 06D-corr,018K 020L,byz.
Var: 01ℵ,02A,03B,04C 06D-org,025P,33,bo. Gries,Lach,Treg,Alf Word,Tisc,We/Ho,Weis Sod,UBS/⋆

2504.1 conj	3450.14 art dat pl fem	5339.5 noun dat pl fem	2541.1 adj sing	840.2 prs-pron dat pl	1498.4 verb 3sing indic pres act
καὶ	ταῖς	χήραις,	καλὸν	αὐτοῖς	⌐a ἐστιν ⌐
kai	*tais*	*chērais*	*kalon*	*autois*	*estin*
and	to the	widows,	good	for them	it is

1430.1 partic	3176.21 verb 3pl subj aor act	5453.1 conj	2476.3 conj		1479.1 conj	1156.2 conj
ἐὰν	μείνωσιν	ὡς	κἀγώ.	**9.**	εἰ	δὲ
ean	*meinōsin*	*hōs*	*kagō*		*ei*	*de*
if	they should remain	as	even I.		If	but

9.a.Txt: 02A,04C,018K 020L,025P,byz.Sod
Var: 01ℵ,03B,06D,33 Lach,Treg,Tisc,We/Ho Weis,UBS/⋆

3620.2 partic	1460.2 verb 3pl indic pres	1053.11 verb 3pl impr aor act	2882.6 adj comp sing neu
οὐκ	ἐγκρατεύονται,	γαμησάτωσαν·	⌐ κρεῖσσον
ouk	*enkrateuontai*	*gamēsatōsan*	*kreisson*
not	they have self control,	let them marry;	better

9.b.Txt: 01ℵ-corr,03B 04C-corr,06D,018K 020L,025P,byz.Weis
Var: 01ℵ-org,02A 04C-org,33,Tisc,We/Ho Sod,UBS/⋆

2882.5 adj comp sing neu	1056.1 conj	1498.4 verb 3sing indic pres act	1053.14 verb inf aor act	1053.5 verb inf pres act
[a⋆ κρεῖττον]	γὰρ	ἐστιν	⌐ γαμῆσαι	[b γαμεῖν]
kreitton	*gar*	*estin*	*gamēsai*	*gamein*
[idem]	for	it is	to marry	[idem]

2211.1 conj	4306.3 verb inf pres pass	3450.4 art dat pl	1156.2 conj	1053.15 verb dat pl masc part perf act
ἢ	πυροῦσθαι.	**10.** Τοῖς	δὲ	γεγαμηκόσιν
ē	*purousthai*	*Tois*	*de*	*gegamēkosin*
than	to be burned.	To the	but	having married

3715.1 verb 1sing indic pres act	3620.2 partic	1466.1 prs-pron nom 1sing	233.1 conj	233.2 conj	3450.5 art sing masc
παραγγέλλω,	οὐκ	ἐγώ,	⌐ ἀλλ'	[⋆ ἀλλὰ]	ὁ
parangellō	*ouk*	*egō*	*all'*	*alla*	*ho*
I charge,	not	I,	but	[idem]	the

2935.1 noun nom sing masc	1129.4 noun acc sing fem	570.3 prep gen	433.2 noun gen sing masc	3231.1 partic	5398.10 verb inf aor pass
κύριος,	γυναῖκα	ἀπὸ	ἀνδρὸς	μὴ	χωρισθῆναι
kurios	*gunaika*	*apo*	*andros*	*mē*	*chōristhēnai*
Lord,	wife	from	husband	not	to be separated;

1430.1 partic	1156.2 conj	2504.1 conj	5398.8 verb 3sing subj aor pass	3176.9 verb 3sing impr pres act	22.1 noun nom sing
11. ἐὰν	δὲ	καὶ	χωρισθῇ,	μενέτω	ἄγαμος,
ean	*de*	*kai*	*chōristhē*	*menetō*	*agamos*
if	but	also	she be separated,	let her remain	unmarried,

2211.1 conj	3450.3 art dat sing	433.3 noun dat sing masc	2614.4 verb 3sing impr aor pass	2504.1 conj	433.4 noun acc sing masc
ἢ	τῷ	ἀνδρὶ	καταλλαγήτω·	καὶ	ἄνδρα
ē	*tō*	*andri*	*katallagētō*	*kai*	*andra*
or	to the	husband	be reconciled;	and	husband

1129.4 noun acc sing fem	3231.1 partic	856.7 verb inf pres act	3450.4 art dat pl	1156.2 conj	3036.2 adj dat pl
γυναῖκα	μὴ	ἀφιέναι.	**12.** Τοῖς	δὲ	λοιποῖς
gunaika	*mē*	*aphienai*	*Tois*	*de*	*loipois*
wife	not	to leave.	To the	but	rest

1466.1 prs-pron nom 1sing	2978.1 verb 1sing pres act	2978.1 verb 1sing pres act	1466.1 prs-pron nom 1sing	3620.1 partic	3450.5 art sing masc
⌐ ἐγώ	λέγω,	[⋆ λέγω	ἐγώ,]	οὐχ	ὁ
egō	*legō*	*legō*	*egō*	*ouch*	*ho*
I	say,	[say	I,]	not	the

7:8. Having established basic principles regarding marriage, Paul now applied these principles to individual situations. He spoke first to the unmarried and widows. "Unmarried" probably refers to unmarried men, the article being masculine, and the widows are especially mentioned because of their dependence and vulnerability. The principle of verse 1 is seen. It is good for them to remain as they are—unmarried.

7:9. The controlling rule depends on the gift of continence. Otherwise, "let them marry" appears as a command, not as permission. It is better to marry than to continually burn with sexual desire. Paul did not regard the suppression of sexual desire as meritorious in itself. There had to be a greater purpose. "To burn" is in the present, indicating a continuous urge, while the answer lies in the single definite act of marriage. The principle is that whatever is morally better, within God's call, should be the determining factor.

7:10. Paul turned his attention next to those who had Christian marriages. This time Paul gave his advice on the basis of a direct command of the Lord (Matthew 5:32; Mark 10:11,12). He was emphasizing the correct attitudes believers should have toward marriage.

Paul mentioned the wife first. In the gospel passages referred to, Christ was speaking primarily to Jews. In that society it was the husband who put away his wife, not the wife her husband. In Corinth, women were more liberated. Paul wanted it understood that neither partner had the right to leave.

7:11. If a woman did depart, however, one of two things should happen. Paul was not approving divorce here; instead he was saying if it happened in spite of everything done to prevent it, the wife must remain alone or be reconciled to her husband. He offered no other alternatives. Reconciliation would probably have to begin with the party who did the departing or divorcing. God made one husband for one wife, and anything contrary was, in this setting, breaking Christ's command.

Similarly the husband was not to separate from his wife. The verb is different but the result is the same.

7:12. Paul now began his application of the principles already cited to what he termed the "rest," which specifically involved various mixed marriage relationships, that is, where a believer and an unbeliever were married. He expressly dealt with a situation where the unbeliever was willing to continue the marriage relationship.

8. I say therefore to the unmarried and widows: ... to single people, *SEB*.

It is good for them if they abide even as I: ... that it is ideal, *Concordant* ... that it is advantageous, *Murdock* ... would be a fine thing, *Williams* ... if they so continue, *Douay* ... is an excellent thing if like me they remain as they are, *Moffatt*.

9. But if they cannot contain, let them marry: But if they have not the gift of continency, *Locke* ... are not excercising self-control, *Montgomery* ... have not self-restraint, *Fenton* ... cannot control themselves, *Wilson*.

for it is better to marry than to burn: ... preferred to the flames of lust, *Locke* ... than to be on fire, *Concordant* ... than to be incontinent, *Sawyer* ... than to be feverish, *Fenton* ... than the fever of passion, *Weymouth* ... than be aflame with passion, *Moffatt* ... to be burning with sexual desire, *SEB*.

10. And unto the married I command, [yet] not I, but the Lord: ... to them that be ioyned in matrimonie, *Rheims* ... I give charge, *Rotherham* ... I give this authoritative instruction, *Wilson* ... but by the Lord's inspiration, *Way*.

Let not the wife depart from [her] husband: ... not to separate, *Moffatt* ... be separated from, *Cranmer*.

11. But and if she depart, let her remain unmarried: ... or if she has already left him, *Weymouth* ... remain without a husband, *Murdock* ... remain single, *Moffatt*.

or be reconciled to [her] husband: ... or be conciliated, *Concordant* ... or let her return, *Fenton* ... or come back to, *SEB*.

and let not the husband put away [his] wife:

12. But to the rest speak I, not the Lord: To other people, *Moffatt* ... To the remnant, *Geneva* ... on my own private judgment, *Way* ... The rest is from me and not from the Lord, *JB*.

1 Corinthians 7:13

2935.1 noun nom sing masc	1479.1 conj	4948.3 indef-pron nom sing	79.1 noun nom sing masc	1129.4 noun acc sing fem	2174.4 verb 3sing indic pres act
κύριος,	εἰ	τις	ἀδελφὸς	γυναῖκα	ἔχει
kurios	ei	tis	adelphos	gunaika	echei
Lord,	If	any	brother	wife	has

566.1 adj sing	2504.1 conj	840.9 prs-pron nom sing fem	3642.9 dem-pron nom sing fem	4759.1 verb 3sing indic pres act
ἄπιστον,	καὶ	⸀ αὐτὴ	[✶ αὕτη]	συνευδοκεῖ
apiston	kai	autē	hautē	suneudokei
an unbelieving,	and	she	[this]	consents

3474.4 verb inf pres act	3196.2 prep	840.3 prs-pron gen sing	3231.1 partic	856.6 verb 3sing impr pres act	840.12 prs-pron acc sing fem
οἰκεῖν	μετ'	αὐτοῦ,	μὴ	ἀφιέτω	αὐτήν·
oikein	met'	autou	mē	aphietō	autēn
to dwell	with	him,	not	let him leave	her.

13.a.**Txt:** 02A,03B 06D-corr2,044,byz. **Var:** p46,01ℵ,06D-org 012G,025P,sa.

2504.1 conj	1129.1 noun nom sing fem	3610.3 rel-pron nom sing fem	1479.1 conj	4948.3 indef-pron nom sing	2174.4 verb 3sing indic pres act
13. καὶ	γυνὴ	⸀ ἥτις	[a✶ εἴ	τις]	ἔχει
kai	gunē	hētis	ei	tis	echei
And	a woman	who	[if	someone]	has

13.b.**Txt:** 06D-corr,018K 020L,byz. **Var:** p11,01ℵ,02A,03B 04C,06D-org,025P,bo. Lach,Treg,Alf,Word Tisc,We/Ho,Weis,Sod UBS/✶

433.4 noun acc sing masc	566.1 adj sing	2504.1 conj	840.5 prs-pron nom sing masc	3642.4 dem-pron nom sing masc
ἄνδρα	ἄπιστον,	καὶ	⸀ αὐτὸς	[b✶ οὗτος]
andra	apiston	kai	autos	houtos
husband	an unbelieving,	and	he	[this]

4759.1 verb 3sing indic pres act	3474.4 verb inf pres act	3196.2 prep	840.10 prs-pron gen sing fem	3231.1 partic	856.6 verb 3sing impr pres act
συνευδοκεῖ	οἰκεῖν	μετ'	αὐτῆς,	μὴ	ἀφιέτω
suneudokei	oikein	met'	autēs	mē	aphietō
consents	to dwell	with	her,	not	let her leave

13.c.**Txt:** 018K,020L 025P,byz. **Var:** p11,01ℵ,02A,03B 04C,06D,33,bo.Lach Treg,Alf,Word,Tisc We/Ho,Weis,Sod UBS/✶

840.6 prs-pron acc sing masc	3450.6 art acc sing masc	433.4 noun acc sing masc	37.16 verb 3sing indic perf pass	1056.1 conj
⸀ αὐτόν.	[c✶ τὸν	ἄνδρα.]	**14.** ἡγίασται	γὰρ
auton	ton	andra	hēgiastai	gar
him.	[the	husband.]	Is made holy	for

3450.5 art sing masc	433.1 noun nom sing masc	3450.5 art sing masc	566.2 adj sing	1706.1 prep	3450.11 art dat sing fem
ὁ	ἀνὴρ	ὁ	ἄπιστος	ἐν	τῇ
ho	anēr	ho	apistos	en	tē
the	husband	the	unbelieving	in	the

14.a.**Var:** 06D,010F 012G,629

1129.3 noun dat sing fem	3450.11 art dat sing fem	3963.5 noun dat sing fem	2504.1 conj	37.16 verb 3sing indic perf pass	3450.9 art nom sing fem
γυναικί,	[a+ τῇ	πίστῃ]	καὶ	ἡγίασται	ἡ
gunaiki	tē	pistē	kai	hēgiastai	hē
wife,	[by the	faith]	and	is made holy	the

1129.1 noun nom sing fem	3450.9 art nom sing fem	566.2 adj sing	1706.1 prep	3450.3 art dat sing	433.3 noun dat sing masc
γυνὴ	ἡ	ἄπιστος	ἐν	τῷ	⸀ ἀνδρί·
gunē	hē	apistos	en	tō	andri
wife	the	unbelieving	in	the	husband;

14.b.**Txt:** 01ℵ-corr 06D-corr,018K,020L byz. **Var:** p46,01ℵ-org,02A 03B,04C,06D-org,025P 33,sa.bo.Lach,Treg,Alf Word,Tisc,We/Ho,Weis Sod,UBS/✶

79.3 noun dat sing masc	1878.1 conj	679.1 partic	3450.17 art pl neu	4891.4 noun pl neu	5050.2 prs-pron gen 2pl	167.5 adj pl neu
[b✶ ἀδελφῷ·]	ἐπεὶ	ἄρα	τὰ	τέκνα	ὑμῶν	ἀκάθαρτά
adelphō	epei	ara	ta	tekna	humōn	akatharta
[brother;]	else	then	the	children	your	unclean

It also apparently referred to one partner who became a believer after marriage. There is no legitimate basis for a Christian marrying a non-Christian in order to win him to the Lord.

Paul said, " . . . speak I, not the Lord." Verse 10 carries an express command of Christ. Here Paul did not have such words of Christ directly; but he was speaking by divine authority and under the inspiration of the Holy Spirit.

7:13. Some Corinthians thought it was necessary to divorce a mate when the latter remained pagan. There was concern that such pagan contact would defile the new Christian. But "if he be pleased" or content rendered this action unnecessary and even forbidden. The decision of the believer depended on the attitude of the pagan partner.

In a mixed marriage, the believing partner is not to take the initiative for a divorce. The reason for this is given in 7:14-16. Verse 14 speaks of the believing partner sanctifying the other spouse, and verse 16 speaks of the possibility of the other spouse being saved by the believing partner. This does not mean, of course, that a marriage partner is automatically converted by a believing spouse; rather, it means that the believing partner's Christian life will influence the other partner.

7:14. Paul offered an explanation for what he had said. He referred to a sanctifying influence, which pertained to a certain relationship to God, not moral uprightness. It did not mean the unbeliever was holy before God in Christ. He used the word in the same sense in 1 Timothy 4:5. The believer was set apart to God. His relation to God was not diminished because before believing he married an unbeliever. Rather, the believer exerts an influence on the unbelieving partner and the home. If they live together in love, the unbeliever showed externally that he belonged with believers. Being one flesh with the believer is very important for the unbeliever. Such scriptural blessings from a fellowship with God also extended to others, not just to the immediate recipients (Genesis 15:18; 17:7; 18:26; 1 Kings 15:4; Isaiah 37:4).

The children of such a union also served as examples. Through the sanctified life of the believer the children would be brought into contact with Christian influences. Until the age when a child was able to make a personal decision in the matter, his life was influenced and to an extent controlled by the faith of his parents. Indeed, the believing partner exerted a holy, sanctifying influence on the whole family. This did not mean that each member of the family automatically had a personal relationship or salvation experience with Jesus Christ. That remained in the domain of personal choice. But it did mean that a holy influence was brought to bear on the members of the family, and they enjoyed some of the blessings of a Christian presence.

If any brother hath a wife that believeth not: . . . haue an vnfeithful wiif, *Wyclif* . . . an infidel, *Rheims.*

and she be pleased to dwell with him, let him not put her away: . . . if she agrees to, *Adams* . . . yf she be content to dwell, *Tyndale* . . . consents to live, *Moffatt* . . . is well pleased, *Rotherham* . . . she approves of making a home, *Concordant* . . . is willing to live with him, *Norlie* . . . and she agrees to live with him, *Fenton* . . . let him not dismiss her, *HistNT* . . . he must not divorce her, *Williams* . . . he should not divorce her, *TCNT* . . . he must not send her away, *JB.*

13. And the woman which hath an husband that believeth not, and if he be pleased to dwell with her, let her not leave him: . . . but he likes being married to her, *SEB* . . . he agrees to live with her, *Beck* . . . he consents to live with her, *Confraternity* . . . to dwell with her, *HistNT* . . . let her not forsake, *Murdock* . . . let her not separate from him, *Weymouth* . . . put her husband away, *Moffatt.*

14. For the unbelieving husband is sanctified by the wife: An unbelieving man married to such a woman serves a holy purpose, *Beck* . . . is hallowed, *Concordant* . . . is, so to speak, sanctified, *Norlie* . . . has become holy, *Rotherham* . . . has become consecrated, *TCNT* . . . is made one with the saints through his wife, *JB* . . . is purified, *Fenton* . . . is consecrated, *Moffatt* . . . consecrated through union, *Montgomery* . . . by union, *Williams.*

and the unbelieving wife is sanctified by the husband: . . . is halowid bi, *Wyclif* . . . is made acceptable to God by being united to her Christian husband, *TEV.*

else were your children unclean; but now are they holy: . . . or else the children would be defiled; but now they are pure, *Fenton, Murdock* . . . are im-

1498.4 verb 3sing indic pres act
ἐστιν,
estin
are,

3431.1 adv
νῦν
nun
now

1156.2 conj
δὲ
de
but

39.16 adj pl neu
ἅγιά
hagia
holy

1498.4 verb 3sing indic pres act
ἐστιν.
estin
are.

15. **1479.1** conj
εἰ
ei
If

1156.2 conj
δὲ
de
but

3450.5 art sing masc
ὁ
ho
the

566.2 adj sing
ἄπιστος
apistos
unbeliever

5398.4 verb 3sing indic pres pass
χωρίζεται,
chōrizetai
separates himself,

5398.5 verb 3sing impr pres pass
χωριζέσθω·
chōrizesthō
let him separate himself;

3620.3 partic
οὐ
ou
not

1396.5 verb 3sing indic perf pass
δεδούλωται
dedoulōtai
having been bound

3450.5 art sing masc
ὁ
ho
the

79.1 noun nom sing masc
ἀδελφὸς
adelphos
brother

2211.1 conj
ἢ
ē
or

3450.9 art nom sing fem
ἡ
hē
the

78.1 noun nom sing fem
ἀδελφὴ
adelphē
sister

1706.1 prep
ἐν
en
in

3450.4 art dat pl
τοῖς
tois
the

4955.3 dem-pron dat pl
τοιούτοις·
toioutois
such,

1706.1 prep
ἐν
en
in

1156.2 conj
δὲ
de
but

1503.3 noun dat sing fem
εἰρήνῃ
eirēnē
peace

2535.19 verb 3sing indic perf act
κέκληκεν
keklēken
has called

2231.4 prs-pron acc 1pl
⌐ ἡμᾶς
hēmas
us

5050.4 prs-pron acc 2pl
[a⋆ ὑμᾶς]
humas
[you]

3450.5 art sing masc
ὁ
ho
the

2296.1 noun nom sing masc
θεός.
theos
God.

15.a.**Txt:** p46,01ℵ-corr 03B,06D,020L,044,byz. it.sa.Weis
Var: 01ℵ-org,02A,04C 018K,bo.Tisc,We/Ho Sod,UBS/⋆

16. **4949.9** intr-pron sing neu
τί
ti
What

1056.1 conj
γὰρ
gar
for

3471.3 verb 2sing indic perf act
οἶδας,
oidas
know you,

1129.5 noun voc sing fem
γύναι,
gunai
wife,

1479.1 conj
εἰ
ei
if

3450.6 art acc sing masc
τὸν
ton
the

433.4 noun acc sing masc
ἄνδρα
andra
husband

4834.12 verb 2sing indic fut act
σώσεις;
sōseis
you shall save?

2211.1 conj
ἢ
ē
or

4949.9 intr-pron sing neu
τί
ti
what

3471.3 verb 2sing indic perf act
οἶδας,
oidas
know you,

433.5 noun voc sing masc
ἄνερ,
aner
husband,

1479.1 conj
εἰ
ei
if

3450.12 art acc sing fem
τὴν
tēn
the

1129.4 noun acc sing fem
γυναῖκα
gunaika
wife

4834.12 verb 2sing indic fut act
σώσεις;
sōseis
you shall save?

17. Εἰ **1479.1** conj
Ei
If

3231.1 partic
μὴ
mē
not

1524.4 adj dat sing masc
ἑκάστῳ
hekastō
to each

17.a.**Txt:** 01ℵ-corr,02A 04C,06D,018K,020L,etc. byz.Sod
Var: 01ℵ-org,03B,Treg Tisc,We/Ho,Weis UBS/⋆

5453.1 conj
ὡς
hōs
as

3177.1 verb 3sing indic aor act
⌐ ἐμέρισεν
emerisen
divided

3177.7 verb 3sing indic perf act
[a μεμέρικεν]
memeriken
[has divided]

3450.5 art sing masc
⌐ ὁ
ho
the

2296.1 noun nom sing masc
Θεός,
Theos
God,

17.b.**Txt:** 018K,020L,byz.
Var: 01ℵ,02A,03B,04C 06D,bo.Gries,Lach,Treg Alf,Word,Tisc,We/Ho Weis,Sod,UBS/⋆

3450.5 art sing masc
[b⋆ ὁ
ho
[the

2935.1 noun nom sing masc
κύριος,]
kurios
Lord,]

1524.1 adj sing
ἕκαστον
hekaston
each

5453.1 conj
ὡς
hōs
as

2535.19 verb 3sing indic perf act
κέκληκεν
keklēken
has called

17.c.**Txt:** 018K,020L,byz.
Var: 01ℵ,02A,03B,04C 06D,bo.Gries,Lach,Treg Alf,Word,Tisc,We/Ho Weis,Sod,UBS/⋆

3450.5 art sing masc
⌐ ὁ
ho
the

2935.1 noun nom sing masc
κύριος,
kurios
Lord,

3450.5 art sing masc
[c⋆ ὁ
ho
[

2296.1 noun nom sing masc
θεός,]
theos
[God,]

3643.1 adv
οὕτως
houtōs
so

7:15. But the unbeliever could choose not to remain with the believing partner. The fact that the unbeliever is the subject places the full burden of separation on his shoulders. "Depart" is in the middle voice—"take himself off." If the unbeliever chose not to abide willingly and peacefully with the believer but to depart, he should be allowed to go. In such cases the believer was not under bondage. The question of remarriage did not technically appear here. On the basis of verse 11, it would seem that for the divorced to remain unmarried was the proper course. The divine Author of Scripture who inspired Paul would not contradict a command of Christ, who allowed divorce only on the grounds of unfaithfulness. Some believe, however, that if the unbeliever formed a new union then the exception of Matthew 5:32 would come into play and the divorced believer might remarry a believer.

The Christian spouse now forsaken was free from the former yoke. What should be the guiding attitude? A desire for peace. The work of Christ resulted in peace with God, as Romans 5:1 tells us. This causes internal peace to prevail in all aspects of life.

7:16. Some would argue that the marriage should be preserved because the unbelieving partner might be saved. But Paul said this is uncertain, and marriage is more than a tool of evangelism. Conflict causes tension and frustration and the aim should be peace. The argument of this verse hinges on the "if" (*ei* in Greek), which should probably be interpreted or translated as "whether." Salvation requires a personal decision. Paul did not exclude the possibility of the unbeliever's salvation at any time here. The emphasis was on the believer and maintaining inner peace (verse 15). Marriage is an intimate, deep, lasting relationship that joins spirit as well as body. Ultimately, a relationship with God is individual and must take priority.

Paul was not advocating divorce or separation. He listed certain qualifications, and this was the last possible move after all steps had been taken to maintain the relationship under God, and after the conscience had been totally absolved of blame. The situation was specifically limited and again the unbeliever must initiate the action.

7:17. In summary, Paul reminded the Corinthians of what he had been saying and allowed an enlargement of this basic principle to apply to all of life. One must remain in one's calling. In Corinth, there had been a disregard for the Christian's station in life. Paul called them back to contentment and service.

God both calls and maintains. He distributes blessings and gifts. "Hath distributed" implies God's governing influence. In the marriage relationship, freedom is not license. Opposed to liberty is the fact that the Christian has certain marital obligations, including the maintenance of one's present state as normal Christian practice.

pure, *Rotherham* . . . in reality they have a place among God's people, *Weymouth* . . . they belong to God, *TCNT*.

15. But if the unbelieving depart, let him depart: . . . the unbelieving companion, *Sawyer* . . . be determined to leave, *Montgomery* . . . be determined to separate, *Moffatt* . . . seeks for separation, *Conybeare* . . . let the separation take place, *Way* . . . let him separate, *Adams*.

A brother or a sister is not under bondage in such [cases]: . . . is not subject to servitude, *Rheims* . . . is not enslaved, *Concordant* . . . is not under servitude, *Douay* . . . is not tied to marriage, *Moffatt* . . . is not bound to remain under the yoke, *Conybeare* . . . is not enslaved in such a case, *Locke* . . . is fettered in such a case, *Way*.

but God hath called us to peace:

16. For what knowest thou, O wife, whether thou shalt save [thy] husband?: For what assurance have you, *Weymouth* . . . What reasonable expectation have you, *Way* . . . you might convert, *SEB* . . . whether thou wilt procure life, *Murdock*.

or how knowest thou, O man, whether thou shalt save [thy] wife?:

17. But as God hath distributed to every man: The Lord has given a role to each person, *SEB* . . . the Lord has imparted to each one, *Sawyer* . . . has apportioned to each, *Wilson* . . . originally allotted to him, *Way* . . . whatever be the condition in life, *Weymouth* . . . whatever be the lot in life, *Montgomery* . . . assigned him by the Lord, *Moffatt*.

as the Lord hath called every one, so let him walk: . . . let each man walk in the same path which God alloted, *Conybeare* . . . walk as the Lord has assigned him, *Adams* . . . everyone must lead the lot, *Moffatt* . . . continue to walk in the lot which the Lord appointed him, *Noyes* . . . when he heard God's call, *Way*.

3906.10 verb 3sing impr pres act	2504.1 conj	3643.1 adv	1706.1 prep	3450.14 art dat pl fem	1564.7 noun dat pl fem
περιπατείτω·	καὶ	οὕτως	ἐν	ταῖς	ἐκκλησίαις
peripateitō	kai	houtōs	en	tais	ekklēsiais
let him walk;	and	thus	in	the	assemblies

3820.15 adj dat pl fem	1293.5 verb 1sing indic pres mid	3919.12 verb nom sing masc part perf pass	4948.3 indef-pron nom sing
πάσαις	διατάσσομαι.	**18.** περιτετμημένος	τις
pasais	diatassomai	peritetmēmenos	tis
all	I order.	Having been circumcised	anyone

2535.37 verb 3sing indic aor pass	3231.1 partic	1970.1 verb 3sing impr pres	1706.1 prep	201.3 noun dat sing fem
ἐκλήθη;	μὴ	ἐπισπάσθω.	ἐν	ἀκροβυστίᾳ
eklēthē	mē	epispasthō	en	akrobustia
was called?	not	let him be uncircumcised:	in	uncircumcision

4948.3 indef-pron nom sing	2535.37 verb 3sing indic aor pass	2535.55 verb 3sing indic perf pass	4948.3 indef-pron nom sing	3231.1 partic
⸂ τις	ἐκλήθη;	[ᵃ☆ κέκληταί	τις;]	μὴ
tis	eklēthē	keklētai	tis	mē
anyone	was called?	[has been called	anyone?]	not

18.a.**Txt**: 06D-corr,018K 020L,byz.
Var: 01ℵ,02A,03B,025P 33,Lach,Treg,Alf,Word Tisc,We/Ho,Weis,Sod UBS/☆

3919.6 verb 3sing impr pres pass	3450.9 art nom sing fem	3921.1 noun nom sing fem	3625.6 num card neu	1498.4 verb 3sing indic pres act
περιτεμνέσθω.	**19.** ἡ	περιτομὴ	οὐδέν	ἐστιν,
peritemnesthō	hē	peritomē	ouden	estin
let him be circumcised.	The	circumcision	nothing	is,

2504.1 conj	3450.9 art nom sing fem	201.1 noun nom sing fem	3625.6 num card neu	1498.4 verb 3sing indic pres act	233.2 conj
καὶ	ἡ	ἀκροβυστία	οὐδέν	ἐστιν,	ἀλλὰ
kai	hē	akrobustia	ouden	estin	alla
and	the	uncircumcision	nothing	is,	but

4932.1 noun nom sing fem	1769.5 noun gen pl fem	2296.2 noun gen sing masc	1524.3 adj nom sing masc	1706.1 prep
τήρησις	ἐντολῶν	θεοῦ.	**20.** ἕκαστος	ἐν
tērēsis	entolōn	theou	hekastos	en
keeping	commandments	God's.	Each	in

3450.11 art dat sing fem	2794.3 noun dat sing fem	3614.11 rel-pron dat sing fem	2535.37 verb 3sing indic aor pass	1706.1 prep
τῇ	κλήσει	ᾗ	ἐκλήθη,	ἐν
tē	klēsei	hē	eklēthē	en
the	calling	in which	he was called,	in

3642.11 dem-pron dat sing fem	3176.9 verb 3sing impr pres act	1395.1 noun nom sing masc	2535.36 verb 2sing indic aor pass
ταύτῃ	μενέτω.	**21.** δοῦλος	ἐκλήθης;
tautē	menetō	doulos	eklēthēs
this	let him remain.	Slave	were you called,

3231.1 partic	4622.3 prs-pron dat 2sing	3169.2 verb 3sing impr pres act	233.1 conj	1479.1 conj	2504.1 conj
μή	σοι	μελέτω·	ἀλλ'	εἰ	καὶ
mē	soi	meletō	all'	ei	kai
not	to you	let it be a care;	but	if	and

1404.3 verb 2sing indic pres	1645.1 adj nom sing masc	1090.63 verb inf aor mid	3095.1 adv comp	5366.8 verb 2sing impr aor mid
δύνασαι	ἐλεύθερος	γενέσθαι,	μᾶλλον	χρῆσαι.
dunasai	eleutheros	genesthai	mallon	chrēsai
you are able	free	to become,	rather	use.

"Hath called" denotes that when God chooses, He expects one to live the pattern of life He sets before him, using the gifts He gives. This was a consistent message with Paul.

7:18,19. Paul applied the principle stated above to the racial distinction of circumcision and uncircumcision. Paul said this is a matter of the outer man and of no importance. The Jews demanded circumcision, but the Gentiles often thought it a sign of liberty when, as sometimes happened, a Jewish youth underwent surgery to remove the marks of circumcision, to better please the Greek culture within which he lived. It is difficult to say whether there were those in Corinth who were trying to conceal their Jewish origin. Perhaps they thought circumcision necessary to obey God more fully. Paul's point was this: Men find themselves in various circumstances when they are called by the Lord. This outward distinction is of no importance. The important thing is to keep the commandments of God. A person should not worry over his circumstances or seek to be what he is not. He is simply to walk according to his calling from God.

7:20. Paul here reiterates the principle he stated in verse 17. Believers in the First Century came from highly varied backgrounds. Most of them were from the middle or lower classes. As he stated earlier: "Ye see your calling, brethren, how that not many wise men after the flesh, not many mighty, not many noble, are called" (1:26). Often, even slaves found salvation through Christ.

This undoubtedly caused severe problems. What now was the relationship between the Christian master and his Christian slave? In Christ they were equals, but the customs of the day still had to be observed.

7:21,22. Slaves may have thought natural freedom was their first concern, but Paul's advice was that believers accept the circumstances they were in when they first found Christ. He said to the slaves, "You were a slave when God called you to become His child. Accept your present social status." He used an interesting phrase, *mallon chrēsai*. Literally, it means "rather use (it)." This could mean a number of things, but most likely it has the import of "make use of your present position as a slave." Although the slave was serving his master from a state of bondage, he could serve as though it was for Christ (see Colossians 3:22,23).

Paul was consistent in his treatment of the master/servant relationship. While he recognized that in Christ all were one, and there were no class distinctions (see Galatians 3:28; Colossians 3:11), he did not advocate change by society by radical methods. He even sent the converted Onesimus back to his master Philemon. Though

And so ordain I in all churches: And thus am I prescribing, *Concordant* . . . I order the same, *Fenton* . . . This is what I command, *Weymouth* . . . Such is the rule I lay down for all, *Moffatt* . . . in all congregacyons, *Cranmer*.

18. Is any man called being circumcised?:

let him not become uncircumcised: Let it not be rejected, *Fenton* . . . let him not revert, *Murdock* . . . let him not adde vncircumcisyon, *Cranmer* . . . be de-circumcised, *Concordant* . . . he is not to efface the marks of it, *Moffatt* . . . Let him not have recourse to the surgeons, *Weymouth*.

Is any called in uncircumcision? let him not be circumcised:

19. Circumcision is nothing, and uncircumcision is nothing: . . . counts for nothing, *Moffatt*.

but the keeping of the commandments of God: . . . but observing Divine commands, *Fenton* . . . of the precepts of God, *Concordant* . . . obedience to God's commands is everything, *Moffatt*.

20. Let every man abide in the same calling wherein he was called: Whatever be the condition in life in which a man was, *Weymouth* . . . remain in the condition of life, *Moffatt* . . . in the same state, *Geneva* . . . in the condition, *Fenton*.

21. Art thou called [being] a servant?: . . . called when in slavery, *Montgomery* . . . a bondman? *Rheims*.

care not for it: Never mind, *Moffatt* . . . Let not that trouble you, *Montgomery* . . . let it not trouble thee, *Murdock* . . . Let not that weigh on your mind, *Weymouth*.

but if thou mayest be made free, use [it] rather: . . . then prefer it, *Fenton* . . . make use of the opportunity, *Montgomery* . . . you had better avail yourself of the opportunity, *Moffatt* . . . yet prefer freedom to slavery, if thou canst obtain it, *Locke*.

1 Corinthians 7:22

22. ὁ γὰρ ἐν κυρίῳ κληθεὶς δοῦλος,
ho *gar* *en* *kuriō* *klētheis* *doulos*
The for in Lord having been called a slave,

3450.5 art sing masc / 1056.1 conj / 1706.1 prep / 2935.3 noun dat sing masc / 2535.42 verb nom sing masc part aor pass / 1395.1 noun nom sing masc

22.a.Txt: 018K,020L,byz.
Sod
Var: 01א,02A,03B,025P
33,Lach,Treg,Alf,Word
Tisc,We/Ho,Weis
UBS/⋆

ἀπελεύθερος κυρίου ἐστίν· ὁμοίως ⸂ καὶ ⸃
apeleutheros *kuriou* *estin* *homoiōs* *kai*
a freedman of Lord is; likewise also

555.1 adj nom sing masc / 2935.2 noun gen sing masc / 1498.4 verb 3sing indic pres act / 3532.1 adv / 2504.1 conj

ὁ ἐλεύθερος κληθεὶς, δοῦλός ἐστιν
ho *eleutheros* *klētheis* *doulos* *estin*
the free having been called, a slave is

3450.5 art sing masc / 1645.1 adj nom sing masc / 2535.42 verb nom sing masc part aor pass / 1395.1 noun nom sing masc / 1498.4 verb 3sing indic pres act

Χριστοῦ. **23.** τιμῆς ἠγοράσθητε· μὴ γίνεσθε
Christou *timēs* *ēgorasthēte* *mē* *ginesthe*
of Christ. With a price you were bought; not become

5382.2 name gen masc / 4940.2 noun gen sing fem / 58.18 verb 2pl indic aor pass / 3231.1 partic / 1090.19 verb 2pl impr pres

δοῦλοι ἀνθρώπων. **24.** ἕκαστος ἐν ᾧ
douloi *anthrōpōn* *hekastos* *en* *hō*
slaves of men. Each in which

1395.6 noun pl masc / 442.7 noun gen pl masc / 1524.3 adj nom sing masc / 1706.1 prep / 3614.3 rel-pron dat sing

ἐκλήθη, ἀδελφοί, ἐν τούτῳ μενέτω παρὰ
eklēthē *adelphoi* *en* *toutō* *menetō* *para*
he was called, brothers, in that let him abide with

2535.37 verb 3sing indic aor pass / 79.6 noun pl masc / 1706.1 prep / 3642.5 dem-pron dat sing masc / 3176.9 verb 3sing impr pres act / 3706.2 prep

24.a.Txt: 02A,Steph
Var: 01א,03B,06D
018K,020L,025P,byz.
Gries,Lach,Treg,Alf
Word,Tisc,We/Ho,Weis
Sod,UBS/⋆

⸂ τῷ ⸃ θεῷ. **25.** Περὶ δὲ τῶν παρθένων
tō *theō* *Peri* *de* *tōn* *parthenōn*
God. Concerning now the virgins,

3450.3 art dat sing / 2296.3 noun dat sing masc / 3875.1 prep / 1156.2 conj / 3450.1 art gen pl / 3795.5 noun gen pl masc

ἐπιταγὴν κυρίου οὐκ ἔχω· γνώμην δὲ
epitagēn *kuriou* *ouk* *echō* *gnōmēn* *de*
commandment of Lord not I have: judgment but

1987.2 noun acc sing fem / 2935.2 noun gen sing masc / 3620.2 partic / 2174.1 verb 1sing pres act / 1100.4 noun acc sing fem / 1156.2 conj

δίδωμι, ὡς ἠλεημένος ὑπὸ κυρίου πιστὸς
didōmi *hōs* *eleēmenos* *hupo* *kuriou* *pistos*
I give, as having received mercy from Lord faithful

1319.1 verb 1sing indic pres act / 5453.1 conj / 1640.17 verb nom sing masc part perf pass / 5097.3 prep / 2935.2 noun gen sing masc / 3964.2 adj nom sing masc

εἶναι. **26.** Νομίζω οὖν τοῦτο καλὸν ὑπάρχειν
einai *Nomizō* *oun* *touto* *kalon* *huparchein*
to be. I think then this good to be

1498.32 verb inf pres act / 3406.1 verb 1sing indic pres act / 3631.1 conj / 3642.17 dem-pron sing neu / 2541.1 adj sing / 5062.11 verb inf pres act

διὰ τὴν ἐνεστῶσαν ἀνάγκην, ὅτι καλὸν
dia *tēn* *enestōsan* *anankēn* *hoti* *kalon*
because of the present necessity, that good

1217.2 prep / 3450.12 art acc sing fem / 1748.4 verb acc sing fem part perf act / 316.4 noun acc sing fem / 3617.1 conj / 2541.1 adj sing

Paul did not support slavery, he was not aiming for social revolution, but spiritual reformation. He pointed out that it is possible to be a Christian in any situation.

If the slave had an opportunity to be free, he should take advantage of it. But the slave was not to worry for he had been called by Christ. The world does not determine a man's position before God. In Christ all are equal.

7:23. Paul returned to his thesis of 6:20. Believers have been bought with the blood of Jesus Christ. This is the reason for prompt obedience. One might be a slave, but he was free from sin and guilt. Another might be free, but he was bound to obedience and service in Christ. They dared not become captive to worldly distinctions or philosophies.

7:24. Paul repeated the principle of this section: A man is to serve God where he is until God calls somewhere else. "Was called" is an aorist, pointing back to the time of God's call; "therein abide" is present continuous, indicating continuity. The ever-present God, who is also faithful, is the One with whom we are able to "abide." The will and pleasure of God must be consulted in every change and type of work: "Abide with God."

7:25. "Now concerning" indicates yet another matter on which the Corinthians had apparently submitted questions. "Virgins" refers to women (and includes the question of daughters at home and the father's responsibility). As before where there are no specific commandments or words of Christ, the position is made clear. There is no distinction here between rule and advice. "Judgment" does not leave the case open to doubt or uncertainty. What was said was based on the risen Christ's mercy to Paul. It points out Paul's significance while giving the glory to God. When Paul gave this advice it was done in faithfulness to the Lord; it must, therefore, be pleasing to Him. It could, then, be trusted. God's grace had made Paul a trustworthy servant and apostle.

7:26. Paul stressed two things: It is a good thing to be a virgin because of the present need, and it is a good thing in itself. The "present distress" was a general reference to the circumstances and pressures all Christians faced in that era of history. The context includes descriptions like "tribulation in the flesh" (verse 28, ASV), "time is short" (verse 29), and "fashion of this world passeth away" (verse 31). The Christian, whether married or unmarried, was caught in struggles and pressures, which are not closely defined,

22. For he that is called in the Lord, [being] a servant, is the Lord's freeman: likewise also he that is called, [being] free, is Christ's servant: . . . is Christ's bondman, *Panin.*

23. Ye are bought with a price: Christ paid a price for you, *SEB* . . . you were dearly bought, *Berkeley.*

be not ye the servants of men: . . . you must not turn slaves to any man, *Moffatt.*

24. Brethren, let every man, wherein he is called, therein abide with God: . . . remain in the position, *TCNT* . . . remain in the presence of God, *Berkeley* . . . let him stay, close to God, *Montgomery.*

25. Now concerning virgins I have no commandment of the Lord: I have no command, *TCNT* . . . I have no orders from, *Moffatt* . . . I have no divine injunction, *Berkeley* . . . unmarried women, *Weymouth* . . . the young girls, *Fenton* . . . the celibates...I have no injunction, *Concordant* . . . I have no ordinance, *Sawyer.*

yet I give my judgment, as one that hath obtained mercy of the Lord to be faithful: . . . but counsel I giue, *Rheims* . . . but I give counsel, *Murdock, Douay* . . . I will give you the opinion, *Moffatt* . . . that I be trewe, *Wyclif* . . . to be trustworthy, *Hanson* . . . is deserving of your confidence, *Weymouth, Montgomery.*

26. I suppose therefore that this is good for the present distress: I judge a single life to be convenient, *Locke* . . . to encounter more easily the present distress, *Fenton* . . . on account of, *Murdock* . . . owing to the imminence of distressful times, *Way* . . . the imminent distress in these days, *Moffatt* . . . this is well in consequence of the present distress, *Hanson* . . . is suitable on account of the necessity of the times, *Murdock* . . . time of suffering now imminent, *Montgomery* . . . in view of the impending distress, *Berkeley* . . . of the existing distress, *Rotherham.*

442.3 noun dat sing masc	3450.16 art sing neu	3643.1 adv	1498.32 verb inf pres act	1204.14 verb 2sing indic perf pass
ἀνθρώπῳ	τὸ	οὕτως	εἶναι.	27. δέδεσαι
anthrōpō	to	houtōs	einai	dedesai
for a man	the	so	to be.	Have you been bound

1129.3 noun dat sing fem	3231.1 partic	2195.6 verb 2sing impr pres act	3052.1 noun acc sing fem	3061.23 verb 2sing indic perf pass
γυναικί;	μὴ	ζήτει	λύσιν.	λέλυσαι
gunaiki	mē	zētei	lusin	lelusai
to a wife?	not	seek	divorce.	Have you been loosed

570.3 prep gen	1129.2 noun gen sing fem	3231.1 partic	2195.6 verb 2sing impr pres act	1129.4 noun acc sing fem	1430.1 partic
ἀπὸ	γυναικός;	μὴ	ζήτει	γυναῖκα.	28. ἐὰν
apo	gunaikos	mē	zētei	gunaika	ean
from	a wife?	not	seek	a wife.	If

28.a.Txt: 018K,020L,byz.
Var: 01ℵ,03B,025P,33
Lach,Treg,Alf,Tisc
We/Ho,Weis,Sod
UBS/⋆

1156.2 conj	2504.1 conj	1053.8 verb 2sing subj aor act	1053.19 verb 2sing subj aor act	3620.1 partic
δὲ	καὶ	῾ γήμῃς,	[ᵃ⋆ γαμήσῃς,]	οὐχ
de	kai	gēmēs	gamēsēs	ouch
but	also	you may have married,	[idem]	not

28.b.Txt: p46,01ℵ,02A
06D,08E,018K,020L
025P,We/Ho,byz.UBS/⋆
Var: 03B,010F,012G
429

262.12 verb 2sing indic aor act	2504.1 conj	1430.1 partic	1053.10 verb 3sing subj aor act	3450.9 art nom sing fem
ἥμαρτες·	καὶ	ἐὰν	γήμῃ	῾ᵇ ἡ ῾
hēmartes	kai	ean	gēmē	hē
you did sin;	and	if	may have married	the

3795.1 noun nom sing masc	3620.1 partic	262.13 verb 3sing indic aor act	2324.4 noun acc sing fem	1156.2 conj	3450.11 art dat sing fem
παρθένος,	οὐχ	ἥμαρτεν·	θλῖψιν	δὲ	τῇ
parthenos	ouch	hēmarten	thlipsin	de	tē
virgin,	not	she did sin:	tribulation	but	in the

4418.3 noun dat sing fem	2174.41 verb 3pl indic fut act	3450.7 art pl masc	4955.7 dem-pron nom pl masc	1466.1 prs-pron nom 1sing	1156.2 conj
σαρκὶ	ἕξουσιν	οἱ	τοιοῦτοι·	ἐγὼ	δὲ
sarki	hexousin	hoi	toioutoi	egō	de
flesh	shall have	the	such;	I	but

5050.2 prs-pron gen 2pl	5177.1 verb 1sing indic pres	3642.17 dem-pron sing neu	1156.2 conj	5183.1 verb 1sing indic pres act
ὑμῶν	φείδομαι.	29. Τοῦτο	δέ	φημι,
humōn	pheidomai	Touto	de	phēmi
you	spare.	This	but	I say,

79.6 noun pl masc	3450.5 art sing masc	2511.1 noun nom sing masc	4810.2 verb nom sing masc part perf pass	3450.16 art sing neu
ἀδελφοί,	ὁ	καιρὸς	συνεσταλμένος·	῾ τὸ
adelphoi	ho	kairos	sunestalmenos	to
brothers,	the	season	having been shortened.	The

29.a.Txt: 06D-corr,018K
020L,byz.
Var: 01ℵ,02A,03B
06D-org,33,bo.Lach,Tisc
We/Ho,Weis,Sod
UBS/⋆

3036.8 adj acc sing neu	1498.4 verb 3sing indic pres act	1498.4 verb 3sing indic pres act	3450.16 art sing neu	3036.8 adj acc sing neu
λοιπὸν	ἐστίν,	[ᵃ⋆ ἐστίν·	τὸ	λοιπὸν]
loipon	estin	estin	to	loipon
remaining	is,	[is:	the	remaining]

2419.1 conj	2504.1 conj	3450.7 art pl masc	2174.19 verb nom pl masc part pres act	1129.9 noun acc pl fem	5453.1 conj	3231.1 partic
ἵνα	καὶ	οἱ	ἔχοντες	γυναῖκας,	ὡς	μὴ
hina	kai	hoi	echontes	gunaikas	hōs	mē
that	even	the	having	wives,	as	not

but the reference is to difficult circumstances. Paul's advice was to remain, then, as they were.

7:27. Paul enlarged on the thought. The moment he recommended remaining single under the "present distress," he had to answer questions concerning those already married. Should they separate? The answer was no. And such unity was a command of the Lord (verse 10). The application here is to men. "Art thou loosed" means simply unmarried.

7:28. This verse makes it clear first to men, then to virgins, that marriage is not a sin. Perhaps some Corinthians had misinterpreted Paul's words and had this view of marriage. Paul made no absolute prohibitions concerning marriage. Marriage may produce distress, but it is a barrier to immorality. The Corinthians appeared to have a strong antipathy toward marriage. Paul must deal with this wrong attitude. Repeatedly the apostle Paul, directed by the Holy Spirit, made clear that marriage in and of itself is not a sin or sinful. Paul acknowledged that the marriage relationship entailed difficulties, but observation teaches us that it is not possible to escape difficulties or anxiety just by remaining single.

Some claim that the phrase "trouble in the flesh" refers to bodily difficulties of married women. But this appears too limited. "Such" is masculine, embracing more than married women. Some see a reference to complications with regard to the ministry, problems which are increased by a man's regard for his wife and children. Such blessings enrich a man's life, but mishaps to them are more difficult to handle. Sometimes a decision must be made between God and family. It was Paul's intention to spare them these difficulties, to aid and help rather than to add pressure.

7:29. By saying "brethren" Paul addressed the whole congregation with this important message. In "the time is short" some see a reference to the Second Coming, others to a crisis in Corinth. Christians live between the descent of the Holy Spirit and the return of Jesus Christ. The Second Coming leads to the end of all things and hastens us toward that end. This does not necessarily mean Paul was certain of the coming of the Lord in his own lifetime, though his writings indicate it was his constant hope. He lived expectantly, while always planning for the future. "It remaineth" or "henceforth" (ASV) carries the idea that there remained only one thing necessary: the eye must be directed toward heaven.

From this point Paul listed five examples of the Christian's freedom from the transient world. Each item can be connected with the married state. "As though they had none" is not an exhortation to marital neglect, but an indication that marriage must be kept in proper perspective, with the advance of the gospel always having top priority.

[I say], that [it is] good for a man so to be: . . . to remain as he is, *Noyes.*

27. Art thou bound unto a wife? seek not to be loosed: Art thou tied to a vvife? *Rheims* . . . in the bonds of wedlock? *Locke* . . . do not attempt to be free, *Fenton* . . . Seek not release, *Murdock* . . . Never try to untie the knot, *Moffatt.*

Art thou loosed from a wife? seek not a wife: Are you unattached to a woman? *Berkeley.*

28. But and if thou marry, thou hast not sinned: . . . if perchance thou even marry, *Rotherham.*

and if a virgin marry, she hath not sinned: . . . if your virgin daughters marry, *Conybeare* . . . if a maid marries, *Moffatt* . . . she has not done wrong, *Montgomery.*

Nevertheless such shall have trouble in the flesh: but I spare you: Yet affliction in the flesh, *Concordant, Campbell* . . . will have outward trouble, *Weymouth* . . . will have tribulation, *Rotherham* . . . they will have bodily privations, *Fenton* . . . will have added troubles, *Norlie* . . . will have trouble in worldly affairs, *Montgomery* . . . will have sorrows in the flesh, *Conybeare* . . . many troubles at this time, and I would like to protect you, *SEB* . . . my wish is to spare you, *TCNT* . . . and I am trying to spare you, *Adams.*

29. But this I say, brethren, the time [is] short: I warn you, brethren, *Weymouth* . . . the era is limited, *Concordant* . . . the interval has been shortened, *Moffatt.*

it remaineth, that both they that have wives be as though they had none: . . . behave as if they had none, *Berkeley.*

2174.19 verb nom pl masc part pres act	1498.12 verb 3pl subj pres act	2504.1 conj	3450.7 art pl masc	2772.6 verb pl masc part pres act
ἔχοντες	ὦσιν·	**30.** καὶ	οἱ	κλαίοντες,
echontes	ōsin	kai	hoi	klaiontes
having	may be;	and	the	weeping,

5453.1 conj	3231.1 partic	2772.6 verb pl masc part pres act	2504.1 conj	3450.7 art pl masc	5299.9 verb nom pl masc part pres act	5453.1 conj
ὡς	μὴ	κλαίοντες·	καὶ	οἱ	χαίροντες,	ὡς
hōs	mē	klaiontes	kai	hoi	chairontes	hōs
as	not	weeping;	and	the	rejoicing,	as

3231.1 partic	5299.9 verb nom pl masc part pres act	2504.1 conj	3450.7 art pl masc	58.2 verb nom pl masc part pres act	5453.1 conj
μὴ	χαίροντες·	καὶ	οἱ	ἀγοράζοντες,	ὡς
mē	chairontes	kai	hoi	agorazontes	hōs
not	rejoicing;	and	the	buying,	as

3231.1 partic	2692.5 verb nom pl masc part pres act	2504.1 conj	3450.7 art pl masc	5366.4 verb nom pl masc part pres act	3450.3 art dat sing
μὴ	κατέχοντες·	**31.** καὶ	οἱ	χρώμενοι	τῷ
mē	katechontes	kai	hoi	chrōmenoi	tō
not	possessing;	and	the	using	the

31.a.Txt: 01ℵ-corr 06D-corr,018K,020L 025P,byz.
Var: 01ℵ-org,02A,03B bo.Lach,Treg,Alf,Tisc We/Ho,Weis,Sod UBS/★

2862.3 noun dat sing masc	3450.6 art acc sing masc	2862.4 noun acc sing masc	3642.5 dem-pron dat sing masc	5453.1 conj	3231.1 partic
κόσμῳ	[ᵃ☆ τὸν	κόσμον]	τούτῳ,	ὡς	μὴ
kosmō	ton	kosmon	toutō	hōs	mē
world	[the	world]	this,	as	not

2679.1 verb nom pl masc part pres	3717.1 verb 3sing indic pres act	1056.1 conj	3450.16 art sing neu	4828.1 noun nom sing neu	3450.2 art gen sing
καταχρώμενοι.	παράγει	γὰρ	τὸ	σχῆμα	τοῦ
katachrōmenoi	paragei	gar	to	schēma	tou
using as their own;	passes away	for	the	fashion	of the

2862.2 noun gen sing masc	3642.1 dem-pron gen sing	2286.1 verb 1sing pres act	1156.2 conj	5050.4 prs-pron acc 2pl	273.1 adj acc pl masc
κόσμου	τούτου.	**32.** θέλω	δὲ	ὑμᾶς	ἀμερίμνους
kosmou	toutou	thelō	de	humas	amerimnous
world	this.	I wish	but	you	without care

1498.32 verb inf pres act	3450.5 art sing masc	22.1 noun nom sing	3179.3 verb 3sing indic pres act	3450.17 art pl neu	3450.2 art gen sing
εἶναι.	ὁ	ἄγαμος	μεριμνᾷ	τὰ	τοῦ
einai	ho	agamos	merimna	ta	tou
to be.	The	unmarried	cares for	the things	of the

32.a.Txt: 018K,020L 025P,byz.
Var: 01ℵ,02A,03B,06D 33,Lach,Treg,Alf,Tisc We/Ho,Weis,Sod UBS/★

2935.2 noun gen sing masc	4316.1 adv	694.10 verb 3sing indic fut act	694.7 verb 3sing subj aor act	3450.3 art dat sing	2935.3 noun dat sing masc
κυρίου,	πῶς	ἀρέσει	[ᵃ☆ ἀρέσῃ]	τῷ	κυρίῳ·
kuriou	pōs	aresei	aresē	tō	kuriō
Lord,	how	he shall please	[he may please]	the	Lord;

3450.5 art sing masc	1156.2 conj	1053.12 verb nom sing masc part aor act	3179.3 verb 3sing indic pres act	3450.17 art pl neu	3450.2 art gen sing
33. ὁ	δὲ	γαμήσας	μεριμνᾷ	τὰ	τοῦ
ho	de	gamēsas	merimna	ta	tou
the	but	having married	cares for	the things	of the

33.a.Txt: 018K,020L 025P,byz.
Var: 01ℵ,02A,03B,06D Lach,Treg,Alf,Tisc We/Ho,Weis,Sod UBS/★

2862.2 noun gen sing masc	4316.1 adv	694.10 verb 3sing indic fut act	694.7 verb 3sing subj aor act	3450.11 art dat sing fem
κόσμου,	πῶς	ἀρέσει	[ᵃ☆ ἀρέσῃ]	τῇ
kosmou	pōs	aresei	aresē	tē
world,	how	he shall please	[he may please]	the

7:30. Every Christian is going to weep, rejoice, and buy as he shares in the events of his world and time. But these are not to be the determinants in the character or actions of the Christian. In each situation the heart must be directed heavenward for guidance. The Christian is not acquiring lasting possessions here. The world has merely the passing fashion of the theater or stage. As J.H. Newman wrote: "Then what this world to thee, my heart? Its gifts nor feed thee nor can bless. Thou hast no owner's part in all its fleetingness" (Nicoll, *Expositor's Greek Testament*, 2:831).

7:31. This addition and summary appears with an air of detachment. "Use this world" (to the full) indicates a man who uses the world in that manner and then has nothing left when the world passes. Rather it should be as the song tells us, "This world is not my home, I'm just passing through." For the world has a transitory nature and form, and it will pass away. This is inevitable. This world has been judged and stands condemned. A present action is involved in this "passing away." What a solemn warning this comment provides. Attachments in this world will pass away.

7:32. Instead of assigning value to this passing world, Paul desired unworried service for the Lord. Paul once again criticized the ascetic tendency found in Corinth; people were fooling themselves if they thought that singleness would release them from anxiety. The New Testament resounds with commands to be free from anxiety (e.g., Matthew 6:25; 1 Peter 5:7) because Christ by His death has delivered us, justified us, and given us peace with God (cf. Romans 5:1). Because of this, Paul made it clear (cf. Romans 8:15) that any *human* attempt to escape anxiety (i.e., celibacy) is insufficient.

Paul wanted his friends to be free from care and unnecessary pressure. This care would detract from perfect service toward God. The unmarried man does not have such "cares" or hindrances to serving the Lord as marriage sometimes brings; hence, Paul's preference for celibacy. His whole aim and guiding principle was what would provide the best service for the Lord whom he loved. He aimed to see how this service might best be accomplished. He desired undistracted service for the Lord.

7:33. The cares of the married and the "freedom" of the single are further compared. Paul said that the married man cannot help but have some concern for "the things that are of the world." This does not denote "worldliness" or sin. It is rather a note that the married man must face the question of "how he may please his wife," which is a direct contrast with "how he may please the Lord." Such a man is divided in interest and purpose between God and wife. He cannot be as intense or "devoted" in his service for the Lord.

30. And they that weep, as though they wept not: People who are crying must act, *SEB* . . . let mourners live, *Moffatt* . . . those lamenting, *Concordant*.

and they that rejoice, as though they rejoiced not: . . . let the joyful live, *Moffatt*.

and they that buy, as though they possessed not: . . . as if they acquired not, *Murdock* . . . had no hold on their goods, *Moffatt*.

31. And they that use this world, as not abusing [it]: Those who do business with the world must act as though they don't care, *SEB* . . . though using it sparingly, *Montgomery* . . . not going beyond the just using, *Murdock* . . . must not be overly absorbed in them, *Norlie*.

for the fashion of this world passeth away: . . . for the arrangement, *Fenton* . . . the present phase, *Moffatt* . . . as it now exists is passing away, *Weymouth*.

32. But I would have you without carefulness: I want you to be free from all preoccupation, *Way* . . . free from worldly anxiety, *Weymouth, Montgomery* . . . to be free from cares, *Alford* . . . to be without worry, *Concordant* . . . be without bidyness, *Wyclif* . . . be without solicitude, *Douay* . . . be without anxiety, *Fenton*.

He that is unmarried careth for the things that belong to the Lord: The syngle man careth, *Geneva* . . . He that is without a vvife, *Rheims* . . . is solicitous about, *Concordant, Douay* . . . has time and liberty to mind things of religion, *Locke* . . . is anxious about the Lord's affairs, *Moffatt* . . . is concerned about the Lord's things, *SEB* . . . the Lord's business, *Montgomery*.

how he may please the Lord:

33. But he that is married careth for the things that are of the world: . . . concerns himself with the business of the world, *Weymouth* . . . is anxious about worldly affairs, *Montgomery*.

how he may please [his] wife: . . . how best to satisfy his wife— so he is torn in two directions, *Moffatt*.

1 Corinthians 7:34

34.a.Var: p15,p46,01ℵ 02A,03B,06D-org,025P 33,sa.bo.Alf,Tisc,We/Ho Weis,Sod,UBS/☆

34.b.Var: p15,p46,01ℵ 02A,03B,06D-corr,018K 020L,025P,sa.bo.Alf Tisc,We/Ho,Weis,Sod UBS/☆

34.c.Var: p15,p46,01ℵ 02A,03B,025P,sa.bo. Lach,Treg,We/Ho,Weis Sod,UBS/☆

34.d.Txt: p46,01ℵ,02A 06D,018K,020L,byz. Tisc,Sod **Var:** p15,03B,025P,sa. bo.Treg,We/Ho,Weis UBS/☆

34.e.Var: 01ℵ,02A,03B 025P,33,Lach,Treg,Alf Tisc,We/Ho,Weis,Sod UBS/☆

34.f.Var: 01ℵ,02A,03B 025P,33,Lach,Treg,Alf Tisc,We/Ho,Weis,Sod UBS/☆

1129.3 noun dat sing fem	2504.1 conj	3177.6 verb 3sing indic perf pass	2504.1 conj	
γυναικί,	**34.** [ᵃ☆+ καὶ]	μεμέρισται.	[ᵇ☆+ καὶ]	
gunaiki	kai	memeristai	kai	
wife.	[and]	Has been divided	[the]	
3450.9 art nom sing fem	1129.1 noun nom sing fem	3450.9 art nom sing fem	22.1 noun nom sing	2504.1 conj
ἡ	γυνὴ	[ᶜ☆+ ἡ	ἄγαμος]	καὶ
hē	gunē	hē	agamos	kai
the	wife	[the	unmarried]	and
3450.9 art nom sing fem	3795.1 noun nom sing masc	3450.9 art nom sing fem	22.1 noun nom sing	3179.3 verb 3sing indic pres act
ἡ	παρθένος.	⸀ᵈ ἡ	ἄγαμος ⸍	μεριμνᾷ
hē	parthenos	hē	agamos	merimna
the	virgin.	The	unmarried	cares for
3450.17 art pl neu	3450.2 art gen sing	2935.2 noun gen sing masc	2419.1 conj	1498.10 verb 3sing subj pres act	39.10 adj nom sing fem
τὰ	τοῦ	κυρίου,	ἵνα	ᾖ	ἁγία
ta	tou	kuriou	hina	ē	hagia
the things	of the	Lord,	that	she may be	holy
2504.1 conj	3450.3 art dat sing	4835.3 noun dat sing neu	2504.1 conj	3450.3 art dat sing	4011.3 noun dat sing neu
καὶ	[ᵉ☆+ τῷ]	σώματι	καὶ	[ᶠ☆+ τῷ]	πνεύματι·
kai	tō	sōmati	kai	tō	pneumati
both	[in the]	in body	and	[in the]	spirit;
3450.9 art nom sing fem	1156.2 conj	1053.13 verb nom sing fem part aor act	3179.3 verb 3sing indic pres act	3450.17 art pl neu	3450.2 art gen sing
ἡ	δὲ	γαμήσασα	μεριμνᾷ	τὰ	τοῦ
hē	de	gamēsasa	merimna	ta	tou
the	but	having married	cares for	the things	of the

34.g.Txt: 018K,020L 025P,byz. **Var:** 01ℵ,02A,03B,06D 33,Lach,Treg,Alf,Tisc We/Ho,Weis,Sod UBS/☆

2862.2 noun gen sing masc	4316.1 adv	694.10 verb 3sing indic fut act	694.7 verb 3sing subj aor act	3450.3 art dat sing
κόσμου,	πῶς	⸀ ἀρέσει	[ᵍ☆ ἀρέσῃ]	τῷ
kosmou	pōs	aresei	aresē	tō
world,	how	she shall please	[she may please]	the
433.3 noun dat sing masc	3642.17 dem-pron sing neu	1156.2 conj	4242.1 prep	3450.16 art sing neu	5050.2 prs-pron gen 2pl	840.1 prs-pron gen pl
ἀνδρί.	**35.** τοῦτο	δὲ	πρὸς	τὸ	ὑμῶν	αὐτῶν
andri	touto	de	pros	to	humōn	autōn
husband.	This	but	for	the	your	selves

35.a.Txt: 01ℵ-corr 06D-corr,018K,020L 025P,byz. **Var:** 01ℵ-org,02A,03B 06D-org,33,Lach,Treg Alf,Tisc,We/Ho,Weis Sod,UBS/☆

4702.2 verb sing neu part pres act	4703.1 adj acc sing	2978.1 verb 1sing pres act	3620.1 partic	2419.1 conj	1022.1 noun acc sing masc
⸀ σύμφερον	[ᵃ☆ σύμφορον]	λέγω·	οὐχ	ἵνα	βρόχον
sumpheron	sumphoron	legō	ouch	hina	brochon
profiting	[profit]	I say;	not	that	a noose
5050.3 prs-pron dat 2pl	1896.5 verb 1sing subj aor act	233.2 conj	4242.1 prep	3450.16 art sing neu	2139.4 adj acc sing neu
ὑμῖν	ἐπιβάλω,	ἀλλὰ	πρὸς	τὸ	εὔσχημον
humin	epibalō	alla	pros	to	euschēmon
you	I may cast before,	but	for	the	seemly,

35.b.Txt: 018K,byz. **Var:** 01ℵ,02A,03B,06D 025P,Gries,Lach,Treg Alf,Word,Tisc,We/Ho Weis,Sod,UBS/☆

2504.1 conj	2125.1 adj acc sing neu	2117.1 adj acc sing	3450.3 art dat sing	2935.3 noun dat sing masc
καὶ	⸀ εὐπρόσεδρον	[ᵇ☆ εὐπάρεδρον]	τῷ	κυρίῳ
kai	euprosedron	euparedron	tō	kuriō
and	waiting	[idem]	on the	Lord

7:34. The difference that exists between married and unmarried men is also found sometimes between married and unmarried women. Often the unmarried can more fully concentrate on the things of God (unless, as in some cases in today's world, they too have family responsibilities). The unmarried can have a singleness of purpose regarding consecration and the pursuit of holiness. This does not make the virgin any more righteous than the wife. But since the wife must take into account the needs of her husband, her consecration is "modified" by her dual purpose. For example, at some point she might want to do an act of charity. But her commitment is also to her husband, and if he is not agreeable, it may be difficult or impossible for her to perform that good act. She may wish to spend much time in prayer, but it may be difficult with family responsibilities calling to her. Thus Paul was stressing one obvious difference between the two states. The married individual has more responsibilities, usually, than the unmarried person, making it harder to find time for serving God.

Paul was speaking in a general sense. We must remember Paul's admonitions elsewhere about the sanctity of marriage (Ephesians 5 and 6) and the needs for which it provides.

The expression "that she may be holy both in body and in spirit" is applied directly to the unmarried woman. Elsewhere in Paul's letters when he speaks of holiness he makes it a requirement for all Christians, not just one group of Christians. It may be, therefore, that this expression was used by ascetics in Corinth to keep women from marriage, since intercourse in their view defiled the body.

Although Paul did not agree with this asceticism, he certainly agreed in general with the necessity of being holy in body and in spirit. Even a casual glance at his epistles indicates his overwhelming concern with purity. He urges Christians, "Present your bodies a living sacrifice, holy, acceptable unto God" (Romans 12:1). Paul says much the same elsewhere in Romans with his exhortation, "Let not sin therefore reign in your mortal body, that ye should obey it in the lusts thereof" (Romans 6:12).

The very first letters Paul wrote show that from the beginning of his ministry he was concerned about immorality. In 1 Thessalonians he wrote, "And the very God of peace sanctify you wholly; and I pray God your whole spirit and soul and body be preserved blameless unto the coming of our Lord Jesus Christ" (1 Thessalonians 5:23). Most of his statements concerning holiness, however, are found here in 1 Corinthians (6:13,15,19,20; 15:44).

7:35. Paul's purpose was not to place undue restraints or absolutes on the Corinthians. Rather, his advice was for the purpose of gaining their best, undistracted service to the Lord. Paul was speaking of spiritual matters. For the third time they were advised that he was writing for their welfare. He was not insisting on celibacy; he was only reminding them of principles to consider in service for the Lord. "Snare" means the noose or lasso by which a wild creature is snared.

34. There is difference [also] between a wife and a virgin: And there has been a distinction, *Clementson.*

The unmarried woman careth for the things of the Lord: The single woman careth for the thinges, *Tyndale* . . . should attend to the wishes, *Fenton* . . . concerns herself with the Lord's business, *Weymouth* . . . can be absorbed in her duties to her Lord, *Way* . . . care for the Master's interests, *TCNT.*

that she may be holy both in body and in spirit: . . . how to be consecrated, *Moffatt* . . . how she may be pure, *Montgomery.*

but she that is married careth for the things of the world: . . . about worldly affairs, *Moffatt.*

how she may please [her] husband:

35. And this I speak for your own profit: . . . your own application, *Fenton* . . . your own benefit, *Campbell* . . . your own advantage, *HistNT* . . . in your own interests, *Moffatt.*

not that I may cast a snare upon you: I'm not trying to add an extra burden to you, *SEB* . . . not to make it harder for you, *Norlie* . . . not to lay a trap for you, *Weymouth* . . . not with any intention of putting a halter round your necks, *TCNT* . . . to bridle you by it, *Adams* . . . to restrict your freedom, *Moffatt* . . . be casting a noose over you, *Concordant* . . . restraint upon you, *Worrell.*

but for that which is comely: . . . but with a view, *Rotherham* . . . but for that which is honest, *Tyndale* . . . but to promote propriety, *HistNT* . . . to promote choice behavior, *Berkeley* . . . to secure decorum and concentration, *Moffatt* . . . rather to promote decency, *Adams.*

and that ye may attend upon the Lord without distraction: . . . that ye may qvyetly cleaue vnto the Lord without separation, *Geneva* . . . and enable you to wait, *Weymouth* . . . vvithout impediment, *Rheims, Douay* . . . in a suitable manner, while not minding worldly things, *Murdock* . . . undivided devotion to the Lord, *Adams* . . . with a seemly and undivided service, *Conybeare.*

1 Corinthians 7:36

560.1 adv		**1479.1** conj	**1156.2** conj	**4948.3** indef-pron nom sing	**801.2** verb inf pres act
ἀπερισπάστως.		**36.** Εἰ	δέ	τις	ἀσχημονεῖν
aperispastōs		Ei	de	tis	aschēmonein
without distraction.		If	but	anyone	to behave unseemly

1894.3 prep	**3450.12** art acc sing fem	**3795.3** noun acc sing masc	**840.3** prs-pron gen sing	**3406.2** verb 3sing indic pres act	**1430.1** partic
ἐπὶ	τὴν	παρθένον	αὐτοῦ	νομίζει,	ἐὰν
epi	tēn	parthenon	autou	nomizei	ean
to	the	virgin	his	thinks,	if

1498.10 verb 3sing subj pres act		**5067.1** adj nom sing	**2504.1** conj	**3643.1** adv	**3648.3** verb 3sing indic pres act
ᾖ		ὑπέρακμος,	καὶ	οὕτως	ὀφείλει
ē		huperakmos	kai	houtōs	opheilei
she be		past the bloom of life,	and	so	it ought

1090.28 verb inf pres	**3614.16** rel-pron sing neu	**2286.3** verb 3sing indic pres act	**4020.12** verb 3sing impr pres act	**3620.1** partic
γίνεσθαι,	ὃ	θέλει	ποιείτω,	οὐχ
ginesthai	ho	thelei	poieitō	ouch
to be,	what	he wills	let him do,	not

262.2 verb 3sing indic pres act	**1053.2** verb 3pl impr pres act	**3614.5** rel-pron nom sing masc	**1156.2** conj	**2449.18** verb 3sing indic perf act
ἁμαρτάνει·	γαμείτωσαν.	**37.** ὃς	δὲ	ἕστηκεν
hamartanei	gameitōsan	hos	de	hestēken
he does sin:	let them marry.	Who	but	stands

37.a.**Txt:** 018K,020L,byz. **Var:** 01ℵ-org,02A,03B 06D,025P,33,Lach,Treg Alf,Tisc,We/Ho,Weis Sod,UBS/✶

1469.1 adj nom sing masc	**1706.1** prep	**3450.11** art dat sing fem	**2559.3** noun dat sing fem	**1706.1** prep	**3450.11** art dat sing fem
⸂ ἑδραῖος	ἐν	τῇ	καρδίᾳ,	[ᵃ✶ ἐν	τῇ
hedraios	en	tē	kardia	en	tē
firm	in	the	heart,	[in	the

2559.3 noun dat sing fem	**840.3** prs-pron gen sing	**1469.1** adj nom sing masc	**3231.1** partic	**2174.17** verb nom sing masc part pres act
καρδίᾳ	αὐτοῦ	ἑδραῖος,]	μὴ	ἔχων
kardia	autou	hedraios,]	mē	echōn
heart	his	firm,]	not	having

37.b.**Var:** 01ℵ,02A,03B 025P,Treg,Alf,Tisc We/Ho,Weis,Sod UBS/✶

316.4 noun acc sing fem	**1833.4** noun acc sing fem	**1156.2** conj	**2174.4** verb 3sing indic pres act	**3875.1** prep	**3450.2** art gen sing
ἀνάγκην,	ἐξουσίαν	δὲ	ἔχει	περὶ	τοῦ
anankēn	exousian	de	echei	peri	tou
necessity,	authority	but	has	over	the

37.c.**Txt:** 06D,018K 020L,byz. **Var:** 01ℵ,02A,03B,025P Lach,Treg,Alf,Tisc We/Ho,Weis,Sod UBS/✶

2375.2 adj gen sing	**2284.2** noun gen sing neu	**2504.1** conj	**3642.17** dem-pron sing neu	**2892.22** verb 3sing indic perf act	**1706.1** prep
ἰδίου	θελήματος,	καὶ	τοῦτο	κέκρικεν	ἐν
idiou	thelēmatos	kai	touto	kekriken	en
his own	will,	and	this	has judged	in

37.d.**Txt:** 06D,018K 020L,byz. **Var:** 01ℵ,02A,03B,025P Lach,Treg,Alf,Tisc We/Ho,Weis,Sod UBS/✶

3450.11 art dat sing fem	**2375.10** adj dat sing fem	**2559.3** noun dat sing fem	**840.3** prs-pron gen sing	**3450.2** art gen sing
τῇ	[ᵇ✶+ ἰδίᾳ]	καρδίᾳ	⸂ᶜ αὐτοῦ ⸃	⸂ᵈ τοῦ ⸃
tē	idia	kardia	autou	tou
the	[his own]	heart	his	the

4931.11 verb inf pres act	**3450.12** art acc sing fem	**1431.4** prs-pron gen 3sing	**3795.3** noun acc sing masc	**2544.1** adv	**4020.5** verb 3sing indic pres act
τηρεῖν	τὴν	ἑαυτοῦ	παρθένον,	καλῶς	⸂ ποιεῖ·
tērein	tēn	heautou	parthenon	kalōs	poiei
to keep	the	of himself	virgin,	well	he does.

7:36. It is admittedly difficult to discover the meaning of verses 36 through 38. Numerous explanations have been offered.

Some have interpreted the passage to mean that a man and a woman had agreed to a "spiritual marriage." They would go through the marriage ceremony but would remain celibates. However, the first examples of this sort of reasoning did not appear until the Second Century, almost 150 years after Paul wrote this letter.

Others have stated that the word *parthenos* ("virgin") may be translated "virgin state" or "celibacy" and be applied to either a man or woman. So, they say, the situation is that of a man or woman who gives up marriage in order to serve God more effectively. This may have influenced the system that developed that called for priests and nuns to remain unmarried.

Some believe that "any man" refers to one who was betrothed (in those days betrothals were contracts usually arranged by parents, often years before the marriage was to take place). This view pictures the man as undecided what to do. He feels he is not behaving honorably toward his fiancee by not marrying her, but will he be sinning if he goes against Paul's advice on celibacy?

The problem with this view is the meaning of the two Greek words whose translations are similar but importantly different. *Gameō* is the word used throughout this chapter, except in verse 38, where the word *gamizō* occurs. *Gameō* has the meaning of "marry," while *gamizō* means "give in marriage." Thus it is incorrect to refer to them as synonyms. Note that a husband-to-be could not give his fiancee in marriage.

The interpretation which has received most wide acceptance in the past is that "any man" refers to the father of a virgin daughter. In those times a daughter was under the absolute control of her father, who had the power to give her in marriage or to refuse to let her do so. The term might also apply in the case of a slave girl and her master, for he also had power to make the decision.

Related to the problem of who the "any man" and "virgin" are, is the problem of the word *huperakmos* which can mean either "past the prime of age," "of marriageable age," or more usually, "given to strong physical passions." If the first meaning is intended here, that is added weight for the view that "any man" refers to a father. However, this requires *parthenon* to mean daughter, which it does not usually do. If *huperakmos* has here its more usual meaning, then "any man" and "his virgin" probably refers to an engaged couple which would explain Paul's concern for their not sinning. It is verse 38, however, which provides the strongest case for the father/daughter option.

7:37. Paul indicates that the man must be fully convinced in his own mind. In making his earlier decision that the girl should remain a virgin, he may have failed to realize she might not want to remain single. He had "power over his own will." He was free to make the decision. If he insisted she remain single, or if he allowed her to marry, it was not sin.

36. But if any man think that he behaveth himself uncomely toward his virgin: ... he acts improperly, *Wilson, Campbell* ... he is not behaving properly to the maid, *Moffatt* ... not treating his unmarried daughter properly, *HistNT* ... it is not suitable for his daughter, *Fenton* ... toward his betrothed, *Norlie.*

if she pass the flower of [her] age, and need so require: ... if she passe the tyme of mariage, *Tyndale* ... if she is getting on in years, *Norlie* ... be beyond marriageable age, *Adams* ... be over her meridian, *Concordant* ... beyond-the-bloom of youth, *Rotherham* ... and he hath not presented her to a husband, *Murdock* ... and is under engagement to do thus, *Fenton* ... if there are good reasons for the proposed match, *Way* ... so the matter is urgent, *Montgomery.*

let him do what he will, he sinneth not: let them marry: ... let him do what she desires...she and her suitor should be allowed to marry, *Weymouth* ... let them be coupled in mariage, *Geneva.*

37. Nevertheless he that standeth stedfast in his heart: ... if a father stands firm, *Weymouth* ... he that hath determined, *Rheims* ... already firmly decided, *SEB.*

having no necessity, but hath power over his own will: ... he is not obliged, *Fenton* ... being under no constraint, *Confraternity* ... is under no compulsion, *Berkeley* ... finds himself under no necessity of marrying, *Locke* ... complete control of his sexual will-power, *SEB* ... a sure control over his desires, *Norlie* ... but is free to act as he will, *Noyes* ... as regards his own wish, *Rotherham.*

and hath so decreed in his heart that he will keep his virgin, doeth well: ... has determined privately, *Rotherham* ... to retain the girl at home, *Fenton* ... keep his unmarried daughter at home, *TCNT* ... to keep his betrothed untouched, *Norlie* ... to preserve his virgin as a virgin, *Berkeley* ... keep his maid a spiritual bride, *Moffatt* ... he will keep his virginity, *Locke* ... to maintain his Celibacy, *Wilson* ... he doeth commendably, *Murdock.*

1 Corinthians 7:38

37.e.Txt: 06D,018K 020L,025P,byz.
Var: 01ℵ,02A,03B,33 bo.Lach,Treg,Alf,Tisc We/Ho,Weis,Sod UBS/☆

4020.52 verb 3sing indic fut act	5452.1 conj	2504.1 conj	3450.5 art sing masc	1534.2 verb nom sing masc part pres act
[ᵉ☆ ποιήσει˙]	**38.** ὥστε	καὶ	ὁ	ʿ ἐκγαμίζων
poiēsei	hōste	kai	ho	ekgamizōn
[he will do.]	So that	also	the	giving in marriage

38.a.Txt: 018K,020L,byz.
Var: 01ℵ,02A,33,Tisc We/Ho,Sod,UBS/☆

1053.1 verb nom sing masc part pres act	3450.12 art acc sing fem	1431.4 prs-pron gen 3sing	3795.3 noun acc sing masc	2544.1 adv
[ᵃ☆ γαμίζων	τὴν	ἑαυτοῦ	παρθένον]	καλῶς
gamizōn	tēn	heautou	parthenon	kalōs
[giving in marriage	the	of himself	virgin]	well

38.b.Txt: 01ℵ-corr,018K 020L,025P,byz.
Var: 01ℵ-org,02A,03B 06D,33,Gries,Lach,Treg Alf,Word,Tisc,We/Ho Weis,Sod,UBS/☆

4020.5 verb 3sing indic pres act	3450.5 art sing masc	1156.2 conj	2504.1 conj	3450.5 art sing masc	3231.1 partic
ποιεῖ˙	ʿ ὁ	δὲ	[ᵇ☆ καὶ	ὁ]	μὴ
poiei	ho	de	kai	ho	mē
does;	the	and	[and	the]	not

38.c.Txt: 01ℵ-corr,018K 020L,025P,byz.
Var: 01ℵ-org,02A,03B 06D,33,Gries,Lach,Treg Tisc,We/Ho,Weis,Sod UBS/☆

1534.2 verb nom sing masc part pres act	1053.1 verb nom sing masc part pres act	2882.6 adj comp sing neu	4020.5 verb 3sing indic pres act
ʿ ἐκγαμίζων	[ᶜ☆ γαμίζων]	κρεῖσσον	ʿ ποιεῖ.
ekgamizōn	gamizōn	kreisson	poiei
giving in marriage	[idem]	better	does.

38.d.Txt: 06D,018K 020L,025P,etc.byz.
Var: 01ℵ,02A,03B,bo. Lach,Treg,Alf,Tisc We/Ho,Weis,Sod UBS/☆

4020.52 verb 3sing indic fut act	1129.1 noun nom sing fem	1204.15 verb 3sing indic perf pass	3414.3 noun dat sing masc	1894.1 prep
[ᵈ☆ ποιήσει.]	**39.** Γυνὴ	δέδεται	ʿᵃ νόμῳ ʾ	ἐφ᾽
poiēsei	Gunē	dedetai	nomō	eph᾽
[will do.]	A wife	is bound	by law	for

39.a.Txt: 01ℵ-corr 06D-corr,020L,025P,byz.
Var: 01ℵ-org,02A,03B 06D-org,Gries,Lach Treg,Alf,Word,Tisc We/Ho,Weis,Sod UBS/☆

3607.1 rel-pron sing acc	5385.4 noun acc sing masc	2180.1 verb sing indic pres	3450.5 art sing masc	433.1 noun nom sing masc	840.10 prs-pron gen sing fem
ὅσον	χρόνον	ζῇ	ὁ	ἀνὴρ	αὐτῆς˙
hoson	chronon	zē	ho	anēr	autēs
as long as	time	may live	the	husband	her:

1430.1 partic	1156.2 conj	2810.7 verb 3sing subj aor pass	3450.5 art sing masc	433.1 noun nom sing masc
ἐὰν	δὲ	κοιμηθῇ	ὁ	ἀνὴρ
ean	de	koimēthē	ho	anēr
if	but	may have fallen asleep	the	husband

39.b.Txt: 06D,020L,byz.
Var: 01ℵ,02A,03B 018K,025P,Lach,Treg Alf,Tisc,We/Ho,Weis Sod,UBS/☆

840.10 prs-pron gen sing fem	1645.5 adj nom sing fem	1498.4 verb 3sing indic pres act	3614.3 rel-pron dat sing	2286.3 verb 3sing indic pres act
ʿᵇ αὐτῆς, ʾ	ἐλευθέρα	ἐστὶν	ᾧ	θέλει
autēs	eleuthera	estin	hō	thelei
her,	free	she is	to whom	she wills

1053.18 verb inf aor pass	3303.1 adv	1706.1 prep	2935.3 noun dat sing masc	3079.8 adj comp nom sing fem
γαμηθῆναι,	μόνον	ἐν	κυρίῳ.	**40.** μακαριωτέρα
gamēthēnai	monon	en	kuriō	makariōtera
to be married,	only	in	Lord.	Happier

1156.2 conj	1498.4 verb 3sing indic pres act	1430.1 partic	3643.1 adv	3176.19 verb 3sing subj aor act	2567.3 prep
δέ	ἐστιν	ἐὰν	οὕτως	μείνῃ,	κατὰ
de	estin	ean	houtōs	meinē	kata
but	she is	if	so	she should remain,	according to

3450.12 art acc sing fem	1684.9 adj acc 1sing fem	1100.4 noun acc sing fem	1374.3 verb 1sing indic pres act	1156.2 conj	2476.3 conj
τὴν	ἐμὴν	γνώμην˙	δοκῶ	δὲ	κἀγὼ
tēn	emēn	gnōmēn	dokō	de	kagō
the	my	judgment;	I think	and	I also

7:38. Verse 38 gives the strongest evidence for the view that verse 36 is addressing a father and his daughter. The reason for this is that Paul here used a different word for marriage (*ekgamizōn*) than he did in verses 28 and 36 (*gameitōsan* and *gēmē*). In Mark 12:25 *gamizō* means "given in marriage" and this is its use in classical Greek. It is also true, however, that the classical distinction between *-eō* and *-izō* verbs (e.g., *gameō* and *gamizō*) was no longer consistently held to in Koine Greek.

To recapitulate this complex section, in verse 25 Paul addressed himself to an issue the Corinthians had brought to Paul's attention (either in the letter they sent to him, cf. 7:1, or else by the representatives from Chloe's household, cf. 1:11), namely, *parthenon* (virgins). Although there are several particular kinds of situations that Paul has addressed, the bottom line to all of Paul's comments, given as they were by the Holy Spirit, is that there is nothing inherently good or evil regarding singleness or marriage. Each is an option; each can be positive; each can be negative.

The only concern that Paul has is that when people make their choice (and it must be a choice) for singleness or marriage they are obedient to God and do not take undue concern for this world which is passing away.

Paul returns to his original theme, that because of circumstances which he calls "the present distress" (probably the persecutions through which the church was going) that the unmarried state would be better. So he says that marriage is acceptable, but the single state is better.

Notice that Paul was not encouraging celibacy on moral grounds, that it is morally better to remain celibate. It is better only because it would make possible greater service for Christ.

7:39. In conclusion, Paul advised regarding widows and remarriage. The last group to fall under the heading of "virgins" in chapter 7 is widows. Paul has asserted all along that marriage and singleness are both legitimate options; that is the case here as well. In one of Paul's final letters, he once again took up the issue of widows (1 Timothy 5:9-15) and took the same stance that he took here. A wife is obligated as long as her husband lives. If her husband should die, the woman is free to marry according to her choice and will, with one exception. Her new spouse must be a believer, one "in the Lord." This would also require seeking the Lord's will in the matter.

7:40. But Paul was of the opinion that she would be happier if she remained a widow. She would be, in particular, happier in her undisturbed devotion to the Lord. And Paul concluded that in these matters he had not merely been bending to personal bias, but had been advised by the Spirit of God, in his position as a called apostle. He voiced not merely private opinion, but that which had come from divine enablement.

38. So then he that giveth [her] in marriage doeth well: If, then, he marries his girl, *Beck* . . . So the man who marries does well, *TEV* . . . the one who consents to his daughter's marriage, *TCNT* . . . gives his unmarried daughter in marriage, *HistNT* . . . marries his bride-to-be, *SEB* . . . his virgyn in matrymonye, *Wyclif* . . . will be doing the right thing, *Moffatt* . . . does right, *NIV*.

but he that giveth [her] not in marriage doeth better: . . . the one who opts against her marriage, *Adams* . . . will do better, *Weymouth* . . . does even better, *NIV*.

39. The wife is bound by the law as long as her husband liveth: . . . bound by the law of wedlock, *Conybeare* . . . during the whole period that he lives, *Weymouth*.

but if her husband be dead, she is at liberty to be married to whom she will: . . . but if her husband sleepe, *Rheims* . . . if he be fallen asleep, *HistNT* . . . should be reposing, *Concordant* . . . anyone she pleases, *Moffatt*.

only in the Lord: . . . only in a Christian way, *Berkeley* . . . provided he is not an unbeliever, *TCNT* . . . provided that he is a Christian, *Weymouth* . . . provided he be a believer, *Way* . . . it must be a Christian, *Moffatt*, *Williams*.

40. But she is happier if she so abide, after my judgment: But more blessed shall she be, *Douay* . . . But she'll be happier, *Beck* . . . her state is a more enviable one if she remains as she is, *Weymouth* . . . if she continue as she is, *Campbell* . . . if she stays as she is, *NIV* . . . if she stayed a widow, *SEB* . . . according to my opinion, *Hanson* . . . that is my opinion, *Moffatt* . . . in my opinion, *Murdock*.

and I think also that I have the Spirit of God: I, too, lay claim, *Norlie* . . . I also know God's intention, *Fenton*.

1 Corinthians 8:1

4011.1 noun sing neu
πνεῦμα
pneuma
Spirit

2296.2 noun gen sing masc
θεοῦ
theou
God's

2174.29 verb inf pres act
ἔχειν.
echein
to have.

8:1. **3875.1** prep
Περὶ
Peri
Concerning

1156.2 conj
δὲ
de
now

3450.1 art gen pl
τῶν
tōn
the

1484.2 adj gen pl neu
εἰδωλοθύτων,
eidōlothutōn
sacrificed to idols,

3471.5 verb 1pl indic perf act
οἴδαμεν,
oidamen
we know,

3617.1 conj
ὅτι
hoti
for

3820.7 adj pl masc
πάντες
pantes
all

1102.4 noun acc sing fem
γνῶσιν
gnōsin
knowledge

2174.5 verb 1pl indic pres act
ἔχομεν.
echomen
we have:

3450.9 art nom sing fem
ἡ
hē
the

1102.1 noun nom sing fem
γνῶσις
gnōsis
knowledge

5284.1 verb 3sing indic pres act
φυσιοῖ,
phusioi
puffs up,

3450.9 art nom sing fem
ἡ
hē
the

1156.2 conj
δὲ
de
but

26.1 noun nom sing fem
ἀγάπη
agapē
love

3481.3 verb 3sing indic pres act
οἰκοδομεῖ.
oikodomei
builds up.

2. **1479.1** conj
εἴ
ei
If

1156.2 conj
⟨a δέ⟩
de
but

4948.3 indef-pron nom sing
τις
tis
anyone

1374.5 verb 3sing indic pres act
δοκεῖ
dokei
thinks

3471.25 verb inf perf act
⟨ εἰδέναι
eidenai
to have known

1091.56 verb inf perf act
[b☆ ἐγνωκέναι]
egnōkenai
[idem]

4948.10 indef-pron sing neu
τι,
ti
anything,

3627.1 adv
⟨ οὐδέπω
oudepō
not yet

3625.6 num card neu
οὐδὲν
ouden
nothing

1091.32 verb 3sing indic perf act
ἔγνωκεν
egnōken
he has known

3632.1 adv
[c☆ οὔπω
oupō
[not yet

1091.17 verb 3sing indic aor act
ἔγνω]
egnō
he knew]

2503.1 conj
καθὼς
kathōs
just as

1158.1 verb 3sing indic pres act
δεῖ
dei
it is necessary

1091.29 verb inf aor act
γνῶναι.
gnōnai
to know.

3. **1479.1** conj
εἴ
ei
If

1156.2 conj
δέ
de
but

4948.3 indef-pron nom sing
τις
tis
anyone

25.2 verb 3sing pres act
ἀγαπᾷ
agapa
love

3450.6 art acc sing masc
τὸν
ton

2296.4 noun acc sing masc
θεόν,
theon
God,

3642.4 dem-pron nom sing masc
οὗτος
houtos
this

1091.46 verb 3sing indic perf pass
ἔγνωσται
egnōstai
is known

5097.2 prep
ὑπ᾽
hup'
by

840.3 prs-pron gen sing
αὐτοῦ.
autou
him:

4. **3875.1** prep
Περὶ
Peri
concerning

3450.10 art gen sing fem
τῆς
tēs
the

1028.2 noun gen sing fem
βρώσεως
brōseōs
eating

3631.1 conj
οὖν
oun
then

3450.1 art gen pl
τῶν
tōn
of the

1484.2 adj gen pl neu
εἰδωλοθύτων,
eidōlothutōn
things sacrificed to idols,

3471.5 verb 1pl indic perf act
οἴδαμεν
oidamen
we know

3617.1 conj
ὅτι
hoti
that

3625.6 num card neu
οὐδὲν
ouden
nothing

1487.1 noun nom sing neu
εἴδωλον
eidōlon
an idol

1706.1 prep
ἐν
en
in

2862.3 noun dat sing masc
κόσμῳ,
kosmō
world,

2504.1 conj
καὶ
kai
and

3617.1 conj
ὅτι
hoti
that

3625.2 num card nom masc
οὐδεὶς
oudeis
no

2296.1 noun nom sing masc
θεὸς
theos
God

2066.5 adj nom sing masc
⟨a ἕτερος ⟩
heteros
other

8:1. The Scriptures approve some things as always right for the Christian; others are always wrong. In between are questions of conscience, considered wrong by some, right by others. The problem at Corinth was the eating of meat that had been sacrificed to idols. The Corinthian Christians were continually confronted with it. Such meat could appear on nearly any table.

In dealing with this problem, and others, Paul set forth certain principles which are valid and useful to this day (1 Corinthians 6:12; Romans 14:1 to 15:13). The phrases "now concerning" or "now as touching" remind us that this was a question which came from the Corinthians themselves. In pursuit of the answer they had begun with a wrong premise. Paul had to correct them. Knowledge was of great value to the Corinthians, and Paul agreed with the importance and exercise of knowledge, but the Corinthians tried to solve their problems with knowledge alone. Paul made it clear that knowledge must be tempered with love.

Paul contrasted knowledge and love. He reminded the Corinthians that "knowledge puffeth up"; it can create pride, intellectual snobbery, and a "party spirit." Love, on the other hand, "edifieth" or builds up. The great Corinthian flaw was their poverty of love. The verb "edifieth" really refers to the putting up of buildings. Paul used it figuratively to mean the building of Christian character and the church. Knowledge alone could destroy the church; love and knowledge together could build it. Edification is the natural outgrowth of love (Ephesians 4:15f.; Matthew 22:37-40; 1 John 4:16-21).

8:2. Knowledge by itself has limitations. No matter how much a man thinks he knows, he still does not know fully. Paul used the perfect tense of the verb, implying full and complete knowledge.

8:3. What really matters is not our knowledge but God's (2 Timothy 2:19; Galatians 4:9). For to be known (*egnōstai*) by God means to share in His grace, having first been recognized by Him. "Is known" implies a knowledge that is complete and full. Proper knowledge, in the hand of love, gives a right foundation for our actions.

8:4. Paul then returned to the immediate question. "We know" (*oidamen*) continues the thought from verse 1. This is typical of Paul's style of writing.

When Paul wrote that "an idol is nothing," he was really saying it had no real place in the world; it had no power over the elements of nature. Rather, there is one God who controls earth and sky. Belief in the truth that the world is controlled by Him will deliver any Christian from superstition and fear. An idol is the product of man and thus has no real influence in the realm in which God Jehovah operates.

1. Now as touching things offered unto idols: And concerning, *Rheims* . . . Relative to food that has been offered to idols, *Berkeley* . . . With regard to food, *Moffatt* . . . about idol-offerings, *Fenton* . . . sacrificed vnto, *Geneva.*

we know that we all have knowledge: . . . we are aware, *Rotherham, HistNT.*

Knowledge puffeth up, but charity edifieth: Understanding makes you vain, *Fenton* . . . tends to make people conceited, *Weymouth* . . . maketh a man swell, *Cranmer* . . . Knowledge breeds conceit, while love builds up character, *TCNT* . . . love edifieth, *Murdock* . . . love builds up, *Moffatt.*

2. And if any man think that he knoweth any thing: Someone may seem to know a lot, *SEB* . . . is confident, *Campbell* . . . is presuming to know, *Concordant* . . . fancies he knows anything, *TCNT* . . . thinks that he knows a lot, *Norlie.*

he knoweth nothing yet as he ought to know: . . . he still has a lot to learn, *Norlie* . . . he still has something to learn, *Beck* . . . as it ought to be comprehended, *Fenton.*

3. But if any man love God, the same is known of him:

4. As concerning therefore the eating of those things that are offered in sacrifice unto idols: In regard to eating food, *HistNT* . . . offered to false gods, *SEB.*

we know that an idol [is] nothing in the world: . . . we are fully aware, *Weymouth* . . . that they really don't exist, *SEB* . . . that the fictitious gods, *Locke* . . . has no true being, *Conybeare* . . . has no real existence, *RSV* . . . existence in the world, *Norlie* . . . existence in the universe, *Montgomery, TCNT.*

and that [there is] none other God but one:

1479.1 conj	3231.1 partic	1518.3 num card nom masc		2504.1 conj	1056.1 conj	1499.1 conj	1498.7 verb 3pl indic pres act
εἰ	μὴ	εἷς.	**5.** καὶ	γὰρ	εἴπερ	εἰσὶν
ei	*mē*	*heis*	*kai*	*gar*	*eiper*	*eisin*
if	not	one.	Even	for	if indeed	there are

2978.32 verb nom pl masc part pres pass	2296.6 noun nom pl masc	1521.1 conj	1706.1 prep	3636.3 noun dat sing masc	1521.1 conj	1894.3 prep
λεγόμενοι	θεοὶ,	εἴτε	ἐν	οὐρανῷ	εἴτε	ἐπὶ
legomenoi	*theoi*	*eite*	*en*	*ourano*	*eite*	*epi*
being called	gods,	whether	in	heaven	or	on

5.a.Txt: Steph
Var: 01ℵ,02A,03B,06D
018K,025P,Gries,Lach
Treg,Alf,Word,Tisc
We/Ho,Weis,Sod
UBS/✶

3450.10 art gen sing fem	1087.2 noun gen sing fem	5450.1 adv	1498.7 verb 3pl indic pres act	2296.6 noun nom pl masc	4044.7 adj nom pl masc
[a τῆς]	γῆς·	ὥσπερ	εἰσὶν	θεοὶ	πολλοὶ
tēs	*gēs*	*hōsper*	*eisin*	*theoi*	*polloi*
the	earth,	as	there are	gods	many

2504.1 conj	2935.6 noun pl masc	4044.7 adj nom pl masc	233.1 conj	2231.3 prs-pron dat 1pl	1518.3 num card nom masc
καὶ	κύριοι	πολλοί·	**6.** ἀλλ'	ἡμῖν	εἷς
kai	*kurioi*	*polloi*	*all'*	*hēmin*	*heis*
and	lords	many,	but	to us	one

2296.1 noun nom sing masc	3450.5 art sing masc	3824.1 noun nom sing masc	1523.1 prep gen	3614.2 rel-pron gen sing	3450.17 art pl neu
θεὸς	ὁ	πατήρ,	ἐξ	οὗ	τὰ
theos	*ho*	*patēr*	*ex*	*hou*	*ta*
God	the	Father,	of	whom	the

3820.1 adj	2504.1 conj	2231.1 prs-pron nom 1pl	1519.1 prep	840.6 prs-pron acc sing masc	2504.1 conj	1518.3 num card nom masc
πάντα,	καὶ	ἡμεῖς	εἰς	αὐτόν·	καὶ	εἷς
panta	*kai*	*hēmeis*	*eis*	*auton*	*kai*	*heis*
all,	and	we	for	him;	and	one

2935.1 noun nom sing masc	2400.1 name nom masc	5382.1 name nom masc	1217.1 prep	3614.2 rel-pron gen sing	3450.17 art pl neu
κύριος	Ἰησοῦς	Χριστός,	δι'	οὗ	τὰ
kurios	*Iēsous*	*Christos*	*di'*	*hou*	*ta*
Lord	Jesus	Christ,	by	whom	the

3820.1 adj	2504.1 conj	2231.1 prs-pron nom 1pl	1217.1 prep	840.3 prs-pron gen sing	233.1 conj	3620.2 partic
πάντα,	καὶ	ἡμεῖς	δι'	αὐτοῦ.	**7.** Ἀλλ'	οὐκ
panta	*kai*	*hēmeis*	*di'*	*autou*	*All'*	*ouk*
all things,	and	we	by	him.	But	not

1706.1 prep	3820.5 adj dat pl	3450.9 art nom sing fem	1102.1 noun nom sing fem	4948.7 indef-pron nom pl masc	1156.2 conj
ἐν	πᾶσιν	ἡ	γνῶσις·	τινὲς	δὲ
en	*pasin*	*hē*	*gnōsis*	*tines*	*de*
in	all	the	knowledge:	some	but

7.a.Txt: 01ℵ-corr,06D
020L,byz.it.
Var: 01ℵ-org,02A,03B
025P,044,33,sa.bo.Lach
Treg,Tisc,We/Ho,Weis
Sod,UBS/✶

3450.11 art dat sing fem	4743.3 noun dat sing fem	4764.3 noun dat sing fem	3450.2 art gen sing	1487.2 noun gen sing neu
τῇ	συνειδήσει	[a✶ συνηθείᾳ]	τοῦ	εἰδώλου
tē	*suneidēsei*	*sunētheia*	*tou*	*eidōlou*
with the	conscience	[habit]	of the	idol,

2175.1 conj	732.1 adv	2175.1 conj	732.1 adv	3450.2 art gen sing	1487.2 noun gen sing neu	5453.1 conj
ἕως	ἄρτι	[✶ ἕως	ἄρτι	τοῦ	εἰδώλου]	ὡς
heōs	*arti*	*heōs*	*arti*	*tou*	*eidōlou*	*hōs*
until	now	[until	now	the	idol]	as

8:5. It is true there are claims to the godship (deity) and lordship (dominion) of idols. In point of fact, there are literally multitudes of these claims. The devil makes lying claims and performs lying wonders. But this very multitude proves inadequacy on their part. "Many" (*polloi*) shows the desire to compensate for truth and authority by numbers. But the fact remains that there is only one true God whether or not He is acknowledged in heathen societies.

8:6. On this hinge of the concept of one true God Paul hangs an important argument. Christians contrast sharply with idolaters. "Father" (*patēr*) denotes a special relationship to God as Creator and spiritual Father. All things exist by Him. Believers are reserved for His purposes and glory. He will reap in "us" His glory, as a father would through his children.

This relationship is possible through the "Lord Jesus Christ" who is seen in His functions of Master, Mediator, and Friend. Such faith leaves no place for false deities. The sacrificial rites were hollow and ineffective.

The central conviction governing Paul's remarks here about food offered to so-called gods is the fact that God is one. This statement is based on Deuteronomy 6:4,5, the Shema, which all faithful Jews recite twice a day. So important are the words of this passage, "Hear, O Israel: The Lord our God is one Lord: and thou shalt love the Lord thy God with all thine heart, and with all thy soul, and with all thy might," that Jesus himself called this the first and greatest commandment in Mark 12:29-31. One scholar has appropriately labeled the Shema "the most important word" for Christian life and doctrine (Miller, p.17).

The oneness of God is the most important word for Christians because it encompasses and explains how every facet of life belongs to God. Because God is one, our loyalty must be exclusive to Him alone. This is why the first commandment says, "Thou shalt have none other gods before me" (Deuteronomy 5:7) because there are no other gods—period. Thus, for Israel, "the absence of faith was not seen as a possibility. The only options for human existence are faith in the living God or idolatry" (Miller, p.25).

The Shema, then, has a twofold significance. The theological implication is that "there is only one ultimate or absolute—the power that undergirds all reality is one" (Miller, p.28). The anthropological implication means "God is that which keeps our lives from being chaotic and divided beyond the limits of human management . . . (and therefore) is that one and absolute object of our allegiance and loyalty" (Miller, p.29).

8:7. But there is another consideration. Not everyone in Corinth understood this. What knowledge these had did not rid them of the consciousness that what they ate was sacrificial idol meat and that they had somehow become connected with the idol. In verse 1 Paul said knowledge was not confined to a certain group in Cor-

5. For though there be that are called gods: For if so-called gods do exist, *Weymouth* . . . there be many imaginary nominal gods, *Locke* . . . there are so-called gods, *Adams* . . . there are nominal gods, *Campbell* . . . those being termed gods, *Concordant.*

whether in heaven or in earth: . . . either in the sky or on the earth, *TCNT* . . . either celestial or terrestrial, *Conybeare.*

(as there be gods many, and lords many,): . . . there are plenty of them, *Moffatt* . . . indeed, a vast number, *Williams* . . . and many demi-gods, *Fenton* . . . but they are not real, *SEB.*

6. But to us [there is but] one God, the Father, of whom [are] all things, and we in him: He is the Source of everything, *SEB* . . . who is the source of all things and the goal of our living, *Williams* . . . for whose service we exist, *Weymouth* . . . and we live for him, *Beck.*

and one Lord Jesus Christ: by whom [are] all things, and we by him: He made everything, *Beck* . . . through whom everything was made, *Williams* . . . through Whom all things exist, including us who ourselves exist through Him, *Adams* . . . and for whom we exist, *Moffatt* . . . and we exist through him, *HistNT.*

7. Howbeit [there is] not in every man that knowledge: But everybody doesn't know this, *Adams* . . . all believers do not recognize these facts, *Weymouth* . . . this knowledge of God is not shared by everyone, *Norlie* . . . by [their] familiarity, until even now, *Rotherham.*

for some with conscience of the idol unto this hour: Some, having been accustomed to idol worship, *Norlie* . . . because of their past habits with idols, *Williams* . . . still idol-conscious, *Confraternity* . . . think in terms of idols, *Berkeley* . . . their quite recent familiarity with idols, *TCNT* . . . by familiarity with the idol, *Worrell* . . . accustomed until now, *Montgomery* . . . still have the habit of treating idols, *SEB.*

355

1 Corinthians 8:8

1484.1 adj sing neu	2052.3 verb 3pl indic pres act	2504.1 conj	3450.9 art nom sing fem	4743.1 noun nom sing fem
εἰδωλόθυτον	ἐσθίουσιν,	καὶ	ἡ	συνείδησις
eidōlothuton	esthiousin	kai	hē	suneidēsis
a thing sacrificed to an idol	eat,	and	the	conscience

840.1 prs-pron gen pl	766.1 adj nom sing	1498.26 verb nom sing fem part pres act	3298.2 verb 3sing indic pres pass	1026.1 noun sing neu
αὐτῶν	ἀσθενὴς	οὖσα	μολύνεται.	8. βρῶμα
autōn	asthenēs	ousa	molunetai	brōma
their,	weak	being,	is being defiled.	Food

1156.2 conj	2231.4 prs-pron acc 1pl	3620.3 partic	3798.2 verb 3sing indic pres act	3798.21 verb 3sing indic fut act
δὲ	ἡμᾶς	οὐ	ʿ παρίστησιν	[ᵃ⋆ παραστήσει]
de	hēmas	ou	paristēsin	parastēsei
but	us	not	does commend	[will commend]

3450.3 art dat sing	2296.3 noun dat sing masc	3641.1 conj	1056.1 conj	1430.1 partic	2052.18 verb 1pl subj aor act
τῷ	θεῷ·	οὔτε	ʿᵇ γὰρ ʾ	ἐὰν	ʿ φάγωμεν
tō	theō	oute	gar	ean	phagōmen
to God;	to God;	neither	for	if	we eat

3915.3 verb 1pl indic pres act	3641.1 conj	1430.1 partic	3231.1 partic	2052.18 verb 1pl subj aor act
περισσεύομεν·	οὔτε	ἐὰν	μὴ	φάγωμεν
perisseuomen	oute	ean	mē	phagōmen
have we an advantage;	neither	if	not	we eat

5139.9 verb 1pl indic pres pass	3231.1 partic	2052.18 verb 1pl subj aor act	5139.9 verb 1pl indic pres pass	3641.1 conj
ὑστερούμεθα.	[⋆ μὴ	φάγωμεν	ὑστερούμεθα,	οὔτε
husteroumetha	mē	phagōmen	husteroumetha	oute
do we come short.	[not	we eat	do we come short,	neither

1430.1 partic	2052.18 verb 1pl subj aor act	3915.3 verb 1pl indic pres act	984.1 verb 2pl pres act	1156.2 conj
ἐὰν	φάγωμεν	περισσεύομεν.]	9. βλέπετε	δὲ
ean	phagōmen	perisseuomen	blepete	de
if	we eat	do we excel.]	Beware	but

3248.1 conj	3231.1 partic	4315.1 adv	3450.9 art nom sing fem	1833.2 noun nom sing fem	5050.2 prs-pron gen 2pl
ʿ μήπως	[⋆ μή	πως]	ἡ	ἐξουσία	ὑμῶν
mēpōs	mē	pōs	hē	exousia	humōn
lest	[not	somehow]	the	right	your

3642.9 dem-pron nom sing fem	4206.1 noun sing neu	1090.40 verb 3sing subj aor mid	3450.4 art dat pl
αὕτη	πρόσκομμα	γένηται	τοῖς
hautē	proskomma	genētai	tois
this	an occasion of stumbling	become	to the

764.5 verb dat pl part pres act	766.6 adj dat pl masc	1430.1 partic	1056.1 conj	4948.3 indef-pron nom sing
ʿ ἀσθενοῦσιν.	[ᵃ⋆ ἀσθενέσιν.]	10. ἐὰν	γὰρ	τις
asthenousin	asthenesin	ean	gar	tis
being weak.	[weak ones.]	If	for	anyone

1481.10 verb 3sing subj aor act	4622.4 prs-pron acc 2sing	3450.6 art acc sing masc	2174.15 verb part pres act	1102.4 noun acc sing fem	1706.1 prep
ἴδῃ	ʿᵃ σὲ, ʾ	τὸν	ἔχοντα	γνῶσιν,	ἐν
idē	se	ton	echonta	gnōsin	en
see	you,	the	having	knowledge,	in

inth. But that did not mean all Christians possessed it. If a person lived with a haunting sense that what he ate belonged to idols, he was associated with idols; he had sinned (Romans 14:23). This one with the weak conscience, unable to discern whether the act was right or wrong, lived with guilt.

8:8. Paul made the point that neither partaking nor abstaining would affect the relationship of the Corinthians to God. Food is too small a matter and God is too great to allow it to determine a believer's relationship to Him. Abstinence will not bring him closer to God, nor drive him away, as the weak might have been led to believe. In like manner indulgence would not make him better as the proud might have wished. This was not the heart of the problem. What Paul was leading up to was having the right motive toward God and others.

8:9. Paul issued a solemn warning about asserting one's personal rights. This can affect one's standing with God. Jesus made it abundantly clear that love toward God shows itself in the way we treat the stranger, our enemies, and our brother. Love is essential in our relationship with God; therefore it is vital in our relationship with our Christian brothers.

The issue is not that we are strong or have a good knowledge of the things of Christ. Nor is the issue that of our wonderful freedom in Christ. The point is that we must consider the frailties of the weak. The stronger we are, the more that attitude is demanded of us.

Meat in itself is a neutral item and may be refrained from for the good of another. "Stumblingblock" (*proskomma*) is something that lies in the path, over which an unwary, unsuspecting foot might trip or stumble. Naturally, this could cause the person to fall. From a spiritual viewpoint a "stumblingblock" is anything that can cause another to sin, to act outside of faith, and so injure his soul or Christian life.

8:10. To reinforce his point, Paul presented an illustration for the Corinthians. He pictured the example of a knowledgeable, strong Christian at a temple feast. He might be there from obligation or for an official ceremony, for such an event in a pagan city would not occur apart from a meal in the temple. Or it might be the result of the general conduct of a Corinthian who considered idol meat as merely ordinary.

Paul censured this because of its effect on others. In 10:18-22 he opposed it on its own account. A "weak" brother, as was possible in open feasts, might observe the actions of the "stronger" brother. By use of a question, Paul pointed out that the weak brother, seeing the example of the stronger brother, might eat thinking it was permissible for him also.

eat [it] as a thing offered unto an idol:

and their conscience being weak is defiled: . . . their moral sense, being still weak, receives a shock, *TCNT* . . . is polluted, *Rheims* . . . are polluted, *Weymouth* . . . is contaminated, *Moffatt* . . . is being guilt-stained, *Way*.

8. But meat commendeth us not to God: But food will not bring us before God, *Adams* . . . Now our food cannot change our place in God's sight, *Conybeare* . . . will not give us a standing, *Concordant* . . . does not recommend us, *Campbell, Berkeley* . . . doth not bring us near to God, *Murdock* . . . does not bring us nearness to God, *Montgomery*.

for neither, if we eat, are we the better; neither, if we eat not, are we the worse: We are not any better off, *SEB* . . . if we abstain we do not lose anything, *Moffatt* . . . we are neither inferior to others if we abstain from it, nor superior to them if we eat it, *Weymouth* . . . are we the richer...are we the poorer, *Geneva* . . . are we lacking, *Worrell* . . . are we deficient, *Macknight* . . . shal vve abound...shal vve lacke, *Rheims* . . . do we come short, *Rotherham* . . . shall we have the less, *Douay* . . . we do not fall short by abstaining, *Norlie* . . . are we worse Christians, *Locke*.

9. But take heed lest by any means this liberty of yours become a stumblingblock to them that are weak: Now beware, *Concordant, Sawyer* . . . lest this same strength of yours, *Fenton* . . . lest this your authority, *Murdock* . . . that this mastery of yours, *Berkeley* . . . that the exercise of your right, *Moffatt* . . . your freedom in this matter, *TCNT* . . . cause not the weake to faule, *Tyndale* . . . be an offense to, *Rheims* . . . be an occasyone of falling, *Cranmer*.

10. For if any man see thee which hast knowledge sit at meat in the idol's temple: . . . the possessor of comprehension, *Fenton* . . . sit feasting in an idol-temple, *Locke* . . . an idol's shrine, *Concordant*.

1 Corinthians 8:11

1483.1 noun dat sing neu	2591.2 verb acc sing masc part pres	3644.1 adv	3450.9 art nom sing fem	4743.1 noun nom sing fem
εἰδωλείῳ	κατακείμενον,	οὐχὶ	ἡ	συνείδησις
eidōleiō	katakeimenon	ouchi	hē	suneidēsis
an idol temple	reclining,	not	the	conscience

840.3 prs-pron gen sing	766.3 adj gen sing masc	1498.19 verb gen sing part pres act	3481.20 verb 3sing indic fut pass	1519.1 prep
αὐτοῦ	ἀσθενοῦς	ὄντος	οἰκοδομηθήσεται	εἰς
autou	asthenous	ontos	oikodomēthēsetai	eis
his	weak	being	will be built up	to

3450.16 art sing neu	3450.17 art pl neu	1484.3 adj acc pl neu	2052.14 verb inf pres act	2504.1 conj
τὸ	τὰ	εἰδωλόθυτα	ἐσθίειν;	**11.** ʿ καὶ
to	ta	eidōlothuta	esthiein	kai
the	the	things sacrificed to idols	to eat?	and

11.a.Txt: 06D-corr,020L byz.
Var: 01א-org,03B,33,bo. Lach,Treg,Tisc,We/Ho Weis,Sod,UBS/☆

616.27 verb 3sing indic fut mid	616.33 verb 3sing indic pres pass	1056.1 conj	3450.5 art sing masc	764.6 verb nom sing masc part pres act
ἀπολεῖται	[ᵃ☆ ἀπόλλυται	γὰρ]	ὁ	ἀσθενῶν
apoleitai	apollutai	gar	ho	asthenōn
will perish	[is being destroyed	for]	the	being weak

11.b.Txt: 020L,byz.
Var: 01א-org,02A,03B 33,Lach,Treg,Alf,Word Tisc,We/Ho,Weis,Sod UBS/☆

79.1 noun nom sing masc	1894.3 prep	3450.11 art dat sing fem	4528.6 adj dat 2sing fem	1102.3 noun dat sing fem	1706.1 prep
ʿ ἀδελφὸς	ἐπὶ	τῇ	σῇ	γνώσει,	[ᵇ☆ ἐν
adelphos	epi	tē	sē	gnōsei	en
brother	on	the	your	knowledge,	[by

3450.11 art dat sing fem	4528.6 adj dat 2sing fem	1102.3 noun dat sing fem	3450.5 art sing masc	79.1 noun nom sing masc	1217.1 prep
τῇ	σῇ	γνώσει,	ὁ	ἀδελφὸς]	δι'
tē	sē	gnōsei	ho	adelphos	di'
the	your	knowledge,	the	brother]	for

3614.6 rel-pron acc sing masc	5382.1 name nom masc	594.10 verb 3sing indic aor act	3643.1 adv	1156.2 conj
ὃν	Χριστὸς	ἀπέθανεν.	**12.** οὕτως	δὲ
hon	Christos	apethanen	houtōs	de
whom	Christ	died.	Thus	now

262.6 verb nom pl masc part pres act	1519.1 prep	3450.8 art acc pl masc	79.9 noun acc pl masc	2504.1 conj
ἁμαρτάνοντες	εἰς	τοὺς	ἀδελφοὺς,	καὶ
hamartanontes	eis	tous	adelphous	kai
sinning	against	the	brothers,	and

5021.2 verb nom pl masc part pres act	840.1 prs-pron gen pl	3450.12 art acc sing fem	4743.4 noun acc sing fem	764.10 verb acc sing fem part pres act
τύπτοντες	αὐτῶν	τὴν	συνείδησιν	ἀσθενοῦσαν,
tuptontes	autōn	tēn	suneidēsin	asthenousan
wounding	their	the	conscience	weak,

1519.1 prep	5382.4 name acc masc	262.1 verb 2pl pres act	1349.1 conj	1479.1 conj	1026.1 noun sing neu
εἰς	Χριστὸν	ἁμαρτάνετε.	**13.** διόπερ	εἰ	βρῶμα
eis	Christon	hamartanete	dioper	ei	brōma
against	Christ	you sin.	Wherefore	if	food

4479.1 verb 3sing indic pres act	3450.6 art acc sing masc	79.4 noun acc sing masc	1466.2 prs-pron gen 1sing	3620.3 partic	3231.1 partic
σκανδαλίζει	τὸν	ἀδελφόν	μου,	οὐ	μὴ
skandalizei	ton	adelphon	mou	ou	mē
cause to offend	the	brother	my,	not	not

Paul said the weaker brother might be "emboldened" (*oikodom-ēthēsetai*) or strengthened; that is, encouraged, to partake of the idol meat. This same word is translated as "edifieth" in verse 1. The phrase is full of irony. Perhaps the stronger brother thought of "building" up by his poor example. But faith was not built, and the result was destruction.

The "stronger" Corinthians in their pride no doubt assumed that by their example they could show the weaker brothers "a better way." The problem with this is that Paul said that "whatsoever is not of faith is sin" (Romans 14:23). It is important to note that Romans 14:1 to 15:5 (which was written while Paul was in Corinth) also deals with the issue of the strong and the weak. Both in Romans and 1 Corinthians Paul personally favors the stronger position, but he would not prescribe this for any who might be offended. As with the issue of singleness and marriage, Paul did not make absolute assertions; Paul's task as an apostle of Jesus Christ and a willing tool of the Holy Spirit was to teach that any and all actions must come from faith, not from the well-meaning (or not so well-meaning) advice of other Christians. God is not glorified by actions performed under duress; rather God looks at the inner motivation of a person and judges on that basis (Romans 15:5,6).

8:11. The result of such an action was that the weak brother perished or "is perishing"; he sinned. What compounded this picture was that this was one for whom Christ died. If Christ would die for the "weak," what should the "stronger" brother be willing to do.

8:12. The sin of wounding a weak conscience is against the brethren, the Church as a whole. A wound is inflicted, because the conscience of the weaker believer is influenced to make a decision which it would not have done on its own and which it should not make. Sin then occurs.

Worst of all, it is a sin against Christ. He is robbed of the soul for which He died. Christ's work on the cross is not appreciated properly.

8:13. In conclusion, Paul's admonition was clear. Abstinence, under such circumstances, was best. But a warning must be offered. Not just any situation demands such forbearance, for some go to an opposite extreme. Nonetheless, Paul would under no circumstances bear the awful burden of causing someone to stumble and sin; that must be prevented at all costs.

Actually, Paul's statement was more comprehensive than some would think; the word "meat" (*brōma*) is a general term relating to food, not just to idol meat. The issue was vital to Paul; he used "brother" four times in these last three verses. It should be important to all Christians to care for the weaker brother. Paul said he

shall not the conscience of him which is weak be emboldened to eat those things which are offered to idols: . . . his conscience, uncertain as it is, *Berkeley* . . . won't you be encouraging him, *Beck* . . . embolden him to violate his scruples of conscience, *Moffatt* . . . be encouraged to eat, *Fenton.*

11. And through thy knowledge shall the weak brother perish: In consequence, *Berkeley* . . . you may bring spiritual destruction upon this weaker man, *Norlie* . . . ruining the weak fellow Christian, *Beck* . . . he who is feeble, *Murdock* . . . the weak man is ruined, *TCNT* . . . is ruined by your enlightenment, *Berkeley* . . . by your so-called knowledge, *Williams* . . . will perish because of your "knowledge"! *TEV* . . . is utterly lost, *Fenton.*
for whom Christ died?:

12. But when ye sin so against the brethren: . . . against your fellow Christians, *Beck.*
and wound their weak conscience: . . . and striking their vveake conscience, *Rheims* . . . injuring their moral sense, *TCNT* . . . and smiting their conscience, *Rotherham, Worrell.*
ye sin against Christ: . . . in reality, sinning, *Weymouth* . . . you are actually sinning against Christ, *Williams.*

13. Wherefore, if meat make my brother to offend: . . . if food is any hindrance to my brother's welfare, *Moffatt* . . . if meat causes my brother to sin, *SEB* . . . if food makes my brother sin, *TEV* . . . is the cause of my brother's downfall, *Norlie* . . . a cause of my brother's falling, *RSV* . . . I shall never eat meat again, *Adams* . . . so that I may not cause my brother to stumble, *Fenton* . . . to fall, *Weymouth.*

1 Corinthians 9:1

2052.15 verb 1sing subj aor act	2880.1 noun acc pl neu	1519.1 prep	3450.6 art acc sing masc	163.3 noun acc sing masc	2419.1 conj
φάγω	κρέα	εἰς	τὸν	αἰῶνα,	ἵνα
phagō	krea	eis	ton	aiōna	hina
should I eat	flesh	unto	the	age,	that

3231.1 partic	3450.6 art acc sing masc	79.4 noun acc sing masc	1466.2 prs-pron gen 1sing	4479.3 verb 1sing subj aor act
μὴ	τὸν	ἀδελφόν	μου	σκανδαλίσω.
mē	ton	adelphon	mou	skandalisō
not	the	brother	my	I may cause to offend.

1.a.Txt: 06D,018K,020L byz.
Var: 01ℵ,02A,03B,025P 33,bo.Gries,Lach,Treg Alf,Word,Tisc,We/Ho Weis,Sod,UBS/☆

3620.2 partic	1498.2 verb 1sing indic pres act	646.1 noun nom sing masc	1645.1 adj nom sing masc
9:1. Οὐκ	εἰμὶ	‹ ἀπόστολος;	[ᵃ☆ ἐλεύθερος;]
Ouk	eimi	apostolos	eleutheros
Not	am I	an apostle?	[free?]

1.b.Txt: 06D,018K,020L byz.
Var: 01ℵ,02A,03B,025P 33,bo.Gries,Lach,Treg Alf,Word,Tisc,We/Ho Weis,Sod,UBS/☆

3620.2 partic	1498.2 verb 1sing indic pres act	1645.1 adj nom sing masc	646.1 noun nom sing masc	3644.1 adv
οὐκ	εἰμὶ	‹ ἐλεύθερος;	[ᵇ☆ ἀπόστολος;]	οὐχὶ
ouk	eimi	eleutheros	apostolos	ouchi
not	am I	free?	[an apostle?]	not

1.c.Txt: 06D,018K,020L 025P,byz.
Var: 01ℵ,02A,03B,Lach Treg,Alf,Tisc,We/Ho Weis,Sod,UBS/☆

2400.3 name acc masc	5382.4 name acc masc	3450.6 art acc sing masc	2935.4 noun acc sing masc	2231.2 prs-pron gen 1pl
Ἰησοῦν	‹ᶜ Χριστὸν ›	τὸν	κύριον	ἡμῶν
Iēsoun	Christon	ton	kurion	hēmōn
Jesus	Christ	the	Lord	our

1.d.Txt: 02A,03B-corr 06D-org,018K,020L,byz. Sod
Var: 01ℵ,03B-org 06D-corr,025P,Tisc We/Ho,Weis,UBS/☆

3571.9 verb 1sing indic perf act	3571.35 verb 1sing indic perf act	3620.3 partic	3450.16 art sing neu	2024.1 noun sing neu	1466.2 prs-pron gen 1sing
‹ ἑώρακα;	[ᵈ ἑόρακα;]	οὐ	τὸ	ἔργον	μου
heōraka	heoraka	ou	to	ergon	mou
have I seen?	[idem]	not	the	work	my

5050.1 prs-pron nom 2pl	1498.6 verb 2pl indic pres act	1706.1 prep	2935.3 noun dat sing masc	1479.1 conj	241.7 adj dat pl masc	3620.2 partic
ὑμεῖς	ἐστε	ἐν	κυρίῳ;	**2.** εἰ	ἄλλοις	οὐκ
humeis	este	en	kuriō	ei	allois	ouk
you	are	in	Lord?	If	to others	not

1498.2 verb 1sing indic pres act	646.1 noun nom sing masc	233.2 conj	1058.1 partic	5050.3 prs-pron dat 2pl	1498.2 verb 1sing indic pres act
εἰμὶ	ἀπόστολος,	ἀλλά	γε	ὑμῖν	εἰμι·
eimi	apostolos	alla	ge	humin	eimi
I am	an apostle,	but	yet	to you	I am;

3450.9 art nom sing fem	1056.1 conj	4825.1 noun nom sing fem	3450.10 art gen sing fem	1684.7 adj gen 1sing fem	645.1 noun gen sing fem
ἡ	γὰρ	σφραγίς	‹ τῆς	ἐμῆς	ἀποστολῆς
hē	gar	sphragis	tēs	emēs	apostolēs
the	for	seal	of the	my	apostleship

2.a.Txt: 06D,018K,020L byz.
Var: 01ℵ,03B,025P,33 Lach,Treg,Alf,Tisc We/Ho,Weis,Sod UBS/☆

1466.2 prs-pron gen 1sing	3450.10 art gen sing fem	645.1 noun gen sing fem	5050.1 prs-pron nom 2pl	1498.6 verb 2pl indic pres act
[ᵃ☆ μου	τῆς	ἀποστολῆς]	ὑμεῖς	ἐστε
mou	tēs	apostolēs	humeis	este
[my	of the	apostleship]	you	are

1706.1 prep	2935.3 noun dat sing masc	3450.9 art nom sing fem	1684.6 adj nom 1sing fem	621.1 noun nom sing fem	3450.4 art dat pl
ἐν	κυρίῳ.	**3.** Ἡ	ἐμὴ	ἀπολογία	τοῖς
en	kuriō	Hē	emē	apologia	tois
in	Lord.	The	my	defense	to the

would abstain, if need be, "while the world standeth." Paul was willing to do this, and the Corinthians needed to follow his example in Christ. There is a certain freedom of knowledge in Christ, but it must be tempered by love. Paul intended to have a clear conscience in liberty and love.

As a summary to chapter 8, let us recall the Gnostic problem at Corinth. The Gnostics, here associated with the strong position, believed that the "spiritual" and the "physical" realms were completely unrelated. Consequently any act involving the body could not detract from their spirituality. This gave them a kind of superiority over other Christians because their freedom was unhindered.

The strong position can be identified particularly in three slogans: "We all have knowledge" (8:1); "there is no . . . idol in the world" (8:4, NASB) and "all things are lawful" (10:23, also in the context of meat offered to idols). Although these statements may appear to be true in and of themselves, the Holy Spirit cannot condone the attitude of pride that lurks behind them. This is why Paul begins the following chapter with the statement that even though he has freedom as an apostle, he is actually subject to God and to his brothers.

9:1. Having suggested his own example, Paul set out to show that his example could be trusted and followed. With "am I not free?" to which Paul expected a positive reply, he asserted that, like other Christians, he had certain Christian rights and privileges. Paul was not bound by Mosaic restrictions. He knew liberty in Christ. The positive response expected to "Am I not an apostle?" also indicated his privileges in the special position of God's called apostle. He had seen "Jesus Christ our Lord." The use of "Jesus" alone (cf. variant c) is rare with Paul. He may have been thinking of his Damascus Road experience or maybe of Christ's humanity.

Paul's work had borne fruit. While the emphasis was still clearly on God, the Corinthians were visible proof of the effectiveness of Paul's labors. They should be the last to doubt Paul's apostleship because he was their spiritual father. They were living proof of the effectiveness of his work.

Paul built his argument to a telling conclusion. Step by step, in thorough and convincing fashion, he involved the Corinthians in the process and presented such a strong base for his conclusions that when he finished, the Corinthian Christians understood what was right in the Lord.

9:2. The Corinthians were the "seal" of Paul's apostleship. The seal (*sphragis*) was important in a day when many could not read. The mark stamped on clay or wax was first a mark of ownership and then a means of authentication (Morris, *Tyndale New Testament Commentaries*, 7:132). This was not only a defense to Paul's critics, it also bore directly on the question of rights.

I will eat no flesh while the world standeth: . . . under no circumstances, *Concordant* . . . I eat flesh to the latest age, *Rotherham* . . . will I touch any kind of animal food, *Weymouth*.

lest I make my brother to offend: . . . for fear I should cause my brother to fall, *Weymouth* . . . I should be snaring my, *Concordant*.

1. Am I not an apostle?:
am I not free?: . . . a freeman? *Campbell*.

have I not seen Jesus Christ our Lord?: . . . with my own eyes? *Norlie*.

are not ye my work in the Lord?: I have accomplished in, *Moffatt* . . . You are the result of my efforts, *SEB* . . . that you are the fruits of my labor, *Conybeare* . . . products of my work in the Lord? *Norlie*.

2. If I be not an apostle unto others, yet doubtless I am to you: . . . yet I am certainly so to you, *Fenton* . . . certainly at least to you I am, *Rotherham* . . . I certainly am one to you, *Beck* . . . At least to you, *SEB*.

for the seal of mine apostleship are ye in the Lord: . . . for your very existence as a Christian church, *Weymouth* . . . for you are the seal set, *Moffatt* . . . for you are the stamp of my apostleship, *Fenton* . . . the seal which stamps the reality of my apostleship, *Conybeare* . . . are the proof of...by virtue of your union with the Lord, *Williams* . . . the actual seal set on my mission-work, *Way*.

1 Corinthians 9:4

1466.7 prs-pron acc 1sing
ἐμὲ
eme
me

348.5 verb dat pl masc part pres act
ἀνακρίνουσίν
anakrinousin
examining

3642.9 dem-pron nom sing fem
ʽ αὕτη
hautē
this

1498.4 verb 3sing indic pres act
ἐστιν,
estin
is:

1498.4 verb 3sing indic pres act
[☆ ἐστιν
estin
[is

3642.9 dem-pron nom sing fem
αὕτη.]
hautē
this.]

3231.1 partic
4. Μὴ
Mē
Not

3620.2 partic
οὐκ
ouk
not

2174.5 verb 1pl indic pres act
ἔχομεν
echomen
have we

1833.4 noun acc sing fem
ἐξουσίαν
exousian
authority

2052.25 verb inf aor act
φαγεῖν
phagein
to eat

2504.1 conj
καὶ
kai
and

3956.23 verb inf aor act
ʽ πιεῖν;
piein
to drink?

3956.29 verb inf aor act
[☆ πεῖν;]
pein
[idem]

3231.1 partic
5. μὴ
mē
not

3620.2 partic
οὐκ
ouk
not

2174.5 verb 1pl indic pres act
ἔχομεν
echomen
have we

1833.4 noun acc sing fem
ἐξουσίαν
exousian
authority

78.4 noun acc sing fem
ἀδελφὴν
adelphēn
a sister,

1129.4 noun acc sing fem
γυναῖκα
gunaika
a wife,

3876.3 verb inf pres act
περιάγειν,
periagein
to take about,

5453.1 conj
ὡς
hōs
as

2504.1 conj
καὶ
kai
also

3450.7 art pl masc
οἱ
hoi
the

3036.3 adj nom pl masc
λοιποὶ
loipoi
remaining

646.4 noun pl masc
ἀπόστολοι,
apostoloi
apostles,

2504.1 conj
καὶ
kai
and

3450.7 art pl masc
οἱ
hoi
the

79.6 noun pl masc
ἀδελφοὶ
adelphoi
brothers

3450.2 art gen sing
τοῦ
tou
of the

2935.2 noun gen sing masc
κυρίου,
kuriou
Lord,

2504.1 conj
καὶ
kai
and

2758.1 name nom masc
Κηφᾶς;
Kēphas
Cephas?

2211.1 conj
6. ἢ
ē
Or

3304.2 adj nom sing masc
μόνος
monos
only

1466.1 prs-pron nom 1sing
ἐγὼ
egō
I

2504.1 conj
καὶ
kai
and

915.1 name nom masc
Βαρναβᾶς
Barnabas
Barnabas

3620.2 partic
οὐκ
ouk
not

2174.5 verb 1pl indic pres act
ἔχομεν
echomen
have we

1833.4 noun acc sing fem
ἐξουσίαν
exousian
authority

3450.2 art gen sing
ʽa τοῦ ʼ
tou
the

3231.1 partic
μὴ
mē
not

2021.12 verb inf pres
ἐργάζεσθαι;
ergazesthai
to work?

4949.3 intr-pron nom sing
7. Τίς
Tis
Who

4605.1 verb 3sing indic pres mid
στρατεύεται
strateuetai
serves as a soldier

2375.5 adj dat pl
ἰδίοις
idiois
at his own

3664.3 noun dat pl neu
ὀψωνίοις
opsōniois
expenses

4077.1 adv
ποτέ;
pote
at any time?

4949.3 intr-pron nom sing
τίς
tis
who

5288.1 verb 3sing indic pres act
φυτεύει
phuteuei
plants

288.3 noun acc sing fem
ἀμπελῶνα,
ampelōna
a vineyard,

2504.1 conj
καὶ
kai
and

1523.2 prep gen
ʽ ἐκ
ek
of

3450.2 art gen sing
τοῦ
tou
the

2561.2 noun gen sing masc
καρποῦ
karpou
fruit

3450.6 art acc sing masc
[a☆ τὸν
ton
[the

2561.3 noun acc sing masc
καρπὸν]
karpon
fruit]

840.3 prs-pron gen sing
αὐτοῦ
autou
of it

3620.2 partic
οὐκ
ouk
not

2052.2 verb 3sing indic pres act
ἐσθίει;
esthiei
does eat?

2211.1 conj
ʽb ἢ
ē
or

4949.3 intr-pron nom sing
τίς
tis
who

6.a.Txt: 06D-corr,018K 020L,byz.
Var: 01א,02A,03B 06D-org,025P,33,Lach Treg,Tisc,We/Ho,Weis Sod,UBS/☆

7.a.Txt: 04C-corr 06D-corr,018K,020L byz.bo.
Var: 01א-org,02A,03B 04C-org,06D-org,025P 33,sa.Lach,Treg,Alf Word,Tisc,We/Ho,Weis Sod,UBS/☆

7.b.Txt: p46,01א,02A 04C-org,018K,020L 025P,We/Ho,UBS/☆
Var: 03B,04C-corr2,06D 08E,010F,012G

362

9:3. "This" relates to the two previous verses. It appears that what was really under attack was Paul's apostleship, not the rights of apostleship. Paul defended this to make his argument accepted. Even if Paul's use of his rights had been criticized, it would have been much easier to accept if he were regarded as a true apostle. Both "answer" and "examine" are legal words, as though defending against a charge. If Paul had established his apostleship, the rights should be granted as well.

The point that Paul was coming to was that all must be an example of love in liberty as he had been.

9:4. Paul had the right or freedom to "eat and to drink." Probably he was speaking of the right to maintenance at the church's expense, or support in other ways. Or he may still have been discussing the matter of food.

9:5. Paul did expect, if he so chose, to be able to "lead about . . . a wife." But this particular question was not limited to marriage only. That would not have been argued. The question with its positive response expected led not only to support for the apostle but to the implication that the wife too should be supported by the church. To support his argument Paul pointed to the actions of other Christian leaders. The reference to "other apostles" would suggest that a number of them were married. The examples used were those who had a special place in the eyes of the Corinthians. This strengthened the general argument.

9:6. The questions continued, each anticipating a positive answer. Paul had the right, along with Barnabas, to refrain from working to support himself while preaching the gospel. His point was that he should be able to desist from manual labor, in order to spend full time spreading the gospel. This would mean that the church would find it necessary to support him.

Certainly, this church could not argue that these two alone were not to be offered such support, or did not have this right, when the many others did.

9:7. Having defended his rights and privileges by the acts of other Christian teachers, Paul now turned to the custom of society. Paul pointed to the examples of the soldier, the vinedresser, and the shepherd. Like Christ before him, Paul found great power in these simple illustrations (Matthew 20:1; 21:28; Luke 11:21,22; 12:32; 14:31; John 10:1-16; 21:15; 1 Corinthians 3:6; 14:8; Ephesians 4:11; 6:10; 1 Thessalonians 5:8). Each one mentioned had a different place in life; one was an employee, one an owner, the shepherd was perhaps a slave. But each was fed from his occupation, each shared in the harvest of his work.

3. Mine answer to them that do examine me is this: My defence to, *Rotherham* . . . My defence to my accusers is this, *Fenton* . . . And [my] apology to my judgers, *Murdock* . . . My defense against those who question me, *Confraternity* . . . my reply to my inquisitors, *Moffatt* . . . how I vindicate myself, *Weymouth* . . . who question my authority, *Noyes* . . . who are investigating my claims is this, *Adams* . . . who set up an inquisition upon me, *Locke*.

4. Have we not power to eat and to drink?: Have we not liberty, *Campbell* . . . my right to be maintained, *Conybeare*.

5. Have we not power to lead about a sister, a wife: May we not take along with us on our journeys, *Norlie*.
as well as other apostles, and [as] the brethren of the Lord, and Cephas?: . . . like the rest of the apostles, *Adams*.

6. Or I only and Barnabas, have not we power to forbear working?: . . . not liberty to, *Campbell* . . . are denied the right of abstaining from work, *Moffatt* . . . right to forbear working? *Rotherham* . . . to abstain from labor? *Wilson* . . . have no right to be maintained, except by the labor of our own hands? *Conybeare* . . . excluded from the privilege of being maintained without working? *Locke*.

7. Who goeth a warfare any time at his own charges?: Vvho euer plaieth the souldiar, *Rheims* . . . Who campaigns, *Fenton* . . . Who serveth as a soldier, *Douay* . . . Who serveth in the wars, *Macknight* . . . goes on a military expedition at his own expense? *Sawyer* . . . at his owne cost? *Geneva* . . . provide his own supplies? *Moffatt* . . . serves at his own cost? *Weymouth* . . . serves at his private cost? *Conybeare*.
who planteth a vineyard, and eateth not of the fruit thereof?: . . . debarred from eating of the produce of it? *Way* . . . without eating its fruit? *Noyes* . . . does not eat any of its grapes? *Norlie*.

1 Corinthians 9:8

4025.1 verb 3sing indic pres act	4027.3 noun acc sing fem	2504.1 conj	1523.2 prep gen	3450.2 art gen sing	1044.1 noun gen sing neu
ποιμαίνει	ποίμνην	καὶ	ἐκ	τοῦ	γάλακτος
poimainei	poimnēn	kai	ek	tou	galaktos
shepherds	a flock,	and	of	the	milk

3450.10 art gen sing fem	4027.2 noun gen sing fem	3620.2 partic	2052.2 verb 3sing indic pres act	3231.1 partic	2567.3 prep
τῆς	ποίμνης	οὐκ	ἐσθίει;	**8.** μὴ	κατὰ
tēs	poimnēs	ouk	esthiei	mē	kata
of the	flock	not	does eat?	not	according to

442.4 noun acc sing masc	3642.18 dem-pron pl neu	2953.1 verb 1sing pres act	2211.1 conj	3644.1 adv	2504.1 conj
ἄνθρωπον	ταῦτα	λαλῶ·	ἢ	⸀ οὐχὶ	καὶ
anthrōpon	tauta	lalō	ē	ouchi	kai
a man	these things	do I speak,	or	not	also

8.a.**Txt:** 018K,020L
025P,byz.
Var: 01ℵ,02A,03B,04C
06D,bo.Lach,Treg,Alf
Word,Tisc,We/Ho,Weis
Sod,UBS/✩

3450.5 art sing masc	3414.1 noun nom sing masc	3642.18 dem-pron pl neu	2504.1 conj	3450.5 art sing masc	3414.1 noun nom sing masc
ὁ	νόμος	ταῦτα	[ᵃ✩ καὶ	ὁ	νόμος
ho	nomos	tauta	kai	ho	nomos
the	law	these things	[also	the	law

3642.18 dem-pron pl neu	3620.3 partic	2978.5 verb 3sing indic pres act	1706.1 prep	1056.1 conj	3450.3 art dat sing
ταῦτα	οὐ]	λέγει;	**9.** ἐν	γὰρ	τῷ
tauta	ou	legei	en	gar	tō
these	not]	says?	In	for	the

3337.2 name gen masc	3338.2 name gen masc	3414.3 noun dat sing masc	1119.22 verb 3sing indic perf pass
⸀ Μωσέως	[✩ Μωϋσέως]	νόμῳ	γέγραπται,
Mōseōs	Mōuseōs	nomō	gegraptai
of Moses	[idem]	law	it has been written,

9.a.**Txt:** p46,01ℵ,02A
03B-corr,04C,06D-corr
018K,020L,025P,byz.
We/Ho,Sod
Var: 03B-org,06D-org
1739,Treg,Alf,Tisc
Weis,UBS/✩

3620.3 partic	5229.3 verb 2sing indic fut act	2749.1 verb 2sing indic fut act	1009.2 noun acc sing masc	246.2 verb acc sing masc part pres act
Οὐ	⸀ φιμώσεις	[ᵃ✩ κημώσεις]	βοῦν	ἀλοῶντα.
Ou	phimōseis	kēmōseis	boun	aloōnta
Not	you shall muzzle	[idem]	an ox	threshing.

3231.1 partic	3450.1 art gen pl	1009.3 noun gen pl masc	3169.1 verb 3sing indic pres act	3450.3 art dat sing	2296.3 noun dat sing masc	2211.1 conj
μὴ	τῶν	βοῶν	μέλει	τῷ	θεῷ;	**10.** ἢ
mē	tōn	boōn	melei	tō	theō	ē
Not	of the	oxen	is there care		with God?	or

1217.1 prep	2231.4 prs-pron acc 1pl	3705.1 adv	2978.5 verb 3sing indic pres act	1217.1 prep	2231.4 prs-pron acc 1pl
δι'	ἡμᾶς	πάντως	λέγει;	δι'	ἡμᾶς
di'	hēmas	pantōs	legei	di'	hēmas
because of	us	altogether	says he?	Because of	us

1056.1 conj	1119.21 verb 3sing indic aor pass	3617.1 conj	1894.2 prep	1667.3 noun dat sing fem	3648.3 verb 3sing indic pres act
γὰρ	ἐγράφη,	ὅτι	⸀ ἐπ'	ἐλπίδι	ὀφείλει
gar	egraphē	hoti	ep'	elpidi	opheilei
for	it was written,	that	in	hope	ought

3648.3 verb 3sing indic pres act	1894.2 prep	1667.3 noun dat sing fem	3450.5 art sing masc	716.1 verb nom sing masc part pres act
[✩ ὀφείλει	ἐπ'	ἐλπίδι]	ὁ	ἀροτριῶν
opheilei	ep'	elpidi	ho	arotriōn
[ought	in	hope]	the	plowing

To this point through the first six verses of the chapter Paul, by three questions and answers, has asserted that he has the right to have his daily needs met, to have a wife to minister with him, and not to have to do manual labor. Paul then supported these claims with several analogies. In verse 7 the analogies are human. If every soldier goes to war with his needs met, why cannot Paul have his met? If it is to be expected that a vinedresser can nourish himself from his own produce, why cannot Paul expect to have his produce, his church, support him? If a shepherd drinks milk while tending the sheep, why should not Paul be fed for tending to his flock?

9:8. Paul wanted to make it clear that he was not speaking from the standpoint of human wisdom alone. Some might have accused him of this on the basis of his previous "natural" illustrations. So Paul proceeded a step further, to a link with divine truth and legal justice. The conjunction *ē* ("or") both combines and contrasts the two major clauses of this sentence which are "I speak" (*lalō*) and "the law says" (*ho nomos . . . legei*). The conjunction *ē* lends emphasis to the second clause which makes clear that Paul speaks not on his own but by authority of the Scriptures.

Paul expected a negative answer to the first question in this verse and a positive answer to the second question. "The law" was regarded as authoritative. This did not mean the Christian was under the power of the Law, but it did acknowledge the truth of principles in the Law and that it had God's blessing. It was a source of truth and right, and Paul used it for Christian guidance.

9:9. The reference is to Deuteronomy 25:4. The "law of Moses" properly refers to the first five books of the Old Testament. Whether it was intended to be so limited or so specific here is difficult to say, but the reference is clear. It is to the ox who, while tramping the corn, shook the grain loose from its husk. After that the mixture was tossed in the air. The wind carried the lighter chaff away. The heavier grain fell back to the floor, and the animal was allowed to eat some of the grain which lay on the floor.

On the basis of this Paul asked, "Doth God take care for oxen?" This question raises an interesting problem. The Greek text contains a *mē* plus an indicative verb, and this normally requires a negative response. But Paul is surely not saying that God does not care for oxen. All through the Scriptures God's care is shown for all the creatures He created, as well as for man. And in itself the Old Testament reference Paul quotes shows God's care for oxen. It appears, then, that here the apostle was making an important point: If God made provision for even an animal, would He not be concerned about those who were ministering for Him?

9:10. The quote and application were made first and foremost to preachers of the gospel, to laborers in the ministry. God provides

or who feedeth a flock, and eateth not of the milk of the flock?: Does a shepherd get no drink, *Moffatt* . . . who shepherds a flock, *Adams* . . . Who takes care of sheep, *Norlie* . . . look after a herd and not get his living from the milk? *TCNT* . . . and does not drink any of the milk the flock produces? *Williams.*

8. Say I these things as a man?: Speake I these things according to man? *Rheims* . . . Am I making use of merely worldly illustrations? *Weymouth* . . . Am I stating only a human rule? *Beck* . . . Am I speaking from a human viewpoint, *Adams* . . . Human arguments, *Moffatt* . . . by way of human illustrations, *Williams* . . . from human examples, *SEB* . . . purely from a human standpoint, *Berkeley* . . . am I guided only by human customs? *TCNT.*

or saith not the law the same also?: Does not the Law speak in the same tone? *Weymouth* . . . or does not the Law mention these matters? *Berkeley* . . . too lay down the same principle? *Way.*

9. For it is written in the law of Moses:

Thou shalt not muzzle the mouth of the ox that treadeth out the corn: . . . thou schalt not bynde the mouth, *Wyclif* . . . that is treading out your grain, *Williams* . . . the threshing bullock, *Fenton.*

Doth God take care for oxen?: Is it the bullocks that God is thinking of? *TCNT* . . . thinking in terms of oxen, *Berkeley.*

10. Or saith he [it] altogether for our sakes?: Isn't He really speaking about us? *Adams* . . . doth he command this chiefly for our sakes, *Macknight* . . . Is it not especially for our sakes? *Norlie* . . . or does he care particularly for us? *Klingensmith* . . . Surely He has us in mind, *Beck* . . . is it really in our interest, *Weymouth* . . . in our behalf? *Williams.*

For our sakes, no doubt, [this] is written: . . . certainly, it was written, *Campbell* . . . to teach us something, *SEB.*

that he that ploweth should plow in hope:

716.3 verb inf pres act	2504.1 conj	3450.5 art sing masc	246.1 verb nom sing masc part pres act	3450.10 art gen sing fem	1667.2 noun gen sing fem
ἀροτριᾶν,	καὶ	ὁ	ἀλοῶν	⸀ τῆς	ἐλπίδος
arotrian	kai	ho	aloōn	tēs	elpidos
to plow,	and	the	threshing,	of the	hope

10.a.Txt: 02A,03B,04C 044,byz.UBS/✦
Var: 01א,06D,010F 012G,33,bo.

840.3 prs-pron gen sing	3218.5 verb inf pres act	1894.2 prep	1667.3 noun dat sing fem	1894.2 prep	1667.3 noun dat sing fem
αὐτοῦ	μετέχειν	ἐπ'	ἐλπίδι.	[ᵃ✦ ἐπ'	ἐλπίδι
autou	metechein	ep'	elpidi.	ep'	elpidi
his	to partake	in	hope.	[in	hope

3450.2 art gen sing	3218.5 verb inf pres act	1479.1 conj	2231.1 prs-pron nom 1pl	5050.3 prs-pron dat 2pl	3450.17 art pl neu
τοῦ	μετέχειν.]	**11.** Εἰ	ἡμεῖς	ὑμῖν	τὰ
tou	metechein.]	Ei	hēmeis	humin	ta
of the	to partake.]	If	we	to you	the

4012.10 adj acc pl neu	4540.12 verb 1pl indic aor act	3144.16 adj sing neu	1479.1 conj	2231.1 prs-pron nom 1pl	
πνευματικὰ	ἐσπείραμεν,	μέγα	εἰ	ἡμεῖς	
pneumatika	espeiramen,	mega	ei	hēmeis	
spiritual things	did sow,	a great thing	if	we	

5050.2 prs-pron gen 2pl	3450.17 art pl neu	4416.7 adj pl neu	2302.10 verb 1pl indic fut act	1479.1 conj	241.6 adj nom pl masc
ὑμῶν	τὰ	σαρκικὰ	θερίσομεν;	**12.** εἰ	ἄλλοι
humōn	ta	sarkika	therisomen;	ei	alloi
your	the	fleshly things	shall reap?	If	others

3450.10 art gen sing fem	1833.1 noun fem	5050.2 prs-pron gen 2pl	5050.2 prs-pron gen 2pl	1833.1 noun fem	
τῆς	⸀ ἐξουσίας	ὑμῶν	[✦ ὑμῶν	ἐξουσίας]	
tēs	exousias	humōn	humōn	exousias	
of the	authority	of you	[of you	authority]	

3218.3 verb 3pl indic pres act	3620.3 partic	3095.1 adv comp	2231.1 prs-pron nom 1pl	233.1 conj	3620.2 partic
μετέχουσιν,	οὐ	μᾶλλον	ἡμεῖς;	Ἀλλ'	οὐκ
metechousin	ou	mallon	hēmeis;	All'	ouk
partake,	not	rather	we?	But	not

5366.6 verb 1pl indic aor mid	3450.11 art dat sing fem	1833.3 noun dat sing fem	3642.11 dem-pron dat sing fem	233.2 conj	
ἐχρησάμεθα	τῇ	ἐξουσίᾳ	ταύτῃ	ἀλλὰ	
echrēsametha	tē	exousia	tautē	alla	
we did use	the	authority	this;	but	

3820.1 adj	4573.2 verb 1pl indic pres act	2419.1 conj	3231.1 partic	1457.1 noun acc sing fem	4948.5 indef-pron
πάντα	στέγομεν,	ἵνα	μὴ	⸀ ἐγκοπὴν	τινα
panta	stegomen,	hina	mē	enkopēn	tina
all things	we bear,	that	not	hindrance	any

4948.5 indef-pron	1457.1 noun acc sing fem	1319.21 verb 1pl subj aor act	3450.3 art dat sing	2077.3 noun dat sing neu	
[✦ τινα	ἐγκοπὴν]	δῶμεν	τῷ	εὐαγγελίῳ	
tina	enkopēn	dōmen	tō	euangeliō	
[any	an obstacle]	we should give	to the	gospel	

3450.2 art gen sing	5382.2 name gen masc	3620.2 partic	3471.6 verb 2pl indic perf act	3617.1 conj	3450.7 art pl masc
τοῦ	Χριστοῦ.	**13.** οὐκ	οἴδατε	ὅτι	οἱ
tou	Christou.	ouk	oidate	hoti	hoi
of the	Christ.	Not	you know	that	the

for the needs of the Christian laborer from the fruits of his labor; thus, "plowing" (sowing and caring for the seed) and "threshing" (the harvest process) should be done in hope and expectation.

Notice again that Paul was building the argument carefully so that the resulting application was the more forceful and binding.

9:11. Paul also argued from the standpoint of natural justice. The opening conditional clause of this verse implies that the condition had been fulfilled. The man who labors to produce the harvest is entitled to share in the proceeds. Paul had labored in the things of the Spirit; he had shown himself a profitable servant. But one cannot eat "spiritual" things. Therefore, Paul was entitled to material and bodily, not sinful, benefits. Considering the vast gulf between "spiritual" and "carnal," it is no wonder that Paul could ask "Is it a great thing?" and expect a negative answer.

Material things are not intended to be the final or suitable reward for spiritual labors. But supply for basic needs is a natural part of the process, and those who have benefited from the spiritual labor of the ministry may be expected to provide the basic elements of life to one who has been called of God to share "spiritual" life on a free and generous basis.

9:12. "Others" had exercised this right of maintenance and Paul did not begrudge them this, for it was right and proper. Yet they had a lesser claim on the Corinthians than Paul; he was their spiritual father.

But Paul and others had not exercised these rights. Rather they had "suffered" (*stegomen*) for the gospel. They had endured patiently and put up with wrong and poor treatment without complaining. It had not been easy to support themselves and continue the heavy load of spreading the gospel. But Paul and his coworkers had done it.

Some thought Paul had not claimed maintenance because his calling and ministry were somehow "inferior." But his motive had been unselfish; he did not want to "hinder the gospel of Christ." "Hinder" (*enkopēn*) means literally "a cutting into" and was used of breaking up a road to prevent an enemy's advance (Morris, *Tyndale New Testament Commentaries*, 7:135,136). Some would claim Paul was preaching only to make a living, and that would hinder the gospel. So Paul renounced his right.

9:13. Paul added to the point. He referred to the example of the "ministers" of the temple. It is doubtful that he was referring to heathen practices because Paul would give no merit to what God had renounced and from which the Christian had turned away.

and that he that thresheth in hope should be partaker of his hope: . . . it should be in the hope of sharing, *Weymouth* . . . should have some hope of a share in the harvest, *Norlie* . . . in hope of partaking of the fruits, *Confraternity* . . . to share in the produce of his toil, *Conybeare* . . . we should expect to get a share of the crop, *Beck* . . . to receive fruit, *Douay*.

11. If we have sown unto you spiritual things: . . . been busy planting spiritual seed in you, *Norlie* . . . Since we planted spiritual things among you, *SEB* . . . sown spiritually for you, *Fenton*.

[is it] a great thing if we shall reap your carnal things?: . . . is it a great matter, *Rheims* . . . is it unreasonable that we should expect, *Locke* . . . if we reap the necessaries of life, *Fenton* . . . reap your worldly goods, *Moffatt* . . . that we should reap a temporal harvest, *Weymouth* . . . we reape youre bodely thynges? *Cranmer* . . . to reap a material support from you? *Williams* . . . reap material benefits from you? *Adams*.

12. If others be partakers of [this] power over you, [are] not we rather?: . . . if others have this prerogative, *Murdock* . . . do not we still more? *Noyes* . . . have we not a stronger claim? *Williams* . . . Shouldn't we have it, too? *SEB*.

Nevertheless we have not used this power; but suffer all things: . . . have not used this right, *Fenton* . . . but forego every claim, *Conybeare* . . . We endure all of these things, *SEB*.

lest we should hinder the gospel of Christ: . . . lest vve should giue any offence, *Rheims* . . . that we might in nothing impede the announcement of, *Murdock* . . . rather than place any obstacle in the way of the good news, *Adams* . . . to keep from hindering the progress, *Williams* . . . that we may cause no impediment to the good news of the Christ, *Hanson*.

13. Do ye not know that they which minister about holy things: . . . the priests who perform the temple-services, *Way* . . . they

367

1 Corinthians 9:14

13.a.**Var:** 01א,03B
06D-org,sa.bo.Treg,Alf
Tisc,We/Ho,Weis,Sod
UBS/✶

3450.17 art pl neu	2393.1 adj acc pl neu	2021.10 verb pl masc part pres	3450.17 art pl neu	1523.2 prep gen
τὰ	ἱερὰ	ἐργαζόμενοι,	[ᵃ✯+ τὰ]	ἐκ
ta	hiera	ergazomenoi	ta	ek
the	sacred things	laboring,	[the]	of

3450.2 art gen sing	2387.1 adj gen sing neu	2052.3 verb 3pl indic pres act	3450.7 art pl masc	3450.3 art dat sing
τοῦ	ἱεροῦ	ἐσθίουσιν·	οἱ	τῷ
tou	hierou	esthiousin	hoi	tō
the	temple	eat;	the	at the

13.b.**Txt:** 01א-corr,018K
020L,byz.
Var: 01א-org,02A,03B
04C,06D,025P,33,Lach
Treg,Alf,Word,Tisc
We/Ho,Weis,Sod
UBS/✶

2356.3 noun dat sing neu	4190.1 verb nom pl masc part pres act	3778.1 verb nom pl masc part pres act
θυσιαστηρίῳ	(προσεδρεύοντες,	[ᵇ✯ παρεδρεύοντες]
thusiastēriō	prosedreuontes	paredreuontes
altar	attending,	[idem]

3450.3 art dat sing	2356.3 noun dat sing neu	4680.1 verb 3pl indic pres mid	3643.1 adv	2504.1 conj
τῷ	θυσιαστηρίῳ	συμμερίζονται;	**14.** οὕτως	καὶ
tō	thusiastēriō	summerizontai	houtōs	kai
with the	alter	partake?	So	also

3450.5 art sing masc	2935.1 noun nom sing masc	1293.3 verb 3sing indic aor act	3450.4 art dat pl	3450.16 art sing neu	2077.1 noun sing neu
ὁ	κύριος	διέταξεν	τοῖς	τὸ	εὐαγγέλιον
ho	kurios	dietaxen	tois	to	euangelion
the	Lord	did order	to the	the	gospel

2576.1 verb dat pl masc part pres act	1523.2 prep gen	3450.2 art gen sing	2077.2 noun gen sing neu	2180.19 verb inf pres act
καταγγέλλουσιν,	ἐκ	τοῦ	εὐαγγελίου	ζῆν.
katangellousin	ek	tou	euangeliou	zēn
announcing,	of	the	gospel	to live.

15.a.**Txt:** 018K,byz.
Var: 01א-org,02A,03B
04C,06D-org,025P,33
Gries,Lach,Treg,Alf
Word,Tisc,We/Ho,Weis
Sod,UBS/✶

1466.1 prs-pron nom 1sing	1156.2 conj	3625.7 num card dat neu	5366.5 verb 1sing indic aor mid	3620.3 partic	5366.11 verb 1sing indic perf
15. ἐγὼ	δὲ	(οὐδενὶ	ἐχρησάμην	[ᵃ✯ οὐ	κέχρημαι
egō	de	oudeni	echrēsamēn	ou	kechrēmai
I	but	none	used	[not	have used

3625.7 num card dat neu	3642.2 dem-pron gen pl	3620.2 partic	1119.7 verb 1sing indic aor act	1156.2 conj	3642.18 dem-pron pl neu
οὐδενὶ]	τούτων·	οὐκ	ἔγραψα	δὲ	ταῦτα
oudeni	toutōn	ouk	egrapsa	de	tauta
none]	of these things.	Not	I did write	now	these things

2419.1 conj	3643.1 adv	1090.40 verb 3sing subj aor mid	1706.1 prep	1466.5 prs-pron dat 1sing	2541.1 adj sing	1056.1 conj
ἵνα	οὕτως	γένηται	ἐν	ἐμοί·	καλὸν	γάρ
hina	houtōs	genētai	en	emoi	kalon	gar
that	thus	it should be	with	me;	good	for

1466.4 prs-pron dat 1sing	3095.1 adv comp	594.20 verb inf aor act	2211.1 conj	3450.16 art sing neu	2715.1 noun sing neu
μοι	μᾶλλον	ἀποθανεῖν,	ἢ	τὸ	καύχημά
moi	mallon	apothanein	ē	to	kauchēma
for me	rather	to die,	than	the	boasting

15.b.**Txt:** 01א-corr,04C
06D-corr,018K,020L
025P,byz.
Var: p46,01א-org,03B
06D-org,33,sa.Lach
Treg,Tisc,We/Ho,Weis
Sod,UBS/✶

1466.2 prs-pron gen 1sing	2419.1 conj	4948.3 indef-pron nom sing	3625.2 num card nom masc	2729.2 verb 3sing subj aor act
μου	(ἵνα	τις	[ᵇ✯ οὐδεὶς]	(κενώσῃ.
mou	hina	tis	oudeis	kenōsē
my	that	any one	[no one]	should make void.

"Do ye not know . . . ?" suggests familiar knowledge, and it was well known that those who worked in sacred things also received their livelihood. Those who regularly served in the temple received a portion of the altar sacrifice. Part was burned on the altar, part was given to the priests.

which vvorke in the holy place, *Rheims* . . . those who work with the sacred things, *Adams* . . . perform temple-rites, *Moffatt*.

live [of the things] of the temple?: . . . eat food from the temple, *Adams* . . . lyue of the sacrifice? *Cranmer* . . . live upon the revenues of the temple, *Conybeare*.

and they which wait at the altar are partakers with the altar?: . . . they that serue the altar, participat, *Rheims* . . . are partakers of the temple, *Cranmer* . . . with the altar share, *Rotherham* . . . have their portion with the altar, *Concordant* . . . get their share of the sacrifices, *Moffatt* . . . all alike share with the altar? *Weymouth* . . . share in what is sacrificed on the altar? *Adams* . . . are maintained from the altar? *Fenton*.

9:14. Lastly, Paul considered an argument from the Lord's command. This was the strongest and highest consideration. God himself had established this arrangement. Jesus had said workers deserve adequate pay (Luke 10:7).

All of these arguments united to make a point about "rights." Paul had renounced his own rights to advance the spread of the gospel. He stresses this theme through the rest of the chapter. He records the principles which motivated him as a preacher of the gospel.

Thus far in his argument, Paul had made an appeal to reason and common sense, to Old Testament Scripture, to Jewish temple practices, and finally to the words of Jesus himself to support the claim that apostles are absolutely entitled to support and remuneration. There is a strange irony to this chapter because Paul has argued strongly and vigorously on behalf of his fellow apostles (such as Barnabas) that they should be supported; yet in the rest of the chapter Paul proceeded to deny any of that support for himself.

In the church of today, the issue of support for ministers has to do largely with salary and benefits. Sadly, few Christians heed both aspects of Paul's arguments in chapter 9. Many clamor loudly for money and large salaries because they deserve it, and yet they ignore the example set by Paul himself who eschewed a salary. There are also others, however, who begrudge ministers their due and require them to be "servants" in a way not intended by Paul. These people need to realize that ministers are highly called of God and deserve their due. All Christians today need to hear *all* of what Paul said in chapter 9.

14. Even so hath the Lord ordained: . . . so the Lord's instructions, *Moffatt* . . . So also the Lord commanded, *Conybeare* . . . has appointed to those, *Sawyer* . . . also prescribes, *Concordant* . . . directed that those, *Confraternity*.

that they which preach the gospel should live of the gospel: . . . those who announce the good news, *Adams* . . . to maintain themselves, *Weymouth* . . . get their living by the gospel? *Moffatt* . . . to be maintained thereby, *Conybeare*.

9:15. Paul had not exercised his rights or liberty, and his refusal to do so had become a rule of life for him. Nor was he writing to establish these rights for himself in the future. Fiercely, strongly, and with much emotion he announced that "it were better for me to die"—in the Greek original, Paul left this incompleted. He would hold to his claim; he would never be so dependent.

Paul did not boast in the wrong sense. He was not speaking from a sense of pride or selfish egotism. His motives were pure. He was speaking in the context of the progress of the gospel, of its furtherance and its success. He was not referring to his own accomplishments.

15. But I have used none of these things: I have availed myself of none, *Fenton* . . . I have used none of these privileges, *Campbell* . . . my full rights, *Weymouth*.

neither have I written these things, that it should be so done unto me: . . . any such provision for myself, *Moffatt* . . . so done in my case, *Clementson*.

for [it were] better for me to die: . . . for I prefer to die, *Hanson*.

than that any man should make my glorying void: . . . shuld take this reioysinge from me, *Tyndale* . . . make this boast of mine an empty one, *Weymouth* . . . deprive me of this, my source of pride, *Moffatt* . . . deprive me of this reason for boasting, *Adams*.

1 Corinthians 9:16

15.c.**Txt**: 018K,044,byz.
Var: p46,01ℵ,02A,03B
04C,06D,020L,025P,33
Lach,Treg,Alf,Tisc
We/Ho,Weis,Sod
UBS/✶

2729.5 verb 3sing indic fut act	16.	1430.1 partic	1056.1 conj	2076.7 verb 1sing subj pres mid
[c☆ κενώσει.]	**16.** ἐὰν	γὰρ	εὐαγγελίζωμαι,
kenōsei	ean	gar	euangelizōmai
[will make void.]	If	for	I announce the good news,

3620.2 partic	1498.4 verb 3sing indic pres act	1466.4 prs- pron dat 1sing	2715.1 noun sing neu	316.1 noun nom sing fem	1056.1 conj
οὐκ	ἔστιν	μοι	καύχημα·	ἀνάγκη	γὰρ
ouk	estin	moi	kauchēma	anankē	gar
not	there is	to me	boasting;	necessity	for

16.a.**Txt**: 01ℵ-corr,018K
020L,byz.
Var: 01ℵ-org,02A,03B
04C,06D,025P,it.sa.bo.
Gries,Lach,Treg,Alf
Word,Tisc,We/Ho,Weis
Sod,UBS/✶

1466.4 prs- pron dat 1sing	1930.1 verb 3sing indic pres	3622.1 partic	1156.2 conj	1056.1 conj
μοι	ἐπίκειται·	οὐαὶ	(δέ	[a☆ γὰρ]
moi	epikeitai	ouai	de	gar
me	is being laid upon;	woe	but	[for]

1466.4 prs- pron dat 1sing	1498.4 verb 3sing indic pres act	1430.1 partic	3231.1 partic	2076.7 verb 1sing subj pres mid
μοί	ἐστιν	ἐὰν	μὴ	(εὐαγγελίζωμαι.
moi	estin	ean	mē	euangelizōmai
to me	it is	if	not	I should announce the good news.

16.b.**Txt**: 01ℵ,02A,018K
byz.Tisc,Sod
Var: 03B,04C,06D,Lach
Treg,Alf,Word,We/Ho
Weis,UBS/✶

2076.28 verb 1sing subj aor mid	17.	1479.1 conj	1056.1 conj	1622.1 adj nom sing masc	3642.17 dem- pron sing neu
[b☆ εὐαγγελίσωμαι.]	**17.** εἰ	γὰρ	ἑκὼν	τοῦτο
euangelisōmai	ei	gar	hekōn	touto
[idem]	If	for	willingly	this

4097.1 verb 1sing indic pres act	3272.3 noun acc sing masc	2174.1 verb 1sing pres act	1479.1 conj	1156.2 conj	208.1 adj nom sing masc
πράσσω,	μισθὸν	ἔχω·	εἰ	δὲ	ἄκων
prassō	misthon	echō	ei	de	akōn
I do,	a reward	I have;	if	but	unwillingly

3484.2 noun acc sing fem	3961.61 verb 1sing indic perf pass	18.	4949.3 intr- pron nom sing	3631.1 conj
οἰκονομίαν	πεπίστευμαι.	**18.** τίς	οὖν
oikonomian	pepisteumai	tis	oun
an administration	I am entrusted with.	What	then

18.a.**Txt**: 01ℵ-corr,03B
06D,020L,025P,byz.
Var: 01ℵ-org,02A,04C
018K,33,sa.bo.Treg,Alf
Tisc,We/Ho,Weis,Sod
UBS/✶

1466.4 prs- pron dat 1sing	1466.2 prs- pron gen 1sing	1498.4 verb 3sing indic pres act	3450.5 art sing masc	3272.1 noun nom sing masc	2419.1 conj
(μοι	[a☆ μού]	ἐστιν	ὁ	μισθός;	ἵνα
moi	mou	estin	ho	misthos	hina
my	[idem]	is	the	reward?	That

2076.9 verb nom sing masc part pres mid	76.1 adj acc sing neu	4935.21 verb 1sing indic fut act	3450.16 art sing neu
εὐαγγελιζόμενος	ἀδάπανον	θήσω	τὸ
euangelizomenos	adapanon	thēsō	to
announcing the good news	without expense	I will make	the

18.b.**Txt**: 06D-corr,018K
020L,025P,byz.
Var: 01ℵ,02A,03B,04C
06D-org,33,Lach,Treg
Alf,Word,Tisc,We/Ho
Weis,Sod,UBS/✶

2077.1 noun sing neu	3450.2 art gen sing	5382.2 name gen masc	1519.1 prep	3450.16 art sing neu	3231.1 partic
εὐαγγέλιον	(τοῦ	Χριστοῦ,)	εἰς	τὸ	μὴ
euangelion	tou	Christou	eis	to	mē
good news	of the	Christ,	to	the	not

2679.2 verb inf aor mid	3450.11 art dat sing fem	1833.3 noun dat sing fem	1466.2 prs- pron gen 1sing	1706.1 prep
καταχρήσασθαι	τῇ	ἐξουσίᾳ	μου	ἐν
katachrēsasthai	tē	exousia	mou	en
to use as my own	the	authority	my	in

9:16. Even in the preaching of the gospel, Paul did not "glory." He could claim no real credit. Rather "necessity" was laid heavily on him. The Greeks considered it ruin to fight against "necessity." Paul thought of the message of the gospel of Christ as laying so heavily upon him that some undefined disaster would come upon him if he did not preach what had been so gloriously given to him. This did not, however, violate the part Paul's free will played in the process.

Paul was a man of duty, motivated by mercy and grace. He had once been an enemy, opposed to the message of the Cross. But that was changed by the call of Christ. He was now an ambassador for the Lord. This speaks of the deep impact and responsibility the call of God brings to a minister's life.

9:17. In this verse Paul may have been saying that the man who preaches willingly merits a reward; whereas, if he does it unwillingly, he is nevertheless not excused. But perhaps the idea in this verse is carefully built on the previous one. If Paul preached from choice he would merit a reward. As it was, it was not his own choice; he had been chosen to preach. The following verse would then begin, "What reward is possible under these circumstances?"

The picture is one of a servant whose work is determined for him and his merit is in his faithfulness. The picture is of a sovereign Lord and an obedient slave. The Lord had given Paul an assignment. Some find a hint of predestination in such a view, but if so, it is in the matter of apostleship, not in the matter of salvation. It is God's choice that is involved. He chooses special vessels for special service.

9:18. Paul's real reward was that while he had to preach, he did not have to preach without pay. He did not have to give up this right and privilege. But from his Master's example, Paul too had learned to be gracious and giving, though in a lesser sense. If Christ could give up His life, Paul could certainly surrender his right to support.

Thus Paul rejected reward in the mercenary sense, to claim it in the wider ethical sense. Again, the purpose was not to "abuse" or make full use of his power or right in the gospel, but to provide a way in which the gospel might be more powerfully and successfully spread. Liberty bowed to love.

These comments reveal a continuous life of love and sacrifice. Paul had caught the gracious spirit of his Lord and Master Jesus Christ. The Master's motivation was the salvation of men. To this end, everything was committed. His disciples saw the motives behind His actions and caught the same dedicated, committed spirit. They were moved to yield everything to the same great cause, the salvation of men. Now Paul was calling the Church to the same spirit and purpose.

16. For though I preach the gospel, I have nothing to glory of: . . . it is no credit to me, *Fenton*.

for necessity is laid upon me: . . . for I cannot help doing it, *Williams* . . . Necessity compels me to do that, *Norlie* . . . is imposed upon me, *Weymouth* . . . I am constrained to do, *Moffatt*.

yea, woe is unto me, if I preach not the gospel!: . . . because it is a punishment for me, *Fenton* . . . woe awaits me if I declare not the gospel, *Campbell* . . . I am accursed if I do not preach, *Williams* . . . if I euangelize not, *Rheims*.

17. For if I do this thing willingly, I have a reward: . . . if I am engaging in this voluntarily, *Concordant* . . . if I do This voluntarily, *Wilson* . . . of my own accord, *Moffatt* . . . And if I preach willingly, *Weymouth*.

but if against my will: . . . but if, not by choice, *Rotherham* . . . but if unwillingly, *Noyes*.

a dispensation [of the gospel] is committed unto me: I have been entrusted with an office, *Fenton* . . . a steward to discharge his trust, *Moffatt* . . . entrusted with a Stewardship reluctantly, *Wilson* . . . I still am entrusted with trusteeship, *Williams* . . . a stewardship has nevertheless been entrusted to me, *Weymouth*.

18. What is my reward then? [Verily] that, when I preach the gospel:

I may make the gospel of Christ without charge: I may deliver the gospel, *Douay* . . . will cost my hearers nothing, *Weymouth* . . . vvithout cost, *Rheims*, . . . without expense, *Concordant, Sawyer* . . . without expense to anybody, *Williams* . . . free of charge, *Moffatt* . . . free to all, *Norlie* . . . without compensation, *Adams*.

that I abuse not my power in the gospel: . . . so as not to use to the full my authority, *Panin* . . . that I misuse not myne auctoritie, *Geneva* . . . and use not the prerogative given me, *Murdock* . . . from insisting on all my rights, *Moffatt* . . . forego my right as an Evangelist, *Conybeare*.

371

1 Corinthians 9:19

3450.3 art dat sing	2077.3 noun dat sing neu	1645.1 adj nom sing masc	1056.1 conj	1498.21 verb sing masc part pres act
τῷ	εὐαγγελίῳ.	19. Ἐλεύθερος	γὰρ	ὢν
tō	euangeliō	Eleutheros	gar	ōn
the	good news.	Free	for	being

1523.2 prep gen	3820.4 adj gen pl	3820.5 adj dat pl	1670.3 prs-pron acc 1sing masc	1396.1 verb 1sing indic aor act	2419.1 conj
ἐκ	πάντων,	πᾶσιν	ἐμαυτὸν	ἐδούλωσα,	ἵνα
ek	pantōn	pasin	emauton	edoulōsa	hina
from	all,	to all	myself	I became a slave,	that

3450.8 art acc pl masc	3979.4 adj comp acc pl masc	2741.4 verb 1sing subj aor act	2504.1 conj	1090.30 verb 1sing indic aor mid
τοὺς	πλείονας	κερδήσω·	20. καὶ	ἐγενόμην
tous	pleionas	kerdēsō	kai	egenomēn
the	more	I might gain.	And	I became

3450.4 art dat pl	2428.4 name-adj dat pl masc	5453.1 conj	2428.6 name-adj nom masc	2419.1 conj	2428.5 name-adj acc pl masc
τοῖς	Ἰουδαίοις	ὡς	Ἰουδαῖος,	ἵνα	Ἰουδαίους
tois	Ioudaiois	hōs	Ioudaios	hina	Ioudaious
to the	Jews	as	a Jew,	that	Jews

2741.4 verb 1sing subj aor act	3450.4 art dat pl	5097.3 prep	3414.4 noun acc sing masc	5453.1 conj	5097.3 prep	3414.4 noun acc sing masc
κερδήσω·	τοῖς	ὑπὸ	νόμον	ὡς	ὑπὸ	νόμον,
kerdēsō	tois	hupo	nomon	hōs	hupo	nomon
I might gain:	to the	under	law	as	under	law,

	3231.1 partic	1498.21 verb sing masc part pres act	840.5 prs-pron nom sing masc	5097.3 prep	3414.4 noun acc sing masc	2419.1 conj
	[a☆+ μὴ	ὢν	αὐτὸς	ὑπὸ	νόμον,]	ἵνα
	mē	ōn	autos	hupo	nomon	hina
	[not	being	self	under	law,]	that

3450.8 art acc pl masc	5097.3 prep	3414.4 noun acc sing masc	2741.4 verb 1sing subj aor act	3450.4 art dat pl	456.1 adj dat pl
τοὺς	ὑπὸ	νόμον	κερδήσω·	21. τοῖς	ἀνόμοις
tous	hupo	nomon	kerdēsō	tois	anomois
the	under	law	I might gain:	to the	without law

5453.1 conj	456.2 adj nom sing masc	3231.1 partic	1498.21 verb sing masc part pres act	456.2 adj nom sing masc	2296.3 noun dat sing masc
ὡς	ἄνομος,	μὴ	ὢν	ἄνομος	⸀ θεῷ,
hōs	anomos	mē	ōn	anomos	theō
as	without law,	not	being	without law	to God,

2296.2 noun gen sing masc	233.1 conj	1756.1 adj nom sing masc	5382.3 name dat masc	5382.2 name gen masc
[a☆ θεοῦ]	ἀλλ’	ἔννομος	⸀ Χριστῷ,	[b☆ Χριστοῦ,]
theou	all’	ennomos	Christō	Christou
[of God]	but	within law	to Christ,	[of Christ,]

2419.1 conj	2741.4 verb 1sing subj aor act	2741.10 verb 1sing subj aor act	3450.8 art acc pl masc	456.4 adj acc pl masc
ἵνα	⸀ κερδήσω	[c☆ κερδάνω	τοὺς]	ἀνόμους·
hina	kerdēsō	kerdanō	tous	anomous
that	I might gain	[I may gain	the]	without law.

1090.30 verb 1sing indic aor mid	3450.4 art dat pl	766.6 adj dat pl masc	5453.1 conj	766.1 adj nom sing
22. ἐγενόμην	τοῖς	ἀσθενέσιν	⸀a ὡς ⸀	ἀσθενής,
egenomēn	tois	asthenesin	hōs	asthenēs
I became	to the	weak	as	weak,

20.a.Var: p46,01א,02A 03B,04C,06D,025P,33 it.sa.bo.Gries,Lach,Treg Alf,Word,Tisc,We/Ho Weis,Sod,UBS/☆

21.a.Txt: 06D-corr,018K 020L,byz.sa.
Var: 01א,02A,03B,04C 06D-org,025P,33,bo. Lach,Treg,Alf,Word Tisc,We/Ho,Weis,Sod UBS/☆

21.b.Txt: 06D-corr,018K 020L,byz.sa.
Var: 01א,02A,03B,04C 06D-org,025P,33,bo. Lach,Treg,Alf,Word Tisc,We/Ho,Weis,Sod UBS/☆

21.c.Txt: 01א-corr,018K 020L,byz.
Var: 01א-org,02A,03B 04C,025P,33,Lach,Treg Alf,Word,Tisc,We/Ho Weis,Sod,UBS/☆

22.a.Txt: 01א-corr,04C 06D,018K,020L,025P byz.sa.bo.Sod
Var: 01א-org,02A,03B Treg,Alf,Word,Tisc We/Ho,Weis,UBS/☆

9:19. Paul's real aim now comes into view. He had established his right to have liberty, so he could choose self-abnegation. He had not become unnecessarily encumbered by the demands of men. Rather, he freed himself from everyone so that he might truly be everyone's servant. Paul had been accused of "gainseeking"; but the gain he sought was winning many to Christ.

9:20. Paul "became" to the Jews as a Jew. He had been rejected by many of them, but he would not unnecessarily antagonize them. The fact that Paul used the article here with "Jews" (*tois Ioudaiois*) is highly unusual in Paul and is thought therefore to be referring to a particular incident, such as the circumcision of Timothy in Acts 16:3. Blass and Debrunner suggest that it might even be translated "those with whom I had to deal on each occasion" (section 262). Another example of where Paul adapted himself to Judaism was over the issue of purification in Acts 21:23-26. Paul did not believe the law of Moses could save a man, nor could the Jewish ceremonies and traditions. He was under grace, not "law." But he respected Jewish scruples and conformed to practices that would enable him to approach the Jew more acceptably.

This was not a case of "watering down" his belief. Rather, it was a subjection of accommodation not of principle. He was not bound to obey the Law, but he did so voluntarily. Because he ministered to those "under the law," Paul was accused of still preaching circumcision. But Paul's goal was to "gain them" for Christ.

This highlights something quite important regarding what it meant for Paul to be a Jew. For Paul, Judaism was tied in with the Law and the Pharisees' hedge around the Law which had perverted God's original intention for the Law. Paul therefore repudiated legalism but did not dispense with the Law because Jesus Christ fulfilled the Law (Matthew 5:17-20). Paul wrote in Romans 10:4, "Christ is the end of the law for righteousness to every one that believeth." Paul, then, was not a "Jew" as such in his theology, but he could use the Law and the beliefs of Judaism *insofar* as it won Jews to Christ. Note that in this paragraph (9:19-23) Paul used *hina* ("in order that") seven times to show that his personal manner was subservient to winning people to Christ.

9:21. Paul next mentioned the Gentiles, or those "without law," the Jewish designation for all outside the cover of the Mosaic covenant. Paul did not practice the law of Moses or make it the basis for his preaching among the Gentiles. But in a true Christian sense, Paul was not "without law." He had advanced to the "law of Christ" which is certain of fulfillment because it is by the Spirit and is governed by "an implanted life," not by an external yoke.

9:22. Paul refers to the weak, reminding the Corinthians of the matters dealt with in chapter 8. He left his position of strength and

19. For though I be free from all [men]: I was not the slave of any one, *TCNT* ... free from any human power, *Williams* ... from all human control, *Weymouth* ... I submit to restrictions, *Way* ... no one has any claim on me, *Norlie.*

yet have I made myself servant unto all: I have made myself a veritable bondman, *Way* ... I enslave myself to all, *Concordant.*

that I might gain the more: ... and yet, to win more converts, *TCNT* ... win over as many, *Moffatt* ... in order to win a larger number, *Berkeley* ... that I might benefit the greatest possible number, *Fenton* ... winning as many converts as possible, *Weymouth* ... that I might gain the most, *Conybeare.*

20. And unto the Jews I became as a Jew: I met the Jews on the footing of a fellow-Jew, *Way* ... I became more Jewish, *SEB.*

that I might gain the Jews: ... that I might benefit the Jews, *Fenton* ... for the winning of Jews, *Williams* ... that I might win Jews for Christ, *Norlie.*

to them that are under the law, as under the law: To those who are subject to Law, *TCNT* ... I became like a man under the Law, *Beck.*

that I might gain them that are under the law: ... so as to gain the devotees of the Law, *Way.*

21. To them that are without law, as without law: To those who have no Law, *TCNT* ... those outside the Law, *Moffatt.*

(being not without law to God, but under the law to Christ,): ... although not lawless toward God but committed to Christ's Law, *Berkeley* ... but closer bound in Messiah's law, *Way* ... but specially under Christ's law, *Williams.*

that I might gain them that are without law: ... so that I might gain those not possessing a law, *Fenton* ... who have no written law, *Williams* ... without any moral law, *Norlie.*

22. To the weak became I as weak: I am made sike to sike men, *Wyclif.*

1 Corinthians 9:23

2419.1 conj	3450.8 art acc pl masc	766.4 adj pl masc	2741.4 verb 1sing subj aor act	3450.4 art dat pl	3820.5 adj dat pl
ἵνα	τοὺς	ἀσθενεῖς	κερδήσω.	τοῖς	πᾶσιν
hina	tous	astheneis	kerdēsō	tois	pasin
that	the	weak	I might gain.	To the	all

1090.1 verb 1sing indic perf act	3450.17 art pl neu	3820.1 adj	2419.1 conj	3705.1 adv	4948.9 indef-pron acc pl masc
γέγονα	⌐ τὰ ⌐b	πάντα,	ἵνα	πάντως	τινὰς
gegona	ta	panta	hina	pantōs	tinas
I have become	the	all things,	that	by all means	some

4834.4 verb 1sing act		3642.17 dem-pron sing neu	3820.1 adj	1156.2 conj	4020.1 verb 1sing pres act
σώσω.	23. ⌐ τοῦτο	[a☆ πάντα]		δὲ	ποιῶ
sōsō	touto	panta		de	poiō
I might save.	This	[all]		and	I do

1217.2 prep	3450.16 art sing neu	2077.1 noun sing neu	2419.1 conj	4642.1 noun nom sing masc
διὰ	τὸ	εὐαγγέλιον,	ἵνα	συγκοινωνὸς
dia	to	euangelion	hina	sunkoinōnos
on account of	the	good news,	that	a fellow partaker

840.3 prs-pron gen sing	1090.39 verb 1sing subj aor mid	3620.2 partic	3471.6 verb 2pl indic perf act	3617.1 conj	3450.7 art pl masc
αὐτοῦ	γένωμαι.	24. Οὐκ	οἴδατε	ὅτι	οἱ
autou	genōmai	Ouk	oidate	hoti	hoi
of it	I might be.	Not	know you	that	the

1706.1 prep	4563.1 noun dat sing	4983.8 verb nom pl masc part pres act	3820.7 adj pl masc	3173.1 conj	4983.3 verb 3pl indic pres act
ἐν	σταδίῳ	τρέχοντες	πάντες	μὲν	τρέχουσιν,
en	stadiō	trechontes	pantes	men	trechousin
in	a race course	running	all	men	run,

1518.3 num card nom masc	1156.2 conj	2956.4 verb 3sing indic pres act	3450.16 art sing neu	1010.1 noun acc sing neu	3643.1 adv
εἷς	δὲ	λαμβάνει	τὸ	βραβεῖον;	οὕτως
heis	de	lambanei	to	brabeion	houtōs
one	but	receives	to	prize?	Thus

4983.6 verb 2pl impr pres act	2419.1 conj	2608.4 verb 2pl subj aor act	3820.6 adj sing masc	1156.2 conj	3450.5 art sing masc
τρέχετε,	ἵνα	καταλάβητε.	25. πᾶς	δὲ	ὁ
trechete	hina	katalabēte	pas	de	ho
run,	that	you may obtain.	Everyone	but	the

74.3 verb nom sing masc part pres	3820.1 adj	1460.1 verb 3sing indic pres	1552.6 dem-pron nom pl masc
ἀγωνιζόμενος,	πάντα	ἐγκρατεύεται·	ἐκεῖνοι
agōnizomenos	panta	enkrateuetai	ekeinoi
striving,	all things	controls himself:	those

3173.1 conj	3631.1 conj	2419.1 conj	5186.1 adj sing	4586.2 noun acc sing masc	2956.21 verb 3pl subj aor act
μὲν	οὖν	ἵνα	φθαρτὸν	στέφανον	λάβωσιν,
men	oun	hina	phtharton	stephanon	labōsin
indeed	then	that	a corruptible	crown	they may receive,

2231.1 prs-pron nom 1pl	1156.2 conj	855.2 adj acc sing	1466.1 prs-pron nom 1sing	4953.1 conj	3643.1 adv
ἡμεῖς	δὲ	ἄφθαρτον.	26. ἐγὼ	τοίνυν	οὕτως
hēmeis	de	aphtharton	egō	toinun	houtōs
we	but	an incorruptible.	I	therefore	thus

felt their weakness in order to gain them.

Note the thrice-repeated "all." In all these actions there was no compromise or compliance with unchristian principles, but rather love and self-denial. Paul did not bend before opposition. But where no principle was at stake, he would go to extreme lengths to meet people and win them to Christ. "Some" indicated that not all would accept Paul's message, but that did not deter him from attempting to reach as many as possible.

9:23. In "all things" Paul's governing aim was "for the gospel's sake." His one purpose was to fulfill his stewardship of the gospel. Determined and versatile in his approach to his assignment, Paul's goal and personal ambition was that he might be a joint partaker in winning people to salvation and leading them to Christ and then to spiritual maturity.

This prepared the stage for the remarks following on discipline and spoke to the Corinthians of the rewards that were available to them if they followed the right way.

9:24. That which had been suggested was now openly expressed. Self-discipline was necessary for both Paul's mission and his salvation. He drew an illustration from the Isthmian games which got their name from the isthmus on which Corinth stood.

Every second or third year, huge crowds gathered to watch the athletic contests. Only free men could participate in the games, and they had to provide proof that for 10 months before the contest they had participated in the necessary preliminary training, as well as spending the last 30 days in exercises in the gymnasium. The winner and his family were honored, and when he returned to his native city, a breach was made in the city walls to allow him to enter, indicating that with such a man they had no need of walls for defense. He also received a prominent seat at all future contests.

In the Greek games only one won the prize. In the Christian race the prize is open to all. The emphasis is on the disciplined, purposeful, hard-running winner. The Christian should run as the winner runs.

9:25. The point made was not mere abstinence, but strong control of appetite and passion. The crown won at the games was the most coveted honor in the Greek world. If these athletes would strive and discipline themselves for something so unenduring as a leafy wreath, how much harder should Christians be willing to strive for a prize that is "incorruptible" or lasts forever. To achieve this prize, the participant must discipline himself in "all things."

that I might gain the weak:
I am made all things to all [men]: I fasshyoned my selfe to all men, *Cranmer* . . . To all these I adapted myself, *Fenton* . . . I became all things, *Douay* . . . I have become all sorts of things to all sorts of people, *Adams*.

that I might by all means save some: . . . by all and every means, *Moffatt* . . . to saue at the least some, *Geneva*.

23. And this I do for the gospel's sake:
that I might be partaker thereof with [you]: . . . that I myght haue my parte therof, *Cranmer* . . . so that I may become a partner with others in it, *Adams*.

24. Know ye not that they which run in a race run all: . . . racing in a stadium, *Concordant*.

but one receiveth the prize?: . . . but a single one, *Fenton* . . . gains the prize? *Moffatt*.

So run, that ye may obtain: . . . so as to win, *Moffatt* . . . so that you may win it, *Fenton* . . . in order to win with certainty, *Weymouth* . . . in such a way that you will get it! *Adams* . . . that you may win, *Conybeare*.

25. And every man that striveth for the mastery is temperate in all things: And every competitor restrains himself, *Fenton* . . . contending in the games...uses self control, *Rotherham* . . . practices self-restraint all round, *Moffatt* . . . who competes in a contest exercises self-control, *Adams* . . . who strives in the matches trains himself by all manner of self-restraint, *Conybeare* . . . refraineth himself from all things, *Douay* . . . abstaineth from all thinges, *Tyndale* . . . readily submit themselves to severe rules of exercise and abstinence, *Locke*.

Now they [do it] to obtain a corruptible crown: . . . for the sake of securing a perishable wreath, *Weymouth* . . . to win a fading wreath, *Moffatt*.

but we an incorruptible: . . . to obtayne an euerlasting crowne, *Cranmer* . . . an unfading, *Moffatt*.

1 Corinthians 9:27

4983.1 verb 1sing pres act	5453.1 conj	3620.2 partic	83.1 adv	3643.1 adv	4296.1 verb 1sing indic pres act
τρέχω,	ὡς	οὐκ	ἀδήλως·	οὕτως	πυκτεύω,
trechō	hōs	ouk	adēlōs	houtōs	pukteuō
run,	as	not	uncertainly;	so	I treat roughly,

5453.1 conj	3620.2 partic	108.3 noun acc sing masc	1188.3 verb nom sing masc part pres act		233.1 conj
ὡς	οὐκ	ἀέρα	δέρων·	27. ⸂	ἀλλ᾽
hōs	ouk	aera	derōn		all'
as	not	air	beating.		But

233.2 conj	5137.1 verb 1sing indic pres act	1466.2 prs-pron gen 1sing	3450.16 art sing neu	4835.1 noun sing neu	2504.1 conj
[✶ ἀλλὰ]	ὑπωπιάζω	μου	τὸ	σῶμα,	καὶ
alla	hupōpiazō	mou	to	sōma	kai
[idem]	I buffet	my	the	body,	and

1390.1 verb 1sing indic pres act	3248.1 conj	3231.1 partic	4315.1 adv	241.7 adj dat pl masc
δουλαγωγῶ,	⸂ μήπως	[✶ μή	πως]	ἄλλοις
doulagōgō	mēpōs	mē	pōs	allois
bring into servitude,	lest	[not	somehow]	to others

2756.17 verb nom sing masc part aor act	840.5 prs-pron nom sing masc	95.1 adj nom sing	1090.39 verb 1sing subj aor mid	3620.3 partic
κηρύξας	αὐτὸς	ἀδόκιμος	γένωμαι.	10:1. Οὐ
kēruxas	autos	adokimos	genōmai	Ou
having preached	myself	rejected	I might be.	Not

2286.1 verb 1sing pres act	1156.2 conj	1056.1 conj	5050.4 prs-pron acc 2pl	49.9 verb inf pres act
θέλω	⸂ δὲ	[ᵃ✶ γὰρ]	ὑμᾶς	ἀγνοεῖν,
thelō	de	gar	humas	agnoein
I wish	now	[for]	you	to be ignorant,

79.6 noun pl masc	3617.1 conj	3450.7 art pl masc	3824.6 noun pl masc	2231.2 prs-pron gen 1pl	3820.7 adj pl masc
ἀδελφοί,	ὅτι	οἱ	πατέρες	ἡμῶν	πάντες
adelphoi	hoti	hoi	pateres	hēmōn	pantes
brothers,	that	the	fathers	our	all

5097.3 prep	3450.12 art acc sing fem	3369.4 noun acc sing fem	1498.37 verb 3pl indic imperf act	2504.1 conj	3820.7 adj pl masc
ὑπὸ	τὴν	νεφέλην	ἦσαν,	καὶ	πάντες
hupo	tēn	nephelēn	ēsan	kai	pantes
under	the	cloud	were,	and	all

1217.2 prep	3450.10 art gen sing fem	2258.2 noun gen sing fem	1324.1 verb indic aor act	2504.1 conj	3820.7 adj pl masc
διὰ	τῆς	θαλάσσης	διῆλθον,	2. καὶ	πάντες
dia	tēs	thalassēs	diēlthon	kai	pantes
through	the	sea	passed,	and	all

1519.1 prep	3450.6 art acc sing masc	3337.6 name acc masc	3338.4 name acc masc	901.18 verb 3pl indic aor mid
εἰς	τὸν	⸂ Μωσῆν	[✶ Μωϋσῆν]	⸂ ἐβαπτίσαντο
eis	ton	Mōsēn	Mousēn	ebaptisanto
to	ton	Moses	[idem]	were baptized

901.17 verb 3pl indic aor pass	1706.1 prep	3450.11 art dat sing fem	3369.3 noun dat sing fem	2504.1 conj	1706.1 prep
[ᵃ ἐβαπτίσθησαν]	ἐν	τῇ	νεφέλῃ	καὶ	ἐν
ebaptisthēsan	en	tē	nephelē	kai	en
[idem]	in	the	cloud	and	in

1.a.**Txt**: 01‭א‬-corr,018K 020L,byz.
Var: 01‭א‬-org,02A,03B 04C,06D,025P,it.sa.bo. Gries,Lach,Treg,Alf Word,Tisc,We/Ho,Weis Sod,UBS/✶

2.a.**Var**: 01‭א‬,02A,04C 06D,044,33,Lach,Tisc Sod

9:26. This concept leads to thoughts of the runner and the boxer. In similar fashion, Paul did not act without purpose or aim. He knew where the finish line was. Nor was he shadowboxing; his opponent was real and he fought "not as one that beateth the air." Only by such effort would Paul win.

9:27. Paul disciplined his body to gain a permanent victory, to meet the test, and qualify for his reward. It appears that Paul accepted his severe bodily suffering as needful for his own sanctification. He dared not lose his crown through failure to satisfy his Lord, or through carelessness and lack of discipline.

The verb *hupōpiazō* literally means "to strike under the eye" and therefore carried the connotation of giving someone "a black eye," certainly a vivid metaphor of what Paul was willing to endure in order to accomplish his ultimate objective of gaining the prize— not only for himself but for the Corinthians as well.

This should not be taken at all as if Paul regarded the physical body as evil; that was Gnostic thought. Rather, Paul's meaning here is similar to Romans 6:13,19 where the body is spoken of as a servant who must serve one of two masters: righteousness or unrighteousness. As with many other things in life (e.g., money, cf. Luke 16:13) what matters most is how we use what we have at our disposal and that it is used for God.

10:1. Indulgence is dangerous to others and one's effectiveness in service. It is also dangerous to one's own soul. To illustrate, Paul turned to Old Testament history. He stressed the importance of what he was saying and its vital nature to the Corinthians with the warning, "I would not . . . should be ignorant" (*agnoein*) or unaware. "All our fathers," without exception, received of the blessings of God. "All" is repeated five times in the first four verses.

The events referred to seem most directly related to the time of the Exodus. The fate of the fathers should warn the children. They knew about the cloud of divine guidance (Exodus 13:20-22; 14:19) and the sea of deliverance (Exodus 14). These were glorious signs of God's presence, blessing, and salvation.

10:2. Together these experiences constituted the inauguration of Israel's national covenant life. Israel was born into its divine estate. They were "baptized (*ebaptisanto*) unto Moses" since in these acts they committed themselves to the leadership of Moses, and "through" him entered acknowledged fellowship with God.

The Corinthians had also been symbolically "baptized into Christ" (Galatians 3:27). The Israelites were united to Moses, but this relationship was in no way as close as the union between Christ and the believer.

26. I therefore so run, not as uncertainly: . . . thus am I racing, not as dubious, *Concordant* . . . I am not just running in one spot, *SEB* . . . run without swerving, *Moffatt* . . . not like a trifler, *Fenton* . . . but not aimlessly, *Norlie* . . . with a clear goal ahead of me, *Beck.*

so fight I, not as one that beateth the air: . . . not as the pugilist who strikes out against the air, *Conybeare* . . . I'm not shadowboxing, *SEB* . . . thus am boxing, as not thrashing air, *Rotherham* . . . does not inflict blows on the air, *Weymouth* . . . not punching the air, *Berkeley.*

27. But I keep under my body, and bring [it] into subjection: I tame my body, *Tyndale* . . . I beat my body, *Geneva* . . . I subdue my body, *Murdock* . . . I exercise my own body and make it serve me, *Norlie* . . . bringing it under complete control, *SEB* . . . I chastise my body, *Rheims, Douay* . . . I severely discipline...make it subservient, *Wilson* . . . master my body, *Moffatt* . . . and lead it captive, *Macknight.*

lest that by any means, when I have preached to others: . . . lest perhaps, *Macknight* . . . after having trained others, *Fenton* . . . while heralding to others, *Berkeley.*

I myself should be a castaway: I should myself be a reprobate, *Sawyer* . . . I my selfe sholde be reproued, *Geneva* . . . I am disqualified myself, *Moffatt* . . . be rejected as unworthy, *Noyes* . . . become disqualified, *Concordant* . . . become unfit to run, *Williams* . . . and be thrown out myself, *Klingensmith.*

1. Moreover, brethren, I would not that ye should be ignorant:
how that all our fathers were under the cloud: . . . sheltered by the cloud, *Weymouth.*

and all passed through the sea: . . . got safely through, *Weymouth* . . . crossed through, *Moffatt.*

2. And were all baptized unto Moses: . . . and all as companions of Moses, *Berkeley.*

in the cloud and in the sea:

1 Corinthians 10:3

3450.11 art dat sing fem	2258.3 noun dat sing fem	2504.1 conj	3820.7 adj pl masc	3450.16 art sing neu	840.15 prs- pron sing neu
τῇ tē the	θαλάσσῃ, thalassē sea,	**3.** καὶ kai and	πάντες pantes all	τὸ to the	αὐτὸ auto same

1026.1 noun sing neu	4012.8 adj sing neu	2052.27 verb indic aor pass	4012.8 adj sing neu	1026.1 noun sing neu
ʹ βρῶμα brōma food	πνευματικὸν pneumatikon spiritual	ἔφαγον, ephagon ate,	[✶ πνευματικὸν pneumatikon [spiritual	βρῶμα brōma food

2052.27 verb indic aor pass	2504.1 conj	3820.7 adj pl masc	3450.16 art sing neu	840.15 prs- pron sing neu	4048.1 noun acc sing neu
ἔφαγον,] ephagon ate,]	**4.** καὶ kai and	πάντες pantes all	τὸ to the	αὐτὸ auto same	ʹ πόμα poma drink

4012.8 adj sing neu	3956.13 verb 3pl indic aor act	4012.8 adj sing neu	3956.13 verb 3pl indic aor act
πνευματικὸν pneumatikon spiritual	ἔπιον· epion drank;	[✶ πνευματικὸν pneumatikon [spiritual	ἔπιον epion drank

4048.1 noun acc sing neu	3956.25 verb 3pl indic imperf act	1056.1 conj	1523.2 prep gen	4012.4 adj gen sing fem
πόμα·] poma drink;]	ἔπινον epinon they were drinking	γὰρ gar for	ἐκ ek of	πνευματικῆς pneumatikēs a spiritual

188.10 verb gen sing fem part pres act	3934.1 noun fem	3450.9 art nom sing fem	1156.2 conj	3934.2 noun nom sing fem
ἀκολουθούσης akolouthousēs following	πέτρας· petras rock,	ἡ hē the	ʹ δὲ de and	πέτρα petra rock

3934.2 noun nom sing fem	1156.2 conj	1498.34 verb sing indic imperf act	3450.5 art sing masc	5382.1 name nom masc	233.1 conj
[✶ πέτρα petra [rock	δὲ] de and]	ἦν ēn was	ὁ ho the	Χριστός. Christos Christ:	**5.** ἀλλ' all' yet

3620.2 partic	1706.1 prep	3450.4 art dat pl	3979.6 adj comp dat pl masc	840.1 prs- pron gen pl	2085.7 verb 3sing indic aor act
οὐκ ouk not	ἐν en with	τοῖς tois the	πλείοσιν pleiosin most	αὐτῶν autōn of them	εὐδόκησεν eudokēsen was well pleased

3450.5 art sing masc	2296.1 noun nom sing masc	2689.1 verb 3pl indic aor pass	1056.1 conj	1706.1 prep	3450.11 art dat sing fem
ὁ ho	θεός· theos God;	κατεστρώθησαν katestrōthēsan they were spread out	γὰρ gar for	ἐν en in	τῇ tē the

2031.2 noun dat sing fem	3642.18 dem- pron pl neu	1156.2 conj	5020.3 noun nom pl masc	2231.2 prs- pron gen 1pl	1090.37 verb 3pl indic aor pass
ἐρήμῳ. erēmō desert.	**6.** ταῦτα tauta These things	δὲ de but	τύποι tupoi types	ἡμῶν hēmōn for us	ἐγενήθησαν, egenēthēsan became,

1519.1 prep	3450.16 art sing neu	3231.1 partic	1498.32 verb inf pres act	2231.4 prs- pron acc 1pl	1923.1 noun acc pl masc
εἰς eis for	τὸ to the	μὴ mē not	εἶναι einai to be	ἡμᾶς hēmas us	ἐπιθυμητὰς epithumētas desirers

10:3,4. The Israelites were sustained by manna from heaven (Exodus 16:11-15) and water from the rocks at Rephidim and Kadesh (Exodus 17:1-7; Numbers 20:1-11). These carried a spiritual meaning for the believing partakers. Paul called the water "spiritual." He did not say the rock from which it issued was spiritual and not material, but that there was a "spiritual Rock" following them; their spirits drank while their bodies drank. "That (other) Rock was Christ." Paul was calling attention to the food's supernatural origin.

This verse indicates that Christ existed in Old Testament times and was spiritually present with Old Testament Israel. It is necessary that the divine Head be so identified to relate the Old Testament example to the New Testament Church.

Christ existed amid this ancient people and yet they perished. How can Christians believe themselves totally secure from such a fate? In passing, the apostle suggested that the Lord's Supper is spiritual food and drink by the first analogy to baptism in 10:2-4 and by the reference to the same observance in 10:16-22. Nowhere else in the New Testament are the two so closely related.

By calling attention to Israel's equivalent of baptism in verses 1 and 2, and Israel's equivalent of the Lord's Supper in verse 3, Paul offered a warning against a false emphasis on the sacraments. As important as baptism and the Eucharist are, they are not of themselves guarantors of salvation. Paul elsewhere evidenced a noncommittal attitude toward baptism at 1:14-16 and 15:29. It must be remembered, however, that Paul was writing here to a congregation who overemphasized the sacraments. For a more complete view of Paul's perspective on baptism it is also necessary to consult passages such as Romans 6:3,4.

10:5. Instead of recognizing Christ's presence and blessings, Israel murmured and disobeyed. The contrasted "but" is strong. Therefore, God was displeased and Israel was judged in the wilderness. The greater part died in the wilderness; only Caleb and Joshua reached the Promised Land (Numbers 14:30).

"Many" of the "all" of verse 4, so highly favored and blessed, received only God's dire judgment. Why? Because of wrong attitudes which resulted in disobedience. The point should have been clear to the Corinthians.

10:6. These were to serve as examples and warnings to the Corinthians and to us to avoid similar disobedience. At the very heart of these disobedient actions were disobedient attitudes, which Paul proceeded to enumerate.

The first refers to attitude and desire: "We should not lust." It recalls Numbers 11:4 and the Israelites' desire for the old diet of Egypt and at the same time refers to the attraction of the idol feasts in Corinth. These incidents were repeated. Evil passions desire evil things.

3. And did all eat the same spiritual meat: ... ate the same spiritual food, *Moffatt* ... the same supernatural food, *RSV*.

4. And did all drink the same spiritual drink: ... all drank of the same spiritual stream, *Conybeare, Montgomery* ... the same supernatural water, *TCNT*.

for they drank of that spiritual Rock that followed them: ... that flowed from the spiritual rock, *Weymouth* ... a supernatural rock, *TCNT* ... from the attending spiritual rock, *Berkeley* ... that went with them, *Beck* ... that attended them, *Murdock* ... which accompanied them, *Moffatt, Williams*.

and that Rock was Christ: ... which rock typified Christ, *Locke* ... was the Messiah, *Fenton*.

5. But with many of them God was not well pleased: Yet, in spite of these privileges, *Way* ... But with most of them, *Weymouth, Adams* ... with the greater part of them, *Panin, Campbell* ... Yet most of them disappointed God, *Norlie* ... with a multitude of them, *Murdock* ... not with the majority of them, *Rotherham* ... in the more part of them, *Rheims* ... Yet most of them lost God's favor, *Conybeare* ... had God no delyte, *Cranmer* ... was not at all satisfied, *Williams* ... God took no pleasure, *Worrell*.

for they were overthrown in the wilderness: ... for they were strewed, *Rotherham* ... laid low in the desert, *Moffatt, Montgomery* ... they were laid prostrate, *Wilson* ... were struck down in the desert, *TCNT* ... and were destroyed in the wilderness, *Locke* ... Their dead bodies were scattered all over the desert, *SEB*.

6. Now these things were our examples: ... they became a warning to us, *Weymouth* ... these became types for us, *Fenton* ... took place as a warning for us, *Moffatt*.

to the intent we should not lust after evil things, as they also lusted: ... that we might not be Cravers, *Wilson* ... to keep us

1 Corinthians 10:7

2527.1 adj gen pl
κακῶν,
kakōn
of evil things,

2503.1 conj
καθὼς
kathōs
just as

2519.4 conj
κἀκεῖνοι
kakeinoi
those also

1922.7 verb 3pl indic aor act
ἐπεθύμησαν.
epethumēsan
desired.

3234.1 adv
7. μηδὲ
mēde
Neither

1486.2 noun nom pl masc
εἰδωλολάτραι
eidōlolatrai
idolaters

1090.19 verb 2pl impr pres
γίνεσθε,
ginesthe
you be,

2503.1 conj
καθώς
kathōs
just as

4948.7 indef-pron nom pl masc
τινες
tines
some

840.1 prs-pron gen pl
αὐτῶν·
autōn
of them;

5453.1 conj
῾ ὡς
hōs
as

5450.1 adv
[ª☆ ὥσπερ]
hōsper
[idem]

1119.22 verb 3sing indic perf pass
γέγραπται,
gegraptai
it has been written,

2495.3 verb 3sing indic aor act
Ἐκάθισεν
Ekathisen
Sat down

3450.5 art sing masc
ὁ
ho
the

2967.1 noun sing masc
λαὸς
laos
people

2052.25 verb inf aor act
φαγεῖν
phagein
to eat

2504.1 conj
καὶ
kai
and

3956.23 verb inf aor act
῾ πιεῖν,
piein
to drink,

3956.29 verb inf aor act
[☆ πεῖν,]
pein
[idem]

2504.1 conj
καὶ
kai
and

448.4 verb 3pl indic aor act
ἀνέστησαν
anestēsan
rose up

3678.1 verb inf pres act
παίζειν.
paizein
to play.

3234.1 adv
8. μηδὲ
mēde
Neither

4062.1 verb 1pl subj pres act
πορνεύωμεν,
porneuōmen
should we commit fornication,

2503.1 conj
καθὼς
kathōs
as

4948.7 indef-pron nom pl masc
τινες
tines
some

840.1 prs-pron gen pl
αὐτῶν
autōn
of them

4062.3 verb 3pl indic aor act
ἐπόρνευσαν,
eporneusan
committed fornication,

2504.1 conj
καὶ
kai
and

3959.3 verb indic aor act
῾ ἔπεσον
epeson
fell

3959.6 verb 3pl indic aor act
[ª☆ ἔπεσαν]
epesan
[idem]

1706.1 prep
῾b ἐν ῾
en
in

1518.7 num card dat fem
μιᾷ
mia
one

2232.3 noun dat sing fem
ἡμέρᾳ
hēmera
day

1492.1 num card
εἰκοσιτρεῖς
eikositreis
twenty three

5342.1 noun nom pl fem
χιλιάδες.
chiliades
thousand.

3234.1 adv
9. μηδὲ
mēde
Neither

1585.1 verb 1pl subj pres act
ἐκπειράζωμεν
ekpeirazōmen
should we tempt

3450.6 art acc sing masc
τὸν
ton
the

5382.4 name acc masc
῾ Χριστόν
Christon
Christ,

2935.4 noun acc sing masc
[ª☆ κύριον,]
kurion
[Lord,]

2503.1 conj
καθὼς
kathōs
just as

2504.1 conj
῾b καὶ ῾
kai
also

4948.7 indef-pron nom pl masc
τινες
tines
some

840.1 prs-pron gen pl
αὐτῶν
autōn
of them

3847.7 verb 3pl indic aor act
ἐπείρασαν,
epeirasan
tempted,

2504.1 conj
καὶ
kai
and

5097.3 prep
ὑπὸ
hupo
by

3450.1 art gen pl
τῶν
tōn
the

3653.5 noun gen pl masc
ὄφεων
opheōn
serpents

616.23 verb 3pl indic aor mid
῾ ἀπώλοντο.
apolonto
perished.

616.35 verb 3pl indic imperf mid
[ᶜ☆ ἀπώλλυντο.]
apōllunto
[were being destroyed.]

3234.1 adv
10. μηδὲ
mēde
Neither

1105.2 verb 2pl impr pres act
῾☆ γογγύζετε,
gonguzete
murmur you,

10:7. From the general admonition, Paul enlarged his discussion to cover certain specific matters. He admonished against idolatry. This urgent warning was repeated in verse 14. Paul was referring to Exodus 32:18-20, and he quoted Exodus 32:6. Remember that the Israelites did this at a time when they were waiting to receive the divine law from God by Moses. Idolatry was a real and continuous problem for the Israelites.

It was a real danger for the Corinthians also. They had been delivered from the superstitions of heathen religion, but they were still drawn by its festivities. They should have stopped their association with such completely, because enjoying this wild, careless merriment could lead rather easily to idolatry again.

When Israel should have been turning to spiritual matters and concentrating on the Lord, they were tempted to treat their salvation carelessly. The same could happen to the Corinthians.

One of the most consistent messages of the entire Bible is that idolatry and sexual immorality are always linked together. The one always results in the other. This is the case here where Paul spoke not only of eating food offered to idols but also of "play." Both the Hebrew *qahas* and the Greek *paizein* have the meaning of sexual play (cf. Genesis 26:8).

10:8. The progression moves from lust and desire to idolatry to fornication. Paul's primary reference appears to be Numbers chapter 25. This verse records that 23,000 died, while Numbers 25:9 records that 24,000 died. However, since Deuteronomy 4:3 indicates that all those connected with Baal-peor were under God's judgment, it seems probable that 23,000 actually died in the plague and Moses included those executed by the judges in Numbers 25:5 to make the total of 24,000 killed. Other writers (such as Hodge) believe both Moses and Paul were using round numbers. The important thing is the very serious danger that Paul was warning his readers about.

10:9. The natural progression in such a path is simply and clearly stated by Paul. The next step is tempting Christ. First comes sensuality, then unbelief. The path remains the same in every generation. The Corinthians would commit this same sin of presuming on divine forbearance if they continued to trifle with idolatry and these related sins.

It is extremely foolish to try God to see how far He will let a person go in sin before He brings judgment to bear. Israel tempted God; the result was judgment from God in the form of fiery serpents. At Corinth it was not so much the participation in pagan feasts as it was dissatisfaction with the discipline of their new faith that caused the problem.

In a sense, because of their disregard for the principles of faith and love, the Corinthians were close to rebelling in the same way that produced such disastrous results for Israel.

from hankering after what is evil, *Williams* . . . that we should not covet, *Douay* . . . we might not covet evil things, *Worrell* . . . we should not hanker after, *Murdock* . . . in pursuit of what is evil, *Weymouth* . . . as they craved, *Moffatt* . . . as they longed, *Montgomery.*

7. Neither be ye idolaters, as [were] some of them: Neither should we serve idols, *Murdock* . . . So do not worship false gods, *Norlie* . . . be ye worshippers of Images, *Tyndale* . . . Don't worship idols, *Beck.*

as it is written, The people sat down to eat and drink:

and rose up to play: . . . rose up to sport, *Noyes* . . . rose up thence for idol-dances, *Way* . . . rose up for idol dances, *Montgomery* . . . got up to dance, *Williams* . . . got up to play around, *SEB* . . . stood up to revel, *Adams* . . . to be making sport, *Rotherham* . . . to make sport, *Moffatt* . . . to act like children, *Klingensmith.*

8. Neither let us commit fornication: Nor must we act licentiously, *Montgomery* . . . let vs be defyled with fornicacion, *Cranmer* . . . Let us stop practicing immorality, *Williams* . . . commit lewdness, *Berkeley.*

as some of them committed:

and fell in one day three and twenty thousand: . . . fell dead in one day, *TCNT.*

9. Neither let us tempt Christ: Neither let us try the long-suffering of Christ, *Conybeare* . . . let us grievously tempt Christ, *Campbell* . . . must we presume upon the Lord, *Moffatt* . . . not go too far in testing the Lord's patience, *Beck* . . . must we presume upon the patience of our Lord, *Montgomery* . . . Nor should we try the patience, *TCNT* . . . stop trying the Lord's patience, *Williams.*

as some of them also tempted:

and were destroyed of serpents: . . . and perished by, *Rheims* . . . They were killed by snakes, *SEB.*

381

1 Corinthians 10:11

10.a.Txt: 02A,03B,04C 044,byz.UBS/☆
Var: 01א,06D,010F 012G,33,bo.

1105.6 verb 1pl subj pres act	**2503.1** conj	**2481.1** conj	**2504.1** conj
[ᵃ γογγύζωμεν,]	ʹ καθὼς	[ᵇ☆ καθάπερ]	ʹᶜ καὶ ʹ
gonguzōmen	kathōs	kathaper	kai
[let us murmur,]	just as	[idem]	also

10.b.Txt: 02A,04C,06D 018K,020L,byz.
Var: 01א,03B,025P Treg,Tisc,We/Ho,Weis Sod,UBS/☆

4948.7 indef-pron nom pl masc	**840.1** prs-pron gen pl	**1105.4** verb 3pl indic aor act	**2504.1** conj	**616.23** verb 3pl indic aor mid	**5097.3** prep
τινὲς	αὐτῶν	ἐγόγγυσαν,	καὶ	ἀπώλοντο	ὑπὸ
tines	autōn	egongusan	kai	apōlonto	hupo
some	of them	murmured,	and	perished	by

10.c.Txt: 018K,020L,byz.
Var: 01א,02A,03B,04C 06D,025P,it.sa.bo.Lach Treg,Alf,Word We/Ho,Weis,Sod UBS/☆

3450.2 art gen sing	**3507.1** noun gen sing masc	**3642.18** dem-pron pl neu	**1156.2** conj	**3820.1** adj
τοῦ	ὀλοθρευτοῦ.	**11.** ταῦτα	δὲ	ʹᵃ πάντα ʹ
tou	olothreutou	tauta	de	panta
the	destroyer.	These things	now	all

11.a.Txt: 04C,018K 020L,025P,044,byz.it.bo. Sod
Var: 02A,03B,33,sa. Treg,Tisc,We/Ho,Weis UBS/☆

5020.3 noun nom pl masc	**5019.1** adv	**4670.8** verb 3pl indic imperf act	**4670.9** verb 3sing indic imperf act
ʹ τύποι	[ᵇ☆ τυπικῶς]	ʹ συνέβαινον	[ᶜ☆ συνέβαινεν]
tupoi	tupikōs	sunebainon	sunebainen
types	[typically]	were happening	[was happening]

11.b.Txt: 06D,020L,byz. sa.bo.
Var: 01א,02A,03B,04C 018K,025P,Lach,Treg Alf,Word,Tisc,We/Ho Weis,Sod,UBS/☆

1552.7 dem-pron dat pl masc	**1119.21** verb 3sing indic aor pass	**1156.2** conj	**4242.1** prep	**3422.2** noun acc sing fem	**2231.2** prs-pron gen 1pl
ἐκείνοις·	ἐγράφη	δὲ	πρὸς	νουθεσίαν	ἡμῶν
ekeinois	egraphē	de	pros	nouthesian	hēmōn
to those,	were written	and	for	admonition	our

11.c.Txt: 02A,06D,byz. 018K,Treg,Tisc,We/Ho Weis,Sod,UBS/☆
Var: 01א,03B,04C

1519.1 prep	**3614.8** rel-pron acc pl masc	**3450.17** art pl neu	**4904.3** noun pl neu	**3450.1** art gen pl	**163.4** noun gen pl masc
εἰς	οὓς	τὰ	τέλη	τῶν	αἰώνων
eis	hous	ta	telē	tōn	aiōnōn
on	whom	the	ends	of the	ages

11.d.Txt: 02A,04C 06D-corr,018K,020L byz.
Var: 01א,03B,06D-org Lach,Treg,Alf,Word Tisc,We/Ho,Weis,Sod UBS/☆

2628.1 verb 3sing indic aor act	**2628.8** verb 3sing indic perf act	**5452.1** conj	**3450.5** art sing masc
ʹ κατήντησεν.	[ᵈ☆ κατήντηκεν.]	**12.** ὥστε	ὁ
katēntēsen	katēntēken	hōste	ho
arrived.	[has arrived.]	So that	the

1374.8 verb nom sing masc part pres act	**2449.38** verb inf perf act	**984.11** verb 3sing impr pres act	**3231.1** partic	**3959.7** verb 3sing subj aor act
δοκῶν	ἑστάναι,	βλεπέτω	μὴ	πέσῃ.
dokōn	hestanai	blepetō	mē	pesē
thinking	to stand,	let him take heed	not	he fall.

3848.1 noun nom sing masc	**5050.4** prs-pron acc 2pl	**3620.2** partic	**2956.34** verb 3sing indic perf act	**1479.1** conj	**3231.1** partic
13. Πειρασμὸς	ὑμᾶς	οὐκ	εἴληφεν	εἰ	μὴ
Peirasmos	humas	ouk	eilēphen	ei	mē
Temptation	you	not	has taken	if	not

440.1 adj nom sing masc	**3964.2** adj nom sing masc	**1156.2** conj	**3450.5** art sing masc	**2296.1** noun nom sing masc
ἀνθρώπινος·	πιστὸς	δὲ	ὁ	θεός,
anthrōpinos	pistos	de	ho	theos
what belongs to man;	faithful	and	ho	God,

3614.5 rel-pron nom sing masc	**3620.2** partic	**1432.7** verb 3sing indic fut act	**5050.4** prs-pron acc 2pl	**3847.19** verb inf aor pass	**5065.1** prep
ὃς	οὐκ	ἐάσει	ὑμᾶς	πειρασθῆναι	ὑπὲρ
hos	ouk	easei	humas	peirasthēnai	huper
who	not	will allow	you	to be tempted	above

10:10. A fifth item was listed: murmuring (*gonguzete*) or grumbling. This amounts to disbelief in God's goodness. It is the complete opposite of faith in God. Paul may have been referring to the rebellion of Korah recorded in Numbers 16:40. Such murmuring was visited by the destroyer or "death angel" (2 Samuel 24:16; Isaiah 37:36; Exodus 12:23; Hebrews 11:28). Murmuring is a sin of dissatisfaction and rebellion that will not stop until it ends in disaster. It is defiance that God will not tolerate.

10:11. Having looked at the Old Testament, Paul proceeded to apply the lessons taught by these incidents. "Now" indicates summary and application. These admonitions are for those "upon whom the ends of the world are come." Jewish and pagan history converge at the point of Christianity. All history finds its apex in the Christian Era. For the lessons of history to go unheeded by this generation would be disastrous.

10:12. Paul wanted his readers to be spiritually alert to the dangers of sin. "Standeth" refers to the believer's position in Christ. The problem is one of pride. The Corinthians had the same proud attitudes as did the ancient Israelites; and unless they were corrected, the results would be similar. They would "fall" morally, that is, sin. "Take heed" that you do stand.

10:13. This verse may be one of the most frequently quoted passages in all of Paul's letters, and indeed, it is one that offers hope in time of trial. Following verse 12 as it does, these words offer encouragement and assurance that it is not necessary, after all, to fall as did the Israelites. If the Corinthians were willing to heed the Old Testament examples, God would be with them to help them stand.

There is more than just hope to this verse however. The "wherefore" (*Dioper*) which begins verse 14 is a warning that if the Corinthians continued to test God (hence Paul's warning in verse 9 not to tempt [test] Christ) and did not flee from idolatry, then God would not help them stand and instead would destroy them.

It is important to note that *peirasmos* ("temptation") is capable of three different meanings. First of all, it may mean temptation to sin. This can only come from Satan; never from God. Secondly, people may test God, as Israel did in the wilderness and as the Corinthians were doing. Finally, there is a testing from God that is not enticement to sin but purposes refinement and purification (Deuteronomy 8:2).

The example that alarms the proud may give hope to the burdened and discouraged; this temptation is bearable. Paul offered consolation first in the fact that this temptation is common to man; it is such as can be borne; it is measured by the strength of the tempted. It is not so strong it cannot be resisted.

10. Neither murmur ye: . . . do you complain as, *Sawyer* . . . nether grucche ye, *Wyclif*.

as some of them also murmured:

and were destroyed of the destroyer: . . . perished by the exterminator, *Concordant* . . . by the Destroying angel, *Moffatt*.

11. Now all these things happened unto them for ensamples: . . . these came upon them typically, *Fenton* . . . by way of warning for others, *Moffatt*.

and they are written for our admonition: . . . and were recorded, *Noyes* . . . for our correction, *Confraternity, Douay*.

upon whom the ends of the world are come: . . . to whom the consummations of the eons have attained, *Concordant* . . . who stand at the meeting of the ages, *Montgomery* . . . upon whom the final age of the world has come, *Confraternity* . . . the perfection of the ages has come, *Fenton* . . . in the closing hours of the world, *Moffatt*.

12. Wherefore let him that thinketh he standeth: . . . who is supposing, *Concordant* . . . whoever imagines he stands, *Fenton* . . . let him that thinks himself safe, *Locke* . . . is standing so securely, *Montgomery*.

take heed lest he fall: . . . lest he fall into sin, *Locke*.

13. There hath no temptation taken you: Trial has not overtaken you, *Fenton* . . . No Trial has assailed You, *Wilson* . . . Only human temptation hath overtaken you, *Panin* . . . has waylaid you, *Moffatt* . . . apprehend you, *Rheims*.

but such as is common to man: . . . as foloweth the nature of man, *Tyndale* . . . except what is human, *Concordant* . . . but such as appartayneth to man, *Geneva*.

but God [is] faithful:

who will not suffer you to be tempted above that ye are able: Who will not permit you, *Fenton* . . . above youre strenght, *Tyndale* . . . above your ability, *Hanson* . . . beyond what you can stand, *Moffatt* . . . beyond your strength, *Confraternity*.

1 Corinthians 10:14

3614.16 rel-pron sing neu	1404.6 verb 2pl indic pres	233.2 conj	4020.52 verb 3sing indic fut act	4713.1 prep dat	3450.3 art dat sing
ὃ	δύνασθε,	ἀλλὰ	ποιήσει	σὺν	τῷ
ho	dunasthe	alla	poiēsei	sun	tō
what	you are able,	but	will make	with	the

3848.3 noun dat sing masc	2504.1 conj	3450.12 art acc sing fem	1532.1 noun acc sing fem	3450.2 art gen sing	1404.22 verb inf pres
πειρασμῷ	καὶ	τὴν	ἔκβασιν,	τοῦ	δύνασθαι
peirasmō	kai	tēn	ekbasin	tou	dunasthai
temptation	also	the	way out,	the	to be able

13.a.Txt: 01ℵ-corr,018K byz.
Var: 01ℵ-org,02A,03B 04C,06D-org,020L,025P Gries,Lach,Treg,Alf Word,Tisc,We/Ho,Weis Sod,UBS/✱

5050.4 prs-pron acc 2pl	5135.3 verb inf aor act	1349.1 conj	27.6 adj pl masc	1466.2 prs-pron gen 1sing
⌐a ὑμᾶς ⌐	ὑπενεγκεῖν.	14. Διόπερ,	ἀγαπητοί	μου,
humas	hupenenkein	Dioper	agapētoi	mou
you	to bear.	Wherefore,	beloved	my,

5180.3 verb 2pl impr pres act	570.3 prep gen	3450.10 art gen sing fem	1485.2 noun gen sing fem	5453.1 conj
φεύγετε	ἀπὸ	τῆς	εἰδωλολατρείας.	15. ὡς
pheugete	apo	tēs	eidōlolatreias	hōs
flee	from	the	idolatry.	As

5265.2 adj dat pl	2978.1 verb 1sing pres act	2892.16 verb 2pl impr aor act	5050.1 prs-pron nom 2pl	3614.16 rel-pron sing neu
φρονίμοις	λέγω·	κρίνατε	ὑμεῖς	ὃ
phronimois	legō	krinate	humeis	ho
to intelligent ones	I speak:	judge	you	what

5183.1 verb 1sing indic pres act	3450.16 art sing neu	4080.1 noun sing neu	3450.10 art gen sing fem	2110.2 noun gen sing fem	3614.16 rel-pron sing neu
φημι.	16. τὸ	ποτήριον	τῆς	εὐλογίας	ὃ
phēmi	to	potērion	tēs	eulogias	ho
I say.	The	cup	of the	blessing	which

2108.1 verb 1pl indic pres act	3644.1 adv	2815.1 noun nom sing fem	3450.2 art gen sing	129.2 noun gen sing neu	3450.2 art gen sing
εὐλογοῦμεν,	οὐχὶ	κοινωνία	⌐ τοῦ	αἵματος	τοῦ
eulogoumen	ouchi	koinōnia	tou	haimatos	tou
we bless,	not	fellowship	of the	blood	of the

5382.2 name gen masc	1498.4 verb 3sing indic pres act	1498.4 verb 3sing indic pres act	3450.2 art gen sing	129.2 noun gen sing neu	3450.2 art gen sing
Χριστοῦ	ἐστιν·	[✱ ἐστιν	τοῦ	αἵματος	τοῦ
Christou	estin	estin	tou	haimatos	tou
Christ	is it?	[is it	of the	blood	of the

5382.2 name gen masc	3450.6 art acc sing masc	735.4 noun acc sing masc	3614.6 rel-pron acc sing masc	2779.1 verb 1pl indic pres act	3644.1 adv
Χριστοῦ;]	τὸν	ἄρτον	ὃν	κλῶμεν,	οὐχὶ
Christou	ton	arton	hon	klōmen	ouchi
Christ?]	The	bread	which	we break,	not

2815.1 noun nom sing fem	3450.2 art gen sing	4835.2 noun gen sing neu	3450.2 art gen sing	5382.2 name gen masc	1498.4 verb 3sing indic pres act
κοινωνία	τοῦ	σώματος	τοῦ	Χριστοῦ	ἐστιν;
koinōnia	tou	sōmatos	tou	Christou	estin
fellowship	of the	body	of the	Christ	is it?

3617.1 conj	1518.3 num card nom masc	735.1 noun nom sing masc	1518.9 num card neu	4835.1 noun sing neu	3450.7 art pl masc
17. ὅτι	εἷς	ἄρτος,	ἓν	σῶμα	οἱ
hoti	heis	artos	hen	sōma	hoi
Because	one	loaf,	one	body	the

Further consolation is found in the fact that God does not originate the temptation, but He does control it. God is faithful to help. God not only limits temptation, He supplies the means of escape. The purpose of seeing the escape is that the tempted may be able to bear the trial and hold up under it. The Corinthians faced the temptation of idolatry and, if resisted, the possibility of persecution. But the door of help stood open in Christ.

10:14. This verse fits so well with what precedes and with what follows that it serves as a hinge on which the whole chapter hangs and turns.

"My dearly beloved" showed Paul's deep concern for his readers and the problems discussed. As he had counseled regarding fornication in 6:18, he did now regarding idolatry. "Flee" (*pheugete*) or "run from" was the admonition. The Corinthians were not to view this matter casually and linger nearby; they were to fly from its presence. They were not to see how far they could go with sin, but have nothing to do with it. Paul had promised them God would sustain them in time of temptation, but this was not a license to play with sin; rather it was an admonition to run fast away, flee.

10:15. The Corinthians prided themselves on their wisdom. Whether Paul mixed sarcasm into this statement or not, he wrote in such a way as to appeal to their attitude and thereby achieve his point. If his readers were really sensible, if they were wise, they would judge and see the wisdom of what Paul wrote.

10:16. Fellowship and communion are important words in this discussion: communion with Christ and communion with demons, which are incompatible. Two elements are involved in such fellowship: one has to do with the sacred object or person honored; the other has to do with the common association among the celebrants.

"Cup of blessing" was the name given to the third cup of the Passover meal and may have been the cup with which our Lord instituted the ordinance of Holy Communion. It seems natural to refer to it at this point. The blessing said over this cup by Jews was, "Blessed are thou, O Lord our God who givest us the fruit of the vine."

But Paul had a wider view than just "blessing" the cup and "breaking" the bread. He had in view the whole sacred means by which we have communion with Christ. The emphasis is on the breaking by which "one" was given to "many" and by which they in turn become one. These elements are a "communion" of the blood and body of Christ and represent a covenant.

10:17. Unity is emphasized. A single loaf was used at Communion, which symbolized unity. The ordinance stems from unity and

but will with the temptation also make a way to escape: . . . but shal in the middes, *Geneva* . . . provide the escape by, *Fenton* . . . provide the way out of it, *Moffatt* . . . furnish also the way, *Noyes.*

that ye may be able to bear [it]: . . . that you may be able to susteine, *Rheims* . . . be enabled to hold out, *Rotherham* . . . you to undergo it, *Concordant* . . . you will be able to come out of it, *Fenton* . . . that you may be able to withstand, *Montgomery.*

14. Wherefore, my dearly beloved, flee from idolatry: . . . ye moost dereworthe to me, *Wyclif* . . . continually flee, *Montgomery* . . . fly from, *Cranmer* . . . Shun idolatry, *Moffatt* . . . flee from the worship of idols, *Confraternity* . . . flee from the seruing of Idols, *Rheims* . . . avoid idolatry, *Fenton.*

15. I speak as to wise men: . . . as to prudent [men], *Rotherham* . . . I speak as to men of understanding, *Conybeare* . . . I am speaking to men of sense, *Montgomery* . . . to intelligent [persons], *PNT* . . . to reflective men, *Fenton* . . . which haue discrecyon, *Cranmer.*

judge ye what I say: . . . use your own judgment upon my words, *Conybeare* . . . weigh my words for yourselves, *Moffatt.*

16. The cup of blessing which we bless: The chalice of benediction, *Rheims, Douay* . . . The cup of thanksgiving, *Murdock.*

is it not the communion of the blood of Christ?: . . . is not a fellowship, *Rotherham* . . . partakinge of the bloude, *Cranmer* . . . not participating in the blood, *Moffatt.*

The bread which we break, is it not the communion of the body of Christ?: . . . a common participation, *Montgomery* . . . the participation of the body, *Rheims* . . . partetakynge of the body of Christ? *Tyndale.*

17. For we [being] many are one bread, [and] one body: . . . are a single body, *Fenton.*

1 Corinthians 10:18

4044.7 adj nom pl masc	**1498.5** verb 1pl indic pres act	**3450.7** art pl masc	**1056.1** conj	**3820.7** adj pl masc	**1523.2** prep gen	**3450.2** art gen sing
πολλοί	ἐσμεν·	οἱ	γὰρ	πάντες	ἐκ	τοῦ
polloi	esmen	hoi	gar	pantes	ek	tou
many	we are;	the	for	all	of	the

1518.1 num card gen	**735.2** noun gen sing masc	**3218.2** verb 1pl indic pres act	**984.1** verb 2pl pres act	**3450.6** art acc sing masc
ἑνὸς	ἄρτου	μετέχομεν.	**18.** βλέπετε	τὸν
henos	artou	metechomen	blepete	ton
one	loaf	we partake.	See	

2447.1 name masc	**2567.3** prep	**4418.4** noun acc sing fem	**3644.1** adv	**3620.1** partic	**3450.7** art pl masc
Ἰσραὴλ	κατὰ	σάρκα·	΄ οὐχὶ	[☆ οὐχ]	οἱ
Israēl	kata	sarka	ouchi	ouch	hoi
Israel	according to	flesh:	not	[idem]	the

2052.11 verb nom pl masc part pres act	**3450.15** art acc pl fem	**2355.1** noun fem	**2817.3** noun nom pl masc	**3450.2** art gen sing
ἐσθίοντες	τὰς	θυσίας,	κοινωνοὶ	τοῦ
esthiontes	tas	thusias	koinōnoi	tou
eating	the	sacrifices,	fellow partakers	with the

2356.2 noun gen sing neu	**1498.7** verb 3pl indic pres act	**4949.9** intr- pron sing neu	**3631.1** conj	**5183.1** verb 1sing indic pres act	**3617.1** conj
θυσιαστηρίου	εἰσίν;	**19.** τί	οὖν	φημι;	ὅτι
thusiastēriou	eisin	ti	oun	phēmi	hoti
altar	are?	What	then	say I?	that

19.a.Txt: 018K,020L,byz. **Var:** 01א-corr,03B 04C-corr,06D,025P Lach,Treg,Alf,Word Tisc,We/Ho,Weis,Sod UBS/☆

1487.1 noun nom sing neu	**1484.1** adj sing neu	**4949.9** intr- pron sing neu	**1498.4** verb 3sing indic pres act
΄ εἴδωλον	[ᵃ☆ εἰδωλόθυτόν]	τί	ἐστιν;
eidōlon	eidōlothuton	ti	estin
an idol	[what is sacrificed to an idol]	anything	is,

19.b.Txt: 018K,020L,byz. **Var:** 01א-corr,03B 04C-corr,06D,025P Lach,Treg,Alf,Word Tisc,We/Ho,Weis,Sod UBS/☆

2211.1 conj	**3617.1** conj	**1484.1** adj sing neu	**1487.1** noun nom sing neu	**4949.9** intr- pron sing neu	
ἢ	ὅτι	΄ εἰδωλόθυτον	[ᵇ☆ εἴδωλόν]	τί	
ē	hoti	eidōlothuton	eidōlon	ti	
or	that	what is sacrificed to an idol	[an idol]	anything	

20.a.Txt: 018K,020L,byz. **Var:** p46,01א,02A,03B 04C,06D,025P,33,Lach Treg,Alf,Word,Tisc We/Ho,Weis,Sod UBS/☆

1498.4 verb 3sing indic pres act	**233.1** conj	**3617.1** conj	**3614.17** rel- pron pl neu	**2357.1** verb 3sing indic pres act	**2357.12** verb 3pl indic pres act
ἐστιν;	**20.** ἀλλ'	ὅτι	ἃ	΄ θύει	[ᵃ☆ θύουσιν]
estin	all'	hoti	ha	thuei	thuousin
is?	but	that	what	sacrifices	[sacrifice]

20.b.Txt: p46,01א,02A 04C,018K,020L,025P 33,byz.sa.bo.We/Ho,Sod **Var:** 03B,06D,Lach,Alf Tisc,Weis,UBS/☆

3450.17 art pl neu	**1477.4** noun pl neu	**1134.5** noun dat pl neu	**2357.1** verb 3sing indic pres act	**2504.1** conj	**3620.3** partic
⁽ᵇ τὰ	ἔθνη, ΄	δαιμονίοις	⁽ᶜ θύει, ΄	καὶ	οὐ
ta	ethnē	daimoniois	thuei	kai	ou
the	nations,	to demons	he sacrifices,	and	not

20.c.Txt: 018K,020L,byz. **Var:** p46,01א,02A,03B 04C,025P,33,Lach,Treg Alf,Tisc,We/Ho,Weis Sod,UBS/☆

2296.3 noun dat sing masc	**2357.12** verb 3pl indic pres act	**3620.3** partic	**2286.1** verb 1sing pres act	**1156.2** conj	**5050.4** prs- pron acc 2pl
θεῷ·	[ᵈ☆+ θύουσιν,]	οὐ	θέλω	δὲ	ὑμᾶς
theō	thuousin	ou	thelō	de	humas
to God.	[they sacrifice.]	Not	I do wish	but	you

20.d.Var: p46,01א,02A 03B,04C,(06D),025P,33 Lach,Treg,Alf,Tisc We/Ho,Weis,Sod UBS/☆

2817.4 noun acc pl masc	**3450.1** art gen pl	**1134.4** noun gen pl neu	**1090.28** verb inf pres	**3620.3** partic
κοινωνοὺς	τῶν	δαιμονίων	γίνεσθαι.	**21.** οὐ
koinōnous	tōn	daimoniōn	ginesthai	ou
fellow partakers	of the	demons	to be.	Not

creates unity for those who partake. They are one in spirit, one in faith, and one in worship. "Bread" suggests also the idea of a common nourishment, sustaining and strengthening an identical life.

It is instructive to note Paul's use of "body" in relation to the Eucharist and to the Corinthian congregation. In the Synoptic Gospels Jesus identifies His actual physical body with the bread of the Last Supper. In 10:17 and 11:17-34 Paul makes a shift from viewing the body of Christ as the physical body which died on the cross to the Church, the Body, i.e., believers, for which He died. This is especially important for chapter 11 where the Corinthians, while partaking of the Eucharist in a wrong manner, were not discerning the body of the Lord (11:29). This means that the Corinthians were not only despising the actual physical body of Christ which was broken for them, but were also despising the body of Christ (believers) for which He died.

The Lord's Supper, therefore, has both a Christological meaning (the sacrificial aspect of Christ's death) as well as an ecclesiastical dimension (the way in which it affects relations among fellow believers). This ecclesiastical concern is present both in chapters 10 and 11 where Paul stressed the need for unity in the body of Christ.

10:18. To enlarge his discussion, Paul turned to the observances of "Israel after the flesh" for illustration. This expression distinguishes the nation of Israel from the Church, the "true Israel." Paul pointed to the fact that those who "eat of the sacrifices" are "partakers" or have communion with the altar.

Going further, participation in the sacrificial feast means fellowship in the sacrifice. Paul's mind is on the total Israelite communion (Leviticus 7:15,16). In these celebrations, there was a recognition of fellowship and service. It was no small thing to eat of the sacrifices offered on the burnt altar in the Jewish temple.

10:19,20. Paul was building to his point. He had noted the meaning of the Lord's Supper and the "communion" involved to show the danger of attending idol feasts. Certain of those with "knowledge" at Corinth would argue that idolatry was merely illusion; that there was no genuine ground of reality, especially for the Christian. They would argue further that these idol feasts had no religious meaning and, therefore, did not touch the conscience; so, friendship or social obligation should allow them to go.

Paul had admitted the truth of the nonreality of the idol in itself as early as 8:4. But he realized the terrible presences behind the idol. Demons were worshiped and communicated with at these idol feasts. The riot and perversion attending the festivals showed evil spirits presided over the events. Therefore, the sacrifice was really being offered to evil spirits (Deuteronomy 32:17), and fellowship was established by the sharing of food.

for we are all partakers of that one bread: . . . since we all have a share of the one loaf, *Adams* . . . are we not all partakers, *Conybeare* . . . all of the one loaf partake, *Rotherham* . . . for we all do share in the one loaf, *Montgomery.*

18. Behold Israel after the flesh: Observe Israel, *Concordant* . . . Look at the Israelites in their practices, *Williams* . . . See how the Jews do it! *Norlie, Beck* . . . the corporate Israel! *Fenton* . . . Look at the rites of Israel, *Moffatt* . . . which walketh carnally, *Tyndale* . . . by natural descent, *Noyes* . . . according to the flesh, *Rheims.*

are not they which eat of the sacrifices partakers of the altar?: . . . they who eat the victims, *Murdock* . . . joint partakers of the altar? *Campbell* . . . are in partnership with the altar? *Conybeare* . . . participate in the altar, *Moffatt.*

19. What say I then?: What, then, do I affirm? *Campbell* . . . Now, what do I mean? *Norlie* . . . Then what do I mean? *Williams.*

that the idol is any thing: . . . that an idol-god really exists, *Norlie* . . . itself means anything, *Moffatt.*

or that which is offered in sacrifice to idols is any thing?: . . . is really changed thereby? *Conybeare.*

20. But I [say], that the things which the Gentiles sacrifice: . . . what the heathen sacrifice, *Fenton.*

they sacrifice to devils, and not to God: . . . is sacrificed to daemons, *Moffatt.*

and I would not that ye should have fellowship with devils: I do not want you to have, *Montgomery* . . . and be in league with devils, *Locke* . . . to participate in daemons, *Moffatt* . . . to become communicants with demons, *Fenton* . . . that ye should be associates of demons, *Murdock* . . . would not have you become partners with the demons, *Conybeare* . . . to become joint partakers, *Campbell.*

1 Corinthians 10:22

1404.6 verb 2pl indic pres	4080.1 noun sing neu	2935.2 noun gen sing masc	3956.10 verb inf pres act	2504.1 conj	4080.1 noun sing neu
δύνασθε	ποτήριον	κυρίου	πίνειν,	καὶ	ποτήριον
dunasthe	potērion	kuriou	pinein,	kai	potērion
you can	cup	of Lord	to drink,	and	cup

1134.4 noun gen pl neu	3620.3 partic	1404.6 verb 2pl indic pres	4971.2 noun gen sing fem	2935.2 noun gen sing masc	3218.5 verb inf pres act
δαιμονίων·	οὐ	δύνασθε	τραπέζης	κυρίου	μετέχειν
daimoniōn	ou	dunasthe	trapezēs	kuriou	metechein
of demons:	not	you can	of table	of Lord	to partake

2504.1 conj	4971.2 noun gen sing fem	1134.4 noun gen pl neu	2211.1 conj	3725.1 verb 1pl indic pres act
καὶ	τραπέζης	δαιμονίων.	22. ἢ	παραζηλοῦμεν
kai	trapezēs	daimoniōn.	ē	parazēloumen
and	of table	of demons.	Or,	do we provoke to jealousy

3450.6 art acc sing masc	2935.4 noun acc sing masc	3231.1 partic	2451.11 adj comp nom pl masc	840.3 prs-pron gen sing	1498.5 verb 1pl indic pres
τὸν	κύριον;	μὴ	ἰσχυρότεροι	αὐτοῦ	ἐσμεν;
ton	kurion;	mē	ischuroteroi	autou	esmen
the	Lord?	not	stronger	of him	are we?

23.a.**Txt**: 01ℵ-corr 04C-corr,018K,020L 044,byz.
Var: p46,01ℵ-org,02A 03B,04C-org,06D,025P sa.bo.Gries,Lach,Treg Alf,Word,Tisc,We/Ho Weis,Sod,UBS/✩

3820.1 adj	1466.4 prs-pron dat 1sing	1815.1 verb 3sing indic pres act	233.1 conj	3620.3 partic	3820.1 adj
23. Πάντα	(a μοι)	ἔξεστιν,	ἀλλ'	οὐ	πάντα
Panta	moi	exestin,	all'	ou	panta
All things	for me	are lawful,	but	not	all things

23.b.**Txt**: 01ℵ-corr,018K 020L,044,byz.
Var: p46,01ℵ-org,02A 03B,04C,06D,sa.bo. Gries,Lach,Treg,Alf Word,Tisc,We/Ho,Weis Sod,UBS/✩

4702.1 verb 3sing indic pres act	3820.1 adj	1466.4 prs-pron dat 1sing	1815.1 verb 3sing indic pres act	233.1 conj	3620.3 partic
συμφέρει·	πάντα	(b μοι)	ἔξεστιν,	ἀλλ'	οὐ
sumpherei	panta	moi	exestin,	all'	ou
are profitable;	all things	for me	are lawful,	but	not

3820.1 adj	3481.3 verb 3sing indic pres act	3235.3 num card nom masc	3450.16 art sing neu	1431.4 prs-pron gen 3sing
πάντα	οἰκοδομεῖ.	24. μηδεὶς	τὸ	ἑαυτοῦ
panta	oikodomei	mēdeis	to	heautou
all	do build up.	No one	to	of himself

24.a.**Txt**: 06D-corr,018K 020L,byz.
Var: 01ℵ,02A,03B,04C 06D-org,015H,025P,33 sa.bo.Gries,Lach,Treg Alf,Word,Tisc,We/Ho Weis,Sod,UBS/✩

2195.7 verb 3sing impr pres act	233.2 conj	3450.16 art sing neu	3450.2 art gen sing	2066.6 adj gen sing masc	1524.3 adj nom sing masc
ζητείτω,	ἀλλὰ	τὸ	τοῦ	ἑτέρου	(a ἕκαστος.)
zēteitō,	alla	to	tou	heterou	hekastos
let seek,	but	the	of the	other	each one.

3820.17 adj sing neu	3450.16 art sing neu	1706.1 prep	3083.1 noun dat sing neu	4310.14 verb acc sing neu part pres pass	2052.1 verb 2pl pres act
25. Πᾶν	τὸ	ἐν	μακέλλῳ	πωλούμενον	ἐσθίετε,
Pan	to	en	makellō	pōloumenon	esthiete,
Everything	to	in	a market	being sold	eat,

3235.6 num card neu	348.4 verb nom pl masc part pres act	1217.2 prep	3450.12 art acc sing fem	4743.4 noun acc sing fem
μηδὲν	ἀνακρίνοντες	διὰ	τὴν	συνείδησιν·
mēden	anakrinontes	dia	tēn	suneidēsin
nothing	inquiring	on account of	the	conscience.

3450.2 art gen sing	1056.1 conj	2935.2 noun gen sing masc	2935.2 noun gen sing masc	1056.1 conj	3450.9 art nom sing fem
26. τοῦ	(γὰρ	κυρίου	[✩ κυρίου	γὰρ]	ἡ
tou	gar	kuriou	kuriou	gar	hē
The	for	Lord's	[Lord's	for]	the

10:21,22. The position of the Corinthian Christians who ate the Lord's Supper and still chose to participate in idol feasts was contradictory and unacceptable. Paul was speaking of the moral and spiritual impossibility of real participation in both the Lord's Communion and the devil's communion.

There cannot be two masters in one life; there cannot be two communions. The distinct reference to "cup" and "table" emphasizes the strength of this admonition. "Cup of the Lord" and other such phrases point to both possession and leadership. The Lord distributes "the cup," and it denotes true fellowship with Him.

In like manner, participation in the idol feasts was wrong because of the fellowship with demons which it allowed. To do this was to break fellowship with the Lord and provoke Him to jealousy. Israel did this often, as we see from Deuteronomy 32:21. To oppose God in this manner and provoke Him to jealousy suggests that we are stronger than He is. Such an idea is foolish and completely wrong.

To participate in both feasts would only cause confusion and spiritual apathy initially. As the matter progressed, it would cause spiritual rebellion and rejection of Christ because allegiances and desires were divided between the Lord Jesus Christ and Satan.

10:23. There must be expedient and edifying profit in our actions. "All things are lawful" states the great, general principle of liberty. It was repeated twice just in this verse. Paul also repeated part of the statement in 6:12.

But not everything that is "lawful" is in our best interest, or another's. "Expedient" (*sumpherei*) refers to what is wise, beneficial, and most proper at the moment. "Edify" (*oikodomei*) refers to building up, especially in the Christian faith.

The point is not whether it is allowable or not, but whether it is profitable in a genuine Christian sense. The pervading theme in Paul's conclusion on the eating of sacrificial meats, the questions of conscience, was the supremacy of love in church life, which is expressed by edification of others.

Note that when Paul spoke of edifying, he had more than just the weak in mind. The whole Church, the entire Christian community, must be safeguarded by love, and thus edified.

10:24. Paul narrowed the principle even more. The Christian is to seek the good of others and promote their interests.

10:25. On the basis of these principles, Paul explained that idol meat offered in the market for sale should not be argued over or worried over, but accepted as from God.

10:26. Idol meat was often difficult to avoid because the butcher generally burnt at least a few hairs of an animal as a sacrifice, and

21. Ye cannot drink the cup of the Lord, and the cup of devils: . . . and the chalice of deuils, *Rheims.*

ye cannot be partakers of the Lord's table, and of the table of devils: You cannot be a guest at both, *Norlie* . . . are not able to share the Lord's table, *Fenton* . . . You can't share the Lord's table, *Beck.*

22. Do we provoke the Lord to jealousy?: . . . do we intend to rouse the Lord's jealousy? *Moffatt* . . . are we trying to incite the Lord, *Williams.*

are we stronger than he?: Are we mightier, *Rotherham.*

23. All things are lawful for me: Everything is permitted, *Fenton* . . . All sorts of things, *Adams* . . . Every thing is in my power, *Murdock.*

but all things are not expedient: . . . everything does not benefit, *Fenton* . . . all things are not beneficial, *Wilson* . . . but not all are good for us, *Moffatt* . . . but not all things are advantageous, *Adams* . . . but not everything is constructive, *Norlie.*

all things are lawful for me:

but all things edify not: . . . but not everything builds up their personality, *Williams.*

24. Let no man seek his own: . . . his own advantage, *Adams* . . . his own private, particular interest alone, *Locke* . . . be looking after his own welfare, *Williams.*

but every man another's [wealth]: . . . but the benefit of others, *Fenton* . . . but each his neighbor's good, *Clementson* . . . but also that of his neighbor, *Williams.*

25. Whatsoever is sold in the shambles, [that] eat: . . . in the market, *Moffatt* . . . in the flesh-market, *Murdock.*

asking no question for conscience sake: . . . never inquiring about it, *Fenton* . . . without any inquiry, or scruple, *Locke.*

26. For the earth [is] the Lord's: . . . belongs to the Lord, *SEB.*

1 Corinthians 10:27

27.a.**Txt:** 04C,06D-corr
015H,018K,020L,byz.sa.
Var: 01א,02A,03B
06D-org,025P,it.bo.Lach
Treg,Alf,Word,Tisc
We/Ho,Weis,Sod
UBS/✫

1087.1 noun sing fem	2504.1 conj	3450.16 art sing neu	3998.1 noun sing neu	840.10 prs-pron gen sing fem	1479.1 conj	1156.2 conj
γῆ	καὶ	τὸ	πλήρωμα	αὐτῆς.	27. εἰ	(a δὲ)
gē	kai	to	plērōma	autēs	ei	de
earth	and	the	fulness	of it.	If	but

4948.3 indef-pron nom sing	2535.1 verb 3sing indic pres act	5050.4 prs-pron acc 2pl	3450.1 art gen pl	566.5 adj gen pl masc	2504.1 conj
τις	καλεῖ	ὑμᾶς	τῶν	ἀπίστων,	καὶ
tis	kalei	humas	tōn	apistōn	kai
anyone	invites	you	of the	unbelieving,	and

2286.5 verb 2pl indic pres act	4057.15 verb inf pres	3820.17 adj sing neu	3450.16 art sing neu	3769.10 verb acc sing neu part pres pass
θέλετε	πορεύεσθαι,	πᾶν	τὸ	παρατιθέμενον
thelete	poreuesthai	pan	to	paratithemenon
you wish	to go,	all	the	being set before

5050.3 prs-pron dat 2pl	2052.1 verb 2pl pres act	3235.6 num card neu	348.4 verb nom pl masc part pres act	1217.2 prep
ὑμῖν	ἐσθίετε,	μηδὲν	ἀνακρίνοντες	διὰ
humin	esthiete	mēden	anakrinontes	dia
you	eat,	nothing	inquiring	on account of

3450.12 art acc sing fem	4743.4 noun acc sing fem	1430.1 partic	1156.2 conj	4948.3 indef-pron nom sing	5050.3 prs-pron dat 2pl
τὴν	συνείδησιν.	28. ἐὰν	δέ	τις	ὑμῖν
tēn	suneidēsin	ean	de	tis	humin
the	conscience.	If	but	anyone	to you

28.a.**Txt:** 04C,06D,018K
020L,025P,byz.bo.
Var: 01א,02A,03B
015H,Lach,Treg,Alf
Tisc,We/Ho,Weis,Sod
UBS/✫

1500.8 verb 3sing subj aor act	3642.17 dem-pron sing neu	1484.1 adj sing neu	2386.1 adj acc sing masc
εἴπῃ,	Τοῦτο	εἰδωλόθυτόν	[ᵃ✫ ἱερόθυτόν]
eipē	Touto	eidōlothuton	hierothuton
says,	This	offered to an idol	[offered in sacrifice]

1498.4 verb 3sing indic pres act	3231.1 partic	2052.1 verb 2pl pres act	1217.1 prep	1552.5 dem-pron acc sing masc	3450.6 art acc sing masc
ἐστιν·	μὴ	ἐσθίετε	δι'	ἐκεῖνον	τὸν
estin	mē	esthiete	di'	ekeinon	ton
is,	not	do eat,	on account of	that one	the

28.b.**Txt:** 015H-corr
018K,020L,044,byz.
Var: 01א,02A,03B,04C
06D,015H-org,025P,33
Gries,Lach,Treg,Alf
Word,Tisc,We/Ho,Weis
Sod,UBS/✫

3245.3 verb acc sing masc part aor act	2504.1 conj	3450.12 art acc sing fem	4743.4 noun acc sing fem	3450.2 art gen sing	1056.1 conj
μηνύσαντα	καὶ	τὴν	συνείδησιν·	(b τοῦ	γὰρ
mēnusanta	kai	tēn	suneidēsin	tou	gar
pointing out	and	the	conscience;	the	for

2935.2 noun gen sing masc	3450.9 art nom sing fem	1087.1 noun sing fem	2504.1 conj	3450.16 art sing neu	3998.1 noun sing neu
κυρίου	ἡ	γῆ	καὶ	τὸ	πλήρωμα
kuriou	hē	gē	kai	to	plērōma
Lord's	the	earth	and	the	fulness

840.10 prs-pron gen sing fem	4743.4 noun acc sing fem	1156.2 conj	2978.1 verb 1sing pres act	3644.1 adv	3450.12 art acc sing fem
αὐτῆς.)	29. συνείδησιν	δὲ	λέγω,	οὐχὶ	τὴν
autēs	suneidēsin	de	legō	ouchi	tēn
its.	Conscience	but,	I say,	not	the

1431.4 prs-pron gen 3sing	233.2 conj	3450.12 art acc sing fem	3450.2 art gen sing	2066.6 adj gen sing masc	2419.1 conj	4949.9 intr-pron sing neu
ἑαυτοῦ,	ἀλλὰ	τὴν	τοῦ	ἑτέρου.	ἵνα	τί
heautou	alla	tēn	tou	heterou	hina	ti
of yourself,	but	the	of the	other;	that	why

the priest would often sell extra meat in the market. Paul wrote that the Corinthians were to ask no question, but rather to accept the fact that their food was a blessing from the Lord, "for the earth is the Lord's." This comes from Psalm 24:1. It would have been difficult to discover the nature of the meat in such a shop without causing a disturbance. In such a situation, the Corinthian Christians were to recognize the divine origin of meat and the goodness of the Lord, and to rest in that. Such things may be used within the framework of the law of Christ.

10:27. A second specific situation was presented. This involved being invited to a dinner by an unsaved host. If the invitation was accepted, the believer was to eat whatever was set before him without questioning the origin of the food. (This involved a private meal, not a meal in an idol temple.)

Before an unbelieving host or family, the Christian would be closely watched. One of the great dangers of such a situation was offense or unprofitable action. Under such circumstances, the Corinthian Christian was not to ask foolish questions because of scruples that have no merit. He should eat what was set on the table. There was no more need to raise the question of conscience in the one case than in the other.

10:28. But at some time at such a dinner or in a marketplace, someone might approach the Christian and explain that the meat had been sacrificed first to an idol. The Corinthians were told specifically how this should be handled. The situation was changed, and the strong Christian should refrain from eating. The meat was not now simply a gift of God, having passed through unknown sources. Rather, it was known as the end product of idolatry and some believed that to then eat it would mean idolatry. The Christian must not eat "for conscience' sake."

Paul did not mean the conscience of the eater, but the conscience of the speaker. The speaker, or another, could not see or grasp this. In deference to this weaker conscience, the strong Christian should not eat such meat.

In summation, whether the speaker was a weak Christian or a pagan, and whether the intent was to warn or embarrass, at such a point the Christian was to announce his faith and for the sake of another, abstain from eating "sacrifice meat."

10:29. Two interconnected questions arise out of this discussion. One of them relates to why anyone else should be able to guide and limit my actions? Can freedom be restricted even when motives are pure? The motive for Paul's using this question in the text is to point out that the exercise of liberty must not be made the means

and the fulness thereof: . . . and all its contents, *Moffatt* . . . and every last thing in it, *Adams* . . . everything in it, *SEB* . . . and all its store, *Way.*

27. If any of them that believe not bid you [to a feast], and ye be disposed to go: . . . some unbelieving heathen, *Williams* . . . invite you, *Fenton* . . . invites some of you to his house, *TCNT* . . . invites you to his house, *Montgomery* . . . to an entertainment, *Locke* . . . and if ye be disposed to go, *Geneva* . . . you want to go, *Concordant* . . . ye are wishing to go, *Rotherham.*

whatsoever is set before you, eat: . . . eat everything which is presented to you, *Wilson.*

asking no question for conscience sake: . . . never examining it, *Fenton* . . . without an inquiry, *Murdock* . . . without raising any question, *Williams, RSV* . . . instead of letting scruples of conscience induce you to ask any questions about it, *Moffatt.*

28. But if any man say unto you, This is offered in sacrifice unto idols: But if somebody tells you, *Beck* . . . if someone informs you, *Berkeley* . . . This is dedicate vnto idols, *Geneva* . . . is an idol offering, *Fenton.*

eat not for his sake that showed it, and for conscience sake: Don't eat it, *SEB* . . . make it your rule not to eat it, *Williams* . . . because of that one who divulges, *Concordant* . . . for the sake of him who pointed it out, *Conybeare* . . . for hurtynge of conscience, *Tyndale* . . . of the person who brought up the issue, *Adams* . . . considering your informant, *Norlie.*

for the earth [is] the Lord's, and the fulness thereof:

29. Conscience, I say, not thine own, but of the other: I mean not yours, but his! *SEB* . . . his conscience, not your own, *Montgomery* . . . but his who told you, *Murdock.*

1056.1 conj	3450.9 art nom sing fem	1644.1 noun nom sing fem	1466.2 prs-pron gen 1sing	2892.29 verb 3sing indic pres pass	5097.3 prep
γὰρ	ἡ	ἐλευθερία	μου	κρίνεται	ὑπὸ
gar	hē	eleutheria	mou	krinetai	hupo
for	the	freedom	my	is being judged	by

241.10 adj gen sing fem	4743.2 noun gen sing fem	1479.1 conj	1156.2 conj	1466.1 prs-pron nom 1sing
ἄλλης	συνειδήσεως;	**30.** εἰ	⟨a δὲ ⟩	ἐγὼ
allēs	suneidēseōs	ei	de	egō
another's	conscience?	If	but	I

30.a.**Txt:** Steph
Var: 01ℵ,02A,03B,04C 06D,018K,020L,025P byz.it.sa.bo.Gries,Lach Treg,Alf,Word,Tisc We/Ho,Weis,Sod UBS/✰

5322.3 noun dat sing fem	3218.1 verb 1sing indic pres act	4949.9 intr-pron sing neu	980.16 verb 1sing indic pres pass	5065.1 prep
χάριτι	μετέχω,	τί	βλασφημοῦμαι	ὑπὲρ
chariti	metechō	ti	blasphēmoumai	huper
with thanks	partake,	why	am I evil spoken of	for

3614.2 rel-pron gen sing	1466.1 prs-pron nom 1sing	2149.1 verb 1sing indic pres act	1521.1 conj	3631.1 conj
οὗ	ἐγὼ	εὐχαριστῶ;	**31.** Εἴτε	οὖν
hou	egō	eucharistō	Eite	oun
what	I	give thanks?	Whether	therefore

2052.1 verb 2pl pres act	1521.1 conj	3956.3 verb 2pl indic pres act	1521.1 conj	4948.10 indef-pron sing neu	4020.2 verb 2pl pres act
ἐσθίετε,	εἴτε	πίνετε,	εἴτε	τι	ποιεῖτε,
esthiete	eite	pinete	eite	ti	poieite
you eat,	or	you drink	or	anything	you do,

3820.1 adj	1519.1 prep	1385.4 noun acc sing fem	2296.2 noun gen sing masc	4020.2 verb 2pl pres act
πάντα	εἰς	δόξαν	θεοῦ	ποιεῖτε.
panta	eis	doxan	theou	poieite
all things	to	glory	God's	do.

671.2 adj nom pl	1090.19 verb 2pl impr pres	2504.1 conj	2428.4 name-adj dat pl masc	2504.1 conj
32. ἀπρόσκοποι	⟨ γίνεσθε	καὶ	Ἰουδαίοις	[✰ καὶ
aproskopoi	ginesthe	kai	Ioudaiois	kai
Without offense	be you	both	to Jews	[both

2428.4 name-adj dat pl masc	1090.19 verb 2pl impr pres	2504.1 conj	1659.6 name dat pl masc	2504.1 conj	3450.11 art dat sing fem
Ἰουδαίοις	γίνεσθε]	καὶ	Ἕλλησιν	καὶ	τῇ
Ioudaiois	ginesthe	kai	Hellēsin	kai	tē
to Jesus	be you]	and	Greeks	and	to the

1564.3 noun dat sing fem	3450.2 art gen sing	2296.2 noun gen sing masc	2503.1 conj	2476.3 conj	3820.1 adj
ἐκκλησίᾳ	τοῦ	θεοῦ·	**33.** καθὼς	κἀγὼ	πάντα
ekklēsia	tou	theou	kathōs	kagō	panta
assembly	of God.		Just as	I also	all

3820.5 adj dat pl	694.1 verb 1sing indic pres act	3231.1 partic	2195.8 verb nom sing masc part pres act	3450.16 art sing neu	1670.1 prs-pron gen 1sing masc
πᾶσιν	ἀρέσκω,	μὴ	ζητῶν	τὸ	ἐμαυτοῦ
pasin	areskō	mē	zētōn	to	emautou
in all things	please;	not	seeking	to	of myself

33.a.**Txt:** 01ℵ-corr,06D 018K,020L,025P,etc.byz.
Var: 01ℵ-org,02A,03B 04C,Lach,Treg,Alf,Tisc We/Ho,Weis,Sod UBS/✰

4702.2 verb sing neu part pres act	4703.1 adj acc sing	233.2 conj	3450.16 art sing neu	3450.1 art gen pl
⟨ σύμφερον,	[a✰ σύμφορον]	ἀλλὰ	τὸ	τῶν
sumpheron	sumphoron	alla	to	tōn
profiting,	[profit]	but	the	of the

of offense to another. Actions done in the right spirit must have a profitable result.

Several alternatives have been posed to explain the question raised by verse 29. Some have suggested that this was an actual complaint of the strong, namely, "Why should I allow my liberty to be infringed on?" This is unlikely: (1) because Paul did not answer this question in the following verse, and (2) this clause begins with *gar* ("for") instead of "but" which would be more likely if Paul were dealing with an interjection by the "strong."

A better suggestion is that Paul, by use of a rhetorical question, elaborated further on why a person might limit his own liberty. Paul, then, was simply reinforcing the meaning of verses 28 and 29 by saying that if a Christian voluntarily restricts his freedom for the sake of another person's conscience, that Christian has not lost his freedom. He has merely put it "on hold" temporarily.

10:30. A second question is added. As long as I eat with a heart of thankfulness to God, why should I be discredited for doing so? The answer is that the believer is responsible not only for a thankful heart but also for the effect his actions may have on a weaker brother. Definite harm could result. A person with a sensitive conscience could regard the act as sacrilegious and hypocritical, and the cause of Christ could be damaged. While there is a limit to which another's conscience should be regarded, nevertheless, consideration for others must be added to our free personal conscience and our true thanksgiving to God.

10:31,32. Paul gave two major reasons for acting as he had presented. The first is that all believers' actions should redound to the glory of God. Anything and everything, "all" without exclusion, must be subordinate to the supreme maxim of Christian duty: bringing glory to God.

The second reason is that there be no occasion to stumble for anyone, in or outside the Church. "Jews" and "Gentiles" include everyone. Causing another to stumble would result in that one sinning. That would affect his salvation and bring dishonor to the Lord.

10:33. Paul concluded by using himself as an example. The apostle attempted to teach not only from knowledge, but from personal life and example. No personal advantage was sought; he always sought the profit of others, and he urged Christians to imitate him. His aim was the highest; his goal the best. This is the proper balance of liberty and love.

for why is my liberty judged of another [man's] conscience?: ... why is my freedom limited, *Sawyer* ... why should my freedom be determined by another man's conscience? *Norlie* ... why should one's own freedom be called into question, *Moffatt* ... "But," you may object, "why should my freedom be decided upon another's scruples of conscience?" *Montgomery.*

30. For if I by grace be a partaker: If I participate with thankes, *Rheims* ... If I partake with thankfulness, *Fenton, Noyes, ASV* ... If I partake with thanksgiving, *Confraternity* ... with gratitude, *Rotherham.*

why am I evil spoken of for that for which I give thanks?: ... why am I blamed, *Sawyer* ... why should I be slandered about that, *Fenton* ... why am I called a sinner for that which I eat with thanksging? *Conybeare* ... why am I reproached for that, *Murdock* ... why am I denounced, *Montgomery.*

31. Whether therefore ye eat, or drink, or whatsoever ye do: do all to the glory of God: ... do everything for God's glory, *Adams* ... do all to the prayse of God, *Tyndale.*

32. Give none offence, neither to the Jews: You should be inoffensive, *Fenton* ... Put no stumblingblock in the way, *Moffatt* ... Give no cause of stumbling, *Conybeare* ... Be without offence to the Jews, *Douay.*

nor to the Gentiles, nor to the church of God: ... nether to the congregacion, *Cranmer.*

33. Even as I please all [men] in all [things]: Such is my own rule, *Moffatt* ... as I also strive, *Noyes* ... just as I also make everything pleasant to every one, *Fenton.*

not seeking mine own profit, but the [profit] of many: I do not strive for personal profit, *Norlie* ... my own expedience, *Concordant* ... my own advantage, *Adams, Campbell* ... the advantage of the greater number, *Moffatt.*

1 Corinthians 11:1

4044.1 adj gen pl	2419.1 conj	4834.27 verb 3pl subj aor pass		3266.1 noun nom pl masc	1466.2 prs-pron gen 1sing
πολλῶν,	ἵνα	σωθῶσιν.		11:1. μιμηταί	μου
pollōn	hina	sōthōsin		mimētai	mou
many,	that	they may be saved.		Imitators	of me

1090.19 verb 2pl impr pres	2503.1 conj	2476.3 conj	5382.2 name gen masc	1852.1 verb 1sing indic pres act	1156.2 conj
γίνεσθε,	καθὼς	κἀγὼ	Χριστοῦ.	2. Ἐπαινῶ	δὲ
ginesthe	kathōs	kagō	Christou	Epainō	de
be,	just as	I also	of Christ.	I praise	now

2.a.Txt: 06D,018K,020L 044,33,byz.it.
Var: p46,01א,02A,03B 04C,025P,sa.bo.Lach Treg,Alf,Word,Tisc We/Ho,Weis,Sod UBS/⋆

5050.4 prs-pron acc 2pl	79.6 noun pl masc	3617.1 conj	3820.1 adj	1466.2 prs-pron gen 1sing
ὑμᾶς,	⌐a ἀδελφοί, ⌐	ὅτι	πάντα	μου
humas	adelphoi	hoti	panta	mou
you,	brothers,	that	in all things	me

3279.10 verb 2pl indic perf	2504.1 conj	2503.1 conj	3722.8 verb 1sing indic aor act	5050.3 prs-pron dat 2pl
μέμνησθε,	καὶ	καθὼς	παρέδωκα	ὑμῖν,
memnēsthe	kai	kathōs	paredōka	humin
you have remembered;	and	just as	I delivered	to you,

3450.15 art acc pl fem	3724.4 noun acc pl fem	2692.1 verb 2pl pres act	2286.1 verb 1sing pres act	1156.2 conj	5050.4 prs-pron acc 2pl
τὰς	παραδόσεις	κατέχετε.	3. θέλω	δὲ	ὑμᾶς
tas	paradoseis	katechete	thelō	de	humas
the	traditions	you keep.	I wish	but	you

3471.25 verb inf perf act	3617.1 conj	3820.2 adj gen sing	433.2 noun gen sing masc	3450.9 art nom sing fem	2747.1 noun nom sing fem
εἰδέναι,	ὅτι	παντὸς	ἀνδρὸς	ἡ	κεφαλὴ
eidenai	hoti	pantos	andros	hē	kephalē
to know,	that	of every	man	the	head

3.a.Txt: p46,01א,02A 03B-corr3,06D-corr,08E 018K,020L,025P,We/Ho UBS/⋆
Var: 03B-org,06D-org 010F,012G,103,462 1926

3450.5 art sing masc	5382.1 name nom masc	1498.4 verb 3sing indic pres act	2747.1 noun nom sing fem	1156.2 conj	1129.2 noun gen sing fem
⌐a ὁ ⌐	Χριστός	ἐστιν·	κεφαλὴ	δὲ	γυναικὸς
ho	Christos	estin	kephalē	de	gunaikos
the	Christ	is,	head	but	of woman

3.b.Var: 01א,02A,03B 06D,33,Lach,Treg,Alf Tisc,We/Ho,Weis,Sod UBS/⋆

3450.5 art sing masc	433.1 noun nom sing masc	2747.1 noun nom sing fem	1156.2 conj	3450.2 art gen sing	5382.2 name gen masc
ὁ	ἀνήρ·	κεφαλὴ	δὲ	[b⋆+ τοῦ]	Χριστοῦ,
ho	anēr	kephalē	de	tou	Christou
the	man,	head	and	[of the]	of Christ,

3450.5 art sing masc	2296.1 noun nom sing masc	3820.6 adj sing masc	433.1 noun nom sing masc	4195.11 verb nom sing masc part pres	2211.1 conj
ὁ	θεός.	4. πᾶς	ἀνὴρ	προσευχόμενος	ἢ
ho	theos	pas	anēr	proseuchomenos	ē
the	God.	Every	man	praying	or

4253.4 verb nom sing masc part pres act	2567.3 prep	2747.2 noun gen sing fem	2174.17 verb nom sing masc part pres	2587.1 verb 3sing indic pres act
προφητεύων,	κατὰ	κεφαλῆς	ἔχων,	καταισχύνει
prophēteuōn	kata	kephalēs	echōn	kataischunei
prophesying,	on	head	having,	puts to shame

3450.12 art acc sing fem	2747.4 noun acc sing fem	840.3 prs-pron gen sing	3820.9 adj nom sing fem	1156.2 conj	1129.1 noun nom sing fem
τὴν	κεφαλὴν	αὐτοῦ.	5. πᾶσα	δὲ	γυνὴ
tēn	kephalēn	autou	pasa	de	gunē
the	head	his.	Every	but	woman

11:1. Paul next turned to matters related to public worship. His teaching is closely related to what has just preceded. The main concern should always be to "do all to the glory of God" (10:31).

11:2. Paul begins with praise for the Corinthian believers. They had faithfully obeyed the rules for behavior he had laid down for them. These were new converts. They needed detailed instructions, and Paul had carefully outlined how they should conduct themselves.

11:3. Some have denounced Paul as a woman hater, but we must remember it was Paul who insisted that in Christ all distinctions were to be removed between Jew and Greek, bond and free, and male and female (Galatians 3:28). Those are some of the most radical words ever uttered concerning social and religious matters.

The context shows that in the Corinthian church women took an active part in the worship services, unlike those in the Jewish synagogue who were not allowed such freedom. Some of these women may have misunderstood their newfound Christian freedom and refrained from wearing the head covering, which custom dictated they should wear when prophesying or praying in public. This is the problem which Paul now addresses.

The apostle stated the "chain of command" for that First Century church. God is the head of Christ, Christ is the head of man, and man is the head of woman. If this principle is examined closely, it reveals an important fact: subordination does not mean inferiority. The sexes are equal mentally, morally, and spiritually.

"Head" refers to a governing, controlling, ruling organ. It indicates a relationship of authority. "The head of every man is Christ" began the discussion. Every man has one head, Christ.

"The head of the woman is the man" establishes the order of authority God has ordained. Man holds headship directly from his Creator and is brought by his manhood into direct responsibility to Christ. The very law of marriage and the social order are grounded in Christ.

On the side of submission, the Lord set the pattern with His perfect loyalty and obedience to the Father. This should make it easier to submit, when we see that Christ is subject to God the Father and man to the Head, Christ. In nature there is equality; in office and work there is submission.

11:4. This principle applied directly to the covering of women. Paul first wrote of the uncovered man. This was a strictly Christian matter, for the Jewish male covered his head.

Man's only head is Christ, and while both sexes worship Him in common, woman also has man as her head. The man who wore a covering dishonored his own place and this reflected on Christ, for he shamed Christ whose lordship he represented.

that they may be saved: ... that I may be instrumental to the salvation of as many as is possible, *Locke* ... that they may live, *Murdock.*

1. Be ye followers of me, even as I also [am] of Christ: Copy me, as I copy Christ, *Moffatt* ... Pattern after me, as I pattern after Christ, *Berkeley* ... Imitate me, as I myself imitate Christ, *TCNT.*

2. Now I praise you, brethren, that ye remember me in all things: I commende you, *Cranmer* ... Now I am applauding you, *Concordant* ... for remembering me in everything, *Montgomery* ... for remembering all my orders, *Locke* ... ye are mindful of me, *Murdock, TCNT.*

and keep the ordinances, as I delivered [them] to you: ... and that you retain the traditions, *Sawyer* ... and hold fast my precepts, *Confraternity* ... You are loyal to the teaching that I passed on to you, *SEB* ... for maintaining the traditions I passed on, *Moffatt* ... in what I instructed you, you observe my instructions, *Fenton* ... you are always mindful of my teaching, *Conybeare* ... you the instructions, *Rotherham* ... you keepe my precepts, *Rheims* ... the suggestions I transmitted to you, *Berkeley.*

3. But I would have you know, that the head of every man is Christ; and the head of the woman [is] the man; and the head of Christ [is] God: ... and of a wife her husband is head, *Montgomery* ... the head of every woman is her husband, *Norlie* ... Christ is over every male, *SEB* ... God is the Head of Christ, *Williams.*

4. Every man praying or prophesying: ... when publicly praying or preaching, *TCNT.*

having [his] head covered: ... havynge eny thynge on his heed, *Tyndale.*

dishonoureth his head: ... disgraces his own head, *Fenton* ... shameth his head, *Geneva* ... puts to shame his head, *PNT.*

395

1 Corinthians 11:6

4195.14 verb nom sing fem part pres	2211.1 conj	4253.5 verb nom sing fem part pres act	175.1 adj dat sing fem
προσευχομένη	ἤ	προφητεύουσα	ἀκατακαλύπτῳ
proseuchomenē	ē	prophēteuousa	akatakaluptō
praying	or	prophesying	uncovered

3450.11 art dat sing fem	2747.3 noun dat sing fem	2587.1 verb 3sing indic pres act	3450.12 art acc sing fem	2747.4 noun acc sing fem
τῇ	κεφαλῇ,	καταισχύνει	τὴν	κεφαλὴν
tē	kephalē	kataischunei	tēn	kephalēn
with the	head,	puts to shame	the	head

5.a.Txt: 03B,06D-corr 018K,byz.Weis
Var: 01ℵ,02A,04C 06D-org,020L,025P Lach,Treg,Alf,Tisc We/Ho,Sod,UBS/✩

1431.9 prs-pron gen 3sing fem	840.10 prs-pron gen sing fem	1518.9 num card neu	1056.1 conj	1498.4 verb 3sing indic pres act	2504.1 conj
(ἑαυτῆς·	[ᵃ✩ αὐτῆς·]	ἓν	γὰρ	ἐστιν	καὶ
heautēs	autēs	hen	gar	estin	kai
herself;	[her;]	one	for	it is	and

3450.16 art sing neu	840.15 prs-pron sing neu	3450.11 art dat sing fem	3449.3 verb dat sing fem part perf pass	1479.1 conj	1056.1 conj
τὸ	αὐτὸ	τῇ	ἐξυρημένη.	6. εἰ	γὰρ
to	auto	tē	exurēmenē	ei	gar
the	same	with the	having been shaven.	If	for

3620.3 partic	2589.1 verb 3sing indic pres mid	1129.1 noun nom sing fem	2504.1 conj	2721.2 verb 3sing impr aor mid
οὐ	κατακαλύπτεται	γυνή,	καὶ	κειράσθω·
ou	katakaluptetai	gunē	kai	keirasthō
not	be covered	a woman,	also	let her be shorn.

1479.1 conj	1156.2 conj	149.1 adj nom sing neu	1129.3 noun dat sing fem	3450.16 art sing neu	2721.4 verb inf aor mid	2211.1 conj
εἰ	δὲ	αἰσχρὸν	γυναικὶ	τὸ	κείρασθαι	ἤ
ei	de	aischron	gunaiki	to	keirasthai	ē
If	but	shameful	to a woman	the	to be shorn	or

3449.1 verb inf	2589.2 verb 3sing impr pres mid	433.1 noun nom sing masc	3173.1 conj	1056.1 conj
ξυρᾶσθαι,	κατακαλυπτέσθω.	7. ἀνὴρ	μὲν	γὰρ
xurasthai	katakaluptesthō	anēr	men	gar
to be shaven,	let her be covered.	Man	indeed	for

3620.2 partic	3648.3 verb 3sing indic pres act	2589.3 verb inf pres mid	3450.12 art acc sing fem	2747.4 noun acc sing fem
οὐκ	ὀφείλει	κατακαλύπτεσθαι	τὴν	κεφαλήν,
ouk	opheilei	katakaluptesthai	tēn	kephalēn
not	ought	to have covered	the	head,

7.a.Var: 01ℵ-corr,02A 03B,06D-org,025P,Lach Treg,Alf,Word,Tisc We/Ho,Weis,Sod UBS/✩

1494.1 noun nom sing fem	2504.1 conj	1385.1 noun nom sing fem	2296.2 noun gen sing masc	5062.6 verb nom sing masc part pres act	3450.9 art nom sing fem
εἰκὼν	καὶ	δόξα	θεοῦ	ὑπάρχων·	[ᵃ✩+ ἡ]
eikōn	kai	doxa	theou	huparchōn	hē
image	and	glory	of God	being;	[the]

1129.1 noun nom sing fem	1156.2 conj	1385.1 noun nom sing fem	433.2 noun gen sing masc	1498.4 verb 3sing indic pres act	3620.3 partic
γυνὴ	δὲ	δόξα	ἀνδρός	ἐστιν·	8. οὐ
gunē	de	doxa	andros	estin	ou
woman	but	glory	of man	is.	Not

1056.1 conj	1498.4 verb 3sing indic pres act	433.1 noun nom sing masc	1523.2 prep gen	1129.2 noun gen sing fem	233.2 conj
γὰρ	ἐστιν	ἀνὴρ	ἐκ	γυναικός,	ἀλλὰ
gar	estin	anēr	ek	gunaikos	alla
for	is	man	of	woman,	but

11:5. The identical situation was repeated for the woman. It seems likely the reference ("prayeth or prophesieth") is to women who participated in public worship. It is important to recognize that verse 5 makes it quite apparent that women were in fact praying and prophesying in church. The problem Paul dealt with was not the fact of women praying and prophesying, but the way they did it. If Paul disapproved of women praying and prophesying in church, he could have explicitly said so. Instead Paul corrected the disorderly manner of their praying and prophesying by telling them that when they did pray and prophesy, they must do so with their heads covered. This is the background by which to better understand 14:33-36. It was necessary for the woman to have her head covered as a sign of submission to the man. If she did not do so she dishonored her "head." The dishonor done to the man fell on her and the shame came home to her. Again, it also reflected on Christ's lordship. For her to submit detracted nothing from her equality with man.

The head-cover, in verse 10 called "power," may seem to have a paradoxical meaning of standing under authority and being endowed with authority.

11:6. It was agreed that it was shameful for a woman to be shaved or shorn. According to Deuteronomy 21:12, for instance, women captured in war were to have their heads shaved as a sign of shame. It was unwomanly, rather manly. The woman who began to act like a man by unveiling should be consistent and be shorn also. But having the head shorn or shaved was a shame. Therefore, being unveiled was also a shame. Thus the veil was to be used.

11:7. Paul drew support for his position from the story of creation (Genesis 1:26,27). Man was made in the direct image of God. Woman appeared, in creation, as derived and auxiliary. It was as wrong for the man to cover his head as it was for the woman not to. For man to cover himself would be to hide the "image and glory of God." Man is the pinnacle of creation and should reveal God's glory. Therefore, there should be no outward sign of subordination when a man worships.

Woman, in her right, stands in a position, singular in nature, to the man and therefore is "the glory of the man." This affords her a high position and at the same time protects man's place. Faith, purity, and beauty show most excellently and proportionately in her. The man who degrades a woman degrades his manhood.

11:8,9. Two more "fors" are added to a chain beginning with verse 6. Paul was speaking of origin and purpose in creation (see Genesis 2:21-24). In origin woman came from Adam's rib, and in

5. But every woman that prayeth or prophesieth: . . . or speaks God's Word, *Beck.*

with [her] head uncovered dishonoureth her head: . . . bareheaded, *Williams* . . . without a veil, *Moffatt* . . . she brings shame upon her head, *Conybeare.*

for that is even all one as if she were shaven: . . . for she is like the abandoned shorn woman, *Fenton* . . . for she is on a level with her whose head is shaven, *Murdock* . . . for it is exactly the same as if she had her hair cut short, *Weymouth* . . . she is no better than a shaven woman, *Moffatt* . . . She might as well have her head shaven, *Norlie.*

6. For if the woman be not covered, let her also be shorn: . . . let her also cut off her hair, *Weymouth* . . . let her shave her head at once, *Conybeare* . . . she should cut off all her hair! *SEB* . . . let her hair be cut off too, *Adams.*

but if it be a shame for a woman to be shorn or shaven: . . . it is disgraceful, *Moffatt* . . . it be a foule thing for a vvoman to be polled or made balde, *Rheims.*

let her be covered: . . . let her wear a veil, *Weymouth.*

7. For a man indeed ought not to cover [his] head:

forasmuch as he is the image and glory of God: . . . since he exists in the image, *Adams* . . . for he represents the likeness and supremacy of God, *Moffatt* . . . being inherently the image, *Concordant* . . . and the manifestation of God's glory, *Conybeare* . . . and reflected glory, *Williams* . . . he is the image and representative of God, *Locke.*

but the woman is the glory of the man: . . . the female is the glory of the male, *SEB* . . . is man's honour, *Fenton.*

8. For the man is not of the woman; but the woman of the man: As a matter of fact, *Adams* . . . For it was not man who was taken from woman, *TCNT* . . . man did not originate from woman, *Williams* . . . does not take his origin from woman, *Weymouth* . . . woman was made from man, *Moffatt.*

| 1129.1 noun
nom sing fem
γυνὴ
gunē
woman | 1523.1
prep gen
ἐξ
ex
of | 433.2 noun
gen sing masc
ἀνδρός·
andros
man. | **9.** καὶ
2504.1
conj
kai
Also | 1056.1
conj
γὰρ
gar
for | 3620.2
partic
οὐκ
ouk
not | 2908.7 verb 3sing
indic aor pass
ἐκτίσθη
ektisthē
was created |

| 433.1 noun
nom sing masc
ἀνὴρ
anēr
man | 1217.2
prep
διὰ
dia
on account of | 3450.12 art
acc sing fem
τὴν
tēn
the | 1129.4 noun
acc sing fem
γυναῖκα,
gunaika
woman, | 233.2
conj
ἀλλὰ
alla
but | 1129.1 noun
nom sing fem
γυνὴ
gunē
woman |

| 1217.2
prep
διὰ
dia
on account of | 3450.6 art
acc sing masc
τὸν
ton
the | 433.4 noun
acc sing masc
ἄνδρα·
andra
man. | **10.** διὰ
1217.2
prep
dia
Because of | 3642.17 dem-
pron sing neu
τοῦτο
touto
this |

| 3648.3 verb 3sing
indic pres act
ὀφείλει
opheilei
ought | 3450.9 art
nom sing fem
ἡ
hē
the | 1129.1 noun
nom sing fem
γυνὴ
gunē
woman | 1833.4 noun
acc sing fem
ἐξουσίαν
exousian
authority | 2174.29 verb
inf pres act
ἔχειν
echein
to have | 1894.3
prep
ἐπὶ
epi
on |

| 3450.10 art
gen sing fem
τῆς
tēs
the | 2747.2 noun
gen sing fem
κεφαλῆς,
kephalēs
head, | 1217.2
prep
διὰ
dia
on account of | 3450.8 art
acc pl masc
τοὺς
tous
the | 32.8 noun
acc pl masc
ἀγγέλους.
angelous
angels. | **11.** πλὴν
3993.1
prep gen
plēn
However |

| 3641.1
conj
οὔτε
oute
neither | 433.1 noun
nom sing masc
ἀνὴρ
anēr
man | 5400.1
prep gen
χωρὶς
chōris
apart from | 1129.2 noun
gen sing fem
γυναικὸς
gunaikos
woman, | 3641.1
conj
οὔτε
oute
nor | 1129.1 noun
nom sing fem
γυνὴ
gunē
woman |

| 5400.1
prep gen
χωρὶς
chōris
apart from | 433.2 noun
gen sing masc
ἀνδρὸς,
andros
man, | 1129.1 noun
nom sing fem
[✶ γυνὴ
gunē
[woman | 5400.1
prep gen
χωρὶς
chōris
without | 433.2 noun
gen sing masc
ἀνδρὸς
andros
man | 3641.1
conj
οὔτε
oute
nor |

| 433.1 noun
nom sing masc
ἀνὴρ
anēr
man | 5400.1
prep gen
χωρὶς
chōris
without | 1129.2 noun
gen sing fem
γυναικὸς]
gunaikos
woman] | 1706.1
prep
ἐν
en
in | 2935.3 noun
dat sing masc
κυρίῳ·
kuriō
Lord. | **12.** ὥσπερ
5450.1
adv
hōsper
As |

| 1056.1
conj
γὰρ
gar
for | 3450.9 art
nom sing fem
ἡ
hē
the | 1129.1 noun
nom sing fem
γυνὴ
gunē
woman | 1523.2
prep gen
ἐκ
ek
of | 3450.2 art
gen sing
τοῦ
tou
the | 433.2 noun
gen sing masc
ἀνδρός,
andros
man, | 3643.1
adv
οὕτως
houtōs
so |

| 2504.1
conj
καὶ
kai
also | 3450.5 art
sing masc
ὁ
ho
the | 433.1 noun
nom sing masc
ἀνὴρ
anēr
man | 1217.2
prep
διὰ
dia
by | 3450.10 art
gen sing fem
τῆς
tēs
the | 1129.2 noun
gen sing fem
γυναικός,
gunaikos
woman; | 3450.17
art pl neu
τὰ
ta
the |

| 1156.2
conj
δὲ
de
but | 3820.1
adj
πάντα
panta
all things | 1523.2
prep gen
ἐκ
ek
of | 3450.2 art
gen sing
τοῦ
tou
the | 2296.2 noun
gen sing masc
θεοῦ.
theou
God. | **13.** ἐν
1706.1
prep
en
In | 5050.3 prs-
pron dat 2pl
ὑμῖν
humin
you |

purpose she was to be his helper and companion. Originally, in creation, man did not come from woman, nor was he created for her. To ignore or discredit this arrangement of God is to invite problems.

11:10. The phrases "power on her head" and "because of the angels" must be explained. An important factor is the context. Paul had been speaking of the principle of subordination, and particularly of the design and purpose of woman in creation. The first phrase would seem to refer to that to which she submits, the covering being its symbol. This might be said, for example, about the soldier who wears his ruler's colors, proudly identifying with him.

It is interesting, however, that the only time the word "power" ("authority," *exousian*) is used in this passage, it is something which belongs to women. Although the context speaks of subordination, it is the woman here who has the sign of authority. The New International Version tries to solve this problem by translating *exousian echein epi* in a passive sense (to "have authority *over*" [her head]); but if so, this is the only time out of 103 New Testament appearances that it is passive.

Others see "authority" in terms of the newfound liberty/authority that the women experienced in Christ, but this interpretation is not readily apparent in the context. Whatever "authority" means, it must be consistent with the following statement regarding "angels."

"Because of the angels" has been looked at in various ways, some of them impossible. Paul could not have meant evil angels subject to sensual temptation. Some have seen in these angels: pious men, prophets, church officers, and matchmakers.

But the better explanation seems to be as follows. In 4:9 Paul mentioned the angels as interested observers of Christian conduct. In 6:3 he spoke of the judgment of certain angels by the saints. Scripture is filled with the fact that angels are associated with God's earthly kingdom and the maintenance of creational laws and limits. It is consistent that angels are present at divine worship and are disturbed by irreverence at such worship. No unseemliness should come before them.

11:11. Paul, at the same time, wanted to insure the position of both man and woman, their need for each other, and their equality under God. There is a basic responsibility of both to each other and to God. The woman is subordinate but not inferior. In the higher things, "in the Lord" and in faith, man and woman exist in partnership and equality.

11:12. There is a balance between equality and subordination. Man is the initial cause; woman the instrumental cause. But the original Source and Ruler, to whom reverence is due, is God.

9. Neither was the man created for the woman: **but the woman for the man:** ... but the woman for the man's sake, *Murdock.*

10. For this cause ought the woman to have power on [her] head: Consequently, *Fenton* ... For this reason...to have on her head a sign of man's authority, *Norlie* ... to have permission upon, *Rotherham* ... a token of authority, *Berkeley* ... to have on her head a symbol of subjection, *Weymouth* ... a symbol of man's authority, *Williams* ... ought to show some sign on her head that she is respecting authority, *SEB* ... wear on her head a sign of man's authority, *TCNT* ... must wear a symbol of subjection on her head, *Moffatt.*
because of the angels: ... especially out of respect to the angels, *Williams* ... out of respect for the angels, *Beck* ... because of her [guardian] angels, *Montgomery.*

11. Nevertheless neither is the man without the woman: ... neither is man independent of woman, *Confraternity* ... and a man needs a woman, *Beck.*
neither the woman without the man, in the Lord: ... is not separate, *Fenton* ... she is not independent, *SEB* ... is not independent of man, *Weymouth, Williams.*

12. For as the woman [is] of the man: ... as woman originates from man, *Weymouth* ... as woman was made from man, *Conybeare.*
even so [is] the man also by the woman: ... so also is the man, *Montgomery* ... so a man is born of a woman, *Beck* ... man comes by means of the woman, *TCNT.*
but all things of God: ... but alle thingis ben of god, *Wyclif* ... but everything proceeds from God, *Fenton* ... and everything, including humankind, *Norlie* ... and they all have their origin from God, *Berkeley* ... Everything comes from God, *SEB* ... and all things spring from God, *Conybeare.*

1 Corinthians 11:14

840.2 prs-pron dat pl	2892.16 verb 2pl impr aor act	4100.2 verb nom sing neu part pres act	1498.4 verb 3sing indic pres act	1129.4 noun acc sing fem
αὐτοῖς	κρίνατε·	πρέπον	ἐστὶν	γυναῖκα
autois	*krinate*	*prepon*	*estin*	*gunaika*
selves	judge:	fitting	is it	for a woman

	175.2 adj acc sing fem	3450.3 art dat sing	2296.3 noun dat sing masc	4195.15 verb inf pres
	ἀκατακάλυπτον	τῷ	θεῷ	προσεύχεσθαι;
	akatakalupton	*tō*	*theō*	*proseuchesthai*
	uncovered		to God	to pray?

14.a.Txt: 06D-corr,018K 020L,byz.sa.
Var: 01א,02A,03B,04C 06D-org,015H,025P,33 bo.Lach,Treg,Alf,Word Tisc,We/Ho,Weis,Sod UBS/✱

	2211.1 conj	3624.1 adv	840.9 prs-pron nom sing fem	3450.9 art nom sing fem	5285.1 noun nom sing fem	3450.9 art nom sing fem
14.	⟨a ἢ⟩	οὐδὲ	⟨ αὐτὴ	ἡ	φύσις	[✱ ἡ
	ē	*oude*	*autē*	*hē*	*phusis*	*hē*
	Or	not even	itself	the	nature	[the

5285.1 noun nom sing fem	840.9 prs-pron nom sing fem	1315.3 verb 3sing indic pres act	5050.4 prs-pron acc 2pl	3617.1 conj	433.1 noun nom sing masc
φύσις	αὐτὴ]	διδάσκει	ὑμᾶς,	ὅτι	ἀνὴρ
phusis	*autē*	*didaskei*	*humas*	*hoti*	*anēr*
nature	itself]	does teach	you,	that	a man

3173.1 conj	1430.1 partic	2835.1 verb 3sing subj pres act	813.1 noun nom sing fem	840.4 prs-pron dat sing	1498.4 verb 3sing indic pres act
μὲν	ἐὰν	κομᾷ,	ἀτιμία	αὐτῷ	ἐστιν,
men	*ean*	*koma*	*atimia*	*autō*	*estin*
	if	have long hair	a dishonor	to him	it is?

1129.1 noun nom sing fem	1156.2 conj	1430.1 partic	2835.1 verb 3sing subj pres act	1385.1 noun nom sing fem	840.11 prs-pron dat sing fem
15. γυνὴ	δὲ	ἐὰν	κομᾷ,	δόξα	αὐτῇ
gunē	*de*	*ean*	*koma*	*doxa*	*autē*
A woman	but	if	have long hair,	glory	to her

1498.4 verb 3sing indic pres act	3617.1 conj	3450.9 art nom sing fem	2836.1 noun nom sing fem	470.2 prep gen	3881.1 noun gen sing neu
ἐστιν;	ὅτι	ἡ	κόμη	ἀντὶ	περιβολαίου
estin	*hoti*	*hē*	*komē*	*anti*	*peribolaiou*
it is;	for	the	long hair	instead	of a covering

15.a.Txt: 01א,02A,03B 33,We/Ho
Var: p46,04C,010F 012G,018K,020L,025P

1319.54 verb 3sing indic perf pass	840.11 prs-pron dat sing fem	1479.1 conj	1156.2 conj	4948.3 indef-pron nom sing	1374.5 verb 3sing indic pres act
δέδοται	⟨a αὐτῇ⟩	**16.** Εἰ	δέ	τις	δοκεῖ
dedotai	*autē*	*Ei*	*de*	*tis*	*dokei*
is given	to her.	If	but	anyone	thinks

5217.1 adj nom sing masc	1498.32 verb inf pres act	2231.1 prs-pron nom 1pl	4955.10 dem-pron acc sing fem	4764.2 noun acc sing fem
φιλόνεικος	εἶναι,	ἡμεῖς	τοιαύτην	συνήθειαν
philoneikos	*einai*	*hēmeis*	*toiautēn*	*sunētheian*
contentious	to be,	we	such	custom

3620.2 partic	2174.5 verb 1pl indic pres act	3624.1 adv	3450.13 art pl fem	1564.5 noun nom pl fem	3450.2 art gen sing
οὐκ	ἔχομεν,	οὐδὲ	αἱ	ἐκκλησίαι	τοῦ
ouk	*echomen*	*oude*	*hai*	*ekklēsiai*	*tou*
not	have,	nor	the	assemblies	

2296.2 noun gen sing masc	3642.17 dem-pron sing neu	1156.2 conj	3715.5 verb nom sing masc part pres act	3620.2 partic	1852.1 verb 1sing indic pres act
θεοῦ.	**17.** Τοῦτο	δὲ	παραγγέλλων	οὐκ	ἐπαινῶ,
theou	*Touto*	*de*	*parangellōn*	*ouk*	*epainō*
of God.	This	but	charging	not	I do praise,

11:13. Paul asked his readers to look at this carefully and judge; the inference was that they would come up with the same conclusion. "Yourselves" is emphatic. They could discover the truth for themselves. There is an appeal both to the fitness and suitability of things to nature or character and common sense.

The matter hinges on general propriety and the Christian influence involved with it, and Paul was sure when the Corinthians rightly considered this custom they would not find it improper.

11:14,15. Paul appealed to the instincts and teaching of nature to support a related item—that of a man's moral constitution. This reference to the moral nature of the world, is true of other times Paul used *phusis* ("nature") such as Romans 1:26 where Paul condemns homosexuality because it is against nature; i.e., against God's moral ordering of the world.

The preference for a man to wear short hair has prevailed in modern times as it did in ancient eras. It is true, there have been exceptions. Homer's warriors wore long hair and the fashion was retained at Sparta. But the Athenian cropped his head when 18 and, except for the aristocratic knights, it was a mark of effeminacy to let the hair grow long. The Nazarite of the Old Testament times was another exception.

On the other hand, a woman's long hair is her glory. It is the crown of her beauty. Her hair served as a natural covering, in addition to the physical covering to be worn in public meetings. Paul's reasoning was that it is necessary that there be a clear distinction of the sexes in appearance as well as every other natural and scriptural way. And there remains this principle of subordination: the man to Christ and the woman to the man.

11:16. Abruptly Paul cut off the discussion with his reference to custom (*sunētheian*) and contention (*philoneikos*). "Contentious" refers to a quarrelsome person, one who disputes for the sake of disputation. It seems this attitude among the Corinthians touched everything, a woman's veil or the position of an apostle.

Many arguments have come over Paul's use of the word "custom" here. Paul seems to be saying, "We have no such custom as women praying or prophesying with head uncovered." Paul appealed to universal custom and to the fact that this was the habit in the Christian churches. To adopt another view would suggest that Paul was doing away with what he had just spent 15 verses asserting.

Paul was not supporting a custom per se but a principle with which the custom was linked. There must be a clear distinction of the sexes, the clear recognition of roles, and the proper order of authority that God established.

11:17. The problem Paul now turned to was a glaring fault that had to be corrected. He did so with authority. The Corinthians

13. Judge in yourselves: Consider about these yourselves, *Fenton* . . . Judge of this matter by your own feeling, *Conybeare*.

is it comely that a woman pray unto God uncovered?: . . . is it proper, *Moffatt, Adams, PNT* . . . is it decent, *Campbell*.

14. Doth not even nature itself teach you, that, if a man have long hair, it is a shame unto him?: . . . if a man should have long tresses, *Fenton* . . . it is an ignominie for him, *Rheims* . . . while it is unmanly for a man to wear long hair, *Way* . . . is disgraceful, *Moffatt* . . . it is a dishonour to him, *Weymouth* . . . to wear his hair long is degrading, *Confraternity*.

15. But if a woman have long hair, it is a glory to her: . . . if her hair is abundant, *Murdock* . . . And a prayse to a woman, *Geneva* . . . but glorious for a woman? *Berkeley*.

for [her] hair is given her for a covering: Her hair is God's gift to her, a natural veil, *Way* . . . instead of a Veil, *Wilson*.

16. But if any man seem to be contentious: . . . assumes to be censorious, *Fenton* . . . is seyn to be ful of striif, *Wyclif* . . . If any man luste to stryue, *Cranmer* . . . presumes to raise objections on this point, *Moffatt* . . . is inclined to be disputatious regarding such a custom, *Montgomery* . . . seems to be quarrelsome, *Hanson* . . . thinks to be contentious in defence of such a custom, *Conybeare*.

we have no such custom: . . . we have no such usage, *Concordant*.

neither the churches of God:

17. Now in this that I declare [unto you] I praise [you] not: And this I commaund, *Rheims* . . . I must announce this, *Berkeley* . . . But while giving you these instructions, *Weymouth* . . . in giving these authoritative instructions, *Adams* . . . But in giving this charge, I do not commend you, *Confraternity* . . . I consider this not to be estimable, *Fenton* . . . I cannot commend you, *Moffatt*.

1 Corinthians 11:18

3617.1 conj	3620.2 partic	1519.1 prep	3450.16 art sing neu	2882.5 adj comp sing neu	2882.6 adj comp sing neu
ὅτι	οὐκ	εἰς	τὸ	ʿ κρεῖττον,	[✶ κρεῖσσον]
hoti	ouk	eis	to	kreitton	kreisson
that	not	for	the	better,	[idem]

233.1 conj	233.2 conj	1519.1 prep	3450.16 art sing neu	2254.1 adj comp	2247.1 adj comp acc sing neu
ʿ ἀλλ'	[✶ ἀλλὰ]	εἰς	τὸ	ʿ ἧττον	[✶ ἧσσον]
all'	alla	eis	to	hētton	hēsson
but	[idem]	for	the	worse	[idem]

4755.15 verb 2pl indic pres		4270.1 adv	3173.1 conj	1056.1 conj	4755.19 verb gen pl masc part pres
συνέρχεσθε.	**18.**	πρῶτον	μὲν	γὰρ	συνερχομένων
sunerchesthe		prōton	men	gar	sunerchomenōn
you come together.		First	indeed	for	coming together

18.a.Txt: byz.
Var: 01א,02A,03B,04C 06D,018K,020L,025P Gries,Lach,Treg,Alf Word,Tisc,We/Ho,Weis Sod,UBS/✶

5050.2 prs-pron gen 2pl	1706.1 prep	3450.11 art dat sing fem	1564.3 noun dat sing fem	189.1 verb 1sing pres act	4830.2 noun pl neu
ὑμῶν	ἐν	ʿa τῇ ʾ	ἐκκλησίᾳ,	ἀκούω	σχίσματα
humōn	en	tē	ekklēsia	akouō	schismata
you	in	the	assembly,	I hear	divisions

1706.1 prep	5050.3 prs-pron dat 2pl	5062.11 verb inf pres act	2504.1 conj	3183.1 noun sing neu	4948.10 indef-pron sing neu
ἐν	ὑμῖν	ὑπάρχειν,	καὶ	μέρος	τι
en	humin	huparchein	kai	meros	ti
among	you	to be,	and	partly	some

3961.4 verb 1sing indic pres act		1158.1 verb 3sing indic pres act	1056.1 conj	2504.1 conj	138.4 noun pl fem	1706.1 prep
πιστεύω·	**19.**	δεῖ	γὰρ	καὶ	αἱρέσεις	ἐν
pisteuō		dei	gar	kai	haireseis	en
I believe.		There must	for	also	sects	among

19.a.Var: 03B,06D-org Lach,Treg,Alf,We/Ho Weis,UBS/✶

5050.3 prs-pron dat 2pl	1498.32 verb inf pres act	2419.1 conj	2504.1 conj	3450.7 art pl masc	1378.3 adj nom pl masc
ὑμῖν	εἶναι,	ἵνα	[a✶+ καὶ]	οἱ	δόκιμοι
humin	einai	hina	kai	hoi	dokimoi
you	to be,	that	[also]	the	approved

5156.2 adj nom pl masc	1090.43 verb 3pl subj aor mid	1706.1 prep	5050.3 prs-pron dat 2pl		4755.19 verb gen pl masc part pres
φανεροὶ	γένωνται	ἐν	ὑμῖν.	**20.**	Συνερχομένων
phaneroi	genōntai	en	humin		Sunerchomenōn
manifest	may become	among	you.		Coming together

3631.1 conj	5050.2 prs-pron gen 2pl	1894.3 prep	3450.16 art sing neu	840.15 prs-pron sing neu	3620.2 partic	1498.4 verb 3sing indic pres act
οὖν	ὑμῶν	ἐπὶ	τὸ	αὐτὸ,	οὐκ	ἔστιν
oun	humōn	epi	to	auto	ouk	estin
therefore	you	into	the	same,	not	it is

2933.2 adj acc sing neu	1168.1 noun sing neu	2052.25 verb inf aor act		1524.3 adj nom sing masc	1056.1 conj	3450.16 art sing neu
κυριακὸν	δεῖπνον	φαγεῖν·	**21.**	ἕκαστος	γὰρ	τὸ
kuriakon	deipnon	phagein		hekastos	gar	to
Lord's	supper	to eat.		Each one	for	the

2375.4 adj acc sing	1168.1 noun sing neu	4160.1 verb 3sing indic pres act	1706.1 prep	3450.3 art dat sing	2052.25 verb inf aor act
ἴδιον	δεῖπνον	προλαμβάνει	ἐν	τῷ	φαγεῖν,
idion	deipnon	prolambanei	en	tō	phagein
his own	supper	takes first	in	the	to eat,

came together "for the worse" instead of the better. Their meetings and the Lord's Supper were a desecration.

11:18. Paul specified the causes of this disgraceful gathering. "When ye come together" indicated repeated occurrence. The trouble was chronic. A contentious spirit was consistently present.

Paul had heard various reports on the Corinthians' actions. He did not believe everything he heard, but he did accept as truth what he listed here. The proper Christian attitude is to believe and hope for the best possible (13:7).

11:19. There were factions in the Corinthian church. Paul was not advocating factions, but in this sinful world they do happen. Men get things out of balance sometimes. Such factions do serve the purpose of sifting the loyal from the disloyal, the good from the bad. The factions leave the genuine believers standing out ("approved") by their loyalty, strength, and constancy. Those approved by God become manifest to other men.

11:20. The "therefore" in this verse anticipates a conclusion on what has already been said and, at the same time, lays a foundation for further remarks.

These divisions had produced a visible rift at this common meal, detracting from the real meaning of the Lord's Supper. It is impossible to relate what was done among the Corinthians with the true sacrament of the Lord's Supper.

11:21. Paul's description reveals scandalous behavior. The problem was one of gluttonous, self-centered disregard for anyone else. The "Lord's supper" here noted was a united supper with which the meeting of the church commenced, apparently taking place as often as once a week. This church supper, later called the Agape (Love Feast) was akin to the dinners held by the guilds. It began as a kind of enlarged family meal. It accorded so well with the social custom that it was a universal Christian custom in the First Century. Later the Communion was separated from the meal for greater decorum, and the Agape faded into extinction.

Each guest brought contributions to supply the table; the poor brought whatever meager amount they had, the rich brought out of their abundance. Greedily, the Corinthians consumed their own supply as soon as they arrived. The poor man with insufficient supply might arrive late, because his time was not his own, and find the table empty, the fellowship gone, and he remained hungry.

that ye come together not for the better, but for the worse: . . . your solemn assemblies do more harm than good, *Montgomery* . . . not with proffit, but with hurt, *Geneva* . . . with bad rather than good results, *Weymouth* . . . are for evil rather than for good, *Conybeare* . . . not to your improvement, but to your deterioration, *Way* . . . but for discomfiture, *Concordant* . . . ye have not made progress, but have deteriorated, *Murdock*.

18. For first of all, when ye come together in the church: . . . in the first place, *PNT* . . . when you meet as a church, *Adams* . . . as you meet in church session, *Berkeley*.

I hear that there be divisions among you: I hear there are differences, *Fenton* . . . there are schismes among you, *Rheims* . . . ther is dissencion amonge you, *Tyndale* . . . that cliques prevail, *Moffatt*.

and I partly believe it:

19. For there must be also heresies among you: . . . you should have parties, *Fenton* . . . be differences of opinion among you, *Weymouth* . . . but also adverse sects, *Conybeare*.

that they which are approved may be made manifest among you: . . . who are the men of sterling worth, *Weymouth* . . . the tried and true may be recognized among you, *Berkeley* . . . who are qualified, *Concordant*.

20. When ye come together therefore into one place: . . . you hold your gatherings, *Moffatt*.

[this] is not to eat the Lord's supper: . . . there is no true eating of the Lord's Supper, *Montgomery* . . . there is no eating of the Lord's Supper, *Alford*.

21. For in eating every one taketh before [other] his own supper: . . . prepares his own individual meal to eat alone, *Fenton* . . . is getting his own dinner, *Concordant* . . . personally to eat it, *Berkeley* . . . Each one hastens to eat the supper that he has prepared for himself, *Norlie*.

2504.1 conj	3614.5 rel-pron nom sing masc	3173.1 conj	3845.1 verb 3sing pres act	3614.5 rel-pron nom sing masc	1156.2 conj	3155.1 verb 3sing indic pres act
καὶ	ὃς	μὲν	πεινᾷ	ὃς	δὲ	μεθύει.
kai	hos	men	peina	hos	de	methuei
and	who	men	hungers	who	and	is drunken.

3231.1 partic	1056.1 conj	3477.1 noun fem	3620.2 partic	2174.2 verb 2pl pres act	1519.1 prep	3450.16 art sing neu
22. μὴ	γὰρ	οἰκίας	οὐκ	ἔχετε	εἰς	τὸ
mē	gar	oikias	ouk	echete	eis	to
Not	for	houses	not	have you	for	the

2052.14 verb inf pres act	2504.1 conj	3956.10 verb inf pres act	2211.1 conj	3450.10 art gen sing fem	1564.1 noun fem	3450.2 art gen sing
ἐσθίειν	καὶ	πίνειν;	ἢ	τῆς	ἐκκλησίας	τοῦ
esthiein	kai	pinein	ē	tēs	ekklēsias	tou
to eat	and	to drink?	or	the	assembly	

2296.2 noun gen sing masc	2675.2 verb 2pl indic pres act	2504.1 conj	2587.2 verb 2pl indic pres act	3450.8 art acc pl masc	3231.1 partic
θεοῦ	καταφρονεῖτε,	καὶ	καταισχύνετε	τοὺς	μὴ
theou	kataphroneite	kai	kataischunete	tous	mē
of God	do you despise,	and	put to shame	the	not

2174.21 verb acc pl masc part pres act	4949.9 intr-pron sing neu	5050.3 prs-pron dat 2pl	1500.6 verb 1sing subj aor act	1500.6 verb 1sing subj aor act
ἔχοντας;	τί	ὑμῖν	εἴπω;	[☆ εἴπω
echontas	ti	humin	eipō	eipō
having?	What	to you	should I say?	[should I say

5050.3 prs-pron dat 2pl	1852.3 verb 1sing subj aor act	5050.4 prs-pron acc 2pl	1706.1 prep	3642.5 dem-pron dat sing masc	3620.2 partic
ὑμῖν;]	ἐπαινέσω	ὑμᾶς	ἐν	τούτῳ;	οὐκ
humin	epainesō	humas	en	toutō	ouk
to you?]	shall I praise	you	in	this?	Not

5050.4 prs-pron acc 2pl	1706.1 prep	3642.5 dem-pron dat sing masc	3620.2 partic	1852.1 verb 1sing indic pres act	1466.1 prs-pron nom 1sing
[☆ ὑμᾶς;	ἐν	τούτῳ	οὐκ]	ἐπαινῶ.	23. Ἐγὼ
humas	en	toutō	ouk	epainō	Egō
[you?	In	this	not]	I do praise.	I

1056.1 conj	3741.4 verb indic aor act	570.3 prep gen	3450.2 art gen sing	2935.2 noun gen sing masc	3614.16 rel-pron sing neu	2504.1 conj
γὰρ	παρέλαβον	ἀπὸ	τοῦ	κυρίου,	ὃ	καὶ
gar	parelabon	apo	tou	kuriou	ho	kai
for	received	from	the	Lord	which	also

3722.8 verb 1sing indic aor act	5050.3 prs-pron dat 2pl	3617.1 conj	3450.5 art sing masc	2935.1 noun nom sing masc	2400.1 name nom masc	1706.1 prep
παρέδωκα	ὑμῖν,	ὅτι	ὁ	κύριος	Ἰησοῦς	ἐν
paredōka	humin	hoti	ho	kurios	Iēsous	en
I delivered	to you,	that	the	Lord	Jesus	in

3450.11 art dat sing fem	3433.3 noun dat sing fem	3614.11 rel-pron dat sing fem	3722.43 verb 3sing indic imperf pass	2956.14 verb 3sing indic aor act
τῇ	νυκτὶ	ᾗ	παρεδίδοτο,	ἔλαβεν
tē	nukti	hē	paredidoto	elaben
the	night	in which	he was delivered up	took

735.4 noun acc sing masc	2504.1 conj	2149.11 verb nom sing masc part aor act	2779.4 verb 3sing indic aor act	2504.1 conj
ἄρτον,	24. καὶ	εὐχαριστήσας	ἔκλασεν,	καὶ
arton	kai	eucharistēsas	eklasen	kai
bread,	and	having given thanks	he broke,	and

Further, hunger and drunkenness sat together. To call such the Lord's Supper would have been a travesty.

11:22. Paul spoke pointedly. His first question proved that home is the place to satisfy such hunger and thirst. His irony attacked their greed and pride. Paul here condemned the rich for their attitude toward the poor ("them that have not"). If those who had plenty of food wished to indulge themselves, then according to Paul they should at least have the consideration to do so at home and not shame those less fortunate.

Apparently this arrogant attitude of rich believers toward the poor was not limited to Corinth. The apostle James had to reprimand the church to which he wrote for showing partiality toward the rich and ignoring the poor (James 2:1-7).

Such inhospitality toward the poor was not only wrong in general, but it was especially shocking since this activity was taking place at a meal honoring the death of Christ. In Paul's second letter to the Corinthians he told them that the significance of the death of Christ is that it made reconciliation between God and man, and between man and man. The Corinthians obviously needed to be told about reconciliation, since their own actions fell deplorably below the expectations of a believer who claimed to partake of the new nature of Christ (cf. 2 Corinthians 5:17-19). The whole letter of First Corinthians, in fact, reveals that every facet of the Corinthians' lives exhibited a lack of reconciliation with other believers.

His second question exposed the fact that if this action was deliberate, then they were scorning and despising "the church of God" and they were shaming and insulting the poorer brethren.

The last two questions and the declaration showed remarkable restraint. Clearly, their actions needed reprimand, not praise.

11:23. Because Paul wished to correct such behavior, he held up before them, as a mirror, the institution, design, and meaning of the Supper as begun by the Lord himself.

What Paul passed on came "of the Lord." What Paul received he gave out. He delivered truth correctly, openly, and positively and fulfilled his trust.

The phrase "same night . . . betrayed . . ." displays more than a necessary time element in a historical sense. It speaks of the character of Jesus who determined to make this new covenant with His people and fulfill the entire will of God even in the dark shadow of betrayal and death.

Note the detail in Paul's teaching. Jesus "took bread," the unleavened cakes of Passover. But the Corinthians were not following Christ's example and Paul's teaching.

11:24. The words "this is my body" have initiated a long dispute between those who favor the idea of a "real" or literal body, those

and one is hungry, and another is drunken: . . . so that one man goes away hungry, *Norlie* . . . and one eats like a hungry man, *Weymouth* . . . one has too little to eat, and another has too much to drink! *TCNT* . . . and another is satisfied, *Wilson* . . . and another drinks overmuch, *Confraternity* . . . and that one imbibes too freely, *Berkeley* . . . again, gorged, *Fenton.*

22. What? have ye not houses to eat and to drink in?:

or despise ye the church of God, and shame them that have not?: Or have ye a contempt for the church, *Locke* . . . or do ye think amiss of the church, *Macknight* . . . show disrespect to, *Moffatt* . . . or do you look with contempt upon, *Fenton* . . . and to shame the poor? *Conybeare* . . . and to humiliate the poor? *TCNT* . . . do you wish to show your contempt...and make those who have no homes feel ashamed? *Weymouth* . . . mortifying those, *Concordant* . . . and put to shame the needy? *Confraternity* . . . Do you want to make poor people ashamed? *SEB* . . . and wish to humiliate those who have nothing? *Adams* . . . those who don't have anything? *Beck.*

What shall I say to you? shall I praise you in this? I praise [you] not: Shall I approve of you? *Fenton* . . . Commend you? *Moffatt* . . . In this I certainly do not praise you, *Montgomery* . . . No, I cannot approve, *Norlie.*

23. For I have received of the Lord that which also I delivered unto you: I accepted from, *Concordant* . . . I received this account from the Lord, *Norlie* . . . what I taught you, *Beck* . . . what I passed on to you, *SEB* . . . that which I imparted to you, *Murdock.*

That the Lord Jesus the [same] night in which he was betrayed took bread: . . . took a loaf, *Moffatt, Campbell.*

24. And when he had given thanks, he brake [it], and said: . . . and broke off some of it, *SEB* . . . broke it in pieces, saying, as he did so, *TCNT.*

1 Corinthians 11:25

1500.5 verb 3sing indic aor act	2956.24 verb 2pl impr aor act	2052.23 verb 2pl impr aor act	3642.17 dem-pron sing neu	1466.2 prs-pron gen 1sing
εἶπεν,	⌐a Λάβετε,	Φάγετε⌐	Τοῦτό	μού
eipen	Labete	Phagete	Touto	mou
said,	Take,	eat,	this	my

1498.4 verb 3sing indic pres act	3450.16 art sing neu	4835.1 noun sing neu	3450.16 art sing neu	5065.1 prep	5050.2 prs-pron gen 2pl
ἐστιν	τὸ	σῶμα	τὸ	ὑπὲρ	ὑμῶν
estin	to	sōma	to	huper	humōn
is	the	body	the	for	you

2779.7 verb nom sing neu part pres pass	3642.17 dem-pron sing neu	4020.2 verb 2pl pres act	1519.1 prep	3450.12 art acc sing fem	1684.9 adj acc 1sing fem
⌐b κλώμενον·⌐	τοῦτο	ποιεῖτε	εἰς	τὴν	ἐμὴν
klōmenon	touto	poieite	eis	tēn	emēn
being broken:	this	do	in	the	of me

363.2 noun acc sing fem	5447.1 adv	2504.1 conj	3450.16 art sing neu	4080.1 noun sing neu
ἀνάμνησιν.	**25.** Ὡσαύτως	καὶ	τὸ	ποτήριον,
anamnēsin	Hōsautōs	kai	to	potērion
remembrance.	In like manner	also	the	cup,

3196.3 prep	3450.16 art sing neu	1167.2 verb inf aor act	2978.15 verb sing masc part pres act	3642.17 dem-pron sing neu	3450.16 art sing neu
μετὰ	τὸ	δειπνῆσαι,	λέγων,	Τοῦτο	τὸ
meta	to	deipnēsai	legōn	Touto	to
after	the	to dine,	saying,	This	the

4080.1 noun sing neu	3450.9 art nom sing fem	2508.3 adj nom sing fem	1236.1 noun nom sing fem	1498.4 verb 3sing indic pres act	1706.1 prep
ποτήριον	ἡ	καινὴ	διαθήκη	ἐστιν	ἐν
potērion	hē	kainē	diathēkē	estin	en
cup	the	new	covenant	is	in

3450.3 art dat sing	1684.2 adj dat 1sing	129.3 noun dat sing neu	3642.17 dem-pron sing neu	4020.2 verb 2pl pres act	3602.1 conj
τῷ	ἐμῷ	αἵματι·	τοῦτο	ποιεῖτε,	ὁσάκις
tō	emō	haimati	touto	poieite	hosakis
the	my	blood:	this	do,	as often as

300.1 partic	1430.1 partic	3956.6 verb 2pl subj pres act	1519.1 prep	3450.12 art acc sing fem	1684.9 adj acc 1sing fem
⌐ ἂν	[a✩ ἐὰν]	πίνητε,	εἰς	τὴν	ἐμὴν
an	ean	pinēte	eis	tēn	emēn
		you may drink,	in	the	of me

363.2 noun acc sing fem	3602.1 conj	1056.1 conj	300.1 partic	1430.1 partic
ἀνάμνησιν.	**26.** Ὁσάκις	γὰρ	⌐ ἂν	[a✩ ἐὰν]
anamnēsin	Hosakis	gar	an	ean
remembrance.	As often as	for		

2052.5 verb 2pl subj pres act	3450.6 art acc sing masc	735.4 noun acc sing masc	3642.6 dem-pron acc sing masc	2504.1 conj	3450.16 art sing neu
ἐσθίητε	τὸν	ἄρτον	τοῦτον,	καὶ	τὸ
esthiēte	ton	arton	touton	kai	to
you should eat	the	bread	this,	and	the

4080.1 noun sing neu	3642.17 dem-pron sing neu	3956.6 verb 2pl subj pres act	3450.6 art acc sing masc	2265.4 noun acc sing masc
ποτήριον	⌐b τοῦτο⌐	πίνητε,	τὸν	θάνατον
potērion	touto	pinēte	ton	thanaton
cup	this	should drink,	the	death

who favor a "representative" presence of the Lord, and those who regard the ordinance primarily as a memorial service.

Those who favor the real presence of Christ argue that the word "this" (neuter pronoun), a reference to the bread, equals "body" (neuter noun). Furthermore, *is* means "is the same thing as" and not "symbolizes or represents." Christ is actually present in the bread; the bread literally is His body. Therefore, eating the bread "unworthily" (verse 29) brings guilt and damnation.

Those who support a view of "representative" or symbolic Communion explain the wording differently. They also maintain that "this" refers to the bread. However, they link the phrase "given for you" to "body"; that is, Christ said He was giving His own body in their behalf. Therefore, the word "is" does not imply a complete identity of bread and body, but rather a close connection. Nevertheless, Christ is present in some mystical or mysterious way.

A third group views the Lord's Supper primarily as a rite of worship instituted by Christ. It serves to commemorate His death, to provide ongoing instruction (as an object lesson) and exhortation, and to function as a source of inspiration. The elements are a means of grace by which believers are inspired to grow in their faith and faithfulness to the Lord.

11:25. Paul referred next to the place and purpose of "the cup." "When he had supped" emphasizes the distinction and special importance of the meal. The impression is that the bread was partaken of during the meal and the cup at the end, although both were necessary to the Communion. This forged a new "testament" or covenant, initiated by God (Jeremiah 31:31-34). The shedding of Christ's blood established the new covenant and all it guarantees. The Communion celebration should be often and reverently observed.

11:26. Christ commanded His disciples to perpetually commemorate Him by Communion. But in the Corinthian church familiarity had made the service seem common. Paul reminded the Corinthians that they showed forth the Lord's death and all it means every time they partook of the sacrament.

The celebration of Communion is to show "the Lord's death till he come." It looks not only back to Calvary, but also ahead to Christ's return and the Marriage Supper of the Lamb. We know not the time nor the date of Christ's return, but we may be assured of its factual nature and certainty.

Each time we participate in the Lord's Supper we are reminded that all the activities and ordinances in the Church are to center around the person of Jesus Christ. The ordinances of water baptism

Take, eat: this is my body, which is broken for you: . . . which shall be delivered for you, *Douay* . . . which is about to be broken, *Weymouth* . . . broken for your sakes, *Concordant, Murdock* . . . which is for you, *Sawyer* . . . which is given for you, *Williams* . . . my body given on your behalf, *TCNT* . . . broken on your behalf, *Berkeley*.

this do in remembrance of me: . . . thus do ye, *Murdock* . . . do for a recollection of Me, *Concordant* . . . for the commemoration of me, *Rheims, Douay* . . . in memory, *Moffatt* . . . in memory of me, *Williams*.

25. After the same manner also [he took] the cup, when he had supped, saying: Similarly, *Concordant, Berkeley* . . . In the same way, *Moffatt* . . . In like manner also the cup, *Sawyer* . . . the same way also the cup, *RSV* . . . the chalice, *Rheims* . . . the chalice, after he had supped, *Douay* . . . after the supper, *Hanson*.

This cup is the new testament in my blood: . . . the new agreement with God, *SEB* . . . the new covenant ratified by my blood, *Moffatt* . . . is the new institution, *Campbell* . . . of which my blood is the pledge, *Weymouth* . . . is the New Settlement, *Fenton* . . . is the new Agreement, *Klingensmith* . . . ratified by my blood, *Williams* . . . [sealed] with my blood, *Sawyer* . . . for the remission of sins, *Norlie*.

this do ye, as oft as ye drink [it], in remembrance of me: . . . do this, whenever you drink it, *Montgomery* . . . as often as ye do it, *Locke* . . . for my Remembrance, *Wilson*.

26. For as often as ye eat this bread, and drink this cup: Every time you eat, *SEB* . . . For every time, *Williams* . . . So that the eating of this bread, and the drinking of this cup of the Lord's supper, *Locke*.

1 Corinthians 11:27

| 3450.2 art
gen sing
τοῦ
tou
of the | 2935.2 noun
gen sing masc
κυρίου
kuriou
Lord | 2576.4 verb 2pl
indic pres act
καταγγέλλετε,
katangellete
you announce, | 884.1
conj
῾ ἄχρις
achris
until | 884.2
conj
[ἄχρι]
achri
[idem] |

26.c.Txt: 01א-corr
06D-corr,018K,020L
025P,byz.
Var: 01א-org,02A,03B
04C,06D-org,33,Gries
Lach,Treg,Alf,Tisc
We/Ho,Weis,Sod
UBS/✱

| 3614.2 rel-
pron gen sing
οὗ
hou
which | 300.1
partic
῾c ἄν ῾
an
an | 2048.8 verb 3sing
subj aor act
ἔλθῃ.
elthē
he should come. | **27.** ῞Ωστε
Hōste
So that | 3614.5 rel-pron
nom sing masc
ὃς
hos
whoever |

27.a.Txt: 018K,020L
025P,byz.bo.
Var: 01א,02A,03B,04C
06D,33,sa.Gries,Lach
Treg,Alf,Word,Tisc
We/Ho,Weis,Sod
UBS/✱

| 300.1
partic
ἄν
an
an | 2052.4 verb 3sing
subj pres act
ἐσθίῃ
esthiē
should eat | 3450.6 art
acc sing masc
τὸν
ton
the | 735.4 noun
acc sing masc
ἄρτον
arton
bread | 3642.6 dem-pron
acc sing masc
῾a τοῦτον ῾
touton
this | 2211.1
conj
ἢ
ē
or |

| 3956.5 verb 3sing
subj pres act
πίνῃ
pinē
should drink | 3450.16 art
sing neu
τὸ
to
the | 4080.1 noun
sing neu
ποτήριον
potērion
cup | 3450.2 art
gen sing
τοῦ
tou
of the | 2935.2 noun
gen sing masc
κυρίου
kuriou
Lord |

| 370.1
adv
ἀναξίως,
anaxiōs
unworthily, | 1761.1 adj
nom sing masc
ἔνοχος
enochos
guilty | 1498.40 verb 3sing
indic fut mid
ἔσται
estai
shall be | 3450.2 art
gen sing
τοῦ
tou
of the | 4835.2 noun
gen sing neu
σώματος
sōmatos
body | 2504.1
conj
καὶ
kai
and |

27.b.Var: 01א,02A,03B
04C,06D,018K,020L
025P,Gries,Lach,Treg
Alf,Word,Tisc,We/Ho
Weis,Sod,UBS/✱

| 3450.2 art
gen sing neu
[b✱+ τοῦ]
tou
[of the] | 129.2 noun
gen sing neu
αἵματος
haimatos
blood | 3450.2 art
gen sing
τοῦ
tou
of the | 2935.2 noun
gen sing masc
κυρίου.
kuriou
Lord. | **28.** δοκιμαζέτω
dokimazetō
Let test |

| 1156.2
conj
δὲ
de
but | 442.1 noun
nom sing masc
ἄνθρωπος
anthrōpos
a man | 1431.6 prs-pron
acc 3sing masc
ἑαυτόν,
heauton
himself, | 2504.1
conj
καὶ
kai
and | 3643.1
adv
οὕτως
houtōs
thus | 1523.2
prep gen
ἐκ
ek
of | 3450.2 art
gen sing
τοῦ
tou
the |

| 735.2 noun
gen sing masc
ἄρτου
artou
bread | 2052.7 verb 3sing
impr pres act
ἐσθιέτω,
esthietō
let him eat, | 2504.1
conj
καὶ
kai
and | 1523.2
prep gen
ἐκ
ek
of | 3450.2 art
gen sing
τοῦ
tou
the | 4080.2 noun
gen sing neu
ποτηρίου
potēriou
cup |

29.a.Txt: 01א-corr
04C-corr,06D,018K
020L,025P,044,etc.byz.
it.
Var: p46,01א-org,02A
03B,04C-org,33,sa.bo.
Lach,Treg,Alf,Tisc
We/Ho,Weis,Sod
UBS/✱

| 3956.7 verb 3sing
impr pres act
πινέτω·
pinetō
let him drink. | **29.** ὁ
ho
The | 1056.1
conj
γὰρ
gar
for | 2052.8 verb nom sing
masc part pres act
ἐσθίων
esthiōn
eating | 2504.1
conj
καὶ
kai
and | 3956.8 verb nom sing
masc part pres act
πίνων
pinōn
drinking |

29.b.Txt: 01א-corr
04C-corr,06D,018K
020L,025P,byz.it.
Var: p46,01א-org,02A
03B,04C-org,33,sa.bo.
Lach,Treg,Alf,Tisc
We/Ho,Weis,Sod
UBS/✱

| 370.1
adv
῾a ἀναξίως, ῾
anaxiōs
in an unworthy manner, | 2890.1 noun
sing neu
κρίμα
krima
judgment | 1431.5 prs-pron
dat 3sing masc
ἑαυτῷ
heautō
to himself | 2052.2 verb 3sing
indic pres act
ἐσθίει
esthiei
eats | 2504.1
conj
καὶ
kai
and |

| 3956.2 verb 3sing
indic pres act
πίνει,
pinei
drinks, | 3231.1
partic
μὴ
mē
not | 1246.3 verb nom sing
masc part pres act
διακρίνων
diakrinōn
discerning | 3450.16 art
sing neu
τὸ
to
the | 4835.1 noun
sing neu
σῶμα
sōma
body | 3450.2 art
gen sing
῾b τοῦ
tou
of the |

and Communion point us consistently to either the finished work of Christ on the cross or the anticipated work in which "all things" shall be summed up in Christ. In trouble, debate, or doctrine, all is to point directly to Christ, and all our actions are to be consistent with the fact that He is our Lord.

11:27. "Wherefore" leads to certain conclusions. A judgment of sorts was necessary on those who were violating the table of the Lord. Throughout this passage the verbs speak of continued practice and habit. "Whosoever" excludes no one. Everyone, rich or poor, high or low, must approach Communion in a reverent, humble manner. By doing violence to the sacraments, the Corinthians were actually desecrating the sacrifice and person of the Lord himself. The magnitude of such a sin is measured by the magnitude of the gift. The penalty is decided by the same measure.

11:28. Great care in behavior should be taken toward the Communion. It was important that the Corinthian Christians honestly and carefully examine themselves before they partook of the elements of the Lord's Supper.

Any truly honest and serious attempt at self-probing would make the scene of verses 20-22 impossible. Such greed and selfishness could not hide under the self-examination that allowed the Holy Spirit to do the probing. Examination would properly involve confession, repentance over anything that weakened the importance of the Lord's Supper and its full significance, and an analysis of one's true faith in Christ.

This is something that must be done regularly by all believers. The implication is that such examination will prove fruitful and favorable. Paul reminds us yet again of the importance of this ordinance invoked by the Lord, of the tremendous reverence that must accompany our approach to His table, and of how terrible is unworthy participation.

11:29. Paul emphasized the need of worthy conduct at the Lord's Supper by stressing the judgment that rested on those who had not properly discerned the "Lord's body." "Discerning" (*diakrinōn*) involves the idea of judging clearly and rightly. In this case it refers to the Lord's Supper, rather than any other eating and drinking.

Because the Corinthians did not judge or act rightly regarding the ordinance, a sentence of judgment rested on them. "Damnation" (*krima*) does not refer to the final judgment, but to a judicial sentence of any kind.

ye do show the Lord's death till he come: . . . you are announcing, *Concordant* . . . you proclaim, *Moffatt, Adams* . . . you openly publish, *Campbell, Macknight* . . . you openly show forth, *Conybeare* . . . you declare the death, *Wilson* . . . until He returns, *Fenton.*

27. Wherefore whosoever shall eat this bread:
and drink [this] cup of the Lord, unworthily: . . . in an unworthy manner, *Weymouth* . . . carelessly, *Moffatt.*
shall be guilty of the body and blood of the Lord: . . . will be liable, *Concordant* . . . shall be responsible for, *Rotherham* . . . will be responsible for, *Fenton* . . . will be held guilty of an offense against the body, *Adams* . . . will be an offender against, *Wilson* . . . must answer for, *Montgomery* . . . shall be guilty of profaning the body, *Conybeare* . . . will have to answer for a sin against the body and the blood of the Lord, *Moffatt.*

28. But let a man examine himself: Let each man scrutinize himself, *Montgomery* . . . proue him self, *Rheims* . . . let a man prove himself, *Sawyer, Douay, Confraternity* . . . let a man test himself, *Fenton, Moffatt* . . . be putting himself to-the-test, *Rotherham.*
and so let him eat of [that] bread, and drink of [that] cup:

29. For he that eateth and drinketh unworthily: . . . without a proper sense of the Body, *Moffatt* . . . not discriminating the body, *Hanson.*
eateth and drinketh damnation to himself: . . . eateth and drinketh iudgement to him self, *Rheims* . . . and drinks judgement, *Weymouth* . . . drinks to his own judgment, *Adams.*
not discerning the Lord's body: . . . not distinguishing the body, *Campbell* . . . without distinguishing the body, *Confraternity* . . . setting apart the body, *Rotherham* . . . not discriminating the body, *Wilson* . . . when not distinguishing the body, *Fenton* . . . if he fails to estimate the body aright, *Weymouth.*

2935.2 noun gen sing masc
κυρίου. \
kuriou
Lord.

30.

1217.2 prep
διὰ
dia
Because of

3642.17 dem-pron sing neu
τοῦτο
touto
this

1706.1 prep
ἐν
en
among

5050.3 prs-pron dat 2pl
ὑμῖν
humin
you

4044.7 adj nom pl masc
πολλοὶ
polloi
many

766.4 adj pl masc
ἀσθενεῖς
astheneis
weak

2504.1 conj
καὶ
kai
and

726.1 adj nom pl masc
ἄρρωστοι,
arrhōstoi
sick,

2504.1 conj
καὶ
kai
and

2810.1 verb 3pl indic pres
κοιμῶνται
koimōntai
are fallen asleep

2401.6 adj nom pl masc
ἱκανοί.
hikanoi
many.

31.a.**Txt:** 01ℵ-corr,04C 018K,020L,025P,byz.sa. bo.
Var: 01ℵ-org,02A,03B 06D,33,Lach,Treg,Alf Word,Tisc,We/Ho,Weis Sod,UBS/☆

31.

1479.1 conj
εἰ
ei
If

1056.1 conj
γὰρ
gar
for

1156.2 conj
[a☆ δὲ]
de
[but]

1431.8 prs-pron acc pl masc
ἑαυτοὺς
heautous
ourselves

1246.7 verb 1pl indic imperf act
διεκρίνομεν,
diekrinomen
we were examining,

3620.2 partic
οὐκ
ouk
not

300.1 partic
ἂν
an
an

2892.42 verb 1pl indic imperf pass
ἐκρινόμεθα·
ekrinometha
we were being judged.

32.

2892.31 verb nom pl masc part pres pass
κρινόμενοι
krinomenoi
Being judged

1156.2 conj
δὲ,
de
but,

5097.3 prep
ὑπὸ
hupo
by

32.a.**Var:** 01ℵ,03B,04C 33,Treg,Alf,Word,Tisc We/Ho,Weis,Sod UBS/☆

3450.2 art gen sing
[a☆+ τοῦ]
tou
[the]

2935.2 noun gen sing masc
κυρίου
kuriou
Lord

3674.7 verb 1pl indic pres pass
παιδευόμεθα,
paideuometha
we are being disciplined,

2419.1 conj
ἵνα
hina
that

3231.1 partic
μὴ
mē
not

4713.1 prep dat
σὺν
sun
with

3450.3 art dat sing
τῷ
tō
the

2862.3 noun dat sing masc
κόσμῳ
kosmō
world

2602.9 verb 1pl subj aor pass
κατακριθῶμεν.
katakrithōmen
we should be condemned.

33.

5452.1 conj
Ὥστε,
Hōste
So that,

79.6 noun pl masc
ἀδελφοί
adelphoi
brothers

1466.2 prs-pron gen 1sing
μου,
mou
my,

4755.18 verb nom pl masc part pres
συνερχόμενοι
sunerchomenoi
coming together

1519.1 prep
εἰς
eis
for

3450.16 art sing neu
τὸ
to
the

2052.25 verb inf aor act
φαγεῖν,
phagein
to eat,

34.a.**Txt:** 01ℵ-corr 04C-corr,018K,020L 025P,byz.
Var: 01ℵ-org,02A,03B 04C,06D-org,it.sa.bo. Gries,Lach,Treg,Alf Word,Tisc,We/Ho,Weis Sod,UBS/☆

238.3 prs-pron acc pl masc
ἀλλήλους
allēlous
one another

1538.3 verb 2pl impr pres
ἐκδέχεσθε·
ekdechesthe
wait for.

34.

1479.1 conj
εἴ
ei
If

1156.2 conj
⟨a δέ ⟩
de
but

4948.3 indef-pron nom sing
τις
tis
anyone

3845.1 verb 3sing pres act
πεινᾷ,
peina
hungers,

1706.1 prep
ἐν
en
at

3486.3 noun dat sing masc
οἴκῳ
oikō
home

2052.7 verb 3sing impr pres act
ἐσθιέτω·
esthietō
let him eat,

2419.1 conj
ἵνα
hina
that

3231.1 partic
μὴ
mē
not

1519.1 prep
εἰς
eis
for

2890.1 noun sing neu
κρίμα
krima
judgment

4755.17 verb 2pl subj pres
συνέρχησθε.
sunerchēsthe
you may come together;

3450.17 art pl neu
Τὰ
Ta
the

1156.2 conj
δὲ
de
and

3036.9 adj acc pl neu
λοιπὰ,
loipa
remaining things

5453.1 conj
ὡς
hōs
when

300.1 partic
ἂν
an
an

2048.6 verb 1sing subj aor act
ἔλθω,
elthō
I may come,

1293.13 verb 1sing indic fut mid
διατάξομαι.
diataxomai
I will set in order.

12:1.

3875.1 prep
Περὶ
Peri
Concerning

1156.2 conj
δὲ
de
now

11:30. A literal physical affliction had settled on some in the church because they had desecrated the Lord's table. However, "sleep" would indicate death "in Christ," which would appear to justify the view that this visitation had affected more than just the desecrators of the Communion; the church community was suffering for their widespread offense. Paul had in mind, not "natural" effects of excesses, but a special chastening of the Lord. This is further proof of their disturbing behavior at the Lord's table.

11:31,32. Paul provided the antidote in a two-step sequence. First, believers should judge themselves. That would solve problems immediately. But if they do not, the Lord will judge and chasten so they will repent and avoid final condemnation with the "world" of unbelievers. Even in the middle of such sinful activity, Paul had positive advice. The Lord has no desire to see His children fall, so He disciplines in order to turn them back to Him.

Once again we are reminded that the ultimate goal of judgment is redemptive and not destructive. In chapter 5 Paul wrote that the man who had committed fornication with his stepmother should be delivered to Satan "that the spirit may be saved in the day of the Lord Jesus" (5:5). The word *paideuometha* ("being chastened") is also used by Paul in 2 Corinthians 6:9 and 1 Timothy 1:20. This is consistent with Hebrews 12:6 which says that "whom the Lord loveth he chasteneth" (cf. Hebrews 12:5-11).

Paul, in his loving manner, with his great pastor's heart, uses "we" to associate himself with his readers. A tremendous amount of hope and faith is present. Christ is overshadowing His church and is concerned about each member. He will accomplish His will and pleasure in the believer.

11:33,34. "Wherefore" shows us the second step in Paul's antidote. It is a practical admonition that includes a note of warmth and closeness ("my brethren") after his severe rebuke. The actions of the feast and the Lord's Supper were to be governed by a loving and reverent spirit.

Self-examination will result in care for others. Therefore, Paul admonished the Corinthians to wait for each other. Those who arrived early should wait for those arriving later. Each individual must be considered of equal importance in the church. Waiting for the others would presume wanting to eat with them.

Someone might raise the objection that he was hungry when he arrived and could not wait. Paul quieted the objection by directing that he first eat something at home. The church supper was more for fellowship than for eating. Otherwise, it would exclude Christian thought and charity. The spirit of love must prevail.

Paul added a footnote, "and the rest ... when I come." Paul was probably referring to other features of the administration of the ordinance which were not so pressing and could await his visit with them.

30. For this cause many [are] weak and sickly among you: Consequently, *Fenton* ... are infirm and ailing, *Concordant* ... and feble, *Rheims* ... and out of health, *Weymouth*.

and many sleep: ... and a number even dead, *Moffatt* ... a considerable number, *Concordant, Campbell*.

31. For if we would judge ourselves: ... if we wolde trye our selues, *Geneva* ... if we tested ourselves, *Fenton* ... If, however, we estimated ourselves aright, *Weymouth* ... we were judging ourselves aright, *Montgomery*.

we should not be judged: ... we would not come under the Lord's judgment, *Moffatt*.

32. But when we are judged: we are chastened of the Lord: ... we are trained, *Montgomery* ... we are being corrected, *Fenton* ... are we being disciplined, *Rotherham*.

that we should not be condemned with the world:

33. Wherefore, my brethren, when ye come together to eat: tarry one for another: ... wait for one another, *Moffatt* ... entertain one another, *Fenton* ... cordially receive each other, *Wilson*.

34. And if any man hunger, let him eat at home: that ye come not together unto condemnation: ... so as not to assemble in an improper manner, *Fenton* ... so that your meetings do not bring condemnation upon you, *Montgomery* ... your coming together may not lead to judgement, *Weymouth* ... only to incur condemnation, *Moffatt*.

And the rest will I set in order when I come: The other matters I will deal with, *Weymouth* ... The other things I will arrange, *Sawyer* ... other matters I will adjust when I come, *Montgomery* ... instructions upon the other matters, *Moffatt* ... and I schal dispose other thingis, *Wyclif* ... I will arrange the rest when I come, *Fenton*.

3450.1 art gen pl	4012.9 adj gen pl neu	79.6 noun pl masc	3620.3 partic	2286.1 verb 1sing pres act	5050.4 prs-pron acc 2pl
τῶν	πνευματικῶν,	ἀδελφοί,	οὐ	θέλω	ὑμᾶς
tōn	pneumatikōn	adelphoi	ou	thelō	humas
the	spiritual things,	brothers,	not	I do wish	you

	49.9 verb inf pres act	3471.6 verb 2pl indic perf act	3617.1 conj	3616.1 conj	1477.4 noun pl neu
	ἀγνοεῖν.	**2.** Οἴδατε	ὅτι	[ᵃ☆+ ὅτε]	ἔθνη
	agnoein	Oidate	hoti	hote	ethnē
	to be ignorant.	You know	that	[when]	Gentiles

2.a.**Var:** 01אּ,02A,03B 04C,06D,020L,025P,sa. Lach,Treg,Alf,Tisc We/Ho,Weis,Sod UBS/☆

1498.1 verb 2pl act	4242.1 prep	3450.17 art pl neu	1487.5 noun acc pl neu	3450.17 art pl neu	873.3 adj acc pl neu	5453.1 conj	300.1 partic
ἦτε,	πρὸς	τὰ	εἴδωλα	τὰ	ἄφωνα	ὡς	ἂν
ēte	pros	ta	eidōla	ta	aphōna	hōs	an
you were,	to	the	idols	the	dumb	as	you

70.29 verb 2pl indic imperf pass	516.7 verb nom pl masc part pres pass	1346.1 conj	1101.1 verb 1sing indic pres act	5050.3 prs-pron dat 2pl
ἤγεσθε,	ἀπαγόμενοι·	**3.** διὸ	γνωρίζω	ὑμῖν,
ēgesthe	apagomenoi	dio	gnōrizō	humin
might be led,	being led away.	Therefore	I reveal	to you,

3617.1 conj	3625.2 num card nom masc	1706.1 prep	4011.3 noun dat sing neu	2296.2 noun gen sing masc	2953.12 verb nom sing masc part pres act
ὅτι	οὐδεὶς	ἐν	πνεύματι	θεοῦ	λαλῶν
hoti	oudeis	en	pneumati	theou	lalōn
that	no one	in	Spirit	of God	speaking

3.a.**Txt:** 06D,018K,020L 025P,byz.sa. **Var:** 01אּ,02A,03B,04C 33-org,bo.Lach,Treg,Alf Word,Tisc,We/Ho,Weis Sod,UBS/☆

2978.5 verb 3sing indic pres act	329.1 noun nom sing neu	2400.3 name acc masc	2400.1 name nom masc	2504.1 conj
λέγει	Ἀνάθεμα	῾ Ἰησοῦν·	[ᵃ☆ Ἰησοῦς,]	καὶ
legei	Anathema	Iēsoun	Iēsous	kai
says	accursed	Jesus;	[idem]	and

3625.2 num card nom masc	1404.4 verb 3sing indic pres	1500.21 verb inf aor act	2935.4 noun acc sing masc	2400.3 name acc masc
οὐδεὶς	δύναται	εἰπεῖν,	῾ Κύριον	Ἰησοῦν,
oudeis	dunatai	eipein	Kurion	Iēsoun
no one	is able	to say	Lord	Jesus,

3.b.**Txt:** 06D,018K,020L 025P,byz. **Var:** 01אּ,02A,03B,04C 33,sa.Lach,Treg,Alf Word,Tisc,We/Ho,Weis Sod,UBS/☆

2935.1 noun nom sing masc	2400.1 name nom masc	1479.1 conj	3231.1 partic	1706.1 prep	4011.3 noun dat sing neu
[ᵇ☆ Κύριος	Ἰησοῦς,]	εἰ	μὴ	ἐν	πνεύματι
Kurios	Iēsous	ei	mē	en	pneumati
[Lord	Jesus]	if	not	in	Spirit

39.3 adj dat sing	1237.1 noun nom pl fem	1156.2 conj	5321.4 noun gen pl neu	1498.7 verb 3pl indic pres act
ἁγίῳ.	**4.** Διαιρέσεις	δὲ	χαρισμάτων	εἰσίν.
hagiō	Diaireseis	de	charismatōn	eisin
Holy.	Varieties	but	of gifts	there are,

3450.16 art sing neu	1156.2 conj	840.15 prs-pron sing neu	4011.1 noun sing neu	2504.1 conj	1237.1 noun nom pl fem
τὸ	δὲ	αὐτὸ	πνεῦμα·	**5.** καὶ	διαιρέσεις
to	de	auto	pneuma	kai	diaireseis
the	but	same	Spirit;	and	varieties

1242.5 noun gen pl fem	1498.7 verb 3pl indic pres act	2504.1 conj	3450.5 art sing masc	840.5 prs-pron nom sing masc	2935.1 noun nom sing masc
διακονιῶν	εἰσιν,	καὶ	ὁ	αὐτὸς	κύριος·
diakoniōn	eisin	kai	ho	autos	kurios
of services	there are,	and	the	same	Lord;

12:1,2. With the words "now concerning," Paul turned to a new area of discussion, one of much interest to him. The expression *peri de* ("now concerning") appears six times in First Corinthians and each time addresses a concern raised by the Corinthians themselves. He wished his readers to be knowledgeable and understanding in the matters that followed (*pneumatikōn*, literally "spirituals").

Paul reminded the Corinthian believers of what they used to be: "Gentiles," heathens, pagans, men following dumb idols. They were helpless, for they had been "carried away" by their worship of these dead and useless idols.

12:3. A comparison of their former heathen condition and their present Christian state shows a change had taken place. A Christian at all times acknowledges the lordship of Jesus Christ.

It is possible, in the public worship, that someone under ecstatic influence may have cried, "Jesus is accursed," and because of the excitement under which the statement was made, some were tempted to believe this came from God. Another view is that the statement might be made by a false teacher.

Such a statement denied the lordship of Jesus Christ. An utterance under the influence of the Holy Spirit is different; it asserts the lordship of Jesus Christ. If this particular utterance involved glossolalia, it would also have involved interpretation (or be a prophecy), for the statement to be understood publicly.

12:4. Having laid down the cornerstone of lordship, Paul turned his thoughts to the matter of "spirituals" (*pneumatikōn*) or "spiritual matters."

The manifestations of the Holy Spirit have both unity and variety. They have not the same purpose or magnitude, but each is given by one and the same Holy Spirit. These manifestations of the Spirit are called "gifts," but the idea of gift lies in their quality and ground and must be carefully used. These, like salvation, are a work of grace, but they still reside in the Holy Spirit.

In other words, their presence in someone does not necessarily signify great holiness, sanctification, or maturity. The word "diversities" (*diaireseis*) or "varieties" gives the idea of distribution and (as is made clear throughout the discussion) this is done by the choice of the Spirit.

12:5. "Administrations" (*diakoniōn*) or "ministries" also differ according to God's decisions. These refer to the functions and services of those having the "gifts." The word also indicates the purpose of spiritual manifestations; these are for the help and strength of the Church. It is a useful service. Notice, it is always "the same Lord" who is served.

---

1 Corinthians 12:5

1. Now concerning spiritual [gifts], brethren: Concerning those who exercise Spiritual Gifts, *Conybeare* . . . the spiritual endowments, *Concordant*.
I would not have you ignorant: I do not wish you to be, *Worrell*.

2. Ye know that ye were Gentiles: . . . whanne ye weren hethen men, *Wyclif* . . . when you were pagans, *Moffatt*.
carried away unto these dumb idols: . . . dragged to speechless idols, *Fenton* . . . the voiceless idols, *Concordant*.
even as ye were led: . . . even as ye happened to be led, *Macknight* . . . you were blindly led astray, *Conybeare* . . . being seduced, *Rotherham*.

3. Wherefore I give you to understand: I inform you, *Fenton* . . . I make known to you, *Worrell*.
that no man speaking by the Spirit of God calleth Jesus accursed: . . . no one can affirm, *Rotherham* . . . Anathema is Jesus, *Concordant* . . . under the influence, *Weymouth* . . . calleth Iesus execrable, *Geneva* . . . defieth Iesus, *Tyndale, Cranmer*.
and [that] no man can say that Jesus is the Lord, but by the Holy Ghost: . . . whoever is brought to own Jesus to be the Messiah, *Locke* . . . can declare Jesus Lord, *Macknight* . . . unless he be inspired by, *Conybeare*.

4. Now there are diversities of gifts: But distributions, *Rotherham* . . . different talents, *Fenton* . . . diuisions of graces, *Rheims* . . . various kinds, *Weymouth* . . . varieties of talents, *Moffatt* . . . apportionments of graces, *Concordant*.
but the same Spirit: . . . yet the selfe same Spirit, *Geneva*.

5. And there are differences of administrations: . . . apportionments of service, *Concordant* . . . there are diversities of ministries, *Worrell* . . . various forms of official service, *Weymouth* . . . of ministrations, *Rheims*.
but the same Lord:

6. | **2504.1** conj | **1237.1** noun nom pl fem | **1739.2** noun gen pl neu | **1498.7** verb 3pl indic pres act | **3450.5** art sing masc | **1156.2** conj

καὶ — kai — and
διαιρέσεις — diaireseis — varieties
ἐνεργημάτων — energēmatōn — of operations
εἰσίν, — eisin — there are,
ὁ — ho — the
δὲ — de — but

6.a.Txt: 01א-corr,018K 020L,byz.Sod **Var:** 01א-org,02A,04C 06D,025P,sa.Gries,Lach Treg,Alf,Word,Tisc We/Ho,Weis,UBS/✶

840.5 prs-pron nom sing masc | **1498.4** verb 3sing indic pres act | **2296.1** noun nom sing masc | **3450.5** art sing masc | **1738.4** verb nom sing masc part pres act | **3450.17** art pl neu

αὐτὸς — autos — same
[a ἐστιν] — estin — it is
θεός, — theos — God,
ὁ — ho — the
ἐνεργῶν — energōn — operating
τὰ — ta — the

3820.1 adj | **1706.1** prep | **3820.5** adj dat pl | **1524.4** adj dat sing masc | **1156.2** conj | **1319.42** verb 3sing indic pres pass

πάντα — panta — all things
ἐν — en — in
πᾶσιν. — pasin — all.
7. ἑκάστῳ — hekastō — To each
δὲ — de — but
δίδοται — didotai — is being given

3450.9 art nom sing fem | **5158.1** noun nom sing | **3450.2** art gen sing | **4011.2** noun gen sing neu | **4242.1** prep

ἡ — hē — the
φανέρωσις — phanerōsis — manifestation
τοῦ — tou — of the
πνεύματος — pneumatos — Spirit
πρὸς — pros — for

3450.16 art sing neu | **4702.2** verb sing neu part pres act | **3614.3** rel-pron dat sing | **3173.1** conj | **1056.1** conj | **1217.2** prep | **3450.2** art gen sing

τὸ — to — the
συμφέρον. — sumpheron — profiting.
8. ᾧ — hō — To whom
μὲν — men — men
γὰρ — gar — for
διὰ — dia — by
τοῦ — tou — the

4011.2 noun gen sing neu | **1319.42** verb 3sing indic pres pass | **3030.1** noun nom sing masc | **4531.2** noun gen sing fem | **241.3** adj dat sing

πνεύματος — pneumatos — Spirit
δίδοται — didotai — is being given
λόγος — logos — a word
σοφίας, — sophias — of wisdom;
ἄλλῳ — allō — to another

1156.2 conj | **3030.1** noun nom sing masc | **1102.2** noun gen sing fem | **2567.3** prep | **3450.16** art sing neu | **840.15** prs-pron sing neu

δὲ — de — and
λόγος — logos — a word
γνώσεως, — gnōseōs — of knowledge,
κατὰ — kata — according to
τὸ — to — the
αὐτὸ — auto — same

9.a.Txt: 01א-corr,02A 06D-corr,018K,020L 025P,byz.sa.bo.Sod **Var:** 01א-org,03B 06D-org,Treg,Tisc We/Ho,Weis,UBS/✶

4011.1 noun sing neu | **2066.2** adj dat sing | **1156.2** conj | **3963.1** noun nom sing fem | **1706.1** prep | **3450.3** art dat sing

πνεῦμα· — pneuma — Spirit;
9. ἑτέρῳ — heterō — to a different one
[a δὲ] — de — and
πίστις, — pistis — faith,
ἐν — en — in
τῷ — tō — the

9.b.Txt: 01א,04C-corr 06D,018K,020L,025P 0201,byz.sa.bo. **Var:** 02A,03B,33,it. Lach,Treg,Alf,Tisc We/Ho,Weis,Sod UBS/✶

840.4 prs-pron dat sing | **1518.2** num card dat | **4011.3** noun dat sing neu | **241.3** adj dat sing | **1156.2** conj | **5321.3** noun pl neu

[αὐτῷ — autō — same
[b✶ ἑνὶ] — heni — [one]
πνεύματι· — pneumati — Spirit;
ἄλλῳ — allō — to another
δὲ — de — but
χαρίσματα — charismata — gifts

2363.1 noun gen pl neu | **1706.1** prep | **3450.3** art dat sing | **840.4** prs-pron dat sing | **4011.3** noun dat sing neu | **241.3** adj dat sing

ἰαμάτων, — iamatōn — of healings,
ἐν — en — by
τῷ — tō — the
αὐτῷ — autō — same
πνεύματι· — pneumati — Spirit;
10. ἄλλῳ — allō — to another

10.a.Txt: 01א,02A,04C 044,byz. **Var:** 03B,06D,010F 012G,0201,6,630,1739 p46

1156.2 conj | **1739.1** noun nom pl neu | **1405.6** noun gen pl fem | **241.3** adj dat sing | **1156.2** conj

δὲ — de — and
ἐνεργήματα — energēmata — operations
δυνάμεων, — dunameōn — of works of power;
ἄλλῳ — allō — to another
[a δὲ] — de — and

12:6. "Operations" (*energēmatōn*) are also diversified, these workings revealing both the availability and the effect of divine power. They result from gifts and ministrations and are workings in virtue of the power operative therein.

But again "it is the same God," as the context shows, that "worketh all (things) in all" (people). Notice the strong Trinitarian bent in "Spirit," "Lord" (which is generally Christ in Paul's epistles), and "God."

12:7. These gifts are given for the purpose of spiritual "profit." "Manifestation" (*phanerōsis*) is a vital word; it clarifies the meaning of "gift" and helps to define this entire section. On the basis of context, it appears as a subjective genitive and means to make evident to the understanding by proof. It is a shining forth, as light makes manifest.

The exercise of the gifts makes the Spirit's presence evident. This is a "manifestation of the Spirit" and not a manifestation of a gift. He is the Source, and in Him these charismata reside. The result is worship, not admiration of the gift. The final purpose is that all the Church may profit. On this basis, the gifts are as needed now as they were then.

12:8. "Wisdom" (*sophias*) by itself includes practical skill in the affairs of life, and in particular in the things of Christ. It is the supernatural ability to see how to handle a particular situation as the Spirit directs. "Word" denotes not only expression, but time and place, beginning and end. The gift operates in a particular setting and time. See the *Greek-English Dictionary* for added helps.

"Word of knowledge" (*gnōseōs*) involves a supernatural utterance of facts, including fundamental principles of the Word. It would include understanding of the great facts of life as they are known by God. See the *Greek-English Dictionary* for further information.

12:9. "Faith" (*pistis*) is infinite trust and belief in God and often appears in times of great crisis or opportunity. It is divine certainty (Matthew 17:20; 1 Kings 18:30-46; Acts 3:1-10).

"Gifts of healing(s)" suggests different healings for different diseases. It is used of God in ministering health to the sick, appears as a sign gift, and is involved in the work of evangelism.

12:10. The word "miracles" involves an orderly intervention in the regular operations of nature. These "works of power" may be negative and destructive as well as positive.

There are those who doubt the validity of miracles today, but if the experience of the Early Church and Scripture itself have any meaning for Christians, then we must believe in the continuing miracle-working power of God. Jesus, as well as Peter, Paul, and

6. And there are diversities of operations: . . . and the working whereby they are wrought is various, *Conybeare* . . . varieties of workings, *Confraternity* . . . varieties of effects, *Moffatt* . . . diversities of energies, *Murdock.*

but it is the same God which worketh all in all: . . . which worketh all thinges that are wrought, in all creatures, *Tyndale* . . . Who is operating all in all, *Concordant* . . . energizing everything in them all, *Fenton* . . . that inwardly works all things in all, *Rotherham* . . . who effects everything in everyone, *Moffatt* . . . that works all these extraordinary gifts, *Locke.*

7. But the manifestation of the Spirit is given to every man to profit withal: The declaration, *Geneva* . . . to proffit the congregacion, *Tyndale* . . . with a view to expedience, *Concordant* . . . but for the good and advantage of the church, *Locke* . . . for the common good, *Moffatt* . . . that it may aid him, *Murdock.*

8. For to one is given by the Spirit the word of wisdom: On one is bestowed through the channel of the Spirit philosophic eloquence, *Way* . . . the vtterance of, *Geneva.*

to another the word of knowledge by the same Spirit: . . . the utterance of spiritual illumination, *Way* . . . comprehension of thought, *Fenton.*

9. To another faith by the same Spirit: . . . special faith, *Weymouth.*

to another the gifts of healing by the same Spirit: . . . the grace of doing cures in one Spirit, *Rheims.*

10. To another the working of miracles: . . . inward workings of deeds of power, *Rotherham* . . . operations of powerful deeds, *Concordant* . . . the exercise of miraculous powers, *Weymouth* . . . workings of mighty deeds, *Worrell.*

to another prophecy: . . . while to another eloquence, *Fenton* . . . inspired oratory, *Way.*

1 Corinthians 12:11

10.b.**Txt:** 01ℵ,02A,04C
044,byz.
Var: 03B,06D,010F
012G,0201,6,630,1739
p46

4252.2 noun nom sing fem	**241.3** adj dat sing	**1156.2** conj	**1247.2** noun pl fem	**4011.5** noun gen pl neu
προφητεία,	ἄλλῳ	⟨b δὲ ⟩	διακρίσεις	πνευμάτων,
prophēteia	allō	de	diakriseis	pneumatōn
prophecy;	to another	and	discerning	of spirits;

10.c.**Txt:** 01ℵ-corr,02A
04C,018K,020L,byz.bo.
Sod
Var: 01ℵ-org,03B,06D
025P,Lach,Treg,Tisc
We/Ho,Weis,UBS/✶

2066.2 adj dat sing	**1156.2** conj	**1079.4** noun pl neu	**1094.6** noun gen pl fem	**241.3** adj dat sing
ἑτέρῳ	⟨c δὲ ⟩	γένη	γλωσσῶν,	ἄλλῳ
heterō	de	genē	glōssōn	allō
to a different one	and	kinds	of tongues;	to another

1156.2 conj	**2042.1** noun nom sing fem	**1094.6** noun gen pl fem	**3820.1** adj	**1156.2** conj	**3642.18** dem-pron pl neu
δὲ	ἑρμηνεία	γλωσσῶν·	**11.** πάντα	δὲ	ταῦτα
de	hermēneia	glōssōn	panta	de	tauta
and	interpretation	of tongues.	All	but	these things

1738.1 verb 3sing indic pres act	**3450.16** art sing neu	**1518.9** num card neu	**2504.1** conj	**3450.16** art sing neu	**840.15** prs-pron sing neu
ἐνεργεῖ	τὸ	ἓν	καὶ	τὸ	αὐτὸ
energei	to	hen	kai	to	auto
operates	the	one	and	the	same

4011.1 noun sing neu	**1238.1** verb nom sing neu part pres act	**2375.10** adj dat sing fem	**1524.4** adj dat sing masc	**2503.1** conj
πνεῦμα,	διαιροῦν	ἰδίᾳ	ἑκάστῳ	καθὼς
pneuma	diairoun	idia	hekastō	kathōs
Spirit,	dividing	his own	to each	just as

1007.3 verb 3sing indic pres	**2481.1** conj	**1056.1** conj	**3450.16** art sing neu	**4835.1** noun sing neu	**1518.9** num card neu
βούλεται.	**12.** Καθάπερ	γὰρ	τὸ	σῶμα	ἓν
bouletai	Kathaper	gar	to	sōma	hen
he wills.	Even as	for	the	body	one

1498.4 verb 3sing indic pres act	**2504.1** conj	**3166.2** noun pl neu	**2174.4** verb 3sing indic pres act	**4044.17** adj pl neu	**4044.17** adj pl neu
ἐστιν	καὶ	μέλη	⟨ ἔχει	πολλά,	[✶ πολλὰ
estin	kai	melē	echei	polla	polla
is	and	members	has	many,	[many

2174.4 verb 3sing indic pres act	**3820.1** adj	**1156.2** conj	**3450.17** art pl neu	**3166.2** noun pl neu	**3450.2** art gen sing
ἔχει,]	πάντα	δὲ	τὰ	μέλη	τοῦ
echei	panta	de	ta	melē	tou
has,]	all	but	the	members	of the

12.a.**Txt:** 01ℵ-corr,06D
byz.
Var: 01ℵ-org,02A,03B
04C,018K,020L,025P
33,bo.Lach,Treg,Alf
Word,Tisc,We/Ho,Weis
Sod,UBS/✶

4835.2 noun gen sing neu	**3450.2** art gen sing	**1518.1** num card gen	**4044.17** adj pl neu	**1498.18** verb part pres act	**1518.9** num card neu
σώματος	⟨a τοῦ	ἑνός, ⟩	πολλὰ	ὄντα,	ἓν
sōmatos	tou	henos	polla	onta	hen
body	of the	one,	many	being,	one

1498.4 verb 3sing indic pres act	**4835.1** noun sing neu	**3643.1** adv	**2504.1** conj	**3450.5** art sing masc	**5382.1** name nom masc
ἐστιν	σῶμα·	οὕτως	καὶ	ὁ	Χριστός.
estin	sōma	houtōs	kai	ho	Christos
are	body:	so	also	the	Christ.

2504.1 conj	**1056.1** conj	**1706.1** prep	**1518.2** num card dat	**4011.3** noun dat sing neu	**2231.1** prs-pron nom 1pl
13. καὶ	γὰρ	ἐν	ἑνὶ	πνεύματι	ἡμεῖς
kai	gar	en	heni	pneumati	hēmeis
Also	for	by	one	Spirit	we

other apostles, lived their lives with the continual expectation of the miraculous. This century has witnessed many validated miracles.

Matthew 8:17, which quotes Isaiah 53:4, shows that one sign of the coming of the kingdom of God was to be miraculous healing. It is also true that some references to "healing" in the Gospels are metaphors for salvation and that Christ's death on the cross, although it brought physical healing, did not bring about healing in precisely the same way in which it brought about salvation. Nevertheless, Jesus' ministry, the apostolic ministry recorded in Acts, and prophecies regarding God's future activity for His people all reveal that miracles (especially, but not exclusively, healing) can be expected by all the people of God in every era of New Testament times.

"Prophecy" (*prophēteia*) means literally "to speak for another" (in this case, to speak for God). With the Day of Pentecost Joel's prophecy of the outpouring of the Holy Spirit was fulfilled (Joel 2:28-30), and it could now be expected that all believers would exercise the gift of prophecy. This gift, which includes forthtelling as well as foretelling, is a supernaturally inspired utterance by the Holy Spirit in one's own language. Its purpose (14:3) is to upbuild, instruct, and comfort.

"Discerning of spirits" is the policeman of the group and is to distinguish among three possible sources of operation: the Spirit, Satan, or the human spirit (1 John 4:1-6; Matthew 7:15-23).

"Kinds of tongues" is defined as the power to speak by the Holy Spirit in a language the speaker has not learned. "Interpretation of tongues" is to render glossolalia understandable to the audience in their language, producing profit. It must be judged by the Word of God for spiritual quality and scriptural correctness.

12:11. Once more Paul emphasizes this theme: these are gifts of the one Holy Spirit. He distributes to each individual as He wills and chooses. The choice is His, and the glory is God's.

12:12. As Paul considers the operation of these manifestations of the Spirit within the Church, he is moved to think of the operation of the Church itself. The analogy used is that of the body; one body with many functions. He is moved to consider the Church as the body of Christ.

He notes in comparison that the body is single, but has many parts. These various parts cannot be separated from the one body. The same is true of Christ's body. "Christ" here means the body of Christ, for the person of Christ is not divided.

12:13. Believers are initiated into Christ's body (meaning the Church) "by one Spirit" or "in one Spirit" (ASV). This cannot be water baptism, because clearly the baptizer is the Holy Spirit, and

to another discerning of spirits: . . . iudgement of spretes, *Tyndale*. . . the power of discriminating between prophetic utterances, *Weymouth* . . . discernment of character, *Fenton* . . . iudgement to discerne, *Cramer* . . . the gift of distinguishing spirits, *Moffatt* . . . the faculty of detecting the truth or falsity of any inspiration, *Way*.

to another [divers] kinds of tongues: . . . species of languages, *Concordant*.

to another the interpretation of tongues: . . . the ability to interpret languages, *Adams* . . . to another expownynge of wordis, *Wyclif* . . . translating languages, *Fenton*.

11. But all these worketh that one and the selfsame Spirit: . . . effectively work, *Campbell* . . . that is the energising source, *Way*.

dividing to every man severally as he will: . . . distributing peculiarly to each one, according as it is disposed, *Rotherham* . . . who bestows His gifts upon each of us in accordance with His own will, *Weymouth* . . . distributing to each his proper gifts as he pleaseth, *Macknight* . . . apportioning them severally to each individual as he pleases, *Moffatt* . . . according as He is intending, *Concordant* . . . distributing to each person as He considers best, *Fenton* . . . as he thinks fit, *Locke* . . . as He determines, *Adams*.

12. For as the body is one, and hath many members: . . . yet it has many limbs, *Fenton* . . . it has many organs, *Way*.

and all the members of that one body, being many, are one body: . . . many as they are, form one body, *Confraternity* . . . comprise but the one body, *Way* . . . together make up one body, *Adams*.

so also [is] Christ: . . . so it is with the church of Christ, *Weymouth*.

13. For by one Spirit are we all baptized into one body: For in the communion of one Spirit, *Conybeare* . . . we were all immersed into One Body, *Wilson*,

3820.7 adj pl masc	1519.1 prep	1518.9 num card neu	4835.1 noun sing neu	901.15 verb 1pl indic aor pass	1521.1 conj
πάντες	εἰς	ἓν	σῶμα	ἐβαπτίσθημεν,	εἴτε
pantes	eis	hen	sōma	ebaptisthēmen	eite
all	into	one	body	were baptized,	whether

2428.2 name-adj pl masc	1521.1 conj	1659.4 name nom pl masc	1521.1 conj	1395.6 noun pl masc	1521.1 conj
Ἰουδαῖοι	εἴτε	Ἕλληνες,	εἴτε	δοῦλοι	εἴτε
Ioudaioi	eite	Hellēnes	eite	douloi	eite
Jews	or	Greeks,	whether	slaves	or

13.a.Txt: 06D-corr,018K byz.
Var: 01ℵ,03B,04C-org 06D-org,025P,33,bo. Lach,Treg,Alf,Word Tisc,We/Ho,Weis,Sod UBS/⋆

1645.2 adj nom pl masc	2504.1 conj	3820.7 adj pl masc	1519.1 prep	1518.9 num card neu	4011.1 noun sing neu
ἐλεύθεροι·	καὶ	πάντες	(a εἰς)	ἓν	πνεῦμα
eleutheroi	kai	pantes	eis	hen	pneuma
free	and	all	into	one	Spirit

4081.11 verb 1pl indic aor pass	2504.1 conj	1056.1 conj	3450.16 art sing neu	4835.1 noun sing neu	3620.2 partic
ἐποτίσθημεν.	**14.** Καὶ	γὰρ	τὸ	σῶμα	οὐκ
epotisthēmen	Kai	gar	to	sōma	ouk
were made to drink.	Also	for	the	body	not

1498.4 verb 3sing indic pres act	1518.9 num card neu	3166.1 noun nom sing neu	233.2 conj	4044.17 adj pl neu	1430.1 partic
ἔστιν	ἓν	μέλος,	ἀλλὰ	πολλά.	**15.** ἐὰν
estin	hen	melos	alla	polla	ean
is	one	member,	but	many.	If

1500.8 verb 3sing subj aor act	3450.5 art sing masc	4087.1 noun nom sing masc	3617.1 conj	3620.2 partic	1498.2 verb 1sing indic pres act
εἴπῃ	ὁ	πούς,	Ὅτι	οὐκ	εἰμὶ
eipē	ho	pous	Hoti	ouk	eimi
should say	the	foot,	Because	not	I am

5331.1 noun nom sing fem	3620.2 partic	1498.2 verb 1sing indic pres act	1523.2 prep gen	3450.2 art gen sing	4835.2 noun gen sing neu	3620.3 partic
χείρ,	οὐκ	εἰμὶ	ἐκ	τοῦ	σώματος·	οὐ
cheir	ouk	eimi	ek	tou	sōmatos	ou
a hand,	not	I am	of	the	body:	not

3706.2 prep	3642.17 dem-pron sing neu	3620.2 partic	1498.4 verb 3sing indic pres act	1523.2 prep gen	3450.2 art gen sing
παρὰ	τοῦτο	οὐκ	ἔστιν	ἐκ	τοῦ
para	touto	ouk	estin	ek	tou
on account of	this	not	is	of	the

4835.2 noun gen sing neu	2504.1 conj	1430.1 partic	1500.8 verb 3sing subj aor act	3450.16 art sing neu	3640.1 noun sing neu
σώματος;	**16.** καὶ	ἐὰν	εἴπῃ	τὸ	οὖς,
sōmatos	kai	ean	eipē	to	ous
body?	And	if	should say	the	ear,

3617.1 conj	3620.2 partic	1498.2 verb 1sing indic pres act	3652.1 noun nom sing masc	3620.2 partic	1498.2 verb 1sing indic pres act
Ὅτι	οὐκ	εἰμὶ	ὀφθαλμός	οὐκ	εἰμὶ
Hoti	ouk	eimi	ophthalmos	ouk	eimi
Because	not	I am	an eye	not	I am

1523.2 prep gen	3450.2 art gen sing	4835.2 noun gen sing neu	3620.3 partic	3706.2 prep	3642.17 dem-pron sing neu
ἐκ	τοῦ	σώματος·	οὐ	παρὰ	τοῦτο
ek	tou	sōmatos	ou	para	touto
of	the	body:	not	on account of	this

418

the element is the body of Christ. Therefore it is regeneration as in Galatians 3:27.

Some say that the Spirit is not the agent. But He cannot be the element of baptism here because the body of Christ is. Thus it has to mean "in virtue of His operation." This would make the phrase "by one Spirit" a dative of instrumentality rather than a dative of location.

This work is accomplished regardless of station or place in life. "Jews or Gentiles" (Greeks) probably refers to nationality and birth. Such hereditary matters do not influence or affect the work of God in our lives. He is available to "whosoever" will come.

"Bond or free" refers to rank or position. God is no respecter of persons. He does not look on the social attainment, the economic status, or the hereditary influence. He looks on the heart.

Representatives of all these were made to "drink into (or of) one Spirit." While some see a reference to Communion here, it is more than possible that this is a reference to the baptism in the Holy Spirit. Certainly, God has poured out His Spirit on all flesh, according to His promise (Acts chapters 2 and 10).

It is the one Spirit who does all this, working, organizing, administrating, bringing about the effective work of Christ in believers' lives.

The work of the one Spirit brings a common bond to each life. There is a sense of unity with Him and each other, a sense of close contact and fellowship, deep, lasting, eternal. When it is the Spirit doing the work, it produces certain specific results and fruit all the time.

12:14. This one Body (of Christ), which has been so established, has many members, from many backgrounds, and each one is necessary and important.

12:15. This diversity in unity is illustrated in several ways. Paul used the illustration of the foot and the hand. The foot might feel inadequate in comparison with the dexterity of the hand. But the foot has a function that is vital.

12:16. Paul added comparison of the ear and the eye. Again, the sense of inadequacy and inferiority might arise. The eye carries a great deal of responsibility and is an obvious part of the body. Should that make the ear feel uninvolved or unimportant because its function is less obvious? Or can it say that because it is not another member of the body that it is not a part of the body? The obvious answer is "No," it cannot say that.

Hanson . . . we have through baptism been made members, *Norlie . . .* into one church, *Locke.*

whether [we be] Jews or Gentiles, whether [we be] bond or free: . . . slaves or freemen, *Fenton, Moffatt.*

and have been all made to drink into one Spirit: . . . and we were all nourished by that one Spirit, *Weymouth . . .* were all made to drink of [the] one spirit, *Hanson . . .* we have all been imbued with one Spirit, *Moffatt.*

14. For the body is not one member, but many: Since, therefore, *Macknight . . .* So, too, the body, *PNT . . .* For a body also, *Murdock . . .* does not have only one part, *SEB . . .* is not one sole member, *Locke . . .* does not consist of one part, *Weymouth, Williams . . .* is not a single organ, *Fenton . . .* does not have only one member, *Adams . . .* the body is not one organ, *Way.*

15. If the foot shall say, Because I am not the hand: Since I am not a hand, *Williams.*

I am not of the body: . . . not a part of the body, *Adams, Montgomery . . .* I am no part of the body, *Wilson . . .* I do not belong to the body, *RSV.*

is it therefore not of the body?: . . . would it not indeed be a part of the body? *Montgomery . . .* would that constitute it no part of the body? *Way . . .* is it for this not of the body? *Wilson . . .* is it for this reason, *Noyes . . .* is it, on that account, *Murdock . . .* does it therefore not belong to the body? *Fenton . . .* would not make it any the less a part of the body, *Weymouth . . .* that does not make it no part of the body, *Moffatt.*

16. And if the ear shall say, Because I am not the eye, I am not of the body: And if the ear may say, *Clementson . . .* As I am not an eye, *PNT . . .* I am not a part of the body, *Williams.*

is it therefore not of the body?: . . . does it thereby sever itself, *Conybeare . . .* would it be any less a part of the body? *Montgomery.*

3620.2 partic	1498.4 verb 3sing indic pres act	1523.2 prep gen	3450.2 art gen sing	4835.2 noun gen sing neu	1479.1 conj	3513.1 adj sing
οὐκ	ἔστιν	ἐκ	τοῦ	σώματος;	**17.** εἰ	ὅλον
ouk	estin	ek	tou	sōmatos	ei	holon
not	is it	of	the	body?	If	whole

3450.16 art sing neu	4835.1 noun sing neu	3652.1 noun nom sing masc	4085.1 adv	3450.9 art nom sing fem	187.1 noun nom sing fem
τὸ	σῶμα	ὀφθαλμός,	ποῦ	ἡ	ἀκοή;
to	sōma	ophthalmos	pou	hē	akoē
the	body	an eye,	where	the	hearing?

1479.1 conj	3513.1 adj sing	187.1 noun nom sing fem	4085.1 adv	3450.9 art nom sing fem	3612.1 noun nom sing fem
εἰ	ὅλον	ἀκοή,	ποῦ	ἡ	ὄσφρησις;
ei	holon	akoē	pou	hē	osphrēsis
if	whole	hearing,	where	the	smelling?

3432.1 adv	3431.1 adv	1156.2 conj	3450.5 art sing masc	2296.1 noun nom sing masc	4935.30 verb 3sing indic aor mid
18. ⸀ νυνὶ	[νῦν]	δὲ	ὁ	θεὸς	ἔθετο
nuni	nun	de	ho	theos	etheto
Now	[idem]	but	ho	God	set

3450.17 art pl neu	3166.2 noun pl neu	1518.9 num card neu	1524.1 adj sing	840.1 prs-pron gen pl	1706.1 prep	3450.3 art dat sing
τὰ	μέλη,	ἓν	ἔκαστον	αὐτῶν	ἐν	τῷ
ta	melē	hen	hekaston	autōn	en	tō
the	members,	one	each	of them	in	the

4835.3 noun dat sing neu	2503.1 conj	2286.22 verb 3sing indic aor act	1479.1 conj	1156.2 conj	1498.34 verb sing indic imperf act
σώματι,	καθὼς	ἠθέλησεν.	**19.** εἰ	δὲ	ἦν
sōmati	kathōs	ēthelēsen	ei	de	ēn
body,	just as	he would.	If	but	were

3450.17 art pl neu	3820.1 adj	1518.9 num card neu	3166.1 noun nom sing neu	4085.1 adv	3450.16 art sing neu	4835.1 noun sing neu
τὰ	πάντα	ἓν	μέλος,	ποῦ	τὸ	σῶμα;
ta	panta	hen	melos	pou	to	sōma
the	all	one	member,	where	to	body?

3431.1 adv	1156.2 conj	4044.17 adj pl neu	3173.1 conj	3166.2 noun pl neu	1518.9 num card neu	1156.2 conj
20. νῦν	δὲ	πολλὰ	μὲν	μέλη,	ἓν	δὲ
nun	de	polla	men	melē	hen	de
Now	but	many	men	members,	one	but

4835.1 noun sing neu	3620.3 partic	1404.4 verb 3sing indic pres	1156.2 conj	3450.5 art sing masc	3652.1 noun nom sing masc
σῶμα.	**21.** οὐ	δύναται	δὲ	[ᵃ☆+ ὁ]	ὀφθαλμὸς
sōma	ou	dunatai	de	ho	ophthalmos
body.	Not	is able	and	[the]	eye

21.a.**Var:** 01ℵ,02A,03B
04C,06D,020L,025P
Gries,Lach,Treg,Alf
Word,Tisc,We/Ho,Weis
Sod,UBS/☆

1500.21 verb inf aor act	3450.11 art dat sing fem	5331.3 noun dat sing fem	5367.3 noun acc sing fem	4622.2 prs-pron gen 2sing	3620.2 partic
εἰπεῖν	τῇ	χειρί,	Χρείαν	σου	οὐκ
eipein	tē	cheiri	Chreian	sou	ouk
to say	to the	hand,	Need	of you	not

2174.1 verb 1sing pres act	2211.1 conj	3687.1 adv	3450.9 art nom sing fem	2747.1 noun nom sing fem	3450.4 art dat pl	4087.6 noun dat pl masc
ἔχω·	ἢ	πάλιν	ἡ	κεφαλὴ	τοῖς	ποσίν,
echō	ē	palin	hē	kephalē	tois	posin
I have;	or	again	the	head	to the	feet,

12:17. In carrying the analogy to its proper conclusion, Paul offered some insights on unity. First, he noted that in the human body each member is important because if some part is missing, some important function of the body is missing, and the body is incapable of performing as a healthy body should and would.

Any time a member of the body of Christ ceases to function, the cause of Christ is hurt because something vital is absent. The Church was formed very carefully to do the whole work of God in this world.

12:18. Secondly, Paul noted that the individual members of the human body do not choose their function or place. They do not reach into some grab bag and pull out a function to please themselves.

The human body was designed very carefully by God. He had a specific plan in mind when He did the work. Nothing was left to chance or accident. The plan was followed very carefully.

The plan was the one God desired. It was according to His delight and was grounded in wisdom, practicality, and love. It therefore pleases His heart to see the body working well and in unity.

That plan and design was intended to profit the rest of the body. He placed each member in order that together they would make the body function properly. And what is true of the physical body is true also of the Church, the body of Christ.

12:19. Thirdly, Paul argued that if the whole body were one member such as an eye or an ear, then the body would not really be a body. Without certain members and functions, there is no complete body. It has lost its purpose and identity. Again, Paul's question anticipated a set response.

12:20. By repetition, Paul drove his point home. Division has no part in a united body of members.

12:21. The individual members must respect one another, because each has a necessary function in a healthy body.

Once more the illustration of eye and hand appears in Paul's discussion. The eye is a powerful, long-range, controlling member. It is valuable to the total body. Being blind is a deficiency, no matter how the other members may try to compensate.

Sometimes members in such positions in the body of Christ think they can do everything themselves. But the eye, despite its visionary work cannot get along without the menial working of the hand. Someone must bring the eye's vision into reality. "Hand" is singular and generally refers to the right or main hand. The body needs both the long-range and the close-at-work member to accomplish its purposes.

17. If the whole body [were] an eye, where [were] the hearing?: . . . where would be the hearing? *Douay, Noyes, PNT* . . . sense of hearing? *Fenton.*

If the whole [were] hearing: If all were hearing, *Montgomery* . . . were all ear, *Moffatt.*

where [were] the smelling?: . . . where would the nostrils be? *Weymouth* . . . where were the scent? *Concordant.*

18. But now hath God set the members every one of them in the body: But as it is, *Noyes* . . . the fact is that God set each one, *Adams* . . . has arranged the parts in the body, *Weymouth* . . . has placed the members, each One of them, *Wilson.*

as it hath pleased him: . . . with the best adaptation, *Fenton* . . . as He has seen fit, *Weymouth* . . . as he willed, *Confraternity, Panin, Clementson* . . . as He wished, *Adams* . . . just as He wanted them to be, *Williams* . . . according to his pleasure, *Murdock* . . . according as he thought fit, *PNT* . . . as He chose to do, *SEB.*

19. And if they were all one member: And if the whole were One Member, *Wilson.*

where [were] the body?: . . . what would become of the body? *Moffatt* . . . where would the body be? *Montgomery* . . . there would be no body! *SEB.*

20. But now [are they] many members: . . . now indeed they are many members, *Clementson* . . . now there are many members indeed, *Douay* . . . though we are many members, *Williams.*

yet but one body: . . . but a single body, *Fenton.*

21. And the eye cannot say unto the hand, I have no need of thee: It is also impossible, *Weymouth* . . . The eye is not able to say to the hand, *Wilson* . . . So the eye cannot say to the hand, *PNT* . . . You are not necessarie for me, *Rheims* . . . Thou art not needful to me, *Murdock* . . . I do not need thy help, *Confraternity* . . . I do not need you, *Williams.*

421

5367.3 noun acc sing fem	5050.2 prs-pron gen 2pl	3620.2 partic	2174.1 verb 1sing pres act	233.2 conj	4044.3 adj dat sing
Χρείαν	ὑμῶν	οὐκ	ἔχω.	22. ἀλλὰ	πολλῷ
Chreian	humōn	ouk	echō	alla	pollō
Need	of you	not	I have.	But	much

3095.1 adv comp	3450.17 art pl neu	1374.13 verb nom pl neu part pres act	3166.2 noun pl neu	3450.2 art gen sing	4835.2 noun gen sing neu
μᾶλλον	τὰ	δοκοῦντα	μέλη	τοῦ	σώματος
mallon	ta	dokounta	melē	tou	sōmatos
rather	the	seeming	members	of the	body

766.9 adj comp nom pl neu	5062.11 verb inf pres act	314.4 adj nom pl neu	1498.4 verb 3sing indic pres act	2504.1 conj
ἀσθενέστερα	ὑπάρχειν,	ἀναγκαῖά	ἐστιν·	23. καὶ
asthenestera	huparchein	anankaia	estin	kai
weaker	to be,	necessary	are;	and

3614.17 rel-pron pl neu	1374.6 verb 1pl indic pres act	814.3 adj comp acc pl neu	1498.32 verb inf pres act	3450.2 art gen sing	4835.2 noun gen sing neu
ἃ	δοκοῦμεν	ἀτιμότερα	εἶναι	τοῦ	σώματος,
ha	dokoumen	atimotera	einai	tou	sōmatos
which	we think	less honorable	to be	of the	body,

3642.3 dem-pron dat pl	4940.4 noun acc sing fem	3916.5 adj comp acc sing fem	3920.1 verb 1pl indic pres act	2504.1 conj
τούτοις	τιμὴν	περισσοτέραν	περιτίθεμεν·	καὶ
toutois	timēn	perissoteran	peritithemen	kai
these	honor	more abundant	we put about;	and

3450.17 art pl neu	803.1 adj nom pl neu	2231.2 prs-pron gen 1pl	2138.1 noun acc sing fem	3916.5 adj comp acc sing fem
τὰ	ἀσχήμονα	ἡμῶν	εὐσχημοσύνην	περισσοτέραν
ta	aschēmona	hēmōn	euschēmosunēn	perissoteran
the	unpresentable	of us	presentability	more abundant

2174.4 verb 3sing indic pres act	3450.17 art pl neu	1156.2 conj	2139.5 adj acc sing fem	2231.2 prs-pron gen 1pl	3620.3 partic
ἔχει·	24. τὰ	δὲ	εὐσχήμονα	ἡμῶν	οὐ
echei	ta	de	euschēmona	hēmōn	ou
has;	the	but	presentable	our	no

5367.3 noun acc sing fem	2174.4 verb 3sing indic pres act	233.1 conj	233.2 conj	3450.5 art sing masc	2296.1 noun nom sing masc
χρείαν	ἔχει.	ʻ ἀλλ'	[☆ ἀλλὰ]	ὁ	θεὸς
chreian	echei	all'	alla	ho	theos
need	has.	But	[idem]	ho	God

4637.1 verb 3sing indic aor act	3450.16 art sing neu	4835.1 noun sing neu	3450.3 art dat sing	5139.4 verb dat sing masc part pres act
συνεκέρασεν	τὸ	σῶμα,	τῷ	ʻ ὑστεροῦντι
sunekerasen	to	sōma	tō	husterounti
blended together	the	body,	to the	lacking

24.a.Txt: 01ℵ-corr,06D 018K,020L,byz. **Var:** 01ℵ-org,02A,03B 04C,33,Lach,Treg,Alf Tisc,We/Ho,Weis,Sod UBS/☆

5139.14 verb dat sing neu part pres pass	3916.5 adj comp acc sing fem	1319.28 verb nom sing masc part aor act	4940.4 noun acc sing fem
[ᵃ☆ ὑστερουμένῳ]	περισσοτέραν	δοὺς	τιμήν,
husteroumenō	perissoteran	dous	timēn
[being deficient]	more abundant	having given	honor,

2419.1 conj	3231.1 partic	1498.10 verb 3sing subj pres act	4830.1 noun nom sing neu	1706.1 prep	3450.3 art dat sing	4835.3 noun dat sing neu
25. ἵνα	μὴ	ᾖ	σχίσμα	ἐν	τῷ	σώματι,
hina	mē	ē	schisma	en	tō	sōmati
that	not	might be	divisions	in	the	body,

422

12:22. No member of the body is sufficient in itself. It is impossible in the physical body; it is impossible in the spiritual Body.

In fact, in contrast to what is often thought, the weaker members are essential to the proper functioning of the body. These may only seem to be weaker; they may actually be weaker. But the point is that they are a part of the body and they are there for a specific purpose, without which the body simply cannot function properly. They are necessary. They are vital. They are a part of the body.

12:23,24. There must be a mutual respect and honoring of lesser members. Delicate but vital organs must be cared for. In verses 23 and 24 Paul used two sets of puns to further his point. Those bodily parts which are less honorable (*atimotera*) must be given more honor (*timēn*), and those parts which are unpresentable (*ta aschē-mona*) must be made presentable (*euschēmona*). "Less honorable" members must be given more honor. How do we do this? Simply, we give them special attention; they are provided with special care and we take the time to clothe them.

"Uncomely parts," within the framework of the analogy, may refer to organs of procreation and excretion. The reference to sexual organs is indicated by the word *peritithemen* ("we put about" = clothe) which recalls Genesis 3:7,21 where God clothed Adam and Eve to cover their nakedness and shame. If this is true, we understand their vital nature, and yet they are weaker, and we must give them special attention to make them honorable in their function.

Whether Paul's point is intended to go this far or not, the point is clear that some parts are more and less attractive, probably because of function. But that does not make them not part of the body. Rather, each has a place and honor in the body.

The more attractive parts we make sure are noticed. They receive honor and attention from others. We do not hide them nor forget them. We provide them with honor and care.

But each member must receive equal honor and care, for God ordained the bodily operations as they are, and He has equalized the gaining and receiving of honor.

If this is the way God has planned for the human body, and He intends that each member function correctly and be a part of the whole, is it not more than reasonable to believe that He has done the same excellent thing in His spiritual body, the Church?

Paul's message could not have been made any clearer. He was writing to a church wracked by internal division, squabbling, and bitterness over such false notions as stronger or weaker, greater or lesser Christians. Just as every member of the physical body has an important function, so every believer (even if he is weak!) has a vital role to fulfill.

12:25,26. God equalized the gaining and receiving of honor to prevent division and argument in the Body and to promote concern

nor again the head to the feet, I have no need of you:

22. Nay, much more those members of the body: Quite the contrary, *Moffatt.*

which seem to be more feeble, are necessary: . . . those very organs which might seem to have least influence are really indispensable, *Way* . . . are considered rather delicate, *Moffatt.*

23. And those [members] of the body, which we think to be less honourable: . . . the least estimable, *Fenton* . . . to be the baser members, *Rheims.*

upon these we bestow more abundant honour: . . . clothe with, *Weymouth* . . . surround with, *Confraternity* . . . accord greater honor, *Adams.* . . invest with special honour, *Moffatt.*

and our uncomely [parts] have more abundant comeliness: And oure vngodly parties have most beauty on, *Tyndale* . . . and so our ungraceful parts, *Weymouth* . . . the less beautiful parts, *Conybeare* . . . and we exert greater effort to make the ugly members attractive, *Adams* . . . our plainest organ, *Fenton* . . . our indecent members have more exceeding respectability, *Concordant* . . . on them we put the more decoration, *Murdock.*

24. For our comely [parts] have no need: . . . than we do for the more beautiful ones that do not need it, *Adams* . . . have no deficiency, *Fenton.*

but God hath tempered the body together: . . . it was God who built up the body, *Weymouth.*

having given more abundant honour to that [part] which lacked: . . . giving supreme honour, *Fenton* . . . with a special dignity for the inferior parts, *Moffatt* . . . and given to the lowlier parts the higher honor, *Conybeare* . . . which is deficient, *Concordant.*

25. That there should be no schism in the body: . . . that debate be not, *Wyclif* . . . might be no disunion, *Murdock* . . . may be no division, *Adams.*

233.2 conj	3450.16 art sing neu	840.15 prs-pron sing neu	5065.1 prep	238.1 prs-pron gen pl	3179.4 verb 3pl subj pres act
ἀλλὰ	τὸ	αὐτὸ	ὑπὲρ	ἀλλήλων	μεριμνῶσιν
alla	to	auto	huper	allēlōn	merimnōsin
but	the	same	for	one another	might have concern

3450.17 art pl neu	3166.2 noun pl neu		2504.1 conj	1521.1 conj	3819.2 verb 3sing indic pres act	1518.9 num card neu	3166.1 noun nom sing neu
τὰ	μέλη·	**26.**	καὶ	εἴτε	πάσχει	ἓν	μέλος,
ta	melē		kai	eite	paschei	hen	melos
the	members.		And	if	suffers	one	member,

4692.1 verb 3sing indic pres act	3820.1 adj	3450.17 art pl neu	3166.2 noun pl neu	1521.1 conj	1386.19 verb 3sing indic pres pass
συμπάσχει	πάντα	τὰ	μέλη·	εἴτε	δοξάζεται
sumpaschei	panta	ta	melē	eite	doxazetai
suffers with	all	the	members;	if	is being glorified

1518.9 num card neu	3166.1 noun nom sing neu	4647.2 verb 3sing indic pres act	3820.1 adj	3450.17 art pl neu	3166.2 noun pl neu
[a ἓν]	μέλος,	συγχαίρει	πάντα	τὰ	μέλη.
hen	melos	sunchairei	panta	ta	melē
one	member,	rejoice with	all	the	members.

5050.1 prs-pron nom 2pl	1156.2 conj	1498.6 verb 2pl indic pres act	4835.1 noun sing neu	5382.2 name gen masc	2504.1 conj
27. Ὑμεῖς	δέ	ἐστε	σῶμα	Χριστοῦ,	καὶ
Humeis	de	este	sōma	Christou	kai
You	now	are	body	of Christ,	and

3166.2 noun pl neu	1523.2 prep gen	3183.2 noun gen sing neu	2504.1 conj	3614.8 rel-pron acc pl masc	3173.1 conj
μέλη	ἐκ	μέρους.	**28.** Καὶ	οὓς	μὲν
melē	ek	merous	Kai	hous	men
members	in	particular.	And	whom	

4935.30 verb 3sing indic aor mid	3450.5 art sing masc	2296.1 noun nom sing masc	1706.1 prep	3450.11 art dat sing fem	1564.3 noun dat sing fem
ἔθετο	ὁ	θεὸς	ἐν	τῇ	ἐκκλησίᾳ
etheto	ho	theos	en	tē	ekklēsia
did set		God	in	the	assembly:

4272.2 num ord sing	646.7 noun acc pl masc	1202.8 num ord sing neu	4254.7 noun acc pl masc	4995.1 num ord sing
πρῶτον	ἀποστόλους,	δεύτερον	προφήτας,	τρίτον
prōton	apostolous	deuteron	prophētas	triton
first,	apostles;	secondly,	prophets;	thirdly,

1314.6 noun acc pl masc	1884.1 adv	1405.5 noun pl fem	1520.1 adv	1884.1 adv
διδασκάλους,	ἔπειτα	δυνάμεις,	[εἶτα	[a✶ ἔπειτα]
didaskalous	epeita	dunameis	eita	epeita
teachers;	then	works of power;	then	[idem]

5321.3 noun pl neu	2363.1 noun gen pl neu	481.1 noun acc pl fem	481.2 noun acc pl fem
χαρίσματα	ἰαμάτων,	[ἀντιλήψεις,	[✶ ἀντιλήμψεις,]
charismata	iamatōn	antilēpseis	antilēmpseis
gifts	of healings;	helps;	[idem]

2913.1 noun acc pl fem	1079.4 noun gen pl neu	1094.6 noun gen pl fem	3231.1 partic	3820.7 adj pl masc
κυβερνήσεις,	γένη	γλωσσῶν.	**29.** μὴ	πάντες
kubernēseis	genē	glōssōn	mē	pantes
guidance;	kinds	of tongues.	Not	all

among the members for each other. This way, suffering and loss are shared, as well as joy and honor. The Body becomes a tightly-knit unity, affected by everything its individual members do and feel.

12:27,28. Paul used the human body as an example to illustrate his point; now he directly applied what he had said to the Corinthians. As elsewhere, there is individuality in unity. All of these workers are called and ordained by God.

It must be remembered that the context for Paul's statements that all members of the Body are to rejoice and suffer together is spiritual gifts. This means that if a church member does not have a prominent gift, he should not be looked down on, but accepted as a member of the Body. Similarly, no one is to think that being used for a special manifestation makes him better in the church than another person.

What about the order, then, that Paul offered. Does listing them as he does tear down what he has been saying about equality? Paul was not talking about the essential nature of the items listed in verses 27-31, but about their relative importance in some of the work of the Church. It should also be noted that the list begins with persons and proceeds to gifts or items, so it is difficult to carry a list of importance too far.

"Apostles" were chief ministers entrusted with the powers necessary to found the Church and make an entire revelation of God's will known to the body of Christ. They were certainly authoritative witnesses to the fact of the gospel and especially to the Resurrection. "Apostles" were and are designated by God for a set task.

The word "prophets" (*prophētas*) seems to have in mind a settled office rather than an occasional manifestation. Their ministry was Holy Spirit inspired speech. They were enabled to speak in their own language by a supernatural anointing. (See 14:1-5.)

"Teachers" (*didaskalous*) labor in word and doctrine with or without a pastoral charge. The word itself lends us some help. In the Ancient Church they played an important role due to the extremely high cost of hand-copied books. In some cases this ministry was local (Acts 13:1; Ephesians 4:11).

"Then" transfers the discussion from people to gifts. Miracles, healings, and tongues have been discussed earlier. "Helps" is a ministry not found elsewhere. It appears to be those who have compassion and ministry to the sick, weak, or helpless in some fashion. Special persons without set offices may render special assistance in needy cases. There are those who parallel "he that giveth" (Romans 12:8) with "helps" and "he that ruleth" (idem) with "governments."

"Governments" (*kubernēseis*) or administrations, while not fully defined, apparently has to do with some type of higher department of leadership. First Timothy 5:17 indicates it may refer to elders who not only labor in teaching and doctrine, but also are charged with some form of leadership.

but [that] the members should have the same care one for another: . . . same anxious care for one another's welfare, *Weymouth* . . . might mutually attend to each other, *Fenton* . . . have a common concern, *Moffatt* . . . are sympathizing, *Concordant* . . . should care equally for one another, *Adams.*

26. And whether one member suffer, all the members suffer with it: . . . if one organ be in pain, all the organs sympathise, *Way* . . . share its suffering, *Moffatt.*
or one member be honoured: . . . is being esteemed, *Concordant.*
all the members rejoice with it: . . . share its honour, *Moffatt* . . . share its pleasure, *Way.*

27. Now ye are the body of Christ:
and members in particular: . . . and individually you are members of it, *Weymouth* . . . and participating members, *Fenton* . . . and severally members of it, *Moffatt.*

28. And God hath set some in the church: . . . by God's appointment there are, *Weymouth* . . . set in the assembly, *Rotherham.*
first apostles:
secondarily prophets: . . . after them, *Murdock* . . . inspired preachers, *Way.*
thirdly teachers: . . . doctors, *Rheims* . . . expounders, *Way.*
after that miracles: . . . then men of power, *Fenton* . . . thereupon powers, *Concordant* . . . next, powers, *Campbell.*
then gifts of healings: . . . then the graces of doing cures, *Rheims* . . . then talent for healing, *Fenton* . . . then ability to cure diseases, *Weymouth.*
helps: . . . or render loving service, *Weymouth* . . . Serviceable Ministrations, *Conybeare* . . . services of help, *Confraternity.*
governments: . . . governors, *Locke* . . . guidings, *Rotherham* . . . and leaders, *Murdock* . . . power of administration, *Confraternity.*
diversities of tongues: . . . the ability to speak different kinds of languages, *Adams.*

1 Corinthians 12:30

646.4 noun pl masc	3231.1 partic	3820.7 adj pl masc	4254.4 noun pl masc	3231.1 partic	3820.7 adj pl masc
ἀπόστολοι;	μὴ	πάντες	προφῆται;	μὴ	πάντες
apostoloi	mē	pantes	prophētai	mē	pantes
apostles?	not	all	prophets?	not	all

1314.4 noun nom pl masc	3231.1 partic	3820.7 adj pl masc	1405.5 noun pl fem	3231.1 partic
διδάσκαλοι;	μὴ	πάντες	δυνάμεις;	**30.** μὴ
didaskaloi	mē	pantes	dunameis	mē
teachers?	not	all	works of power?	not

3820.7 adj pl masc	5321.3 noun pl neu	2174.6 verb 3pl indic pres act	2363.1 noun gen pl neu	3231.1 partic	3820.7 adj pl masc
πάντες	χαρίσματα	ἔχουσιν	ἰαμάτων;	μὴ	πάντες
pantes	charismata	echousin	iamatōn	mē	pantes
all	gifts	have	of healings?	not	all

1094.7 noun dat pl fem	2953.5 verb 3pl indic pres act	3231.1 partic	3820.7 adj pl masc	1323.1 verb 3pl indic pres act
γλώσσαις	λαλοῦσιν;	μὴ	πάντες	διερμηνεύουσιν;
glōssais	lalousin	mē	pantes	diermēneuousin
with tongues	do speak?	not	all	do interpret?

2189.1 verb 2pl pres act	1156.2 conj	3450.17 art pl neu	5321.3 noun pl neu	3450.17 art pl neu	2882.3 adj comp acc
31. Ζηλοῦτε	δὲ	τὰ	χαρίσματα	τὰ	⸀κρείττονα·
Zēloute	de	ta	charismata	ta	kreittona
Be eager for	but	the	gifts	the	better,

31.a.**Txt:** 018K,020L,byz. Sod
Var: 01א,02A,03B,04C 33,Lach,Treg,Alf,Tisc We/Ho,Weis,UBS/✶

3157.1 adj comp acc	2504.1 conj	2068.1 adv	2567.2 prep	5073.3 noun acc sing fem	3461.4 noun acc sing fem
[ᵃ✶ μείζονα.]	καὶ	ἔτι	καθ'	ὑπερβολὴν	ὁδὸν
meizona	kai	eti	kath'	huperbolēn	hodon
[greater,]	and	yet	according to	excellence	a way

5050.3 prs-pron dat 2pl	1161.1 verb 1sing indic pres act	1430.1 partic	3450.14 art dat pl fem	1094.7 noun dat pl fem	3450.1 art gen pl
ὑμῖν	δείκνυμι.	**13:1.** Ἐὰν	ταῖς	γλώσσαις	τῶν
humin	deiknumi	Ean	tais	glōssais	tōn
to you	I show.	If	with the	tongues	of the

442.7 noun gen sing masc	2953.1 verb 1sing pres act	2504.1 conj	3450.1 art gen pl	32.6 noun gen pl masc	26.4 noun acc sing fem
ἀνθρώπων	λαλῶ	καὶ	τῶν	ἀγγέλων,	ἀγάπην
anthrōpōn	lalō	kai	tōn	angelōn	agapēn
men	I speak	and	of the	angels,	love

1156.2 conj	3231.1 partic	2174.1 verb 1sing pres act	1090.1 verb 1sing indic perf act	5311.1 noun nom sing masc	2255.1 verb nom sing masc part pres act
δὲ	μὴ	ἔχω,	γέγονα	χαλκὸς	ἠχῶν
de	mē	echō	gegona	chalkos	ēchōn
but	not	have,	I have become	brass	sounding

2211.1 conj	2923.1 noun nom sing neu	212.2 verb nom sing neu part pres act	2504.1 conj	1430.1 partic	2174.1 verb 1sing pres act
ἢ	κύμβαλον	ἀλαλάζον.	**2.** καὶ	ἐὰν	ἔχω
ē	kumbalon	alalazon	kai	ean	echō
or	a cymbal	clanging.	And	if	I have

4252.4 noun acc sing fem	2504.1 conj	3471.14 verb 1sing subj perf act	3450.17 art pl neu	3328.5 noun acc pl neu	3820.1 adj
προφητείαν,	καὶ	εἰδῶ	τὰ	μυστήρια	πάντα
prophēteian	kai	eidō	ta	mustēria	panta
prophecy,	and	know	the	mysteries	all

12:29. These questions expect a negative answer. They point to what Paul has said earlier. God has put diversity in the body of Christ; He has set in order a variety of functions and gifts for the good of the Church.

12:30. Again the questions beg a "No" answer. Not everyone manifests these particular gifts. Paul was stressing diversity, not exclusiveness. It must be remembered that it is the Spirit who distributes as He wishes and manifests as He chooses.

12:31. Paul concludes with an exhortation to "covet . . . the best gifts." How is this determined, and does it mean one gift is worth more than others? The criterion of worth is use; purpose determines value. Those most serviceable to others are the most valuable and thus the greater or best gifts.

This naturally leads to that "more excellent way." Paul did not abolish gifts; he just showed the environment in which they are to exist and the force by which they are to be guided. That environment and force is love.

13:1. Henry Drummond called love the "summum bonum," the supreme good (p.11). It comes from and is, at best, a part of God. "Love is more than a characteristic of God, it is His character." (See 1 John 4:7,8.)

Love is discussed in many parts of the Word of God. It was a vital part of Jesus' ministry and thought. Yet it never reaches a fuller, stronger, deeper presentation than in this chapter. Inspired by the Holy Spirit, with Christ in full view, Paul wrote this stirring description of love.

The supremacy of love is quickly established. It is supreme over "tongues" and speech. No language in heaven or earth can be compared with the practice of love. The art of oratory, so highly valued at Corinth, could not surpass love.

"Brass" (*chalkos*) denotes first metal, copper, and then any object made from it. Here it probably refers to a gong. "Sounding" (*ēchōn*) might be rendered "resounding."

"Tinkling" (*alalazon*) is rather clashing like the sound of heavy cymbals. The sound may be attractive and entertaining; it may be alluring and persuasive. But if action is not motivated by love, it is only noise, "sound without soul."

13:2. To understand the contrast Paul put forth between love and tongues, prophecy, understanding, knowledge, and faith in verses 1 and 2, it is necessary to take into consideration why chapter 13 is sandwiched between chapters 11 to 14. The larger context of chapters 11 to 14 is that of public worship. In chapter 11 Paul was concerned to draw limits for the proper role of women in church

29. [Are] all apostles?: Not all are apostles, *Concordant* . . . Are they all legates? *Murdock.*
[are] all prophets?:
[are] all teachers? [are] all workers of miracles?: . . . can all be marvel-workers? *Way.*

30. Have all the gifts of healing?: Are all endowed, *Moffatt.*
do all speak with tongues?:
do all interpret?: Are all able to interpret? *Moffatt* . . . all do not translate, *Fenton.*

31. But covet earnestly the best gifts: But pursue the better giftes, *Rheims* . . . But always seek to excel in the greater gifts, *Weymouth* . . . Yet strive after the greater gifts, *Confraternity* . . . if ye are emulous of the superior gifts, *Murdock* . . . I would have you delight in the best gifts, *Conybeare* . . . But be envying the greater gifts, *Rotherham* . . . Yet be zealous for the greater graces, *Concordant* . . . Set your hearts on the higher talents, *Moffatt.*
and yet show I unto you a more excellent way: But now, I am going to show you a far better way, *Adams* . . . now I will point out to you a way of life which transcends all others, *Weymouth* . . . I will show you a path wherein to walk, *Conybeare.*

1. Though I speak with the tongues of men and of angels: If I can speak all the languages of men, *Weymouth* . . . If I could speak in every tongue of men, *Murdock.*
and have not charity: . . . but have not friendship, *Fenton* . . . but am destitute of Love, *Weymouth.*
I am become [as] sounding brass, or a tinkling cymbal: I should become an echoing trumpet, or a resounding drum, *Fenton* . . . a noisy gong or a clanging cymbal, *Moffatt* . . . a loud-sounding trumpet, *Weymouth* . . . resounding copper, *Concordant.*

2. And though I have [the gift of] prophecy:
and understand all mysteries, and all knowledge: . . . and see, in the law and the prophets, all

1 Corinthians 13:3

2.a.Txt: 01א,04C,06D 018K,020L,byz.Tisc,Sod
Var: 02A,03B,33,Treg Alf,We/Ho,Weis,UBS/✶

2504.1 conj	3820.12 adj acc sing fem	3450.12 art acc sing fem	1102.4 noun acc sing fem	2504.1 conj	1430.1 partic	2550.1 conj
καὶ	πᾶσαν	τὴν	γνῶσιν,	ʾ καὶ	ἐὰν	[ᵃ✶ κἂν]
kai	pasan	tēn	gnōsin,	kai	ean	kan
and	all	the	knowledge,	and	if	[and if]

2174.1 verb 1sing pres act	3820.12 adj acc sing fem	3450.12 art acc sing fem	3963.4 noun acc sing fem	5452.1 conj	3598.4 noun pl neu
ἔχω	πᾶσαν	τὴν	πίστιν,	ὥστε	ὄρη
echō	pasan	tēn	pistin,	hōste	orē
I have	all	the	faith,	so as	mountains

2.b.Txt: 02A,04C,018K 020L,byz.We/Ho
Var: 01א,03B,06D,33 Lach,Treg,Tisc,Weis Sod,UBS/✶

3150.1 verb inf pres act	3150.5 verb inf pres act	26.4 noun acc sing fem	1156.2 conj	3231.1 partic
ʾ μεθιστάνειν,	[ᵇ✶ μεθιστάναι,]	ἀγάπην	δὲ	μὴ
methistanein,	methistanai,	agapēn	de	mē
to remove,	[idem]	love	but	not

3.a.Txt: 01א,06D,018K 020L,byz.Tisc
Var: 02A,03B,04C,33 Lach,Treg,Alf,We/Ho Weis,Sod,UBS/✶

2174.1 verb 1sing pres act	3628.1 num card neu	1498.2 verb 1sing indic pres act	2504.1 conj	1430.1 partic	2550.1 conj
ἔχω,	οὐθέν	εἰμι.	3. ʾ καὶ	ἐὰν	[ᵃ✶ κἂν]
echō,	outhen	eimi.	kai	ean	kan
have,	nothing	I am.	And	if	[and if]

5430.2 verb 1sing subj aor act	3820.1 adj	3450.17 art pl neu	5062.4 verb part pres act	1466.2 prs-pron gen 1sing
ψωμίσω	πάντα	τὰ	ὑπάρχοντά	μου,
psōmisō	panta	ta	huparchonta	mou,
I give away in food	all	the	goods	my,

2504.1 conj	1430.1 partic	3722.15 verb 1sing subj aor act	3450.16 art sing neu	4835.1 noun sing neu	1466.2 prs-pron gen 1sing
καὶ	ἐὰν	παραδῶ	τὸ	σῶμά	μου
kai	ean	paradō	to	sōma	mou
and	if	I deliver up	the	body	my

3.b.Txt: 018K,044,byz.
Var1: 04C,06D,020L Tisc,Weis,Sod,UBS/✶
Var2: p46,01א,03B,048 6,33,69

2419.1 conj	2516.11 verb 1sing subj fut pass	2516.13 verb 1sing indic fut pass	2714.11 verb 1sing subj aor mid
ἵνα	ʾ καυθήσωμαι,	[¹ᵇ καυθήσομαι,	² καυχήσωμαι,]
hina	kauthēsōmai,	kauthēsomai,	kauchēsōmai
that	I may be burned,	[I shall be burned,	I may boast,]

26.4 noun acc sing fem	1156.2 conj	3231.1 partic	2174.1 verb 1sing pres act	3625.6 num card neu	5456.6 verb 1sing indic pres pass
ἀγάπην	δὲ	μὴ	ἔχω,	οὐδὲν	ὠφελοῦμαι.
agapēn	de	mē	echō,	ouden	ōpheloumai.
love	but	not	have,	nothing	I am being profited.

3450.9 art nom sing fem	26.1 noun nom sing fem	3086.1 verb 3sing indic pres act	5376.1 verb 3sing indic pres	3450.9 art nom sing fem
4. Ἡ	ἀγάπη	μακροθυμεῖ,	χρηστεύεται·	ἡ
Hē	agapē	makrothumei,	chrēsteuetai	hē
The	love	has patience,	is kind;	the

4.a.Txt: 01א,02A,04C 06D,010F,012G,044 048,byz.
Var: 03B,33,104,629 1175,2464

26.1 noun nom sing fem	3620.3 partic	2189.3 verb 3sing indic pres act	3450.9 art nom sing fem	26.1 noun nom sing fem	3620.3 partic
ἀγάπη	οὐ	ζηλοῖ·	ʾᵃ ἡ	ἀγάπη ʾ	οὐ
agapē	ou	zēloi	hē	agapē	ou
love	not	is envious;	the	love	not

3928.1 verb 3sing indic pres	3620.3 partic	5284.2 verb 3sing indic pres pass	3620.2 partic	801.1 verb 3sing indic pres act
περπερεύεται,	οὐ	φυσιοῦται,	5. οὐκ	ἀσχημονεῖ,
perpereuetai,	ou	phusioutai,	ouk	aschēmonei,
is boastful,	not	is puffed up,	not	is not indecent,

worship and how Christians should conduct themselves at the Lord's Supper. Chapters 12 and 14 have to do with the proper exercise of the gifts of the Spirit in church worship.

The apostle Paul was forced to deal with these issues specifically because various Corinthian Christians were exalting their "Christian liberty" and "knowledge" to such a degree that they made a mockery of orderly Christian worship. Paul insisted in chapter 13 that the model of Christian worship is love, not knowledge or any other special gift in which the Corinthians thought they excelled.

First Corinthians 13, therefore, is not a general treatise on the nature of love; it is a very specific instruction explaining how people are to relate to one another in public worship. Paul did not condemn the gifts of tongues or prophecy; rather, he insisted that they cannot be used indiscriminately or boastfully but must be subordinated to love.

Love is superior to great knowledge and understanding. This involves inspiration and prophecy: the work of the seer. Mysteries are known, truths that men could never learn and penetrate for themselves, but only because it pleased God to reveal them. "All" explains the extent of the knowledge. It is "nothing" without love.

Love is superior to great faith, the kind of faith that moves mountain after mountain. Without love as the motive, even such miracle-working faith as this, exciting and successful though it may be, is of no value.

13:3. Love surpasses great generosity of goods and self. There may be generosity to the point of becoming a pauper and yet be without love. Men of the First Century, as today, saw great merit in deeds of charity and suffering. But these without love have no merit. To be of value love must be the motive.

If one gave one's self as a martyr, which is as far as this point could be carried, without love as the motive, there would be no gain of any kind.

13:4. Love is supreme in its position and practical in its display. It has great patience toward evil and is kind when doing good. Love is long-suffering (Ephesians 4:1-3; 2 Peter 3:9). It has an infinite capacity for endurance and patience.

Love is "kind" (Luke 6:27-35; James 3:17). It shows goodness toward those who ill-treat it. It gives itself in the service of others.

It "envieth not" (James 3:14-16); it is not jealous. It has no petty feelings toward those, for instance, who are doing the same work, only better. Love is not displeased at the success of others. Love "vaunteth not" itself. The root of this word points to a "windbag." It is "not puffed up." Humility is an ingredient of love.

13:5. Love is concerned with giving itself rather than asserting itself. It does not "behave itself unseemly." This phrase carries the

the mysteries contained in them, *Locke* . . . perceiving all secrets, *Concordant* . . . and am versed in all mysteries, *Weymouth* . . . fathom all mysteries and secret lore, *Moffatt* . . . and every science, *Murdock*.

and though I have all faith: . . . and have such absolute faith, *Weymouth* . . . if I possessed perfect faith, *Fenton* . . . faith to the highest degree, *Locke*.

so that I could remove mountains: . . . so as to transport mountains, *Concordant* . . . so that I meue hillis fro her place, *Wyclif*.

and have not charity:

I am nothing: I am of no value, *Locke*.

3. And though I bestow all my goods to feed [the poor]: . . . if I should distribute, *Rheims* . . . I morsel out, *Rotherham* . . . if I bestow all I have in relief of the poor, *Locke* . . . if I should feed out to the destitute all I possess, *Murdock*.

and though I give my body to be burned: . . . deliver my body, *Fenton*.

and have not charity:

it profiteth me nothing: . . . nothing do I benefit, *Concordant* . . . I gain nothing, *Fenton*.

4. Charity suffereth long, [and] is kind: . . . patient, is gracious, *Rotherham* . . . Friendship forbears, *Fenton* . . . is courteous, *Geneva* . . . is gentle and benign, *Locke*.

charity envieth not: . . . nor jealousy, *Weymouth* . . . without emulation, *Locke*.

charity vaunteth not itself: . . . is not forward and self-assertive, *Weymouth* . . . is not vainglorious, *Fenton, PNT* . . . not bragging, *Concordant* . . . love is not boisterous, *Murdock*.

is not puffed up: . . . gives itself no airs, *Moffatt* . . . swelleth not, *Geneva* . . . is not pompous, *Fenton*.

5. Doth not behave itself unseemly: . . . is not ambitious, *Rheims* . . . is never rude, *Moffatt* . . . is not indecent, *Concordant* . . . dealeth not dishonestly, *Cranmer* . . . does not behave unbecomingly, *Weymouth*.

1 Corinthians 13:6

3620.3 partic	2195.5 verb 3sing indic pres act	3450.17 art pl neu	1431.9 prs-pron gen 3sing fem	3620.3 partic	3809.1 verb 3sing indic pres pass
οὐ	ζητεῖ	τὰ	ἑαυτῆς,	οὐ	παροξύνεται,
ou	zētei	ta	heautēs	ou	paroxunetai
not	seeks	the things	of itself,	not	is quickly provoked,

3620.3 partic	3023.4 verb 3sing indic pres	3450.16 art sing neu	2527.7 adj sing neu	3620.3 partic	5299.2 verb 3sing indic pres act
οὐ	λογίζεται	τὸ	κακόν,	**6.** οὐ	χαίρει
ou	logizetai	to	kakon	ou	chairei
not	reckons	the	evil,	not	rejoices

1894.3 prep	3450.11 art dat sing fem	92.3 noun dat sing fem	4647.2 verb 3sing indic pres act	1156.2 conj	3450.11 art dat sing fem
ἐπὶ	τῇ	ἀδικίᾳ,	συγχαίρει	δὲ	τῇ
epi	tē	adikia	sunchairei	de	tē
at	the	unrighteousness,	rejoices with	in	the

223.3 noun dat sing fem	3820.1 adj	4573.1 verb 3sing indic pres act	3820.1 adj	3961.6 verb 3sing indic pres act
ἀληθείᾳ,	**7.** πάντα	στέγει,	πάντα	πιστεύει,
alētheia	panta	stegei	panta	pisteuei
truth;	all things	covers,	all things	believes,

3820.1 adj	1666.2 verb 3sing indic pres act	3820.1 adj	5116.3 verb 3sing indic pres act	3450.9 art nom sing fem
πάντα	ἐλπίζει,	πάντα	ὑπομένει.	**8.** Ἡ
panta	elpizei	panta	hupomenei	Hē
all things	hopes,	all things	endures.	The

26.1 noun nom sing fem	3626.1 adv	1588.1 verb 3sing indic pres act	3959.1 verb 3sing indic pres act	1521.1 conj
ἀγάπη	οὐδέποτε	(ἐκπίπτει.	[a☆ πίπτει.]	εἴτε
agapē	oudepote	ekpiptei	piptei	eite
love	never	falls;	[idem]	whether

1156.2 conj	4252.5 noun nom pl fem	2643.19 verb 3pl indic fut pass	1521.1 conj	1094.5 noun nom pl fem
δὲ	προφητεῖαι,	καταργηθήσονται·	εἴτε	γλῶσσαι,
de	prophēteiai	katargēthēsontai	eite	glōssai
but	prophecies,	they shall be done away;	whether	tongues,

3835.11 verb 3pl indic fut mid	1521.1 conj	1102.1 noun nom sing fem	2643.18 verb 3sing indic fut pass
παύσονται·	εἴτε	γνῶσις,	καταργηθήσεται.
pausontai	eite	gnōsis	katargēthēsetai
they shall cease;	whether	knowledge	it shall be done away.

1523.2 prep gen	3183.2 noun gen sing neu	1056.1 conj	1091.4 verb 1pl indic pres act	2504.1 conj	1523.2 prep gen
9. ἐκ	μέρους	γὰρ	γινώσκομεν,	καὶ	ἐκ
ek	merous	gar	ginōskomen	kai	ek
In	part	for	we know,	and	in

3183.2 noun gen sing neu	4253.1 verb 1pl indic pres act	3615.1 conj	1156.2 conj	2048.8 verb 3sing subj aor act
μέρους	προφητεύομεν·	**10.** ὅταν	δὲ	ἔλθῃ
merous	prophēteuomen	hotan	de	elthē
part	we prophesy;	when	but	may come

3450.16 art sing neu	4894.1 adj sing	4966.1 adv	3450.16 art sing neu	1523.2 prep gen	3183.2 noun gen sing neu
τὸ	τέλειον,	(a τότε)	τὸ	ἐκ	μέρους
to	teleion	tote	to	ek	merous
the	perfect,	then	the	in	part

8.a.**Txt:** 01א-corr
04C-corr,06D,018K
020L,025P,byz.Sod
Var: 01א-org,02A,03B
04C-org,33,Lach,Treg
Alf,Tisc,We/Ho,Weis
UBS/☆

10.a.**Txt:** 06D-corr,018K
020L,byz.
Var: 01א,02A,03B
06D-org,33,it.bo.Lach
Treg,Alf,Word,Tisc
We/Ho,Weis,Sod
UBS/☆

idea of anything disgraceful, dishonorable, or indiscreet.

Further, it is "not easily provoked." It "thinketh no evil." It imputes no evil to anyone nor does it hold anything against anyone. "Thinketh" (*logizetai*) is a word Paul used frequently for the reckoning or imputing of righteousness to believers. Here it is connected with the keeping of accounts, recording them, and reckoning them to someone.

13:6,7. Love "rejoiceth in the truth" (John 14:6; Romans 14:17; Ephesians 4:21). Even love cannot rejoice when the truth is denied. Love rejoices in the gospel.

Love "beareth all things" (Ephesians 4:2; Colossians 3:13). It endures, without disclosing to the world its stress or complaint. There is no bragging.

It "believeth all things." With a good conscience it puts good to another's credit. In trust and faith it believes the very best it honestly can at all times.

Love "endureth all things." It is steadfast even in difficult circumstances. There is a patient, loving spirit.

13:8,9. This love shall endure forever. It is compared with prophecy, tongues, and knowledge, all items of value in this life, but in a sense "temporary."

The painfully acquired knowledge of earthly things will "vanish away" in light of the overwhelming knowledge of God. Its incompleteness will be evident to everyone. The knowledge of the Lord shall be full.

To "prophesy in part" probably means that the prophet has only a partial glimpse of truth; his prophecy is accurate but incomplete. God does not reveal everything. This is the pattern in the Old Testament, as we discover from Hebrews 1:1-3. What the prophets of old spoke was accurate and true, but there was a fuller revelation to come, a final revelation in the Son of God, God's Word to man. We are learning about and from that Word; we seek truth and wisdom; we grow in knowledge. But when He restores all things and human limitations are removed, the veil will be lifted to show understanding beyond our reach now, understanding rich, full, and final.

13:10. That is exactly Paul's point as this verse indicates. When He who is perfect is fully revealed in His glory, then anything and everything partial will be swallowed up in that fullness.

A day of completeness and perfection is coming. Everything partial, temporary, or inadequate shall vanish in the light of Christ's brilliant power and glory.

seeketh not her own: . . . never selfish, *Moffatt*.

is not easily provoked, thinketh no evil: . . . nor blaze out in passionate anger, *Weymouth* . . . not exasperated, *Rotherham* . . . not incensed, *Concordant* . . . never irritated, never resentful, *Moffatt* . . . nor brooding over injury, *Fenton*.

6. Rejoiceth not in iniquity: . . . love is never glad when others go wrong, *Moffatt* . . . finds no pleasure in injustice done to others, *Weymouth*.

but rejoiceth in the truth: . . . joyfully sides with, *Weymouth* . . . rejoices with the right, *Fenton*.

7. Beareth all things, believeth all things: . . . slow to expose . . . eager to believe the best, *Moffatt* . . . knows how to be silent . . . full of trust, *Weymouth*.

hopeth all things:

endureth all things: . . . waits for all, *Fenton*.

8. Charity never faileth: Love never disappears, *Moffatt*.

but whether [there be] prophecies, they shall fail: . . . as for eloquence it will cease, *Fenton* . . . shalbe abolished, *Geneva* . . . be made voide, *Rheims* . . . will be discarded, *Concordant*.

whether [there be] tongues, they shall cease: . . . they will be silent, *Fenton*.

whether [there be] knowledge, it shall vanish away: . . . will be brought to an end, *Weymouth*.

9. For we know in part: For out of an installment are we knowing, *Concordant* . . . we only know bit by bit, *Moffatt*.

and we prophesy in part: . . . we teach with imperfection, *Fenton*.

10. But when that which is perfect is come: . . . when the perfect state of things, *Weymouth*.

then that which is in part shall be done away: . . . all that is imperfect will be brought to an end, *Weymouth* . . . will be superseded, *Moffatt* . . . will become useless, *Fenton*.

1 Corinthians 13:11

2643.18 verb 3sing indic fut pass	3616.1 conj	1498.46 verb 1sing indic imperf mid	3378.1 adj nom sing masc	5453.1 conj
καταργηθήσεται.	11. ὅτε	ἤμην	νήπιος,	ʽ ὡς
katargēthēsetai	hote	ēmēn	nēpios	hōs
shall be done away.	When	I was	an infant,	as

3378.1 adj nom sing masc	2953.44 verb indic imperf act	2953.44 verb indic imperf act	5453.1 conj	3378.1 adj nom sing masc
νήπιος	ἐλάλουν,	[✩ ἐλάλουν	ὡς	νήπιος,]
nēpios	elaloun	elaloun	hōs	nēpios
an infant	I was speaking,	[I was speaking	as	an infant,]

5453.1 conj	3378.1 adj nom sing masc	5262.11 verb 1sing indic imperf act	5453.1 conj	3378.1 adj nom sing masc
ʽ ὡς	νήπιος,	ἐφρόνουν,	ὡς	νήπιος
hōs	nēpios	ephronoun	hōs	nēpios
as	an infant	I was thinking,	as	an infant

3023.19 verb 1sing indic imperf	5262.11 verb 1sing indic imperf act	5453.1 conj	3378.1 adj nom sing masc	3023.19 verb 1sing indic imperf
ἐλογιζόμην·	[✩ ἐφρόνουν	ὡς	νήπιος,	ἐλογιζόμην
elogizomēn	ephronoun	hōs	nēpios	elogizomēn
I was reasoning;	[I was thinking	as	an infant,	I was reasoning

5453.1 conj	3378.1 adj nom sing masc	3616.1 conj	1156.2 conj	1090.1 verb 1sing indic perf act	433.1 noun nom sing masc
ὡς	νήπιος·]	ὅτε	ʽa δὲ ʼ	γέγονα	ἀνήρ,
hōs	nēpios	hote	de	gegona	anēr
as	an infant;]	when	but	I became	a man,

11.a.Txt: 01ℵ-corr 06D-corr,018K,020L 025P,byz.bo.Sod **Var:** 01ℵ-org,02A,03B 06D-org,Lach,Treg,Alf Tisc,We/Ho,Weis UBS/✩

2643.7 verb 1sing indic perf act	3450.17 art pl neu	3450.2 art gen sing	3378.2 adj gen sing masc	984.5 verb 1pl indic pres act
κατήργηκα	τὰ	τοῦ	νηπίου,	12. βλέπομεν
katērgēka	ta	tou	nēpiou	blepomen
I did away with	the things	of the	infant.	We see

1056.1 conj	732.1 adv	1217.1 prep	2054.1 noun gen sing neu	1706.1 prep	135.1 noun dat sing neu	4966.1 adv
γὰρ	ἄρτι	δι'	ἐσόπτρου	ἐν	αἰνίγματι,	τότε
gar	arti	di'	esoptrou	en	ainigmati	tote
for	now	through	a mirror	in	a riddle,	then

1156.2 conj	4241.1 noun sing neu	4242.1 prep	4241.1 noun sing neu	732.1 adv	1091.1 verb 1sing indic pres act
δὲ	πρόσωπον	πρὸς	πρόσωπον·	ἄρτι	γινώσκω
de	prosōpon	pros	prosōpon	arti	ginōskō
but	face	to	face;	now	I know

1523.2 prep gen	3183.2 noun gen sing neu	4966.1 adv	1156.2 conj	1906.20 verb 1sing indic fut mid	2503.1 conj
ἐκ	μέρους,	τότε	δὲ	ἐπιγνώσομαι	καθὼς
ek	merous	tote	de	epignōsomai	kathōs
in	part,	then	but	I shall know	just as

2504.1 conj	1906.19 verb 1sing indic aor pass	3432.1 adv	1156.2 conj	3176.1 verb 3sing indic act	3963.1 noun nom sing fem
καὶ	ἐπεγνώσθην.	13. νυνὶ	δὲ	μένει	πίστις,
kai	epegnōsthēn	nuni	de	menei	pistis
also	I have been known.	Now	and	remain	faith,

1667.1 noun nom sing fem	26.1 noun nom sing fem	3450.17 art pl neu	4980.4 num card neu	3642.18 dem-pron pl neu	3157.2 adj comp nom sing
ἐλπίς,	ἀγάπη,	τὰ	τρία	ταῦτα·	μείζων
elpis	agapē	ta	tria	tauta	meizōn
hope,	love;	the	three	these;	the greater

432

13:11. To explain more fully, Paul gave us the illustration of a child becoming a man. "Put away" is an indication of the determination on Paul's part not to be ruled by childish attitudes. The tense is perfect, which shows that Paul put away childish things with decision and finality. This is a normal process for normal growth. The child strives to be a man and works at becoming one with clear deliberation. The spiritual process is also like that. Out of a spiritual nature comes the desire for maturity, fullness, and "manhood."

13:12. To express it by yet another figure, Paul included the illustration of the mirror reflection. Mirrors were a specialty of Corinth, but they were made of polished brass so the image was dim at best. Silvering glass was not discovered until the 13th Century. This makes the point of Paul's illustration more obvious.

Here on earth our sight of eternal things is at best indistinct. Human limitations make the fullness of our spiritual destiny hazy. But that will change. Sometime, in eternity, we shall know as we are now known, and we will understand redemption and our Redeemer fully.

Paul's use of "mirror" as a metaphor or analogy for "seeing" has been the subject of much debate. Most frequently it has been taken in a negative sense implying that our knowledge of God is skewed and warped. The Hellenistic Jew Philo, for example, used the mirror in this way. C.K. Barrett, however, suggests that the metaphor "must take its sense from the context; always the glass is an instrument of revelation . . . " (*Harper's New Testament Commentaries*, p.307). The fact that "mirror," by itself, was not a negative image is suggested by the following *en ainigmati* (literally, "in a riddle").

The most likely background for *ainigmati* (which occurs only here in the New Testament) is the Septuagint of Numbers 12:8 where God spoke "mouth to mouth" with Moses (i.e., directly), not *en ainigmati*, in "dark speeches" or riddles as He did to the prophets. The point is not so much the inadequacy of God's revelation to the prophets as it is the indirectness of it. Thus, the understanding here in verse 12 should focus on the indirectness of the knowledge of God's revelation more than on our utter inability to understand His revelation. By stressing its indirectness, and the fact that we will understand in full only later, Paul was counteracting the Gnostic view that God can be fully known in the present.

13:13. Love stands above faith and hope, both of which are essential in the plan and work of salvation. The reason is that love will not fail or "fall" in the sense of cessation. Love surpasses its companions, since it is the character of God. Love is the fruition of faith's efforts and hope's anticipations.

Fittingly, love is the last word of the chapter. The heart needs love, and the Christian must allow every thought, action, and attitude to be ruled by love, which is the greatest in all of life.

1 Corinthians 13:13

11. When I was a child, I spake as a child: . . . a litle one, *Rheims* . . . a minor, *Concordant* . . . in the imperfect state of childhood, *Locke.*

I understood as a child, I thought as a child: I reflected like, *Fenton* . . . I had the feelings of, *Noyes* . . . reasoned like, *Weymouth* . . . I argued like, *Moffatt.*

but when I became a man, I put away childish things: . . . came to the state and perfection of manhood, *Locke* . . . I have laid aside, *Rotherham* . . . I have discarded childish manners, *Hanson* . . . outworn for me are the things of the child, *Way.*

12. For now we see through a glass, darkly: For at present, *Concordant* . . . we see as yet the Vision glassed in a mirror—it is a dark riddle, *Way* . . . we only see the baffling reflections in a mirror, *Moffatt* . . . a mirror obscurely, *Rotherham, Clementson* . . . the dim, and, as it were, enigmatical representation of things, *Locke* . . . in a dark manner, *Douay* . . . and are puzzled, *Weymouth* . . . and are baffled, *Montgomery.*

but then face to face: . . . as a man sees another, *Locke* . . . shall we gaze, *Way.*

now I know in part; but then shall I know even as also I am known: Now I knowe vnparfectly, *Tyndale* . . . now I know partially, *Fenton, Murdock* . . . now I know in fragments, but then shall I understand even as I also have been understood, *Montgomery* . . . Now my knowledge comes from seeing but a part, *Way* . . . then I shall recognize, *Concordant* . . . then shall I know fully, *Clementson, Panin* . . . even as I am fully known, *Weymouth.*

13. And now abideth faith, hope, charity, these three: And now exist, *Fenton* . . . endure, *Montgomery* . . . these abide unperishing...These three Gifts alone, *Way* . . . now are remaining faith, expectation, *Concordant.*

but the greatest of these [is] charity: . . . but the chiefest of these, *Geneva* . . . the greatest of them is friendship, *Fenton.*

1 Corinthians 14:1

| 1156.2 conj **δὲ** *de* but | 3642.2 dem-pron gen pl **τούτων** *toutōn* of these | 3450.9 art nom sing fem **ἡ** *hē* the | 26.1 noun nom sing fem **ἀγάπη.** *agapē* love. | | 1371.6 verb 2pl impr pres act **14:1. Διώκετε** *Diōkete* Pursue | 3450.12 art acc sing fem **τὴν** *tēn* the |

| 26.4 noun acc sing fem **ἀγάπην·** *agapēn* love, | 2189.1 verb 2pl pres act **ζηλοῦτε** *zēloute* be eager for | 1156.2 conj **δὲ** *de* and | 3450.17 art pl neu **τὰ** *ta* the | 4012.10 adj acc pl neu **πνευματικά,** *pneumatika* spiritual things, | 3095.1 adv comp **μᾶλλον** *mallon* rather |

| 1156.2 conj **δὲ** *de* but | 2419.1 conj **ἵνα** *hina* that | 4253.2 verb 2pl subj pres act **προφητεύητε.** *prophēteuēte* you may prophesy. | 3450.5 art sing masc **2. ὁ** *ho* The | 1056.1 conj **γὰρ** *gar* for | 2953.12 verb nom sing masc part pres act **λαλῶν** *lalōn* speaking |

| 1094.3 noun dat sing fem **γλώσσῃ,** *glōssē* in a tongue, | 3620.2 partic **οὐκ** *ouk* not | 442.8 noun dat pl masc **ἀνθρώποις** *anthrōpois* to men | 2953.2 verb sing indic pres act **λαλεῖ,** *lalei* speaks, | 233.2 conj **ἀλλὰ** *alla* but | 3450.3 art dat sing (a **τῷ**) *tō* to |

2.a.**Txt:** 01א-corr,02A 06D-corr,018K,020L byz.Sod
Var: 01א-org,03B 06D-org,025P,Lach Treg,Tisc,We/Ho,Weis UBS/*

| 2296.3 noun dat sing masc **θεῷ,** *theō* to God: | 3625.2 num card nom masc **οὐδεὶς** *oudeis* no one | 1056.1 conj **γὰρ** *gar* for | 189.5 verb 3sing indic pres act **ἀκούει,** *akouei* hears; | 4011.3 noun dat sing neu **πνεύματι** *pneumati* in spirit | 1156.2 conj **δὲ** *de* but |

| 2953.2 verb sing indic pres act **λαλεῖ** *lalei* he speaks | 3328.5 noun acc pl neu **μυστήρια·** *mustēria* mysteries. | 3450.5 art sing masc **3. ὁ** *ho* The | 1156.2 conj **δὲ** *de* but | 4253.4 verb nom sing masc part pres act **προφητεύων,** *prophēteuōn* prophesying, |

| 442.8 noun dat pl masc **ἀνθρώποις** *anthrōpois* to men | 2953.2 verb sing indic pres act **λαλεῖ** *lalei* speaks | 3482.3 noun acc sing fem **οἰκοδομὴν** *oikodomēn* building up | 2504.1 conj **καὶ** *kai* and | 3735.4 noun acc sing fem **παράκλησιν** *paraklēsin* encouragement |

| 2504.1 conj **καὶ** *kai* and | 3750.1 noun acc sing fem **παραμυθίαν.** *paramuthian* consolation. | 3450.5 art sing masc **4. ὁ** *ho* The | 2953.12 verb nom sing masc part pres act **λαλῶν** *lalōn* speaking | 1094.3 noun dat sing fem **γλώσσῃ,** *glōssē* with a tongue, |

| 1431.6 prs-pron acc 3sing masc **ἑαυτὸν** *heauton* himself | 3481.3 verb 3sing indic pres act **οἰκοδομεῖ·** *oikodomei* builds up; | 3450.5 art sing masc **ὁ** *ho* the | 1156.2 conj **δὲ** *de* but | 4253.4 verb nom sing masc part pres act **προφητεύων** *prophēteuōn* prophesying, |

| 1564.4 noun acc sing fem **ἐκκλησίαν** *ekklēsian* assembly | 3481.3 verb 3sing indic pres act **οἰκοδομεῖ.** *oikodomei* builds up. | 2286.1 verb 1sing pres act **5. θέλω** *thelō* I want | 1156.2 conj **δὲ** *de* now | 3820.8 adj acc pl masc **πάντας** *pantas* all | 5050.4 prs-pron acc 2pl **ὑμᾶς** *humas* you |

| 2953.24 verb inf pres act **λαλεῖν** *lalein* to speak | 1094.7 noun dat pl fem **γλώσσαις,** *glōssais* with tongues, | 3095.1 adv comp **μᾶλλον** *mallon* rather | 1156.2 conj **δὲ** *de* but | 2419.1 conj **ἵνα** *hina* that | 4253.2 verb 2pl subj pres act **προφητεύητε·** *prophēteuēte* you should prophesy: |

14:1. Now begins an analysis of the utterance gifts: tongues, interpretation, and prophecy. The emphasis on prophecy is due to the pride of the Corinthians over tongues and their neglect of the other gifts of the Spirit. Paul was not speaking against tongues (14:5,18) but emphasizing the need for edification in utterance.

He encouraged believers to "follow after charity (love)." Love is not to be pursued to the neglect of everything else but in the interest of all else. The constant need is that everything be done out of love.

"Desire" (*zēloute*) is the same word which is translated "covet earnestly" in 12:31. It is proper and good to desire these spiritual gifts (12:8-10). They should be earnestly sought within the framework of love. Every believer is to be Spirit-filled; therefore, any Spirit-filled believer may manifest these spiritual gifts.

Paul emphasized prophecy because of the principle of edification. The Corinthians overemphasized tongues. Paul was showing the need for balance and edification.

14:2. Paul first explained the action and communion of tongues. There is adequate sound in "tongues," but there is not understanding. "Tongues" do not edify anyone else because no one can understand what is being said unless there is interpretation or, as occasionally happens, the "tongues" are in a foreign language understood by someone present. Only God understands.

"Not unto men" shows that, whatever the intention, the person speaking in tongues still speaks only to God. If there is no interpretation, and no one present understood the language, then only God understands. "In the spirit," on the basis of context and verses 14 and 15, may refer to the believer's spirit which is quickened and sanctified by the Holy Spirit. It is possible to speak "in the spirit" without the aid of the understanding. The public assembly is not the place for such "private" communion, unless the gift of interpretation is operating to produce edification.

14:3,4. Prophecy will result in edification. Its results are noted. "Comfort" touches sorrow and fear and is found only here in the New Testament. "Exhortation" refers to duty, and "edification" to knowledge, character, and progress of the Church.

"Tongues" in prayer and praise bring personal edification and therefore have value for the individual, but prophecy edifies to a greater extent because it edifies the whole church.

Speaking in a tongue is edifying to the speaker himself, because it is an exercise of his spirit with the Holy Spirit, Godward. It adds a new dimension to one's devotional life. Prophecy has a larger effect, because it reaches a larger audience.

14:5. In this verse Paul summarized what he had said by establishing the good of tongues but the greater good of prophecy.

1. Follow after charity: Labour for loue, *Cranmer* . . . Be eager in your pursuit, *Weymouth* . . . Make love your aim, *Moffatt*.
and desire spiritual [gifts]: . . . nevertheless, be envious, *Rotherham* . . . be zealous for spiritual endowments, *Concordant* . . . earnestly pursue spiritual things, *Rheims* . . . and then set your heart on, *Moffatt* . . . mental powers, *Fenton*.
but rather that ye may prophesy: . . . but most chefly, *Cranmer* . . . especially those enabling you to instruct, *Fenton* . . . but let it be chiefly so in order that you may prophesy, *Weymouth*.

2. For he that speaketh in an [unknown] tongue speaketh not unto men:
but unto God: for no man understandeth [him]: . . . addresses God not men, *Moffatt* . . . for no man heareth, *Rheims* . . . for no one is listening, *Rotherham*.
howbeit in the spirit he speaketh mysteries: . . . he speaketh secret things, *Geneva* . . . he is speaking secrets, *Concordant*.

3. But he that prophesieth: On the other hand, *Moffatt* . . . but the preacher, *Fenton*.
speaketh unto men [to] edification:
and exhortation, and comfort: . . . encouragement, *Weymouth* . . . and consolation and comfort, *Concordant* . . . encourage, and console them, *Moffatt*.

4. He that speaketh in an [unknown] tongue edifieth himself: The linguist instructs himself, *Fenton* . . . speaketh strange langage, *Geneva* . . . is building up, *Rotherham* . . . does good to himself, *Weymouth*.
but he that prophesieth edifieth the church: . . . the congregacion, *Tyndale* . . . instructs the assembly, *Fenton* . . . does good to the church, *Weymouth*.

5. I would that ye all spake with tongues: I want you all, *Concordant*.
but rather that ye prophesied: . . . but I would prefer you, *Moffatt*.

5.a.Txt: 01ℵ-corr,06D 018K,020L,byz.
Var: 01ℵ-org,02A,03B 025P,bo.Lach,Treg,Alf Tisc,We/Ho,Weis,Sod UBS/✶

3157.2 adj comp nom sing	1056.1 conj	1156.2 conj	3450.5 art sing masc	4253.4 verb nom sing masc part pres act	2211.1 conj
μείζων	ʹ γὰρ	[ᵃ✶ δὲ]	ὁ	προφητεύων	ἢ
meizōn	*gar*	*de*	*ho*	*prophēteuōn*	*ē*
greater	for	[and]	the	prophesying	than

3450.5 art sing masc	2953.12 verb nom sing masc part pres act	1094.7 noun dat pl fem	1609.1 prep gen	1479.1 conj	3231.1 partic
ὁ	λαλῶν	γλώσσαις,	ἐκτὸς	εἰ	μὴ
ho	*lalōn*	*glōssais*	*ektos*	*ei*	*mē*
the	speaking	with tongues,	except	if	not

1323.2 verb 3sing subj pres act	2419.1 conj	3450.9 art nom sing fem	1564.2 noun nom sing fem	3482.3 noun acc sing fem
διερμηνεύῃ,	ἵνα	ἡ	ἐκκλησία	οἰκοδομὴν
diermēneuē	*hina*	*hē*	*ekklēsia*	*oikodomēn*
he should interpret,	that	the	assembly	building up

2956.18 verb 3sing subj aor act		3432.1 adv	3431.1 adv	1156.2 conj	79.6 noun pl masc	1430.1 partic
λάβῃ.	6. ʹ	Νυνὶ	[✶ Νῦν]	δέ,	ἀδελφοί,	ἐὰν
labē		*Nuni*	*Nun*	*de*	*adelphoi*	*ean*
may receive.		Now	[idem]	and,	brothers,	if

2048.6 verb 1sing subj aor act	4242.1 prep	5050.4 prs-pron acc 2pl	1094.7 noun dat pl fem	2953.12 verb nom sing masc part pres act	4949.9 intr-pron sing neu
ἔλθω	πρὸς	ὑμᾶς	γλώσσαις	λαλῶν,	τί
elthō	*pros*	*humas*	*glōssais*	*lalōn*	*ti*
I come	to	you	in tongues	speaking,	what

5050.4 prs-pron acc 2pl	5456.4 verb 1sing indic fut act	1430.1 partic	3231.1 partic	5050.3 prs-pron dat 2pl	2953.25 verb 1sing act
ὑμᾶς	ὠφελήσω,	ἐὰν	μὴ	ὑμῖν	λαλήσω
humas	*ōphelēsō*	*ean*	*mē*	*humin*	*lalēsō*
you	shall I benefit,	if	not	to you	I shall speak

2211.1 conj	1706.1 prep	597.3 noun dat sing fem	2211.1 conj	1706.1 prep	1102.3 noun dat sing fem	2211.1 conj
ἢ	ἐν	ἀποκαλύψει,	ἢ	ἐν	γνώσει,	ἢ
ē	*en*	*apokalupsei*	*ē*	*en*	*gnōsei*	*ē*
either	in	revelation,	or	in	knowledge,	or

6.a.Txt: 01ℵ-corr,02A 03B,06D-corr,018K 020L,025P,byz.We/Ho Sod
Var: 01ℵ-org,06D-org Tisc,Weis,UBS/✶

1706.1 prep	4252.3 noun dat sing fem	2211.1 conj	1706.1 prep	1316.3 noun dat sing fem	3539.1 adv	3450.17 art pl neu
ἐν	προφητείᾳ,	ἢ	ʹᵃ ἐν ʹ	διδαχῇ;	7. ὅμως	τὰ
en	*prophēteia*	*ē*	*en*	*didachē*	*homōs*	*ta*
in	prophesy,	or	in	teaching?	Even	the

889.1 adj nom pl neu	5292.4 noun acc sing fem	1319.8 verb acc sing masc part pres act	1521.1 conj	830.1 noun nom sing masc
ἄψυχα	φωνὴν	διδόντα,	εἴτε	αὐλὸς
apsucha	*phōnēn*	*didonta*	*eite*	*aulos*
lifeless things	a sound	giving,	whether	flute

1521.1 conj	2760.1 noun nom sing fem	1430.1 partic	1287.2 noun acc sing fem	3450.4 art dat pl	5190.2 noun dat pl masc	3231.1 partic
εἴτε	κιθάρα,	ἐὰν	διαστολὴν	τοῖς	φθόγγοις	μὴ
eite	*kithara*	*ean*	*diastolēn*	*tois*	*phthongois*	*mē*
or	harp,	if	distinction	to the	sounds	not

1319.19 verb 3sing subj aor act	4316.1 adv	1091.49 verb 3sing indic fut pass	3450.16 art sing neu	826.2 verb nom sing neu part pres pass	2211.1 conj
δῷ,	πῶς	γνωσθήσεται	τὸ	αὐλούμενον	ἢ
dō	*pōs*	*gnōsthēsetai*	*to*	*auloumenon*	*ē*
gives,	how	shall be known	the	being piped	or

Prophecy, or the combination of tongues and interpretation, edifies the Church because it is an understandable message.

In doing this, Paul adds another reason for the excellence of prophecy. The one who prophesies, giving a message that can be understood, is of greater value to the Church than the speaker in tongues, unless there is an interpretation. Tongues plus interpretation accomplishes in two steps what prophecy accomplishes in one. In that case, they are on equal footing, for the same end is accomplished: edification for the body of gathered believers.

A general principle is clear: The gifts of the Spirit are intended for the edification of the members of the body of Christ.

14:6. Paul used a series of illustrations to show the profit provided to the Church by understandable words and messages. He referred to those gifts that carry clear messages. Paul was not depreciating the value of "tongues," but placing it in proper perspective.

The term "brethren" indicates his close relationship and feelings for the Corinthian believers.

Paul used himself as an illustration. If he came to them ministering by "speaking with tongues" it would be impossible for the congregation to understand the message (except by interpretation); therefore, it would be profitless to the church body. What help would he be if he brought a sound that could not be understood?

Paul was speaking about four ways a minister could convey truth: revelation, knowledge, prophesying, and doctrine. These had been demonstrated in his own ministry. Paul's use of *revelation* (*apokalupsei*) varied considerably depending on the context. Frequently it refers to the end times and Christ's coming (Romans 2:5; 8:19; 1 Corinthians 1:7; 2 Thessalonians 1:7), but it can also refer to the gospel of preaching Christ (Romans 16:25), or to visions (2 Corinthians 12:1,7). Whichever of these possibilities might be in mind here, the coupling of revelation with teaching suggests that this revelation must be taught and understood. In 2:10-12 he had referred to the revelation and knowledge he had received from the Lord. He had also ministered prophetically and in doctrine. However, all these had come to the Corinthians in intelligible speech, so all could profit. Again Paul was emphasizing that tongues that are not understood are unprofitable to those who hear.

14:7. Paul used another illustration, this time from the inanimate world of music. "Pipe" (*aulos*) is a flute and represents the wind instruments. "Harp" (*kithara*), from which we get *guitar*, represents the stringed instruments (Morris, *Tyndale New Testament Commentaries*, 7:192). Music rightly presented will speak to the very heart of man. But for this to happen, there must be a variety and balance of harmony, expression, and chord.

Without purpose, balance, and clear expression, there is mere noise—aimless, profitless jangle. Sound and speech must communicate meaning and message in an understandable, receivable way.

for greater [is] he that prophesieth than he that speaketh with tongues: ... the preacher is greater than the linguist, *Fenton* ... the man who prophesies is superior, *Weymouth*.

except he interpret, that the church may receive edifying: ... vnlesse perhaps he interpret, *Rheims, Douay* ... except he expound it also, *Geneva* ... unless, indeed, the latter adds a running interpretation, *Way* ... in order that the church may get a blessing, *Weymouth* ... that the assembly may receive edification, *Sawyer* ... may receive instruction, *Fenton* ... may benefit by being built up, *Adams* ... he edifieth the church, *Murdock*.

6. Now, brethren, if I come unto you speaking with tongues: ... if I should come among you, *Murdock* ... should I apply myself to you in a tongue you knew not, *Locke* ... speaking foreign languages, *Fenton*.

what shall I profit you, except I shall speak to you either by revelation: ... what shall I be benefiting you, *Concordant* ... if the utterance is neither, *Weymouth* ... what good could I do you, *Moffatt* ... unless I can communicate to you, *Adams*.

or by knowledge, or by prophesying, or by doctrine?: ... ether in techinge, *Wyclif* ... or science, or in a sermon, *Fenton* ... no inspired address, no exposition? *Way*.

7. And even things without life giving sound, whether pipe or harp: ... if lifeless instruments, *Montgomery* ... So of irrational objects making a sound, *Sawyer* ... Inanimate instruments...the flute, *Moffatt* ... soulless things, *Concordant* ... when yielding a sound, *Weymouth*.

except they give a distinction in the sounds: ... if they make no distinction between one sound and another, *Murdock* ... a distinction in the notes, *Rotherham* ... a distinction to the utterances, *Concordant*.

how shall it be known what is piped or harped?: ... how shall it be ascertained, *Rotherham* ... whereby the tune and composure are understood, *Locke*.

1 Corinthians 14:8

3450.16 art sing neu	2761.2 verb nom sing neu part pres pass	2504.1 conj	1056.1 conj	1430.1 partic	81.1 adj acc sing fem
τὸ	κιθαριζόμενον;	8. καὶ	γὰρ	ἐὰν	ἄδηλον
to	kitharizomenon	kai	gar	ean	adēlon
the	being harped?	Also	for	if	an uncertain

5292.4 noun acc sing fem	4393.1 noun nom sing fem	4393.1 noun nom sing fem	5292.4 noun acc sing fem	1319.19 verb 3sing subj aor act
φωνὴν	σάλπιγξ	[☆ σάλπιγξ	φωνὴν]	δῷ,
phōnēn	salpinx	salpinx	phōnēn	dō
sound	a trumpet	[a trumpet	sound]	gives,

4949.3 intr-pron nom sing	3764.4 verb 3sing indic fut mid	1519.1 prep	4031.3 noun acc sing masc	3643.1 adv
τίς	παρασκευάσεται	εἰς	πόλεμον;	9. οὕτως
tis	paraskeuasetai	eis	polemon	houtōs
who	shall prepare himself	for	war?	So

2504.1 conj	5050.1 prs-pron nom 2pl	1217.2 prep	3450.10 art gen sing fem	1094.2 noun gen sing fem	1430.1 partic	3231.1 partic
καὶ	ὑμεῖς	διὰ	τῆς	γλώσσης	ἐὰν	μὴ
kai	humeis	dia	tēs	glōssēs	ean	mē
also	you,	by means	of the	tongue	if	not

2135.1 adj acc sing masc	3030.4 noun acc sing masc	1319.22 verb 2pl subj aor act	4316.1 adv	1091.49 verb 3sing indic fut pass
εὔσημον	λόγον	δῶτε,	πῶς	γνωσθήσεται
eusēmon	logon	dōte	pōs	gnōsthēsetai
an intelligible	speech	you give,	how	shall be known

3450.16 art sing neu	2953.48 verb sing part pres pass	1498.42 verb 2pl indic fut mid	1056.1 conj	1519.1 prep	108.3 noun acc sing masc
τὸ	λαλούμενον;	ἔσεσθε	γὰρ	εἰς	ἀέρα
to	laloumenon	esesthe	gar	eis	aera
the	being spoken?	you will be	for	into	air

2953.16 verb nom pl masc part pres act	4965.9 dem-pron pl neu	1479.1 conj	5018.4 verb 3sing opt aor act	1079.4 noun pl neu
λαλοῦντες.	10. Τοσαῦτα,	εἰ	τύχοι,	γένη
lalountes	Tosauta	ei	tuchoi	genē
speaking.	So many,	if	may be,	kinds

10.a.Txt: 018K,020L,byz.
Var: 01ℵ,02A,03B,06D 025P,Lach,Treg,Alf Word,Tisc,We/Ho,Weis Sod,UBS/☆

5292.6 noun gen pl fem	1498.4 verb 3sing indic pres act	1498.7 verb 3pl indic pres act	1706.1 prep	2862.3 noun dat sing masc	2504.1 conj
φωνῶν	ἐστιν	[ᵃ☆ εἰσιν]	ἐν	κόσμῳ,	καὶ
phōnōn	estin	eisin	en	kosmō	kai
of sounds	there is	[there are]	in	world,	and

10.b.Txt: 01ℵ-corr 06D-corr,018K,020L byz.
Var: 01ℵ-org,02A,03B 06D-org,025P,33,sa.bo. Lach,Treg,Alf,Word Tisc,We/Ho,Weis,Sod UBS/☆

3625.6 num card neu	840.1 prs-pron gen pl	873.2 adj nom sing neu	1430.1 partic	3631.1 conj
οὐδὲν	ᵇ αὐτῶν	ἄφωνον·	11. ἐὰν	οὖν
ouden	autōn	aphōnon	ean	oun
none	of them	without sound.	If	therefore

3231.1 partic	3471.14 verb 1sing subj perf act	3450.12 art acc sing fem	1405.4 noun acc sing fem	3450.10 art gen sing fem	5292.2 noun gen sing fem
μὴ	εἰδῶ	τὴν	δύναμιν	τῆς	φωνῆς,
mē	eidō	tēn	dunamin	tēs	phōnēs
not	I know	the	power	of the	sound,

1498.38 verb 1sing indic fut mid	3450.3 art dat sing	2953.14 verb dat sing masc part pres act	910.1 adj nom sing masc	2504.1 conj	3450.5 art sing masc
ἔσομαι	τῷ	λαλοῦντι	βάρβαρος·	καὶ	ὁ
esomai	tō	lalounti	barbaros	kai	ho
I shall be	to the	speaking	a barbarian;	and	the

14:8. From the inanimate world Paul also drew the illustration of the battle trumpet. One melody was for reveille, another for taps, another for advance in battle, another for retreat.

If there was no clear distinction in sound, the troops would not understand nor react in the proper manner. Then who would prepare for the battle? The answer is no one.

14:9. From the living world, Paul used yet another illustration and applied it directly to the situation at Corinth. "Likewise ye" means "take a lesson here"; understand and apply it. "By the tongue" appears to refer to the physical tongue, setting this verse in marked contrast to the inanimate realm of verses 7 and 8. What is true of the inanimate is true to a larger degree of the human tongue: it articulates as it is directed.

This was the problem at Corinth. The "words" had no meaning; they were not "intelligible" (RSV). They were like one speaking "into the air." This proverbial expression noted ineffectiveness and profitlessness.

14:10. In his last illustration, Paul summarized all he had been saying. He drew from the widest possible source: "in the world." There are many hundreds of languages and many dialects within general language groups. There are a multitude of sounds in the world. None of them is without "signification." Paul asserted that each voice carries the real nature of a voice. In other words, the sounds mean something to somebody.

14:11. There must be an existing understanding between speaker and listener, or each will view the other as a "barbarian." "Meaning" (*dunamin*) has the idea of "force" or "power."

Speech is a persuasive and communicative force. But speech that is not understood is powerless, futile, and useless. The listener may hear, but try as he may he cannot understand. The speaker may repeat his message, but he cannot make his listener understand.

It is as Paul wrote in 14:2, "He speaketh mysteries." The result is that each considers the other a "barbarian." The Greeks divided the world into Greeks and barbarians. While Paul had in mind primarily unintelligent speech and the lack of communication, the fuller sense of the term "barbarian" (*barbaros*), one beyond the limits of civilization, was implied. In such a case, nothing profitable or edifying could be accomplished. What a tragic ending to something filled with promise and value.

The one clear conclusion is that something unintelligible should not be part of public worship. What is done, whether prophecy or tongues and interpretation, must be of more than personal value; it must profit the whole body of Christ.

8. For if the trumpet give an uncertain sound: . . . should be giving a dubious sound, *Concordant* . . . sounds indistinct, *Moffatt.*

who shall prepare himself to the battle?: . . . what soldier will be prepared for battle? *Montgomery* . . . to the warre? *Cranmer* . . . who shal prepare him selfe to fyght? *Geneva.*

9. So likewise ye, except ye utter by the tongue words easy to be understood: . . . unless you produce an intelligible speech, *Fenton* . . . if you should not be giving an intelligible expression, *Concordant* . . . except ye speake wordes that haue signification, *Geneva* . . . ye give intelligible discourse, *Rotherham* . . . you fail to utter intelligible words, *Weymouth* . . . if ye utter a discourse, *Murdock* . . . that is readily understood, *Moffatt.*

how shall it be known what is spoken?: . . . how can people make out what you say? *Moffatt.*

for ye shall speak into the air: . . . for ye schuln be spekynge in veyn, *Wyclif* . . . You will be talking to the winds, *Weymouth.*

10. There are, it may be, so many kinds of voices in the world: . . . let us say, *Montgomery* . . . we will suppose, a great number of languages, *Weymouth* . . . so many species of sounds in the world, *Concordant* . . . many kinds of language in the world, *Moffatt.*

and none of them [is] without signification: . . . and no creature is without a language, *Weymouth* . . . and none meaningless, *Fenton* . . . and not one unspoken, *Rotherham* . . . without distinct pronunciation, *PNT.*

11. Therefore if I know not the meaning of the voice: . . . the meaning of the particular language, *Weymouth* . . . I do not know the force of the expression, *Montgomery* . . . if I do not know the import of the sound, *Murdock.*

I shall be unto him that speaketh a barbarian: . . . to be talking gibberish, *Moffatt.*

1 Corinthians 14:12

2953.12 verb nom sing masc part pres act
λαλῶν,
lalōn
speaking,

1706.1 prep
ἐν
en
for

1466.5 prs-pron dat 1sing
ἐμοὶ
emoi
me

910.1 adj nom sing masc
βάρβαρος·
barbaros
a barbarian.

3643.1 adv
12. οὕτως
houtōs
So

2504.1 conj
καὶ
kai
also

5050.1 prs-pron nom 2pl
ὑμεῖς,
humeis
you,

1878.1 conj
ἐπεὶ
epei
since

2190.3 noun nom pl masc
ζηλωταί
zēlōtai
eager

1498.6 verb 2pl indic pres act
ἐστε
este
you are

4011.5 noun gen pl neu
πνευμάτων,
pneumatōn
of spiritual things,

4242.1 prep
πρὸς
pros
for

3450.12 art acc sing fem
τὴν
tēn
the

3482.3 noun acc sing fem
οἰκοδομὴν
oikodomēn
building up

3450.10 art gen sing fem
τῆς
tēs
of the

1564.1 noun fem
ἐκκλησίας
ekklēsias
assembly

13.a.**Txt:** 01ℵ-corr,018K
020L,byz.Sod
Var: 01ℵ-org,02A,03B
06D,025P,33,Lach,Treg
Alf,Tisc,We/Ho,Weis
UBS/★

2195.1 verb 2pl pres act
ζητεῖτε
zēteite
seek

2419.1 conj
ἵνα
hina
that

3915.7 verb 2pl subj pres act
περισσεύητε.
perisseuēte
you may abound.

1349.1 conj
13. ⸀ Διόπερ
Dioper
Wherefore

1346.1 conj
[ᵃ★ διὸ]
dio
[idem]

3450.5 art sing masc
ὁ
ho
the

2953.12 verb nom sing masc part pres act
λαλῶν
lalōn
speaking

1094.3 noun dat sing fem
γλώσσῃ,
glōssē
with a tongue,

4195.9 verb 3sing impr pres
προσευχέσθω
proseuchesthō
let him pray

2419.1 conj
ἵνα
hina
that

1323.2 verb 3sing subj pres act
διερμηνεύῃ.
diermēneuē
he may interpret.

1430.1 partic
14. ἐὰν
ean
If

1056.1 conj
γὰρ
gar
for

4195.6 verb 1sing subj pres
προσεύχωμαι
proseuchōmai
I pray

1094.3 noun dat sing fem
γλώσσῃ,
glōssē
with a tongue,

3450.16 art sing neu
τὸ
to
the

4011.1 noun sing neu
πνεῦμά
pneuma
spirit

1466.2 prs-pron gen 1sing
μου
mou
my

4195.3 verb 3sing indic pres
προσεύχεται,
proseuchetai
prays,

3450.5 art sing masc
ὁ
ho
the

1156.2 conj
δὲ
de
but

3426.1 noun nom sing masc
νοῦς
nous
understanding

1466.2 prs-pron gen 1sing
μου
mou
my

173.1 adj nom sing masc
ἄκαρπός
akarpos
unfruitful

1498.4 verb 3sing indic pres act
ἐστιν.
estin
is.

4949.9 intr-pron sing neu
15. τί
ti
What

3631.1 conj
οὖν
oun
then

1498.4 verb 3sing indic pres act
ἐστιν;
estin
is it?

4195.27 verb 1sing indic fut mid
προσεύξομαι
proseuxomai
I will pray

3450.3 art dat sing
τῷ
tō
in the

4011.3 noun dat sing neu
πνεύματι,
pneumati
Spirit,

4195.27 verb 1sing indic fut mid
προσεύξομαι
proseuxomai
I will pray.

1156.2 conj
δὲ
de
but

2504.1 conj
καὶ
kai
also

3450.3 art dat sing
τῷ
tō
with the

3426.3 noun dat sing masc
νοΐ·
noi
understanding.

5402.3 verb 1sing indic fut act
ψαλῶ
psalō
I will sing praise

3450.3 art dat sing
τῷ
tō
in the

4011.3 noun dat sing neu
πνεύματι,
pneumati
Spirit,

5402.3 verb 1sing indic fut act
ψαλῶ
psalō
I will sing praise

1156.2 conj
δὲ
de
but

2504.1 conj
καὶ
kai
also

3450.3 art dat sing
τῷ
tō
with the

14:12. The application was made to the Corinthians. "Even so ye" indicated the need to understand and apply these instructions to their situation. The Corinthians coveted spiritual gifts; they were zealous and desirous of such, which was good as long as their aim was the profit of others. From his heart, Paul exhorted the Corinthians, who sometimes acted out of selfish motives, to excel in the gifts of the Spirit for the edification of believers.

Verse 12 is a reminder that chapter 13 presents not so much an abstract treatise on love, but the way in which individual Christians are to exercise their gifts. Paul encouraged the Corinthians to seek spiritual gifts, but only insofar as they were used in love to edify the body, rather than as a means of exulting in their own private, self-serving gifts.

14:13. Paul next dealt with the use of tongues. If the church body was to be edified by an "unknown" tongue, they must understand what was said. Therefore, the admonition was for the person who spoke in tongues to pray for the interpretation.

These spiritual gifts are not static. A man who is used in the gift of tongues may also be used in another gift, such as interpretation. To this end he should pray.

14:14. This verse explains further why one should pray to interpret what he has said in a tongue. At the same time, Paul established the need for understanding and the place of tongues and prophecy.

"Spirit" (*pneuma*) refers to a man's spirit. It is contrasted with "understanding." Normally man works through his understanding. But with the gift of tongues this is not so. And this is where the problem arises. One's "spirit" does not communicate the clear messages with another's spirit that one's "understanding" does with another's understanding. Now he that prays and speaks in a tongue does well, but because the interpretation is not given it is comprehensible to no one else. Paul was not presenting man's spirit and understanding as opposed to each other. God works with men by either avenue. The point is that it is necessary to recognize the proper place of each.

14:15. How does the matter stand? Paul answered the question by calling attention to two activities: praying and singing. The singing is of praise to God, perhaps even using some of the psalms. Paul indicated he would pray and sing "with the spirit" and "with the understanding." Paul recognized both the gift of tongues and the value of understandable speech. His motive was to edify the body of Christ. In this context, that meant he would interpret his "tongue" in a public gathering.

and he that speaketh [shall be] a barbarian unto me: . . . a foreigner to me, *Fenton, Adams* . . . is all gibberish to me, *Locke* . . . will seem a mere jargon to me, *Way.*

12. Even so ye, forasmuch as ye are zealous of spiritual [gifts]: . . . ye are envious of spirits, *Rotherham* . . . you are ambitious for spiritual gifts, *Weymouth.*

seek that ye may excel to the edifying of the church: . . . try to proceed so as to promote, *Fenton* . . . that you may be superabounding to, *Concordant* . . . be zealous to abound in what builds up the church, *Adams* . . . make the edification of the church your aim, *Moffatt* . . . so as to benefit the church, *Weymouth* . . . of the congregacion, *Tyndale.*

13. Wherefore let him that speaketh in an [unknown] tongue pray that he may interpret: . . . pray for the power of interpreting them, *Weymouth* . . . ask God to enable him to give a concurrent interpretation, *Way.*

14. For if I pray in an [unknown] tongue:
my spirit prayeth: . . . my spirit is praying, *Concordant* . . . my spirit, it is true, accompanies my words, *Locke.*
but my understanding is unfruitful: . . . yet my mind is unfruitful, *Concordant* . . . my meaning is unintelligible, *Fenton* . . . but my mind is no use to anyone, *Moffatt* . . . is barren, *Weymouth, Montgomery* . . . is without fruit, *Douay.*

15. What is it then?: How then does the matter stand? *Weymouth* . . . What is the answer to the problem? *Adams.*
I will pray with the spirit, and I will pray with the understanding also: I may pray, *Fenton* . . . with my mind, *Moffatt.*
I will sing with the spirit, and I will sing with the understanding also: I will sing in the Spirit's rapture, *Way* . . . sing praise with my mind, *Moffatt* . . . will I be playing music, *Concordant.*

1 Corinthians 14:16

16.a.Txt: 018K,020L,byz.
Var: 01א,02A,03B,06D
025P,33,Lach,Treg,Alf
Tisc,We/Ho,Weis,Sod
UBS/✶

16.b.Var: 01א-corr,03B
06D,025P,sa.bo.We/Ho
Weis,Sod,UBS/✶

16.c.Txt: 018K,020L,byz.
Var: 01א,02A,03B,06D
025P,33,Lach,Treg,Alf
Tisc,We/Ho,Weis,Sod
UBS/✶

3426.3 noun dat sing masc	1878.1 conj	1430.1 partic	2108.8 verb 2sing subj aor act	2108.18 verb 2sing subj pres act
νοῖ.	16. ἐπεὶ	ἐὰν	ʽ εὐλογήσῃς	[a☆ εὐλογῇς
noi	epei	ean	eulogēsēs	eulogēs
understanding.	Else	if	you bless	[idem]

1706.1 prep	3450.3 art dat sing	4011.3 noun dat sing neu	3450.5 art sing masc	376.1 verb nom sing masc part pres act
[b☆+ ἐν]	ʽc τῷ	πνεύματι,	ὁ	ἀναπληρῶν
en	tō	pneumati	ho	anaplērōn
[in]	with the	spirit,	the	occupying

3450.6 art acc sing masc	4964.4 noun acc sing masc	3450.2 art gen sing	2376.2 noun gen sing masc	4316.1 adv	2029.11 verb 3sing indic fut act
τὸν	τόπον	τοῦ	ἰδιώτου	πῶς	ἐρεῖ
ton	topon	tou	idiōtou	pōs	erei
the	place	of the	uninstructed	how	shall he say

3450.16 art sing neu	279.1 partic	1894.3 prep	3450.11 art dat sing fem	4528.6 adj dat 2sing fem	2150.3 noun dat sing fem
τὸ	Ἀμήν	ἐπὶ	τῇ	σῇ	εὐχαριστίᾳ,
to	Amēn	epi	tē	sē	eucharistia
the	Amen	at	the	you	giving of thanks,

1879.1 conj	4949.9 intr-pron sing neu	2978.4 verb 2sing indic pres act	3620.2 partic	3471.4 verb 3sing indic perf act	4622.1 prs-pron nom 2sing
ἐπειδὴ	τί	λέγεις	οὐκ	οἶδεν;	17. σὺ
epeidē	ti	legeis	ouk	oiden	su
since	what	you say	not	he knows?	You

3173.1 conj	1056.1 conj	2544.1 adv	2149.2 verb 2sing indic pres act	233.1 conj	3450.5 art sing masc	2066.5 adj nom sing masc
μὲν	γὰρ	καλῶς	εὐχαριστεῖς,	ἀλλ'	ὁ	ἕτερος
men	gar	kalōs	eucharisteis	all'	ho	heteros
for		well	give thanks,	but	the	other

3620.2 partic	3481.15 verb 3sing indic pres pass	2149.1 verb 1sing indic pres act	3450.3 art dat sing	2296.3 noun dat sing masc
οὐκ	οἰκοδομεῖται.	18. εὐχαριστῶ	τῷ	θεῷ
ouk	oikodomeitai	eucharistō	tō	theō
not	is being built up.	I thank		God

18.a.Txt: 018K,020L,byz.
Var: 01א,02A,03B,06D
025P,33,Gries,Lach
Treg,Alf,Word,Tisc
We/Ho,Weis,Sod
UBS/✶

1466.2 prs-pron gen 1sing	3820.4 adj gen pl	5050.2 prs-pron gen 2pl	3095.1 adv comp	1094.7 noun dat pl fem
ʽa μου, ʼ	πάντων	ὑμῶν	μᾶλλον	γλώσσαις
mou	pantōn	humōn	mallon	glōssais
my,	all	of you	more	in tongues

18.b.Txt: 018K,020L,byz.
Var: 01א,03B,06D,025P
33,Lach,Treg,Alf,Tisc
We/Ho,Weis,Sod
UBS/✶

2953.12 verb nom sing masc part pres act	2953.1 verb 1sing pres act	233.1 conj	233.2 conj	1706.1 prep
ʽ λαλῶν·	[b☆ λαλῶ·]	19. ʽ ἀλλ'	[☆ ἀλλὰ]	ἐν
lalōn	lalō	all'	alla	en
speaking;	[I speak;]	but	[idem]	in

1564.3 noun dat sing fem	2286.1 verb 1sing pres act	3864.1 num card	3030.8 noun acc pl masc	1217.2 prep	3450.2 art gen sing
ἐκκλησίᾳ	θέλω	πέντε	λόγους	διὰ	τοῦ
ekklēsia	thelō	pente	logous	dia	tou
assembly	I desire	five	words	with	the

19.a.Txt: 018K,020L
048,byz.Sod
Var: p46,01א,02A,03B
06D,025P,044,33,Lach
Treg,Alf,Word,Tisc
We/Ho,Weis,UBS/✶

3426.2 noun gen sing masc	3450.3 art dat sing	3426.3 noun dat sing masc	1466.2 prs-pron gen 1sing	2953.37 verb inf aor act
νοός	[a☆ τῷ	νοῖ]	μου	λαλῆσαι,
noos	tō	noi	mou	lalēsai
understanding	[with the	understanding]	my	to speak,

14:16. "Unlearned" (*idiōtou*) denotes a private individual, a layman, not necessarily a non-Christian, but one who is unskilled or ignorant in these matters. This word was used in some pagan associations to denote nonmembers who were allowed to participate in the sacrifices. Clearly, whether a non-Christian or an unlearned believer, this one was unlearned and unable to participate in the same way as mature believers.

Those who maintain that the *idiōtēs* of this verse is the same as the *idiōtēs* of verse 23, and therefore an unbeliever, argue that Paul had in view a proselyte or a catechumen (cf. *BAGD*, "idiōtēs"). It is true in the following centuries the Church had a special place for nonbaptized converts, but this kind of specialized meaning is highly unlikely for the situation of the Church in A.D. 54.

Another drawback to understanding *idiōtēs* in this instance is that the context is concerned with the edification of the church body. Since Paul was concerned that the *idiōtēs* be edified, the *idiōtēs* must be part of the Body.

The expression *ho anaplērōn ton topon*, "he that occupieth the room of," should be understood as "the one who fills the role" or "the one who takes the place of." Paul, therefore, was suggesting to those involved in the gift of tongues that they put themselves in the place of someone unlearned in the operations of the Spirit in worship. By doing so, they would realize that by not being interpreted their utterances would be unintelligible, and therefore unedifying, to outsiders.

By not understanding the utterance of tongues, an *idiōtēs* would be unable to respond with "Amen," the customary response to a prayer in both Jewish synagogue services and Christian worship services. Deuteronomy 27:14-26 contains an example of a communal "amen" said after individual prayers of blessing and curse. In the New Testament "amen" occurs frequently in places of praise and doxology (e.g., Romans 11:36).

He could not say "Amen" to the blessing of the Spirit because he could not understand it. By such an "Amen," the worshiper made another's prayer his own; assent is given. Others would have the same problem, but special concern was expressed for "the unlearned."

14:17. There was nothing wrong with the prayer in relationship to God. Praising God or praying in other tongues provides a special liberty of expression. "Thou . . . givest thanks well." The problem was that there was no edification. The person listening did not profit because there was no understanding on his part.

14:18,19. Paul restressed the place of tongues and prophecy and their relationship. He used the first person singular. Speaking in tongues was widespread at Corinth. Yet Paul acknowledged that he exercised it to an even greater extent. Far from decrying it, he thanked God for it because it comes by the Holy Spirit for the aid

16. Else when thou shalt bless with the spirit: Otherwise...in spirit only, *Weymouth* . . . If you bless God in spirit only, *TCNT* . . . if you pronounce a blessing in the Spirit, *Norlie* . . . by the impulse of the Spirit, *Locke*.

how shall he that occupieth the room of the unlearned say Amen at thy giving of thanks: . . . how can one of an uneducated condition express his assent, *Fenton* . . . how is the outsider to say, *Moffatt* . . . how is he who occupies the position of the uninspired to add his 'Amen!' *Way* . . . how shall he that holdeth the place of the unlearned say, Amen, to thy blessing? *Douay* . . . who is filling up the place of a plain person, *Concordant* . . . who is in the position of being ungifted, *Adams* . . . how can those in the congregation who are without your gift say, *TCNT*.

seeing he understandeth not what thou sayest?: . . . he is not aware, *Concordant* . . . since he knows not what you say? *Sawyer.*

17. For thou verily givest thanks well: Thou blessest, indeed, very well, *Murdock* . . . Your thanksgiving may be excellent, *TCNT* . . . It is well enough for you to give thanks that way, *Norlie* . . . appropriately enough, *Adams.*

but the other is not edified: . . . but it is of no value to the man who cannot understand you, *Norlie* . . . and yet your neighbour is not benefited, *Weymouth* . . . but others are not helped by it, *TCNT.*

18. I thank my God: Thank God, *TCNT* . . . I am thankful to God, *Norlie.*

I speak with tongues more than ye all: I am a better linguist, *Fenton* . . . I use the gift of 'tongues,' *TCNT* . . . that I speak in more languages than all of you, *Adams* . . . with all your tongues, *Douay* . . . in an [unknown] tongue, *Noyes.*

19. Yet in the church I had rather speak five words with my understanding: Still, in public worship, *Norlie* . . . I would rather speak five words intelligently, *TCNT.*

1 Corinthians 14:20

2419.1 conj	2504.1 conj	241.8 adj acc pl masc	2697.2 verb 1sing subj aor act	2211.1 conj	3325.1 adj acc pl masc	3030.8 noun acc pl masc
ἵνα	καὶ	ἄλλους	κατηχήσω,	ἢ	μυρίους	λόγους
hina	kai	allous	katēchēsō,	ē	murious	logous
that	also	others	I may instruct,	than	ten thousand	words

1706.1 prep	1094.3 noun dat sing fem		79.6 noun pl masc	3231.1 partic	3676.3 noun pl masc	1090.19 verb 2pl impr pres
ἐν	γλώσσῃ.	**20.** Ἀδελφοί,		μὴ	παιδία	γίνεσθε
en	glōssē.	Adelphoi,		mē	paidia	ginesthe
in	a tongue.	Brothers,		not	children	be

3450.14 art dat pl fem	5260.1 noun dat pl fem	233.2 conj	3450.11 art dat sing fem	2520.3 noun dat sing fem	3377.1 verb 2pl impr pres act
ταῖς	φρεσίν·	ἀλλὰ	τῇ	κακίᾳ	νηπιάζετε,
tais	phresin	alla	tē	kakia	nēpiazete,
in the	minds,	but	in the	malice	be babes;

3450.14 art dat pl fem	1156.2 conj	5260.1 noun dat pl fem	4894.3 adj nom pl masc	1090.19 verb 2pl impr pres	1706.1 prep	3450.3 art dat sing
ταῖς	δὲ	φρεσὶν	τέλειοι	γίνεσθε.	**21.** ἐν	τῷ
tais	de	phresin	teleioi	ginesthe.	en	tō
in the	but	minds	mature	be.	In	the

3414.3 noun dat sing masc	1119.22 verb 3sing indic perf pass	3617.1 conj	1706.1 prep	2063.1 adj dat pl masc
νόμῳ	γέγραπται,	Ὅτι	ἐν	ἑτερογλώσσοις,
nomō	gegraptai,	Hoti	en	heteroglōssois,
law	it has been written,	By	other tongues,	

2504.1 conj	1706.1 prep	5327.3 noun dat pl neu	2066.4 adj dat pl	2066.3 adj gen pl	2953.25 verb 1sing act
καὶ	ἐν	χείλεσιν	ʼ ἑτέροις,	[a☆ ἑτέρων]	λαλήσω
kai	en	cheilesin	heterois,	heterōn	lalēsō
and	by	lips	other	[of others]	I will speak

3450.3 art dat sing	2967.3 noun dat sing masc	3642.5 dem-pron dat sing masc	2504.1 conj	3624.2 adv	3643.1 adv
τῷ	λαῷ	τούτῳ,	καὶ	οὐδ'	οὕτως
tō	laō	toutō,	kai	oud'	houtōs
to the	people	this,	and	not even	thus

1508.4 verb 3pl indic fut mid	1466.2 prs-pron gen 1sing	2978.5 verb 3sing indic pres act	2935.1 noun nom sing masc	5452.1 conj
εἰσακούσονταί	μου,	λέγει	κύριος.	**22.** Ὥστε
eisakousontai	mou,	legei	kurios.	Hōste
will they hear	me,	says	Lord.	So that

3450.13 art pl fem	1094.5 noun nom pl fem	1519.1 prep	4447.1 noun sing neu	1498.7 verb 3pl indic pres act	3620.3 partic	3450.4 art dat pl
αἱ	γλῶσσαι	εἰς	σημεῖόν	εἰσιν,	οὐ	τοῖς
hai	glōssai	eis	sēmeion	eisin,	ou	tois
the	tongues	for	a sign	are,	not	to the

3961.3 verb dat pl masc part pres act	233.2 conj	3450.4 art dat pl	566.6 adj dat pl masc	3450.9 art nom sing fem	1156.2 conj
πιστεύουσιν,	ἀλλὰ	τοῖς	ἀπίστοις·	ἡ	δὲ
pisteuousin	alla	tois	apistois	hē	de
believing,	but	to the	unbelievers;	the	but

4252.2 noun nom sing fem	3620.3 partic	3450.4 art dat pl	566.6 adj dat pl masc	233.2 conj	3450.4 art dat pl
προφητεία,	οὐ	τοῖς	ἀπίστοις,	ἀλλὰ	τοῖς
prophēteia,	ou	tois	apistois,	alla	tois
prophecy,	not	to the	unbelievers,	but	to the

21.a.**Txt:** 06D,018K
020L,025P,byz.
Var: 01א,02A,03B,33
Lach,Treg,Alf,Tisc
We/Ho,Weis,Sod
UBS/☆

and strength of the individual. He probably was referring to his private devotional times.

But Paul added a specific note regarding their use in the church assembly. Again, edification was to be the aim. Some of the Corinthians gloried in their ability to speak in a "tongue." Paul could have done the same. But he stressed what served the most. His thought was how best to benefit his brethren in the Lord. That meant speaking in an understandable language.

14:20. Another major reason for the excellence of prophecy in the public assembly has to do with spiritual persuasion, or the conviction to even the more skeptical that God is truly present. This should be the aim of everything done and said in the assembly: to see men convicted of their sin or immaturity and persuaded of the power of God in Christ to transform and mature them.

"In understanding" reflects reasoning. It refers to the midriff or diaphragm, for this is where the Greeks located thought. Proper understanding of spiritual matters is one sign of Christian maturity.

In malice or wrong believers should be children. Innocence, simplicity, and distaste for evil should be clear always. But in "understanding" they should be mature.

14:21. Paul turned to the Old Testament to teach a truth. "The law" (*nomos*) in Jewish usage extended to Scripture in general—for them, the Old Testament. He referred to the prophecy in Isaiah 28:11,12. Isaiah said that God would speak to His people "with stammering lips and another tongue," perhaps alluding to the judgment coming in the Assyrian invasion. But he added, "They would not hear."

There seems to be a further meaning, referring to the coming of the Holy Spirit upon the Early Church. Even though it was accompanied by a miracle of language and some believed, some would not respond. The moving of the Spirit has always had a dual result, turning to God in repentance or rejection of His message.

14:22. "Wherefore" indicates a conclusion and application of what has just been said. Tongues are for a sign to the unbeliever: it would seem that surely he would be touched, and he would respond to this phenomenon of "tongues." It does not seem, however, that even this will affect some people enough to turn them to God.

Paul points out that the purpose of prophecy is to minister to believers especially. In verse 3 he had said it produces edification, exhortation, and comfort. Notice, however, that the results of tongues for the unbeliever or of prophecy for the believer depends upon the hearer. The manifestation comes from God, but the hearer must respond in a proper way.

1 Corinthians 14:22

that [by my voice] I might teach others also: . . . so as to instruct others, *Weymouth* . . . to the teaching of other, *Geneva* . . . to the informacion of other, *Cranmer* . . . for the instruction of other people, *Moffatt.*

than ten thousand words in an [unknown] tongue: . . . than myriads of words, *Rotherham.*

20. Brethren, be not children in understanding: . . . do not become childish, *Fenton* . . . in your thoughts, *Murdock.*

howbeit in malice be ye children: But in evil be minors, *Concordant* . . . but in baseness become babes, *Rotherham* . . . as concerning maliciousnes, *Geneva* . . . to evil things be ye infants, *Murdock* . . . in evil be mere infants, *Moffatt* . . . be utter babes, *Weymouth.*

but in understanding be men: . . . but be mature, *Moffatt* . . . prove yourselves to be men of ripe years, *Weymouth* . . . be of a ripe age, *Geneva.*

21. In the law it is written:

With [men of] other tongues and other lips will I speak unto this people: By men of alien tongues, *Moffatt* . . . with strange lips, *Fenton* . . . With a foreign speech, *Murdock.*

and yet for all that will they not hear me, saith the Lord: . . . neither thus will they be hearkening, *Concordant* . . . even so also they will not hearken to me, *Murdock* . . . and then they will never understand Me, *Fenton* . . . even then they will not listen to Me, *Weymouth, Montgomery.*

22. Wherefore tongues are for a sign, not to them that believe: . . . is intended as a sign, *Weymouth* . . . are for a warning, *Fenton* . . . not to the faithful, but to infidels, *Rheims* . . . to those that have faith, *Rotherham.*

but to them that believe not: . . . but to those who disbelieve, *Clementson.*

but prophesying [serveth] not for them that believe not: . . . contrariwyse, *Geneva.*

but for them which believe: . . . is meant for believers, *Moffatt.*

3961.3 verb dat pl masc part pres act	1430.1 partic	3631.1 conj	4755.4 verb 3sing subj aor act	3450.9 art nom sing fem
πιστεύουσιν.	**23.** Ἐὰν	οὖν	συνέλθῃ	ἡ
pisteuousin	Ean	oun	sunelthē	hē
believing.	If	therefore	come together	the

1564.2 noun nom sing fem	3513.6 adj nom sing fem	1894.3 prep	3450.16 art sing neu	840.15 prs-pron sing neu	2504.1 conj	3820.7 adj pl masc
ἐκκλησία	ὅλη	ἐπὶ	τὸ	αὐτὸ,	καὶ	πάντες
ekklēsia	holē	epi	to	auto	kai	pantes
assembly	whole	in	the	same,	and	all

1094.7 noun dat pl fem	2953.7 verb 3pl subj pres act	2953.7 verb 3pl subj pres act	1094.7 noun dat pl fem
ʽ γλώσσαις	λαλῶσιν,	[✶ λαλῶσιν	γλώσσαις,]
glōssais	lalōsin	lalōsin	glōssais
with tongues	should speak,	[should speak	in tongues,]

1511.10 verb 3pl subj aor act	1156.2 conj	2376.3 noun nom pl masc	2211.1 conj	566.4 adj nom pl masc	3620.2 partic
εἰσέλθωσιν	δὲ	ἰδιῶται	ἢ	ἄπιστοι,	οὐκ
eiselthōsin	de	idiōtai	ē	apistoi	ouk
come in	and	uninstructed ones	or	unbelievers,	not

2029.14 verb 3pl indic fut act	3617.1 conj	3077.4 verb 2pl indic pres	1430.1 partic	1156.2 conj	3820.7 adj pl masc
ἐροῦσιν	ὅτι	μαίνεσθε;	**24.** ἐὰν	δὲ	πάντες
erousin	hoti	mainesthe	ean	de	pantes
will they say	that	you are mad?	If	but	all

4253.3 verb 3pl subj pres act	1511.7 verb 3sing subj aor act	1156.2 conj	4948.3 indef-pron nom sing	566.2 adj sing
προφητεύωσιν,	εἰσέλθῃ	δέ	τις	ἄπιστος
prophēteuōsin	eiselthē	de	tis	apistos
prophesy,	should come in	and	some	unbeliever

2211.1 conj	2376.1 noun nom sing masc	1638.8 verb 3sing indic pres pass	5097.3 prep	3820.4 adj gen pl
ἢ	ἰδιώτης,	ἐλέγχεται	ὑπὸ	πάντων,
ē	idiōtēs	elenchetai	hupo	pantōn
or	uninstructed,	he is being convicted	by	all,

25.a.**Txt**: (06D-corr) 018K,(020L),byz.
Var: 01ℵ,02A,03B 06D-org,bo.Gries,Lach Treg,Alf,Word,Tisc We/Ho,Weis,Sod UBS/✶

348.8 verb 3sing indic pres pass	5097.3 prep	3820.4 adj gen pl	2504.1 conj	3643.1 adv
ἀνακρίνεται	ὑπὸ	πάντων,	**25.** ʽa καὶ	οὕτως ʼ
anakrinetai	hupo	pantōn	kai	houtōs
he is being examined	by	all;	and	thus

3450.17 art pl neu	2899.4 adj pl neu	3450.10 art gen sing fem	2559.1 noun fem	840.3 prs-pron gen sing	5156.4 adj nom
τὰ	κρυπτὰ	τῆς	καρδίας	αὐτοῦ	φανερὰ
ta	krupta	tēs	kardias	autou	phanera
the	secrets	of the	heart	his	manifest

1090.14 verb 3sing indic pres	2504.1 conj	3643.1 adv	3959.11 verb nom sing masc part aor act	1894.3 prep	4241.1 noun sing neu
γίνεται·	καὶ	οὕτως	πεσὼν	ἐπὶ	πρόσωπον,
ginetai	kai	houtōs	pesōn	epi	prosōpon
becomes;	and	thus,	having fallen	upon	face,

4210.20 verb 3sing indic fut act	3450.3 art dat sing	2296.3 noun dat sing masc	514.3 verb nom sing masc part pres act	3617.1 conj	3450.5 art sing masc
προσκυνήσει	τῷ	θεῷ,	ἀπαγγέλλων	ὅτι	ʽ ὁ
proskunēsei	tō	theō	apangellōn	hoti	ho
he will worship	to	God,	declaring	that	

14:23. Paul added detail to what he had just written. He visualized the whole congregation gathering and all speaking in tongues. If an unbeliever or one "unlearned" walked in, and did not understand or see the spiritual sense in the scene, he would feel justified in declaring these Christians "mad" or raving (*mainesthe*).

A note aside, the text says "into one place." This is a support for the regular Lord's Day services and regular attendance at them.

The fact that Paul spoke of the whole assembly gathering together into "one place" has led many to wonder what kind of service is in mind here. It may be that this single gathering is the same as at 11:17 where the Corinthians gathered together for the love meal. It is not impossible that their worship service took place outside (since it is unlikely that all the believers met together in one house) and at the same time as the love feast. This would explain how unbelievers and others could happen to come to a service and hear people speaking in tongues.

If, as the Corinthians thought, tongues is the highest gift of the Spirit, then nothing could be better than to have the whole church speaking "with tongues." But the result was not what they had expected. There was a marked lack of edification for the "unlearned" or unbelieving who came in, and as a result they claimed madness and irrationality on the part of the Christians. This drove them away from the church, rather than drawing them into its fellowship.

14:24. The aim of prophecy stood in clear contrast to this. The direct, understandable message from God would have powerful results. The "outsider" would be "convinced of all." This means the unbeliever would be convicted; the prophetic word would show him his condition and state.

The phrase "judged of all" means to put on trial, to sift judicially, to examine by question after penetrating question. The Word of the Lord throws a searchlight into hidden recesses of the heart. The unbeliever would then realize, through the work of the Holy Spirit, that he was guilty of sin and was under the judgment of God.

14:25. The secrets of his heart would be "made manifest." That which he thought safely hidden in his own being would be brought to light. "Made manifest" may carry a double meaning. Perhaps some particular sin would be mentioned, or the unlearned or unbelieving would see an image of himself in a general prophecy on sin. In these cases, the sin might be manifested to the congregation or simply to the individual. In any case, profit and edification was the intention.

Generally, there appears first the inward work, then the outward product. First comes the penetration of the Law, the measuring stick of righteousness and morality. Then comes the gospel with its presentation of mercy, faith, and grace. The results are worship and witness.

23. If therefore the whole church be come together into one place: . . . the whole church to be holding a united meeting, *Way* . . . if the whole congregation is assembled, *Norlie.*

and all speak with tongues, and there come in [those that are] unlearned, or unbelievers: . . . if all present use the gift of 'tongues,' *TCNT* . . . and everybody is speaking, *Montgomery* . . . in private persons, *Rotherham* . . . unlearned persons or infidels, *Douay* . . . or such as believe not, *Murdock.*

will they not say that ye are mad?: . . . would they not imagine you were mad? *Fenton* . . . won't they say that you are crazy? *Adams* . . . would they not say that you are demented? *Norlie* . . . ye are out of youre wites? *Cranmer* . . . you are insane, *Moffatt* . . . you are raving? *Way.*

24. But if all prophesy: . . . if all could preach, *Fenton* . . . every one is prophesying, *Weymouth* . . . if all those present use the 'prophetic' gift, *TCNT.*

and there come in one that believeth not, or [one] unlearned: . . . and one unlearned or an unbeliever should come among you, *Murdock* . . . or a man without the gift, *TCNT.*

he is convinced of all, he is judged of all: . . . one by one they probe his thoughts, *Way* . . . he is convicted...and closely examined by all, *Weymouth* . . . he is being exposed by all, he is being examined by all, *Concordant, Moffatt* . . . he becomes conscious of his sin and is called to account, *TCNT* . . . he is rebuked of all men, *Tyndale* . . . and all will put questions to him, *Norlie.*

25. And thus are the secrets of his heart made manifest: . . . so are the secretes...opened, *Geneva* . . . the hidden evils...are brought to light, *Moffatt* . . . and the secrets...are laid open [to him], *Murdock* . . . will be revealed, *Norlie* . . . will be disclosed, *Adams.*

and so falling down on [his] face he will worship God: . . . throwing himself, *TCNT* . . . pay homage to God, *Fenton, Way* . . . he will adore God, *Douay.*

2296.1 noun
nom sing masc
θεὸς
theos
God

3552.1 adv
ὄντως
ontōs
indeed

3552.1 adv
[ὄντως
ontōs
[indeed

3450.5 art
sing masc
ὁ
ho
the

2296.1 noun
nom sing masc
θεὸς]
theos
God]

1706.1 prep
ἐν
en
among

5050.3 prs-
pron dat 2pl
ὑμῖν
humin
you

1498.4 verb 3sing
indic pres act
ἐστιν.
estin
is.

3552.1 adv

26. Τί
Ti
What

3631.1 conj
οὖν
oun
then

1498.4 verb 3sing
indic pres act
ἐστιν,
estin
is it,

79.6 noun
pl masc
ἀδελφοί;
adelphoi
brothers?

26.a.**Txt:** 01ℵ-corr,06D
018K,020L,byz.it.
Var: p46,01ℵ-org,02A
03B,025P,33,sa.bo.Lach
Treg,Tisc,We/Ho,Weis
Sod,UBS/⋆

3615.1 conj
ὅταν
hotan
when

4755.17 verb
2pl subj pres
συνέρχησθε,
sunerchēsthe
you may come together,

1524.3 adj
nom sing masc
ἕκαστος
hekastos
each

5050.2 prs-
pron gen 2pl
⌐a ὑμῶν ⌐
humōn
of you

5403.2 noun
acc sing masc
ψαλμὸν
psalmon
a psalm

2174.4 verb 3sing
indic pres act
ἔχει,
echei
has,

1316.4 noun
acc sing fem
διδαχὴν
didachēn
a teaching

2174.4 verb 3sing
indic pres act
ἔχει,
echei
has,

1094.4 noun
acc sing fem
⌐ γλῶσσαν
glōssan
a tongue

2174.4 verb 3sing
indic pres act
ἔχει,
echei
has,

597.4 noun
acc sing fem
ἀποκάλυψιν
apokalupsin
a revelation

2174.4 verb 3sing
indic pres act
ἔχει,
echei
has,

597.4 noun
acc sing fem
[⋆ ἀποκάλυψιν
apokalupsin
[a revelation

2174.4 verb 3sing
indic pres act
ἔχει,
echei
has,

1094.4 noun
acc sing fem
γλῶσσαν
glōssan
a tongue

2174.4 verb 3sing
indic pres act
ἔχει,]
echei
has,]

2042.2 noun
acc sing fem
ἑρμηνείαν
hermēneian
an interpretation

2174.4 verb 3sing
indic pres act
ἔχει·
echei
has.

3820.1 adj
πάντα
panta
All things

26.b.**Txt:** Steph
Var: 01ℵ,02A,03B,06D
018K,020L,byz.Gries
Lach,Treg,Alf,Word
Tisc,We/Ho,Weis,Sod
UBS/⋆

4242.1 prep
πρὸς
pros
for

3482.3 noun
acc sing fem
οἰκοδομὴν
oikodomēn
building up

1090.46 verb
3sing impr aor mid
⌐ γενέσθω.
genesthō
let be done.

1090.18 verb
3sing impr pres
[b⋆ γινέσθω.]
ginesthō
[idem]

1521.1 conj
27. εἴτε
eite
If

1094.3 noun
dat sing fem
γλώσσῃ
glōssē
with a tongue

4948.3 indef-
pron nom sing
τις
tis
anyone

2953.2 verb sing
indic pres act
λαλεῖ,
lalei
speaks,

2567.3 prep
κατὰ
kata
by

1411.3 num card
δύο
duo
two

2211.1 conj
ἢ
ē
or

3450.16 art
sing neu
τὸ
to
the

3978.3 adj sup
acc sing neu
πλεῖστον
pleiston
most

4980.1 num
card nom
τρεῖς,
treis
three,

2504.1 conj
καὶ
kai
and

301.1 adv
ἀνὰ
ana
in

3183.1 noun
sing neu
μέρος,
meros
succession,

2504.1 conj
καὶ
kai
and

1518.3 num
card nom masc
εἷς
heis
one

1323.3 verb 3sing
impr pres act
διερμηνευέτω.
diermēneuetō
let interpret;

1430.1 partic
28. ἐὰν
ean
if

1156.2 conj
δὲ
de
and

3231.1 partic
μὴ
mē
not

1498.10 verb 3sing
subj pres act
ᾖ
ē
there be

1322.1 noun
nom sing masc
ʹ διερμηνευτής,
diermēneutēs
an interpreter,

4456.1 verb 3sing
impr pres act
σιγάτω
sigatō
let him be silent

1706.1 prep
ἐν
en
in

1564.3 noun
dat sing fem
ἐκκλησίᾳ·
ekklēsia
an assembly;

1431.5 prs-pron
dat 3sing masc
ἑαυτῷ
heautō
to himself

The last part of this verse is reminiscent of Isaiah 45:14. So powerful would be the effect of the divine message and presence that the unbeliever would prostrate himself before God. There would be humility, confession, and surrender, as the man worshiped God. The once unbelieving person would leave the congregation announcing "God is in you." Such a church is successful.

14:26. Paul next turned from the subject of edification to the difficult matter of order in the church assembly. Accordingly, any member of the church might be expected to take part in the service.

Generally, the Corinthians were energetic in their involvement. But this exuberance also created a problem in that everyone tried to speak at the same time. The result was disorder. One had a psalm, which could mean one of the 150 in the Psalms, but it could also denote a song with instrumental accompaniment. One had a "doctrine," which involved lessons in Christian truth. One had a "tongue," a "revelation" which might involve prophecy, an "interpretation." This was fine as long as the rules were remembered. The manifestation must be of a kind that edified, and it must be brought in an edifying manner.

14:27. Having set the standard for an orderly service, Paul showed the specific procedure regarding the exercise of "a tongue." He indicated a situation in the assembly where a man could speak aloud in an unknown tongue. The order was to be "by two, or at the most by three." This has generally been considered the number of times this particular manifestation should be exercised during one service. It appears that some had tried to speak at the same time as another. The result was disorder. Paul strongly opposed such action.

If one or more spoke "in an unknown tongue" there must be an interpretation, for the congregation must be edified. The presentation was to be clear, orderly, and spiritual. There seems no reason to stress this to mean only one person should interpret for the two or three speakers in tongues. What Paul was indicating was prompt interpretation. As one speaks in a tongue, one should then interpret.

14:28. If there was no interpreter present in the assembly, Paul gave specific instruction to the speaker in a tongue: He must refrain from public utterance and be content to speak in tongues in solitude unto God. Or, according to verse 13, he should pray that God will give him the interpretation.

The reason for this prohibition was that such public unintelligible utterance would not edify the congregation. It also showed that God does not operate through robots, but through a person's will and personality.

and report that God is in you of a truth: . . . announcing, *Fenton* . . . declaring, *Sawyer* . . . affirming that God is among you indeed, *Douay* . . . God is really among you, *Moffatt.*

26. How is it then, brethren?: What follows, then, brothers? *Montgomery* . . . What then is [to be done] brothers? *Sawyer* . . . what is the upshot of all of this? *Adams.*

when ye come together, every one of you hath: . . . each contributes something, *Moffatt.*

a psalm: . . . has a hymn, *Fenton.*

hath a doctrine: . . . has a lesson, *Fenton* . . . another piece of exposition, *Way.*

hath a tongue, hath a revelation:

hath an interpretation: . . . has an explanation, *Fenton.*

Let all things be done unto edifying: . . . with a view to the building up of faith and character, *Weymouth* . . . with a view to the spiritual advancement of the church, *Way.*

27. If any man speak in an [unknown] tongue:

[let it be] by two, or at the most [by] three, and [that] by course: . . . at one meeting, and that in turn, *Moffatt* . . . and that separately, one after another, *Locke* . . . not simultaneously, but in turn, *Way* . . . and they should do so in turn, *Adams* . . . and by turns, *Sawyer* . . . and let them speak one by one, *Murdock.*

and let one interpret: . . . let someone interpret, *Moffatt, Montgomery* . . . and let those who have the gift of discernment of inspiration then exercise it, *Way* . . . let one be translating, *Rotherham.*

28. But if there be no interpreter: . . . if there is nobody who can fully interpret, *Adams* . . . not a translator, *Fenton.*

let him keep silence in the church: . . . let him hold his peace, *Rheims* . . . let him hush in the ecclesia, *Concordant* . . . let not any one use his gift of tongues in the congregation, *Locke.*

1 Corinthians 14:29

| 1156.2 conj δὲ *de* and | 2953.9 verb 3sing impr pres act λαλείτω *laleitō* let him speak | 2504.1 conj καὶ *kai* and | 3450.3 art dat sing τῷ *tō* to | 2296.3 noun dat sing masc θεῷ. *theō* to God. | 4254.4 noun pl masc 29. προφῆται *prophētai* Prophets |

| 1156.2 conj δὲ *de* and | 1411.3 num card δύο *duo* two | 2211.1 conj ἢ *ē* or | 4980.1 num card nom τρεῖς *treis* three | 2953.11 verb 3pl impr pres act λαλείτωσαν, *laleitōsan* let speak, | 2504.1 conj καὶ *kai* and | 3450.7 art pl masc οἱ *hoi* the |

| 241.6 adj nom pl masc ἄλλοι *alloi* others | 1246.2 verb 3pl impr pres act διακρινέτωσαν· *diakrinetōsan* let discern. | 1430.1 partic 30. ἐὰν *ean* If | 1156.2 conj δὲ *de* but | 241.3 adj dat sing ἄλλῳ *allō* to another |

| 596.8 verb 3sing subj aor pass ἀποκαλυφθῇ *apokaluphthē* should be a revelation | 2493.8 verb dat sing masc part pres καθημένῳ, *kathēmenō* sitting by, | 3450.5 art sing masc ὁ *ho* the | 4272.5 num ord nom sing masc πρῶτος *prōtos* first |

| 4456.1 verb 3sing impr pres act σιγάτω. *sigatō* let be silent. | 1404.6 verb 2pl indic pres 31. δύνασθε *dunasthe* You can | 1056.1 conj γὰρ *gar* for | 2567.2 prep καθ' *kath'* by | 1518.4 num card acc masc ἕνα *hena* one | 3820.7 adj pl masc πάντες *pantes* all |

| 4253.7 verb inf pres act προφητεύειν, *prophēteuein* prophesy, | 2419.1 conj ἵνα *hina* that | 3820.7 adj pl masc πάντες *pantes* all | 3101.2 verb 3pl subj pres act μανθάνωσιν, *manthanōsin* may learn, | 2504.1 conj καὶ *kai* and |

| 3820.7 adj pl masc πάντες *pantes* all | 3731.23 verb 3pl subj pres pass παρακαλῶνται· *parakalōntai* may be exhorted. | 2504.1 conj 32. καὶ *kai* And | 4011.4 noun pl neu πνεύματα *pneumata* spirits | 4254.5 noun gen pl masc προφητῶν *prophētōn* of prophets |

| 4254.6 noun dat pl masc προφήταις *prophētais* to prophets | 5131.7 verb 3sing indic pres pass ὑποτάσσεται· *hupotassetai* is being subject. | 3620.3 partic 33. οὐ *ou* Not | 1056.1 conj γὰρ *gar* for | 1498.4 verb 3sing indic pres act ἐστιν *estin* he is |

| 179.1 noun fem ἀκαταστασίας *akatastasias* of disorder | 3450.5 art sing masc ὁ *ho* the | 2296.1 noun nom sing masc θεὸς, *theos* God, | 233.1 conj ʹ ἀλλ' *all'* but | 233.2 conj [✶ ἀλλὰ] *alla* [idem] |

| 1503.2 noun gen sing fem εἰρήνης, *eirēnēs* of peace, | 5453.1 conj ὡς *hōs* as | 1706.1 prep ἐν *en* in | 3820.15 adj dat pl fem πάσαις *pasais* all | 3450.14 art dat pl fem ταῖς *tais* the | 1564.7 noun dat pl fem ἐκκλησίαις *ekklēsiais* assemblies | 3450.1 art gen pl τῶν *tōn* of the |

34.a.Txt: 06D,018K 020L,byz.Sod
Var: p46,018,02A,03B 04C,025P,33,sa.bo.Lach Treg,Alf,Tisc,We/Ho Weis,UBS/✶

| 39.4 adj gen pl ἁγίων. *hagiōn* saints. | 3450.13 art pl fem 34. Αἱ *Hai* The | 1129.6 noun pl fem γυναῖκες *gunaikes* women | 5050.2 prs-pron gen 2pl ʹa ὑμῶν ʹ *humōn* your | 1706.1 prep ἐν *en* in | 3450.14 art dat pl fem ταῖς *tais* the |

14:29. This order is universal. Prophecy should be subjected to the same standard as tongues. Everything must edify the congregation. Again we see the order of two or three in a service.

"The other" is plural. The utterance was not to be accorded uncritical acceptance. It was to be "judged" or discerned.

14:30. A spirit of love and gracious consideration should be manifested in relation to the utterance manifestations. Paul suggests a situation where one person has been speaking, and the Holy Spirit impresses another person to say something that has been revealed to him. The first speaker should be willing to give way to the other person. It has been said that the Holy Spirit is a gentleman and will not bring disorder and disruption. The edifying of the congregation is the objective all should seek.

14:31. Paul was establishing an orderly, loving, edifying exercise of prophecy. As each person was moved on by the Spirit, in wisdom he would have the opportunity to exercise the gift. He would not be slighted, but would minister within the framework of order and "preferring one another."

Anyone filled with the Spirit has the potential and opportunity of being used in any of these gifts of the Spirit. With due order and self-discipline each would have an opportunity to minister and profit the assembly.

The purpose is that "all may learn, and all may be comforted." If there is equal opportunity for utterance, then all the hearers will benefit. The result will be blessing, benefit, and learning.

14:32. Paul explained how the order of verses 29-31 is possible. The speaker is in control of himself. The "spirits of the prophets are subject to the prophets." This adds a subjective reason for regulation to the objective reason of verse 31. The speaker's will is important. The gift must be exercised in wisdom and love to accomplish the best possible ends. A false prophet will not so speak or act.

14:33. The submissiveness Paul urged is founded on the virtue and desire of God himself. He is a God of peace. In the character of God, there is a guarantee against disorderliness. He wanted to pass this on to the Church.

The laws of nature show a marked lack of confusion. It is foolish to suppose God's spiritual laws and works would be different. Paul infers order by indicating God's underlying motive: peace.

14:34. Understanding the customs of the times helps to understand the reason for Paul's instruction for the women to "keep

and let him speak to himself, and to God: . . . let him, silently, within himself, *Locke.*

29. Let the prophets speak two or three:
and let the other judge: . . . let the others discriminate, *Concordant* . . . the others should reflect, *Fenton* . . . exercise their judgment upon what is said, *Moffatt* . . . let the others examine and discuss it, *Locke.*

30. If [any thing] be revealed to another that sitteth by: . . . if something is suggested, *Fenton.*
let the first hold his peace: . . . let the first be silent, *Weymouth* . . . the first speaker must be quiet, *Moffatt* . . . let the first hush, *Concordant* . . . let the first stop speaking, *Murdock.*

31. For ye may all prophesy one by one: . . . eche bi hym silf, *Wyclif.*
that all may learn:
and all may be comforted: . . . all be consoled, *Concordant* . . . all be encouraged, *Moffatt.*

32. And the spirits of the prophets: . . . the spiritual endowments of prophets, *Concordant.*
are subject to the prophets: . . . are regulated by, *Fenton* . . . yield submission to prophets, *Weymouth* . . . are in the power of the Prophets, *Geneva* . . . are masters of their own actions, *Locke* . . . can control their own prophetic spirits, *Moffatt.*

33. For God is not [the author] of confusion, but of peace: . . . is not disturbance, *Fenton* . . . is not for turbulence, *Concordant* . . . is not causer of stryfe, *Cranmer* . . . of disorder, *Weymouth* . . . of tumult, *Murdock* . . . but of harmony, *Moffatt.*
as in all churches of the saints: This custom prevails, *Montgomery.*

34. Let your women keep silence in the churches: Let youre wyves, *Tyndale* . . . Let married

451

1564.7 noun dat pl fem
ἐκκλησίαις
ekklēsiais
assemblies

4456.2 verb 3pl impr pres act
σιγάτωσαν·
sigatōsan
let them be silent,

3620.3 partic
οὐ
ou
not

1056.1 conj
γὰρ
gar
for

1994.9 verb 3sing indic perf pass
⌐ ἐπιτέτραπται
epitetraptai
it is allowed

1994.7 verb 3sing indic pres pass
[b✶ ἐπιτρέπεται]
epitrepetai
[is being allowed]

840.14 prs-pron dat pl fem
αὐταῖς
autais
to them

2953.24 verb inf pres act
λαλεῖν·
lalein
to speak;

233.1 conj
⌐ ἀλλ'
all'
but

233.2 conj
[✶ ἀλλὰ
alla
[idem]

5131.15 verb inf pres pass
⌐ ὑποτάσσεσθαι,
hupotassesthai
to be in subjection,

5131.25 verb 3pl impr pres pass
[c✶ ὑποτασσέσθωσαν,]
hupotassesthōsan
[let them be subject,]

2503.1 conj
καθὼς
kathōs
according as

2504.1 conj
καὶ
kai
also

3450.5 art sing masc
ὁ
ho
the

3414.1 noun nom sing masc
νόμος
nomos
law

2978.5 verb 3sing indic pres act
λέγει.
legei
says.

35. **1479.1** conj
εἰ
ei
If

1156.2 conj
δέ
de
but

4948.10 indef-pron sing neu
τι
ti
anything

3101.13 verb inf aor act
μαθεῖν
mathein
to learn

2286.6 verb 3pl indic pres act
θέλουσιν,
thelousin
they wish,

1706.1 prep
ἐν
en
at

3486.3 noun dat sing masc
οἴκῳ
oikō
home

3450.8 art acc pl masc
τοὺς
tous
the

2375.8 adj acc pl masc
ἰδίους
idious
own

433.9 noun acc pl masc
ἄνδρας
andras
husbands

1890.3 verb 3pl impr pres act
ἐπερωτάτωσαν·
eperōtatōsan
let them ask;

149.1 adj nom sing neu
αἰσχρὸν
aischron
a shame

1056.1 conj
γάρ
gar
for

1498.4 verb 3sing indic pres act
ἐστιν
estin
it is

1129.8 noun dat pl fem
⌐ γυναιξὶν
gunaixin
for women

1706.1 prep
ἐν
en
in

1564.3 noun dat sing fem
ἐκκλησίᾳ·
ekklēsia
assembly

2953.24 verb inf pres act
λαλεῖν.
lalein
to speak.

1129.3 noun dat sing fem
[a✶ γυναικὶ
gunaiki
[for a woman

2953.24 verb inf pres act
λαλεῖν
lalein
to speak

1706.1 prep
ἐν
en
in

1564.3 noun dat sing fem
ἐκκλησίᾳ.]
ekklēsia
assembly.]

36. **2211.1** conj
Ἢ
Ē
Or

570.1 prep gen
ἀφ'
aph'
from

5050.2 prs-pron gen 2pl
ὑμῶν
humōn
you

3450.5 art sing masc
ὁ
ho
the

3030.1 noun nom sing masc
λόγος
logos
word

3450.2 art gen sing
τοῦ
tou

2296.2 noun gen sing masc
θεοῦ
theou
of God

1814.3 verb 3sing indic aor act
ἐξῆλθεν·
exēlthen
went out,

2211.1 conj
ἢ
ē
or

1519.1 prep
εἰς
eis
to

5050.4 prs-pron acc 2pl
ὑμᾶς
humas
you

3304.7 adj acc pl masc
μόνους
monous
only

2628.1 verb 3sing indic aor act
κατήντησεν;
katēntēsen
did it arrive?

37. **1479.1** conj
Εἴ
Ei
If

4948.3 indef-pron nom sing
τις
tis
anyone

1374.5 verb 3sing indic pres act
δοκεῖ
dokei
thinks

4254.1 noun nom sing masc
προφήτης
prophētēs
a prophet

1498.32 verb inf pres act
εἶναι
einai
to be

2211.1 conj
ἢ
ē
or

4012.2 adj nom sing masc
πνευματικός,
pneumatikos
spiritual,

1906.4 verb 3sing impr pres act
ἐπιγινωσκέτω
epiginōsketō
let him recognize

3614.17 rel-pron pl neu
ἃ
ha
the things

silence in the churches." He was not forbidding participation by women, for he had already mentioned praying and prophesying by women (11:5). He was speaking to married women, for he mentions their husbands in the next verse. In that era men and women sat apart. Sometimes the women had legitimate questions about what was being said. In such cases, Paul suggested they not disturb the meeting.

Paul's reference to the "law" is uncertain. Usually when he quoted from the Law he identified the citation but did not do so here. Usually Genesis 3:16 is taken as the source for Paul's statement.

14:35. Paul advised the proper procedure. If the woman's motive was a true desire to learn, she should not interrupt the service by asking her husband. Rather than cause a disturbance she should wait and ask her husband at home. This was the rule to be followed. To do otherwise would be disruptive, against custom, and would not be edifying.

14:36. Paul reproved the situation with the use of irony and questions to which he expected a negative answer. He reminded the Corinthians that they had not originated the Word, nor were they the only ones to receive it. Therefore they must conform to the Biblical pattern and Christian custom.

Selfishness and pride were rebuked. Paul suggested that the haughty Corinthians were desiring to take the place of God and were thinking they knew better than God by trying to make His Word mean what they thought it should. This could not be allowed.

14:37. What remained now was for Paul to establish his authority for what he had written. While in the context this summation belongs particularly to the words of chapter 14, in a wider sense it belongs to the whole of Paul's discussion on public worship.

Paul asserted his apostolic position and authority and the source of the truths he presented and then once again reaffirmed the directives concerning orderly manifestations and the overall theme of edification.

Paul stated that what he had written were the "commandments of the Lord." This provides insight into how the New Testament writers viewed their inspiration; no greater claim could be made.

If a man thinks himself to be spiritual he will acknowledge the inspired truth of what is said here. Paul made no personal judgments. He left the answer as to possession of gifts, etc., to the individual. Whatever the case, he was to obey these commands from the Lord. And his reception of Paul's words would decide the nature and quality of his prophecy or spirituality.

women, *Weymouth* . . . must keep quiet at gatherings, *Moffatt* . . . hold their peace, *Rheims* . . . in the assemblies, *Sawyer.*

for it is not permitted unto them to speak: . . . since they are not allowed to speak, *Adams* . . . to discourse there, *Locke.*

but [they are commanded] to be under obedience, as also saith the law: . . . let them be in submission, *Rotherham* . . . must take a subordinate place, *Moffatt* . . . but to be subject, *Douay* . . . but to be in subjection, *Murdock* . . . be content with a subordinate place, *Weymouth* . . . as stated in the law, *Fenton.*

35. And if they will learn any thing: . . . wish to ask questions, *Weymouth* . . . wish to be informed on any subject, *Murdock.*

let them ask their husbands at home: . . . let them be inquiring, *Concordant.*

for it is a shame for women to speak in the church: For it is a foule thing, *Rheims* . . . it is scandalous, *Fenton* . . . it is improper, *Adams* . . . it is unbecoming, *Murdock* . . . it is disgraceful for a married woman to speak at a church assembly, *Weymouth, Moffatt* . . . to be addressing a public meeting, *Way* . . . to discourse and debate with men publicly, *Locke.*

36. What? came the word of God out from you?: Consider this, *Adams* . . . was it from you that the word of God came forth? *Murdock.*

or came it unto you only?: . . . are you the only ones that it ever got to? *Adams* . . . as if the Gospel began at Corinth, *Locke* . . . Or did it reach only to you? *Murdock.*

37. If any man think himself to be a prophet, or spiritual: If any one deems himself . . . or a man with spiritual gifts, *Weymouth* . . . imagine himself to be an orator, or inspired, *Fenton* . . . or gifted, *Moffatt.*

let him acknowledge that the things that I write unto you: . . . let him be recognizing that, *Concordant* . . . that these rules, *Locke.*

1 Corinthians 14:38

37.a.**Txt:** Steph
Var: 01ℵ,03B,018K
020L,byz.Gries,Lach
Treg,Alf,Word,Tisc
We/Ho,Weis,Sod
UBS/✶

37.b.**Txt:** 06D-corr,018K
020L,byz.sa.
Var: p46,01ℵ,02A,03B
06D-org,048,33,bo.Lach
Treg,Alf,Word,Tisc
We/Ho,Weis,Sod
UBS/✶

37.c.**Txt:** 06D-corr,018K
020L,byz.sa.
Var: p46,01ℵ,02A,03B
048,33,bo.Lach,Treg
Alf,Word,We/Ho,Weis
Sod,UBS/✶

38.a.**Txt:** p46,01ℵ-corr
02A-corr,03B,06D-corr
018K,020L,byz.Weis
Var: 01ℵ-org,02A-org
06D-org,048,Lach,Tisc
We/Ho,Sod,UBS/✶

39.a.**Var:** 01ℵ,02A
03B-org,06D-corr,Lach
Treg,Alf,Tisc,We/Ho
Weis,Sod,UBS/✶

1119.1 verb 1sing indic pres act	5050.3 prs-pron dat 2pl	3617.1 conj	3450.2 art gen sing	2935.2 noun gen sing masc	1498.7 verb 3pl indic pres act
γράφω	ὑμῖν,	ὅτι	⟨a τοῦ ⟩	κυρίου	⟨ εἰσὶν
graphō	humin	hoti	tou	kuriou	eisin
I write	to you,	that	of the	Lord	they are

1498.4 verb 3sing indic pres act	1769.4 noun nom pl fem	1769.1 noun nom sing fem	1479.1 conj	1156.2 conj
[b✶ ἐστὶν]	⟨ ἐντολαί·	[c✶ ἐντολή·]	**38.** εἰ	δέ
estin	entolai	entolē	ei	de
[it is]	commands.	[a command.]	If	but

4948.3 indef-pron nom sing	49.1 verb 3sing indic pres act	49.5 verb 3sing impr pres act	49.14 verb 3sing indic pres pass
τις	ἀγνοεῖ,	⟨ ἀγνοείτω.	[a✶ ἀγνοεῖται.]
tis	agnoei	agnoeitō	agnoeitai
any	be ignorant,	let him be ignorant.	[he is being disregarded.]

5452.1 conj	79.6 noun pl masc	1466.2 prs-pron gen 1sing	2189.1 verb 2pl pres act	3450.16 art sing neu
39. Ὥστε,	ἀδελφοί,	[a✶+ μου,]	ζηλοῦτε	τὸ
Hōste	adelphoi	mou	zēloute	to
So that,	brothers,	[my,]	be eager	the

4253.7 verb inf pres act	2504.1 conj	3450.16 art sing neu	2953.24 verb inf pres act	1094.7 noun dat pl fem	3231.1 partic
προφητεύειν,	καὶ	τὸ	λαλεῖν	⟨ γλώσσαις	μὴ
prophēteuein	kai	to	lalein	glōssais	mē
to prophesy,	and	the	to speak	with tongues	not

2940.2 verb 2pl impr pres act	3231.1 partic	2940.2 verb 2pl impr pres act	1094.7 noun dat pl fem	3820.1 adj
κωλύετε.	[✶ μὴ	κωλύετε	γλώσσαις·]	**40.** πάντα
kōluete	mē	kōluete	glōssais	panta
do forbid.	[not	forbid	in tongues.]	All things

40.a.**Var:** 01ℵ,02A,03B
06D,025P,bo.Gries,Lach
Treg,Alf,Word,Tisc
We/Ho,Weis,Sod
UBS/✶

1156.2 conj	2137.1 adv	2504.1 conj	2567.3 prep	4861.2 noun acc sing fem	1090.18 verb 3sing impr pres
[a✶+ δὲ	εὐσχημόνως	καὶ	κατὰ	τάξιν	γινέσθω.
de	euschēmonōs	kai	kata	taxin	ginesthō
[but]	decently	and	with	order	let be done.

1101.1 verb 1sing indic pres act	1156.2 conj	5050.3 prs-pron dat 2pl	79.6 noun pl masc	3450.16 art sing neu
15:1. Γνωρίζω	δὲ	ὑμῖν,	ἀδελφοί,	τὸ
Gnōrizō	de	humin	adelphoi	to
I make known	but	to you,	brothers,	the

2077.1 noun sing neu	3614.16 rel-pron sing neu	2076.15 verb 1sing indic aor mid	5050.3 prs-pron dat 2pl	3614.16 rel-pron sing neu
εὐαγγέλιον	ὃ	εὐηγγελισάμην	ὑμῖν,	ὃ
euangelion	ho	euēngelisamēn	humin	ho
good news	which	I announced	to you;	which

2504.1 conj	3741.7 verb 2pl indic aor act	1706.1 prep	3614.3 rel-pron dat sing	2504.1 conj	2449.20 verb 2pl indic perf act
καὶ	παρελάβετε,	ἐν	ᾧ	καὶ	ἑστήκατε,
kai	parelabete	en	hō	kai	hestēkate
also	you received,	in	which	also	you stand,

1217.1 prep	3614.2 rel-pron gen sing	2504.1 conj	4834.16 verb 2pl indic pres pass	4949.2 intr-pron dat sing	3030.3 noun dat sing masc
2. δι'	οὗ	καὶ	σῴζεσθε.	τίνι	λόγῳ
di'	hou	kai	sōzesthe	tini	logō
by	which	also	you are being saved,	what	word

Paul was following Jesus' viewpoint as expressed in John 8:47. Some have thought that "spiritual" must refer to "tongues" because Paul first mentioned "prophet" and because of the context. But the word is more general than that. Anyone who possessed a spiritual gift or was genuinely spiritual would acknowledge the validity of Paul's statements.

14:38. This verse has been variously interpreted. But whether it is viewed as a response by Paul, the Corinthian church, or some future indictment, the fact is presented that to refuse Paul's directives carried disastrous consequences. Paul's relationship with the Corinthian Christians seemed always to be tenuous. In 4:21 Paul told them that if they did not heed his words he would come to them with the rod. Apparently this became necessary since he later paid them a painful visit (cf. 2 Corinthians 2:1-4). Paul, as an apostle and representative of Jesus Christ, had no choice but to seek His commands regardless of the opposition he might receive.

The words of verse 38 that "if any man be ignorant, let him be ignorant" represent the unequivocal stance of a man of God who proclaims God's Word even if it be rejected. This may be compared with the prophetic commission of Isaiah 6:9,10. Rejection of truth leads to spiritual ignorance, and that can be tragic.

14:39. In conclusion, Paul wanted believers to desire and treasure spiritual manifestations. Notice that despite the problems associated with tongues he concludes by endorsing them.

14:40. At the same time Paul reminded the Corinthians these manifestations of the Spirit are to remain within the framework of edification and order. Good taste and proper procedure are to be the standards always.

15:1. The resurrection of Jesus Christ is the indisputable rock on which Christianity and the gospel stand. This chapter sets forth this great truth and the problems of denying it as well as the promise in affirming it.

Paul began with a gentle rebuke. Rather than reminding the Corinthians of the gospel he had preached, he declared it to them again. Some did not seem to realize the importance of the gospel Paul had preached to them even though they had received it.

15:2. The gospel is the means used to bring salvation. "Ye are saved" is present continuous, indicating continuing activity: "You are being saved." From God's standpoint there is both a permanent,

are the commandments of the Lord: ... it is an order, *Fenton* ... is a precept of the Lord, *Concordant.*

38. But if any man be ignorant: ... if any man know not, *Douay* ... But if anybody disregards this, *Adams.*

let him be ignorant: ... disregard him, *Adams* ... he shall not be known, *Douay.*

39. Wherefore, brethren, covet to prophesy: The conclusion, my brethren, *Weymouth* ... be envious of, *Rotherham* ... desire earnestly to prophesy, *Sawyer* ... desire the talent for oratory, *Fenton* ... be emulous of prophesying, *Murdock* ... be ambitious for the gift, *Montgomery* ... let prophecy have the preference, *Locke.*

and forbid not to speak with tongues: ... and do not prohibit, *Fenton* ... and do not check speaking with tongues, *Weymouth* ... prohibit not, *Murdock* ... to speak in other languages, *Adams.*

40. Let all things be done decently and in order: ... let all occur respectably, *Concordant* ... in a becoming and orderly manner, *Weymouth* ... with comeliness and arrangement, *Rotherham* ... decorously, *Moffatt* ... and according to order among you, *Rheims* ... let everything be conducted with due regard to decorum and discipline, *Way* ... and regularity, *Murdock.*

1. Moreover, brethren, I declare unto you the gospel which I preached unto you: ... the joyful message which I myself announced to you, *Rotherham* ... I imparted to you, *Fenton.*

which also ye have received: ... which you accepted also, *Concordant.*

and wherein ye stand: ... you have your footing, *Moffatt* ... and in the which ye continue, *Tyndale.*

2. By which also ye are saved: ... you are being saved, *SEB.*

1 Corinthians 15:3

2076.15 verb 1sing indic aor mid
εὐηγγελισάμην
euēngelisamēn
I announced

5050.3 prs-pron dat 2pl
ὑμῖν
humin
to you

1479.1 conj
εἰ
ei
if

2692.1 verb 2pl pres act
κατέχετε,
katechete
you hold fast,

1609.1 prep gen
ἐκτὸς
ektos
except

1479.1 conj
εἰ
ei
if

3231.1 partic
μὴ
mē
not

1488.1 adv
εἰκῇ
eikē
in vain

3961.22 verb 2pl indic aor act
ἐπιστεύσατε.
episteusate
you believed.

3. **3722.8** verb 1sing indic aor act
Παρέδωκα
Paredōka
I delivered

1056.1 conj
γὰρ
gar
for

5050.3 prs-pron dat 2pl
ὑμῖν
humin
to you

1706.1 prep
ἐν
en
in

4272.4 num ord dat pl
πρώτοις,
prōtois
the first place,

3614.16 rel-pron sing neu
ὃ
ho
what

2504.1 conj
καὶ
kai
also

3741.4 verb indic aor act
παρέλαβον,
parelabon
I received,

3617.1 conj
ὅτι
hoti
that

5382.1 name nom masc
Χριστὸς
Christos
Christ

594.10 verb 3sing indic aor act
ἀπέθανεν
apethanen
died

5065.1 prep
ὑπὲρ
huper
for

3450.1 art gen pl
τῶν
tōn
the

264.6 noun gen pl fem
ἁμαρτιῶν
hamartiōn
sins

2231.2 prs-pron gen 1pl
ἡμῶν,
hēmōn
our,

2567.3 prep
κατὰ
kata
according to

3450.15 art acc pl fem
τὰς
tas
the

1118.8 noun acc pl fem
γραφάς·
graphas
scriptures;

4. **2504.1** conj
καὶ
kai
and

3617.1 conj
ὅτι
hoti
that

2267.4 verb 3sing indic aor pass
ἐτάφη,
etaphē
he was buried;

2504.1 conj
καὶ
kai
and

3617.1 conj
ὅτι
hoti
that

1446.29 verb 3sing indic perf pass
ἐγήγερται
egēgertai
he is raised

3450.11 art dat sing fem
τῇ
tē
the

4995.6 num ord dat sing fem
΄ τρίτῃ
tritē
third

2232.3 noun dat sing fem
ἡμέρᾳ,
hēmera
day,

4.a.Txt: 018K,020L 025P,byz.
Var: 01אּ,02A,03B,06D 33,bo.Lach,Treg,Alf Word,Tisc,We/Ho,Weis Sod,UBS/✱

2232.3 noun dat sing fem
[ᵃ✱ ἡμέρᾳ
hēmera
[day

3450.11 art dat sing fem
τῇ
tē
on the

4995.6 num ord dat sing fem
τρίτῃ]
tritē
third]

2567.3 prep
κατὰ
kata
according to

3450.15 art acc pl fem
τὰς
tas
the

1118.8 noun acc pl fem
γραφάς,
graphas
scriptures;

5. **2504.1** conj
καὶ
kai
and

3617.1 conj
ὅτι
hoti
that

3571.21 verb 3sing indic aor pass
ὤφθη
ōphthē
he appeared

2758.3 name dat masc
Κηφᾷ,
Kēpha
to Cephas,

1520.1 adv
εἶτα
eita
then

5.a.Var: 06D-org,010F 012G,330,464-org

3450.4 art dat pl
τοῖς
tois
to the

1420.1 num card
΄✱ δώδεκα.
dōdeka
twelve.

1717.1 num card
[ᵃ ἕνδεκα.]
hendeka
[eleven.]

6. **1884.1** adv
ἔπειτα
epeita
Then

3571.21 verb 3sing indic aor pass
ὤφθη
ōphthē
he appeared

1868.1 prep gen
ἐπάνω
epanō
to above

3863.1 num card dat
πεντακοσίοις
pentakosiois
five hundred

79.8 noun dat pl masc
ἀδελφοῖς
adelphois
brothers

2160.1 adv
ἐφάπαξ,
ephapax
at once,

1523.1 prep gen
ἐξ
ex
of

6.a.Txt: 018K,020L 025P,byz.
Var: 01אּ,02A,03B,06D Lach,Treg,Alf,Word Tisc,We/Ho,Weis,Sod UBS/✱

3614.1 rel-pron gen pl
ὧν
hōn
whom

3450.7 art pl masc
οἱ
hoi
the

3979.3 adj comp pl
΄ πλείους
pleious
greater part

3979.5 adj comp nom pl masc
[ᵃ✱ πλείονες]
pleiones
[majority]

3176.6 verb 3pl indic pres act
μένουσιν
menousin
remain

once-for-all sense and a progressive sense. Salvation is a growing, deepening, inexhaustible experience. However, believers have the obligation to maintain their walk with God.

If the Corinthians held to it, this gospel would save them unless they had "believed in vain." This phrase could refer to belief on an inadequate basis. If men are not really trusting Christ, their belief is empty. "Vain" (*eikē*) includes the idea of at random, or without serious apprehension. Paul may also have been making an early reference to what he would refute in verses 12-19.

15:3,4. Paul was a faithful steward, and he had delivered to the Corinthians the very essence and substance of the gospel. This he did "first of all." Preaching the gospel had first place on Paul's list of priorities. Necessity lay heavily upon him.

Paul delivered what he had "received." Galatians 1:12 says he received it by direct revelation. The three basic truths he preached were: (1) Christ's death for our sins, (2) Christ's burial, and (3) Christ's resurrection.

The second of these truths links the others together, for it certified the completeness of Christ's death and the reality of His resurrection. His death and burial are presented in the aorist tense as historical events; the Resurrection is emphatically placed in the perfect tense, as an abiding power. The perfect tense appears in this manner six more times in this chapter.

The Resurrection occurred on the third day, fulfilling the prophecies of Holy Writ as well as indicating restoration of life when, under normal circumstances, decay would have begun.

15:5. There were many witnesses to this great event. Jesus appeared to Peter (Luke 24:34). It was not a vision; He was seen by human eyes. Peter was one of the leading apostles, and his witness would have a profound effect on the Church and the world.

Jesus appeared to "the twelve." This was a designation for this group without regard to number. Judas was gone.

15:6. After that He was seen of "above five hundred brethren." The word used for "at once" (*ephapax*) is not so translated elsewhere and is perhaps better translated "once for all," indicating that this was the culminating manifestation of the risen Christ, made at the general gathering of His brethren (Nicoll, *Expositor's Greek Testament*, 2:920).

The majority of the group of over 500 remained alive when this epistle was written. There was a continuing witness to the Resurrection. Only a few had "fallen asleep." This was indeed one of the effects of the Resurrection: death was transformed into sleep in Christ.

if ye keep in memory what I preached unto you: ... if you grasp it, *Fenton* ... if you bear in mind the words in which I proclaimed, *Weymouth* ... if you retain those joyful tidings which I delivered to you, *Campbell*.

unless ye have believed in vain: ... your faith was all haphazard, *Moffatt* ... unless your faith was empty, *Adams* ... has been unreal from the very first, *Weymouth* ... to no purpose, *Confraternity, Campbell* ... you believed inconsiderately, *Wilson*.

3. For I delivered unto you first of all that which I also received: ... the first thing I taught you, *Conybeare*.

how that Christ died for our sins according to the scriptures: ... died on account of our sins, *Murdock* ... as the scripture had said, *Moffatt* ... agreing to the Scriptures, *Geneva*.

4. And that he was buried: He was entombed, *Concordant*.

and that he rose again the third day according to the scriptures: ... in agreement with, *Adams* ... in accordance with, *Fenton*.

5. And that he was seen of Cephas: ... he appeared to, *Rotherham*.

then of the twelve: ... afterwards by the twelve, *Fenton* ... thereupon by the twelve, *Concordant* ... and after that to the Eleven, *Confraternity*.

6. After that, he was seen of above five hundred brethren at once: Afterwards He was seen by more, *Weymouth* ... appeared openly, *Fenton* ... more then fiue hundred brethren together, *Rheims* ... over five hundred, *Adams*.

of whom the greater part remain unto this present: ... most of whom are still alive, *Weymouth* ... most of whom still remain alive, *Adams* ... the majority of whom survive to this day, *Moffatt* ... of whiche many lyuen yit but summe ben deede, *Wyclif* ... the greater number remain, *Fenton* ... many of whom are with us still, *Confraternity*.

6.b.**Txt:** 01ℵ-corr
02A-corr,06D-corr,018K
020L,025P,byz.Sod
Var: 01ℵ-org,02A-org
03B,06D-org,it.sa.bo.
Lach,Treg,Tisc,We/Ho
Weis,UBS/✱

2175.1 conj	732.1 adv	4948.7 indef-pron nom pl masc	1156.2 conj	2504.1 conj	2810.6 verb 3pl indic aor pass
ἕως	ἄρτι,	τινὲς	δὲ	⌐b καὶ ⌐	ἐκοιμήθησαν.
heōs	arti	tines	de	kai	ekoimēthēsan
until	now,	some	but	also	are fallen asleep.

1884.1 adv	3571.21 verb 3sing indic aor pass	2362.3 name dat masc	1520.1 adv	3450.4 art dat pl	646.6 noun dat pl masc
7. ἔπειτα	ὤφθη	Ἰακώβῳ,	εἶτα	τοῖς	ἀποστόλοις
epeita	ōphthē	Iakōbō	eita	tois	apostolois
Then	he appeared	to James;	then	to the	apostles

3820.5 adj dat pl	2057.3 adj acc sing	1156.2 conj	3820.4 adj gen pl	5451.1 adv	3450.3 art dat sing
πᾶσιν.	**8.** ἔσχατον	δὲ	πάντων,	ὡσπερεὶ	τῷ
pasin	eschaton	de	pantōn	hōsperei	tō
all;	last	and	of all,	as	to the

1612.1 noun dat sing neu	3571.21 verb 3sing indic aor pass	2476.1 conj	1466.1 prs-pron nom 1sing	1056.1 conj
ἐκτρώματι	ὤφθη	κἀμοί.	**9.** Ἐγὼ	γάρ
ektrōmati	ōphthē	kamoi	Egō	gar
miscarriage,	he appeared	also to me.	I	for

1498.2 verb 1sing indic pres act	3450.5 art sing masc	1633.2 adj sup nom sing masc	3450.1 art gen pl	646.5 noun gen pl masc
εἰμι	ὁ	ἐλάχιστος	τῶν	ἀποστόλων,
eimi	ho	elachistos	tōn	apostolōn
am	the	least	of the	apostles,

3614.5 rel-pron nom sing masc	3620.2 partic	1498.2 verb 1sing indic pres act	2401.3 adj nom sing masc	2535.35 verb inf pres pass
ὃς	οὐκ	εἰμὶ	ἱκανὸς	καλεῖσθαι
hos	ouk	eimi	hikanos	kaleisthai
who	not	am	fit	to be called

646.1 noun nom sing masc	1354.1 conj	1371.12 verb 1sing indic aor act	3450.12 art acc sing fem	1564.4 noun acc sing fem
ἀπόστολος,	διότι	ἐδίωξα	τὴν	ἐκκλησίαν
apostolos	dioti	ediōxa	tēn	ekklēsian
apostle,	because	I persecuted	the	assembly

3450.2 art gen sing	2296.2 noun gen sing masc	5322.3 noun dat sing fem	1156.2 conj	2296.2 noun gen sing masc	1498.2 verb 1sing indic pres act
τοῦ	θεοῦ.	**10.** χάριτι	δὲ	θεοῦ	εἰμι
tou	theou	chariti	de	theou	eimi
	of God.	By grace	but	of God	I am

3614.16 rel-pron sing neu	1498.2 verb 1sing indic pres act	2504.1 conj	3450.9 art nom sing fem	5322.1 noun nom sing fem	840.3 prs-pron gen sing
ὃ	εἰμι,	καὶ	ἡ	χάρις	αὐτοῦ
ho	eimi	kai	hē	charis	autou
what	I am,	and	the	grace	his

3450.9 art nom sing fem	1519.1 prep	1466.7 prs-pron acc 1sing	3620.3 partic	2727.6 adj nom sing fem	1090.32 verb 3sing indic aor pass
ἡ	εἰς	ἐμὲ	οὐ	κενὴ	ἐγενήθη,
hē	eis	eme	ou	kenē	egenēthē
the	towards	me	not	void	was,

233.2 conj	3917.3 adv comp	840.1 prs-pron gen pl	3820.4 adj gen pl	2844.10 verb 1sing indic aor act	3620.2 partic
ἀλλὰ	περισσότερον	αὐτῶν	πάντων	ἐκοπίασα·	οὐκ
alla	perissoteron	autōn	pantōn	ekopiasa	ouk
but	more abundantly	of them	all	I labored,	not

15:7. Jesus appeared to James. The most fitting conclusion is that this was James, the brother of the Lord. This appearance, only mentioned here, explains the presence of "his brethren" (Acts 1:14) among the 120 at Jerusalem and James' subsequent leadership of the Jerusalem church. When Paul wrote this epistle, James held a high position and would have been an impressive witness.

Then Jesus appeared to "all the apostles." Interpretation depends on whether the stricter or looser sense of "apostles" is used. Paul, presumably aware of the absence of Thomas on the occasion of verse 5 and his consequent skepticism, may have written of this appearance to show that all the apostles saw Christ, and the resultant witness was complete and unqualified. Most likely he was speaking of the original apostles.

"Apostles" also could have a general meaning. Paul indicates in 9:1,2 that the seal of his apostleship, a sign that he was an apostle, was his founding of the church at Corinth ("for the seal of mine apostleship are ye in the Lord" [9:2]). A second factor in determining the meaning of *apostle* is that the 12 disciples of Christ were regarded as a special and distinct group known as "the Twelve" who were separate from the other apostles. Another indication that "apostle" could be a loose term is that words like *deacon* and *presbyter* designated general functions and not particular offices or hierarchical designations (especially since the Church was only 20 years old).

15:8. Lastly, Jesus appeared to Paul. Paul described himself as an untimely child in this reference to Christ's appearance to him. "Of me also" lends emphasis to the matter. Even to Paul, the Lord appeared in resurrection power.

Some find in this an indication of the suddenness and violence of Paul's birth into Christ. Some see here the unripe birth of one changed in a moment from persecutor to apostle instead of maturing normally for his work. It may have been one of the insults the Judaists threw at Paul. Perhaps his opponents took note of his personal appearance and his doctrine of free grace and called him an abortion. Paul adopted the title and gave it a deeper meaning.

15:9. The emphatic personal pronoun "I" shows the great grace and condescension of Christ. Paul held staunchly to two points: One was the high dignity of his position as an apostle; the other was his profound sense of unworthiness in the matter. He felt himself unworthy because he had "persecuted the church of God." He had been active in the greatest of injustices; he had willfully persecuted the "church of God."

15:10. But the grace of God worked a marvelous transformation in Paul's life. He was a sinner saved by grace; an apostle and servant of Jesus Christ by grace.

but some are fallen asleep: ... some were put to repose also, *Concordant.*

7. After that, he was seen of James: Next He was seen by, *Conybeare.*
then of all the apostles:

8. And last of all he was seen of me also: ... and finally he, *Moffatt.*
as of one born out of due time: ... even as if a premature birth, *Concordant* ... as to one of untimely birth, *Weymouth* ... unto the untimely birth, *Rotherham* ... as if to a laggard, *Fenton* ... as if by the one prematurely born, *Wilson* ... the one whose birth was an abnormality, *Adams.*

9. For I am the least of the apostles: I am the most insignificant of, *Fenton* ... Yes, I am the meanest of His apostles, *Way.*
that am not meet to be called an apostle: ... one who doesn't deserve to be called, *Adams* ... am not fit, *Weymouth* ... and am not worthy, *Conybeare* ... who am not competent to be called, *Concordant* ... unfit to bear the name, *Moffatt.*
because I persecuted the church of God:

10. But by the grace of God I am what I am:
and his grace which [was bestowed] upon me was not in vain: ... his grace in me hath not been void, *Rheims* ... His grace, which stooped to me, has not proved ineffectual, *Way* ... he showed me did not go for nothing, *Moffatt* ... did not come to be for naught, *Concordant* ... did not prove ineffectual, *Weymouth* ... has not been useless, *Fenton* ... was not fruitless, *Conybeare, Wilson* ... was not found void, *Panin* ... His grace to me wasn't wasted, *Adams.*
but I laboured more abundantly than they all: On the contrary, *Adams* ... but I toiled more abundantly, *Panin* ... in fact I have labored more than any of them, *Confraternity* ... more strenuously than all the rest, *Weymouth.*

1 Corinthians 15:11

1466.1 prs-pron nom 1sing	1156.2 conj	233.1 conj	233.2 conj	3450.9 art nom sing fem	5322.1 noun nom sing fem
ἐγὼ	δὲ,	ʼ ἀλλ'	[☆ ἀλλὰ]	ἡ	χάρις
egō	de	all'	alla	hē	charis
I	but,	but	[idem]	the	grace

3450.2 art gen sing	2296.2 noun gen sing masc	3450.9 art nom sing fem	4713.1 prep dat	1466.5 prs-pron dat 1sing	1521.1 conj
τοῦ	θεοῦ	ʼᵃ ἡ ʼ	σὺν	ἐμοί.	**11.** εἴτε
tou	theou	hē	sun	emoi	eite
	of God	the	with	me.	Whether

3631.1 conj	1466.1 prs-pron nom 1sing	1521.1 conj	1552.6 dem-pron nom pl masc	3643.1 adv	2756.3 verb 1pl indic pres act
οὖν	ἐγὼ	εἴτε	ἐκεῖνοι,	οὕτως	κηρύσσομεν,
oun	egō	eite	ekeinoi	houtōs	kērussomen
therefore	I	or	those,	so	we preach,

2504.1 conj	3643.1 adv	3961.22 verb 2pl indic aor act	1479.1 conj	1156.2 conj	5382.1 name nom masc
καὶ	οὕτως	ἐπιστεύσατε.	**12.** Εἰ	δὲ	Χριστὸς
kai	houtōs	episteusate	Ei	de	Christos
and	so	you believed.	If	now	Christ

2756.22 verb 3sing indic pres pass	3617.1 conj	1523.2 prep gen	3361.2 adj gen pl	1446.29 verb 3sing indic perf pass
κηρύσσεται,	ὅτι	ἐκ	νεκρῶν	ἐγήγερται,
kērussetai	hoti	ek	nekrōn	egēgertai
is being preached,	that	from among	dead	he has been raised,

4316.1 adv	2978.3 verb 3pl indic pres act	4948.7 indef-pron nom pl masc	1706.1 prep	5050.3 prs-pron dat 2pl	1706.1 prep
πῶς	λέγουσιν	ʼ τινες	ἐν	ὑμῖν	[☆ ἐν
pōs	legousin	tines	en	humin	en
how	say	some	among	you	[among

5050.3 prs-pron dat 2pl	4948.7 indef-pron nom pl masc	3617.1 conj	384.1 noun nom sing fem	3361.2 adj gen pl	3620.2 partic
ὑμῖν	τινες]	ὅτι	ἀνάστασις	νεκρῶν	οὐκ
humin	tines	hoti	anastasis	nekrōn	ouk
you	some]	that	a resurrection	of dead	not

1498.4 verb 3sing indic pres act	1479.1 conj	1156.2 conj	384.1 noun nom sing fem	3361.2 adj gen pl	3620.2 partic
ἔστιν;	**13.** εἰ	δὲ	ἀνάστασις	νεκρῶν	οὐκ
estin	ei	de	anastasis	nekrōn	ouk
there is?	If	but	a resurrection	of dead	not

1498.4 verb 3sing indic pres act	3624.1 adv	5382.1 name nom masc	1446.29 verb 3sing indic perf pass	1479.1 conj	1156.2 conj
ἔστιν,	οὐδὲ	Χριστὸς	ἐγήγερται·	**14.** εἰ	δὲ
estin	oude	Christos	egēgertai	ei	de
there is,	neither	Christ	has been raised:	if	but

5382.1 name nom masc	3620.2 partic	1446.29 verb 3sing indic perf pass	2727.1 adj sing	679.1 partic	3450.16 art sing neu
Χριστὸς	οὐκ	ἐγήγερται,	κενὸν	ἄρα	τὸ
Christos	ouk	egēgertai	kenon	ara	to
Christ	not	has been raised,	void	then	the

2754.1 noun sing neu	2231.2 prs-pron gen 1pl	2727.6 adj nom sing fem	1156.2 conj	2504.1 conj	3450.9 art nom sing fem
κήρυγμα	ἡμῶν,	κενὴ	ʼᵃ δὲ ʼ	καὶ	ἡ
kērugma	hēmōn	kenē	de	kai	hē
proclamation	our,	void	and	also	the

If at the outset Paul appeared last and least, his ministry gave him the premier position. By his efforts he extended the kingdom of Christ over a larger area than any other person. Yet "not I," he asserted. Grace did the work; Paul was the instrument.

15:11. Concluding his comparison of himself and the other apostles, Paul noted that whether it was he or another, "we preach" and "ye believed." On the crucial matters of verses 1-4 and on the matter of the Resurrection there was not the slightest variation. The authoritative witness of Paul or Peter, Jerusalem or Corinth, was unified and in one accord.

15:12. Paul had asserted the fact of Christ's resurrection with barely a clue as to his purpose in so beginning. Now he made it clear. If the resurrection of Christ is true, how could anyone say the resurrection of the dead was not also a fact?

Some at Corinth had doubted the resurrection of the dead. Such skepticism wrecked the faith of the church, just as party divisions had damaged its love. But these people did not, apparently, doubt the personal resurrection of Jesus Christ. They just would not admit the recovery of the body.

This argument had its parallels with the doctrine of the Sadducees (Acts 23:8) and countless illustrations from the superstitions of the Greeks. Some Greek philosophies theorized that the soul continued to exist, but the body died forever. Their idea belonged to the "wisdom of this age."

Paul's opposing argument followed two basic lines: If the Resurrection is untrue, then the Christian faith and its witnesses are false; and if the Resurrection is not real, then neither are the effects derived from it.

15:13. The resurrection of Jesus Christ was logically impossible if there was a denial of bodily resurrection. Christ's resurrection was not even an exception; it was a pattern for many who would follow. If there was no resurrection of the dead, neither had Christ been raised. However, we know that though He was dead, that God raised Him to life. A universal negative cannot be accepted if one fact to the contrary exists.

15:14. If the fact is untrue, the testimony is untrue. If the message is hollow, building on an untrue fact, then the faith is also hollow, building on an untrue message and fact. Such reasoning robbed the gospel of its vitality. The Corinthians must agree with Paul, for they knew of their own faith; they had believed and accepted the apostles' preaching.

yet not I, but the grace of God which was with me: . . . yet I do not ascribe to any thing of myself, but to the favour of God, which accompanied me, *Locke* . . . but the gift of God, *Fenton* . . . God's unmerited favor, *Williams* . . . God's love that was with me, *Beck* . . . that is joined with me, *Berkeley*.

11. Therefore whether [it were] I or they: At any rate, *Moffatt* . . . whether I did it or they, *Beck* . . . or the other apostles, *Locke*.

so we preach, and so ye believed: . . . this is what we preach, and this is what you believed, *Beck*.

12. Now if Christ be preached that he rose from the dead: . . . if what we proclaim about Christ, *TCNT* . . . is being heralded, *Concordant*.

how say some among you that there is no resurrection of the dead?: . . . individuals among you assert, *Moffatt* . . . There is no reviviscence of the dead? *Murdock*.

13. But if there be no resurrection of the dead:

then is Christ not risen: . . . the Messiah also hath not risen, *Murdock*.

14. And if Christ be not risen:

then [is] our preaching vain: . . . false certainly is our preaching, *Macknight* . . . both our preaching is worthless, *Fenton* . . . our proclamation is groundless, *TCNT* . . . what we preach is a delusion, *Weymouth* . . . our preaching is idle talk, *Locke* . . . the message which we preach has nothing in it, *Williams* . . . then our preaching amounts to nothing, *Berkeley* . . . our preaching is wasted, *Klingensmith*.

and your faith [is] also vain: . . . and our faith is equally so! *TCNT* . . . there is nothing in our faith either, *Williams* . . . your faith is an idle dream, you are still sunk in your sins, *Way* . . . and your believing it is to no purpose, *Locke* . . . and your faith is futile, *Berkeley* . . . You have believed in something which is false! *SEB* . . . is groundless, *Norlie*.

1 Corinthians 15:15

14.b.Var: 03B,06D-org
0243,0270-org,6,33,81
1241,1739,1881

3963.1 noun nom sing fem	**5050.2** prs-pron gen 2pl	**2231.2** prs-pron gen 1pl	**2128.30** verb 1pl indic pres pass	**1156.2** conj
πίστις	⸌☆ ὑμῶν.	[b ἡμῶν.]	15. εὑρισκόμεθα	δὲ
pistis	*humōn*	*hēmōn*	*heuriskometha*	*de*
faith	your.	[our.]	We are being found	and

2504.1 conj	**5412.1** noun nom pl masc	**3450.2** art gen sing	**2296.2** noun gen sing masc	**3617.1** conj	**3113.17** verb 1pl indic aor act
καὶ	ψευδομάρτυρες	τοῦ	θεοῦ,	ὅτι	ἐμαρτυρήσαμεν
kai	*pseudomartures*	*tou*	*theou*	*hoti*	*emarturēsamen*
also	false witnesses		of God;	for	we witnessed

2567.3 prep	**3450.2** art gen sing	**2296.2** noun gen sing masc	**3617.1** conj	**1446.5** verb 3sing indic aor act	**3450.6** art acc sing masc
κατὰ	τοῦ	θεοῦ	ὅτι	ἤγειρεν	τὸν
kata	*tou*	*theou*	*hoti*	*ēgeiren*	*ton*
concerning		God	that	he raised up	the

5382.4 name acc masc	**3614.6** rel-pron acc sing masc	**3620.2** partic	**1446.5** verb 3sing indic aor act	**1499.1** conj	**679.1** partic
Χριστόν,	ὃν	οὐκ	ἤγειρεν	εἴπερ	ἄρα
Christon	*hon*	*ouk*	*ēgeiren*	*eiper*	*ara*
Christ,	whom	not	he raised	if	then

3361.5 adj nom pl masc	**3620.2** partic	**1446.16** verb 3pl indic pres pass	**1479.1** conj	**1056.1** conj	**3361.5** adj nom pl masc	**3620.2** partic
νεκροὶ	οὐκ	ἐγείρονται·	16. εἰ	γὰρ	νεκροὶ	οὐκ
nekroi	*ouk*	*egeirontai*	*ei*	*gar*	*nekroi*	*ouk*
dead	not	are being raised.	If	for	dead	not

1446.16 verb 3pl indic pres pass	**3624.1** adv	**5382.1** name nom masc	**1446.29** verb 3sing indic perf pass	**1479.1** conj
ἐγείρονται,	οὐδὲ	Χριστὸς	ἐγήγερται·	17. εἰ
egeirontai	*oude*	*Christos*	*egēgertai*	*ei*
are being raised,	neither	Christ	has been raised:	if

1156.2 conj	**5382.1** name nom masc	**3620.2** partic	**1446.29** verb 3sing indic perf pass	**3124.3** adj nom sing fem	**3450.9** art nom sing fem
δὲ	Χριστὸς	οὐκ	ἐγήγερται,	ματαία	ἡ
de	*Christos*	*ouk*	*egēgertai*	*mataia*	*hē*
but	Christ	not	has been raised,	vain	the

17.a.Var: 03B,06D-org
Lach,We/Ho,Weis
UBS/☆

3963.1 noun nom sing fem	**5050.2** prs-pron gen 2pl	**1498.4** verb 3sing indic pres act	**2068.1** adv	**1498.6** verb 2pl indic pres act	**1706.1** prep
πίστις	ὑμῶν·	[a+ ἐστίν·]	ἔτι	ἐστὲ	ἐν
pistis	*humōn*	*estin*	*eti*	*este*	*en*
faith	your;	[is;]	still	you are	in

3450.14 art dat pl fem	**264.7** noun dat pl fem	**5050.2** prs-pron gen 2pl	**679.1** partic	**2504.1** conj	**3450.7** art pl masc
ταῖς	ἁμαρτίαις	ὑμῶν.	18. ἄρα	καὶ	οἱ
tais	*hamartiais*	*humōn*	*ara*	*kai*	*hoi*
the	sins	your.	Then	and	the

2810.8 verb nom pl masc part aor pass	**1706.1** prep	**5382.3** name dat masc	**616.23** verb 3pl indic aor mid	**1479.1** conj	**1706.1** prep
κοιμηθέντες	ἐν	Χριστῷ	ἀπώλοντο.	19. εἰ	ἐν
koimēthentes	*en*	*Christō*	*apōlonto*	*ei*	*en*
having fallen asleep	in	Christ	perished.	If	in

3450.11 art dat sing fem	**2205.3** noun dat sing fem	**3642.11** dem-pron dat sing fem	**1666.12** verb nom pl masc part perf act	**1498.5** verb 1pl indic pres act
τῇ	ζωῇ	ταύτῃ	⸌ ἠλπικότες	ἐσμὲν
tē	*zōē*	*tautē*	*ēlpikotes*	*esmen*
the	life	this	having hope	we are

15:15. Additionally, Paul argued, if the dead are not raised, Paul and his fellow witnesses would be giving lying testimony of the worst kind about God. They would be literally testifying against Him. Either Christ arose from the dead or the apostles had lied in affirming it. There was no other solution. The second possibility never entered Paul's mind.

15:16. This verse serves as a hinge for the section. What had already been said was repeated with minor adjustment. Paul then turned to a discussion of the unreality of effect if there is no raising of the dead.

15:17. The effects of denying the resurrection of Jesus Christ included the fact that faith would be ineffective because it is built on a false foundation; therefore, our sin has not been removed, and we are still sinners. A faith is useless which does not save from sin. But without Christ's resurrection, both our justification and sanctification are meaningless.

But this was contrary to experience; the Corinthians had experienced salvation; therefore Christ had been raised from the dead.

15:18. Paul moved through this morbid maze to other necessary conclusions if Christ had not been raised from the dead. He spoke of those who had "fallen asleep in Christ." The sense of Christ's presence and His promises had turned death into sleep. But if the Resurrection was denied, then they had really perished "in sins," in ruin and damnation. Lying down to "rest" untroubled, they would find the promises they had believed were a lie.

In such a case, there would be no hope beyond the grave. This would make Christianity no better than the worst paganism. Death would be the final victor.

15:19. The bitterness of the last step in this argument now showed itself. Misery would be the conclusion of such negative reasoning. It is possible for the adverb "only" to modify either the phrase "in this life" or the verb "hope." It appears it modifies the phrase, since "hope" usually appears in the New Testament as a positive term for the certain future joy of Christians, and the second alternative gives "hope" a tentative, negative connotation. These words do not mean that there is no significance to this life but that if Christ is not risen neither this life nor the future life has any meaning. If hope in Christ exists in this world and life only, there is no present

15. Yea, and we are found false witnesses of God: . . . we are detected bearing false witness, *Moffatt* . . . we are found guilty of false witness against God, *Conybeare* . . . guilty of lying about God, *Williams* . . . we, who pretend to be witnesses for God and his truth, shall be found liars, *Locke* . . . found false witnesses concerning God, *Fenton*.

because we have testified of God that he raised up Christ: . . . we gave evidence respecting, *Fenton* . . . by affirming of him, *Moffatt* . . . concerning God, *Murdock* . . . that He resurrected Christ, *Berkeley*.

whom he raised not up, if so be that the dead rise not: . . . whom He did not raise in case no dead are actually raised, *Berkeley*.

16. For if the dead rise not: For if the dead are never raised, *Williams*.

then is not Christ raised:

17. And if Christ be not raised: your faith [is] vain: . . . your faith is futile, *Moffatt* . . . your faith is delusive, *Hanson* . . . your faith is deceptive, *Wilson* . . . your faith is inane, *Murdock* . . . is a mere delusion, *Williams* . . . is to no purpose, *Locke, Alford* . . . is mere folly, *TCNT*.

ye are yet in your sins: . . . your sins are not forgiven, but you are still liable to the punishment due to them, *Locke* . . . you are still under the penalty of your sins, *Williams*.

18. Then they also which are fallen asleep in Christ are perished: It follows also that, *Weymouth* . . . More than that, *Montgomery* . . . they also, who died in the belief of the Gospel, are perished and lost, *Locke* . . . those who went to their rest trusting in Christ perished! *TCNT* . . . those who died trusting in Christ, *Norlie*.

19. If in this life only we have hope in Christ: If in this present life, *Weymouth* . . . If the advantages we expect from Christ are confined to this life, *Locke*.

1 Corinthians 15:20

19.a.Txt: 06D-corr,018K 020L,025P,byz.sa.bo. **Var:** 01א,02A,03B 06D-org,33,Lach,Treg Alf,Word,Tisc,We/Ho Weis,Sod,UBS/✶

1706.1 prep	5382.3 name dat masc	1706.1 prep	5382.3 name dat masc	1666.12 verb nom pl masc part perf act	1498.5 verb 1pl indic pres act
ἐν	Χριστῷ	[ᵃ✶ ἐν	Χριστῷ	ἠλπικότες	ἐσμὲν]
en	Christō	en	Christō	ēlpikotes	esmen
in	Christ	[in	Christ	having hope	we are]

3303.1 adv	1639.2 adj comp nom pl masc	3820.4 adj gen pl	442.7 noun gen pl masc	1498.5 verb 1pl indic pres act
μόνον,	ἐλεεινότεροι	πάντων	ἀνθρώπων	ἐσμέν.
monon	eleeinoteroi	pantōn	anthrōpōn	esmen
only,	more miserable	of all	men	we are.

	3432.1 adv	1156.2 conj	5382.1 name nom masc	1446.29 verb 3sing indic perf pass	1523.2 prep gen
20.	Νυνὶ	δὲ	Χριστὸς	ἐγήγερται	ἐκ
	Nuni	de	Christos	egēgertai	ek
	Now	but	Christ	has been raised	from among

20.a.Txt: 06D-corr,018K 020L,byz. **Var:** 01א,02A,03B 06D-org,025P,33,sa.bo. Gries,Lach,Treg,Alf Word,Tisc,We/Ho,Weis Sod,UBS/✶

3361.2 adj gen pl	532.1 noun nom sing fem	3450.1 art gen pl	2810.11 verb gen pl masc part perf	1090.33 verb 3sing indic aor mid
νεκρῶν,	ἀπαρχὴ	τῶν	κεκοιμημένων	⌈ᵃ ἐγένετο. ⌉
nekrōn	aparchē	tōn	kekoimēmenōn	egeneto
dead,	first fruit	of the	having fallen asleep	he became.

21.a.Txt: 06D-corr,020L 025P,byz. **Var:** 01א,02A,03B 06D-org,018K,33,Lach Treg,Word,Tisc,We/Ho Weis,Sod,UBS/✶

	1879.1 conj	1056.1 conj	1217.1 prep	442.2 noun gen sing masc	3450.5 art sing masc	2265.1 noun nom sing masc	2504.1 conj
21.	ἐπειδὴ	γὰρ	δι'	ἀνθρώπου	⌈ᵃ ὁ ⌉	θάνατος,	καὶ
	epeidē	gar	di'	anthrōpou	ho	thanatos	kai
	Since	for	by	man	the	death,	also

1217.1 prep	442.2 noun gen sing masc	384.1 noun nom sing fem	3361.2 adj gen pl	5450.1 adv	1056.1 conj
δι'	ἀνθρώπου	ἀνάστασις	νεκρῶν.	**22.** ὥσπερ	γὰρ
di'	anthrōpou	anastasis	nekrōn	hōsper	gar
by	man	resurrection	of dead.	As	for

1706.1 prep	3450.3 art dat sing	75.1 name masc	3820.7 adj pl masc	594.4 verb 3pl indic pres act	3643.1 adv
ἐν	τῷ	Ἀδὰμ	πάντες	ἀποθνήσκουσιν,	οὕτως
en	tō	Adam	pantes	apothnēskousin	houtōs
in	the	Adam	all	die,	so

2504.1 conj	1706.1 prep	3450.3 art dat sing	5382.3 name dat masc	3820.7 adj pl masc	2210.8 verb 3pl indic fut pass
καὶ	ἐν	τῷ	Χριστῷ	πάντες	ζωοποιηθήσονται.
kai	en	tō	Christō	pantes	zōopoiēthēsontai
also	in	the	Christ	all	shall be made alive.

	1524.3 adj nom sing masc	1156.2 conj	1706.1 prep	3450.3 art dat sing	2375.3 adj dat sing	4852.1 noun dat sing neu
23.	ἕκαστος	δὲ	ἐν	τῷ	ἰδίῳ	τάγματι·
	hekastos	de	en	tō	idiō	tagmati
	Each	but	in	the	his own	rank:

23.a.Var: 01א,02A,03B 06D,018K,020L,025P byz.Gries,Lach,Treg,Alf Word,Tisc,We/Ho,Weis Sod,UBS/✶

532.1 noun nom sing fem	5382.1 name nom masc	1884.1 adv	3450.7 art pl masc	3450.2 art gen sing
ἀπαρχὴ	Χριστός,	ἔπειτα	οἱ	[ᵃ✶+ τοῦ
aparchē	Christos	epeita	hoi	tou
first fruit	Christ,	then	the	[of the]

5382.2 name gen masc	1706.1 prep	3450.11 art dat sing fem	3814.3 noun dat sing fem	840.3 prs-pron gen sing	1520.1 adv
Χριστοῦ	ἐν	τῇ	παρουσίᾳ	αὐτοῦ·	**24.** εἶτα
Christou	en	tē	parousia	autou	eita
of Christ	at	the	coming	his.	Then

deliverance from sin and no future inheritance in heaven, and believers are of all men most to be pitied. If there is no resurrection Christians have made great sacrifices for an empty, fruitless hope without foundation. If such were the case, it is no wonder the Christian would be the object of great pity.

we are of all men most miserable: ... most to be pitied, *Rotherham* ... to be pitied most, *Moffatt* ... the most wretched of all men, *Fenton.*

15:20. "But now" Paul broke into song and unconditionally asserted the resurrection of Christ. The ugly consequences of verses 12-19 are untrue because there *is* a resurrection of the dead; Christ *has* been raised. Paul used the perfect tense of the verb *to rise*. Not only did Christ rise, He is alive forever.

Christ's resurrection makes the resurrection of the members of His church inevitable. He is the "firstfruits" of many who shall follow. There is an allusion to the first harvest sheaf of the Passover which was presented in the sanctuary on the 16th Nisan (possibly the day of Christ's resurrection). The first ripe sheaf was an earnest of the harvest and was consecrated to God and given to Him in thankfulness and anticipation of what was to come.

Christ was not the first to rise from the dead. But the others died again. His resurrection was to a life that knows no death. His is the life and truth that conquered death.

20. But now is Christ risen from the dead: But the fact is that, *Adams* ... But, in reality, Christ has risen from the dead, *Weymouth* ... in truth, Christ is actually risen, *Locke.*
[and] become the firstfruits of them that slept: ... a Fore-runner of the sleepers, *Fenton.*

21. For since by man [came] death, by man [came] also the resurrection of the dead:

15:21,22. Christ is identified with those sleeping in death because He is the antitype of Adam. He is the One through whom life comes as Adam was the one through whom death came. When Adam sinned he passed into a new state, one controlled and symbolized by death. But Christ brought life. Christ then is the principle and root of resurrection life.

There is also the suggestion here that death is not a law or necessity of fate. Man brought it on himself by an event in history, and it is removable, in degree, by another event in history: the Resurrection.

Adam is pictured as the natural, earthly founder of humanity of which Christ is the spiritual, heavenly counterpart and the giver of new life. However, Paul was not here linking all the dead, even the sinful dead, with Christ. He was linking the risen Christ with the Christian dead, as yet unresurrected. As death in every case is established in Adam, so life in all cases is established in Christ.

22. For as in Adam all die: ... as the death that all men suffer is owing to Adam, *Locke* ... as it was by Adam, *Murdock* ... through Adam, *Weymouth.*
even so in Christ shall all be made alive: ... alle men schulen (shall) be quykened, *Wyclif* ... all will be revived, *Fenton* ... so also by the Messiah they all live, *Murdock* ... is procured them by Christ, *Locke.*

15:23. But while there is a unity in nature and principle, there is a difference in agreement and a distinction in order. Christ was raised as the firstfruit, then at His coming those who are His shall be raised. The thought is of a military division. There is the Captain, above all in His solitary glory; and there is His army, now sleeping, which shall rise at His trumpet's sound (1 Thessalonians 4:16).

23. But every man in his own order: But each in his own turn, *Confraternity* ... in his proper rank, *Rotherham* ... each in his own class, *Concordant* ... every one in his order, *Murdock* ... in the right order, *Weymouth* ... in his own vision, *Moffatt* ... in his proper band, *Macknight.*
Christ the firstfruits: ... the first to rise, *Weymouth* ... to be reaped, *Moffatt.*
afterward they that are Christ's at his coming: ... then those who belong to Christ at his appearing, *Montgomery* ... next after him shall rise those, who are his people, his church, *Locke* ... that beleeued in his comming, *Rheims* ... who have believed, at his coming, *Confraternity* ... Christ's people rising at His return, *Weymouth* ... in His presence thereafter the consummation, *Concordant* ... at his arrival, *Moffatt.*

1 Corinthians 15:25

24.a.Txt: 018K,020L,byz.
Var: 03B,Lach,Treg,Alf
Tisc,Weis,UBS/★

3450.16 art sing neu	4904.1 noun sing neu	3615.1 conj	3722.16 verb 3sing subj aor act	3722.50 verb 3sing subj pres act
τὸ	τέλος,	ὅταν	ʼ παραδῷ	[a παραδιδοῖ]
to	telos	hotan	paradō	paradidoi
the	end,	when	he shall have given up	[he delivers]

3450.12 art acc sing fem	926.4 noun acc sing fem	3450.3 art dat sing	2296.3 noun dat sing masc	2504.1 conj	3824.3 noun dat sing masc
τὴν	βασιλείαν	τῷ	θεῷ	καὶ	πατρί,
tēn	basileian	tō	theō	kai	patri
the	kingdom	to the	God	and	Father;

3615.1 conj	2643.3 verb 3sing subj aor act	3820.12 adj acc sing fem	741.4 noun acc sing fem	2504.1 conj
ὅταν	καταργήσῃ	πᾶσαν	ἀρχὴν	καὶ
hotan	katargēsē	pasan	archēn	kai
when	he shall have brought to nothing	all	rule	and

3820.12 adj acc sing fem	1833.4 noun acc sing fem	2504.1 conj	1405.4 noun acc sing fem	1158.1 verb 3sing indic pres act	1056.1 conj
πᾶσαν	ἐξουσίαν	καὶ	δύναμιν·	**25.** δεῖ	γὰρ
pasan	exousian	kai	dunamin	dei	gar
all	authority	and	power.	It is necessary	for

840.6 prs-pron acc sing masc	929.4 verb inf pres act	884.1 conj	884.2 conj	3614.2 rel-pron gen sing
αὐτὸν	βασιλεύειν,	ʼ ἄχρις	[★ ἄχρι]	οὗ
auton	basileuein	achris	achri	hou
him	to reign,	until	[idem]	which

25.a.Txt: 01ℵ-corr
06D-corr,018K,020L
byz.
Var: 01ℵ-org,02A,03B
06D-org,025P,33,sa.bo.
Lach,Treg,Alf,Word
Tisc,We/Ho,Weis,Sod
UBS/★

300.1 partic	4935.13 verb 3sing subj aor act	3820.8 adj acc pl masc	3450.8 art acc pl masc	2172.7 adj acc pl masc
ʼa ἄν ʼ	θῇ	πάντας	τοὺς	ἐχθροὺς
an	thē	pantas	tous	echthrous
	he shall have put	all	the	enemies

5097.3 prep	3450.8 art acc pl masc	4087.7 noun acc pl masc	840.3 prs-pron gen sing	2057.4 adj nom sing masc	2172.1 adj nom sing masc
ὑπὸ	τοὺς	πόδας	αὐτοῦ.	**26.** ἔσχατος	ἐχθρὸς
hupo	tous	podas	autou	eschatos	echthros
under	the	feet	his.	Last	enemy

2643.9 verb 3sing indic pres pass	3450.5 art sing masc	2265.1 noun nom sing masc	3820.1 adj	1056.1 conj
καταργεῖται	ὁ	θάνατος.	**27.** Πάντα	γὰρ
katargeitai	ho	thanatos	Panta	gar
is being abolished	the	death.	All things	for

5131.2 verb 3sing indic aor act	5097.3 prep	3450.8 art acc pl masc	4087.7 noun acc pl masc	840.3 prs-pron gen sing	3615.1 conj
ὑπέταξεν	ὑπὸ	τοὺς	πόδας	αὐτοῦ·	ὅταν
hupetaxen	hupo	tous	podas	autou	hotan
he put in subjection	under	the	feet	his.	When

1156.2 conj	1500.8 verb 3sing subj aor act	3617.1 conj	3820.1 adj	5131.21 verb 3sing indic perf pass
δὲ	εἴπῃ	ὅτι	πάντα	ὑποτέτακται,
de	eipē	hoti	panta	hupotetaktai
but	it be said	that	all things	have been put in subjection,

1206.1 adj sing	3617.1 conj	1609.1 prep gen	3450.2 art gen sing	5131.3 verb gen sing masc part aor act	840.4 prs-pron dat sing
δῆλον	ὅτι	ἐκτὸς	τοῦ	ὑποτάξαντος	αὐτῷ
dēlon	hoti	ektos	tou	hupotaxantos	autō
clear	that	except	the	having put in subjection	to him

466

15:24. Christ's second advent, of which the Rapture is a part, concludes the present history of the world. "Then cometh (is) the end," which indicates the end of the drama of sin and redemption. "Then" indicates taking place at an unspecified time afterward.

The end will be culminated by Christ's delivering the Kingdom to God the Father before which He shall have abolished all opposition, "all rule, and all authority and power." The two verbs (*paradō* and *katargēsē*) indicate distinct but related actions. When every opposing force has been destroyed, then Christ shall lay His kingdom at the Father's feet.

"To God, even the Father" explains the reason for Christ's act of submission. The thought is not one of loss, but of giving to another what was designed for Him. This does not indicate a demotion of Christ; it is not the cessation of Christ's dominion, but the inauguration of Christ's eternal kingdom; it is not the termination of Christ's rule but of the reign of sin and death. "All" is complete.

15:25. There is a compelling necessity about the word "must." God decides finally on the matter and no uncertainty is involved. There is a reference to Psalm 110:1 which indicates the Messiah's obligation and power. This general eschatology indicates Christ's kingship and points to the task He fulfills today. His work is a prelude to and notice of the end.

15:26. Paul had spoken of the event occurring at the "end" of earthly history and of the event preceding that, which is the subjection of all rule and power to that of Christ. Death is the last enemy to be totally destroyed. This stands in opposition to the position held by "some" in verse 12. These said there is no resurrection; Paul countered that there is to be no death. Death shall be robbed of all its control and power. It shall be abolished.

This was the climax of Paul's argument. In fact, in experience and in principle, Paul had shown the victory of the Resurrection over death.

15:27. Acting as a supplement to Paul's main thought in verses 20-26, this verse reaffirms the unlimited dominion of Christ and the fact that only through His absolute victory can the kingdom of God be consummated.

There is a reference to Psalm 8, which promised man complete rule over his domain. As man, Christ is the Deliverer and Conqueror for man; He has conquered death. "When all things shall be subdued unto him (the Son)," His commission will be ended and the travail of His soul will be satisfied (Isaiah 53:11).

"But" adds a self-evident assertion concerning God the Father. Behind the messianic reign is the absolute supremacy of God.

24. Then [cometh] the end: Then the end shall be, *Macknight* . . . will be the perfection, *Fenton* . . . And then will be the end, *Murdock.*

when he shall have delivered up the kingdom to God, even the Father: . . . when he shall resign the kingdom, *Campbell* . . . when he hands over his royal power, *Moffatt* . . . when He delivers the empire, *Adams* . . . surrender the Kingship to God, *Weymouth.*

when he shall have put down all rule and all authority and power: . . . he shall have abrogated All Government, *Wilson* . . . when he shall have abolished all government, *Campbell* . . . whensoever He may abolish all rule, *Clementson* . . . when he will destroy every principality, *Sawyer* . . . whenever He should be nullifying all sovereignty, *Concordant* . . . when every prince, and every sovereign, and all powers shall have come to naught, *Murdock* . . . overthrown all other government, *Weymouth* . . . all his foes are put under, *Moffatt* . . . having destroyed all other dominion, *Conybeare.*

25. For he must reign: . . . must continue King, *Weymouth.*
till he hath put all enemies under his feet:

26. The last enemy [that] shall be destroyed [is] death: Death is to be done away with, *Rotherham* . . . being abolished, *Concordant* . . . is to be overthrown is Death, *Weymouth* . . . will be rendered powerless, *Wilson.*

27. For he hath put all things under his feet: For He subjects, *Concordant* . . . he made subject under, *Rotherham* . . . he hath subjected all under, *Murdock.*
But when he saith all things are put under [him: All things are in subjection, *Weymouth* . . . are subdued to him, *Rheims.*
it is] manifest that he is excepted, which did put all things under him:** . . . it is evident, *Hanson, Montgomery* . . . that God is excepted, *Conybeare* . . . it is clear that this doesn't include the One Who subjected everything to Him, *Adams.*

467

1 Corinthians 15:28

3450.17 art pl neu	3820.1 adj		3615.1 conj	1156.2 conj	5131.18 verb 3sing subj aor pass
τὰ	πάντα·	**28.** ὅταν	δὲ		ὑποταγῇ
ta	panta	hotan	de		hupotagē
the	all things.	When	but		shall have been put in subjection

28.a.Txt: 01‭א‬,02A 06D-corr2,044,byz. **Var:** 03B,06D-org,010F 012G,0243,33,1175 1739,sa.

840.4 prs-pron dat sing	3450.17 art pl neu	3820.1 adj	4966.1 adv	2504.1 conj	840.5 prs-pron nom sing masc	3450.5 art sing masc
αὐτῷ	τὰ	πάντα,	τότε	⌐a καὶ	αὐτὸς	ὁ
autō	ta	panta	tote	kai	autos	ho
to him	the	all things,	then	also	himself	the

5048.1 noun nom sing masc	5131.23 verb 3sing indic fut pass	3450.3 art dat sing	5131.4 verb dat sing masc part aor act
υἱὸς	ὑποταγήσεται	τῷ	ὑποτάξαντι
huios	hupotagēsetai	tō	hupotaxanti
Son	will be put in subjection	to the	having put in subjection

840.4 prs-pron dat sing	3450.17 art pl neu	3820.1 adj	2419.1 conj	1498.10 verb 3sing subj pres act	3450.5 art sing masc
αὐτῷ	τὰ	πάντα,	ἵνα	ᾖ	ὁ
autō	ta	panta	hina	ē	ho
to him	the	all things,	that	may be	the

28.b.Txt: 01‭א‬,06D-corr 018K,020L,025P,byz. Tisc,Sod **Var:** 02A,03B,06D-org 33,Lach,Treg,Alf We/Ho,Weis,UBS/☆

2296.1 noun nom sing masc	3450.17 art pl neu	3820.1 adj	1706.1 prep	3820.5 adj dat pl	1878.1 conj
θεὸς	⌐b τὰ ⌐	πάντα	ἐν	πᾶσιν.	**29.** Ἐπεὶ
theos	ta	panta	en	pasin	Epei
God	the	all	in	all.	Since

4949.9 intr-pron sing neu	4020.55 verb 3pl indic fut act	3450.7 art pl masc	901.13 verb nom pl masc part pres pass	5065.1 prep
τί	ποιήσουσιν	οἱ	βαπτιζόμενοι	ὑπὲρ
ti	poiēsousin	hoi	baptizomenoi	huper
what	shall they do	the	being baptized	for

3450.1 art gen pl	3361.2 adj gen pl	1479.1 conj	3517.1 adv	3361.5 adj nom pl masc	3620.2 partic	1446.16 verb 3pl indic pres pass
τῶν	νεκρῶν	εἰ	ὅλως	νεκροὶ	οὐκ	ἐγείρονται·
tōn	nekrōn	ei	holōs	nekroi	ouk	egeirontai
the	dead	if	at all	dead	not	are being raised?

4949.9 intr-pron sing neu	2504.1 conj	901.12 verb 3pl indic pres pass	5065.1 prep	3450.1 art gen pl	3361.2 adj gen pl
τί	καὶ	βαπτίζονται	ὑπὲρ	⌐ τῶν	νεκρῶν;
ti	kai	baptizontai	huper	tōn	nekrōn
why	also	are they being baptized	for	the	dead?

29.a.Txt: 06D-corr,020L byz. **Var:** 01‭א‬,02A,03B 06D-org,018K,025P,sa. bo.Gries,Lach,Treg,Alf Word,Tisc,We/Ho,Weis Sod,UBS/☆

840.1 prs-pron gen pl	4949.9 intr-pron sing neu	2504.1 conj	2231.1 prs-pron nom 1pl	2765.2 verb 1pl indic pres act
[a☆ αὐτῶν;]	**30.** τί	καὶ	ἡμεῖς	κινδυνεύομεν
autōn	ti	kai	hēmeis	kinduneuomen
[them?]	Why	also	we	are in danger

3820.12 adj acc sing fem	5443.4 noun acc sing fem		2567.2 prep	2232.4 noun acc sing fem	594.1 verb 1sing indic pres act
πᾶσαν	ὥραν;	**31.** καθ'		ἡμέραν	ἀποθνῄσκω,
pasan	hōran	kath'		hēmeran	apothnēskō
every	hour?	By		day	I die,

31.a.Txt: 02A,Steph **Var:** p46,01‭א‬,03B,06D 018K,020L,025P,etc.byz. Elzev,Gries,Lach,Treg Alf,Word,Tisc,We/Ho Weis,Sod,UBS/☆

3375.1 partic	3450.12 art acc sing fem	2233.6 adj acc 1sing fem	5052.7 adj acc 2sing fem	2716.3 noun acc sing fem
νὴ	τὴν	⌐ ἡμετέραν	[a☆ ὑμετέραν]	καύχησιν,
nē	tēn	hēmeteran	humeteran	kauchēsin
by	the	our	[your]	boasting,

468

15:28. The first part of the next verse reaffirms objectively what was issued subjectively as the verdict by Christ himself on His own finished work. When this subjection of "all things" to Christ has been completed, then Christ shall be subjected to God the Father. This simply involves the subjection of sonship. There is no inferiority of nature or removal of power, but the free submission of love.

This was the spirit that motivated Christ in His earthly ministry. His intention was always to glorify the Father, who in turn glorified the Son. And the purpose of all this is fixed in conclusion: "that God may be all in all"; that God's will may be everywhere observed and His being everywhere immanent.

15:29. "Baptized for the dead" has been much debated for many centuries. To what was he referring? William Barclay, in his commentary on 1 Corinthians, has a plausible explanation of this verse. He says, " . . . this phrase can refer to only one custom, which has quite correctly passed out of Church practice altogether. In the Early Church there was vicarious baptism. If a person died who had intended to become a member of the Church and was actually under instruction, sometimes someone else underwent baptism for him. The custom sprang from a superstitious view of baptism that, without it, a person was necessarily excluded from the bliss of heaven. It was to safeguard against this exclusion that sometimes people volunteered to be baptized literally on behalf of those who had died. Here Paul neither approves or disapproves that practice. He merely asks if there can be any point in it if there is no resurrection and the dead never rise again" (*The Daily Study Bible*, p.171).

The fact that Paul only parenthetically referred to this practice suggests that it held no importance for him at all. He was merely using it as an example to show that the Corinthians were being inconsistent in their view of the afterlife: if there is no future resurrection, what was the point of baptizing for the dead?

15:30. The New Testament refers often to the peril of the apostles and other Christian workers. They daily faced hazards with the hope of future joy and security because of the resurrection of the dead. If the resurrection of the dead is not a fact, this constant exposure to danger was foolhardy, even madness.

15:31. Lest the Corinthians think Paul was exaggerating his situation, he offered his exclamation. *Kath' hēmeran apothnēskō* (literally, "daily I die") comes first in the Greek for emphasis. His danger was real and constant. As well as daily facing danger, he in himself daily abandoned his life.

28. And when all things shall be subdued unto him: . . . whenever all may be subjected to Him, *Concordant* . . . when He has subjugated all to Him, *Fenton* . . . the whole universe has been made subject to Him, *Weymouth*.

then shall the Son also himself be subject unto him that put all things under him:

that God may be all in all: . . . may be everything to everyone, *Moffatt*.

29. Else what shall they do which are baptized for the dead: . . . what do they obtain, *Fenton* . . . on behalf of their dead? *Moffatt*.

if the dead rise not at all? why are they then baptized for the dead?: . . . if the dead are not absolutely raised? *Fenton*.

30. And why stand we in jeopardy every hour?: . . . why should we run a risk every hour? *Fenton* . . . are vve in danger euery houre? *Rheims, Moffatt* . . . running into peril, *Rotherham* . . . are we also in danger every hour? *Concordant* . . . expose ourselves to danger every hour, *Weymouth*.

31. I protest by your rejoicing which I have in Christ Jesus our Lord:

I die daily: . . . but I am at death's door! *Moffatt*.

1 Corinthians 15:32

31.b.**Var:** 01א,02A,03B
018K,025P,33,sa.bo.
Lach,Treg,Alf,Tisc
We/Ho,Weis,Sod
UBS/✶

79.6 noun pl masc	3614.12 rel-pron acc sing fem	2174.1 verb 1sing pres act	1706.1 prep	5382.3 name dat masc
[b✶+ ἀδελφοί,]	ἣν	ἔχω	ἐν	Χριστῷ
adelphoi	hēn	echō	en	Christō
[brothers,]	which	I have	in	Christ

2400.2 name masc	3450.3 art dat sing	2935.3 noun dat sing masc	2231.2 prs-pron gen 1pl	1479.1 conj	2567.3 prep
Ἰησοῦ	τῷ	κυρίῳ	ἡμῶν.	**32.** εἰ	κατὰ
Iēsou	tō	kuriō	hēmōn.	ei	kata
Jesus	the	Lord	our.	If	according to

442.4 noun acc sing masc	2318.1 verb 1sing indic aor act	1706.1 prep	2163.2 name dat fem	4949.9 intr-pron sing neu
ἄνθρωπον	ἐθηριομάχησα	ἐν	Ἐφέσῳ,	τί
anthrōpon	ethēriomachēsa	en	Ephesō	ti
man	I fought with beasts	in	Ephesus,	what

1466.4 prs-pron dat 1sing	3450.16 art sing neu	3650.1 noun nom sing neu	1479.1 conj	3361.5 adj nom pl masc	3620.2 partic
μοι	τὸ	ὄφελος,	εἰ	νεκροὶ	οὐκ
moi	to	ophelos,	ei	nekroi	ouk
to me	the	profit,	if	dead	not

1446.16 verb 3pl indic pres pass	2052.18 verb 1pl subj aor act	2504.1 conj	3956.16 verb 1pl subj aor act	833.1 adv
ἐγείρονται;	Φάγωμεν	καὶ	πίωμεν,	αὔριον
egeirontai	Phagōmen	kai	piōmen,	aurion
are being raised?	We may eat	and	we may drink;	tomorrow

1056.1 conj	594.3 verb 1pl indic pres act	3231.1 partic	3966.11 verb 2pl indic pres pass	5188.2 verb 3pl indic pres act
γὰρ	ἀποθνήσκομεν.	**33.** μὴ	πλανᾶσθε·	Φθείρουσιν
gar	apothnēskomen.	mē	planasthe	Phtheirousin
for	we die.	Not	be misled:	corrupt

33.a.**Txt:** Steph,Lach
Var: 01א,02A,03B,06D
018K,020L,025P,byz.
Gries,Treg,Alf,Word
Tisc,We/Ho,Weis,Sod
UBS/✶

2222.1 noun acc pl neu	5378.4 adj acc pl neu	5378.6 adj acc pl neu	3520.1 noun nom pl fem	2527.6 adj nom pl fem
ἤθη	ʿ χρήσθʾ	[a✶ χρηστὰ]	ὁμιλίαι	κακαί.
ēthē	chrēsth'	chrēsta	homiliai	kakai
manners	good	[idem]	companionships	evil.

1581.1 verb 2pl impr aor act	1341.1 adv	2504.1 conj	3231.1 partic	262.1 verb 2pl pres act
34. ἐκνήψατε	δικαίως,	καὶ	μὴ	ἁμαρτάνετε·
eknēpsate	dikaiōs	kai	mē	hamartanete
Become sober	righteously,	and	not	sin;

54.1 noun acc sing fem	1056.1 conj	2296.2 noun gen sing masc	4948.7 indef-pron nom pl masc	2174.6 verb 3pl indic pres act	4242.1 prep
ἀγνωσίαν	γὰρ	θεοῦ	τινες	ἔχουσιν·	πρὸς
agnōsian	gar	theou	tines	echousin	pros
ignorance	for	of God	some	have:	to

34.a.**Txt:** 02A,018K
020L,byz.
Var: 01א,03B,06D,025P
Lach,Treg,Alf,Tisc
We/Ho,Weis,Sod
UBS/✶

1775.1 noun acc sing fem	5050.3 prs-pron dat 2pl	2978.1 verb 1sing pres act	2953.1 verb 1sing pres act	233.1 conj
ἐντροπὴν	ὑμῖν	ʿ λέγω.	[a✶ λαλῶ.]	**35.** ʿ Ἀλλʾ
entropēn	humin	legō	lalō	All'
shame	to you	I speak.	[idem]	But

233.2 conj	2029.11 verb 3sing indic fut act	4948.3 indef-pron nom sing	4316.1 adv	1446.16 verb 3pl indic pres pass
[✶ Ἀλλὰ]	ἐρεῖ	τις,	Πῶς	ἐγείρονται
Alla	erei	tis,	Pōs	egeirontai
[idem]	will say	someone,	How	are being raised

In the process Paul boasted of the results of his apostolic work, which was the very reason for which he died daily. It was this glorying in the work of the Lord and his commitment to it that caused Paul to die daily.

15:32. Paul experienced poverty and pain; if there is no "day of Christ," he had been a fool. It is believed by some that Paul actually fought in the Ephesian arena. However, since Paul was a Roman citizen, he could not ordinarily be compelled to fight in the arena. No such experience is listed in 2 Corinthians 11. It appears from Acts 19:31-40 that Paul had friends among the ranking officials at Ephesus who probably would have prevented such a thing. Paul probably had in mind those men in Ephesus who had fiercely opposed him. Thus "I have fought with beasts at Ephesus" is probably used somewhat figuratively.

Morbid unbelief will produce a certain desperation and sensuality. Paul quoted from Isaiah 22:13 which reveals the recklessness bred by the absence of a hope of life after death. This citation might have provided an axiom for the popular Epicureanism. It is also an excellent example of ancient popular morals and attitudes. This was the best that could be had, they thought. But it was not so if there is a resurrection from the dead.

15:33. Paul charged the Corinthian believers, "Be not deceived." They were attempting to be too broad in allowing tenets that produced skepticism and were demoralizing in their effect. The line the apostle quoted, "evil . . . manners," has been attributed to Menander's *Thais* (ca. 322 B.C.). But it was probably used even before that time.

15:34. Paul exhorted the Christians in Corinth to "awake . . . and sin not." *Awake* originally had the sense of becoming sober after drunkenness. Paul urged the believers to sober righteousness.

"Some" of the Corinthians had no "knowledge of God." This statement indicated a characteristic, persistent condition which these "some" shared with the heathen. Paul spoke this to move the Corinthian believers to shame. The error that had arisen among them was caused by a lack of real knowledge of God.

15:35. Having established the fact of the resurrection, Paul turned to questions regarding the nature and experiential side of the resurrection of the body. The recorded questions in this verse refer to the possibility and conceivability of the resurrection of the body. They imply that the resurrection of the body is absurd. But Paul answered each one.

32. If after the manner of men I have fought with beasts at Ephesus: . . . from merely human motives, *Weymouth.*

what advantageth it me, if the dead rise not?: If dead men do not rise, *Moffatt* . . . vvhat doth it profit me, *Rheims* . . . what is my gain, *Fenton.*

let us eat and drink; for to-morrow we die:

33. Be not deceived: Be not seduced, *Rheims* . . . Be not misled, *Fenton* . . . Make no mistake about this, *Moffatt.*

evil communications corrupt good manners: Evil companionships corrupt good morals, *Weymouth* . . . vile teachings, *Fenton* . . . evil conversations, *Concordant.*

34. Awake to righteousness, and sin not: . . . to perfect sobriety, *Fenton.*

for some have not the knowledge of God: . . . some of you are insensible, *Moffatt.*

I speak [this] to your shame: I speake this to your rebuke, *Geneva* . . . I speak reproving you, *Fenton* . . . in order to move you to shame, *Weymouth.*

35. But some [man] will say, How are the dead raised up?:

1 Corinthians 15:36

3450.7 art pl masc	3361.5 adj nom pl masc	4029.2 intr- pron dat sing	1156.2 conj	4835.3 noun dat sing neu	2048.36 verb 3pl indic pres
οἱ	νεκροί;	ποίῳ	δὲ	σώματι	ἔρχονται;
hoi	*nekroi*	*poiō*	*de*	*sōmati*	*erchontai*
the	dead?	with what	and	body	do they come?

36.a.Txt: 018K,020L,byz.
Var: 01א,02A,03B,06D
025P,Lach,Treg,Alf
Tisc,We/Ho,Weis,Sod
UBS/✷

871.3 adj voc sing masc	871.1 adj sing masc	4622.1 prs- pron nom 2sing	3614.16 rel- pron sing neu	4540.2 verb 2sing indic pres act
36. ἄφρον,	[ᵃ✷ ἄφρων,]	σὺ	ὃ	σπείρεις,
aphron	*aphrōn*	*su*	*ho*	*speireis*
Fool;	[idem]	you	what	sow,

3620.3 partic	2210.6 verb 3sing indic pres pass	1430.1 partic	3231.1 partic	594.13 verb 3sing subj aor act	2504.1 conj
οὐ	ζωοποιεῖται	ἐὰν	μὴ	ἀποθάνῃ·	**37.** καὶ
ou	*zōopoieitai*	*ean*	*mē*	*apothanē*	*kai*
not	is being made alive	if	not	it die.	And

3614.16 rel- pron sing neu	4540.2 verb 2sing indic pres act	3620.3 partic	3450.16 art sing neu	4835.1 noun sing neu	3450.16 art sing neu
ὃ	σπείρεις,	οὐ	τὸ	σῶμα	τὸ
ho	*speireis*	*ou*	*to*	*sōma*	*to*
what	you sow,	not	the	body	the

1090.71 verb acc sing neu part fut mid	4540.2 verb 2sing indic pres act	233.2 conj	1125.2 adj acc sing masc	2821.3 noun acc sing masc
γενησόμενον	σπείρεις,	ἀλλὰ	γυμνὸν	κόκκον,
genēsomenon	*speireis*	*alla*	*gumnon*	*kokkon*
going to become	you sow,	but	a bare	grain,

1479.1 conj	5018.4 verb 3sing opt aor act	4476.1 noun gen sing neu	2211.1 conj	4948.1 indef- pron gen sing	3450.1 art gen pl
εἰ	τύχοι,	σίτου	ἢ	τινος	τῶν
ei	*tuchoi*	*sitou*	*ē*	*tinos*	*tōn*
if	it may be	of wheat	or	of someone	of the

3036.1 adj gen pl	3450.5 art sing masc	1156.2 conj	2296.1 noun nom sing masc	840.4 prs- pron dat sing	1319.2 verb 3sing indic pres act
λοιπῶν·	**38.** ὁ	δὲ	θεὸς	ʿαὐτῷ	δίδωσιν
loipōn	*ho*	*de*	*theos*	*autō*	*didōsin*
rest;		and	God	to it	gives

1319.2 verb 3sing indic pres act	840.4 prs- pron dat sing	4835.1 noun sing neu	2503.1 conj	2286.22 verb 3sing indic aor act	2504.1 conj
[✷ δίδωσιν	αὐτῷ]	σῶμα	καθὼς	ἠθέλησεν,	καὶ
didōsin	*autō*	*sōma*	*kathōs*	*ēthelēsen*	*kai*
[gives	to it]	a body	just as	he willed,	and

38.a.Txt: 01א-corr,018K
020L,byz.
Var: 01א-org,02A,03B
06D,025P,33,Lach,Treg
Alf,Tisc,We/Ho,Weis
Sod,UBS/✷

1524.4 adj dat sing masc	3450.1 art gen pl	4543.4 noun gen pl neu	3450.16 art sing neu	2375.4 adj acc sing	4835.1 noun sing neu
ἑκάστῳ	τῶν	σπερμάτων	ʿᵃ τὸ ʾ	ἴδιον	σῶμα.
hekastō	*tōn*	*spermatōn*	*to*	*idion*	*sōma*
to each	of the	seeds	the	its own	body.

3620.3 partic	3820.9 adj nom sing fem	4418.1 noun nom sing fem	3450.9 art nom sing fem	840.9 prs-pron nom sing fem	4418.1 noun nom sing fem
39. οὐ	πᾶσα	σὰρξ	ἡ	αὐτὴ	σάρξ·
ou	*pasa*	*sarx*	*hē*	*autē*	*sarx*
Not	every	flesh	the	same	flesh,

39.a.Txt: byz.bo.
Var: 01א,02A,03B,06D
018K,020L,025P,Gries
Lach,Treg,Alf,Word
Tisc,We/Ho,Weis,Sod
UBS/✷

233.2 conj	241.9 adj nom sing fem	3173.1 conj	4418.1 noun nom sing fem	442.7 noun gen pl masc	241.9 adj nom sing fem
ἀλλὰ	ἄλλη	μὲν	ʿᵃ σὰρξ ʾ	ἀνθρώπων,	ἄλλη
alla	*allē*	*men*	*sarx*	*anthrōpōn*	*allē*
but	another	men	flesh	of men,	another

15:36. "Thou fool" showed Paul's estimate of the skepticism involved in the questions. Paul may have been reflecting the Old Testament definition of a fool as a man who has no regard for God (cf. Psalm 14:1, "The fool hath said in his heart, There is no God"). The Biblical fool is not simply unintelligent, he is morally reprehensible. He involved the objector personally in the discussion. If this foolish man would only look at the fields, at his own work, he would realize that nature carries an analogy. The farmer plants a seed in the ground. But it cannot produce a plant or crop or enhance itself unless it first dies. Thus life comes out of death. The seed does not give itself life; God gives it life.

Jesus himself used the analogy of wheat being planted, dying, and sprouting to speak of His own death (John 12:24). Although Jesus was there speaking primarily of the necessity of His death, the passage strongly maintains that in death a transformation takes place and that the final product is more glorious than the initial one.

Paul did not explain the modus operandi, but what he did show is that the mystery creates no doubt or prejudice against the reality, for the same mystery is present in the vegetating seed. With this example from nature so evident, why should anyone think the transformation of a dead body impossible?

15:37. The purpose of the sower is to receive a different (new) form or product from his seed. Yet the sower knows it is the same body or seed. The truth of this lower "resurrection" supports the conceivability of the higher resurrection. "It may chance . . . grain" refers to the fact that the grain of wheat gives no more promise of a future body than any other seed or grain. But the raised "body" will be more wonderful than the "body" (seed) that was buried.

15:38. That which arises from the dead seed is a God-given body, as is the resurrection one. God gives the body as He wills. This is the connection between seed and plant.

Additionally, as God finds a fit body for each of the numberless planted seeds, so He will provide a fit body for man's redeemed, glorified nature. The man sows; the seed dies; the plant is raised by the power of God. It is an ordained rising; so shall it be with the resurrection of the body. God gives continually the proper body to each seed.

15:39. Paul spoke of the varied forms in nature and the appropriateness of each for the life it clothes. For example, in the zoological realm there is countless differentiation rather than uniformity. The corporeity of each division listed has been established by God according to individual constitution and needs. If God can

1 Corinthians 15:39

and with what body do they come?: . . . with what sort of body, *Adams* . . . in what form will they come? *TCNT* . . . do they come back, *Weymouth.*

36. [Thou] fool, that which thou sowest is not quickened, except it die: Imprudent one! *Concordant* . . . Simpleton! what you sow is not made alive, *Campbell* . . . Foolish man!...unless it dies, *Montgomery* . . . Senseless man, *Douay* . . . Senseless!...unless it arises from its bed, *Fenton* . . . does not daily experience teach thee, *Locke* . . . is not brought to life, *Noyes* . . . is not made alive, *Panin* . . . does not burst into life, *TCNT* . . . till it hath partaken of death, *Conybeare.*

37. And that which thou sowest, thou sowest not that body that shall be:
but bare grain, it may chance of wheat, or of some other [grain]: . . . but a mere kernel, *Hanson* . . . but a naked grain, *Fenton* . . . but a naked kernel, *Concordant, Rotherham* . . . or some other seed, *Moffatt.*

38. But God giveth it a body as it hath pleased him: . . . an appropriate body, *Rotherham* . . . at his pleasure, *Geneva* . . . such as He intended, *Fenton* . . . such as God has thought fit to give it, *Locke.*
and to every seed his own body: . . . and to each of the seeds, *Macknight* . . . its proper body, *Campbell, Douay* . . . its natural body, *Murdock* . . . a plant, of a particular shape and size, *Locke* . . . he gives the form peculiar to itself, *TCNT.*

39. All flesh [is] not the same flesh: . . . even now, all flesh is not identical in composition, *Way* . . . And every body is not alike, *Murdock* . . . there are different kinds of flesh, *Locke* . . . differ the one from the other, *Conybeare.*
but [there is] one [kind of] flesh of men: . . . but there is one kind for human beings, *Adams* . . . for the body of a man is one thing, *Murdock.*

39.b.**Var:** 01א,03B,06D
33,bo.Lach,Treg,Alf
Tisc,We/Ho,Weis,Sod
UBS/✶

1156.2 conj	4418.1 noun nom sing fem	2906.2 noun gen pl neu	241.9 adj nom sing fem	1156.2 conj	4418.1 noun nom sing fem
δὲ	σάρξ	κτηνῶν,	ἄλλη	δὲ	[ᵇ✶+ σὰρξ]
de	sarx	ktēnōn	allē	de	sarx
and	flesh	of beasts,	another	and	[flesh]

2459.4 noun gen pl masc	241.9 adj nom sing fem	1156.2 conj	4279.1 adj gen pl neu	4279.1 adj gen pl neu	241.9 adj nom sing fem
‛ ἰχθύων,	ἄλλη	δὲ	πτηνῶν.	[✶ πτηνῶν,	ἄλλη
ichthuōn	allē	de	ptēnōn	ptēnōn	allē
of fish,	another	and	of birds.	[of birds,	another

1156.2 conj	2459.4 noun gen pl masc	2504.1 conj	4835.4 noun pl neu	2016.7 adj pl neu	2504.1 conj
δὲ	ἰχθύων.]	**40.** καὶ	σώματα	ἐπουράνια,	καὶ
de	ichthuōn	kai	sōmata	epourania	kai
and	of fish.]	And	bodies	heavenly,	and

4835.4 noun pl neu	1904.3 adj pl neu	233.1 conj	233.2 conj	2066.9 adj	3173.1 conj
σώματα	ἐπίγεια·	‛ ἀλλ’	[✶ ἀλλὰ]	ἑτέρα	μὲν
sōmata	epigeia	all’	alla	hetera	men
bodies	earthly:	but	[idem]	different	men

3450.9 art nom sing fem	3450.1 art gen pl	2016.2 adj gen pl	1385.1 noun nom sing fem	2066.9 adj	1156.2 conj
ἡ	τῶν	ἐπουρανίων	δόξα,	ἑτέρα	δὲ
hē	tōn	epouraniōn	doxa	hetera	de
the	of the	heavenly	glory,	different	and

3450.9 art nom sing fem	3450.1 art gen pl	1904.1 adj gen pl	241.9 adj nom sing fem	1385.1 noun nom sing fem	2229.2 noun gen sing masc
ἡ	τῶν	ἐπιγείων.	**41.** ἄλλη	δόξα	ἡλίου,
hē	tōn	epigeiōn	allē	doxa	hēliou
that	of the	earthly:	another	glory	of sun,

2504.1 conj	241.9 adj nom sing fem	1385.1 noun nom sing fem	4437.2 noun gen sing fem	2504.1 conj	241.9 adj nom sing fem	1385.1 noun nom sing fem
καὶ	ἄλλη	δόξα	σελήνης,	καὶ	ἄλλη	δόξα
kai	allē	doxa	selēnēs	kai	allē	doxa
and	another	glory	of moon,	and	another	glory

786.5 noun gen pl masc	786.1 noun nom sing masc	1056.1 conj	786.2 noun gen sing masc	1302.1 verb 3sing indic pres act	1706.1 prep
ἀστέρων	ἀστὴρ	γὰρ	ἀστέρος	διαφέρει	ἐν
asterōn	astēr	gar	asteros	diapherei	en
of stars;	star	for	from star	differs	in

1385.3 noun dat sing fem	3643.1 adv	2504.1 conj	3450.9 art nom sing fem	384.1 noun nom sing fem	3450.1 art gen pl
δόξῃ.	**42.** Οὕτως	καὶ	ἡ	ἀνάστασις	τῶν
doxē	Houtōs	kai	hē	anastasis	tōn
glory.	So	also	the	resurrection	of the

3361.2 adj gen pl	4540.15 verb 3sing indic pres pass	1706.1 prep	5193.3 noun dat sing fem	1446.15 verb 3sing indic pres pass
νεκρῶν.	σπείρεται	ἐν	φθορᾷ,	ἐγείρεται
nekrōn	speiretai	en	phthora	egeiretai
dead.	It is being sown	in	corruption,	it is being raised

1706.1 prep	854.1 noun dat sing fem	4540.15 verb 3sing indic pres pass	1706.1 prep	813.3 noun dat sing fem
ἐν	ἀφθαρσίᾳ·	**43.** σπείρεται	ἐν	ἀτιμίᾳ,
en	aphtharsia	speiretai	en	atimia
in	incorruptibility.	It is being sown	in	dishonor,

find the precise body necessary for these lower forms, and even for mortal man, can He not also provide the proper body for the resurrected man?

15:40. Paul added to his illustrations by comparing celestial and terrestrial bodies. Again, countless differentiation is noted. While the heavenly and earthly bodies are alike in the sense that they are both bodies, there is a vast difference in "glory" between the two. Each is taken care of and provided for by God.

Although it is only implied in English, the Greek noun *doxa* ("glory") governs not only the phrase "celestial (heavenly) bodies" but also bodies "terrestrial (earthly)." It is true that Paul was drawing a distinction between the glory of the heavenly bodies in their brilliance (i.e., the sun, moon, and stars all reveal brightness) and that of earthly bodies, but it must still be recognized that Paul spoke of the earthly bodies (*sōmata*) as having glory.

It must be noted that the word for "bodies" here (*sōmata*) refers to the physical flesh and blood of a body in contrast to *sarx* which also means "body" but was used by Paul metaphorically to speak of human sinful nature (as, e.g., in Romans 7:5). The difference between *sōmata* and *sarx* must be considered when speaking of the "body."

15:41. Paul specifically mentioned the sun, moon, and stars as examples of the point of differentiation in body and "glory." Each has a glory distinctly its own, ordained by God. Each has its unique function and place. All are glorious, but there are degrees of glory.

15:42. "So also ... of the dead" serves as both a summary and transitional sentence. Paul made a direct application to his theme, the resurrection body. From there, he began to describe its change more directly and specifically.

Paul first noted the states of both natural and resurrection bodies and the changes involved. There will be a change from corruption to incorruption. The figure of sowing suggests our mortal bodies which shall conclude with death and out of which a different body will emerge.

"Corruption" (*phthora*) refers most correctly to the perishableness of man's actual body. The word refers primarily to the physical body's gradual decaying tendency.

The "incorruption" (*aphtharsia*) of the resurrection state is well placed here. The major objection of the Greeks to this thought was that the body is basically corruptible. They thought only of the body of flesh and blood. Paul agreed that corruption is a property of the earthly body. But the resurrection body will be a transformed body of which incorruption is a characteristic.

another flesh of beasts: ... and that of a beast is another, *Murdock* ... another is animal, *Berkeley* ... another flesh for cattle, *Fenton* ... Flesh of Cattle, *Wilson*.

another of fishes, [and] another of birds: ... and another of fowls, *Campbell* ... is essentially different, *Way* ... is of a peculiar sort, different from them all, *Locke*.

40. [There are] also celestial bodies, and bodies terrestrial: To look yet farther into the difference of bodies, *Locke* ... heavenly bodies...earthly bodies, *Moffatt* ... bodies peculiar to the heavens, *TCNT*.

but the glory of the celestial [is] one: ... the splendour of, *Moffatt* ... differs, *Fenton*.

and the [glory] of the terrestrial [is] another:

41. [There is] one glory of the sun, and another glory of the moon: One kind of splendor belongs to, *Williams* ... the glory of the sun is one thing, *Murdock*.

and another glory of the stars: for [one] star differeth from [another] star in glory: ... for star is excelling star in glory, *Concordant* ... moreover, star excelleth star in glory, *Macknight* ... star excels star in glory, *Campbell* ... and one star exceedeth another star in glory, *Murdock* ... does one star differ, *Berkeley* ... in brilliancy, *Fenton*.

42. So also [is] the resurrection of the dead: It is the same with, *Weymouth* ... So likewise is, *Conybeare*.

It is sown in corruption: ... what is sown is mortal, *Moffatt* ... in a state of decay, *Weymouth* ... sown in decay, *Williams* ... in destruction, *Sawyer* ... is a poor, weak, contemptible, corruptible thing, *Locke* ... sown in decomposition, *Berkeley*.

it is raised in incorruption: When it is raised again, it shall be powerful, glorious, *Locke* ... they arise without corruption, *Murdock* ... raised free from decay, *Weymouth* ... it is raised in indestructableness, *Sawyer*.

1 Corinthians 15:44

1446.15 verb 3sing indic pres pass	1706.1 prep	1385.3 noun dat sing fem	4540.15 verb 3sing indic pres pass	1706.1 prep
ἐγείρεται	ἐν	δόξῃ·	σπείρεται	ἐν
egeiretai	en	doxē	speiretai	en
it is being raised	in	glory.	It is being sown	in

763.3 noun dat sing fem	1446.15 verb 3sing indic pres pass	1706.1 prep	1405.3 noun dat sing fem	4540.15 verb 3sing indic pres pass
ἀσθενείᾳ,	ἐγείρεται	ἐν	δυνάμει·	**44.** σπείρεται
astheneia	egeiretai	en	dunamei	speiretai
weakness,	it is being raised	in	power.	It is being sown

4835.1 noun sing neu	5426.4 adj nom sing neu	1446.15 verb 3sing indic pres pass	4835.1 noun sing neu	4012.8 adj sing neu
σῶμα	ψυχικόν,	ἐγείρεται	σῶμα	πνευματικόν.
sōma	psuchikon	egeiretai	sōma	pneumatikon
a body	natural,	it is being raised	a body	spiritual:

44.a.Var: 01א,02A,03B 04C,06D-org,33,Lach Treg,Alf,Word,Tisc We/Ho,Weis,Sod UBS/✶

1479.1 conj	1498.4 verb 3sing indic pres act	4835.1 noun sing neu	5426.4 adj nom sing neu	2504.1 conj	1498.4 verb 3sing indic pres act
[ᵃ✩+ εἰ]	ἔστιν	σῶμα	ψυχικόν,	⸆ καὶ	ἔστιν
ei	estin	sōma	psuchikon	kai	estin
[if]	there is	a body	physical,	and	there is

44.b.Txt: 018K,020L,byz. Var: 01א,02A,03B,04C 06D,33,Lach,Treg,Alf Word,Tisc,We/Ho,Weis Sod,UBS/✶

1498.4 verb 3sing indic pres act	2504.1 conj	4835.1 noun sing neu	4012.8 adj sing neu	3643.1 adv
[✩ ἔστιν	καὶ]	⸀ᵇ σῶμα ⸃	πνευματικόν.	**45.** οὕτως
estin	kai	sōma	pneumatikon	houtōs
[there is	and]	a body	spiritual.	So

2504.1 conj	1119.22 verb 3sing indic perf pass	1090.33 verb 3sing indic aor mid	3450.5 art sing masc	4272.5 num ord nom sing masc
καὶ	γέγραπται,	Ἐγένετο	ὁ	πρῶτος
kai	gegraptai	Egeneto	ho	prōtos
also	it has been written,	Became	the	first

442.1 noun nom sing masc	75.1 name masc	1519.1 prep	5425.4 noun acc sing fem	2180.17 verb acc sing fem part pres act	3450.5 art sing masc
ἄνθρωπος	Ἀδὰμ	εἰς	ψυχὴν	ζῶσαν·	ὁ
anthrōpos	Adam	eis	psuchēn	zōsan	ho
man	Adam	to	a soul	living;	the

2057.4 adj nom sing masc	75.1 name masc	1519.1 prep	4011.1 noun sing neu	2210.3 verb sing neu part pres act	233.1 conj
ἔσχατος	Ἀδὰμ	εἰς	πνεῦμα	ζωοποιοῦν.	**46.** ἀλλ'
eschatos	Adam	eis	pneuma	zōopoioun	all'
last	Adam	to	a spirit	life-giving.	But

3620.3 partic	4272.2 num ord sing	3450.16 art sing neu	4012.8 adj sing neu	233.2 conj	3450.16 art sing neu
οὐ	πρῶτον	τὸ	πνευματικὸν,	ἀλλὰ	τὸ
ou	prōton	to	pneumatikon	alla	to
not	first	the	spiritual,	but	the

5426.4 adj nom sing neu	1884.1 adv	3450.16 art sing neu	4012.8 adj sing neu	3450.5 art sing masc
ψυχικόν,	ἔπειτα	τὸ	πνευματικόν.	**47.** ὁ
psuchikon	epeita	to	pneumatikon	ho
natural,	then	the	spiritual:	the

4272.5 num ord nom sing masc	442.1 noun nom sing masc	1523.2 prep gen	1087.2 noun gen sing fem	5353.1 adj nom sing masc
πρῶτος	ἄνθρωπος	ἐκ	γῆς,	χοϊκός·
prōtos	anthrōpos	ek	gēs	choikos
first	man	out of	earth,	made of dust;

476

15:43. Paul spoke of a second change, that from dishonor to glory. There is nothing honorable about the body that is put into the grave without rights and left to decay. Its decomposition would in a short time cause us to shrink back in horror. But the Greeks' rising doubts on the dishonorable nature of the present body were unjustified; it shall be changed into a glorious body. As the beautiful plant far surpasses the seed from which it sprang, so shall the resurrection body far surpass this present one in glory.

15:44. There are distinctions in nature between the natural and the spiritual body. Paul added another "it is sown." "Natural" has to do with the present life in all its aspects, especially as it stands in opposition to the supernatural life. The human body is suited to this life, not the heavenly.

"Spiritual" refers to the type of body needed for the world to come. A change will take place.

15:45. The different natures are contrasted in the reference to Adam and Christ. The basic characteristic of man from the beginning has been the "soul." The first Adam passed on his nature to all who followed. As the father of the human race his nature was stamped on it.

Christ, in comparison, "was made a quickening spirit." He is the progenitor of the spiritual race. As such, He stamps His nature on those who are "in Him." But not only is this "last Adam" the pattern for all those in Him, He is also the source of that life which will result in the resurrection body. The "last Adam" indicates Christ's humanity and our bodily relationship to Him.

The best view on "life-giving spirit" (NASB) seems to be that it is a reference to the resurrection of Christ. Not only did He then enter a "spiritual" form, He will pass that spiritual form (body) on to His followers in the resurrection (John 11:25; Romans 8:10f.).

15:46. However, there is a logical and necessary order: first natural, then spiritual. This does not mean that Paul was equating the two; he was simply establishing the order. The spiritual outweighs the natural even in the context of the body.

15:47. Paul then spoke of the origin of the two natures. The first man had an earthly origin. While Paul had in mind specifically the idea of bodily origin, the words "of the earth, earthy" denote the whole quality of this life. This first man refers to Adam (Genesis 2:7). "Earthy" (*choikos*) is different from "earth" and means "made of dust." The first man was bound to this earth.

43. It is sown in dishonour; it is raised in glory: . . . that which is sown is disfigured, that which rises is beautiful, *TCNT* . . . sown in contempt, *Fenton* . . . sown inglorious, *Moffatt* . . . sown in a state of dishonor, *Adams* . . . sown in humiliation, it is raised in splendor, *Williams*.

it is sown in weakness; it is raised in power: . . . in a state of helplessness, *Adams* . . . it is raised in strength, *Williams*.

44. It is sown a natural body: . . . it is sowen a beestli bodi, *Wyclif* . . . sown an animate body, *Moffatt* . . . an animal body, *Weymouth, Murdock*.

it is raised a spiritual body:

There is a natural body, and there is a spiritual body: For there is a body of the animal life, *Murdock*.

45. And so it is written, The first man Adam was made a living soul: . . . was a living nature, *Fenton* . . . became a living animal, *Weymouth* . . . became an animate being, *Moffatt* . . . became a living being, *Montgomery* . . . became a living creature, *Williams*.

the last Adam [was made] a quickening spirit: . . . the second Adam [became], *Murdock* . . . a life-giving, *Moffatt, Sawyer, PNT, Montgomery* . . . is a Life-producing Spirit, *Fenton* . . . made of a spiritual constitution, with a power to give life to others, *Locke*.

46. Howbeit that [was] not first which is spiritual: . . . the spiritual was not first, *Sawyer*.

but that which is natural: . . . but the animal, *Locke*.

and afterward that which is spiritual: . . . and only then, *Moffatt*.

47. The first man [is] of the earth, earthy: . . . was from the Ground, *Wilson* . . . of the ground, *Rotherham* . . . was made of earthly clay, *Conybeare* . . . made of dust, *PNT, Norlie* . . . dust, or earthy particles, *Locke* . . . was made of the dust of the earth, *Williams* . . . material, *Moffatt*.

1 Corinthians 15:48

47.a.Txt: 01א-corr,02A
06D-corr,018K,020L
025P,044,byz.
Var: 01א-org,03B,04C
06D-org,33,it.bo.Lach
Treg,Alf,Tisc,We/Ho
Weis,Sod,UBS/☆

3450.5 art sing masc	1202.2 num ord nom sing masc	442.1 noun nom sing masc	3450.5 art sing masc	2935.1 noun nom sing masc	1523.1 prep gen
ὁ	δεύτερος	ἄνθρωπος,	⟨a ὁ	κύριος ⟩	ἐξ
ho	deuteros	anthrōpos,	ho	kurios	ex
the	second	man,	the	Lord	out of

3636.2 noun gen sing masc	3497.2 rel-pron nom sing masc	3450.5 art sing masc	5353.1 adj nom sing masc	4955.7 dem-pron nom pl masc	2504.1 conj
οὐρανοῦ.	48. οἷος	ὁ	χοϊκός,	τοιοῦτοι	καὶ
ouranou.	hoios	ho	choïkos,	toioutoi	kai
heaven.	Such as	the	made of dust,	such	also

3450.7 art pl masc	5353.3 adj nom pl masc	2504.1 conj	3497.2 rel-pron nom sing masc	3450.5 art sing masc	2016.3 adj nom sing masc
οἱ	χοϊκοί·	καὶ	οἷος	ὁ	ἐπουράνιος,
hoi	choïkoi	kai	hoios	ho	epouranios,
the	made of dust;	and	such as	the	heavenly,

4955.7 dem-pron nom pl masc	2504.1 conj	3450.7 art pl masc	2016.4 adj nom pl masc	2504.1 conj	2503.1 conj
τοιοῦτοι	καὶ	οἱ	ἐπουράνιοι·	49. καὶ	καθὼς
toioutoi	kai	hoi	epouranioi	kai	kathōs
such	also	the	heavenly.	And	just as

5246.5 verb 1pl indic aor act	3450.12 art acc sing fem	1494.4 noun acc sing fem	3450.2 art gen sing	5353.2 adj gen sing masc
ἐφορέσαμεν	τὴν	εἰκόνα	τοῦ	χοϊκοῦ,
ephoresamen	tēn	eikona	tou	choïkou,
we bore	the	image	of the	made of dust,

49.a.Txt: 03B,016I,6,38
88,206,218,242,630
915,919,999,etc.
Var: p46,01א,02A,04C
06D,010F,012G,044
075,0243,byz.bo.

5246.6 verb 1pl indic fut act	5246.7 verb 1pl subj aor act	2504.1 conj	3450.12 art acc sing fem	1494.4 noun acc sing fem
⟨☆ φορέσομεν	[a φορέσωμεν]	καὶ	τὴν	εἰκόνα
phoresomen	phoresōmen	kai	tēn	eikona
we shall bear	[let us bear]	also	the	image

3450.2 art gen sing	2016.1 adj gen sing	3642.17 dem-pron sing neu	1156.2 conj	5183.1 verb 1sing indic pres act
τοῦ	ἐπουρανίου.	50. Τοῦτο	δέ	φημι,
tou	epouraniou.	Touto	de	phēmi,
of the	heavenly.	This	but	I say,

79.6 noun pl masc	3617.1 conj	4418.1 noun nom sing fem	2504.1 conj	129.1 noun sing neu	926.4 noun acc sing fem	2296.2 noun gen sing masc
ἀδελφοί,	ὅτι	σὰρξ	καὶ	αἷμα	βασιλείαν	θεοῦ
adelphoi,	hoti	sarx	kai	haima	basileian	theou
brothers,	that	flesh	and	blood	kingdom	of God

50.a.Txt: 02A,04C,06D
018K,020L,byz.Gries
Lach,Sod
Var: 01א,03B,025P
Treg,Tisc,We/Ho,Weis
UBS/☆

2789.8 verb inf aor act	3620.3 partic	1404.7 verb 3pl indic pres	1404.4 verb 3sing indic pres	3624.1 adv
κληρονομῆσαι	οὐ	⟨ δύνανται,	[a☆ δύναται,]	οὐδὲ
klēronomēsai	ou	dunantai,	dunatai,	oude
inherit	not	are able,	[is able,]	nor

3450.9 art nom sing fem	5193.1 noun nom sing fem	3450.12 art acc sing fem	854.2 noun acc sing fem	2789.1 verb 3sing indic pres act
ἡ	φθορὰ	τὴν	ἀφθαρσίαν	κληρονομεῖ.
hē	phthora	tēn	aphtharsian	klēronomei.
the	corruption	the	incorruptibility	does inherit.

51.a.Txt: 01א,02A
04C-corr,06D-corr,018K
020L,025P,byz.bo.Sod
Var: 03B,04C-org
06D-org,Treg,Alf,Tisc
We/Ho,Weis,UBS/☆

1481.20 verb 2sing impr aor mid	3328.1 noun sing neu	5050.3 prs-pron dat 2pl	2978.1 verb 1sing pres act	3820.7 adj pl masc	3173.1 conj
51. Ἰδοὺ	μυστήριον	ὑμῖν	λέγω·	Πάντες	⟨a μὲν ⟩
Idou	mustērion	humin	legō	Pantes	men
Lo	a mystery	to you	I tell:	All	

The "second man" refers to Jesus Christ. The first use of the word "man" is contrasted with the second "man." "First" and "second" suggest that both Adam and Christ had great significance for others. But while Christ appeared on this earth (Philippians 2:7) and lived, died, and rose again, His origin was not of this earth, but of heaven. Most specifically, within a historical relationship, Paul was presenting Christ as following and displacing Adam in the course of human history. He came from heaven to do it. Since there is no verb in either clause of this verse, some scholars have inserted a form of "come" to suggest that the first Adam came from the ground and the second from heaven (although earth and heaven may be taken adverbially suggesting an earthly or heavenly nature).

15:48. All of Adam's descendants are in Adam's image just as all of Christ's followers are in His image. It seems that more than just a physical distinction between pre- and post-resurrection states is involved. There is some moral connotation (Romans 6:4; Philippians 3:17-21; Colossians 3:1-4).

All men are patterned after the first Adam in that they have "earthy" bodies. But Christians enjoy another relationship also. Their relationship with Christ indicates that they are also "heavenly." This involves both the present implication and the future certainty. In the words of 1 John 3:2, "We shall be like him . . . ."

15:49. "We have borne" (*ephoresamen*) involves the idea of what is continual and habitual. "Image" (*eikona*) is used of man being made in God's image. "Image" may denote simply representation, or it may be used more precisely to indicate the original.

Paul assured us that we shall be given a spiritual or resurrection body. The image we have borne is evidence of the one we will bear.

15:50. Paul also quieted the minds of the living and exhorted the Corinthians to worthy accomplishment in Christ because of the fact and hope of the resurrection.

In the process, Paul made two important assertions. The first was that "flesh and blood cannot inherit the kingdom of God." "Flesh and blood" denote first substance (flesh), then the life-giving principle (blood) of the physical body.

The natural body is unsuited for the kingdom of God. It must be changed. "Inherit" (*klēronomēsai*) points to the rights and possessions of believers, as yet unrealized.

The second assertion, built on the first, was that corruption (perishableness) cannot inherit incorruption (imperishableness). There must be a necessary change.

15:51. Paul applied this to those who might have wondered if they had to die before they could be changed. "Behold" calls for

the second man [is] the Lord from heaven:

48. As [is] the earthy, such [are] they also that are earthy: As he was of the dust, so also those who are of the dust, *Murdock* . . . have barely an animal life and constitution, *Locke*.

and as [is] the heavenly, such [are] they also that are heavenly: . . . and as was he who was from heaven, so also are the heavenly, *Murdock*.

49. And as we have borne the image of the earthy: . . . as we resembled the earthly, *Fenton* . . . even as we have borne the likeness of the earthy, *Confraternity* . . . as we have worn the likeness of him from the dust, *Murdock* . . . a resemblance to the earthly, *Weymouth* . . . the likeness of material man, *Moffatt* . . . as in the animal, corruptible, mortal state, we were born in, *Locke*.

we shall also bear the image of the heavenly: . . . so shall we wear the likeness of him from heaven, *Murdock* . . . of the heavenly one, *PNT*.

50. Now this I say, brethren: And this I affirm, brethren, *Campbell*.

that flesh and blood cannot inherit the kingdom of God: . . . our mortal bodies, *Weymouth* . . . can not possesse, *Rheims* . . . can obtain no part in the kingdom, *Confraternity* . . . cannot possess God's reign, *Hanson* . . . is not able to enjoy an allotment in the kingdom, *Concordant* . . . a Divine Kingdom, *Fenton*.

neither doth corruption inherit incorruption: . . . perishable inherit what is imperishable, *Weymouth* . . . the perishing inherit the imperishable, *Moffatt* . . . nor shall destruction inherit indestructibleness, *Sawyer*.

51. Behold, I show you a mystery: Listen! I tell you a secret, *Fenton* . . . Here is a secret truth for you, *Moffatt* . . . a Secret I disclose to you, *Wilson* . . . To which let me add, what has not been hitherto discovered, *Locke*.

3620.3 partic	2810.12 verb 1pl indic fut pass	3820.7 adj pl masc	1156.2 conj	234.4 verb 1pl indic fut pass
οὐ	κοιμηθησόμεθα·	πάντες	δὲ	ἀλλαγησόμεθα,
ou	koimēthēsometha	pantes	de	allagēsometha
not	we shall fall asleep,	all	but	we shall be changed,

1706.1 prep	817.1 adj dat sing neu	1706.1 prep	4349.1 noun dat sing fem	3652.2 noun gen sing masc	1706.1 prep
52. ἐν	ἀτόμῳ,	ἐν	ῥιπῇ	ὀφθαλμοῦ,	ἐν
en	atomō	en	rhipē	ophthalmou	en
in	an instant,	in	twinkling	of an eye,	at

3450.11 art dat sing fem	2057.9 adj dat sing fem	4393.3 noun dat sing fem	4394.5 verb 3sing indic fut act	1056.1 conj
τῇ	ἐσχάτῃ	σάλπιγγι·	σαλπίσει	γάρ,
tē	eschatē	salpingi	salpisei	gar
the	last	trumpet;	a trumpet shall sound	for,

2504.1 conj	3450.7 art pl masc	3361.5 adj nom pl masc	1446.32 verb 3pl indic fut pass	855.4 adj nom pl masc	2504.1 conj
καὶ	οἱ	νεκροὶ	ἐγερθήσονται	ἄφθαρτοι,	καὶ
kai	hoi	nekroi	egerthēsontai	aphthartoi	kai
and	the	dead	shall be raised	incorruptible,	and

2231.1 prs-pron nom 1pl	234.4 verb 1pl indic fut pass	1158.1 verb 3sing indic pres act	1056.1 conj	3450.16 art sing neu
ἡμεῖς	ἀλλαγησόμεθα.	53. δεῖ	γὰρ	τὸ
hēmeis	allagēsometha	dei	gar	to
we	shall be changed.	It is necessary	for	the

5186.1 adj sing	3642.17 dem-pron sing neu	1730.11 verb inf aor mid	854.2 noun acc sing fem	2504.1 conj
φθαρτὸν	τοῦτο	ἐνδύσασθαι	ἀφθαρσίαν,	καὶ
phtharton	touto	endusasthai	aphtharsian	kai
corruption	this	to put on	incorruptibility,	and

3450.16 art sing neu	2326.2 adj sing neu	3642.17 dem-pron sing neu	1730.11 verb inf aor mid	110.1 noun acc sing fem
τὸ	θνητὸν	τοῦτο	ἐνδύσασθαι	ἀθανασίαν.
to	thnēton	touto	endusasthai	athanasian
the	mortal	this	to put on	immortality.

54.a.Txt: 01א-corr2,03B 06D,044,075,byz. Var: p46,01א-org,088 0121,0243,1175 1739-org,bo.

3615.1 conj	1156.2 conj	3450.16 art sing neu	5186.1 adj sing	3642.17 dem-pron sing neu
54. ὅταν	δὲ	τὸ	⌜ᵃ φθαρτὸν	τοῦτο
hotan	de	to	phtharton	touto
When	but	the	corruptible	this

1730.5 verb 3sing subj aor mid	854.2 noun acc sing fem	2504.1 conj	3450.16 art sing neu	2326.2 adj sing neu
ἐνδύσηται	ἀφθαρσίαν,	καὶ	τὸ ⌝	θνητὸν
endusētai	aphtharsian	kai	to	thnēton
shall have put on	incorruptibility,	and	the	mortal

54.b.Txt: 01א-corr2,03B 06D,044,075,byz. Var: 01א-org,02A,088 33

3642.17 dem-pron sing neu	1730.5 verb 3sing subj aor mid	3450.12 art acc sing fem	110.1 noun acc sing fem	4966.1 adv
τοῦτο	ἐνδύσηται	[ᵇ+ τὴν]	ἀθανασίαν,	τότε
touto	endusētai	tēn	athanasian	tote
this	shall have put on	[the]	immortality,	then

1090.69 verb 3sing indic fut mid	3450.5 art sing masc	3030.1 noun nom sing masc	3450.5 art sing masc	1119.24 verb nom sing masc part perf pass
γενήσεται	ὁ	λόγος	ὁ	γεγραμμένος,
genēsetai	ho	logos	ho	gegrammenos
shall come to pass	the	word	the	having been written:

emphatic attention to the declaration that would follow. "Mystery" speaks of a secret that is impossible for man to penetrate. Man can only know it as God has chosen to make it known. Man could never have discovered what will happen at the resurrection, but God has revealed it.

"We" is used generally. Paul lived as though Christ might come at any time, even though he did not know when He was coming, nor did he claim to. Some believers will not die, but whether among that group or not, dead or alive, "we shall all be changed."

15:52. Paul used three vivid phrases to describe this change that will take place. "In a moment" is "that which cannot be cut or divided," the smallest possible. We get our word *atom* from it. It describes the instantaneousness of the event. "Twinkling" (*rhipē*) suggests the idea of throwing. It refers to the time it takes to cast a glance or flutter an eyelid.

"At the last trump" represents the solemn finality of this transformation. In the Scriptures and contemporary Judaism, the trumpet was often associated with both festivals and the events of the end time (Morris, *Tyndale New Testament Commentaries*, 7:233). The Christian dead shall be raised incorruptible.

15:53. The necessity of change was reaffirmed as being due to our nature and condition. The human body, of which Paul was painfully conscious, must put on incorruption and immortality. It is bound to do so. But the power to make this happen comes from God. "To put on" (*endusasthai*) is the usual word for putting on clothing. This change is represented as an investiture with incorruption and immortality.

15:54. It is characteristic of Paul to see fulfillment of Scripture in all of this. "When" indicates time. When these things shall have taken place, then certain Old Testament prophecies will be fulfilled. "Corruption" putting on "incorruption" and "mortal" putting on "immortality" are what must come to pass to fulfill the Old Testament. The quotation is from Isaiah 25:8 and there is a parallel with 1 Corinthians 15:24,27.

The destruction of this last enemy, this "king of terrors," indicates absolute victory for Christ and His followers. "Swallowed" (*katepothē*) presents a dramatic figure and expresses complete destruction. Not only will death be destroyed so that it can do no more harm, all of its apparent victories in days and years past will be undone, reversed, destroyed. Those who are in Christ shall live in absolute victory!

We shall not all sleep, but we shall all be changed: . . . we shall not, indeed, all die, *Campbell* . . . Vve shal al in deede rise againe, *Rheims* . . . We are not all going to die, *Norlie* . . . but we shall all undergo a change, *TCNT*.

52. In a moment, in the twinkling of an eye, at the last trump: for the trumpet shall sound: It will come about suddenly, quickly, *Norlie* . . . for the trumpet shal blowe, *Geneva* . . . in an eye's glance, *Fenton* . . . in the flash of an eye, *Way, Adams*.

and the dead shall be raised incorruptible: . . . incapable of decay, *Weymouth*.

and we shall be changed: . . . we, also, shall undergo a change, *TCNT*.

53. For this corruptible must put on incorruption: For so it must be: this perishable nature must clothe itself, *Weymouth* . . . this corruptible frame and constitution of ours, *Locke* . . . perishing body must be invested with, *Moffatt* . . . this destructible must put on indestructibleness, *Sawyer* . . . must be endowed, *Fenton* . . . must needs clothe itself, *Rotherham* . . . must be clothed with, *Montgomery*.

and this mortal [must] put on immortality: . . . and that which dieth, *Murdock* . . . this deedly thing to putte aweye vndeedlynesse, *Wyclif*.

54. So when this corruptible shall have put on incorruption, and this mortal shall have put on immortality: . . . when this corruptible body shall, *Macknight* . . . and this that dieth, immortality, *Murdock*.

then shall be brought to pass the saying that is written: . . . then will take place the word that is written, *Murdock* . . . the written declaration, *Fenton* . . . then the saying that was written will come true, *Adams* . . . then indeed will the words of Scripture come true, *TCNT* . . . then shall be fulfilled what was foretold, *Locke* . . . then shall the word be accomplished that is written, *Sawyer* . . . will be realized, *Moffatt* . . . shall be accomplished, *Campbell*.

1 Corinthians 15:55

2636.4 verb 3sing indic aor pass	**3450.5** art sing masc	**2265.1** noun nom sing masc	**1519.1** prep	**3396.1** noun sing neu	**4085.1** adv
Κατεπόθη	ὁ	θάνατος	εἰς	νῖκος.	**55.** Ποῦ
Katepothē	ho	thanatos	eis	nikos	Pou
Was swallowed up	the	death	in	victory.	Where

4622.2 prs-pron gen 2sing	**2265.5** noun voc sing masc	**3450.16** art sing neu	**2730.1** noun nom sing neu	**3396.1** noun sing neu
σου,	θάνατε,	τὸ	ʽ κέντρον;	[ᵃ☆ νῖκος;]
sou,	thanate,	to	kentron;	nikos;
your,	death,	to the	sting?	[victory?]

4085.1 adv	**4622.2** prs-pron gen 2sing	**85.4** noun voc sing masc	**2265.5** noun voc sing masc	**3450.16** art sing neu
ποῦ	σου,	ʽ ᾅδη,	[ᵇ☆ θάνατε,]	τὸ
pou	sou,	hadē,	thanate,	to
Where	your,	hades,	[death,]	to the

3396.1 noun sing neu	**2730.1** noun nom sing neu	**3450.16** art sing neu	**1156.2** conj	**2730.1** noun nom sing neu
ʽ νῖκος;	[ᶜ☆ κέντρον;]	**56.** Τὸ	δὲ	κέντρον
nikos;	kentron;	To	de	kentron
victory?	[sting?]	The	now	sting

3450.2 art gen sing	**2265.2** noun gen sing masc	**3450.9** art nom sing fem	**264.2** noun nom sing fem	**3450.9** art nom sing fem	**1156.2** conj
τοῦ	θανάτου	ἡ	ἁμαρτία·	ἡ	δὲ
tou	thanatou	hē	hamartia	hē	de
of the	death	the	sin,	the	and

1405.1 noun nom sing fem	**3450.10** art gen sing fem	**264.1** noun fem	**3450.5** art sing masc	**3414.1** noun nom sing masc	**3450.3** art dat sing
δύναμις	τῆς	ἁμαρτίας	ὁ	νόμος·	**57.** τῷ
dunamis	tēs	hamartias	ho	nomos	tō
power	of the	sin	the	law;	tō

1156.2 conj	**2296.3** noun dat sing masc	**5322.1** noun nom sing fem	**3450.3** art dat sing	**1319.7** verb dat sing masc part pres act	**2231.3** prs-pron dat 1pl
δὲ	θεῷ	χάρις	τῷ	διδόντι	ἡμῖν
de	theō	charis	tō	didonti	hēmin
but	to God	thanks,	the	giving	us

3450.16 art sing neu	**3396.1** noun sing neu	**1217.2** prep	**3450.2** art gen sing	**2935.2** noun gen sing masc	**2231.2** prs-pron gen 1pl	**2400.2** name masc
τὸ	νῖκος	διὰ	τοῦ	κυρίου	ἡμῶν	Ἰησοῦ
to	nikos	dia	tou	kuriou	hēmōn	Iēsou
to the	victory	by	the	Lord	our	Jesus

5382.2 name gen masc	**5452.1** conj	**79.6** noun pl masc	**1466.2** prs-pron gen 1sing	**27.6** adj pl masc
Χριστοῦ.	**58.** Ὥστε,	ἀδελφοί	μου	ἀγαπητοί,
Christou.	Hōste,	adelphoi	mou	agapētoi,
Christ.	So that,	brothers	my	beloved,

1469.2 adj nom pl masc	**1090.19** verb 2pl impr pres	**275.1** adj nom pl masc	**3915.8** verb nom pl masc part pres act	**1706.1** prep
ἑδραῖοι	γίνεσθε,	ἀμετακίνητοι,	περισσεύοντες	ἐν
hedraioi	ginesthe,	ametakinētoi,	perisseuontes	en
firm	be,	immovable,	increasing	in

3450.3 art dat sing	**2024.3** noun dat sing neu	**3450.2** art gen sing	**2935.2** noun gen sing masc	**3704.1** adv	**3471.20** verb nom pl masc part perf act
τῷ	ἔργῳ	τοῦ	κυρίου	πάντοτε,	εἰδότες
tō	ergō	tou	kuriou	pantote,	eidotes
the	work	of the	Lord	always,	knowing

55.a.**Txt:** 01ℵ-corr 02A-corr,06D,018K 020L,025P,byz. **Var:** p46,01ℵ-org,03B 04C,088,33,sa.bo.Lach Treg,Tisc,We/Ho,Weis Sod,UBS/☆

55.b.**Txt:** 01ℵ-corr 02A-corr,018K,020L 025P,044,byz. **Var:** 01ℵ-org,03B,04C 06D-org,bo.Lach,Treg Alf,Tisc,We/Ho,Weis Sod,UBS/☆

55.c.**Txt:** 01ℵ-corr 02A-corr,06D,018K 020L,025P,byz. **Var:** p46,01ℵ-org,03B 04C,088,33,sa.bo.Lach Treg,Tisc,We/Ho,Weis Sod,UBS/☆

15:55. Paul could contain himself no longer. He broke forth into a song of triumph over death. It is in the strain of Hosea's anticipation of Israel's resurrection from national death (see Hosea 13:14). The words of Hosea are freely adapted. "Sting" (*kentron*) gives us the picture of death as a creature with a deadly sting. The great harmfulness of death is pictured. But there is more than a question here. "Where" denotes an exclamation of victory, a challenge, that must be answered by "Nowhere!" Death holds no permanent victory. Believers are victors over death and its sting.

15:56. Sin gives death its power; it is its sting. It gives death its penal character, its humiliating form, and its bondage of corruption. To those who fall "asleep" in Jesus Christ, however, the sting of death has been removed because Christ has taken their sense of guilt and fear of judgment.

Sin in turn receives its power from the Law. In a few words Paul gave a condensation of his teaching concerning the relation between sin and the Law. The Law imposed on sinful man necessary but impossible requirements, promising salvation on fulfillment of impossible terms and death on nonfulfillment. This in effect extended sin and involved the sinner in hopeless guilt. When death is "the wages of sin" it has a deadly sting. When death, because of pardoned sin, ushers the believer into the immediate presence of the Lord it is gain, not loss. The believer can sing with the hymn writer, "O the joy of sins forgiven" because they have been washed away by the death and resurrection of Christ.

15:57. Paul ended his song of triumph by asserting the Source of our victory. The apostle finally linked his doctrine of the bodily resurrection and transformation of the believer to his basic teaching on justification and forgiveness of sins.

The use of the present participle may carry the idea that it is God's characteristic to give victory. This is daily victory. "Victory" is just one word, but it sums up all Paul had written in this chapter. It denotes enemies and a battle, but not ours. This great victory is being given to believers by God because of the Victor, "our Lord Jesus Christ," who is the One through whom their victory comes.

15:58. The word "therefore" brings the matter to the point of conclusion and application. "My beloved brethren" not only showed Paul's concern for them, it also called on them to prove themselves brothers. They were urged negatively not to be flighty, movable, or unstable in their Christian beliefs and actions, but steadfast and unmovable. Positively, they were urged to be "abounding" or overflowing in the work of the Lord.

Death is swallowed up in victory: . . . is consumed in to victory, *Tyndale* . . . is swallowed up forever, *Campbell, Macknight* . . . is absorbed in victory, *Murdock.*

55. O death, where [is] thy sting?:
O grave, where [is] thy victory?: Hell where is thy victory? *Cranmer* . . . Hades! where is thy victory? *Campbell.*

56. The sting of death [is] sin: . . . but the pricke of deeth: is synne, *Wyclif.*
and the strength of sin [is] the law: . . . and sin derives its power from, *Weymouth* . . . the power of sin is the law, *Concordant, Confraternity* . . . and sin's power is, *Berkeley* . . . and the law gives sin its power, *Williams* . . . and the povver of sinne, *Rheims.*

57. But thanks [be] to God:
which giveth us the victory through our Lord Jesus Christ: The victory is ours, *Moffatt.*

58. Therefore, my beloved brethren, be ye stedfast, unmoveable: Consequently, *Berkeley* . . . be firm, *Fenton, Weymouth* . . . hold your ground, *Moffatt* . . . be stable, *Campbell* . . . stand firm and unshaken, *TCNT* . . . and be not vacillating, *Murdock* . . . incapable of being moved, *Williams.*
always abounding in the work of the Lord: . . . but be ye at all times abundant in the work of the Lord, *Murdock* . . . busily occupied at all times in the Lord's work, *Weymouth* . . . aboundingly active in the Lord's service, *Berkeley* . . . always letting the cup run over in the work of the Lord, *Williams* . . . always diligent in the Lord's work, *TCNT* . . . always abounding in your obedience to the precepts of Christ, and in those duties which are required of us, *Locke* . . . always ryche in the workes, *Geneva* . . . superabounding in the work, *Rotherham.*

1 Corinthians 16:1

3617.1 conj	3450.5 art sing masc	2845.1 noun nom sing masc	5050.2 prs-pron gen 2pl	3620.2 partic	1498.4 verb 3sing indic pres act	2727.2 adj nom sing masc
ὅτι	ὁ	κόπος	ὑμῶν	οὐκ	ἔστιν	κενὸς
hoti	ho	kopos	humōn	ouk	estin	kenos
that	the	toil	you	not	is	empty

1706.1 prep	2935.3 noun dat sing masc		3875.1 prep	1156.2 conj	3450.10 art gen sing fem	3022.1 noun gen sing fem
ἐν	κυρίῳ.	**16:1.** Περὶ	δὲ	τῆς	λογίας
en	kuriō	Peri	de	tēs	logias
in	Lord.	Concerning	now	the	collection

3021.1 noun gen sing fem	3450.10 art gen sing fem	1519.1 prep	3450.8 art acc pl masc	39.9 adj acc pl masc	5450.1 adv
[✶ λογείας]	τῆς	εἰς	τοὺς	ἁγίους,	ὥσπερ
logeias	tēs	eis	tous	hagious	hōsper
[idem]	the	for	the	saints,	as

1293.2 verb 1sing indic aor act	3450.14 art dat pl fem	1564.7 noun dat pl fem	3450.10 art gen sing fem	1046.1 name gen fem
διέταξα	ταῖς	ἐκκλησίαις	τῆς	Γαλατίας,
dietaxa	tais	ekklēsiais	tēs	Galatias
I directed	the	assemblies	of the	of Galatia,

3643.1 adv	2504.1 conj	5050.1 prs-pron nom 2pl	4020.36 verb 2pl impr aor act	2567.3 prep	1518.8 num card acc fem
οὕτως	καὶ	ὑμεῖς	ποιήσατε.	**2.** κατὰ	μίαν
houtōs	kai	humeis	poiēsate	kata	mian
so	also	you	do.	By	first

2.a.Txt: 018K,020L,byz. bo.
Var: 02A,03B,04C,06D 025P,33,Lach,Treg,Alf Word,Tisc,We/Ho,Weis Sod,UBS/✶

4378.4 noun gen pl neu	4378.2 noun gen sing neu	1524.3 adj nom sing masc	5050.2 prs-pron gen 2pl	3706.1 prep
σαββάτων	[a ✶ σαββάτου]	ἕκαστος	ὑμῶν	παρ'
sabbatōn	sabbatou	hekastos	humōn	par'
of weeks	[of week]	each	of you	by

1431.5 prs-pron dat 3sing masc	4935.4 verb 3sing impr pres act	2320.3 verb nom sing masc part pres act	3614.16 rel-pron sing neu	4948.10 indef-pron sing neu
ἑαυτῷ	τιθέτω,	θησαυρίζων	ὃ	τι
heautō	tithetō	thēsaurizōn	ho	ti
himself	let put,	treasuring up	which	whatever

2.b.Txt: 01ℵ,02A,04C 06D,018K,020L,025P etc.byz.Tisc,Sod
Var: 03B,Treg,We/Ho Weis,UBS/✶

300.1 partic	1430.1 partic	2117.2 verb 3sing subj pres pass	2419.1 conj	3231.1 partic	3615.1 conj
ἂν	[b ✶ ἐὰν]	εὐοδῶται·	ἵνα	μὴ	ὅταν
an	ean	euodōtai	hina	mē	hotan
an	ean	he may be prospered in,	that	not	when

2048.6 verb 1sing subj aor act	4966.1 adv	3022.2 noun nom pl fem	3021.2 noun nom pl fem	1090.17 verb 3pl subj pres
ἔλθω	τότε	λογῖαι	[✶ λογεῖαι]	γίνωνται.
elthō	tote	logiai	logeiai	ginōntai
I may come	then	collections	[idem]	there should be.

3615.1 conj	1156.2 conj	3716.5 verb 1sing subj aor mid	3614.8 rel-pron acc pl masc	1430.1 partic
3. ὅταν	δὲ	παραγένωμαι,	οὓς	ἐὰν
hotan	de	paragenōmai	hous	ean
When	and	I shall have arrived,	whomever	ean

1375.11 verb 2pl subj aor act	1217.1 prep	1976.6 noun gen pl fem	3642.8 dem-pron acc pl masc	3854.4 verb 1sing act
δοκιμάσητε	δι'	ἐπιστολῶν	τούτους	πέμψω
dokimasēte	di'	epistolōn	toutous	pempsō
you may approve	by	epistles	these	I will send

Believers should always be "abounding" in the Lord's work because their labor is not in vain. Labor "in the Lord" is not illusion, not profitless, but profitable, rewarding, promised success, which should spur those who are Christ's to greater work.

16:1. Paul has almost completed his letter. Items of large importance have been discussed. But there were a few general items that were still on his heart; thus in shorter but necessary comments he added these needful reminders.

"Now concerning" introduced a new topic. The phrase is used in this letter to mark topics mentioned by the Corinthians in their letter to Paul.

The matter in question touched on the offering which was to be taken to Jerusalem to help those who had been totally devastated by severe economic conditions. Paul had not only made a promise concerning them (Galatians 2:10), he saw this as an opportunity to unite the Jewish and Gentile elements of the Church.

Paul urged this giving to come from the highest motives. It was a part of the work of the Lord in which Christians should abound because of their victory through the Lord Jesus Christ. The fact that this collection was being made for the saints should recommend it to saints everywhere.

16:2. Paul gave instructions concerning this collection. It was to be generous and systematically arranged "upon the first day of the week." This was a support for the regular observance of that day (Sunday) as the time for the Church as a whole to gather. Also, the giving was to be regular, not just emotional.

Further, everyone should make a contribution, however large or small, and the giving was to be proportionate as "God hath prospered him." The blessing would determine the amount.

16:3. Another New Testament principle of giving was that financial gifts must be carefully administered. Reputable, honest, trusted individuals were to be picked by the Corinthians to carry these funds to the Jerusalem church.

This was an area of church administration that needed great care, and any hint of mismanagement must be guarded against. This arrangement would protect Paul from the accusation of an unhealthy interest in the offering. Moreover, those who did the giving should be able to have a voice in who would take their gift. This trip would bring the Corinthians into personal contact with the Jerusalem believers and strengthen the unity of the Church.

In the Greek there is nothing corresponding to the first "your" of the verse. Therefore the comma might come after "approve."

forasmuch as ye know that your labour is not in vain in the Lord: . . . your labour will not be lost, *Locke* . . . is not futile, *Fenton* . . . is not worthless, *Adams* . . . your toil is not fruitless, *Weymouth* . . . that what you do in the service of the Lord is labor not thrown away! *Norlie.*

1. Now concerning the collection for the saints: With regard to, *Moffatt* . . . of the gaderingis of money, *Wycliff* . . . the tax collected, *Fenton* . . . for the converts to Christianity, *Locke.*

as I have given order to the churches of Galatia, even so do ye: . . . you must carry out the same arrangements, *Moffatt* . . . as I have enjoined, *Conybeare* . . . as I arranged with, *Fenton* . . . even as I prescribe, *Concordant* . . . as I directed, *Rotherham* . . . as I haue ordeined, *Rheims* . . . do you also, *Confraternity.*

2. Upon the first [day] of the week: . . . some sondaye, *Tyndale.*

let every one of you lay by him in store: . . . put aside a sum, *Moffatt* . . . each of you set apart a certain portion of his profits, *Way* . . . let each of you set apart whatever his gains may enable him to spare, *Conybeare.*

as [God] hath prospered him: . . . according as he thrives, *Locke* . . . depositing as he may be prospered, *Wilson* . . . accumulating as he may prosper, *Clementson* . . . putting it into the treasury, *Campbell* . . . whatever gain has been granted to him, *Weymouth.*

that there be no gatherings when I come: . . . that there may be no need of, *Locke* . . . there may be no collections, *Conybeare.*

3. And when I come, whomsoever ye shall approve by [your] letters: On my arrival, *Montgomery* . . . whomsoever you should be attesting through letters, *Concordant* . . . you shall authorize, *Hanson* . . . whoever you may choose, *Fenton* . . . whomsoever you shall judge to be fitted for the trust I will furnish with letters, *Conybeare* . . . you accredit by letter, *Weymouth* . . . will furnish credentials for, *Moffatt.*

1 Corinthians 16:4

661.3 verb inf aor act	3450.12 art acc sing fem	5322.4 noun acc sing fem	5050.2 prs-pron gen 2pl	1519.1 prep	2395.2 name fem
ἀπενεγκεῖν	τὴν	χάριν	ὑμῶν	εἰς	Ἰερουσαλήμ·
apenenkein	tēn	charin	humōn	eis	Ierousalēm
to carry	the	gift	your	to	Jerusalem:

1430.1 partic	1156.2 conj	1498.10 verb 3sing subj pres act	510.1 adj sing	510.1 adj sing	1498.10 verb 3sing subj pres act
4. ἐὰν	δὲ	ᾖ	ἄξιον	[☆ ἄξιον	ᾖ]
ean	de	ē	axion	axion	ē
if	and	it be	suitable	[suitable	it be]

3450.2 art gen sing	2476.2 conj	4057.15 verb inf pres	4713.1 prep dat	1466.5 prs-pron dat 1sing
τοῦ	κἀμὲ	πορεύεσθαι,	σὺν	ἐμοὶ
tou	kame	poreuesthai	sun	emoi
the	me also	to go,	with	me

4057.34 verb 3pl indic fut mid	2048.54 verb 1sing indic fut mid	1156.2 conj	4242.1 prep	5050.4 prs-pron acc 2pl
πορεύσονται.	**5.** Ἐλεύσομαι	δὲ	πρὸς	ὑμᾶς
poreusontai	Eleusomai	de	pros	humas
they shall go.	I will come	but	to	you

3615.1 conj	3081.4 name acc fem	1324.3 verb 1sing subj aor act	3081.4 name acc fem
ὅταν	Μακεδονίαν	διέλθω·	Μακεδονίαν
hotan	Makedonian	dielthō	Makedonian
when	Macedonia	I shall have gone through;	Macedonia

1056.1 conj	1324.10 verb 1sing indic pres	4242.1 prep	5050.4 prs-pron acc 2pl	1156.2 conj	5018.8 verb acc sing neu part aor act
γὰρ	διέρχομαι.	**6.** πρὸς	ὑμᾶς	δὲ	τυχὸν
gar	dierchomai	pros	humas	de	tuchon
for	I do go through.	With	you	and	perhaps

6.a.**Txt**: 01א,02A,04C 06D,018K,020L,025P etc.byz.Tisc,Sod **Var**: 03B,We/Ho,Weis UBS/☆

3748.3 verb 1sing indic fut act	2620.2 verb 1sing indic fut act	2211.1 conj	2504.1 conj	3775.3 verb 1sing indic fut act
(παραμενῶ,	[a καταμενῶ]	ἢ	καὶ	παραχειμάσω,
paramenō	katamenō	ē	kai	paracheimasō
I shall stay,	[I will remain]	or	even	I shall winter,

2419.1 conj	5050.1 prs-pron nom 2pl	1466.6 prs-pron acc 1sing	4170.2 verb 2pl subj aor act	3619.1 adv	1430.1 partic
ἵνα	ὑμεῖς	με	προπέμψητε	οὖ	ἐὰν
hina	humeis	me	propempsēte	hou	ean
that	you	me	may set forward	where ever	

4057.3 verb 1sing subj pres	3620.3 partic	2286.1 verb 1sing pres act	1056.1 conj	5050.4 prs-pron acc 2pl	732.1 adv	1706.1 prep
πορεύωμαι.	**7.** οὐ	θέλω	γὰρ	ὑμᾶς	ἄρτι	ἐν
poreuōmai	ou	thelō	gar	humas	arti	en
I may go.	Not	I will	for	you	now	in

7.a.**Txt**: 018K,020L,byz. **Var**: 01א,02A,03B,04C 06D,025P,it.bo.Gries Lach,Treg,Alf,Word Tisc,We/Ho,Weis,Sod UBS/☆

3800.1 noun dat sing fem	1481.19 verb inf aor act	1666.1 verb 1sing indic pres act	1156.2 conj	1056.1 conj	5385.4 noun acc sing masc
παρόδῳ	ἰδεῖν·	ἐλπίζω	(δὲ	[a☆ γὰρ]	χρόνον
parodō	idein	elpizō	de	gar	chronon
passing	to see,	I hope	but	[for]	a time

4948.5 indef-pron	1946.9 verb inf aor act	4242.1 prep	5050.4 prs-pron acc 2pl	1430.1 partic	3450.5 art sing masc	2935.1 noun nom sing masc
τινὰ	ἐπιμεῖναι	πρὸς	ὑμᾶς,	ἐὰν	ὁ	κύριος
tina	epimeinai	pros	humas	ean	ho	kurios
certain	to remain	with	you,	if	the	Lord

The meaning then would be that after the Corinthians had picked men for the responsibility, Paul would write letters of commendation to be sent with them.

16:4. A thought was added on the possibility of Paul's going to Jerusalem with those who would be chosen to carry this gift. Paul inserted "if" because he was uncertain as to whether or not he would go.

The giving of Christians should be such as to indicate the blessings of God and their own proper stewardship of the things of this earth. They are to be generously given and shared. Paul was not certain of the liberality of the Corinthians, thus he was guarding his position as an apostle and their respect for him.

16:5. Paul indicated that he would come to visit the Corinthians, although at the time of this writing the time was uncertain. In 4:18,19, Paul had remarked on those who did not think he would actually come to them. Now he stated the fact with certainty.

The time was set as "when I shall pass through Macedonia." "When" is indefinite again. In Acts "pass through" regularly denotes an evangelistic tour. The last part of this verse appears to give new information to the Corinthians, as though they had not known before of Paul's trip.

16:6. But Paul did not wish to visit Corinth just in passing. Rather, he desired to abide with them for awhile. Both "it may be" and "whithersoever I go" indicate clear uncertainty as to the apostle's future plans.

Winter was the time when travel was normally suspended. This extended visit during the winter would allow the Corinthians opportunity to "bring (Paul) on (his) journey." In other words, it would give them a chance to provide what he had need of for the journey. "You" is emphatic.

It is interesting that this is what Paul finally did. Acts 20:1-3 records that he traveled from Ephesus to Macedonia, and after "much exhortation" he went to Greece where he stayed for 3 months.

Paul's writings show that balance between what he desired and thought he might do, and the certain will of God.

16:7. Paul indicated he would not do this immediately. He did not wish to make a quick visit. The Corinthians had requested his speedy arrival and this could have been arranged. But such a visit could only have been "by the way" in passing and would have been of little help.

There remained a greater leading than the apostle's own wish and will. That was the Lord's will; "if the Lord permit." Paul was above all a servant, and he went where his Master, the Lord, directed.

them will I send to bring your liberality unto Jerusalem: . . . to carry your gift, *Fenton, Campbell* . . . convey your bounty, *Moffatt* . . . to carry your benevolence, *Conybeare* . . . your kind gift, *Weymouth, Clementson.*

4. And if it be meet that I go also: Which if it deserves, *Locke* . . . or if there shall seem sufficient reason, *Conybeare* . . . if it be vvorthie, *Rheims* . . . if it is important enough for me also to go, *Confraternity* . . . is worth while for me also to make the journey, *Weymouth* . . . if it be suitable, *PNT* . . . Or, if it be proper, *Campbell.*
they shall go with me:

5. Now I will come unto you, when I shall pass through Macedonia: for I do pass through Macedonia: . . . when I traverse, *Fenton* . . . for my plan will be to pass, *Weymouth* . . . for I intend to take that, *Locke* . . . after my tour, *Moffatt.*

6. And it may be that I will abide: . . . perhaps I shall make some stay, *Locke* . . . perhaps I shall remain with you, *Conybeare.*
yea, and winter with you: . . . or els tary all wynter, *Cranmer* . . . or even spend the winter, *PNT* . . . possibly spending the winter, *Montgomery* . . . perhaps remain or even winter, *Confraternity.*
that ye may bring me on my journey whithersoever I go: I may sojourn, *Rotherham* . . . you may speed me, *Moffatt* . . . that ye may accompany me, *Murdock.*

7. For I will not see you now by the way: . . . to pay you a brief visit now, *Fenton* . . . on this occasion merely in passing, *Weymouth* . . . to call in upon you, as I pass by, *Locke* . . . now for a passing visit, *Conybeare.*
but I trust to tarry a while with you: . . . since I hope to stay, *Conybeare* . . . for I hope to continue some time with you, *Sawyer.*
if the Lord permit: . . . yf God shal suffre me, *Geneva.*

1 Corinthians 16:8

7.b.**Txt**: 06D,018K,byz.
Var: 01ℵ,02A,03B,04C
Lach,Treg,Alf,Word
Tisc,We/Ho,Weis,Sod
UBS/✶

1994.2 verb 3sing subj pres act	1994.4 verb 3sing subj aor act	1946.10 verb 1sing indic fut act	1156.2 conj	1706.1 prep
ʹ ἐπιτρέπῃ.	[ᵇ✶ ἐπιτρέψῃ.]	8. ἐπιμενῶ	δὲ	ἐν
epitrepē	epitrepsē	epimenō	de	en
permit.	[idem]	I shall remain	but	in

2163.2 name dat fem	2175.1 conj	3450.10 art gen sing fem	3868.1 noun gen sing fem	2351.2 noun nom sing fem	1056.1 conj
Ἐφέσῳ	ἕως	τῆς	πεντηκοστῆς·	9. θύρα	γάρ
Ephesō	heōs	tēs	pentēkostēs	thura	gar
Ephesus	till		Pentecost.	A door	for

1466.4 prs-pron dat 1sing	453.12 verb 3sing indic perf act	3144.9 adj sing fem	2504.1 conj	1740.1 adj nom sing	2504.1 conj
μοι	ἀνέῳγεν	μεγάλη	καὶ	ἐνεργής,	καὶ
moi	aneōgen	megalē	kai	energēs	kai
to me	has been opened	great	and	efficient,	and

477.4 verb nom pl masc part pres	4044.7 adj nom pl masc	1430.1 partic	1156.2 conj	2048.8 verb 3sing subj aor act
ἀντικείμενοι	πολλοί.	10. Ἐὰν	δὲ	ἔλθῃ
antikeimenoi	polloi	Ean	de	elthē
opposers	many.	If	now	come

4943.1 name nom masc	984.1 verb 2pl pres act	2419.1 conj	863.1 adv	1090.40 verb 3sing subj aor mid	4242.1 prep
Τιμόθεος,	βλέπετε	ἵνα	ἀφόβως	γένηται	πρὸς
Timotheos	blepete	hina	aphobōs	genētai	pros
Timothy,	see	that	without fear	he may be	with

5050.4 prs-pron acc 2pl	3450.16 art sing neu	1056.1 conj	2024.1 noun sing neu	2935.2 noun gen sing masc	2021.4 verb 3sing indic pres
ὑμᾶς·	τὸ	γὰρ	ἔργον	κυρίου	ἐργάζεται,
humas	to	gar	ergon	kuriou	ergazetai
you;	the	for	work	of Lord	he works,

10.a.**Txt**: 06D,byz.
Var: 01ℵ,02A,04C
018K,020L,025P,Lach
Treg,Alf,Tisc,Weis,Sod
UBS/✶

5453.1 conj	2504.1 conj	1466.1 prs-pron nom 1sing	2476.3 conj	3231.1 partic	4948.3 indef-pron nom sing
ὡς	ʹ καὶ	ἐγώ.	[ᵃ✶ κἀγώ·]	11. μή	τις
hōs	kai	egō	kagō	mē	tis
as	even	I.	[even I.]	Not	anyone

3631.1 conj	840.6 prs-pron acc sing masc	1832.6 verb 3sing subj aor act	4170.4 verb 2pl impr aor act	1156.2 conj
οὖν	αὐτὸν	ἐξουθενήσῃ·	προπέμψατε	δὲ
oun	auton	exouthenēsē	propempsate	de
therefore	him	should despise;	set forward	but

840.6 prs-pron acc sing masc	1706.1 prep	1503.3 noun dat sing fem	2419.1 conj	2048.8 verb 3sing subj aor act	4242.1 prep	1466.6 prs-pron acc 1sing
αὐτὸν	ἐν	εἰρήνῃ,	ἵνα	ἔλθῃ	πρός	με
auton	en	eirēnē	hina	elthē	pros	me
him	in	peace,	that	he may come	to	me;

1538.1 verb 1sing indic pres	1056.1 conj	840.6 prs-pron acc sing masc	3196.3 prep	3450.1 art gen pl	79.7 noun gen pl masc
ἐκδέχομαι	γὰρ	αὐτὸν	μετὰ	τῶν	ἀδελφῶν.
ekdechomai	gar	auton	meta	tōn	adelphōn
I await	for	him	with	the	brothers.

3875.1 prep	1156.2 conj	619.2 name acc masc	3450.2 art gen sing	79.2 noun gen sing masc	4044.17 adj pl neu
12. Περὶ	δὲ	Ἀπολλῶ	τοῦ	ἀδελφοῦ,	πολλὰ
Peri	de	Apollō	tou	adelphou	polla
Concerning	and	Apollos	the	brother,	much

488

16:8,9. In connection with this, Paul explained when he would leave Ephesus and gave a brief testimony concerning his work there. He would remain until Pentecost, the 50th day from the 16th Nisan in the Passover Feast. Some scholars have made capital out of the apparent contradiction between Paul's words in verse 8 that he would "tarry" and his words in 4:19, "I will come to you shortly." The solution (as if there were even a problem!) is to be discerned from the context of each chapter. In chapter 4, Paul was filled with anger at the Corinthian divisiveness and was admonishing them that if they didn't improve their behavior he would come to deal severely with them. Paul's admonition has been paraphrased by C.K. Barrett: "Anyone would think I was never going to set foot in Corinth again; but look out! I'll be there sooner than you think" (*Harper's New Testament Commentaries*, p.390).

In chapter 16, however, Paul had an entirely different purpose in mind. Although Paul was listing his itinerary to the Corinthians, his personal itinerary was always subject to the will of God.

"Door" is a figurative expression. "Effectual" (*energēs*) is unusual here, especially in regard to its modification of door. It means "active" or "effective," and speaks of the influence gained by entering. "Great" (*megalē*) speaks of the door's width and the region into which it opened. "Is opened" (*aneōgen*) indicates present and continuous opportunity.

But Paul also called the Corinthians' attention to the fact of great opposition. Wherever the work of the Lord goes forth, it increases and flourishes despite opposition and adversity.

16:10,11. Paul might not come immediately, but others would, such as Timothy. Paul therefore put in a good word for his young associate. His direction to make Timothy feel at ease pointed to the disposition both of Timothy and the Corinthian church. It shows Timothy's youth, sensitivity, and possibly his timidity. It may have indicated wrong attitudes on the part of the church at Corinth.

Paul was concerned about Timothy in the midst of such a situation. Therefore, he reminded his readers that he and Timothy were engaged in the same work, "the work of the Lord." They had the same purpose, the same calling, and the same Lord. If Timothy attempted the task of 4:17, there was the possibility of trouble.

Rather, Timothy was to be sent forward on his journey in peace. "Conduct him forth" uses the same verb as that in verse 6, of Paul being sent on his journey. The Corinthians were to arrange and obtain that which was necessary for Timothy's journey. It appears Paul expected Timothy's return before he departed from Ephesus.

The Church is to treat its messengers with equal care and concern. Such treatment is not to be based on personality or expertise, but on the messenger's calling and the value of the message he has been called to present.

16:12. Paul added a word concerning Apollos. His use of the phrase "as touching . . . Apollos" suggests that his coming had been

8. But I will tarry at Ephesus until Pentecost: For I shall continue at, *Murdock* . . . the time of the Harvest Festival, *Weymouth* . . . i.e. Whitsuntide, *Locke*.

9. For a great door and effectual is opened unto me: I have wide opportunities here for active service, *Moffatt* . . . a wide door stands open before me which demands great efforts, *Weymouth* . . . a great wide open door, *Fenton* . . . promising opportunity given me, *Locke* . . . and operative, *Concordant*.

and [there are] many adversaries: . . . yet there are many opposers, *Campbell* . . . there are many to thwart me, *Moffatt* . . . and many are they who are trying to shut it in my face, *Way*.

10. Now if Timotheus come, see that he may be with you without fear: . . . make him feel quite at home, *Moffatt* . . . pray take care that he be easy, *Locke* . . . be careful to give him no cause of fear, *Conybeare* . . . he is free from fear in his relations with you, *Weymouth* . . . that he is not troubled by you, *Fenton* . . . without trepidation, *Montgomery*.

for he worketh the work of the Lord, as I also [do]: . . . he is engaged in the Master's work, *Weymouth* . . . he promotes, *Locke*.

11. Let no man therefore despise him: . . . let no one slight him, *Weymouth* . . . let no one disparage him, *Montgomery* . . . should be scorning him, *Concordant* . . . Don't let anyone make light of him, *Adams*.

but conduct him forth in peace, that he may come unto me: . . . but send him forward, *Campbell* . . . But set him forward on his journey, *Panin* . . . but speed him on his way, *Confraternity*.

for I look for him with the brethren: . . . for I expect him, *Campbell* . . . with his companions, *Fenton*.

12. As touching [our] brother Apollos, I greatly desired him to come unto you with the brethren: Now concerning . . . I besought

3731.11 verb 1sing indic aor act	840.6 prs-pron acc sing masc	2419.1 conj	2048.8 verb 3sing subj aor act	4242.1 prep	5050.4 prs-pron acc 2pl
παρεκάλεσα	αὐτὸν	ἵνα	ἔλθῃ	πρὸς	ὑμᾶς
parekalesa	*auton*	*hina*	*elthē*	*pros*	*humas*
I exhorted	him	that	he should go	to	you

3196.3 prep	3450.1 art gen pl	79.7 noun gen pl masc	2504.1 conj	3705.1 adv	3620.2 partic	1498.34 verb sing indic imperf act
μετὰ	τῶν	ἀδελφῶν·	καὶ	πάντως	οὐκ	ἦν
meta	*tōn*	*adelphōn*	*kai*	*pantōs*	*ouk*	*ēn*
with	the	brothers;	and	at all	not	was

2284.1 noun sing neu	2419.1 conj	3431.1 adv	2048.8 verb 3sing subj aor act	2048.55 verb 3sing indic fut mid	1156.2 conj	3615.1 conj
θέλημα	ἵνα	νῦν	ἔλθῃ,	ἐλεύσεται	δὲ	ὅταν
thelēma	*hina*	*nun*	*elthē*	*eleusetai*	*de*	*hotan*
will	that	now	he should come;	he will come	but	when

2100.1 verb 3sing subj aor act	1121.3 verb 2pl impr pres act	4590.1 verb 2pl pres act	1706.1 prep	3450.11 art dat sing fem
εὐκαιρήσῃ.	**13.** Γρηγορεῖτε,	στήκετε	ἐν	τῇ
eukairēsē	*Grēgoreite*	*stēkete*	*en*	*tē*
he shall have opportunity.	Watch you;	stand fast	in	the

3963.3 noun dat sing fem	405.1 verb 2pl impr pres	2874.1 verb 2pl impr pres pass	3820.1 adj
πίστει,	ἀνδρίζεσθε,	κραταιοῦσθε·	**14.** πάντα
pistei	*andrizesthe*	*krataiousthe*	*panta*
faith,	show yourselves like men,	be strong.	All things

5050.2 prs-pron gen 2pl	1706.1 prep	26.3 noun dat sing fem	1090.18 verb 3sing impr pres	3731.1 verb 1sing indic pres act	1156.2 conj
ὑμῶν	ἐν	ἀγάπῃ	γινέσθω.	**15.** Παρακαλῶ	δὲ
humōn	*en*	*agapē*	*ginesthō*	*Parakalō*	*de*
your	in	love	let be done.	I exhort	but

5050.4 prs-pron acc 2pl	79.6 noun pl masc	3471.6 verb 2pl indic perf act	3450.12 art acc sing fem	3477.4 noun acc sing fem
ὑμᾶς,	ἀδελφοί·	οἴδατε	τὴν	οἰκίαν
humas	*adelphoi*	*oidate*	*tēn*	*oikian*
you,	brothers,	you know	the	house

4585.1 name gen masc	3617.1 conj	1498.4 verb 3sing indic pres act	532.1 noun nom sing fem	3450.10 art gen sing fem	875.2 name gen fem
Στεφανᾶ,	ὅτι	ἐστὶν	ἀπαρχὴ	τῆς	Ἀχαΐας,
Stephana	*hoti*	*estin*	*aparchē*	*tēs*	*Achaias*
of Stephanas,	that	it is	first fruit		Achaia's,

2504.1 conj	1519.1 prep	1242.4 noun acc sing fem	3450.4 art dat pl	39.8 adj dat pl masc	4872.1 verb 3pl indic aor act
καὶ	εἰς	διακονίαν	τοῖς	ἁγίοις	ἔταξαν
kai	*eis*	*diakonian*	*tois*	*hagiois*	*etaxan*
and	for	service	to the	saints	they appointed

1431.8 prs-pron acc pl masc	2419.1 conj	2504.1 conj	5050.1 prs-pron nom 2pl	5131.8 verb 2pl subj pres pass	3450.4 art dat pl
ἑαυτούς·	**16.** ἵνα	καὶ	ὑμεῖς	ὑποτάσσησθε	τοῖς
heautous	*hina*	*kai*	*humeis*	*hupotassesthe*	*tois*
themselves,	that	also	you	be subject	to the

4955.3 dem-pron dat pl	2504.1 conj	3820.3 adj dat sing	3450.3 art dat sing	4753.3 verb dat sing masc part pres act	2504.1 conj
τοιούτοις,	καὶ	παντὶ	τῷ	συνεργοῦντι	καὶ
toioutois	*kai*	*panti*	*tō*	*sunergounti*	*kai*
such,	and	to everyone	the	working with	and

mentioned in the Corinthian letter to Paul. Considering the factions in Corinth and the fact that Apollos was viewed as Paul's rival there, it is valuable to note that Paul urged him to go to Corinth. It gives an insight into Paul's character and his concerns.

16:13,14. In these two verses Paul wrote a series of short, powerful phrases that ring like military commands and are filled with clear direction. "Watch" is a present imperative. Paul was speaking of a continuing state. All the imperatives, in fact, in these two verses are present imperatives. More is meant than the mere absence of sleep. There is the idea of determined wakefulness and alertness. In Scripture there is both the warning to watchfulness against temptation and sin and also for the second coming of the Lord. Speaking against the Corinthians' lack of stability, Paul directed them to a particular steadfastness: "Stand fast in the faith"; in the person and power of Jesus Christ and His love (13:2,13; 15:14-17).

Further, they were urged to be mature and courageous. There was a challenge to "play the man" (Moffatt) in all the activities of the Christian life. It was a charge against the childishness of the Corinthians. They had not been able to succeed because of their entanglement with heathen society and influence. The fight over sin and opposition of every sort is not one for children; it is for men.

Paul instructed the Corinthians to be strong. Christians may feel weak, but then is the time to go to the Strong One for strength. They must be "mighty" in Christian activity, by the power of the Lord. This contrasted with the Corinthian tendency to moral weakness and unsteadiness.

They were also charged to love. The Greek states it better: "in love." It refers to agape love, the highest, complete love. It stands as more than an equal or companion to Christian action. It is the realm and atmosphere within which the Christian thinks, moves, and lives. It is the fountain out of which all proper action flows (1 Peter 4:8).

16:15. Paul set before the Corinthians men to pattern themselves after and to respect, such as the household of Stephanas. "Ministry" is a general term for service. It does not indicate clergy.

16:16. Paul noted the manner in which the Corinthians were to treat such as the house of Stephanas. Again the indication is not that the men mentioned were church officials.

Paul was asking for willing submission to the direction of those willing and able to lead in profitable and excellent work. Such extensive work and sacrifice deserves respect in the Church as a whole. Paul included in this sweeping statement not only the house of Stephanas, but also all who helped and labored in the church.

him much, *PNT* . . . I have often requested, *Fenton* . . . I have repeatedly urged, *Weymouth*.

but his will was not at all to come at this time: . . . he is quite resolved not to do so at present, *Weymouth* . . . he was quite unwilling to come at present, *Confraternity*.

but he will come when he shall have convenient time: . . . when there is a good opportunity, *Fenton* . . . he will come when he shall have opportunity, *Hanson*.

13. Watch ye, stand fast in the faith: Stand firm, *Concordant* . . . Be vigilant, *PNT* . . . Be on the alert, *Weymouth*.

quit you like men, be strong: Be manly! Be staunch! *Concordant* . . . doe manfully, and be strengthened, *Rheims* . . . be manly; be self-restrained, *Fenton* . . . play the man, *Moffatt*.

14. Let all your things be done with charity: Let all your actions occur in love! *Concordant* . . . be done in love, *PNT* . . . from motives of love, *Weymouth*.

15. I beseech you, brethren, (ye know the house of Stephanas: Now I am entreating you, brethren—you are acquainted, *Concordant* . . . I ask this favour of you, *Moffatt* . . . But I advise you, *Fenton*.

that it is the firstfruits of Achaia: . . . they were the pioneers of Achaia, *Fenton* . . . were the earliest Greek converts to Christ, *Weymouth*.

and [that] they have addicted themselves to the ministry of the saints,): . . . they have appointed themselves, *PNT* . . . for service to the saints, *Fenton*.

16. That ye submit yourselves unto such: . . . to such as these do you also be subject, *Confraternity* . . . you to put yourselves under people like that, *Moffatt* . . . to show deference to such, *Montgomery*.

and to every one that helpeth with [us], and laboureth:

1 Corinthians 16:17

2844.5 verb dat sing masc part pres act	5299.1 verb 1sing indic pres act	1156.2 conj	1894.3 prep	3450.11 art dat sing fem	3814.3 noun dat sing fem
κοπιῶντι.	17. χαίρω	δὲ	ἐπὶ	τῇ	παρουσίᾳ
kopiōnti	chairō	de	epi	tē	parousia
laboring.	I rejoice	but	at	the	coming

	4585.1 name gen masc	2504.1 conj	5251.1 name gen masc		5251.2 name gen masc
17.a.Txt: 018K,025P,byz. **Var:** 01ℵ,02A,03B,04C 06D,020L,33,Lach,Treg Alf,Word,Tisc,We/Ho Weis,Sod,UBS/☆	Στεφανᾶ	καὶ	ʽ Φουρτουνάτου	[ᵃ☆ Φορτουνάτου]	
	Stephana	kai	Phourtounatou	Phortounatou	
	of Stephanas	and	Fortunatus	[idem]	

2504.1 conj	876.1 name gen sing	3617.1 conj	3450.16 art sing neu	5050.2 prs-pron gen 2pl
καὶ	᾿Αχαϊκοῦ,	ὅτι	τὸ	ʽ ὑμῶν
kai	Achaikou	hoti	to	humōn
and	Achaicus;	because	to	your

	5052.2 adj acc 2sing	5140.2 noun acc sing neu	3642.7 dem-pron nom pl masc	376.3 verb 3pl indic aor act
17.b.Txt: 01ℵ,02A,018K 020L,byz. **Var:** 03B,04C,06D,025P 33,Lach,Treg,Alf,Word Tisc,We/Ho,Weis,Sod UBS/☆	[ᵇ☆ ὑμέτερον]	ὑστέρημα	οὗτοι	ἀνεπλήρωσαν·
	humeteron	husterēma	houtoi	aneplērōsan
	[idem]	absence	these	filled up.

372.1 verb 3pl indic aor act	1056.1 conj	3450.16 art sing neu	1684.1 adj 1sing	4011.1 noun sing neu	2504.1 conj	3450.16 art sing neu
18. ἀνέπαυσαν	γὰρ	τὸ	ἐμὸν	πνεῦμα	καὶ	τὸ
anepausan	gar	to	emon	pneuma	kai	to
They refreshed	for	the	my	spirit	and	the

5050.2 prs-pron gen 2pl	1906.1 verb 2pl pres act	3631.1 conj	3450.8 art acc pl masc	4955.8 dem-pron acc pl masc
ὑμῶν,	ἐπιγινώσκετε	οὖν	τοὺς	τοιούτους.
humōn	epiginōskete	oun	tous	toioutous
yours;	recognize	therefore	the	such.

776.3 verb 3pl indic pres	5050.4 prs-pron acc 2pl	3450.13 art pl fem	1564.5 noun nom pl fem	3450.10 art gen sing fem
19. ᾿Ασπάζονται	ὑμᾶς	αἱ	ἐκκλησίαι	τῆς
Aspazontai	humas	hai	ekklēsiai	tēs
Greet	you	the	assemblies	tēs

	767.2 name gen fem	776.3 verb 3pl indic pres	776.2 verb 3sing indic pres	5050.4 prs-pron acc 2pl
19.a.Txt: 03B,020L,byz. **Var:** 01ℵ,04C,06D 018K,025P,Alf,Tisc We/Ho,Weis,Sod UBS/☆	᾿Ασίας·	ʽ ἀσπάζονται	[ᵃ☆ ἀσπάζεται]	ὑμᾶς
	Asias	aspazontai	aspazetai	humas
	of Asia.	Greet	[greets]	you

1706.1 prep	2935.3 noun dat sing masc	4044.17 adj pl neu	205.1 name nom masc	2504.1 conj	4111.1 name nom fem
ἐν	κυρίῳ	πολλὰ	᾿Ακύλας	καὶ	ʽ Πρίσκιλλα,
en	kuriō	polla	Akulas	kai	Priskilla
in	Lord	much	Aquila	and	Priscilla,

	4110.2 name nom fem	4713.1 prep dat	3450.11 art dat sing fem	2567.1 prep	3486.4 noun acc sing masc	840.1 prs-pron gen pl
19.b.Txt: 02A,04C,06D 018K,020L,byz. **Var:** 01ℵ,03B,025P,33 sa.bo.Treg,Tisc,We/Ho Weis,Sod,UBS/☆	[ᵇ☆ Πρίσκα]	σὺν	τῇ	κατ᾿	οἶκον	αὐτῶν
	Priska	sun	tē	kat'	oikon	autōn
	[Prisca,]	with	the	by	house	their

1564.3 noun dat sing fem	776.3 verb 3pl indic pres	5050.4 prs-pron acc 2pl	3450.7 art pl masc	79.6 noun nom pl masc
ἐκκλησίᾳ·	20. ἀσπάζονται	ὑμᾶς	οἱ	ἀδελφοὶ
ekklēsia	aspazontai	humas	hoi	adelphoi
assembly.	Greet	you	the	brothers

16:17,18. Paul admonished the Corinthians about their manner toward Stephanas, Fortunatus, and Achaicus when they returned home. But at present, he expressed his joy over their being with him.

Fortunatus was a common Latin name. *Achaicus* was a rare Greek name. Because of their names, some have supposed one or both were slaves, although there is little to support this. These three men probably carried the church letter to Paul. And since Paul commended them at the close of this letter, it is probable they would carry his letter back to Corinth.

Paul said that these three had made up to him for the absence of the Corinthians. In other words, they had representatively supplied him with the desired fellowship of the Corinthians. This would fit Paul's nature and satisfies the word "coming." It expressed the tenderness and depth of his feeling for the Corinthians even though they had not always treated him in a fitting or proper manner.

The coming of these men had been enjoyable not only because they had supplied a need but also because they had refreshed Paul's spirit and, therefore, that of the Corinthians. It would please and cheer them to know this visit had such desirable effects.

16:19. Paul delighted in binding the churches together with real expressions of love. This was the purpose of the following greetings.

Paul specifically noted Aquila and Priscilla and the believers who met in their home. "Asia" referred to what was then the Roman province of Asia and what is now western Asia Minor. These two were well-known to the Corinthians (Acts 18:1-3).

Originally from Rome, Aquila and Priscilla had been a large part of Paul's life. Priscilla and Aquila had been forced to leave Rome in A.D. 49 when the Roman Emperor Claudius banished all Jews from the city of Rome. This edict was lifted in A.D. 50, allowing the Jews to return. When Paul wrote his letter to the Romans in A.D. 54 Priscilla and Aquila were once again residing in Rome (cf. Romans 16:3). When Paul first came to Corinth, he worked and lodged with them. They had been generous to him. Because they, like Paul, were tentmakers by trade, they worked together in this craft to support themselves.

At the time of Paul's writing this epistle Priscilla (or Prisca as she was also known) and Aquila were living in Ephesus where they had their own house-church.

Further, they had at some time risked their lives for him. They had instructed and encouraged Apollos in the Faith. They are mentioned six times in the New Testament.

"Salute you much" is a deep, warm, affectionate Christian greeting. "With the church . . . in their house" can hardly mean the whole Ephesian church. Perhaps it meant a neighboring section of it.

16:20. Paul added a comprehensive salute and then indicated the proper response. "All the brethren" is not specific, but appears to be all-inclusive.

17. I am glad of the coming of Stephanas and Fortunatus and Achaicus: I reioyce in the presence of, *Rheims, Douay* . . . I was very happy, *SEB* . . . at the arrival of, *Fenton.*

for that which was lacking on your part they have supplied: . . . for they have made up for your absence, *Moffatt, Beck* . . . they have supplied what was deficient on your side, *Locke* . . . they have accomplished your instructions, *Fenton.*

18. For they have refreshed my spirit and yours: . . . they gave rest, *Rotherham* . . . they soothe my spirit, *Concordant* . . . they have lightened my spirit, *Conybeare* . . . they have quieted my mind, *Locke.*

therefore acknowledge ye them that are such: . . . therefore honour such men, *Fenton* . . . So cultivate the acquaintance of such men, *Montgomery* . . . You should appreciate men like that, *Beck* . . . You should give special recognition, *SEB* . . . Cultivate friendships with such men as these, *TCNT* . . . To such render due acknowledgment, *Conybeare* . . . have a regard to such men, *Locke.*

19. The churches of Asia salute you: The assemblies, *Hanson* . . . The congregations, *Campbell* . . . send greetings, *Klingensmith* . . . send regards to you all, *Fenton* . . . greet you heartily in the Lord, *Confraternity.*

Aquila and Priscilla salute you much in the Lord: . . . send you a hearty Christian greeting, *TCNT* . . . Salute you most heartily, *Berkeley* . . . in hearty Christian love, *Weymouth* . . . with much Christian affection, *Locke* . . . greetings in the Lord, *Beck.*

with the church that is in their house: . . . the congregacion, *Cranmer* . . . the church at their home, *Beck* . . . which assembles at their house, *Conybeare.*

20. All the brethren greet you: All the brotherhood salutes you, *Moffatt* . . . All the Christians greet you, *Beck* . . . send you good wishes, *TCNT.*

493

3820.7 adj pl masc	776.9 verb 2pl impr aor mid	238.3 prs-pron acc pl masc	1706.1 prep	5207.1 noun dat sing neu
πάντες.	Ἀσπάσασθε	ἀλλήλους	ἐν	φιλήματι
pantes	Aspasasthe	allēlous	en	philēmati
all.	Greet you	one another	with	a kiss

39.3 adj dat sing	3450.5 art sing masc	777.1 noun nom sing masc	3450.11 art dat sing fem	1684.8 adj dat 1sing fem	5331.3 noun dat sing fem
ἁγίῳ.	21. Ὁ	ἀσπασμὸς	τῇ	ἐμῇ	χειρὶ
hagiō	Ho	aspasmos	tē	emē	cheiri
holy.	The	greeting	by the	my	hand

3834.2 name gen masc	1479.1 conj	4948.3 indef-pron nom sing	3620.3 partic	5205.3 verb 3sing indic pres act	3450.6 art acc sing masc
Παύλου·	22. εἴ	τις	οὐ	φιλεῖ	τὸν
Paulou	ei	tis	ou	philei	ton
of Paul.	If	anyone	not	love	the

2935.4 noun acc sing masc	2400.3 name acc masc	5382.4 name acc masc	1498.16 verb 3sing impr pres act	329.1 noun nom sing neu
κύριον	⌐a Ἰησοῦν	Χριστόν, ⌐	ἤτω	ἀνάθεμα·
kurion	Iēsoun	Christon	ētō	anathema
Lord	Jesus	Christ,	let him be	accursed:

3106.1 noun masc	109.1 verb 2sing impr	3106.2 noun masc	109.2 verb 3sing indic	3450.9 art nom sing fem
⌐ Μαρὰν	ἀθά.	[✶ Μαρανα	θα.]	23. ἡ
Maran	atha	Marana	tha	hē
Maran	atha.	[Marana	tha.]	The

22.a.**Txt**: 01א-corr 04C-corr,06D,018K 020L,025P,byz.bo. **Var**: 01א-org,02A,03B 04C-org,33,Lach,Treg Alf,Tisc,We/Ho,Weis Sod,UBS/✶

23.a.**Txt**: 01א-corr,02A 04C,06D,018K,020L 025P,byz.sa.bo. **Var**: 01א-org,03B,33 Treg,Alf,Tisc,We/Ho Weis,Sod,UBS/✶

24.a.**Txt**: 01א,02A,04C 06D,018K,020L,025P byz.it.bo.Gries,Word Sod **Var**: 03B,33,sa.Treg Tisc,We/Ho,Weis UBS/✶

24.b.**Txt**: (018K),(020L) Steph **Var**: Gries,Lach,Treg Word,Tisc,We/Ho,Weis Sod,UBS/✶

5322.1 noun nom sing fem	3450.2 art gen sing	2935.2 noun gen sing masc	2400.2 name masc	5382.2 name gen masc	3196.1 prep
χάρις	τοῦ	κυρίου	Ἰησοῦ	⌐a Χριστοῦ ⌐	μεθ'
charis	tou	kuriou	Iēsou	Christou	meth'
grace	of the	Lord	Jesus	Christ	with

5050.2 prs-pron gen 2pl	3450.9 art nom sing fem	26.1 noun nom sing fem	1466.2 prs-pron gen 1sing	3196.3 prep	3820.4 adj gen pl
ὑμῶν.	24. ἡ	ἀγάπη	μου	μετὰ	πάντων
humōn	hē	agapē	mou	meta	pantōn
you.	The	love	my	with	all

5050.2 prs-pron gen 2pl	1706.1 prep	5382.3 name dat masc	2400.2 name masc	279.1 partic	4242.1 prep
ὑμῶν	ἐν	Χριστῷ	Ἰησοῦ.	⌐a ἀμήν. ⌐	⌐b Πρὸς
humōn	en	Christō	Iēsou	amēn	Pros
you	in	Christ	Jesus.	Amen.	To

2854.3 name acc pl masc	4272.9 num ord nom sing fem	1119.21 verb 3sing indic aor pass	570.3 prep gen	5212.1 name gen masc
Κορινθίους	πρώτη	ἐγράφη	ἀπὸ	Φιλίππων,
Korinthious	prōtē	egraphē	apo	Philippōn
Corinthians	first	was written	from	Philippi,

1217.2 prep	4585.1 name gen masc	2504.1 conj	5251.1 name gen masc	2504.1 conj	876.1 name gen sing
διὰ	Στεφανᾶ	καὶ	Φουρτουνάτου	καὶ	Ἀχαϊκοῦ,
dia	Stephana	kai	Phourtounatou	kai	Achaikou
by	Stephanas	and	Fortunatus	and	Achaicus

2504.1 conj	4943.2 name gen masc
καὶ	Τιμοθέου. ⌐
kai	Timotheou
and	Timothy.

The admonition from Paul on a "holy kiss" has caused much discussion. The custom was common in Paul's day, and in some countries a kiss on both cheeks is common in our day. Such a greeting would be a rebuke to any division or haughtiness; it would note that they were in accord.

16:21. It was Paul's custom to dictate his letters to an amanuensis. But to mark the letter's genuineness he would, at the end, sign and close it himself. This was what he did now. This was his letter and personal greeting.

16:22. With great feeling, Paul closed the epistle. If a man falsely pretended to love the Lord, let him be "Anathema" (*anathema*), Paul wrote. Such a one is accursed. "Love not" (*ou philei*) is a strong note of accusation. It declares the individual to be heartless, lacking even human affection for Jesus. Such men, as the apostle John pointed out, neither love nor know God.

The second clause is "Maranatha" (*Maran atha*). This is an Aramaic word translated into Greek. Dividing the word, it breaks down roughly like this: *Mar* means "Lord"; *an* or *ana* denotes "our," and the latter part is from the verb *atha*, which means "to come" (Morris, *Tyndale New Testament Commentaries*, 7:247,248). This seems best translated, "Our Lord cometh." This accords with Philippians 4:5; 1 Thessalonians 4:14; James 5:7; Revelation 1:7; 3:11; 22:20. It fits the immediate context; it is in harmony with 1 Corinthians 15, and it agrees with the New Testament attitude towards Christ's return.

16:23,24. Paul desired that the Corinthians should be constantly attended by the marvelous grace of "our Lord Jesus Christ," that it should be the constant source of ministry and blessing to them. It was a common farewell from Paul and was expanded in 2 Corinthians 13:14.

Paul also added a note of affection peculiar to this letter, but it was fitting in light of some of the harsh directives he had to give the Corinthians. He noted his love for them all, and he desired it in an abiding sense ("with you").

He noted the foundation and bond for love among them all: the bond of Jesus Christ. Division, bigotry, and non-Christian behavior were all products of the Corinthians' living. It should be otherwise.

It is fitting that the last words should show the great heart of the apostle and, even more importantly, the bond of all things, the person of Jesus Christ. Paul's last word was "Jesus."

Greet ye one another with an holy kiss: Give one another, *BB* . . . with a sacred kiss, *TCNT, Goodspeed* . . . with the kiss of peace, *Barclay* . . . I should like you to shake hands all round as a sign of Christian love, *Phillips.*

21. The salutation of [me] Paul with mine own hand: That which followeth is, *Locke* . . . The good wishes, *Fenton* . . . The final greeting of me, *Weymouth* . . . I, Paul, add this farewell in my own handwriting, *TCNT* . . . Here is the greeting that I, Paul, write with my own hand, *Beck* . . . send you these words of love in my writing, *BB* . . . The salutation, with my hand, of Paul, *Rotherham* . . . Here is my own greeting, written by me, *Phillips.*

22. If any man love not the Lord Jesus Christ, let him be Anathema, Maranatha: If any one is destitute of love, *Weymouth* . . . If any one is not a friend to the Lord, *Sawyer* . . . If any one be an enemy to...let him be accursed, or devoted to destruction, *Locke* . . . If any one is not loving the Lord, *Rotherham* . . . has not love for the Lord, *BB* . . . A curse upon anyone who has no love for the Lord. Lord come quickly! *Goodspeed* . . . excommunicate to death, *Geneva* . . . let him be delivered to the Lord coming in Judgment, *Fenton* . . . a curse on him! Our Lord, come! *Beck* . . . he should be condemned! *SEB* . . . let him be accursed, when the Lord cometh! *Worrell* . . . Our Lord is coming, *Weymouth, Adams* . . . may the Lord soon come! *Phillips.*

23. The grace of our Lord Jesus Christ [be] with you: The favour of, *Locke, Klingensmith, Rotherham* . . . the blessing of, *TCNT, Goodspeed* . . . May the Lord Jesus love you! *Beck.*

24. My love [be] with you all in Christ Jesus. Amen: My Christian love to all of you, *TCNT* . . . My love to you all, *Barclay* . . . My love is with you all in Christ Jesus, *Fenton* . . . through Christ Jesus, *Goodspeed* . . . So be it, *BB.*

THE SECOND EPISTLE
OF PAUL TO THE
CORINTHIANS

Expanded Interlinear

Textual Critical Apparatus

Verse-by-Verse Commentary

Various Versions

Πρὸς
Pros
To

2854.3 name
acc pl masc

Κορινθίους
Korinthious
Corinthians

1976.1 noun
nom sing fem

ἐπιστολὴ
epistolē
letter

1202.4 num ord
nom sing fem

δευτέρα.
deutera
second.

**Textual
Apparatus**

3834.1 name
nom masc

1:1. Παῦλος
Paulos
Paul,

646.1 noun
nom sing masc

ἀπόστολος
apostolos
apostle

2400.2
name masc

ʼ Ἰησοῦ
Iēsou
of Jesus

5382.2 name
gen masc

Χριστοῦ
Christou
Christ

5382.2 name
gen masc

[☆ Χριστοῦ
Christou
[of Christ

2400.2
name masc

Ἰησοῦ]
Iēsou
Jesus]

1217.2
prep

διὰ
dia
by

2284.2 noun
gen sing neu

θελήματος
thelēmatos
will

2296.2 noun
gen sing masc

θεοῦ,
theou
of God,

2504.1
conj

καὶ
kai
and

4943.1 name
nom masc

Τιμόθεος
Timotheos
Timothy

3450.5 art
sing masc

ὁ
ho
the

79.1 noun
nom sing masc

ἀδελφός,
adelphos
brother,

3450.11 art
dat sing fem

τῇ
tē
to the

1564.3 noun
dat sing fem

ἐκκλησίᾳ
ekklēsia
assembly

3450.2 art
gen sing

τοῦ
tou

2296.2 noun
gen sing masc

θεοῦ
theou
of God

3450.11 art
dat sing fem

τῇ
tē
the

1498.28 verb dat
sing fem part pres act

οὔσῃ
ousē
being

1706.1
prep

ἐν
en
in

2855.1
name dat fem

Κορίνθῳ,
Korinthō
Corinth,

4713.1
prep dat

σὺν
sun
with

3450.4
art dat pl

τοῖς
tois
the

39.8 adj
dat pl masc

ἁγίοις
hagiois
saints

3820.5
adj dat pl

πᾶσιν
pasin
all

3450.4
art dat pl

τοῖς
tois
the

1498.24 verb dat pl
masc part pres act

οὖσιν
ousin
being

1706.1
prep

ἐν
en
in

3513.8 adj
dat sing fem

ὅλῃ
holē
whole

3450.11 art
dat sing fem

τῇ
tē

875.3 name
dat fem

Ἀχαΐᾳ·
Achaia
Achaia.

5322.1 noun
nom sing fem

2. χάρις
charis
Grace

5050.3 prs-
pron dat 2pl

ὑμῖν
humin
to you

2504.1
conj

καὶ
kai
and

1503.1 noun
nom sing fem

εἰρήνη
eirēnē
peace

570.3
prep gen

ἀπὸ
apo
from

2296.2 noun
gen sing masc

θεοῦ
theou
God

3824.2 noun
gen sing masc

πατρὸς
patros
Father

2231.2 prs-
pron gen 1pl

ἡμῶν
hēmōn
our

2504.1
conj

καὶ
kai
and

2935.2 noun
gen sing masc

κυρίου
kuriou
Lord

2400.2
name masc

Ἰησοῦ
Iēsou
Jesus

5382.2 name
gen masc

Χριστοῦ.
Christou
Christ.

2109.1 adj
nom sing masc

3. Εὐλογητὸς
Eulogētos
Blessed

3450.5 art
sing masc

ὁ
ho
the

2296.1 noun
nom sing masc

θεὸς
theos
God

2504.1
conj

καὶ
kai
and

3824.1 noun
nom sing masc

πατὴρ
patēr
Father

3450.2 art
gen sing

τοῦ
tou
of the

2935.2 noun
gen sing masc

κυρίου
kuriou
Lord

2231.2 prs-
pron gen 1pl

ἡμῶν
hēmōn
our

2400.2
name masc

Ἰησοῦ
Iēsou
Jesus

5382.2 name
gen masc

Χριστοῦ,
Christou
Christ,

THE SECOND EPISTLE OF PAUL TO THE
CORINTHIANS

1:1. In the salutation of all his epistles except 1 and 2 Thessalonians, Paul referred to himself as either an apostle, a servant, or a prisoner of Jesus Christ. His favorite word to describe himself, however, was "apostle" or "sent one." The phrase "of Jesus Christ by the will of God" qualified his office as a "sent one." He had been called and sent out by the Lord Jesus himself. Paul's calling was not of his own choosing. It was by God's will (Acts 9:15).

Paul's emphasis on being an apostle by the will of God here focuses on the privilege that was his in being sent on a mission as an ambassador by the King of heaven. In other places he qualified the reference to his apostleship by declaring he had the office "by the commandment" of God (1 Timothy 1:1). In this case he thought more of the responsibility the Lord laid on him than of the opportunity God afforded him in sending him out. In either case, though, Paul made it clear he did not initiate his entrance into the ministry. No man in the natural would have chosen for himself the kind of life Paul lived. He stated emphatically that God put him into the ministry (1 Timothy 1:12). Paul did not choose the ministry; God chose him for the ministry.

In these opening words Paul identified himself with Timothy "our brother." The word *brother* was also used in pagan societies, but the Christian gospel gave it new meaning. Here it means "our fellow Christian." Not only was Timothy Paul's brother in the Lord, he was also his son in the Christian faith (1 Corinthians 4:17; 1 Timothy 1:2; 2 Timothy 1:2). The closest of bonds united Paul and Timothy in the ministry of the gospel.

1:2. This verse has been called a Christian version of a Jewish blessing. Here, and in the first part of verse 3, Paul gives a Christian sense to Jewish liturgy. God is more than just the God of the Old Testament patriarchs and of Israel. God is the Father of Jesus Christ, the Son whom God sent to redeem the world. Implied very plainly in these verses is the deity of Christ.

1:3. Also implied is the fact that God is not only the Father of the Lord Jesus Christ, He is *our* Father, the Father of *our* Lord Jesus. Believers are united to the Father and the Son through faith (1 John 1:3) and are given power to become sons of God (John

Various Versions

1. Paul, an apostle of Jesus Christ by the will of God: This letter comes to you from Paul, *Phillips* . . . Paul a legate, *Murdock* . . . appointed by God, *JB* . . . chosen by God, *NLT* . . . a special messenger, *RPNT* . . . missionary, *Klingensmith* . . . of Yeshua Mashiach, *MJV* . . . an ambassador belonging to Christ Jesus through the desire of God, *Wuest* . . . by the purpose, *BB* . . . by the good pleasure of God, *Murdock* . . . because God willed it so, *Barclay*.

and Timothy [our] brother: . . . our colleague, *JB, Barclay* . . . our fellow worker, *Beck*.

unto the church of God which is at Corinth: . . . to God's congregation, *Barclay* . . . to the community of God, *HistNT* . . . assembly of God, *Young*.

with all the saints which are in all Achaia: . . . together with all who are dedicated to him, *JB* . . . in conjunction with, *Rotherham* . . . with all God's people, *Weymouth* . . . to all the faithful, *Greber* . . . to all Christ's people throughout Greece, *TCNT* . . . the holy people everywhere in Greece, *Beck* . . . who are throughout Achaia, *NASB*.

2. Grace [be] to you and peace from God our Father, and [from] the Lord Jesus Christ: May unconditional love be yours, *RPNT* . . . spiritual blessing and peace to you, *Williams* . . . the Lord Jesus Christ bless you and give you peace, *TCNT* . . . favour to you, *Rotherham* . . . and every blessing from God, *Barclay*.

3. Blessed [be] God, even the Father of our Lord Jesus Christ: Give praise to God, *SEB* . . . Let us praise, *Beck* . . . a gentle Father, *JB*.

2 Corinthians 1:4

| 3450.5 art
sing masc
ὁ
ho
the | 3824.1 noun
nom sing masc
πατὴρ
patēr
Father | 3450.1
art gen pl
τῶν
tōn
of the | 3490.2 noun
gen pl masc
οἰκτιρμῶν
oiktirmōn
compassions, | 2504.1
conj
καὶ
kai
and | 2296.1 noun
nom sing masc
θεὸς
theos
God |

| 3820.10 adj
gen sing fem
πάσης
pasēs
of all | 3735.2 noun
gen sing fem
παρακλήσεως,
paraklēseōs
encouragement; | 3450.5 art
sing masc
4. ὁ
ho
the | 3731.7 verb nom sing
masc part pres act
παρακαλῶν
parakalōn
encouraging | 2231.4 prs-
pron acc 1pl
ἡμᾶς
hēmas
us |

| 1894.3
prep
ἐπὶ
epi
in | 3820.11 adj
dat sing fem
πάσῃ
pasē
all | 3450.11 art
dat sing fem
τῇ
tē
the | 2324.3 noun
dat sing fem
θλίψει
thlipsei
tribulation | 2231.2 prs-
pron gen 1pl
ἡμῶν,
hēmōn
our, | 1519.1
prep
εἰς
eis
for | 3450.16 art
sing neu
τὸ
to
the |

| 1404.22
verb inf pres
δύνασθαι
dunasthai
to be able | 2231.4 prs-
pron acc 1pl
ἡμᾶς
hēmas
us | 3731.10 verb
inf pres act
παρακαλεῖν
parakalein
to encourage | 3450.8 art
acc pl masc
τοὺς
tous
the | 1706.1
prep
ἐν
en
in | 3820.11 adj
dat sing fem
πάσῃ
pasē
every |

| 2324.3 noun
dat sing fem
θλίψει,
thlipsei
tribulation, | 1217.2
prep
διὰ
dia
through | 3450.10 art
gen sing fem
τῆς
tēs
the | 3735.2 noun
gen sing fem
παρακλήσεως
paraklēseōs
encouragement | 3614.10 rel-
pron gen sing fem
ἧς
hēs
with which |

| 3731.22 verb 1pl
indic pres pass
παρακαλούμεθα
parakaloumetha
we are being encouraged | 840.7 prs-pron
nom pl masc
αὐτοὶ
autoi
ourselves | 5097.3
prep
ὑπὸ
hupo
by | 3450.2 art
gen sing
τοῦ
tou | 2296.2 noun
gen sing masc
θεοῦ·
theou
God. |

| 3617.1
conj
5. ὅτι
hoti
Because | 2503.1
conj
καθὼς
kathōs
just as | 3915.2 verb 3sing
indic pres act
περισσεύει
perisseuei
abounds | 3450.17
art pl neu
τὰ
ta
the | 3667.2
noun pl neu
παθήματα
pathēmata
sufferings | 3450.2 art
gen sing
τοῦ
tou
of the |

5.a.Var: 01ℵ,02A,03B
04C,06D,018K,Gries
Lach,Treg,Alf,Word
Tisc,We/Ho,Weis,Sod
UBS/⋆

| 5382.2 name
gen masc
Χριστοῦ
Christou
Christ | 1519.1
prep
εἰς
eis
toward | 2231.4 prs-
pron acc 1pl
ἡμᾶς,
hēmas,
us, | 3643.1
adv
οὕτως
houtōs
so | 1217.2
prep
διὰ
dia
through | 3450.2 art
gen sing
[a⋆+ τοῦ]
tou
[the] |

| 5382.2 name
gen masc
Χριστοῦ
Christou
Christ | 3915.2 verb 3sing
indic pres act
περισσεύει
perisseuei
abounds | 2504.1
conj
καὶ
kai
also | 3450.9 art
nom sing fem
ἡ
hē
the | 3735.1 noun
nom sing fem
παράκλησις
paraklēsis
encouragement | 2231.2 prs-
pron gen 1pl
ἡμῶν.
hēmōn.
our. |

| 1521.1
conj
6. εἴτε
eite
Whether | 1156.2
conj
δὲ
de
but | 2323.3 verb 1pl
indic pres pass
θλιβόμεθα,
thlibometha,
we are being troubled, | 5065.1
prep
ὑπὲρ
huper
for | 3450.10 art
gen sing fem
τῆς
tēs
the | 5050.2 prs-
pron gen 2pl
ὑμῶν
humōn
your |

6.a.Var: 06D,018K,byz.
Steph

| 3735.2 noun
gen sing fem
παρακλήσεως
paraklēseōs
encouragement | 2504.1
conj
καὶ
kai
and | 4843.2 noun
gen sing fem
σωτηρίας,
sōtērias,
salvation, | 3450.10 art
gen sing fem
[a τῆς
tēs
the | 1738.10 verb gen
sing fem part pres mid
ἐνεργουμένης
energoumenēs
being effective |

1:12). As God's sons Christians are recipients of His mercies and His comfort. God is the divine source of the believer's help. He is the channel through whom all blessings are communicated to men.

1:4. Some form of the word *comfort* occurs 10 times in verses 3-7. All are derived from the Greek *parakaleō* from which we get *comforter*. Paul declared here that God comforts His children in times of tribulations. How? We are not told; possibly through the ministry of Christian friends, certainly through the Scriptures. Christ promised He would not leave His followers orphans but that He would send the Holy Spirit to be their Comforter (John 14:16-18; 15:26). The emphasis here is on the constancy of that comfort. It is not to be temporary or spasmodic. This verse could just as well read: "who *always* comforts us . . . ."

Several times this epistle expresses a paradox, i.e., affliction and comfort appear to go together, but not without a purpose. The very comfort that is received in times of suffering brings with it an understanding of why the comfort is sent in the first place. It is not only for the one who is comforted, it will also through that one benefit others.

1:5. It is a reassuring thought that the constant comfort of God attends the overflowing sufferings that may come the believer's way. The Greek adverbs *kathōs* ("for as") and *houtōs* ("so also") express a comparison in which the second element matches the first. "For as" the sufferings of Christ may be present in abundance (*perisseuei*), "so . . . also" is the encouragement and comfort present in abundance (*perisseuei*) for enduring the trial. This word means "to provide in superabundance." It is used in Matthew 14:20 to describe the fragments taken up "over and above" what had been eaten. It is also used by Jesus in the Parable of the Prodigal Son to describe the "bread enough and to spare" in the father's house (Luke 15:17).

Paul was saying here that although the sufferings of Christ seem to be present in abundance, even to overflowing, the comfort and encouragement for enduring the trial is just as abundant if only the Corinthians were spiritually sensitive enough to recognize it.

Paul was not necessarily referring only to what he suffered in his own body. These "sufferings" are those common to all who are united with Christ (Romans 8:17; 2 Corinthians 1:7; 1 Peter 4:13). "For as" union with Christ may be the cause of affliction, "so also" is its source of consolation. Apart from Christ, suffering often leads to despair rather than comfort.

1:6. The conditional "if" found in some versions does not imply any doubt regarding the sufferings. It is a simple way of stating the case. The verse has been translated "whenever we suffer" or "every time we suffer." The affliction that came to Paul and his

the Father of mercies: . . . of all consolation, *Fenton, Worrell* . . . of tender mercies, *HistNT, Montgomery* . . . compassionate mercies, *Wuest* . . . the compassionate Father, *TCNT.*

and the God of all comfort: . . . of all encouragement, *Klingensmith* . . . of every comfort, *Norlie.*

4. Who comforteth us in all our tribulation: He encourages us, *SEB* . . . who consoles us, *Rotherham* . . . comfort in all our trials, *Phillips* . . . in all our distress, *HistNT* . . . in all our afflictions, *Confraternity, Wesley, RSV* . . . in all my troubles, *Montgomery.*

that we may be able to comfort them which are in any trouble: . . . to make us capable, *Adams* . . . give the same sort of strong sympathy to others, *Phillips* . . . in all distress, *Douay* . . . in any kind of distress, *Berkeley* . . . having all kinds of trouble, *SEB* . . . in any distress, *Confraternity.*

by the comfort wherewith we ourselves are comforted of God: . . . the same comfort, *Norlie* . . . with the very comfort which we ourselves receive from him, *TCNT* . . . God is ever comforting me, *Montgomery* . . . we are divinely sustained, *Berkeley.*

5. For as the sufferings of Christ abound in us, so our consolation also aboundeth by Christ: . . . the more we share Christ's suffering, *Phillips* . . . we have more than our share of comfort, *Weymouth* . . . my sufferings for Christ are running over the cup, *Williams* . . . overflowed to us, *Fenton* . . . are overflowing towards us, *Rotherham* . . . come into our lives plentifully, *Norlie* . . . through Christ, *Wesley* . . . through the Christ, *Panin.*

6. And whether we be afflicted: . . . if we have trials to endure, *Norlie* . . . we be in tribulation, *Young, Douay* . . . we are grieved, *Fenton* . . . we are in tribulation, *Rotherham.*

[it is] for your consolation and salvation: . . . for your instruction, *Confraternity* . . . deliverance, and preservation, *Wuest* . . . and be saved, *SEB.*

2 Corinthians 1:7

1706.1 prep	5119.3 noun dat sing fem	3450.1 art gen pl	840.1 prs-pron gen pl	3667.3 noun gen pl neu	3614.1 rel-pron gen pl	2504.1 conj
ἐν	ὑπομονῇ	τῶν	αὐτῶν	παθημάτων	ὧν	καὶ
en	hupomonē	tōn	autōn	pathēmatōn	hōn	kai
in	endurance	of the	same	sufferings	which	also

6.b.Var: 01ℵ,02A,04C 025P,044,Gries,Tisc We/Ho,Sod,UBS/✱

2231.1 prs-pron nom 1pl	3819.3 verb 1pl indic pres act	1521.1 conj	3731.22 verb 1pl indic pres pass
ἡμεῖς	πάσχομεν.	εἴτε	παρακαλούμεθα,
hēmeis	paschomen	eite	parakaloumetha
we	suffer,	whether	we are being encouraged,

6.c.Txt: 03B,06D,018K 020L,byz.
Var: 01ℵ,02A,04C,025P 044,Gries,Tisc,We/Ho Weis,Sod,UBS/✱

5065.1 prep	3450.10 art gen sing fem	5050.2 prs-pron gen 2pl	3735.2 noun gen sing fem	2504.1 conj
ὑπὲρ	τῆς	ὑμῶν	παρακλήσεως	καὶ
huper	tēs	humōn	paraklēseōs	kai
for	the	your	encouragement	and

4843.2 noun gen sing fem	2504.1 conj	3450.9 art nom sing fem	1667.1 noun nom sing fem	2231.2 prs-pron gen 1pl	942.2 adj nom sing fem
σωτηρίας	καὶ	ἡ	ἐλπὶς	ἡμῶν	βεβαία
sōtērias	kai	hē	elpis	hēmōn	bebaia
salvation;	and	the	hope	our	sure

7.a.Txt: 06D-corr,018K 020L,byz.
Var: 01ℵ,02A,03B,04C 06D-org,025P,33,Lach Treg,Alf,Word,Tisc We/Ho,Weis,Sod UBS/✱

5065.1 prep	5050.2 prs-pron gen 2pl	3471.20 verb nom pl masc part perf act	3617.1 conj	5450.1 adv	5453.1 conj
ὑπὲρ	ὑμῶν·	**7.** εἰδότες	ὅτι	ὥσπερ	[a✱ ὡς]
huper	humōn	eidotes	hoti	hōsper	hōs
for	you;	knowing	that	as	[idem]

2817.3 noun nom pl masc	1498.6 verb 2pl indic pres act	3450.1 art gen pl	3667.3 noun gen pl neu	3643.1 adv	2504.1 conj
κοινωνοί	ἐστε	τῶν	παθημάτων,	οὕτως	καὶ
koinōnoi	este	tōn	pathēmatōn	houtōs	kai
partners	you are	of the	sufferings,	so	also

3450.10 art gen sing fem	3735.2 noun gen sing fem	3620.3 partic	1056.1 conj	2286.4 verb 1pl indic pres act	5050.4 prs-pron acc 2pl
τῆς	παρακλήσεως.	**8.** Οὐ	γὰρ	θέλομεν	ὑμᾶς
tēs	paraklēseōs	Ou	gar	thelomen	humas
of the	encouragement.	Not	for	do we wish	you

8.a.Txt: p46,03B,018K 020L,044,0121,0243 byz.
Var: 01ℵ,02A,04C,06D 08E,010F,012G,025P 33,81,104,365,1175 2495

49.9 verb inf pres act	79.6 noun pl masc	5065.1 prep	3875.1 prep	3450.10 art gen sing fem
ἀγνοεῖν,	ἀδελφοί,	ὑπὲρ	[a περὶ]	τῆς
agnoein	adelphoi	huper	peri	tēs
to be ignorant	brothers,	as to	[concerning]	the

8.b.Txt: 01ℵ-corr 06D-corr,018K,020L byz.bo.
Var: 01ℵ-org,02A,03B 04C,06D-org,025P,33 Lach,Treg,Alf,Word Tisc,We/Ho,Weis,Sod UBS/✱

2324.2 noun gen sing fem	2231.2 prs-pron gen 1pl	3450.10 art gen sing fem	1090.57 verb gen sing fem part aor mid	2231.3 prs-pron dat 1pl	1706.1 prep
θλίψεως	ἡμῶν	τῆς	γενομένης	ἡμῖν	ἐν
thlipseōs	hēmōn	tēs	genomenēs	hēmin	en
tribulation	our	the	having happened	to us	in

3450.11 art dat sing fem	767.3 name dat fem	3617.1 conj	2567.2 prep	5073.3 noun acc sing fem	911.3 verb 1pl indic aor pass
τῇ	Ἀσίᾳ,	ὅτι	καθ'	ὑπερβολὴν	ἐβαρήθημεν
tē	Asia	hoti	kath'	huperbolēn	ebarēthēmen
	Asia,	that	in	excess	we were burdened

5065.1 prep	1405.4 noun acc sing fem	5065.1 prep	1405.4 noun acc sing fem	911.3 verb 1pl indic aor pass
ὑπὲρ	δύναμιν,	[✱ ὑπὲρ	δύναμιν	ἐβαρήθημεν,]
huper	dunamin	huper	dunamin	ebarēthēmen
beyond	power,	[beyond	power	we were burdened,]

companions enabled them to share this comfort with the saints at Corinth in such a way that it resulted in the strengthening of their faith, patience, and endurance as they went through similar trials. One of the wider results of suffering is the ability to comfort others.

Paul began here to distinguish between himself and his companions and his readers. He endured distress, trouble, and afflictions for the consolation and salvation of the Corinthians. In this sense their salvation became effective as they endured the same kinds of sufferings Paul and his party were going through.

"Salvation" here means more than conversion. The term *salvation* (Greek, *sōtēria*) also implies the following: (1) deliverance (material, temporal, spiritual, and eternal); (2) present experience of God's power to deliver from the bondage of sin; (3) future deliverance of believers at the return of Christ; (4) inclusively, to sum up all the blessings given by God to men through Christ by the Holy Spirit.

Thus the comfort ministered abundantly by God to His children in times of suffering extends beyond this present life into eternity. Our Heavenly Father plans all on our behalf with eternity in view while we tend to think in terms of time. Seeing things with temporal eyes we conclude God's chief aim for us is constant health, wealth, and happiness in this world. Instead, His major concern is our spiritual growth. Paul told the Romans that tribulation—suffering—works patience or perseverance, and patience produces experience or character (Romans 5:3,4). Character motivated by godly love as described in 1 Corinthians 13 is the one thing we will take with us into eternity (1 Corinthians 13:13).

1:7. Comfort does not mean suffering will be taken away. But it can be understood as suffering for Christ with the result being *hupomonē* (verse 6), i.e., patient endurance in suffering. Paul's knowledge of this caused him to regard the believers with an unshakable hope despite their deficiencies in love and loyalty.

He calls them fellow participants (*koinōnoi*) of the sufferings. This term means "to share with someone in something." For Paul, the law of fellowship with Christ meant that as they participated in the sufferings of Christ, so also would they share the divine comfort.

1:8. Verses 8-10 indicate the reality of the sufferings of which Paul had been speaking. Although it is not certain the trouble which Paul and his companions faced in Asia, some conjectures are shipwreck, rebellion and division in the Corinthian church, severe illness, some unrecorded problem from which there seemed to be no escape, and the riot at Ephesus (Acts 19). It does not appear that Paul was writing to tell the Corinthians *what* the trouble was, but to tell *how* they had been affected. In the last part of this verse Paul used graphic language to describe the utter hopelessness of their situation. They were prostrated beyond all power of endur-

which is effectual in the enduring of the same sufferings which we also suffer: ... enabling you to bear patiently, *Noyes* ... endure patiently, *Phillips* ... through your patient fortitude, *Weymouth* ... your energetic endurance, *Fenton* ... we ourselves are enduring, *Murdock*.

or whether we be comforted, [it is] for your consolation and salvation:

7. And our hope of you [is] stedfast: Our hopes for you do not waver, *TCNT* ... concerning you, *Wesley* ... respecting you is firm, *PNT* ... is unshaken, *Berkeley, RSV* ... constant, *Wuest* ... is firmly grounded, *NASB*.

knowing, that as ye are partakers of the sufferings: ... you are comrades, *Montgomery* ... that as you are sharing our sufferings, *TCNT*.

so [shall ye be] also of the consolation: ... as you are participators, *Fenton* ... ye are joint-partakers, *Rotherham* ... so you share also, *HistNT*.

8. For we would not, brethren, have you ignorant of our trouble which came to us in Asia: ... we do not want you to be, *RSV* ... you to be uninformed, *Williams* ... of our affliction, *Hanson* ... which happened to us, *Alford* ... which befell us, *Wesley, Clementson*.

that we were pressed out of measure, above strength: We were crushed, *Confraternity* ... we were completely overwhelmed, *Phillips* ... I was burdened altogether beyond my strength, *Montgomery* ... The burdens were heavier than we could carry, *SEB* ... burdened far beyond human ability, *Adams* ... that our strength could not hold out, *Norlie* ... afflicted exceedingly, *Murdock* ... exceedingly burdened, *Young* ... were excessively loaded, *Fenton* ... exceedingly weighed down, *Weymouth* ... exceedingly oppressed, *PNT* ... beyond our power, *Wuest, Sawyer* ... past our strength, *HistNT* ... exceedingly, beyond power, were we weighed down, *Rotherham*.

503

5452.1 conj	1804.2 verb inf aor pass	2231.4 prs-pron acc 1pl	2504.1 conj	3450.2 art gen sing	2180.19 verb inf pres act
ὥστε	ἐξαπορηθῆναι	ἡμᾶς	καὶ	τοῦ	ζῆν·
hōste	*exaporēthēnai*	*hēmas*	*kai*	*tou*	*zēn*
so as	to despair	for us	even	of the	to live.

233.2 conj	840.7 prs-pron nom pl masc	1706.1 prep	1431.7 prs-pron dat pl masc	3450.16 art sing neu	605.1 noun acc sing neu
9. ἀλλὰ	αὐτοὶ	ἐν	ἑαυτοῖς	τὸ	ἀπόκριμα
alla	*autoi*	*en*	*heautois*	*to*	*apokrima*
But	ourselves	in	ourselves	the	sentence

3450.2 art gen sing	2265.2 noun gen sing masc	2174.36 verb 1pl indic perf act	2419.1 conj	3231.1 partic	3844.14 verb nom pl masc part perf act
τοῦ	θανάτου	ἐσχήκαμεν,	ἵνα	μὴ	πεποιθότες
tou	*thanatou*	*eschēkamen*	*hina*	*mē*	*pepoithotes*
of the	death	we have had,	that	not	having trusted

1498.11 verb 1pl subj pres act	1894.1 prep	1431.7 prs-pron dat pl masc	233.1 conj	1894.3 prep	3450.3 art dat sing	2296.3 noun dat sing masc
ὦμεν	ἐφ'	ἑαυτοῖς,	ἀλλ'	ἐπὶ	τῷ	θεῷ
ōmen	*eph'*	*heautois*	*all'*	*epi*	*tō*	*theō*
we might be	in	ourselves,	but	in	the	God

3450.3 art dat sing	1446.3 verb dat sing masc part pres act	3450.8 art acc pl masc	3361.7 adj acc pl masc	3614.5 rel-pron nom sing masc	1523.2 prep gen
τῷ	ἐγείροντι	τοὺς	νεκρούς·	**10.** ὃς	ἐκ
tō	*egeironti*	*tous*	*nekrous*	*hos*	*ek*
the	raising	the	dead;	who	from

10.a.**Txt:** 01ℵ,02A,03B 04C,06D,012G,018K 025P,044,33,614 1739-org,byz.
Var: p46,630,1739-corr1

4930.2 dem-pron gen sing masc	2265.2 noun gen sing masc	4930.5 dem-pron gen pl masc	2265.7 noun gen pl masc
⌐✶ τηλικούτου	θανάτου	[ᵃ τηλικούτων	θανάτων]
tēlikoutou	*thanatou*	*tēlikoutōn*	*thanatōn*
so great	a death	[so great	deaths]

10.b.**Txt:** 06D-corr,018K 020L,byz.
Var: p46,01ℵ,03B,04C 025P,33,sa.bo.Lach Treg,Alf,Tisc,We/Ho Weis,Sod,UBS/✶

4363.6 verb 3sing indic aor mid	2231.4 prs-pron acc 1pl	2504.1 conj	4363.1 verb 3sing indic pres mid	4363.12 verb 3sing indic fut mid
ἐρρύσατο	ἡμᾶς	⌐ καὶ	ῥύεται,	[ᵇ✶ ῥύσεται,]
errhusato	*hēmas*	*kai*	*rhuetai*	*rhusetai*
delivered	us	and	does deliver;	[will deliver;]

10.c.**Txt:** 01ℵ,02A,04C 06D-corr2,044,byz.
Var: p46,03B,06D-org 0121,0243,1739,1881

1519.1 prep	3614.6 rel-pron acc sing masc	1666.10 verb 1pl indic perf act	3617.1 conj	2504.1 conj	2068.1 adv
εἰς	ὃν	ἠλπίκαμεν	⌐ᶜ ὅτι ⌐	καὶ	ἔτι
eis	*hon*	*ēlpikamen*	*hoti*	*kai*	*eti*
in	whom	we have hoped	that	also	still

4363.12 verb 3sing indic fut mid	4795.1 verb gen pl masc part pres act	2504.1 conj	5050.2 prs-pron gen 2pl	5065.1 prep
ῥύσεται,	**11.** συνυπουργούντων	καὶ	ὑμῶν	ὑπὲρ
rhusetai	*sunupourgountōn*	*kai*	*humōn*	*huper*
he will deliver;	laboring together	also	you	for

2231.2 prs-pron gen 1pl	3450.11 art dat sing fem	1157.3 noun dat sing fem	2419.1 conj	1523.2 prep gen	4044.1 adj gen pl	4241.5 noun gen pl neu
ἡμῶν	τῇ	δεήσει,	ἵνα	ἐκ	πολλῶν	προσώπων
hēmōn	*tē*	*deēsei*	*hina*	*ek*	*pollōn*	*prosōpōn*
us	by the	prayer,	that	by	many	persons

3450.16 art sing neu	1519.1 prep	2231.4 prs-pron acc 1pl	5321.1 noun sing neu	1217.2 prep	4044.1 adj gen pl
τὸ	εἰς	ἡμᾶς	χάρισμα	διὰ	πολλῶν
to	*eis*	*hēmas*	*charisma*	*dia*	*pollōn*
the	towards	us	gift	through	many

ance. They were like an overloaded ship that was gradually sinking. They were utterly at a loss, absolutely without a way of escape.

1:9. Paul even went so far as to say he and his companions had the *apokrima* of death passed on them. This Greek word is found only here in the New Testament. They were like men condemned to death who, having made a petition for mercy, had instead received the sentence that they must die.

Now we have the paradox. The weakening of Paul's self-confidence and the self-despair to which it led resulted in the growth of a radical confidence in God. In the depths of his despair suddenly Paul seemed to grasp the divine purpose and was inspired with a new trust in God. The word "trust" is from the Greek *peithō* from which we also get the words *faith, believe,* and *confidence.* It has a solid equivalence in the Hebrew, namely, *batach.* The concept of hope and trust in God in both Old and New Testaments carries with it the idea not only of God's help in present distress but also the thought of eschatological help that puts an end to all distress.

Here again the importance of looking beyond the confines of this life becomes apparent. The faith the Lord looks for seems always to be of the resurrection variety. Abraham believed Jehovah would raise Isaac from the dead when he sacrificed him (Hebrews 11:17-19). Only a faith that declares God indeed raised Jesus from the dead brings deliverance from sin (Romans 10:9).

1:10. Paul was inspired with a strong confidence in God who could not only *keep* from death but was also able to *raise* from the dead. In fact, the deliverance that God brought to them was so great it was tantamount to a resurrection from the dead. Here, deliverance appears to rise above all else. God has delivered us; He is still delivering us. He will continue to deliver us. What a hope!

1:11. Paul's deliverance was conditioned by two things: his own trust and the continual intercession of the Church. That intercession seemed of the essence. God may not have acted on Paul's behalf if they had not prayed. The Psalmist noted how critical Moses' petition for Israel was. He wrote, "Therefore he said that he would destroy them, had not Moses his chosen stood before him in the breach, to turn away his wrath, lest he should destroy them" (Psalm 106:23).

Here we have the manward and Godward aspect of deliverance. Paul's trust, born in the depths of despair, along with the Corinthian believers' help (*sunupourgountōn*—help and cooperation in prayer), resulted in *to eis hēmas charisma.* Most commentators take the *charisma* here to refer to "the gracious gift of rescue from mortal danger."

The word "persons" is from the Greek *prosōpon* in most places translated "face" or "presence." This meaning could be retained

insomuch that we despaired even of life: ... we actually despaired of life, *TCNT* ... we lost hope of life, *Klingensmith* ... we told ourselves that this was the end, *Phillips.*

9. But we had the sentence of death in ourselves: Yes, we felt sentenced to death, *Beck* ... feel like men condemned to death, *NAB* ... We thought we would die, *NLT* ... we decided the end must be death, *HistNT* ... the answer of death, *Hanson, Douay.*

that we should not trust in ourselves, but in God which raiseth the dead: ... that we might learn to trust, *Phillips* ... that I might not rely on myself, *Montgomery* ... might not rely on ourselves, *TCNT* ... might not have confidence, *Clementson* ... might not repose confidence, *Rotherham.*

10. Who delivered us from so great a death, and doth deliver: Who rescued us, *Fenton* ... rescued us from imminent death, *Murdock* ... He saved us from imminent death, *Norlie* ... from so imminent a death, *Weymouth* ... from such great perils, *Confraternity* ... from a death so horrible, *Williams* ... and is rescuing, *Wilson* ... He will rescue us in the future, *SEB.*

in whom we trust that he will yet deliver [us]: He is our hope, *Beck* ... we have set our hope, *Sawyer* ... we have fixed our hope, *Rotherham.*

11. Ye also helping together by prayer for us: ... striving together for us, *Sawyer* ... working together...by your supplication, *Young, Alford* ... cooperating by prayer, *Wilson* ... co-operating on our behalf by your supplication, *Hanson* ... cooperate on our behalf by prayer, *HistNT* ... at the intercession of many, *Weymouth.*

that for the gift [bestowed] upon us by the means of many persons: ... for the mercy bestowed upon us, *Worrell* ... obtained for us, *Douay* ... the blessings vouchsafed to me through the intercession of many, *Montgomery.*

11.a.Txt: p46-corr3,01ℵ
02A,04C,06D-org,012G
044,1739
Var: p46-org,03B
06D-corr3,018K,025P
614

2149.13 verb 3sing subj aor pass	5065.1 prep	2231.2 prs-pron gen 1pl	5050.2 prs-pron gen 2pl	3450.9 art nom sing fem
εὐχαριστηθῇ	ὑπὲρ	ʼ☆ ἡμῶν.	[ᵃ ὑμῶν.]	12. Ἡ
eucharistethe	huper	hēmōn	humōn	Hē
thanks may be given	for	us.	[you]	The

1056.1 conj	2716.1 noun nom sing fem	2231.2 prs-pron gen 1pl	3642.9 dem-pron nom sing fem	1498.4 verb 3sing indic pres act	3450.16 art sing neu
γὰρ	καύχησις	ἡμῶν	αὕτη	ἐστίν,	τὸ
gar	kauchēsis	hēmōn	hautē	estin	to
for	boasting	our	this	is,	the

12.a.Txt: 01ℵ-corr,06D
020L,byz.it.
Var: p46,01ℵ-org,02A
03B,04C,018K,025P,33
sa.bo.Lach,Treg,Alf,Tisc
We/Ho,Weis,Sod
UBS/☆

3115.1 noun sing neu	3450.10 art gen sing fem	4743.2 noun gen sing fem	2231.2 prs-pron gen 1pl	3617.1 conj	1706.1 prep
μαρτύριον	τῆς	συνειδήσεως	ἡμῶν,	ὅτι	ἐν
marturion	tēs	suneidēseōs	hēmōn	hoti	en
testimony	of the	conscience	our,	that	in

12.b.Var: 01ℵ,02A,03B
04C,06D,33,Lach,Treg
Alf,Word,Tisc,We/Ho
Weis,Sod,UBS/☆

567.2 noun dat sing fem	40.2 noun dat sing fem	2504.1 conj	1495.2 noun dat sing fem	3450.2 art gen sing
ʼ ἁπλότητι	[ᵃ ἁγιότητι]	καὶ	εἰλικρινείᾳ	[ᵇ☆+ τοῦ]
haplotēti	hagiotēti	kai	eilikrineia	tou
simplicity	[holiness]	and	sincerity	

12.c.Txt: 01ℵ,02A,04C
06D,010F,012G,044,byz.
Var: p46,03B,0121,6,33
630,1175,1739,1881
2464

2296.2 noun gen sing masc	2504.1 conj	3620.2 partic	1706.1 prep	4531.3 noun dat sing fem	4416.5 adj dat sing fem	233.1 conj
θεοῦ,	[ᶜ+ καὶ]	οὐκ	ἐν	σοφίᾳ	σαρκικῇ	ἀλλʼ
theou	kai	ouk	en	sophia	sarkikē	allʼ
of God,	[and]	not	in	wisdom	fleshly,	but

1706.1 prep	5322.3 noun dat sing fem	2296.2 noun gen sing masc	388.7 verb 1pl indic aor pass	1706.1 prep	3450.3 art dat sing
ἐν	χάριτι	θεοῦ,	ἀνεστράφημεν	ἐν	τῷ
en	chariti	theou	anestraphēmen	en	tō
in	grace	of God,	we had our conduct	in	the

2862.3 noun dat sing masc	3917.2 adv comp	1156.2 conj	4242.1 prep	5050.4 prs-pron acc 2pl	3620.3 partic
κόσμῳ,	περισσοτέρως	δὲ	πρὸς	ὑμᾶς.	13. οὐ
kosmō	perissoterōs	de	pros	humas	ou
world,	more abundantly	and	toward	you.	Not

1056.1 conj	241.15 adj pl neu	1119.3 verb 1pl indic pres act	5050.3 prs-pron dat 2pl	233.1 conj	2211.1 conj	3614.17 rel-pron pl neu
γὰρ	ἄλλα	γράφομεν	ὑμῖν	ἀλλʼ	ἢ	ἃ
gar	alla	graphomen	humin	allʼ	ē	ha
for	other things	do we write	to you	but	or	what

312.2 verb 2pl indic pres act	2211.1 conj	2504.1 conj	1906.1 verb 2pl pres act	1666.1 verb 1sing indic pres act
ἀναγινώσκετε,	ἢ	καὶ	ἐπιγινώσκετε,	ἐλπίζω
anaginōskete	ē	kai	epiginōskete	elpizō
you read,	or	even	recognize;	I hope

13.a.Txt: 06D-corr,018K
020L,025P,byz.
Var: 01ℵ,02A,03B,04C
06D-org,33,Lach,Treg
Alf,Tisc,We/Ho,Weis
Sod,UBS/☆

1156.2 conj	3617.1 conj	2504.1 conj	2175.1 conj	4904.2 noun gen sing neu	1906.21 verb 2pl indic fut mid
δὲ	ὅτι	ʼᵃ καὶ ʼ	ἕως	τέλους	ἐπιγνώσεσθε,
de	hoti	kai	heōs	telous	epignōsesthe
and	that	even	to	end	you will recognize,

2503.1 conj	2504.1 conj	1906.5 verb 2pl indic aor act	2231.4 prs-pron acc 1pl	570.3 prep gen
14. καθὼς	καὶ	ἐπέγνωτε	ἡμᾶς	ἀπὸ
kathōs	kai	epegnōte	hēmas	apo
just as	also	you did recognize	us	from

here, e.g., "thanks from many upturned faces" or "from many persons." Since many had interceded, many would be thankful.

1:12. With verse 11 Paul ended the introduction of this letter. He then turned immediately to the main concern of the correspondence. In the body of the epistle the apostle felt compelled to defend his ministry against a series of false charges. That requirement made this the most painful to write of all his letters.

Verses 12-14 imply there either was or had been a different atmosphere at Corinth, at least on the part of some, with regard to Paul's ministry. They said he was insincere and fickle.

Paul dealt with these charges by offering a twofold defense. First, he affirmed his absolute and complete sincerity. The two Greek words *haplotēti* and *eilikrineia* have been called a hendiadys, i.e., the expression of one idea by the use of two independent words connected by the word *and* (*kai*). These two words together refer to the moral purity and godly sincerity of Paul's inner motives and outward conduct.

The apostle recognized the conscience as a creature of God intended to serve commendable moral purposes. In his several letters he spoke of a conscience that is weak (1 Corinthians 8:7-12); good (1 Timothy 1:5,19); pure (1 Timothy 3:9); and seared (1 Timothy 4:2). Paul valued the approval of his conscience, though he placed the ministry of the Holy Spirit above it (Romans 9:1).

Paul's conscience bore witness to the fact that he had never deceived anyone. The sincerity and integrity of his behavior became the very grounds for his rejoicing (*kauchēsis* = "boasting"). However, here the term picks up the good sense of praise of God found in the Hebrew *halal* (see Psalms 34:2; 44:8).

Paul had no confidence in the flesh or the wisdom of this world (1 Corinthians 2:1-5). He was careful to give all credit to the grace of God. His cry was, "By the grace of God I am what I am" (1 Corinthians 15:10). The exceptional effects produced by God's grace in the life of Paul had never been more clearly manifested than in his dealings with the Corinthian church.

1:13. Paul's second defense had to do with his letters. He had been accused of writing one thing, saying another, and doing something else. But Paul indicated that he had always been perfectly honest. He meant exactly what he wrote.

The play on words is not discernible in English, but Paul indicated that there was no difference in what they read (*anaginōskete*) in his letters and what they acknowledged (*epiginōskete*) or observed firsthand in his conduct. His actions and his words were in complete harmony.

1:14. Paul had spent 18 months at Corinth preaching and teaching the Word of God. The thought here is that the Corinthian

---

thanks may be given by many on our behalf: . . . on our account, *Murdock.*

12. For our rejoicing is this, the testimony of our conscience: For this is our proud claim, *NTPE* . . . The reason for our exultation, *Berkeley* . . . our chief satisfaction is this, *TCNT* . . . our glorying, *Young* . . . For our pride is the exact evidence of our conscience, *Fenton* . . . our conscience backs us up, *Norlie.*

that in simplicity and godly sincerity: . . . we have been absolutely aboveboard and sincere, *Phillips* . . . was one of holy living, *Norlie* . . . acted from pure motives, *Williams* . . . marked by a purity of motive, *TCNT* . . . frankness and honesty, *Fenton* . . . holiness and with pure motives, *Weymouth* . . . holiness, purity, and unsullied character of God, *Wuest.*

not with fleshly wisdom, but by the grace of God: . . . without human cleverness, *Beck* . . . not with fleshly cunning, *HistNT* . . . the gracious help of God, *Weymouth.*

we have had our conversation in the world: . . . we behaved ourselves, *ASV, Hanson* . . . we had our behaviour, *Rotherham* . . . I have conducted myself, *Montgomery* . . . we did conduct, *Young* . . . we have conducted ourselves, *Confraternity.*

and more abundantly to you-ward: . . . especially with you, *Beck* . . . more especially toward you, *PNT.*

13. For we write none other things unto you, than what ye read or acknowledge: . . . and very well recognize, *Montgomery.*

and I trust ye shall acknowledge even to the end: . . . get a complete understanding, *SEB* . . . that you will understand it perfectly, *Williams* . . . you will admit this even to the end, *Norlie.*

14. As also ye have acknowledged us in part: . . . you have understood, *Confraternity.*

2 Corinthians 1:15

3183.2 noun gen sing neu	3617.1 conj	2715.1 noun sing neu	5050.2 prs-pron gen 2pl	1498.5 verb 1pl indic pres act	2481.1 conj
μέρους,	ὅτι	καύχημα	ὑμῶν	ἐσμεν,	καθάπερ
merous	hoti	kauchēma	humōn	esmen	kathaper
part,	that	boasting	your	we are,	even as

2504.1 conj	5050.1 prs-pron nom 2pl	2231.2 prs-pron gen 1pl	1706.1 prep	3450.11 art dat sing fem	2232.3 noun dat sing fem	3450.2 art gen sing
καὶ	ὑμεῖς	ἡμῶν	ἐν	τῇ	ἡμέρα	τοῦ
kai	humeis	hēmōn	en	tē	hēmera	tou
also	you	ours	in	the	day	of the

14.a.Var: 01ℵ,03B,025P 33,it.sa.bo.Lach,Alf,Tisc We/Ho,Weis,Sod UBS/☆

2935.2 noun gen sing masc	2231.2 prs-pron gen 1pl	2400.2 name masc		2504.1 conj	3642.11 dem-pron dat sing fem
κυρίου	[ª+ ἡμῶν]	Ἰησοῦ.	**15.**	Καὶ	ταύτῃ
kuriou	hēmōn	Iēsou		Kai	tautē
Lord	[our]	Jesus.		And	with this

3450.11 art dat sing fem	3870.1 noun dat sing fem	1007.16 verb 1sing indic imperf	4242.1 prep	5050.4 prs-pron acc 2pl
τῇ	πεποιθήσει	ἐβουλόμην	ʿ πρὸς	ὑμᾶς
tē	pepoithēsei	eboulomēn	pros	humas
the	confidence	was deciding	to	you

15.a.Txt: 02A,06D,018K 020L,byz. **Var:** 01ℵ,03B,04C,025P Treg,Alf,Tisc,We/Ho Weis,Sod,UBS/☆

2048.23 verb inf aor act	4245.2 adj comp acc sing neu	4245.2 adj comp acc sing neu	4242.1 prep	5050.4 prs-pron acc 2pl
ἐλθεῖν	πρότερον,	[ª☆ πρότερον	πρὸς	ὑμᾶς
elthein	proteron	proteron	pros	humas
to come	previously,	[previously	to	you

15.b.Txt: 01ℵ-org,02A 04C,06D,012G,018K 044,33,1739,byz. **Var:** 01ℵ-corr3,03B 020L,025P,88,614,915 1175,2464

2048.23 verb inf aor act	2419.1 conj	1202.7 num ord acc sing fem	5322.4 noun acc sing fem	5315.4 noun acc sing fem
ἐλθεῖν,]	ἵνα	δευτέραν	ʿ☆ χάριν	[ᵇ χαράν]
elthein	hina	deuteran	charin	charan
to come,]	that	a second	benefit	[occasion for joy]

2174.9 verb 2pl subj pres act	2504.1 conj	1217.1 prep	5050.2 prs-pron gen 2pl	1324.8 verb inf aor act	1519.1 prep
ἔχητε·	**16.** καὶ	δι'	ὑμῶν	διελθεῖν	εἰς
echēte	kai	di'	humōn	dielthein	eis
you might have;	and	by	you	to pass through	to

3081.4 name acc fem	2504.1 conj	3687.1 adv	570.3 prep gen	3081.2 name gen fem	2048.23 verb inf aor act
Μακεδονίαν,	καὶ	πάλιν	ἀπὸ	Μακεδονίας	ἐλθεῖν
Makedonian	kai	palin	apo	Makedonias	elthein
Macedonia,	and	again	from	Macedonia	to come

4242.1 prep	5050.4 prs-pron acc 2pl	2504.1 conj	5097.1 prep	5050.2 prs-pron gen 2pl	4170.8 verb inf aor pass	1519.1 prep
πρὸς	ὑμᾶς,	καὶ	ὑφ'	ὑμῶν	προπεμφθῆναι	εἰς
pros	humas	kai	huph'	humōn	propemphthēnai	eis
to	you,	and	by	you	to be sent off	to

3450.12 art acc sing fem	2424.4 name acc fem	3642.17 dem-pron sing neu	3631.1 conj	1003.3 verb nom sing masc part pres mid
τὴν	Ἰουδαίαν.	**17.** τοῦτο	οὖν	ʿ βουλευόμενος,
tēn	Ioudaian	touto	oun	bouleuomenos
the	Judea.	This	therefore	purposing,

17.a.Txt: 06D,018K,byz. **Var:** 01ℵ,02A,03B,04C 025P,bo.Lach,Treg,Alf Word,Tisc,We/Ho,Weis Sod,UBS/☆

1007.8 verb nom sing masc part pres	3231.1 partic	4948.10 indef-pron sing neu	3252.1 partic	679.1 partic
[ª☆ βουλόμενος]	ʿ μή	τι	[☆ μήτι]	ἄρα
boulomenos	mē	ti	mēti	ara
[idem]	not	any	[not]	indeed

508

saints had once been proud of Paul and Timothy. However, their confidence had been shaken by a minority of rebellious church members and ad hominem remarks by false teachers regarding Paul's ministry.

Paul told the Corinthians they could still be proud. Neither he nor Timothy had changed. Their ministry had always been in the light of "that day" and when that day comes the Corinthians will know more fully the veracity of Paul's ministry to them. As they understood him more fully they would appreciate what God's grace was doing through him.

The Corinthians may have only partially understood Paul and his companions during the time the church was being established. The time would come when both Paul and the Corinthians would rejoice together. He would be their rejoicing as the one who had introduced them to Christ. They would be his rejoicing as converts.

1:15,16. Paul's original itinerary included sea travel from Ephesus to Corinth, a journey by land north into Macedonia, then a second visit to Corinth on the return trip. Regarding the apostle's explanation here Carver wrote, "He desired that they should have 'the benefit of a double visit' (15, NEB; lit., 'have a second grace'). The expression is peculiar. Wendland notes that 'a tremendous awareness of power comes to light in these words: The apostle is the bearer of divine grace, and his presence in the church signifies a time when grace is at work (see Romans 1:11; 15:29).' Paul wanted to be a blessing to them both going and coming" (*Beacon Bible Commentary*, 8:509).

However, the apostle had no unwholesome view of himself as the sole source of blessing. After declaring a similar desire to impart grace to the Romans by visiting them, he said, "That is, that I may be comforted together with you by the mutual faith both of you and me" (Romans 1:12). Likewise, the blessing was to flow in two directions during his trip to Corinth. Brethren of the congregation there would have opportunity to assist Paul in his missionary ministry. They would bring him on his way toward Judea by seeing he had needed funds and supplies. As he wrote Titus, "Bring Zenas the lawyer and Apollos on their journey diligently, that nothing be wanting unto them" (Titus 3:13,14).

When Paul altered his plans to revisit the church at Corinth his opponents used his perfectly legitimate change from two short visits to one long visit as an excuse to charge him with insincerity and unreliability. Paul insisted that the modification of his original travel plan had been in good faith. In reality it was loving consideration that had caused this revision. A previous visit (12:14; 13:1) may have been unpleasant. For their sake Paul did not want to come in the same manner again.

1:17. Paul took this opportunity to point out that he had not changed his plans without a reason. In his question "did I use

that we are your rejoicing: ... we are your theme of boasting, *Rotherham* ... as your reason for boasting, *Weymouth*.

even as ye also [are] ours in the day of the Lord Jesus: ... when Christ reveals all secrets, *Phillips*.

15. And in this confidence I was minded to come unto you before: With this assurance, *Confraternity, Berkeley* ... with this conviction, *TCNT* ... after mature consideration, *Wuest* ... I was purposing, *Young, Wilson* ... I purposed, *PNT* ... I had planned at first, *Adams* ... was I disposed, *Rotherham*.

that ye might have a second benefit: ... ye might receive the grace doubly, *Murdock* ... would be helped two times, *NLT* ... so that you would enjoy two visits, *Norlie* ... you would be helped twice, *SEB* ... be having a second bestowment, *Wuest* ... a second pleasure, *Fenton* ... a second gift, *Campbell* ... a double delight, *Williams* ... a pleasure twice over, *Montgomery* ... a double blessing, *Berkeley*.

16. And to pass by you into Macedonia, and to come again out of Macedonia unto you:

and of you to be brought on my way toward Judaea: ... to be sent forward, *Young* ... helped forward by you, *Weymouth* ... and be sped by you, *HistNT* ... be escorted from you, *Berkeley* ... sent with full provisions by you to Judea, *Adams* ... on my journey, *Clementson*.

17. When I therefore was thus minded: Because we had to change this plan, *Phillips* ... Yes, I changed my mind, *NLT* ... I therefore intended thus, *Panin* ... In purposing this did I display, *Montgomery* ... being my intention, *Wilson* ... in this my intention, *Confraternity*.

did I use lightness?: ... did I act thoughtlessly, *Greber* ... Was I vacillating when I wanted to do

3450.11 art dat sing fem	1631.1 noun dat sing fem	5366.5 verb 1sing indic aor mid	2211.1 conj	3614.17 rel-pron pl neu	1003.1 verb 1sing indic pres
τῇ	ἐλαφρίᾳ	ἐχρησάμην;	ἢ	ἃ	βουλεύομαι
tē	elaphria	echrēsamēn	ē	ha	bouleuomai
the	lightness	did I use?	or	what	I intend,

2567.3 prep	4418.4 noun acc sing fem	1003.1 verb 1sing indic pres	2419.1 conj	1498.10 verb 3sing subj pres act
κατὰ	σάρκα	βουλεύομαι,	ἵνα	ᾖ
kata	sarka	bouleuomai	hina	ē
according to	flesh	do I determine,	that	there should be

3706.1 prep	1466.5 prs-pron dat 1sing	3450.16 art sing neu	3346.1 partic	3346.1 partic	2504.1 conj	3450.16 art sing neu	3620.3 partic
παρ'	ἐμοὶ	τὸ	Ναὶ	ναὶ,	καὶ	τὸ	Οὒ
par'	emoi	to	Nai	nai	kai	to	Ou
with	me	the	yes	yes,	and	the	no

3620.3 partic	**18.** 3964.2 adj nom sing masc	1156.2 conj	3450.5 art sing masc	2296.1 noun nom sing masc	3617.1 conj	3450.5 art sing masc
οὔ;	πιστὸς	δὲ	ὁ	θεὸς,	ὅτι	ὁ
ou	pistos	de	ho	theos	hoti	ho
no?	Faithful	now	the	God,	that	the

3030.1 noun nom sing masc	2231.2 prs-pron gen 1pl	3450.5 art sing masc	4242.1 prep	5050.4 prs-pron acc 2pl	3620.2 partic	1090.33 verb 3sing indic aor mid
λόγος	ἡμῶν	ὁ	πρὸς	ὑμᾶς	οὐκ	ἐγένετο
logos	hēmōn	ho	pros	humas	ouk	egeneto
word	our	the	to	you	not	was

1498.4 verb 3sing indic pres act	3346.1 partic	2504.1 conj	3620.3 partic	**19.** 3450.5 art sing masc	1056.1 conj	3450.2 art gen sing
[ᵃ☆ ἔστιν]	Ναὶ	καὶ	Οὒ.	ὁ	γὰρ	τοῦ
estin	Nai	kai	Ou	ho	gar	tou
[is]	yes	and	no.	The	for	

2296.2 noun gen sing masc	3450.2 art gen sing	2296.2 noun gen sing masc	1056.1 conj	5048.1 noun nom sing masc	2400.1 name nom masc
θεοῦ	[☆ τοῦ	θεοῦ	γὰρ]	υἱὸς	Ἰησοῦς
theou	tou	theou	gar	huios	Iēsous
of God		[God	for]	Son,	Jesus

5382.1 name nom masc	5382.1 name nom masc	2400.1 name nom masc	3450.5 art sing masc	1706.1 prep	5050.3 prs-pron dat 2pl
Χριστὸς	[Χριστὸς	Ἰησοῦς]	ὁ	ἐν	ὑμῖν
Christos	Christos	Iēsous	ho	en	humin
Christ,	[Christ	Jesus]	the	among	you

1217.1 prep	2231.2 prs-pron gen 1pl	2756.25 verb nom sing masc part aor pass	1217.1 prep	1466.3 prs-pron gen 1sing	2504.1 conj
δι'	ἡμῶν	κηρυχθείς,	δι'	ἐμοῦ	καὶ
di'	hēmōn	kēruchtheis	di'	emou	kai
by	us	having been proclaimed,	by	me	and

4465.2 name gen masc	2504.1 conj	4943.2 name gen masc	3620.2 partic	1090.33 verb 3sing indic aor mid	3346.1 partic
Σιλουανοῦ	καὶ	Τιμοθέου,	οὐκ	ἐγένετο	Ναὶ
Silouanou	kai	Timotheou	ouk	egeneto	Nai
Silvanus	and	Timothy,	not	was	yes

2504.1 conj	3620.3 partic	233.2 conj	3346.1 partic	1706.1 prep	840.4 prs-pron dat sing	1090.3 verb 3sing indic perf act
καὶ	Οὒ,	ἀλλὰ	Ναὶ	ἐν	αὐτῷ	γέγονεν·
kai	Ou	alla	Nai	en	autō	gegonen
and	no,	but	yes	in	him	has been.

18.a.Txt: 01ℵ-corr 06D-corr,018K,020L byz. Var: 01ℵ-org,02A,03B 04C,06D-org,025P,33 Lach,Treg,Alf,Word Tisc,We/Ho,Weis,Sod UBS/☆

lightness" (i.e., "Was I vacillating and fickle?"), the use of the interrogative particle *mē* strengthens the expected negative answer. The change hadn't been a whim of his carnal nature, but a deliberate purpose—possibly to spare them a rebuke (cf. 1:23; 2:4).

Paul was not the kind to say "yes" and "no" in the same breath. In fact, his deep love and concern for the Corinthians was one of the reasons for his delay in coming to them. They should have known him well enough from previous experience to have realized this. When Paul's evangelistic party had preached Christ to the Corinthians, they had not proclaimed one thing out of one corner of their mouths and something contradictory out of the other side.

These two parallel rhetorical questions imply that Paul's ministry had not been carried out *kata sarka* ("according to flesh"), i.e., he had not been controlled by worldly or selfish considerations. Paul's ministry was always "according to the Spirit." This was in keeping with what he professed and what he lived.

In determining where he went in his ministry Paul followed a rule based on his missionary call to take the gospel to the Gentiles (Acts 9:15; 22:21; 26:17). He always selected sites where Christ had not yet been preached (Romans 15:20,21). His burden for souls took him to the area of his hometown in his first missionary journey. A pastoral concern caused him to return there to begin his second trip (Acts 15:36). Yet he was always open to specific direction of the Holy Spirit as to where he should go (Acts 16:6-10). He never carelessly chose his own way.

1:18. Paul found it difficult to believe that anyone could have thought changed plans indicated changed character. The charge of the Corinthians against Paul reflected back, not only on his message, but also on God himself. They were actually the fickle ones.

Paul then made a transition from his trustworthiness as a person to his consistency as a preacher. He pointed out that God is true (*pistos*, meaning "trustworthy, faithful, dependable"). In verse 12 Paul mentioned his conscience as a witness. Here he indicated that God also bore witness to Paul's integrity. Just as God could be fully trusted, so also could the Word of God preached by Paul and his companions be considered trustworthy. Paul took a solemn vow, appealing to the unchanging nature of God as he affirmed that their message was not inconsistent or contradictory.

1:19. Paul reminded the Corinthian believers that the Jesus Christ they knew was the same Jesus Christ that he and Silvanus (Silas) and Timothy had preached to them during the 18 months of their ministry in Corinth. In essence Paul wrote, "We were the instruments God used when we preached the gospel and you believed." Their message and their character went together. A positive Christ could scarcely have been preached by negative preachers.

this? *RSV* . . . I was not vacillating, *NASB* . . . am I, therefore, to be condemned of fickleness? *Locke* . . . did I show fickleness? *Confraternity, Hanson* . . . as one inconsiderate? *Murdock* . . . because it was not carried out? *Way.*

or the things that I purpose, do I purpose according to the flesh: . . . thought to be an uncertain man, *Locke* . . . do I form them on worldly principles, *Weymouth* . . . determined by self-interest, *NAB* . . . in planning that? *Williams.*

that with me there should be yea yea, and nay nay?: . . . saying "yes" and meaning "no"? *Phillips* . . . Yes, yes, and No, no? *Young* . . . It is and It is not, *Douay* . . . "Yes, yes!" equals "No, no"? *Berkeley* . . . to have my "Yes" mean "No," if I want it so? *Williams* . . . and changing to "no, no," according to circumstance? *Norlie.*

18. But [as] God [is] true, our word toward you was not yea and nay: God is faithful, *Young, Hanson* . . . as God can be trusted, *NTPE* . . . is dependable, *Adams, SEB* . . . my message to you, *Montgomery* . . . our language to you, *Weymouth* . . . our object towards you, *Fenton.*

19. For the Son of God, Jesus Christ, who was preached among you by us: . . . who was proclaimed to you, *Wilson.*

[even] by me and Silvanus and Timotheus, was not yea and nay: . . . was not wavering between, *Montgomery* . . . was not inconsistent! *SEB* . . . showed no wavering between 'Yes' and 'No,' *TCNT* . . . did not show himself a waverer between "Yes" and "No," *Weymouth.*

but in him was yea: . . . in Christ is the confirming 'Yes,' *TCNT* . . . it has always been yes in Him, *Adams* . . . it was ever one consistent affirmative, *Way* . . . he is the divine "Yes," *Phillips.*

20. ὅσαι γὰρ ἐπαγγελίαι θεοῦ, ἐν αὐτῷ
3607.5 rel-pron nom pl fem / 1056.1 conj / 1845.5 noun nom pl fem / 2296.2 noun gen sing masc / 1706.1 prep / 840.4 prs-pron dat sing
hosai / gar / epangeliai / theou / en / autō
Whatever / for / promises / of God, / in / him

τὸ Ναί, ʿκαὶ ἐν αὐτῷ [ªᵃ☆ διὸ καὶ
3450.16 art sing neu / 3346.1 partic / 2504.1 conj / 1706.1 prep / 840.4 prs-pron dat sing / 1346.1 conj / 2504.1 conj
to / Nai / kai / en / autō / dio / kai
the / yes, / and / in / him / [werefore / also

20.a.Txt: 06D-corr,018K 020L,byz.
Var: 01א,02A,03B,04C 025P,33,bo.Lach,Treg Alf,Word,Tisc,We/Ho Weis,Sod,UBS/☆

δι' αὐτοῦ] τὸ Ἀμὴν, τῷ θεῷ
1217.1 prep / 840.3 prs-pron gen sing / 3450.16 art sing neu / 279.1 partic / 3450.3 art dat sing / 2296.3 noun dat sing masc
di' / autou / to / Amēn / tō / theō
through / him] / the / Amen, / to God

πρὸς δόξαν δι' ἡμῶν. **21.** ὁ δὲ
4242.1 prep / 1385.4 noun acc sing fem / 1217.1 prep / 2231.2 prs-pron gen 1pl / 3450.5 art sing masc / 1156.2 conj
pros / doxan / di' / hēmōn / ho / de
for / glory / by / us. / The / now

βεβαιῶν ἡμᾶς σὺν ὑμῖν εἰς Χριστὸν,
943.1 verb nom sing masc part pres act / 2231.4 prs-pron acc 1pl / 4713.1 prep dat / 5050.3 prs-pron dat 2pl / 1519.1 prep / 5382.4 name acc masc
bebaiōn / hēmas / sun / humin / eis / Christon
confirming / us / with / you / unto / Christ,

καὶ χρίσας ἡμᾶς θεός· **22.** ὁ καὶ
2504.1 conj / 5383.3 verb nom sing masc part aor act / 2231.4 prs-pron acc 1pl / 2296.1 noun nom sing masc / 3450.5 art sing masc / 2504.1 conj
kai / chrisas / hēmas / theos / ho / kai
and / having anointed / us, / God, / the / also

σφραγισάμενος ἡμᾶς, καὶ δοὺς τὸν
4824.7 verb nom sing masc part aor mid / 2231.4 prs-pron acc 1pl / 2504.1 conj / 1319.28 verb nom sing masc part aor act / 3450.6 art acc sing masc
sphragisamenos / hēmas, / kai / dous / ton
having sealed / us, / and / having given / the

ἀρραβῶνα τοῦ πνεύματος ἐν ταῖς καρδίαις
722.2 noun acc sing masc / 3450.2 art gen sing / 4011.2 noun gen sing neu / 1706.1 prep / 3450.14 art dat pl fem / 2559.7 noun dat pl fem
arrhabōna / tou / pneumatos / en / tais / kardiais
earnest / of the / Spirit / in / the / hearts

ἡμῶν. **23.** Ἐγὼ δὲ μάρτυρα τὸν θεὸν
2231.2 prs-pron gen 1pl / 1466.1 prs-pron nom 1sing / 1156.2 conj / 3116.3 noun acc sing masc / 3450.6 art acc sing masc / 2296.4 noun acc sing masc
hēmōn / Egō / de / martura / ton / theon
our. / I / but / a witness / the / of God

ἐπικαλοῦμαι ἐπὶ τὴν ἐμὴν ψυχήν, ὅτι
1926.1 verb 1sing indic pres mid / 1894.3 prep / 3450.12 art acc sing fem / 1684.9 adj acc 1 sing fem / 5425.4 noun acc sing fem / 3617.1 conj
epikaloumai / epi / tēn / emēn / psuchēn, / hoti
call / upon / the / my / soul, / that

φειδόμενος ὑμῶν οὐκέτι ἦλθον εἰς Κόρινθον·
5177.2 verb nom sing masc part pres / 5050.2 prs-pron gen 2pl / 3629.1 adv / 2048.1 verb indic aor act / 1519.1 prep / 2855.2 name acc fem
pheidomenos / humōn / ouketi / ēlthon / eis / Korinthon
sparing / you / no longer / did I come / to / Corinth.

512

1:20. The apostles preached a positive gospel. Their preaching was confirmed by positive proofs (Mark 16:20). They emphatically declared that God was working according to the Scriptures. Jesus Christ has added "yea" and "Amen" to every promise of God. He is God's guarantee that all of God's promises are true. God shows His faithfulness in keeping His promises to the letter. Jesus Christ is the grand affirmation to all of God's promises.

1:21. To recapitulate then, Paul wrote to his converts: here is God—absolutely trustworthy; here is Christ—always "yes"; here is our message—as unchanging and dependable as God himself; here are Paul and his companions, God's instruments along with the Corinthians, all "stablished" or firmly united in Christ and made faithful disciples. Not only have they been established, but they have also been anointed for divine service just as Christ (the Anointed One) was.

1:22. In these verses (21,22) four statements are made about what God has done to and for the apostles and the Corinthian believers. Note the Trinitarian implications: God *established* them in Christ. He *anointed* or commissioned them for service. They were *sealed* and *given the Holy Spirit.*

The Greek aorist middle participle *sphragisamenos,* translated "sealed," conveys a twofold idea; namely, to *mark* (with a seal) as a means of identification. This mark not only denoted ownership but also carried with it the protection of the owner. From this definition we can better understand the symbolic use of the term describing those who became Christians as being sealed with or by the Holy Spirit (Ephesians 1:13; 4:30).

However, many feel that it means more here than to just provide with a mark of identification. It also includes an endowment with power from heaven as denoted by God's giving the *arrhabōna* of the Spirit. In modern Greek *arrhabōna* is an engagement ring. Here it refers to a pledge or partial payment that is only a small fraction of the future endowment. What is given in the partial payment is the same in kind as can be expected in the future endowment. It is not the promising of one thing and the giving of another.

1:23. In this verse Paul returned to his explanation of why he changed his original plans. He used the language of the law court to give weight to his truthfulness. Some translate the first part of this verse "I stake my life on it." The Greek phrase "upon my soul" could mean "as one who knows my inmost thoughts." Paul's motives for not coming were love and concern. Deep down he had not wished to come to them "with a rod" (1 Corinthians 4:21) even though he had been ready to do so if necessary.

20. For all the promises of God in him [are] yea: He is the yes that makes them come true, *Beck* . . . But with Him it is always "Yes," *Williams* . . . finds it affirmative in him, *Phillips.*

and in him Amen, unto the glory of God by us: . . . to the honor of God, *HistNT.*

21. Now he which stablisheth us with you in Christ: For he that establisheth, *Wesley* . . . He Who supports us, *Fenton* . . . has securely united us together, *RPNT* . . . he who confirms us, *Rotherham, PNT* . . . who is confirming you, *Young* . . . into union with Christ, *TCNT.*

and hath anointed us, [is] God: God has chosen us, *SEB* . . . and has commissioned us, *RSV.*

22. Who hath also sealed us: He attested us, *Fenton* . . . He who consecrated us and set his mark on us, *TCNT* . . . stamped us with his seal, *Confraternity.*

and given the earnest of the Spirit in our hearts: . . . as down payment, *Adams* . . . security deposit, *Berkeley* . . . as a pledge, *Confraternity* . . . a first installment, *Williams* . . . the first-fruits, *KJII* . . . the token payment guaranteeing, *Wuest* . . . the living guarantee of the Spirit, *Phillips* . . . the pledge and installment of the Spirit, *HistNT* . . . foretaste of future blessing, *Weymouth.*

23. Moreover I call God for a record upon my soul: But I invoke God as a witness, *Rotherham, Wilson* . . . I for a witness, *Young* . . . a witness upon my life, *Hanson* . . . putting my soul on trial, *Adams* . . . to give evidence to my life, *Fenton* . . . against my spirit, *Klingensmith.*

that to spare you I came not as yet unto Corinth: . . . in order not to hurt you, *Beck* . . . to spare you pain, *Weymouth.*

24.

3620.1 partic	3617.1 conj	2934.2 verb 1pl indic pres act	5050.2 prs-pron gen 2pl	3450.10 art gen sing fem	3963.2 noun gen sing fem
οὐχ	ὅτι	κυριεύομεν	ὑμῶν	τῆς	πίστεως,
ouch	hoti	kurieuomen	humōn	tēs	pisteōs
Not	that	we rule over	your	the	faith,

233.2 conj	4754.4 adj nom pl masc	1498.5 verb 1pl indic pres act	3450.10 art gen sing fem	5315.2 noun gen sing fem	5050.2 prs-pron gen 2pl
ἀλλὰ	συνεργοί	ἐσμεν	τῆς	χαρᾶς	ὑμῶν,
alla	sunergoi	esmen	tēs	charas	humōn
but	fellow workers	are	of the	joy	your:

3450.11 art dat sing fem	1056.1 conj	3963.3 noun dat sing fem	2449.20 verb 2pl indic perf act		2892.13 verb 1sing indic aor act
τῇ	γὰρ	πίστει	ἑστήκατε.	**2:1.**	ἔκρινα
tē	gar	pistei	hestēkate		ekrina
by the	for	faith	you have stood.		I judged

1156.2 conj	1056.1 conj	1670.2 prs-pron dat 1sing masc	3642.17 dem-pron sing neu	3450.16 art sing neu	3231.1 partic
ʿ δὲ	[a☆ γὰρ]	ἐμαυτῷ	τοῦτο,	τὸ	μὴ
de	gar	emautō	touto	to	mē
but	[for]	with myself	this,	to	not

3687.1 adv	2048.23 verb inf aor act	1706.1 prep	3049.3 noun dat sing fem	4242.1 prep	5050.4 prs-pron acc 2pl	1706.1 prep
πάλιν	ʿ ἐλθεῖν	ἐν	λύπῃ	πρὸς	ὑμᾶς.	[b☆ ἐν
palin	elthein	en	lupē	pros	humas	en
again	to come	in	grief	to	you.	[in

3049.3 noun dat sing fem	4242.1 prep	5050.4 prs-pron acc 2pl	2048.23 verb inf aor act	1479.1 conj	1056.1 conj	1466.1 prs-pron nom 1sing
λύπῃ	πρὸς	ὑμᾶς	ἐλθεῖν·]	**2.** εἰ	γὰρ	ἐγὼ
lupē	pros	humas	elthein	ei	gar	egō
grief	to	you	to come.]	If	for	I

3048.1 verb 1sing indic pres act	5050.4 prs-pron acc 2pl	2504.1 conj	4949.3 intr-pron nom sing	1498.4 verb 3sing indic pres act	3450.5 art sing masc
λυπῶ	ὑμᾶς,	καὶ	τίς	ʿa ἐστιν ʾ	ὁ
lupō	humas	kai	tis	estin	ho
grieve	you,	also	who	is it	the

2146.1 verb nom sing masc part pres act	1466.6 prs-pron acc 1sing	1479.1 conj	3231.1 partic	3450.5 art sing masc	3048.8 verb nom sing masc part pres pass
εὐφραίνων	με,	εἰ	μὴ	ὁ	λυπούμενος
euphrainōn	me	ei	mē	ho	lupoumenos
gladdening	me,	if	not	the	being grieved

1523.1 prep gen	1466.3 prs-pron gen 1sing	2504.1 conj	1119.7 verb 1sing indic aor act	5050.3 prs-pron dat 2pl	3642.17 dem-pron sing neu
ἐξ	ἐμοῦ;	**3.** καὶ	ἔγραψα	ʿa ὑμῖν ʾ	τοῦτο
ex	emou	kai	egrapsa	humin	touto
by	me?	And	I wrote	to you	this

840.15 prs-pron acc neu	2419.1 conj	3231.1 partic	2048.13 verb nom sing masc part aor act	3049.4 noun acc sing fem	2174.1 verb 1sing pres act
αὐτό,	ἵνα	μὴ	ἐλθὼν	λύπην	ʿ ἔχω
auto	hina	mē	elthōn	lupēn	echō
same,	that	not	having come	grief	I might have

2174.33 verb 1sing subj aor act	570.1 prep gen	3614.1 rel-pron gen pl	1158.6 verb 3sing indic imperf act	1466.6 prs-pron acc 1sing
[b☆ σχῶ]	ἀφ'	ὧν	ἔδει	με
schō	aph'	hōn	edei	me
[idem]	from	whom	it is necessary for	me

1.a.Txt: 01א,02A,04C 06D-corr1,010F,012G 044,081,byz.
Var: p46,03B,0223,0243 33,630,1175,1739,1881 2495

1.b.Txt: 01א,02A,04C 06D-corr,010F,012G 044,081,byz.
Var: p46,03B,0223,0243 33,630,1175,1739,1881 2495

2.a.Txt: 01א-corr,06D 018K,020L,025P,byz.it. Sod
Var: 01א-org,02A,03B 04C,bo.Lach,Treg,Alf Word,Tisc,We/Ho,Weis UBS/☆

3.a.Txt: 01א-corr 04C-corr,06D,018K 020L,byz.it.
Var: 01א-org,02A,03B 04C-org,025P,bo.Lach Treg,Alf,Word,Tisc We/Ho,Weis,Sod UBS/☆

3.b.Txt: 01א-corr,04C 06D,018K,020L,byz.
Var: 01א-org,02A,03B 025P,Treg,Alf,Tisc We/Ho,Weis,Sod UBS/☆

1:24. Paul knew that faith could not be demanded. Nor could holiness be legislated. This is determined by God, not man. Paul did not wish to be a tyrant who made men tremble. His desire was to be a helper to strengthen faith.

2:1,2. Verse 2 provides a basis for verse 1. The Corinthian converts were the source of Paul's joy. How then could he have caused pain to those who were the very source of his happiness! The sorrow in view here is that which Paul would have experienced if there had been no repentance on the part of the Corinthians.

Pondering these facts, Zahniser declared, "Paul gives here what is heralded as a new doctrine in missionary service, a helpful rather than a directive role" (*The Wesleyan Bible Commentary*, 5:271). He observed further, "Administrative power is never exercised properly in displaying itself, but is only an aid to the spiritual progress of the Church" (ibid., 5:270,271). He concluded, "Paul was a man who worked with concern (Acts 20:19,31), administered his churches with a sense of burden (11:28), and rent his soul almost in twain as his fatherly spirit yearned over his erring children" (ibid., 5:271).

The apostle displayed here the same attitude toward leadership that Peter did. He wrote instructions to church elders of his day saying simply, "The elders which are among you I exhort, who am also an elder" (1 Peter 5:1). He claimed no higher office than that of a fellow elder. His charge to other leaders was that they take the oversight of the congregation not "as being lords over God's heritage, but being ensamples to the flock" (1 Peter 5:3).

Paul also demonstrated the spirit of Jesus here in showing a concern over the joy of his converts. To His students the Master said, "These things have I spoken unto you, that my joy might remain in you, and that your joy might be full" (John 15:11). He made provision for it through prayer. He declared, "Hitherto have ye asked nothing in my name: ask, and ye shall receive, that your joy may be full" (John 16:24). He gave the Spirit, in part, for the same reason. Thus Luke recorded on various occasions that "the disciples were filled with joy, and with the Holy Ghost" (Acts 13:52).

Though doing all he possibly could on their behalf, the apostle realized in the end relationship with God is a highly personal matter. When the final word was said the Corinthians would stand or fall before the Lord on the basis of individual faith. He would not dominate as to their position in the presence of Jesus.

2:3. Many scholars feel verse 1 refers to a painful visit Paul had made to the church at an earlier date (see 12:14; 13:1). The implications are that this visit had been under circumstances painful to both Paul and the church. In addition to a "painful visit" there is also the feeling that verse 3 refers to what some scholars have called the "Severe Letter" Paul had written instead of visiting the church at Corinth (see also 2:9; 7:8,12).

24. Not for that we have dominion over your faith: Not that we excercise lordship, *HistNT* . . . Not that we exercise dominion, *Alford* . . . we do not dictate your faith, *Klingensmith* . . . that we domineer over your faith, *Hanson.*

but are helpers of your joy: . . . we are joint promoters, *Campbell* . . . to promote your joy, *Williams* . . . we are fellow-workers, *Confraternity* . . . associates of your joy, *Wilson* . . . we are partners in your pleasure, *Fenton.*

for by faith ye stand: . . . ye have stood, *Wesley* . . . you have already gained a firm footing, *Greber* . . . you are standing firm, *NASB, Weymouth, TCNT.*

1. But I determined this with myself: In thinking it through, *Norlie* . . . I decided this, *Young* . . . I have definitely decided, *Williams* . . . So far as I am concerned, I have resolved, *Weymouth.*

that I would not come again to you in heaviness: . . . that my next visit, *Noyes* . . . make you another distressing visit, *Berkeley* . . . make you sorrowful, *Douay* . . . again in grief, *Wesley* . . . again in displeasure, *Norlie* . . . pay you another painful visit, *Adams, TCNT, Williams* . . . with sorrow, *ASV* . . . with distress, *Fenton.*

2. For if I make you sorry, who is he then that maketh me glad: For what point is there in my depressing the very people, *Phillips* . . . I cause you grief, *Wuest* . . . that cheereth me, *Wesley.*

but the same which is made sorry by me?: . . . but he that is grieved by me? *Wesley* . . . except the very ones whom I have offended? *Norlie* . . . save him on whom I have inflicted sorrow, *Kleist* . . . that is grieved, *Confraternity.*

3. And I wrote this same unto you: . . . about this very matter, *Noyes.*

lest, when I came, I should have sorrow from them of whom I ought to rejoice:

2 Corinthians 2:4

5299.11 verb inf pres act	3844.13 verb nom sing masc part perf act	1894.3 prep	3820.8 adj acc pl masc	5050.4 prs-pron acc 2pl	3617.1 conj
χαίρειν·	πεποιθὼς	ἐπὶ	πάντας	ὑμᾶς,	ὅτι
chairein	pepoithōs	epi	pantas	humas,	hoti
to rejoice;	having trusted	in	all	you,	that

3450.9 art nom sing fem	1684.6 adj nom 1sing fem	5315.1 noun sing fem	3820.4 adj gen pl	5050.2 prs-pron gen 2pl	1498.4 verb 3sing indic pres act
ἡ	ἐμὴ	χαρὰ	πάντων	ὑμῶν	ἐστιν.
hē	emē	chara	pantōn	humōn	estin
the	my	joy	of all	you	is.

	1523.2 prep gen	1056.1 conj	4044.10 adj gen sing fem	2324.2 noun gen sing fem	2504.1 conj	4779.2 noun gen sing fem
4.	ἐκ	γὰρ	πολλῆς	θλίψεως	καὶ	συνοχῆς
	ek	gar	pollēs	thlipseōs	kai	sunochēs
	Out of	for	much	tribulation	and	distress

2559.1 noun fem	1119.7 verb 1sing indic aor act	5050.3 prs-pron dat 2pl	1217.2 prep	4044.1 adj gen pl	1139.2 noun gen pl neu
καρδίας	ἔγραψα	ὑμῖν	διὰ	πολλῶν	δακρύων,
kardias	egrapsa	humin	dia	pollōn	dakruōn,
of heart	I wrote	to you	through	many	tears;

3620.1 partic	2419.1 conj	3048.14 verb 2pl subj aor pass	233.2 conj	3450.12 art acc sing fem	26.4 noun acc sing fem
οὐχ	ἵνα	λυπηθῆτε,	ἀλλὰ	τὴν	ἀγάπην
ouch	hina	lupēthēte,	alla	tēn	agapēn
not	that	you might be grieved,	but	the	love

2419.1 conj	1091.19 verb 2pl aor act	3614.12 rel-pron acc sing fem	2174.1 verb 1sing pres act	3917.2 adv comp
ἵνα	γνῶτε	ἣν	ἔχω	περισσοτέρως
hina	gnōte	hēn	echō	perissoterōs
that	you might know	which	I have	more abundantly

1519.1 prep	5050.4 prs-pron acc 2pl		1479.1 conj	1156.2 conj	4948.3 indef-pron nom sing	3048.5 verb 3sing indic perf act
εἰς	ὑμᾶς.	**5.**	Εἰ	δέ	τις	λελύπηκεν,
eis	humas.		Ei	de	tis	lelupēken,
towards	you.		If	but	anyone	has grieved,

3620.2 partic	1466.7 prs-pron acc 1sing	3048.5 verb 3sing indic perf act	233.1 conj	233.2 conj	570.3 prep gen
οὐκ	ἐμὲ	λελύπηκεν,	ʼ ἀλλʼ	[✶ ἀλλὰ]	ἀπὸ
ouk	eme	lelupēken,	allʼ	alla	apo
not	me	he has grieved,	but	[idem]	in

3183.2 noun gen sing neu	2419.1 conj	3231.1 partic	1897.1 verb 1sing subj pres act	3820.8 adj acc pl masc	5050.4 prs-pron acc 2pl
μέρους,	ἵνα	μὴ	ἐπιβαρῶ,	πάντας	ὑμᾶς.
merous	hina	mē	epibarō	pantas	humas.
part	that	not	I may bear heavily	all	you.

	2401.2 adj sing	3450.3 art dat sing	4955.6 dem-pron dat sing masc	3450.9 art nom sing fem	1993.1 noun nom sing fem
6.	ἱκανὸν	τῷ	τοιούτῳ	ἡ	ἐπιτιμία
	hikanon	tō	toioutō	hē	epitimia
	Enough	to the	such a one	the	rebuke

3642.9 dem-pron nom sing fem	3450.9 art nom sing fem	5097.3 prep	3450.1 art gen pl	3979.2 adj comp gen pl	5452.1 conj
αὕτη	ἡ	ὑπὸ	τῶν	πλειόνων·	**7.** ὥστε
hautē	hē	hupo	tōn	pleionōn	hōste
this	which	by	the	greater part;	so that

Paul had asked the church to discipline an offender (1 Corinthians 5:13). It seems that at first the church had refused to do this. However, after the severe letter they did so, and the man humbly confessed and quit his sinning. Paul had written to the church for that very reason. He had hoped his letter would result in proper discipline in Christian love, repentance on the part of the offender, and changed attitudes on the part of some in the church. In terms of both sadness and happiness Paul stressed how closely he and his readers were joined in Christian love and fellowship.

2:4. Paul had written this previous letter out of *pollēs* ("great, strong, deep") *thlipseōs* ("trouble and anguish of heart"). The words Paul used reveal some of his deep inner feelings. He had come to the Corinthians once *en lupē* or in deep grief, sorrow, and pain of mind and spirit (2:1), and he did not want to go through such an experience again. Thus, he had written to them "with many tears." The word "with" denotes attending circumstances, i.e., "I was (actually) crying when I wrote the previous letter to you."

Paul had not written in order to cause the Corinthians the same hurt (*lupē*) they had caused him. He did not mean to inflict grief for its own sake. He *did* desire that a heaviness might be produced that would lead to repentance rather than simply remorse. Paul had not written to hurt but to heal. The very grief caused by his severe letter was a manifestation of his love for them.

This *agapē* love is described by the comparative adverb *perissoterōs*, which is taken to mean "especially" here. Paul's special love for the Corinthians was a deep and abiding kind. It was a love of understanding and purpose. It was also a love that might at times cause pain in order to bless and benefit.

2:5. Here the apostle began a defense against the second charge directed at him in Corinth, that of harshness in the case of discipline. Apparently some member of the congregation opposed him, perhaps hinting he sought personal vengeance in the matter. He showed a delicacy of feeling by not naming the offender. The negation (*ouk . . . alla*), i.e., "not . . . but," is used in the absolute sense, not to render void the first conception but to direct undivided attention to the second. Someone had indeed grieved Paul, but it was primarily the congregation at Corinth that had been grieved.

2:6. Evidently the majority of the church had decided to discipline the offender. The "of many" implies the decision was not unanimous. Some felt the punishment was not severe enough. Paul says that this *epitimia* was sufficient. This Greek term is used only here in the New Testament. It is a technical term relating to congregational discipline for censure by the church.

having confidence in you all, that my joy is [the joy] of you all: . . . being persuaded concerning you all, *Wesley.*

4. For out of much affliction and anguish of heart: I was much troubled, *Norlie* . . . in deep suffering and depression of spirit, *Weymouth* . . . in deep distress, *Berkeley* . . . agony of heart, *Fenton* . . . distress of heart, *Wilson* . . . a most unhappy heart, *Phillips* . . . and pressure of heart, *Young.*

I wrote unto you with many tears:

not that ye should be grieved: . . . not to pain you, *Montgomery* . . . should be distressed, *Fenton.*

but that ye might know the love which I have more abundantly unto you: No, I wanted to show you the great love, *SEB* . . . but to convince you of my love, *Montgomery* . . . come to know experientially, *Wuest* . . . how very much I love you, *Beck* . . . the great love, *Confraternity* . . . I so richly bear you, *Berkeley* . . . I have for you especially, *HistNT* . . . I have especially for you, *NASB.*

5. But if any have caused grief:
he hath not grieved me, but in part: . . . he has not made me sorry, *Concordant* . . . but to some extent at least, *Berkeley.*

that I may not overcharge you all: I don't want to be too unkind, *SEB* . . . not to be too severe, *PNT, Confraternity* . . . may not burden you, *Young* . . . may not lay a load on you all, *Campbell* . . . not to overstate the case, *Norlie, Montgomery.*

6. Sufficient to such a man [is] this punishment: . . . has been sufficient, *Phillips* . . . punishment enough, *Norlie.*

which [was inflicted] of many: The majority of you have censured him for his misdeeds, *Norlie* . . . inflicted by the majority, *Wuest, Hanson* . . . imposed by the majority, *Montgomery* . . . the majority of you, *Weymouth.*

2 Corinthians 2:8

7.a.Txt: p46,01**ℵ**,04C
018K,020L,025P,byz.
Var: 02A,03B,We/Ho

4967.1 noun acc sing neu	3095.1 adv comp	5050.4 prs- pron acc 2pl	5319.10 verb inf aor mid	2504.1 conj
τοὐναντίον	⌈a μᾶλλον ⌉	ὑμᾶς	χαρίσασθαι	καὶ
tounantion	mallon	humas	charisasthai	kai
on the contrary	rather	you	to forgive	and

3731.15 verb inf aor act	3248.1 conj	3231.1 partic	4315.1 adv	3450.11 art dat sing fem
παρακαλέσαι,	⌈ μήπως	[☆ μή	πως ⌉	τῇ
parakalesai,	mēpōs	mē	pōs	tē
to encourage,	lest	[not	how]	with the

3916.4 adj comp dat sing fem	3049.3 noun dat sing fem	2636.6 verb 3sing subj aor pass	3450.5 art sing masc
περισσοτέρα	λύπη	καταποθῇ	ὁ
perissotera	lupē	katapothē	ho
more abundant	grief	should be swallowed up	the

4955.4 dem-pron nom sing masc	1346.1 conj	3731.1 verb 1sing indic pres act	5050.4 prs- pron acc 2pl	2937.1 verb inf aor act
τοιοῦτος.	**8.** διὸ	παρακαλῶ	ὑμᾶς	κυρῶσαι
toioutos	dio	parakalō	humas	kurōsai
such a one.	Wherefore	I exhort	you	to confirm

1519.1 prep	840.6 prs-pron acc sing masc	26.4 noun acc sing fem	1519.1 prep	3642.17 dem- pron sing neu	1056.1 conj	2504.1 conj
εἰς	αὐτὸν	ἀγάπην.	**9.** εἰς	τοῦτο	γὰρ	καὶ
eis	auton	agapēn	eis	touto	gar	kai
towards	him	love.	For,	this	for	also

1119.7 verb 1sing indic aor act	2419.1 conj	1091.20 verb 1sing subj aor act	3450.12 art acc sing fem	1376.4 noun acc sing fem	5050.2 prs- pron gen 2pl
ἔγραψα,	ἵνα	γνῶ	τὴν	δοκιμὴν	ὑμῶν,
egrapsa,	hina	gnō	tēn	dokimēn	humōn,
did I write,	that	I might know	the	proof	of you,

1479.1 conj	1519.1 prep	3820.1 adj	5093.2 adj nom pl masc	1498.6 verb 2pl indic pres act	3614.3 rel- pron dat sing	1156.2 conj
εἰ	εἰς	πάντα	ὑπήκοοί	ἐστε.	**10.** ᾧ	δέ
ei	eis	panta	hupēkooi	este.	hō	de
if	to	everything	obedient	you are.	To whom	but

10.a.Txt: 01**ℵ**-corr
04C-org,018K,020L,byz.
Var: 01**ℵ**-org,02A,03B
04C-corr,06D,025P,33
Lach,Treg,Alf,Word
Tisc,We/Ho,Weis,Sod
UBS/☆

4948.10 indef- pron sing neu	5319.1 verb 2pl indic pres	2504.1 conj	1466.1 prs- pron nom 1sing	2476.3 conj	2504.1 conj
τι	χαρίζεσθε,	⌈ καὶ	ἐγώ	[a☆ κἀγώ ⌉	καὶ
ti	charizesthe,	kai	egō	kagō	kai
anything	you forgive,	also	I;	[also I;]	also

1056.1 conj	1466.1 prs- pron nom 1sing	1479.1 conj	4948.10 indef- pron sing neu	5319.11 verb 1sing indic perf	3614.3 rel- pron dat sing
γὰρ	ἐγὼ	⌈ εἴ	τι	κεχάρισμαι,	ᾧ
gar	egō	ei	ti	kecharismai,	hō
for	I	if	anything	I have forgiven,	of whom

10.b.Txt: 06D-corr,018K
020L,33,byz.
Var: 01**ℵ**,02A,03B,04C
Gries,Lach,Treg,Alf
Word,Tisc,We/Ho,Weis
Sod,UBS/☆

5319.11 verb 1sing indic perf	3614.16 rel- pron sing neu	5319.11 verb 1sing indic perf	1479.1 conj	4948.10 indef- pron sing neu
κεχάρισμαι,	[b☆ ὃ	κεχάρισμαι,	εἴ	τι
kecharismai	ho	kecharismai	ei	ti
I have forgiven,	[which	I have forgiven,	if	anything

5319.11 verb 1sing indic perf	1217.1 prep	5050.4 prs- pron acc 2pl	1706.1 prep	4241.3 noun dat sing neu
κεχάρισμαι,]	δι'	ὑμᾶς	ἐν	προσώπῳ
kecharismai	di'	humas	en	prosōpō
I have forgiven,]	because of	you,	in	person

2:7. Whatever the censure was, the offender had deserved it. But discipline should not go beyond what is fair. It must also leave room for repentance. Forgiveness and reconciliation should then follow with the result being comfort and renewed fellowship (cf. Luke 17:3). Undue severity is to be avoided as much as undue leniency.

In a case of laziness deserving discipline at Thessalonica the apostle gave similar instructions. He considered refusing to work in support of oneself the height of selfishness. As such it cuts across the core of unselfishness in Christianity. Christ came not to have others serve Him but to serve others (Mark 10:45). The offender's laziness was so serious that Paul instructed, "Have no company with him, that he may be ashamed" (2 Thessalonians 3:14f.). Then he quickly added, "Yet count him not as an enemy, but admonish him as a brother."

2:8. Paul appealed to the Corinthian church members to confirm (*kurōsai*) their love to the offender. This Greek word is a legal term meaning "to enforce" or "to validate." Combining the two somewhat opposite concepts of *agapē* ("love") and *kuroun* (the legal term of developing church law) was not accidental. The church had made the decision to discipline one of its members. Paul now begged them earnestly to reverse the disciplinary process by confirming or deciding in favor of love for the repentant offender. This practical assurance of their love was to be shown in forgiveness and restoration.

2:9. In a former letter Paul had set forth a course of action to be taken in dealing with an erring member. The reaction of the Corinthians would serve as a *dokimēn* ("proof") of their willingness to obey his authority as an apostle of Jesus Christ. The Greek word meaning proof that is the result of testing is unique in that it expresses both the fact that a test was made and that it was successfully passed.

2:10. If the church was ready to reinstate the offender, Paul was satisfied with their decision. The perfect tense found here in *kecharismai* ("forgive," see also verse 9) indicates a present condition resulting from a past action. If any forgiveness was necessary on Paul's part it could be considered already given. If the Corinthians had forgiven the offender they could include Paul's forgiveness as having been given along with theirs. Paul felt deeply his responsibility as an apostle. Thus the action he had taken had for its main object the total welfare of the Corinthian church. Paul strengthened his position by appealing to Christ as a witness to the sincerity of his forgiveness "in (the) *prosōpō* (literally 'face') of Christ," i.e., as though Christ were looking on. His action had been performed as though he were in the presence of Christ.

7. So that contrariwise ye [ought] rather to forgive [him], and comfort [him]: On the other hand, *Wilson, Campbell* . . . Now you should turn around, *Beck* . . . so, instead of further rebuke, *Berkeley* . . . is better to forgive and encourage, *Klingensmith* . . . show him that you still love him, *Norlie.*

lest perhaps such a one should be swallowed up with overmuch sorrow: . . . lest by any means, *ASV* . . . may overpower him, *Norlie* . . . be overwhelmed by too much sorrow, *Confraternity* . . . overwhelmed by despair, *Berkeley* . . . be driven to despair, *Weymouth* . . . be completely overwhelmed by remorse, *Phillips* . . . with his excessive grief, *Hanson* . . . by excessive sorrow, *HistNT* . . . by more excessive sorrow, *Concordant* . . . abundant sorrow, *Young* . . . that excessive reproof may drown him, *Fenton.*

8. Wherefore I beseech you that ye would confirm [your] love toward him: I entreat you publicly, *Wilson* . . . I beseech you fully to restore him to your love, *Conybeare* . . . to reaffirm, *NASB* . . . to ratify your love, *HistNT* . . . fully reinstate him in your love, *Weymouth, Montgomery* . . . in your affection, *Berkeley.*

9. For to this end also did I write:

that I might know the proof of you: . . . was something of a test, *Phillips.*

whether ye be obedient in all things: . . . whether respecting all things, *Rotherham* . . . you meet the specifications laid down, *Wuest* . . . you would follow my orders implicitly, *Phillips* . . . you are prepared to be obedient in every respect, *Weymouth* . . . in carrying out my orders, *Norlie.*

10. To whom ye forgive any thing, I [forgive] also: . . . you grant pardon, *Fenton.*

for if I forgave any thing, to whom I forgave [it]:

for your sakes [forgave I it] in the person of Christ: . . . in the presence of Christ, *Weymouth, PNT.*

5382.2 name gen masc				3982.5 verb 1pl subj aor pass	5097.3 prep
Χριστοῦ,	11. ἵνα	μὴ		πλεονεκτηθῶμεν	ὑπὸ
Christou	2419.1 conj hina	3231.1 partic mē		pleonektēthōmen	hupo
of Christ;	that	not		we should be taken advantage of	by

3450.2 art gen sing	4423.2 noun sing masc	3620.3 partic	1056.1 conj	840.3 prs-pron gen sing	3450.17 art pl neu	3402.2 noun pl neu
τοῦ	Σατανᾶ·	οὐ	γὰρ	αὐτοῦ	τὰ	νοήματα
tou	Satana	ou	gar	autou	ta	noēmata
	Satan,	not	for	his	the	thoughts

49.2 verb 1pl indic pres act	2048.13 verb nom sing masc part aor act	1156.2 conj	1519.1 prep	3450.12 art acc sing fem
ἀγνοοῦμεν.	12. Ἐλθὼν	δὲ	εἰς	τὴν
agnooumen	Elthōn	de	eis	tēn
are we ignorant.	Having come	now	to	

5015.3 name acc fem	1519.1 prep	3450.16 art sing neu	2077.1 noun sing neu	3450.2 art gen sing	5382.2 name gen masc
Τρῳάδα	εἰς	τὸ	εὐαγγέλιον	τοῦ	Χριστοῦ,
Trōada	eis	to	euangelion	tou	Christou
Troas	for	the	good news	of the	Christ,

2504.1 conj	2351.1 noun fem	1466.4 prs-pron part perf dat 1sing	453.29 verb gen sing fem part perf pass	1706.1 prep	2935.3 noun dat sing masc
καὶ	θύρας	μοι	ἀνεῳγμένης	ἐν	κυρίῳ,
kai	thuras	moi	aneōgmenēs	en	kuriō
also	a door	to me	having been opened	in	Lord,

3620.2 partic	2174.34 verb 1sing indic perf act	423.2 noun acc sing fem	3450.3 art dat sing	4011.3 noun dat sing neu	1466.2 prs-pron gen 1sing
13. οὐκ	ἔσχηκα	ἄνεσιν	τῷ	πνεύματί	μου
ouk	eschēka	anesin	tō	pneumati	mou
not	I have had	rest	in the	spirit	my

3450.3 art dat sing	3231.1 partic	2128.21 verb inf aor act	1466.6 prs-pron acc 1sing	4951.4 name acc masc	3450.6 art acc sing masc
τῷ	μὴ	εὑρεῖν	με	Τίτον	τὸν
tō	mē	heurein	me	Titon	ton
at the	not	to find	my	Titus	the

79.4 noun acc sing masc	1466.2 prs-pron gen 1sing	233.2 conj	651.3 verb nom sing masc part aor mid	840.2 prs-pron dat pl
ἀδελφόν	μου·	ἀλλὰ	ἀποταξάμενος	αὐτοῖς,
adelphon	mou	alla	apotaxamenos	autois
brother	my;	but	having taken leave	of them,

1814.1 verb indic aor act	1519.1 prep	3081.4 name acc fem	3450.3 art dat sing	1156.2 conj	2296.3 noun dat sing masc
ἐξῆλθον	εἰς	Μακεδονίαν.	14. Τῷ	δὲ	θεῷ
exēlthon	eis	Makedonian	Tō	de	theō
I went out	into	Macedonia.	To the	but	God

5322.1 noun nom sing fem	3450.3 art dat sing	3704.1 adv	2335.1 verb dat sing masc part pres act	2231.4 prs-pron acc 1pl
χάρις	τῷ	πάντοτε	θριαμβεύοντι	ἡμᾶς
charis	tō	pantote	thriambeuonti	hēmas
thanks,	the	always	leading in triumph	us

1706.1 prep	3450.3 art dat sing	5382.3 name dat masc	2504.1 conj	3450.12 art acc sing fem	3606.3 noun acc sing fem	3450.10 art gen sing fem
ἐν	τῷ	Χριστῷ,	καὶ	τὴν	ὀσμὴν	τῆς
en	tō	Christō	kai	tēn	osmēn	tēs
in	the	Christ,	and	the	odor	of the

2:11. Unwillingness on the part of the Corinthians to forgive and comfort the offender and to confirm their love toward him could cause him to be *katapothē* (swallowed up with total extinction as a possible result) with excessive sorrow (see 2:7). If this happened there would be the danger that the church would be outwitted by Satan and robbed of a member of its fellowship. This should never happen because both Paul and the Corinthian believers were well aware of Satan's *noēmata*. This term (in the plural here) carries a sinister connotation meaning "evil schemings."

For the Corinthians to display ignorance of the strength of their enemy made them poor soldiers. These devices, designs, and plots the devil uses against Christians all stem from his basic character. His major name which Paul used here, *Satana*, reveals him as the chief "adversary" of the work of God. Paul showed his opposition is most real and not just imagined, as some suggest. In his first letter Peter said his plans include devouring every believer he possibly can (1 Peter 5:8). In an effort to do that he accuses them both to their face and before God constantly (Revelation 12:9,10). Another of his names, devil (*diabolos*), speaks of this diabolic work of "slandering" people.

2:12. Paul now returned to his report regarding his change of travel plans. His purpose in coming to Troas had been to preach the gospel. While there "a door was opened." The metaphor of the open door means to "make possible" or "feasible."

2:13. An unusual opportunity for Christian service had opened up for Paul. However, Paul's anxiety regarding the affairs at Corinth seems to have kept him from taking advantage of the open door at Troas. The distress he experienced is pictured in a very forceful way by the use of the perfect tense for the verb here, namely, "I *had* no rest (relaxation, relief) in my spirit." Even as he wrote, Paul still had a vivid realization of the agony of spirit he had felt at Troas when Titus failed to arrive with news from Corinth. Again, the perfect tense also shows the continuation of Paul's tension until it grew so strong that he said good-bye to his friends and converts and hurried on to Macedonia.

2:14. Scholars differ in their opinions as to whether these verses (2:14 to 7:4) are an actual digression or not. It appears very possible that Paul at last met with Titus, possibly at Philippi, and received a very favorable report. Paul did not report this meeting but implied it by breaking into a doxology (2:14).

In verse 13 we see Paul's anxiety. In verses 14 and following we see his gratitude to God for divine deliverance and continual triumph "in Christ" as the gospel was being spread abroad in every place.

11. Lest Satan should get an advantage of us: Then Satan won't fool us, *SEB* ... to keep the devil from getting the best of us, *Beck* ... that we may not be circumvented, *Sawyer* ... that we may not be overmastered, *Fenton* ... that we may not be defeated by Satan, *Confraternity* ... that we may not be overreached by Satan, *Rotherham* ... the Adversary, *Young*.

for we are not ignorant of his devices: We know what he has in mind, *Beck* ... not ignorant of his purposes, *Wuest* ... of his designs, *Adams, RSV* ... of his schemes, *NASB* ... of his schemings, *Berkeley* ... of his tricks, *Klingensmith* ... well we know his methods! *Phillips*.

12. Furthermore, when I came to Troas to [preach] Christ's gospel: ... for the joyful message, *Rotherham*.

and a door was opened unto me of the Lord:

13. I had no rest in my spirit: I was on edge the whole time, *Phillips* ... I have had no relaxation, *Wuest* ... I had no ease, *Fenton* ... I was still very worried, *SEB* ... no peace of mind, *Norlie, Montgomery* ... no relief for my spirit, *Weymouth* ... but my mind could not rest, *RSV*.

because I found not Titus my brother: I did not meet, *Berkeley* ... I failed to find Titus, *TCNT*.

but taking my leave of them, I went from thence into Macedonia: I bade them farewell, *Weymouth* ... bidding them farewell, *Confraternity* ... so that I parted from them, *Conybeare* ... I proceeded into Macedonia, *Fenton*.

14. Now thanks [be] unto God, which always causeth us to triumph in Christ: ... who at all times leads us, *Rotherham*, ... always leads us, *Hanson* ... exhibiteth us, *Noyes* ... leads us in one continual triumph, *TCNT* ... leads us on triumphantly, *Beck* ... heads our triumphal procession, *Weymouth* ... to victory, *Norlie* ... to celebrate his victory over the enemies of Christ, *Conybeare* ... who ever makes our life a pageant of triumph, *HistNT*.

1102.2 noun gen sing fem	840.3 prs-pron gen sing	5157.1 verb dat sing masc part pres act	1217.1 prep	2231.2 prs-pron gen 1pl
γνώσεως	αὐτοῦ	φανεροῦντι	δι'	ἡμῶν
gnōseōs	autou	phanerounti	di'	hēmōn
knowledge	of him	making manifest	through	us

1706.1 prep	3820.3 adj dat sing	4964.3 noun dat sing masc	3617.1 conj	5382.2 name gen sing	2156.1 noun nom sing fem
ἐν	παντὶ	τόπῳ.	**15.** ὅτι	Χριστοῦ	εὐωδία
en	panti	topō	hoti	Christou	euōdia
in	every	place.	For	of Christ	a sweet aroma

1498.5 verb 1pl indic pres act	3450.3 art dat sing	2296.3 noun dat sing masc	1706.1 prep	3450.4 art dat pl	4834.19 verb dat pl masc part pres pass	2504.1 conj
ἐσμὲν	τῷ	θεῷ	ἐν	τοῖς	σωζομένοις	καὶ
esmen	tō	theō	en	tois	sōzomenois	kai
we are		to God	in	the	being saved	and

1706.1 prep	3450.4 art dat pl	616.19 verb dat pl masc part pres	3614.4 rel-pron dat pl	3173.1 conj	3606.1 noun nom sing fem
ἐν	τοῖς	ἀπολλυμένοις·	**16.** οἷς	μὲν,	ὀσμὴ
en	tois	apollumenois	hois	men	osmē
in	the	perishing;	to whom	men	an odor

16.a.Var: 01**ℵ**,02A,03B 04C,33,Lach,Treg,Alf Tisc,We/Ho,Weis,Sod UBS/✸

1523.2 prep gen	2265.2 noun gen sing masc	1519.1 prep	2265.4 noun acc sing masc	3614.4 rel-pron dat pl	1156.2 conj
[a✰+ ἐκ]	θανάτου	εἰς	θάνατον·	οἷς	δὲ,
ek	thanatou	eis	thanaton	hois	de
[out of]	of death	to	death,	to whom,	but

16.b.Var: 01**ℵ**,02A,03B 04C,33,Lach,Treg,Alf Tisc,We/Ho,Weis,Sod UBS/✸

3606.1 noun nom sing fem	1523.2 prep gen	2205.2 noun gen sing fem	1519.1 prep	2205.4 noun acc sing fem	2504.1 conj	4242.1 prep
ὀσμὴ	[b✰+ ἐκ]	ζωῆς	εἰς	ζωήν.	καὶ	πρὸς
osmē	ek	zōēs	eis	zōēn	kai	pros
an odor	[out of]	of life	to	life;	and	for

3642.18 dem-pron pl neu	4949.3 intr-pron nom sing	2401.3 adj nom sing masc	3620.3 partic	1056.1 conj	1498.5 verb 1pl indic pres act
ταῦτα	τίς	ἱκανός;	**17.** οὐ	γάρ	ἐσμεν
tauta	tis	hikanos	ou	gar	esmen
these things	who	competent?	Not	for	we are

17.a.Txt: 01**ℵ**,02A,03B 04C,044,0243,byz. **Var:** p46,06D,010F 012G,020L,6,326,630 945,2495

5453.1 conj	3450.7 art pl masc	4044.7 adj nom pl masc	3036.3 adj nom pl masc	2556.1 verb nom pl masc part pres act
ὡς	οἱ	′✰ πολλοὶ,	[a λοιποί,]	καπηλεύοντες
hōs	hoi	polloi	loipoi	kapēleuontes
as	the	many,	[remaining,]	making gain by peddling

17.b.Txt: 01**ℵ**-corr,06D 018K,020L,byz. **Var:** 01**ℵ**-org,02A,03B 04C,025P,33,Lach,Treg Alf,Tisc,We/Ho,Weis Sod,UBS/✸

3450.6 art acc sing masc	3030.4 noun acc sing masc	3450.2 art gen sing	2296.2 noun gen sing masc	233.1 conj	5453.1 conj	1523.1 prep gen
τὸν	λόγον	τοῦ	θεοῦ,	ἀλλ'	ὡς	ἐξ
ton	logon	tou	theou	all'	hōs	ex
the	word		of God,	but	as	of

17.c.Txt: 01**ℵ**-corr 06D-corr,018K,020L 025P,byz. **Var:** 01**ℵ**-org,02A,03B 04C,06D-org,Lach,Treg Tisc,We/Ho,Weis,Sod UBS/✸

1495.1 noun gen sing fem	233.1 conj	5453.1 conj	1523.2 prep gen	2296.2 noun gen sing masc	2684.1 prep
εἰλικρινείας,	ἀλλ'	ὡς	ἐκ	θεοῦ,	′ κατενώπιον
eilikrineias	all'	hōs	ek	theou	katenōpion
sincerity,	but	as	of	God,	before

2683.1 prep gen	3450.2 art gen sing	2296.2 noun gen sing masc	1706.1 prep	5382.3 name dat masc
[b✰ κατέναντι]	′c τοῦ ′	θεοῦ,	ἐν	Χριστῷ
katenanti	tou	theou	en	Christō
[idem]		God,	in	Christ

The Greek term *thriambeuonti* ("cause to triumph") is given various meanings. Whether Paul was envisioning himself and his co-workers as soldiers of the Lord or prisoners of Christ, a basic thought here is that of display in a triumphal procession. Every place Paul ministered God gave him the victory regardless of the circumstances. The knowledge (*gnōseos*) spoken of here is specifically Christian knowledge and understanding of the Scriptures given by God. It is opposed to Gnosticism and the mystery religions of the First Century.

2:15. This was not a special knowledge communicated *by* a favored few *to* a favored few. The fragrance (*osmē*) of the knowledge of God (2:14) was spread throughout the New Testament world by the preaching and works of the apostles. In spreading the fragrance of Christ the apostles themselves became a sweet perfume (*euōdia*, i.e., from *eu* meaning "well," and *ozō*, meaning "to smell"). This word is used of the fragrance from a sacrifice pleasing to God. A tradition states that when Polycarp was burned at the stake a similar fragrance was noted.

2:16. Here the primary thought is not so much sacrifice as it is the dual effect produced through the ministry of the gospel. A graphic example of this is in Mark 16:16, namely, "He that believeth . . . shall be saved; but he that believeth not shall be damned" (see also John 3:18; Luke 2:34). In a sense Paul saw ministers of the gospel as messengers of both life and death, of salvation and judgment. Little wonder he asked, "And who is sufficient for these things?"

2:17. Two words stand out in relation to Paul's solemn view of his position as a gospel preacher. First, there is *kapēleuontes* ("corrupt"). The word occurs only here in the New Testament. It comes from the world of merchandising, suggesting trickery and avarice. The *kapelos* was often suspected of things like putting the best fruit on top of the basket or adulterating pure wine with water.

Paul was no peddler of spiritual goods for material gain. He refused to make merchandise of the gospel. Nor would he ever cheapen it by diluting it with foreign elements.

The second word to note here is *eilikrineias* ("sincerity"). It is derived from *eile* which refers to the "warmth or the light of the sun" and *krinō*. Thus the full sense is often given as "tested by the light of the sun," "completely pure." This word always denotes moral purity. Thus Paul contrasted the deceitfulness of the religious "hucksters" of his day with his pure motives and honorable methods in preaching the gospel. He received his message from God, ministered before Him, and was answerable to Him.

and maketh manifest the savour of his knowledge by us in every place: . . . he shows forth, *Klingensmith* . . . the sweet aroma, *NASB* . . . an odor of incense everywhere, *Montgomery* . . . penetrate every place, *Norlie.*

15. For we are unto God a sweet savour of Christ, in them that are saved, and in them that perish: . . . a sweet perfume, *Fenton* . . . a fragrant odor, *Clementson* . . . the pleasant smell of Christ, *SEB* . . . the unmistakable "scent" of Christ, *Phillips* . . . fragrance of Christ to God, *Concordant* . . . among the destroyed, *Campbell.*

16. To the one [we are] the savour of death unto death; and to the other the savour of life unto life: . . . we are the deadly scent of death, *Adams* . . . To the latter, it is the smell of doom and death, *Norlie* . . . to these a fatal odor, *Berkeley* . . . odour of deadily death...an odour of living life, *Fenton* . . . odour of death predicitive of death, *Weymouth* . . . of death that kills, *Beck* . . . to the former the odor of life, *Noyes.*
And who [is] sufficient for these things?: . . . who is equal to this? *Fenton* . . . who is competent? *Weymouth, Concordant* . . . who is qualified for this? *HistNT, Berkeley.*

17. For we are not as many, which corrupt the word of God: For we are not as the majority, *Concordant* . . . profiting by corrupting, *KJII* . . . secondhand dealers in God's word, *Kleist* . . . bartering the word, *Panin* . . . making merchandise of the word, *Worrell* . . . peddling the word, *NASB* . . . trafficking in the word, *Montgomery, Wilson* . . . making profit by teaching God's Word falsely, *Norlie.*
but as of sincerity, but as of God, in the sight of God speak we in Christ: . . . but I speak from a single heart, *Conybeare* . . . but from the purest motives, *Berkeley* . . . but as of full strength, *PNT* . . . but with transparent motives, as commissioned by God, *Weymouth* . . . in the very presence of God, *Montgomery.*

2 Corinthians 3:1

2953.4 verb 1pl indic pres act		751.2 verb 1pl indic pres mid	3687.1 adv	1431.8 prs-pron acc pl masc	4771.7 verb inf pres act
λαλοῦμεν.	3:1.	Ἀρχόμεθα	πάλιν	ἑαυτοὺς	συνιστάνειν;
laloumen		Archometha	palin	heautous	sunistanein
we speak.		Do we begin	again	ourselves	to commend?

1479.1 conj	2211.1 conj	3231.1 partic	5370.2 verb 1pl indic pres act	5453.1 conj	4948.7 indef-pron nom pl masc
εἰ	[ᵃ⋆ ἢ]	μὴ	χρῄζομεν,	ὥς	τινες
ei	ē	mē	chrēzomen	hōs	tines
if	[or]	not	we need,	as	some,

4808.1 adj gen pl fem	1976.6 noun gen pl fem	4242.1 prep	5050.4 prs-pron acc 2pl	2211.1 conj	1523.1 prep gen
συστατικῶν	ἐπιστολῶν	πρὸς	ὑμᾶς,	ἢ	ἐξ
sustatikōn	epistolōn	pros	humas	ē	ex
recommendation	letters	to	you,	or	from

5050.2 prs-pron gen 2pl	4808.1 adj gen pl fem	3450.9 art nom sing fem	1976.1 noun nom sing fem	2231.2 prs-pron gen 1pl
ὑμῶν	(ᵇ συστατικῶν;)	2. ἡ	ἐπιστολὴ	ἡμῶν
humōn	sustatikōn	hē	epistolē	hēmōn
you	introductory?	The	epistle	our

5050.1 prs-pron nom 2pl	1498.6 verb 2pl indic pres act	1442.1 verb nom sing fem part perf pass	1706.1 prep	3450.14 art dat pl fem	2559.7 noun dat pl fem
ὑμεῖς	ἐστε,	ἐγγεγραμμένη	ἐν	ταῖς	καρδίαις
humeis	este	engegrammenē	en	tais	kardiais
you	are,	having been inscribed	in	the	hearts

2231.2 prs-pron gen 1pl	1091.42 verb nom sing fem part pres pass	2504.1 conj	312.15 verb nom sing fem part pres pass	5097.3 prep
ἡμῶν,	γινωσκομένη	καὶ	ἀναγινωσκομένη	ὑπὸ
hēmōn	ginōskomenē	kai	anaginōskomenē	hupo
our,	being known	and	being read	by

3820.4 adj gen pl	442.7 noun gen pl masc	5157.8 verb nom pl masc part pres pass	3617.1 conj	1498.6 verb 2pl indic pres act
πάντων	ἀνθρώπων·	3. φανερούμενοι	ὅτι	ἐστὲ
pantōn	anthrōpōn	phaneroumenoi	hoti	este
all	men,	being manifested	that	you are

1976.1 noun nom sing fem	5382.2 name gen masc	1241.18 verb nom sing fem part aor pass	5097.1 prep	2231.2 prs-pron gen 1pl
ἐπιστολὴ	Χριστοῦ	διακονηθεῖσα	ὑφ'	ἡμῶν,
epistolē	Christou	diakonētheisa	huph'	hēmōn
epistle	Christ's,	having been ministered	by	us;

1442.1 verb nom sing fem part perf pass	3620.3 partic	3158.2 adj dat sing neu	233.2 conj	4011.3 noun dat sing neu
ἐγγεγραμμένη	οὐ	μέλανι,	ἀλλὰ	πνεύματι
engegrammenē	ou	melani	alla	pneumati
having been inscribed,	not	with ink,	but	with Spirit

2296.2 noun gen sing masc	2180.11 verb gen sing part pres act	3620.2 partic	1706.1 prep	3970.2 noun dat pl fem	3009.2 adj dat pl fem
θεοῦ	ζῶντος,	οὐκ	ἐν	πλαξὶν	λιθίναις,
theou	zōntos	ouk	en	plaxin	lithinais
of God	living;	not	on	tablets	of stone,

233.1 conj	1706.1 prep	3970.2 noun dat pl fem	2559.1 noun fem	2559.7 noun dat pl fem
ἀλλ'	ἐν	πλαξὶν	(καρδίας	[ᵃ⋆ καρδίαις]
all'	en	plaxin	kardias	kardiais
but	on	tablets	of heart	[hearts]

3:1. One of the charges brought against Paul by his enemies had been self-assertion and pride. Some feel these charges may have been made in connection with Paul's words in 1 Corinthians 4:16; 11:1, namely, "Follow me." However, lest his words in 2 Corinthians 2:17 be misinterpreted as self-praise he quickly assured the Corinthians that he needed no letters of recommendation either to them or from them. In the Greek the form of this question indicates that a negative answer is expected. Paul was not against letters of recommendation. Later on these letters became quite necessary because of large numbers of charlatans.

Indeed the apostle himself wrote such letters of recommendation on behalf of others. In fact, before he closed this very epistle he included several lines to commend Titus and other fellow workers to the Corinthians (8:16-19,22,23). This Early Church practice provided a pattern for the licensing of ministers in the Church of today.

3:2. Paul used the pronoun "Ye" (*humeis*) with the verb *este* ("ye are"). When this is done it expresses a certain emphasis because the subject is already in the verb. This construction is used to express a special relationship between the subject "Ye" and the predicate noun "epistle." Paul's recommendation was not *letters*, but *lives* that were known and read by everybody. The implication is that the authenticity of the letters produced by other so-called apostles was suspect and would not stand close scrutiny.

3:3. The words "manifestly declared" (*phaneroumenoi*) mean "to make known or be shown." The connotation is that of public display. Some think Paul may have had in mind a letter engraved on a monument displayed to public gaze where all who passed by could read it.

In a sense believers themselves are *epistolē* or authoritative letters of Christ "known and read of all men." Paul's work was not his own but that of Christ. He was simply a *diakonos*, or one of the King's "servants."

A second metaphor grows out of the first. So close to the hearts of Paul and his companions were the interests of the Corinthians that Paul wrote, "You are a letter of Christ inscribed upon our hearts." Their being a "letter" was the work of the Spirit of God in their hearts. Paul used two comparisons to show this. First, he compared the miracle-working power of God with human letters of recommendation written with ink. Paul's "letters" of recommendation were vastly superior to the scrolls of his rivals. The contrast between "ink" and "Spirit" takes on added meaning when it is remembered that the ink used in Paul's day washed off easily.

The second comparison deals with how the messages were written. The Ten Commandments were written on "tables of stone" (Exodus 24:12). The message of the gospel Paul preached was written by the Spirit of God in their hearts.

1. Do we begin again to commend ourselves?: Is this going to be more self-advertisement, *Phillips* . . . Am I falling into self-recommendation again? *Goodspeed* . . . Are we beginning to flourish our credentials all over again? *Barclay* . . . attempting to put ourselves in the right? *BB* . . . like a new attempt to commend ourselves to you? *JB* . . . as if we were again boasting about ourselves? *TEV* . . . to pat ourselves on the back, *SEB*.

or need we, as some [others], epistles of commendation to you: Unlike other people, we need no letters, *JB* . . . that we, like some people, need letters of introduction, *Barclay* . . . letters of approval, *BB*.

or [letters] of commendation from you?: . . . commentary letters, *Concordant*.

2. Ye are our epistle written in our hearts, known and read of all men: Our letter of recommendation is yourselves, *Weymouth* . . . Credentials! you, you are my credentials, *Way* . . . you are all the letter we need, *NEB* . . . my commendatory epistle, *Locke* . . . inscribed in our hearts, *Rotherham*, *PNT* . . . open to everyone to know and to read, *Barclay*.

3. [Forasmuch as ye are] manifestly declared to be the epistle of Christ: It is clear that Christ himself wrote this letter, *TEV* . . . it is plain that you are a letter that has come from Christ, *NEB*.

ministered by us: . . . drawn up by us, *JB* . . . produced by my service, *Williams* . . . transcribed by me, *Montgomery* . . . transmitted by us, *Fenton* . . . delivered by us, *Sawyer, Wilson, Barclay* . . . committed to my charge, *Conybeare* . . . entrusted to our care, *TCNT* . . . executed by our ministry, *HistNT* . . . the result of our ministry, *NIV*.

written not with ink, but with the Spirit of the living God: . . . recorded not with ink, *BB*.

not in tables of stone, but in fleshly tables of the heart: . . . not on slabs, *Adams* . . . not in the tablets, *Young* . . . not on stone plates, *Beck* . . . but on the pages of the human heart, *NEB*.

2 Corinthians 3:4

4417.1 adj dat pl fem	3870.2 noun acc sing fem	1156.2 conj	4955.10 dem- pron acc sing fem	2174.5 verb 1pl indic pres act
σαρκίναις.	**4.** Πεποίθησιν	δὲ	τοιαύτην	ἔχομεν
sarkinais	Pepoithēsin	de	toiautēn	echomen
fleshy.	Confidence	and	such	have we

1217.2 prep	3450.2 art gen sing	5382.2 name gen masc	4242.1 prep	3450.6 art acc sing masc	2296.4 noun acc sing masc
διὰ	τοῦ	Χριστοῦ	πρὸς	τὸν	θεόν·
dia	tou	Christou	pros	ton	theon
through	the	Christ	towards	ton	God:

3620.1 partic	3617.1 conj	2401.6 adj nom pl masc	1498.5 verb 1pl indic pres act	570.1 prep gen	1431.2 prs- pron gen pl
5. οὐχ	ὅτι	⸂ ἱκανοί	ἐσμεν	ἀφ᾽	ἑαυτῶν
ouch	hoti	hikanoi	esmen	aph'	heautōn
not	that	competent	we are	from	ourselves

3023.17 verb inf aor mid	4948.10 indef- pron neu	570.1 prep gen	1431.2 prs- pron gen pl	2401.6 adj nom pl masc
λογίσασθαί	τι	[✷ ἀφ᾽	ἑαυτῶν	ἱκανοί
logisasthai	ti	aph'	heautōn	hikanoi
to reckon	anything	[from	ourselves	competent

1498.5 verb 1pl indic pres act	3023.17 verb inf aor mid	4948.10 indef- pron sing neu	5453.1 conj	1523.1 prep gen	1431.2 prs- pron gen pl
ἐσμεν	λογίσασθαί	τι]	ὡς	ἐξ	ἑαυτῶν,
esmen	logisasthai	ti	hōs	ex	heautōn
we are	to reckon	anything]	as	of	ourselves,

233.1 conj	3450.9 art nom sing fem	2402.1 noun nom sing fem	2231.2 prs- pron gen 1pl	1523.2 prep gen	3450.2 art gen sing	2296.2 noun gen sing masc
ἀλλ᾽	ἡ	ἱκανότης	ἡμῶν	ἐκ	τοῦ	θεοῦ·
all'	hē	hikanotēs	hēmōn	ek	tou	theou
but	the	competency	our	of	tou	God;

3614.5 rel-pron nom sing masc	2504.1 conj	2403.1 verb 3sing indic aor act	2231.4 prs- pron acc 1pl	1243.5 noun acc pl masc	2508.4 adj gen sing fem
6. ὃς	καὶ	ἱκάνωσεν	ἡμᾶς	διακόνους	καινῆς
hos	kai	hikanōsen	hēmas	diakonous	kainēs
who	also	made competent	us	servants	of a new

1236.2 noun gen sing fem	3620.3 partic	1115.2 noun gen sing neu	233.2 conj	4011.2 noun gen sing neu	3450.16 art sing neu
διαθήκης,	οὐ	γράμματος,	ἀλλὰ	πνεύματος·	τὸ
diathēkēs	ou	grammatos	alla	pneumatos	to
covenant;	not	of letter,	but	of Spirit;	the

6.a.Txt: p46-org,02A 04C,06D,byz.
Var: p46-corr3,01ℵ,03B 010F,012G,018K,025P 044,0243,6,33,104,326 etc.co.

1056.1 conj	1115.1 noun sing neu	609.1 verb 3sing indic pres act	609.1 verb 3sing indic pres act	3450.16 art sing neu
γὰρ	γράμμα	⸂ ἀποκτείνει,	[ᵃ✷ ἀποκτέννει,]	τὸ
gar	gramma	apokteinei	apoktennei	to
for	letter	kills,	[idem]	the

1156.2 conj	4011.1 noun sing neu	2210.1 verb 3sing indic pres act	1479.1 conj	1156.2 conj	3450.9 art nom sing fem	1242.1 noun nom sing fem
δὲ	πνεῦμα	ζωοποιεῖ.	**7.** Εἰ	δὲ	ἡ	διακονία
de	pneuma	zōopoiei	Ei	de	hē	diakonia
but	Spirit	makes alive.	If	but	the	service

3450.2 art gen sing	2265.2 noun gen sing masc	1706.1 prep	1115.5 noun dat pl neu	1779.1 verb nom sing fem part perf pass
τοῦ	θανάτου	ἐν	γράμμασιν,	ἐντετυπωμένη
tou	thanatou	en	grammasin	entetupōmenē
of the	death	in	letters,	having been engraven

3:4,5. Paul could say what he did because of the confidence given him through Christ. His was not self-confidence or arrogance. He claimed nothing for himself—all was God. His confidence would endure in the sight of God. His trust was not in his own ability to think out something: "as (if) of ourselves." It was God who made Paul and his companions adequate for any task. One of the great Old Testament titles for God was *El Shaddai*, sometimes interpreted to mean "The All-Sufficient One." It was the All-Sufficient One who made Paul more than adequate for his work as a minister of the gospel. With these words the apostle answers his question of 2:16, "And who is sufficient for these things?"

Paul's theology here is the same as that expressed by Peter in his exhortation to those who serve in the church. He wrote, "If any man minister, let him do it as of the ability which God giveth" (1 Peter 4:11). He recognized one could serve with human talents in such a way as to draw attention to self. Thus the reason he gave for his instruction was "that God in all things may be glorified through Jesus Christ: to whom be praise and dominion for ever and ever."

3:6. The verb "hath made . . . able" is from the same word as "sufficient" in verse 5. Paul and his companions had been made able ministers of the new covenant. This new covenant is spoken of as early as Jeremiah 31:31. God's *diathēkēs* ("decree" or "covenant") which He directed toward Christians is described as *kainēs* ("new," Ezekiel 11:19; 36:26). Some feel the prophecy in Ezekiel 36:26 was fulfilled in the outpouring of the Holy Spirit on the Day of Pentecost and in the apostolic proclamation of the gospel which followed.

The letter of the Law which causes men to die (Romans 7:9-11) is contrasted with the life-giving Spirit (John 6:63). Note in this passage (3:3-6) it is not stone *but* flesh, not letter *but* Spirit, not external *but* internal, not Law *but* grace.

3:7. These verses continue the contrast made between the letter and the Spirit. Paul was careful not to leave the impression that the Law was bad (Romans 7:7) or against the promises of God (Galatians 3:21). It was not designed to kill, but to bring believers to Christ (Galatians 3:24). The greatness of the glory of the old covenant is described in such a way that the glory of the new covenant appears more striking in contrast.

Beginning with these lines the apostle addressed still another charge against him. His critics apparently claimed he despised or at least neglected the Law in his preaching. But how could he? The messages of both the Law and grace came from God; therefore both are good. The brilliance in the teachings of Moses dims in the presence of the truths of the gospel, as the light of the moon dims when the sun rises. One does not despise the moon when there is

4. And such trust have we through Christ to God-ward: This is the sort of confidence, *SEB* . . . Such is the confidence, *Weymouth* . . . Such is the assurance I have, *Confraternity* . . . we have this great confidence, *Fenton* . . . such confidence have we through the Christ, *Hanson*.

5. Not that we are sufficient of ourselves to think any thing as of ourselves: . . . not because we possess self-sufficiency, *Berkeley* . . . not that we are personally qualified, *HistNT* . . . not that we are competent, *Concordant* . . . that we could accomplish anything by ourselves, *Adams* . . . by our own reasonings, *Weymouth*.

but our sufficiency [is] of God: . . . but our competency, *Campbell* . . . our capacity is, *Fenton* . . . but God gives us our ability, *Beck* . . . Our ability is of God, *Klingensmith* . . . but our qualification is from God, *Hanson, HistNT* . . . has its source in God, *Wuest*.

6. Who also hath made us able ministers of the new testament: Who also qualified us, *Worrell* . . . makes us competent administrators, *Phillips* . . . competent to serve, *Weymouth* . . . sufficient to be ministrants, *Young* . . . sufficient as ministers, *Alford* . . . efficient ministers, *PNT* . . . dispensers of a new covenant, *Concordant* . . . of a new institution, *Campbell* . . . of a New Settlement, *Fenton* . . . of a New Way of Worship, *NLT*.

not of the letter, but of the spirit: . . . but a spiritual principle, *TCNT*.

for the letter killeth, but the spirit giveth life: . . . for the letter slays, *Rotherham* . . . for the writing kills, *Sawyer* . . . the written law puts to death, *HistNT* . . . for the letter destroys, but the Spirit restores to life, *Fenton* . . . the spirit makes the dead to live, *Conybeare* . . . doth make alive, *Young*.

7. But if the ministration of death: Now, if the dispensation of death, *Wilson, Concordant* . . . served to bring death penalties, *Norlie*.

2 Corinthians 3:8

7.a.Txt: 01ℵ-corr
06D-corr,018K,020L
byz.
Var: 01ℵ-org,02A,03B
04C,06D-org,025P,33
Lach,Treg,Alf,Word
Tisc,We/Ho,Weis,Sod
UBS/✱

1706.1 prep	3012.7 noun dat pl masc	1090.32 verb 3sing indic aor pass	1706.1 prep	1385.3 noun dat sing fem	5452.1 conj
[a ἐν ⟩	λίθοις,	ἐγενήθη	ἐν	δόξῃ,	ὥστε
en	lithois	egenēthē	en	doxē	hōste
in	stones,	was produced	with	glory,	so as

3231.1 partic	1404.22 verb inf pres	810.6 verb inf aor act	3450.8 art acc pl masc	5048.9 noun acc pl masc	2447.1 name masc
μὴ	δύνασθαι	ἀτενίσαι	τοὺς	υἱοὺς	Ἰσραὴλ
mē	dunasthai	atenisai	tous	huious	Israēl
not	to be able	to look intently	the	children	of Israel

1519.1 prep	3450.16 art sing neu	4241.1 noun sing neu	3337.2 name gen masc	3338.2 name gen masc
εἰς	τὸ	πρόσωπον	ʽΜωσέως,	[✱ Μωϋσέως]
eis	to	prosōpon	Mōseōs	Mouseōs
into	to the	face	of Moses,	[idem]

1217.2 prep	3450.12 art acc sing fem	1385.4 noun acc sing fem	3450.2 art gen sing	4241.2 noun gen sing neu	840.3 prs-pron gen sing
διὰ	τὴν	δόξαν	τοῦ	προσώπου	αὐτοῦ,
dia	tēn	doxan	tou	prosōpou	autou
on account of	the	glory	of the	face	his,

3450.12 art acc sing fem	2643.11 verb acc sing fem part pres pass	4316.1 adv	3644.1 adv	3095.1 adv comp	3450.9 art nom sing fem
τὴν	καταργουμένην·	8. πῶς	οὐχὶ	μᾶλλον	ἡ
tēn	katargoumenēn	pōs	ouchi	mallon	hē
the	being nullified;	how	not	rather	the

1242.1 noun nom sing fem	3450.2 art gen sing	4011.2 noun gen sing neu	1498.40 verb 3sing indic fut mid	1706.1 prep	1385.3 noun dat sing fem
διακονία	τοῦ	πνεύματος	ἔσται	ἐν	δόξῃ;
diakonia	tou	pneumatos	estai	en	doxē
service	of the	Spirit	shall be	in	glory?

9.a.Txt: 03B,06D-corr2
bo.byz.
Var: p46,01ℵ,02A,04C
06D-org,010F,012G,044
0243,33,104,326,630
1175,1739,bo.UBS/✱

1479.1 conj	1056.1 conj	3450.9 art nom sing fem	1242.1 noun nom sing fem	3450.11 art dat sing fem	1242.1 noun nom sing fem
9. εἰ	γὰρ	ʽ ἡ	διακονία	[a✱ τῃ	διακονίᾳ]
ei	gar	hē	diakonia	tē	diakonia
If	for	the	service	[by the	service]

3450.10 art gen sing fem	2603.1 noun gen sing fem	1385.1 noun nom sing fem	4044.3 adj dat sing	3095.1 adv comp
τῆς	κατακρίσεως	δόξα,	πολλῷ	μᾶλλον
tēs	katakriseōs	doxa	pollō	mallon
of the	condemnation	glory,	much	rather

9.b.Txt: 01ℵ-corr,06D
018K,020L,025P,byz.it.
Sod
Var: 01ℵ-org,02A,03B
04C,33,Lach,Treg,Alf
Tisc,We/Ho,Weis
UBS/✱

3915.2 verb 3sing indic pres act	3450.9 art nom sing fem	1242.1 noun nom sing fem	3450.10 art gen sing fem	1336.2 noun gen sing fem
περισσεύει	ἡ	διακονία	τῆς	δικαιοσύνης
perisseuei	hē	diakonia	tēs	dikaiosunēs
abounds	the	service	of the	righteousness

10.a.Txt: Steph
Var: 01ℵ,02A,03B,04C
06D,018K,020L,025P
byz.Gries,Lach,Treg,Alf
Word,Tisc,We/Ho,Weis
Sod,UBS/✱

1706.1 prep	1385.3 noun dat sing fem	2504.1 conj	1056.1 conj	3624.1 adv	3620.3 partic
[b ἐν ⟩	δόξῃ.	10. καὶ	γὰρ	ʽ οὐδὲ	[a✱ οὐ]
en	doxē	kai	gar	oude	ou
in	glory.	Even	for	neither	[not]

1386.26 verb 3sing indic perf pass	3450.16 art sing neu	1386.28 verb nom sing neu part perf pass	1706.1 prep
δεδόξασται	τὸ	δεδοξασμένον	ἐν
dedoxastai	to	dedoxasmenon	en
has been made glorious	to the	having been made glorious	in

no sun. Nor does he depise the light of the lowly lamp he burns to illuminate his room when he has neither sun nor moon.

The Greek *kainēs* in verse 6 is used to describe the "new" covenant everywhere in the New Testament except Hebrews 12:24. In Hebrews 12:24 the word is *neos*. This latter word refers to "what is new and distinctive." *Kainos* suggests a difference in nature and it is this difference Paul sought to emphasize.

In the New Testament the Law is represented in Moses (cf. Jesus' words in Luke 16:29, "They have Moses . . . ," also Luke 24:27, "and beginning at Moses . . . "). Moses was called the minister of an external covenant that produced death because of the condemnation under which offenders were placed. Paul referred back to the giving of the Law on Sinai. The accompanying circumstances then were so glorious that when Moses came down from the mount his face reflected the very glory of God. The Israelites could not "look intently" (NASB) at Moses' face.

3:8. We are not told how long Moses' face shone. The implications are that it was outward and transient in contrast with the "ministration of the spirit" which is internal and lasting. This contrast is strengthened by the grammatical form of the negative. Rather than simply *ou* ("not"), it is *ouchi mallon*, "not to a greater degree."

More understanding comes regarding Paul's comparison between the blessings of the Law and grace by considering his statements of like nature in addressing the Romans. He used *mallon* repeatedly there to contrast the death that came to man through the first Adam and the life he may have through the second Adam, Jesus. As real as the death is that comes to all through Adam, the apostle declared the life Jesus provides is "much more" (*pollō mallon*) available to all who believe (verse 9). Thus the "rather more glorious" here becomes the "much more" of Romans.

3:9. Notice again the antitheses. The Law ministers death, but to a greater degree the Spirit ministers life. The Law ministers condemnation, but to a *much* greater degree (*pollō mallon*) the Spirit ministers righteousness. The old order faded away. The Holy Spirit is working in the new order to bring about what the old order could not do because of the weakness of the flesh (Romans 8:3). In this area the righteousness (*dikaiosunēs*) bestowed by God closely approximates salvation. Keeping the Law could never produce *dikaiosunēs*.

3:10. Mount Sinai was a scene of awesome glory. However, it was nothing in comparison to the glory of Mount Calvary. When Moses came down from Sinai after receiving the Ten Commandments, his face shone with God's glory. But this glory faded and

written [and] engraven in stones, was glorious: . . . was brought into existence in glory, *Rotherham* . . . came with glory, *Weymouth, Worrell* . . . was inaugurated with glory, *PNT* . . . accompanied with such splendour, *HistNT* . . . came with a blaze of glory, *NTPE*.

so that the children of Israel could not stedfastly behold the face of Moses for the glory of his countenance: . . . the sons of Israel could not continue looking at, *SEB* . . . could not gaze steadily on, *Montgomery* . . . could not stare at, *Klingensmith* . . . to look unflinchingly at, *Phillips* . . . on account of the brightness, *Sawyer* . . . because of the brightness of his face—a vanishing brightness, *Weymouth* . . . the transient glory that shone upon it, *Confraternity* . . . due to his facial brilliance, *Berkeley*.

which [glory] was to be done away: . . . a glory even then fading, *Montgomery* . . . a splendour that was waning, *HistNT* . . . which was being nullified, *Concordant* . . . its brightness, fading as this was, *RSV* . . . even though transitory, *Phillips* . . . was soon to fade, *Conybeare*.

8. How shall not the ministration of the spirit be rather glorious?: But how much more glorious will be the ministry of the Spirit? *SEB* . . . be more luminous? *RPNT* . . . be still more glorious, *Murdock*.

9. For if the ministration of condemnation [be] glory: . . . that announces doom, *Berkeley* . . . which pronounces doom had glory, *Weymouth*.

much more doth the ministration of righteousness exceed in glory: . . . how much greater and more glorious, *Norlie* . . . far more is the religion that sets men right with God rich in splendor, *TCNT* . . . the dispensation of righteousness, *Concordant* . . . radiant in glory, *Montgomery* . . . exceed in splendour, *Fenton*.

10. For even that which was made glorious had no glory in this respect: . . . once resplendent in glory, *Weymouth*.

2 Corinthians 3:11

10.b.Txt: 04C,018K
020L,byz.
Var: 01א,02A,03B,06D
025P,Lach,Treg,Alf
Tisc,We/Ho,Weis,Sod
UBS/✶

3642.5 dem-pron dat sing masc	3450.3 art dat sing	3183.3 noun dat sing neu	1736.2 prep	1736.1 prep
τούτῳ	τῷ	μέρει,	῝ ἕνεκεν	[b✶ εἵνεκεν]
toutō	tō	merei	heneken	heineken
this	the	respect,	on account of	[idem]

3450.10 art gen sing fem	5072.2 verb gen sing fem part pres act	1385.2 noun gen sing fem	1479.1 conj	1056.1 conj	3450.16 art sing neu
τῆς	ὑπερβαλλούσης	δόξης.	11. εἰ	γὰρ	τὸ
tēs	huperballousēs	doxēs	ei	gar	to
the	surpassing	glory.	If	for	the

2643.12 verb nom sing neu part pres pass	1217.2 prep	1385.2 noun gen sing fem	4044.3 adj dat sing	3095.1 adv comp	3450.16 art sing neu
καταργούμενον	διὰ	δόξης,	πολλῷ	μᾶλλον	τὸ
katargoumenon	dia	doxēs	pollō	mallon	to
being nullified	through	glory,	much	rather	the

3176.14 verb sing neu part pres act	1706.1 prep	1385.3 noun dat sing fem	2174.19 verb nom pl masc part pres act	3631.1 conj	4955.10 dem- pron acc sing fem
μένον	ἐν	δόξῃ.	12. Ἔχοντες	οὖν	τοιαύτην
menon	en	doxē	Echontes	oun	toiautēn
remaining	in	glory.	Having	therefore	such

1667.4 noun acc sing fem	4044.11 adj dat sing fem	3816.3 noun dat sing fem	5366.1 verb 1pl indic pres	2504.1 conj	3620.3 partic
ἐλπίδα,	πολλῇ	παῤῥησίᾳ	χρώμεθα·	13. καὶ	οὐ
elpida	pollē	parrhēsia	chrōmetha	kai	ou
hope,	much	boldness	we use:	and	not

2481.1 conj	3337.1 name nom masc	3338.1 name nom masc	4935.24 verb 3sing indic imperf act	2542.1 noun sing neu
καθάπερ	῝ Μωσῆς	[✶ Μωϋσῆς]	ἐτίθει	κάλυμμα
kathaper	Mōsēs	Mōusēs	etithei	kalumma
as	Moses	[idem]	was putting	a veil

13.a.Txt: 01א,06D,018K
byz.Tisc
Var: 02A,03B,04C,020L
025P,33,Lach,Treg,Alf
Word,We/Ho,Weis,Sod
UBS/✶

1894.3 prep	3450.16 art sing neu	4241.1 noun sing neu	1431.4 prs- pron gen 3sing	840.3 prs- pron gen sing	4242.1 prep
ἐπὶ	τὸ	πρόσωπον	῝ ἑαυτοῦ,	[a✶ αὐτοῦ,]	πρὸς
epi	to	prosōpon	heautou	autou	pros
on	the	face	of himself,	[his,]	for

3450.16 art sing neu	3231.1 partic	810.6 verb inf aor act	3450.8 art acc pl masc	5048.9 noun acc pl masc	2447.1 name masc
τὸ	μὴ	ἀτενίσαι	τοὺς	υἱοὺς	Ἰσραὴλ
to	mē	atenisai	tous	huious	Israēl
the	not	to look intently	the	sons	of Israel

1519.1 prep	3450.16 art sing neu	4904.1 noun sing neu	3450.2 art gen sing	2643.13 verb gen sing neu part pres pass	233.1 conj
εἰς	τὸ	τέλος	τοῦ	καταργουμένου·	14. ῝ ἀλλ'
eis	to	telos	tou	katargoumenou	all'
to	the	end	of the	being nullified.	But

233.2 conj	4313.2 verb 3sing indic aor pass	3450.17 art pl neu	3402.2 noun pl neu	840.1 prs- pron gen pl
[✶ ἀλλὰ]	ἐπωρώθη	τὰ	νοήματα	αὐτῶν.
alla	epōrōthē	ta	noēmata	autōn
[idem]	were hardened	the	thoughts	their,

14.a.Var: 01א,02A,03B
04C,06D,025P,it.bo.
Lach,Treg,Alf,Word
Tisc,We/Ho,Weis,Sod
UBS/✶

884.2 conj	1056.1 conj	3450.10 art gen sing fem	4449.1 adv	2232.1 noun fem	3450.16 art sing neu
ἄχρι	γὰρ	τῆς	σήμερον	[a✶+ ἡμέρας]	τὸ
achri	gar	tēs	sēmeron	hēmeras	to
unto	for	the	present	[day]	the

later Moses died. The glory ministered by the Spirit will never fade. Christ is alive and Christians are "changed into the same image from glory to glory" (3:18).

3:11. Verses 7-11 assert three conclusions which use the comparative degree. The comparative is sometimes strengthened by the use of *mallon*, meaning here "very far better." This is *bad* English, but *good* Greek. Verses 7 and 8 conclude that if the dispensation of the Law which ministered death was attended by glory, then now to a *greater degree* is life ministered by the Spirit.

The second conclusion is similar. The Corinthians knew how glorious the ministry of Moses was. But if the ministry of Moses that brought condemnation was glorious, it is exceeded in glory to a *much greater degree* by the righteousness God provided.

The third conclusion is almost identical with that in verse 9. For if the old covenant existed with a genuine glory even though it was transitory, then now to a *much greater degree* there is the glory of the new covenant which is permanent.

3:12. Paul expressed his confidence in the abiding permanence of the gospel message. On this the Christian's hope is based, and in this hope there is no element of uncertainty. Several commentators connect this hope (*elpida*) with the gift of the Holy Spirit and all that results from it.

Paul's confidence was grounded in the abiding glory of the new covenant. Because of this he used *parrhēsia* ("boldness"). This Greek word was used in the political sphere, and some of the shades of meaning persist in later Christian usage. Some of these are the right to say anything and the truth of what is said. There is also the interesting idea that such freedom of speech may be opposed by those to whom it may apply. However, in the face of such opposition *parrhēsia* is the candor that opposes any who would hamper or limit the unveiling of the truth.

3:13. The use of *parrhēsia* implied a face that was uncovered before men. The contrast here is between the openness brought in by the new covenant and the transitory character of the Mosaic dispensation. The glory on the face of Moses was real, so bright Moses had to cover his face (Exodus 34:29-35). But it was also a glory that would fade away.

3:14. The vacillating conduct of the Israelites in the Old Testament revealed that they did not understand the ministry of Moses. Their minds became dull and callous. They were unable, perhaps even unwilling, to understand. The situation had not changed in Paul's day. The Jews still failed to recognize the transitory character of the Law: that it was only a schoolmaster to bring them to Christ

by reason of the glory that excelleth: . . . on account of the surpassing glory, *Rotherham* . . . the glory which surpasses it, *Weymouth* . . . because of the superior glory, *Young.*

11. For if that which is done away [was] glorious: If what passed away, *Berkeley* . . . which was fading away, *Montgomery.*
much more that which remaineth [is] glorious: . . . that which is permanent, *Beck* . . . the present permanent plan, *Phillips* . . . which abides, *Confraternity, Berkeley* . . . will exist in much greater magnificence, *Fenton.*

12. Seeing then that we have such hope: Having, then, such an expectation, *Concordant.*
we use great plainness of speech: I speak and act without disguise, *Conybeare* . . . we use much freedom, *Young* . . . great openness of speech, *Rotherham* . . . we speak quite unreservedly, *Berkeley* . . . we can be very bold, *Adams.*

13. And not as Moses, [which] put a veil over his face: . . . we do not imitate Moses, *Weymouth.*
that the children of Israel could not stedfastly look to the end of that which is abolished: . . . to prevent the Israelites gazing at the disappearance of what was passing away, *TCNT* . . . were not to look intently, *Concordant* . . . could not stare at, *Klingensmith* . . . might not observe the glory of his countenance, *Confraternity* . . . until the final fading of the glory, *Adams* . . . the last rays of the fading glory, *Beck* . . . until the brightness faded away, *SEB.*

14. But their minds were blinded: But their conceptions, *Rotherham* . . . their senses, *Douay* . . . their apprehensions were calloused, *Concordant* . . . their minds had become dense, *TCNT* . . . were hardened, *Young, NASB* . . . were dulled, *Berkeley* . . . were made dull, *Weymouth, Montgomery* . . . it dimmed their thoughts, *Fenton.*

2 Corinthians 3:15

840.15 prs-pron sing neu	2542.1 noun sing neu	1894.3 prep	3450.11 art dat sing fem	318.1 noun dat sing fem	3450.10 art gen sing fem
αὐτὸ	κάλυμμα	ἐπὶ	τῇ	ἀναγνώσει	τῆς
auto	kalumma	epi	tē	anagnōsei	tēs
same	veil	at	the	reading	of the

3683.5 adj gen sing fem	1236.2 noun gen sing fem	3176.1 verb 3sing indic act	3231.1 partic	341.1 verb nom sing neu part pres pass
παλαιᾶς	διαθήκης	μένει,	μὴ	ἀνακαλυπτόμενον,
palaias	diathēkēs	menei	mē	anakaluptomenon
old	covenant	remains,	not	uncovered,

3614.16 rel-pron sing neu	4948.10 indef-pron sing neu	3617.1 conj	1706.1 prep	5382.3 name dat masc	2643.9 verb 3sing indic pres pass
ὃ	τι	[✶ ὅτι]	ἐν	Χριστῷ	καταργεῖται·
ho	ti	hoti	en	Christō	katargeitai
which	some	[that]	in	Christ	is being nullified.

233.1 conj	2175.1 conj	4449.1 adv	2237.1 conj	312.13 verb 3sing indic pres mid
15. ἀλλ'	ἕως	σήμερον,	ἡνίκα	ἀναγινώσκεται
all'	heōs	sēmeron	hēnika	anaginōsketai
But	unto	this day,	when	is being read

312.19 verb 3sing subj pres pass	3337.1 name nom masc	3338.1 name nom masc	2542.1 noun sing neu
[ᵃ✶ ἀναγινώσκηται]	Μωσῆς	[✶ Μωϋσῆς]	κάλυμμα
anaginōskētai	Mōsēs	Mōusēs	kalumma
[idem]	Moses,	[idem]	a veil

15.a.Txt: 018K,020L,byz.
Var: 01א,02A,03B,04C
Lach,Treg,Alf,Tisc
We/Ho,Weis,Sod
UBS/✶

1894.3 prep	3450.12 art acc sing fem	2559.4 noun acc sing fem	840.1 prs-pron gen pl	2719.2 verb 3sing indic pres	2237.1 conj
ἐπὶ	τὴν	καρδίαν	αὐτῶν	κεῖται·	16. ἡνίκα
epi	tēn	kardian	autōn	keitai	hēnika
upon	the	heart	their	lies.	When

16.a.Txt: 01א-corr,03B
06D,018K,020L,025P
byz.Weis,Sod
Var: 01א-org,02A,Tisc
We/Ho,UBS/✶

1156.1 conj	300.1 partic	1156.2 conj	1430.1 partic	1978.7 verb 3sing subj aor act	4242.1 prep
δ'	ἂν	[ᵃ✶ δὲ	ἐὰν]	ἐπιστρέψῃ	πρὸς
d'	an	de	ean	epistrepsē	pros
but	an	[but	if]	it shall have turned	to

2935.4 noun acc sing masc	3877.3 verb 3sing indic pres pass	3450.16 art sing neu	2542.1 noun sing neu	3450.5 art sing masc
κύριον,	περιαιρεῖται	τὸ	κάλυμμα.	17. Ὁ
kurion	periaireitai	to	kalumma	Ho
Lord,	is being taken away	the	veil.	The

1156.2 conj	2935.1 noun nom sing masc	3450.16 art sing neu	4011.1 noun sing neu	1498.4 verb 3sing indic pres act	3619.1 adv
δὲ	κύριος	τὸ	πνεῦμά	ἐστιν·	οὗ
de	kurios	to	pneuma	estin	hou
now	Lord	the	Spirit	is;	where

17.a.Txt: 01א-corr
06D-corr,018K,020L
025P,byz.sa.
Var: p46,01א-org,02A
03B,04C,06D-org,33,bo.
Lach,Treg,Alf,Word
Tisc,We/Ho,Weis,Sod
UBS/✶

1156.2 conj	3450.16 art sing neu	4011.1 noun sing neu	2935.2 noun gen sing masc	1550.1 adv	1644.1 noun nom sing fem
δὲ	τὸ	πνεῦμα	κυρίου,	[ᵃ ἐκεῖ]	ἐλευθερία.
de	to	pneuma	kuriou	ekei	eleutheria
and	the	Spirit	of Lord,	there	freedom.

2231.1 prs-pron nom 1pl	1156.2 conj	3820.7 adj pl masc	341.2 verb dat sing neu part perf pass	4241.3 noun dat sing neu
18. ἡμεῖς	δὲ	πάντες	ἀνακεκαλυμμένῳ	προσώπῳ
hēmeis	de	pantes	anakekalummenō	prosōpō
We	but	all	having been uncovered	face

(Galatians 3:24). It is only through Christ that the veil is removed. Only through Him could the Jews and all others really understand the true meaning of the Law and the gospel.

3:15. Those of Paul's day still could not see the glory of God in His Word. The Judaizers at Corinth pointed people back to the Law, taking care to always read publicly "Moses." The name of the writer stood not only for his writings but also included all the Old Testament. Abraham said to the rich man, "They have Moses and the prophets; let them hear them" (Luke 16:29). The most complete title for the Old Testament was "Moses, . . . the prophets, and . . . the psalms" (Luke 24:44).

As Moses descended the mount, of necessity he covered his face. Israel could not stand to look upon the glory of the Lord reflected on his countenance (3:7). Even in Paul's day the veil of unbelief concealed the truth from their minds. The fault did not lie with the Law (Romans 7:7), but with its readers.

3:16. Instead of returning to the Law, Israel needed to turn back to the Lord. Then He would take away (remove) the veil just as Moses did when he returned to the mountain to commune with Jehovah (Exodus 34:34). With the covering removed, they could see Christ as the theme of the Word.

The teachers of Saul of Tarsus interpreted Scripture in such a way as to keep him from seeing the truth until he met Jesus near Damascus. However, Paul's conversion experience quickly removed the veil, and he saw the Messiah in the passage, much as the Ethiopian eunuch had (Acts 8:32-35).

3:17. Like Jesus, Paul declared God is Spirit (John 4:24). Indeed, He is Father, Son, and Spirit. Those who worship Him must worship in the Spirit and according to truth. The illumination of the Spirit makes alive the truth of Scripture. The Spirit enables one to find liberty instead of bondage as he reads the Bible. The sincere Israelite discovers freedom from slavery to the ritual of the Law.

However, this liberty is not license to sin, as Paul made clear in addressing the Galatians. He explained, "For, brethren, ye have been called unto liberty; only use not liberty for an occasion to the flesh" (Galatians 5:13). Proctor expressed a similar sentiment in commenting on liberty in 3:17. He said it consists in the fact that "the consciousness of the restraining and condemning nature of the law is taken away. Christians no longer desire to break the law; they are imbued with the spirit of the law" (*The New Bible Commentary*, p.992).

3:18. The face of the Christian is open, unveiled. He beholds (contemplates) the glory of the Lord which he sees as if looking in

for until this day remaineth the same veil: . . . the same veil remaineth unremoved, *Wesley* . . . the same covering remains, *Wuest* . . . remains unmoved, *Fenton*.

untaken away in the reading of the old testament: . . . when they read in their synagogues the ancient covenant, *Conybeare* . . . when the old contract is read, *Klingensmith* . . . during the reading of the book of the ancient Covenant, the same veil remains unlifted, *Weymouth*.

which [veil] is done away in Christ: . . . because it is removed in Christ, *NASB* . . . it is only removed by Christ, *Fenton*.

15. But even unto this day, when Moses is read:
the veil is upon their heart: . . . a covering is lying on their heart, *Concordant* . . . a veil over their minds, *Phillips*.

16. Nevertheless when it shall turn to the Lord, the veil shall be taken away: Yet if they "turned to the Lord," *Phillips* . . . when they shall be converted, *Douay* . . . the veil is rent away, *Conybeare* . . . is stripped away, *Montgomery* . . . is removed, *Williams* . . . will be withdrawn, *Weymouth*.

17. Now the Lord is that Spirit: This is the God's Spirit at work, *RPNT* . . . By the word 'Lord' is to be understood the Spirit, *TCNT*.
and where the Spirit of the Lord [is], there [is] liberty: . . . there is freedom, *Fenton* . . . freedom is enjoyed, *Weymouth*.

18. But we all, with open face: . . . with unveiled face, *Young*.

2 Corinthians 4:1

3450.12 art acc sing fem τὴν *tēn* the	1385.4 noun acc sing fem δόξαν *doxan* glory	2935.2 noun gen sing masc κυρίου *kuriou* of Lord	2704.1 verb nom pl masc part pres mid κατοπτριζόμενοι, *katoptrizomenoi* beholding as in a mirror,	3450.12 art acc sing fem τὴν *tēn* the
840.12 prs-pron acc sing fem αὐτὴν *autēn* same	1494.4 noun acc sing fem εἰκόνα *eikona* image	3209.1 verb 1pl indic pres pass μεταμορφούμεθα *metamorphoumetha* are being transformed	570.3 prep gen ἀπὸ *apo* from	1385.2 noun gen sing fem δόξης *doxēs* glory
1519.1 prep εἰς *eis* to	1385.4 noun acc sing fem δόξαν, *doxan* glory,	2481.1 conj καθάπερ *kathaper* even as	570.3 prep gen ἀπὸ *apo* from	2935.2 noun gen sing masc κυρίου *kuriou* Lord 4011.2 noun gen sing neu πνεύματος. *pneumatos* Spirit.

1217.2 prep **4:1.** Διὰ *Dia* Because of	3642.17 dem- pron sing neu τοῦτο, *touto* this,	2174.19 verb nom pl masc part pres act ἔχοντες *echontes* having	3450.12 art acc sing fem τὴν *tēn* the	1242.4 noun acc sing fem διακονίαν *diakonian* service
3642.12 dem- pron acc sing fem ταύτην, *tautēn* this,	2503.1 conj καθὼς *kathōs* according as	1640.13 verb 1pl indic aor pass ἠλεήθημεν, *ēleēthēmen* we received mercy,	3620.2 partic οὐκ *ouk* not	1560.1 verb 1pl indic pres act ʿ ἐκκακοῦμενˑ *ekkakoumen* we faint.

1.a.Txt: 04C,06D-corr
018K,020L,025P,byz.
Var: 01ℵ,02A,03B
06D-org,33,Lach,Treg
Alf,Word,Tisc,We/Ho
Weis,Sod,UBS/✩

	1450.5 verb 2pl aor act [ᵃ✩ ἐγκακοῦμεν,] *enkakoumen* [idem]	233.1 conj **2.** ʿ ἀλλ᾽ *all'* But	233.2 conj [✩ ἀλλὰ] *alla* [idem]	546.1 verb 1pl indic aor mid ἀπειπάμεθα *apeipametha* we renounced
3450.17 art pl neu τὰ *ta* the	2899.4 adj pl neu κρυπτὰ *krupta* hidden things	3450.10 art gen sing fem τῆς *tēs* of the	151.2 noun gen sing fem αἰσχύνης, *aischunēs* shame,	3231.1 partic μὴ *mē* not 3906.15 verb nom pl masc part pres act περιπατοῦντες *peripatountes* walking
1706.1 prep ἐν *en* in	3696.1 noun dat sing fem πανουργίᾳ *panourgia* craftiness,	3234.1 adv μηδὲ *mēde* nor	1383.1 verb nom pl masc part pres act δολοῦντες *dolountes* falsifying	3450.6 art acc sing masc τὸν *ton* the 3030.4 noun acc sing masc λόγον *logon* word
3450.2 art gen sing τοῦ *tou*	2296.2 noun gen sing masc θεοῦ, *theou* of God,	233.2 conj ἀλλὰ *alla* but	3450.11 art dat sing fem τῇ *tē* by the	5158.2 noun dat sing fem φανερώσει *phanerōsei* manifestation 3450.10 art gen sing fem τῆς *tēs* of the

2.a.Txt: 06D-corr,018K
020L,byz.
Var: 02A,03B,025P
We/Ho,Weis,Sod
UBS/✩

223.2 noun gen sing fem ἀληθείας *alētheias* truth	4771.5 verb nom pl masc part pres act ʿ συνιστῶντες *sunistōntes* commending	4771.16 verb nom pl masc part pres act [ᵃ✩ συνιστάνοντες] *sunistanontes* [idem]		1431.8 prs-pron acc pl masc ἑαυτοὺς *heautous* ourselves
4242.1 prep πρὸς *pros* to	3820.12 adj acc sing fem πᾶσαν *pasan* every	4743.4 noun acc sing fem συνείδησιν *suneidēsin* conscience	442.7 noun gen pl masc ἀνθρώπων *anthrōpōn* of men	1783.1 prep gen ἐνώπιον *enōpion* before 3450.2 art gen sing τοῦ *tou*

a mirror. Like mirrors of polished brass in Paul's day, the Bible offers the reader an image of Jesus.

As the believer contemplates Jesus through prayer and the reading of the Word, the Spirit of the Lord changes (Greek, *metamorphoumetha*, cf. English, *metamorphosis*) him into the likeness and appearance he beholds. He is transformed (Romans 12:2 where the same Greek verb appears) into that image from one glorious level to another. The complete likeness to Jesus will come when he sees Him face-to-face (1 John 3:2).

4:1. God put Paul in the ministry. He did not choose it for himself. He always considered he received that honor as an act of mercy and grace (1 Timothy 1:12,13).

His ministry offered life for death (3:7f.), justification for condemnation (3:9), and something permanent for the temporary (3:11). The Law, given by Moses, provided far less. Accordingly, the apostle stood strong in the face of opposition at Corinth. He did not lose heart.

4:2. The false teachers in the church at Corinth had stooped to low levels in their efforts to discredit Paul's ministry. All that they practiced he had renounced. These included hidden, secret, shameful things. He detested the basic dishonesty which motivated them. The craftiness (*panourgia*, literally, "readiness to do anything without scruples") they used was a stench in his nostrils. Paul's critics even handled the Word of God deceitfully, in a distorted manner. They adulterated it, as the wine seller of the day who weakened his merchandise by diluting it with water.

By contrast, Paul openly proclaimed the truth of the gospel. He stated its concepts plainly with no intent or attempt to deceive or trick anyone.

Paul's ministerial critics who sought to draw disciples to themselves acted as if the end justifies the means. He simply relied on the manifestation of the truth to accomplish the task. He used nothing deceptive nor secretive. As he explained in his defense before Agrippa, "This thing was not done in a corner" (Acts 26:26).

Sincere ministers of the gospel have nothing to hide. They preach no esoteric truths understood only by the initiated, as Paul's Gnostic enemies claimed. When the high priest asked Jesus of His teaching as if it were secretive, He replied, "I spake openly to the world; I ever taught in the synagogue, and in the temple, whither the Jews always resort; and in secret have I said nothing" (John 18:20).

The apostle needed to do no more to recommend himself to those of a sincere conscience. Certainly such ministerial conduct left him acceptable (commendable in the sight of, before the presence of) to God.

beholding as in a glass the glory of the Lord: . . . reflecting as in a mirror, *Confraternity* . . . reflecting the glory, *Rotherham.*
are changed into the same image from glory to glory: . . . are being transformed, *Young* . . . will be transformed into the same resemblance, *Fenton* . . . the same likeness, *Weymouth* . . . from one degree of glory to another, *Wuest.*
[even] as by the Spirit of the Lord:

1. Therefore seeing we have this ministry: For this cause, *Alford* . . . Discharging therefore this ministry, *Confraternity* . . . being engaged in this service, *Weymouth* . . . having this service, *Fenton.*
as we have received mercy:
we faint not: I never give up, *Williams* . . . we do not get discouraged, *PNT* . . . we shrink not back, *Alford.*

2. But have renounced the hidden things of dishonesty: . . . we have repudiated, *Hanson* . . . put a ban on secret and disgraceful methods, *Norlie* . . . We use no hocus-pocus, *Phillips* . . . the secrecy which marks a feeling of shame, *Weymouth* . . . the hidden things of shame, *ASV* . . . the secret dealings of shame, *Fenton.*
not walking in craftiness: . . . no clever tricks, *Phillips* . . . not wandering in villainy, *Fenton* . . . we avoid unscrupulous conduct, *Confraternity* . . . the sphere of craftiness, *Wuest.*
nor handling the word of God deceitfully: . . . no dishonest manipulation, *Phillips* . . . nor yet counterfeiting, *Rotherham* . . . nor falsifying the word of God, *Hanson.*
but by manifestation of the truth: But, by an open statement of the truth, *Norlie* . . . but with openness of the truth, *Fenton.*
commending ourselves to every man's conscience in the sight of God: . . . in presence of God, *Rotherham.*

2 Corinthians 4:3

2296.2 noun gen sing masc	1479.1 conj	1156.2 conj	2504.1 conj	1498.4 verb 3sing indic pres act	2543.5 verb nom sing neu part perf pass
θεοῦ.	3. εἰ	δὲ	καὶ	ἔστιν	κεκαλυμμένον
theou	ei	de	kai	estin	kekalummenon
God.	If	but	also	is	having been covered

3450.16 art sing neu	2077.1 noun sing neu	2231.2 prs- pron gen 1pl	1706.1 prep	3450.4 art pl masc	616.19 verb dat pl masc part pres
τὸ	εὐαγγέλιον	ἡμῶν,	ἐν	τοῖς	ἀπολλυμένοις
to	euangelion	hēmōn	en	tois	apollumenois
the	good news	our,	in	the	perishing

1498.4 verb 3sing indic pres act	2543.5 verb nom sing neu part perf pass	1706.1 prep	3614.4 rel- pron dat pl	3450.5 art sing masc
ἐστὶν	κεκαλυμμένον·	4. ἐν	οἷς	ὁ
estin	kekalummenon	en	hois	ho
it is	having been covered;	in	whom	the

2296.1 noun nom sing masc	3450.2 art gen sing	163.1 noun gen sing masc	3642.1 dem- pron gen sing	5027.1 verb 3sing indic aor act	3450.17 art pl neu
θεὸς	τοῦ	αἰῶνος	τούτου	ἐτύφλωσεν	τὰ
theos	tou	aiōnos	toutou	etuphlōsen	ta
god	of the	age	this	blinded	the

3402.2 noun pl neu	3450.1 art gen pl	566.5 adj gen pl masc	1519.1 prep	3450.16 art sing neu	3231.1 partic	820.1 verb inf aor act
νοήματα	τῶν	ἀπίστων,	εἰς	τὸ	μὴ	αὐγάσαι
noēmata	tōn	apistōn	eis	to	mē	augasai
thoughts	of the	unbelieving,	to	the	not	to beam forth

840.2 prs- pron dat pl	3450.6 art acc sing masc	5298.1 noun acc sing masc	3450.2 art gen sing	2077.2 noun gen sing neu
⌐a αὐτοῖς ⌐	τὸν	φωτισμὸν	τοῦ	εὐαγγελίου
autois	ton	phōtismon	tou	euangeliou
to them	the	illumination	of the	good news

3450.10 art gen sing fem	1385.2 noun gen sing fem	3450.2 art gen sing	5382.2 name gen masc	3614.5 rel-pron nom sing masc	1498.4 verb 3sing indic pres act
τῆς	δόξης	τοῦ	Χριστοῦ,	ὅς	ἐστιν
tēs	doxēs	tou	Christou	hos	estin
of the	glory	of the	Christ,	who	is

1494.1 noun nom sing fem	3450.2 art gen sing	2296.2 noun gen sing masc	3620.3 partic	1056.1 conj	1431.8 prs- pron acc pl masc
εἰκὼν	τοῦ	θεοῦ.	5. οὐ	γὰρ	ἑαυτοὺς
eikōn	tou	theou	ou	gar	heautous
image	of the	of God.	Not	for	ourselves

2756.3 verb 1pl indic pres act	233.2 conj	5382.4 name acc masc	2400.3 name acc masc	2935.4 noun acc sing masc	1431.8 prs- pron acc pl masc
κηρύσσομεν,	ἀλλὰ	Χριστὸν	Ἰησοῦν	κύριον·	ἑαυτοὺς
kērussomen	alla	Christon	Iēsoun	kurion	heautous
do we proclaim,	but	Christ	Jesus	Lord,	ourselves

1156.2 conj	1395.9 noun acc pl masc	5050.2 prs- pron gen 2pl	1217.2 prep	2400.3 name acc masc	3617.1 conj
δὲ	δούλους	ὑμῶν	διὰ	Ἰησοῦν.	6. ὅτι
de	doulous	humōn	dia	Iēsoun	hoti
and	slaves	your	for the sake of	Jesus.	Because

3450.5 art sing masc	2296.1 noun nom sing masc	3450.5 art sing masc	1500.15 verb nom sing masc part aor act	1523.2 prep gen	4510.3 noun gen sing neu
ὁ	θεὸς	ὁ	εἰπών	ἐκ	σκότους
ho	theos	ho	eipōn	ek	skotous
	God	the	having spoken	out of	darkness

4:3. Though some of Paul's critics at Corinth accused him otherwise, he exerted every effort to see that men heard the unadulterated truth of the gospel. He was careful that his behavior did not nullify the message he preached. He presented its precepts as clearly as possible. Bold in the process, he wrote, "Seeing then that we have such hope, we use great plainness of speech" (3:12). In spite of this some said Paul's preaching was too difficult for the common person to comprehend. Even Peter declared that in Paul's writings there were "some things hard to be understood" (2 Peter 3:16). However, Paul acknowledged the fact with all due respect, unlike the opposition in Corinth.

In such a setting the apostle explained that any failure to receive his message was not due to any fault of his. If his gospel was hidden (*kekalummenon*, "veiled," from the same root as in 3:18), it was veiled from those who were lost, namely those who were already in a state of perishing.

4:4. The fault was in the fact that Satan, the god of this world (*aiōnos*, "this present age"), had blinded those who refused to accept Paul's message. The adversary is always ready to darken the minds of those who resist the gospel. In his letter to the Ephesians Paul wrote of people who have their understanding darkened through the blindness of their hearts (Ephesians 4:18). However, they could not escape personal responsibility by blaming their sinful state on the devil. The apostle further described them as those "who being past feeling have given themselves over" to a wicked way of life (Ephesians 4:19). They would not see; therefore, they could not see. Willful blindness became penal blindness.

Thus spiritual forces hindered those at Corinth from seeing the light of the gospel. They failed to recognize Jesus as the very image (likeness, exact representation) of God.

4:5. The false apostles at Corinth apparently promoted themselves to a shameful degree. They chose a poor substitute in focusing on their own example rather than that of Jesus. By way of contrast, Paul declared he preached (*kērussomen*, "publicly proclaimed") Christ, not self. Some preached Moses (Acts 15:21); the apostle preached Jesus (1 Corinthians 2:2).

Paul constantly identified himself simply as a servant (*doulos*, a "slave" in contrast to a hired servant) of the Lord and of His people. In his first letter to the Corinthians Paul wrote, "Let a man so account of us, as of the ministers of Christ, and stewards of the mysteries of God" (1 Corinthians 4:1).

4:6. The Lord had done too much for Paul for him to ever stoop to the low level of preaching himself. God had performed a miracle

3. But if our gospel be hid: ... the meaning of our Good News, *Weymouth*.
it is hid to them that are lost:

4. In whom the god of this world hath blinded the minds of them which believe not: ... the God of this aeon, *Hanson* ... blinded the understanding, *Montgomery* ... darkened the thoughts with unbelief, *Fenton* ... their minds have been kept in the dark, *TEV* ... the conceptions of the unbelieving, *Rotherham*.
lest the light of the glorious gospel of Christ, who is the image of God, should shine unto them: ... that they should not see, *Hanson* ... so as to shut out the sunshine, *Weymouth* ... kept from seeing the radiant light, *Norlie* ... to stop them seeing the light shed by the Good News, *JB* ... the illumination of the evangel of the glory of Christ, *Concordant* ... to prevent the illumination of the gospel...from penetrating, *Berkeley* ... should not dawn upon them, *Montgomery* ... Who is the representative of God, *Fenton* ... who is the exact likeness of God, *TEV* ... should not shine forth, *Alford* ... cannot dawn upon them, *NEB* ... from dawning upon them, *Goodspeed*.

5. For we preach not ourselves, but Christ Jesus the Lord: For we have not heralded, *Berkeley* ... For I am not proclaiming myself, *Williams* ... It is not ourselves that we preach, *Barclay* ... is not about ourselves, *BB*.
and ourselves your servants for Jesus' sake: ... your bond-servants, *Noyes*.

6. For God, who commanded the light to shine out of darkness:

2 Corinthians 4:7

6.a.Txt: 01א-corr,04C
06D-corr,018K,020L
025P,byz.Sod
Var: 01א-org,02A,03B
06D-org,Lach,Treg,Alf
Tisc,We/Ho,Weis
UBS/✱

5295.1 noun sing neu	2962.4 verb inf aor act	2962.5 verb 3sing indic fut act	3614.5 rel-pron nom sing masc	2962.2 verb 3sing indic aor act
φῶς	ʽ λάμψαι,	[ᵃ✱ λάμψει,]	ὃς	ἔλαμψεν
phōs	*lampsai*	*lampsei*	*hos*	*elampsen*
light	to shine,	[will shine,]	who	shone

1706.1 prep	3450.14 art dat pl fem	2559.7 noun dat pl fem	2231.2 prs-pron gen 1pl	4242.1 prep	5298.1 noun acc sing masc
ἐν	ταῖς	καρδίαις	ἡμῶν,	πρὸς	φωτισμὸν
en	*tais*	*kardiais*	*hēmōn*	*pros*	*phōtismon*
in	the	hearts	our,	for	illumination

3450.10 art gen sing fem	1102.2 noun gen sing fem	3450.10 art gen sing fem	1385.2 noun gen sing fem	3450.2 art gen sing	2296.2 noun gen sing masc
τῆς	γνώσεως	τῆς	δόξης	τοῦ	θεοῦ
tēs	*gnōseōs*	*tēs*	*doxēs*	*tou*	*theou*
of the	knowledge	of the	glory		of God

6.b.Txt: p46,01א,04C
(06D),015H,018K,020L
025P,byz.bo.Sod
Var: 02A,03B,33,sa.
Lach,Treg,Alf,Tisc
We/Ho,Weis,UBS/✱

1706.1 prep	4241.3 noun dat sing neu	2400.2 name masc	5382.2 name gen masc	2174.5 verb 1pl indic pres act
ἐν	προσώπῳ	ʽᵇ Ἰησοῦ ʾ	Χριστοῦ.	7. Ἔχομεν
en	*prosōpō*	*Iēsou*	*Christou*	*Echomen*
in	face	of Jesus	Christ.	We have

1156.2 conj	3450.6 art acc sing masc	2321.4 noun acc sing masc	3642.6 dem-pron acc sing masc	1706.1 prep	3611.2 adj dat pl neu
δὲ	τὸν	θησαυρὸν	τοῦτον	ἐν	ὀστρακίνοις
de	*ton*	*thēsauron*	*touton*	*en*	*ostrakinois*
but	the	treasure	this	in	earthen

4487.4 noun dat pl neu	2419.1 conj	3450.9 art nom sing fem	5073.1 noun nom sing fem	3450.10 art gen sing fem	1405.2 noun gen sing fem
σκεύεσιν,	ἵνα	ἡ	ὑπερβολὴ	τῆς	δυνάμεως
skeuesin	*hina*	*hē*	*huperbolē*	*tēs*	*dunameōs*
vessels,	that	the	excellence	of the	power

1498.10 verb 3sing subj pres act	3450.2 art gen sing	2296.2 noun gen sing masc	2504.1 conj	3231.1 partic	1523.1 prep gen	2231.2 prs-pron gen 1pl
ᾖ	τοῦ	θεοῦ,	καὶ	μὴ	ἐξ	ἡμῶν·
ē	*tou*	*theou*	*kai*	*mē*	*ex*	*hēmōn*
may be		of God,	and	not	from	us:

1706.1 prep	3820.3 adj dat sing	2323.4 verb nom pl masc part pres pass	233.1 conj	3620.3 partic	4580.2 verb nom pl masc part pres pass
8. ἐν	παντὶ	θλιβόμενοι,	ἀλλ'	οὐ	στενοχωρούμενοι·
en	*panti*	*thlibomenoi*	*all'*	*ou*	*stenochōroumenoi*
in	every	being oppressed,	but	not	being restricted;

633.3 verb nom pl masc part pres mid	233.1 conj	3620.2 partic	1804.1 verb nom pl masc part pres	1371.24 verb nom pl masc part pres pass
ἀπορούμενοι,	ἀλλ'	οὐκ	ἐξαπορούμενοι·	9. διωκόμενοι,
aporoumenoi	*all'*	*ouk*	*exaporoumenoi*	*diōkomenoi*
being perplexed,	but	not	being in despair;	being persecuted,

233.1 conj	3620.2 partic	1452.7 verb nom pl masc part pres pass	2569.1 verb nom pl masc part pres	233.1 conj
ἀλλ'	οὐκ	ἐγκαταλειπόμενοι·	καταβαλλόμενοι,	ἀλλ'
all'	*ouk*	*enkataleipomenoi*	*kataballomenoi*	*all'*
but	not	being forsaken;	being cast down,	but

3620.2 partic	616.18 verb nom pl masc part pres	3704.1 adv	3450.12 art acc sing fem	3363.1 noun acc sing fem
οὐκ	ἀπολλύμενοι·	10. πάντοτε	τὴν	νέκρωσιν
ouk	*apollumenoi*	*pantote*	*tēn*	*nekrōsin*
not	being destroyed;	always	the	dying

in Paul's life like that of the Creation. In the beginning God said, "Let there be light: and there was light" (Genesis 1:3). The great Creator had also commanded the light to shine in the darkness of the heart of the former Saul of Tarsus, symbolized by the bright light he saw the moment of his conversion (Acts 9:3). It brought him the knowledge of the glory of God which radiated from the face of Jesus who knew no covering of the face as did Moses (3:13). The countenance of the Saviour shone brightly.

4:7. The Lord committed the treasure of the gospel to the apostle for careful management as a steward of God. Men of that day sometimes kept priceless objects in earthen jars. Of all the things held in store, the truths of the gospel were the most valuable.

With that analogy Paul recognized the greatness of the message committed to him as standing in sharp contrast to his frailty as its container. God arranged it that way so men would realize the extraordinary quality of what Paul possessed was of the Lord and not of man. Paul ministered by the power (ability) which God gave, so the Lord was glorified in all (1 Peter 4:11).

4:8. Among the many charges brought against Paul by the opposition at Corinth was the claim he lived a life of relative ease as a preacher. The defense which builds as this letter unfolds makes that increasingly clear. The false teachers told tales of their hardships to make themselves appear the true ministers and Paul the doubtful one.

To explain, the apostle used a series of paradoxes in which he revealed he knew some of the worst and some of the best of times in his ministry. He experienced trouble and was hard-pressed on every side. Yet he was never crushed by his afflictions. He was sometimes perplexed as to the exact course of action he should take. He had no ready solution to some of his problems. In spite of it all, Paul never came to the point of despair.

4:9. Further, Paul was constantly persecuted (*diōkomenoi*, with the original meaning of "chase after, drive away, drive out"). He was pursued and hunted like a wild animal. Yet he never felt deserted or abandoned. Shortly after his conversion he was driven out of Damascus to escape certain death. Later, enemies of the gospel chased him from Antioch of Pisidia to Iconium and then to Lystra where they stoned him and left him for dead. They hunted him from Philippi to Thessalonica to Berea and then to Athens.

He was often cast down, but he was not left in despair (ruined, lost, destroyed). In the figure of a boxer in the ring, he was knocked down but never knocked out. The servant of the Lord in the will of God is indestructible in the ultimate view.

hath shined in our hearts: to [give] the light of the knowledge of the glory of God in the face of Jesus Christ: . . . to enlighten the knowledge, *Fenton* . . . which is radiant on the face of Christ, *Weymouth.*

7. But we have this treasure in earthen vessels: But we possess, *Fenton* . . . This priceless treasure we hold, *Phillips* . . . within utensils of mere clay, *Berkeley* . . . in a fragile case of clay, *Weymouth* . . . in bodies of clay, *Norlie.*
that the excellency of the power may be of God, and not of us: That the pre-eminence, *HistNT* . . . the exceeding greatness, *Hanson* . . . the surpassing greatness, *Montgomery* . . . the grandeur of the power, *Fenton* . . . not to originate in us, *Weymouth.*

8. [We are] troubled on every side, yet not distressed: We are hedged in, *Berkeley* . . . We are handicapped on all sides, *Phillips* . . . In everything distressed yet not straitened, *HistNT* . . . afflicted in every way, but not crushed, *NASB* . . . pressed hard, but not hemmed in, *Rotherham* . . . yet not suppressed, *Hanson* . . . but not overpowered, *Fenton.*
[we are] perplexed, but not in despair: We were without resources, *Klingensmith* . . . we suffer embarrassments, *Berkeley* . . . we are puzzled, *Phillips* . . . yet not over-perplexed, *Panin* . . . not destitute, *Confraternity* . . . we are never at a loss, *Norlie* . . . yet never utterly baffled, *Weymouth.*

9. Persecuted, but not forsaken: We are hunted but not caught, *Klingensmith* . . . pursued, yet never left unsuccoured, *Weymouth* . . . yet not deserted, *Hanson* . . . yet not abandoned, *Worrell* . . . not left in the lurch, *Wuest.*
cast down, but not destroyed: . . . prostrate, *HistNT* . . . smitten down, *Panin* . . . struck to the ground, *Weymouth* . . . repulsed, but not exterminated, *Fenton* . . . we may be knocked down but we are never knocked out! *Phillips* . . . but we do not perish, *Confraternity.*

539

2 Corinthians 4:11

10.a.Txt: 018K,020L,byz.
Var: 01א,02A,03B,04C
06D,025P,33,Gries
Lach,Treg,Alf,Word
Tisc,We/Ho,Weis,Sod
UBS/⋆

3450.2 art gen sing	2935.2 noun gen sing masc	2400.2 name masc	1706.1 prep	3450.3 art dat sing	4835.3 noun dat sing neu
τοῦ	⌐a Κυρίου ⌐	Ἰησοῦ	ἐν	τῷ	σώματι
tou	Kuriou	Iēsou	en	tō	sōmati
of the	Lord	Jesus	in	the	body

3924.1 verb nom pl masc part pres act	2419.1 conj	2504.1 conj	3450.9 art nom sing fem	2205.1 noun nom sing fem	3450.2 art gen sing
περιφέροντες,	ἵνα	καὶ	ἡ	ζωὴ	τοῦ
peripherontes	hina	kai	hē	zōē	tou
bearing about,	that	also	the	life	

2400.2 name masc	1706.1 prep	3450.3 art dat sing	4835.3 noun dat sing neu	2231.2 prs-pron gen 1pl	5157.12 verb 3sing subj aor pass
Ἰησοῦ	ἐν	τῷ	σώματι	ἡμῶν	φανερωθῇ.
Iēsou	en	tō	sōmati	hēmōn	phanerōthē
of Jesus	in	the	body	our	may be manifested;

103.1 adv	1056.1 conj	2231.1 prs-pron nom 1pl	3450.7 art pl masc	2180.13 verb nom pl masc part pres act	1519.1 prep
11. ἀεὶ	γὰρ	ἡμεῖς	οἱ	ζῶντες	εἰς
aei	gar	hēmeis	hoi	zōntes	eis
always	for	we	the	living	to

2265.4 noun acc sing masc	3722.29 verb 1pl indic pres pass	1217.2 prep	2400.3 name acc masc	2419.1 conj
θάνατον	παραδιδόμεθα	διὰ	Ἰησοῦν,	ἵνα
thanaton	paradidometha	dia	Iēsoun	hina
death	are being delivered	on account of	Jesus,	that

2504.1 conj	3450.9 art nom sing fem	2205.1 noun nom sing fem	3450.2 art gen sing	2400.2 name masc	5157.12 verb 3sing subj aor pass
καὶ	ἡ	ζωὴ	τοῦ	Ἰησοῦ	φανερωθῇ
kai	hē	zōē	tou	Iēsou	phanerōthē
also	the	life		of Jesus	may be manifested

1706.1 prep	3450.11 art dat sing fem	2326.1 adj dat sing fem	4418.3 noun dat sing fem	2231.2 prs-pron gen 1pl	5452.1 conj	3450.5 art sing masc
ἐν	τῇ	θνητῇ	σαρκὶ	ἡμῶν.	**12.** Ὥστε	ὁ
en	tē	thnētē	sarki	hēmōn	Hōste	ho
in	the	mortal	flesh	our;	so that	the

12.a.Txt: 018K,020L,byz.
Var: 01א,02A,03B,04C
06D,025P,33,bo.Gries
Lach,Treg,Alf,Word
Tisc,We/Ho,Weis,Sod
UBS/⋆

3173.1 conj	2265.1 noun nom sing masc	1706.1 prep	2231.3 prs-pron dat 1pl	1738.8 verb 3sing indic pres mid	3450.9 art nom sing fem
⌐a μὲν ⌐	θάνατος	ἐν	ἡμῖν	ἐνεργεῖται,	ἡ
men	thanatos	en	hēmin	energeitai	hē
	death	in	us	works,	the

1156.2 conj	2205.1 noun nom sing fem	1706.1 prep	5050.3 prs-pron dat 2pl	2174.19 verb nom pl masc part pres act	1156.2 conj	3450.16 art sing neu
δὲ	ζωὴ	ἐν	ὑμῖν·	**13.** ἔχοντες	δὲ	τὸ
de	zōē	en	humin	echontes	de	to
and	life	in	you.	Having	and	the

840.15 prs-pron sing neu	4011.1 noun sing neu	3450.10 art gen sing fem	3963.2 noun gen sing fem	2567.3 prep	3450.16 art sing neu
αὐτὸ	πνεῦμα	τῆς	πίστεως,	κατὰ	τὸ
auto	pneuma	tēs	pisteōs	kata	to
same	spirit	of the	faith,	according to	the

1119.29 verb sing neu part perf pass	3961.18 verb 1sing indic aor act	1346.1 conj	2953.26 verb 1sing indic aor act
γεγραμμένον,	Ἐπίστευσα,	διὸ	ἐλάλησα,
gegrammenon	Episteusa	dio	elalēsa
having been written,	I believed,	therefore	I spoke;

540

4:10. Paul always carried in his own body the stigma associated with the crucifixion of Jesus. To the Jewish person such a man was cursed of God (Galatians 3:13). Because Paul identified himself as one with Christ, men sought to kill him too. The abuse Paul's physical body took left him with scars to prove this identification to those who questioned whether or not he knew hardships in the ministry. He wrote to the Galatians, "I bear in my body the marks of the Lord Jesus" (Galatians 6:17). He proudly wore them because in a sense they identified him as belonging to the Lord much as the branding of cattle shows ownership.

However, just as God raised Jesus from the dead following His crucifixion, so He manifested (made known, showed in a visible way) life in the apostle's body following his suffering. The death was his, but the life was that of Jesus.

4:11. Paul knew what it was like to be constantly handed over to the custody of the police or the court for the testimony of Jesus. He concluded, though, that such was necessary in order that the life of Christ might be demonstrated in his mortal (subject to death, destined to die) body. Without death there can be no resurrection. Where there is no cross there is no crown.

4:12. In verses 10 and 11 the paradoxical existence of both death and life at the same time relates to Paul's personal experiences. He referred to what he described later in this letter where he concluded, "For when I am weak, then am I strong" (12:10). However, he changed the application of his analogy in verse 12. Death still worked in him, but the resurrection life which resulted worked in those to whom he ministered. No doubt the desire for this caused him to pray as he did in Philippians. He wrote, "That I may know him, and the power of his resurrection, and the fellowship of his sufferings, being made conformable unto his death" (Philippians 3:10).

Harris stressed the changed figure when he wrote, "Here his thought seems to be 'I suffer exposure to physical death for your sakes (cf. v. 15a); you enjoy more of the risen life of Christ as a consequence.' He apparently saw not only a causal but also a proportional relation between his 'death' and the 'life' of the Corinthian believers. The deeper his experience of the trials and sufferings of the apostolic life, the richer their experience of the joys and privileges of Christian existence (cf. Colossians 1:24; 2 Timothy 2:10). The 'middle term' between his experience and theirs was the divine comfort that, having received, he could then dispense (cf. 1:4)" (*The Expositor's Bible Commentary*, 10:343).

4:13. Faith put Paul at ease even in the face of severe persecution. He declared he had the same spirit of faith as the Psalmist whom men subjected to similar mistreatment. David kept his confidence

10. Always bearing about in the body the dying of the Lord Jesus: . . . always being exposed to death, *Williams* . . . the mortification, *Douay* . . . the marks of a death like that of Jesus, *TCNT* . . . the putting to death of Jesus, *Hanson.*

that the life also of Jesus might be made manifest in our body: . . . that it may be clearly shown, *Weymouth, Williams* . . . Jesus may be displayed, *Fenton* . . . may be disclosed, *HistNT* . . . may also be set forth in our lives, *Norlie.*

11. For we which live are alway delivered unto death for Jesus' sake: . . . surrendered for the sake of Jesus, *Fenton.*

that the life also of Jesus might be made manifest in our mortal flesh: . . . that the living power of Jesus, *Norlie* . . . may yet be evidenced, *Berkeley* . . . may be revealed, *NAB.*

12. So then death worketh in us, but life in you: In us then death is active, *HistNT* . . . death is active in us, *SEB* . . . So that the preaching of the Gospel procures sufferings and danger of death to me, *Locke* . . . while death is wearing down my frame, a new life is animating you, *Way* . . . Life is active within you, *TCNT* . . . energizes in us, *Fenton* . . . is operating in us, *Concordant* . . . we are constantly dying, while you are in full enjoyment of Life, *Weymouth.*

13. We having the same spirit of faith: In the same spirit of faith, *TEV* . . . We have the same kind of faith as David had, *NLT.*

according as it is written: . . . that was recorded, *Berkeley* . . . as he who said in the Scriptures, *Williams* . . . in the Writings, *BB.*

I believed, and therefore have I spoken: . . . from the faith in my heart, *BB* . . . and consequently speak, *Fenton* . . . therefore did I speak, *Worrell* . . . and therefore speak out, *NEB.*

2504.1 conj	2231.1 prs-pron nom 1pl	3961.7 verb 1pl indic pres act	1346.1 conj	2504.1 conj
καὶ	ἡμεῖς	πιστεύομεν,	διὸ	καὶ
kai	hēmeis	pisteuomen	dio	kai
also	we	believe,	therefore	also

2953.4 verb 1pl indic pres act	3471.20 verb nom pl masc part perf act	3617.1 conj	3450.5 art sing masc	1446.7 verb nom sing masc part aor act
λαλοῦμεν·	14. εἰδότες	ὅτι	ὁ	ἐγείρας
laloumen	eidotes	hoti	ho	egeiras
we speak;	knowing	that	the	having raised up

14.a.Txt: 01ℵ,04C,06D 010F,012G,044,bo.byz. **Var:** p46,03B,629,1739

3450.6 art acc sing masc	2935.4 noun acc sing masc	2400.3 name acc masc	2504.1 conj	2231.4 prs-pron acc 1pl	1217.2 prep
τὸν	⌐a κύριον ⌐	Ἰησοῦν,	καὶ	ἡμᾶς	⌐ διὰ
ton	kurion	Iēsoun	kai	hēmas	dia
the	Lord	Jesus,	also	us	through

14.b.Txt: 01ℵ-corr 06D-corr,018K,020L byz. **Var:** 01ℵ-org,03B,04C 06D-org,025P,33,bo. Lach,Treg,Alf,Word Tisc,We/Ho,Weis,Sod UBS/✱

4713.1 prep dat	2400.2 name masc	1446.13 verb 3sing indic fut act	2504.1 conj	3798.21 verb 3sing indic fut act	4713.1 prep dat
[b✱ σὺν]	Ἰησοῦ	ἐγερεῖ,	καὶ	παραστήσει	σὺν
sun	Iēsou	egerei	kai	parastēsei	sun
[with]	Jesus	will raise up,	and	will present,	with

5050.3 prs-pron dat 2pl	3450.17 art pl neu	1056.1 conj	3820.1 adj	1217.1 prep	5050.4 prs-pron acc 2pl
ὑμῖν.	15. τὰ	γὰρ	πάντα	δι'	ὑμᾶς,
humin	ta	gar	panta	di'	humas
you.	The	for	all things	for the sake of	you,

2419.1 conj	3450.9 art nom sing fem	5322.1 noun nom sing fem	3981.6 verb nom sing fem part aor act	1217.2 prep	3450.1 art gen pl
ἵνα	ἡ	χάρις	πλεονάσασα	διὰ	τῶν
hina	hē	charis	pleonasasa	dia	tōn
that	the	grace,	having abounded	through	the

3979.2 adj comp gen pl	3450.12 art acc sing fem	2150.4 noun acc sing fem	3915.14 verb 3sing subj aor act	1519.1 prep
πλειόνων	τὴν	εὐχαριστίαν	περισσεύσῃ	εἰς
pleionōn	tēn	eucharistian	perisseusē	eis
most,	the	thanksgiving	may cause to exceed	to

3450.12 art acc sing fem	1385.4 noun acc sing fem	3450.2 art gen sing	2296.2 noun gen sing masc	1346.1 conj	3620.2 partic
τὴν	δόξαν	τοῦ	θεοῦ.	16. Διὸ	οὐκ
tēn	doxan	tou	theou	Dio	ouk
the	glory		of God.	Wherefore	not

16.a.Txt: 04C,06D-corr 018K,020L,025P,byz. **Var:** 01ℵ,03B,06D-org 33,Lach,Treg,Alf,Word Tisc,We/Ho,Weis,Sod UBS/✱

1560.1 verb 1pl indic pres act	1450.5 verb 2pl aor act	233.1 conj	1479.1 conj	2504.1 conj
⌐ ἐκκακοῦμεν·	[a✱ ἐγκακοῦμεν,]	ἀλλ'	εἰ	καὶ
ekkakoumen	enkakoumen	all'	ei	kai
we faint;	[idem]	but	if	indeed

3450.5 art sing masc	1838.1 prep gen	2231.2 prs-pron gen 1pl	442.1 noun nom sing masc	1305.4 verb 3sing indic pres pass
ὁ	ἔξω	ἡμῶν	ἄνθρωπος	διαφθείρεται,
ho	exō	hēmōn	anthrōpos	diaphtheiretai
the	outward	our	man	is being brought to decay,

16.b.Txt: 06D-corr,018K 020L,byz. **Var:** 01ℵ,03B,04C 06D-org,025P,Lach Treg,Tisc,We/Ho,Weis Sod,UBS/✱

233.1 conj	3450.5 art sing masc	2060.1 adv	2059.1 prep gen	2231.2 prs-pron gen 1pl
ἀλλ'	ὁ	⌐ ἔσωθεν	[b✱ ἔσω	ἡμῶν]
all'	ho	esōthen	esō	hēmōn
yet	the	inward	[inward	our]

in God in spite of adverse circumstances. "The sorrows of death compassed me," he wrote (Psalm 116:3). He proclaimed his faith before men, and the Lord delivered him from certain destruction. He said simply, "He helped me" (Psalm 116:6). Even so the apostle believed and continued to declare his faith.

4:14. Thoughts of suffering repeatedly on the brink of death for the sake of the gospel brought to mind for Paul the certainty of death sooner or later for all men, even for believers (cf. Hebrews 9:27). The sole exception will be in the translation of Christians who still live at the return of Christ (1 Corinthians 15:51f.).

However, death holds no terror for the child of God. Paul declared Christ's resurrection from the dead guaranteed that of the believer. The One who raised His only begotten Son will just as surely raise all His spiritual children one day. The apostle wrote to the Romans, "But if the Spirit of him that raised up Jesus from the dead dwell in you, he that raised up Christ from the dead shall also quicken (make alive) your mortal bodies by his Spirit that dwelleth in you" (Romans 8:11).

Triumphantly Paul pictured the morning of the resurrection as leading to the presentation of all believers before God. He declared both he and the faithful Corinthians would be in the number. In view of the current problems in the Corinthian church, the confidence Paul expressed was a compliment to them.

4:15. Again Paul noted God intended his ministerial trials to benefit believers such as those at Corinth. He wrote the Romans that "all things work together for good to them that love God" (Romans 8:28).

Hardships provide a perfect setting for the grace of God to become abundant (*pleonasasa*, "to grow, spread to more and more people"). At the same time thanksgiving increases as it arises to the Lord from the many (*pleionōn*, comparative of *polus*, thus "more and more") yet to be won to Christ. All will redound or cause to overflow to the glory of God.

4:16. These glorious facts gave Paul sufficient reason not to faint or lose heart. True, the difficulties encountered in his ministry wore his physical strength away. He knew well his outward man was decaying. At the same time, though, his inward man was renewed day by day.

The apostle realized what all aging believers know. They too find comfort in the fact that both decay and renewal go on at the same time within their being. They receive the answer to the prayer of the Psalmist, "Cast me not off in the time of old age; forsake me not when my strength faileth" (Psalm 71:9).

we also believe, and therefore speak: ... that is why we speak, *SEB*.

14. Knowing that he which raised up the Lord Jesus: Because we are certain, *BB* ... knowing that he, who resuscitated our Lord Jesus, *Murdock* ... assured that He, *Berkeley*.

shall raise up us also by Jesus: and shall present [us] with you: ... will give us a place in his glory, *BB* ... and will bring us into his presence along with you, *Barclay* ... to stand in His own presence, *Weymouth* ... and bring me side by side with you, *Goodspeed* ... into his presence, *TEV*.

15. For all things [are] for your sakes: Everything happens for your good, *SEB* ... all things are ordered, *NEB* ... Everything is for your sakes, *Barclay* ... for your benefit, *TCNT*.

that the abundant grace might through the thanksgiving of many redound to the glory of God: ... it may result in an overflowing, *Adams* ... the exuberant favour of God, *Locke* ... the grace being multiplied, *Panin* ... reaches greater and greater numbers, *Goodspeed* ... the favour abounding, *Rotherham* ... being more richly bestowed...and more and more promote the glory of God, *Weymouth* ... may overflow, *Fenton*.

16. For which cause we faint not: That is why, *Beck* ... Wherefore we lose not heart, *HistNT* ... Therefore we never flinch, *Way* ... we are not discouraged, *Berkeley* ... we do not get discouraged, *PNT* ... we never give up, *SEB* ... we never collapse, *Phillips*.

but though our outward man perish: ... our nature, *TCNT* ... our outer nature is wasting away, *Williams* ... outer man is decaying, *Confraternity* ... is impaired, *Campbell* ... is corrupted, *Douay* ... is exhausted, *Fenton*.

yet the inward [man] is renewed day by day: ... is being renewed, *Concordant* ... receives fresh strength, *Phillips*.

339.1 verb 3sing indic pres pass	**2232.3** noun dat sing fem	**2504.1** conj	**2232.3** noun dat sing fem	**3450.16** art sing neu	**1056.1** conj
ἀνακαινοῦται	ἡμέρα	καὶ	ἡμέρᾳ.	**17.** τὸ	γὰρ
anakainoutai	hēmera	kai	hēmera	to	gar
is being renewed	day	by	day.	The	for

17.a.**Txt**: 01ℵ,04C,06D 018K,020L,025P,byz. Tisc,Sod
Var: p46,03B,We/Ho Weis,UBS/✻

3771.1 adv	**1632.1** adj nom sing neu	**3450.10** art gen sing fem	**2324.2** noun gen sing fem	**2231.2** prs-pron gen 1pl
παραυτίκα	ἐλαφρὸν	τῆς	θλίψεως	⟨a ἡμῶν ⟩
parautika	elaphron	tēs	thlipseōs	hēmōn
momentary	lightness	of the	tribulation	our

2567.2 prep	**5073.3** noun acc sing fem	**1519.1** prep	**5073.3** noun acc sing fem	**164.1** adj sing	**916.2** noun acc sing neu
καθ'	ὑπερβολὴν	εἰς	ὑπερβολὴν	αἰώνιον	βάρος
kath'	huperbolēn	eis	huperbolēn	aiōnion	baros
in	excess	to	surpassing	an eternal	weight

1385.2 noun gen sing fem	**2686.2** verb 3sing indic pres	**2231.3** prs-pron dat 1pl	**3231.1** partic	**4503.4** verb gen pl masc part pres act
δόξης	κατεργάζεται	ἡμῖν,	**18.** μὴ	σκοπούντων
doxēs	katergazetai	hēmin	mē	skopountōn
of glory	works out	for us;	not	noticing

2231.2 prs-pron gen 1pl	**3450.17** art pl neu	**984.25** verb pl neu part pres pass	**233.2** conj	**3450.17** art pl neu	**3231.1** partic
ἡμῶν	τὰ	βλεπόμενα,	ἀλλὰ	τὰ	μὴ
hēmōn	ta	blepomena	alla	ta	mē
we	the things	being seen,	but	the things	not

984.25 verb pl neu part pres pass	**3450.17** art pl neu	**1056.1** conj	**984.25** verb pl neu part pres pass	**4199.4** adj nom pl neu
βλεπόμενα·	τὰ	γὰρ	βλεπόμενα	πρόσκαιρα·
blepomena	ta	gar	blepomena	proskaira
being seen;	the things	for	being seen	temporary,

3450.17 art pl neu	**1156.2** conj	**3231.1** partic	**984.25** verb pl neu part pres pass	**164.8** adj nom pl neu	**3471.5** verb 1pl indic perf act
τὰ	δὲ	μὴ	βλεπόμενα	αἰώνια.	**5:1.** Οἴδαμεν
ta	de	mē	blepomena	aiōnia	Oidamen
the things	but	not	being seen	eternal.	We know

1056.1 conj	**3617.1** conj	**1430.1** partic	**3450.9** art nom sing fem	**1904.2** adj nom sing fem	**2231.2** prs-pron gen 1pl
γὰρ	ὅτι	ἐὰν	ἡ	ἐπίγειος	ἡμῶν
gar	hoti	ean	hē	epigeios	hēmōn
for	that	if	the	earthly	our

					3477.2 noun nom sing fem
					οἰκία
					oikia
					house

3450.2 art gen sing	**4491.1** noun gen sing neu	**2617.8** verb 3sing subj aor pass	**3482.3** noun acc sing fem	**1523.2** prep gen	**2296.2** noun gen sing masc
τοῦ	σκήνους	καταλυθῇ,	οἰκοδομὴν	ἐκ	θεοῦ
tou	skēnous	kataluthē	oikodomēn	ek	theou
of the	tabernacle	be destroyed,	a building	from	God

2174.5 verb 1pl indic pres act	**3477.4** noun acc sing fem	**879.1** adj acc sing	**164.1** adj sing	**1706.1** prep	**3450.4** art dat pl
ἔχομεν,	οἰκίαν	ἀχειροποίητον,	αἰώνιον	ἐν	τοῖς
echomen	oikian	acheiropoiēton	aiōnion	en	tois
we have,	a house	not made with hands,	eternal	in	the

3636.8 noun dat pl masc	**2504.1** conj	**1056.1** conj	**1706.1** prep	**3642.5** dem-pron dat sing masc	**4578.1** verb 1pl indic pres act
οὐρανοῖς.	**2.** καὶ	γὰρ	ἐν	τούτῳ	στενάζομεν,
ouranois	kai	gar	en	toutō	stenazomen
heavens.	Indeed	for	in	this	we groan,

4:17. The Spirit within Paul brought him to the conclusion that his relatively insignificant affliction which brought distress because of the pressure of outward circumstances actually worked for his good. As something which was momentary, it brought about for him a far more exceeding (*huperbolēn eis huperbolēn*, literally "excess to excess"), beyond all measure or comparison, weight or fullness of glory. That glory would be eternal and would never fade away. To the Romans he wrote, "For I reckon that the sufferings of this present time are not worthy to be compared with the glory which shall be revealed in us" (Romans 8:18).

4:18. One of the things which kept Paul true to his calling was holding the proper perspective in life. He did not look (*skopeō*, "to gaze upon," or "to fix one's eyes upon") or concentrate his attention upon the things which are seen. Instead, the apostle fixed his gaze on the things which are not seen. His reason was the things which are seen are transitory, lasting only for time, while the things which are not seen are eternal.

The choice of verbs (*skopeō* [see above] versus *blepō*, "to look or see") is significant in this verse for Paul intends to convey a contrast. He indicates that he deliberately shifted his "gaze" (*skopeō*) or attention from that which is visible, i.e., "the things are *seen* (*ta blepomena*)," to that which is invisible. The verse is an attempt to teach the Corinthians that the eternal realities which should motivate believers are beyond the perception of the senses. Faith in the world of the unseen spiritual realities should be occupying the attention of those claiming to possess faith in Christ.

5:1. With knowledge of the eternal, Paul could say he knew (*oidamen*, which can mean either "to know" or "to have insight provided by intuition or revelation") what comes at the end of life for the Christian. He ceases to live in his tabernacle, the physical body which is like a tent. The apostle knew well just how transitory and fragile such temporary dwelling places were since he made tents with his own hands. Peter also spoke of the day when he would "put off" his tent (2 Peter 1:14). At death, man's physical body is taken down and folded up like a tent.

Just as certain as death for Paul was the fact that afterward he would live in a house not made with human hands. In that world where temporal things no longer exist, his dwelling would be an eternal one in the heavens.

Life in the world to come is no less real than this one. It is no imaginary existence in a fog where one drifts in and out of consciousness. John recognized regarding the afterlife that "it doth not yet appear what we shall be" (1 John 3:2). However, he quickly added, "But we know that, when he shall appear, we shall be like him." After His resurrection Jesus demonstrated He was as real as before (Luke 24:26-43). He was no ghostly person, but a real one.

17. For our light affliction, which is but for a moment: We have trials, *Norlie* . . . For the fleeting trifle, *Fenton* . . . transitory burden of suffering, *Weymouth.*

worketh for us a far more exceeding [and] eternal weight of glory: . . . preparing for us an everlasting weight of glory, greater than anything we can imagine, *Beck* . . . is producing for us, *Berkeley* . . . an enormously erupting everlasting, *Klingensmith* . . . weight of majesty, *HistNT* . . . burden of glory, *Concordant* . . . great beyond expression, *Campbell.*

18. While we look not at the things which are seen, but at the things which are not seen: . . . we aiming not at, *Wilson, Campbell* . . . we do not fasten our eyes on the visible, *Berkeley* . . . what is not being observed, *Concordant* . . . not looking for the visible things, but the invisible, *Rotherham.*

for the things which are seen [are] temporal; but the things which are not seen [are] eternal: For the seen is for a time, *HistNT* . . . things that are seen pass away, *Conybeare* . . . are transitory, *Phillips* . . . What is seen is only temporary, but what is unseen lasts forever, *SEB* . . . things that are unseen, *Worrell* . . . are everlasting, *Klingensmith.*

1. For we know that if our earthly house of [this] tabernacle were dissolved: . . . that if perchance, *Rotherham* . . . this earthly house of our soul, *Norlie* . . . if this poor tent, our earthly house, is taken down, *Weymouth* . . . terrestrial tabernacle house should be demolished, *Concordant* . . . may be thrown down, *Young* . . . is torn down, *Beck* . . . should be dismantled, *Berkeley* . . . be destroyed, *Confraternity.*

we have a building of God: I have a mansion built, *Montgomery* . . . a mansion built by God, *Conybeare.*

an house not made with hands: eternal in the heavens: . . . everlasting, *Campbell* . . . It lasts forever, *SEB* . . . age-abiding, *Rotherham.*

3450.16 art sing neu	3476.1 noun acc sing neu	2231.2 prs-pron gen 1pl	3450.16 art sing neu	1523.1 prep gen	3636.2 noun gen sing masc
τὸ	οἰκητήριον	ἡμῶν	τὸ	ἐξ	οὐρανοῦ
to	oikētērion	hēmōn	to	ex	ouranou
the	dwelling	our	the	from	heaven

1887.1 verb inf aor mid	1955.4 verb nom pl masc part pres act	1480.1 partic	1479.1 conj	1058.1 partic
ἐπενδύσασθαι	ἐπιποθοῦντες	3. ꞈ εἴγε	[☆ εἴ	γε]
ependusasthai	epipothountes	eige	ei	ge
to be clothed with	longing;	if indeed	[if	indeed]

3.a.Txt: p46,01א,03B 04C,06D-corr2,044 0243,byz.
Var: 06D-org

2504.1 conj	1730.10 verb nom pl masc part aor mid	1549.4 verb nom pl masc part aor mid	3620.3 partic	1125.3 adj nom pl masc
καὶ	ꞈ ἐνδυσάμενοι,	[ᵃ☆ ἐκδύσαμενοι,]	οὐ	γυμνοὶ
kai	endusamenoi,	ekdusamenoi,	ou	gumnoi
also	having been clothed,	[having put off,]	not	naked

2128.42 verb 1pl indic fut pass	2504.1 conj	1056.1 conj	3450.7 art pl masc	1498.23 verb nom pl masc part pres act	1706.1 prep
εὑρεθησόμεθα.	4. καὶ	γὰρ	οἱ	ὄντες	ἐν
heurethēsometha.	kai	gar	hoi	ontes	en
we shall be found.	Indeed	for	the	being	in

3450.3 art dat sing	4491.2 noun dat sing neu	4578.1 verb 1pl indic pres act	911.2 verb nom pl masc part pres pass	1879.1 conj
τῷ	σκήνει	στενάζομεν	βαρούμενοι·	ꞈ ἐπειδὴ
tō	skēnei	stenazomen	baroumenoi	epeidē
the	tabernacle	we groan	being burdened;	since

4.a.Txt: Steph
Var: 01א,03B,04C,06D 018K,020L,025P,Elzev Gries,Lach,Treg,Alf Word,Tisc,We/Ho,Weis Sod,UBS/☆

1894.1 prep	3614.3 rel-pron dat sing	3620.3 partic	2286.4 verb 1pl indic pres act	1549.3 verb inf aor mid	233.1 conj
[ᵃ☆ ἐφ'	ᾧ]	οὐ	θέλομεν	ἐκδύσασθαι,	ἀλλ'
eph'	hō	ou	thelomen	ekdusasthai,	all'
[upon	which]	not	we do wish	to be unclothed,	but

1887.1 verb inf aor mid	2419.1 conj	2636.6 verb 3sing subj aor pass	3450.16 art sing neu	2326.2 adj sing neu
ἐπενδύσασθαι,	ἵνα	καταποθῇ	τὸ	θνητὸν
ependusasthai,	hina	katapothē	to	thnēton
to be clothed upon,	that	may be swallowed up	the	mortal

5097.3 prep	3450.10 art gen sing fem	2205.2 noun gen sing fem	3450.5 art sing masc	1156.2 conj	2686.10 verb nom sing masc part aor mid
ὑπὸ	τῆς	ζωῆς.	5. ὁ	δὲ	κατεργασάμενος
hupo	tēs	zōēs.	ho	de	katergasamenos
by	the	life.	The	now	having wrought out

2231.4 prs-pron acc 1pl	1519.1 prep	840.15 prs-pron sing neu	3642.17 dem-pron sing neu	2296.1 noun nom sing masc	3450.5 art sing masc
ἡμᾶς	εἰς	αὐτὸ	τοῦτο	θεός,	ὁ
hēmas	eis	auto	touto	theos	ho
us	for	same	this thing	God,	the

5.a.Txt: 01א-corr 06D-corr,018K,020L byz.
Var: 01א-org,03B,04C 06D-org,025P,bo.Lach Treg,Alf,Word,Tisc We/Ho,Weis,Sod UBS/☆

2504.1 conj	1319.28 verb nom sing masc part aor act	2231.3 prs-pron dat 1pl	3450.6 art acc sing masc	722.2 noun acc sing masc
ꞈᵃ καὶ ꞈ	δοὺς	ἡμῖν	τὸν	ἀρραβῶνα
kai	dous	hēmin	ton	arrhabōna
also	having given	to us	the	down payment

3450.2 art gen sing	4011.2 noun gen sing neu	2269.3 verb nom pl masc part pres act	3631.1 conj
τοῦ	πνεύματος.	6. Θαρροῦντες	οὖν
tou	pneumatos.	Tharrhountes	oun
of the	Spirit.	Being confident	therefore

5:2. In the meantime some discomfort remains for the believer. He experiences a certain groaning because of undesirable circumstances in this life. He is not really "at home" in this world. In his letter to the Romans Paul said, "We . . . groan within ourselves, waiting for the adoption, to wit, the redemption of our body" (Romans 8:23). As Abraham of old, the Christian is a sojourner rather than a permanent resident on earth. Abraham "looked for a city which hath foundations, whose builder and maker is God" (Hebrews 11:10).

With the apostle the child of God earnestly desires and longs for the day when he will be clothed upon (*ependusasthai*, from the same root as the English word *endue*) with his house from heaven. That house, of course, is the glorified body of the transfigured Christian. The resurrection body alone can provide a proper covering for the soul's nakedness.

5:3,4. For the person of modesty, nothing could bring greater distress than appearing naked in public. Even so the soul shies away from being unclothed, without a body. Paul used this fact to explain that his desire, along with all Christians who still abide in their present physical bodies, was not to be unclothed. They do not seek death as such, whether by ordinary means, accidental means, or suicide. Despite the teachings of Freudian psychology, the apostle expressed no "death wish" here.

The sting of death has been removed for the Christian, but he finds no pleasure in the prospects of dying. He has no morbid fear of death, but it is still repulsive to his flesh.

What the believer anticipates in connection with death is being clothed upon with a new body. He knows the joy of having a redeemed soul, but he must await the day when his redemption applies to his body in the resurrection (Romans 8:23). Come that day, both the body and soul will agree in the pursuit of the things of God. Fleshly appetites will no longer pull in an opposite direction. The spirit-flesh conflict will cease.

Besides all this, any dread of death will be forever gone in the resurrection. The present state of mortality where man bears the burden of being subject to death will be "swallowed up" in a life that is eternal for the Christian.

5:5. Worshipfully Paul declared God has prepared believers for this selfsame thing (this very purpose). To demonstrate His plan for our future He has given us an earnest, a down payment or the first installment, as a guarantee of the rest that is to follow. The realities of experiences such as new birth by the Spirit and the baptism in the Spirit serve that purpose for believers. To the Ephesians Paul wrote that after they believed they "were sealed with that Holy Spirit of promise, which is the earnest of our inheritance until the redemption of the purchased possession" (Ephesians 1:13,14).

2. For in this we groan: earnestly desiring to be clothed upon with our house which is from heaven: . . . longing to be clothed, *Hanson, Worrell* . . . to be endowed with our little cottage, *Fenton* . . . to be invested with that habitation, *Wilson* . . . with our heavenly mansion, *Campbell* . . . with our dwelling, *NASB* . . . the cover of my heavenly habitation, *Montgomery* . . . to put on our heavenly dwelling, *RSV* . . . the glorified body from heaven, *Norlie* . . . the Heavenly home, *Phillips*.

3. If so be that being clothed we shall not be found naked: . . . we shall not be found destitute, *Wilson* . . . be found naked [a disembodied spirit], *Wuest* . . . be found without bodies, *TCNT*.

4. For we that are in [this] tabernacle do groan, being burdened: . . . we who are in this tent sigh, *Confraternity* . . . groaning in deep trouble, *Montgomery*.

not for that we would be unclothed, but clothed upon: . . . because we do not want to take it off, *Murdock* . . . but rather to be invested with the other coverings, *Berkeley* . . . to be unclothed [divested of our mortal body] but clothed upon [invested with our heavenly body], *Wuest*.

that mortality might be swallowed up of life: . . . that this our dying nature might, *Conybeare* . . . what is mortal may, *Montgomery* . . . may be absorbed by immortal life, *Norlie* . . . may be absorbed in Life, *Weymouth, Murdock*.

5. Now he that hath wrought us for the selfsame thing [is] God: And he that prepareth us for this thing, *Murdock* . . . prepared us for this very end, *Norlie* . . . has prepared us for this change, *TCNT* . . . this very thing, *Hanson*.

who also hath given unto us the earnest of the Spirit: . . . as a down payment, *Adams* . . . as a guarantee, *RSV* . . . a pledge and foretaste of that bliss, *Weymouth* . . . a guarantee that we will live again, *SEB*.

| 3704.1
adv
πάντοτε,
pantote
always, | 2504.1
conj
καὶ
kai
and | 3471.20 verb nom pl
masc part perf act
εἰδότες
eidotes
knowing | 3617.1
conj
ὅτι
hoti
that | 1720.1 verb nom pl
masc part pres act
ἐνδημοῦντες
endēmountes
being at home | 1706.1
prep
ἐν
en
in |

| 3450.3
art dat sing
τῷ
tō
the | 4835.3 noun
dat sing neu
σώματι
sōmati
body | 1540.1 verb 1pl
indic pres act
ἐκδημοῦμεν
ekdēmoumen
we are from home | 570.3
prep gen
ἀπὸ
apo
away from | 3450.2
art gen sing
τοῦ
tou
the |

| 2935.2 noun
gen sing masc
κυρίου·
kuriou
Lord, | 1217.2
prep
7. διὰ
dia
by | 3963.2 noun
gen sing fem
πίστεως
pisteōs
faith | 1056.1
conj
γὰρ
gar
for | 3906.5 verb 1pl
indic pres act
περιπατοῦμεν,
peripatoumen
we walk, | 3620.3
partic
οὐ
ou
not |

| 1217.2
prep
διὰ
dia
by | 1482.2 noun
gen sing neu
εἴδους
eidous
sight; | 2269.2 verb 1pl
indic pres act
8. θαρῥοῦμεν
tharrhoumen
we are confident, | 1156.2
conj
δὲ,
de
but | 2504.1
conj
καὶ
kai
and | 2085.3 verb 1pl
indic pres act
εὐδοκοῦμεν
eudokoumen
are pleased |

| 3095.1
adv comp
μᾶλλον
mallon
rather | 1540.3 verb
inf aor act
ἐκδημῆσαι
ekdēmēsai
to be from home | 1523.2
prep gen
ἐκ
ek
out of | 3450.2
art gen sing
τοῦ
tou
the | 4835.2 noun
gen sing neu
σώματος
sōmatos
body | 2504.1
conj
καὶ
kai
and |

| 1720.2 verb
inf aor act
ἐνδημῆσαι
endēmēsai
to be at home | 4242.1
prep
πρὸς
pros
with | 3450.6 art
acc sing masc
τὸν
ton
the | 2935.4 noun
acc sing masc
κύριον.
kurion
Lord. | 1346.1
conj
9. Διὸ
Dio
Wherefore | 2504.1
conj
καὶ
kai
also |

| 5226.1 verb
1pl indic pres
φιλοτιμούμεθα,
philotimoumetha
we are ambitious, | 1521.1
conj
εἴτε
eite
whether | 1720.1 verb nom pl
masc part pres act
ἐνδημοῦντες
endēmountes
being at home | 1521.1
conj
εἴτε
eite
or | 1540.2 verb nom pl
masc part pres act
ἐκδημοῦντες,
ekdēmountes
being from home, |

| 2080.2 adj
nom pl masc
εὐάρεστοι
euarestoi
well pleasing | 840.4 prs-
pron dat sing
αὐτῷ
autō
to him | 1498.32 verb
inf pres act
εἶναι.
einai
to be. | 3450.8 art
acc pl masc
10. τοὺς
tous
The | 1056.1
conj
γὰρ
gar
for | 3820.8 adj
acc pl masc
πάντας
pantas
all |

| 2231.4 prs-
pron acc 1pl
ἡμᾶς
hēmas
we | 5157.17 verb
inf aor pass
φανερωθῆναι
phanerōthēnai
to be manifested | 1158.1 verb 3sing
indic pres act
δεῖ
dei
must | 1699.1
prep gen
ἔμπροσθεν
emprosthen
before | 3450.2
art gen sing
τοῦ
tou
the |

| 961.1 noun
gen sing neu
βήματος
bēmatos
judgment seat | 3450.2
art gen sing
τοῦ
tou
of the | 5382.2 name
gen masc
Χριστοῦ,
Christou
Christ, | 2419.1
conj
ἵνα
hina
that | 2837.6 verb 3sing
subj aor mid
κομίσηται
komisētai
may receive |

| 1524.3 adj
nom sing masc
ἕκαστος
hekastos
each | 3450.17
art pl neu
τὰ
ta
the things | 1217.2
prep
διὰ
dia
in | 3450.2
art gen sing
τοῦ
tou
the | 4835.2 noun
gen sing neu
σώματος,
sōmatos
body, | 4242.1
prep
πρὸς
pros
according to |

5:6,7. The apostle found reason to be confident and courageous because of these truths. His faith rested on facts. He could face hardships and even the threat of death without flinching. He knew that as long as he remained in his physical body he was absent from the Lord. Sight may not say such things, but faith does; and Paul ordered his life by its realities.

5:8. So significant was it that the apostle repeated the fact of his confident and courageous attitude in the face of death. Strange as it may seem to some, he was actually willing and even wished to be absent from the body so he could be present with the Lord. In writing to the Philippians, the Spirit moved him to say, "For to me to live is Christ, and to die is gain" (Philippians 1:21). Except for his ministry, he thought it better to depart and be with Christ (Philippians 1:23,24).

5:9. The choice of living or dying did not rest with the man Paul, of course. He committed his way to the Lord. His concern was that of pleasing the Saviour, whether present (*endēmountes*, "at home," same as in verses 6 and 8) or absent (*ekdēmountes*, "away from home," same as in verses 6 and 8) from the physical body. He labored, strived earnestly for, and held as his chief ambition that very thing.

The ambition of the false teachers at Corinth was to please people and gain a following. Paul wanted peace with men too, but he aspired more to be accepted of the Lord.

5:10. The prospect of having to give an account to God for his conduct in the ministry kept the apostle on the right track. He faced the fact that all believers must one day appear (*phanerōthēnai*, "to show or reveal," i.e., "reveal themselves, be made known, stand openly") before the Lord. Each will be summoned to appear before the judgment seat (*bēma*, "judicial bench") of Christ, to be judged as to the quality of their Christian service on earth.

Paul pictured that judicial bench as being at the top of a set of steps such as was the case in his day. The Romans not only believed crime must be punished, but they also held the penalty must be administered publicly. Accordingly, the judge sat openly at the top of the stairs to a governmental building to hear cases that came before him.

The believer's hearing before Christ will examine the nature of his service to the Master during his earthly life. Ministers especially will be judged according to the quality of the work they have done. If the spiritual buildings they have erected were made of wood, hay, or stubble, they will stand before Jesus without reward (1 Corinthians 3:12-15).

The judgment seat of Christ concerns rewards for past service as well as assignments for future service to the Master during the

6. Therefore [we are] always confident: Having good courage, *Rotherham* . . . we always behave undauntedly, *Wesley* . . . always courageous, *Hanson.*

knowing that, whilst we are at home in the body: . . . while we are sojourning, *Wesley.*

we are absent from the Lord: I am in banishment from, *Montgomery* . . . is to be abroad from the Lord, *HistNT.*

7. (For we walk by faith, not by sight:): . . . we are living a life of faith, *Weymouth* . . . We live by trusting Him, without seeing Him, *Beck* . . . is faith, not appearances, *HistNT* . . . not by appearance, *Alford, Hanson.*

8. We are confident: We are cheerful, *Norlie.*

[I say], and willing rather to be absent from the body: . . . we prefer to be, *Berkeley* . . . would prefer to leave the body, *Adams.*

and to be present with the Lord: . . . to be at home, *Clementson, Hanson* . . . and go home to be with the Lord, *Adams* . . . to come home unto the Lord, *Rotherham.*

9. Wherefore we labour: Therefore we are ambitious, *Wesley, Hanson, Clementson* . . . we are desirous, *Fenton* . . . I strive earnestly, *Conybeare* . . . we make it our ambition, *HistNT, Adams.*

that, whether present or absent, we may be accepted of him: . . . we always want to please God, *SEB* . . . to please Him, *Adams, Douay* . . . to be well pleasing to Him, *Concordant* . . . to please Him perfectly, *Weymouth* . . . we may be approved by him, *Noyes* . . . we may be well pleasing unto him, *Alford.*

10. For we must all appear before the judgment seat of Christ: . . . all be reviewed, *Fenton* . . . all be exposed, *HistNT* . . . all must needs be made manifest before the tribunal, *Rotherham.*

that every one may receive the things [done] in [his] body: . . . may be requited, *Berkeley* . . . the things practiced in the body, *Klingensmith.*

2 Corinthians 5:11

3614.17 rel-pron pl neu	4097.15 verb 3sing indic aor act	1521.1 conj	18.3 adj sing	1521.1 conj	2527.7 adj sing neu
ἃ	ἔπραξεν,	εἴτε	ἀγαθὸν	εἴτε	⸀ κακόν.
ha	epraxen	eite	agathon	eite	kakon
what	he did,	whether	good	or	evil.

5175.1 adj sing neu	3471.20 verb nom pl masc part perf act	3631.1 conj	3450.6 art acc sing masc	5238.4 noun acc sing masc
[ᵃ☆ φαῦλον.]	11. Εἰδότες	οὖν	τὸν	φόβον
phaulon	Eidotes	oun	ton	phobon
[worthless.]	Knowing	therefore	the	terror

3450.2 art gen sing	2935.2 noun gen sing masc	442.9 noun acc pl masc	3844.3 verb 1pl indic pres act	2296.3 noun dat sing masc	1156.2 conj
τοῦ	κυρίου,	ἀνθρώπους	πείθομεν,	θεῷ	δὲ
tou	kuriou	anthrōpous	peithomen	theō	de
of the	Lord,	men	we persuade,	to God	but

5157.19 verb 1pl indic perf pass	1666.1 verb 1sing indic pres act	1156.2 conj	2504.1 conj	1706.1 prep	3450.14 art dat pl fem
πεφανερώμεθα·	ἐλπίζω	δὲ	καὶ	ἐν	ταῖς
pephanerōmetha	elpizō	de	kai	en	tais
we have been manifested,	I hope	and	also	in	the

4743.5 noun dat pl fem	5050.2 prs-pron gen 2pl	5157.20 verb inf perf pass	3620.3 partic
συνειδήσεσιν	ὑμῶν	πεφανερῶσθαι.	12. οὐ
suneidēsesin	humōn	pephanerōsthai	ou
consciences	your	to have been manifested.	Not

1056.1 conj	3687.1 adv	1431.8 prs-pron acc pl masc	4771.3 verb 1pl indic pres act	5050.3 prs-pron dat 2pl	233.2 conj
⸀ γὰρ ⸀	πάλιν	ἑαυτοὺς	συνιστάνομεν	ὑμῖν,	ἀλλὰ
gar	palin	heautous	sunistanomen	humin	alla
for	again	ourselves	do we commend	to you,	but

867.1 noun acc sing fem	1319.9 verb nom pl masc part pres act	5050.3 prs-pron dat 2pl	2715.2 noun gen sing neu	5065.1 prep
ἀφορμὴν	διδόντες	ὑμῖν	καυχήματος	ὑπὲρ
aphormēn	didontes	humin	kauchēmatos	huper
occasion	giving	to you	of boasting	in behalf of

2231.2 prs-pron gen 1pl	2419.1 conj	2174.9 verb 2pl subj pres act	4242.1 prep	3450.8 art acc pl masc	1706.1 prep
ἡμῶν,	ἵνα	ἔχητε	πρὸς	τοὺς	ἐν
hēmōn	hina	echēte	pros	tous	en
us,	that	you may have	towards	the	in

4241.3 noun dat sing neu	2714.9 verb acc pl masc part pres	2504.1 conj	3620.3 partic	3231.1 partic	1706.1 prep
προσώπῳ	καυχωμένους	καὶ	⸀ οὐ	[ᵇ☆ μὴ	ἐν]
prosōpō	kauchōmenous	kai	ou	mē	en
appearance	boasting	and	not	[not	in]

2559.3 noun dat sing fem	1521.1 conj	1056.1 conj	1822.3 verb 1pl indic aor act	2296.3 noun dat sing masc
καρδίᾳ.	13. εἴτε	γὰρ	ἐξέστημεν,	θεῷ·
kardia	eite	gar	exestēmen	theō
in heart.	Whether	for	we were beside ourselves,	to God;

1521.1 conj	4845.1 verb 1pl indic pres act	5050.3 prs-pron dat 2pl	3450.9 art nom sing fem	1056.1 conj	26.1 noun nom sing fem
εἴτε	σωφρονοῦμεν,	ὑμῖν.	14. ἡ	γὰρ	ἀγάπη
eite	sōphronoumen	humin	hē	gar	agapē
or	are sober minded	for you.	The	for	love

Millennium and the Eternal Age. To those who have erected a quality building in Christian service the Lord will say, "Well done, thou good and faithful servant: thou hast been faithful over a few things, I will make thee ruler over many things" (Matthew 25:21).

Those who appear at that tribunal will not be at the Great White Throne Judgment where unbelievers will answer to God regarding matters of sin and salvation (Revelation 20:11-15). A thousand years separate the two judgments (Revelation 20:5,6).

5:11. Paul feared coming before God unprepared, and he held an equal concern for others. He knew well the terror (*phobon*, "fear," here that which causes fear) of the Lord. As the author of Hebrews wrote, "It is a fearful thing to fall into the hands of the living God" (Hebrews 10:31). For this very reason Paul did his best to persuade men to turn from sin.

The apostle realized, of course, that already he himself stood openly before the Lord. His Master knew he was genuine, and he hoped his sincerity was equally clear at Corinth in the face of false accusations against him.

5:12. Here, as elsewhere in this letter, Paul emphasized his reasons for defending his ministry. He intended not to recommend himself personally to them. As he explained earlier (3:1ff.), surely that was not necessary. He did not defend his person but his ministry. He persuaded men of his integrity for the sake of the Church.

Persons attracted to preachers who opposed Paul were taking pride in external things rather than the internal realities of character. They boasted of the accomplishments of their favorite ministers who tried to remove the apostle from his position of honor in the Church.

Then out of concern for the welfare of sincere Christians at Corinth, Paul gave them an opportunity to respond to his critics in kind. He did not want them to feel they followed an inferior apostle and thus become discouraged along the way.

5:13. Some hinted Paul was mentally unbalanced. They suggested he went to such extremes that he even sought hardships. Only a religious maniac would do such. Festus suggested something similar (Acts 26:24). He thought much study drove the apostle to the border of insanity. Even Jesus' family feared He was losing His senses at one time (Mark 3:21).

Paul answered that any apparent fanaticism was for God and any sound thinking was for the Corinthians' good. He did all for the Lord and others, not self.

according to that he hath done: whether [it be] good or bad: ... or worthless, *Weymouth, Adams.*

11. Knowing therefore the terror of the Lord, we persuade men: Consequently, knowing how to reverence the Lord, *Fenton* ... how greatly the Lord is to be feared, *Weymouth* ... the fearfulness of the Lord's judgment, *Conybeare* ... we "try to win over men," *HistNT* ... we are trying to win our fellow men, *TCNT* ... we try to win men for Him, *Norlie.*

but we are made manifest unto God:

and I trust also are made manifest in your consciences: ... we shine forth, *Fenton.*

12. For we commend not ourselves again unto you: ... to your favour, *Weymouth.*

but give you occasion to glory on our behalf: ... but are giving you an opportunity, *Wilson* ... a ground of boasting, *Conybeare* ... opportunity to exult, *HistNT* ... to be proud of us, *SEB* ... who on the surface are proud, *Berkeley* ... respecting us, *PNT.*

that ye may have somewhat to [answer] them which glory in appearance, and not in heart: ... may have an answer ready, *Montgomery* ... who are proud of outward things, *SEB* ... with whom superficial appearances are everything, *Weymouth* ... rather than the inward qualification, *Phillips.*

13. For whether we be beside ourselves, [it is] to God: For if we are extravagant, *Murdock* ... if we are mad, *Fenton* ... if we are transported beyond ourselves, *Wesley* ... were out of our mind, *Confraternity* ... taken leave of our senses, *Adams* ... it was in God's service! *TCNT.*

or whether we be sober, [it is] for your cause: ... if we are sane, *Confraternity, Beck* ... are rational, *Fenton* ... if we are discreet, *Murdock* ... are "in our senses," *HistNT* ... be of sound mind, *Alford* ... or are soberminded, *Rotherham.*

3450.2 art gen sing	5382.2 name gen masc	4762.1 verb 3sing indic pres act	2231.4 prs-pron acc 1pl	2892.19 verb acc pl masc part aor act	3642.17 dem-pron sing neu
τοῦ	Χριστοῦ	συνέχει	ἡμᾶς,	κρίναντας	τοῦτο,
tou	Christou	sunechei	hēmas	krinantas	touto
of the	Christ	compels	us,	having judged	this,

3617.1 conj	1479.1 conj	1518.3 num card nom masc	5065.1 prep	3820.4 adj gen pl	594.10 verb 3sing indic aor act	679.1 partic
ὅτι	⌜a εἰ ⌝	εἷς	ὑπὲρ	πάντων	ἀπέθανεν,	ἄρα
hoti	ei	heis	huper	pantōn	apethanen	ara
that	if	one	for	all	died,	then

14.a.Txt: 01ℵ-corr 04C-org,byz.bo. **Var:** 01ℵ-org,03B 04C-corr,06D,018K 020L,025P,Lach,Treg Alf,Word,Tisc,We/Ho Weis,Sod,UBS/⋆

3450.7 art pl masc	3820.7 adj pl masc	594.9 verb indic aor act		2504.1 conj	5065.1 prep	3820.4 adj gen pl
οἱ	πάντες	ἀπέθανον·	**15.**	καὶ	ὑπὲρ	πάντων
hoi	pantes	apethanon		kai	huper	pantōn
the	all	died;		and	for	all

594.10 verb 3sing indic aor act	2419.1 conj	3450.7 art pl masc	2180.13 verb nom pl masc part pres act	3239.1 adv	1431.7 prs-pron dat pl masc
ἀπέθανεν,	ἵνα	οἱ	ζῶντες	μηκέτι	ἑαυτοῖς
apethanen	hina	hoi	zōntes	mēketi	heautois
he died,	that	the	living	no longer	to themselves

2180.4 verb 3pl pres act	233.2 conj	3450.3 art dat sing	5065.1 prep	840.1 prs-pron gen pl	594.17 verb dat sing masc part aor act
ζῶσιν,	ἀλλὰ	τῷ	ὑπὲρ	αὐτῶν	ἀποθανόντι
zōsin	alla	tō	huper	autōn	apothanonti
should live,	but	to the	for	them	having died

2504.1 conj	1446.26 verb dat sing masc part aor pass		5452.1 conj	2231.1 prs-pron nom 1pl	570.3 prep gen
καὶ	ἐγερθέντι.	**16.**	Ὥστε	ἡμεῖς	ἀπὸ
kai	egerthenti		Hōste	hēmeis	apo
and	having been raised again.		So that	we	from

3450.2 art gen sing	3431.1 adv	3625.3 num card acc masc	3471.5 verb 1pl indic perf act	2567.3 prep	4418.4 noun acc sing fem
τοῦ	νῦν	οὐδένα	οἴδαμεν	κατὰ	σάρκα·
tou	nun	oudena	oidamen	kata	sarka
the	now	no one	know	according to	flesh;

16.a.Txt: 01ℵ-corr 04C-corr,06D-corr,020L 025P,byz. **Var:** 01ℵ-org,03B 06D-org,33,Lach,Treg Alf,Tisc,We/Ho,Weis Sod,UBS/⋆

1479.1 conj	1156.2 conj	2504.1 conj	1091.33 verb 1pl indic perf act	2567.3 prep	4418.4 noun acc sing fem
εἰ	⌜a δὲ ⌝	καὶ	ἐγνώκαμεν	κατὰ	σάρκα
ei	de	kai	egnōkamen	kata	sarka
if	but	even	we have known	according to	flesh

5382.4 name acc masc	233.2 conj	3431.1 adv	3629.1 adv	1091.4 verb 1pl indic pres act	5452.1 conj
Χριστόν,	ἀλλὰ	νῦν	οὐκέτι	γινώσκομεν	**17.** ὥστε
Christon	alla	nun	ouketi	ginōskomen	hōste
Christ,	yet	now	no longer	we know.	So that

1479.1 conj	4948.3 indef-pron nom sing	1706.1 prep	5382.3 name dat masc	2508.3 adj nom sing fem	2909.1 noun nom sing fem	3450.17 art pl neu
εἴ	τις	ἐν	Χριστῷ,	καινὴ	κτίσις·	τὰ
ei	tis	en	Christō	kainē	ktisis	ta
if	anyone	in	Christ	a new	creation:	the

739.7 adj nom pl neu	3790.2 verb 3sing indic aor act	1481.20 verb 2sing impr aor mid	1090.3 verb 3sing indic perf act	2508.9 adj pl neu
ἀρχαῖα	παρῆλθεν,	ἰδοὺ	γέγονεν	καινά
archaia	parēlthen	idou	gegonen	kaina
old things	passed away;	lo,	have become	new

5:14. Far from being motivated selfishly, Paul protested that the love of Christ compelled him. Since Jesus died for him, how could he live for himself?

Inspired by the Spirit, Paul declared the core of the gospel here. Christ died for all as a substitute; He was actually executed for the sins of others. It logically follows that everyone who accepts that substitute should view himself as dead.

5:15. From the moment of conversion every believer should live for Christ, not self. Paul had written earlier, "Ye are not your own ... ye are bought with a price: therefore glorify God in your body, and in your spirit, which are God's" (1 Corinthians 6:19,20).

5:16. Those who viewed Paul as a self-seeking minister thought in human terms. They drew conclusions by the standards of worldly men. With spiritually blinded eyes people in general evaluate things falsely. They see through dark-colored, badly distorted glasses.

In contrast, the apostle had ceased to think in a worldly manner long before this. When he viewed Christ from a human point of view, he saw Him as a blasphemer. But after meeting the Master on the road to Damascus he knew Jesus as the Saviour of men.

As to the previous view of Paul and others concerning Jesus, Kent commented, "They thought of Him as a religious teacher from Galilee, untrained in any rabbinical school, who made messianic claims and was alleged to work miracles. Now, however, Paul no longer regarded Christ from this 'worldly point of view' (NIV)" (p.88). He also noted that the apostle's remark here has nothing to do with the question of whether or not he saw Christ in flesh on earth.

After meeting Jesus personally near Damascus Paul also looked at all men with a different set of values. He judged them and knew them no longer as an unregenerate man knows them. He related to them no more as persons distinguished by color of skin, country of origin, or station in life. He knew the truth that all equally need salvation.

5:17. Paul's radical change becomes the experience of all born-again believers. Once dead, now they are alive. Formerly blind, they see! Christ makes new creations of those who believe, as real as God made Adam in the beginning.

Biblical salvation not only brings something new, but it also subtracts something old. One's former set of values and his way of thinking disappear. His new outlook on life dictates a new life-style; the old becomes unworthy in his eyes.

The perfect tense of "become" (*gegonen*) indicates the results of the new birth at some point of time in the past remain current for the Christian. Through an experience as real as life he has been translated from the old world to the new.

14. For the love of Christ constraineth us: Christ is our motivation, *Adams* ... Christ's love controls us, *SEB* ... sustains us, *Fenton* ... overmasters us, *Weymouth* ... overmasters me, *Montgomery* ... impels us, *Confraternity, Berkeley* ... that urges us, *HistNT* ... controls us, *NASB* ... keeps us in harmony, *Klingensmith*.

because we thus judge, that if one died for all, then were all dead: ... having concluded this, *NASB* ... the conclusion at which we have arrived being this, *Weymouth* ... consequently all died, *Concordant* ... So, everyone died, *SEB*.

15. And [that] he died for all: that they which live should not henceforth live unto themselves: ... should live no longer, *Alford*.

but unto him which died for them, and rose again: ... for their sakes, *Concordant* ... on their behalf, *NASB*.

16. Wherefore henceforth know we no man after the flesh: Consequently, *Berkeley* ... we esteem him no more on that account, *Campbell* ... are acquainted with no one, *Concordant* ... we do not evaluate a person from a worldly point of view, *Norlie* ... view no man carnally, *Conybeare* ... only as a human being, *Beck*.

yea, though we have known Christ after the flesh: ... we know Christ personally, *Fenton* ... as a man, *Weymouth*.

yet now henceforth know we [him] no more: ... we don't evaluate Him this way, *Adams*.

17. Therefore if any man [be] in Christ, [he is] a new creature: ... there is a new creation, *Montgomery* ... a new creation altogether, *Norlie*.

old things are passed away; behold, all things are become new: The old is gone. Look! the new has come, *Berkeley* ... The old life has passed away, *Montgomery* ... the old state of things has passed away; a new state of things has come into existence, *Weymouth*.

17.a.Txt: 06D-corr,018K 020L,025P,044,byz. **Var:** p46,01א,03B,04C 06D-org,it.sa.bo.Lach Treg,Alf,Tisc,We/Ho Weis,Sod,UBS/✩

18.a.Txt: 06D-corr,018K 020L,byz. **Var:** 01א,03B,04C 06D-org,025P,33,it.bo. Lach,Treg,Alf,Word Tisc,We/Ho,Weis,Sod UBS/✩

3450.17 art pl neu	3820.1 adj	3450.17 art pl neu	1156.2 conj	3820.1 adj	1523.2 prep gen	3450.2 art gen sing
ʳᵃ τὰ	πάντα. ˋ	**18.** τὰ	δὲ	πάντα	ἐκ	τοῦ
ta	panta	ta	de	panta	ek	tou
the	all things:	the	and	all things	of	the

2296.2 noun gen sing masc	3450.2 art gen sing	2614.2 verb gen sing masc part aor act	2231.4 prs-pron acc 1pl	1431.5 prs-pron dat 3sing masc
θεοῦ,	τοῦ	καταλλάξαντος	ἡμᾶς	ἑαυτῷ
theou	tou	katallaxantos	hēmas	heautō
God,	the	having reconciled	us	to himself

1217.2 prep	2400.2 name masc	5382.2 name gen masc	2504.1 conj	1319.29 verb gen sing masc part aor act	2231.3 prs-pron dat 1pl
διὰ	ʳᵃ Ἰησοῦ ˋ	Χριστοῦ,	καὶ	δόντος	ἡμῖν
dia	Iēsou	Christou	kai	dontos	hēmin
by	Jesus	Christ,	and	having given	to us

3450.12 art acc sing fem	1242.4 noun acc sing fem	3450.10 art gen sing fem	2613.2 noun gen sing fem	5453.1 conj
τὴν	διακονίαν	τῆς	καταλλαγῆς·	**19.** ὡς
tēn	diakonian	tēs	katallagēs	hōs
the	ministry	of the	reconciliation:	how

3617.1 conj	2296.1 noun nom sing masc	1498.34 verb sing indic imperf act	1706.1 prep	5382.3 name dat masc	2862.4 noun acc sing masc
ὅτι	θεὸς	ἦν	ἐν	Χριστῷ	κόσμον
hoti	theos	ēn	en	Christō	kosmon
that	God	was	in	Christ	world

2614.1 verb nom sing masc part pres act	1431.5 prs-pron dat 3sing masc	3231.1 partic	3023.7 verb nom sing masc part pres	840.2 prs-pron dat pl
καταλλάσσων	ἑαυτῷ,	μὴ	λογιζόμενος	αὐτοῖς
katallassōn	heautō	mē	logizomenos	autois
reconciling	to himself,	not	reckoning	to them

3450.17 art pl neu	3761.6 noun acc pl neu	840.1 prs-pron gen pl	2504.1 conj	4935.37 verb nom sing masc part aor mid
τὰ	παραπτώματα	αὐτῶν,	καὶ	θέμενος
ta	paraptōmata	autōn	kai	themenos
the	offenses	their,	and	having put

1706.1 prep	2231.3 prs-pron dat 1pl	3450.6 art acc sing masc	3030.4 noun acc sing masc	3450.10 art gen sing fem	2613.2 noun gen sing fem
ἐν	ἡμῖν	τὸν	λόγον	τῆς	καταλλαγῆς.
en	hēmin	ton	logon	tēs	katallagēs
in	us	the	word	of the	reconciliation.

5065.1 prep	5382.2 name gen masc	3631.1 conj	4102.2 verb 1pl indic pres act	5453.1 conj
20. ὑπὲρ	Χριστοῦ	οὖν	πρεσβεύομεν,	ὡς
huper	Christou	oun	presbeuomen	hōs
For	Christ	therefore	we are ambassadors,	as

3450.2 art gen sing	2296.2 noun gen sing masc	3731.8 verb gen sing masc part pres act	1217.1 prep	2231.2 prs-pron gen 1pl	1183.2 verb 1pl indic pres
τοῦ	θεοῦ	παρακαλοῦντος	δι'	ἡμῶν·	δεόμεθα
tou	theou	parakalountos	di'	hēmōn	deometha
the	God	exhorting	by	us,	we beseech

5065.1 prep	5382.2 name gen masc	2614.5 verb 2pl impr aor pass	3450.3 art dat sing	2296.3 noun dat sing masc	3450.6 art acc sing masc
ὑπὲρ	Χριστοῦ,	καταλλάγητε	τῷ	θεῷ·	**21.** τὸν
huper	Christou	katallagēte	tō	theō	ton
for	Christ,	Be reconciled	to	God.	The

5:18. That new life leads to the realization that all things are of God. Paul said reconciliation especially is by His initiative.

Man's sins alienated him from his Maker. Disobedience to God always brings distance in relationship with Him. Paul's good news was that God took the initiative to restore fallen man to fellowship with himself. If He had not, surely man would not. Indeed, he could not.

A gracious God gave this message to Paul to share with mankind. In a faithful ministry (*diakonia*, "service") he did what his Master told him to do.

5:19. Having declared the doctrine of reconciliation as the center of Christian theology, Paul, directed by the Spirit, returned to the subject. The Corinthians, and indeed all men, must clearly understand the truth of the teaching.

The gospel begins with the fact that God was in Christ even while He was on earth. The fullness of the Deity dwelt in the body of Jesus (Colossians 2:9). Jesus was no ordinary man. If He had been, His death would have paid the penalty for His sins alone.

As it is, the Incarnation made reconciliation possible. Because Christ died for man's sins, his fellowship with God can be restored. The Father's righteousness demands each man pay the penalty for his sins. Since Jesus had none, He offered himself as a substitute for others. God accepted His death as such. Then God can stop imputing (counting against them) the sins of those who believe and still be true to His nature. In rebellion mankind committed many trespasses (took many false steps) on the road to destruction. Now because of Christ's obedience the record of all the believer's trespasses has been erased.

The Lord committed or deposited this message with Paul for careful handling. Paul managed this word of reconciliation as a steward of an estate entrusted to his care.

5:20. Being a steward of the gospel treasure, the apostle was also an ambassador (from *presbeuō*, "travel [or] work as an ambassador") for Christ. The Greek "for Christ" (*huper Christou*) appears first in the sentence for the sake of emphasis. Paul had the full authority any ambassador on earth does. He was the personal representative of the Majesty who sent him from the heavenly kingdom to the earthly one. Jesus said to the 12 apostles, "He that receiveth you receiveth me" (Matthew 10:40). Any contempt or injury toward the apostle was an offense against the Head of State who dispatched him. His message was not his own but that of his Sovereign. When he shared it with men it was with the same authority as if God spoke.

Paul realized God pleaded directly with men through him. In Christ's place he begged men to be reconciled to God. The Lord provided for man's fellowship with Him to be restored, but he must accept that offer.

18. And all things [are] of God: This has all originated with God, *Williams.*

who hath reconciled us to himself by Jesus Christ: Who restored us to Himself, *Fenton.*

and hath given to us the ministry of reconciliation: . . . and gave to us the office of restoration, *Fenton* . . . the work of bringing people back to Himself, *SEB* . . . the ministry of peacemaking, *NTPE.*

19. To wit, that God was in Christ:

reconciling the world unto himself: . . . personally reconciling, *Phillips* . . . getting rid of the enmity between Himself and the people of the world, *Beck* . . . with his majesty, *Murdock.*

not imputing their trespasses unto them: . . . not reckoning to them, *Young, HistNT* . . . not counting to them their offences, *Wilson* . . . not invoicing against them their falling aside, *Klingensmith* . . . not counting people's trespasses against them, *Adams* . . . not charging men's transgressions, *Weymouth* . . . their offences, *Rotherham* . . . not counting up their sins against them, *Berkeley* . . . instead of debiting men's offenses against them, *Williams.*

and hath committed unto us the word of reconciliation: He has entrusted, *Weymouth, Norlie, TCNT* . . . deposited with us, *Fenton* . . . the message, *Confraternity.*

20. Now then we are ambassadors for Christ: We are representing Christ, *SEB* . . . we are envoys, *HistNT* . . . We are Christ's missionaries, *NLT* . . . I am an envoy to represent Christ, *Williams.*

as though God did beseech [you] by us: God making his appeal through us, *RSV.*

we pray [you] in Christ's stead: So we plead, on behalf of Christ, *Norlie* . . . we implore you, *Fenton* . . . on Christ's behalf, *Hanson.*

be ye reconciled to God: Come and be God's friends, *Beck* . . . be gathered again to God! *Fenton.*

2 Corinthians 6:1

21.a.Txt: 01א-corr
06D-corr,018K,020L
025P,byz.
Var: 01א-org,03B,04C
06D-org,33,bo.Lach
Treg,Alf,Word,Tisc
We/Ho,Weis,Sod
UBS/✫

1056.1 conj	3231.1 partic	1091.27 verb acc sing masc part aor act	264.4 noun acc sing fem	5065.1 prep	2231.2 prs-pron gen 1pl
⸂a γὰρ ⸃	μὴ	γνόντα	ἁμαρτίαν	ὑπὲρ	ἡμῶν
gar	mē	gnonta	hamartian	huper	hēmōn
for	not	having known	sin	for	us

264.4 noun acc sing fem	4020.24 verb 3sing indic aor act	2419.1 conj	2231.1 prs-pron nom 1pl	1090.16 verb 1pl subj pres
ἁμαρτίαν	ἐποίησεν,	ἵνα	ἡμεῖς	⸀ γινώμεθα
hamartian	epoiēsen	hina	hēmeis	ginōmetha
sin	he made,	that	we	might become

21.b.Txt: Steph
Var: 01א,03B,04C,06D
018K,020L,025P,byz.
Lach,Treg,Alf,Word
Tisc,We/Ho,Weis,Sod
UBS/✫

1090.41 verb 1pl subj aor mid	1336.1 noun nom sing fem	2296.2 noun gen sing masc	1706.1 prep	840.4 prs-pron dat sing
[b✫ γενώμεθα]	δικαιοσύνη	θεοῦ	ἐν	αὐτῷ.
genōmetha	dikaiosunē	theou	en	autō
[idem]	righteousness	of God	in	him.

4753.4 verb nom pl masc part pres act	1156.2 conj	2504.1 conj	3731.2 verb 1pl indic pres act
6:1. Συνεργοῦντες	δὲ	καὶ	⸂✫ παρακαλοῦμεν
Sunergountes	de	kai	parakaloumen
Working together	but	also	we encourage

1.a.Txt: 01א,03B,04C
044,byz.
Var: p46,06D,010F
012G,2495

3731.9 verb nom pl masc part pres act	3231.1 partic	1519.1 prep	2727.1 adj sing	3450.12 art acc sing fem	5322.4 noun acc sing fem
[a παρακαλοῦντες]	μὴ	εἰς	κενὸν	τὴν	χάριν
parakalountes	mē	eis	kenon	tēn	charin
[encouraging]	not	in	vain	the	grace

3450.2 art gen sing	2296.2 noun gen sing masc	1203.16 verb inf aor mid	5050.4 prs-pron acc 2pl	2978.5 verb 3sing indic pres act	1056.1 conj
τοῦ	θεοῦ	δέξασθαι	ὑμᾶς	**2.** λέγει	γάρ,
tou	theou	dexasthai	humas	legei	gar
	of God	to receive	you:	he says	for,

2511.3 noun dat sing masc	1178.2 adj dat sing masc	1858.1 verb 1sing indic aor act	4622.2 prs-pron gen 2sing	2504.1 conj	1706.1 prep	2232.3 noun dat sing fem
Καιρῷ	δεκτῷ	ἐπήκουσά	σου,	καὶ	ἐν	ἡμέρᾳ
Kairō	dektō	epēkousa	sou	kai	en	hēmera
In a time	accepted	I listened to	you,	and	in	a day

4843.2 noun gen sing fem	990.3 verb 1sing indic aor act	4622.3 prs-pron dat 2sing	1481.20 verb 2sing impr aor mid	3431.1 adv	2511.1 noun nom sing masc
σωτηρίας	ἐβοήθησά	σοι·	ἰδοὺ	νῦν	καιρὸς
sōtērias	eboēthēsa	soi	idou	nun	kairos
of salvation	I helped	you:	lo,	now	time

2124.1 adj nom sing	1481.20 verb 2sing impr aor mid	3431.1 adv	2232.2 noun nom sing fem	4843.2 noun gen sing fem
εὐπρόσδεκτος,	ἰδοὺ	νῦν	ἡμέρα	σωτηρίας·
euprosdektos	idou	nun	hēmera	sōtērias
well accepted;	behold,	now	day	of salvation:

3235.5 num card acc fem	1706.1 prep	3235.2 num card dat	1319.9 verb nom pl masc part pres act	4207.1 noun acc sing fem
3. μηδεμίαν	ἐν	μηδενὶ	διδόντες	προσκοπήν,
mēdemian	en	mēdeni	didontes	proskopēn
not one	in	not anything	giving	offense,

2419.1 conj	3231.1 partic	3331.1 verb 3sing subj aor pass	3450.9 art nom sing fem	1242.1 noun nom sing fem	233.1 conj
ἵνα	μὴ	μωμηθῇ	ἡ	διακονία·	**4.** ἀλλ'
hina	mē	mōmēthē	hē	diakonia	all'
that	not	be blamed	the	service;	but

5:21. To further explain the doctrine of reconciliation, the apostle declared it involved Jesus' becoming sin for mankind. The One who knew no sin (*hamartia*, to miss the mark, to be in error) God reckoned as bearing the sins of man at Calvary. As Isaiah said, "The Lord hath laid on him the iniquity of us all" (Isaiah 53:6).

As to the fact that Jesus knew no sin Meyer observed: "This does not merely mean that Christ never committed a sin in thought, word, or deed; that every thought which He ever conceived, every pleasure that He ever felt, every desire that ever stirred in His heart, was absolutely without stain of sin, sweet and pure; not merely that He was free from every stain of original sin: it means that He was the One whom sin could not reach, the One who could not be tempted with sin, as St. James expresses it (James 1:13), the One who was 'holy, harmless, undefiled, *separate from sinners,* and higher than the heavens' (Hebrews 7:26)" (pp.118,119).

Unthinkable as it was, God accounted such an One a sinner because it was necessary to make possible man's becoming righteous. Man's sins were charged to Christ's account. Christ's righteousness was credited to the account of all who would believe on Him. Paul announced this truth in 1 Corinthians 1:30.

Then under the inspiration of the Spirit the apostle pronounced history's greatest double paradox. God arranged both for Jesus to be made sin and for man to be made righteous!

6:1. Paul was not only a steward or manager and an ambassador, but he was also a worker together with God. He used the same analogy in his earlier letter (1 Corinthians 3:9). There he pictured himself as a worker with God on a farm.

In such a responsible partnership the apostle pleaded with those in the church he founded not to receive the grace of God in vain or to no purpose. He feared they might depart from the Faith and surrender their confidence in his message because of what his critics said against him.

6:2. With the words of Isaiah to the Gentiles (Isaiah 49:8), Paul reminded the Corinthians God had heard them in an acceptable or favorable time (*kairos*, "fitting season," contrasted with *chronos*, which usually refers to time itself). In the day of salvation the Lord had succored (*eboēthēsa*, of its eight times in the New Testament, it is translated "help" six times) them. They must never take these things lightly.

6:3. Indeed, let all at Corinth beware lest they cause any to stumble (*proskopēn*, "make a misstep," used here only in the New Testament). Paul declared he did his best to avoid such a tragedy lest the ministry be discredited.

21. For he hath made him [to be] sin for us: . . . was regarded as sin, *Fenton* . . . a sin offering, *Wesley* . . . actually to be sin for our sakes, *Phillips* . . . in our behalf, *Young, Hanson.*

who knew no sin: Christ never sinned, *SEB* . . . who knew nothing of sin, *Confraternity.*

that we might be made the righteousness of God in him: . . . that we might be changed into the righteousness of God, *Conybeare* . . . receive justification from God, *Norlie.*

1. We then, [as] workers together [with him]: As God's coworkers, *SEB.*

beseech [you] also that ye receive not the grace of God in vain: Don't let God's love be wasted on you, *Beck* . . . we further appeal to you, *Berkeley* . . . the gift of God in vain, *Fenton* . . . to no purpose, *Weymouth.*

2. (For he saith, I have heard thee in a time accepted: In a favourable season, *Fenton* . . . At a time of welcome I have listened to you, *Weymouth* . . . I listened to you at the right time, *Norlie* . . . In an approved season, I hearkened to thee, *Rotherham, ASV.*

and in the day of salvation have I succoured thee: I aided thee, *Hanson* . . . I assisted thee, *Wilson* . . . I have helped thee, *Confraternity, HistNT.*

behold, now [is] the accepted time: . . . the present is a very favourable time, *Fenton* . . . the highly acceptable time! *HistNT* . . . Now is the right time, *SEB* . . . the time of loving welcome, *Weymouth.*

behold, now [is] the day of salvation.):

3. Giving no offence in any thing: Giving no cause of offence, *Alford* . . . We do not want to give offense, *Norlie* . . . we put no obstacle whatever in anyone's way, *Berkeley* . . . no single occasion of stumbling, *Rotherham.*

that the ministry be not blamed: . . . may not be impugned, *HistNT* . . . may not be discredited, *Berkeley* . . . should fall into discredit, *Weymouth.*

2 Corinthians 6:5

4.a.Txt: 01ℵ-corr
06D-corr,018K,020L
byz.
Var1: 03B,025P,We/Ho
Weis,Sod,UBS/☆
Var2: 01ℵ-org,04C
06D-org,33,Lach,Treg
Alf,Word,Tisc

1706.1 prep	3820.3 adj dat sing	4771.5 verb nom pl masc part pres act	4771.16 verb nom pl masc part pres act
ἐν	παντὶ	ʿ συνιστῶντες	[¹ᵃ☆ συνιστάνοντες
en	panti	sunistōntes	sunistanontes
in	everything	commending	[idem

4771.15 verb nom pl masc part pres act	1431.8 prs-pron acc pl masc	5453.1 conj	2296.2 noun gen sing masc	1243.3 noun nom pl masc
² συνιστάντες]	ἑαυτοὺς	ὡς	θεοῦ	διάκονοι,
sunistantes	heautous	hōs	theou	diakonoi
idem]	ourselves	as	God's	servants,

1706.1 prep	5119.3 noun dat sing fem	4044.11 adj dat sing fem	1706.1 prep	2324.7 noun dat pl fem	1706.1 prep
ἐν	ὑπομονῇ	πολλῇ,	ἐν	θλίψεσιν,	ἐν
en	hupomonē	pollē	en	thlipsesin	en
in	endurance	much,	in	tribulations,	in

316.5 noun dat pl fem	1706.1 prep	4581.2 noun dat pl fem	1706.1 prep	3987.7 noun dat pl fem	1706.1 prep
ἀνάγκαις,	ἐν	στενοχωρίαις,	5. ἐν	πληγαῖς,	ἐν
anankais	en	stenochōriais	en	plēgais	en
necessities,	in	difficulties,	in	stripes,	in

5274.5 noun dat pl fem	1706.1 prep	179.4 noun dat pl fem	1706.1 prep	2845.6 noun dat pl masc	1706.1 prep
φυλακαῖς,	ἐν	ἀκαταστασίαις,	ἐν	κόποις,	ἐν
phulakais	en	akatastasiais	en	kopois	en
imprisonments,	in	riots,	in	labors,	in

69.1 noun dat pl fem	1706.1 prep	3383.4 noun dat pl fem	1706.1 prep	53.1 noun dat sing fem	1706.1 prep
ἀγρυπνίαις,	ἐν	νηστείαις,	6. ἐν	ἁγνότητι,	ἐν
agrupniais	en	nēsteiais	en	hagnotēti	en
watchings,	in	fastings,	in	pureness,	in

1102.3 noun dat sing fem	1706.1 prep	3087.3 noun dat sing fem	1706.1 prep	5379.3 noun dat sing fem	1706.1 prep
γνώσει,	ἐν	μακροθυμίᾳ,	ἐν	χρηστότητι,	ἐν
gnōsei	en	makrothumia	en	chrēstotēti	en
knowledge,	in	patience,	in	kindness,	in

4011.3 noun dat sing neu	39.3 adj dat sing	1706.1 prep	26.3 noun dat sing fem	502.3 adj dat sing fem	1706.1 prep
πνεύματι	ἁγίῳ,	ἐν	ἀγάπῃ	ἀνυποκρίτῳ,	7. ἐν
pneumati	hagiō	en	agapē	anupokritō	en
Spirit	Holy,	in	love	sincere,	in

3030.3 noun dat sing masc	223.2 noun gen sing fem	1706.1 prep	1405.3 noun dat sing fem	2296.2 noun gen sing masc	1217.2 prep
λόγῳ	ἀληθείας,	ἐν	δυνάμει	θεοῦ,	διὰ
logō	alētheias	en	dunamei	theou	dia
word	of truth,	in	power	of God;	through

3450.1 art gen pl	3559.2 noun gen pl neu	3450.10 art gen sing fem	1336.2 noun gen sing fem	3450.1 art gen pl	1182.7 adj gen pl neu
τῶν	ὅπλων	τῆς	δικαιοσύνης	τῶν	δεξιῶν
tōn	hoplōn	tēs	dikaiosunēs	tōn	dexiōn
the	weapons	of the	righteousness	on the	right hand

2504.1 conj	704.2 adj gen pl neu	1217.2 prep	1385.2 noun gen sing fem	2504.1 conj	813.2 noun gen sing fem
καὶ	ἀριστερῶν,	8. διὰ	δόξης	καὶ	ἀτιμίας,
kai	aristerōn	dia	doxēs	kai	atimias
and	left,	through	glory	and	dishonor,

6:4. Not only did Paul's motives and message validate his ministry, but so did his conduct. He related specifically how he labored to keep from contributing to the backsliding of anyone and to maintain the integrity of the ministry. In all things he sought to demonstrate he was a worthy preacher of the gospel.

He did so with much patience (steadfastness, endurance). The way he faced up to ministerial hardships indicated his genuineness. This was true in the affliction or difficulty he encountered because of outward circumstances. The various necessities and dire straits (*stenochōria*, "narrowness") he faced provided further opportunities for God to manifest His grace to Paul. So did the distresses and calamities he knew.

6:5. Further, the apostle understood what it means to suffer stripes or blows for Jesus' sake. He had even been imprisoned because he preached the gospel. He and Silas were both beaten and placed behind bars at Philippi. The jailer sensed their suffering so that immediately upon his miraculous conversion he "took them the same hour of the night, and washed their stripes" (Acts 16:33). Later Paul spent long periods in jail at Caesarea and Rome. Sometimes he barely escaped, and at other times he was left for dead in tumults or riots caused by enemies of the gospel where he preached.

None except the truly called and fully dedicated would labor as hard as Paul did. By day he toiled at his tentmaking trade to support himself and those with him. By night he shared with men the Bread of Life. When his long day ended, even what remained of some of his nights was sleepless because his prayer burden had him watching over the souls of men. He knew what it was to fast too, both voluntarily and involuntarily, when he had no food to eat.

6:6. By pureness (the word includes sincerity and integrity) the apostle proved himself a genuine servant of the Lord. The knowledge God had imparted to him demonstrated it also. He learned it through the study of Scripture, but God revealed the correct understanding where his Jewish teachers had incorrectly interpreted the Word to him (Galatians 1:11,12).

Through the power and fruit of the Spirit Paul showed longsuffering or forbearance toward weaknesses and wrongs of others, even when at times he could have retaliated. By the Holy Spirit he was full of kindness and generosity to others. He possessed that all-important attribute of love that was unfeigned, genuine and without hypocrisy.

6:7. The apostle always spoke the word of truth in the power of God. As a warrior he wore the whole armor of God with weapons of defense in his left hand and offense in his right.

4. But in all [things] approving ourselves as the ministers of God: . . . commending ourselves, *ASV.*

in much patience, in afflictions:

in necessities, in distresses: . . . in straits, *Rotherham* . . . by helplessness, *Weymouth* . . . or even disasters, *Phillips* . . . amid troubles, *HistNT* . . . calamities, *Norlie.*

5. In stripes, in imprisonments: . . . in lashes, *Berkeley.*

in tumults, in labours: . . . in riots, *Fenton* . . . in the midst of political instability, *Wuest* . . . by facing riots, *Weymouth* . . . mobbings, *Berkeley* . . . being mobbed, having to work like slaves, *Phillips* . . . in toilings, *Rotherham.*

in watchings, in fastings: . . . in sleepless nights, *Confraternity.*

6. By pureness, by knowledge: . . . though innocence, *Berkeley* . . . in innocence, *Confraternity* . . . in chastity, *Rotherham.*

by longsuffering, by kindness: . . . in patience, *NASB* . . . in forbearance, *Hanson, Norlie* . . . when conferring benefits, *Fenton.*

by the Holy Ghost, by love unfeigned: . . . by sincere love, *Weymouth* . . . in unaffected love, *Confraternity* . . . unpretended love, *Berkeley* . . . in genuine love, *NASB* . . . by unpretended love, *Fenton* . . . a love devoid of hypocrisy, *Wuest.*

7. By the word of truth, by the power of God: . . . by true reason, *Fenton* . . . the proclamation of the truth, *Weymouth.*

by the armour of righteousness on the right hand and on the left: . . . with the armor of justice, *Confraternity* . . . the weapons of righteousness, *Rotherham* . . . our only weapon is a life of integrity, *Phillips.*

8. By honour and dishonour: . . . ignominy, *Weymouth* . . . and disgrace, *Fenton.*

1217.2 prep	1419.1 noun gen sing fem	2504.1 conj	2143.1 noun gen sing fem	5453.1 conj	3969.2 adj nom sing masc	2504.1 conj
διὰ	δυσφημίας	καὶ	εὐφημίας·	ὡς	πλάνοι,	καὶ
dia	dusphēmias	kai	euphēmias	hōs	planoi	kai
through	evil report	and	good report:	as	deceivers,	and

225.3 adj nom pl masc	5453.1 conj	49.13 verb nom pl masc part pres pass	2504.1 conj	1906.18 verb nom pl masc part pres pass
ἀληθεῖς·	**9.** ὡς	ἀγνοούμενοι,	καὶ	ἐπιγινωσκόμενοι·
alētheis	hōs	agnooumenoi	kai	epiginōskomenoi
true;	as	being unknown,	and	being well known;

5453.1 conj	594.7 verb nom pl masc part pres act	2504.1 conj	1481.20 verb 2sing impr aor mid	2180.3 verb 1pl pres act	5453.1 conj
ὡς	ἀποθνήσκοντες,	καὶ	ἰδοὺ	ζῶμεν·	ὡς
hōs	apothnēskontes	kai	idou	zōmen	hōs
as	dying,	and	lo	we live;	as

3674.8 verb nom pl masc part pres pass	2504.1 conj	3231.1 partic	2266.6 verb nom pl masc part pres pass	5453.1 conj
παιδευόμενοι,	καὶ	μὴ	θανατούμενοι·	**10.** ὡς
paideuomenoi	kai	mē	thanatoumenoi	hōs
being disciplined,	and	not	being put to death;	as

3048.9 verb nom pl masc part pres pass	103.1 adv	1156.2 conj	5299.9 verb nom pl masc part pres act	5453.1 conj	4292.4 adj pl masc
λυπούμενοι,	ἀεὶ	δὲ	χαίροντες·	ὡς	πτωχοὶ
lupoumenoi	aei	de	chairontes	hōs	ptōchoi
being sorrowful,	always	but	rejoicing;	as	poor,

4044.8 adj acc pl masc	1156.2 conj	4008.1 verb nom pl masc part pres act	5453.1 conj	3235.6 num card neu	2174.19 verb nom pl masc part pres act
πολλοὺς	δὲ	πλουτίζοντες·	ὡς	μηδὲν	ἔχοντες,
pollous	de	ploutizontes	hōs	mēden	echontes
many	but	enriching;	as	nothing	having,

2504.1 conj	3820.1 adj	2692.5 verb nom pl masc part pres act	3450.16 art sing neu	4601.1 noun sing neu	2231.2 prs-pron gen 1pl
καὶ	πάντα	κατέχοντες.	**11.** Τὸ	στόμα	ἡμῶν
kai	panta	katechontes	To	stoma	hēmōn
and	all things	possessing.	The	mouth	our

453.12 verb 3sing indic perf act	4242.1 prep	5050.4 prs-pron acc 2pl	2854.2 name voc pl masc	3450.9 art nom sing fem	2559.2 noun nom sing fem
ἀνέῳγεν	πρὸς	ὑμᾶς,	Κορίνθιοι,	ἡ	καρδία
aneōgen	pros	humas	Korinthioi	hē	kardia
has been opened	to	you,	Corinthians,	the	heart

2231.2 prs-pron gen 1pl	3975.3 verb 3sing indic perf pass	3620.3 partic	4580.1 verb 2pl indic pres pass	1706.1 prep
ἡμῶν	πεπλάτυνται·	**12.** οὐ	στενοχωρεῖσθε	ἐν
hēmōn	peplatuntai	ou	stenochōreisthe	en
our	has been enlarged.	Not	you are being cramped	in

2231.3 prs-pron dat 1pl	4580.1 verb 2pl indic pres pass	1156.2 conj	1706.1 prep	3450.4 art dat pl	4551.2 noun dat pl neu
ἡμῖν,	στενοχωρεῖσθε	δὲ	ἐν	τοῖς	σπλάγχνοις
hēmin	stenochōreisthe	de	en	tois	splanchnois
us,	you are being cramped	but	in	the	bowels

5050.2 prs-pron gen 2pl	3450.12 art acc sing fem	1156.2 conj	840.12 prs-pron acc sing fem	486.1 noun acc sing fem	5453.1 conj
ὑμῶν.	**13.** τὴν	δὲ	αὐτὴν	ἀντιμισθίαν,	ὡς
humōn	tēn	de	autēn	antimisthian	hōs
your;	the	but	same	recompense,	as

6:8. Paul continued his list in discussing his conduct stating several paradoxes he had experienced as a preacher. He was honored by his friends and dishonored by his enemies. Some spread evil reports about him and slandered him while others gave good reports. However, Paul knew he always spoke the truth.

6:9. Sometimes the apostle experienced human sorrow, but in it all he had cause for rejoicing. From his prison cell in later years he wrote, "Rejoice in the Lord always: and again I say, Rejoice" (Philippians 4:4).

6:10. Paul knew poverty too. He could feel with those who went hungry and suffered need (Philippians 4:12). In fact, it was in discussing times of need he declared, "I can do all things through Christ which strengtheneth me" (Philippians 4:13). However, the apostle was willing to be in financial want at times if through devotion to duty regardless of circumstances he could make others rich spiritually. In this he was like Christ. Later in this second letter to the Corinthians Paul wrote that "though he (Christ) was rich, yet for your sakes he became poor, that ye through his poverty might be rich" (8:9). The apostle could say he had nothing, yet he possessed all things.

6:11. Suddenly, with great feeling the apostle shouted out the address, "O ye Corinthians!" Only twice elsewhere did he do such a thing in his letters. After crying "O foolish Galatians," he chided them for having turned away so soon from a faith in Christ to the ritualistic worship of Judaism again (Galatians 3:1). He addressed the Philippians by name while commending them for sending him a missionary offering (Philippians 4:15).

The expression showed deep emotion as he wrote these words. With a passion one can feel as he reads these lines, the apostle cried out he had opened wide his mouth to them. He had spoken freely and honestly to them on all occasions. He had opened his heart toward them also. His was no mere professional relationship. He loved them with all his heart.

6:12. Paul made clear there was no distance between him and his audience as far as he was concerned. The relationship was not straitened (restricted, strained) on his part. They had broken the fellowship. If they continued to remain apart from him, the trouble was in their own "bowels." The word is a synonym for heart. Paul used it to speak of the seat of the emotions or affections.

6:13. With as strong a plea as it is possible for man to make, the apostle begged the Corinthians who had turned against him to

by evil report and good report: . . . through blame and praise, *Berkeley* . . . through calumny and praise, *Weymouth.*

as deceivers, and [yet] true: They call us imposters, *Norlie* . . . looked upon as impostors, *Weymouth.*

9. As unknown, and [yet] well known:
as dying, and, behold, we live: Never far from death, *Phillips.*
as chastened, and not killed: . . . as punished, *NASB* . . . seemingly crushed, *Fenton* . . . and not put to death, *Young.*

10. As sorrowful, yet alway rejoicing: . . . yet our joy is inextinguishable, *Phillips.*
as poor, yet making many rich: . . . as destitute, *Rotherham* . . . as indigent but making many wealthy, *Berkeley* . . . but we bestow wealth on many, *Weymouth.*
as having nothing, and [yet] possessing all things: . . . we have everything worth having, *Phillips.*

11. O [ye] Corinthians, our mouth is open unto you: We keep nothing back from you, *HistNT* . . . I am unsealing my lips to you, *Montgomery* . . . we address you frankly, *Berkeley* . . . We have spoken freely to you, *Norlie.*
our heart is enlarged: . . . is expanded, *Weymouth* . . . is wide open to you, *Confraternity.*

12. Ye are not straitened in us: In us there is no lack of room for you, *Confraternity* . . . Our affections toward you are not restricted, *Norlie* . . . There is no narrowness in our love to you, *Weymouth* . . . You are not restrained by us, *NASB.*
but ye are straitened in your own bowels: . . . in your own affections, *Fenton* . . . in your own souls, *Sawyer* . . . in your hearts' afflictions, *Rotherham.*

13. Now for a recompense in the same: . . . now as a return of benefits, *Sawyer* . . . you should widen your affections toward us, *Norlie.*

4891.6 noun dat pl neu	2978.1 verb 1sing pres act	3975.2 verb 2pl impr aor pass	2504.1 conj	5050.1 prs-pron nom 2pl	3231.1 partic
τέκνοις	λέγω,	πλατύνθητε	καὶ	ὑμεῖς.	14. Μὴ
teknois	legō	platunthēte	kai	humeis	Mē
to children	I speak,	be enlarged	also	you.	Not

1090.19 verb 2pl impr pres	2065.1 verb nom pl masc part pres act	566.6 adj dat pl masc	4949.3 intr-pron nom sing	1056.1 conj
γίνεσθε	ἑτεροζυγοῦντες	ἀπίστοις·	τίς	γὰρ
ginesthe	heterozugountes	apistois	tis	gar
be	yoking unevenly	with unbelievers;	what	for

3222.1 noun nom sing fem	1336.3 noun dat sing fem	2504.1 conj	455.3 noun dat sing fem	4949.3 intr-pron nom sing	1156.2 conj
μετοχὴ	δικαιοσύνῃ	καὶ	ἀνομίᾳ;	῾ τίς	δὲ
metochē	dikaiosunē	kai	anomia	tis	de
participation	righteousness	and	lawlessness?	what	and

14.a.**Txt**: 018K,byz.
Var: 01ℵ,03B,04C,06D
020L,025P,33,it.bo.
Lach,Treg,Alf,Word
Tisc,We/Ho,Weis,Sod
UBS/⋆

2211.1 conj	4949.3 intr-pron nom sing	2815.1 noun nom sing fem	5295.3 noun dat sing neu	4242.1 prep	4510.1 noun sing
[ᵃ⋆ ἢ	τίς]	κοινωνία	φωτὶ	πρὸς	σκότος;
ē	tis	koinōnia	phōti	pros	skotos
[or	what]	fellowship	light	with	darkness?

4949.3 intr-pron nom sing	1156.2 conj	4708.1 noun nom sing fem	5382.3 name dat masc	5382.2 name gen masc
15. τίς	δὲ	συμφώνησις	῾ Χριστῷ	[ᵃ⋆ Χριστοῦ]
tis	de	sumphōnēsis	Christō	Christou
what	and	agreement	Christ	[idem]

15.a.**Txt**: 06D,018K
020L,byz.
Var: 01ℵ,03B,025P,33
Lach,Treg,Alf,Tisc
We/Ho,Weis,Sod
UBS/⋆

4242.1 prep	948.2 name masc	2211.1 conj	4949.3 intr-pron nom sing	3182.1 noun nom sing fem	3964.4 adj dat sing masc	3196.3 prep
πρὸς	Βελίαρ·	ἢ	τίς	μερὶς	πιστῷ	μετὰ
pros	Beliar	ē	tis	meris	pistō	meta
with	Belial,	or	what	part	to a believer	with

566.3 adj gen sing masc	4949.3 intr-pron nom sing	1156.2 conj	4634.1 noun nom sing fem	3348.3 noun dat sing masc
ἀπίστου;	16. τίς	δὲ	συγκατάθεσις	ναῷ
apistou	tis	de	sunkatathesis	naō
an unbeliever?	what	and	agreement	a temple

16.a.**Txt**: p46,01ℵ-corr
04C,06D-corr,018K,byz.
it.
Var: 01ℵ-org,03B
06D-org,020L,025P,33
sa.bo.Lach,Treg,Tisc
We/Ho,Weis,Sod
UBS/⋆

2296.2 noun gen sing masc	3196.3 prep	1487.4 noun gen pl neu	5050.1 prs-pron nom 2pl	2231.1 prs-pron nom 1pl	1056.1 conj
θεοῦ	μετὰ	εἰδώλων;	῾ ὑμεῖς	[ᵃ⋆ ἡμεῖς]	γὰρ
theou	meta	eidōlon	humeis	hēmeis	gar
of God	with	idols?	you	[we]	for

16.b.**Txt**: p46,01ℵ-corr
04C,06D-corr,018K,byz.
it.
Var: 01ℵ-org,03B
06D-org,020L,025P,33
sa.bo.Lach,Treg,Tisc
We/Ho,Weis,Sod
UBS/⋆

3348.1 noun nom sing masc	2296.2 noun gen sing masc	1498.6 verb 2pl indic pres act	1498.5 verb 1pl indic pres act	2180.11 verb gen sing part pres act
ναὸς	θεοῦ	῾ ἐστε	[ᵇ⋆ ἐσμεν	ζῶντος,
naos	theou	este	esmen	zōntos
a temple	of God	are	[idem]	living,

2503.1 conj	1500.5 verb 3sing indic aor act	3450.5 art sing masc	2296.1 noun nom sing masc	3617.1 conj	1758.5 verb 1sing indic fut act
καθὼς	εἶπεν	ὁ	θεὸς,	῞Οτι	ἐνοικήσω
kathōs	eipen	ho	theos	Hoti	enoikēsō
according as	said		God,		I will dwell

1706.1 prep	840.2 prs-pron dat pl	2504.1 conj	1688.1 verb 1sing indic fut act	2504.1 conj	1498.38 verb 1sing indic fut mid
ἐν	αὐτοῖς,	καὶ	ἐμπεριπατήσω	καὶ	ἔσομαι
en	autois	kai	emperipatēsō	kai	esomai
among	them,	and	will walk among;	and	I will be

return his steadfast love for them. He urged a recompence of the same affection he had shown them. He asked only for a fair exchange of enlarged hearts. He wanted a return of their confidence, to be sure, but more than that, he wanted their love.

In all this Paul spoke tenderly to his readers as his children in the Faith. He reminded them in his earlier letter they had many teachers but only one father (1 Corinthians 4:15).

6:14. Concern for evil in the hearts of the critical faction at Corinth caused Paul to call for a separation between them and true Christians in the church. His plea was for a pure congregation divorced from the sins of society, whether in the lives of pagans about them or in the professing believers in their fellowship.

He began with a command that genuine disciples not be unequally yoked with unbelievers. Under the Law the Lord did not allow the mismatching of uneven teams of animals. No one should plow an ox and an ass together (Deuteronomy 22:10). How much less should unequal men be yoked?

In his first letter to Corinth the apostle instructed that fellowship cease between sincere and hypocritical Christians. Real disciples should keep no company with any man who was called a brother who practiced fornication or who was covetous, an idolater, a railer, a drunkard, or an extortioner (1 Corinthians 5:11). Paul likewise told Titus to withdraw from a factious person who constantly caused division in the body (Titus 3:10,11).

To further make his point Paul asked a series of rhetorical questions. What do righteousness and lawlessness have in common to share with each other? What fellowship can light and darkness have together?

6:15. What concord (*sumphōnēsis*, "agreement" here only in the New Testament) does Christ have with Belial ("worthlessness")? What part or portion does a believer share with an infidel (*apistos*, same as in verse 14) or unbeliever?

6:16. What agreement or union does the temple (*naos*) of God have with idols? In regard to the communion service Paul wrote earlier, "Ye cannot drink the cup of the Lord, and the cup of devils: ye cannot be partakers of the Lord's table, and of the table of devils" (1 Corinthians 10:21).

The apostle declared Christians are the temple of God, again using *naos*, the abiding place of Jehovah. From Leviticus 26:12 he quoted the promise that the Lord would both dwell with and walk among His people.

What relationship can there be then between each of these items in the five questions? The obvious answer is none. In every case the two stand as opposite because they belong to different realms. The logical conclusion is believers and unbelievers can have no

(I speak as unto [my] children,) be ye also enlarged: . . . let your hearts also be wide open to me, *Montgomery* . . . open wide your hearts, *Berkeley* . . . with the same complete candor! *Phillips.*

14. Be ye not unequally yoked together with unbelievers: Do not be mismated, *Norlie, RSV* . . . Don't be mismatched, *SEB* . . . Don't be hooked up with, *Klingensmith* . . . Be not getting diversely-yoked, *Rotherham, PNT* . . . unequally connected, *Fenton* . . . Share no incongruous yoke, *HistNT* . . . Don't link up with unbelievers, *Phillips* . . . like oxen yoked with asses, *Weymouth.*

for what fellowship hath righteousness with unrighteousness?: What participation, *Wilson* . . . How can right and wrong be partners? *Beck* . . . for what common ground, *Berkeley* . . . what partnership, *Norlie* . . . for what partaking is there to righteousness and lawlessness? *Young* . . . and iniquity, *Alford, Panin* . . . what do righteousness and lawlessness share in common? *Adams.*

and what communion hath light with darkness?: . . . what partnership, *Weymouth* . . . what in common, *PNT.*

15. And what concord hath Christ with Belial?: What harmony is there, *Confraternity*

or what part hath he that believeth with an infidel?: . . . what partnership, *Berkeley* . . . or what portion, *Hanson* . . . who can classify faith with unbelief? *Fenton.*

16. And what agreement hath the temple of God with idols?: What common ground, *Phillips* . . . What connection, *Wilson* . . . what compact, *Weymouth* . . . what alliance, *Norlie* . . . has God's sanctuary, *HistNT* . . . the sanctuary, *Young.*

for ye are the temple of the living God; as God hath said:

I will dwell in them, and walk in [them]: . . . live and walk among them, *Beck* . . . move among them, *Confraternity* . . . travel with them, *Fenton.*

2 Corinthians 6:17

16.c.Txt: 06D,018K
020L,byz.it.Sod
Var: 01א,03B,04C,025P
33,Lach,Treg,Tisc
We/Ho,Weis,UBS/⋆

17.a.Txt: 06D,018K
020L,025P,byz.
Var: 01א,03B,04C,33
Lach,Treg,Alf,Tisc
We/Ho,Weis,Sod
UBS/⋆

840.1 prs-pron gen pl	2296.1 noun nom sing masc	2504.1 conj	840.7 prs-pron nom pl masc	1498.43 verb 3pl indic fut mid	1466.4 prs-pron dat 1sing
αὐτῶν	θεός,	καὶ	αὐτοὶ	ἔσονταί	ʹ μοι
autōn	theos	kai	autoi	esontai	moi
their	God,	and	they	shall be	to me

1466.2 prs-pron gen 1sing	2967.1 noun sing masc	1346.1 conj	1814.44 verb 2pl impr pres act	1814.10 verb 2pl impr aor act
[c⋆ μου]	λαός.	**17.** διὸ	ʹ ἐξέλθετε	[a⋆ ἐξέλθατε]
mou	laos	dio	exelthete	exelthate
[my]	a people.	Wherefore	come out	[idem]

1523.2 prep gen	3189.4 adj gen sing neu	840.1 prs-pron gen pl	2504.1 conj	866.9 verb 2pl impr aor pass	2978.5 verb 3sing indic pres act
ἐκ	μέσου	αὐτῶν	καὶ	ἀφορίσθητε,	λέγει
ek	mesou	autōn	kai	aphoristhēte	legei
from	the midst	their	and	be separated,	says

2935.1 noun nom sing masc	2504.1 conj	167.3 adj gen sing neu	3231.1 partic	674.7 verb 2pl impr pres mid	2476.3 conj
κύριος,	καὶ	ἀκαθάρτου	μὴ	ἅπτεσθε·	κἀγὼ
kurios	kai	akathartou	mē	haptesthe	kagō
Lord,	and	unclean	not	touch,	and I

1509.1 verb 1sing indic fut mid	5050.4 prs-pron acc 2pl	2504.1 conj	1498.38 verb 1sing indic fut mid	5050.3 prs-pron dat 2pl	1519.1 prep
εἰσδέξομαι	ὑμᾶς,	**18.** καὶ	ἔσομαι	ὑμῖν	εἰς
eisdexomai	humas	kai	esomai	humin	eis
will receive	you;	and	I will be	to you	for

3824.4 noun acc sing masc	2504.1 conj	5050.1 prs-pron nom 2pl	1498.42 verb 2pl indic fut mid	1466.4 prs-pron dat 1sing	1519.1 prep	5048.9 noun acc pl masc
πατέρα,	καὶ	ὑμεῖς	ἔσεσθέ	μοι	εἰς	υἱοὺς
patera	kai	humeis	esesthe	moi	eis	huious
a father,	and	you	shall be	to me	for	sons

2504.1 conj	2341.8 noun acc pl fem	2978.5 verb 3sing indic pres act	2935.1 noun nom sing masc	3703.1 noun nom sing masc
καὶ	θυγατέρας,	λέγει	κύριος	παντοκράτωρ.
kai	thugateras	legei	kurios	pantokratōr
and	daughters,	says	Lord	Almighty.

3642.15 dem-pron acc pl fem	3631.1 conj	2174.19 verb nom pl masc part pres act	3450.15 art acc pl fem	1845.1 noun fem
7:1. Ταύτας	οὖν	ἔχοντες	τὰς	ἐπαγγελίας,
Tautas	oun	echontes	tas	epangelias
These	therefore	having	the	promises,

27.6 adj pl masc	2483.6 verb 1pl subj aor act	1431.8 prs-pron acc pl masc	570.3 prep gen	3820.2 adj gen sing
ἀγαπητοί,	καθαρίσωμεν	ἑαυτοὺς	ἀπὸ	παντὸς
agapētoi	katharisōmen	heautous	apo	pantos
beloved,	we should cleanse	ourselves	from	every

3299.1 noun gen sing masc	4418.2 noun gen sing fem	2504.1 conj	4011.2 noun gen sing neu	1989.2 verb nom pl masc part pres act
μολυσμοῦ	σαρκὸς	καὶ	πνεύματος,	ἐπιτελοῦντες
molusmou	sarkos	kai	pneumatos	epitelountes
defilement	of flesh	and	spirit,	perfecting

41.3 noun acc sing fem	1706.1 prep	5238.3 noun dat sing masc	2296.2 noun gen sing masc	5397.6 verb 2pl impr aor act	2231.4 prs-pron acc 1pl
ἁγιωσύνην	ἐν	φόβῳ	θεοῦ.	**2.** Χωρήσατε	ἡμᾶς·
hagiōsunēn	en	phobō	theou	Chōrēsate	hēmas
holiness	in	fear	of God.	Receive	us:

close communion, whether in the church, in marriage, or in business. Any association a believer has with an unbeliever should have the goal of winning him to Christ.

6:17. To "come out from among them" should be an automatic reaction in view of the above reasoning. Still, Paul used the aorist imperative to issue his call for separation to indicate urgency. His words are from Isaiah 52:11. Once they leave the world behind, God's children should then touch no unclean thing. If they "come out" and "touch not," the Lord will receive (*eisdexomai*, here only in the New Testament) or welcome them.

6:18. The apostle had one more promise for the faithful at Corinth. As they lived in faith and obedience to Him, God would be their Father and they would be His sons and daughters. This promise is specifically from the Lord Almighty (*pantokratōr*, used as a part of God's name 10 times in the New Testament and always translated "Almighty").

7:1. On the basis of these promises Paul had a new appeal for the converts at Corinth. It concerned the doctrine of sanctification. The doctrine has both its positive and negative aspects. It involves separation from the secular on the one hand and dedication to the sacred on the other. Neither a legalistic separation from sin nor an empty profession of dedication to God constitutes sanctification. Here the apostle's emphasis is on the separation side of the doctrine. He exhorted a cleansing of self from sin.

In one sense it is God who sanctifies (1 Thessalonians 5:23,24). However, man must participate in it as Paul made clear here. In Leviticus 20:7,8 Jehovah instructed the people of Israel to sanctify themselves, though a moment later He declared, "I am the Lord which sanctify you."

With an emphasis on man's responsibility in sanctification Paul stated he must rid himself of filthiness, that which defiles the flesh in outward acts such as drunkenness, stealing, and murder. He cannot afford to take less care as to what soils his spirit, the inner sins of pride, envy, and jealousy.

When the believer accepts what Christ did for him, he is immediately sanctified (1 Corinthians 6:11). However, he has a continuous duty of perfecting (maintaining, completing) holiness in his life. He is under obligation to do so in the fear of God, with appropriate awe and respect for Him.

7:2. Continuing his plea of 6:11-13, the apostle again begged the Corinthians to receive or make room for him in their hearts. Thus

and I will be their God, and they shall be my people:

17. Wherefore come out from among them, and be ye separate, saith the Lord: So, come away, *SEB* ... Come out of company with them, *Williams* ... depart from the midst of them, *Wilson* ... from the heathen, *TCNT*.

and touch not the unclean [thing]: ... touch nothing impure, *Weymouth* ... Touch nothing that is sinful, *NLT*.

and I will receive you: Then I will accept you, *SEB* ... I will give you welcome, *Rotherham* ... I will welcome you with favor, *HistNT*.

18. And will be a Father unto you, and ye shall be my sons and daughters:
saith the Lord Almighty: The Lord the Ruler of all, *Weymouth* ... the All-Ruling Lord, *Fenton* ... the All-powerful God, *NLT* ... The Lord Omnipotent speaks, *Berkeley*.

1. Having therefore these promises, dearly beloved: Dear friends, *SEB* ... In possession, *Berkeley* ... As we possess these promises, *HistNT*.
let us cleanse ourselves from all filthiness of the flesh and spirit: ... let us purify, *Sawyer* ... we should purify ourselves, *Fenton* ... from all defilement, *Weymouth* ... every pollution, *Young, Concordant* ... all contamination, *Wuest* ... from all polution of flesh, *Rotherham*.
perfecting holiness in the fear of God: Let us be completely holy, showing respect for God, *SEB* ... and complete our dedication by reverence, *Berkeley* ... progressively accomplishing holiness, *Wuest* ... secure perfect holiness, *Weymouth* ... completing our holiness, *Adams* ... perfecting purity in reverence, *Fenton* ... by consecrating ourselves to him completely, *Phillips*.

2. Receive us: Make room for us, *Panin* ... Take us into your hearts, *HistNT* ... Open your hearts to us, *ASV* ... Give us a favorable hearing, *Conybeare*.

3625.3 num card acc masc	90.7 verb 1pl indic aor act	3625.3 num card acc masc	5188.3 verb 1pl indic aor act	3625.3 num card acc masc
οὐδένα	ἠδικήσαμεν,	οὐδένα	ἐφθείραμεν,	οὐδένα
oudena	ēdikēsamen	oudena	ephtheiramen	oudena
no one	did we wrong,	no one	did we corrupt,	no one

3982.4 verb 1pl indic aor act		3620.3 partic	4242.1 prep	2603.2 noun acc sing fem	4242.1 prep
ἐπλεονεκτήσαμεν.	3. ʹ	οὐ	πρὸς	κατάκρισιν	[☆ πρὸς
epleonektēsamen		ou	pros	katakrisin	pros
did we defraud.		Not	for	condemnation	[for

2603.2 noun acc sing fem	3620.3 partic	2978.1 verb 1sing pres act	4136.1 verb 1sing indic perf act	1056.1 conj	3617.1 conj
κατάκρισιν	οὐ]	λέγω·	προείρηκα	γὰρ	ὅτι
katakrisin	ou	legō	proeirēka	gar	hoti
condemnation	not]	I speak,	I have before said	for	that

1706.1 prep	3450.14 art dat pl fem	2559.7 noun dat pl fem	2231.2 prs-pron gen 1pl	1498.6 verb 2pl indic pres act	1519.1 prep
ἐν	ταῖς	καρδίαις	ἡμῶν	ἐστε	εἰς
en	tais	kardiais	hēmōn	este	eis
in	the	hearts	our	you are,	for

3450.16 art sing neu	4731.2 verb inf aor act	2504.1 conj	4651.1 verb inf pres act	4044.9 adj nom sing fem
τὸ	συναποθανεῖν	καὶ	συζῆν.	4. πολλή
to	sunapothanein	kai	suzēn	pollē
the	to die together	and	to live together.	Great

1466.4 prs-pron dat 1sing	3816.1 noun nom sing fem	4242.1 prep	5050.4 prs-pron acc 2pl	4044.9 adj nom sing fem	1466.4 prs-pron dat 1sing
μοι	παρρησία	πρὸς	ὑμᾶς,	πολλή	μοι
moi	parrhēsia	pros	humas	pollē	moi
to me	boldness	towards	you,	great	to me

2716.1 noun nom sing fem	5065.1 prep	5050.2 prs-pron gen 2pl	3997.28 verb 1sing indic perf pass	3450.11 art dat sing fem
καύχησις	ὑπὲρ	ὑμῶν·	πεπλήρωμαι	τῇ
kauchēsis	huper	humōn	peplērōmai	tē
boasting	in respect of	you;	I have been filled	with the

3735.3 noun dat sing fem	5086.2 verb 1sing indic pres pass	3450.11 art dat sing fem	5315.3 noun dat sing fem	1894.3 prep
παρακλήσει,	ὑπερπερισσεύομαι	τῇ	χαρᾷ	ἐπὶ
paraklēsei	huperperisseuomai	tē	chara	epi
encouragement;	I overabound	with the	joy	at

3820.11 adj dat sing fem	3450.11 art dat sing fem	2324.3 noun dat sing fem	2231.2 prs-pron gen 1pl	2504.1 conj	1056.1 conj
πάσῃ	τῇ	θλίψει	ἡμῶν.	5. Καὶ	γὰρ
pasē	tē	thlipsei	hēmōn	Kai	gar
all	the	tribulation	our.	Indeed	for,

2048.17 verb gen pl masc part aor act	2231.2 prs-pron gen 1pl	1519.1 prep	3081.4 name acc fem	3625.5 num card acc fem
ἐλθόντων	ἡμῶν	εἰς	Μακεδονίαν,	οὐδεμίαν
elthontōn	hēmōn	eis	Makedonian	oudemian
having come	we	into	Macedonia,	not any

2174.35 verb 3sing indic perf act	423.2 noun acc sing fem	3450.9 art nom sing fem	4418.1 noun nom sing fem	2231.2 prs-pron gen 1pl	233.1 conj
ἔσχηκεν	ἄνεσιν	ἡ	σὰρξ	ἡμῶν,	ἀλλ᾽
eschēken	anesin	hē	sarx	hēmōn	all'
has had	rest	the	flesh	our,	but

he had not departed from the overall discussion of his relationship with them. His earlier treatment of the subjects of sins and holiness showed the Corinthians' attitude toward them affected their fellowship with him as well as with God.

In renewed defense of his ministry Paul protested that he had not wronged or treated any man unjustly. Nor had he corrupted or defrauded (taken advantage of, cheated) anyone. Possibly some whispered he had misused church funds, a charge he would soon answer in detail in chapters 8 and 9. At the direction of the Spirit Paul used the aorist tense with each of the three verbs to say he had never at any time done any of these things.

7:3. Anticipating possible misunderstanding of his purpose in writing as he did, the apostle declared his aim was not to condemn all the Corinthian believers with the few who had made the false charges. Justifiably he hated evil, without or within the church in the Greek city, but he was angry at no person. He repeated again that those of the congregation in Corinth were his very life. He would live with them, sharing their joys and sorrows, and if necessary he would even die with them. Along with his converts elsewhere, the hope of seeing them stand acceptably before the Lord on judgment day was the major reward he anticipated. His converts were his joy and crown (1 Thessalonians 2:19,20). No wonder they filled his heart.

7:4. Precisely because he loved the Corinthians so much Paul felt he could be fearless in his speech toward them. In case any among them counted his straightforward preaching as harshness, he wanted them to know also that he was just as forward in praising them among Christians wherever he went. As a faithful father, he showed great boldness in correcting them, but he took great pride in them too.

In fact, thoughts of them brought him much comfort. The inspiration he drew from their lives caused his joy to overflow even in the distress brought on by outward circumstances he experienced. True ministers always draw much strength from those they serve.

7:5. Among the troubles he experienced were those he had in the province of Macedonia just before he wrote this letter. At Ephesus he wrote 1 Corinthians and sent it with Titus as his personal messenger. Paul was so anxious to know how they had received it he started toward Corinth to meet Titus on his return. Taking the land route, he stopped briefly at Troas. When the young minister did not arrive as soon as expected, the apostle hastened to Macedonia. All this he explained earlier in 2:12,13.

we have wronged no man: We injure no one, *Concordant*.

we have corrupted no man: . . . ruined, *Phillips, HistNT*.

we have defrauded no man: We tricked no one, *Klingensmith* . . . we took advantage of no one, *NASB, ASV, PNT* . . . we didn't take advantage of anybody, *Adams* . . . we have imposed on no one, *Greber* . . . we have plundered none, *Fenton* . . . cheated, *Phillips* . . . gained any selfish advantage, *Weymouth* . . . we have exploited no one, *Berkeley*.

3. I speak not [this] to condemn [you]:
for I have said before: I have previously said, *Hanson, Wilson*.
that ye are in our hearts to die and live with [you]: . . . are ready to live and die with you, *Greber*.

4. Great [is] my boldness of speech toward you, great [is] my glorying of you: I trust you; I am proud of you, *Norlie* . . . Great is my confidence, *Confraternity* . . . is my freedom, *Young* . . . very loudly do I boast of you, *Weymouth* . . . To your face I talk to you with utter frankness, *Phillips* . . . on your behalf, *Rotherham* . . . for I am very proud of you, *Fenton*.
I am filled with comfort: I'm very much encouraged, *Beck* . . . I am quite content, *Fenton*.
I am exceeding joyful in all our tribulation: I'm overjoyed, *Beck, RSV* . . . Overbound with, *Young* . . . I am overloaded with joy, *Klingensmith* . . . I am thoroughly delighted, *Adams* . . . supremely delighted, *Fenton* . . . greatly superabounding with the joy, *Rotherham* . . . filled with good cheer, *PNT* . . . I overflow with joy in all our affliction, *Hanson* . . . my heart overflows with joy amid all our affliction, *Weymouth*.

5. For, when we were come into Macedonia:
our flesh had no rest: . . . our bodies had no rest at all, *SEB* . . . enjoyed no respite at all, *Berkeley* . . . no relief at all had our flesh, *Rotherham* . . . such as human nature craves, *Weymouth*.

1706.1 prep
ἐν
en
in

3820.3 adj dat sing
παντὶ
panti
every

2323.4 verb nom pl masc part pres pass
θλιβόμενοι·
thlibomenoi
being oppressed;

1839.1 prep gen
ἔξωθεν
exōthen
without

3135.1 noun nom pl fem
μάχαι,
machai
contentions,

2060.1 adv
ἔσωθεν
esōthen
within

5238.5 noun nom pl masc
φόβοι.
phoboi
fears.

233.1 conj
6. ἀλλ'
all'
But

3450.5 art sing masc
ὁ
ho
the

3731.7 verb nom sing masc part pres act
παρακαλῶν
parakalōn
encouraging

3450.8 art acc pl masc
τοὺς
tous
the

4862.3 adj acc pl masc
ταπεινοὺς
tapeinous
brought low

3731.13 verb 3sing indic aor act
παρεκάλεσεν
parekalesen
encouraged

2231.4 prs-pron acc 1pl
ἡμᾶς
hēmas
us

3450.5 art sing masc
ὁ
ho
the

2296.1 noun nom sing masc
θεὸς
theos
God

1706.1 prep
ἐν
en
by

3450.11 art dat sing fem
τῇ
tē
the

3814.3 noun dat sing fem
παρουσίᾳ
parousia
coming

4951.2 name gen masc
Τίτου·
Titou
of Titus;

3620.3 partic
7. οὐ
ou
not

3303.1 adv
μόνον
monon
only

1156.2 conj
δὲ
de
and

1706.1 prep
ἐν
en
by

3450.11 art dat sing fem
τῇ
tē
the

3814.3 noun dat sing fem
παρουσίᾳ
parousia
coming

840.3 prs-pron gen sing
αὐτοῦ,
autou
his,

233.2 conj
ἀλλὰ
alla
but

2504.1 conj
καὶ
kai
also

1706.1 prep
ἐν
en
by

3450.11 art dat sing fem
τῇ
tē
the

3735.3 noun dat sing fem
παρακλήσει
paraklēsei
encouragement

3614.11 rel-pron dat sing fem
ᾗ
hē
with which

3731.25 verb 3sing indic aor pass
παρεκλήθη
pareklēthē
he was encouraged

1894.1 prep
ἐφ'
eph'
as to

5050.3 prs-pron dat 2pl
ὑμῖν,
humin
you;

310.2 verb nom sing masc part pres act
ἀναγγέλλων
anangellōn
relating

2231.3 prs-pron dat 1pl
ἡμῖν
hēmin
to us

3450.12 art acc sing fem
τὴν
tēn
the

5050.2 prs-pron gen 2pl
ὑμῶν
humōn
your

1956.1 noun acc sing fem
ἐπιπόθησιν,
epipothēsin
longing,

3450.6 art acc sing masc
τὸν
ton
the

5050.2 prs-pron gen 2pl
ὑμῶν
humōn
your

3465.2 noun acc sing masc
ὀδυρμόν,
odurmon
mourning,

3450.6 art acc sing masc
τὸν
ton
the

5050.2 prs-pron gen 2pl
ὑμῶν
humōn
your

2188.4 noun acc sing neu
ζῆλον
zēlon
zeal

5065.1 prep
ὑπὲρ
huper
for

1466.3 prs-pron gen 1sing
ἐμοῦ,
emou
me;

5452.1 conj
ὥστε
hōste
so that

1466.6 prs-pron acc 1sing
με
me
me

3095.1 adv comp
μᾶλλον
mallon
the more

5299.21 verb inf aor pass
χαρῆναι.
charēnai
to be rejoiced.

3617.1 conj
8. Ὅτι
Hoti
For

1479.1 conj
εἰ
ei
if

2504.1 conj
καὶ
kai
also

3048.3 verb 1sing indic aor act
ἐλύπησα
elupēsa
I grieved

5050.4 prs-pron acc 2pl
ὑμᾶς
humas
you

1706.1 prep
ἐν
en
in

3450.11 art dat sing fem
τῇ
tē
the

1976.3 noun dat sing fem
ἐπιστολῇ,
epistolē
epistle,

3620.3 partic
οὐ
ou
not

3208.1 verb 1sing indic pres
μεταμέλομαι,
metamelomai
I do regret,

1479.1 conj
εἰ
ei
if

2504.1 conj
καὶ
kai
even

3208.5 verb 1sing indic imperf
μετεμελόμην·
metemelomēn
I was regretting;

Of course Paul ministered while he waited. He found no rest for his weary body. Outwardly he dealt with quarreling and strife in Macedonia as in other places. Inwardly he wrestled with anxieties and concerns as to the condition of the church at Corinth.

7:6. However, the God of all comfort, He who provides consolation for all the humbled, met Paul's personal needs. God providentially arranged for Titus to arrive just at the right time with priceless encouragement. His personal presence (*parousia*) wonderfully refreshed the apostle.

7:7. While renewed fellowship with a much-loved brother meant a lot to Paul, Titus' arrival brought news which strengthened him more than ever. The young preacher himself had been greatly refreshed through his visit to the Corinthian church. The grace of God he saw in their lives comforted him to no small extent. The fire of this enthusiastic report warmed Paul's heart immediately.

However, the apostle was interested in more than just the welfare of Titus. Imagine the thrill as his youthful partner rehearsed events at Corinth which spoke loudly of the believers' earnest desire, their longing to see the apostle. Titus told also of the love for Paul they manifested with tears of sorrow. The old warrior listened intently as Titus told him about the believers' fervent mind or zeal for him. With the load of not knowing how they might respond to his earlier letter lifted, Paul rejoiced greatly.

That the Corinthians earnestly desired to see him, mourned because they had pained him, and remained devoted friends though false teachers exerted so evil an influence to the contrary, meant a great deal to Paul.

7:8. The apostle referred to the earlier letter in 2:4. He said he shed many tears as he wrote it. Its corrective content caused fears he might overburden the Corinthians with grief when his intent was simply to demonstrate his love and concern for them. As a matter of fact, Paul even wrote a letter before that one. He mentioned it in 1 Corinthians 5:9 where he revealed a small portion of its subject matter.

Of the extent to which Paul went previously, and again here to close the distance between himself and the Corinthians, Carver wrote, "In a most delicate manner Paul attempts to perfect his reconciliation with the church. If all the misunderstandings, suspicions, and bitterness are to be removed from their relationship, the past must be opened up, not just covered over only to rise again in some future circumstances. Love that is spiritual seeks a reconciliation so real that the relation can actually be the same again even though the healed wound will ever bear a scar" (*Beacon Bible Commentary*, 8:569,570).

but we were troubled on every side: . . . in utter distress, *HistNT* . . . oppressed, *PNT.*

without [were] fightings, within [were] fears: . . . it was wrangles without, *HistNT* . . . wranglings outside, *Berkeley* . . . contentions without, *Fenton* . . . conflicts without, *Kleist* . . . and anxiety within, *Phillips.*

6. Nevertheless God, that comforteth those that are cast down: . . . who consoleth the lowly, *Worrell* . . . who comforts the downhearted, *Montgomery, Williams* . . . who encourages the weary, *Klingensmith* . . . who lifts up the downcast, *Norlie* . . . those who feel miserable, *Beck* . . . the disconsolate, *Wilson* . . . the depressed, *Murdock.*

comforted us by the coming of Titus: . . . has encouraged us, *TCNT.*

7. And not by his coming only: . . . not only in his presence, *Young.*

but by the consolation wherewith he was comforted in you:

when he told us your earnest desire: . . . narrating to us, *Wilson* . . . rehearsing to us, *Rotherham, Worrell* . . . declaring to us your longing desire, *Clementson* . . . how much you yearned to see me, *SEB.*

your mourning, your fervent mind toward me: . . . of your penitence, *TCNT* . . . your deep sorrow, *Sawyer* . . . your lamentation, your zeal for me, *Young* . . . how loyal you were to me, *Williams.*

so that I rejoiced the more: . . . was happier still, *Montgomery* . . . so that my sorrow has been turned into joy, *Conybeare* . . . I was gladder still, *Williams.*

8. For though I made you sorry with a letter: For even though I hurt your feelings, *NTPE* . . . I caused you pain, *Adams.*

I do not repent: I am not regretting it, *Concordant* . . . and now I am glad I sent it, *Phillips.*

though I did repent: Even if I was inclined to regret it, *TCNT.*

2 Corinthians 7:9

8.a.Txt: 01ℵ,04C
06D-corr,018K,020L
025P,33,etc.byz.bo.Tisc
Sod
Var: p46,03B,06D-org,it.
sa.Treg,We/Ho,Weis
UBS/✱

984.2 verb 1sing indic pres act	1056.1 conj	3617.1 conj	3450.9 art nom sing fem	1976.1 noun nom sing fem	1552.9 dem-pron nom sing fem
βλέπω	⸆ γὰρ ⸄	ὅτι	ἡ	ἐπιστολὴ	ἐκείνη
blepō	gar	hoti	hē	epistolē	ekeinē
I see	for	that	the	epistle	that,

1479.1 conj	2504.1 conj	4242.1 prep	5443.4 noun acc sing fem	3048.4 verb 3sing indic aor act	5050.4 prs-pron acc 2pl	3431.1 adv
εἰ	καὶ	πρὸς	ὥραν	ἐλύπησεν	ὑμᾶς,	9. νῦν
ei	kai	pros	hōran	elupēsen	humas,	nun
if	even	for	an hour,	grieved	you.	Now

5299.1 verb 1sing indic pres act	3620.1 partic	3617.1 conj	3048.12 verb 2pl indic aor pass	233.1 conj	3617.1 conj
χαίρω,	οὐχ	ὅτι	ἐλυπήθητε,	ἀλλ'	ὅτι
chairō	ouch	hoti	elupēthēte	all'	hoti
I rejoice,	not	that	you were grieved,	but	that

3048.12 verb 2pl indic aor pass	1519.1 prep	3211.2 noun acc sing fem	3048.12 verb 2pl indic aor pass	1056.1 conj
ἐλυπήθητε	εἰς	μετάνοιαν·	ἐλυπήθητε	γὰρ
elupēthēte	eis	metanoian	elupēthēte	gar
you were grieved	to	repentance;	you were grieved	for

2567.3 prep	2296.4 noun acc sing masc	2419.1 conj	1706.1 prep	3235.2 num card dat	2193.3 verb 2pl subj aor pass
κατὰ	θεόν,	ἵνα	ἐν	μηδενὶ	ζημιωθῆτε
kata	theon,	hina	en	mēdeni	zēmiōthēte
according to	God,	that	in	nothing	you might suffer loss

1523.1 prep gen	2231.2 prs-pron gen 1pl	3450.9 art nom sing fem	1056.1 conj	2567.3 prep	2296.4 noun acc sing masc
ἐξ	ἡμῶν.	10. ἡ	γὰρ	κατὰ	θεὸν
ex	hēmōn.	hē	gar	kata	theon
by	us.	The	for	according to	God

3049.1 noun nom sing fem	3211.2 noun acc sing fem	1519.1 prep	4843.3 noun acc sing fem	276.1 adj acc sing fem
λύπη	μετάνοιαν	εἰς	σωτηρίαν	ἀμεταμέλητον
lupē	metanoian	eis	sōtērian	ametamelēton
grief	repentance	to	salvation	not to be regretted

10.a.Txt: 01ℵ-corr,018K
020L,byz.
Var: 01ℵ-org,03B,04C
06D,025P,Lach,Treg
Alf,Word,Tisc,We/Ho
Weis,Sod,UBS/✱

2686.2 verb 3sing indic pres	2021.4 verb 3sing indic pres	3450.9 art nom sing fem	1156.2 conj	3450.2 art gen sing
⸄ κατεργάζεται·	[ᵃ✱ ἐργάζεται·]	ἡ	δὲ	τοῦ
katergazetai	ergazetai	hē	de	tou
works out;	[works;]	the	but	of the

2862.2 noun gen sing masc	3049.1 noun nom sing fem	2265.4 noun acc sing masc	2686.2 verb 3sing indic pres	1481.20 verb 2sing impr aor mid
κόσμου	λύπη	θάνατον	κατεργάζεται.	11. ἰδοὺ
kosmou	lupē	thanaton	katergazetai.	idou
world	grief	death	works out.	Lo

1056.1 conj	840.15 prs-pron sing neu	3642.17 dem-pron sing neu	3450.16 art sing neu	2567.3 prep	2296.4 noun acc sing masc
γὰρ	αὐτὸ	τοῦτο	τὸ	κατὰ	θεὸν
gar	auto	touto	to	kata	theon
for,	same	this thing,	to	according to	God

11.a.Txt: 01ℵ-corr,06D
018K,020L,025P,byz.
Var: 01ℵ-org,03B,04C
33,Lach,Treg,Tisc
We/Ho,Weis,Sod
UBS/✱

3048.16 verb inf aor pass	5050.4 prs-pron acc 2pl	4073.4 intr-pron acc sing fem	2686.9 verb 3sing indic aor mid
λυπηθῆναι	⸆ ὑμᾶς ⸄	πόσην	κατειργάσατο
lupēthēnai	humas	posēn	kateirgasato
to have been grieved	you,	how much	it worked out

Titus truthfully reported the second letter made the Corinthians sorry and caused them pain. In spite of that the apostle declared he had not repented (*metamelomai*, not the usual word for repent), i.e., he did not regret he had sent it. However, he experienced the human emotion of regretting temporarily the corrective tone of his message. Any who have duties in discipline, parents included, understand what he felt. Without it, the disciplinarian should examine his motives. Paul was glad after it was all over that the letter had caused pain for only a season (a short while, even a moment).

7:9. Now Paul could rejoice, though he found no pleasure in causing them pain. The happiness he experienced was over their sorrow which led them to repentance (*metanoia*, "change of mind or attitude," the more usual word for repentance). It relieved him to know the Corinthians had not sustained injury through the corrective ministry of his letter.

7:10. The apostle revealed much about the doctrine of repentance here. He stressed that sorrow is not repentance. In fact, only godly sorrow works toward repentance. It is from God, produced by the Holy Spirit. It is also directed toward Him for having offended Him through sin. In his farewell to the Ephesian elders Paul declared he regularly preached repentance toward God and faith toward Jesus (Acts 20:21).

King David experienced godly sorrow after his sin with Bathsheba. He recorded his prayer of repentance in Psalm 51:4: "Against thee, thee only, have I sinned, and done this evil in thy sight." With that attitude he found pardon from God.

By contrast, the sorrow of this world regrets only sin's discovery and leads merely to dread of the consequence of sin. Since it does not work repentance, it ends in eternal death in the lake of fire. It can also adversely affect a person's health in this life and lead to physical death. Depression flowing from worldly sorrow can result in suicide.

King Saul sensed only the sorrow of this world at his rejection by Jehovah. It caused him concern lest he lose respect in the eyes of the men of the army he commanded. When the prophet Samuel refused to help him keep up appearances, Saul sought to physically restrain the man of God (1 Samuel 15:22-30). In the end he committed suicide (1 Samuel 31:4).

7:11. Paul experienced a worshipful spirit as he contemplated the fact that the Corinthians had known godly sorrow. He knew that is what produces true repentance. The change of mind it involves is by no means a surface action. Rather, it is a deep-seated alteration in the inner man. Its product is a basic change of attitude. It brings a totally new outlook on life.

for I perceive that the same epistle hath made you sorry: . . . that I grieved you by the letter, *Wesley*.

though [it were] but for a season: . . . temporarily, *Fenton* . . . even for an hour, *Rotherham* . . . though only momentarily, *Berkeley* . . . only for a while, *RSV* . . . only for a time, *HistNT*.

9. Now I rejoice, not that ye were made sorry, but that ye sorrowed to repentance: . . . you were sad enough to change your hearts, *SEB* . . . brought you to repentance, *TCNT* . . . led you to repentance, *Confraternity* . . . to reformation, *Young, Hanson* . . . to change of thinking, *Klingensmith* . . . had a salutary effect, *Weymouth*.

for ye were made sorry after a godly manner: . . . grieved unto a return to God, *Fenton* . . . grieved after a godly sort, *Hanson* . . . such as God intended you to have, *Greber*.

that ye might receive damage by us in nothing: . . . that ye might suffer loss, *Clementson, ASV* . . . might suffer no loss through us, *HistNT* . . . no detriment from us, *Murdock* . . . so that you were not punished by it uselessly, *Fenton* . . . not merely to make you offended by what we said, *Phillips* . . . you were not in the least damaged by us, *Berkeley*.

10. For godly sorrow worketh repentance to salvation not to be repented of: For, sorrowing on account of God worketh a conversion, *Murdock* . . . There are no regrets, *SEB* . . . a repentance not to be regretted, *Weymouth* . . . never to be regretted, *Noyes*.

but the sorrow of the world worketh death: . . . results in death, *HistNT* . . . produces death, *Confraternity, Weymouth*.

11. For behold this selfsame thing: Look at this very fact, *HistNT* . . . For mark the effects of this very thing, *Weymouth*.

that ye sorrowed after a godly sort: . . . your Divine grief, *Fenton* . . . God's type of sorrow, *SEB* . . . suffered in accordance with the will of God, *Williams*.

5050.3 prs-pron dat 2pl	4561.3 noun acc sing fem	233.2 conj	621.4 noun acc sing fem	233.2 conj
ὑμῖν	σπουδήν,	ἀλλὰ	ἀπολογίαν,	ἀλλὰ
humin	spouden	alla	apologian	alla
in you	eagerness,	but	defense,	but

24.1 noun acc sing fem	233.2 conj	5238.4 noun acc sing masc	233.2 conj	1956.1 noun acc sing fem	233.2 conj
ἀγανάκτησιν,	ἀλλὰ	φόβον,	ἀλλὰ	ἐπιπόθησιν,	ἀλλὰ
aganaktēsin	alla	phobon	alla	epipothēsin	alla
indignation,	but	fear,	but	longing,	but

2188.4 noun acc sing neu	233.1 conj	233.2 conj	1544.3 noun acc sing fem	1706.1 prep	3820.3 adj dat sing
ζῆλον,	(ἀλλ'	[✶ ἀλλὰ]	ἐκδίκησιν,	ἐν	παντὶ
zēlon	all'	alla	ekdikēsin	en	panti
zeal,	but	[idem]	vengeance!	in	every

11.b.Txt: 06D-corr,018K 020L,025P,byz.Lach **Var:** 01א,03B,04C 06D-org,33,Treg,Alf Word,Tisc,We/Ho,Weis Sod,UBS/✶

4771.8 verb 2pl indic aor act	1431.8 prs-pron acc pl masc	52.3 adj acc pl masc	1498.32 verb inf pres act	1706.1 prep	3450.3 art dat sing
συνεστήσατε	ἑαυτοὺς	ἁγνοὺς	εἶναι	(ᵇ ἐν)	τῷ
sunestēsate	heautous	hagnous	einai	en	tō
you proved	yourselves	pure	to be	in	the

4088.3 noun dat sing neu	679.1 partic	1479.1 conj	2504.1 conj	1119.7 verb 1sing indic aor act	5050.3 prs-pron dat 2pl	3620.1 partic
πράγματι.	**12.** ἄρα	εἰ	καὶ	ἔγραψα	ὑμῖν,	οὐχ
pragmati	ara	ei	kai	egrapsa	humin	ouch
matter.	Then	if	also	I wrote	to you,	not

12.a.Txt: byz. **Var:** 01א,03B,04C,06D 018K,(020L),Lach,Treg Alf,Tisc,We/Ho,Weis Sod,UBS/✶

1736.1 prep	1736.2 prep	3450.2 art gen sing	90.13 verb gen sing masc part aor act	3624.1 adv
(εἵνεκεν	[ᵃ✶ ἕνεκεν]	τοῦ	ἀδικήσαντος,	οὐδὲ
heineken	heneken	tou	adikēsantos	oude
for the sake of	[idem]	the	having done wrong,	nor

12.b.Txt: byz. **Var:** 01א,03B,04C,06D 018K,(020L),Lach,Treg Alf,Tisc,We/Ho,Weis Sod,UBS/✶

1736.1 prep	1736.2 prep	3450.2 art gen sing	90.19 verb gen sing masc part aor pass
(εἵνεκεν	[ᵇ✶ ἕνεκεν]	τοῦ	ἀδικηθέντος·
heineken	heneken	tou	adikēthentos
for the sake of	[idem]	the	having suffered wrong,

12.c.Txt: byz. **Var:** 01א,03B,04C,06D 018K,(020L),Lach,Treg Alf,Tisc,We/Ho,Weis Sod,UBS/✶

233.1 conj	1736.1 prep	1736.2 prep	3450.2 art gen sing	5157.17 verb inf aor pass
ἀλλ'	(εἵνεκεν	[ᶜ✶ ἕνεκεν]	τοῦ	φανερωθῆναι
all'	heineken	heneken	tou	phanerōthēnai
but	for the sake of	[idem]	the	to be manifested

3450.12 art acc sing fem	4561.3 noun acc sing fem	5050.2 prs-pron gen 2pl	3450.12 art acc sing fem	5065.1 prep	2231.2 prs-pron gen 1pl
τὴν	σπουδὴν	ὑμῶν	τὴν	ὑπὲρ	ἡμῶν
tēn	spouden	humōn	tēn	huper	hēmōn
the	diligence	your	the	for	us

4242.1 prep	5050.4 prs-pron acc 2pl	1783.1 prep gen	3450.2 art gen sing	2296.2 noun gen sing masc	1217.2 prep
πρὸς	ὑμᾶς	ἐνώπιον	τοῦ	θεοῦ.	**13.** Διὰ
pros	humas	enōpion	tou	theou	Dia
to	you	before	the	God.	On account of

13.a.Var: 01א,03B,04C 06D,018K,020L,025P 33,Lach,Treg,Alf,Word Tisc,We/Ho,Weis,Sod UBS/✶

3642.17 dem-pron sing neu	3731.30 verb 1pl indic perf pass	1894.3 prep	1156.2 conj	3450.11 art dat sing fem
τοῦτο	παρακεκλήμεθα	ἐπὶ	[ᵃ✶+ δὲ]	τῇ
touto	parakeklēmetha	epi	de	tē
this	we have been encouraged	in	[and]	the

With repentance comes a change of mind about God and His holy demands. It alters a person's attitude about sin. The penitent comes to realize he has greatly offended the Lord by his wicked deeds. That sense, that knowledge becomes so real the repentant one weeps over his sins. True repentance is so radical in experience it is part of the process of the new birth.

Godly sorrow leads to repentance; repentance plus faith in Christ culminates in regeneration; and regeneration produces conversion where the believer turns from sin to live a new life. The apostle illustrated this truth as he marveled at what repentance produced at Corinth.

Paul noted that repentance produced a strong desire to correct the wrongs at Corinth. It produced in the believers an eagerness to clear themselves, to present a true defense (*apologia*) by attending to the problem of sin in their ranks. It brought indignation or anger against the sin of the member of their church who had an incestuous affair with his stepmother (1 Corinthians 5:1).

Further, repentance stirred fear (reverence, respect) for God in the hearts of the Corinthians. Pondering truth as to the judgment of the Lord on sin brought about a wholesome awe in His presence. It gave them a vehement desire for restoration to full fellowship with the Lord and the apostle Paul. The zeal they felt in repentance caused them to adminster discipline on the offender.

In the end repentance propelled the believers at Corinth into such action that they demonstrated they were now clear and innocent in the matter. They responded very differently to the apostle's original letter of instruction that they attend to the problem. Instead of weeping over the sin among them then, they had proudly declared their conduct acceptable to God (1 Corinthians 5:2). After all, didn't they have all the gifts of the Spirit in operation in their services?

7:12. With deep appreciation for the way the Corinthians had responded to the ministry of correction in his letter, Paul had a final word of explanation. He had not written with any ill will toward the one who had done the wrong, even though that one had treated another, his father, unjustly. Nor had Paul addressed the issue just to defend the one who had suffered the injustice to his wife. Paul's cause was more basic. He intended to show the care and devotion to them that he maintained before God.

7:13. Returning to the matter of Titus' report, Paul said once more it brought him much encouragement. He wrote again also of the blessing those at Corinth were to Titus. Above his own comfort, the apostle was even more pleased at what he saw in his young partner. Titus' spirit was refreshed, his mind set at rest through his visit to the troubled church. He had gone, wondering how the believers would receive him as a disciplinarian. Their reception soon relieved him of all anxiety over the matter.

what carefulness it wrought in you: ... what earnestness, *Confraternity* ... how great diligence it produced in you, *Sawyer*.

yea, [what] clearing of yourselves: ... what explanations, *TCNT* ... what eagerness to defend yourselves, *Norlie*.

yea, [what] indignation: What strong feeling! *TCNT*.

yea, [what] fear: ... what alarm, *Weymouth*.

yea, [what] vehement desire: ... earnest longing! *TCNT* ... longing affection, *Weymouth* ... what yearning, *Confraternity*.

yea, [what] zeal: ... what fervor, *Montgomery* ... what enthusiasm, *Adams*.

yea, [what] revenge!: You wanted to make it right, *SEB* ... you punished the guilty, *Greber* ... what concern for justice, *Adams* ... what exacting of punishment! *Alford* ... what a decision it produced from you! *Fenton*.

In all [things] ye have approved yourselves to be clear in this matter: In every respect, *PNT* ... Upon the whole, *Campbell* ... You have completely wiped away reproach, *Weymouth* ... you demonstrated yourselves, *NASB* ... ye evinced yourselves to be chaste, *Rotherham* ... to be innocent, *Montgomery* ... to be pure in the matter, *Hanson* ... from every stain of guilt, *Conybeare*.

12. Wherefore, though I wrote unto you: Consequently, even if I write to you, *Concordant*.

[I did it] not for his cause that had done the wrong: ... not to punish the offender, *Weymouth* ... not on account of the profligate, *Fenton*.

nor for his cause that suffered wrong:

but that our care for you in the sight of God might appear unto you: ... our diligent care over you, *Wesley* ... how deep your devotion to us really is, *TEV*.

13. Therefore we were comforted in your comfort: On this account, *Berkeley* ... That is why we have been so comforted and encouraged, *Barclay* ... your own concern for us, *JB*.

2 Corinthians 7:14

13.b.Txt: 018K,020L,byz.
bo.
Var: 01ℵ,03B,04C,06D
025P,33,it.Lach,Treg
Alf,Word,Tisc,We/Ho
Weis,Sod,UBS/☆

13.c.Txt: byz.
Var: 01ℵ,03B,04C,06D
018K,020L,025P,33
Lach,Treg,Alf,Word
Tisc,We/Ho,Weis,Sod
UBS/☆

3735.3 noun dat sing fem	5050.2 prs-pron gen 2pl	2231.2 prs-pron gen 1pl	3917.2 adv comp
παρακλήσει	ʽ ὑμῶν	[ᵇ☆ ἡμῶν]	περισσοτέρως
paraklēsei	humōn	hēmōn	perissoterōs
encouragement	your,	[our]	the more abundantly

1156.2 conj	3095.1 adv comp	5299.17 verb 1pl indic aor pass	1894.3 prep	3450.11 art dat sing fem	5315.3 noun dat sing fem
ʽᶜ δὲ ʼ	μᾶλλον	ἐχάρημεν	ἐπὶ	τῇ	χαρᾷ
de	mallon	echarēmen	epi	tē	chara
and	rather	we rejoiced	at	the	joy

4951.2 name gen masc	3617.1 conj	372.8 verb 3sing indic perf pass	3450.16 art sing neu	4011.1 noun sing neu
Τίτου,	ὅτι	ἀναπέπαυται	τὸ	πνεῦμα
Titou	hoti	anapepautai	to	pneuma
of Titus,	because	has been refreshed	the	spirit

840.3 prs-pron gen sing	570.3 prep gen	3820.4 adj gen pl	5050.2 prs-pron gen 2pl	3617.1 conj	1479.1 conj
αὐτοῦ	ἀπὸ	πάντων	ὑμῶν·	**14.** ὅτι	εἰ
autou	apo	pantōn	humōn	hoti	ei
his	by	all	of you.	Because	if

4948.10 indef-pron sing neu	840.4 prs-pron dat sing	5065.1 prep	5050.2 prs-pron gen 2pl	2714.15 verb 1sing indic perf	3620.3 partic
τι	αὐτῷ	ὑπὲρ	ὑμῶν	κεκαύχημαι,	οὐ
ti	autō	huper	humōn	kekauchēmai	ou
anything	to him	about	you	I have boasted,	not

2587.4 verb 1sing indic aor pass	233.1 conj	5453.1 conj	3820.1 adj	1706.1 prep	223.3 noun dat sing fem
κατῃσχύνθην·	ἀλλ'	ὡς	πάντα	ἐν	ἀληθείᾳ
katēschunthēn	all'	hōs	panta	en	alētheia
I was put to shame;	but	as	all things	in	truth

2953.28 verb 1pl indic aor act	5050.3 prs-pron dat 2pl	3643.1 adv	2504.1 conj	3450.9 art nom sing fem	2716.1 noun nom sing fem
ἐλαλήσαμεν	ὑμῖν,	οὕτως	καὶ	ἡ	καύχησις
elalēsamen	humin	houtōs	kai	hē	kauchēsis
we spoke	to you,	so	also	the	boasting

14.a.Txt: 01ℵ-corr,04C
06D,018K,020L,025P
byz.Sod
Var: 01ℵ-org,03B,Tisc
We/Ho,Weis,UBS/☆

2231.2 prs-pron gen 1pl	3450.9 art nom sing fem	1894.3 prep	4951.2 name gen masc	223.1 noun nom sing fem	1090.32 verb 3sing indic aor pass
ἡμῶν	ʽᵃ ἡ ʼ	ἐπὶ	Τίτου	ἀλήθεια	ἐγενήθη·
hēmōn	hē	epi	Titou	alētheia	egenēthē
our	the	to	Titus	truth	became;

2504.1 conj	3450.17 art pl neu	4551.1 noun pl neu	840.3 prs-pron gen sing	3917.2 adv comp
15. καὶ	τὰ	σπλάγχνα	αὐτοῦ	περισσοτέρως
kai	ta	splanchna	autou	perissoterōs
and	the	bowels	his	more abundantly

1519.1 prep	5050.4 prs-pron acc 2pl	1498.4 verb 3sing indic pres act	362.4 verb gen sing masc part pres pass	3450.12 art acc sing fem
εἰς	ὑμᾶς	ἐστιν,	ἀναμιμνῃσκομένου	τὴν
eis	humas	estin	anamimnēskomenou	tēn
towards	you	are,	being remembered	the

3820.4 adj gen pl	5050.2 prs-pron gen 2pl	5056.4 noun acc sing fem	5453.1 conj	3196.3 prep	5238.2 noun gen sing masc	2504.1 conj
πάντων	ὑμῶν	ὑπακοήν,	ὡς	μετὰ	φόβου	καὶ
pantōn	humōn	hupakoēn	hōs	meta	phobou	kai
of all	your	obedience,	as	with	fear	and

As Paul's associate, Titus knew controversy from the beginning (Galatians 2:1,3). Both his experience and gifts from God appeared to suit him for ministry to churches with problems. His service to Corinth as Paul's partner on this occasion suggests that. Later, he was also sent to Crete to handle administrative difficulties in the churches there (Titus 1:5). The apostle dispatched him on a mission to Dalmatia while he, Paul, was confined to prison at Rome (2 Timothy 4:10). For these reasons scholars often picture Titus as being a more forceful figure in church matters than Timothy.

7:14. Paul had often boasted to Titus of the wonderful believers at Corinth. His "if I have boasted" here could be read "since I have." The personal attack against Paul by the few did not blind him to the greatness of the many. As the youthful minister departed on his unpleasant journey, no doubt Paul assured him genuine Christians in the church would prove true though things looked dark at the moment.

As to his use of compliment in ministry to men, Hughes saw Paul "not hesitating to reprove what is amiss, but yet warmly and sympathetically encouraging them in the true emotions of those whose hearts are regenerate, which is the best way of ensuring that their past errors will not be repeated. A minister who keeps the main end in view, the glorious goal to which he wishes to guide his people, will realize that to be truly faithful in his dealings with them means to encourage them lovingly in that which is good as well as to correct and discipline them when they fall into sin" (*The New London Commentary*, p.280).

The founder of the church at Corinth had not overstated the case. He thanked its members in this follow-up letter for not humiliating him before Titus. What he had told his traveling companion about them proved to be true, just as everything he had preached to them about Jesus was true. As he wrote earlier, he was not among those ministers who dilute the gospel in the way some wine merchants cheapen their product by mixing it with water (2:17).

7:15. Upon Titus' return Paul learned he loved the Corinthians more than ever. His former respect for them was based on hearsay evidence. Now he had an abundant inward affection (*splanchna*, English "spleen," the verb form of the word is always translated "compassion") for them based on firsthand acquaintance.

Two things about the faithful at Corinth impressed Titus. Though he was younger and a stranger, they welcomed him with fear and trembling. Such a respect for the ministry spoke well of the founding father of the church. He also took special note of their obedience. First, they were most cooperative with him. Second, they carefully followed every instruction of the letter from Paul he delivered to them in disciplining the sinning member. Third and most

yea, and exceedingly the more joyed we for the joy of Titus: We were more than delighted, *Barclay* . . . we were especially delighted to see, *NIV* . . . by the happiness of Titus, *TCNT* . . . we had the even greater happiness of finding Titus so happy, *JB* . . . also delighted beyond everything by seeing how happy Titus is, *NEB*.

because his spirit was refreshed by you all: This is what comforts me, *Montgomery* . . . because all of you had cheered him up, *Beck* . . . you have all helped to set his mind completely at rest, *NEB* . . . his spirit has been refreshed, *NIV* . . . his spirit had been made glad by you all, *BB* . . . his spirit has been made stronger, *NLT* . . . was soothed by all of you, *Berkeley* . . . the way in which all of you helped to cheer him up! *TEV* . . . by the good disposition he found you all in towards me, *Locke* . . . he has no more worries, *JB*.

14. For if I have boasted any thing to him of you: I had bragged about you, *SEB*.

I am not ashamed: . . . you have not let me down, *Phillips* . . . and you have not disappointed me, *TEV* . . . I was not disgraced, *Fenton, Concordant* . . . my pride in you has been justified, *NEB* . . . I have had no reason to be ashamed of it, *Goodspeed* . . . I am specially gratified by this, *Barclay*.

but as we spake all things to you in truth: . . . bore the mark of truth, *NEB*.

even so our boasting, which [I made] before Titus: . . . just so the proud claims we made, *Barclay* . . . our boasting to Titus has proved to be as true, *JB*.

is found a truth: . . . turned out to be truth, *KJII* . . . is verified, *Campbell*.

15. And his inward affection is more abundant toward you: His heart goes out all the more to you, *Goodspeed* . . . his tender affection, *Young* . . . are especially favourable towards you, *Fenton*.

whilst he remembereth the obedience of you all: . . . as he continues recalling, *Williams* . . . when he calls to mind, *Rotherham* . . . the obedience which all of you manifested, *Weymouth*.

4997.2 noun gen sing masc	1203.7 verb 2pl indic aor mid	840.6 prs-pron acc sing masc	5299.1 verb 1sing indic pres act	3617.1 conj	1706.1 prep
τρόμου	ἐδέξασθε	αὐτόν.	16. χαίρω	ὅτι	ἐν
tromou	edexasthe	auton.	chairō	hoti	en
trembling	you received	him.	I rejoice	that	in

3820.3 adj dat sing	2269.1 verb 1sing indic pres act	1706.1 prep	5050.3 prs-pron dat 2pl	1101.2 verb 1pl indic pres act
παντὶ	θαῤῥῶ	ἐν	ὑμῖν.	8:1. Γνωρίζομεν
panti	tharrhō	en	humin.	Gnōrizomen
everything	I am confident	in	you.	We make known

1156.2 conj	5050.3 prs-pron dat 2pl	79.6 noun pl masc	3450.12 art acc sing fem	5322.4 noun acc sing fem	3450.2 art gen sing	2296.2 noun gen sing masc
δὲ	ὑμῖν,	ἀδελφοί,	τὴν	χάριν	τοῦ	θεοῦ
de	humin,	adelphoi,	tēn	charin	tou	theou
but	to you,	brothers,	the	grace		of God

3450.12 art acc sing fem	1319.55 verb acc sing fem part perf pass	1706.1 prep	3450.14 art dat pl fem	1564.7 noun dat pl fem	3450.10 art gen sing fem
τὴν	δεδομένην	ἐν	ταῖς	ἐκκλησίαις	τῆς
tēn	dedomenēn	en	tais	ekklēsiais	tēs
the	has been given	in	the	assemblies	

3081.2 name gen fem	3617.1 conj	1706.1 prep	4044.11 adj dat sing fem	1376.3 noun dat sing fem	2324.2 noun gen sing fem
Μακεδονίας·	2. ὅτι	ἐν	πολλῇ	δοκιμῇ	θλίψεως
Makedonias	hoti	en	pollē	dokimē	thlipseōs
of Macedonia;	that	in	much	proof	of tribulation

3450.9 art nom sing fem	3913.1 noun nom sing fem	3450.10 art gen sing fem	5315.2 noun gen sing fem	840.1 prs-pron gen pl	2504.1 conj	3450.9 art nom sing fem
ἡ	περισσεία	τῆς	χαρᾶς	αὐτῶν	καὶ	ἡ
hē	perisseia	tēs	charas	autōn	kai	hē
the	abundance	of the	joy	their	and	the

2567.3 prep	893.2 noun gen sing neu	4290.1 noun nom sing fem	840.1 prs-pron gen pl	3915.13 verb 3sing indic aor act
κατὰ	βάθους	πτωχεία	αὐτῶν	ἐπερίσσευσεν
kata	bathous	ptōcheia	autōn	eperisseusen
according to	deep	poverty	their	abounded

1519.1 prep	3450.6 art acc sing masc	4009.3 noun acc sing masc	3450.16 art sing neu	4009.1 noun sing masc	3450.10 art gen sing fem
εἰς	⌐ τὸν	πλοῦτον	[a☆ τὸ	πλοῦτος]	τῆς
eis	ton	plouton	to	ploutos	tēs
to	the	riches	[the	riches]	of the

2.a.Txt: 01ℵ-corr,06D 018K,020L,byz. Var: 01ℵ-org,03B,04C 025P,33,Lach,Treg,Alf Tisc,We/Ho,Weis,Sod UBS/☆

567.1 noun gen sing fem	840.1 prs-pron gen pl	3617.1 conj	2567.3 prep	1405.4 noun acc sing fem	3113.1 verb 1sing pres act
ἁπλότητος	αὐτῶν·	3. ὅτι	κατὰ	δύναμιν,	μαρτυρῶ,
haplotētos	autōn	hoti	kata	dunamin,	marturō,
liberality	their.	For	according to	power,	I bear witness,

2504.1 conj	5065.1 prep	3706.2 prep	1405.4 noun acc sing fem	824.2 adj nom pl masc
καὶ	⌐ ὑπὲρ	[a☆ παρὰ]	δύναμιν	αὐθαίρετοι,
kai	huper	para	dunamin	authairetoi,
and	beyond	[idem]	power	willing of themselves,

3.a.Txt: 018K,020L 025P,byz. Var: 01ℵ,03B,04C,06D 33,Lach,Treg,Alf,Word Tisc,We/Ho,Weis,Sod UBS/☆

3196.3 prep	4044.10 adj gen sing fem	3735.2 noun gen sing fem	1183.4 verb nom pl masc part pres	2231.2 prs-pron gen 1pl
4. μετὰ	πολλῆς	παρακλήσεως	δεόμενοι	ἡμῶν
meta	pollēs	paraklēseōs	deomenoi	hēmōn
with	much	urging	begging	our,

of all, they had a strong determination to do the will of God in every area of responsibility.

7:16. Paul concluded his discussion of the disciplinary case by repeating the fact that the Corinthians' behavior had brought him joy. Furthermore, they had renewed his confidence in them. He knew he could depend on them under every circumstance.

8:1. The apostle had a new subject to discuss at this juncture in his letter. In this section he dealt with the matter of worshipful giving. He used the whole of chapters 8 and 9 for this major division of the epistle.

Paul informed the church at Corinth of the grace of giving which God had granted to Christians in the churches of Macedonia. At least the congregations at Philippi, Thessalonica, and Beroea were included. He used the affectionate term "brethren" to address the Corinthians.

8:2. The apostle told the Corinthian believers that Macedonian churches had given an offering for needy brethren in Jerusalem. They did this in spite of the great trial of affliction they themselves had endured. Zahniser wrote, "This region had suffered the ravages of civil war between Caesar and Pompey, between Brutus and Cassius and the triumvirs, and finally between Augustus and Antonius. They actually made a petition for a surcease of their burdens of taxation in the reign of Tiberius and were granted the favor as a depleted area" (*The Wesleyan Bible Commentary*, 5:298).

Yet they had abundant joy despite their need. Their abundant liberality or generosity matched their joy. In their giving they followed the example of the widow who gave out of her poverty while others gave of their surplus (Mark 12:43,44).

Then how can the apostle write of "the riches of their liberality"? As Hughes asked, "How could the Macedonians have wealth if they lived in deep poverty? They gave from their ability (defined in 8:11-12)—that is, their giving was commensurate with their resources, small though they were. But the Macedonians also gave *beyond* their ability. They gave until it hurt. For that reason, Paul used them as a model for the Corinthians when he discussed equality and heart-level giving" (*Everyman's Bible Commentary*, p.75).

8:3. Paul bore them record (was their witness, *marturia*) that they gave in the offering beyond their ability. They did so willingly of themselves with no appeals from the apostle for contributions.

8:4. In fact, they had asked Paul earnestly for the privilege of participation in the project. Paul did not beg them, but they begged

how with fear and trembling ye received him: . . . with respect and reverence, *Norlie* . . . by the timidity and nervous anxiety with which you welcomed him, *Weymouth.*

16. I rejoice therefore that I have confidence in you in all [things]: I have good courage concerning you, *Worrell* . . . I do celebrate the fact that in all your affairs, *RPNT* . . . you have justified my good opinion of you in every way, *Norlie* . . . because I relied upon you in everything, *Fenton.*

1. Moreover, brethren, we do you to wit of the grace of God: . . . we make you acquainted with, *Wilson.*
bestowed on the churches of Macedonia:

2. How that in a great trial of affliction: . . . how, under ordeal of terrible affliction, *Berkeley* . . . much proof of tribulation, *Panin* . . . while passing through great trouble, *Weymouth* . . . Amid a severe ordeal of distress, *HistNT.*
the abundance of their joy: . . . because of the overflow of their kindness, *Fenton* . . . their boundless joy, *Weymouth.*
and their deep poverty abounded unto the riches of their liberality: . . . have had an abundant issue in rich generosity upon their part, *HistNT* . . . in the wealth of their liberality, *NASB.*

3. For to [their] power, I bear record, yea: I can testify that to the utmost of their power, *Weymouth* . . . and I give evidence beyond their ability, *Fenton.*
and beyond [their] power [they were] willing of themselves: . . . yes, beyond their means, they gave, *Confraternity* . . . gave of their own accord, *ASV* . . . they voluntarily have given, *Berkeley* . . . of their own free will, *Norlie.*

4. Praying us with much entreaty: In fact they simply begged us, *Phillips* . . . they insistently begged, *Kleist.*

2 Corinthians 8:5

3450.12 art acc sing fem	5322.4 noun acc sing fem	2504.1 conj	3450.12 art acc sing fem	2815.4 noun acc sing fem	3450.10 art gen sing fem
τὴν *tēn* the	χάριν *charin* grace	καὶ *kai* and	τὴν *tēn* the	κοινωνίαν *koinōnian* fellowship	τῆς *tēs* of the

1242.2 noun gen sing fem	3450.10 art gen sing fem	1519.1 prep	3450.8 art acc pl masc	39.9 adj acc pl masc	1203.16 verb inf aor mid
διακονίας *diakonias* service	τῆς *tēs* the	εἰς *eis* for	τοὺς *tous* the	ἁγίους *hagious* saints	⌐a δὲξασθαι *dexasthai* to receive

4.a.Txt: Steph
Var: 01א,03B,04C,06D
018K,020L,025P,byz.
Gries,Lach,Treg,Alf
Word,Tisc,We/Ho,Weis
Sod,UBS/✶

2231.4 prs- pron acc 1pl	2504.1 conj	3620.3 partic	2503.1 conj	1666.7 verb 1pl indic aor act	233.1 conj
ἡμᾶς· ⌐\ *hēmas* for us.	5. καὶ *kai* And	οὐ *ou* not	καθὼς *kathōs* according as	ἠλπίσαμεν, *ēlpisamen* we hoped,	⌐ ἀλλ' *all'* but

233.2 conj	1431.8 prs- pron acc pl masc	1319.17 verb 3pl indic aor act	4270.1 adv	3450.3 art dat sing	2935.3 noun dat sing masc
[ἀλλὰ] *alla* [idem]	ἑαυτοὺς *heautous* themselves	ἔδωκαν *edōkan* they gave	πρῶτον *prōton* first	τῷ *tō* to the	κυρίῳ, *kuriō* Lord,

2504.1 conj	2231.3 prs- pron dat 1pl	1217.2 prep	2284.2 noun gen sing masc	2296.2 noun gen sing masc	1519.1 prep	3450.16 art sing neu
καὶ *kai* and	ἡμῖν *hēmin* to us	διὰ *dia* by	θελήματος *thelēmatos* will	θεοῦ, *theou* of God.	6. εἰς *eis* To	τὸ *to* the

3731.15 verb inf aor act	2231.4 prs- pron acc 1pl	4951.4 name acc masc	2419.1 conj	2503.1 conj	4138.1 verb 3sing indic aor mid
παρακαλέσαι *parakalesai* to exhort	ἡμᾶς *hēmas* we	Τίτον, *Titon* Titus,	ἵνα *hina* that	καθὼς *kathōs* just as	προενήρξατο *proenērxato* he before began,

3643.1 adv	2504.1 conj	1989.4 verb 3sing subj aor act	1519.1 prep	5050.4 prs- pron acc 2pl	2504.1 conj
οὕτως *houtōs* so	καὶ *kai* also	ἐπιτελέσῃ *epitelesē* he might complete	εἰς *eis* among	ὑμᾶς *humas* you	καὶ *kai* also

3450.12 art acc sing fem	5322.4 noun acc sing fem	3642.12 dem- pron acc sing fem	233.1 conj	5450.1 adv	1706.1 prep	3820.3 adj dat sing
τὴν *tēn* the	χάριν *charin* grace	ταύτην. *tautēn* this.	7. Ἀλλ' *All'* But	ὥσπερ *hōsper* even as	ἐν *en* in	παντὶ *panti* every

3915.4 verb 2pl indic pres act	3963.3 noun dat sing fem	2504.1 conj	3030.3 noun dat sing masc	2504.1 conj	1102.3 noun dat sing fem
περισσεύετε, *perisseuete* you abound,	πίστει, *pistei* in faith,	καὶ *kai* and	λόγῳ, *logō* word,	καὶ *kai* and	γνώσει, *gnōsei* knowledge,

2504.1 conj	3820.11 adj dat sing fem	4561.2 noun dat sing fem	2504.1 conj	3450.11 art dat sing fem	1523.1 prep gen	5050.2 prs- pron gen 2pl
καὶ *kai* and	πάσῃ *pasē* all	σπουδῇ, *spoudē* diligence,	καὶ *kai* and	τῇ *tē* in the	ἐξ *ex* from	⌐ ὑμῶν *humōn* you

7.a.Txt: 01א,04C,06D
018K,020L,025P,byz.it.
Tisc
Var: p46,03B,sa.bo.
We/Ho,Weis,Sod
UBS/✶

1706.1 prep	2231.3 prs- pron dat 1pl	2231.2 prs- pron gen 1pl	1706.1 prep	5050.3 prs- pron dat 2pl	26.3 noun dat sing fem	2419.1 conj
ἐν *en* to	ἡμῖν *hēmin* us	[a✶ ἡμῶν *hēmōn* [our	ἐν *en* to	ὑμῖν] *humin* you]	ἀγάπῃ, *agapē* love,	ἵνα *hina* that

578

him! They insisted that he accept their money and take it with him to pass on to the Christians in financial straits in Jerusalem. They urged him to take on the true fellowship of such a ministry (service, *diakonias*). Being poor themselves they knew how to feel with others in great need.

Of course the apostle was not opposed to the effort. Nor was he unconcerned about brethren short of life's necessities in Jerusalem. He and Barnabas had already taken a similar offering for needy Christians to Jerusalem (Acts 11:27-30). The money came from the young Gentile church at Antioch of Syria. The Jerusalem church itself had demonstrated generosity toward needy members from the start (Acts 4:34,35).

8:5. The way the Macedonians went about presenting their offering was beyond anything the apostle could have hoped for. They exceeded all his expectations. First, they gave themselves in full devotion to the Lord. Giving of money to God apart from that would be pointless. Their worshipful giving was certainly in the will of God.

8:6. With thanksgiving in his own spirit at the grace of giving in the hearts of the Macedonians, Paul responded to their request to head up the project. It fitted with his burden and some preliminary preparations he had made earlier to collect funds for the same purpose at Corinth and in Galatia. Titus was instrumental in assisting the apostle in that he took his previous letter to the Corinthians. It contained instructions on how to raise the funds (1 Corinthians 16:1-3).

Since Titus had already worked on the project at Corinth, Paul requested him to return there to finish what he had started. It may be the apostle's critics and the trouble they caused in the Corinthian church had slowed the effort. Regardless, Paul was anxious that God perfect the grace of giving in the hearts of Corinthian believers as they completed collecting funds for the needy.

8:7. Their spiritual father praised the Corinthians that they abounded in possessing many of God's gifts and graces. In the gifts of faith and knowledge they ranked high among the churches. In their meetings the Spirit often granted utterances, tongues, interpretation, and prophecy. They showed much diligence (eagerness, zeal) about the things of God. Above all they were full of love which they had frequently manifested toward Paul. In his first letter to them he offered similar commendation saying, "Ye come behind

that we would receive the gift, and [take upon us] the fellowship of the ministering to the saints: . . . that they might participate in the beneficence, *Murdock* . . . to accept their gifts, *Phillips* . . . to convey the gift, *Fenton* . . . being rendered to God's people, *Weymouth* . . . supporting their fellow-Christians, *Norlie* . . . the fund for their fellow-Christians, *TCNT*.

5. And [this they did], not as we hoped: And they surpassed our expectations, *HistNT* . . . not according as we expected, *Young* . . . beyond our expectations, *Campbell* . . . more than we expected, *Beck* . . . a mere cash payment, *Phillips*.

but first gave their own selves to the Lord, and unto us by the will of God:

6. Insomuch that we desired Titus, that as he had begun: We therefore encouraged Titus, *Fenton* . . . so that I insisted that, *Williams* . . . so that we exhorted, *Hanson* . . . the one who commenced the work, *Weymouth*.

so he would also finish in you the same grace also: . . . he should also see to the completion of this expression of your sympathy, *TCNT* . . . to bring it to successful completion, *NAB* . . . to get this bounty completed, *HistNT* . . . to complete this gracious arrangement, *Berkeley* . . . this gracious work, *RSV*.

7. Therefore, as ye abound in every [thing, in] faith: You are rich in so many things, *Norlie* . . . you are already very rich in faith, *Weymouth*.

and utterance, and knowledge: . . . and discourse, *Rotherham* . . . of eloquence, of spiritual illumination, *Way* . . . and doctrine, *PNT* . . . and a ready exposition, *Wuest*.

and [in] all diligence, and [in] your love to us: . . . perfect enthusiasm, *Williams* . . . enthusiasm in every form, *Way* . . . all earnestness, *Hanson*, *NASB* . . . every kind of zeal, *Beck* . . . unwearied zeal, *Weymouth* . . . and in complete eagerness, *Adams* . . . and all careful work, *Klingensmith*.

2 Corinthians 8:8

2504.1 conj	1706.1 prep	3642.11 dem-pron dat sing fem	3450.11 art dat sing fem	5322.3 noun dat sing fem	3915.7 verb 2pl subj pres act
καὶ	ἐν	ταύτῃ	τῇ	χάριτι	περισσεύητε.
kai	en	tautē	tē	chariti	perisseuēte
also	in	this	the	grace	you should abound.

	3620.3 partic	2567.1 prep	1987.2 noun acc sing fem	2978.1 verb 1sing pres act	233.2 conj	1217.2 prep
8.	Οὐ	κατ'	ἐπιταγὴν	λέγω,	ἀλλὰ	διὰ
	Ou	kat'	epitagēn	legō	alla	dia
	Not	according to	a command	do I speak,	but	through

3450.10 art gen sing fem	2066.3 adj gen pl	4561.1 noun gen sing fem	2504.1 conj	3450.16 art sing neu	3450.10 art gen sing fem
τῆς	ἑτέρων	σπουδῆς	καὶ	τὸ	τῆς
tēs	heterōn	spoudēs	kai	to	tēs
the	of others	diligence	and	the	of the

5052.5 adj gen 2sing fem	26.2 noun gen sing fem	1097.3 adj acc sing neu	1375.5 verb nom sing masc part pres act		1091.5 verb 2pl indic pres act
ὑμετέρας	ἀγάπης	γνήσιον	δοκιμάζων·	**9.**	γινώσκετε
humeteras	agapēs	gnēsion	dokimazōn		ginōskete
your	love	genuineness	proving.		You know

1056.1 conj	3450.12 art acc sing fem	5322.4 noun acc sing fem	3450.2 art gen sing	2935.2 noun gen sing masc	2231.2 prs-pron gen 1pl	2400.2 name masc
γὰρ	τὴν	χάριν	τοῦ	κυρίου	ἡμῶν	Ἰησοῦ
gar	tēn	charin	tou	kuriou	hēmōn	Iēsou
for	the	grace	of the	Lord	our	Jesus

9.a.**Txt:** p46,01א,04C 06D,010F,012G **Var:** 03B,sa.

5382.2 name gen masc	3617.1 conj	1217.1 prep	5050.4 prs-pron acc 2pl	4291.1 verb 3sing indic aor act
⸂ᵃ Χριστοῦ, ⸃	ὅτι	δι'	ὑμᾶς	ἐπτώχευσεν
Christou	hoti	di'	humas	eptōcheusen
Christ,	that	for the sake of	you	he became poor

4004.1 adj nom sing masc	1498.21 verb sing masc part pres act	2419.1 conj	5050.1 prs-pron nom 2pl	3450.11 art dat sing fem	1552.2 dem-pron gen sing
πλούσιος	ὤν,	ἵνα	ὑμεῖς	τῇ	ἐκείνου
plousios	ōn	hina	humeis	tē	ekeinou
rich	being,	that	you	by the	of that

4290.2 noun dat sing fem	4007.7 verb 2pl subj aor act		2504.1 conj	1100.4 noun acc sing fem	1706.1 prep
πτωχείᾳ	πλουτήσητε.	**10.**	καὶ	γνώμην	ἐν
ptōcheia	ploutēsēte		kai	gnōmēn	en
poverty	might be enriched.		And	a judgment	in

3642.5 dem-pron dat sing masc	1319.1 verb 1sing indic pres act	3642.17 dem-pron sing neu	1056.1 conj	5050.3 prs-pron dat 2pl	4702.1 verb 3sing indic pres act
τούτῳ	δίδωμι·	τοῦτο	γὰρ	ὑμῖν	συμφέρει,
toutō	didōmi	touto	gar	humin	sumpherei
this	I give,	this	for	for you	is profitable,

3610.2 rel-pron nom pl masc	3620.3 partic	3303.1 adv	3450.16 art sing neu	4020.41 verb inf aor act	233.2 conj
οἵτινες	οὐ	μόνον	τὸ	ποιῆσαι,	ἀλλὰ
hoitines	ou	monon	to	poiēsai	alla
who	not	only	the	to do,	but

2504.1 conj	3450.16 art sing neu	2286.19 verb inf pres act	4138.2 verb 2pl indic aor mid	570.3 prep gen	3930.1 adv
καὶ	τὸ	θέλειν	προενήρξασθε	ἀπὸ	πέρυσι·
kai	to	thelein	proenērxasthe	apo	perusi
also	the	to will	began before	from	last year.

in no gift" (1 Corinthians 1:5-7). In like manner, he now wanted them also to abound in the grace of giving.

8:8. Paul preferred not to speak by commandment on the matter of this offering even though in his apostolic office he could have. He wrote the same to Philemon whom he chose to beseech rather than to enjoin (Philemon 8,9). God is more pleased when His people give on some other basis than obedience to law, though the grace of giving should provoke one to give more than the law requires.

Paul had better ways of appealing to the believers at Corinth for these funds. For one, he challenged them by the forward, zealous example of others in giving, namely, the Macedonians. Then he appealed to their love for God and the brethren. The offering allowed them to demonstrate its sincerity and genuineness.

8:9. Another basis of appeal Paul used in stirring Christians at Corinth to give was the example of Jesus. It, of course, was the greatest of all. The apostle declared it was grace even on His part that caused Him to surrender His riches in becoming poor that all who believe on Him might be rich.

A more complete account of what Jesus left behind to come to earth is in Philippians 2:5-8. Possessing the wealth of the universe in His preincarnate state, He gave it all up to be born a man. He experienced that birth in abject poverty. The humble inn in the town of His birth had no room as a decent place for Him to come into the world. His mother bore Him, attended only by Joseph. She lay on a straw-covered dirt floor of a stable. His only crib was the feeding trough for the animals who shared the place of His birth, probably a cave stable in Bethlehem.

During His stay of 30 years on earth He never owned a place to lay His head (Matthew 8:20). When He came to the end of His earthly life the only provisions He could offer for the care of His mother came through the kindness He requested of a friend with His dying breath (John 19:26,27). Before they crucified Him they stripped Him of the meager clothing He wore. Soldiers gambled to see who would get the garments of pitifully small value He left behind (Mark 15:24).

In death they buried Him in a borrowed tomb (Matthew 27:60). Others provided the customary burial cloths and spices, and they were relative strangers (John 19:38-42). Thus He lived and died owning nothing of this world's goods.

8:10. Paul appealed to the most noble motives as godly reasons for worshiping the Lord through giving. Instead of giving orders, he offered advice and presented his opinion. He concluded that approach was expedient (advantageous, better) for the Corinthians. His suggestion was that since they were eager to start the worthy project of collecting funds for needy brethren in Jerusalem "a year ago," now they should complete it.

[see] that ye abound in this grace also: . . . in this gracious work also, *NASB* . . . this grace of liberal giving also flourishes in you, *Weymouth* . . . in this work of kindness, *Beck.*

8. I speak not by commandment: Not by way of injunction, *Rotherham* . . . I don't want you to read this as an order, *Phillips* . . . I do not speak imperatively, *Fenton* . . . I am not issuing an order, *Berkeley.*

but by occasion of the forwardness of others: . . . but as testing the sincerity, *Confraternity* . . . through the earnest zeal of others, *PNT.*

and to prove the sincerity of your love: . . . but to test the genuineness of your love, *Norlie* . . . want a genuine proof of your friendship, *Fenton* . . . the reality of your Love, *Wilson* . . . the dependability of, *Klingensmith* . . . the good disposition of your charity, *Douay.*

9. For ye know the grace of our Lord Jesus Christ: . . . the graciousness of, *Confraternity* . . . the condescending goodness, *Weymouth* . . . the bounteous grace of our Lord, *HistNT.*

that, though he was rich, yet for your sakes he became poor: Who, when existing in wealth, impoverished Himself for you, *Fenton* . . . he became destitute, *Rotherham.*

that ye through his poverty might be rich: . . . you might be made wealthy, *Wuest.*

10. And herein I give [my] advice: In this matter, then, I offer my counsel, *Norlie* . . . But in this matter I give you an opinion, *Weymouth* . . . Still, on this subject, *HistNT* . . . I give judgment, *Hanson.*

for this is expedient for you, who have begun before: It is to your interest, *Confraternity* . . . for this thing is profitable, *PNT* . . . for this is beneficial for you, *Wilson* . . . this is to your advantage, *NASB* . . . who not only originated the work, *Fenton.*

not only to do, but also to be forward a year ago: . . . also to do it willingly, *Wesley.*

2 Corinthians 8:11

11.

3432.1 adv	1156.2 conj	2504.1 conj	3450.16 art sing neu	4020.41 verb inf aor act	1989.5 verb 2pl impr aor act	3567.1 conj
νυνὶ	δὲ	καὶ	τὸ	ποιῆσαι	ἐπιτελέσατε,	ὅπως
nuni	de	kai	to	poiēsai	epitelesate	hopōs
Now	but	also	the	to do	complete;	so that

2481.1 conj	3450.9 art nom sing fem	4147.1 noun nom sing fem	3450.2 art gen sing	2286.19 verb inf pres act	3643.1 adv
καθάπερ	ἡ	προθυμία	τοῦ	θέλειν,	οὕτως
kathaper	hē	prothumia	tou	thelein	houtōs
even as	the	readiness	of the	to will,	so

2504.1 conj	3450.16 art sing neu	1989.7 verb inf aor act	1523.2 prep gen	3450.2 art gen sing	2174.29 verb inf pres act	1479.1 conj
καὶ	τὸ	ἐπιτελέσαι	ἐκ	τοῦ	ἔχειν.	**12.** Εἰ
kai	to	epitelesai	ek	tou	echein	Ei
also	the	to complete	out of	the	to have.	If

1056.1 conj	3450.9 art nom sing fem	4147.1 noun nom sing fem	4154.1 verb 3sing indic pres	2498.1 conj	1430.1 partic
γὰρ	ἡ	προθυμία	πρόκειται,	καθὸ	ἐὰν
gar	hē	prothumia	prokeitai	katho	ean
for	the	readiness	is present,	according as	if

2174.7 verb 3sing subj pres act	4948.3 indef-pron nom sing	2124.1 adj nom sing	3620.3 partic	2498.1 conj
ἔχῃ	⌜a τις⌝	εὐπρόσδεκτος,	οὐ	καθὸ
echē	tis	euprosdektos	ou	katho
may have	anyone	acceptable,	not	according as

3620.2 partic	2174.4 verb 3sing indic pres act	3620.3 partic	1056.1 conj	2419.1 conj	241.7 adj dat pl masc	423.1 noun nom sing fem
οὐκ	ἔχει.	**13.** οὐ	γὰρ	ἵνα	ἄλλοις	ἄνεσις,
ouk	echei	ou	gar	hina	allois	anesis
not	he has.	Not	for	that	to others	case,

5050.3 prs-pron dat 2pl	1156.2 conj	2324.1 noun nom sing fem	233.1 conj	1523.1 prep gen	2444.2 noun gen sing fem	1706.1 prep
ὑμῖν	⌜a δὲ⌝	θλῖψις·	ἀλλ'	ἐξ	ἰσότητος	ἐν
humin	de	thlipsis	all'	ex	isotētos	en
for you	but	hardship,	but	of	equality,	in

3450.3 art dat sing	3431.1 adv	2511.3 noun dat sing masc	3450.16 art sing neu	5050.2 prs-pron gen 2pl	3914.1 noun nom sing neu
τῷ	νῦν	καιρῷ	τὸ	ὑμῶν	περίσσευμα
tō	nun	kairō	to	humōn	perisseuma
the	now	time	the	your	abundance

1519.1 prep	3450.16 art sing neu	1552.1 dem-pron gen pl	5140.2 noun acc sing neu	2419.1 conj	2504.1 conj
εἰς	τὸ	ἐκείνων	ὑστέρημα,	**14.** ἵνα	καὶ
eis	to	ekeinōn	husterēma	hina	kai
for	the	of those	deficiency,	that	also

3450.16 art sing neu	1552.1 dem-pron gen pl	3914.1 noun nom sing neu	1090.40 verb 3sing subj aor mid	1519.1 prep	3450.16 art sing neu
τὸ	ἐκείνων	περίσσευμα	γένηται	εἰς	τὸ
to	ekeinōn	perisseuma	genētai	eis	to
to	of those	abundance	may be	for	the

5050.2 prs-pron gen 2pl	5140.2 noun acc sing neu	3567.1 conj	1090.40 verb 3sing subj aor mid	2444.1 noun nom sing fem
ὑμῶν	ὑστέρημα·	ὅπως	γένηται	ἰσότης·
humōn	husterēma	hopōs	genētai	isotēs
your	deficiency,	so that	there should be	equality.

12.a.**Txt:** 04C-corr,020L
byz.bo.
Var: 01א,03B,04C-org
06D,018K,025P,it.Lach
Treg,Alf,Word,Tisc
We/Ho,Weis,Sod
UBS/∗

13.a.**Txt:** 01א-corr,06D
018K,020L,025P,byz.
Sod
Var: 01א-org,03B,04C
33,Lach,Treg,Tisc
We/Ho,Weis,UBS/∗

8:11. The apostle commended the Corinthians for their readiness of mind to raise money for the needy. However, it was more than a mental assent toward a worthy cause. It moved them to will (*thelein*) to work on the project.

Now Paul exhorted them to complete it. Each should give according to what he had. In his earlier letter he stated the same principle. Every believer at Corinth was to contribute to this offering according as God had prospered him (1 Corinthians 16:2). From the first, such offerings in the church were in keeping with each one's ability to give (Acts 11:29).

8:12. As the Spirit moved on him, the apostle emphasized that the attitude of the heart is the important thing in Christian giving. That is what God accepts as worship rather than the money presented. Certainly the amount given is not what the Lord looks for. Instead, He receives any servant who approaches Him in giving on the basis of what he has to offer. If in his heart he would give much but has little, heaven's record shows a large offering. God expects no one to give what he does not have. None must be asked to give above his ability.

Of course, those who have much and offer little find small favor with the Lord. They make the mistake of trying to worship grudgingly with the hand rather than in spirit and in truth. With them God is not well pleased.

As Ironside explained, "It was not a question of saying, 'Well, I would do something but am not able,' but a question of doing what they could. If you can give only a little to the Lord, give that, and He will multiply it. If you can give a great deal, give it to Him. He looks into the heart. Many a one puts in a dime, and on the books of heaven it goes down as though it were a dollar, but do not put in a dime if you could give the dollar, for that won't go down at all!" (p.199).

8:13. The apostle declared it was not his intent that those who received this offering should be relieved financially while at the same time those who gave it were burdened by it. God's plan does not call for some to give to the extent they do without basic necessities so others may live in abundance.

8:14. What the apostle preached here about sharing with others was the principle of equality. It seemed reasonable that at a time when Christians in Jerusalem suffered want, their brethren in other parts of the world should share their abundance with them. At another time (*kairos,* "season," rather than *chronos,* measured time) the situation would be reversed. Then those in Jerusalem would have the opportunity to return the favor.

11. Now therefore perform the doing [of it]: So now finish, *Klingensmith* . . . also complete what you must do, *Adams* . . . complete the doing, *Hanson* . . . complete the enterprise, *Berkeley* . . . complete the deed, *HistNT.*

that as [there was] a readiness to will: . . . to purpose it, *PNT.*

so [there may be] a performance also out of that which ye have: . . . so there may be the completion, *Clementson* . . . your desire to carry it through, *Confraternity* . . . so [shall be] the completion also, *Hanson* . . . the completion out of what ye have, *Worrell* . . . in proportion to what ye have, *Wesley* . . . to what you possess, *HistNT.*

12. For if there be first a willing mind: For if the desire exists, *Fenton.*

[it is] accepted according to that a man hath: . . . it is acceptable according to what one may possess, *Fenton.*

[and] not according to that he hath not:

13. For [I mean] not that other men be eased, and ye burdened: . . . and ye pressured, *Young* . . . and you loaded down, *Klingensmith* . . . and you distressed, *Conybeare.*

14. But by an equality, [that] now at this time your abundance [may be a supply] for their want: You have a surplus right now, *Klingensmith* . . . Your present abundance, *Adams* . . . but to make your burdens equal, *Conybeare* . . . by the rule of equality, *Alford* . . . at the present time, *Confraternity* . . . for their deficiency, *Rotherham, Wilson.*

that their abundance also may be [a supply] for your want: . . . what they will not need will relieve your need, *Beck* . . . for your deficiency later on, *Weymouth.*

that there may be equality: . . . rather share fairly, *Klingensmith* . . . and so it will be fair, *Beck* . . . so that there may be equalization of burdens, *Weymouth* . . . and thus conditions become equalized, *Berkeley.*

2 Corinthians 8:15

15. καθὼς γέγραπται, Ὁ τὸ πολὺ
kathōs *gegraptai,* *Ho* *to* *polu*
According as it has been written, The to the much

οὐκ ἐπλεόνασεν· καὶ ὁ τὸ ὀλίγον οὐκ
ouk *epleonasen·* *kai* *ho* *to* *oligon* *ouk*
not had over, and the to the little not

ἠλαττόνησεν. **16.** Χάρις δὲ τῷ θεῷ, τῷ
ēlattonēsen. *Charis* *de* *tō* *theō,* *tō*
did lack. Thanks but to the to God, the

ʹ διδόντι [a☆ δόντι] τὴν αὐτὴν σπουδὴν
didonti *donti* *tēn* *autēn* *spoudēn*
giving [idem] the same diligence

ὑπὲρ ὑμῶν ἐν τῇ καρδίᾳ Τίτου· **17.** ὅτι
huper *humōn* *en* *tē* *kardia* *Titou·* *hoti*
for you in the heart of Titus. For

τὴν μὲν παράκλησιν ἐδέξατο, σπουδαιότερος
tēn *men* *paraklēsin* *edexato,* *spoudaioteros*
the indeed exhortation he received, more diligent

δὲ ὑπάρχων, αὐθαίρετος ἐξῆλθεν πρὸς
de *huparchōn,* *authairetos* *exēlthen* *pros*
but being, of his own accord he went out to

ὑμᾶς. **18.** συνεπέμψαμεν δὲ μετ᾽ αὐτοῦ τὸν
humas. *sunepempsamen* *de* *met'* *autou* *ton*
you. We sent but with him the

ἀδελφὸν οὗ ὁ ἔπαινος ἐν τῷ
adelphon *hou* *ho* *epainos* *en* *tō*
brother of whom the praise in the

εὐαγγελίῳ διὰ πασῶν τῶν ἐκκλησιῶν·
euangeliō *dia* *pasōn* *tōn* *ekklēsiōn·*
good news through all the assemblies;

19. οὐ μόνον δὲ, ἀλλὰ καὶ χειροτονηθεὶς
ou *monon* *de,* *alla* *kai* *cheirotonētheis*
not only and, but also having been chosen

16.a.**Txt:** 01א,03B,04C
016I,044,0243,sa.byz.
Var: p46,06D,010F
012G,020L,6,323,326
1241,2496,bo.

8:15. Instead of communism, the apostle's instructions encouraged a certain thermostatic principle of equality as illustrated in Israel's gathering of the manna in the wilderness. If a person collected much or little, it all measured the same (Exodus 16:18)! The greedy person found his surplus weighed no more than the one who tried to honestly bring in his share. The individual who was unable to collect his due portion discovered it measured what God allowed anyway.

No one was to save any manna gathered as the day's supply for the day following. Those who disobeyed the command found what they kept over spoiled (Exodus 16:20). In the same way corruption always accompanies the hoarding of wealth.

8:16. This offering presented as an act of worship provoked other praise to the Lord. For one thing, Paul thanked God for putting the same zealous concern for the Corinthians in the heart of Titus.

8:17. Titus readily welcomed Paul's "exhortation" (request) (8:6) to proceed to Corinth to assist in completing the giving project there. Indeed Titus felt a sense of special urgency toward the matter. In reality he went to the Greek city voluntarily, even more than in response to the apostle's appeal.

Hughes has noted the oneness of the apostle and his associate and wrote: " 'The same earnestness' (8:16) linked Titus' heart to Paul's. Not only did Titus share the same earnestness for the offering, but he went of his own accord (8:17). Titus was a true self-starter and was motivated first by his own desire and, second, by Paul's appeal. Paul stressed that fact to support the genuineness of Titus' ministry" (*Everyman's Bible Commentary*, p.81).

8:18. Wisdom dictated that Paul ask others to join Titus in this money-raising project. That was his plan from the beginning. In a previous letter to Corinth he stated, "Whomsoever ye shall approve by your letters, them will I send to bring your liberality unto Jerusalem" (1 Corinthians 16:3).

Paul included a letter of recommendation for these brethren within his letter to the Corinthians. Such documents were an important part of the world of the First Century just as they are today. Paul referred to their prevalent use earlier (3:1-3). Ministerial credentials serve the purpose of letters of recommendation.

The apostle commended one he sent with Titus as a "brother" known well among the churches of the area. Everyone spoke highly of his work in the gospel, perhaps as a preacher.

8:19. Further, this "brother" had been chosen by the churches for this particular assignment. The election process involved voting

15. As it is written, He that [had gathered] much had nothing over: . . . had no surplus, *Hanson, Wilson* . . . had not more than enough, *Rotherham* . . . were not over-fed, *Fenton.*

and he that [had gathered] little had no lack: . . . had not less, *Rotherham.*

16. But thanks [be] to God:
which put the same earnest care into the heart of Titus for you: Who is imparting the same diligence, *Concordant* . . . who kindles in the heart of, *Williams* . . . who has an equal zeal for you, *NAB* . . . who has inspired Titus, *Confraternity* . . . who putteth the same diligence for you, *Panin* . . . the same devotion for you, *Berkeley.*

17. For indeed he accepted the exhortation: . . . has responded to my appeals, *TCNT* . . . he accepted the call, *KJII* . . . welcomed our request, *Weymouth* . . . welcomed my request, *Beck* . . . our appeal, *NASB, Norlie, Adams.*

but being more forward: . . . and, impatient to begin, *Fenton* . . . being already more diligent, *Rotherham* . . . but was so enthusiastic about it that, *Norlie* . . . because he is so enthusiastic for you, *Williams* . . . but being very earnest, *Noyes, Wilson* . . . and being extremely diligent, *Sawyer.*

of his own accord he went unto you: . . . by his own volition, *Berkeley.*

18. And we have sent with him the brother:
whose praise [is] in the gospel throughout all the churches: . . . whose fame in the service of, *TCNT* . . . who is so well known for his preaching, *Klingensmith* . . . whose applause in the evangel, *Concordant* . . . whose fame as a herald of the Glad-tidings has spread through all the churches, *Way.*

19. And not [that] only:
but who was also chosen of the churches to travel with us with

5097.3 prep	3450.1 art gen pl	1564.6 noun gen pl fem	4748.1 noun nom sing masc	2231.2 prs-pron gen 1pl
ὑπὸ	τῶν	ἐκκλησιῶν	συνέκδημος	ἡμῶν
hupo	tōn	ekklēsiōn	sunekdēmos	hēmōn
by	the	assemblies	fellow traveller	our

19.a.**Txt:** p46,01ℵ,06D 018K,020L,044,byz.Tisc **Var:** 03B,04C,025P,sa. bo.Lach,Treg,Alf,Word We/Ho,Weis,Sod UBS/✱

4713.1 prep dat	1706.1 prep	3450.11 art dat sing fem	5322.3 noun dat sing fem	3642.11 dem-pron dat sing fem	3450.11 art dat sing fem
ˊ σὺν	[ᵃ ἐν]	τῇ	χάριτι	ταύτῃ	τῇ
sun	en	tē	chariti	tautē	tē
with	[in]	the	grace	this,	the

1241.17 verb dat sing fem part pres pass	5097.1 prep	2231.2 prs-pron gen 1pl	4242.1 prep	3450.12 art acc sing fem	840.3 prs-pron gen sing
διακονουμένῃ	ὑφ'	ἡμῶν	πρὸς	τὴν	αὐτοῦ
diakonoumenē	huph'	hēmōn	pros	tēn	autou
being served	by	us	to	the	himself

3450.2 art gen sing	2935.2 noun gen sing masc	1385.4 noun acc sing fem	2504.1 conj	4147.3 noun acc sing fem	5050.2 prs-pron gen 2pl
τοῦ	κυρίου	δόξαν	καὶ	προθυμίαν	ˊ ὑμῶν·
tou	kuriou	doxan	kai	prothumian	humōn
of the	Lord	glory	and	readiness	your;

19.b.**Txt:** Steph **Var:** 01ℵ,03B,04C,06D 018K,020L,025P,byz. Gries,Lach,Treg,Alf Word,Tisc,We/Ho,Weis Sod,UBS/✱

2231.2 prs-pron gen 1pl	4575.1 verb nom pl masc part pres mid	3642.17 dem-pron sing neu	3231.1 partic	4948.3 indef-pron nom sing
[ᵇ✱ ἡμῶν]	**20.** στελλόμενοι	τοῦτο,	μὴ	τις
hēmōn	stellomenoi	touto,	mē	tis
[our]	avoiding	this,	not	anyone

2231.4 prs-pron acc 1pl	3331.2 verb 3sing subj aor mid	1706.1 prep	3450.11 art dat sing fem	99.1 noun dat sing fem
ἡμᾶς	μωμήσηται	ἐν	τῇ	ἁδρότητι
hēmas	mōmēsētai	en	tē	hadrotēti
us	should blame	in	the	abundance

3642.11 dem-pron dat sing fem	3450.11 art dat sing fem	1241.17 verb dat sing fem part pres pass	5097.1 prep	2231.2 prs-pron gen 1pl
ταύτῃ	τῇ	διακονουμένῃ	ὑφ'	ἡμῶν·
tautē	tē	diakonoumenē	huph'	hēmōn
this	the	being served	by	us;

21.a.**Txt:** (04C),018K 020L,byz. **Var:** 01ℵ,03B,06D,025P Lach,Treg,Alf,Tisc We/Ho,Weis,Sod UBS/✱

4165.2 verb nom pl masc part pres mid	4165.3 verb 1pl indic pres act	1056.1 conj	2541.11 adj pl neu
21. ˊ προνοούμενοι	[ᵃ✱ προνοοῦμεν	γὰρ]	καλὰ
pronooumenoi	pronooumen	gar	kala
providing	⌠ we provide	for]	things right

3620.3 partic	3303.1 adv	1783.1 prep gen	2935.2 noun gen sing masc	233.2 conj	2504.1 conj
οὐ	μόνον	ἐνώπιον	κυρίου,	ἀλλὰ	καὶ
ou	monon	enōpion	kuriou,	alla	kai
not	only	before	Lord,	but	also

1783.1 prep gen	442.7 noun gen pl masc	4693.1 verb 1pl indic aor act	1156.2 conj	840.2 prs-pron dat pl
ἐνώπιον	ἀνθρώπων.	**22.** Συνεπέμψαμεν	δὲ	αὐτοῖς
enōpion	anthrōpōn.	Sunepempsamen	de	autois
before	men.	We sent with	and	them

3450.6 art acc sing masc	79.4 noun acc sing masc	2231.2 prs-pron gen 1pl	3614.6 rel-pron acc sing masc	1375.9 verb 1pl indic aor act
τὸν	ἀδελφὸν	ἡμῶν	ὃν	ἐδοκιμάσαμεν
ton	adelphon	hēmōn	hon	edokimasamen
the	brother	our	whom	we proved

by a show of hands (*cheirotoneō*, "to stretch out the hand"). His duty was to "travel with us with this grace." *Charis* is usually translated "grace," but here and in verse 4 it means "gift," referring to the financial offering being collected.

Of this "brother" Meyer observed, "Evidently this man was not one of Paul's regular assistants" (p.183). The churches of Macedonia chose him. As earlier, churches near Timothy recommended him to Paul, "So now the congregations of Macedonia had engaged the services of this brother, and on the basis of their observation had elected him as a traveling companion for Paul to deliver the collection in Jerusalem" (ibid., p.184).

Paul took seriously the charge to administer (*diakoneō*) these funds. The offering accomplished purposes other than just meeting the needs of brethren in financial straits. Everyone participating did so in worship, to the glory of God. The offering also demonstrated the grace of giving the Lord had worked in the hearts of believers at Corinth. It showed their ready mind and willingness to love their brethren in Christ in deed as well as word.

8:20. The sacredness of the assignment produced carefulness in administrative procedure for the apostle. He determined to avoid anything that might lead someone to find fault with what was done. He had already suffered enough unjust criticism from his enemies at Corinth. They were always ready to suggest he intended to personally profit from the money in this offering. He needed no more such censure.

Nor did the apostle want anyone to credit him as the source of this lavish gift. God's people gave it all. He simply administered (*diakoneō*, "served") in it.

8:21. Some preachers conclude they do not care what people think as long as they know their ministry is acceptable with God. Paul was of a different opinion. His carefulness as a church administrator led him to plan ahead with due consideration for things honest before men and God. Of course, he and the others must first actually be praiseworthy before God; but he felt they must also appear that way in the presence of men. This was especially true regarding church finances. He determined that everything would be both honest and open. He left no room for suspicion or criticism.

8:22. Paul had already named Titus as the chairman of the finance committee as well as one of its members (8:6,16). He added another and wrote a recommendation of him here also. He is called

this grace: . . . he was also appointed, *HistNT* . . . he was also ordained by, *Douay* . . . had been expressly chosen...to accompany me with this beneficence, *Murdock* . . . as appointee, *Berkeley* . . . who was also appointed by vote by the assemblies, *Young* . . . has been selected, *Adams* . . . as our fellow-traveller, *Rotherham*.

which is administered by us: . . . which we are undertaking, *NTPE* . . . we're doing, *Beck*.

to the glory of the same Lord: . . . to honor the Lord, *Beck*.

and [declaration of] your ready mind: . . . demonstrates also the willingness, *Phillips* . . . and to our cordiality, *Murdock*.

20. Avoiding this, that no man should blame us in this abundance which is administered by us: Thus we shall avoid any criticism, *Norlie* . . . We take this precaution, *Berkeley* . . . guarding against this, *Sawyer* . . . We are taking precautions to prevent anyone from impugning us in reference to this munificence, *HistNT* . . . We're trying to avoid any criticism of the way we're handling this great gift, *Beck* . . . that no one should discredit us, *NASB* . . . that no one should cast censure on us, in [respect to], *Murdock* . . . of this generous amount, *Confraternity* . . . which is being dispensed, *Wilson*.

21. Providing for honest things: . . . for we take forethought, *Noyes* . . . providing honourable things, *Rotherham* . . . for in forethought, *PNT* . . . we are attentive to things commendable, *Murdock* . . . for we take thought for things honorable, *ASV* . . . so we plan ahead to do good, *Adams* . . . and to be absolutely aboveboard, *Phillips*.

not only in the sight of the Lord: God's approval of our integrity, *Weymouth* . . . not only before God, *Murdock*.

but also in the sight of men: . . . but also before men, *Murdock* . . . but man's also, *Weymouth*.

22. And we have sent with them our brother:

1706.1 prep	4044.4 adj dat pl	4038.1 adv	4558.1 adj acc sing masc	1498.18 verb part pres act	3432.1 adv
ἐν	πολλοῖς	πολλάκις	σπουδαῖον	ὄντα,	νυνὶ
en	pollois	pollakis	spoudaion	onta	nuni
in	many things	often	diligent	being,	now

1156.2 conj	4044.16 adj sing neu	4559.1 adj comp acc sing	3870.1 noun dat sing fem	4044.11 adj dat sing fem
δὲ	πολὺ	σπουδαιότερον	πεποιθήσει	πολλῇ
de	polu	spoudaioteron	pepoithēsei	pollē
and	much	more diligent	by the confidence	great

3450.11 art dat sing fem	1519.1 prep	5050.4 prs-pron acc 2pl		1521.1 conj	5065.1 prep	4951.2 name gen masc
τῇ	εἰς	ὑμᾶς.	**23.**	εἴτε	ὑπὲρ	Τίτου,
tē	eis	humas		eite	huper	Titou
the	towards	you.		Whether	as regards	Titus,

2817.1 noun nom sing masc	1684.3 adj nom 1sing masc	2504.1 conj	1519.1 prep	5050.4 prs-pron acc 2pl	4754.1 adj nom sing masc
κοινωνὸς	ἐμὸς	καὶ	εἰς	ὑμᾶς	συνεργός·
koinōnos	emos	kai	eis	humas	sunergos
partner	my	and	for	you	a fellow worker;

1521.1 conj	79.6 noun pl masc	2231.2 prs-pron gen 1pl	646.4 noun pl masc	1564.6 noun gen pl fem	1385.1 noun nom sing fem
εἴτε	ἀδελφοὶ	ἡμῶν,	ἀπόστολοι	ἐκκλησιῶν,	δόξα
eite	adelphoi	hēmōn	apostoloi	ekklēsiōn	doxa
or	brothers	our,	messengers	of assemblies,	glory

5382.2 name gen masc		3450.12 art acc sing fem	3631.1 conj	1716.2 noun acc sing fem	3450.10 art gen sing fem	26.2 noun gen sing fem
Χριστοῦ.	**24.**	Τὴν	οὖν	ἔνδειξιν	τῆς	ἀγάπης
Christou		Tēn	oun	endeixin	tēs	agapēs
Christ's.		The	therefore	proof	of the	love

5050.2 prs-pron gen 2pl	2504.1 conj	2231.2 prs-pron gen 1pl	2716.2 noun gen sing fem	5065.1 prep	5050.2 prs-pron gen 2pl	1519.1 prep
ὑμῶν,	καὶ	ἡμῶν	καυχήσεως	ὑπὲρ	ὑμῶν,	εἰς
humōn	kai	hēmōn	kauchēseōs	huper	humōn	eis
your,	and	of our	boasting	about	you,	to

840.8 prs-pron acc pl masc	1715.9 verb 2pl mid	1715.10 verb nom pl masc part pres mid	2504.1 conj
αὐτοὺς	⸂ ἐνδείξασθε	[a☆ ἐνδεικνύμενοι]	⸃b καὶ ⸃
autous	endeixasthe	endeiknumenoi	kai
them	you show	[manifesting]	and

1519.1 prep	4241.1 noun sing neu	3450.1 art gen pl	1564.6 noun gen pl fem		3875.1 prep	3173.1 conj
εἰς	πρόσωπον	τῶν	ἐκκλησιῶν.	**9:1.**	Περὶ	μὲν
eis	prosōpon	tōn	ekklēsiōn		Peri	men
in	face	of the	assemblies.		Concerning	men

1056.1 conj	3450.10 art gen sing fem	1242.2 noun gen sing fem	3450.10 art gen sing fem	1519.1 prep	3450.8 art acc pl masc	39.9 adj acc pl masc
γὰρ	τῆς	διακονίας	τῆς	εἰς	τοὺς	ἁγίους
gar	tēs	diakonias	tēs	eis	tous	hagious
for	the	service	the	for	the	saints

3916.1 adj sing neu	1466.4 prs-pron dat 1sing	1498.4 verb 3sing indic pres act	3450.16 art sing neu	1119.5 verb inf pres act
περισσόν	μοί	ἐστιν	τὸ	γράφειν
perisson	moi	estin	to	graphein
superfluous	for me	it is	the	to write

24.a.**Txt**: 01ℵ,04C
06D-corr,018K,020L
025P,byz.bo.We/Ho,Sod
Var: 03B,06D-org,33
Lach,Treg,Alf,Tisc
Weis,UBS/☆

24.b.**Txt**: Steph
Var: 01ℵ,03B,04C,06D
018K,020L,025P,byz.
Gries,Lach,Treg,Alf
Word,Tisc,We/Ho,Weis
Sod,UBS/☆

simply "our brother." Often challenging circumstances had tested him, and in every case they proved him diligent, zealous for the cause of Christ. Sensing Paul's love for Corinth, he was eager to serve there.

8:23. Next the apostle wrote his letter of recommendation for Titus. He was a full partner in the apostle's work. He shared (*koinōnos*) totally in all responsibilities. He was a fellow helper, a true working companion.

Titus and the other two brethren were messengers (*apostoloi*, "sent ones") of the churches. They were missionary representatives of their congregations. Their lives radiated the glory of Christ. Their ministerial conduct brought honor to His name.

8:24. With such impressive credentials, it is little wonder the apostle recommended these men to the church at Corinth without reservation. Obviously, the congregation must give them an appropriate reception.

Paul called for a proper demonstration of Christian love toward these traveling ministers upon their arrival at Corinth. No doubt he also expected the people to attend to their needs for room, board, and other expenses while they were there assisting in the money-raising project. He had taught the church about adequate support for the ministry in his first letter to its members (1 Corinthians 9:6-14). His masterful treatise argued that logic, the Law, and the Lord Jesus all instruct proper care for the ministry. Paul's concluding statement was, "Even so hath the Lord ordained that they which preach the gospel should live of the gospel" (1 Corinthians 9:14). The apostle expressed confidence that the church would at this time set a good example "before the churches" as to the way ministers should be treated.

Once more Paul asked believers at Corinth to justify all the favorable things he had been saying about them. They had not disappointed him during Titus' visit (7:14). No doubt he was more concerned for their reputation than his embarrassment.

9:1. As if to pause yet renew his discussion of the project for the needy in Israel, the apostle spoke of it as a "ministry" to the saints. He no longer referred to it as a "collection" as in his first letter (1 Corinthians 16:1). In this epistle he constantly wrote of it in connection with the "grace" of giving. The Spirit inspired Paul to keep the subject of money in the church on a high plane. Ministers today would do well to follow his example.

Confidently, the apostle said it was really unnecessary for him to write about the offering. Everything he said about it was already in their hearts. He wrote in the spirit of Peter who wanted to put his audience in remembrance, though they were already established in the truth he presented (2 Peter 1:12).

whom we have oftentimes proved diligent in many things: . . . we have frequently put to the test on various occasions, *Berkeley* . . . and found dependable, *Klingensmith*.

but now much more diligent, upon the great confidence which [I have] in you:

23. Whether [any do inquire] of Titus:

[he is] my partner and fellowhelper concerning you: . . . he is my comrade, *HistNT* . . . my mate, *Concordant* . . . he is my intimate companion, *TCNT* . . . my associate, *Berkeley* . . . and assistant, *Murdock* . . . in your behalf, *Worrell*.

or our brethren [be inquired of, they are] the messengers of the churches: . . . and both the brothers are official messengers, *Phillips* . . . they are missionaries, *Wuest* . . . they are delegates, *Weymouth* . . . the apostles of the ecclesias, *Concordant* . . . apostles of assemblies, *Rotherham*.

[and] the glory of Christ: . . . a credit to Christ, *HistNT*.

24. Wherefore show ye to them, and before the churches: Indicate therefore to them, *Hanson* . . . Display to them, *Noyes* . . . exhibit ye to them, *Murdock* . . . demonstrate to the churches, *Adams*.

the proof of your love: . . . the exhibition of, *Rotherham*.

and of our boasting on your behalf: . . . and the truth of our boasting, *Adams* . . . and a justification of our boasting, *Weymouth* . . . and justify my boasting, *Conybeare* . . . ground for my praising you so highly, *Williams* . . . respecting you, *Murdock*.

1. For as touching the ministering to the saints: For, respecting the, *Worrell* . . . concerning the ministration by the saints, *Murdock* . . . as regards giving or withholding relief from the members of the church, *Way*.

it is superfluous for me to write to you: It may seem a waste of time for me to write to you, *Norlie* . . . it is really unnecessary for me, *Weymouth* . . . it is needless that, *Conybeare*.

5050.3 prs-pron dat 2pl
ὑμῖν.
humin
to you.

2. 3471.2 verb 1sing indic perf act
οἶδα
oida
I know

1056.1 conj
γὰρ
gar
for

3450.12 art acc sing fem
τὴν
tēn
the

4147.3 noun acc sing fem
προθυμίαν
prothumian
readiness

5050.2 prs-pron gen 2pl
ὑμῶν
humōn
your

3614.12 rel-pron acc sing fem
ἣν
hēn
which

5065.1 prep
ὑπὲρ
huper
concerning

5050.2 prs-pron gen 2pl
ὑμῶν
humōn
you

2714.1 verb 1sing indic pres
καυχῶμαι
kauchōmai
I boast of

3082.4 name dat pl masc
Μακεδόσιν,
Makedosin
to Macedonians;

3617.1 conj
ὅτι
hoti
that

875.1 name nom fem
Ἀχαΐα
Achaia
Achaia

3764.2 verb 3sing indic perf mid
παρεσκεύασται
pareskeuastai
has been prepared

570.3 prep gen
ἀπὸ
apo
from

3930.1 adv
πέρυσι·
perusi
last year,

2504.1 conj
καὶ
kai
and

3450.5 art sing masc
ὁ
ho
the

2.a.Txt: 04C,06D,018K
020L,025P,etc.byz.Lach
Sod
Var: 01א,03B,33,Treg
Tisc,We/Ho,Weis
UBS/✱

2.b.Txt: 06D,018K,020L
byz.
Var: 01א,03B,04C,025P
33,Lach,Treg,Tisc
We/Ho,Weis,Sod
UBS/✱

3450.16 art sing neu
[ᵃ✱ τὸ]
to
[idem]

1523.1 prep gen
⸀ᵇ ἐξ ⸃
ex
of

5050.2 prs-pron gen 2pl
ὑμῶν
humōn
you

2188.1 noun sing neu
ζῆλος
zēlos
zeal

2025.2 verb 3sing indic aor act
ἠρέθισεν
ērethisen
provoke

3450.8 art acc pl masc
τοὺς
tous
the

3979.4 adj comp acc pl
πλείονας.
pleionas
greater number.

3. 3854.5 verb 1sing indic aor act
ἔπεμψα
epempsa
I sent

1156.2 conj
δὲ
de
but

3450.8 art acc pl masc
τοὺς
tous
the

79.9 noun acc pl masc
ἀδελφούς,
adelphous
brothers,

2419.1 conj
ἵνα
hina
that

3231.1 partic
μὴ
mē
not

3450.16 art sing neu
τὸ
to
the

2715.1 noun sing neu
καύχημα
kauchēma
boasting

2231.2 prs-pron gen 1pl
ἡμῶν
hēmōn
our

3450.16 art sing neu
τὸ
to
the

5065.1 prep
ὑπὲρ
huper
about

5050.2 prs-pron gen 2pl
ὑμῶν
humōn
you

2729.3 verb 3sing subj aor pass
κενωθῇ
kenōthē
should be made void

1706.1 prep
ἐν
en
in

3450.3 art dat sing
τῷ
tō
the

3183.3 noun dat sing neu
μέρει
merei
respect

3642.5 dem-pron dat sing masc
τούτῳ·
toutō
this,

2419.1 conj
ἵνα
hina
that

2503.1 conj
καθὼς
kathōs
according as

2978.25 verb indic imperf act
ἔλεγον,
elegon
I was saying,

3764.3 verb nom pl masc part perf mid
παρεσκευασμένοι
pareskeuasmenoi
having prepared

1498.1 verb 2pl act
ἦτε,
ēte
you may be;

4. 3248.1 conj
⸀ μήπως
mēpōs
lest perhaps

3231.1 partic
[✱ μή
mē
[not

4315.1 adv
πως]
pōs
how]

1430.1 partic
ἐὰν
ean
if

2048.9 verb 3pl subj aor act
ἔλθωσιν
elthōsin
should come

4713.1 prep dat
σὺν
sun
with

1466.5 prs-pron dat 1sing
ἐμοὶ
emoi
me

3082.3 name nom pl masc
Μακεδόνες,
Makedones
Macedonians,

2504.1 conj
καὶ
kai
and

2128.15 verb 3pl subj aor act
εὕρωσιν
heurōsin
found

5050.4 prs-pron acc 2pl
ὑμᾶς
humas
you

528.1 adj acc pl masc
ἀπαρασκευάστους,
aparaskeuastous
unprepared,

2587.6 verb 1pl subj aor pass
καταισχυνθῶμεν
kataischunthōmen
should be put to shame

2231.1 prs-pron nom 1pl
ἡμεῖς,
hēmeis
we,

2419.1 conj
ἵνα
hina
that

9:2. Paul knew well the Corinthians' willingness in the matter of the offering. In fact he had boasted of their attitude about it to the Macedonians. He declared those of Achaia, Greece, were prepared to give to the fund the year before. Complimenting them, he told the Corinthians their zeal had provoked (aroused, stirred) many others to contribute.

Then the apostle praised the Corinthians to the Macedonians, and he praised the Macedonians to the Corinthians (8:1-6). He had a wholesome rivalry going between the churches. Sometimes congregations today enjoy friendly competition as a means of stirring themselves to do their best in supporting worthy causes.

True, as Hughes noted, Paul elsewhere condemned glorying in men (*The New London Commentary*, p.323). In his first letter to the Corinthians he said "that no flesh should glory in his (God's) presence" (1 Corinthians 1:29). The instruction came in the form of condemnation because various factions in the church had been picking favorite preachers solely on the basis of differing personalities. Their choice bore no relation to differences in doctrine or practice. To end the discussion he declared, "Therefore let no man glory in men: for all things are yours" (1 Corinthians 3:21). God gave different ministers with various abilities and talents. Believers need them all.

However, Hughes explained, "Paul's glorying here is neither in men nor in human achievements as such, but in the grace of God manifested in and through the lives of men. Thus he has already gloried to the Corinthians of the amazing liberality of the Macedonians, but in doing so he has attributed everything to 'the grace of God which hath been given in the churches of Macedonia' (8:1). True Christian giving flows from the prior giving of God's grace, and Paul's glorying in the goodness of God" (*The New London Commentary*, p.323).

9:3. Still, the apostle did not want the pace of the project to slow. So he appointed a "finance committee" and sent its chairman and members to Corinth. Again he expressed mild concern that his boasting about his converts in Corinth might prove to be in vain. He wanted to make sure that his talk of their being ready with their offering was completely true. Certainly they were prepared to give the year before, as he had said. Now he desired their readiness to include money in hand.

9:4. Sending the brethren on ahead, Paul himself planned to go to Corinth later. He foresaw the possibility that some Macedonian believers might accompany him. If they arrived with him and found the church unprepared with its offering, what a source of embarrassment that would be to the apostle. He thought of all the boasting he had done to the Macedonians about how aggressive the Corinthians were when it came to giving! He shuddered to think of how humiliated he would be to find their offering incomplete.

2. For I know the forwardness of your mind: . . . for I have known your readiness of mind, *Young* . . . I know your readiness, *Worrell* . . . I know your willingness, *Campbell.*

for which I boast of you to them of Macedonia: . . . you in Greece, *Weymouth.*

that Achaia was ready a year ago: . . . was prepared, *Fenton* . . . has been prepared for a year back, *HistNT* . . . has been prepared since last year, *Norlie* . . . hath been prepared for a year, *Panin.*

and your zeal hath provoked very many: . . . and the zeal of you did stir up the more part, *Young* . . . has stimulated the majority, *Hanson* . . . has consequently been a stimulus, *Phillips* . . . through your zeal many were aroused, *Fenton* . . . your enthusiasm has stimulated more than yourselves, *Way* . . . has excited many, *Wilson* . . . stirred up the majority, *Rotherham* . . . a goodly number, *Berkeley.*

3. Yet have I sent the brethren: My reason for sending our Brothers, *TCNT.*

lest our boasting of you should be in vain in this behalf: . . . may not be made void in this respect, *Alford, ASV, Hanson* . . . in this particular be proved empty, *PNT* . . . in this particular matter an empty boast, *TCNT* . . . may not be made empty in this case, *NASB* . . . you may not turn out to have been an idle one, *Weymouth* . . . turned into an empty boast, *Conybeare* . . . you should be found empty in this instance, *Confraternity* . . . should be made void in this respect, *Rotherham.*

that, as I said, ye may be ready: . . . ye may be prepared, *Macknight.*

4. Lest haply if they of Macedonia come with me, and find you unprepared: . . . accompany me, *HistNT* . . . and find that you are not ready, *Williams.*

2 Corinthians 9:5

4.a.Txt: 01א,03B
04C-corr2,044,0209
0243,bo.byz.
Var: p46,04C-org,06D
010F,012G,048

3231.1 partic	2978.8 verb 1pl subj pres act	2978.1 verb 1sing pres act	5050.1 prs-pron nom 2pl	1706.1 prep	3450.11 art dat sing fem
μὴ	ʿ λέγωμεν	[ᵃ☆ λέγω]	ὑμεῖς,	ἐν	τῇ
mē	legōmen	legō	humeis	en	tē
not	we may say	[I say]	you,	in	the

4.b.Txt: 01א-corr
06D-corr,018K,020L
025P,byz.
Var: 01א-org,03B,04C
06D-org,33,it.bo.Gries
Lach,Treg,Alf,Word
Tisc,We/Ho,Weis,Sod
UBS/☆

5125.3 noun dat sing fem	3642.11 dem-pron dat sing fem	3450.10 art gen sing fem	2716.2 noun gen sing fem
ὑποστάσει	ταύτῃ	ʿᵇ τῆς	καυχήσεως. ˎ
hupostasei	tautē	tēs	kauchēseōs
confidence	this	of the	boasting.

314.3 adj nom sing neu	3631.1 conj	2216.12 verb 1sing indic aor mid	3731.15 verb inf aor act	3450.8 art acc pl masc
5. ἀναγκαῖον	οὖν	ἡγησάμην	παρακαλέσαι	τοὺς
anankaion	oun	hēgēsamēn	parakalesai	tous
Necessary	therefore	I thought	to exhort	the

79.9 noun acc pl masc	2419.1 conj	4140.2 verb 3pl subj aor act	1519.1 prep	5050.4 prs-pron acc 2pl	2504.1 conj
ἀδελφοὺς	ἵνα	προέλθωσιν	εἰς	ὑμᾶς,	καὶ
adelphous	hina	proelthōsin	eis	humas	kai
brothers	that	they should go before	to	you,	and

4153.1 verb 3pl subj aor act	3450.12 art acc sing fem	4152.4 verb acc sing fem part perf pass
προκαταρτίσωσιν	τὴν	ʿ προκατηγγελμένην
prokatartisōsin	tēn	prokatēngelmenēn
should arrange beforehand	the	having been foreannounced

5.a.Txt: 018K,020L,byz.
Var: 01א,03B,04C,06D
025P,Lach,Treg,Alf
Word,Tisc,We/Ho,Weis
Sod,UBS/☆

4139.2 verb acc sing fem part perf pass	2110.4 noun acc sing fem	5050.2 prs-pron gen 2pl	3642.12 dem-pron acc sing fem
[ᵃ☆ προεπηγγελμένην]	εὐλογίαν	ὑμῶν	ταύτην
proepēngelmenēn	eulogian	humōn	tautēn
[having been before promised]	blessing	your	this

2071.4 adj acc sing fem	1498.32 verb inf pres act	3643.1 adv	5453.1 conj	2110.4 noun acc sing fem	2504.1 conj	3231.1 partic
ἑτοίμην	εἶναι	οὕτως	ὡς	εὐλογίαν,	καὶ	μὴ
hetoimēn	einai	houtōs	hōs	eulogian	kai	mē
ready	to be	thus	as	a blessing,	and	not

5.b.Txt: Steph
Var: 01א,03B,04C,06D
018K,020L,025P,byz.
Gries,Lach,Treg,Alf
Word,Tisc,We/Ho,Weis
Sod,UBS/☆

5450.1 adv	5453.1 conj	3984.4 noun acc sing fem	3642.17 dem-pron sing neu	1156.2 conj
ʿ ὥσπερ	[ᵇ☆ ὡς]	πλεονεξίαν.	**6.** Τοῦτο	δέ,
hōsper	hōs	pleonexian	Touto	de
as	[idem]	covetousness.	This	but,

3450.5 art sing masc	4540.5 verb nom sing masc part pres act	5178.1 adv	5178.1 adv	2504.1 conj
ὁ	σπείρων	φειδομένως,	φειδομένως	καὶ
ho	speirōn	pheidomenōs	pheidomenōs	kai
the	sowing	sparingly,	sparingly	also

2302.9 verb 3sing indic fut act	2504.1 conj	3450.5 art sing masc	4540.5 verb nom sing masc part pres act	1894.2 prep	2110.5 noun dat pl fem
θερίσει·	καὶ	ὁ	σπείρων	ἐπ'	εὐλογίαις,
therisei	kai	ho	speirōn	ep'	eulogiais
shall reap;	and	the	sowing	on	blessings,

1894.2 prep	2110.5 noun dat pl fem	2504.1 conj	2302.9 verb 3sing indic fut act	1524.3 adj nom sing masc	2503.1 conj
ἐπ'	εὐλογίαις	καὶ	θερίσει.	**7.** ἕκαστος	καθὼς
ep'	eulogiais	kai	therisei	hekastos	kathōs
on	blessings	also	shall reap:	each	according as

592

The apostle made a parenthetic comment about his not mentioning the possibility of embarrassment for the believers at Corinth in case they had not completed the fund-raising project. Modestly, he would rather speak of the possibility of his failure than theirs. Either way, an appeal to avoid humiliation is an acceptable motivation to Christian service.

9:5. Paul's tact in handling the delicate financial project in the church at Corinth is evidence he was clothed by the Spirit as he wrote and as he engaged in the administrative functions of the pastor. With the remote prospect that the congregation was not ready with its offering, he explained he thought it necessary (considered it his duty, felt a compulsion) to send the brethren on ahead. They would arrange to receive the offering in advance of his arrival. Their aim was to guide the people in gathering their contribution beforehand (*prokatartizō*, here only in the New Testament).

The apostle reminded the Corinthians they had received notice of this offering well in advance. This gave ample time for everyone to give his fair share without placing a hardship on any. The tithing system fits perfectly into Paul's teaching here on the grace of giving. It provides for both equitable and systematic giving. True worshipers paid tithes from grateful hearts long before the law of Moses required it, as did Abraham (Genesis 14:20) and Jacob (Genesis 28:20-22).

Paul was concerned that the offering be one of bounty (*eulogias*, "good words"), a gift of blessing. He did not want it to be one of covetousness or miserliness. Take note that covetousness manifests itself in many, subtle ways. Men usually associate it with amassing wealth, but Paul shows here it can reveal itself in hoarding wealth, giving grudgingly in an offering. For him the offering was a means of enhancing their relationship with God. Right attitude meant everything in view of that purpose.

9:6. Though the apostle was determined not to encourage any to give above his ability, he did promote generosity of heart. To do so he recalled the law of harvest. Sow sparingly, and reap accordingly; sow bountifully, and reap plenteously.

Under God Paul selected powerful words to encourage generous giving. He employed *eulogias*, "blessing," with a play on words here. His message, then, was that those who sow seeds of blessing will reap a harvest of blessing. To warn against stinginess he recalled words of the wise man: "There is that scattereth, and yet increaseth; and there is that withholdeth more than is meet, but it tendeth to poverty" (Proverbs 11:24).

The apostle applied the law of harvest to giving in his epistle to the Galatians also. He instructed support of the ministry saying he that was taught must "communicate" or share with "him that teacheth in all good things" (Galatians 6:6). Then he spoke of reaping what is sown as true whether the sowing is to the flesh or Spirit.

we (that we say not, ye) should be ashamed in this same confident boasting: . . . we would feel humiliated, *Berkeley* . . . not to say yourselves, *Confraternity* . . . ashamed in this matter, *Douay* . . . in this assertion, *Fenton* . . . should be put to shame for that glorying, *Murdock*.

5. Therefore I thought it necessary to exhort the brethren: I have therefore considered it needful, *HistNT* . . . I was careful to request these my brethren, *Murdock* . . . necessary to urge, *Adams* . . . to entreat, *ASV*.

that they would go before unto you: . . . so that they might proceed to you, *Fenton*.

and make up before hand your bounty: . . . arrange in advance, *Beck, RSV* . . . and get your promised love-offering ready beforehand, *Williams* . . . your previously promised blessing, *Hanson* . . . this your before-promised blessing, *Rotherham* . . . your aforepromised bounty, *Panin* . . . your long-promised liberality, *HistNT* . . . this previously announced gift, *Wilson*.

whereof ye had notice before, that the same might be ready:

as [a matter of] bounty, and not as [of] covetousness: . . . be spontaneous, *Fenton* . . . as a free gift, *Sawyer* . . . as a blessing, *Young* . . . as money that was gladly given and not forced out of you, *Beck* . . . to be a spontaneous gift, and not money squeezed out of you, *Phillips* . . . and not of grudging avarice, *HistNT* . . . but gives grudgingly under pressure, *Wuest* . . . not a matter of stinginess, *Klingensmith* . . . and not something extorted from you, *Berkeley* . . . not as something exacted under pressure, *Adams*.

6. But this [I say], He which soweth sparingly shall reap also sparingly: Mark this! *HistNT, Confraternity* . . . he that sows thinly, *Klingensmith*.

and he which soweth bountifully shall reap also bountifully: But if you sow generously, *Beck* . . . who sows liberally, *Berkeley* . . . and the generous sower will also reap, *Fenton* . . . with blessings also shall reap, *Rotherham*.

2 Corinthians 9:8

7.a.Txt: 06D,018K,020L
byz.
Var: 01ℵ,03B,04C,025P
Lach,Treg,Alf,Word
Tisc,We/Ho,Weis,Sod
UBS/★

4114.1 verb 3sing indic pres mid
ʽ προαιρεῖται
proaireitai
he decides

4114.2 verb 3sing indic perf mid
[ᵃ☆ προῄρηται]
proērētai
[he has chosen]

3450.11 art dat sing fem
τῇ
tē
in the

2559.3 noun dat sing fem
καρδίᾳ·
kardia
heart;

3231.1 partic
μὴ
mē
not

1523.2 prep gen
ἐκ
ek
of

1523.2 noun gen sing fem
λύπης
lupēs
grief,

2211.1 conj
ἢ
ē
or

1523.1 prep gen
ἐξ
ex
of

316.2 noun gen sing fem
ἀνάγκης·
anankēs
necessity;

2407.1 adj acc sing masc
ἱλαρὸν
hilaron
a cheerful

1056.1 conj
γὰρ
gar
for

1389.1 noun acc sing masc
δότην
dotēn
giver

25.2 verb 3sing pres act
ἀγαπᾷ
agapa
loves

3450.5 art sing masc
ὁ
ho

2296.1 noun nom sing masc
θεός.
theos
God.

8. ʽ **1409.1** adj nom sing masc
δυνατὸς
dunatos
Able

8.a.Txt: 04C-corr
06D-corr,018K,020L
025P,byz.Sod
Var: 01ℵ,03B,04C-org
06D-org,Lach,Treg,Alf
Tisc,We/Ho,Weis
UBS/★

1408.1 verb 3sing indic pres act
[ᵃ☆ δυνατεῖ]
dunatei
[is able]

1156.2 conj
δὲ
de
for

3450.5 art sing masc
ὁ
ho

2296.1 noun nom sing masc
θεὸς
theos
God

3820.12 adj acc sing fem
πᾶσαν
pasan
every

5322.4 noun acc sing fem
χάριν
charin
grace

3915.18 verb inf aor act
περισσεῦσαι
perisseusai
to make abound

1519.1 prep
εἰς
eis
towards

5050.4 prs-pron acc 2pl
ὑμᾶς,
humas
you,

2419.1 conj
ἵνα
hina
that

1706.1 prep
ἐν
en
in

3820.3 adj dat sing
παντὶ
panti
every

3704.1 adv
πάντοτε
pantote
always

3820.12 adj acc sing fem
πᾶσαν
pasan
all

835.2 noun acc sing fem
αὐτάρκειαν
autarkeian
sufficiency

2174.19 verb nom pl masc part pres act
ἔχοντες,
echontes
having,

3915.7 verb 2pl subj pres act
περισσεύητε
perisseuēte
you may abound

1519.1 prep
εἰς
eis
to

3820.17 adj sing neu
πᾶν
pan
every

2024.1 noun sing neu
ἔργον
ergon
work

18.3 adj sing
ἀγαθόν·
agathon
good:

9. **2503.1** conj
καθὼς
kathōs
just as

1119.22 verb 3sing indic perf pass
γέγραπται,
gegraptai
it has been written,

4505.2 verb 3sing indic aor act
Ἐσκόρπισεν,
Eskorpisen
He scattered abroad,

1319.14 verb 3sing indic aor act
ἔδωκεν
edōken
he gave

3450.4 art dat pl
τοῖς
tois
to the

3855.1 adj dat pl masc
πένησιν·
penēsin
poor,

3450.9 art nom sing fem
ἡ
hē
the

1336.1 noun nom sing fem
δικαιοσύνη
dikaiosunē
righteousness

840.3 prs-pron gen sing
αὐτοῦ
autou
his

3176.1 verb 3sing indic act
μένει
menei
abides

1519.1 prep
εἰς
eis
unto

3450.6 art acc sing masc
τὸν
ton
the

163.3 noun acc sing masc
αἰῶνα.
aiōna
age.

10.a.Txt: 01ℵ,04C
06D-corr2,044,048,0209
0243,byz.
Var: p46,03B,06D-org
010F,012G,1175

10. **3450.5** art sing masc
ʽΟ
Ho
The

1156.2 conj
δὲ
de
now

2007.1 verb nom sing masc part pres act
ἐπιχορηγῶν
epichorēgōn
supplying

4543.1 noun sing neu
ʽ σπέρμα
sperma
seed

4556.2 noun acc sing masc
[ᵃ☆ σπόρον]
sporon
[idem]

3450.3 art dat sing
τῷ
tō
to the

4540.7 verb dat sing masc part pres act
σπείροντι
speironti
sowing

2504.1 conj
καὶ
kai
and

735.4 noun acc sing masc
ἄρτον
arton
bread

1519.1 prep
εἰς
eis
for

1028.4 noun acc sing fem
βρῶσιν
brōsin
eating

9:7. Paul's next principle on giving is basic. Let each man contribute to worthy causes as he purposes or decides in his heart and makes up his mind before the Lord to do. Elsewhere Paul emphasized giving according to financial blessings God has granted (1 Corinthians 16:2). In short, ability for sharing equals responsibility to give.

The apostle advised against giving grudgingly or reluctantly. Certainly Christ did not give His all with that attitude. Paul wanted none to contribute to this offering with a feeling of necessity or compulsion.

Paul never employed high-pressure methods in raising church funds. In his former letter to Corinth he asked that monies be given systematically, on a regular weekly basis, specifically so that there would be no pressure to collect an offering when he arrived (1 Corinthians 16:2). If one contributes in the excitement or pressure of the moment, he may later regret it. The apostle realized that such an attitude kills worship.

On the other hand, a cheerful (Greek, *hilaros*) spirit enhances worship. God loves those who give gladly.

9:8. The apostle not only declared God loves a cheerful giver, but he promised the Lord would make it possible for His children to give generously. Writing of "grace" (*charis*) abounding so as to provide a sufficiency for every good work, he used the word in a new sense. The promise implies an ability to contribute to every cause. Grace works in financial matters so that the believers will have sufficient to make giving possible.

God's blessings rested on Israel to give both cheerfully and generously at the building of the tabernacle. The people actually gave so much they had to be restrained (Exodus 36:5-7). This is one of the unusual instances in history when people gave "more than enough for the service" of the Lord.

9:9. Paul spoke next of spiritual blessings which accompany generous giving. He took the words of Psalm 112:9 as a text for his comments. The Psalmist sings the praises of the man of means who freely disperses abroad and shares generously of his goods with others. He especially distributes what he has among the poor and needy. Consequently, God's favor is upon him so his righteousness remains forever, literally "unto the age."

Jesus spoke the same beautiful truth in the Sermon on the Mount. He exhorted men to lay up treasures in heaven rather than on earth. Thus they concentrate on that which remains forever.

9:10. Paul's meditation on the truth of the Psalmist stirred a prayer in his heart. Remembering what Isaiah said, he addressed the One who gives seed to the sower and bread for food (see Isaiah 55:10). He asked that One to multiply the seed sown, both of the

7. Every man according as he purposeth in his heart: . . . what he has decided upon in his own mind, *Weymouth* . . . as he has predetermined, *Rotherham* . . . he had planned, *Berkeley.*

[so let him give]:

not grudgingly, or of necessity: . . . not of grief, *Hanson* . . . not regretting his gift, as if it were wrung from him, *Way* . . . not sorrowfully, *Williams* . . . and not do it reluctantly or under compulsion, *Weymouth* . . . not with sadness, not by constraint, *Murdock.*

for God loveth a cheerful giver: . . . loves a hilarious, *Berkeley.*

8. And God [is] able to make all grace abound toward you: God has power to shower upon you every kind of blessing in abundance, *TCNT* . . . able to lavish all grace, *Concordant* . . . give you every free gift in full measure, *NTPE* . . . to make your every spiritual blessing overflow for you, *Williams* . . . to reward you abundantly for every gift, *Greber.*

that ye, always having all sufficiency in all [things]: . . . under all circumstances, *Berkeley.*

may abound to every good work: . . . you may have ample means for all good works, *Weymouth* . . . you may have a surplus, *Klingensmith.*

9. (As it is written, He hath dispersed abroad: The Bible says of such a person, *Beck* . . . He distributed freely, *Greber.*

he hath given to the poor: He has lavished his gifts on the needy, *NEB* . . . gave generously, *Barclay.*

his righteousness remaineth for ever: His almsgiving remains, *Weymouth* . . . His acts of love last forever, *NLT* . . . abides to the remotest age, *Rotherham* . . . continues for ever, *TCNT* . . . his good deeds will never be forgotten, *JB* . . . his kindness lasts forever, *Barclay.*

10. Now he that ministereth seed to the sower both minister bread for [your] food: . . . may He who is supplying seed to, *Young* . . . he who gives seed for putting into the field, *BB.*

2 Corinthians 9:11

5359.2 verb 3sing opt aor act	5359.3 verb 3sing indic fut act	2504.1 conj	3989.3 verb 3sing opt aor act
ʹ χορηγῆσαι	[ᵇ★ χορηγήσει]	καὶ	ʹ πληθῦναι
chorēgēsai	chorēgēsei	kai	plēthunai
may he supply	[he will provide]	and	may he multiply

3989.10 verb 3sing indic fut act	3450.6 art acc sing masc	4556.2 noun acc sing masc	5050.2 prs-pron gen 2pl	2504.1 conj
[ᶜ★ πληθυνεῖ]	τὸν	σπόρον	ὑμῶν,	καὶ
plēthunei	ton	sporon	humōn	kai
[he will multiply]	the	sowing	your,	and

831.9 verb 3sing opt aor act	831.16 verb 3sing indic fut act	3450.17 art pl neu	1075.2 noun voc pl neu
ʹ αὐξῆσαι	[ᵈ★ αὐξήσει]	τὰ	ʹ γεννήματα
auxēsai	auxēsei	ta	gennēmata
may he increase	[he will increase]	the	fruits

1073.1 noun acc pl neu	3450.10 art gen sing fem	1336.2 noun gen sing fem	5050.2 prs-pron gen 2pl	1706.1 prep
[★ γενήματα]	τῆς	δικαιοσύνης	ὑμῶν.	**11.** ἐν
genēmata	tēs	dikaiosunēs	humōn	en
[idem]	of the	righteousness	your:	in

3820.3 adj dat sing	4008.2 verb nom pl masc part pres pass	1519.1 prep	3820.12 adj acc sing fem	567.3 noun acc sing fem
παντὶ	πλουτιζόμενοι	εἰς	πᾶσαν	ἁπλότητα,
panti	ploutizomenoi	eis	pasan	haplotēta
every	being enriched	to	all	liberality,

3610.3 rel-pron nom sing fem	2686.2 verb 3sing indic pres	1217.1 prep	2231.2 prs-pron gen 1pl	2150.4 noun acc sing fem
ἥτις	κατεργάζεται	δι'	ἡμῶν	εὐχαριστίαν
hētis	katergazetai	di'	hēmōn	eucharistian
which	works out	through	us	thanksgiving

3450.3 art dat sing	2296.3 noun dat sing masc	3617.1 conj	3450.9 art nom sing fem	1242.1 noun nom sing fem	3450.10 art gen sing fem
τῷ	θεῷ·	**12.** ὅτι	ἡ	διακονία	τῆς
tō	theō	hoti	hē	diakonia	tēs
to God.		Because	the	ministry	of the

2983.1 noun gen sing fem	3642.10 dem-pron gen sing fem	3620.3 partic	3303.1 adv	1498.4 verb 3sing indic pres act
λειτουργίας	ταύτης	οὐ	μόνον	ἐστὶν
leitourgias	tautēs	ou	monon	estin
service	this	not	only	is

4180.1 verb nom sing fem part pres act	3450.17 art pl neu	5140.3 noun acc pl neu	3450.1 art gen pl	39.4 adj gen pl
προσαναπληροῦσα	τὰ	ὑστερήματα	τῶν	ἁγίων,
prosanaplērousa	ta	husterēmata	tōn	hagiōn
completely filling up	the	shortages	of the	saints,

233.2 conj	2504.1 conj	3915.9 verb nom sing fem part pres act	1217.2 prep	4044.1 adj gen pl	2150.5 noun gen pl fem
ἀλλὰ	καὶ	περισσεύουσα	διὰ	πολλῶν	εὐχαριστιῶν
alla	kai	perisseuousa	dia	pollōn	eucharistiōn
but	also	abounding	through	many	thanksgivings

3450.3 art dat sing	2296.3 noun dat sing masc	1217.2 prep	3450.10 art gen sing fem	1376.2 noun gen sing fem	3450.10 art gen sing fem
τῷ	θεῷ·	**13.** διὰ	τῆς	δοκιμῆς	τῆς
tō	theō	dia	tēs	dokimēs	tēs
to God;		through	the	proof	of the

natural and the spiritual kind. Multiplying natural seed supplies the sower's need and makes it possible for him to share with others. Then Paul prayed that God would increase the fruits of righteousness for all of His people, in keeping with the song the apostle quoted in verse 9.

9:11. Again the apostle promised the Lord will enrich the believer to all bountifulness or generosity. As he gives to meet the needs of others, such as ministers like Paul, the apostle declared in turn, "My God shall supply all your need according to his riches in glory by Christ Jesus" (Philippians 4:19). However, in a word specifically for the rich, the apostle said God not only gives them all things richly to enjoy, but He also intended they be ready to distribute and willing to share what they have with others (1 Timothy 6:17,18).

Good things follow spiritually when one relates to God financially according to Paul's teaching. Experiencing the realities of the promises the apostle recalled here caused him to offer thanksgiving to God. Giving in worship then is not a temporal matter only but an eternal one. It relates not only to material but to spiritual things. It belongs in the sanctuary and is vital in all that transpires in the life of the Church.

9:12. At this point Paul reached the climax of his message. Certainly his concern in discussing the offering for the needy had been hungry people whom he wanted to see fed. Naturally he desired those dressed in rags to be properly clothed, and those without housing to have adequate shelter. He emphasized again one good from this service was that it would supply the needs of the saints. However, he finally focused on what his highest aims were.

What follows here fits the same mold of what the apostle wrote on church finances in a note of thanks to the Philippians (Philippians 4:10-19). Though he expressed appreciation for an offering they had sent, he was careful to show giving in the church does much more than just help pay the bills or feed the preacher. Their offering demonstrated their love for him, and the love behind it meant more than its contents. Through it they commendably shared the burden of his financial straits. But he did not write with a hint they send another offering soon. What he encouraged was their laying up treasure in heaven. They needed to have fruit credited to their account there. Most of all, though, the presentation of their gift resembled the worship of old when men burnt sacrifices before Jehovah. It was "an odor of a sweet smell, a sacrifice acceptable, well-pleasing to God" (Philippians 4:18).

Then in a similar way here, going beyond the important matter of meeting human need, the apostle first declared the offering would produce much thanksgiving to God. He had drawn attention to the fact that the giver is blessed and worships. Now he stated those receiving the offering also would respond with abundant thanksgiving.

and multiply your seed sown: . . . shall multiply your store, *Way* . . . your store of seed, *NIV* . . . will furnish you with plenteous store of seed, *Conybeare* . . . will take care of the growth of your seed, *BB*.

and increase the fruits of your righteousness;): . . . at the same time increasing the fruits of your righteousness, *BB* . . . he will multiply it and swell the harvest of your benevolence, *NEB* . . . to yield a plentiful harvest, *Weymouth* . . . increase the products, *Campbell* . . . and he will make it grow into a plentiful harvest, *Barclay* . . . increase your generous yield, *NAB* . . . and make your righteousness grow into a fine harvest, *SEB* . . . make the harvest of your good deeds a larger one, *JB* . . . and enlarge the harvest of your uprightness, *Goodspeed* . . . and produce a rich harvest, *TEV*.

11. Being enriched in every thing to all bountifulness: You will grow rich in every way, *Goodspeed* . . . He will always make you rich enough to be generous at all times, *TEV* . . . in every respect, *Berkeley* . . . to every kind of generous giving, *KJII* . . . for all liberality, *Campbell* . . . so that you can be generous on every occasion, *NIV*.

which causeth through us thanksgiving to God: . . . so that through me you can show perfect liberality, *Goodspeed* . . . will evoke thanksgiving, *Berkeley* . . . wakes a chorus of thanksgiving to God, *Way*.

12. For the administration of this service not only supplieth the want of the saints: For the rendering of a public service like this, *TCNT* . . . It is like a serving ministry which does two things, *SEB* . . . not only is replenishing the wants, *Concordant* . . . filling up the deficiencies of the saints, *Rotherham*.

but is abundant also by many thanksgivings unto God: . . . but is also rich, *Murdock* . . . overflows also in much gratitude, *Confraternity* . . . also results in abundant thanksgiving, *TCNT* . . . Many people will thank God, *SEB*.

1242.2 noun gen sing fem	3642.10 dem-pron gen sing fem	1386.5 verb nom pl masc part pres act	3450.6 art acc sing masc	2296.4 noun acc sing masc
διακονίας	ταύτης	δοξάζοντες	τὸν	θεὸν
diakonias	*tautēs*	*doxazontes*	*ton*	*theon*
service	this	glorifying		God

1894.3 prep	3450.11 art dat sing fem	5130.1 noun dat sing fem	3450.10 art gen sing fem	3534.1 noun gen sing fem	5050.2 prs-pron gen 2pl
ἐπὶ	τῇ	ὑποταγῇ	τῆς	ὁμολογίας	ὑμῶν
epi	*tē*	*hupotagē*	*tēs*	*homologias*	*humōn*
at	the	subjection,	by the	confession	your,

1519.1 prep	3450.16 art sing neu	2077.1 noun sing neu	3450.2 art gen sing	5382.2 name gen masc	2504.1 conj
εἰς	τὸ	εὐαγγέλιον	τοῦ	Χριστοῦ,	καὶ
eis	*to*	*euangelion*	*tou*	*Christou*	*kai*
to	the	good news	of the	Christ,	and

567.2 noun dat sing fem	3450.10 art gen sing fem	2815.2 noun gen sing fem	1519.1 prep	840.8 prs-pron acc pl masc	2504.1 conj
ἁπλότητι	τῆς	κοινωνίας	εἰς	αὐτοὺς	καὶ
haplotēti	*tēs*	*koinōnias*	*eis*	*autous*	*kai*
liberality	of the	fellowship	towards	them	and

1519.1 prep	3820.8 adj acc pl masc	2504.1 conj	840.1 prs-pron gen pl	1157.3 noun dat sing fem	5065.1 prep
εἰς	πάντας,	**14.** καὶ	αὐτῶν	δεήσει	ὑπὲρ
eis	*pantas*	*kai*	*autōn*	*deēsei*	*huper*
towards	all;	and	their	in request	for

14.a.Var: 01א-org,03B 1881,2495

5050.2 prs-pron gen 2pl	1955.5 verb gen pl masc part pres act	5050.4 prs-pron acc 2pl	2231.4 prs-pron acc 1pl	1217.2 prep
ὑμῶν,	ἐπιποθούντων	⟨☆ ὑμᾶς	[a ἡμᾶς]	διὰ
humōn	*epipothountōn*	*humas*	*hēmas*	*dia*
you,	longing	for you,	[us,]	on account of

3450.12 art acc sing fem	5072.3 verb acc sing fem part pres act	5322.4 noun acc sing fem	3450.2 art gen sing	2296.2 noun gen sing masc	1894.1 prep
τὴν	ὑπερβάλλουσαν	χάριν	τοῦ	θεοῦ	ἐφ'
tēn	*huperballousan*	*charin*	*tou*	*theou*	*eph'*
the	surpassing	grace		of God	upon

15.a.Txt: 01א-corr 04C-corr,06D-corr,018K 020L,025P,byz.bo. **Var:** 01א-org,03B 04C-org,06D-org,33 Lach,Treg,Alf,Tisc We/Ho,Weis,Sod UBS/☆

5050.3 prs-pron dat 2pl	5322.1 noun nom sing fem	1156.2 conj	3450.3 art dat sing	2296.3 noun dat sing masc	1894.3 prep
ὑμῖν.	**15.** χάρις	⟨a δὲ ⟩	τῷ	θεῷ	ἐπὶ
humin	*charis*	*de*	*tō*	*theō*	*epi*
you.	Thanks	now		to God	for

3450.11 art dat sing fem	409.1 adj dat sing fem	840.3 prs-pron gen sing	1424.3 noun dat sing fem	840.5 prs-pron nom sing masc	1156.2 conj
τῇ	ἀνεκδιηγήτῳ	αὐτοῦ	δωρεᾷ.	**10:1.** Αὐτὸς	δὲ
tē	*anekdiēgētō*	*autou*	*dōrea*	*Autos*	*de*
the	indescribable	his	gift.	Myself	now

1466.1 prs-pron nom 1sing	3834.1 name nom masc	3731.1 verb 1sing indic pres act	5050.4 prs-pron acc 2pl	1217.2 prep	3450.10 art gen sing fem
ἐγὼ	Παῦλος	παρακαλῶ	ὑμᾶς	διὰ	τῆς
egō	*Paulos*	*parakalō*	*humas*	*dia*	*tēs*
I	Paul	encourage	you	by	the

1.a.Txt: 01א-corr,04C 06D,018K,020L,byz. **Var:** 01א-org,03B,025P 33,Lach,Treg,Alf,Word Tisc,We/Ho,Weis,Sod UBS/☆

4095.2 noun gen sing fem	4099.1 noun gen sing fem	2504.1 conj	1917.1 noun gen sing fem	3450.2 art gen sing
⟨ πραότητος	[a☆ πραΰτητος]	καὶ	ἐπιεικείας	τοῦ
praotētos	*prautētos*	*kai*	*epieikeias*	*tou*
humility	[meekness]	and	gentleness	of the

9:13. Paul understood the "experiment of this ministration," or better "the approved character of their service," would have a second desirable effect. It would inspire the recipients to glorify God at the evidence of the Gentiles' subjection to the gospel. The offering would provide tangible proof to the Jewish Christians that Gentile conversions were real. Theirs was no mere "professed," or more correctly merely an expressed subjection. It was genuine.

Thirdly, the recipients would thank God for the Corinthians' liberal distribution (*koinōnias*, here "unselfishness, devotion to others"). They would appreciate the gift, but more, they would recognize it came from hearts where a work of grace had been done.

9:14. Fourth, the Jewish brethren would pray for the Gentile members of the body of Christ. Though miles separated them, they were united in a common spirit of prayer.

Fifth, the recipients of their gift would have a deep affection for their benefactors. The offering would serve to cement the bond of love between them. For Paul nothing was more valuable than unity in the Church. How he preached, taught, worked, and prayed for it, especially between Jewish and Gentile believers. Now it would be furthered through this gift.

The "longing" of the recipients of the offering toward those who gave would also include a desire to follow the example of the contributors. They would see the exceeding (*huperballousan*, one of Paul's several superlatives) grace of God in them. That would cause a burning desire for the Lord to do a similar work in their hearts.

In Romans 15:25,26 the apostle gave the exciting conclusion of the matter discussed in Second Corinthians chapters 8 and 9. He wrote, "But now I go unto Jerusalem to minister unto the saints. For it hath pleased them of Macedonia and Achaia to make a certain contribution for the poor saints which are at Jerusalem."

9:15. Paul reached a peak experience in meditation on giving here. Stirred deeply, he exclaimed, "Thanks be unto God for his unspeakable gift!" "Thanks" is another meaning of *charis*. The superlative *anekdiēgētos* ("unspeakable, indescribable") appears only here in the New Testament.

10:1. Paul began a new section of his letter here. He returned to the matter of his relationship to the church at Corinth. Earlier he defended his office; now he defends more himself. This then is the most personal part of the most personal letter of the apostle.

The apostle emphatically identified himself anew, "I Paul myself." The pleas, the appeals, and the entreaties he was about to make rested on the meekness and gentleness of Christ. The fact that Paul followed Christ's example led his enemies to charge he

13. Whiles by the experiment of this ministration they glorify God for your professed subjection unto the gospel of Christ: In the way that you stand the test of this service, *Norlie* ... they are praising God for your loyalty, *Berkeley* ... to your professed adherence to the Good News, *Weymouth* ... for your fidelity to your profession of faith, *TCNT* ... for the alliance of your profession, *Fenton.*

and for [your] liberal distribution unto them, and unto all [men]: ... and for the generosity of your contribution, *HistNT* ... and, by your generous sharing with them, *Klingensmith.*

14. And by their prayer for you: ... with warm affection, *Adams.*

which long after you for the exceeding grace of God in you: ... elicited by God's surpassing grace bestowed on you, *Kleist* ... who ardently love you, *Campbell* ... because of the unusual measure, *Berkeley* ... because of the excellent grace, *Douay* ... surpassing grace which is resting upon you, *Weymouth.*

15. Thanks [be] unto God for his unspeakable gift: ... for His indescribable gift! *NASB* ... His unexpected bounty! *Fenton* ... for his indescribable bounty! *Rotherham* ... for his inexpressible free Gift! *Wilson* ... for his inestimable gift! *TCNT* ... for His indescribable gratuity! *Concordant* ... more priceless than words can tell! *Norlie* ... precious beyond description, *Way.*

1. Now I Paul myself beseech you by the meekness and gentleness of Christ: I personally make this appeal before you, *Greber* ... make a personal appeal to you, *TCNT* ... appeal to you personally, *Norlie, Berkeley* ... advise you, *Fenton* ... and yieldedness of Christ, *Clementson* ... and considerateness of the Christ, *Rotherham* ... and clemency of Christ, *Macknight* ... and modesty of Christ, *Douay* ... and leniency of Christ, *Concordant.*

5382.2 name gen masc	3614.5 rel-pron nom sing masc	2567.3 prep	4241.1 noun sing neu	3173.1 conj	4862.2 adj nom sing masc
Χριστοῦ,	ὃς	κατὰ	πρόσωπον	μὲν	ταπεινὸς
Christou	hos	kata	prosōpon	men	tapeinos
Christ,	who	according to	face	men	humble

1706.1 prep	5050.3 prs- pron dat 2pl	544.2 verb nom sing masc part pres act	156.2 conj	2269.1 verb 1sing indic pres act	1519.1 prep
ἐν	ὑμῖν,	ἀπὼν	δὲ	θαρρῶ	εἰς
en	humin	apōn	de	tharrhō	eis
among	you,	being absent	but	am bold	towards

5050.4 prs- pron acc 2pl	1183.1 verb 1sing indic pres	1156.2 conj	3450.16 art sing neu	3231.1 partic	3780.6 verb nom sing masc part pres act
ὑμᾶς·	2. δέομαι	δὲ	τὸ	μὴ	παρὼν
humas	deomai	de	to	mē	parōn
you;	I beg	but	the	not	being present

2269.5 verb inf aor act	3450.11 art dat sing fem	3870.1 noun dat sing fem	3614.11 rel- pron dat sing fem		3023.2 verb 1sing indic pres
θαρρῆσαι	τῇ	πεποιθήσει	ᾗ		λογίζομαι
tharrhēsai	tē	pepoithēsei	hē		logizomai
to be bold	with the	confidence	with which		I reckon

4958.7 verb inf aor act	1894.3 prep	4948.9 indef- pron acc pl masc	3450.8 art acc pl masc		3023.9 verb acc pl masc part pres
τολμῆσαι	ἐπί	τινας	τοὺς		λογιζομένους
tolmēsai	epi	tinas	tous		logizomenous
to be daring	towards	some	the		reckoning

2231.4 prs- pron acc 1pl	5453.1 conj	2567.3 prep	4418.4 noun acc sing fem		3906.16 verb acc pl masc part pres act
ἡμᾶς	ὡς	κατὰ	σάρκα		περιπατοῦντας.
hēmas	hōs	kata	sarka		peripatountas
us	as	according to	flesh		walking.

1706.1 prep	4418.3 noun dat sing fem	1056.1 conj	3906.15 verb nom pl masc part pres act	3620.3 partic	2567.3 prep
3. ἐν	σαρκὶ	γὰρ	περιπατοῦντες,	οὐ	κατὰ
en	sarki	gar	peripatountes	ou	kata
In	flesh	for	walking,	not	according to

4418.4 noun acc sing fem	4605.2 verb 1pl indic pres mid	3450.17 art pl neu	1056.1 conj	3559.1 noun pl neu	3450.10 art gen sing fem
σάρκα	στρατευόμεθα·	4. τὰ	γὰρ	ὅπλα	τῆς
sarka	strateuometha	ta	gar	hopla	tēs
flesh	do we war.	The	for	weapons	of the

4603.1 noun gen sing fem	2231.2 prs- pron gen 1pl	3620.3 partic	4416.7 adj pl neu	233.2 conj	1409.4 adj nom pl neu
στρατείας	ἡμῶν	οὐ	σαρκικὰ,	ἀλλὰ	δυνατὰ
strateias	hēmōn	ou	sarkika	alla	dunata
warfare	our	not	fleshly,	but	powerful

3450.3 art dat sing	2296.3 noun dat sing masc	4242.1 prep	2478.1 noun acc sing fem		3658.1 noun gen pl neu
τῷ	θεῷ	πρὸς	καθαίρεσιν		ὀχυρωμάτων·
tō	theō	pros	kathairesin		ochurōmatōn
to	through God	to	overthrow		of strongholds;

3027.2 noun acc pl masc	2479.1 verb nom pl masc part pres act	2504.1 conj	3820.17 adj sing neu		5151.1 noun sing neu
5. λογισμοὺς	καθαιροῦντες	καὶ	πᾶν		ὕψωμα
logismous	kathairountes	kai	pan		hupsōma
reasonings	overthrowing	and	every		high thing

appeared base, overly humble, and subservient as a preacher. They sarcastically said he was bold only when he was absent and writing letters to them.

10:2. However, they made the mistake of thinking Paul's meekness was weakness. They did not understand that the weak do not have the strength to be meek. Meekness is strength under perfect control. In meekness Paul patiently besought and entreated the offenders to correct the error of their ways, or else the next time he was present he would demonstrate his confidence and boldness against his critics.

One offense they had committed against the apostle was to say he walked according to the flesh. Their fleshly behavior showed they were the ones who did so. They were wrong to conclude Paul thought and lived on a worldly plane just because they did. But they loudly, though falsely, proclaimed theirs was a walk in the Spirit in contrast to Paul.

10:3. Almost as if to throw back at them some of their words against him, the apostle stated he certainly did "walk in the flesh" in the sense that he lived as all human beings do. He grew tired, weary, and hungry as all men; therefore he needed food, clothing, and shelter as all others. And to be sure, Paul experienced the same physical hardships his critics gloried in.

However, he denied he warred "after the flesh." As a veteran soldier of the Cross he was too wise for that. He would no more go to battle with fleshly weapons than David would have dressed in Saul's armor (1 Samuel 17:38,39).

10:4. Paul emphatically denied his weapons, including any piece of his armor for spiritual warfare, were of a carnal, physical, or fleshly nature. He took no undue advantage of unsuspecting men through any misuse of personal charm. He refused to use dishonest flattery in attempts to manipulate men. No intellectually appealing philosophical discussion fell from his lips to draw people to himself personally. Disappointment came to those who sought "excellency of speech" (1 Corinthians 2:1) in his sermons. He purposely excited no one with merely psychologically stimulating material.

Instead, his implements of war were mighty because they were those supplied by God. With them he pulled down, overpowered, conquered, and destroyed spiritual strongholds. Such fortresses were prisons for the minds of men. Since the gods of this world guard the bars that hold them, only spiritual weapons more effective than theirs can set their captives free.

10:5. Indeed, the apostle's war instruments cast down (*kathairountes*, same as in "pulling down" in verse 4) imaginations. These

who in presence [am] base among you: ... am quiet in appearance, *Fenton* ... who am humble when I'm face to face with you, *Beck.*

but being absent am bold toward you:

2. But I beseech [you], that I may not be bold when I am present with that confidence: ... with the assurance, *Rotherham.*

wherewith I think to be bold against some: ... may not have to "make a brave front," *HistNT.*

which think of us as if we walked according to the flesh: ... who entertain the notion, *Berkeley* ... who regard us as if, *Hanson, NASB* ... as working only for human satisfaction, *Norlie* ... who fancy we work for selfish ends, *Fenton* ... we are guided by worldly principles, *Weymouth.*

3. For though we walk in the flesh: ... though we are still living in the world, *Weymouth.*

we do not war after the flesh: ... we do not war with carnal weapons, *Berkeley* ... we do not fight our battles, *Norlie* ... we do not contend for self, *Fenton.*

4. (For the weapons of our warfare [are] not carnal: ... are not of the flesh, *Hanson.*

but mighty through God: ... but powerful through God, *PNT* ... powerful with God, *Rotherham* ... but divinely powerful, *NASB.*

to the pulling down of strong holds;): ... for the purpose of destroying fortresses, *Fenton* ... in overthrowing strong fortresses, *Weymouth* ... to upset defense lines, *Klingensmith* ... for the Demolition of Fortresses, *Wilson.*

5. Casting down imaginations: They upset reasonings, *Klingensmith* ... we tear down calculations, *Berkeley* ... every deceptive fantasy, *Phillips* ... Destroying reasonings, *Wesley* ... defeating opponents, *Fenton* ... casting down [false] speculations, *Hanson* ... we overthrow arrogant 'reckonings,' *Weymouth.*

2 Corinthians 10:6

1854.10 verb acc sing neu part pres mid	2567.3 prep	3450.10 art gen sing fem	1102.2 noun gen sing fem	3450.2 art gen sing
ἐπαιρόμενον	κατὰ	τῆς	γνώσεως	τοῦ
epairomenon	kata	tēs	gnōseōs	tou
lifting itself up	against	the	knowledge	

2296.2 noun gen sing masc	2504.1 conj	161.2 verb nom pl masc part pres act	3820.17 adj sing neu	3402.1 noun acc sing neu	1519.1 prep
θεοῦ,	καὶ	αἰχμαλωτίζοντες	πᾶν	νόημα	εἰς
theou	kai	aichmalōtizontes	pan	noēma	eis
of God,	and	leading captive	every	thought	into

3450.12 art acc sing fem	5056.4 noun acc sing fem	3450.2 art gen sing	5382.2 name gen masc	2504.1 conj	1706.1 prep
τὴν	ὑπακοὴν	τοῦ	Χριστοῦ,	6. καὶ	ἐν
tēn	hupakoēn	tou	Christou	kai	en
the	obedience	of the	Christ;	and	in

2071.5 adj dat sing neu	2174.19 verb nom pl masc part pres act	1543.5 verb inf aor act	3820.12 adj acc sing fem	3737.3 noun acc sing fem
ἑτοίμῳ	ἔχοντες	ἐκδικῆσαι	πᾶσαν	παρακοήν,
hetoimō	echontes	ekdikēsai	pasan	parakoēn
readiness	having	to avenge	all	disobedience,

3615.1 conj	3997.22 verb 3sing subj aor pass	5050.2 prs-pron gen 2pl	3450.9 art nom sing fem	5056.1 noun nom sing fem
ὅταν	πληρωθῇ	ὑμῶν	ἡ	ὑπακοή.
hotan	plērōthē	humōn	hē	hupakoē
when	may have been fulfilled	your	the	obedience.

3450.17 art pl neu	2567.3 prep	4241.1 noun sing neu	984.1 verb 2pl pres act	1479.1 conj
7. Τὰ	κατὰ	πρόσωπον	βλέπετε;	εἴ
Ta	kata	prosōpon	blepete	ei
The things	according to	appearance	do you look at?	If

4948.3 indef-pron nom sing	3844.10 verb 3sing indic perf act	1431.5 prs-pron dat 3sing masc	5382.2 name gen masc	1498.32 verb inf pres act	3642.17 dem-pron sing neu
τις	πέποιθεν	ἑαυτῷ	Χριστοῦ	εἶναι,	τοῦτο
tis	pepoithen	heautō	Christou	einai	touto
anyone	is persuaded	in himself	of Christ	to be,	this

3023.6 verb 3sing impr pres	3687.1 adv	570.1 prep gen	1894.1 prep	1431.4 prs-pron gen 3sing	3617.1 conj
λογιζέσθω	πάλιν	ἀφ'	[a☆ ἐφ']	ἑαυτοῦ	ὅτι
logizesthō	palin	aph'	eph'	heautou	hoti
let him reckon	again	of	[idem]	himself,	that

2503.1 conj	840.5 prs-pron nom sing masc	5382.2 name gen masc	3643.1 adv	2504.1 conj	2231.1 prs-pron nom 1pl
καθὼς	αὐτὸς	Χριστοῦ,	οὕτως	καὶ	ἡμεῖς
kathōs	autos	Christou	houtōs	kai	hēmeis
according as	he	of Christ,	so	also	we

5382.2 name gen masc	1430.1 partic	4885.1 conj	1056.1 conj	2504.1 conj	3917.3 adv comp
b Χριστοῦ. ˎ	8. ἐάν	τε	γὰρ	a καὶ ˎ	περισσότερόν
Christou	ean	te	gar	kai	perissoteron
of Christ.	If	and	for	even	more abundantly

4948.10 indef-pron sing neu	2714.11 verb 1sing subj aor mid	3875.1 prep	3450.10 art gen sing fem	1833.1 noun fem
τι	καυχήσωμαι	περὶ	τῆς	ἐξουσίας
ti	kauchēsōmai	peri	tēs	exousias
somewhat	I should boast	concerning	the	authority

7.a.Txt: 04C,06D,018K
025P,byz.
Var: 01א,03B,020L
Treg,Tisc,We/Ho,Weis
Sod,UBS/☆

7.b.Txt: 06D-corr,018K
020L,byz.bo.
Var: 01א,03B,04C
06D-org,025P,Gries
Lach,Treg,Alf,Word
Tisc,We/Ho,Weis,Sod
UBS/☆

8.a.Txt: 01א-corr
06D-corr,020L,byz.
Var: 01א-org,03B,04C
06D-org,025P,bo.Lach
Treg,Alf,Tisc,We/Ho
Weis,Sod,UBS/☆

included sophistries, philosophical reasonings with a surface and fallacious logic. Such had a basic appeal to a fleshly intellect. Embracing systems of thought of this kind fed an arrogant attitude that exalted itself in opposition to the true knowledge of God.

Paul's reference to "casting down imaginations" and "bringing into captivity every thought" does not encourage mental warfare for the believer. True, things in the mind often trouble the conscientious Christian, and he would like to rid himself of them. He feels condemned by them as the apostle did in Romans 7. But victory comes through the covering of the blood of Jesus, as Paul found in Romans 7:25 and 8:1.

The Christian experience was certainly not simply one of thought warfare for Paul. He determined to bring all non-Biblical teaching he encountered into captivity. He captured and led away as a prisoner of war every philosophical system which was contrary to the view of this world set forth in Scripture. All his conclusions on the great questions of life came into obedience to the gospel of Christ.

10:6. Paul was ready to take revenge on (to punish, to discipline in his apostolic office) every false teacher at Corinth. Their disobedience (*parakoē*, "unwillingness to hear") must be dealt with. However, he put the welfare of believers first. Only when their "obedience" (*hupakoē*, willingness to hear with the intent of obeying) was fulfilled or perfected did he intend to turn to troublesome teachers. Then he would attend to them as in the case of military officers who are court-martialed.

10:7. Though the apostle earlier chided the Corinthians for looking at outward appearances (5:12), now he called on them to observe the obvious. Let them take note of those persons among them who boasted that they were in Christ and yet in so doing left the impression that others were not. They were convinced "in themselves" of that fact. They particularly questioned the spiritual standing of preachers like Paul.

The apostle called on these members of the "Christ Party" at Corinth (1 Corinthians 1:12) to think again. He belonged to the Saviour as much as they did. This should have been obvious to all even by outward appearances!

10:8. However, at this point Paul's modesty called forth a word of explanation. He sensed some might think he went too far in boasting of his authoritative position in Christ. Even if he bragged a little too much, he spoke only honestly of what the Lord had given him.

Besides, his ministerial gifts and graces came from the good hand of God with the intent that they be used to edify or build up

and every high thing that exalteth itself against the knowledge of God: . . . and every height elevating, *Concordant* . . . and every imposing defense, *Phillips* . . . and overthrowing every barrier raised against, *TCNT* . . . and every rampart that erects itself, *HistNT* . . . that towers high in defiance of, *Weymouth* . . . the wisdom of God, *NLT*.

and bringing into captivity every thought to the obedience of Christ: They make prisoners of every thought, *Klingensmith* . . . I can make each rebel purpose my prisoner-of-war, *Way* . . . and subduing, *Fenton* . . . and are bringing captive every intent, *Rotherham* . . . and bringing every intent, *Alford* . . . every understanding, *Douay* . . . bringing them into subjection to Christ, *Locke* . . . and make it yield to Christ, *NTPE*.

6. And having in a readiness to revenge all disobedience: . . . we shall make quick work of punishing, *Kleist* . . . and competent to expel every mutineer, *Fenton* . . . and are prepared to punish, *Campbell* . . . to administer justice, *Berkeley* . . . are prepared to punish all disobedience, *Campbell*.

when your obedience is fulfilled: . . . is complete, *HistNT* . . . is fully shown, *Berkeley* . . . is made complete, *Williams*.

7. Do ye look on things after the outward appearance?: Look at the facts as they are, *NTPE* . . . at the surface of things? *Fenton*.

If any man trust to himself that he is Christ's:

let him of himself think this again: Let him reflect about it, *Norlie* . . . let him consider again, *Sawyer* . . . let him ponder this over in his mind, *Berkeley*.

that, as he [is] Christ's, even so [are] we Christ's:

8. For though I should boast somewhat more of our authority: . . . we boasted excessively about our authority, *Fenton* . . . to boast more loudly of our apostolic authority, *Weymouth* . . . about our authorization, *Berkeley*.

2 Corinthians 10:9

8.b.**Txt:** 06D-corr,018K
020L,byz.
Var: 01ℵ-org,03B,04C
06D-org,33,Lach,Treg
Alf,Tisc,We/Ho,Weis
Sod,UBS/⋆

2231.2 prs-pron gen 1pl	3614.10 rel-pron gen sing fem	1319.14 verb 3sing indic aor act	3450.5 art sing masc	2935.1 noun nom sing masc	2231.3 prs-pron dat 1pl
ἡμῶν,	ἧς	ἔδωκεν	ὁ	κύριος	⁽ᵇ ἡμῖν ⁾
hēmōn,	hēs	edōken	ho	kurios	hēmin
our,	which	gave	the	Lord	to us

1519.1 prep	3482.3 noun acc sing fem	2504.1 conj	3620.2 partic	1519.1 prep	2478.1 noun acc sing fem	5050.2 prs-pron gen 2pl
εἰς	οἰκοδομὴν	καὶ	οὐκ	εἰς	καθαίρεσιν	ὑμῶν,
eis	oikodomēn	kai	ouk	eis	kathairesin	humōn,
for	edification	and	not	for	overthrowing	you,

3620.2 partic	152.4 verb 1sing indic fut pass	2419.1 conj	3231.1 partic	1374.18 verb 1sing subj aor act	5453.1 conj
οὐκ	αἰσχυνθήσομαι	**9.** ἵνα	μὴ	δόξω	⁽ ὡς
ouk	aischunthēsomai	hina	mē	doxō	hōs
not	I shall be put to shame;	that	not	I may seem	as if

300.1 partic	5445.1 conj	1615.1 verb inf pres act	5050.4 prs-pron acc 2pl	1217.2 prep	3450.1 art gen pl
ἂν	[ὡσὰν]	ἐκφοβεῖν	ὑμᾶς	διὰ	τῶν
an	hōsan	ekphobein	humas	dia	tōn
an	[as if]	to frighten	you	by means of	the

1976.6 noun gen pl fem	3617.1 conj	3450.13 art pl fem	3173.1 conj	1976.5 noun nom pl fem	5183.2 verb 3sing indic pres act
ἐπιστολῶν.	**10.** ὅτι	αἱ	⁽ μέν	ἐπιστολαὶ,	φησίν,
epistolōn	hoti	hai	men	epistolai	phēsin,
epistles:	because	the	men	epistles,	says he,

1976.5 noun nom pl fem	3173.1 conj	5183.2 verb 3sing indic pres act	920.2 adj nom pl fem	2504.1 conj	2451.9 adj nom pl fem
[⋆ ἐπιστολαὶ	μέν,	φησίν,]	βαρεῖαι	καὶ	ἰσχυραί·
epistolai	men	phēsin	bareiai	kai	ischurai
[epistles	indeed,	he says,]	weighty	and	strong,

3450.9 art nom sing fem	1156.2 conj	3814.1 noun nom sing fem	3450.2 art gen sing	4835.2 noun gen sing neu	766.1 adj nom sing
ἡ	δὲ	παρουσία	τοῦ	σώματος	ἀσθενὴς,
hē	de	parousia	tou	sōmatos	asthenēs,
the	but	presence	of the	body	weak,

2504.1 conj	3450.5 art sing masc	3030.1 noun nom sing masc	1832.9 verb nom sing masc part perf pass	3642.17 dem-pron sing neu
καὶ	ὁ	λόγος	ἐξουθενημένος.	**11.** τοῦτο
kai	ho	logos	exouthenēmenos	touto
and	the	speech	having been dispised.	This

3023.6 verb 3sing impr pres	3450.5 art sing masc	4955.4 dem-pron nom sing masc	3617.1 conj	3497.3 rel-pron nom pl masc
λογιζέσθω	ὁ	τοιοῦτος,	ὅτι	οἷοί
logizesthō	ho	toioutos,	hoti	hoioi
let reckon	the	such a one,	that	such as

1498.5 verb 1pl indic pres act	3450.3 art dat sing	3030.3 noun dat sing masc	1217.1 prep	1976.6 noun gen pl fem	544.3 verb nom pl masc part pres act
ἐσμεν	τῷ	λόγῳ	δι'	ἐπιστολῶν	ἀπόντες,
esmen	tō	logō	di'	epistolōn	apontes,
we are	in the	word	by	epistles	being absent,

4955.7 dem-pron nom pl masc	2504.1 conj	3780.7 verb nom pl masc part pres act	3450.3 art dat sing	2024.3 noun dat sing neu	3620.3 partic
τοιοῦτοι	καὶ	παρόντες	τῷ	ἔργῳ.	**12.** Οὐ
toioutoi	kai	parontes	tō	ergō	Ou
such	also	being present	in the	deed.	Not

believers in churches such as at Corinth. The Master never meant them for destruction (*kathairesis*, as in verse 4). With them the apostle tore down fortresses of the devil. On the other hand, false preachers in Corinth used their abilities to tear down churches!

Paul felt no shame in this defense of himself. His motives were pure. He knew that if the opposition should be able to discredit him personally, they would nullify his message. Actually, his enemies were the ones who stood in disgrace.

10:9. To clarify things further, Paul stated that he wanted nothing he wrote in this letter to terrify (*ekphobeō*, here only in the New Testament) or frighten anyone. He did not want anything he said to seem that way or have that appearance. The Spirit inspired him to help rather than to hurt.

10:10. Even the apostle's critics at Corinth recognized that his letters were weighty and powerful. They acknowledged their effectiveness, though their words contained no real compliment. Continuing their attack on the apostle, they said only when he wrote letters from a distance did he appear courageous. They claimed when he was in residence at Corinth his bodily presence (*parousia*) was weak and most unimpressive. Again they misinterpreted the meekness and gentleness of Christ which he possessed by the power of the Spirit (10:1).

Paul's ministerial enemies further declared his speech (*logos*, "word") was contemptible. In their opinion it amounted to nothing. They might have admitted the content of his sermons was acceptable, but they judged his delivery of the poorest sort. He had no polish such as they witnessed in the lectures of the graduates of the schools of rhetoric. What he said may have been presentable, but how he said it was almost repulsive to them. They had their eyes on the entertainment of form and cared little for the speaker's actual message.

In his first letter to Corinth (1 Corinthians 2:1-5), Paul had said he refused to cater to the demands of such an audience. No doubt he sought to clothe his message in an attractive form, but not to merely entertain men in the process.

10:11. The apostle had a further word for the opposition to ponder. If they thought the words of his letters severe just because he was absent, he would change all that when he arrived. Once present at Corinth again, his actions would support the word he used in writing to them. He would soon dispel any charge of cowardice against him through the boldness he used in confronting his critics.

which the Lord hath given us for edification: . . . for building up, *Young.*

and not for your destruction: . . . and not for overthrowing it, *TCNT* . . . and not for your ruin, *Berkeley.*

I should not be ashamed: I shall never have to blush for doing so, *Williams.*

9. That I may not seem as if I would terrify you by letters: I do not wish to intimidate you, *NAB* . . . as if I were frightening you, *PNT* . . . that I am trying to frighten you, *Norlie* . . . that I am scaring you, *Klingensmith* . . . as if I wanted to frighten you by my letters, *Weymouth* . . . who writes you terrifying letters, *Phillips* . . . that I am writing empty threats, *Conybeare* . . . to be frightening you, *Adams* . . . merely by my letters, *HistNT.*

10. For [his] letters, say they, [are] weighty and powerful: . . . are impressive, *Beck* . . . and forceful, *Williams* . . . and vigorous, *TCNT.*

but [his] bodily presence [is] weak: . . . is unimpressive, *NASB* . . . is insignificant, *Berkeley* . . . he is feeble, *Norlie.*

and [his] speech contemptible: . . . he is hard to listen to, *NLT* . . . and people despise what he says, *Beck* . . . and the speech despicable, *Young* . . . and the speech insignificant, *Hanson* . . . and his rebukes—who heeds them? *Way* . . . and rhetoric powerless, *Fenton* . . . and there is nothing to his speeches, *Norlie* . . . of no account, *PNT, Panin.*

11. Let such an one think this: Such people should consider this, *Fenton.*

that, such as we are in word by letters when we are absent: . . . in our epistolary discourse, *Murdock.*

such [will we be] also in deed when we are present: . . . no less strong will I be in action, *Way* . . . are we in act, *Concordant* . . . when we are there, *Klingensmith.*

1056.1 conj	4958.3 verb 1pl indic pres act	1462.1 verb inf aor act	2211.1 conj	4644.2 verb inf aor act
γὰρ	τολμῶμεν	ἐγκρῖναι	ἢ	συγκρῖναι
gar	tolmōmen	enkrinai	ē	sunkrinai
for	dare we	to rank among	or	to compare with

1431.8 prs-pron acc pl masc	4948.8 indef-pron dat pl masc	3450.1 art gen pl	1431.8 prs-pron acc pl masc	4771.6 verb gen pl masc part pres act
ἑαυτούς	τισιν	τῶν	ἑαυτοὺς	συνιστανόντων,
heautous	tisin	tōn	heautous	sunistanontōn
ourselves	some	the	themselves	commending;

233.2 conj	840.7 prs-pron nom pl masc	1706.1 prep	1431.7 prs-pron dat pl masc	1431.8 prs-pron acc pl masc	3224.2 verb nom pl masc part pres act
ἀλλὰ	αὐτοὶ	ἐν	ἑαυτοῖς	ἑαυτοὺς	μετροῦντες,
alla	autoi	en	heautois	heautous	metrountes
but	they	by	themselves	themselves	measuring,

2504.1 conj	4644.1 verb nom pl masc part pres act	1431.8 prs-pron acc pl masc	1431.7 prs-pron dat pl masc	3620.3 partic
καὶ	συγκρίνοντες	ἑαυτοὺς	ἑαυτοῖς,	οὐ
kai	sunkrinontes	heautous	heautois	ou
and	comparing	themselves	with themselves,	not

12.a.**Txt**: 06D-corr,018K 020L,025P,044,byz. **Var**: p46,01ℵ-corr,03B 33,Lach,Treg,Alf,Tisc We/Ho,Weis,Sod UBS/★

4770.2 verb 3pl indic pres act	4770.13 verb 3pl indic pres act	2231.1 prs-pron nom 1pl	1156.2 conj	3644.1 adv
⌐ συνιοῦσιν.	[ᵃ★ συνιᾶσιν.]	**13.** ἡμεῖς	δὲ	⌐ οὐχὶ
suniousin	suniasin	hēmeis	de	ouchi
do understand.	[idem]	We	now	not

3620.2 partic	1519.1 prep	3450.17 art pl neu	278.1 adj acc pl neu	2714.17 verb 1pl indic fut mid
[οὐκ]	εἰς	τὰ	ἄμετρα	καυχησόμεθα,
ouk	eis	ta	ametra	kauchēsometha
[idem]	to	the things	beyond measure	will boast,

233.2 conj	2567.3 prep	3450.16 art sing neu	3228.3 noun acc sing neu	3450.2 art gen sing	2554.1 noun gen sing masc
ἀλλὰ	κατὰ	τὸ	μέτρον	τοῦ	κανόνος
alla	kata	to	metron	tou	kanonos
but	according to	the	measure	of the	rule

3614.2 rel-pron gen sing	3177.1 verb 3sing indic aor act	2231.3 prs-pron dat 1pl	3450.5 art sing masc	2296.1 noun nom sing masc	3228.1 noun gen sing neu
οὗ	ἐμέρισεν	ἡμῖν	ὁ	θεὸς	μέτρου
hou	emerisen	hēmin	ho	theos	metrou
which	divided	to us		God	of measure

2167.2 verb inf aor mid	884.2 conj	2504.1 conj	5050.2 prs-pron gen 2pl	3620.3 partic	1056.1 conj	5453.1 conj	3231.1 partic
ἐφικέσθαι	ἄχρι	καὶ	ὑμῶν.	**14.** οὐ	γὰρ	ὡς	μὴ
ephikesthai	achri	kai	humōn	ou	gar	hōs	mē
to reach	to	also	you.	Not	for	as	not

2167.1 verb nom pl masc part pres	1519.1 prep	5050.4 prs-pron acc 2pl	5077.1 verb 1pl indic pres act	1431.8 prs-pron acc pl masc
ἐφικνούμενοι	εἰς	ὑμᾶς	ὑπερεκτείνομεν	ἑαυτούς·
ephiknoumenoi	eis	humas	huperekteinomen	heautous
reaching	to	you	do we overstretch	ourselves,

884.2 conj	1056.1 conj	2504.1 conj	5050.2 prs-pron gen 2pl	5185.2 verb 1pl indic aor act	1706.1 prep	3450.3 art dat sing
ἄχρι	γὰρ	καὶ	ὑμῶν	ἐφθάσαμεν	ἐν	τῷ
achri	gar	kai	humōn	ephthasamen	en	tō
to	for	also	you	we came	in	the

10:12. To further prevent misunderstanding of the focus on himself, Paul declared he dared not join the crowd of preachers who wrote their own letters of recommendation. That was pure presumption. If any thought him lacking the courage to do so, he acknowledged guilt to that charge of cowardice with a touch of sarcasm. He was not brave enough to belong to that group.

Those ministers judged themselves successful by subjective, human standards. They evaluated themselves by themselves. In this they acted unwisely. They lacked insight and understanding in truly spiritual things. These were actually men of ignorance!

10:13. False teachers trying to unseat the apostle at Corinth even took credit for things to which they had contributed nothing. They refused to recognize they had entered into other men's labors. Not even the 12 apostles could claim their work was totally of themselves. Jesus said to them, "I sent you to reap that whereupon ye bestowed no labor" (John 4:38).

By contrast Paul said he determined never to boast of things outside his "measure," beyond the limits set by the call of God on his life. It established for him a sphere of responsible activity in gospel work. The Lord distributed or assigned this rule (*kanonos*, English *canon*) to him.

Paul's original call sent him to Gentiles and kings as well as to the Children of Israel, with emphasis on the former (Acts 9:15). Once in the early part of his ministry he thought he might do a profitable work among his own people in the Jerusalem area. To emphasize the intended direction of his missionary call, the Lord said to him, "Depart: for I will send thee far hence unto the Gentiles" (Acts 22:21).

The rule for him was clear. His mission was to preach the gospel in virgin territory, where Christ had never been named (Romans 15:20). God did not intend him to labor where other preachers had already worked. His assignment was that of planting new churches, not to build on another's foundation.

This designated sphere of influence had brought the apostle to Corinth. When he worshipfully recalled what the Lord did through him in founding the church there, he spoke justifiably of things within the limits God had set for him.

10:14. Accordingly, Paul declared his ministry did not extend beyond the limits the Lord determined for him when he came initially to Corinth. It was not as if his territory did not reach that far, as some of the critics may have suggested. Indeed, he was living by the rule he had made for himself based on his missionary call.

He reminded the Corinthians he was the first to come (*phthanō*, "come before") to them with the gospel. He had the privilege of preaching and announcing the good news to them the first time they heard it.

12. For we dare not make ourselves of the number: For we presume not to equal, *Wesley* . . . we dare not rank, *Hanson*.

or compare ourselves with some that commend themselves: . . . persons distinguished by their self-commendation, *Weymouth* . . . who commend their own qualities, *Berkeley*.

but they measuring themselves by themselves: . . . by their own standards, *Phillips* . . . by their own yardstick, *Beck*.

and comparing themselves among themselves: . . . or by comparisons within their own circle, *Phillips*.

are not wise: . . . are without understanding, *ASV, Panin, Worrell* . . . they do not show good judgment, *Norlie* . . . they don't show good sense, *Beck* . . . are without discernment, *Rotherham* . . . are guilty of folly, *Conybeare*.

13. But we will not boast of things without [our] measure: We are not going to make any extravagant claims, *Norlie* . . . ours will be no immoderate exultation, *HistNT* . . . as regards the unmeasured things, *Rotherham*.

but according to the measure of the rule which God hath distributed to us: Our limit is the field of work to which God has bound us, *Beck* . . . by the sphere of activity that God has assigned to us, *Adams* . . . rule God has set for us, *Klingensmith* . . . which the God of measure, *Hanson* . . . the province...apportioned to us, *ASV* . . . allotted to us, *PNT* . . . hath imparted to us, *Murdock*.

a measure to reach even unto you: . . . a sphere which reaches even to you, *Montgomery*.

14. For we stretch not ourselves beyond [our measure]: . . . we are not overextending ourselves, *NASB* . . . We are not claiming too much, *Norlie* . . . not going beyond our commission, *Confraternity* . . . not overstepping the limits of my authority, *Montgomery*.

as though we reached not unto you:

for we are come as far as to you also in [preaching] the gospel of Christ: . . . for we outstrip others, *Concordant*.

2 Corinthians 10:15

2077.3 noun dat sing neu	3450.2 art gen sing	5382.2 name gen masc	3620.2 partic	1519.1 prep	3450.17 art pl neu
εὐαγγελίῳ *euangeliō* good news	τοῦ *tou* of the	Χριστοῦ· *Christou* Christ;	**15.** οὐκ *ouk* not	εἰς *eis* to	τὰ *ta* the things

278.1 adj acc pl neu	2714.8 verb nom pl masc part pres	1706.1 prep	243.4 adj dat pl masc	2845.6 noun dat pl masc
ἄμετρα *ametra* beyond measure	καυχώμενοι *kauchōmenoi* boasting	ἐν *en* in	ἀλλοτρίοις *allotriois* others'	κόποις, *kopois* labors,

1667.4 noun acc sing fem	1156.2 conj	2174.19 verb nom pl masc part pres act	831.12 verb gen sing fem part pres pass	3450.10 art gen sing	3963.2 noun gen sing fem
ἐλπίδα *elpida* hope	δὲ *de* but	ἔχοντες, *echontes* having,	αὐξανομένης *auxanomenēs* increasing	τῆς *tēs* the	πίστεως *pisteōs* faith

5050.2 prs- pron gen 2pl	1706.1 prep	5050.3 prs- pron dat 2pl	3141.5 verb inf aor pass	2567.3 prep
ὑμῶν, *humōn* your,	ἐν *en* among	ὑμῖν *humin* you	μεγαλυνθῆναι *megalunthēnai* to be enlarged	κατὰ *kata* according to

3450.6 art acc sing masc	2554.3 noun acc sing masc	2231.2 prs- pron gen 1pl	1519.1 prep	3913.2 noun acc sing fem	1519.1 prep
τὸν *ton* the	κανόνα *kanona* rule	ἡμῶν *hēmōn* our	εἰς *eis* to	περισσείαν, *perisseian* abundance,	**16.** εἰς *eis* to

3450.17 art pl neu	5075.1 prep gen	5050.2 prs- pron gen 2pl	2076.25 verb inf aor mid
τὰ *ta* the	ὑπερέκεινα *huperekeina* beyond	ὑμῶν *humōn* you	εὐαγγελίσασθαι, *euangelisasthai* to announce the good news,

3620.2 partic	1706.1 prep	243.1 adj dat sing	2554.2 noun dat sing masc	1519.1 prep	3450.17 art pl neu	2071.7 adj pl neu
οὐκ *ouk* not	ἐν *en* in	ἀλλοτρίῳ *allotriō* another's	κανόνι *kanoni* rule	εἰς *eis* as to	τὰ *ta* things	ἕτοιμα *hetoima* ready

2714.14 verb inf aor mid	3450.5 art sing masc	1156.2 conj	2714.7 verb nom sing masc part pres	1706.1 prep
καυχήσασθαι. *kauchēsasthai* to boast.	**17.** Ὁ *Ho* The	δὲ *de* but	καυχώμενος, *kauchōmenos* boasting,	ἐν *en* in

2935.3 noun dat sing masc	2714.6 verb 3sing impr pres	3620.3 partic	1056.1 conj	3450.5 art sing masc	1431.6 prs-pron acc 3sing masc
κυρίῳ *kuriō* Lord	καυχάσθω· *kauchasthō* let him boast.	**18.** οὐ *ou* Not	γὰρ *gar* for	ὁ *ho* the	ἑαυτὸν *heauton* himself

4771.4 verb nom sing masc part pres act	4771.14 verb nom sing masc part pres act	1552.3 dem-pron nom sing masc	1498.4 verb 3sing indic pres act
⸂ συνιστῶν, *sunistōn* commending,	[ᵃ⋆ συνιστάνων,] *sunistanōn* [idem]	ἐκεῖνός *ekeinos* that	ἐστιν *estin* is

1378.1 adj nom sing masc	233.1 conj	233.2 conj	3614.6 rel-pron acc sing masc	3450.5 art sing masc
δόκιμος, *dokimos* approved,	⸂ ἀλλ' *all'* but	[⋆ ἀλλὰ] *alla* [idem]	ὃν *hon* whom	ὁ *ho* the

10:15. Certainly then, Paul did not boast of things beyond his measure, his sphere of God-appointed influence or action. He did not take credit for what other men had done in the work of the Lord's kingdom. He did not boast of other men's labors as his critics did. They ignored the fact that the one whose influence they were doing their best to ruin was the very one who had founded the church they worked in. In sorrow Paul wrote these words to save the church they would destroy.

As a matter of fact, the apostle held a God-given hope that his sphere of influence would soon extend even further to the west, beyond Corinth. Believers in Corinth would actually assist him in that ministry. As their faith increased, as it matured in successfully resisting the opposition's attempts to destroy it, they would help make possible an increase in his territory. Their missionary support would greatly enlarge his area of action.

10:16. With the help of the Corinthians, Paul knew he would preach the gospel in the regions beyond them. He wrote the Romans a similar message. He said, "Whensoever I take my journey into Spain, I will come to you: for I trust to see you in my journey, and to be brought on my way thitherward by you" (Romans 15:24). Writings of Ancient Church fathers reveal the apostle did indeed minister the gospel in Spain. He went there probably during the period between his first and second Roman imprisonments.

Again Paul indirectly rebuked his critics who sought to steal the hearts of the Corinthians from him. He declared he was not as some who boast of "another man's line of things" or range of actions. Other workers made things ready for their hands, yet they took full credit for the whole project.

10:17. However, no one should conclude the apostle fought on a fleshly plane with his enemies. It is not so much his person he defended as the gospel. He struggled not simply to keep certain Christians loyal to him. He wanted them to remain true to God. Accordingly, he turned back to the previously written Word of God. Jeremiah said none should glory (*kauchaomai*, "boast," as in verse 16 and throughout this passage) in his wisdom, strength, or riches, but men must glory only in the Lord (Jeremiah 9:23,24). In his first letter to Corinth Paul included the same principle (1 Corinthians 1:31).

10:18. To glory, boast, or commend oneself does not necessarily mean one is approved by God. Commendation from the Lord is all that matters. In his previous letter to the Corinthians the apostle said the judgment of others or even his own appraisal of himself was of no consequence (1 Corinthians 4:3,4). The Lord's judgment at the last day will determine all.

15. Not boasting of things without [our] measure: We are not boasting extravagantly, *Norlie*.

[that is], of other men's labours: . . . and take credit for other men's labours, *Weymouth* . . . about the work done by others, *Norlie* . . . in other person's hard work, *Klingensmith*.

but having hope, when your faith is increased: . . . as your faith groweth, *ASV* . . . by a growing of your faith, *Rotherham*.

that we shall be enlarged by you according to our rule abundantly: . . . shall enlarge our sphere of influence, *Berkeley* . . . we shall be magnified, *ASV, Sawyer* . . . to be magnified among you superabundantly, *Concordant*.

16. To preach the gospel in the [regions] beyond you: . . . shall tell the Good News in the districts beyond you, *Weymouth* . . . in places that lie beyond you, *Confraternity*.

[and] not to boast in another man's line of things made ready to our hand: . . . without having to take credit for work done in another's field, *Norlie* . . . work already done in another man's field, *Beck*.

17. But he that glorieth, let him glory in the Lord: . . . the proud should be proud in the Lord, *Fenton*.

18. For not he that commendeth himself is approved: . . . the man of genuine character is not he who commends himself, *HistNT* . . . It is not self-commendation that matters, *Phillips* . . . not who accredits himself, *Way* . . . it is not people who recommend themselves that win approval, *TCNT*.

but whom the Lord commendeth: . . . but whom the Lord establishes, *Fenton* . . . he whom the Lord praiseth, *Murdock*.

2 Corinthians 11:1

2935.1 noun nom sing masc	4771.2 verb 3sing indic pres act		3649.1 partic	428.7 verb 2pl impr imperf mid
κύριος	συνίστησιν.	**11:1.**	Ὄφελον	ἀνείχεσθέ
kurios	sunistēsin		Ophelon	aneichesthe
Lord	commends.		O that	you were bearing with

1.a.Var: 01א,03B,06D 33,Elzev,Lach,Treg,Alf Word,Tisc,We/Ho,Weis Sod,UBS/☆

1466.2 prs-pron gen 1sing	3262.1 adj acc sing	4948.10 indef-pron sing neu	3450.11 art dat sing fem	869.2 noun gen sing fem
μου	μικρόν	[a☆+ τι]	τῇ	(ἀφροσύνῃ·
mou	mikron	ti	tē	aphrosunē
me	a little	[some]	in the	foolishness;

1.b.Txt: 018K,020L 025P,byz. **Var:** 01א,03B,06D,025P 33,Lach,Treg,Alf,Word Tisc,We/Ho,Weis,Sod UBS/☆

869.3 noun gen sing fem	233.2 conj	2504.1 conj	428.1 verb 2pl pres mid	1466.2 prs-pron gen 1sing
[b☆ ἀφροσύνης·]	ἀλλὰ	καὶ	ἀνέχεσθέ	μου.
aphrosunēs	alla	kai	anechesthe	mou
[of foolishness;]	but	indeed	bear with	me.

2189.2 verb 1sing indic pres act	1056.1 conj	5050.4 prs-pron acc 2pl	2296.2 noun gen sing masc	2188.3 noun dat sing masc
2. ζηλῶ	γὰρ	ὑμᾶς	θεοῦ	ζήλῳ·
zēlō	gar	humas	theou	zēlō
I am jealous	for	you	of God	with jealousy,

712.1 verb 1sing indic aor mid	1056.1 conj	5050.4 prs-pron acc 2pl	1518.2 num card dat	433.3 noun dat sing masc	3795.3 noun acc sing masc
ἡρμοσάμην	γὰρ	ὑμᾶς	ἑνὶ	ἀνδρὶ	παρθένον
hērmosamēn	gar	humas	heni	andri	parthenon
I betrothed	for	you	to one	man	a virgin

52.5 adj acc sing fem	3798.12 verb inf aor act	3450.3 art dat sing	5382.3 name dat sing	5236.1 verb 1sing indic pres	1156.2 conj
ἁγνὴν	παραστῆσαι	τῷ	Χριστῷ·	**3.** φοβοῦμαι	δὲ
hagnēn	parastēsai	tō	Christō	phoboumai	de
pure	to present	to the	Christ.	I fear	but

3248.1 conj	3231.1 partic	4315.1 adv	5453.1 conj	3450.5 art sing masc	3653.1 noun nom sing masc
(μήπως	[☆ μή	πως,]	ὡς	ὁ	ὄφις
mēpōs	mē	pōs	hōs	ho	ophis
lest by any means	[not	how]	as	the	serpent

2075.4 name acc fem	1802.3 verb 3sing indic aor act	1802.3 verb 3sing indic aor act	2075.4 name acc fem	1706.1 prep
(Εὔαν	ἐξηπάτησεν	[☆ ἐξηπάτησεν	Εὔαν]	ἐν
Heuan	exēpatēsen	exēpatēsen	Heuan	en
Eve	deceived	[deceived	Eve]	in

3.a.Txt: 06D-corr,018K 020L,byz. **Var:** 01א,03B,06D-org 025P,33,bo.Lach,Treg Alf,Tisc,We/Ho,Weis Sod,UBS/☆

3450.11 art dat sing fem	3696.1 noun dat sing fem	840.3 prs-pron gen sing	3643.1 adv	5188.8 verb 3sing subj aor pass
τῇ	πανουργίᾳ	αὐτοῦ,	(a οὕτως)	φθαρῇ
tē	panourgia	autou	houtōs	phtharē
the	craftiness	his,	so	should be corrupted

3.b.Var: p46,01א-org 03B,33,sa.bo.Lach,Treg Alf,Word,We/Ho,Weis Sod,UBS/☆

3450.17 art pl neu	3402.2 noun pl neu	5050.2 prs-pron gen 2pl	570.3 prep gen	3450.10 art gen sing fem	567.1 noun gen sing fem
τὰ	νοήματα	ὑμῶν	ἀπὸ	τῆς	ἁπλότητος
ta	noēmata	humōn	apo	tēs	haplotētos
the	thoughts	your	from	the	simplicity

3.c.Txt: 03B,06D,018K 020L,025P,byz.We/Ho Sod **Var:** 01א,Tisc,Weis UBS/☆

2504.1 conj	3450.10 art gen sing fem	53.2 noun gen sing fem	3450.10 art gen sing fem	1519.1 prep	3450.6 art acc sing masc
[b☆+ καὶ	τῆς	ἁγνότητος]	τῆς	εἰς	(c τὸν)
kai	tēs	hagnotētos	tēs	eis	ton
[and	the	purity]	the	as to	the

11:1. Once more the Spirit moved the apostle to apologize for the focus on self. He asked his readers to bear with him in his folly (foolishness or seeming lack of sense) and then thanked them that they were already doing just that.

Paul disliked the role of the self-defender. It rubbed against the grain of his modesty. The trait of true modesty displayed itself repeatedly in his ministry. In First Corinthians he said, "I am the least of the apostles, that am not meet to be called an apostle" (1 Corinthians 15:9). In Ephesians he spoke of himself as one who was "less than the least of all saints" (Ephesians 3:8).

11:2. Paul offered a clear reason behind this self-defense which was distasteful to him. He was jealous over his converts at Corinth. Concern for their welfare forced his foolishness. Injured pride had nothing to do with it. It was not even a human emotion that moved him. Instead, it was a jealousy (*zēlos*), a zeal like that of God.

Nothing is more detestable than human jealousy. The author of The Song of Solomon rightly observed, "Jealousy is cruel as the grave" (Song of Solomon 8:6). It brings great strain to many a marriage. However, the Lord makes clear repeatedly in His Word that He is jealous over His people. For example, Zechariah declared, "Thus saith the Lord of hosts; I am jealous for Jerusalem and for Zion with a great jealousy" (Zechariah 1:14). Thus Paul said his was a "godly" jealousy.

Contrasting the two kinds of jealousy, Harris wrote, "Human jealousy is a vice, but to share divine jealousy is a virtue. It is the motive and object of the jealousy that is all-important. There is a place for a spiritual father's passionate concern for the exclusive and pure devotion to Christ of his spiritual children, and also a place for anger at potential violators of that purity (11:29)" (*The Expositor's Bible Commentary*, 10:385).

Behind Paul's feelings was the fact he had espoused (betrothed, engaged) them to be married to Christ. Fathers made full arrangements for marriages in ancient cultures, and this is so even among some societies today. The engagement was to one husband. A love and a relationship of that magnitude could be for only one Person, Christ.

The apostle was also fearful about his converts at Corinth. As any father he anticipated the day he could proudly present his daughter to her husband as a chaste, pure virgin (*parthenon*). Church purity is a valid concern for any pastor.

11:3. However, Paul feared unfaithfulness at Corinth might deny him that privilege. He was not ignorant of the way the flesh and the devil work. Satan in the form of a serpent deceived Eve with his subtilty (*panourgia*, "craftiness, trickery," readiness to do anything). Then Paul's concern was that the minds of the Corinthians might be corrupted and led astray from the simplicity and sincerity that is in Christ.

1. Would to God ye could bear with me a little in [my] folly: Please, put up with a bit of foolishness of mine, *Berkeley* . . . I want you to put up with me while I indulge in a bit of foolishness, *Adams* . . . you would put up with a little folly from me, *Norlie* . . . with a little "senselessness" from me! *HistNT* . . . as to some little imprudence, *Rotherham*.

and indeed bear with me: . . . you will have to tolerate me, *Berkeley*.

2. For I am jealous over you with godly jealousy: . . . for I am zealous, *Young* . . . I rave for you with a Divine madness, *Fenton* . . . For I am ardently devoted to you, *Wilson* . . . For I love you, *Conybeare* . . . I feel a divine jealousy for you, *Williams*.

for I have espoused you to one husband: For I have betrothed you, *Weymouth* . . . I arranged your wedding, *Klingensmith* . . . I promised you in marriage, *Beck* . . . for I affianced you to one, *Hanson* . . . to one Man, *Norlie*.

that I may present [you as] a chaste virgin to Christ: . . . a pure virgin, *Young* . . . like a faithful bride, *Weymouth*.

3. But I fear, lest by any means: I am apprehensive, *Williams*.

as the serpent beguiled Eve through his subtlety: . . . as the snake tricked Eve by his cunning, *Klingensmith* . . . by its trickery seduced Eve, *Beck* . . . completely deceived Eve in his knavery, *Rotherham* . . . by his cunning, *Norlie*.

so your minds should be corrupted from the simplicity that is in Christ: I am afraid that you will be fooled, *NLT* . . . your minds should be led astray, *NASB* . . . your thoughts may be turned aside, *Williams* . . . so your imaginations should be corrupted, *Conybeare* . . . should be seduced from your single-mindedness, *Montgomery* . . . led astray from their simple devotion, *Norlie* . . . from their single-heartedness and their fidelity to Christ, *Weymouth* . . . from that singleness of heart, *HistNT* . . . your simple and pure loyalty, *Beck*.

2 Corinthians 11:4

5382.4 name acc masc	1479.1 conj	3173.1 conj	1056.1 conj	3450.5 art sing masc	2048.44 verb nom sing masc part pres	241.5 adj acc sing masc
Χριστόν.	4. εἰ	μὲν	γὰρ	ὁ	ἐρχόμενος	ἄλλον
Christon	ei	men	gar	ho	erchomenos	allon
Christ.	If	indeed	for	the	coming	another

2400.3 name acc masc	2756.2 verb 3sing indic pres act	3614.6 rel-pron acc sing masc	3620.2 partic	2756.12 verb 1pl indic aor act	2211.1 conj
Ἰησοῦν	κηρύσσει	ὃν	οὐκ	ἐκηρύξαμεν,	ἢ
Iēsoun	kērussei	hon	ouk	ekēruxamen	ē
Jesus	proclaims	whom	not	we did proclaim,	or

4011.1 noun sing neu	2066.1 adj sing	2956.1 verb 2pl pres act	3614.16 rel- pron sing neu	3620.2 partic	2956.16 verb 2pl indic aor act
πνεῦμα	ἕτερον	λαμβάνετε	ὃ	οὐκ	ἐλάβετε,
pneuma	heteron	lambanete	ho	ouk	elabete
a spirit	different	you receive	which	not	you did receive,

2211.1 conj	2077.1 noun sing neu	2066.1 adj sing	3614.16 rel- pron sing neu	3620.2 partic	1203.7 verb 2pl indic aor mid
ἢ	εὐαγγέλιον	ἕτερον	ὃ	οὐκ	ἐδέξασθε,
ē	euangelion	heteron	ho	ouk	edexasthe
or	good news	different	which	not	you did accept,

4.a.Txt: Steph
Var: 01ℵ,06D-corr
018K,020L,025P,byz.
Gries,Treg,Word,Tisc
Sod

4.b.Txt: Steph
Var: 03B,06D-org,33
Lach,Alf,We/Ho,Weis
UBS/⋆

2544.1 adv	428.8 verb 2pl impr imperf mid	428.7 verb 2pl impr imperf mid	428.1 verb 2pl pres mid
καλῶς	(ἠνείχεσθε.	[¹ᵃ ἀνείχεσθε	²ᵇ⋆ ἀνέχεσθε.]
kalōs	ēneichesthe	aneichesthe	anechesthe
well	were you bearing with.	[idem	you endure.]

3023.2 verb 1sing indic pres	1056.1 conj	3235.6 num card neu	5139.8 verb inf perf act	3450.1 art gen pl
5. Λογίζομαι	γὰρ	μηδὲν	ὑστερηκέναι	τῶν
Logizomai	gar	mēden	husterēkenai	tōn
I reckon	for	in nothing	to have been behind	the

5065.1 prep	3003.1 adv	5082.1 adv	646.5 noun gen pl masc	1479.1 conj
(ὑπὲρ	λίαν	[⋆ ὑπερλίαν]	ἀποστόλων·	6. εἰ
huper	lian	huperlian	apostolōn	ei
beyond	exceedingly	[beyond measure]	apostles.	If

1156.2 conj	2504.1 conj	2376.1 noun nom sing masc	3450.3 art dat sing	3030.3 noun dat sing masc	233.1 conj	3620.3 partic	3450.11 art dat sing fem
δὲ	καὶ	ἰδιώτης	τῷ	λόγῳ,	ἀλλ'	οὐ	τῇ
de	kai	idiōtēs	tō	logō	all'	ou	tē
but	even	untrained	in the	speech,	yet	not	in the

1102.3 noun dat sing fem	233.1 conj	1706.1 prep	3820.3 adj dat sing	5157.15 verb nom pl masc part aor pass
γνώσει·	ἀλλ'	ἐν	παντὶ	(φανερωθέντες
gnōsei	all'	en	panti	phanerōthentes
knowledge;	but	in	every	having been made manifest

6.a.Txt: 01ℵ-corr
06D-corr,018K,020L
025P,byz.
Var: 01ℵ-org,03B,33
Lach,Treg,Alf,Tisc
We/Ho,Weis,Sod
UBS/⋆

5157.22 verb nom pl masc part aor act	1706.1 prep	3820.5 adj dat pl	1519.1 prep	5050.4 prs- pron acc 2pl
[ᵃ⋆ φανερώσαντες]	ἐν	πᾶσιν	εἰς	ὑμᾶς.
phanerōsantes	en	pasin	eis	humas
[having manifested]	in	all things	to	you.

7.a.Txt: p34,p46,01ℵ
03B,044,0121,byz.
Var: 06D,010F,012G
018K-org,020L,025P
365

2211.1 conj	264.4 noun acc sing fem	4020.22 verb 1sing indic aor act	1670.3 prs-pron acc 1sing masc	1431.6 prs-pron acc 3sing masc
7. Ἢ	ἁμαρτίαν	ἐποίησα,	(⋆ ἐμαυτὸν	[ᵃ ἑαυτὸν]
Ē	hamartian	epoiēsa	emauton	heauton
Or	sin	did I commit,	myself	[himself]

612

11:4. The apostle was surprised at the ready response Corinthian believers had given to the newcomers (*erchomenos*). They preached or proclaimed another (*allos*, "another of the same kind") interpretation of the same Jesus. Their representation of Christ was different from that which Paul presented to them. They were of another (*heteron*, "another of a different kind") spirit too. It was not the same kind of spirit the apostle projected to them. Theirs was in fact another (*heteron*) gospel. It was not the good news they accepted when Paul, their father in the Faith, first came to them. Then how could they put up with such preachers so easily?

The apostle did not include "ye might well bear with him" in his remarks to the Galatians regarding similar false teachers. There he instructed, "If any man preach any other gospel unto you than that ye have received, let him be accursed" (Galatians 1:9).

11:5. To make his point clear Paul felt compelled to declare he was of the opinion he was not a whit behind or not at all inferior to such chief or super apostles. Interestingly, his words differ markedly from some of his first letter to the Corinthians. In it he judged himself to be "the least of the apostles," and not at all worthy to be called an apostle (1 Corinthians 15:9). Earlier he had compared himself with true apostles while in his second letter he stands in contrast to false teachers.

Though the apostle acknowledged he may have seemed to have no sense in speaking of himself in such terms, instead, under the inspiration of the Spirit he was indeed wise. The sage of old advised at times it is necessary to "answer a fool according to his folly, lest he be wise in his own conceit" (Proverbs 26:5). In the same sense Paul replied to the false charges made against him by the "super apostles" at Corinth.

11:6. As earlier (10:10), the apostle again responded to accusations against his speech. Some declared he was rude (*idiōtēs*, a layman as compared to a specialist), unskilled as a public speaker. Since the claim came from his critics, it was not necessarily a statement of fact. Certainly his sermons as recorded in Acts are reasoned, logical, lucid presentations. Nonetheless, he admitted he was not schooled as a polished lecturer in the art of Greek rhetoric. Such men of his day became popular entertainers and collected considerable sums from the crowds that flocked around them.

However, Paul gave no ground to the opposition when it came to knowledge. In that area he had thoroughly demonstrated his ability among them in every way. Presenting truth was his aim in a public address. His concern was the message, not the manner of its presentation.

11:7. The itinerant lecturers who used their mouths to make a living charged sizable fees for every performance. People paid gladly

4. For if he that cometh preacheth another Jesus: . . . if the newcomer, *Fenton* . . . had proclaimed to you, *Murdock* . . . a pseudo-Jesus, *RPNT*.

whom we have not preached:
or [if] ye receive another spirit: Spirit different from the One, *Weymouth, Williams.*

which ye have not received:
or another gospel, which ye have not accepted: . . . which you did not embrace, *Wilson* . . . different from what you previously welcomed, *Berkeley.*

ye might well bear with [him]: . . . you submit to it readily enough, *RSV.*

5. For I suppose I was not a whit behind the very chiefest apostles: I consider myself to be deficient in nothing, *Fenton* . . . I consider myself not a single bit inferior to those surpassingly superior apostles of yours! *Williams* . . . regard myself as nowise inferior, *Confraternity* . . . behind the very foremost apostles, *Noyes* . . . to these extraspecial messengers of yours, *Phillips.*

6. But though [I be] rude in speech: . . . if in the matter of speech I am no orator, *Weymouth* . . . If I am untrained in speech, *Klingensmith* . . . though I be unskilled in speech, *Montgomery* . . . Even if I lack skill in rhetoric, *Berkeley* . . . even uncultured in [my] discourse, *Rotherham* . . . though I be a common man in my speech, *Alford* . . . even if I am not a polished speaker, *Norlie.*

yet not in knowledge: I know what I'm talking about, *Beck* . . . yet I am not wanting in the gift of knowledge, *Conybeare.*

but we have been thoroughly made manifest among you in all things: . . . we have made that perfectly clear to you in every way, *HistNT* . . . at all events, among you! *Fenton.*

7. Have I committed an offence in abasing myself: Or did I commit a sin, *Hanson* . . . did I commit a fault, *Douay* . . . by humbling myself, *Murdock* . . . thereby degrading myself, *Norlie.*

4864.1 verb nom sing masc part pres act	2419.1 conj	5050.1 prs-pron nom 2pl	5150.7 verb 2pl subj aor pass	3617.1 conj	1425.1 adv
ταπεινῶν	ἵνα	ὑμεῖς	ὑψωθῆτε,	ὅτι	δωρεὰν
tapeinōn	hina	humeis	hupsōthēte	hoti	dōrean
humbling	that	you	might be exalted,	because	freely

3450.16 art sing neu	3450.2 art gen sing	2296.2 noun gen sing masc	2077.1 noun sing neu	2076.15 verb 1sing indic aor mid
τὸ	τοῦ	θεοῦ	εὐαγγέλιον	εὐηγγελισάμην
to	tou	theou	euangelion	euēngelisamēn
the		of God	good news	I announced

5050.3 prs-pron dat 2pl	241.13 adj acc pl fem	1564.1 noun fem	4664.1 verb 1sing indic aor act	2956.25 verb nom sing masc part aor act
ὑμῖν;	8. ἄλλας	ἐκκλησίας	ἐσύλησα,	λαβὼν
humin	allas	ekklēsias	esulēsa	labōn
to you?	Other	assemblies	I robbed,	having received

3664.1 noun acc sing neu	4242.1 prep	3450.12 art acc sing fem	5050.2 prs-pron gen 2pl	1242.4 noun acc sing fem	2504.1 conj
ὀψώνιον	πρὸς	τὴν	ὑμῶν	διακονίαν·	9. καὶ
opsōnion	pros	tēn	humōn	diakonian	kai
wages	for	the	your	service.	And

3780.6 verb nom sing masc part pres act	4242.1 prep	5050.4 prs-pron acc 2pl	2504.1 conj	5139.13 verb nom sing masc part aor pass
παρὼν	πρὸς	ὑμᾶς	καὶ	ὑστερηθεὶς,
parōn	pros	humas	kai	husterētheis
being present	with	you	and	having been deficient,

3620.3 partic	2625.1 verb 1sing indic aor act	3625.1 num card gen	3628.2 num card gen	3450.16 art sing neu
οὐ	κατενάρκησα	⸀ οὐδενός·	[✶ οὐθενός·]	τὸ
ou	katenarkēsa	oudenos	outhenos	to
not	I did burden	no one,	[idem]	the

1056.1 conj	5140.2 noun acc sing neu	1466.2 prs-pron gen 1sing	4180.2 verb 3pl indic aor act	3450.7 art pl masc
γὰρ	ὑστέρημά	μου	προσανεπλήρωσαν	οἱ
gar	husterēma	mou	prosaneplērōsan	hoi
for	deficiency	my	completely filled up	the

79.6 noun pl masc	2048.16 verb nom pl masc part aor act	570.3 prep gen	3081.2 name gen fem	2504.1 conj	1706.1 prep
ἀδελφοὶ	ἐλθόντες	ἀπὸ	Μακεδονίας·	καὶ	ἐν
adelphoi	elthontes	apo	Makedonias	kai	en
brothers	having come	from	Macedonia,	and	in

3820.3 adj dat sing	4.1 adj acc sing masc	5050.3 prs-pron dat 2pl	1670.3 prs-pron acc 1sing masc	1670.3 prs-pron acc 1sing masc
παντὶ	ἀβαρῆ	⸀ ὑμῖν	ἐμαυτὸν	[✶ ἐμαυτὸν
panti	abarē	humin	emauton	emauton
everything	not burdensome	to you	myself	[myself

5050.3 prs-pron dat 2pl	4931.12 verb 1sing indic aor act	2504.1 conj	4931.26 verb 1sing indic fut act	1498.4 verb 3sing indic pres act	223.1 noun nom sing fem
ὑμῖν]	ἐτήρησα	καὶ	τηρήσω.	10. ἔστιν	ἀλήθεια
humin	etērēsa	kai	tērēsō	estin	alētheia
to you]	I kept	and	will keep.	Is	truth

5382.2 name gen masc	1706.1 prep	1466.5 prs-pron dat 1sing	3617.1 conj	3450.9 art nom sing fem	2716.1 noun nom sing fem	3642.9 dem-pron nom sing fem
Χριστοῦ	ἐν	ἐμοὶ	ὅτι	ἡ	καύχησις	αὕτη
Christou	en	emoi	hoti	hē	kauchēsis	hautē
of Christ	in	me	that	the	boasting	this

to hear such "professionals." By way of contrast, while planting a church Paul did not ask the infant congregation to support him financially. Instead he worked with his hands as a tentmaker to supply his own needs (Acts 18:1-3). This caused his critics to say he was not a "professional."

Concerning this issue Hughes wrote, "Among the Greeks the accredited rhetorician or philosopher was a 'professional' man who charged for his services and lived by his art. For a speaker to refuse remuneration, or not demand it, would at once cause his listeners, such as the sophistication of their outlook, to suspect him of being spurious, a mere *poseur*, and his teaching as worthless" (*The New London Commentary*, p.383). Socrates gained repute by standing alone against the Sophists in this practice.

In 1 Corinthians 9:6-14 Paul said established churches should meet the financial needs of their minister. He declared the Law, reason, and Christ all taught this principle. His conclusion was, "Even so hath the Lord ordained that they which preach the gospel should live of the gospel" (1 Corinthians 9:14).

Yet he asked for no such support in pioneering churches (1 Corinthians 9:15-18). He wanted to establish new congregations on a solid foundation. The apostle determined not to be classified with the traveling entertainers. He was not in the ministry for money (Acts 20:33,34). Further, by word and deed he instructed young converts to shun the prevailing notion among Romans that it was beneath the dignity of a free man to work for a living (Acts 20:35). To be truly Christian they must work to meet their own needs and to have extra to give to those who could not supply their own needs.

With some accusing him of being unprofessional because he worked, Paul wondered if he had committed an offense (*hamartian*, "sin") in presenting the good news to them freely (without cost, as a gift). In the eyes of his enemies he degraded himself by doing so. Of course, he made them appear exalted by way of comparison.

11:8,9. As a matter of fact, at times he "robbed" (accepted wages, offerings) from churches he had previously established so he could minister to them. For example, after he left Macedonia and moved on south to plant the churches at Thessalonica and Corinth, the believers at Philippi sent several offerings to the apostle (Philippians 4:15,16). Despite what his critics said, Paul determined to continue his financial policy in planting new churches.

11:10. Protesting by the truth of Christ which he held to, Paul emphatically declared nothing would change his mind in this matter. He would not allow criticism from his enemies to set the criteria for ministerial ethics in his life. Slander would not change his character. If he must boast to match the opposition, he would glory in the fact that he acted correctly concerning finances in planting new churches, especially in the regions of Achaia, Greece. As he wrote

that ye might be exalted: . . . in order that you might be exalted, *Norlie* . . . to push you forward? *Klingensmith.*

because I have preached to you the gospel of God freely?: . . . without charge, *Alford* . . . without a fee, *Phillips* . . . without fee or reward? *Weymouth, Conybeare* . . . to you for nothing? *HistNT* . . . without compensation? *Berkeley* . . . free of charge? *Confraternity* . . . free of cost? *Montgomery* . . . without accepting any pay? *Williams* . . . without payment, *TCNT.*

8. I robbed other churches: I stripped Other Congregations, *Wilson* . . . I sponged on other churches, *Williams.*

taking wages [of them], to do you service: . . . receiving pay from them, *Weymouth* . . . when I took supplies from them to serve you, *Klingensmith* . . . taking rations, *PNT* . . . receiving supplies with a view to the ministering unto you, *Rotherham* . . . for ministering to you, *Panin* . . . to minister to you free of charge, *Phillips* . . . for services to you, *Fenton.*

9. And when I was present with you, and wanted: . . . and being deficient, *Fenton* . . . and my resources failed, *Weymouth* . . . and very hard up, *Phillips* . . . and ran short of funds, *Berkeley* . . . and had needs, *Adams* . . . and in need, *TCNT* . . . when I lacked the actual necessities of life, *Montgomery.*

I was chargeable to no man: I was not a burden on any man, *Hanson* . . . I was burdensome to none of you, *Murdock.*

for that which was lacking to me the brethren which came from Macedonia supplied: . . . supplied beforehand my deficiency, *Wilson.*

and in all [things] I have kept myself from being burdensome unto you, and [so] will I keep [myself]: . . . so in every way, *HistNT* . . . free from troubling you for maintenance, *Fenton* . . . and I shall continue to do so, *TCNT.*

10. As the truth of Christ is in me:

2 Corinthians 11:11

10.a.Txt: Steph
Var: 01ℵ,03B,06D,020L
025P,Elzev,Gries,Lach
Treg,Alf,Word,Tisc
We/Ho,Weis,Sod
UBS/✱

3620.3 partic	4824.10 verb 3sing indic fut pass	5256.3 verb 3sing indic fut pass	1519.1 prep	1466.7 prs-pron acc 1sing
οὐ	ʿ σφραγίσεται	[ᵃ✱ φραγήσεται]	εἰς	ἐμὲ
ou	sphragisetai	phragēsetai	eis	eme
not	shall be sealed up	[idem]	as to	me

1706.1 prep	3450.4 art dat pl	2797.1 noun dat pl neu	3450.10 art gen sing fem	875.2 name gen fem	1296.1 adv
ἐν	τοῖς	κλίμασιν	τῆς	Ἀχαΐας.	11. ʿ διατί;
en	tois	klimasin	tēs	Achaias.	diati;
in	the	regions		of Achaia.	Why?

1217.2 prep	4949.9 intr-pron sing neu	3617.1 conj	3620.2 partic	25.5 verb 1sing indic pres act	5050.4 prs-pron acc 2pl	3450.5 art sing masc
[✱ διὰ τί;]		ὅτι	οὐκ	ἀγαπῶ	ὑμᾶς;	ὁ
dia ti;		hoti	ouk	agapō	humas;	ho
[idem]		because	not	I do love	you?	

2296.1 noun nom sing masc	3471.4 verb 3sing indic perf act	3614.16 rel-pron sing neu	1156.2 conj	4020.1 verb 1sing indic pres act	2504.1 conj
θεὸς	οἶδεν·	12. Ὃ	δὲ	ποιῶ,	καὶ
theos	oiden	Ho	de	poiō,	kai
God	knows.	What	but	I do,	also

4020.21 verb 1sing act	2419.1 conj	1568.1 verb 1sing subj aor act	3450.12 art acc sing fem	867.1 noun acc sing fem	3450.1 art gen pl
ποιήσω,	ἵνα	ἐκκόψω	τὴν	ἀφορμὴν	τῶν
poiēsō,	hina	ekkopsō	tēn	aphormēn	tōn
I will do,	that	I may cut off	the	occasion	of the

2286.17 verb gen pl masc part pres act	867.1 noun acc sing fem	2419.1 conj	1706.1 prep	3614.3 rel-pron dat sing	2714.5 verb 3pl indic pres
θελόντων	ἀφορμήν,	ἵνα	ἐν	ᾧ	καυχῶνται
thelontōn	aphormēn,	hina	en	hō	kauchōntai
wishing	an occasion,	that	in	which	they boast

2128.38 verb 3pl subj aor pass	2503.1 conj	2504.1 conj	2231.1 prs-pron nom 1pl	3450.7 art pl masc
εὑρεθῶσιν	καθὼς	καὶ	ἡμεῖς.	13. οἱ
heurethōsin	kathōs	kai	hēmeis.	hoi
they may be found	according as	also	we.	The

1056.1 conj	4955.7 dem-pron nom pl masc	5405.1 noun nom pl masc	2023.3 noun pl masc	1380.1 adj nom pl masc
γὰρ	τοιοῦτοι	ψευδαπόστολοι,	ἐργάται	δόλιοι,
gar	toioutoi	pseudapostoloi,	ergatai	dolioi,
for	such	false apostles,	workers	deceitful,

3215.5 verb nom pl masc part pres mid	1519.1 prep	646.7 noun acc pl masc	5382.2 name gen masc
μετασχηματιζόμενοι	εἰς	ἀποστόλους	Χριστοῦ·
metaschēmatizomenoi	eis	apostolous	Christou
transforming themselves	into	apostles	of Christ.

14.a.Txt: 06D-corr,018K
020L,byz.
Var: 01ℵ,03B,06D-org
025P,33,Lach,Treg,Alf
Word,Tisc,We/Ho,Weis
Sod,UBS/✱

2504.1 conj	3620.3 partic	2275.2 adj sing neu	2272.1 noun sing neu	840.5 prs-pron nom sing masc
14. καὶ	οὐ	ʿ θαυμαστόν·	[ᵃ✱ θαῦμα,]	αὐτὸς
kai	ou	thaumaston	thauma,	autos
And	not	wonderful,	[wonder,]	himself

1056.1 conj	3450.5 art sing masc	4423.1 noun nom sing masc	3215.3 verb 3sing indic pres mid	1519.1 prep	32.4 noun acc sing masc
γὰρ	ὁ	Σατανᾶς	μετασχηματίζεται	εἰς	ἄγγελον
gar	ho	Satanas	metaschēmatizetai	eis	angelon
for		Satan	transforms himself	into	an angel

earlier, "It were better for me to die, than that any man should make my glorying void" (1 Corinthians 9:15). The false apostles may have made merchandise of the gospel, but he never would.

11:11. Did Paul's personal policy on church finances show a lack of love for his converts in Corinth? No doubt his critics hinted if he really had their welfare at heart he would have treated them more "professionally." To the contrary, it was precisely because he loved them so much that he did not demand their support in pioneering the congregations in Corinth.

Writing another church he planted, and defending himself against the same charge, the apostle said he worked night and day so he would not be a burden to young converts. His conduct concerning ministerial support demonstrated he was "affectionately desirous" of them and that they were "dear" to him (1 Thessalonians 2:5-9). He loved them so much he treated them gently "as a nurse cherisheth her children."

11:12. Once more the founder of the church at Corinth declared his determination to continue doing what he had always done in the way he treated finances as a pioneer pastor. Inspired by the Spirit as he wrote, he aimed to catch those who slandered him in this matter in their own trap. His explanations snatched the occasion for glorying right out of their hands. He "pulled the rug from under their feet." He made them appear as human as the one they criticized, slandering him as the lowly preacher who had to work because his ministry was so poor it did not support him.

11:13. For the first time in his letter Paul plainly called his critics false apostles (*pseudapostoloi*, here only in the New Testament). They were deceitful, dishonest workers. They transformed and disguised themselves so as to appear to be the apostles of Christ. He warned the elders at Ephesus that such false teachers, wolves in sheep's clothing, would arise among them seeking to draw away disciples unto themselves (Acts 20:29,30). Sadly, in the end they would devour the flock they pretended to care for.

11:14. Paul, the true apostle, was not at all surprised at this problem caused by his critics at Corinth. He knew well what worked in the darkened hearts of wicked men. These false teachers were servants of Satan. As true children of the devil they acted like their father. He regularly disguises himself as an angel of light, never appearing as darkness.

no man shall stop me of this boasting in the regions of Achaia: ... that will not be silenced, *Klingensmith* ... will not be silenced anywhere in Greece, *Beck* ... within the boundaries, *Montgomery* ... in the district, *Fenton* ... in the country of Greece, *NLT.*

11. Wherefore? because I love you not? God knoweth:

12. But what I do, that I will do: I will continue to do, *NASB* ... But I will persist, *Weymouth* ... to do what I am doing, *Norlie.*
that I may cut off occasion from them which desire occasion: ... that I may cut off opportunity, *NASB, Campbell* ... that I may deprive them, *Confraternity* ... to eliminate the opportunity, *Berkeley* ... that I may take away any pretext for their boasting, *Adams.*
that wherein they glory, they may be found even as we:

13. For such [are] false apostles, deceitful workers: They are counterfeits of the real thing, dishonest practitioners, *Phillips* ... For these sham apostles— tricksters, *Fenton* ... false missionaries...tricky workmen, *Klingensmith* ... dishonest workmen, *Weymouth* ... cheating workmen, *NTPE.*
transforming themselves into the apostles of Christ: ... fashioning themselves, *Panin* ... assuming the garb of apostles of Christ, *Weymouth* ... clothing themselves in the garb of Christ's Apostles, *Conybeare* ... masquerading as, *HistNT* ... in disguise passing as, *Norlie* ... wearing the masks of Christ's apostles, *Berkeley.*

14. And no marvel: It is no surprise! *NLT* ... and no wonder, *Young* ... And it is not surprising, *Wilson.*
for Satan himself is transformed into an angel of light: ... can disguise himself as, *Weymouth* ... masquerades as, *Berkeley* ... pretends to be, *Klingensmith.*

5295.2 noun gen sing neu	3620.3 partic	3144.16 adj sing neu	3631.1 conj	1479.1 conj	2504.1 conj	3450.7 art pl masc
φωτός·	**15.** οὐ	μέγα	οὖν	εἰ	καὶ	οἱ
phōtos	ou	mega	oun	ei	kai	hoi
of light.	Not	a great thing	therefore	if	also	the

1243.3 noun nom pl masc	840.3 prs-pron gen sing	3215.4 verb 3pl indic pres mid	5453.1 conj	1243.3 noun nom pl masc
διάκονοι	αὐτοῦ	μετασχηματίζονται	ὡς	διάκονοι
diakonoi	autou	metaschēmatizontai	hōs	diakonoi
servants	his	transform themselves	as	servants

1336.2 noun gen sing fem	3614.1 rel-pron gen pl	3450.16 art sing neu	4904.1 noun sing neu	1498.40 verb 3sing indic fut mid
δικαιοσύνης,	ὧν	τὸ	τέλος	ἔσται
dikaiosunēs	hōn	to	telos	estai
of righteousness;	of whom	the	end	shall be

2567.3 prep	3450.17 art pl neu	2024.4 noun pl neu	840.1 prs-pron gen pl	3687.1 adv	2978.1 verb 1sing pres act
κατὰ	τὰ	ἔργα	αὐτῶν.	**16.** Πάλιν	λέγω,
kata	ta	erga	autōn	Palin	legō
according to	the	works	their.	Again	I say,

3231.1 partic	4949.3 intr-pron nom sing	1466.6 prs-pron acc 1sing	1374.19 verb 3sing subj aor act	871.2 adj acc sing masc	1498.32 verb inf pres act
μή	τίς	με	δόξῃ	ἄφρονα	εἶναι·
mē	tis	me	doxē	aphrona	einai
Not	anyone	me	should think	a fool	to be;

1479.1 conj	1156.2 conj	3232.1 partic	3231.1 partic	1058.1 partic	2550.1 conj	5453.1 conj	871.2 adj acc sing masc
εἰ	δὲ	῾ μήγε,	[μή	γε]	κἂν	ὡς	ἄφρονα
ei	de	mēge	mē	ge	kan	hōs	aphrona
if	but	otherwise,	[not	indeed]	even if	as	a fool

1203.12 verb 2pl impr aor mid	1466.6 prs-pron acc 1sing	2419.1 conj	3261.1 adv	4948.10 indef-pron sing neu	2476.3 conj
δέξασθέ	με,	ἵνα	῾ μικρόν	τι	κἀγὼ
dexasthe	me	hina	mikron	ti	kagō
receive	me,	that	little	some	I also

2476.3 conj	3261.1 adv	4948.10 indef-pron sing neu	2714.11 verb 1sing subj aor mid	3614.16 rel-pron sing neu
[✵ κἀγὼ	μικρόν	τι]	καυχήσωμαι.	**17.** ὃ
kagō	mikron	ti	kauchēsōmai	ho
[I also	little	some]	may boast.	What

2953.1 verb 1sing pres act	3620.3 partic	2953.1 verb 1sing pres act	2567.3 prep	2935.4 noun acc sing masc	2567.3 prep
λαλῶ,	οὐ	῾ λαλῶ	κατὰ	κύριον,	[✵ κατὰ
lalō	ou	lalō	kata	kurion	kata
I speak,	not	do I speak	according to	Lord,	[according to

2935.4 noun acc sing masc	2953.1 verb 1sing pres act	233.1 conj	5453.1 conj	1706.1 prep	869.2 noun dat sing fem	1706.1 prep
κύριον	λαλῶ,]	ἀλλ'	ὡς	ἐν	ἀφροσύνῃ,	ἐν
kurion	lalō	all'	hōs	en	aphrosunē	en
Lord	I speak,]	but	as	in	folly,	in

3642.11 dem-pron dat sing fem	3450.11 art dat sing fem	5125.3 noun dat sing fem	3450.10 art gen sing fem	2716.2 noun gen sing fem
ταύτῃ	τῇ	ὑποστάσει	τῆς	καυχήσεως.
tautē	tē	hupostasei	tēs	kauchēseōs
this	the	confidence	of the	boasting.

11:15. Understandably, then, the apostle reasoned it is no great thing for the ministers (*diakonoi*, "servants") of Satan to disguise themselves as promoters of righteousness. They, like the devil, appear to be what they are not. Satan never approaches the Christian as Satan. He came to Eve as one who knew how to help her "be as gods" (Genesis 3:5). In the same way sin rarely tempts as sin. Once recognized for what it is, the temptation to sin loses much of its force. Likewise error often presents itself as truth.

So these false apostles seemed to advance just causes. However, as Paul wrote the Romans, "They that are such serve not our Lord Jesus Christ, but their own belly; and by good words and fair speeches deceive the hearts of the simple" (Romans 16:18).

Their true nature would appear at the end. Their reward would be according to their works. Paul implied they will be dammed on judgment day. He did not teach here contrary to his message elsewhere that men are saved by grace and not works (Ephesians 2:8,9). Still, there is a Biblical sense in which people will be judged, "every man according to their works" (Revelation 20:13).

11:16. The list of charges against the apostle was long; therefore, he continued his defense. However, before turning to the next false claim against him he apologized more for his "foolishness." He did not want to appear as lacking in modesty. The behavior of the braggart was particularly distasteful to him. If he appeared as a fool, though, he asked for tolerance in boasting yet about himself.

Recognizing that modesty should prevail in the ministry of every preacher, Kent reasoned: "There are times, however, when personal explanations are necessary. In order to prevent distorted statements, unfounded gossip, or outright slander, or to protect the welfare or reputation of others, it may be one's duty to set the record straight, even when one must risk feelings of awkwardness. Surely it is essential to defend the truth and prevent the twisting of facts when the Lord's work is involved" (p.173).

11:17. Paul explained that his boasting was not a Christian characteristic. It was "not after the Lord." However, by this he offered no disclaimer to inspiration in writing this paragraph. Noting this Meyer observed: "When Paul in this verse says that he is not speaking *kata kurion*, he is not referring to inspiration. He does not mean to say that the Lord has nothing to do with the matter and is not giving him the very words by His Spirit" (p.274). He concluded, "Paul is simply referring to his method of speaking in the given situation" (ibid., p.274). Indeed, the Spirit directed him in a necessary vindication of truth in order to preserve the integrity of the gospel the apostle preached. On the surface what follows seems the greatest of all Paul's boasting, but in these prefacing remarks he never appeared more humble.

15. Therefore [it is] no great thing if his ministers also be transformed as the ministers of righteousness: So it is nothing extraordinary, *Berkeley* . . . So, it isn't any big thing, *SEB* . . . So it isn't surprising, *Beck* . . . his servants transform themselves, *Fenton.*

whose end shall be according to their works: . . . whose doom, *Williams* . . . whose consummation, *Concordant* . . . correspond to their deeds, *RSV* . . . in accordance with their actions, *Weymouth* . . . In the end they will get exactly what their actions deserve, *TEV* . . . in the end they will get what their conduct deserves, *Barclay* . . . will end up the same way they lived, *SEB* . . . so shall be their fate, *HistNT* . . . be in keeping with their deeds, *Adams.*

16. I say again, Let no man think me a fool: I repeat, *Confraternity* . . . no one should presume me to be imprudent, *Concordant* . . . Let no one imagine me to be imprudent, *Rotherham* . . . that I am vain, *Norlie* . . . a Simpleton, *Wilson.*

if otherwise, yet as a fool receive me: But, if you do, bear with me, *SEB* . . . then treat me as a fool, *JB* . . . put up with me as such, *BB* . . . accept me as a fool, *Barclay* . . . show me at least the patience you would show a fool, *Goodspeed.*

that I may boast myself a little: Then I can brag a little as fools do, *SEB* . . . Give me a chance to do just a little talking about the claims I am proud of, *Barclay.*

17. That which I speak, I speak [it] not after the Lord: When I confidently brag like this, *SEB* . . . When I boast in this reckless way, *Goodspeed* . . . what I am saying now is not what the Lord would have me say, *TEV* . . . is not prompted by, *JB* . . . I am not speaking here as a Christian, *NEB* . . . This isn't a Christian way to talk, *Barclay.*

but as it were foolishly: . . . but as though in delirium, *Fenton* . . . as if in a fit of folly, *JB.*

in this confidence of boasting: . . . in the certainty that I have something to boast about, *JB.*

2 Corinthians 11:18

18.a.Txt: 01**ℵ**-corr2,03B
06D-corr1,015H,044
0121,byz.
Var: p46,01**ℵ**-org
06D-org,010F,012G,098
33,81,104,365,629
1175,1739-org

18. ἐπεὶ — *epei* — Since [1878.1 conj]
πολλοὶ — *polloi* — many [4044.7 adj nom pl masc]
καυχῶνται — *kauchōntai* — boast [2714.5 verb 3pl indic pres]
κατὰ — *kata* — according to [2567.3 prep]
[a] τὴν — *tēn* — the [3450.12 art acc sing fem]
σάρκα, — *sarka,* — flesh, [4418.4 noun acc sing fem]

κἀγὼ — *kagō* — I also [2476.3 conj]
καυχήσομαι. — *kauchēsomai.* — will boast. [2714.16 verb 1sing indic fut mid]
19. ἡδέως — *hēdeōs* — Gladly [2217.1 adv]
γὰρ — *gar* — for [1056.1 conj]
ἀνέχεσθε — *anechesthe* — you bear with [428.1 verb 2pl pres mid]
τῶν — *tōn* — the [3450.1 art gen pl]

ἀφρόνων, — *aphronōn,* — fools [871.5 adj gen pl masc]
φρόνιμοι — *phronimoi* — intelligent [5265.1 adj nom pl]
ὄντες· — *ontes·* — being. [1498.23 verb nom pl masc part pres act]
20. ἀνέχεσθε — *anechesthe* — You bear [428.1 verb 2pl pres mid]
γὰρ — *gar* — for [1056.1 conj]

εἴ — *ei* — if [1479.1 conj]
τις — *tis* — anyone [4948.3 indef-pron nom sing]
ὑμᾶς — *humas* — you [5050.4 prs-pron acc 2pl]
καταδουλοῖ, — *katadouloi,* — brings into bondage, [2585.1 verb 3sing indic pres act]
εἴ — *ei* — if [1479.1 conj]
τις — *tis* — anyone [4948.3 indef-pron nom sing]

κατεσθίει, — *katesthiei,* — devours, [2688.1 verb 3sing indic pres act]
εἴ — *ei* — if [1479.1 conj]
τις — *tis* — anyone [4948.3 indef-pron nom sing]
λαμβάνει, — *lambanei,* — takes, [2956.4 verb 3sing indic pres act]
εἴ — *ei* — if [1479.1 conj]
τις — *tis* — anyone [4948.3 indef-pron nom sing]

ἐπαίρεται, — *epairetai,* — exalts himself, [1854.9 verb 3sing indic pres mid]
εἴ — *ei* — if [1479.1 conj]
τις — *tis* — anyone [4948.3 indef-pron nom sing]
ὑμᾶς — *humas* — you [5050.4 prs-pron acc 2pl]
εἰς — *eis* — on [1519.1 prep]
πρόσωπον — *prosōpon* — the face [4241.1 noun sing neu]

[✶ εἰς — *eis* — [on [1519.1 prep]
πρόσωπον — *prosōpon* — face [4241.1 noun sing neu]
ὑμᾶς] — *humas* — you] [5050.4 prs-pron acc 2pl]
δέρει. — *derei.* — beats. [1188.2 verb 3sing indic pres act]
21. κατὰ — *kata* — As to [2567.3 prep]

ἀτιμίαν — *atimian* — dishonor [813.4 noun acc sing fem]
λέγω, — *legō,* — I speak, [2978.1 verb 1sing pres act]
ὡς — *hōs* — as [5453.1 conj]
ὅτι — *hoti* — that [3617.1 conj]
ἡμεῖς — *hēmeis* — we [2231.1 prs-pron nom 1pl]
ἠσθενήσαμεν· — *esthenēsamen·* — were weak; [764.13 verb 1pl indic aor act]

21.a.Txt: 06D,018K
020L,025P,byz.
Var: 01**ℵ**,03B,33,Lach
Treg,Tisc,We/Ho,Weis
Sod,UBS/✶

[a✶ ἠσθενήκαμεν·] — *esthenēkamen* — [have been weak;] [764.17 verb 1pl indic perf act]
ἐν — *en* — In [1706.1 prep]
ᾧ — *hō* — where [3614.3 rel-pron dat sing]
δ' — *d'* — but [1156.1 conj]
ἄν — *an* — [300.1 partic]
τις — *tis* — anyone [4948.3 indef-pron nom sing]

τολμᾷ, — *tolma,* — may be daring, [4958.1 verb 3sing pres act]
ἐν — *en* — in [1706.1 prep]
ἀφροσύνῃ — *aphrosunē* — folishness [869.2 noun dat sing fem]
λέγω, — *legō,* — I speak, [2978.1 verb 1sing pres act]
τολμῶ — *tolmō* — am daring [4958.2 verb 1sing indic pres act]

κἀγώ. — *kagō.* — I also. [2476.3 conj]
22. Ἑβραῖοί — *Hebraioi* — Hebrews [1439.2 name nom pl masc]
εἰσιν; — *eisin;* — are they? [1498.7 verb 3pl indic pres act]
κἀγώ· — *kagō·* — I also. [2476.3 conj]
Ἰσραηλῖταί — *Israēlitai* — Israelites [2448.2 name pl masc]

11:18. Circumstances forced him to compare himself with those who gloried after the flesh or by human standards. Of course he knew the teaching of the wise man who advised, "Answer not a fool according to his folly, lest thou also be like unto him" (Proverbs 26:4). Yet he was also acquainted with the wise man's instruction to "answer a fool according to his folly, lest he be wise in his own conceit" (Proverbs 26:5). Both exhortations are obviously good. The dilemma is when do you apply which? In this case the Spirit gave Paul the wisdom to know it was now time to apply the second part of the counsel of the sage of old.

11:19. With tongue in cheek the founder of the church at Corinth complimented those he won to Christ for suffering fools gladly. They not only tolerated those who bragged on themselves, but they apparently loved their boasting. This, he said sarcastically, indicated just how wise they were! At the moment he felt the same as Job who chided his "comforters" in saying, "No doubt but ye are the people, and wisdom shall die with you" (Job 12:2).

11:20. Believers in Corinth even allowed these false teachers to bring them into bondage. They seemed to enjoy the fact that such leaders usurped authority over them. Apparently they liked being reduced to slavery.

These gullible Christians put up with preachers who devoured them (consumed them, ate them up). They tolerated men who took of their goods, demanding offerings for their support.

Simple as these believers were, ministers who exalted themselves before them appealed to their fancy. They liked the star on the stage. Men who used what we would call today the Hollywood approach to evangelism attracted and held their attention.

Strange as it seemed, they were so duped they even allowed these preachers to slap them in the face, the highest form of personal insult. By no means did Paul suggest they should do otherwise than "turn the other cheek" when attacked by a persecutor (Luke 6:29). However, the situation at Corinth was entirely different. People there willingly submitted themselves to be exploited.

11:21. Paul reproached himself, admitted to his shame that he might have allowed some to think him weak. He might have appeared powerless because Spirit-produced character made him cautious in speaking out to defend himself. Yet immediately he declared he was ready to be as bold, as courageous as anyone. So he proceeded to boast even more forcefully than earlier of his ministerial experiences (see 6:4-10).

11:22. The apostle found it necessary to defend against the charge his ministry was inferior to that of the false apostles. His critics

18. Seeing that many glory after the flesh: . . . since men generally boast of their personal affairs, *Norlie* . . . Since many boast about their position, *Fenton.*
I will glory also:

19. For ye suffer fools gladly: . . . ye bear with, *Alford, PNT* . . . being tolerant to fools, *Norlie* . . . will gladly tolerate fools, *Berkeley.*
seeing ye [yourselves] are wise:

20. For ye suffer, if a man bring you into bondage: You even put up with those who exploit you, *NAB* . . . if he enslaves you, *Hanson* . . . if a man takes away your liberty, *Phillips.*
if a man devour [you]: . . . if anyone bites you, *Klingensmith* . . . lives at your expense, *Weymouth* . . . spends your money, *Phillips* . . . or imposes on you, *Berkeley.*
if a man take [of you]: . . . if a man seizeth you, *Alford* . . . if he takes advantage of you, *NASB* . . . when they prey upon you, *Norlie* . . . or traps you, *Beck* . . . makes a fool of you, *Phillips* . . . if they rob, *Fenton* . . . or exploits you, *Berkeley.*
if a man exalt himself: . . . if anyone makes himself a tyrant, *Klingensmith* . . . or lords it over you, *Beck* . . . if any one is lifting himself up, *Rotherham* . . . or snubs you, *Berkeley.*
if a man smite you on the face: . . . if he beats you on the face, *Hanson.*

21. I speak as concerning reproach: By way of disparagement I assume that, *Alford* . . . by way of disparagement, *ASV, Hanson* . . . I say this to my discredit, *HistNT* . . . I'm ashamed to admit it, *Beck.*
as though we had been weak: . . . because we have been insulted, *Fenton.*
Howbeit wheresoever any is bold:
(I speak foolishly,) I am bold also: I will match him, *Berkeley.*

22. Are they Hebrews? so [am] I: Are they Jews? *Beck* . . . I also! *Young.*

1498.7 verb 3pl indic pres act	2476.3 conj	4543.1 noun sing neu	11.1 name masc	1498.7 verb 3pl indic pres act	2476.3 conj
εἰσιν;	κἀγώ·	σπέρμα	Ἀβραάμ	εἰσιν;	κἀγώ·
eisin	kagō	sperma	Abraam	eisin	kagō
are they?	I also.	Seed	of Abraham	are they?	I also.

	1243.3 noun nom pl masc	5382.2 name gen masc	1498.7 verb 3pl indic pres act	3773.1 verb nom sing masc part pres act
23.	διάκονοι	Χριστοῦ	εἰσιν;	παραφρονῶν
	diakonoi	Christou	eisin	paraphronōn
	Servants	of Christ	are they?	being beside myself

2953.1 verb 1sing pres act	5065.1 prep	1466.1 prs-pron nom 1sing	1706.1 prep	2845.6 noun dat pl masc	3917.2 adv comp
λαλῶ,	ὑπὲρ	ἐγώ·	ἐν	κόποις	περισσοτέρως,
lalō	huper	egō	en	kopois	perissoterōs
I speak,	above	I;	in	labors	more abundantly,

1706.1 prep	3987.7 noun dat pl fem	5071.1 adv	1706.1 prep	5274.5 noun dat pl fem
⸃ ἐν	πληγαῖς	ὑπερβαλλόντως,	ἐν	φυλακαῖς
en	plēgais	huperballontōs	en	phulakais
in	stripes	above measure,	in	imprisonments

3917.2 adv comp	1706.1 prep	5274.5 noun dat pl fem	3917.2 adv comp	1706.1 prep
περισσοτέρως,	[★ ἐν	φυλακαῖς	περισσοτέρως,	ἐν
perissoterōs	en	phulakais	perissoterōs	en
more abundantly,	[in	prisons	far more,	in

3987.7 noun dat pl fem	5071.1 adv	1706.1 prep	2265.6 noun dat pl masc	4038.1 adv
πληγαῖς	ὑπερβαλλόντως,]	ἐν	θανάτοις	πολλάκις.
plēgais	huperballontōs	en	thanatois	pollakis
stripes	excessively,]	in	deaths	often.

	5097.3 prep	2428.3 name-adj gen pl masc	3862.1 adv	4910.2 num card
24.	ὑπὸ	Ἰουδαίων	πεντάκις	⸃ τεσσαράκοντα
	hupo	Ioudaiōn	pentakis	tessarakonta
	From	Jews	five times	forty

4910.1 num card	3706.2 prep	1518.8 num card acc fem	2956.12 verb indic aor act	4994.1 adv
[τεσσεράκοντα]	παρὰ	μίαν	ἔλαβον,	25. τρὶς
tesserakonta	para	mian	elabon	tris
[idem]	except	one	I received.	Three

4320.3 verb 1sing indic aor pass	526.1 adv	3008.6 verb 1sing indic aor pass	4994.1 adv
ἐρραβδίσθην,	ἅπαξ	ἐλιθάσθην,	τρὶς
errhabdisthēn	hapax	elithasthēn	tris
I was beaten with rods,	once	I was stoned,	three times

3352.1 verb 1sing indic aor act	3436.1 noun acc sing neu	1706.1 prep	3450.3 art dat sing	1030.1 noun dat sing masc
ἐναυάγησα,	νυχθήμερον	ἐν	τῷ	βυθῷ
enauagēsa	nuchthēmeron	en	tō	buthō
I was shipwrecked,	a night and a day	in	the	deep

4020.42 verb 1sing indic perf act		3460.2 noun dat pl fem	4038.1 adv	2766.2 noun dat pl masc
πεποίηκα·	26.	ὁδοιπορίαις	πολλάκις·	κινδύνοις
pepoiēka		hodoiporiais	pollakis	kindunois
I have passed:		in journeyings	often,	in perils

questioned his birth and background. They probably pictured him as not being a "real" Jew. If so he would not have moved in Gentile circles as a minister. The Ebionites, a First Century Jewish sect, spread a rumor that Paul was a Gentile by birth.

In response, the apostle said he was as much a Hebrew, an Israelite (a seed, a descendant of Abraham), as they. As in writing to the Philippians, he reasoned if anyone had a right to brag about the nobility of his birth he had even more (Philippians 3:4-6).

11:23. Paul said, "So they proudly proclaim they are the ministers, servants of Christ, do they? Well, I am even more so!" Yet immediately the apostle's modesty compelled him to apologize again. This time he termed such boasting of self sheer madness. He played the part of a fool (*paraphronōn*, "one beside himself," stronger than *aphron* in verses 16 and 19).

If the opposition wanted a comparison between his ministry and theirs, he would oblige. Was their work demanding? He worked harder. Had they suffered stripes, felt the blows on their back for preaching? He had known the experience "above measure," to a much greater degree than his critics. If they had been behind bars for Jesus' sake, he had been imprisoned more frequently. He had even been near death often as he faced angry mobs.

11:24. Fellow Jews had beaten Paul with 39 stripes on 5 different occasions. The law of Moses limited such punishment to 40 blows, but Jewish custom permitted only 39 lest a miscount go beyond what the Law allowed (Deuteronomy 25:3).

11:25. The apostle also suffered at the hands of the Gentiles. He had been sentenced (likely in a Roman court) to a beating with rods three different times. He knew one such experience as a pioneer pastor at Philippi, though the punishment he received was illegally administered (Acts 16:23-37).

Once the apostle was stoned by those of his own people. At Lystra Jewish rebels persuaded a mob to illegally stone Paul. Afterward they dragged him outside the city leaving him for dead (Acts 14:19). However, wondrously the Lord raised him up. He immediately returned to the city and the next day continued on his journey in ministry (Acts 14:20).

The apostle had also suffered shipwreck. In fact, once he spent a day and night (*nuchthēmeron*, literally 24 hours) adrift in the depth of the sea. Luke did not record the account of this incident in Paul's life in Acts. The story he told of the sea disaster during the voyage to Rome came some time after Paul wrote this epistle.

11:26. The apostle next listed several pairs of perils he faced in his many travels. These dangers that confronted him daily no doubt

Are they Israelites? so [am] I: I too! *Rotherham.*

Are they the seed of Abraham? so [am] I: . . . descendants of, *Weymouth* . . . the offspring of, *HistNT* . . . the posterity, *Sawyer* . . . from the family of, *NLT.*

23. Are they ministers of Christ?: Are they servants of, *Weymouth.*

(I speak as a fool) I [am] more: I [am] above [them], *PNT* . . . as if I were out of my mind, *Weymouth* . . . like one out of his senses, *HistNT* . . . (in defect of understanding, I say it,) I am superior, *Murdock.*

in labours more abundant: Overflowing in hard work, *Klingensmith* . . . I have labored harder, *Adams* . . . with measureless toils, *Berkeley* . . . I have done more work than anyone else, *Norlie.*

in stripes above measure: . . . suffered innumerable lashings, *Adams* . . . in Scourges to excess, *Wilson* . . . by excessively cruel floggings, *Weymouth.*

in prisons more frequent: . . . in bonds, *Murdock* . . . far more imprisonments, *NASB.*

in deaths oft: . . . facing death so frequently, *Berkeley* . . . often exposed to death, *Confraternity* . . . in the jaws of death, *Adams.*

24. Of the Jews five times received I forty [stripes] save one: Five times the Jews gave me a whipping, *Norlie* . . . was I scourged, *Murdock* . . . less one, *Wilson.*

25. Thrice was I beaten with rods: . . . with Roman rods, *Weymouth* . . . I have been scourged by the Romans, *Montgomery.*

once was I stoned, thrice I suffered shipwreck:

a night and a day I have been in the deep: . . . was floating on the open sea, *Weymouth* . . . I have been adrift at sea, *Berkeley* . . . in a swamp, *Concordant.*

26. [In] journeyings often: . . . by frequent travelling, *Weymouth* . . . During frequent Journeys, *Wilson* . . . I've traveled much, *Beck.*

2 Corinthians 11:27

4074.6 noun gen pl masc	2766.2 noun dat pl masc	3001.4 noun gen pl masc	2766.2 noun dat pl masc	1523.2 prep gen
ποταμῶν,	κινδύνοις	λῃστῶν,	κινδύνοις	ἐκ
potamōn	*kindunois*	*lēstōn*	*kindunois*	*ek*
of rivers,	in perils	of robbers,	in perils	from

1079.2 noun gen sing neu	2766.2 noun dat pl masc	1523.1 prep gen	1477.5 noun gen pl neu	2766.2 noun dat pl masc	1706.1 prep
γένους,	κινδύνοις	ἐξ	ἐθνῶν,	κινδύνοις	ἐν
genous	*kindunois*	*ex*	*ethnōn*	*kindunois*	*en*
race,	in perils	from	Gentiles,	in perils	in

4032.3 noun dat sing fem	2766.2 noun dat pl masc	1706.1 prep	2030.2 noun dat sing fem	2766.2 noun dat pl masc	1706.1 prep
πόλει,	κινδύνοις	ἐν	ἐρημίᾳ,	κινδύνοις	ἐν
polei	*kindunois*	*en*	*erēmia*	*kindunois*	*en*
city,	in perils	in	desert,	in perils	in

27.a.**Txt:** 01ℵ-corr,018K 020L,025P,byz.Sod **Var:** 01ℵ-org,03B,06D Lach,Treg,Alf,Word Tisc,We/Ho,Weis UBS/★

2258.3 noun dat sing fem	2766.2 noun dat pl masc	1706.1 prep	5404.1 noun dat pl masc	1706.1 prep
θαλάσσῃ,	κινδύνοις	ἐν	ψευδαδέλφοις·	**27.** ⸂a ἐν ⸃
thalassē	*kindunois*	*en*	*pseudadelphois*	*en*
sea,	in perils	among	false brothers;	in

2845.3 noun dat sing masc	2504.1 conj	3313.1 noun dat sing masc	1706.1 prep	69.1 noun dat pl fem	4038.1 adv
κόπῳ	καὶ	μόχθῳ,	ἐν	ἀγρυπνίαις	πολλάκις,
kopō	*kai*	*mochthō*	*en*	*agrupniais*	*pollakis*
labor	and	toil,	in	sleeplessness	often,

1706.1 prep	3016.2 noun dat sing masc	2504.1 conj	1367.1 noun dat sing neu	1706.1 prep	3383.4 noun dat pl fem
ἐν	λιμῷ	καὶ	δίψει,	ἐν	νηστείαις
en	*limō*	*kai*	*dipsei*	*en*	*nēsteiais*
in	hunger	and	thirst,	in	fastings

4038.1 adv	1706.1 prep	5427.2 noun dat sing neu	2504.1 conj	1126.3 noun dat sing fem	5400.1 prep gen
πολλάκις,	ἐν	ψύχει	καὶ	γυμνότητι·	**28.** χωρὶς
pollakis	*en*	*psuchei*	*kai*	*gumnotēti*	*chōris*
often,	in	cold	and	nakedness.	Besides

3450.1 art gen pl	3786.1 prep gen	3450.9 art nom sing fem	1983.1 noun nom sing fem	1466.2 prs-pron gen 1sing
τῶν	παρεκτὸς,	⸀ ἡ	ἐπισύστασίς	μου
tōn	*parektos*	*hē*	*episustasis*	*mou*
the things	without,	the	crowding	on me

28.a.**Txt:** 018K,020L 025P,byz. **Var:** 01ℵ-org,03B,33 Lach,Treg,Alf,Word Tisc,We/Ho,Weis,Sod UBS/★

3450.9 art nom sing fem	1971.1 noun nom sing fem	1466.4 prs-pron dat 1sing	3450.9 art nom sing fem	2567.2 prep	2232.4 noun acc sing fem
[a★ ἡ	ἐπίστασίς	μοι]	ἡ	καθ'	ἡμέραν,
hē	*epistasis*	*moi*	*hē*	*kath'*	*hēmeran*
[the	pressure	on me]	the	by	day,

3450.9 art nom sing fem	3178.1 noun nom sing fem	3820.14 adj gen pl fem	3450.1 art gen pl	1564.6 noun gen pl fem
ἡ	μέριμνα	πασῶν	τῶν	ἐκκλησιῶν.
hē	*merimna*	*pasōn*	*tōn*	*ekklēsiōn*
the	care	concerning all	the	assemblies.

4949.3 intr-pron nom sing	764.2 verb 3sing indic pres act	2504.1 conj	3620.2 partic	764.1 verb 1sing pres act	4949.3 intr-pron nom sing
29. τίς	ἀσθενεῖ,	καὶ	οὐκ	ἀσθενῶ;	τίς
tis	*asthenei*	*kai*	*ouk*	*asthenō*	*tis*
Who	is weak,	and	not	I am weak?	who

surpassed anything his critics at Corinth could brag about in their experience.

Paul risked his life when his travels demanded he cross swollen streams and rivers without bridges. The more sure footing of the journey on land brought the threat of robbers. He knew what it was to be in danger among his own countrymen, the Jews, as well as to face peril from the heathen, the Gentiles (*ethnōn*). He was not safe whether he was in the city or in the wilderness (uninhabited areas, the countryside). On board ship the storm could swallow him up at any time. The most painful thought of all to Paul, though, was the fact that he faced perils among false brethren.

11:27. Further, the apostle knew weariness from the toil of his labor. He suffered the pain of exertion and hardship. Sleepless nights caused by ministerial care forced their way into his place of sleep. Often he fasted of necessity due to lack of food. Sometimes he was even short of sufficient clothing.

No doubt Paul's fastings were often of a religious nature, though apparently not in this reference. Hughes wrote, "The 'fastings' should not here be taken to refer to self-imposed religious disciplines, but rather to the forgoing of meals in order that his work as a minister of Christ might not be interrupted. Inspired by the example of his Master, the will of God was paramount in his life, far more important than food and drink, for the impulse of his whole ministry was the realization that 'man shall not live by bread alone' and that his meat was to do the will of Him that had sent him, and to accomplish His work (Matthew 4:4; John 4:34)" (*The New London Commentary*, p.413).

11:28. Surely none of the "super apostles" could claim they suffered more than Paul. He was at the forefront of the battle. However, in addition to those items of personal abuse that came from without, the apostle carried a heavy burden for all the churches (*ekklēsiōn*, "assemblies") under his care. No doubt the constant threat of disruption from the false teachers made the load heavier.

The apostle did not just establish congregations and forget them. For example, some time after returning from their first missionary journey he said to Barnabas, "Let us go again and visit our brethren in every city where we have preached the word of the Lord, and see how they do" (Acts 15:36). As Ironside noted, "Paul carried the people of God upon his heart. He could not go into a place and labor for a while and then be through with them. They were still on his heart, and if they got into trouble, into difficulty, into dissension, it burdened him, and he took it to God and wrote letters to them and tried to help and bless" (p.249).

11:29. Paul feared lest any become fainthearted and give up. He felt keenly with people in their weaknesses. If he learned of anyone

[in] perils of waters: . . . amid dangers in crossing rivers, *Weymouth* . . . which I was exposed to danger, *Adams*.

[in] perils of robbers: . . . of bandits, *Montgomery*.

[in] perils by [mine own] countrymen: . . . from kindred, *Young*.

[in] perils by the heathen: . . . from the people who do not know God, *NLT* . . . from the pagans, *Klingensmith*.

[in] perils in the city: . . . in towns, *TCNT*.

[in] perils in the wilderness: . . . in perils in desert, *Rotherham* . . . dangers in the country, *TCNT* . . . in the open country, *Klingensmith* . . . in lonely places, *Way*.

[in] perils in the sea:

[in] perils among false brethren: . . . dangers from spies in our midst, *Weymouth* . . . from traitors disguised as fellow-believers, *Way* . . . among sham brothers, *Berkeley* . . . from false friends, *Beck*.

27. In weariness and painfulness: I have experienced hard work, *Norlie* . . . in labor and travail, *ASV, Hanson* . . . in toil and hardship, *Rotherham*.

in watchings often: . . . often in sleepless watchings, *Conybeare* . . . in vigils many a time, *HistNT*.

in hunger and thirst:

in fastings often: . . . often without food, *RSV*.

in cold and nakedness: . . . poorly clad and exposed to cold, *Williams* . . . and exposure, *NASB*.

28. Beside those things that are without: Apart from all the rest, *HistNT* . . . Besides these experiences, *Berkeley* . . . besides these outward trials, *Adams*.

that which cometh upon me daily: . . . which presseth upon, *ASV* . . . is imposed on me, *Rotherham*.

the care of all the churches: . . . the anxious care, *Wilson* . . . there is my concern for all the churches, *Williams*.

29. Who is weak, and I am not weak?: Who is infirm, *Young* . . . but I share his weakness? *Conybeare*.

4479.6 verb 3sing indic pres pass	2504.1 conj	3620.2 partic	1466.1 prs-pron nom 1sing	4306.1 verb 1sing indic pres pass
σκανδαλίζεται,	καὶ	οὐκ	ἐγὼ	πυροῦμαι;
skandalizetai	kai	ouk	egō	puroumai
is being offended,	and	not	I	am being burned?

1479.1 conj	2714.10 verb inf pres	1158.1 verb 3sing indic pres act	3450.17 art pl neu	3450.10 art gen sing fem
30. Εἰ	καυχᾶσθαι	δεῖ,	τὰ	τῆς
Ei	kauchasthai	dei	ta	tēs
If	to boast	it is necessary,	the things	of the

763.1 noun fem	1466.2 prs-pron gen 1sing	2714.16 verb 1sing indic fut mid	3450.5 art sing masc	2296.1 noun nom sing masc
ἀσθενείας	μου	καυχήσομαι.	**31.** Ὁ	θεὸς
astheneias	mou	kauchēsomai	Ho	theos
weakness	my	I will boast.	The	God

31.a.Txt: 06D,025P,byz. bo.
Var: 01א,03B,018K 020L,Lach,Treg,Alf Word,Tisc,We/Ho,Weis Sod,UBS/★

2504.1 conj	3824.1 noun nom sing masc	3450.2 art gen sing	2935.2 noun gen sing masc	2231.2 prs-pron gen 1pl	2400.2 name masc
καὶ	πατὴρ	τοῦ	κυρίου	⌐a ἡμῶν ⌐	Ἰησοῦ
kai	patēr	tou	kuriou	hēmōn	Iēsou
and	Father	of the	Lord	our	Jesus

31.b.Txt: 06D,018K 020L,025P,byz.
Var: 01א,03B,33,Lach Treg,Alf,Tisc,We/Ho Weis,Sod,UBS/★

5382.2 name gen masc	3471.4 verb 3sing indic perf act	3450.5 art sing masc	1498.21 verb sing masc part pres act	2109.1 adj nom sing masc
⌐b Χριστοῦ ⌐	οἶδεν,	ὁ	ὢν	εὐλογητὸς
Christou	oiden	ho	ōn	eulogētos
Christ	knows,	the	being	blessed

1519.1 prep	3450.8 art acc pl masc	163.6 noun acc pl masc	3617.1 conj	3620.3 partic	5409.1 verb 1sing indic pres	1706.1 prep
εἰς	τοὺς	αἰῶνας,	ὅτι	οὐ	ψεύδομαι.	**32.** ἐν
eis	tous	aiōnas	hoti	ou	pseudomai	en
to	the	ages,	that	not	I do lie.	In

1149.1 name dat fem	3450.5 art sing masc	1474.1 noun nom sing masc	696.2 name gen masc	3450.2 art gen sing	928.2 noun gen sing masc
Δαμασκῷ	ὁ	ἐθνάρχης	Ἁρέτα	τοῦ	βασιλέως
Damaskō	ho	ethnarchēs	Hareta	tou	basileōs
Damascus	the	ethnarch	of Aretas	the	king

5268.2 verb 3sing indic imperf act	3450.12 art acc sing fem	1148.1 name-adj gen pl masc	4032.4 noun acc sing fem	4032.4 noun acc sing fem
ἐφρούρει	τὴν	⌐ Δαμασκηνῶν	πόλιν,	[★ πόλιν
ephrourei	tēn	Damaskēnōn	polin	polin
was guarding	the	of the Damascenes	city,	[city

32.a.Txt: 01א,06D-corr 015H,018K,020L,025P 044,33,byz.Sod
Var: 03B,06D-org,it.sa. Lach,Treg,Word,Tisc We/Ho,Weis,UBS/★

1148.1 name-adj gen pl masc	3945.6 verb inf aor act	1466.6 prs-pron acc 1sing	2286.12 verb nom sing masc part pres act	2504.1 conj
Δαμασκηνῶν]	πιάσαι	με	⌐a θέλων ⌐	**33.** καὶ
Damaskēnōn	piasai	me	thelōn	kai
of the Damascenes]	to take	me	wishing.	And

1217.2 prep	2353.1 noun gen sing fem	1706.1 prep	4410.1 noun dat sing fem	5301.6 verb 1sing indic aor pass	1217.2 prep
διὰ	θυρίδος	ἐν	σαργάνῃ	ἐχαλάσθην	διὰ
dia	thuridos	en	sarganē	echalasthēn	dia
through	a window	in	a basket	I was let down	through

3450.2 art gen sing	4886.2 noun gen sing neu	2504.1 conj	1614.1 verb indic aor act	3450.15 art acc pl fem	5331.8 noun acc pl fem	840.3 prs-pron gen sing
τοῦ	τείχους,	καὶ	ἐξέφυγον	τὰς	χεῖρας	αὐτοῦ.
tou	teichous	kai	exephugon	tas	cheiras	autou
the	wall,	and	escaped	the	hands	his.

who had been offended (*skandalizetai*, English *scandalized*) or caught in a trap, he burned with indignation against sin and its causes. Likely the false apostles at Corinth had wrecked the faith of some.

11:30. In his battle with the critics at Corinth Paul felt compelled to boast about his ministry. However, he again declared he would glory only of those things which revealed his infirmities. Circumstances which made clear his weakness forced him to lean on the Lord for strength. In this way God was glorified.

11:31. The opposition at Corinth had first accused Paul of doing little in the ministry in comparison to them. Now that the apostle had given a long list of his experiences to show them wrong, he realized the next plot to discredit him would probably include suggestions he had exaggerated his case.

Accordingly, he called God to witness that he was telling the truth. He declared the "God and Father of our Lord Jesus Christ" knew he did not lie. He tried to deceive no one in what he wrote. Earlier in this letter he had likewise protested, "I call God for a record upon my soul" (1:23). Elsewhere he affirmed he spoke the truth in Christ and did not lie (Romans 9:1; Galatians 1:20; 1 Timothy 2:7).

Contrary to the thinking of some, Jesus did not forbid the taking of such "oaths" in a legal setting when He said, "Swear not at all" (Matthew 5:34). God instructed His people early on that matter. Moses taught them to "swear by his name" (Deuteronomy 6:13). Then it is not wrong to sincerely say "so help me God" when testifying in court. When Pilate stated, "I adjure thee by the living God," Jesus knew He had been placed under oath and answered accordingly (Matthew 26:63).

Interestingly, as the apostle called upon God to witness his truthfulness, he could not help but insert an exclamation of worship to Him. "May He be blessed (*eulogētos*, 'to speak well of'), praised for evermore," he said.

11:32,33. Paul gave one final example of hardships through which God had been glorified in his life. The experience was from the early days of his ministry. The governor at Damascus sought to arrest him with an intent to turn him over to the Jews. In the attempt he posted guards at every gate of the city watching all who went out, day or night (Acts 9:24).

By the grace of God and the assistance of his fellow believers the apostle escaped. From a house built on the wall of the city through one of its windows they let him down in a hamperlike basket, no doubt under the cover of darkness.

who is offended, and I burn not?: Who is hindered, *HistNT* ... Who is made to stumble, *Confraternity* ... Who is led astray into sin, and I am not aflame with indignation? *Weymouth* ... who is in danger of stumbling, *Noyes* ... without my suffering grief? *Berkeley* ... but I burn with indignation, *Montgomery*.

30. If I must needs glory: If I must boast, *Campbell*.
I will glory of the things which concern mine infirmities: ... boast of what pertains to my weakness, *NASB* ... the things which belong to my weakness, *Noyes* ... that show my weakness! *Williams*.

31. The God and Father of our Lord Jesus Christ, which is blessed for evermore: ... who is blessed throughout the ages, *Weymouth* ... to the remotest ages, *Rotherham*.
knoweth that I lie not: ... is aware that I am not lying, *Concordant* ... knows That I do not falsify, *Wilson*.

32. In Damascus the governor under Aretas the king: ... the big chief, *Klingensmith* ... the commander of the army, *Murdock*.
kept the city of the Damascenes with a garrison: ... had the gates of that city guarded, *TCNT* ... guarded the city, *Fenton* ... kept watch over, *Alford*.
desirous to apprehend me: ... intending to, *Campbell* ... wishing to seize me, *Young* ... wishing to capture me, *Norlie* ... in order to catch me, *Fenton* ... wanting to arrest me, *Concordant*.

33. And through a window in a basket was I let down by the wall: ... through an opening, *Hanson, Weymouth*.
and escaped his hands: ... and fled out of his hands, *Young* ... and ran away from his hands, *Klingensmith* ... and escaped from his grip, *Berkeley* ... escaped from his clutches, *Williams* ... slipped through his fingers, *Way*.

12:1. Καυχᾶσθαι
2714.10 verb inf pres
Kauchasthai
To boast

δὴ
1205.1 partic
dē
indeed

οὐ
3620.3 partic
ou
not

συμφέρον
4702.2 verb sing neu part pres act
sumpheron
being profitable

μοι·
1466.4 prs-pron dat 1sing
moi
to me;

1.a.Txt: 018K,byz.
Var: p46,03B,(025P),33
Lach,Treg,Tisc,We/Ho
Weis,Sod,UBS/☆

[ᵃ☆ δεῖ·
1158.1 verb 3sing indic pres act
dei
[it is necessary

οὐ
3620.3 partic
ou
not

συμφέρον
4702.2 verb sing neu part pres act
sumpheron
being profitable,]

μέν,]
3173.1 conj
men

ἐλεύσομαι
2048.54 verb 1sing indic fut mid
eleusomai
I will come

1.b.Txt: 06D,018K,020L
byz.Sod
Var: 01‭ℵ‬,03B,025P,33
Lach,Treg,Tisc,We/Ho
Weis,UBS/☆

γὰρ
1056.1 conj
gar
for

[ᵇ☆ δὲ]
1156.2 conj
de
[but]

εἰς
1519.1 prep
eis
to

ὀπτασίας
3564.3 noun acc pl fem
optasias
visions

καὶ
2504.1 conj
kai
and

ἀποκαλύψεις
597.6 noun acc pl fem
apokalupseis
revelations

κυρίου·
2935.2 noun gen sing masc
kuriou
of Lord.

2. οἶδα
3471.2 verb 1sing indic perf act
oida
I know

ἄνθρωπον
442.4 noun acc sing masc
anthrōpon
a man

ἐν
1706.1 prep
en
in

Χριστῷ
5382.3 name dat masc
Christō
Christ

πρὸ
4112.1 prep
pro
before

ἐτῶν
2073.4 noun gen pl neu
etōn
years

δεκατεσσάρων,
1175.2 num card gen
dekatessarōn
fourteen,

εἴτε
1521.1 conj
eite
whether

ἐν
1706.1 prep
en
in

σώματι
4835.3 noun dat sing neu
sōmati
body

οὐκ
3620.2 partic
ouk
not

οἶδα·
3471.2 verb 1sing indic perf act
oida
I know,

εἴτε
1521.1 conj
eite
or

ἐκτὸς
1609.1 prep gen
ektos
out of

τοῦ
3450.2 art gen sing
tou
the

σώματος
4835.2 noun gen sing neu
sōmatos
body

οὐκ
3620.2 partic
ouk
not

οἶδα,
3471.2 verb 1sing indic perf act
oida
I know,

ὁ
3450.5 art sing masc
ho

θεὸς
2296.1 noun nom sing masc
theos
God

οἶδεν
3471.4 verb 3sing indic perf act
oiden
knows,

ἁρπαγέντα
720.10 verb acc sing masc part aor pass
harpagenta
having been caught away

τὸν
3450.6 art acc sing masc
ton
the

τοιοῦτον
4955.2 dem-pron acc sing
toiouton
such a one

ἕως
2175.1 conj
heōs
to

τρίτου
4995.2 num ord gen sing
tritou
third

οὐρανοῦ.
3636.2 noun gen sing masc
ouranou
heaven.

3. καὶ
2504.1 conj
kai
And

οἶδα
3471.2 verb 1sing indic perf act
oida
I know

τὸν
3450.6 art acc sing masc
ton
the

τοιοῦτον
4955.2 dem-pron acc sing
toiouton
such

ἄνθρωπον,
442.4 noun acc sing masc
anthrōpon
a man,

εἴτε
1521.1 conj
eite
whether

3.a.Txt: 01‭ℵ‬,06D-corr
018K,020L,025P,byz.
Sod
Var: p46,03B,06D-org
Lach,Treg,Alf,Tisc
We/Ho,Weis,UBS/☆

ἐν
1706.1 prep
en
in

σώματι
4835.3 noun dat sing neu
sōmati
body

εἴτε
1521.1 conj
eite
or

ἐκτός
1609.1 prep gen
ektos
out of

[ᵃ☆ χωρὶς]
5400.1 prep gen
chōris
[apart from]

τοῦ
3450.2 art gen sing
tou
the

σώματος
4835.2 noun gen sing neu
sōmatos
body

οὐκ
3620.2 partic
ouk
not

οἶδα·
3471.2 verb 1sing indic perf act
oida
I know,

ὁ
3450.5 art sing masc
ho

θεὸς
2296.1 noun nom sing masc
theos
God

οἶδεν·
3471.4 verb 3sing indic perf act
oiden
knows:

12:1. Though Paul felt obligated to boast of some of his experiences as a preacher under the present circumstances, he knew the dangers involved. Generally, such was not expedient (helpful, profitable). However, he concluded he must speak further of some of the remarkable things the Lord had done for him. These included visions in which he saw genuine images of heavenly things. They also brought him revelations (disclosures, knowledge) from above. The risen Lord communicated to him his understanding of the gospel in this way (Galatians 1:11,12).

12:2. Again, though, as Paul spoke of one of his most wonderful experiences he did so with extreme modesty. He talked about it in the third person. In that way he took himself out of the picture and gave all credit to the Lord. He rehearsed what happened to "a man" more than 14 years before. Apparently he had told no one of this event. Much less had he ever boasted about it.

Some wonder, though, if Paul was actually writing of himself. Harris responds: "Undoubtedly so, for several reasons: (1) He knew the exact time the revelation took place (v.2) and that its content was beyond words even if it were permissible to try to communicate it (v.4). (2) The revelation was directly related to the receipt of a 'thorn,' which was given, says Paul, 'to me' (v.7). (3) The reference to a lack of awareness whether he was in the body or not (vv.2,3) points to a personal experience. (4) Paul would be unlikely to feel embarrassment (cf.1) about boasting on another person's behalf (cf. v.5a). (5) For Paul to relate a remarkable experience that happened to some Christian unknown to the Corinthians but known to Paul would scarcely fit the context" (*The Expositor's Bible Commentary*, 10:395).

He was not certain whether that man was in the body or out of the body during the experience. Only God knew for sure. At any rate, it was the most sacred and personal event of his life. It took him to the third heaven. The first heaven is the atmosphere. The second is that of outer space. It houses the sun, moon, and stars. The third is the place of God's abode. He later called it paradise (verse 4).

12:3. Certainly, the apostle wrote not of his conversion here, as glorious as that was. That had happened 20 years before, and he often spoke of it. He may have been speaking of what took place at Lystra as he was stoned and dragged out of the city by the mob, "supposing he had been dead" (Acts 14:19). So twice in recalling the matter he declared whether "the man" was dead or alive at the moment, he knew not. Only God did.

To be certain, though, the experience gave him a taste of what all believers will know in eternity. When body and soul are separated at death, blessed consciousness continues. Even more wonderful, death does not interrupt fellowship with God. Actually, that fellowship becomes enhanced.

1. It is not expedient for me doubtless to glory: I must needs boast, *Alford* . . . I have to keep on boasting, *Williams* . . . although there is no advantage in doing so, *Adams* . . . there is nothing to gain by it, *NTPE* . . . I am forced to boast, though it is unprofitable, *Montgomery* . . . I am compelled to boast. It is not a profitable employment, *Weymouth* . . . It is not profitable, *Hanson* . . . it is not proper, *Macknight* . . . It is necessary to glory, though it is not indeed profitable, *Clementson*.

I will come to visions and revelations of the Lord: I will pass on to a worthier subject, *Way* . . . to apparitions, *Concordant* . . . what the Lord has shown and told me, *Beck* . . . that I have had, *Norlie*.

2. I knew a man in Christ above fourteen years ago: . . . all this happened fourteen years ago, *Way*.

(whether in the body, I cannot tell: I have not known, *Young* . . . I know not, *Hanson* . . . whether it was an actual physical experience, *Phillips* . . . I am not aware, *Concordant*.

or whether out of the body, I cannot tell:

God knoweth;): . . . that is known to God alone, *Way*.

such an one caught up to the third heaven: . . . was taken up, *NLT* . . . suddenly conveyed away, *Wilson, Campbell* . . . carried up as far as the third heaven, *Fenton* . . . was snatched away to the third heaven, *Adams, Concordant* . . . to the highest heaven, *Weymouth*.

3. And I knew such a man: But I know such a person, *SEB*.

(whether in the body, or out of the body: Again, I don't know, *SEB* . . . whether in or outside, *NAB* . . . or apart from, *Montgomery* . . . or separated from, *TCNT*.

I cannot tell: God knoweth;):

4. 3617.1 conj
ὅτι
hoti
that

720.8 verb 3sing indic aor pass
ἡρπάγη
hērpagē
he was caught away

1519.1 prep
εἰς
eis
to

3450.6 art acc sing masc
τὸν
ton

3719.3 noun acc sing masc
παράδεισον,
paradeison
Paradise,

2504.1 conj
καὶ
kai
and

189.21 verb 3sing indic aor act
ἤκουσεν
ēkousen
heard

725.1 adj acc pl neu
ἄρρητα
arrhēta
unutterable

4343.4 noun pl neu
ῥήματα,
rhēmata
sayings,

3614.17 rel-pron pl neu
ἃ
ha
which

3620.2 partic
οὐκ
ouk
not

1815.2 verb nom sing neu part pres act
ἐξὸν
exon
being permitted

442.3 noun dat sing masc
ἀνθρώπῳ
anthrōpō
to man

2953.37 verb inf aor act
λαλῆσαι.
lalēsai
to speak.

5. 5065.1 prep
ὑπὲρ
huper
Concerning

3450.2 art gen sing
τοῦ
tou
the

4955.5 dem-pron gen sing masc
τοιούτου
toioutou
such a one

2714.16 verb 1sing indic fut mid
καυχήσομαι·
kauchēsomai
I will boast,

5065.1 prep
ὑπὲρ
huper
concerning

1156.2 conj
δὲ
de
but

1670.1 prs-pron gen 1sing masc
ἐμαυτοῦ
emautou
myself

3620.3 partic
οὐ
ou
not

2714.16 verb 1sing indic fut mid
καυχήσομαι,
kauchēsomai
I will boast,

1479.1 conj
εἰ
ei
if

3231.1 partic
μὴ
mē
not

1706.1 prep
ἐν
en
in

3450.14 art dat pl fem
ταῖς
tais
the

763.6 noun dat pl fem
ἀσθενείαις
astheneiais
weaknesses

5.a.**Txt:** 01א,06D-corr 018K,020L,025P,byz. Tisc,Sod
Var: 03B,06D-org,33,bo. Lach,Treg,We/Ho,Weis UBS/✱

1466.2 prs-pron gen 1sing
[a μου]
mou
my.

6. 1430.1 partic
ἐὰν
ean
If

1056.1 conj
γὰρ
gar
for

2286.26 verb 1sing subj aor act
θελήσω
thelēsō
I should desire

2714.14 verb inf aor mid
καυχήσασθαι,
kauchēsasthai
to boast,

3620.2 partic
οὐκ
ouk
not

1498.38 verb 1sing indic fut mid
ἔσομαι
esomai
I shall be

871.1 adj sing masc
ἄφρων·
aphrōn
a fool;

223.4 noun acc sing fem
ἀλήθειαν
alētheian
truth

1056.1 conj
γὰρ
gar
for

2029.9 verb 1sing indic fut act
ἐρῶ·
erō
I will say;

5177.1 verb 1sing indic pres
φείδομαι
pheidomai
I refrain

1156.2 conj
δέ,
de
but,

3231.1 partic
μή
mē
not

4948.3 indef-pron nom sing
τις
tis
anyone

1519.1 prep
εἰς
eis
as to

1466.7 prs-pron acc 1sing
ἐμὲ
eme
me

6.a.**Txt:** 01א-corr 06D-org,018K,020L 025P,byz.
Var: 01א-org,03B 06D-corr,33,Lach,Treg Tisc,We/Ho,Weis,Sod UBS/✱

3023.13 verb 3sing subj aor mid
λογίσηται
logisētai
should reckon

5065.1 prep
ὑπὲρ
huper
above

3614.16 rel-pron sing neu
ὃ
ho
what

984.4 verb 3sing indic pres act
βλέπει
blepei
he sees

1466.6 prs-pron acc 1sing
με,
me
me,

2211.1 conj
ἤ
ē
or

189.5 verb 3sing indic pres act
ἀκούει
akouei
hears

4948.10 indef-pron sing neu
[a τι]
ti
anything

1523.1 prep gen
ἐξ
ex
of

1466.3 prs-pron gen 1sing
ἐμοῦ
emou
me.

7.a.**Var:** 01א,02A,03B 33,bo.Lach,Treg,Alf We/Ho,Weis,Sod UBS/✱

7. 2504.1 conj
Καὶ
Kai
And

3450.11 art dat sing fem
τῇ
tē
by the

7.b.**Txt:** p46,01א-corr2 044,0243,byz.
Var: 01א-org,02A,06D 010F,012G,33,629-org

5073.2 noun dat sing fem
ὑπερβολῇ
huperbolē
excess

3450.1 art gen pl
τῶν
tōn
of the

597.5 noun gen pl fem
ἀποκαλύψεων
apokalupseōn
revelations

1346.1 conj
[a✱+ διό,]
dio
[wherefore,]

2419.1 conj
[b ἵνα
hina
that

12:4. This marvelous experience took the man into paradise. The word used spoke of a garden, a park. The Septuagint used it for the Garden of Eden. To the dying thief who believed, Jesus said, "Today shalt thou be with me in paradise" (Luke 23:43). Then Jesus himself went immediately there upon His death. To all who overcome, the Lord promised the privilege of eating of the tree of life which "is in the midst of the paradise of God" (Revelation 2:7).

While he was in that beautiful garden in the third heaven, the person of whom Paul wrote heard things too sacred to tell upon his return to earth. What he experienced was simply unspeakable. No human language could ever adequately describe what he saw and heard. Further, it was unlawful to speak of them. God did not permit a full account of it. What took place contained a message for "the man" alone.

12:5. Paul's paradise experience was by grace alone. The apostle could not possibly boast about it as if he accomplished it. Under the Spirit's control, he could but modestly glory of what happened as if he spoke of some other person's heavenly venture. Again he declared he would take pride only in his weaknesses for they forced him to rely on God.

12:6. On the other hand, if Paul were the kind of preacher who wanted to brag about himself, he could do so and not be as some fools were in the process. After all, he could relate some exciting things and just be telling the truth.

However, he refrained from writing of other heavenly experiences. He feared some might evaluate or esteem him more highly than they should. As with all men, to see Paul was to be aware of his humanity. If he spoke too much of wonders in his life and later some learned he was just another mortal, they might lose confidence in him and his gospel.

The apostle was determined that all should understand what he had explained before in this letter. He wrote, "We have this treasure in earthen vessels, that the excellency of the power may be of God, and not of us" (4:7). He wanted the faith of his converts to rest in the Lord, not man (1 Corinthians 2:5).

12:7. In Paul's life the Lord allowed events to combat pride. His eternal plan allows "that no flesh should glory in his presence" (1 Corinthians 1:29). With visions and revelations, there was a danger pride might raise its ugly head. To prevent this God permitted a thorn to come and remain in Paul's flesh. To stick a thorn in the foot is a most painful experience. Not to remove it to relieve the suffering is ordinarily unthinkable.

Many have speculated about Paul's thorn. One guess is it was some illness of the eyes because he wrote the Galatians with large

4. How that he was caught up into paradise:

and heard unspeakable words: . . . inexpressible words, *NASB* . . . unutterable utterances, *Rotherham* . . . indescribable things spoken, *Wilson* . . . unutterable ideas, *Fenton* . . . secret words *Confraternity.*

which it is not lawful for a man to utter: . . . that it is not possible for man to speak, *Young* . . . and that man must not repeat, *Norlie* . . . must not, be translated into human speech, *Phillips* . . . that it is not permissible, *Adams* . . . it is not permitted, *Murdock* . . . it is not granted to man to utter, *Douay* . . . no human being is allowed to repeat, *Berkeley* . . . to relate, *Wilson.*

5. Of such an one will I glory: yet of myself I will not glory:

but in mine infirmities: . . . save in weaknesses, *Panin.*

6. For though I would desire to glory: . . . if I were disposed to glory, *Murdock* . . . should choose to continue boasting, *Montgomery.*

I shall not be a fool: . . . it would not be vanity, *Norlie.*

for I will say the truth:

but [now] I forbear, lest any man should think of me above that which he seeth me [to be]: . . . but I refrain, *Hanson, Murdock* . . . in case anyone should esteem me beyond, *HistNT* . . . than what you see and hear about great revelations, *Klingensmith.*

or [that] he heareth of me:

7. And lest I should be exalted above measure through the abundance of the revelations: . . . keep me from feeling proud, *Beck* . . . be made overbearing by the sublimity of the revelations, *Fenton* . . . to prevent my becoming absurdly conceited, *Phillips* . . . including the superb fact of the revelations, *Berkeley* . . . by the transcendancy, *Wilson* . . . by reason of the exceeding greatness, *Hanson* . . . were so surpassingly wonderful, *Norlie* . . . lest I should be overelated...judging by the stupendous grandeur of the revelations, *Weymouth.*

3231.1 partic	5066.1 verb 1sing subj pres pass	1319.44 verb 3sing indic aor pass	1466.4 prs-pron dat 1sing	4502.1 noun nom sing masc
μὴ	ὑπεραίρωμαι, `	ἐδόθη	μοι	σκόλοψ
mē	huperairōmai	edothē	moi	skolops
not	I might be exalted,	was given	to me	a thorn

3450.11 art dat sing fem	4418.3 noun dat sing fem	32.1 noun nom sing masc	4423.5 noun sing masc	4423.2 noun sing masc
τῇ	σαρκί,	ἄγγελος	` Σατᾶν	[☆ Σατανᾶ,]
tē	sarki	angelos	Satan	Satana
for the	flesh,	a messenger	of Satan,	[idem]

2419.1 conj	1466.6 prs-pron acc 1sing	2826.1 verb 3sing subj pres act	2419.1 conj	3231.1 partic	5066.1 verb 1sing subj pres pass
ἵνα	με	κολαφίζῃ,	ἵνα	μὴ	ὑπεραίρωμαι.
hina	me	kolaphizē	hina	mē	huperairōmai
that	me	he might buffet,	that	not	I might be exalted.

	5065.1 prep	3642.1 dem-pron gen sing	4994.1 adv	3450.6 art acc sing masc	2935.4 noun acc sing masc
8.	ὑπὲρ	τούτου	τρὶς	τὸν	κύριον
	huper	toutou	tris	ton	kurion
	For	this	three times	the	Lord

3731.11 verb 1sing indic aor act	2419.1 conj	861.4 verb 3sing subj aor act	570.2 prep gen	1466.3 prs-pron gen 1sing	2504.1 conj
παρεκάλεσα,	ἵνα	ἀποστῇ	ἀπ'	ἐμοῦ·	**9.** καὶ
parekalesa	hina	apostē	ap'	emou	kai
I made request	that	it might depart	from	me,	And

2029.3 verb 3sing indic perf act	1466.4 prs-pron dat 1sing	708.1 verb 3sing indic pres act	4622.3 prs-pron dat 2sing	3450.9 art nom sing fem
εἴρηκέν	μοι,	Ἀρκεῖ	σοι	ἡ
eirēken	moi	Arkei	soi	hē
he has said	to me,	Sufficient for	you	the

9.a.**Txt**: 01ℵ-corr 02A-corr,06D-corr,018K 020L,025P,byz.bo.Sod
Var: p46,01ℵ-org 02A-org,03B,06D-org,sa. Lach,Treg,Alf,Tisc We/Ho,Weis,UBS/☆

5322.1 noun nom sing fem	1466.2 prs-pron gen 1sing	3450.9 art nom sing fem	1056.1 conj	1405.1 noun nom sing fem	1466.2 prs-pron gen 1sing
χάρις	μου·	ἡ	γὰρ	δύναμις	`a μου
charis	mou	hē	gar	dunamis	mou
grace	my;	the	for	power	my

9.b.**Txt**: 01ℵ-corr 06D-corr,018K,020L 025P,byz.
Var: 01ℵ-org,02A,03B 06D-org,Lach,Treg,Alf Tisc,We/Ho,Weis,Sod UBS/☆

1706.1 prep	763.3 noun dat sing fem	4896.8 verb 3sing indic pres pass	4903.15 verb 3sing indic pres pass	2219.1 adv sup
ἐν	ἀσθενείᾳ	` τελειοῦται.	[b☆ τελεῖται.]	ἥδιστα
en	astheneia	teleioutai	teleitai	hēdista
in	weakness	is being perfected.	[idem]	Most gladly

3631.1 conj	3095.1 adv comp	2714.16 verb 1sing indic fut mid	1706.1 prep	3450.14 art dat pl fem	763.6 noun dat pl fem
οὖν	μᾶλλον	καυχήσομαι	ἐν	ταῖς	ἀσθενείαις
oun	mallon	kauchēsomai	en	tais	astheneiais
therefore	rather	will I boast	in	the	weaknesses

9.c.**Txt**: 01ℵ,02A,06D 018K,020L,025P,byz.it. sa.Tisc,Sod
Var: 03B,bo.We/Ho Weis,UBS/☆

1466.2 prs-pron gen 1sing	2419.1 conj	1965.1 verb 3sing subj aor act	1894.2 prep	1466.7 prs-pron acc 1sing	3450.9 art nom sing fem
`c μου `	ἵνα	ἐπισκηνώσῃ	ἐπ'	ἐμὲ	ἡ
mou	hina	episkēnōsē	ep'	eme	hē
my	that	may dwell	upon	me	the

1405.1 noun nom sing fem	3450.2 art gen sing	5382.2 name gen masc	1346.1 conj	2085.1 verb 1sing indic pres act
δύναμις	τοῦ	Χριστοῦ.	**10.** διὸ	εὐδοκῶ
dunamis	tou	Christou	dio	eudokō
power	of the	Christ.	Wherefore	I take pleasure

letters and they were willing to give him their eyes if they could (Galatians 6:11; 4:15). Some liberals say the thorn was epilepsy and that his conversion experience on the road to Damascus was among his many seizures! This is unthinkable. Others think his problem was one of chronic attacks of malarial fever.

Paul said a messenger of Satan brought the thorn. The spirit buffeted (beat, struck as with the fist) and tortured him. The devil continuously slapped the apostle on the face, as the present subjunctive tense of the verb shows. Thus Paul followed the story of his most blessed experience in life (verses 2-4) with that of his deepest humiliation.

12:8. Little wonder, then, Paul talked to the Lord earnestly about removing such a thorn. He besought (intreated, implored, urgently appealed to) God three times for relief.

Even Jesus had three seasons of prayer for assistance in Gethsemane (Mark 14:35-41). Elijah petitioned for rain seven times before water fell from the sky (1 Kings 18:42-44). Daniel had to remain before the Lord for 21 days before his answer came (Daniel 10:12-14).

12:9. God's answer to Paul's prayer did not remove the thorn. The Lord sometimes gives a negative response to the most earnest petition. Instead it gave him assurance God would provide sufficient grace and divine strength to sustain him regardless of his trials. As the apostle himself declared in 1 Corinthians 10:13, with every temptation the Lord always provides a way of escape making it possible to bear up under the difficulty.

More wonderfully, though, God's power reaches its perfection through human weakness. As the smallest of light shines most brightly in the darkest of nights, the Lord reveals His strength most completely in the face of man's helplessness. As someone has said, Christians are somewhat like tea; their real strength does not show until they are in hot water.

Having learned the lesson Jesus taught him through the thorn, Paul experienced an attitude change. He came to the place where he could gladly glory in his weakness. He knew it was necessary for him to realize his helplessness in order for the power of Christ to rest upon him and become an overshadowing tent to cover him.

Hughes has warned against misusing the apostle's words here in following "the errors of a later ascetic theology which encouraged men to think that by means of self-inflicted bodily sufferings and indignities they could accumulate forgiveness of post-baptismal sins and justifying merit before God. That was a joyless theology of insecurity; whereas Paul's theology is one of unclouded joy and impregnable security . . ." (*The New London Commentary*, p.452). He concluded Paul's thorn was not self-induced but *given*.

there was given to me a thorn in the flesh: . . . like the agony of impalement, *Weymouth* . . . given a chronic pain in my body, *Norlie* . . . a sting of my flesh, *Douay* . . . a sharp spike was sent to pierce my flesh, *TCNT* . . . a splinter in the flesh, *Concordant*.

the messenger of Satan to buffet me: It bothered me like a satanic angel, *Norlie* . . . a messenger of the adversary, *Hanson* . . . an instrument of Satan, for my discipline, *TCNT* . . . the devil's messenger to plague me, *Beck* . . . to correct me, *Fenton* . . . that it might afflict me, *Wilson* . . . to beat me up, *Klingensmith* . . . to maltreat me, *Berkeley* . . . to slap me around, *Adams*.

lest I should be exalted above measure: . . . but it kept me from becoming puffed up, *Norlie* . . . so that I might not be haughty, *Fenton* . . . to keep me from being too much elated, *Way* . . . that I might not be too much lifted up, *Noyes*.

8. For this thing I besought the Lord thrice: Concerning this, *Alford* . . . Three times I begged, *Phillips, Williams* . . . I implored the Lord, *Fenton* . . . I invoked the Lord, *Berkeley*.

that it might depart from me: . . . to rid me of it, *Norlie*.

9. And he said unto me: . . . but His reply has been, *Weymouth* . . . He has protested to me, *Concordant*.

My grace is sufficient for thee: My help is sufficient for you, *Adams* . . . is enough, *HistNT*.

for my strength is made perfect in weakness: . . . for my power is completed, *Klingensmith* . . . for power matures in weakness, *Weymouth* . . . my power is shown the more completely, *Phillips* . . . My power is perfected in weakness, *Fenton* . . . is made complete, *Rotherham* . . . in infirmity, *Douay* . . . in the forge of infirmity, *Way*.

Most gladly therefore will I rather glory in my infirmities:

that the power of Christ may rest upon me: . . . that the strength of, *Hanson, Noyes* . . . that Christ's power might overshadow me, *Adams* . . . may settle upon me, *HistNT* . . . may dwell in me, *Confraternity, Douay*.

1706.1 prep
ἐν
en
in

763.6 noun dat pl fem
ἀσθενείαις,
astheneiais
weaknesses,

1706.1 prep
ἐν
en
in

5038.3 noun dat pl fem
ὕβρεσιν,
hubresin
insults,

1706.1 prep
ἐν
en
in

316.5 noun dat pl fem
ἀνάγκαις,
anankais
necessities,

1706.1 prep
ἐν
en
in

1369.5 noun dat pl masc
διωγμοῖς,
diōgmois
persecutions,

1706.1 prep
ἐν
en
in

2504.1 conj
[ᵃ☆ καὶ]
kai
[and]

4581.2 noun dat pl fem
στενοχωρίαις,
stenochōriais
difficulties

5065.1 prep
ὑπὲρ
huper
for

10.a.Txt: 01א-corr,06D 018K,020L,025P,33,byz. it.bo.Sod
Var: p46,01א-org,03B Tisc,We/Ho,Weis UBS/☆

5382.2 name gen masc
Χριστοῦ·
Christou
Christ:

3615.1 conj
ὅταν
hotan
when

1056.1 conj
γὰρ
gar
for

764.1 verb 1sing pres act
ἀσθενῶ,
asthenō
I may be weak,

4966.1 adv
τότε
tote
then

1409.1 adj nom sing masc
δυνατός
dunatos
powerful

1498.2 verb 1sing indic pres act
εἰμι.
eimi
I am.

1090.1 verb 1sing indic perf act
11. Γέγονα
Gegona
I have become

871.1 adj sing masc
ἄφρων
aphrōn
a fool

2714.7 verb nom sing masc part pres
⸂ᵃ καυχώμενος·⸃
kauchōmenos
boasting;

5050.1 prs-pron nom 2pl
ὑμεῖς
humeis
you

11.a.Txt: 020L,025P,byz.
Var: 01א,02A,03B,06D 018K,Gries,Lach,Treg Alf,Word,Tisc,We/Ho Weis,Sod,UBS/☆

1466.6 prs-pron acc 1sing
με
me
me

313.4 verb 2pl indic aor act
ἠναγκάσατε·
ēnankasate
compelled:

1466.1 prs-pron nom 1sing
ἐγὼ
egō
I

1056.1 conj
γὰρ
gar
for

3648.8 verb 1sing indic imperf act
ὤφειλον
ōpheilon
ought

5097.1 prep
ὑφ'
huph'
by

5050.2 prs-pron gen 2pl
ὑμῶν
humōn
you

4771.12 verb inf pres pass
συνίστασθαι·
sunistasthai
to have been commended;

3625.6 num card neu
οὐδὲν
ouden
nothing

1056.1 conj
γὰρ
gar
for

5139.5 verb 1sing indic aor act
ὑστέρησα
husterēsa
I was behind

3450.1 art gen pl
τῶν
tōn
the

5065.1 prep
⸂ ὑπὲρ
huper
beyond

5082.1 adv
[☆ ὑπερλίαν]
huperlian
[beyond measure]

3003.1 adv
λίαν
lian
exceedingly

646.5 noun gen pl masc
ἀποστόλων,
apostolōn
apostles,

1479.1 conj
εἰ
ei
if

2504.1 conj
καὶ
kai
also

3625.6 num card neu
οὐδέν
ouden
nothing

1498.2 verb 1sing indic pres act
εἰμι.
eimi
I am.

3450.17 art gen pl neu
12. Τὰ
Ta
The

3173.1 conj
μὲν
men
indeed

4447.2 noun pl neu
σημεῖα
sēmeia
signs

12.a.Txt: 06D-corr,018K 020L,025P,byz.bo.
Var: 01א,02A,03B 06D-org,33,Lach,Treg Alf,Word,Tisc,We/Ho Weis,Sod,UBS/☆

3450.2 art gen sing
τοῦ
tou
of the

646.2 noun gen sing masc
ἀποστόλου
apostolou
apostle

2686.8 verb 3sing indic aor pass
κατειργάσθη
kateirgasthē
were worked out

1706.1 prep
ἐν
en
among

5050.3 prs-pron dat 2pl
ὑμῖν
humin
you

1706.1 prep
ἐν
en
in

12.b.Txt: 06D-corr,018K 020L,025P,byz.bo.
Var: 01א-org,03B,33 Alf,Tisc,We/Ho Weis,Sod,UBS/☆

3820.11 adj dat sing fem
πάσῃ
pasē
all

5119.3 noun dat sing fem
ὑπομονῇ,
hupomonē
endurance,

1706.1 prep
⸂ᵃ ἐν ⸃
en
in

4447.4 noun dat pl neu
σημείοις
sēmeiois
signs

2504.1 conj
⸂ καὶ
kai
and

4885.1 conj
[ᵇ☆ τε
te
[both

2504.1 conj
καὶ]
kai
and]

4907.3 noun dat pl neu
τέρασιν
terasin
wonders

2504.1 conj
καὶ
kai
and

1405.7 noun dat pl fem
δυνάμεσιν.
dunamesin
works of power.

4949.9 intr-pron sing neu
13. τί
ti
In what

1056.1 conj
γὰρ
gar
for

12:10. The apostle declared again he delighted in and cheerfully accepted the fact of his human weakness. Then he revealed more of what the thorn involved. It included suffering reproaches (shame, insults, mistreatment) at the hands of his enemies. At times it brought necessities (privations and hardships). Periods of distress (difficulty, anguish) came with it.

Understandably, then, the apostle sought relief from such constant pressures. However, the lesson he learned by carrying a heavy burden was priceless. He came to know man's extremities are God's opportunities. As long as his suffering was for Christ's sake, he rested in the assurance that when circumstances pressed him to helplessness he would then, and only then, experience the help of the Lord. To say "when I am weak, then am I strong" sounds contradictory, but the paradox expresses a truth more valuable than gold.

Of course, not all suffering in the lives of Christians qualifies for such blessings as followed Paul's. As Peter warned, "Let none of you suffer as a murderer, or as a thief, or as an evildoer, or as a busybody in other men's matters" (1 Peter 4:15).

12:11. As if coming down to earth from the heights of ministerial argument, Paul for a final time said he was a fool to boast about himself as he had. The conduct of the opposition at Corinth forced him to it.

Instead of being compelled to self-vindication through circumstances, the apostle reasoned the Corinthians should have been commending him. After all, in nothing was he the least inferior to the "super apostles" among them. In times of conflict Christians can be wrong in failing to take a stand on the side of righteousness.

The "chiefest apostles" with Paul should have engaged in an honest appraisal of themselves. In that case they would have joined in chorus with him in saying "I am nothing" and not have been guilty of any false humility.

12:12. Instead, the critics bragged of miracles in their ministry as if done by their own hands. Paul said he too wrought wonders among them, but not by his strength. God blessed the integrity of his patient, steadfast endurance. The risen Saviour worked with him confirming the Word he preached as with His early followers (Mark 16:20).

The Lord granted signs which pointed men heavenward. The Spirit performed wonders to attract and hold the attention of men. Christ did mighty deeds and miracles, as needed to accomplish good in the lives of people.

The apostle sent a similar message concerning his ministry to the Romans (Romans 15:18,19). The writer of Hebrews also declared the Word "was confirmed unto us by them that heard him; God also bearing them witness, both with signs and wonders, and with divers miracles, and gifts of the Holy Ghost" (Hebrews 2:3,4).

10. Therefore I take pleasure in infirmities: I am contented, *Wilson* . . . That is why I delight in, *TCNT*.

in reproaches, in necessities: . . . in outrage, *Conybeare* . . . in insults, in dire needs, *KJII* . . . with injuries, *Sawyer* . . . with problems, *Klingensmith*.

in persecutions, in distresses for Christs's sake: . . . and calamities, *Norlie* . . . in dire calamities, *Berkeley* . . . and hard pressed for Christ, *Beck* . . . in behalf of Christ, *Noyes*.

for when I am weak, then am I strong: . . . when I am consciously weak, *Williams* . . . then am I powerful, *Rotherham*.

11. I am become a fool in glorying: I have been guilty of folly, *Conybeare* . . . I have been talking like some imbecile, *Way* . . . a Simpleton, *Wilson* . . . I am nutty, *Klingensmith*.

ye have compelled me: You have forced me, *Fenton* . . . You drove me to it, *Klingensmith* . . . You have constrained me to it, *Campbell*.

for I ought to have been commended of you: . . . ought to have been my vindicators, *Weymouth*.

for in nothing am I behind the very chiefest apostles: I am equal to your best missionaries, *Klingensmith* . . . was I inferior to the most eminent apostles, *Worrell* . . . I am not a single bit inferior to your surpassingly superior apostles, *Williams* . . . have I fallen short of the most eminent apostles, *Confraternity* . . . to these super-apostles, *Adams*.

though I be nothing: . . . even if I am rated as a nobody, *Norlie* . . . though I be of no account, *Conybeare*.

12. Truly the signs of an apostle were wrought among you in all patience: Certainly the criteria that distinguish the apostle, *Kleist* . . . The credentials of, *Fenton* . . . The signs that mark a true Apostle, *TCNT* . . . tokens of my apostolate, *Berkeley* . . . were performed, *Sawyer* . . . in all endurance, *Rotherham*.

in signs, and wonders, and mighty deeds: . . . and miraculous powers, *HistNT* . . . and by supernatural works, *Adams*.

2 Corinthians 12:14

13.a.Txt: 01א-corr,02A
06D-corr,018K,020L
025P,byz.Sod
Var: 01א-org,03B
06D-org,33,Lach,Treg
Alf,Tisc,We/Ho,Weis
UBS/✶

1498.4 verb 3sing indic pres act	3614.16 rel-pron sing neu	2252.1 verb 2pl indic aor pass	2056.1 verb 2pl indic aor pass
ἐστιν	ὃ	ʹ ἡττήθητε	[ᵃ✶ ἡσσώθητε]
estin	ho	hēttēthēte	hēssōthēte
is it	that	you were inferior	[idem]

5065.1 prep	3450.15 art acc pl fem	3036.6 adj acc pl fem	1564.1 noun fem	1479.1 conj	3231.1 partic
ὑπὲρ	τὰς	λοιπὰς	ἐκκλησίας,	εἰ	μὴ
huper	tas	loipas	ekklēsias	ei	mē
beyond	the	remaining	assemblies,	if	not

3617.1 conj	840.5 prs-pron nom sing masc	1466.1 prs-pron nom 1sing	3620.3 partic	2625.1 verb 1sing indic aor act	5050.2 prs-pron gen 2pl
ὅτι	αὐτὸς	ἐγὼ	οὐ	κατενάρκησα	ὑμῶν;
hoti	autos	egō	ou	katenarkēsa	humōn
that	myself	I	not	did burden	you?

5319.6 verb 2pl impr aor mid	1466.4 prs-pron dat 1sing	3450.12 art acc sing fem	92.4 noun acc sing fem	3642.12 dem-pron acc sing fem
χαρίσασθέ	μοι	τὴν	ἀδικίαν	ταύτην.
charisasthe	moi	tēn	adikian	tautēn
Forgive	me	the	injustice	this.

14.a.Var: 01א,02A,03B
sa.Gries,Lach,Treg,Alf
Word,Tisc,We/Ho,Weis
Sod,UBS/✶

1481.20 verb 2sing impr aor mid	4995.1 num ord sing	3642.17 dem-pron sing neu	2072.1 adv	2174.1 verb 1sing pres act
14. Ἰδοὺ	τρίτον	[ᵃ✶+ τοῦτο]	ἑτοίμως	ἔχω
Idou	triton	touto	hetoimōs	echō
Lo,	a third time	[this]	ready	I am

2048.23 verb inf aor act	4242.1 prep	5050.4 prs-pron acc 2pl	2504.1 conj	3620.3 partic	2625.2 verb 1sing indic fut act
ἐλθεῖν	πρὸς	ὑμᾶς,	καὶ	οὐ	καταναρκήσω
elthein	pros	humas	kai	ou	katanarkēsō
to come	to	you,	and	not	I will burden

14.b.Txt: 06D-corr,018K
020L,byz.it.
Var: 01א,02A,03B,33
Lach,Treg,Alf,Tisc
We/Ho,Weis,Sod
UBS/✶

5050.2 prs-pron gen 2pl	3620.3 partic	1056.1 conj	2195.3 verb 1sing indic pres act	3450.17 art pl neu	5050.2 prs-pron gen 2pl
[ᵇ ὑμῶν· ʹ	οὐ	γὰρ	ζητῶ	τὰ	ὑμῶν,
humōn	ou	gar	zētō	ta	humōn
you;	not	for	I do seek	the things	your,

233.1 conj	233.2 conj	5050.4 prs-pron acc 2pl	3620.3 partic	1056.1 conj	3648.3 verb 3sing indic pres act
ʹ ἀλλ'	[✶ ἀλλὰ]	ὑμᾶς.	οὐ	γὰρ	ὀφείλει
all'	alla	humas	ou	gar	opheilei
but	[idem]	you;	not	for	ought

3450.17 art pl neu	4891.4 noun pl neu	3450.4 art dat pl	1112.3 noun dat pl masc	2320.4 verb inf pres act	233.1 conj
τὰ	τέκνα	τοῖς	γονεῦσιν	θησαυρίζειν,	ʹ ἀλλ'
ta	tekna	tois	goneusin	thēsaurizein	all'
the	children	for the	parents	to treasure up,	but

233.2 conj	3450.7 art pl masc	1112.1 noun pl masc	3450.4 art dat pl	4891.6 noun dat pl neu	1466.1 prs-pron nom 1sing
[✶ ἀλλὰ]	οἱ	γονεῖς	τοῖς	τέκνοις.	**15.** ἐγὼ
alla	hoi	goneis	tois	teknois	egō
[idem]	the	parents	for the	children.	I

1156.2 conj	2219.1 adv sup	1154.5 verb 1sing indic fut act	2504.1 conj	1537.1 verb 1sing indic fut pass	5065.1 prep
δὲ	ἥδιστα	δαπανήσω	καὶ	ἐκδαπανηθήσομαι	ὑπὲρ
de	hēdista	dapanēsō	kai	ekdapanēthēsomai	huper
now	most gladly	will spend	and	will be utterly spent	for

12:13. The "super apostles" at Corinth said the church there was an inferior one until they came along. Paul asked for the specifics of the charge. In what way were they inferior? To answer his own question, with tongue in cheek he suggested perhaps it was in the fact that he had not asked for a salary while he pastored the Corinthian church. Thus he returned to the subject he discussed earlier at length (11:7-12).

The "I" is emphatic in the sentence. The question was, "Is it that I myself was not burdensome, dead weight on you while planting your church?" This distinguished him from his critics who would not have thought of preaching without pay.

With a touch of irony the apostle asked the Corinthians to forgive him this wrong. If not demanding they meet his financial needs stunted the growth of their church, he was sorry. But, of course, the whole idea was outlandish and nonsense.

12:14. At this point Kent wrote of the crucial conclusion of a letter saying, "Whether it will be accepted and will motivate the readers to appropriate action, or will simply irritate them and thus compound the problem, may depend on the tone of the final paragraphs. Paul had been writing about some sensitive matters. He had spoken of misunderstandings, mistreatment, wrong interpretations placed on his actions, and of a disturbing tendency at Corinth to tolerate wrong teaching. If his apostolic admonition were to be heeded, Paul must make every attempt to leave the impression that he was the Corinthians' friend and sought only their best interests" (p.189).

In the beginning of this letter Paul defended himself against the charge he did not really love the Corinthians or else he would have returned to them by now. In response he explained God directed his way (1:17-23). He did not decide where he would or would not go as any man might. Besides, they needed to correct some errors before he came.

Now near the end of the epistle, the apostle spoke again of his next visit to Corinth. He said it was the third time he was ready to come. Had he made a second trip to Corinth already? Some think he did, but it was such a hurried, unprofitable visit the Bible does not record the details of it. Acts does not mention it. It may have been the "painful visit" Paul alluded to earlier in this letter (2:1).

Whatever the case, once more the apostle declared he would not change his financial policy toward them. He would not demand pay in coming to Corinth again. It was not their money he wanted but their hearts. He was their spiritual father, unlike the false teachers who had come after him (1 Corinthians 4:15). As a parent he did not expect his children to provide for him, but he wanted to store up treasure for them.

12:15. Paul's parental heart opened wide as he declared he would gladly spend all he had for his spiritual children. He was even

13. For what is it wherein ye were inferior to other churches: . . . ye were at disadvantage when compared, *Noyes*.

except [it be] that I myself was not burdensome to you?: . . . except that I did not accept payment, *Fenton* . . . did not burden you with my expenses? *Norlie* . . . never hung as a dead weight upon you? *Weymouth* . . . except that I did not take up offerings among you? *Klingensmith*.

forgive me this wrong: My humblest apologies for this great wrong! *Phillips* . . . Pardon me this unfairness, *Berkeley* . . . Pardon my unfair treatment of you, *Way* . . . this injury, *Douay* . . . this injustice! *Young, Wilson*.

14. Behold, the third time I am ready to come to you: I am preparing, *Montgomery*.

and I will not be burdensome to you: . . . and I shall not be a nuisance to you, *NTPE*.

for I seek not yours, but you: I desire not your money, *Weymouth* . . . I am not hunting for what you have, *Klingensmith* . . . this was my cunning, *Montgomery* . . . I seek not your goods, *HistNT* . . . not your Property, *Wilson* . . . It is you I want, *Phillips*.

for the children ought not to lay up for the parents: . . . should not accumulate wealth, *Berkeley* . . . should not save up, *Confraternity* . . . ought not to be hoarding, *Concordant*.

but the parents for the children:

15. And I will very gladly spend and be spent for you: . . . cheerfully will I both pay [my] expenses, *Murdock* . . . and be entirely spent for your souls, *Young* . . . to invest and be invested for your souls, *Klingensmith* . . . spent out for the sake of, *PNT* . . . and be completely spent on behalf of your souls, *Norlie* . . . be fully spent in behalf of your souls, *Rotherham* . . . and be exhausted, for the sake of, *Fenton* . . . and be bankrupted for the sake of your souls, *Concordant* . . . for your welfare, *TCNT*.

2 Corinthians 12:16

15.a.**Txt:** 01א-corr
06D-corr,018K,020L
025P,byz.Sod
Var: 01א-org,02A,03B
33,sa.bo.Lach,Treg,Alf
Tisc,We/Ho,Weis
UBS/✶

15.b.**Txt:** p46,01א-corr
03B,06D,018K,020L
025P,byz.it.Weis,Sod
Var: 01א-org,02A,33,sa.
bo.Tisc,We/Ho,UBS/✶

3450.1 art gen pl	5425.6 noun gen pl fem	5050.2 prs-pron gen 2pl	1479.1 conj	2504.1 conj	3917.2 adv comp
τῶν	ψυχῶν	ὑμῶν·	εἰ	[a καὶ]	περισσοτέρως
tōn	psuchōn	humōn	ei	kai	perissoterōs
the	souls	your,	if	even	more abundantly

5050.4 prs-pron acc 2pl	25.8 verb nom sing masc part pres act	25.5 verb 1sing indic pres act	2254.1 adj comp	2247.1 adj comp acc sing neu
ὑμᾶς	[ἀγαπῶν,	[b✶ ἀγαπῶ,]	[ἧττον	[✶ ἧσσον]
humas	agapōn	agapō	hētton	hēsson
you	loving,	[I love]	less	[idem]

25.28 verb 1sing indic pres pass	1498.17 verb 3sing impr pres act	1156.2 conj	1466.1 prs-pron nom 1sing	3620.3 partic
ἀγαπῶμαι.	16. Ἔστω	δέ,	ἐγὼ	οὐ
agapōmai	Estō	de	egō	ou
I am being loved.	Be it so	but,	I	not

2570.1 verb 1sing indic aor act	5050.4 prs-pron acc 2pl	233.1 conj	233.2 conj	5062.6 verb nom sing masc part pres act
κατεβάρησα	ὑμᾶς·	[ἀλλ'	[✶ ἀλλὰ]	ὑπάρχων
katebarēsa	humas	all'	alla	huparchōn
did burden	you;	but	[idem]	being

3697.1 adj nom sing masc	1382.3 noun dat sing masc	5050.4 prs-pron acc 2pl	2956.12 verb indic aor act	3231.1 partic	4948.5 indef-pron
πανοῦργος	δόλῳ	ὑμᾶς	ἔλαβον.	17. μή	τινα
panourgos	dolō	humas	elabon	mē	tina
crafty	with deceit	you	I took.	Not	any

3614.1 rel-pron gen pl	643.16 verb 1sing indic perf act	4242.1 prep	5050.4 prs-pron acc 2pl	1217.1 prep	840.3 prs-pron gen sing
ὧν	ἀπέσταλκα	πρὸς	ὑμᾶς,	δι'	αὐτοῦ
hōn	apestalka	pros	humas	di'	autou
of whom	I have sent	to	you,	by	him

3982.2 verb 1sing indic aor act	5050.4 prs-pron acc 2pl	3731.11 verb 1sing indic aor act	4951.4 name acc masc	2504.1 conj
ἐπλεονέκτησα	ὑμᾶς;	18. παρεκάλεσα	Τίτον,	καὶ
epleonektēsa	humas	parekalesa	Titon	kai
did I defrand	you?	I besought	Titus,	and

4733.1 verb 1sing indic aor act	3450.6 art acc sing masc	79.4 noun acc sing masc	3231.1 partic	4948.10 indef-pron sing neu
συναπέστειλα	τὸν	ἀδελφόν·	[μή	τι
sunapesteila	ton	adelphon	mē	ti
sent with	the	brother:	not	some

3252.1 partic	3982.3 verb 3sing indic aor act	5050.4 prs-pron acc 2pl	4951.1 name nom masc	3620.3 partic	3450.3 art dat sing
[✶ μήτι]	ἐπλεονέκτησεν	ὑμᾶς	Τίτος;	οὐ	τῷ
mēti	epleonektēsen	humas	Titos	ou	tō
[not]	Did defrand	you	Titus?	Not	by the

840.4 prs-pron dat sing	4011.3 noun dat sing neu	3906.19 verb 1pl indic aor act	3620.3 partic	3450.4 art dat pl
αὐτῷ	πνεύματι	περιεπατήσαμεν;	οὐ	τοῖς
autō	pneumati	periepatēsamen	ou	tois
same	spirit	walked we?	Not	in the

19.a.**Txt:** 01א-corr,06D
018K,020L,025P,byz.bo.
Var: p46,01א-org,02A
03B,33,Lach,Treg,Alf
Tisc,We/Ho,Weis,Sod
UBS/✶

840.2 prs-pron dat pl	2460.1 noun dat pl neu	3687.1 adv	3682.1 adv	1374.1 verb 2pl pres act
αὐτοῖς	ἴχνεσιν;	19. [Πάλιν	[a✶ Πάλαι]	δοκεῖτε
autois	ichnesin	Palin	Palai	dokeite
same	steps?	Again	[Already]	do you think

willing to be spent, to pour out his own physical life to the last drop in sacrifice for them (*psuchōn*, literally, their "souls"). He felt as when he wrote the Philippians, "Yea, and if I be offered upon the sacrifice and service of your faith, I joy, and rejoice with you all" (Philippians 2:17).

He realized, of course, children do not always repay a parent's love in kind. Sometimes they hurt worst the ones who love them most. Even so, the more he loved the Corinthians the colder they seemed to feel toward him in return.

12:16. However, as far as his conduct toward his converts was concerned, their response to his deeds of kindness did not dictate his behavior. As a true spiritual father he loved, expecting nothing in return. Indeed, no wise parent gives of himself to a child just to be repaid in later years.

For that reason Paul had decided long before this not to be a financial burden to believers at Corinth. They were wrong in being influenced by what the critics said in a slanderous manner of the apostle. To drive the point home, he sarcastically put himself in a class with the opposition for a moment. He said, "Being crafty (clever, sly as they are), I caught you in a trap."

Of this Hughes wrote, "Craftiness was, of course, characteristic of the Apostle's detractors, just as it is pre-eminently characteristic of Satan, whose ministers they were (11:15). As Satan beguiled Eve with his craftiness, so too these deceitful workers (11:13) were seeking to delude and pervert the Corinthian Christians whom Paul had betrothed to Christ (11:2f.)" (*The New London Commentary*, p.464). They said he received money with crafty intent. Then, "The fact was that they would dearly have liked to get their own fingers on that money; but, being unable to do this, they did the next most damaging thing, which was to ascribe to the one whose authority they wished to destroy the designs of their own evil hearts" (ibid., p.465).

12:17. Some of the apostle's enemies suggested that though he asked for no money in planting the church at Corinth, he no doubt profited from the offering he raised for needy brethren in Judea. He responded, "Did any of those I sent ever make a gain, take advantage of, cheat, or defraud you?" The negative particle *mē* expects a "no" answer. Contrary to the charge against him, Paul never used his apostolic office as a "cloak of covetousness" (1 Thessalonians 2:5).

12:18. Specifically, did Titus or the brother sent with him take advantage of them financially? (see 8:16-22). Did not Titus show the same attitude toward money that Paul did? Did they not tread the same footsteps? The *ou* in both of the last questions expects a "yes" answer.

though the more abundantly I love you: If I love you excessively, *Berkeley.*
the less I be loved:

16. But be it so, I did not burden you: I was not a financial burden to you, *Norlie.*
nevertheless, being crafty: . . . but you say that I was crafty all along, *TCNT* . . . was I a clever fellow, *Beck* . . . this was my cunning, *Montgomery* . . . but yet you say that I was crafty, *Norlie* . . . by being a trickster, *Williams* . . . like the cunning knave he is, *Way.*
I caught you with guile: But some say I set a trap for you, *NLT* . . . with which I caught you by a trick, *Montgomery* . . . but, being a rascal, have taken pay of you by a trick! *Fenton* . . . and got the better of you by deceit, *Norlie* . . . I cheated you by my cunning, *Williams* . . . entrapped you, *Way* . . . who trapped you with some trick? *Beck.*

17. Did I make a gain of you by any of them whom I sent unto you?: Did I exploit you through anyone, *NTPE* . . . I did not make any money out of you, *Williams* . . . that I pilfered from you? *Murdock* . . . wrung fraudulent gain from you? *Way* . . . whom I dispatched to you? *HistNT.*

18. I desired Titus, and with [him] I sent a brother: I summoned, *Berkeley* . . . I pleaded with Titus to go, *Adams* . . . I urged Titus to go, *Confraternity* . . . I besought Titus, and I sent forth in conjunction, *Rotherham.*
Did Titus make a gain of you?: Has Titus exploited you? *Greber* . . . take any advantage of you? *ASV, HistNT* . . . plunder you? *Fenton.*
walked we not in the same spirit?: Did he and I not proceed, *HistNT.*
[walked we] not in the same steps?: . . . and in the same course? *Fenton* . . . Did we not act alike? *Klingensmith* . . . And do exactly the same things, *Beck* . . . in the same tracks? *Berkeley.*

3617.1 conj	5050.3 prs-pron dat 2pl	620.2 verb 1pl indic pres	2684.1 prep
ὅτι	ὑμῖν	ἀπολογούμεθα;	(κατενώπιον
hoti	humin	apologoumetha	katenōpion
that	to you	we are making a defense?	before

2683.1 prep gen	3450.2 art gen sing	2296.2 noun gen sing masc	1706.1 prep	5382.3 name dat masc
[b✶ κατέναντι]	(c τοῦ `	θεοῦ	ἐν	Χριστῷ
katenanti	tou	theou	en	Christō
[idem]		God	in	Christ

2953.4 verb 1pl indic pres act	3450.17 art pl neu	1156.2 conj	3820.1 adj	27.6 adj pl masc	5065.1 prep	3450.10 art gen sing fem
λαλοῦμεν·	τὰ	δὲ	πάντα,	ἀγαπητοί,	ὑπὲρ	τῆς
laloumen	ta	de	panta	agapētoi	huper	tēs
we speak;	the	and	all things,	beloved,	for	the

5050.2 prs-pron gen 2pl	3482.2 noun gen sing fem	5236.1 verb 1sing indic pres	1056.1 conj	3248.1 conj
ὑμῶν	οἰκοδομῆς.	20. φοβοῦμαι	γὰρ,	(μήπως
humōn	oikodomēs	phoboumai	gar	mēpōs
your	edification.	I fear	for,	lest perhaps

3231.1 partic	4315.1 adv	2048.13 verb nom sing masc part aor act	3620.1 partic	3497.4 rel-pron acc pl masc	2286.1 verb 1sing pres act
[✶ μή	πως]	ἐλθὼν	οὐχ	οἵους	θέλω
mē	pōs	elthōn	ouch	hoious	thelō
[not	how]	having come	not	such as	I wish

2128.10 verb 1sing subj aor act	5050.4 prs-pron acc 2pl	2476.3 conj	2128.35 verb 1sing subj aor pass	5050.3 prs-pron dat 2pl	3497.1 rel-pron sing
εὕρω	ὑμᾶς,	κἀγὼ	εὑρεθῶ	ὑμῖν	οἷον
heurō	humas	kagō	heurethō	humin	hoion
I should find	you,	and I	be found	by you	such as

3620.3 partic	2286.5 verb 2pl indic pres act	3248.1 conj	3231.1 partic	4315.1 adv	2038.5 noun pl fem
οὐ	θέλετε·	(μήπως	[✶ μή	πως]	(ἔρεις,
ou	thelete	mēpōs	mē	pōs	ereis
not	you do wish:	lest perhaps	[not	how]	rivalries,

2038.1 noun nom sing fem	2188.5 noun nom pl masc	2188.1 noun nom sing neu	2349.4 noun nom pl masc	2036.4 noun nom pl fem
[a✶ ἔρις,	(ζῆλοι,	[b✶ ζῆλος,]	θυμοί,	ἐριθεῖαι,
eris	zēloi	zēlos	thumoi	eritheiai
[strife,]	jealousies,	[jealously,]	indignations,	contentions,

2606.1 noun nom pl fem	5422.1 noun nom pl masc	5286.1 noun nom pl fem	179.3 noun nom pl fem
καταλαλιαί,	ψιθυρισμοί,	φυσιώσεις,	ἀκαταστασίαι·
katalaliai	psithurismoi	phusiōseis	akatastasiai
evil speakings,	whisperings,	conceits,	commotions;

3231.1 partic	3687.1 adv	2048.12 verb part aor act	1466.6 prs-pron acc 1sing	2048.14 verb gen sing masc part aor act
21. μὴ	πάλιν	(ἐλθόντα	με	[a✶ ἐλθόντος
mē	palin	elthonta	me	elthontos
not	again	having come	me	[having come

1466.2 prs-pron gen 1sing	4864.3 verb 3sing subj aor act	1466.6 prs-pron acc 1sing	3450.5 art sing masc	2296.1 noun nom sing masc
μου]	ταπεινώσῃ	[b✶+ με]	ὁ	θεός
mou	tapeinōsē	me	ho	theos
my]	should humble	[me]	ho	God

12:19. Did they think he had returned to excusing (*apologou-metha*, cf. English *apologize*), defending himself before them? With the Spirit moving on Paul as he wrote, he declared he spoke before God pleading the sacrifice of Christ for justification in his case. God was his judge, not men. Further, the cause Paul defended was the Lord's, not his.

Of course, he did minister to man in what he wrote. He intended his letter to edify or build up the Corinthians. He counted the recipients of his epistle as among the "dearly beloved" in spite of the note of rebuke in much of what he wrote. No doubt only a small group had caused his problems.

12:20. The apostle was concerned about what might happen when he arrived at Corinth. He was apprehensive lest they not solve many of their remaining problems before he came. He would like all difficulties to be removed in advance of his arrival. Otherwise, his duty would be that of a disciplinarian. Then they would not find him as they would like either.

He hoped his letter would be enough. To follow Paul's example, today's pastors must also attend to problems rather than ignore them. However, like the apostle they would do well to try mild remedies before turning to more severe ones.

The apostle established another good pattern for ministers of all times in that he went beyond speaking in general terms. He listed specific evils. He feared lest he find the congregations engaged in debates (discord, contentions). He was concerned he would see the subtle sin of envy or jealousy in the assembly. Envy manifests itself in the form of hatred of others because they have something you wish you had.

The apostle was apprehensive lest conditions in the church would become so tense that some would lose control to wrath or outbursts of anger. Also, he did not want to see strifes (disputes, outbreaks of selfishness) which promoted factions in the congregation.

Certainly backbiting (evil speech, defamation of character, or slander) was out of place in a fellowship of believers. And few things are worse than whispering (talebearing, gossip).

With things at Corinth as they were Paul did not know but what he would also discover the sin of "swellings." The word refers to being puffed up through pride. After all, in his first letter to them the apostle had rebuked the congregation at Corinth for having spiritual pride (1 Corinthians 5:2). Such a church would be in a state of tumult (disorder, unruliness).

12:21. If Paul did discover sin like this in the Corinthian church, it would understandably break his heart. The shame and embarrassment would cause him to weep. He would mourn over the many who had sinned already. Obviously, he would rather God not permit him such a humiliating experience.

19. Again, think ye that we excuse ourselves unto you?: You are imagining, all this time, *Weymouth* . . . Do you think we are apologizing to you again? *Fenton* . . . we are trying to justify ourselves in your eyes, *Norlie* . . . we have been defending ourselves before you? *RSV.*

we speak before God in Christ: but [we do] all things, dearly beloved, for your edifying: . . . for your spiritual welfare, *Norlie* . . . for the sake of benefiting you, *Fenton.*

20. For I fear, lest, when I come, I shall not find you such as I would: For I dread, *Montgomery* . . . for I am apprehensive that, *Williams.*

and [that] I shall be found unto you such as ye would not:

lest [there be] debates, envyings: . . . strifes, *Rotherham* . . . wranglings, *Noyes* . . . finding arguments, *Phillips.*

wraths, strifes: . . . animosities, *Confraternity* . . . passions, *Fenton* . . . rivalry, slander, *Norlie* . . . intrigues, *Hanson* . . . ugly temper, sectarianism, *Berkeley* . . . party spirit, *Montgomery* . . . hot tempers, selfishness, *Klingensmith* . . . angry passions, *HistNT* . . . ill-natured talk, *Weymouth* . . . intrigues, *Conybeare* . . . and obstinacy, *Murdock* . . . divided loyalties, *Phillips.*

backbitings, whisperings: . . . detractions, *Confraternity, Douay* . . . bad talk, gossip, *Klingensmith* . . . undue eulogy, *Weymouth* . . . slanderings, inflations, *Fenton.*

swellings, tumults: . . . big heads, *Klingensmith* . . . swollen heads, *NTPE* . . . haughty pride, *Williams* . . . disturbances, *Fenton, Wilson* . . . and insolence, *Murdock* . . . unrest, *Weymouth* . . . arrogance, *Montgomery* . . . self-assertion, *TCNT* . . . insurrections, *Young* . . . conceits, disorders, *Hanson* . . . commotions, *PNT* . . . seditions, *Rotherham* . . . and disharmony, *Phillips* . . . and disorder, *RSV* . . . disorderly behavior, *Beck.*

21. [And] lest, when I come again, my God will humble me among you: . . . may humiliate me before you, *Norlie, Williams.*

2 Corinthians 13:1

1466.2 prs-pron gen 1sing	4242.1 prep	5050.4 prs-pron acc 2pl	2504.1 conj	3858.5 verb 1sing subj aor act	4044.8 adj acc pl masc
μου	πρὸς	ὑμᾶς,	καὶ	πενθήσω	πολλοὺς
mou	pros	humas	kai	penthēsō	pollous
my	as to	you,	and	I should mourn over	many

3450.1 art gen pl	4117.1 verb gen pl masc part perf act	2504.1 conj	3231.1 partic	3210.13 verb gen pl masc part aor act
τῶν	προημαρτηκότων,	καὶ	μὴ	μετανοησάντων
tōn	proēmartēkotōn	kai	mē	metanoēsantōn
of the	having before sinned,	and	not	having repented

1894.3 prep	3450.11 art dat sing fem	165.3 noun dat sing fem	2504.1 conj	4061.3 noun dat sing fem	2504.1 conj
ἐπὶ	τῇ	ἀκαθαρσίᾳ	καὶ	πορνείᾳ	καὶ
epi	tē	akatharsia	kai	porneia	kai
upon	the	uncleanness	and	fornication	and

760.2 noun dat sing fem	3614.11 rel-pron dat sing fem	4097.18 verb 3pl indic aor act	4995.1 num ord sing
ἀσελγείᾳ	ᾗ	ἔπραξαν.	**13:1.** Τρίτον
aselgeia	hē	epraxan	Triton
licentiousness	which	they practiced.	Third time

3642.17 dem-pron sing neu	2048.32 verb 1sing indic pres	4242.1 prep	5050.4 prs-pron acc 2pl	1894.3 prep	4601.2 noun gen sing neu
τοῦτο	ἔρχομαι	πρὸς	ὑμᾶς·	ἐπὶ	στόματος
touto	erchomai	pros	humas	epi	stomatos
this	I am coming	to	you.	In	mouth

1411.3 num card	3116.5 noun gen pl masc	2504.1 conj	4980.2 num card gen	2449.47 verb 3sing indic fut pass	3820.17 adj sing neu
δύο	μαρτύρων	καὶ	τριῶν	σταθήσεται	πᾶν
duo	marturōn	kai	triōn	stathēsetai	pan
of two	witnesses	or	of three	shall be established	every

4343.1 noun sing neu	4136.1 verb 1sing indic perf act	2504.1 conj	4161.1 verb 1sing indic pres act	5453.1 conj
ῥῆμα.	**2.** προείρηκα	καὶ	προλέγω,	ὡς
rhēma	proeirēka	kai	prolegō	hōs
matter.	I have before declared	and	I say beforehand,	as

3780.6 verb nom sing masc part pres act	3450.16 art sing neu	1202.8 num ord sing neu	2504.1 conj	544.2 verb nom sing masc part pres act
παρὼν	τὸ	δεύτερον,	καὶ	ἀπὼν
parōn	to	deuteron	kai	apōn
being present	to the	second time,	and	being absent

2.a.Txt: 06D-corr,018K 020L,025P,byz.sa.
Var: p46,01ℵ,02A,03B 06D-org,33,Gries,Lach Treg,Alf,Word,Tisc We/Ho,Weis,Sod UBS/★

3431.1 adv	1119.1 verb 1sing indic pres act	3450.4 art dat pl	4117.2 verb dat pl masc part perf act	2504.1 conj	3450.4 art dat pl
νῦν	⸂ γράφω ⸃	τοῖς	προημαρτηκόσιν,	καὶ	τοῖς
nun	graphō	tois	proēmartēkosin	kai	tois
now	I write	to the	having before sinned,	and	to the

3036.2 adj dat pl	3820.5 adj dat pl	3617.1 conj	1430.1 partic	2048.6 verb 1sing subj aor act	1519.1 prep	3450.16 art sing neu
λοιποῖς	πᾶσιν,	ὅτι	ἐὰν	ἔλθω	εἰς	τὸ
loipois	pasin	hoti	ean	elthō	eis	to
remaining	all,	that	if	I come	to	the

3687.1 adv	3620.3 partic	5177.6 verb 1sing indic fut mid	1878.1 conj	1376.4 noun acc sing fem	2195.1 verb 2pl pres act
πάλιν	οὐ	φείσομαι.	**3.** ἐπεὶ	δοκιμὴν	ζητεῖτε
palin	ou	pheisomai	epei	dokimēn	zēteite
again	not	I will spare.	Since	a proof	you seek

642

The tactfulness of this Spirit-led minister is inspiring. As he wrote of perhaps finding the Corinthians less than he wanted them to be, he softened the rebuke by adding he didn't want them to be disappointed in him either. Instead of talking of their embarrassment, he spoke of his. He rebuked "with all long-suffering" (2 Timothy 4:2).

The apostle's wisdom also shows in that he could have spoken of the existence rather than just the possibility of sin in the lives of members of the Corinthian assembly. Indeed he continued with a focus on those who had actually committed the sin of uncleanness or immorality. There were also those who had practiced fornication (*porneia*, which refers to all illicit sexual activity). Others were guilty of lasciviousness (licentiousness, sensuality). Even worse, they had not repented of their sins.

13:1. Again Paul informed the Corinthians of the anticipated trip to see them. It would be his third visit to their church (12:14). As such it should confirm the gospel he had shared with them in keeping with the validating laws of Moses. To protect the innocent, under God the leader of Israel decreed the court could convict only "in the mouth of two or three witnesses" (cf. Deuteronomy 17:6; 19:15).

Jesus said believers must use this principle in matters of church discipline (Matthew 18:16). Paul instructed elsewhere that it must apply in trials for ministers (1 Timothy 5:19).

13:2. Thus the apostle warned when he arrived, if necessary, he would follow legal principles, scripturally founded, regarding witnesses in dealing with the offenders at Corinth. He had given them fair warning earlier when he was present with them during his second visit. This could have been the time he went there "in heaviness" (2:1). Once more in advance of his third arrival he made clear his determination to rid the church of evil.

Paul specifically addressed those who had already sinned (12:21). However, he wanted all others who might be tempted to follow their example to also know he would not spare them. He would practice strict discipline. With the congregation assembled he would dismiss them from membership in the church (1 Corinthians 5:4,5), turning them out to the camp of Satan where they belonged. He would put away such evil persons from among the fellowship of believers (1 Corinthians 5:2,13). Under God he would rid the lump of all leaven (1 Corinthians 5:7).

With such a disciplinary stance toward sin, one readily understands why the apostle was incensed that some said his theology allowed Christians to sin with impunity. To the Romans he wrote that was slanderous and declared those who misquoted him would meet a just damnation in the end (Romans 3:8).

and [that] I shall bewail many which have sinned already: . . . and I should mourn over, *Wesley* . . . and I shall lament many of those who had previously sinned, *Rotherham* . . . many whose hearts still cling to their old sins, *Weymouth*.

and have not repented of the uncleanness and fornication and lasciviousness which they have committed: . . . and gross sensuality, of which they have been guilty, *Weymouth* . . . and no self control, *Klingensmith* . . . and whoredom...they did practise, *Young* . . . and prostitution, *Concordant* . . . the wantonness, *Way* . . . impurity, immorality, and licentiousness, *RSV* . . . and sensuality which they practised, *HistNT* . . . for the vice, and profligacy, and excess, which they have practised, *Fenton* . . . which they perpetrated, *Rotherham* . . . in which they have indulged, *TCNT*.

1. This [is] the third [time] I am coming to you: This is my third visit to you, *Berkeley*.

In the mouth of two or three witnesses shall every word be established: On the evidence of, *Weymouth, Fenton* . . . each statement, *TCNT* . . . Every fact is to be confirmed, *NASB* . . . Every charge must be established, *Norlie* . . . every matter shall be decided, *NTPE* . . . must be substantiated, *Adams* . . . shall every declaration, *Rotherham* . . . shall be confirmed, *Berkeley* . . . Everything must be proved, *Beck* . . . be made to stand, *Concordant*.

2. I told you before: I now forewarn you, *Montgomery* . . . the second time, *Campbell*.

and foretell you, as if I were present, the second time: . . . and am saying beforehand, *Rotherham* . . . and I do say beforehand, *Worrell*.

and being absent now I write to them which heretofore have sinned, and to all other:

that, if I come again, I will not spare: I will not let up on you, *Klingensmith* . . . I shall have no mercy, *JB* . . . I will show no leniency, *NEB, Kleist* . . . nobody will escape punishment, *TEV*.

2 Corinthians 13:4

3450.2 art gen sing	1706.1 prep	1466.5 prs-pron dat 1sing	2953.13 verb gen sing masc part pres act	5382.2 name gen masc	3614.5 rel-pron nom sing masc
τοῦ	ἐν	ἐμοὶ	λαλοῦντος	Χριστοῦ,	ὃς
tou	en	emoi	lalountos	Christou	hos
of the	in	me	speaking	Christ,	who

1519.1 prep	5050.4 prs-pron acc 2pl	3620.2 partic	764.2 verb 3sing indic pres act	233.2 conj	1408.1 verb 3sing indic pres act	1706.1 prep
εἰς	ὑμᾶς	οὐκ	ἀσθενεῖ,	ἀλλὰ	δυνατεῖ	ἐν
eis	humas	ouk	asthenei	alla	dunatei	en
towards	you	not	is weak,	but	is powerful	in

4.a.Txt: 01א-corr,02A 06D-corr,020L,byz.Sod **Var:** 01א-org,03B 06D-org,018K,025P,33 Treg,Alf,Tisc,We/Ho Weis,UBS/⋆

5050.3 prs-pron dat 2pl	2504.1 conj	1056.1 conj	1479.1 conj	4568.12 verb 3sing indic aor pass	1523.1 prep gen
ὑμῖν·	**4.** καὶ	γὰρ	⌐a εἰ ⌐	ἐσταυρώθη	ἐξ
humin	kai	gar	ei	estaurōthē	ex
you,	indeed	for	if	he was crucified	in

763.1 noun fem	233.2 conj	2180.1 verb sing indic pres	1523.2 prep gen	1405.2 noun gen sing fem	2296.2 noun gen sing masc
ἀσθενείας,	ἀλλὰ	ζῇ	ἐκ	δυνάμεως	θεοῦ·
astheneias	alla	zē	ek	dunameōs	theou
weakness,	yet	he lives	by	power	God's;

4.b.Txt: 03B,06D,044 0243,sa.byz. **Var:** p46,01א,010F 012G,1311,2495,bo.

2504.1 conj	1056.1 conj	2231.1 prs-pron nom 1pl	764.3 verb 1pl indic pres act	1706.1 prep	4713.1 prep dat
καὶ	γὰρ	ἡμεῖς	ἀσθενοῦμεν	⌐⋆ ἐν	[b σὺν]
kai	gar	hēmeis	asthenoumen	en	sun
indeed	for	we	are weak	in	[with]

4.c.Txt: 06D-corr,018K 020L,byz.Sod **Var:** 01א,02A,03B 06D-org,33,Lach,Treg Alf,Word,Tisc,We/Ho Weis,UBS/⋆

840.4 prs-pron dat sing	233.2 conj	2180.30 verb 1pl indic fut mid	2180.26 verb 1pl indic fut act	4713.1 prep dat
αὐτῷ,	ἀλλὰ	⌐ ζήσομεθα	[c⋆ ζήσομεν]	σὺν
autō	alla	zēsometha	zēsomen	sun
him,	but	we shall live	[idem]	with

840.4 prs-pron dat sing	1523.2 prep gen	1405.2 noun gen sing fem	2296.2 noun gen sing masc	1519.1 prep	5050.4 prs-pron acc 2pl
αὐτῷ,	ἐκ	δυνάμεως	θεοῦ	εἰς	ὑμᾶς·
autō	ek	dunameōs	theou	eis	humas
him	by	power	God's	towards	you,

1431.8 prs-pron acc pl masc	3847.1 verb 2pl pres act	1479.1 conj	1498.6 verb 2pl indic pres act	1706.1 prep	3450.11 art dat sing fem
5. ἑαυτοὺς	πειράζετε	εἰ	ἐστὲ	ἐν	τῇ
heautous	peirazete	ei	este	en	tē
yourselves	test you	if	you are	in	the

3963.3 noun dat sing fem	1431.8 prs-pron acc pl masc	1375.1 verb 2pl pres act	2211.1 conj	3620.2 partic
πίστει,	ἑαυτοὺς	δοκιμάζετε.	ἢ	οὐκ
pistei	heautous	dokimazete	ē	ouk
faith;	yourselves	prove:	or	not

1906.1 verb 2pl pres act	1431.8 prs-pron acc pl masc	3617.1 conj	2400.1 name nom masc	5382.1 name nom masc	1706.1 prep
ἐπιγινώσκετε	ἑαυτοὺς,	ὅτι	Ἰησοῦς	Χριστὸς	ἐν
epiginōskete	heautous	hoti	Iēsous	Christos	en
do you recognize	yourselves,	that	Jesus	Christ	in

5.a.Txt: 01א,02A 06D-corr,018K,020L 025P,byz.it.Sod **Var:** 03B,06D-org,33 Treg,Tisc,We/Ho,Weis UBS/⋆

5050.3 prs-pron dat 2pl	1498.4 verb 3sing indic pres act	1479.1 conj	3231.1 partic	4948.10 indef-pron sing neu	3252.1 partic
ὑμῖν	⌐a ἐστιν; ⌐	εἰ	⌐ μὴ	τι	[⋆ μήτι]
humin	estin	ei	mē	ti	mēti
you	is,	if	not	any	[not]

13:3. Some at Corinth had demanded proof that Paul was a true apostle, that Christ really spoke through him. He announced he would give it when he arrived, though probably not the kind of evidence they would like. He would demonstrate his God-given authority to lead the church in matters of discipline.

As Christ came once as an advocate or defense counsel and will come the next time as Judge, so Paul's next visit would be as a disciplinarian. He might have appeared weak to some, but no more. He would show himself mighty (strong, courageous) for the sake of the gospel and those who truly believed it. The time for forbearance would be past. Further waiting would damage the Lord's cause too much.

13:4. In the case of Christ, it is true He was crucified when He possessed the weakness of His human form. Those who looked on at the cross mocked at the idea He saved others when they thought Him so powerless He could not even save himself (Matthew 27:42). Little did they know what the truth really was. The fact is, if He saved himself, others He could not save. In the end, God bared His mighty arm toward Jesus in that He raised Him from the dead (Ephesians 1:19,20). He demonstrated that Jesus is His Son through the miracle of the Resurrection (Romans 1:4). In like manner, children of the Lord, such as Paul, who may appear weak now will one day live by that same power of God.

13:5. The Corinthians had been so quick to examine and judge Paul that he had a suggestion for them. They should be proving, putting themselves to the test, instead of him. The apostle placed "yourselves" and "your own selves" first in these two sentences for the sake of emphasis. Thus his first sentence began, "Yourselves examine."

Men analyze metal with respect to its purity. They try coins to determine their genuineness. Even more so, Christians ought to often take a careful look at the state of their souls. At least every time they approach the communion table they should examine themselves (1 Corinthians 11:28). With David they must pray, "Search me, O God, and know my heart: try me, and know my thoughts: and see if there be any wicked way in me" (Psalm 139:23,24).

It is imperative for believers to assure their hearts that they are continuing in the Faith. Even when there appears no need to search the inner man, Paul warned, "Let him that thinketh he standeth take heed lest he fall" (1 Corinthians 10:12).

The apostle said believers at Corinth must know (know exactly, completely) that Christ lived within them. Otherwise they might end up as reprobates (not having passed the test, unqualified, rejected, worthless). Paul did not level such serious warnings with an air of superiority. He recognized that unless he continued striving in faith he too might become a "castaway" (1 Corinthians 9:27).

3. Since ye seek a proof of Christ speaking in me: You want proof, *JB* . . . You will have all the proof you want, *TEV* . . . since you are demanding proof, *NIV* . . . You are looking for proof that Christ speaks through me, *Barclay.*

which to you-ward is not weak: When he deals with you, *TEV* . . . he is no weakling, *Barclay.*

but is mighty in you: . . . but is powerful in you, *ASV* . . . makes his power felt among you, *NEB* . . . powerful among you, *SEB.*

4. For though he was crucified through weakness: For he was feeble, *BB* . . . he was a weak mortal when he was crucified, *Greber* . . . in human weakness He died on the cross, *Way* . . . True, it was in weakness that he died, *Barclay* . . . nailed to the cross, *SEB.*

yet he liveth by the power of God: . . . which gives him continuing life, *Barclay.*

For we also are weak in him: but we shall live with him by the power of God toward you: . . . but in our relations with you, *TEV* . . . the source of our life, *Barclay* . . . we will live with Christ for you, *SEB* . . . for your benefit, *JB.*

5. Examine yourselves, whether ye be in the faith: Test yourselves to discover whether you are true believers, *Weymouth* . . . to find out, *SEB* . . . whether you are continuing in the faith, *Williams* . . . are you living the life of faith? *NEB.*

prove your own selves: . . . put your own selves under examination, *Weymouth* . . . Prove it to yourselves, *SEB.*

Know ye not your own selves: Or do ye not recognise yourselves? *Rotherham* . . . Do ye acknowledge, *JB* . . . Surely you recognize, *NEB* . . . You must be well aware, *Barclay.*

how that Jesus Christ is in you: . . . is among you? *SEB.*

except ye be reprobates?: . . . if you are sincere? *Weymouth* . . . unless indeed you fail the test? *NASB* . . . unless you are rejected ones, *KJII* . . . Or are you backsliders? *Norlie* . . . you turn out to be, *Adams* . . . unless you are counterfeits? *Berkeley.*

2 Corinthians 13:6

95.3 adj nom pl masc	**1498.6** verb 2pl indic pres act	**1666.1** verb 1sing indic pres act	**1156.2** conj	**3617.1** conj	**1091.51** verb 2pl indic fut mid
ἀδόκιμοί	ἐστε.	6. ἐλπίζω	δὲ	ὅτι	γνώσεσθε
adokimoi	este	elpizō	de	hoti	gnōsesthe
rejected	you are?	I hope	now	that	you will know

3617.1 conj	**2231.1** prs-pron nom 1pl	**3620.2** partic	**1498.5** verb 1pl indic pres act	**95.3** adj nom pl masc	**2153.1** verb 1sing indic pres
ὅτι	ἡμεῖς	οὐκ	ἐσμὲν	ἀδόκιμοι.	7. ⸀ εὔχομαι
hoti	hēmeis	ouk	esmen	adokimoi	euchomai
that	we	not	are	rejected.	I pray

7.a.Txt: 06D-corr,018K 020L,byz.
Var: 01ℵ,02A,03B 06D-org,025P,33,it.bo. Lach,Treg,Alf,Word Tisc,We/Ho,Weis,Sod UBS/⋆

	2153.2 verb 1pl indic pres	**1156.2** conj	**4242.1** prep	**3450.6** art acc sing masc	**2296.4** noun acc sing masc	**3231.1** partic
	[ᵃ⋆ εὐχόμεθα]	δὲ	πρὸς	τὸν	θεὸν	μὴ
	euchometha	de	pros	ton	theon	mē
	[we pray]	but	to	the	God	not

4020.41 verb inf aor act	**5050.4** prs-pron acc 2pl	**2527.7** adj sing neu	**3235.6** num card neu	**3620.1** partic	**2419.1** conj	**2231.1** prs-pron nom 1pl
ποιῆσαι	ὑμᾶς	κακὸν	μηδέν,	οὐχ	ἵνα	ἡμεῖς
poiēsai	humas	kakon	mēden	ouch	hina	hēmeis
to do	you	evil	nothing;	not	that	we

1378.3 adj nom pl masc	**5154.16** verb 1pl subj aor pass	**233.1** conj	**2419.1** conj	**5050.1** prs-pron nom 2pl	**3450.16** art sing neu
δόκιμοι	φανῶμεν,	ἀλλ᾽	ἵνα	ὑμεῖς	τὸ
dokimoi	phanōmen	all'	hina	humeis	to
approved	may appear,	but	the	you	what

2541.1 adj sing	**4020.9** verb 2pl subj pres act	**2231.1** prs-pron nom 1pl	**1156.2** conj	**5453.1** conj	**95.3** adj nom pl masc
καλὸν	ποιῆτε,	ἡμεῖς	δὲ	ὡς	ἀδόκιμοι
kalon	poiēte	hēmeis	de	hōs	adokimoi
right	may do,	we	and	as	rejected

1498.11 verb 1pl subj pres act	**3620.3** partic	**1056.1** conj	**1404.5** verb 1pl indic pres	**4948.10** indef-pron sing neu	**2567.3** prep
ὦμεν.	8. οὐ	γὰρ	δυνάμεθά	τι	κατὰ
ōmen	ou	gar	dunametha	ti	kata
may be.	Not	for	have we power	any	against

3450.10 art gen sing fem	**223.2** noun gen sing fem	**233.1** conj	**233.2** conj	**5065.1** prep	**3450.10** art gen sing fem
τῆς	ἀληθείας,	⸀ ἀλλ᾽	[⋆ ἀλλὰ]	ὑπὲρ	τῆς
tēs	alētheias	all'	alla	huper	tēs
the	truth,	but	[idem]	for	the

223.2 noun gen sing fem	**5299.3** verb 1pl indic pres act	**1056.1** conj	**3615.1** conj	**2231.1** prs-pron nom 1pl
ἀληθείας.	9. χαίρομεν	γὰρ	ὅταν	ἡμεῖς
alētheias	chairomen	gar	hotan	hēmeis
truth.	We rejoice	for	when	we

764.4 verb 1pl subj pres act	**5050.1** prs-pron nom 2pl	**1156.2** conj	**1409.2** adj nom pl masc	**1498.1** verb 2pl act	**3642.17** dem-pron sing neu
ἀσθενῶμεν,	ὑμεῖς	δὲ	δυνατοὶ	ἦτε·	τοῦτο
asthenōmen	humeis	de	dunatoi	ēte	touto
may be weak,	you	and	powerful	may be.	This

9.a.Txt: 01ℵ-corr 06D-corr,018K,020L byz.
Var: 01ℵ-org,02A,03B 06D-org,025P,33,it.bo. Lach,Treg,Alf,Word Tisc,We/Ho,Weis,Sod UBS/⋆

1156.2 conj	**2504.1** conj	**2153.2** verb 1pl indic pres	**3450.12** art acc sing fem	**5050.2** prs-pron gen 2pl	**2646.1** noun acc sing fem
⸀ᵃ δὲ ⸀	καὶ	εὐχόμεθα,	τὴν	ὑμῶν	κατάρτισιν.
de	kai	euchometha	tēn	humōn	katartisin
but	also	we pray for,	the	your	perfecting.

13:6. Since the Corinthians had spent so much time and effort in examining Paul, he was confident they had come to a correct conclusion of his standing before God. Certainly he was no reprobate. In saying so he was expressing no rash self-confidence. He was as careful in guarding the spiritual state of his own soul as he was to exhort them to be careful to examine themselves. In his first letter to them he wrote, "But I keep under my body, and bring it into subjection: lest that by any means, when I have preached to others, I myself should be a castaway" (*adokimos*, "reprobate") (1 Corinthians 9:27).

13:7. As so often in his letters, from Paul's inner being flowed a spontaneous prayer for the Corinthians. He prayed they would do no evil. He wanted individual believers to live upright lives. He desired the church in Corinth to be free from sin.

Yet his prayer was for their sake instead of his. His motive remained pure. He was not asking that the church he pioneered at Corinth be trouble-free so he would appear approved (tried and true, genuine) as a successful preacher. In fact, he was willing to appear as a reprobate, as a failure, if that would contribute to their salvation. As he wrote the Romans, "I could wish that myself were accursed from Christ for my brethren, my kinsmen according to the flesh," if that would save their souls (Romans 9:3).

What the apostle prayed for was honest (morally good, noble, praiseworthy) living on the part of the Corinthians. He wanted them to stand approved not only before men but more so before God.

13:8. Despite what Paul's critics at Corinth said about him, he was no hypocrite. Something within made it impossible for him to do anything against the truth. As John wrote of the genuine child of God, "His seed remaineth in him: and he cannot sin, because he is born of God" (1 John 3:9). To speak of a sinning Christian is like referring to an honest liar or a trustworthy thief. It is a contradiction of terms. Of course, the impossibility to sin is a moral rather than an absolute one. For both of these apostles, integrity within compelled them to do everything in life in keeping with the truth of God.

13:9. Once more Paul's unselfishness came through. He did not promote self. His concern was the welfare of his converts. He was glad to be weak if that contributed to their being strong. He wished for (*euchometha*, "prayed for") their perfection, that they be complete in their Christian lives. Earlier in this letter he was concerned with their "perfecting holiness in the fear of God" (7:1). He was like the writer of Hebrews who exhorted, "Therefore leaving the principles of the doctrine of Christ, let us go on unto perfection" (Hebrews 6:1). They must pursue maturity.

6. But I trust that ye shall know that we are not reprobates: I hope that we do not flunk out, *Klingensmith* . . . that we are not disapproved, *Rotherham* . . . not unapproved, *Noyes* . . . are not without proof, *Wilson* . . . we haven't failed in our test, *Beck* . . . that we are not false Christians, *Greber*.

7. Now I pray to God that ye do no evil: . . . make supplication to God, *Berkeley*.

not that we should appear approved: . . . not in order that our sincerity may be demonstrated, *Weymouth* . . . not so that we may appear superior, *Fenton* . . . not that we may appear as men of genuine character, *HistNT*.

but that ye should do that which is honest:

though we be as reprobates: . . . though we may appear to have failed, *Norlie*.

8. For we can do nothing against the truth: . . . we have no power against, *Noyes* . . . we have no ability against the truth, *Berkeley*.

but for the truth: . . . but only for the furtherance of the truth, *Weymouth* . . . but only in defense of the truth, *Montgomery* . . . in harmony with it, *RPNT*.

9. For we are glad, when we are weak: And so we rejoice, *Kleist*.

and ye are strong: . . . but ye may be powerful, *Rotherham*.

and this also we wish, [even] your perfection: . . . and we pray for this, *Fenton* . . . What we pray for is your improvement, *RSV* . . . it is your development that we pray for, *HistNT* . . . even your restoration, *Hanson* . . . that you may be made perfect, *Norlie* . . . the perfecting of your characters, *Weymouth* . . . your complete restoration, *Wilson* . . . your perfect reformation, *Conybeare*.

10. 1217.2 prep
διὰ / *dia* / Because of

3642.17 dem-pron sing neu
τοῦτο / *touto* / this

3642.18 dem-pron pl neu
ταῦτα / *tauta* / these things

544.2 verb nom sing masc part pres act
ἀπὼν / *apōn* / being absent

1119.1 verb 1sing indic pres act
γράφω, / *graphō* / I write,

2419.1 conj
ἵνα / *hina* / that

3780.6 verb nom sing masc part pres act
παρὼν / *parōn* / being present

3231.1 partic
μὴ / *mē* / not

658.1 adv
ἀποτόμως / *apotomōs* / with severity

5366.7 verb 1sing subj aor mid
χρήσωμαι, / *chrēsōmai* / I may treat,

2567.3 prep
κατὰ / *kata* / according to

3450.12 art acc sing fem
τὴν / *tēn* / the

1833.4 noun acc sing fem
ἐξουσίαν / *exousian* / authority

3614.12 rel-pron acc sing fem
ἣν / *hēn* / which

1319.14 verb 3sing indic aor act
(ἔδωκέν / *edōken* / gave

1466.4 prs-pron dat 1sing
μοι / *moi* / me

3450.5 art sing masc
ὁ / *ho* / the

2935.1 noun nom sing masc
κύριος / *kurios* / Lord

3450.5 art sing masc
[✶ ὁ / *ho* / [the

2935.1 noun nom sing masc
κύριος / *kurios* / Lord

1319.14 verb 3sing indic aor act
ἔδωκέν / *edōken* / gave

1466.4 prs-pron dat 1sing
μοι,] / *moi* / me,]

1519.1 prep
εἰς / *eis* / for

3482.3 noun acc sing fem
οἰκοδομὴν / *oikodomēn* / edification

2504.1 conj
καὶ / *kai* / and

3620.2 partic
οὐκ / *ouk* / not

1519.1 prep
εἰς / *eis* / for

2478.1 noun acc sing fem
καθαίρεσιν. / *kathairesin* / overthrowing.

11. 3036.8 adj acc sing neu
Λοιπόν, / *Loipon* / Remaining,

79.6 noun pl masc
ἀδελφοί, / *adelphoi* / brothers,

5299.7 verb 2pl impr pres act
χαίρετε, / *chairete* / rejoice;

2645.4 verb 2pl impr pres act
καταρτίζεσθε, / *katartizesthe* / restore yourselves;

3731.24 verb 2pl impr pres pass
παρακαλεῖσθε, / *parakaleisthe* / be encouraged;

3450.16 art sing neu
τὸ / *to* / the

840.15 prs-pron sing neu
αὐτὸ / *auto* / same thing

5262.1 verb 2pl pres act
φρονεῖτε, / *phroneite* / mind;

1502.1 verb 2pl impr pres act
εἰρηνεύετε· / *eirēneuete* / be at peace;

2504.1 conj
καὶ / *kai* / and

3450.5 art sing masc
ὁ / *ho* / the

2296.1 noun nom sing masc
θεὸς / *theos* / God

3450.10 art gen sing fem
τῆς / *tēs* / of the

26.2 noun gen sing fem
ἀγάπης / *agapēs* / love

2504.1 conj
καὶ / *kai* / and

1503.2 noun gen sing fem
εἰρήνης / *eirēnēs* / peace

1498.40 verb 3sing indic fut mid
ἔσται / *estai* / shall be

3196.1 prep
μεθ' / *meth'* / with

5050.2 prs-pron gen 2pl
ὑμῶν. / *humōn* / you.

12. 776.9 verb 2pl impr aor mid
Ἀσπάσασθε / *Aspasasthe* / Greet

238.3 prs-pron acc pl masc
ἀλλήλους / *allēlous* / one another

1706.1 prep
ἐν / *en* / with

39.3 adj dat sing
ἁγίῳ / *hagiō* / a holy

5207.1 noun dat sing neu
φιλήματι. / *philēmati* / kiss.

13. 776.3 verb 3pl indic pres
ἀσπάζονται / *aspazontai* / Greet

5050.4 prs-pron acc 2pl
ὑμᾶς / *humas* / you

3450.7 art pl masc
οἱ / *hoi* / the

39.7 adj pl masc
ἅγιοι / *hagioi* / saints

3820.7 adj pl masc
πάντες. / *pantes* / all.

14. 3450.9 art nom sing fem
Ἡ / *Hē* / The

5322.1 noun nom sing fem
χάρις / *charis* / grace

3450.2 art gen sing
τοῦ / *tou* / of the

2935.2 noun gen sing masc
κυρίου / *kuriou* / Lord

2400.2 name masc
Ἰησοῦ / *Iēsou* / Jesus

5382.2 name gen masc
Χριστοῦ, / *Christou* / Christ,

13:10. Again the apostle declared his hope that his corrective letter would be all he ever needed to do to help them mend their ways. He preferred to rebuke while absent than when present after his arrival. He feared if he waited until then he might use sharpness (*apotomōs*, only here and in Titus 1:13 in the New Testament), proceeding in a more cutting way than he would desire.

Instead, their spiritual father desired to use his God-given abilities to build believers up. To use his authority to tear down gave him no pleasure.

13:11-14. At last the painful letter approached its close. In its final section the Corinthians were still called brethren. None of its chastisement should say otherwise. Its author bade them farewell (*chairete*, a word that exhorted them to rejoice).

Again Paul challenged those he loved to be perfect, complete. He wanted them to be comforted and assured that God cares. They needed to be of one mind, thinking, believing, and speaking in agreement. In his earlier epistle Paul wrote, "Now I beseech you, brethren, by the name of our Lord Jesus Christ, that ye all speak the same thing, and that there be no divisions among you; but that ye be perfectly joined together in the same mind and in the same judgment" (1 Corinthians 1:10). Now they still needed to live in peace, dwelling together in harmony.

All four of Paul's exhortations here are present imperatives, indicating these must go on with continuous action at Corinth. In that case the God of love and peace would abide in their fellowship. Paul wrote often of the God of peace; here he reminded the Corinthian believers that He is also the God of love.

Paul frequently ended his letters with a request that certain ones be greeted in the congregation. Here he merely asked that believers at Corinth greet one another with a holy kiss. The implication was that the salutation be a warm one and included approaching the fellow member of the body of Christ by name.

The custom of greeting with a kiss was prevalent in the ancient world as it is in many places yet today. Paul indicated its frequent use by mentioning it elsewhere (Romans 16:16; 1 Corinthians 16:20; 1 Thessalonians 5:26). Peter brought his first epistle to a close much as Paul did this one, calling it a "kiss of charity" (1 Peter 5:14).

Certainly, New Testament believers did not exchange kisses between the sexes in their meetings. Paul would never have encouraged anything that might possibly be sensuous. Indeed, in the synagogues from which many earlier Christians came, men and women occupied different parts of the building. In some cultures today they do not sit together in church, not even husband and wife. However, despite the fact that they gave the customary kiss with all discretion, the passing of the years saw outsiders accusing believers of promoting unwholesome relations through the practice. Thus it declined. It has been replaced by the handshake in a large part of the world.

10. Therefore I write these things being absent: On this account, *PNT*.

lest being present I should use sharpness: . . . not have to treat you harshly, *Norlie* . . . I may not employ severity, *Fenton*.

according to the power which the Lord hath given me to edification: . . . using the authority, *Beck* . . . in accordance with the authority, *Fenton*.

and not to destruction: . . . and not for casting down, *Young*.

11. Finally, brethren, farewell: To sum it all up, brothers, *Berkeley* . . . In conclusion, *Confraternity*.

Be perfect, be of good comfort: Move on to the best, *Klingensmith* . . . Aim at perfection, take courage, *Montgomery* . . . Mend your ways, pay attention to my appeal, *Adams* . . . Reform what is amiss in yourselves, *Conybeare* . . . be adjusted; receive admonition, *Berkeley* . . . Keep on growing to be perfect, *Beck* . . . perfect yourselves, *Fenton* . . . be at harmony, be encouraged, *HistNT* . . . be joyful, secure perfection of character, *Weymouth* . . . rejoice...take courage, *Norlie* . . . be getting restored to order; be receiving consolation, *Rotherham* . . . be of good cheer, *PNT* . . . be made complete, *NASB*.

be of one mind, live in peace: . . . may harmony and quietness be among you, *Murdock* . . . agree in your thinking; preserve peace, *Berkeley* . . . be like-minded, *NASB* . . . cultivate peace, *Wilson*.

and the God of love and peace shall be with you:

12. Greet one another with an holy kiss: . . . a saint's kiss, *HistNT* . . . a sacred kiss, *Williams* . . . an affectionate hug, *RPNT*.

13. All the saints salute you: All the holy people greet you, *Beck* . . . All God's people here send greetings to you, *Weymouth*.

14. The grace of the Lord Jesus Christ: The favour, *Rotherham* . . . spiritual blessing, *Williams*.

2 Corinthians 13:14

2504.1 conj	3450.9 art nom sing fem	26.1 noun nom sing fem	3450.2 art gen sing	2296.2 noun gen sing masc	2504.1 conj	3450.9 art nom sing fem
καὶ	ἡ	ἀγάπη	τοῦ	θεοῦ,	καὶ	ἡ
kai	*hē*	*agapē*	*tou*	*theou*	*kai*	*hē*
and	the	love		of God,	and	the

14.a.Txt: 01ℵ-corr,06D
018K,025P,byz.bo.
Var: p46,01ℵ-org,02A
03B,33,Gries,Lach,Treg
Alf,Word,Tisc,We/Ho
Weis,Sod,UBS/⋆

2815.1 noun nom sing fem	3450.2 art gen sing	39.2 adj gen sing	4011.2 noun gen sing neu	3196.3 prep	3820.4 adj gen pl
κοινωνία	τοῦ	ἁγίου	πνεύματος	μετὰ	πάντων
koinōnia	*tou*	*hagiou*	*pneumatos*	*meta*	*pantōn*
fellowship	of the	Holy	Spirit	with	all

14.b.Txt: 018K,Steph
Var: Gries,Lach,Word
Tisc,We/Ho,Weis,Sod
UBS/⋆

5050.2 prs-pron gen 2pl	279.1 partic	4242.1 prep	2854.3 name acc pl masc	1202.4 num ord nom sing fem
ὑμῶν.	ᵃ ἀμήν. ⸍	ᵇ Πρὸς	Κορινθίους	δευτέρα
humōn	*amēn*	*Pros*	*Korinthious*	*deutera*
you.	Amen.	To	Corinthians	second

1119.21 verb 3sing indic aor pass	570.3 prep gen	5212.1 name gen masc	3450.10 art gen sing fem	3081.2 name gen fem
ἐγράφη	ἀπὸ	Φιλίππων	τῆς	Μακεδονίας,
egraphē	*apo*	*Philippōn*	*tēs*	*Makedonias*
written	from	Philippi		of Macedonia,

1217.2 prep	4951.2 name gen masc	2504.1 conj	3037.3 name gen masc
διὰ	Τίτου	καὶ	Λουκᾶ. ⸍
dia	*Titou*	*kai*	*Louka*
by	Titus	and	Luke.

Paul also usually closed his letters by sending greetings from those associated with him to the recipients of the communication. Here he simply said, "All the saints salute (*aspazontai*, 'greet,' from the same root as the verb in verse 12) you." This included the Christians of Macedonia where the apostle was when he wrote this letter.

As here, Paul frequently called believers saints. They occupied that position because they were sanctified, separated from sin and dedicated to God. This happened the moment of their conversion, though some were vile sinners an instant before. In the first letter to the Corinthians Paul took note of the "before" and "after" scene in the lives of many of them. The list of sins of which he wrote included fornication, idolatry, homosexuality, thievery, and drunkenness. Then he remarked, "And such were some of you: but ye are washed, but ye are sanctified, but ye are justified in the name of the Lord Jesus, and by the Spirit of our God" (1 Corinthians 6:9-11).

In closing the Roman letter Paul declared in Romans 16:16, "The churches of Christ salute you." He followed this short greeting with salutations from various brethren whom he mentioned by name (Romans 16:21-23). The scribe who wrote the words as the apostle dictated even added, "I Tertius, who wrote this epistle, salute you in the Lord" (Romans 16:22).

The benediction in verse 14 of 2 Corinthians is the most complete of Paul's letters. It includes each member of the Trinity, God the Father, the Lord Jesus Christ, and the Holy Spirit. From each it promised triple blessings, grace, love, and fellowship.

and the love of God, and the communion of the Holy Ghost, [be] with you all. Amen: May you be joined together by the Holy Spirit, *NLT* . . . the fellowship that is ours in the Holy Spirit, *Phillips* . . . the fellowship the Holy Spirit gives, *Barclay* . . . and the companionship of, *TCNT* . . . and the communication of, *Douay* . . . and the sharing of, *SEB* . . . and the common sharing of, *Williams* . . . and the joint participation of, *Wilson* . . . and the participation in the holy Spirit, *Goodspeed* . . . and the partaking of, *Noyes* . . . as you share Him be with you all! *Beck.*

The *Overview* is a significant section of the *Study Bible*. It offers important information describing the major incidents and themes of each book. Its background facts concerning history, customs, geography, economics, and politics provide a splendid backdrop for understanding the events which transpired on the first-century stage. Since it serves as the background, it does not necessarily cover every chapter or section of the book.

The New Testament can be divided into two basic parts. First there is a historical part, the Gospels and Acts; these contain apostolic testimony about Jesus and the Early Church. The second is a didactic (teaching) part consisting of the various letters (epistles) which give the apostolic interpretation of the events surrounding salvation. Just as the literary genre "gospel" was unique and unparalleled in antiquity, so too, the content of the letters is uniquely Christian. That also is due to Christianity's being grounded in history as well as a religion founded upon divine revelation. The oral proclamation of the apostles ceased with time, but through their letters they continue to speak to the Church until the end of time. *Apostle* means "one sent"; *epistle* denotes a "sent letter."

There are 2 groups of New Testament letters: the 13 letters of Paul and the Epistle to the Hebrews as well as the 7 so-called General Epistles. Paul's letters may be broken into four groups: (1) Eschatological Epistles (1 and 2 Thessalonians); (2) The Chief Epistles (sometimes referred to as "soteriological," concerning the doctrine of salvation—Romans, 1 and 2 Corinthians, Galatians); (3) The Prison Epistles (sometimes called ecclesiastical, that is, "church epistles"), written during Paul's imprisonment in Rome (Ephesians, Philippians, Colossians, and Philemon); (4) The Pastoral Epistles (1 and 2 Timothy, Titus).

Paul's letter to the church in Rome is the longest and most structured of the Pauline correspondence. It is regularly ascribed the most importance. There is general consensus that Paul, inspired by the Holy Spirit, authored it; arguments in favor of that include the self-testimony of the letter (1:15), its style, its content, and the tradition of the Early Church.

Apparently the letter was composed during the years A.D. 56–57, and probably from Corinth near the close of Paul's third missionary journey. At this point Paul was nearing the close of an epoch. He could reflect upon 20 years of Christian ministry. On every strategic front of the Roman Empire Christianity had made advances and had planted churches. The great apostle to the Gentiles now set his sights on the West; he intended to go all the way to Spain. On the way he wanted to fulfill his earnest desire to visit Rome, where a church was already thriving.

Just as Antioch was the base camp for the missionary outreach to the Gentiles in the East, now Rome would be the headquarters for the evangelization of the western Roman Empire. Paul wrote to advise them of his upcoming visit; thus Romans is in a sense a letter of introduction to the church. However, it was not a personal introduction but a presentation of the gospel that Paul preached. He outlined the message he hoped they would join him in spreading.

From such a background it becomes understandable why Paul summarized the gospel in such a highly didactic (teaching) way. Luther called Romans "the correct main piece of the New Testament and the 'most evident gospel.'" Chapter 1, verses 16 and 17, capsulize the major theme of the letter: "The gospel . . . is the power of God unto salvation to every one that believeth; to the Jew first, and also to the Greek.

For therein is the righteousness of God revealed from faith to faith."

Romans can be divided into a section on teaching (chapters 1 to 8); a section on the history of salvation that deals with God's plans for Israel and the rest of mankind (chapters 9 to 11); and a section of admonition (chapters 12 to 16). Although dogmatic, Romans is not polemical, as is, for example, Galatians. Several passages address practical problems (chapter 14). In these Paul instructed the church about how to handle its current struggles. By and large, though, basic questions are discussed. The logic of the letter flows smoothly and serenely, despite Paul's natural inclination to preach. (See below for a fuller discussion of the character of the letter as a whole.)

The absence of verses 1-24 in chapter 16 of some manuscripts has caused some consternation. The most likely explanation is that the letter was closed temporarily in 15:33 but it was not sent until Phoebe could take it to Rome (16:1f.). Thus Paul added further greetings to those he knew in Rome—among others Priscilla and Aquila who apparently returned after the edict against Jews was lifted (ca. A.D. 54; cf. Acts 18:2)—then he closed the letter. Origen indicates a knowledge of this section in the oldest manuscripts. Because the passage is of such a personal nature it may have been omitted in those manuscripts that circulated for the Church at large. If the letter was read aloud it might be omitted for the same reason. No person in the Ancient Church denied the authenticity of chapter 16 except for the heretic Marcion, who excised the passage, including chapter 15, for his own dogmatic reasons.

The letter to the Romans is considered by many to be the most significant theological document in the New Testament. Throughout the history of the Church it has maintained its major position. During the Reformation it became the pivotal book for the doctrine of justification by faith alone. The following structure can be presented:

I. OPENING (1:1-17)
  A. Authorship and Greetings (1:1-15)
  B. Major Themes (1:16,17)
    1. The Gospel Is the Power of God Unto Salvation
    2. Through the Gospel God's Righteousness Is Revealed
    3. The Source of the Gospel's Power Is Faith
    4. The Message of the Gospel Is Universal

II. TEACHING SECTION (1:18–8:39)
  A. Concerning Sin (1:18–3:20)
    1. The Guilt of the Gentiles (1:18-32)
      a. Ungodliness, spiritual ignorance, and idolatry (1:18-23)
      b. Unrighteousness and moral decay (1:24-32)
    2. The Guilt of the Jews (2:1–3:20)
      a. The principle of judgment (2:1-16)
        (1) God's judgment rests on the principle of truth (2:1-5)
        (2) God's judgment considers one's works (2:6-10)
        (3) God does not show partiality in His judgment (2:11-15)
        (4) God judges according to the gospel (2:16)
      b. False and true Judaism (2:17-29)
        (1) The claim of the Jews (2:17-20)
        (2) The failure of the Jews (2:21-27)
        (3) The true Jewish religion (2:28,29)
      c. The Jewish advantage (3:1-8)
      d. The world's guilt (3:9-20)
        (1) The accusation (3:9)
        (2) The proof of Scripture (3:10-18)
        (3) The conclusion (3:19,20)
  B. Concerning Justification (3:21–5:21)
    1. The Basis of Justification (3:21-31)
      a. The new revelation of God's righteousness (3:21,22)
        (1) The righteousness of God revealed in the Law.
        (2) Witnessed by the Law and the Prophets.
        (3) The righteousness of God is by faith.
      b. The three metaphors (3:23-26)
        (1) The legal metaphor (3:23)
        (2) The slave market metaphor (3:24)
        (3) The temple metaphor (3:25,26)
      c. The two addenda (3:27-31)
        (1) Boasting is excluded (3:27,28)
        (2) Salvation is for everyone (3:29,30)

I. OPENING (1:1-17)

The letter to the Romans is termed the first great theological work in Christian literature; such a title is fully deserved. But since this major Christian document is in the form of a letter, it has an opening.

A. Authorship and Greetings (1:1-15)

Paul first identified himself as the sender, just as custom dictated. But he did this in a manner totally different from, say, the letter to his friend Philemon. Paul wrote to the church in Rome not so much for personal reasons but as the servant and apostle of Jesus Christ. The letter to Rome outlines the gospel Paul preached. He appealed both to his apostolic authority and to the authority of Scripture as the basis for the veracity of his message. The opening shows by what authority the apostle was writing. Paul did not himself found the church in Rome; however, at the same time he was no "outsider." He was writing as the apostle to the Gentiles and as an instructor in faith and truth (Romans 11:13; cf. 1 Timothy 2:7).

Paul's gospel is the gospel of God, and it is about the Son of God. Jesus Christ is the main character of the gospel story; in fact, He is the story itself. "According to the flesh," according to His human origin, He came from the line of David in keeping with messianic promises. "According to the Spirit of holiness," according to His spiritual heritage, He is the almighty Son of God. He proved this by being raised from the dead. The Pauline portrait of Christ does not simply point to the human and divine natures of Jesus; rather, it directs our attention

655

to the two different positions He assumed in His manifestation: humiliation and exaltation.

B. Major Themes (1:16,17)

With a classic understatement Paul declared that he was not ashamed of the gospel. Actually the cross of Christ was his only glory (Galatians 6:14). At the same time Paul knowingly placed himself at odds with the world's attitude toward the gospel, because the preaching of the Cross is foolishness to those who are perishing (1 Corinthians 1:18). Nothing causes as much offense to the sinful man as the message of the Cross.

1. The Gospel Is the Power of God Unto Salvation

Thus Paul could declare he was not ashamed of it. It is superior to any human claim of personal merit in that it accomplishes something. It is the *dunamis* ("power") in contrast to the "powerlessness" of man to do anything to save himself. The gospel is God's solution to the problem of sin; it makes the dead alive and makes one a new creation in Christ. Salvation is mankind's greatest need, and only God can fulfill it. He alone can save us (Isaiah 35:4). He accomplishes this through Jesus Christ. The gospel then is the vibrant, powerful message of that salvation that has been procured for all mankind.

2. Through the Gospel God's Righteousness Is Revealed

The gospel becomes God's power for our salvation because in it God reveals His righteousness "by faith from first to last," as the apostle says. The phrase "the righteousness of God" appears for the first time in this passage. There is particular significance to that expression here. It does not simply refer to an attribute of God but to an action on God's part (Dodd, *The Moffatt New Testament Commentary*, p.10). God's righteousness is expressed in His action in that He saves mankind: "The Lord hath made known his salvation: his righteousness hath he openly showed in the sight of the heathen" (Psalm 98:2).

The gospel offers the solution to the question of how can God be just in justifying the ungodly (3:26; 4:5). In the Law, God's righteousness is revealed in judgment, but in the gospel it is manifest for salvation. Thus the "righteousness of God" is not only an attribute of God but that which He freely gives to man. This great truth

became apparent to Martin Luther and became a leading force behind the Reformation. Luther realized that what was previously thought to be an expression of God's strict expectations was in fact a declaration that God justifies. His righteousness does not condemn or judge the sinner; it invites him by grace to share in God's life (cf. 8:33).

3. The Source of the Gospel's Power Is Faith

It is for the one who believes "the power of God unto salvation." The righteousness of God that is revealed in the gospel is "first and last of faith," that is, no one can obtain salvation or righteousness through keeping the Law. It can only be received by faith. Faith in this context concerns the gospel itself. This includes the fact that the sinner places his trust in the gospel message; he depends upon it to guide his/her life and puts his trust in its message.

This faith is moreover based upon certain salvation events accomplished by God in Christ: When Jesus rose from the dead He justified those believing in Him (4:25). Faith is the condition upon which the gospel depends. The believer receives God's righteousness "by faith." At the same time the gospel demands that Christians act upon their faith. "Faith cometh by hearing" (10:17). Believers are saved by hearing and not by doing (Acts 11:14). The righteous will live by faith!

4. The Message of the Gospel Is Universal

Although it is "for the Jew first," it is not like the Mosaic covenant whose blessings were restricted to Jews and proselytes of the Jewish religion. The gospel is "to the Jew first, and also to the Greek." When Paul spoke from the Greek perspective the pagans were excluded (1:14). But from a Jewish point of view the Greek was a typical Gentile, i.e., he was excluded and outside of the covenant (Moody, *Broadman Bible Commentary*, 10:168). Paul proclaimed a gospel in which "there is neither Jew nor Greek!" (Galatians 3:28). Before the apostle began to condemn the world before God, his opening words acknowledged that salvation in Christ is just as universally affective as the guilt of mankind.

II. TEACHING SECTION (1:18–8:39)
A. Concerning Sin (1:18–3:20)

The counterpart to God's grace is His wrath. Just as the righteousness of God is revealed in the gospel (1:17), so too, God's wrath is revealed from heaven against sin (1:18). God's kindness is offset by His sternness (11:22). Paul demonstrated how justified God is in His wrath and how necessary the gospel is if we are to escape this wrath. Justification can only be appreciated against the backdrop of God's wrath because of sin. The one not knowing guilt has no comprehension of innocence either. The most serious consequence of sin is not that it leads to Satan's snares; rather, it puts one under the judgment of God (Luke 12:5). Paul shows in 1:18 to 3:20 that both Gentiles and Jews stand before God without excuse; each has incurred the wrath of God.

1. The Guilt of the Gentiles (1:18-32)

God directs His wrath toward two things: ungodliness and unrighteousness (1:18). Ungodliness refers to sin of a religious nature; unrighteousness involves sin in the moral sense of that word.

a. Ungodliness, spiritual ignorance, and idolatry (1:18-23). The ungodly one does not perceive God worthy of knowing (1:28), and he desires no fellowship with God. Ungodliness involves sinning against those commandments on the first table. It also concerns the spurning of the greatest commandment, to "love the Lord thy God with all thy heart, and with all thy soul, and with all thy mind" (Matthew 22:37).

Ungodliness leads to spiritual ignorance (1:18-23), which results from a hardened heart (Ephesians 4:17,18). Because God has afforded men the opportunity to know Him through natural revelation, such as the Creation (1:19,20), as well as through his (man's) conscience (2:14,15), mankind is without excuse before God. He is ignorant of God not because of an intellectual deficiency; rather, it is due to his moral deficiency. It is the evil delusion about which the Bible has so much to say; it is the very essence of sin (Ecclesiastes 7:25). Sin corrupts the cognitive life of man and darkens his heart (1:21). In the end, the mind ruled by sin is utterly worthless (1:28).

Furthermore, spiritual ignorance results in idolatry (1:23-25). The void in the soul of man must be filled by something, and where God is excluded something else moves in and takes His place. At the heart of every denial of God—in one form or another—is a worship of the creation rather than the Creator (1:25). Eventually demonic forces are worshiped (1 Corinthians 10:20); the devil becomes one's god (2 Corinthians 4:4). The most serious aspect of idolatry is not its threat to life; instead it is its essentially sinful character. It offends God and subjects men to God's wrath.

b. Unrighteousness and moral decay (1:24-32). Unrighteousness as well as every other sin is a violation of God's law and a conscious rejection of His will (1 John 3:4). In actuality unrighteousness is rooted in ungodliness—a religious sin results in a wrong moral action. Eventually one discovers that unrighteousness lies at the root of many other sins (Murray, *New International Commentary on the New Testament*, 1:43). Paul's sin lists are paralleled elsewhere in earlier Jewish literature (e.g., Wisdom of Solomon 12 to 14). His own "catalogue of vices" are not that far removed from common social standards found elsewhere in Gentile writings. Paul divided the sins into two groups.

First he spoke of sexual impurity (1:24-28). Idolatry is a source of most immorality, and paganism is characterized by much sexual perversion. Paul indicted the worst kind of immorality—unnatural sexual relations. In an effort to relay the extent of pagan immorality and the degree to which it can control men, Paul first showed he was appalled that "even their women exchanged natural relations for unnatural ones" (1:26).

Three times Paul stressed that because men are held captive to their desires there is implicit judgment; God has handed them over to their own lusts (1:24,26,28). Ultimately, God allows men to choose their own route. Nevertheless, there is an element of God's judgment—active judgment—in this. God punishes sin with sin; the one who loves sin is handed over to his own lusts. This is not to say that God tempts men to sin (James 1:13), but He does permit man free choice. Man receives the due penalty of his sins—in part because of the corrosive, destructive character of sin, and in part because it is a judgment from God.

Second, in 1:29-32 Paul focused upon those sins that defile the spirit of man. These include social sins, sins against the second table of the Law, and sins against the great commandment: love your neighbor. He also mentioned hatred against God.

The list culminates in 1:32, which states that those who live in such sins know very well the judgment of God as well as His sentence for such sins—death. However, these reprobates do not simply live in sins themselves, they also encourage others who participate in like sins.

Thus there is a "fellowship" in sin, an evil unity in which sinners support one another in their rebellion against God. This mystery of lawlessness is fundamental to the superstructure of Satan's realm.

2. The Guilt of the Jews (2:1–3:20)

Paul knew that voices from many sources would agree with his condemnation of the sins of the Gentiles. A contemporary of Paul, Seneca, a Stoic philosopher, wrote a number of pieces on virtue and sin that are entirely compatible with what the apostle to the Gentiles wrote. Paul would have received an even more thoroughgoing endorsement from the Jewish community for his indictment of Gentiles. But when Paul moved into a well-planned dialogue/argument (which never actually occurred) called a diatribe, in which he took the Jewish religiosity to task, they became his opponents rather than advocates. Some—by their own positions—were compelled to agree with this indisputable logic. Using rhetorical questions, Paul virtually "tied up" his opponents. Thus Paul moved the Jew to the center of his readers' field of vision and kept him there, not just in the central portion of this section, but in 2:1-16 and 3:9-20 as well.

a. The principle of judgment (2:1-16).

The Jews must not fall into the error of thinking that if they judged others they themselves would not be judged. In sharp contrast to human judging stands God's judgment. Paul then proceeded to outline the principles used by God.

(1) God's judgment rests upon the principle of truth (2:1-5). "According to truth" (verse 2), the Lord is "the righteous judge" (2 Timothy 4:8). Apparently Paul was referring to the common Jewish misconception that God would use different standards for judging Jews and Gentiles (cf. the Wisdom of Solomon, chapters 11 to 13 especially). Paul denounced such an attitude (2:9,11,27). "Wherein thou judgest another, thou condemnest thyself; for thou that judgest doest the same things" (2:1).

(2) God's judgment considers one's works (2:6-10). Far from getting off easy, the Jews will be judged first, just as they will be rewarded first (2:9,10). At the Judgment words will not replace deeds. Being judged according to deeds does not contradict the doctrine of justification by faith, because judgment based upon works is not the same as judgment by works (Moody, *Broadman Bible Commentary*, 10:174). Being judged according to works is a consistent principle of Scripture (e.g., Psalm 62:3; Proverbs 24:12; Jeremiah 17:10; 2 Corinthians 5:10; 2 Timothy 4:14; 1 Peter 1:17; Revelation 2:23; 20:12). Individuals may be denied not only because of unbelief, but also because of evil deeds. Good works, furthermore, are evidence of faith and salvation. Salvation is solely by faith (Romans 3:28), but faith never stands alone (James 2:14-20). It produces works.

(3) God does not show partiality in His judgment (2:11-15). Precisely because of this each man will be judged according to his own merits. Jews having the Law will be thus judged according to the Law (2:12). But Gentiles also have a law, the law of conscience that teaches them right from wrong. They have the work of law written in their hearts, according to Paul. This thought verbally resembles Jeremiah 31:31, but it has a different meaning.

"There is no nation so lost to everything human that it does not keep within the limits of some laws. Since then all nations, of themselves and without monitor, are disposed to make laws for themselves, it is beyond all question evident that they have some notions of justice" (Calvin, *Calvin's Commentaries: Romans,* p.96).

(4) God judges according to the gospel (2:16). The teaching of a final judgment does not contradict the message of the gospel; in fact, it is integral to the announcement of grace. This was not fully realized until the proclamation of the gospel, thus Paul only infrequently pointed to the gospel as the basis for judgment. Paul suggested that a new principle of judgment is in force: "That they all might be damned who believed not the truth" (2 Thessalonians 2:12; cf. John 16:9 and its context).

b. False and true Judaism (2:17-29).

The next section opens with the words: "Behold, thou art called a Jew . . . " (2:17). At this juncture Paul began a most curious argumentation. In response to the boast of those Jews who pointed to their Jewish heritage Paul questioned their adherence to Judaism: You are called a Jew, but are you really? Thus Paul was redefining "Jewish" not in terms of natural descent, but in terms of a spiritual position.

(1) The claim of the Jews (2:17-20). In short statements Paul summarized some of the privileges the Jews appealed to as an indication of their "superiority" over the Gentiles. His stipulations are not without irony; nevertheless, he did not deny that being Jewish has certain actual advantages. Still, he undermined their basis for such claims to superiority.

(2) The failure of the Jews (2:21-27). Paul posed five questions to the Jewish legal expert or teacher of the Law: First, "Thou therefore which teachest another, teachest thou not thyself?" Paul asserted, just as Jesus had, that the ultimate sin of Judaism was its hypocrisy (cf. Matthew 23:1f.). The adherents knew the Law; they taught others the Law, but they did not themselves do what the Law demanded. Thus Paul could regard their "religion" as useless.

Circumcision meant Jews must keep the Law (cf. Galatians 5:3)—all of it! Perhaps, Paul argued, circumcision was of some small value ("profiteth") if one indeed kept the whole Law. But any violation of the Law, even in its smallest point, was a violation of the whole Law. The violator, thus, must be regarded in the same manner as an uncircumcised Gentile (2:25). This reasoning would not have set well in Jewish ears, for to them circumcision had a value all its own. Some rabbis taught that the sign of circumcision prevented any Jew from going to Gehenna (Moody, *Broadman Bible Commentary*, 10:177). Paul regarded these speculations as empty self-delusion.

(3) The true Jewish religion (2:28,29). Jews regarded themselves superior to Gentiles on the basis of ethnic heritage (nationality) and religion (especially monotheism). They saw themselves certainly on a par with Christians and more typically above. They considered Christians, especially Jewish Christians, as deceivers. However, at a very early stage of development Christianity responded to this charge.

Peter redirected this charge of deceit upon the Jews themselves in his public accusation that they betrayed the Messiah by delivering Him to the Romans (Acts 3:13; cf. 4:27). Even Paul's deep love for his kinsmen did not prevent him from using scathing language against them (1 Thessalonians 2:15).

With words charged with indignation Paul attacked the Judaizers and called them "dogs, those men who do evil, those mutilators of the flesh" (Philippians 3:2, NIV). The kind of Judaism that had crucified the Messiah and had persecuted His disciples ceased being "true Judaism" to Paul. Paul reserved the title *Jew* for those who believe in Christ. Over against those "putting confidence in the flesh" are those of the (true) circumcision, those who "worship God in the spirit" (Philippians 3:3). "For he is not a Jew, which is one outwardly; . . . but he is a Jew, which is one inwardly; and circumcision

is that of the heart, in the spirit, and not in the letter; whose praise is not of men, but of God" (Romans 2:28,29).

There is some dispute over the final words. Jews are named in keeping with their ancestor Judah. Some contend that Judah means "the praised one," and is from the Hebrew word *yadah*, "praise." Leah, who worshiped God because of her son, named him Judah in keeping with her praise of God (Genesis 29:35). His father Jacob blessed him from his death bed with the words: "Thou art he whom thy brethren shall praise" (Genesis 49:8).

c. The Jewish advantage (3:1-8). In this next section Paul gave his imaginary opponent one opportunity to defend himself. It consists of two of the standard arguments against Christianity which Paul undoubtedly met in the synagogues. The first relates to the perception mentioned above: Judaism and circumcision. The second relates to the Jewish objection that God would be unjust if "our unrighteousness brings out God's righteousness more clearly."

(1) Is Judaism actually practiced in vain? Paul's challenger raised an objection which might mistakenly be concluded from Paul's earlier arguments. If what Paul said about the value of "inwardly" belonging to God's people is true, and if only the "circumcision of the heart" by the Spirit has significance, "What advantage then hath the Jew? or what profit is there of circumcision?" (3:1). "What advantage is there in being Jewish and in being circumcised as a sign of the covenant?" asks his imaginary opponent.

Paul, however, did not concede to such reasoning. On the contrary, he responded that the advantage of being Jewish is "much every way" (3:2). The privileges of the Jewish people are actual, although they have been abused and neglected in the past.

One of the main advantages of the Jewish people is that they were entrusted with God's Word in the Holy Scriptures. The Scriptures speak on behalf of God in the same way the prophets did. Circumcision was a sign of God's covenant with Abraham, the patriarch of the nation (Genesis 17). God remains faithful to this covenant in spite of the unfaithfulness of the Jewish people.

(2) The second Jewish objection, that it is "unjust" that "our unrighteousness brings out God's righteousness more clearly" (3:5, NIV)—and hence an invitation to sin that grace may abound, was soundly refuted by Paul. Man-

kind's sin is no less reprehensible because it does not affect God, thus Paul ignored such reasoning. God is the judge of the world and the moral standard of the universe; this is revealed truth. "The reply to objections is proclamation" (Murray, *New International Commentary on the New Testament*, p.99).

Still, Paul had more to say than this. The imaginary opponent rephrased the objection, and this time Paul—in obvious disbelief—admitted that some had erroneously insinuated that this is what he taught. Heralds of the gospel, and especially Paul, were continually suspected of encouraging "lawlessness" (antinomianism). The New Testament is plagued with traces of the struggle against those who pervert the freedom of the gospel into license for immorality (Galatians 5:13-21; Titus 1:16; 2 Peter 2:1f.; 2:18f.; Jude 4).

This distortion of the Christian message afforded the legal experts in Judaism as well as the philosophers of the Gentile world the opportunity to infiltrate the gospel ranks. They asserted that lawlessness was a natural by-product of gospel proclamation. Paul's letters indicate they claimed much of their authority (unjustly) from Paul's own teachings. Paul readdressed himself to this issue in 6:1f., and he took it as a point of departure for his teaching on sanctification. In 3:8 though, he only rejected scornfully such agitators with the words "whose damnation is just."

d. *The world's guilt (3:9-20).* In this section Paul moved toward concluding his argument. He posed the question: "Are we Jews any better than the Gentiles?" Although Jews may have advantage "much in every way," they are "in no wise" better than Gentiles in God's eyes (cf. Bruce, *Tyndale New Testament Commentaries*, 6:92).

(1) *The accusation (3:9).* Paul summarized and restated the accusation he made earlier: Jew and Greek alike are under the condemnation of sin. To be under sin means that sin controls and dominates one's existence. But it also signifies one's guilt before God. One already stands under God's judgment. In the next two sections Paul discussed these two dimensions of sin.

(2) *The proof of Scripture (3:10-18).* Having summarized the charge in the preceding verse, Paul now began his argument with the evidence of Scripture. He employed a method of interpretation commonly used by the rabbis of his day. It derived its name, *charaz*, from the pro-

cess of threading beads on a string, such as a string of pearls. The practice of *charaz* involved using, for example, a Pentateuchal text as a basic text; then one would "string" other texts to this on the basis of corresponding words or phrases. These other texts came from the Prophets, Psalms, and other portions of Scripture (Edersheim).

In this instance Paul created a chain of six citations from the Old Testament which demonstrate man's sinful nature and conduct. Five times it is noted that none are righteous and none seek God (verses 10-12).

In highly metaphorical language Paul noted those physical parts of the body capable of serving unrighteousness (verses 13-15). Fallen man is characterized by his "worthlessness" (verse 12; cf. 1:28). No one does anything good or makes any effort to seek God.

(3) *The conclusion (3:19,20).* The final verses pronounce the sentence: All the world is guilty before God. It is guilty because of sin—actual concrete sin, not some subjective feeling of guilt. This guilt and sin separate man from an offended and holy God. Sin itself devastates man, creating inner conflicts as well as binding him to wrongdoing.

The actual problem of guilt before God places man under His judgment and wrath. Mankind is enabled to recognize this problem only through the convicting power of the Holy Spirit through preaching and the Word of God. Through the power of the Holy Spirit man comes to realize that he needs something more than deliverance from a bad conscience; what he really needs is to be justified—made righteous—before God, so he will not perish eternally.

In no uncertain terms Paul asserted that "by the deeds of the law there shall no flesh be justified in his sight" (3:20). Because the Law permits man to recognize sin he can confess it. However, the Law is not able to release man from the guilt of that sin, nor can it set him free from sin's power. Only the gospel of the "good news" of Jesus Christ has that ability.

B. Concerning Justification (3:21–5:21)

Someone once said that this is the most important section of the most important book in the Bible. Although this is an overstatement, there is something to be said for its element of truth. There is perhaps no other portion of Scripture which condenses so much of the essence of the gospel.

1. The Basis of Justification (3:21-31)

In this section Paul began to proclaim the gospel in the same manner as he had in the opening (see above), having laid the groundwork in between. The thunder of the Law closes every mouth; sin is stilled in silence. It is in this setting that the still voice of the gospel can be heard.

The gospel cannot meet an unrecognized need, but where men are awakened from their worldly slumber and their religious self-righteousness the gospel can penetrate and accomplish mighty things. Jesus himself declared that He had not come for the righteous but for the unrighteous; it is the sinner who needs to be justified.

a. The new revelation of God's righteousness (3:21,22). Section 3:21-26 is actually made up of a hymn of three verses, each containing four lines and arranged in balance.

(1) verses 21,22a
(2) verses 22b-25a
(3) verses 25b,26

The following breakdown, however, is according to content.

The main focus of this section of the letter to Rome is the issue of righteousness—the dispute between the unrighteous man and the righteous God. Prior to this point Paul had stressed that God's righteousness is revealed in His judgment. Here Paul shifted gears and began to describe an entirely different manifestation of the righteousness of God.

(1) The righteousness of God revealed in the Law. The words of the Law announce the arrival of a totally new age and order—what some have called "God's eschatological now." In sharp contrast to the role of the Law in manifesting God's righteousness Paul had previously outlined, now he spoke of a new righteousness that is revealed apart from the Law. This does not concern righteousness in the subjective sense, such as an attribute of God; rather, it involves an objective righteousness that God imputes to those who believe. This is the righteousness that Paul introduced as early as 1:17: "The righteousness of God revealed from faith to faith"—that is, a righteousness by faith in contrast to a righteousness through the Law.

God could not satisfy His demand for righteousness apart from destroying the moral universe. Only the righteous can stand before God (Psalm 15). However, man cannot attain this righteousness through his own efforts; therefore, God gives to man the righteousness he needs by offering him salvation. Even if the path of the Law had been an avenue to righteousness, it was a path no one could follow. Indeed, Paul argued that the Law was never a means of attaining righteousness.

Since man is unable to win righteousness by doing the works of the Law, God gives it to him as a free gift. By His own sovereignty God declares sinners righteous if they accept His provision for their redemption. This enigmatic event is termed "justification" in the Scripture. All those believing in the One who justifies the ungodly may experience it (4:5).

This is a righteousness apart from the Law; that is, it is not something that man earns by keeping the Law. This righteousness is given on a totally different basis—Jesus Christ.

(2) Witnessed by the Law and the Prophets. Whenever Paul spoke of a righteousness apart from the Law it must not be assumed that the gospel contradicts the old covenant and the Holy Scriptures. At its heart even the old covenant was founded upon promise rather than Law (Galatians 3:17). True Judaism is not a legalistic religion but a religion of promise. Thus Paul declared that the righteousness of God that is apart from the Law is nevertheless precisely the righteousness to which the Law and the prophets bore witness. Later Paul offered a series of texts in support of this claim. The very point at which the faith of the Bible differs so radically from every other human religion in the world is that God's righteousness is something He gives, and it cannot be earned.

(3) The righteousness of God is by faith. Over against one's "own righteousness, which is by the law" (Philippians 3:9), the true righteousness, now revealed, is called "the righteousness of God which is by faith of Jesus Christ" (Romans 3:22). Unlike legalistic religions or human religions that depend upon man's own efforts, the righteousness of God depends upon the work of Christ. Man does not deserve it, and yet for Christ's sake it is imputed to those who believe. It rests upon an individual's being forgiven and having repented of his sins. God demands righteousness, but He provides the believer with the very righteousness He wants.

Whereas the "righteousness of the law" was thought to be won through keeping the Law, God's righteousness comes through faith. The centrality of faith is highlighted by the deliberate redundancy of verse 22: "righteousness of God which is by faith of Jesus Christ unto all and upon all them that believe!" Faith here is not some nebulous "faith" without substance; neither is it simply believing that God exists. The faith which justifies is faith in Jesus Christ, the Son of God (1:3,4), who "was delivered over to death for our sins and was raised to life for our justification" (4:25, NIV). The one justified by faith is the one believing in Jesus' person and Christ's work on his behalf.

b. The three metaphors (3:23-26). Justification by faith is the great theological theme in Romans. It stands in sharp contrast to the rabbis' doctrine of justification by works. Paul did not present the arguments for his teaching by mere logic, although what he said is indeed logical. Instead, he used a series of pictures or parables, the language of the prophet and the poet.

The apostle used three metaphors. One comes from the courtroom: The accused is acquitted; although guilty, he is justified by God's own decision. The second metaphor is from the slave market: The one in bondage is released through the price of redemption paid by Jesus Christ. The third metaphor is taken from the temple offerings: The blood of Jesus Christ is the real basis of justification. Through the repentant sinner's faith, the blood of Jesus becomes a propitiation that satisfies God's wrath against sin.

(1) The legal metaphor (3:23). The repentant sinner is justified on the basis of what Paul called "the righteousness of God."

Justification is not synonymous with forgiveness, although it is clearly granted only on the basis of forgiveness of sins. The way the word *justification* is used, it indicates it is not identical with forgiveness. If an individual actually kept the Law he was no sinner and therefore did not need to be forgiven. No one could actually be justified through fulfilling the commands of the Law, but if he could, it could not accurately be described as forgiveness.

Romans 3:4 speaks of God's being justified. The same Greek word for justification is used in Luke 7:29 where it is said the people justified God, i.e., acknowledged God to be in the right. Justifying God means acknowledging His completely righteous character. Thus, justification is something other than forgiveness of sins.

Justification is the opposite of condemnation: "By thy words thou shalt be justified, and by thy words thou shalt be condemned" (Matthew 12:37). See also Romans 5:16; 8:33,34. A court does not make a man a criminal. It simply arrives at a decision about what he already is.

If he is acquitted, this is a public declaration that no guilt can be placed upon him. The term *justification* has the same meaning in the Bible. It means to be acquitted of what one is accused of, to be declared righteous by God (G.H. Clark).

In his teaching about justification, Paul described what takes place in God's courtroom. Here the guilty one is acquitted; the sinner is justified. His sins are canceled, and the righteousness of Christ is imputed to him. If God rendered such a decision only on the basis of what the sinner is himself, it would be unjust. Of course, this would be contrary to the character of God. Proverbs 17:15 says, "He that justifieth the wicked, and he that condemneth the just, even they both are abomination to the Lord."

The main question in the Book of Romans is: how then can a just God acquit and justify the ungodly one? It was of special importance to Paul to defend God's character and actions in the matter, to show that He can be just and still justify the sinner. No doubt Paul encountered objections to this teaching in his discussions with the Jews. They could not understand that the gospel did not contradict the righteousness of God. The apostle's reply to the Jews' opposition was this: God can be just and still justify the person who believes in Jesus because the believer stands before God clothed in Jesus' own righteousness. He has a new relationship with God secured for him by what Paul called "the redemption that is in Christ Jesus" (3:24).

(2) The slave market metaphor (3:24). The Greek word used here for "redemption" is *apolutrōseōs*. The term was used in connection with redeeming a slave or prisoner of war. In the Septuagint *lutroō* is used of God's redemption of His people from Egypt and from Babylon (Deuteronomy 7:8; Isaiah 51:11). In the New Testament the word has the double meaning of being redeemed and being bought by a price, a ransom, *lutron*. This last term is used in Matthew 20:28 and Mark 10:45. In both passages it is said that Jesus would give His life "a ransom for many." This substitutionary atonement is the basis of redemption. Jesus gave His own life as the price paid for that redemption.

God taught His people under the old covenant that He had the right to redeem His people (Rosenius). If an Israelite had been sold into slavery because of a debt, he could be redeemed by a brother. In the Old Testament the subject of redemption already had a distinct spiritual context. It is written in Psalm 49:7,8: "None of them can by any means redeem his brother, nor give to God a ransom for him: (for the redemption of their soul is precious, and it ceaseth for ever)." This passage concerns the relationship between man and God. It requires a ransom, but no man can save his brother from death by paying a price. The ransom is now paid in full by Jesus Christ, and God himself is the One who has actually paid the price so that He and man can have a restored relationship.

(3) The temple metaphor (3:25,26). Paul took his third picture from the temple and the ritual of the old covenant. He used the word *hilastērion.* The only other place the term is used in the New Testament is Hebrews 9:5. There it means the mercy seat, the golden cover of the ark of the covenant where the blood was sprinkled on the great Day of Atonement. The word is also used in such a manner 22 times in the Septuagint. Most scholars agree that in 3:25 Paul wanted to include the symbolism of the mercy seat. Origen and all the Greek fathers of the Church understood the verse this way. In fact, it has always enjoyed widespread support among Bible scholars.

Such a reference to the mercy seat of the old covenant does not limit the meaning of the Greek word since it is used in other ways. Although Paul alluded to the mercy seat by using the word *hilastērion,* there is no reason to believe he confined the meaning of the word only to the mercy seat. The term belongs to a group of words used in connection with atonement and reconciliation.

Besides *hilastērion,* which is used this way twice, three related Greek words are used in the New Testament—each of them twice.

The verb *hilaskomai* stands in Greek usage for soothing an offended person or securing his favor through a gift or an atoning sacrifice. It is the offended party, not the offender, who becomes softened in his attitude. In the New Testament this word is used in Hebrews 2:17, where it refers to Christ who as a high priest made reconciliation for sin. It is also used in Luke 18:13 where the publican prayed that God would be merciful to him. The publican was praying in the temple—the place where atonement must be made. Thus his prayer was consistent with the thought of atonement.

The adjective *hileōs* is used in Matthew 16:22 where Peter rebuked Jesus with the words "Be it far from thee," or more literally, "Have mercy on you." The word is also used in Hebrews 8:12 where the word of the prophet is quoted: "I will be merciful to their unrighteousness."

The noun *hilasmos* is used in 1 John 2:2; 4:10 concerning Christ as the propitiation for our sins.

Thus the usage of these words in the New Testament is consistent with their usual meaning in Greek usage. This is also true in Romans 3:25. Paul could have employed a word used in the New Testament concerning Christ as an atonement, i.e., *hilasmos,* but he did not. Instead, he chose to use the well-known word for mercy seat, *hilastērion,* a word used for the place of the atonement, not the offering made there. It is difficult to believe the Holy Spirit inspired writer did not do this intentionally. It seems clear that he wanted to bring the mercy seat into the picture, thus connecting Christ's sacrifice with the Day of Atonement. The Jews understood the mercy seat to be God's throne on earth. Thus the usage of the mercy seat as a picture of Christ in His sacrifice fits in with the temple metaphor very well.

Paul was also dealing with another basic theological problem: When God justifies sinners, how can it be just when He bore with sins throughout the Old Testament period? Under the old covenant the various sacrifices—and especially those on the Day of Atonement—were to remind the people that God would one day make atonement for sin by one perfect sacrifice (Hebrews 10:3). However, the Jews did not understand this symbolism of the Day of Atonement, for only the high priest saw the blood-sprinkled mercy seat.

Now something new and unheard of had taken place: the mercy seat was displayed openly. It was no more hidden behind the veil of the temple. It was presented publicly, thus demonstrating God's righteousness to the whole universe, to heaven and earth (Manson, *Peake's Commentary on the Bible*). The mercy seat God had now set forth was not an imperfect copy of the one in the tabernacle and temple. The day of types and shadows was past, for reality had now come (Hebrews 9:11). God is gracious and He has shown the reason for it. Paul declared it is Jesus Christ himself "whom God hath set forth to be a propitiation through faith in his blood."

The mystery is not that God punishes sin, but how can He *not* do so? Only the gospel can give the correct answer. Jewish teachers of the Law accused the gospel of contradicting the righteousness of God. Paul, however, showed that the Jews themselves could not really explain how God can be righteous when He has borne with the sins of past generations. In the shedding of His blood, Jesus displayed the answer to God's forbearance in the past and His justifying grace in the present. God has placed His Son not only before His own eyes, but has exhibited Him to all the world.

c. The two addenda (3:27-31). Now Paul returned to the format of the dialogue. However, it is evident that the apostle himself was asking the rhetorical questions as the antagonist. Several facts need to be noted:

(1) Boasting is excluded (3:27,28). In Paul's writings the matter of "boasting" was taken very seriously. First Corinthians 1:29 says God has chosen that which is low in the world so no flesh could boast before Him. In 3:27 Paul resumed the line of thought from the final verse in the preceding chapter. Earlier he had declared men have nothing to boast about. Their violation of the Law has deprived them of all right to boast. Such an attitude is inconsistent with the law of faith. No one can boast about his works, because works are not the basis of salvation. The basis is faith, thus excluding everything about which a believer might boast.

Christians are justified by faith and faith alone. Luther did not add anything to the actual construction of the text when he added his famous "alone" because this is exactly what the verse emphasizes. Unfortunately, the Council of Trent went against the plain meaning of the text by finally deciding to omit "without works of the law" in quoting Paul. The apostle was emphasizing here that believers are justified by faith alone apart from the works of the Law.

(2) Salvation is for everyone (3:29,30). All have sinned, including both Jews and Gentiles and confirmed by Paul in the preceding chapter, but all may be saved. As an argument for this, Paul pointed to the Shema, Israel's great confession of faith: God is one (Deuteronomy 6:4). The one true God is not only the God of the Jews. He is also the God of the whole earth. In other statements Paul emphasized the fact that God chose Abraham and his family in order that He might bless all people, not just the Jews. Now the apostle stressed the truth that this was through faith, not by the Law, proving that salvation has been provided for (all) who believe. Those who have had the Law (the Jews) must come to God the same way as those without the Law (the Gentiles). God justifies by faith the circumcised as well as the uncircumcised.

2. Illustration of Abraham's Faith (4:1–5:11)

Chapters 4 and 5 can be considered as comments on the basic proclamation of justification by faith in the latter part of chapter 3. There are a number of questions and objections which must be answered so that conclusions can be made. Paul treated this material in two sections.

Here the apostle made another of his surprising points. He presented his argument around two prominent Old Testament persons, Abraham as the type of the one justified by faith (chapter 4) and Adam as the type of Christ (5:12-21). By doing this Paul made his presentation lively and clear and gave a series of proofs from the Scripture for justification by faith. He had already done this in 3:21, where he said the Law and the prophets bear testimony to this truth.

In 3:21 Paul explained the real foundation of justification, based on the redemptive work of Christ. In chapter 5 he explained faith more thoroughly as the subjective means by which the righteousness of God is imputed to man. Paul pointed to Abraham the ancestor of Israel, showing from his life that justification is by faith, not by works (4:1-7), not by circumcision (4:9-12), not by the Law (4:13-16). Then Abraham was presented as the father of believers (4:17-25). Following this is a passage which concerns the blessing resulting from justification (5:1-11).

a. Not by works (4:1-8). Abraham was a justified man. Paul here opposed the rabbis' teaching that Abraham fulfilled the Law and therefore was justified by works. The apostle quoted the Scripture, "Abraham believed God, and it was counted unto him for righteousness." Of all the just men in the Old Testament, none surpasses Abraham. Moses was called the servant of God, but Abraham was called the friend of God. From the Lord himself he received testimony that he had kept all His commandments and laws (Genesis 26:5). But even the most righteous and perfect man must be justified by his faith, not by his works. The rabbis listed Abraham's faith among his good works, but Paul placed faith in opposition to works. By faith and by faith only was Abraham justified.

b. Not by circumcision (4:9-12). Some may raise the question, "When Abraham's faith was counted to him for righteousness, did this not take place because he had entered the covenant of circumcision with God?" Paul rejected such a thought by reminding his readers that righteousness by faith was ascribed to Abraham at least 14 years before he was circumcised. Justification is by faith, not by religious rites.

c. *Not by the Law (4:13-16).* Since the covenant of circumcision was not the basis of Abraham's justification, neither can the Law given at Sinai. In Galatians 3:15-22 Paul pointed out that the Law was given 430 years later. In Romans he presented these principal arguments: law and promise are two entirely different categories. God's promise did concern blessing (Genesis 12:2,3; Galatians 3:8,9), but the Law works wrath (Romans 4:15). If Law makes men heirs of God's promise, then faith is made void.

Therefore, Paul declared that Abraham and his family did not receive the promise of being heirs of the world by the Law, but by the righteousness of faith. Abraham received the promise by faith because it was by God's grace. If he had received it from works it would be like a salary which he earned by his labors. But the promise was by grace, not earnings. Works would render grace meaningless. Where does faith enter the picture? It is the means by which an individual accepts and receives the grace of God which is given apart from works.

d. *The father of believers (4:17-25).* When Paul spoke of Abraham as the father of believers, the subject becomes one of spiritual relationship. To a certain extent chapter 4 presents a contrast to chapter 5 where Adam is presented as the ancestor of the human race (according to the flesh). This argument had great relevance to the Jews. They were descendants of Abraham, and they must be saved in the same way as their great ancestor. When Paul insisted that natural descent was not enough to save them, it was language the Jews understood. They must also have a spiritual relationship with Abraham, which meant they must have the same kind of faith he had. Paul was echoing the preaching of John the Baptist (Matthew 3:7-9) and of Jesus himself (John 8:33-58).

Abraham's faith was characterized by his belief that God makes the dead alive and that He is the Creator who by His word brings into existence what did not previously exist. Thus his faith in God concerned His being both Redeemer and Creator. When God promised Abraham posterity as innumerable as dust and stars, he was still childless, but he believed God (4:18-22). When Abraham went to the mountain to sacrifice Isaac, he believed God could raise from the dead the son through whom the promise was to be carried out (compare Hebrews 11:19).

By this faith Abraham was justified, but this is not recorded in Scripture just to honor Abraham's memory. It is written because of all those who have the same faith in God. The faith of Abraham was displayed first because he believed God had power to raise up Isaac the son of promise. The Christian faith leads believers to accept the fact that God gave His Son to die for the sinner and raised Him from the dead for the believer's justification.

e. *The blessings of justification (5:1-11).* In 4:13 the promise to Abraham is interpreted as meaning he would become heir to the world. In 8:17 Paul spoke of believers as "heirs of God, and joint-heirs with Christ." They share with the only begotten Son His undivided inheritance (John 1:14; Revelation 21:7). This inheritance is "all things."

Paul mentioned the believer's inheritance briefly in 4:13, and then proceeded with his series of arguments. In all of this he was focusing on the important subject of salvation. Paul returned to this subject after completing his interpretation of Abraham's justification. In 5:1-11 the apostle dealt with the other blessings resulting from justification. This passage forms a transition to the next section of the epistle which concerns sanctification. Chapter 5 deals with what believers *have* in Christ, while chapter 6 speaks of what they *are* in Christ.

Next Paul summed up the blessings shared by Christ and the believer, and he did it under the headings of three well-known words—faith, hope, and charity (1 Corinthians 13:13).

(1) Faith (5:1,2). The apostle mentioned three things produced by faith. First, as discussed previously, is justification. The first evidence of justification is peace with God. This peace must be understood theologically, not psychologically. The subject is not peace in one's heart and mind, but peace with God. The peace a believer *feels* is simply the result of the peace he has *received* from God. Unsaved man lives in rebellion against his Creator, which is the reason for his restlessness and internal discord. When he is justified by faith, this warfare ceases. The repentant sinner is reconciled to God, so he no longer lives under His wrath. Enmity and revolt are gone. Therefore, peace with God is something much more than a feeling. A total

change in man's relationship with God has taken place.

Furthermore, "we have access by faith into this grace wherein we stand." One commentator says this statement could refer to being introduced to a royal person—a striking and beautiful illustration. The real meaning, however, is that since believers are now in favor with God they have been given great privileges.

(2) Hope (5:2-4). Faith and justification do not only provide rich treasures of peace and grace now, they give hope of enjoying the glory of God in the future. What the believer now possesses is evidence that the future has already begun and is a foretaste and pledge of that which is to come. Even the believer's present tribulations only strengthen and increase this hope.

(3) Charity (love, 5:5-11). A believer is secure in the knowledge that he will not be ashamed in his hope—a security resting in the love of God. This love has been poured out into his heart by the Holy Spirit, who is himself the guarantee of the believer's inheritance until the day of redemption when he actually enters into it. The overwhelming love of God in the believer's heart is the great force which guides his life.

The amazing thing is that this love was shown "when we were still powerless, Christ died for the ungodly" (NIV). Sinners did not win (earn) God's love. His love won and keeps them. Christ died for the ungodly at a time God had already fixed. Much more then, being justified by Christ's blood, believers will be saved from wrath through Him. The believer does not boast of himself or his own works as the basis of his salvation and hope. He boasts of God by the Lord Jesus Christ. This means that in Christ he trusts God as Guarantor that his hope will be realized.

This discussion of love is actually a hymn about love, as 3:21-26 is a hymn about righteousness. In both passages there is a poetic section of three verses, each containing four lines and two parallels. Verse 1 of the hymn says Christ died "when we were . . . without strength" in verse 2 while men were sinners, in verse 3 while they were enemies (Moody, *Broadman Bible Commentary*, 10:193). The hymn in 3:21 exalts the death of Christ as the perfect revelation of God's righteousness, while the hymn in 5:6-11 exalts the Cross as the ultimate proof of God's love.

3. Adam and Christ (5:12-21)

Paul explained the connection between justification and faith in chapter 4. In 5:12-21 he ended that explanation and presented the connection between justification and the Fall. In chapter 4, justification is illustrated by the faith of Abraham. In chapter 5 it is seen in connection with the fall of Adam. Paul built on the truth that the record of the Fall tells of realities, that sin actually entered the world through a man. From this fact Paul declared that Adam is a type and Christ a countertype (5:14). As sin entered the world by one man, God has sent one Man to take away sin.

The focus of Paul's teaching in this section was to answer the question: How can the One take the place of the many? He knew this was an objection some had to the gospel, so he replied to it. This passage does not take form as dialogue, although some of it may be dialogue in a limited sense. Actually it is a rather complicated discourse.

Verse 12 is unfinished, as if the apostle had been suddenly interrupted. He inserted two great parentheses (13,14 and 15-17) and replied to two important questions. First, in verse 18 he resumed the line of thought begun in verse 12 and carried through the explanation which was started there. In verses 20,21 he ended his discussion about justification by establishing that grace is greater than sin and rules in those who are justified. This forms the transition to the next section of the epistle concerning sanctification, i.e., that the believer must not let sin rule him (6:12).

In 5:12-21, justification was still discussed, but the apostle's main intent was to justify God, to show that God is righteous. In chapter 3 this question was addressed: How can God be just when He justifies the ungodly? In chapter 5 the reply is given to another question: How can God be righteous when He allows one Man to bear the punishment for the sins of all humanity?

The apostle gave the answer immediately: "As by one man sin entered into the world, and death by sin; and so death passed upon all men, for that all have sinned." Paul ended the statement without making any conclusion. For the time being he did not clarify it further but inserted his parenthetical remarks.

In the first parenthesis Paul defended his teaching that all sinned when one sinned (verse 12). Adam's influence on the human family was not just his bad example or his creation of a moral climate which made it easy for his descendants to sin. Paul was not emphasizing the fallen nature Adam passed on to his descendants but the sentence God passed on them—an imputed guilt which Adam as the head of the human race brought on every member of the race. God placed the entire family of Adam under sin because of the fall of Adam.

Now Paul moved to prove that the sentence resulting from Adam's sin rests on the human race. He presented the argument that even those who did not bear personal guilt because of breaking God's commandments were under the dominion of death anyway. Such was the case from Adam to Moses, i.e., the period before the Law was given.

This is not mere theory. Paul was discussing a guilt which is demonstrated daily. Each innocent child that dies is a testimony to the sentence of death which rests on mankind.

This imputed guilt can be abolished only when men are granted righteousness by God, i.e., justified. Fundamentally this can happen in two ways, but practically and in reality in only one. Fundamentally man can be justified by the Law, which Paul maintained distinctly (Romans 10:5; Galatians 3:12). This means that the descendant of Adam who fulfills the law of God will not be condemned on the Day of Judgment because of Adam's sin even though in this life he is under judgment because of that sin. Here man stands at the tension point between two declarations of God, i.e., that God visits on children the sin of their fathers (Exodus 20:5) and that a son shall not die because of his father's sin if he is converted (Ezekiel 18:20). However, the Law is a "way of salvation" only in theory. Just as distinctly as Paul said that he who fulfills the Law is justified by it, he also said that *nobody* is justified by works of the Law. The reason is that no such man ever lived. No one has ever fulfilled the Law. "All have sinned, and come short of the glory of God" (Romans 3:23; cf. 3:20; Galatians 2:16; 3:10,11,21).

In addition to judgment because of Adam's sin, there rests over each man the judgment for his personal sins. Therefore, the justification Christ provides is not only to restore what Adam forfeited, but is a "free gift of many offenses unto justification" (5:16). Two interpretations of Paul's arguments are presented. Verses 15-17 consist of two contrasts expressed by the antithesis—not by the Fall but much more (compare verses 9,10). Verses 19,20 consist of

two similarities, expressed by the comparison: as—so (compare verse 12).

To counteract the results of Adam's fall and the "many falls" which have followed this first fall, the work of Christ had to be powerful. Adam is a type of Christ as the head of a creation—Adam, head of the first; Christ, head of the second creation. However, Adam is also a contrast to Christ as shown by their different characters and the totally opposite effects of their works. Anyone can tear down and destroy—this was the work of Adam. But to build up and restore is more difficult, and this is Christ's work. His work is more powerful because it has cancelled the disastrous results of Adam's fall. That fall had terrible repercussions lasting to this present moment, but it did not hinder God from fulfilling His plan. The work of Christ is a work of God; Adam's work was the rebellion of a human against his Creator. In a sense Christ's work is also the work of "the first man" since He as "the second man" and the "last Adam" restored what the first man destroyed (1 Corinthians 15:45).

God's placing the whole human race under sin because of Adam's fall was an act of grace because it enabled Him to have mercy on all (cf. Romans 11:32; Galatians 3:22). If one man, as head and representative of the race, could bring such disaster on all mankind, it is an astounding miracle that Jesus Christ as the new head and representative of the race can bring salvation and blessing to all. If Adam's sinful action had such results, how much greater are the results of Christ's righteous work and obedience. Righteousness is not weaker than evil. Satan's seduction of Adam and Eve brought distress and anguish on mankind, but nothing could prevent God from redeeming those who were seduced!

The sin and guilt of man were real. The offense was great. "But where sin abounded, grace did much more abound" (5:20).

C. Concerning Sanctification (6:1–8:39)

In chapter 6 Paul began a new section of the Epistle to the Romans. Sin needs a "double cure." The sinner needs forgiveness and justification—the theme in chapters 3 to 5. But he also needs deliverance from the power and control of sin. This is the subject Paul discussed in this section of Romans. The theme now is sanctification. While justification is a single decisive act on God's part, sanctification is continuous in the believer's life. The one who is holy must remain holy (cf. Revelation 22:11).

In an epistle as rich and comprehensive as Romans, there will be passages which follow one theme and then there is a break as the apostle began another subject. The following chapters deal with various themes as shown below (chapter 5 has already dealt with freedom from wrath; that is, reconciliation):

Chapter 6: Freedom from sin—or, positively, sanctification.

Chapter 7: Freedom from the Law—or, positively, emancipation.

Chapter 8: Freedom from death—or, positively, the believer's inheritance. (See Nygren, pp.230,265,304.)

Such an outline may help in developing a survey of these chapters. However, the material cannot be squeezed into tight compartments.

We must not lose sight of the fact that Paul, guided by the Spirit, developed a consecutive line of thought from 6:1 to 8:16. The main focus is on emancipation from sin. In 6:1-11 Paul pointed to Christ's death as the basis of emancipation. In 6:14,15 he equated emancipation from sin with liberty from the Law. Since believers are not under the Law, they are not under the dominion of sin.

Then Paul used metaphors to illustrate these truths. To show our freedom from sin, he used the slave or servant analogy (6:16). To show our freedom from the Law, he used the illustration of marriage (7:1-4).

A new section follows in which the apostle explained why it is so important to be free from the Law and why the Law cannot make anyone free (7:5). In this section of the epistle Paul emphasized that emancipation is the work of the Spirit, which is based on the work of Christ (8:1-16).

Finally, the apostle presented the Christian hope. The believer's spiritual emancipation is just the beginning of his complete and eternal emancipation, "the glorious liberty of the children of God" (8:21).

1. Freedom from Sin (6:1-23)

Paul opened the new section of the epistle by mentioning again the question from 3:8, expressing it this way: "Shall we continue in sin, that grace may abound?" There is but one answer: "God forbid!" The question is rhetorical but not just hypothetical. Paul dealt with the objection of Jewish legalists to Christianity.

But it was even more unthinkable that Christians could consider adopting such a lawless principle. It amounted to receiving the grace of God in vain (2 Corinthians 6:1) and turning that grace into lasciviousness (Jude 4). Paul warned against such a delusion (1 Corinthians 6:9,10; Galatians 5:21).

As a reaction against lawless tendencies, some demanded that new converts keep the Mosaic law. This may have been understandable, but it was not a legitimate conclusion. Paul rejected it emphatically. He could never employ legalism as a cure for looseness in conduct (Bruce, *Tyndale New Testament Commentaries*, 6:128). On the contrary, Paul pointed to the Law as the basis for sin's dominion (6:14), a subject on which he enlarged in chapter 7. For Paul the basis for victorious living was not the Law but abiding in Christ.

a. Baptized into His death (6:1-14). As a starting point Paul referred to Christian baptism, which illustrates a spiritual reality in the believer's experience. He has been crucified with Christ, was buried, and has risen with Him.

The death of Christ happened but once and cannot be repeated. Paul was not speaking of a repetition of our Lord's crucifixion when he referred to our being "planted together in the likeness of his death." He was emphasizing the righteousness of Christ that is imputed to the believer as a result of his union with Christ and identification with His death. Christ not only died but He arose and His life is the believer's sanctifying power. Christ for us and we in Him—our righteousness. Christ in us—our sanctification.

Baptism symbolizes a subjective experience in the believer's life—a reality springing from his union with Christ.

He who believes in Christ is "justified from sin" (6:7). This means he is liberated from serving sin as a way of life. Therefore the apostle can command: Let not sin reign! It is a contradictory thought that he who is dead to sin should continue to live in sin. As Christ died *for* sin, the believer dies *to* its dominion and attraction.

b. Analogy of the slave (6:15-23). The second part of the chapter begins in the same manner as the first part. There are four parallel expressions in verses 1-3 and 15,16. Each contains the same opening challenge: "What then?" and the same rhetorical question, "Shall we continue in sin?" Each has the same reply of rejection: "God forbid!" There is also the same appeal: "Know ye not . . . ."

In this chapter "slaves" is a better translation of the word *doulos* than "servants." A slave had no rights. Paul was here describing two kinds of service and two kinds of slaves. Man has a right to decide which he will choose. He can become the slave of sin or the slave of Christ.

There are also two kinds of freedom. The person who is the slave of sin is "free from righteousness," because he is not bound by any kind of moral code. He makes his own rules for living, he sets his own standards, and determines his own conduct. But he who is the slave of Christ is free from the slavery of sin. The believer has changed masters. He has discovered genuine freedom.

This section concludes with verse 23. There Paul declared that while Christ's servants receive eternal life as a gift of grace, the servants of sin receive the wages they deserve—death. Usually it is God who punishes sin, but here is one of the few places in the Bible where sin brings along its own punishment. Compare James 1:15 that teaches us when sin is finished, it brings forth death.

2. Freedom from the Law (7:1-25)

Paul wrote of emancipation from sin in chapter 6. Here in chapter 7 he discussed emancipation from the Law. It is not difficult to understand that we need emancipation from sin, but why is the apostle so concerned that believers must be set free from the Law? The answer is already indicated in 6:14. Being delivered from sin means being delivered from the Law which causes sin's dominion.

This teaching may have been puzzling to some and needed further explanation, so Paul treated the matter thoroughly in chapter 7. As an introduction he wrote that he was addressing those who knew the Law. The entire context shows he was referring to the Law given at Sinai. Those who "know the law" are not just Jews but even believers whose Bible was the Old Testament. Paul wanted all believers to know Christ had emancipated them from the Law. In the Early Church this became a subject of great controversy and disturbed many Gentiles who had turned to Christ. Paul had already shown how powerless the Law is to justify a man. Now he explained it is just as powerless in sanctifying believers.

a. Analogy from marriage (7:1-6). Paul presented a new allegory. He compared man's connection with the Law and the believer's union with Christ to marriage. A woman cannot at the same time be married to two men, and no man can at the same time be under the authority of the Law and the authority of Christ. The believer has no higher authority than Christ, and neither is there any authority equal to Christ. The terms for a person's union with Christ require that he also be emancipated from the Law.

This is a legal matter. As long as a woman's husband is alive, she is bound to him by law. But if the husband dies, the wife is free to marry another man. Paul said that in the same manner he who dies to sin is free from the Law. This was a well-known teaching of the rabbis. It was commonly maintained that such obligations ceased at death.

Paul concluded that as the believer is to be considered as dead with Christ (6:2-11), he is also dead to the Law. By His death Christ has delivered us from the Law so we may belong to Him (cf. Galatians 2:19-21; 2 Corinthians 5:15; Colossians 3:3). For the believer the old, unhappy marriage, with sin as "offspring," has ceased. A new marriage producing the fruits of righteousness has been contracted.

Thus it is through Christ's death that the believer is freed from the Law. What a tremendous price Christ paid! Therefore, to return to the Law is spiritual unfaithfulness to Christ just as idolatry in the Old Testament was considered spiritual adultery. From Galatians 4:3-11 we note that returning to the Law is equivalent to returning to idolatry and worshiping idols "which by nature are no gods." We are set free from the Law by Christ's death and he who returns to the Law crucifies God's Son afresh (Hebrews 6:6), i.e., considers Him as dead and the union with Him dissolved (cf. Galatians 5:2-4).

From verse 7 to the end of the chapter the content falls naturally into two parts: (1) The power of the Law to stir sinful desires and make sin active in the life (7-13); and (2) the conflict between the two "laws" in man (14-25).

b. The Law activates sin (7:7-13). Paul already had shown that the Law's purpose was to reveal and identify sin so that it "abounded" (5:20). Now he went a step further, showing that the Law even stirs up sin, awakening it to life and activity. Thus the Law has an influence on man which is quite contrary to what one might be inclined to think. The Law brings death, not life. It does not produce holiness but sin—deceiving man into believing otherwise. The Law is not the reason for sin, but it shows what sin is, and man's sinful nature automatically rises up against the teaching and leads him to disobedience and sin. Sin is so vicious that it uses what is actually good in order to destroy its victim.

Paul related this conflict in an autobiographical section which is one of the great confessions of Scripture. The apostle's testimony is very personal, but it is also the history of each man who ever lived. It is the history of mankind itself. The apostle made distinct references to the Fall, showing that the enemy, Satan, uses exactly the same tactics today. He takes the holy commandments of God to deceive man and make him fall. "I was alive without the Law once," Paul wrote. This is a picture of the relative innocence of childhood, illustrating the original innocence of man before the Fall.

The first autobiographical verses are rather simple to interpret. Paul spoke in the past tense and what he said seems to belong to his life before he became a believer. The rest of the chapter is totally different and is one of the most controversial passages in Romans.

c. The "man" in Romans 7 (7:14-25). Who is this "wretched man" who is sounding his call of distress? This is the question upon which the correct interpretation of this passage rests.

The interpretation of chapter 7 has a long and interesting history all the way back to the church fathers. Three main views have emerged through the centuries: (1) that Paul is describing his spiritual experience prior to his becoming a Christian; (2) that this is the testimony of a normal Christian experience; (3) that the interpretation is to be found in both of the first two views—a compromise interpretation.

(1) A pre-Christian experience. During the first three centuries the church fathers agreed largely that Paul was describing his experiences under the Law before his conversion. Augustine also had this view at first, but changed his mind later. At the time of the Reformation the Greek fathers in the western church embraced this interpretation. Chief among these were Erasmus, Socinus, and others of similar caliber and level of leadership. Arminius and his followers, including Grotius, held to this view. Later it was maintained by men like Francke, Spencer, and Bengel in Germany, and by John Wesley and Adam Clarke in England. Among recent scholars this view seems to be the one most favored. However, many stand on the other side.

There are a series of arguments supporting the view that this passage relates to Paul's pre-Christian experience. Dodd says it would make all of Paul's teaching ridiculous if he admitted that at the time he was writing his epistles he was "a miserable wretch, a prisoner to sin's law" (*The Moffatt New Testament Commentary*, p.108). M. Black finds Dodd's arguments convincing (*New Century Bible*, pp.101-108). Clarke asks what benefit Paul received by his conversion if he was still a prisoner under the law of sin and death: "He had found no salvation under an inefficient Law; and he was left in thraldom under an equally inefficient Gospel" (*Clarke's Commentary*, 6:92). L. Allen says that in this chapter, Paul dramatically relives his life as a Pharisee.

Those who share this interpretation find it inconceivable that Paul could say concerning himself in his present standing as a Christian that he is "carnal, sold under sin" (verse 14) and that he is a "wretched man," torn by internal conflicts, unable to do the good he wants to do, and forced to commit the evil he does not want to do.

(2) A normal Christian life. Other interpreters find that all the struggles Paul mentioned belong to a normal Christian experience. Augustine was the first church father to maintain forcefully that Paul was describing an aspect of his life as a Christian. Later this became the usual interpretation in the western church and was maintained, for instance, by Thomas Aquinas. The reformers Luther, Melanchthon, Calvin, and Beza agreed with this view of Augustine. Calvinists usually maintain this opinion, which is contrary to the belief of the Arminians. Lutherans are more divided on the question. A number of more recent scholars share this second interpretation (i.e., Hodge, p.246; Nygren, p.301; Barth, pp.266-268; Murray, *New International Commentary on the New Testament*, 1:267-269; G.H. Clark, and others).

These scholars, of course, have a number of arguments to substantiate their view. Some believe it would be contrary to the whole format of the Epistle to the Romans if a prominent passage about the unconverted man suddenly appeared in an explanation of sanctification. They state that it is logical to expect to find the problem about the believer's two natures discussed here. Conflict with sin and fleshly impulses is part of the normal experience of the believer. Chapter 8 speaks just as distinctly about this as chapter 7. A Christian cannot overlook the fact that within himself is a nature to which he cannot yield without losing his spiritual life (8:13). This includes an apostle as well as all other believers. The more holy a Christian becomes, the more painfully he will feel this internal conflict. Paul also spoke of these two conflicting tendencies in other passages (Galatians 5:17). Such an intense contrast between an inner desire to obey God's law and will and the carnal nature's opposition to God's law could not be experienced by an unconverted person. Paul used strong expressions to describe this conflict, but did he really say more than we all have felt when we cried out to God in our private closet of prayer? Haven't we felt the strong spiritual longings of the apostle as well as his weakness? Haven't we experienced the paradox of the cry of distress from the "wretched man" and the joyful praises over being set free: "I thank God through Jesus Christ our Lord!"

(3) A compromise solution. A controversial passage like this naturally leads us to seek a compromise interpretation. Both views have their strong arguments as well as their great difficulties. If Paul was describing a sinner, how could he have such a deep desire to do God's will? Paul said that they who are after the flesh do mind the things of the flesh. He declared the carnal mind is in a state of enmity against God (8:5-7). On the other hand, how can a Christian say he does evil that he does not want to do, committing acts he hates? (7:15,19). Is this not describing slavery to sin? One might say that the "man" in chapter 7 is too spiritual to be a sinner and too bound by sin to be living a true Christian life.

This puzzling section of Romans is closely related to the preceding passage that describes the experience of an awakened conscience under the Law. Is it possible this is an extension and further development of the same theme? Is it not possible that this concerns the experiences of man under the Law but also those experiences with which a Christian grapples? Ramifications of this view vary somewhat with different scholars, but basically the conclusions are the same. A number of commentators, both recent and past, share this view. (See Moody, *Broadman Bible Commentary*, 10:211-213.)

Gerlach claims that the struggle Paul describes is a struggle under the Law. He does not believe it is the struggle of a believer who possesses the spiritual weapons provided by the gospel. He sees it as a powerless attempt to avoid evil and do good with the help of the Law, never the gospel. However, the struggle which is depicted is not just something that happened in the past. It is one which is easily encountered in the present. The Galatians fell back under the Law and were in danger of straying from the gospel. This can happen to anyone who forsakes the liberty of the gospel.

Oivind Andersen maintains that chapters 6 and 7 together create the foundation for chapter 8. Chapter 6 speaks of Christ's death and our death with Him as the basis of sanctification. While the first part of the autobiographical section (7:7-13) is in the past tense, verse 14 speaks in the present. This is not accidental. This section describes an individual's feelings when his conscience has been aroused but he is not yet converted. However, a Christian can also have these experiences because sin and the old nature in us must still be contended with.

The apostle wrote of a Christian's relation to the Law in his struggle to live a holy life. It is not just the construction of the passage in the present tense which makes it clear that Paul spoke as a Christian. It is the content of his statements. The basic attitude toward sin and the law of God described in this section is possible only for the Christian. It is not the believer's normal struggle against sin which is described here. The apostle is showing what a Christian experiences struggling against sin if he uses the Law as his source of power to conquer sin and live a holy life. A Christian cannot conquer sin and the old nature by the Law, but by Jesus Christ.

Since the Church has debated this passage through the centuries, we cannot hope to draw conclusions which all will accept. In fact, we can only present the different views and the arguments for them. It is puzzling that capable, spiritual men can present such important and logical points of view that are so contradictory to each other. This would seem to indicate that the third may be the best. It softens the other two interpretations. Sometimes a compromise solution like this comes the closest to the correct one.

3. Freedom in Christ (8:1-39)

Chapter 8 distinctly marks a new section of Romans. We can tell this even by the first verses, which introduce us to a life of spiritual emancipation, governed by the law of the Spirit of life (8:1-4). In this new section the Spirit stands in contrast to the flesh, not the Law (8:5-13). Adoption stands in contrast to bondage (8:14-17).

a. Justification and freedom (8:1-4). It is remarkable that Paul makes a connection here with the main theme of the epistle, justification: "There is therefore now no condemnation to them which are in Christ Jesus." In contrast, verse 3 says that God "condemned sin in the flesh." God condemned that which condemned us. The sinner is acquitted and justified in Christ because sin has been condemned in the flesh of Christ.

That which was impossible under the Law, God did. This is explained in three short statements in 8:3.

First, He sent His own Son in the likeness of sinful flesh. Paul used an expression here which closely guards the sinlessness of Christ. When he wrote in 1 Timothy 3:16 that Christ put on human flesh he said, "God was manifest in the flesh." Thus he differentiates between Christ's being manifest in the flesh and manifest in the *likeness* of the flesh." To have said that Christ was manifest in the likeness of flesh would have been error, casting doubt about the reality of Christ's humanity. But here in 8:3 another expression is necessary because the topic is sinful flesh. The apostle cannot say that Christ, who knew no sin (2 Corinthians 5:21), came in sinful flesh. Therefore, he added here the word "likeness," *homoiomati.* The subject is also expressed like this: Christ was revealed in flesh, but He came in the likeness of sinful flesh. He came in real flesh, but it was not sinful flesh.

Paul spoke from a Hebrew background in using the term "flesh." To the Hebrews, the Greek dualism between *sarx* (flesh) and *psuchē* (soul) was strange. The Hebrew *basar* and its Greek equivalent *sarx* expressed to a Jew the being and personality of man. Flesh is not something a man has, but something he is (cf. Genesis 6:3). The word often expresses man's being a weak, feeble, earthly person in contrast to the power of the eternal God. Thus in the Incarnation Christ put on flesh, experiencing deep humiliation compared with His place in the Godhead. His putting on flesh was real, not symbolical.

More is implied in Jesus' coming in the likeness of sinful flesh than His coming in flesh. This fact emphasizes that He became united with the fallen, sinful human race. The human nature He put on was not the glorious and perfect nature which Adam possessed before the Fall. It was our human nature, reduced and debased by sin. Yet sin itself was not in Him (Hodge, pp.252f.).

When God sent His Son to partake of our nature (but without sin), it was to deal with the sin in our nature. The expression "for sin" is one used in the Septuagint for "sin offering." The expression is used often in the Old Testament—more than 50 times in Leviticus alone. Paul used this second expression in connection with Christ's offering: "Who gave himself for our sins" (Galatians 1:4). Apparently the expression has the same meaning in 8:3 where the thought of sacrifice is dominant. Through Christ's sacrificial death, God did what the Law could not.

God condemned sin in the flesh. This third statement connects naturally with the two preceding ones. It can have but one meaning—sin has received its judgment and punishment. The Greek term *katakrinō* means "to condemn." God condemned sin in the flesh. He made His Son to be sin in order to justify us (2 Corinthians 5:21). God made Him to become a curse for us in order to be able to bless us (Galatians 3:13,14). It pleased the Lord to bruise Him when He presented the sin offering (Isaiah 53:10).

Jesus suffered in our nature as one of the human race and as the race's representative. He had to partake of flesh and blood and be like His brethren in all things to be able to act as high priest in atoning for sin (Hebrews 2:14-18). He came in the likeness of sinful flesh and in this flesh was condemned. Therefore, there is no condemnation for those who are in Christ Jesus. Having been justified, the believer can now be set free from the power and control of sin.

This passage teaches that emancipation from sin's power objectively is connected with the death of Christ and related subjectively to justification. This is a truth we meet many places in the Epistle to the Romans and elsewhere in the New Testament. However, 7:21-25 especially sheds light on this matter. Here we note that Paul spoke of the power of sin as a law. The law of sin and death rules over men. This is no casual designation, for it is a law in the clearest and deepest meaning. It is a declaration of God which emphasizes that sin rules over the sinner.

The law that declares a sinner the slave of sin is based on the righteousness of God. The one who chooses sin has to take sin with all its consequences. Three times in chapter 1 Paul declared that God gives men up to their sin (1:24,26,28). Man is in double bondage—to the devil and to his own flesh (Ephesians 2:2,3). God has promised to deliver the sinner from this bondage only when he accepts Christ.

The Spirit of God is the only power which can set men free from sin. But the Spirit of God sets them free only when they have been forgiven. Only the one who has been acquitted of the guilt of sin can be set free from the power of sin. Only in Christ Jesus will the law of the Spirit of life set one free from the law of sin and death.

b. The Spirit of liberty (8:5-14). In verse 3 Paul repeated what he said positively in chapter 6 and negatively in chapter 7: "For what the law could not do" (cf. 7:1-25), "God sending His own Son . . . " (cf. 6:1-12). Only the Spirit of God can accomplish the possibilities shown in chapter 6 and conquer the "impossibilities" spoken of in chapter 7. The new life cannot produce itself—this can only come by the Spirit of God.

Paul called this new principle of life the law of the Spirit of life. Jesus had said the Spirit would come as rivers of living water (John 7:37-39). Christianity broke forth as a spiritual river, something new in the history of mankind, different from all other religions and all forms of religion. This is the age of Pentecost which the prophets foretold.

Liberty is the distinct mark of the new age (Galatians 5:1)—liberty from bondage to sin and the Law. "Where the Spirit of the Lord is, there is liberty" (2 Corinthians 3:17). The new servitude is by the Spirit, not the letter (Romans 7:6). The law is written in the heart, not on tables of stone. In chapter 7 the Law stands in contrast to the flesh, but in chapter 8 it is the Spirit who stands in contrast to the flesh. This makes all the difference.

The flesh is still the same. It is not any better in chapter 8 than it was in chapter 7. The flesh is still at war with God and cannot be subject to His law (verse 7). But now the works of the flesh are conquered by the Spirit: "As many as are led by the Spirit of God, they are the sons of God" (verse 14).

c. Our adoption (8:15-39). Believers move from bondage to adoption. Instead of the spirit of bondage which creates fear, they have received the Spirit of adoption which cries Abba, Father. The Spirit himself makes intercession for them and testifies with their spirit that they are the sons of God. Even during the present time of tribulation believers can rejoice because they know these sufferings are not worthy to be compared with the glory which shall be revealed in them.

"And if children, then heirs." Those who have received the Spirit as the firstfruits and pledge sigh for the total possession of that which includes their adoption. This will be achieved fully at the redemption of the body from mortality and death.

"For we are saved by hope." It is not a hope which one can see, but it is firm and secure. "I am persuaded!" the apostle said. Nothing shall be able to separate us from the love of God in Christ Jesus our Lord.

III. HISTORY OF SALVATION SECTION (9:1–11:36)

Chapter 9 begins a new section of the Epistle to the Romans. These 3 chapters belong to what has been termed the teaching part of the epistle, but they differ clearly from the preceding chapters.

It is correct in general to say that chapter 9 relates to Israel's past, chapter 10 relates to Israel's current situation, and chapter 11 deals with Israel's future. The two major subjects discussed in these chapters are God's relationship with Israel and the doctrine of election.

This section must not be considered as an appendage to the epistle. On the contrary, it is related to the major theme of the Epistle to the Romans (1:16,17), that the gospel is the power of God for salvation—explained in the first section of the epistle (chapters 1 to 8). However, what is *not* discussed there is Paul's declaration that the gospel is provided to "the Jew first, and also to the Greek" (1:16).

A. The Doctrine of Election

It has been said that chapter 9 is the most difficult passage in Scripture to interpret. In fact, the difficulties are so great that few will claim to understand the passage thoroughly. This is because the subjects of election and predestination are among the most difficult aspects of the Christian faith. Paul often mentioned the elect, and in his epistles he discussed the matter more thoroughly in three places: Ephesians 1:1-11; Romans 8:28-30; 9 to 11; and especially 9:6-29. This last section is usually considered to be the main passage that deals with the subject of the so-called double predestination doctrine. This teaching maintains that God from eternity has irrevocably chosen a group of people for salvation and another group for perdition. In Bruce's interpretation he regrets that some theological schools formed their election doctrine too quickly from the preliminary stage of Paul's presentation in chapter 9, without paying sufficient attention to his conclusion in 11:25-32. Bruce is undoubtedly correct and in more recent exegetical work, greater care seems to have been taken than was often the case earlier (*Tyndale New Testament Commentaries*, 6:180).

It is not surprising that such conflicting opinions prevail within Protestant Christianity about the doctrine of election. Great denominations and great leaders within them have held opposing views. Rather than being discouraged over this, we should be humbled over it because it reveals how human all of us are even in our attempts to discover God's truth and His will.

Of course it is virtually impossible to draw dogmatic conclusions about this matter. The most we can achieve is probably to find a view that satisfies us in our own mind (14:5)—and many of us must probably settle for less! The matter of election is connected with the eternal counsels of God. We have to accept the fact that God acts "so that no man can find out the work that God maketh from the beginning to the end" (Ecclesiastes 3:11). Then we have to rest satisfied with the knowledge which is now partial but will one day become clear (1 Corinthians 13:9).

Election and predestination are among the most difficult areas of Christian doctrine because they touch on the great mystery: Why has God created man who will finally be lost forever? No doctrine of election gives any satisfactory reply to this question whether it maintains the complete sovereignty of God or gives room for man to influence his own final destiny. In any case it is evident that God knew the end from the beginning. He knew the eternal destiny of the creation of His own hand. The Scripture says God's election took place "before the foundation of the world" (Ephesians 1:4). This implies election in creation itself. God's sovereignty is unquestioned in His work of creation whatever we might think about His sovereignty concerning the destiny of men.

We do not actually avoid the problems of predestination by speaking of "free will." The difficulties are still there, but when we consider man's free will in our search for the correct interpretation, it brings the different opinions close together.

As already mentioned, more recent efforts at exegesis agree that chapters 9 to 11 are a discussion of salvation history rather than a dogmatic statement about predestination and election. Certain portions of Scripture have too often been taken out of their context and used as arguments in religious quarrels. It is evident that the contents of these chapters do not possess the dogmatism sometimes attributed to them.

This section of Scripture containing the most detailed discussion of the subject of election that is found anywhere else in the Bible. This is not coincidental, but appears to be part of Paul's intent in writing the Epistle to the Romans. In the first part of the epistle he discussed such basic truths of the Christian faith as justification and sanctification. It is logical that he then would proceed in the second part of the epistle to explain God's election. We should not overlook the fact that the presentation in chapter 9 connects naturally with the last part of chapter 8 that mentions election. Thus the subject becomes a principal one in the teaching part of the epistle. The theme of election is so central in the Christian faith that it can claim such a prominent place in this epistle.

But the matter is taken up in the context of salvation history. This is logical in more than one way. Israel is the elected nation and it would be inconceivable to overlook it in such a discussion. The history of Israel is a demonstration of God's election. We must have this view of salvation history if we are to understand at least part of what is implied in being elected. We must avoid forcing our interpretation into some kind of dogmatic system. On the contrary, the dogmatic questions should be considered against the background of salvation history.

B. Paul's Grief Because of the Unbelief in Israel (9:1-5)

The beginning of this section (verses 1-5) opens with Paul's expression of sorrow over Israel's unbelief and ends with a doxology of praise for God's plan of salvation.

During Paul's discussion of God's plan of salvation in the first part of the epistle, a central theme is the connection between Law and the gospel. Many times the apostle obviously had the Jews in mind. In the opening words of the epistle Paul said the gospel he preached was something God had promised in the holy Scriptures which were committed to the charge of the Jews (1:2; 3:2). Before he began the "admonishing" part of the letter, he addressed this problem: How can it be explained that the Jews—the people who were especially prepared for God's promise—did not know their Messiah when He came, while so many Gentiles who did not have the messianic promises and prophecies received Him?

This matter was of deep personal interest to Paul. He was a Jew himself, "an Hebrew of the Hebrews," and he had strong ties to his people. He began the discussion with a solemn assurance of the heaviness and continual sorrow he felt because his "kinsmen according to the flesh" rejected the gospel. If it would make a difference for them, Paul was willing to be "accursed from Christ" (9:2,3).

When Paul took up the question about Israel's place in God's plan of salvation, he hinted at a question of current interest to Christians in the Church. Almost everywhere there were Jewish minorities in those local congregations. This was true in Rome where the church from the beginning consisted of "strangers of Rome" who were present on the Day of Pentecost in Jerusalem (Acts 2:10). The Gentiles were in the majority generally where there were Christian congregations. It was important to them as well as to Jewish Christians to have insight into God's plan for His covenant people, the descendants of Abraham. There might be a tendency for the Gentile Christians to hold the Jew in contempt—something to which Paul objected (11:18). On the other hand, Jewish Christians could be in danger of letting loyalty and love for their own people overshadow the glory of belonging to God's *new* covenant people. These problems were later taken up and discussed in the Epistle to the Hebrews. Their existence when Paul wrote to the Romans is surely one of the reasons he focused on this theme here.

However, the main question concerned the situation of Israel at that time. Understanding this was of vital importance in understanding the gospel which Paul had explained in the first main section of the epistle. One of Paul's key arguments was that this gospel had been preached previously in the prophecies of the Old Testament (1:2; 16:26). When the Jews rejected the gospel it meant they rejected the evidences from the Scriptures to which Paul referred. Thus they doubted the trustworthiness of the gospel. How could one expect then that the Gentiles should receive a Jewish Messiah whom the Jews themselves had rejected? The Jews' rejection of the gospel caused problems which required an answer. In the Epistle to the Romans Paul gave a systematic statement of the gospel he preached and its connection with the old covenant, but he could not overlook the problems arising because the people who had received the messianic promises had rejected the Messiah.

In his Epistle to the Romans Paul proclaimed the entire message of the gospel. In the first part he discussed the main truths: sin and grace, the person and work of Christ, justification and sanctification. He also gave a basic presentation of ecclesiology and eschatology. The position of the Church as it related to Israel must also be explained. The connection between the people of the old and new covenants must be discussed. In the first part of the epistle the gospel is shown as applying chiefly to the questions about personal salvation. In the second section the theme is the kingdom of God and its completion. Here in three short chapters the apostle Paul set forth the greatest eschatological perspectives in the entire New Testament.

The section comprised of chapters 9 to 11 is thus not to be considered as an irrelevant parenthesis inserted between the two main parts of the epistle. This section forms an important main section of this most systematic epistle in the New Testament.

Chapters 1 to 5 concern the grace of God in justification; chapters 6 to 8 concern His grace in sanctification; chapters 9 to 11 discuss His grace in election. The place of election is treated nowhere else in the New Testament in such detail as it is here.

The parallelism between chapters 3 and 9 shows how close the connection is between the first and second main parts of the Epistle to the Romans. The objections against the gospel which are discussed in chapter 3 are discussed once more in chapter 9, and here they get their final reply. This involves three particular questions:

(1) The first objection is that the gospel would abolish the privileges which had been given the Jews. "What advantage then hath the Jew? or what profit is there of circumcision?" (3:1). Paul replied in 3:2: "Much every way: chiefly, because that unto them were committed the oracles of God." In 9:4,5 Paul once more discussed the question and showed what privileges are given to the Jewish people.

(2) The second objection in chapter 3 concerns the validity of God's promises to Israel: "For what if some did not believe? shall their

unbelief make the faith of God without effect?" (3:3). Paul rejected such a thought immediately in verse 4: "God forbid: yea, let God be true, but every man a liar." But he took up the objection once more in 9:6 and assured: "Not as though the word of God hath taken none effect."

(3) The third objection made in chapter 3 is the question about the righteousness of God: "But if our unrighteousness commend the righteousness of God, what shall we say? Is God unrighteous who taketh vengeance?" (3:5). Again Paul replied immediately: "God forbid: for then how shall God judge the world?" (verse 6). In 9:14 Paul discussed the same question once more: "What shall we say then? Is there unrighteousness with God? God forbid." The three objections to the gospel which are set forth in chapter 3 are thus fully answered in chapter 9.

We note then that the content of chapters 9 to 11 is related to the theme of Romans (1:16,17) and answers questions arising from the subjects discussed in the first part of the epistle. But actually this section breaks the pattern. Here light is thrown on problems which concern the entire revelation of the Bible, God's sovereignty, and election. In these chapters Paul constantly referred to the Old Testament because the matters on which he threw light have their background and origin in the Old Testament. Now they can be interpreted in the light of fulfillment. But because these themes are among the most difficult that man has struggled with, their interpretation is far from simple.

C. God's Relationship With Israel (9:6-29)

The apostle took up the theme of Israel's rejection very carefully. He knew this was a matter that could seem harsh and hurtful to his Jewish brethren. Therefore, he opened the section with a solemn assurance of his love for his countrymen and relatives. He was the apostle to the Gentiles, and he magnified his office (11:13). But his first desire was to go to his own people with the gospel and he was willing to go to the Gentiles only when the Lord himself warned him the Jews would reject his testimony about Jesus (Acts 22:17-21). Later the Jews had persecuted him from city to city and he knew now they were continually adding to their sins (1 Thessalonians 2:16). It was because of this bitter opposition from his own people that it was very important for Paul to emphasize he did not have any personal grudges against them.

It was of no satisfaction to Paul that the Jewish people were not the sole recipients of God's special favor and that God was choosing a people from among both Jews and Gentiles. On the contrary, Paul would have willingly made the greatest sacrifices if it could have brought his countrymen to Christ.

Paul said he could wish himself "accursed from Christ" if this could be of any profit to his brethren. The form of the statement implies that this would be impossible. It is hypothetical, but the words express a love patterned after the example of Jesus, who was made a curse for our sake (Galatians 3:13). Whatever this desire might mean, it does not indicate that Paul was willing to become an enemy of Christ or live in sin. It is wrong to imagine that good can come from doing evil (3:8), and it is also wrong to suppose that one could serve a good cause by becoming evil. The deep concern of Paul's heart was the suffering and loss the Jews were experiencing by turning away from Christ. If it would save his brethren, he was willing to give up the glory and blessedness he enjoyed through Christ and which Israel forfeited by rejecting Him (cf. Colossians 1:24).

Paul accepted fully the privileges granted the Jews and he set them forth in seven expressions:

(1) The adoption: The Lord calls this people His son (Exodus 4:22; Hosea 11:1). They are His property more than any other people on earth (Exodus 19:5).

(2) The glory: The glory of God was given to Israel by the Lord's personal presence with His people (Exodus 24:16,17; 40:34,35; Leviticus 16:2; 1 Kings 8:10,11).

(3) The covenants: These are the covenants of promise which God made with Abraham (Genesis 12 and 15), the covenant of Law on Sinai (Exodus 19:5), and the covenant with King David (2 Samuel 7; 1 Chronicles 17).

(4) The giving of the Law: Israel received the Law through divine revelation. On Sinai God explained what was good and holy and what was evil and sinful. Only Israel has received such a revelation and through this revelation the will of God has been known among the nations.

(5) The divine service: This includes holy actions—the sacrifice and purification rituals; holy places—the tabernacle and temple; the priesthood—the Levites and the prophets; holy times—the Sabbath and the calendar of feasts. The divine service of the Old Testament illus-

trated and prepared for the salvation provided in the New Testament.

(6) The promises: The promises of God and not the Mosaic law were the basis of salvation for Israel. It was when the Israelites believed the promises God had given that they were saved in ancient times (cf. Hebrews 11).

(7) The fathers: This refers to the first ancestors of the Jewish people—Abraham, Isaac, and Jacob—and also the holy men of God who kept and proclaimed the covenant through the centuries.

Finally Paul mentioned the great climax of Israel's privileges: From this nation Christ came—He who is the fulfillment and realization of the messianic promises. Of course He came from Israel in only one sense—according to the flesh, that is, according to His human nature. Spiritually He is "over all, God blessed for ever" (9:5). That verse is one of the great Christological statements of the New Testament and shows the true humanity of Christ as well as His deity.

This passage has been thus understood from the early days of the Church. Among the church fathers agreement was almost absolute. For three centuries it was unanimous. Then in the Fourth Century another view arose among interpreters under the influence of Arianism, which attempted to explain away Christ's deity. However, the interpretation was completely rejected. Calvin wrote, "They who break off this clause from the previous context, that they may take away from Christ so clear a testimony to his divinity, most presumptuously attempt to introduce darkness in the midst of the clearest light; for the words most evidently mean this, *Christ who is from the Jews according to the flesh, is God blessed forever*" (italics original, *Calvin's Commentaries: Romans,* p.342).

Linguistically there is no doubt that the entire passage proclaims Christ's deity. Among those who tried to make it mean something else were those with wrong motives. Some maintained that Paul could not have meant to say Christ is God. By inserting a period after "the flesh" (*sarx* in the Greek text) one interpreter tried to separate the last part of the verse and change its construction so it had no connection with the preceding part. All of this is farfetched and a completely unnatural exegesis. Westcott said such a change of the subject seems unlikely. Nigel Turner declared it is grammatically unnatural that a participle which goes together with Christ "first be divorced from it

and then be given the force of a wish, receiving a different person as its subject" (p.15). Adam Clarke said with considerable indignation in his comment: "I pass by the groundless and endless conjectures about reversing some of the particles and placing points in different positions, as they have been all invented to get rid of the doctrine of Christ's divinity, which is so obviously acknowledged by the simple text" (6:110).

Linguistically it seems completely unreasonable to conclude that the last sentence in this verse is meant as a disconnected exclamation of praise. No such doxology can be found anyplace in the Bible. The basic text lacks a relative sentence or the relative pronoun which Paul always adds to such praise elsewhere in his writings (Andersen). Also, the succession of words here is different from that used in doxologies. Such passages of praise read like this: "Blessed is he," not—as here—"God blessed." In the Septuagint as well as the New Testament all doxologies are formed this way (Matthew 21:9; 23:39; Mark 11:9,10; Luke 1:42,68; 13:35; 19:38; John 12:13; 2 Corinthians 1:3; Ephesians 1:3; 1 Peter 1:3). In Romans 9:5 the succession of the words is the way it occurs in declarations, not forms of praise, i.e., Romans 1:25; 2 Corinthians 11:31: "He who is blessed for ever" (cf. Hodge, p.300; Barrett, *Harper's New Testament Commentaries*, pp.177f.; Murray, *New International Commentary on the New Testament*, 2:5ff.). Paul is declaring in this verse the deity of Jesus Christ.

For objective reasons and not just because of linguistic and grammatical considerations, "God blessed for ever" must refer to Christ. The context requires it. In this section the apostle wrote of his deep grief because his people were under judgment and curse and it would be absurd for him to conclude with a praise to God. It is also unimaginable that Paul would reduce his testimony concerning Jesus to merely mentioning that He is "according to the flesh." The expression in itself indicates that Jesus in His person possesses something which is higher than flesh (Calvin, *Calvin's Commentaries: Romans*, p.342). We have an antithesis here and something is required to balance the expression "according to the flesh" (Bruce, *Tyndale New Testament Commentaries*, 6:176). The word here is a parallel to 1:3,4 where it is said that Christ "was made of the seed of David according to the flesh, and declared to be the Son of God with power, according to the Spirit of holiness, by the resurrection from the dead." It is typical of Paul that when he spoke of what Christ is according to the flesh, His human side, he also spoke of what Christ is according to the divine side (Andersen). In 1:4 He is called "the Son of God with power." In 9:5 He is called "God blessed for ever."

All of this fits the context. Christ came as the fulfillment of God's revelation and the salvation history of the Old Testament which Paul has outlined briefly. Jesus is that "child" who is born, the "son" who is given, the one the prophet called "mighty God" (Isaiah 9:6). This is the Jewish people's greatest glory and greatest tragedy: "He came unto his own, and his own received him not" (John 1:11). This was the cause of Paul's deep distress for his people—they had rejected their Messiah, their God.

1. Israel's Rejection and God's Promises (9:6-13)

Since God has put aside His people of the old covenant and given His kingdom to a people who bring forth its fruits (Matthew 21:43), has He then broken His covenant promises to the fathers? Paul replied immediately to this question: "Not as though the word of God hath taken none effect" (9:6). This expansion of God's call to all mankind corresponds with the promise itself which was given to Abraham when God called him: "In thee shall all families of the earth be blessed" (Genesis 12:3). But when the great part of the people of Israel are now excluded and receive no share of the promised blessing, it is plainly because they do not belong to "the children of the promise" (9:8). "For they are not all Israel, which are of Israel" (9:6).

The Israel for whom the promises of God shall be fulfilled is not "the children of the flesh." Not all the posterity of Abraham are considered to belong to the family which owns the promise. To prove this, Paul set forth an argument he knew all Jews would accept. He referred to the relationship between Ishmael and Isaac and between Esau and Jacob. Both Ishmael and Esau were descendants of Abraham, but no Jew would claim that their posterity belonged to the nation of promise. Paul transferred this truth to the Jewish people. Already in 2:28,29 he had said that he was not a Jew which was one outwardly but he was a Jew which was one inwardly. In 4:12 Paul also followed this thought. Abraham is "the father of circumcision to them who are not of the circumcision

only, but who also walk in the steps of that faith of our father Abraham."

This is in fact a truth taken from the Old Testament. The true Israelites are those with a clean heart (Psalm 73:1), those who seek God's face (Psalm 24:6). John the Baptist maintained the same view. When the Jews pleaded that they were the children of Abraham, John replied that God could give Abraham children of "these stones." Jesus had a sharp conflict with the unbelieving Jews for His teaching along this same line. He told them He knew they were of Abraham's lineage but He did not accept them as Abraham's children (John 8:37-39). Thus it is no new thought Paul put forth when he maintained that an election takes place among the chosen ones. This is what has taken place throughout the history of the people. Only the believing Israelites inherited the promise, and they were almost always in the minority among their people. What has taken place before is now being repeated. If the great part of the Jewish people reject their Messiah, this does not mean that God's promise has been discarded or that His word has failed.

2. Israel's Rejection and God's Righteousness (9:14-29)

The next objection to Paul's preaching is that God would be unfair to turn away from His people of the old covenant. This was a deeply rooted delusion in Israel—that they had a claim on God which He could not escape. Now Paul showed that everything God gives is of grace, and God is completely sovereign as to whom He will show grace. When Jacob and Esau were still unborn and neither had done good nor bad, God made His choice between them. When Jacob was chosen, this was grace. When Esau was rejected, no wrong was done to him. It is not of him that wills, nor of him that runs, Paul said. Abraham wanted Ishmael to inherit the promise. Isaac wanted Esau to inherit the promise. But God chose otherwise. Esau went hunting to get venison for his father and receive the blessing, but this did not help him. The will of God according to election stood firmly.

Even God's enemies must serve His intentions. Pharaoh was raised up for God to show His power in Him. God handed him over to his reprobate mind and hardened his heart while He had mercy on Israel. "He hath mercy on whom he will have mercy, and whom he will he hardeneth" (9:18). Just as the clay cannot complain to the potter, man cannot say to

God, "Why hast thou made me thus?" (verse 20). God maintains His unrestricted right over His creation to act as He wishes concerning what belongs to Him.

Paul applied this to Israel as the prophets did (Isaiah 45:9). However, when he used this Old Testament picture of God's sovereign power, it was not because he was pleading for any despotic action on God's part. The will of God is for the good of people and those Old Testament passages to which Paul referred speak of the care God has for His people: "But now, O Lord, thou art our father; we are the clay, and thou our potter; and we all are the work of thy hand. Be not wroth very sore, O Lord, neither remember iniquity for ever: behold, see, . . . we are all thy people" (Isaiah 64:8,9).

The picture of the clay in the potter's hand should not cause the Jews to have a fatalistic attitude. They were acquainted with Jeremiah 18:1-10 where it is said that a vessel which was marred was taken up once more and formed into another vessel. "O house of Israel, cannot I do with you as this potter? saith the Lord. Behold, as the clay is in the potter's hand, so are ye in mine hand, O house of Israel. At what instant I shall speak concerning a nation, and concerning a kingdom, to pluck up, and to pull down, and to destroy it; if that nation, against whom I have pronounced, turn from their evil, I will repent of the evil that I thought to do unto them." Just this way Paul described the situation of his people. God has shown His power by rejecting the nation because they rejected His Messiah, but God is also able to graft them in again if they do not continue in their unbelief (11:23).

To sum up, chapters 9 to 11 fall into three sections. In chapter 9 Paul justified God's actions concerning Israel by referring to His sovereignty. He is God and is within His rights to act as He wishes without accounting to any man. Israel's history shows that God dealt with His people this way in the past. Chapter 10 shows that God's rejection of the covenant nation is no casual action. Israel had placed herself outside God's blessing because of her unbelief. But even though Israel as a nation was put aside, there was also a remnant who believed. Paul himself and his brethren who believed in Christ represented this true Israel. Chapter 11 speaks of Israel's future. Israel will eventually be saved, that is, the Jews as a nation will be restored as the people of God.

Paul then summed up the matter in 11:32: "God hath concluded them all in unbelief, that he might have mercy upon all." This corresponds with 5:12-20, which says that God has placed the entire human race under judgment because of Adam's fall. He was the first man, but through the second Man, Jesus Christ, God can justify those who believe and give life to all men who receive His Son. This is the intent and goal of the eternal counsels of God. Here the choice of grace in Christ has its place.

In the Scripture God has pulled aside the veil over the mystery of election just enough to show us that here are some secrets we cannot completely comprehend. But we must keep in focus that the question of election is placed in the context of salvation history where the salvation of both Israel and the Gentiles is concerned. Thus we must view predestination and election in light of God's will and saving love. Everything must finally serve the salvation plan of God. Therefore, Paul concluded by praising God for His wisdom. Paul admits that God's judgments are unsearchable and His ways past finding out. However, those judgments and ways—which are so much higher than ours— lead to the great goal which God has fixed: His eternal kingdom.

IV. ADMONITION SECTION (12:1–13:14)

Paul followed his general practice when he added a section of admonition to his doctrinal presentation. This practical application of Christian doctrine can be found in most of his epistles. The preaching of sound doctrine, declaring the gospel and the person and work of Christ, is basic and must come first. Here in the Epistle to the Romans Paul laid the foundation of the believer's new life-style in chapters 6 to 8. There he taught about the new life the believer has received in Christ. This new life is the source of the new conduct expressed in his daily walk. Christian practice has Christian truth as its origin and the two are inseparably connected. With Paul's "therefore" in 12:1 this final section connects with the first doctrinal section of the epistle. This reference to the gospel (in the first section) is a necessary background to admonition. These admonitions are given in light of "the mercies of God" (12:1). They are also set forth by the authority of Christ and the Holy Spirit (15:30).

The admonition section of the epistle falls into one general part (chapters 12,13) where the teaching concerns basically all age groups, and a special part (14:1 to 15:13) which contains admonitions relating primarily to conditions in the church at Rome but also to matters among all believers.

The general part contains a series of admonitions which cover the greatest area of the Christian life and gives some examples which illuminate different situations. This concerns the believer's body (12:1) and mind (12:2). This is vital to his relationship with God (12:1,2), fellow Christians (12:4), those outside the Church (12:17), and governing authorities (13:1). Paul taught obedience to the laws of the community (13:1) and the faithful fulfillment of God's law (13:10).

A. Personal Life (12:1,2)

The first basic admonition concerns each believer's relation to God and the worship of Him. The expression Paul used about consecration to God is taken from ritual language, but the contrast to the divine service of the Old Testament is striking. Here in Romans the subject is a living sacrifice; the believer should *live* for God. This divine service includes both body and mind (verses 1,2). Paul emphasized that what makes the believer different from the world comes from within through the renewing of his mind.

B. Church Life (12:3-8)

Then Paul wrote about the life of the Church. In verse 1 the subject is the physical body, while in verse 5 it is the spiritual body of Christ, the Church. Christian love should first of all be expressed to those "who are of the household of faith." Proper relationship to those outside the Church depends on brotherly love inside the Church (cf. 2 Peter 1:7).

C. Social Life (12:9-21)

Our love must extend to all men, beginning with our fellow believers. Our love for the world is an extension of our love for those in the Church. A Christian must not be conformed to this world (verse 2), but neither should he be isolated. We have a relationship with all fellow humans. The Christian mind is to be expressed in actions among believers by unfeigned love. This means, among other things, to have willing fellowship with those who are not highly esteemed and even considered "low." In relation to the world the Christian mind will express itself by an attitude of peacemaking which leaves no room for vengeance but conquers evil with good. This section echoes Jesus' preaching distinctly. Some of it reminds us of the Sermon on the Mount. None of the four Gospels had been written at this time, but Paul had a knowledge of Jesus' teachings.

D. Obedience to Authority (13:1-7)

When Paul discussed the social relationships of Christians, their relationship with governing authorities also came into view. Before this, the Roman authorities had been rather indifferent to Christian activity and had even shown considerable tolerance. They considered Christianity a Jewish "denomination" and to a large extent had granted Christians the same privilege and protection the Jews had enjoyed as a legal, registered religious group in the empire. In a few more years this would change, and persecution of Christians would begin. Paul knew from experience how critical the situation was already and how important it was that Christians not challenge their rulers unwisely. This was particularly true in Rome where the Church lived under the eye of the highest authorities. What happened there could produce repercussions for Christians all over the Roman Empire. There had already been some trouble in Rome. The historian Suetonius wrote that Emperor Claudius had exiled all Jews from Rome because they constantly caused turmoil (Acts 18:2). This shows there were controversies among the Jews because of Christianity. This was the background of the emperor's edict.

Paul did not here discuss this question: How shall a Christian behave toward an authority who abuses his power? But the apostle declared that all authorities are the servants of God—dreaded by evil and praised by the good. As long as the governing authority fills its God-given place, it can demand Christians' loyalty. Obedience to the authorities is an extension of the believer's obedience to the Lord. Therefore, it is not just because of the fear of punishment that the Christian should subject himself to the governing authorities. It is a matter of conscience.

E. Fulfillment of the Law (13:8-10)

After speaking about obedience to human law, Paul wrote about fulfilling the law of God. We still hear echoes from Jesus' teaching, and the section concludes with the great declaration: "love is the fulfilling of the law."

F. The Eschatological Section (13:11-14)

Paul, after writing of Christian love, expressed the theme of Christian hope. Everything in this passage emphasizes and reinforces what has been said previously: Romans 12:1 refers to the teaching in chapters 6 to 8 about holy living based on the preaching of the gospel; 13:10 refers to love as the new impelling power that enables us to fulfill the Law; 13:11 looks forward to the return of Christ as the motive for holiness (cf. 1 John 3:3). Salvation, the final salvation, is nearer than when we believed (1 Thessalonians 5:8,9; 1 Peter 1:5; 2:2). The New Testament teaches that the day of redemption is near: Philippians 4:5; James 5:8. The first generation of believers expected the return of Christ in their day (John 21:23; 1 Thessalonians 1:10; 4:17). However, this expectation took into consideration that to the Lord "one day is . . . as a thousand years, and a thousand years as one day" (2 Peter 3:8). When Paul wrote "the night is far spent," he put the present evil age alongside the age to come. "The night" includes all the dark times until the Second Coming, which is "the day." The first coming of Christ took place at the end of the times (Hebrews 9:26; cf. Hebrews 1:1) and the present age belongs to the end of the world (1 Corinthians 10:11). Therefore the night is far spent and the day is at hand.

V. THE STRONG AND THE WEAK (14:1–15:13)

The entire Epistle to the Romans is of course addressed to the church in Rome and clearly shows this background. However, it has a message to all Christians. It seems correct to say that 14:1 to 15:13 treats in a special way questions which presented problems in Rome at that time. There were difficulties about those considered "strong" and others labeled "weak." Those who had a strong conscience and used their Christian liberty freely were in conflict with those who had weak consciences and were confused about questions of food and the observance of certain days. Paul took these matters up in other epistles also. The matters of the Jewish Sabbath and feast days are mentioned in Galatians 4:10 and Colossians 2:16,17. Jewish eating customs are mentioned in Colossians 2:21. What is unusual is that Paul discussed the situation in Rome in a way that shows an entirely different reaction than when he wrote to Galatia and Colossae. The only conclusion we can draw is that there were different backgrounds in those churches. In the Epistle to the Galatians Paul opposed the Judaizers who taught that it was necessary to follow the Law in order to be justified and actually were preaching "another gospel." In the Epistle to the Colossians Paul struggled against a Gnostic error that taught extreme asceticism to discipline the desires of the body and encouraged worship of angels. None of these problems are mentioned in the Epistle to the Romans. There Paul addressed believers who because of a weak conscience had imposed unnecessary burdens on themselves. These "weak" ones in Rome remind us of the "weak" in Corinth who did not dare to eat meat, fearing it may have been offered to idols before being sold in the market (1 Corinthians 8 and 10).

Paul admonished the believers in Rome to be tolerant toward those with different viewpoints in this matter. He told those on both sides not to judge or scorn fellow believers with different opinions (14:1-12). He also cautioned the "strong" not to put a stumbling block or an occasion to fall in the path of the weak brother but rather to sacrifice the use of one's own liberty if necessary (14:13-23). As a motive for such an attitude Paul referred to the example of Christ, who did not live to please himself but honored God by His concern for the well-being of others (15:1-13).

VI. CONCLUSION OF THE EPISTLE (15:14–16:27)

The long ending of the epistle falls into a number of sections. First, Paul discussed personal conditions and told of his own plans (15:14-33). He recommended to them Phoebe, who ministered to the church in Cenchrea (16:1,2), then gave a series of personal greetings which show that Paul had a great circle of friends in the church (16:3-16). He implored them seriously to pay close attention to people trying to cause division and to disassociate themselves from them (16:17-20). The epistle concludes with a doxology in which Paul reiterates what he wrote in the opening verses.

Overview–1 Corinthians

The city of Corinth was located in southern Greece in the province of Achaia, on the narrow isthmus connecting the Greek mainland with Peloponnesus, that peninsula extending into the Mediterranean Sea. Even prior to the Corinth of the New Testament, a strategic city had existed on the site. "Old Corinth," however, was destroyed by the Romans in 146 B.C. Nevertheless, because of its being ideally suited for trade—with harbors on the Aegean Sea on the east and the Gulf of Corinth, which connected to the Ionian Sea on the west—it was eventually rebuilt. Almost all of the east-west trade had to travel through Corinth; the other option was to sail around the Peloponnesus, an option often dangerous and difficult. After the city lay dormant for 100 years, Julius Caesar ordered it rebuilt (46 B.C.). Originally the newer city was settled by army veterans from Italy. These Italian immigrants spoke Greek, so the entire province was Greek-speaking. Later, Greeks returned to populate it. Because of its being a trade center, the population was a composite of people from all over the Mediterranean region. From 27 B.C. on, Corinth was the capital city of Achaia.

Corinth had a bad reputation, even among Gentiles and pagans. To "live like a Corinthian" meant to live licentiously. The expression "Corinthian girls" became an idiom throughout the Roman Empire for "harlots." In the city's temple of Aphrodite there were countless numbers of temple prostitutes. Aphrodite was the Greek goddess of love, beauty, and life and was synonymous with the Roman goddess Venus or the Phoenician deity Astarte.

On his second missionary journey, Paul visited Corinth and conducted his work there for 18 months. During this period he established the Corinthian church composed of Jewish and Gentile Christians. Later, after he had moved to Ephesus for a 3-year period, he apparently made brief visits to the city while he was on his third missionary journey. A third visit to Corinth probably took place towards the end of that missionary journey, just as the Ephesian ministry was coming to a close.

Paul began his ministry in Corinth from the Jewish synagogue. Later, he moved to a house church perhaps adjacent to the synagogue (Acts 18:4-7). Crispus, the ruler of the synagogue, and his family were converted to Christ. Most of the others in the church had a Greek/Gentile background. A few may have belonged to the upper class, for we read of one "Erastus, who

is the city's director of public works" (Romans 16:23, NIV). Most, though, were from the lower classes, such as slaves, freedmen, etc. (1:26ff.; 7:21).

Paul wrote several letters to the church at Corinth; we know of at least three, two of which we have. First Corinthians 5:9 indicates that Paul wrote one letter to the church prior to the one we call "First Corinthians." Paul also received a letter from the Corinthians (7:1). First Corinthians then, is partially a response to that letter, and at the same time, Paul's means of addressing other current issues. Whereas in the Epistle to the Romans we meet Paul the teacher, in 1 Corinthians we encounter Paul the spiritual leader. Just as the Epistle to the Romans contains much doctrinal instruction, 1 Corinthians holds much ethical teaching. Paul discussed the situation at Corinth in a very forthright manner; issues were evaluated and a response was given on the basis of Christian faith and teaching. Because the letter takes such a fundamental approach to resolving issues, it was of utmost importance to the Corinthian believers individually, but also to the Church throughout the ages.

First Corinthians was written from Ephesus, probably a little while before Pentecost, A.D. 55 (cf. 16:8; i.e., toward the end of Paul's 3-year stay in Ephesus). There is general agreement that this is indeed an authentic Pauline letter. Robertson and Plummer remark that those attempting to show Paul was not the author only succeed in proving their own ignorance (*The International Critical Commentary, Corinthians*, p.xvi). The genuineness of the epistle is attested by both external and internal evidence. Among the external witnesses are Clement of Rome, who around A.D. 95 refers to a letter which can only be 1 Corinthians. Irenaeus' writings contain more than 60 quotes or allusions to 1 Corinthians; Clement of Alexandria's around 130; and Tertullian's around 400. Moreover, the authenticity is attested by Ignatius, Polycarp, Hermas, Justin Martyr, Athenagorus, and by the *Didache* (The Teaching of the Twelve Apostles). In the Muratorian Fragment it is placed first among the writings of Paul. The internal witnesses—the style, vocabulary, and content—corroborate the external evidence and coincide with what is known both about Paul and the church to which he wrote.

First Corinthians was a reply to a letter Paul received from believers in Corinth. In that letter questions were raised concerning sexual relations, meat offered to idols, and perhaps the exercise of spiritual gifts in the congregation. The letter may have also inquired about proper procedure in worship (e.g., the Lord's Supper). Paul replied very directly to their questions.

However, before discussing their questions (7:1ff.), Paul devoted six chapters to what he evidently regarded as more crucial and urgent problems in the Corinthian church. Paul had learned from others about these other problems (1:11; 5:1). Divisions had arisen in the church body because some were identifying themselves according to Paul, Apollos, or Peter; some even claimed to be "of Christ" (1:12). The Corinthians seemed not to view these divisions as a serious matter, but Paul thought otherwise. Furthermore, he had received word of adultery in the church of such a morally degenerate nature that it was not even heard of among the Gentiles. It had even caused moral offense among the city's inhabitants, who were otherwise accustomed to moral laxity. Paul had another complaint: believers were taking one another to pagan courts to settle their petty differences.

Paul wrote to correct these problems as well as to answer the questions in the Corinthians' letter. In addition, he addressed certain doctrinal issues, particularly concerning the resurrection of believers, and he affirmed some of the basic tenets of Christian proclamation (cf. 2:2; 15:1ff.). Paul endeavored to prevent two things: the influence of the moral corruption that existed outside the church; and the infiltration of a teaching based upon Greek philosophical ideals which threatened to destroy the heart of the gospel.

Even though the scheme of 1 Corinthians does not follow the same kind of rigid structure as the Epistle to the Romans, the main sections are rather easy to identify:

I. CHRISTIAN PROCLAMATION (1:1–4:21)
  A. Greeting and Thanksgiving (1:1-9)
  B. Dispute Over Preachers (1:10-17)
  C. The Foolishness of Preaching (1:18–2:5)
  D. Preaching Wisdom (2:6-16)
  E. The Role of Preachers (3:1-23)
  F. The Hardships of Ministry (4:1-21)
II. CHRISTIAN MORALITY AND ETHICS (5:1–7:40)
  A. Moral Laxity (5:1–6:20)

  1. Immorality and Congregational Disputes (5:1-13)
  2. Lawsuits Before Pagan Courts (6:1-11)
  3. The Body as the Temple of God (6:12ff.)
  B. Married and Unmarried States (7:1-40)
III. CHRISTIAN FREEDOM (8:1–10:33)
  A. Meat Offered to Idols (8:1-13)
  B. The Proper Use of Freedom (9:1-27)
  C. The Example of Israel (10:1-14)
  D. Practical Advice (10:15ff.)
IV. CHRISTIAN WORSHIP (11:1–14:40)
  A. The Conduct of Women (11:2-16)
  B. Love Feasts and the Lord's Supper (11:17-34)
  C. The Gifts of Grace (12:1-31 and 14:1-40)
  D. The Song of Love (13:1-13)
V. CHRISTIAN HOPE FOR THE FUTURE (15:1-58)
  A. The Resurrection of Christ (15:1-22)
    1. The Essence of the Gospel (15:1-5)
    2. Witnesses of the Resurrection (15:6-11)
    3. The Importance of Christ's Resurrection (15:12-22)
  B. Eschatological Perspectives (15:20-34)
    1. The Fact of the Resurrection (15:20-22)
    2. Stages in the Consummation (15:23-28)
    3. Practical Concerns (15:29-34)
  C. How Do the Dead Rise? (15:35-58)
    1. The Resurrection of the Body (15:35)
    2. Analogies (15:36-41)
    3. Four Antitheses (15:42-44)
    4. The First and Last Adam (15:45-49)
    5. Resurrection and Transformation (15:50-58)

I. CHRISTIAN PROCLAMATION (1:1–4:21)

The first main section of 1 Corinthians concerns Christian proclamation, the most crucial distinctive of the Christian Church. Here that theme is especially discussed in relation to the problem of dissension among the Corinthians and their arguments over which preacher was "better" or "right." Paul's teaching, therefore, did not merely inform about the nature of Christian proclamation, it also reflected the place of heralds of the gospel and the attitude the Church is to exhibit towards them.

First, the apostle addressed the problem of interpersonal strife that had arisen in the church; he rejected it outright (1:10-16). Next he related how such dissension could occur: the Corinthians were indiscriminately accepting preaching modeled after Greek "wisdom" (i.e., rhetoric and persuasion), rather than the word of the Cross (1:17-2:5). Paul wrote that the Corinthians were too immature to handle actual spiritual "wisdom." He then explained that the conflict over preachers was pointless, since every witness sent by God is merely a servant performing those duties for which the Lord has equipped him (3:3-23). Paul lastly commented on the hazards of preaching (chapter 4).

The dispute in Corinth ran far deeper than simple preference for one leader/preacher over another. This attitude reflected a fundamentally defective understanding of the gospel—the message of the Cross. They had allowed interests other than the gospel to affect their judgment; this will always result in schism. Paul exposed the heart of the problem. They had allowed interests other than the word of the Cross to control them. Instead of sorting out the various factions into "correct" and "incorrect" categories, Paul directed their attention to the element necessary for unity in the body—the message of the Cross. At the same time he uncovered the actual reason for the divisions: The church had succumbed to strange teachings and had been deceived by Hellenistic "wisdom." The elevation of human wisdom and human beings resulted in factions and caused dissent in the church at Corinth.

A truth emerges here which applies to almost any conflict over doctrine: many of those involved in conflict do not really grasp the issue or its consequences. The believers in Corinth were not intentionally rejecting the gospel, they merely wanted to modify the message to make it more acceptable. What they failed to recognize, however, was that to dress the gospel in the garments of Greek philosophy would be to rob it of its distinctive character. A gospel preached in "words of human wisdom" is no gospel at all (1:17).

The gospel of the first Christian churches was in risk of being distorted from two sources: paganism and Judaism. The epistolary literature of the New Testament generally reflects such conflict, but 1 Corinthians and Galatians are the clearest responses to this danger.

The Epistle to the Galatians cautions against legalistic Judaism's influence upon the young church. It does not appear that these "Judaizers" were in any way connected with James, the leader of the Jewish-Christian congregation in Jerusalem (Acts 15:24). Further, it seems they did not go so far as to deny Jesus' messiahship and His status as Saviour. Nonetheless, Paul declared that they preached "another gospel" (Galatians 1:6-9). Their teaching is summarized in Acts 15:1: "Except ye be circumcised after the manner of Moses, ye cannot be saved." Verse 5 says that these Judaizers had a pharisaic background but they "believed." Thus, they did not deny that belief in Jesus is essential for salvation, but they asserted that believers must also "keep the law of Moses." This mixture of Law and gospel is a distortion of the gospel, said Paul (Galatians 1:7). He strongly condemned it: "But though we, or an angel from heaven, preach any other gospel unto you than that which we have preached unto you, let him be accursed" (verse 8). Any "gospel" that neutralizes grace and relies upon works is not the gospel but its annulment!

While one main assault on the gospel originated from pharisaic Judaism, the other source of attack came from Gentile/pagan philosophy. Just as Judaism was a legalistic religion, Hellenistic philosophical speculation was the ultimate in pagan religion. "Pagan" here does not mean some simplistic, animistic philosophy; rather, it was one of the most sophisticated philosophies of all time. Hellenistic paganism had sunk into deep idolatry and moral decay, but for Paul it was the Greeks' worship of "wisdom" that typified paganism. Precisely at the point of "wisdom" paganism launches its sharpest attack on Christianity.

The idolatry and immorality surrounding the first Gentile churches had their effect upon the newly converted. Yet even more dangerous was the subtle infiltration of Gentile thoughts and ideas, such as the attack from so-called "wisdom." This is what Paul picked up on in the first section of his letter. Just as he showed in the Epistle to the Galatians that it is impossible to unite Christianity with Jewish legalism, in 1 Corinthians he demonstrated that the gospel and Hellenistic wisdom are altogether incompatible. Any plan of salvation that "unites" law and grace perverts the gospel and becomes "another gospel," and to join Greek philosophy with the gospel strips the gospel of its power. Faith and "wisdom" are as incompatible as faith and works of the Law in relation to receiving salvation. Any compromise between the gospel of God and human wisdom is impossible.

The New Testament renounces the kind of wisdom exposed and denounced here and elsewhere in its pages. The "wisdom cult" originated in the Gnostic mystery religions, which adopted myths from the Orient and mixed them with Hellenistic philosophy. "Christian" Gnosticism mixed the gospel of Jesus Christ with Hellenistic "wisdom," asceticism, and worship of angels. These were merely a "spiritualized" form of idolatry. Such a form of "Christian" Gnosticism may also have been threatening the church at Colossae.

The strange "wisdom" teaching that threatened the early Christian churches surfaced in a variety of forms. While the wisdom at Colossae was decidedly mythological in character, the type in Corinth was more rational and intellectual. But Paul condemned this worldly "wisdom" whatever its form. It is foreign to the gospel and an enemy to it. It was the root of the divisions that emerged in Corinth threatened to destroy the church.

A. Greeting and Thanksgiving (1:1-9)

Paul began his letter with a greeting and an offering of thanks to God for the believers in Corinth. His generous acknowledgment of the good in the church—its richness of doctrine, knowledge, and spiritual gifts—was in no way sarcastic. Neither was it flattery designed to ingratiate the church to himself. That kind of reasoning was foreign to Paul. On the contrary, the apostle stated with great joy that not everything was going badly in Corinth. Much true piety and spiritual abundance existed in the church. Paul's letter addressed the errors and abuses in the Corinthian church but the believers needed to be reminded immediately that there was much that was positive about the church. This would keep them from losing courage and thinking that Paul was denouncing everyone.

Paul wrote with apostolic authority, as one with the authority to act on behalf of the Lord and to speak with the authority of Jesus. His letter was more than a friendly correspondence; it was a holy letter to be read in the church and received as the Word of God.

B. Dispute Over Preachers (1:10-17)

To begin his discussion of the problem of divisiveness in Corinth, Paul opened with an appeal for unity. He explained that he learned of the conflict not from some vague rumor but from reliable witnesses whom he named: "those who are of the house of Chloe."

To say Paul was seriously concerned about divisions in the church would be an understatement. No less than 4 of the 16 chapters are devoted to that issue and its ramifications. Still it is noteworthy that he did not refer to the disputing factions as "sects" (*hairesis*), but as "schisms" (*schismata*, pl.). This denotes "splits," or "divisions."

Paul's choice of words may reflect the state of affairs in Corinth. Perhaps they were not the result of heretical groups; their error may not have gone that far . . . yet. Nevertheless, the seed of division sown among them resulted in a spiritual cleavage in the church. Members had selected their "favorite preacher" and were taking sides against one another—despite the fact that the preachers themselves did not want or encourage such division.

Paul mentioned four such groups, but he did not elaborate on what specifically distinguished each group. A great deal of literature has been devoted to trying to identify the various features of each group; however, such an attempt is ultimately doomed to failure. There is simply not enough hard evidence.

The general consensus argues that those claiming to be "of Paul" or "for Paul" attached a great deal of importance to Paul's teaching on Christian freedom. Those "of Apollos," an eloquent scholar from Alexandria, perhaps put a great deal of emphasis upon a polished, rhetorical style. The members of the Cephas group are regarded by many as representatives of a Jewish-Christian faction; these would naturally affiliate with Peter, the apostle to the circumcised. The above may be true, but it cannot be confirmed.

The greatest conflict of opinion concerns the nature of the fourth group, those "of Christ." Some interpreters regard this to be Paul's reply to the first three groups. Although possible, it is not probable. Paul continued with the indignant rhetorical question, "Is Christ divided?" This would seem to indicate that even the name of Christ was being used by a faction.

Opinions differ as to what characterized this the "Christ group." It may have asserted a special "spirituality" that regarded itself above human authority and the only true followers of Jesus. Their error lay in claiming Christ exclusively for themselves. The very name that should have united all the people had become a party name. Paul rejected it just as he had the others.

Naturally Paul rejected those claiming to be "of Paul." He would not tolerate any group of Pauline "disciples"; he was in the business of making disciples of Jesus Christ and Him alone. Peter and Apollos apparently felt the same as Paul. The question of who was the "greatest" interested Peter no more than Paul (cf. Galatians 2:6). Paul's confidence in Apollos becomes clear when he asked him to go to Corinth (1 Corinthians 16:12).

The conflict in Corinth probably did not concern any actual doctrinal issues, but the consequences of their divisions included their being "puffed up for one against another" (4:6). This kind of conflict was moreover totally unjustified, since the only kind of justifiable dispute would concern doctrine. To contend for the Faith is the obligation of every believer; personal conflict is usually unauthorized. In the eyes of the people the personalities of the preachers overshadowed their message, which was Biblical and in total agreement. As the personalities became the focus of attention the gospel receded into the background. If the gospel had been given its rightful place in the community, those who heard it would not have made the messenger more important than the message. The basis of Christian unity is the cross of Christ; only the preaching of the Cross can lead believers into that unity.

C. The Foolishness of Preaching (1:18–2:5)

For Paul the cross became a religious symbol, a new and radical viewpoint in the ancient world. In fact, "the cross" has become the central symbol in Christian proclamation. Paul spoke of "the preaching of the cross," which equals the gospel itself, the power of God unto salvation (1:18; cf. Romans 1:16). The very gospel the Corinthians believed and by which they were saved is the same gospel received by Paul: Christ died for our sins according to the Scriptures, He was buried, and He rose from the dead (15:1ff.). The message of salvation is the announcement of the reality of what God has done in Christ. This makes the gospel "good news," and its truth cannot be compromised.

"The preaching of the cross" was an offense to the Jews, a stumbling block that made them fall. Paul linked this to their demand for a "sign" before they would believe (1:22). They thought the Messiah would authenticate himself with signs from heaven, like Moses or Elijah. Even though they saw Him heal the sick and raise the dead, they continued to demand a sign from heaven. Jesus told them the only sign they would be given would be the sign of Jonah the prophet. As Jonah was in the belly of the great fish for 3 days, so too would the Son of Man be in the heart of the earth for 3 days. The ultimate sign given to them was the death and resurrection of Jesus, and this was the "sign" Paul preached. Nevertheless, the scandal of "the cross" made it virtually impossible for the Jews to accept its message. The Law stated that "He that is hanged, is accursed of God" (Deuteronomy 21:23; cf. Galatians 3:13). To reconcile the dilemma of a Messiah dying in such total weakness and defeat was virtually impossible. Furthermore, that any "Messiah" should die under the judgment and curse of God was absurd and a contradiction within itself.

The Jewish leaders who later had stoned Stephen and caused the death of so many other believers took care to see that Jesus died a Roman death; that was all the "proof" they needed that Jesus was not the promised Messiah. They could not accept a humiliated Messiah. Their unbelief stemmed directly from a failure to believe the Scriptures. They were blind to the Old Testament's anticipation of the Suffering Servant of God, spoken of in Isaiah 53. They had no use for any Messiah who would allow himself to bear the sin and its penalty of all peoples. However, this is precisely the kind of Messiah Paul preached: Christ crucified (2:2); Christ made sin for us (2 Corinthians 5:21); Christ made a curse for us (Galatians 3:13). There is no other way to salvation than this.

To the Greek "the preaching of the cross" was the ultimate folly. One could not expect its absurdity to be taken seriously. A crucified Jew the saviour of the whole world? Impossible. The Greeks regarded the message of the Cross as an insult to their intelligence. The danger facing the church at Corinth was that it would adopt the world's attitude toward the message of the Cross. Undoubtedly some were urging that the message be adapted to suit the cultural situation and to make it more acceptable to outsiders. Paul was responding to the efforts of some to cloak Christianity in the guise of the wisdom of the world, i.e., Hellenistic rhetorical methods and terminology.

Paul was not against adapting to one's environment; he had done it himself. He became a Jew to the Jews and a Greek to the Greeks (9:19-22). His sermon on Mars Hill in Athens, just before he went to Corinth reflected this (Acts 17:22ff.). But when it came to modifying the gospel according to the Hellenistic "wisdom" philosophy, he was immovable. His solid reluctance to alter the gospel's heart at this point resembles his similar ardor against the Judaizers in Galatians. He would not preach the gospel with "wise words"; his listeners' faith could not rest upon human wisdom but upon the power of God (1:17; 2:4). This explains why Greeks seeking wisdom did not find it in the preaching of the apostles. Instead of human wisdom they met the "foolishness" of preaching, the plain, unaltered truth of the gospel. The preaching of the Cross is carried out in the "demonstration of the Spirit's power" (2:4, NIV). The expression "demonstration" (*apodeixis*) here denotes "proof," a term often appearing in argumentation in which the premise is known to be true and reliable. At the same time, it denotes more than a logical truth, because an argument may be logically sound yet still unconvincing. The "proof" has real power to convince; it has a spiritual impact upon the inner person. This cannot be produced by human eloquence; it comes only from the convicting power of the Holy Spirit (cf. John 16:8). When Paul declared that his preaching was in the demonstration of the Spirit's power, he was probably referring to those supernatural manifestations that accompanied his ministry. He himself observed that signs and wonders were worked in Corinth (2 Corinthians 12:12). In this case, though, there was undoubtedly something more than external miracles; rather, it included the spiritual power that was the key to apostolic preaching.

As Paul's own ministry attests, the power of the Cross is not revealed in human power and ability, but in weakness and humiliation (2:3; cf. 2 Corinthians 10:10; 12:5-9). He therefore avoided any appearance of using "enticing words of man's wisdom" or the methods of philosophers, because human wisdom has already proved inadequate for leading man to God. Through its wisdom the world did not know Him (1:21). With a series of rhetorical questions Paul invites the "wise person" to step forward. Where is the wise? where is the scribe, (the expert in the law)? where is the disputer (debater) of this world (age)? The last expression is somewhat sarcastic. Together the three summarize the essence of what was regarded as "wise." But which of these three understood salvation on the basis of their "wisdom"? The

world might expect them to be at the forefront, but their wisdom had not led them to faith or shown them the way to God.

On the contrary, not many considered "wise" in the world's eyes are called. Neither are many called whom the world regards as powerful or influential. And not many esteemed as "noble" receive the gospel. That which a person might boast about or exalt himself for is captured in these three expressions: intellectual superiority, political and economic power, and social status. Against these the apostle Paul juxtaposed the elect of God. God chooses the "foolish things" of this world, not the "wise." He calls the weak, not the strong; He invites the lowly and even despised, not the exalted. He summons those disowned by human society— "nonpersons" who are not even recognized by the rest of society. These are like slaves, the lowest dregs of society. To be "nothing" or nonexistent was abhorrent to the Greek mind. But for Paul it stood at the crux of God's new act in which He was creating a new creation from nothing. The words of the Old Testament ring out clearly: "Those who were not a people will become a people," the new people of God (Hosea 1:7ff.; cf. Romans 9:25,26; 1 Peter 2:10).

A word of caution is in order here. Paul was not suggesting that the "lowly" are really the "lofty" and the "powerful" the "powerless." God chooses the things which are indeed lowly, not for the purpose of exalting them according to worldly standards, but precisely because they are lowly. None have reason for boasting in the presence of God (1:29). The sole criterion for salvation remains faith (Romans 3:27); no one can take credit for what God's grace accomplishes. Both the exalted and the debased stand in need before God. God's choosing the lowly and humble shows that it is by grace alone that salvation comes. It is altogether the work of God: "Of him are ye in Christ Jesus, who of God is made unto us wisdom, and righteousness, and sanctification, and redemption" (1:30).

Paul made it perfectly clear that the preaching of the Cross is foolishness to those who are perishing, but to those who believe it is the power and wisdom of God (1:18,24). With this as his background, Paul proceeded to explain the nature of true spiritual wisdom.

D. Preaching Wisdom (2:6-16)

Paul's argument revolved around two contrasts: the weakness of God is stronger than men, and the foolishness of God is wiser than men. These two concepts are interlaced with one another continually, but the first section (1:17-2:5) focuses upon how the "weakness" of God accomplishes what the "power" of humanity cannot. The foolishness of preaching is superior to every human philosophy or epistemology because it acts. The preaching of the Cross, which might appear "rough-cut" in the company of "gems" of human oratory, nevertheless has the power to set men and women free and transform their lives.

In 2:6-16 Paul began to discuss the second major contrast: the foolishness of God is wiser than men. Lacking any ability to grasp the foolishness of the preaching of the Cross, fallen man, ruled not by the Spirit of God but by his own corrupt nature, cannot receive the things of the Spirit. They are "folly" to him. To modify the Christian message in order to accommodate Gentiles, therefore, is useless. In fact, it is not the simple, plain presentation of the gospel that prevents men from receiving, but the reality that the gospel is foreign to the natural man. He is hostile to it. Therefore, the gospel must be proclaimed in simple, direct terms. Only then can the Spirit of God use it to convince men of their need to be saved.

This principle applies not only to the evangelistic efforts of proclaiming the gospel, but to the teaching ministry within the Church itself. Just as the kerygma—the essence of the proclamation of the gospel—owes nothing to the world, so too, the Christian teaching or didachē is not to be overly influenced by human teaching. Rather, teaching should be marked by the Spirit's instruction. The Spirit teaches spiritual things which can only be interpreted by spiritual words; spiritual matters must be compared with other spiritual matters (2:13).

The simple message Paul preached could help some to grasp its forthright message. But this does not mean the gospel is not sophisticated, lacks depth, or anything similar. That would be a total misrepresentation. The Christian message is one of the deepest mysteries of all time: God and the human condition, sin and redemption, time and eternity, and the beginning and the consummation. The wisdom given by God can grant insight into the mysteries of the earth never before accessible by merely human methods. Wisdom indeed characterizes the gospel: "But we speak the wisdom of God in a mystery, even the hidden wisdom, which God ordained before the world unto our glory" (2:7).

Related to this, Paul raised two questions: What does the deeper wisdom of Christ consist of? Who participates in this secret wisdom?

When Paul explained the nature of Christian wisdom, he began—quite understandably given the problem of wisdom in Corinth—by setting out very clearly that the hidden wisdom of God is entirely different from the wisdom of the world. Worldly wisdom is an invention of mankind, thus it is colored by sin's influence (cf. Ephesians 4:17,18). Consequently, it is empty and restricted to this present world. Christian wisdom, however, being of a divine origin, consists of the concepts which God "ordained before the world" (2:7), i.e., what God thought before He created. It therefore reflects the wisdom of God himself and His plan of salvation. "Christ . . . the wisdom of God" is the essence of this wisdom, and in Him are "hid all the treasures of wisdom and knowledge" (Colossians 2:2,3). Spiritual wisdom does not lead one away from the Cross, as worldly wisdom does; rather it points toward it, since Christ is what spiritual wisdom is all about.

Because spiritual wisdom comes from God and is hidden in God, it is unobtainable for anyone not having the Spirit of God. Only the Spirit of God knows what dwells in God (2:10ff.). "The princes of this world" did not know this wisdom. If they had known it they would not have crucified the Lord of glory (2:8).

It is not strange that the world and its leaders did not grasp the deep wisdom of God. It is amazing that "the wisdom" is also unknown by carnal and immature believers. Preaching of this wisdom is "meat" in contrast to the "milk" of preaching basic gospel truths. Paul declared that the Corinthians were not able to bear preaching on wisdom (3:1,2). It can be dangerous to immature believers because it can be misinterpreted (cf. 2 Peter 3:15,16). The kind of insight referred to here is more than intellectual. It is closely related to a person's spiritual condition. This wisdom is for the "mature," the "spiritual" (2:6,15). Spiritual maturity in this instance is necessary to comprehend the deep things of God. It also denotes the condition of an individual as "spiritual" rather than "carnal, fleshly" (3:3). These are not just "babes" in Christ, but "carnal Christians," whose lifestyle is inconsistent with their Christian testimony.

The New Testament writings encourage the Christian to grow in knowledge. This is not just mental, but includes the entire personality.

Spiritual immaturity leads to all kinds of destructive influences (Ephesians 4:13,14). To be deficient in Christian knowledge can lead to backsliding (Hebrews 6:1ff.). Against this background Paul desired all believers to obtain "all the riches of the full assurance of understanding" (Colossians 2:1f.). The apostle must not be misunderstood here as saying that wisdom is available only for the mature. By no means would he have endorsed some spiritual hierarchy within the body of Christ. All believers may achieve "the unity of the faith, and of the knowledge of the Son of God" (Ephesians 4:13). Knowledge here is not merely intellectual information, but spiritual growth, maturity (2 Peter 3:18). When Paul stated that the Corinthians were "babes in Christ," he meant that they needed more than teaching to obtain the hidden wisdom of God.

E. The Role of Preachers (3:1-23)

Having explained the essence of Christian proclamation in 1:17 to 2:5 and the nature of Christian wisdom in 2:6-26, Paul returned (chapter 3) to a theme introduced in 1:10-16: divisions in the church over leaders. The apostle explained in this section the role of the preacher and his place in the Church. He showed how utterly pointless was their favoring one preacher over another. Their attitude showed they were still living a fleshly existence; they were still immature and therefore not ready to receive deeper spiritual instruction (3:1-3).

"Who, then is Paul, and who is Apollos, but ministers by whom ye believed?" Paul asked (3:5). They were servants of God, their special ministry was given to them by God alone. Paul used two illustrations. He compared the Church with a field and with the temple of God. In each case His servants have their different roles.

In God's field some plant and others water. How absurd it would be to say "I'm for the planter," or "I'm for the waterer." They are coworkers, not competitors. Together they work for God who alone can grant growth. Apart from Him neither the one who plants nor the one who waters is anything. But because they are working together toward the same objective, it is ridiculous for anyone to align with one and reject the other. It is disastrous when Christians become "puffed up for one against another" (4:6). If the leaders were esteemed for who they truly are—servants of the Lord—there would not be any conflict or division.

The second image Paul utilized is that of the temple, God's holy habitation of old. The Old Testament spoke of a new temple that would be erected in the last days (Isaiah 28:16). The early Christians saw the Church of the New Testament as the spiritual fulfillment of these prophecies. Paul declared that he had laid the foundation of this spiritual building in Corinth. This foundation was none other than that which God himself had laid—Jesus Christ (3:11). He is the cornerstone of the "foundation of the apostles and prophets." In Him the various churches or "buildings" are fitted together into a "holy temple . . . an habitation of God through the Spirit" (Ephesians 2:20-22). Jesus' work and His person are the foundation of the Church. When Jesus said He would build His Church, He associated this with Peter's confession at Caesarea Philippi: "You are the Christ, the Son of the living God" (Matthew 16:16ff.). No one else can lay another foundation, declared Paul. Any organization built on another foundation is not a church. Christ and His presence authenticate the Church.

The "building" rests upon this foundation. Its erection, first and foremost, comes through preaching. To continue the imagery, preaching the gospel, i.e., evangelization, brings new "stones" for the building. Teaching doctrine places and fits the stones properly into the larger structure. The object is that everyone should be presented "perfect" in Christ (Colossians 1:28) and be "thoroughly equipped" for service (Ephesians 4:12ff.). Later Pauline churches had to endure "preachers" who tried to build on another foundation. These were sharply rebuked (Galatians 1:6f.; Philippians 3:2,18; Colossians 2:8). In 1 Corinthians Paul spoke of those who build upon the same foundation but with different materials. Those who build on Christ's foundation, provided their work stands, will be rewarded. But those who build with "cheap" or "worthless" material, will not be rewarded. Instead, their work will burn in the fiery judgment. Nevertheless, the one building upon the proper foundation will not lose his soul, even though he loses his reward. He will be saved, but only as through fire. A genuine believer never relies upon his own efforts to save him, but the work of Christ. Although the believer may fail and his work perish, the work of Christ stands firm. This is what saves him.

It is a different matter when divisions are

caused in the Body of Christ. Paul uses two Greek words, *dichostasia* and *schismata*, which are translated "divisions." He also speaks of *hairesis* ("heresies") as dividing the church (see 11:19 and 2 Peter 2:1) and calls them a work of the flesh (Galatians 5:20).

Paul uses strong language: "If any man destroy the temple of God, him shall God destroy" (3:17), stating that believers are the temple of God. To destroy the Church is a heinous crime. It is like touching the "apple of his eye" (cf. Zechariah 2:8) and defiling the bride of Christ. The larger Church can never be destroyed (Matthew 16:18), but from Revelation (2:5; 3:16; etc.) it is apparent that some individual churches can be. Whether Paul's warning of God's judgment was directed at certain individuals cannot be determined for sure (cf. Galatians 5:10).

Paul concluded this subsection by warning the Corinthians not to "glory in men" (3:21). How could they choose sides or follow a particular teaching, when in actuality everything was theirs? Whether Paul, Apollos, or Cephas, they were all servants given to the Church by God (cf. 12:28; Ephesians 4:11). Indeed, whether the world, life, or death, whether present or future, everything belongs to the children of God and will work for their good (cf. Romans 8:28). Why limit to a part what God has given in totality? Why choose the world's empty wisdom when the eternal wisdom of God—the things "eye hath not seen not ear heard, neither have entered into the heart of man"—are available (cf. 2:7-10).

F. The Hardships of Ministry (4:1-21)

Paul concluded this section on preachers and preaching with a discussion of their low status in the world and the hardships endured by servants of Christ. He opened the section and united it with what had preceded it by asking the Corinthians to regard their leaders not as leaders of factions, but as ministers and stewards of Christ.

The two terms he used express both the low position of the witnesses as well as their uniqueness. The term for servant here, *hepēretas*, originally denoted the rowers who sat on the lowest bench in the ship. From this it came to describe any "assistant" or "helper." The second term, *oikonomous*, signified a slave who was the overseer of his master's household and property. This "steward" was in charge of his fellow slaves, but depending upon the extent of his master's flexibility, he was nevertheless a slave like the rest.

The first obligation of a steward is to be faithful. Where faithfulness was at stake, the opinions of others did not matter to Paul. Indeed, he did not even judge himself; he left that to God. Although he had not knowingly been unfaithful in his service, he realized he could make mistakes. Thus he declared, "He who judges me is the Lord." Paul was not concerned that the Corinthians would look into his record. He knew his record would be evaluated by the One who will bring to light everything that has been hidden in the darkness and the inner motives of hearts. When the Lord returns hidden motives will be exposed—Paul's as well as those of everyone else's. Then all men will praise God. Apparently every believer will receive praise for something. Paul looked confidently, but with a holy respect, toward the time when he would stand before the judgment seat of Christ (2 Corinthians 5:10,11).

Next comes the most biting portion of the entire letter. It contains the harshest rebuke and is marked by a painful irony. But Paul gave it in deep love, calling his listeners "brethren" and his "dear children" (4:6-14). First, he explained why he had referred to himself and Apollos (1:12; 3:4,22). It was not because this was necessarily a Corinthian concern, but because he and Apollos were models of what he was talking about. Paul customarily supported his arguments with references to Scripture (cf. 1:19f.,31; 2:9,16; 3:19f.). Apparently there were some teachers in the Corinthian church who thought their vision was superior in authority to Scripture. They incited division in the church. To supersede what was written was itself divisive. Consequently, the danger of elevating the teaching of men above Scripture by giving them authority and power is plain.

Typically, Paul set things in order with one of his penetrating rhetorical questions. "For who maketh thee to differ from another?" Paul questioned. The only answer could be, "I did it myself!" No one would admit to that, however. But Paul was relentless: "And what hast thou that thou didst not receive?" Only a fool boasts of something he obtained from others.

Within the Corinthian church were individuals who imagined they had already reached a perfection that cannot occur in this life. That perfection belongs to the time of the consummation. They not only judged before the time (verse 5), they also took credit (glory) in advance. They were already satisfied. They had become rich already! But Jesus declared, "Blessed are those who are hungering and thirsting after righteousness." Jesus also said, "Blessed are the poor in spirit."

The Corinthians were acting as if the kingdom of God had already come and they had been appointed rulers. "I truly wish it were so," commented Paul sarcastically. "If that were true," he reasoned, "we apostles could rule with you." The pretense of glory and the illusion of divine living experienced by the Corinthians was entirely foreign to the apostles. While the Corinthians listened to the wisdom of the world, the apostles were preaching the word of the Cross. They lived their lives under the Cross; they followed the rejected Messiah, the humiliated Son of Man.

The church in Corinth, or at least some of its members, was influenced by the deadly teaching of Laodicea. They imagined themselves wealthy to the exclusion of Christ (Revelation 3:17). To shock them into awareness of what was happening, Paul compared them with the apostles: "We are fools for Christ's sake, but ye are wise in Christ; . . . ye are honorable, but we are despised" (4:10). As heralds of the suffering Messiah, the Son of God, the apostles were the most lowly of all. Their fate was as much sealed as those waiting to die in the arena. They were a spectacle to all the world, both angels and mankind. They had not obtained the kingdom of God, and at the present time some were hungry, thirsty, naked, mistreated, homeless, and tired.

The Greeks despised manual labor and those who performed it. Only slaves worked with their hands. However, Paul declared that he and the other apostles had worked with their own hands. He continued, "Being reviled, we bless; being persecuted, we suffer it: being defamed we entreat" (4:12,13). To the Greek such ideas sounded despicable. Aristotle declared that the highest priority was not to endure insult, that it was the characteristic of a big soul. But the apostle endured suffering as "the scum of the earth." Such were the conditions of the servants of Christ. This was the apostolic call to which Paul had been summoned and set apart from the beginning (Acts 9:16; cf. 2 Corinthians 4:11; 11:23f.; 12:10; 1 Thessalonians 2:6). How unfair it was for his own spiritual children to lay further burdens on the already encumbered apostle. How petty divisions and partiality are

when the true servants are enduring affliction on behalf of the Church (Colossians 1:24).

The first main section of the letter concludes with a deeply personal appeal: "For though ye have ten thousand instructors in Christ, yet have ye not many fathers: for in Christ Jesus I have begotten you through the gospel" (4:15). Paul recognized others shared in the upbuilding of the Church through preaching and teaching. But he asked the Corinthians to listen to him as their spiritual father. "Be followers of me!" He did not say, "Do as I tell you!" but rather, "Do as I do." Instead of searching for the wisdom and honor of the world, they were to follow Paul as he followed Christ.

II. CHRISTIAN MORALITY AND ETHICS (5:1–7:40)

The introduction to the second major section may seem abrupt. Omitting any transitional statement, Paul immediately gave the serious charge: "It is reported commonly that there is fornication among you." Far from having any justification for their boasting, because of spirituality or knowledge, the Corinthians should instead have been mourning because of the moral decay of the church (5:2).

A. Moral Laxity (5:1–6:20)

1. Immorality and Congregational Disputes (5:1-13). Paul charged that the Corinthians were tolerating a brand of immorality so decadent that it did not even occur among Gentiles. Apparently a man was living with his step-mother, his own father's wife. Perhaps she was divorced or widowed. We are not told whether they were married, but apparently their relationship was long-term. It is disturbing enough that such a thing would take place in the church at all, but what is truly alarming is that the church did not take any disciplinary action against it. The church, therefore, was also guilty. A church is responsible for what takes place within it and must face God's judgment for laxity. Moreover, its members are exposed to sin, which can spread like a disease: "Know ye not that a little leaven leaveneth the whole lump?" (5:6).

Realizing their irresponsibility, Paul demanded that they rid themselves of this sinner. This was not only for the sake of the church but for the sake of the individual as well. If the church did nothing, the man could only think his conduct was acceptable. This would make him blind to his own sin and make it difficult for him to repent. Consequently, the church must act and remove him from the congregation. They must "deliver such an one unto Satan for the destruction of the flesh, that the spirit may be saved in the day of the Lord Jesus" (5:5).

The expression "deliver unto Satan" also occurs in 1 Timothy 1:20. When a person is expelled from the spiritual refuge of the church, he must face the evil one in his own strength. That one is destined to fall under Satan's power. It is hard to make the "destruction of the flesh" mean anything except physical sickness and suffering brought on by the enemy (cf. Job 2:5-7; 2 Corinthians 12:7-9).

That the church in Corinth could ignore such a flagrant violation of God's commandments reflects the same kind of fleshly nature that caused its members to put value on worldly wisdom and to "glory in men" (3:21). They boasted of their "libertine views" and their "tolerance," which actually ignored a condition that should only be stamped as sin. But Paul cautioned them, "Your glorying is not good" (5:6).

Furthermore, Paul straightened out a misunderstanding in an earlier letter—they were not to have any fellowship with adulterers. He was not referring to those outside the church, however. If Christians avoided contact with such people altogether, they would have to "leave the world." Instead, Paul was referring to "adulterers" who profess Christianity, yet continue in sin. A genuine Christian must not fellowship with such a person. On the other hand, it is not possible to avoid contact with the outside world. Elsewhere the apostle cautioned against having any kind of intimate relationship with the ungodly (2 Corinthians 6:14.).

In an effort to separate themselves from the world, some believers have avoided any contact with it. However, when the issue concerns those inside the church, it is the responsibility and obligation of the church to pass judgment (5:12,13).

2. Lawsuits Before Pagan Courts (6:1-11). The right of the Church to judge its members and in the age to come the world (6:2), and even angels (6:3), was ignored by the Corinthians. Even worse, they were taking their disputes against one another before pagan courts! With biting sarcasm Paul asked, "Is it so, that there is not a wise man among you? no, not one that shall be able to judge between his brethren?" (6:5). While the Corinthians took pride in their "wisdom," in actuality they did not even view themselves as competent to render judgment in trivial matters!

No matter what, it is a tragedy for believers to have lawsuits against one another. Actually a Christian should be willing to be defrauded rather than fight for his "rights" in such a manner (this recalls the Sermon on the Mount, Matthew 5:39ff.). But even more seriously, such a lawsuit would determine one "right" and the other "wrong." Paul thus asked, "Know ye not that the unrighteous shall not inherit the kingdom of God?" (6:9). It is therefore preferable for a Christian to suffer unrighteousness. After all, the unrighteous person excludes himself from the kingdom of God (cf. Matthew 13:41-43).

In addition to this Paul offered a so-called vice list (6:9,10). Sins against the general commandments are listed here, as well as violations of the sixth commandment. Paul placed the same demands upon homosexuals as he did upon unmarried heterosexuals; all married people are warned against adultery. Such sins invite the judgment of God; anyone who thinks differently is headed for destruction.

Some of these sins may lie in the past of some believers, but now they are "washed" (cf. Revelation 7:14; especially Acts 22:16, where the same Greek word is used in connection with washing). This recalls the symbolism of baptism which washes away not only the guilt and feelings of guilt, but the sins themselves (cf. Romans 6:1ff.).

3. The Body as the Temple of God (6:12ff.). Following the parenthetical section about lawsuits, Paul resumed his primary theme: sexual conduct and holiness of believers. He again showed that adultery is a particularly deplorable sin, since it profanes the body of the believer.

Two circumstances made the situation in Corinth critical. First, the morally bankrupt condition of the pagan society around the church might easily have influenced believers' attitudes towards moral issues. Those "living like Corinthians" did not consider immorality a serious problem. An individual's moral conduct was not believed to have any effect upon one's spiritual life at all. Second, some had perverted Christian liberty into a license for immorality and lawlessness. Every ancient congregation had to battle this delusion (cf. Titus 1:16; 2 Peter 2:18; Jude 4; Revelation 2:20). Freedom was being exploited as an "occasion to the flesh" (Galatians 5:13).

When Paul said, "All things are lawful," he was not giving a blanket endorsement of all actions. He qualified it by saying not all things are expedient; that is, for the best. He repeated this statement in 10:23, where he applied it to eating meat sacrificed to idols, which he would not do, if it caused a brother to stumble. The great principle of action is found in 10:31: "Whether therefore ye eat, or drink, or whatsoever ye do, do all to the glory of God."

Freedom is to be used for good. It runs counter to the nature of freedom to use it to permit something else to rule. In the original language the passage has a play on words: "To have the authority to do something must not mean we become under the authority of something else."

Any notion that sexual relations are nothing besides a bodily function like eating and drinking was abhorrent to the apostle. He categorically rejected such an idea by affirming, "Meats for the belly, and the belly for meats: but God shall destroy both it and them" (6:13). However, the body is not for fornication (6:15). His reasoning is virtually identical to Jesus' words in Mark 7:18-23. There the Lord contrasted "that whatsoever thing from without entereth into the man" and does not defile the person, with the evil which comes out of the heart and defiles him. Among the evil things coming from within, Jesus explicitly mentioned lewdness.

When a man and woman live together the two become "one flesh," their bodies joint possessions. The physical union between a man and his wife is according to the will of God and does not prevent the body from belonging to the Lord. But in an adulterous situation, the "members of Christ" join with the members of a prostitute. This disrupts communion with the Lord. "The body is for the Lord"—it is thus a terrible insult to profane that which belongs to Him.

Sexual immorality profanes the very temple of God. When Paul talked about the body as the dwelling place of the human spirit, he called it a house (2 Corinthians 5:1; cf. 2 Peter 1:13,14, tabernacle), but as the residence of the Holy Spirit, it is the temple of God (6:19). When Paul commented that the adulterer sins against one's own body, he apparently had a twofold point. One, it refers to the body of the individual, and two, it refers to the body of Christ, the Church, the true temple of God.

Paul concluded his comments by urging the Corinthians to honor God in their bodies. While those disrupting the community defended adultery and viewed the body as worthless and meaningless, Paul forbade adultery by demonstrating what a high position the body has as the temple of the Holy Spirit.

B. Married and Unmarried States (7:1-40)

Beginning with 7:1 Paul addressed issues raised by the Corinthians in an earlier letter to him. Many divide the letter at this juncture.

Each time Paul discussed a Corinthian issue (from their former letter) he began with the Greek phrase *peri de*, "now concerning." The following topics fall under this category: marriage and divorce (7:1); marriage of young women 7:25; sacrifices to idols (8:1); spiritual gifts (12:1); collection for the saints in Judea (16:1); and, Apollos (16:12).

In chapter 7 Paul answered questions concerning the married and unmarried states. He defended both states as legitimate before God. He said something positive about both being married and unmarried, but he opposed extreme views in either direction.

He began by saying that it is good for a man "not to touch a woman." This phrase, of course, is not intended to be taken literally, and neither was he saying it is better to be unmarried than married. Here, "not to touch a woman" is a euphemism for having sexual relations. Paul fully recognized the temporal and spiritual advantages of being unmarried; spiritual because the unmarried person can devote more time to the things of the Lord (7:32), and temporal because the unmarried person is spared some of the hardships of the married state (7:26-28). But what is best for each individual is a personal decision. It depends on the gift of grace received by each, and thus on God's will for each (7:7). What Paul intended to assert, however, was that avoiding illicit sexual relations (as a single or married person) is good. Being single is not morally inferior to being married. People of that time may have considered singleness and sexual purity as almost mutually exclusive in the morally depraved society in Corinth. Anyone living the single life was naturally assumed to be immoral. Paul rejected such a prejudice.

The other extreme rejected by Paul was that being married is sinful. However, sexual relations outside of matrimony are indeed sinful. To prevent rampant adultery Paul wrote that each was to have his or her own spouse. Marriage is not some "higher," "spiritual" union which rejects sexual relations. Marriage does not become more spiritual if the partners abstain from sex. Neither partner should defraud the other, unless both agree to devote themselves to prayer—and then only for a given period of time. Therefore, Paul distanced himself from any position espousing some artificial union between men and women that claims higher spirituality. Avoiding sex in marriage does not bring about a preferred spiritual condition either; on the contrary, it can lead to greater temptation by Satan and to adultery.

Paul remained consistent in this position when he addressed the issue of virgins and matrimony (7:25ff.). It is absurd to think that the apostle would first distance himself from any "spiritualizing" of matrimony and then turn around and favor what he had just argued against! These kinds or forms of "marriage" were unknown to the Ancient Church, although an ascetic position did at times emerge. The first examples of spiritual marriages come from the Second Century, almost 150 years after Paul wrote 1 Corinthians, and then it appeared only in isolated, fanatical circles. Those joined in such "engagements" or "marriages" mutually pledged to live celibate lives; any union would be "spiritual."

In 7:36-38 it seems that Paul was giving advice to one having custody of a young girl. Ordinarily this is taken to mean a father's normal authority over his unmarried daughter. Other commentators have thought it could refer to a man and his fiancee. At the close of the last century, however, some theologians suggested a new theory that Paul was advising an individual living in the so-called spiritual marriage or engagement condition, who found celibacy increasingly difficult to maintain. According to this new interpretation Paul consented that the man could marry his "fiancee," but he (Paul) contended that he would do better if he sent his "fiancee" away and continued to live in celibacy. Thus according to this theory, Paul advocated some kind of divorce. The theory runs counter in many ways to what Paul wrote earlier in the chapter.

The theory of a spiritual engagement also lacks any contextual support. The original verb in 7:38 is *gamizō*, which means "to give in marriage." This is over against *gameō*, "to marry," which occurs a total of seven times in the chapter (verses 9,10,28,30,34,36,39). (See the commentary for 7:36-38.)

III. CHRISTIAN FREEDOM (8:1–10:33)

One of the dominant issues discussed in 1 Corinthians is the misuse and abuse of Christian freedom. The second major section of the epistle dealt with the moral side of that issue. Next Paul turned to other aspects of the same subject. He warned those who were thinking Christian freedom made adultery acceptable: "*Flee* fornication" (6:18). The third major section examined the Christian's freedom in relation to idolatry. Paul's teaching on that subject concluded with the same admonition: "*Flee* from idolatry" (10:14).

The members of the church in Corinth were not in disagreement about exactly what constituted idolatry. Like many other early assemblies, they had left idolatry when they decided to follow the living and true God (cf. 1 Thessalonians 1:9). What caused difficulties was more practical in nature. The Corinthians lived in a place where idolatry affected every aspect of social existence. Social gatherings often took place in idol temples. In addition, nearly all of the meat sold in the marketplace had at one time been offered to an idol. This raised two questions: One, should a Christian participate in a feast in an idol temple with his Gentile family and friends? And two, could a believer purchase and eat meat that was previously offered to an idol. Paul treated these questions at a very basic level, and offered some practical solutions.

First, Paul opposed the arrogant "knowledge" or "enlightment" concerning these things some in Corinth boasted they had. This kind of "knowledge" is the kind of prideful display Paul had just spent four chapters denouncing. Just as he disavowed false wisdom (3:18): "If any man among you seemeth to be wise . . ."— he now rejected false knowledge: "If any man think that he knoweth any thing" (8:2). Later he warned against a false, fleshly sense of security, "him that thinketh he standeth" (10:12; cf. Romans 11:25; Galatians 6:3). Those who boast of knowledge, he said, never really know anything as they should.

In contrast to a knowledge that is "puffed up," Paul preached a love that "builds up." The one who loves God possesses something greater than knowledge. He himself is known by God (8:3; cf. Galatians 4:9). But those who abuse Christian freedom because they lack love are a stumbling block to their "weaker" brethren. Causing offense means to make another fall, stumble. These are not simple barbs or insults.

The offense was that some who professed knowledge and freedom were enticing others to exceed what their consciences allowed. Such a stance is destructive to the Christian life and faith of those enticed and can result in a fall (10:11). In order to avoid such a situation, Paul argued that it is better to relinquish one's freedom. Paul was himself an example. Throughout most of the chapter he showed how he gave up his rights as an apostle to become the servant of all in order to win souls.

Having thereby emphasized that regard for one's brother was reason enough to avoid anything associated with idolatry, he proceeded to demonstrate that this was also necessary for each individual. Actually, idols do not exist; they are fictions, for there is but one God. But behind the idolatrous image lies an evil power. What is offered in sacrifice to the idol is sacrificed to the evil spirit. Idols are thus indeed linked to evil. This applied to Christians who were partakers in idol feasts.

Paul drew a comparison with the Lord's Supper. He reminded the Corinthians that those eating the bread and drinking the cup were partakers of and shared communion with the body and blood of Christ. The same held true for a pagan sacrificial meal, a religious ceremony signifying commonality and fellowship. Paul conluded, "Ye cannot drink the cup of the Lord, and the cup of devils: ye cannot be partakers of the Lord's table, and of the table of devils" (10:16-21).

The one who may "think that he knoweth any thing" in fact knows nothing as it should be known. He only has a knowledge that leads him astray. Those claiming "knowledge" superior to the weak who do not have such knowledge have themselves been snared by the sin of idolatry—a real enough sin, although idols are nothing and meaningless. With a piercing earnestness, Paul recounted the history of Israel as a warning: "Now all these things happened unto them for ensamples" (10:11).

After giving explicit instructions that Christians were not to share in pagan sacrificial meals, Paul discussed another question raised by the Corinthians: Can a believer eat meat bought at the marketplace or served at another's home? It is quite possible that such meat—almost all meat—had been offered in sacrifice to an idol. In these circumstances the issue was not sharing in a pagan sacrifice, but eating the meat. It was made holy through the Word of God and prayer (cf. 1 Timothy 4:4,5). What God has created is clean.

But, Paul said, if the meat was expressly identified as meat formerly sacrificed to an idol, for the sake of another's conscience, it should not be eaten. A Christian is to strive not to cause offense to any—Jews, Greeks, nor to the household of God (10:32).

IV. CHRISTIAN WORSHIP (11:1–14:40)

The theme of the next major section of this letter is worship in the church. Paul complained about and corrected certain problems. Initially he praised the Corinthians for following his commands—the "traditions" which he passed on to them. He did not want to discourage them with one-sided criticism.

This major section falls into four smaller sections. First Paul commented on the conduct of women during the worship service (11:2-16). Next he reprimanded the church because it was abusing the love feast and Lord's Supper (11:17-34). Then he answered the church's question about spiritual matters, including the use of spiritual gifts (chapters 12 to 14). In the midst of the latter there is Paul's ode to love, one of the most marvelous passages in all of Scripture (chapter 13).

A. The Conduct of Women (11:2-16)

Perhaps one of the most significant changes that took place in the ancient Christian assemblies was the revolutionary shift in the social position of women. While the Greeks commonly regarded women as having no soul, the apostle Peter called them "heirs together of the grace of life" (1 Peter 3:7). Paul's words, "There is neither male nor female" (Galatians 3:28), are perhaps some of the most socially and religiously radical words ever uttered.

In Christian worship services women played an active role, unlike those in the Jewish synagogues where they were entirely passive. Although women were permitted in the synagogue, they were not allowed to share in the service in any way. They were not even counted to obtain the required 10 necessary for a service. However, in the Christian churches women at least shared in both prayer and prophecy (11:5).

Some of the women in the church at Corinth brought the custom of praying without a head covering into the church, perhaps as a misunderstanding of their new-found Christian freedom. As was seen in the two earlier major sections, an "overrealization" of Christian teaching results in a distortion of the gospel. Paul opposed their new custom because it challenged some fundamental principles. He regarded it as more than a forsaking of cultural custom; it violated the order of God's creation. From the most ancient of times, women in the Middle East and Asia grew their hair long and covered their heads as a symbol of their dependence upon the man. Later, Christian churches adopted this custom (11:16).

The Greek word Paul used to denote the woman's head covering is *exousia*, "authority, power." However, underlying this Greek term is the Aramaic word *shaltōnyah*, which has the twofold idea of "covering" and "power" (Kittel, cited by Foerster, "exousia," *TDNT*, 2:574). Paul apparently intended this double meaning when he used *exousia*. It suited his purpose by showing the significance of women's headcoverings: It showed her dependency upon the man, while at the same time it represented authority. The woman was under the authority of her husband, but she maintained her dignity. The context suggests that "authority" here has a passive sense. The interpretation goes as far back as the church father Chrysostom, who also used the term in this manner.

Paul said that the man is the head of the woman. "Head" expresses will and authority. This is a puzzling thought since the common view of that day saw the "bowels, inward parts" as the seat of emotions and contemplation. Paul asserted that the woman is simultaneously subject to the man as well as equal to him. For this logic he appealed to creation (cf. Genesis 2:18) and to Christ's relationship with the Father. Christ is in no way demeaned or called inferior when Paul says God is His "head" (11:3). In the same way, a woman should not be viewed as inferior or less than a man even though God has ordered that man is the "head."

B. Love Feasts and the Lord's Supper (11:17-34)

In this section Paul again referred to the splits within the church (11:18). The kind of division he was now confronting did not concern differences in leaders or doctrines but revolved around the social and cultural differences among the members. Remarkably, Paul considered this kind of division as serious as a doctrinal split. He employed the term *haireseis*, "sects, parties," here; this sin will exclude some from the kingdom of God (Galatians 5:20, 21).

It reflects how seriously Paul viewed the problem of cliques in the church.

The divisions especially appeared in the love feasts and the Lord's Supper (11:20f.). Many had turned these occasions into opportunities to eat and drink; some were even getting drunk! Whatever the situation, this kind of conduct was sinful, but in the context of a sacred meal, the Lord's Supper, it was a profanation of something holy and sacred. The one participating in such an unfitting manner was eating and drinking condemnation upon himself (11:29). The injunction of verse 28 to "examine" oneself is a call to look closely at one's heart before partaking in the Lord's Supper. An outward appearance of reverence is inadequate. What is in question is one's attitude of heart towards Christ.

By recounting the apostolic tradition of the institution of the Lord's Supper (11:23), Paul demonstrated that the event the Corinthians had been profaning was in actuality a truly sacred moment in Christian worship. When Paul commented that he received the words of the Supper from the Lord, he did not use the preposition *para*, "by," which would have indicated a direct communication, but the preposition *apo*, "from," which assures the words originated from the Lord. Nevertheless, the formula did not prevent Paul from referring to a personal revelation (cf. Acts 18:9f.; 22:18; 23:11; 27:23; 2 Corinthians 12:7; Galatians 1:12; 2:2). Moreover, one case does not eliminate the possibility of the other. Paul's words are virtually technical language denoting the reception and transmission of holy tradition, which appears in the Gospel records. It is crucial to realize that only 25 years had passed since Jesus instituted the Supper—and it would be almost as many again before the first Gospel was written. Already there was a detailed record of the institution of the Supper and its centrality in early Christian communities.

C. The Gifts of Grace (12:1-31 and 14:1-40)

One of the major questions the Corinthians asked Paul about in their earlier letter apparently concerned the *charismatōn*, which were experienced regularly in the worship and church services of ancient Christian churches. With respect to the church in Corinth, Paul commented that it lacked no gift (1:7). At the same time, he also said that he did not want them to be ignorant about the exercise and purpose of the gifts of the Spirit. He implied that they actually knew very little about the workings of the Spirit.

Chapter 12 gives a summary description of the gifts of the Spirit, and chapter 14 offers instruction on the proper use of the charismata. Placed between these two chapters are Paul's comments on love. He referred to love as greater than any of the gifts and the only legitimate motive for using the gifts.

First, Paul affirmed that spiritual manifestations in the Christian congregation are much more than the idol trances the Gentile believers had experienced before their conversion. Such pagan phenomena were of course fleshly demonstrations, whereas Christians experience the effects of the Holy Spirit's manifestation. Pagan demonstrations were in part the result of spiritual forces, to the extent that their source was other than what the believer experienced. Before their conversion the Corinthians were drawn to the dumb idols (12:2), now they were driven by the Spirit of God (cf. 8:14). The Triune God was the One causing their spiritual utterances. The charismata, services, and manifestations of power were different, but one and the same Spirit was behind them all. The same Lord, and the same God "worketh" in all (12:4-6).

Different from other more "natural" gifts of the Spirit, the list of the Spirit's workings given in 1 Corinthians 12 are often described as "supernatural" gifts of the Spirit. The term *charismata* is often applied to these "gifts." Such a distinction between supernatural and nonsupernatural is undoubtedly legitimate, but this can easily result in elevating some as more "spiritual" than others. This can lead to some of the gifts being overlooked and underused. Moreover, it is not always easy to distinguish between what is natural and what is supernatural in a world that is led by an almighty and ever-present God. One thing is clear, though; spiritual gifts are in no way a guarantee of spirituality or holiness. The Corinthians were well equipped with the charismata, but they were still oriented towards this world and lacked spiritual maturity.

This in no way negates any argument that the gifts are not important. They are, in fact, God's response to the Church's need for spiritual power in carrying out its mission. The charismata are the basis of the special positions or "offices" that the Lord established for His church (12:28f.; cf. Ephesians 4:20).

The apostle Paul referred to these gifts as "the manifestation of the Spirit." Some have debated whether this is a comprehensive list of the Spirit's workings or a series of examples. Both sides have strong and weak arguments. On the one hand, certainly many different spiritual "effects" or "gifts" exist other than the categories Paul provided, but on the other hand, virtually every gift can be linked to one or more in the list he gave.

Some have attempted to categorize the gifts according to the three dominant properties of the human soul: understanding, will, emotion. Such a breakdown looks like this: (1) gifts of understanding (knowledge, wisdom, and discerning of spirits); (2) gifts of power (faith, healing, working of miracles); (3) gifts of inspired utterance (prophecy, tongues, interpretation of tongues). The gifts can also fall into four groups: (1) the word of wisdom, which gives God's counsel, and the word of knowledge, which affords special insight into the truths of God's Word; (2) faith, which here must refer to miracle-working faith (cf. 13:2; Matthew 17:20), the gifts of healing, and the power to work miracles; (3) the gift of prophecy, which is always to be associated with the ability to discern spirits; and (4) speaking in tongues, which can only be for the blessing of the church when it is interpreted.

According to many interpreters, the way the gifts are listed implies there is some disparity or heirarchy in their character. Thus, it is argued, the gift of tongues is the least worthy, while the word of wisdom and prophecy are among the greatest. But from Paul's point of view, it seems that he may have regarded tongues among the highest (14:1). He considered speaking in tongues plus the interpretation of tongues as equivalent to prophecy (14:5). Even though some might argue tongues is the "least" of the gifts, it cannot be too insignificant, for the apostle Peter received it (Acts 2:4) as did Paul. Paul even thanked God for his gift of speaking in tongues (14:8); it is clearly not to be ignored.

The Corinthian congregation was richly equipped with the charismata, but they lacked wisdom in using the gifts in a sound and fitting manner. Paul instructed them about the nature and number of the charismata. He concluded by saying, "Covet to prophesy, and forbid not to speak with tongues. Let all things be done decently and in order!" (14:39,40).

D. The Song of Love (13:1-13)

Surpassing in importance any of the gifts of the Spirit is the fruit of the Spirit, love ("charity," KJV; cf. Galatians 5:22). The charismata are equipment given to the believer for service. The fruit of the Spirit is the mind and nature of Christ being realized in the character and conduct of the life of the believer who is being conformed to the image of Christ (Galatians 4:19). One cannot be a Christian without producing some of the fruit of the Spirit. Thus Paul could not encourage seeking spiritual gifts without emphasizing that something is more important: i.e., to follow after love (12:31; 14:1). This is the "more excellent way."

This "Song of Love" is unparalleled in its beauty. Harnack referred to it as "the greatest, strongest, and deepest which Paul ever wrote." The lyrical style and rhythmical form of the passage remind one of a hymn. Its very penetrating message is typical of only the loftiest poetry. There is almost nothing elsewhere in the writings of Paul requiring so little explanation.

Some interpreters have conjectured that since this section differs so much from the style and message of its context that it must have been added from another source. True, Paul may have used these thoughts elsewhere, but the way in which it presently appears does not represent any great digression. With his opening words Paul compared love with the charismata; when the end comes love will remain while everything else—including the charismata—will fail.

Paul demonstrated that without love, even the greatest of gifts is meaningless. Speaking in tongues, prophesying, knowing all things, and having all faith—none of these can replace love, not even a great sacrifice. Self-denial without love is as useless as using the gifts of the Spirit without love.

Paul described two great qualities of love: it is patient and it is kind. He then stated in negative terms what love does not do. To the last he added the positive qualifier: Charity (love) "rejoiceth not in iniquity, but rejoiceth in the truth." The kind of love Paul was referring to here is not a kind of moral laxity which sacrifices truth and right for the sake of ease. Rather four short words summarize the extent of love: It *bears* all things, *believes* all things, *hopes* all things, and *endures* all things.

Finally, Paul asserted that love will always remain. He contrasted one group of three items against another group of three. Three will remain until the end, and three will pass away. Prophecy, tongues, and knowledge will end when that which is perfect is come, and believers can know fully. But faith, hope, and love will remain until the end of all things. And of these, "the greatest . . . is love" (13:13).

V. CHRISTIAN HOPE FOR THE FUTURE (15:1-58)

In this final major section of 1 Corinthians, Paul discussed the question of the believer's hope for the future. His immediate reason for this can be detected in 15:12, where he wrote that some of the Corinthians were claiming there was no resurrection of the dead. Paul received word of this and found it necessary to speak to the matter. He demonstrated that the doctrine of the Resurrection is central to the entire Christian message and faith. The Christian's hope for the future does *not* rest in some shadowy, spiritual existence in which the soul is "freed" from the body's prison (to put it in Greek philosophical language). The gospel does not preach that believers are redeemed "from" their physical bodies, rather, it teaches the "redemption of the body" (Romans 8:23). Paul then argued that the power of the Resurrection was proven in Christ whom God raised from the dead (cf. Ephesians 1:18-20). Christ is the "firstfruits of them that slept" (15:20). Thus He is the "guarantee" of the future resurrection awaiting believers. The resurrection of Christ is inseparable from His work of redemption (15:14). Therefore, it follows that the resurrection of the believer is an inseparable element of the redemption in which he participates.

In addition to addressing the pressing problems in Corinth, Paul had already instructed the Corinthians in the fundamental doctrines of the Faith. Now, using the controversy over the Resurrection as a springboard, he offered the most comprehensive discussion of resurrection in the entire New Testament. First, he discussed the importance of Christ's resurrection. Second, he outlined what the future holds for Christians and showed the place of the Resurrection in that hope. Third, he commented on how the dead will rise.

A. The Resurrection of Christ (15:1-22)

1. The Essence of the Gospel (15:1-5). Paul opened his remarks by calling attention to the early portions of the letter, where he discussed the centrality of the "preaching of the cross" to the Christian proclamation of salvation. Now he again "validated" the authenticity of the gospel he had preached to them. That gospel is what had saved them when they believed (cf. Acts 11:14). This is a unique aspect of the Christian faith and differs from every man-made religion or philosophy. The message of the gospel, delivered by Paul to the Corinthians, is that which he himself received: "That Christ died for our sins according to the scriptures" (15:3).

Now Paul proceeded to show that it is not only the death of Jesus, but His resurrection that is an indispensable element of Christian proclamation. The opening verses of chapter 15 summarize the main content of gospel tradition. This involves the death of Christ, His burial, His resurrection, and His appearances as the risen Lord. At the same time, Paul offered the apostolic witness to the historicity of the gospel (verses 6-9), and the apostolic interpretation of the events of salvation, namely, that Christ died for our sins (verse 3).

2. Witnesses of the Resurrection (15:6-11). This section contains the Church's first written testimonies of the resurrection of Christ. It was composed many years prior to any of the Gospels. Jesus revealed himself many times in the time between His resurrection and His ascension; the Gospels record 9 or 10 such events. Paul mentioned only the ones which would have the greatest impact upon the Corinthians. He mentioned in particular Jesus' appearance to Simon Peter, a leader among the apostles, to James, the overseer in the Jerusalem church. He mentioned the large number of witnesses who were apparently still living: "above five hundred brethren at once; of whom the greater part remain unto this present." This was written just 20–25 years after the events, when the first generation of believers was still around to confirm the truth of what was being preached.

At least two of the events Paul referred to are not mentioned in the four Gospels. Both concern people who did not believe Jesus was Messiah until after they encountered the risen Lord. One was James, the brother of Jesus. During Jesus' earthly life, His brothers did not believe in Him (John 7:5), but after the Resurrection we find them together with the apostles in the upper room in Jerusalem (Acts 1:14). Shortly thereafter James became the undisputed leader of the Jerusalem church (Galatians 1:19).

The other appearance of Jesus not mentioned in the Gospel accounts was to Paul. Although this event took place several years after the Resurrection and Ascension, Paul nonetheless joined this appearance with those experienced by the other apostles. He considered this appearance not just a "vision" or "trance"; rather, it was a genuine occurrence. The risen Christ appeared to him just as He had to others following His resurrection. Therefore, Paul declared that he had not received the gospel from another man, but from the risen Lord (Galatians 1:12). Immediately he began to preach the message revealed to him (Acts 9:20-22; Galatians 1:16f.). But this does not imply Paul had no contact with or had adopted apostolic traditions about the life and death and resurrection of Jesus (Galatians 1:18ff.; 2:1ff.). His own encounter with the risen Lord did not cause him to deny the testimony of others. On the contrary, he said that he himself both received and passed on this holy tradition (15:3).

3. The Importance of Christ's Resurrection (15:12-22). Apparently those who denied the final Resurrection, did not deny the resurrection of Christ. Paul, however, pointed out the logical end of their reasoning. If there is no resurrection of the dead, then Christ could not have risen either. And if Christ had not risen, then the very foundation of the Christian faith had been removed. In a dramatic series of "if-then" statements, Paul rehearsed the logical consequences of thinking Christ had not risen from the dead.

First, if Christ had not risen, "then is our preaching vain" (verse 14). The apostolic proclamation would be "emptiness," that is, without any substance or basis. Christian proclamation would thereby be reduced to nothing more than the empty "wisdom" of the world. Christianity would be only one more religion in the world's philosophical and religious systems. Further, their "faith is also vain" (verse 14). Faith comes by hearing (Romans 10:17). Faith can be of no more value than the message it stands on. If preaching is empty, then faith in its message is no more than a miserable emptiness.

Second, if Christ is not risen, then the heralds of the gospel were "false witnesses of God" (verse 15). Their preaching was not just empty, it was a false and fraudulent testimony (the main character of apostolic preaching was that of a witness). The apostles had not defended some concept, philosophy, or human teaching; rather, as witnesses they announced the truth of what they had "seen and heard" (Acts 4:20) in the life and ministry of Jesus. If what they proclaimed was not true, then they were false witnesses, bearing false witness against God himself. Paul was fully aware of the responsibility resting upon those preaching the gospel. If its basis is in real events, then it indeed announces a mighty saving act of God in time and space, whose impact affects all mankind. But the validity of the entire message rests on whether or not it is true. As someone once said, "For Paul, any Christianity that is not based on reality does not benefit the life of the community, but becomes a tragic self-delusion."

If Christ is not risen, "your faith is vain" (verse 17). Thus Paul found it inconceivable that an empty or false faith could have any positive benefit for a believer. From his perspective, the advantage of faith depends completely on the fact that it receives and participates in the actual gifts of salvation: the forgiveness of sins and salvation from the judgment of sin. This depends altogether on the truth of the gospel message: Christ died to atone for our sins; He was raised for our justification (cf. Romans 4:25).

This enabled Paul to argue further that if Christ was not risen, "ye are yet in your sins" (verse 17). The forgiveness of sins was a reality to Paul. It involved much more than being released from the feeling of guilt. It involved actual forgiveness from the one God, who alone can forgive sin and nullify its consequences. The individual who believes moves from being under the judgment of God to being in His grace; it is the difference between being saved and being lost. If the gospel's offering of grace is not founded upon the facts of God's saving act in Christ, then those who believe the gospel remain in their sins. This applies not only to those believers who are living, but also to those who have died. If Christ is not risen, then they died in their sins, deluded into putting faith in a false hope.

False hope is worse than no hope: "If in this life only we have hope in Christ, we are of all men most miserable" (verse 19). Paul admitted, in fact, in verse 32 that a life without hope for eternal life is reflected in the pagan proverb recorded in Isaiah 22:13: "Let us eat and drink; for tomorrow we shall die." Of course, for Paul, the fear of God offered something for this life also (cf. 1 Timothy 4:8). He realized that the joy of the world is empty and temporary. Not much is lost in relinquishing what the world offers. Nevertheless, a Christianity that exists only for the present life and which has no hope for the future—because it involves a delusion—was unimaginable to Paul. He did not see any advantage in exchanging a worldly life "without hope" (Ephesians 2:12) for a "false religious hope" that is just as deceived. Hence, if Christ is not risen, then the Christian hope is just as false as the Christian faith.

Paul's argument in this section is designed to show how the entire Christian faith would crumble if some of the Corinthians' claim that the dead did not rise were true. If it were so, faith in Christ's resurrection must also be relinquished (verses 12,13). Also, the veracity of the apostolic witness would be called into question (verses 14,15), and finally salvation itself, and the Christian hope of eternal life would be regarded as false (verses 16-19). But such reasoning is based upon a faulty foundation, and Paul demolished such logic in verse 20 with the triumphant cry, "But now Christ is risen!" Thereby he confirmed the truth of the gospel. He secured the reality of salvation; and demonstrated that the resurrection of the dead is a fact because Christ has been raised, "the firstfruit" from the dead. He is the beginning of the resurrection awaiting all who belong to Christ. "But now" marks the shift from the hypothetical to the actual.

B. Eschatological Perspectives (15:20-34)

1. The Fact of Resurrection (15:20-22). The fact that Christ rose from the dead guarantees the resurrection of believers. Just as those who believe in Christ have been in a spiritual sense "crucified with" and "risen with" their Lord (cf. Galatians 2:20; Colossians 3:1), they will also in the consummation share in bodily resurrection together with Christ. Paul thus drew a parallel between Adam and Christ: Adam, the ancestor and head of the human race, and Christ, the progenitor and head of a new race (cf. Romans 5:12-19). All coming from Adam—those "in Adam"—come under the power of death because of Adam's fall. In the same way, all those "in Christ" share in His victory over death. Just as Adam's sin affected the rest of the human race, so too, Christ's resurrection affects those for whom He died and rose. The resurrection for salvation or condemnation takes place at the directive of Christ (cf. John 5:28,29). But to be "alive in Christ" involves more than merely the resurrection. It must also point to what is called "the resurrection of life." This includes the abundance of life that is in

Christ which is shared by those who are in Him (cf. Romans 8:11).

2. Stages in the Consummation (15:23-28). Next Paul proceeded to show that being made fully alive in Christ takes place step by step and in various stages. These verses provide a rich glimpse into the future. The last days began with the first coming of Christ (Hebrews 1:1; 9:26) and cover a long period of time prior to the consummation. At various stages God manifests His kingdom. Not all are made alive simultaneously; each is raised according to his own "turn" (NIV). The term for "turn" here is *tagmati*, originally a military technical term, which later had a more general usage. Originally it meant a "division" of an army; later a "class" or "group" of any kind. The implication of *tagmati*'s use here is that the individual is being made alive together with the "division" to which he belongs.

Opinions differ among interpreters whether Paul was thinking of two or three stages in the resurrection. Those who maintain there are only two stages—Christ the firstfruit and the believers as the rest of the harvest—point to Paul's comments in verse 54 that "Death is swallowed up in victory," when the mortal puts on immortality. This may suggest that Paul regarded death, as the last enemy, as vanquished by the Parousia. But the picture in verses 23-28 suggest that there are three stages in the eschatological program. Paul outlined them in this manner: First, Christ rose as the firstfruit, the firstborn from the dead (Colossians 1:18). His resurrection initiated and guaranteed the resurrection of believers. Second, those who belong to Christ will be made alive at His coming, i.e., His parousia (verse 23). And third, as indicated by another "then" in verse 24, "Then cometh the end, when he shall have delivered up the kingdom to God, even the Father." It is difficult to interpret this "then" as anything but a third stage. Similarly "then" functions in verse 23 to show the distance of time between the Parousia and the "End" (cf. Revelation 20:1ff.). During the interim between the return and the final judgment, Christ will destroy all the spiritual powers that resist God (verse 25). Three expressions for these "spiritual powers" occur: *archēn*, "rulers"; *exousian*, "authorities"; and *dunamin*, "powers." All three designations occur in Ephesians 1:21; the first and last occur in Romans 8:38; and the first two occur in Ephesians 6:12; Colossians 1:16; 2:10. When all these forces are overcome, Christ will

hand over the purified and cleansed Kingdom to His Father, and God shall be all in all.

This highly significant prophetic word concludes with the puzzling words in verse 28 that the Son himself will be subject to the Father. All theories of interpretation aside, this undoubtedly involves a relationship between the Persons of the Godhead; we cannot expect to grasp fully this divine mystery. But when such a theme recurs throughout Holy Scriptures, we should do our best to consider what this divine disclosure does tell us. Many of Christianity's greatest teachers have debated the issue; their comments are pertinent. Augustine, Beza, and Theodoret understood this text as reflecting Paul's understanding that when Christ presents the Church to the Father the saints will share fully in God's salvation. Because His work as mediator of salvation is complete, Christ lays aside His role as the revelation mediator between God and mankind.

Luther, Melanchthon, Bengel, and many others agree that the passage speaks of the end of Christ's mediatorial role—where there is no more sin there is no longer need of redemption or intercession. Interpreters like Meyer (*Meyer's Commentary on the New Testament*, 6:362f.) maintain that it alludes to the kingly dominion and the authority to judge which Christ has exercised over the enemy (also discussed in the preceding verses). Hofmann argues that when the Son subjects himself to the Father, it involves, from a human standpoint, the fact that He no longer assumes the role of mediator between God and the world.

None of these interpretations alter the trinitarian picture of God. However, a number of them imply that the passage about the Son's subjection to the Father does not merely reflect the mission of the Son, but the interrelationship between the Persons of the Godhead. Here some have attempted to differentiate between the divine and human natures of Christ, and have argued that the Son can be subject only at the human level. Others, though, do not regard the Son's being subject to the Father as inconsistent with the trinitarian understanding that the members of the Trinity are identical in nature and substance.

Godet reminds us that Paul previously in this letter stated that "Christ is God's" (3:23), that "the head of Christ is God" (11:3), and that both of these refer to Christ's status in glory, (pp.795-804). He suggests, therefore, that the idea that the Son was subject to the Father was an inherent aspect of the writings of Paul, just as the preexistence of the Son was an established fact. Both concepts are conveyed by the term "Son," which simultaneously expresses equality in essence and yet the possibility of being in subjection. According to this view, subjection thus is in keeping with the relationship between the Father and Son during both His divine and human existence.

Others echo the same opinion. The other Person in the Trinity, in keeping with His nature, must accept the authority, will, and desires, of the First Person. Therefore, He declares himself the Son and the First Person His Father. Although identical to the Father in eternality, power, and honor, the Son finds His joy in doing the will of the Father; that is His desire. The obedience of the God-man on earth to the Father above did not reflect a new relationship effected by the Incarnation, but it continued the eternal fellowship that existed between the Son and Father in heaven. The submission of the Son to the will of the Father does not deprive Him of any of His divine honor and glory. As far as His personal humility in the Incarnation (cf. Philippians 2:5ff.) and His handing over of the Kingdom to the Father are concerned, they are totally of His own free will. These acts express His love for the Father (cf. John 14:31). The kingdom of the Father is dear to Jesus. Because of this He does not seek a personal eternal kingdom; rather, He joins His Father on His throne and invites His followers to sit with Him (Revelation 3:21).

3. Practical Concerns (15:29-34). After presenting these tremendous prospects, and before he dealt with the question of how the dead rise, Paul included in the passage some practical arguments for the reality of the resurrection. Next he reviewed some of the ethical consequences of resurrection faith.

First, Paul reminded the Corinthians that baptism implies a belief in the resurrection. Within the rite of baptism is a drama of the Resurrection: we are "raised together with Christ" (Colossians 2:12; cf. Romans 6:3-5). When Paul introduced baptism here it is with the phrase "they which are baptized for the dead." This is either referring to some kind of substitutional baptism for the dead practiced by some of the Corinthians, or, more likely, it is a reference to those who were baptized in order to be reunited with their deceased Christian friends or family. In either case such a baptism was meaningless. Substitutional bap-

tism is of no avail to the dead if the dead do not indeed rise; and there is no possibility of being reunited with fellow believers after death unless there is a resurrection. Chrysostom rejected substitutionary baptism for the dead as outside of orthodoxy. He interpreted it instead by noting that in the baptismal rite the one being baptized confesses, "I believe in the resurrection of the dead." He continued, "And on this faith we are baptized." By speaking of baptism Paul was confirming the basic and commonly accepted tenet of the Church that the dead will rise.

As far as he was concerned, Paul demonstrated in both word and practice that he believed in the resurrection. Why else would he have risked serious danger and trials for the sake of the gospel? Paul then continued to show how doctrine influences behavior. The resurrection is indeed a doctrine of the Church, and it has ethical consequences. If there is no resurrection then the rally cry of the hedonists of this age, "Eat drink, and be merry, for tomorrow we die!" is justified. It may be that some of those in Corinth who were denying the resurrection had already adopted such a moral stance. To deny the reality of the resurrection is in itself a sin and it leads to greater sin. "Be not deceived!" the apostle warned. As the Greek proverb says, "Evil communications corrupt good manners" (Menander, *Thais*). The Greek followers of "wisdom" denied the resurrection. A Christian risks much when he fellowships with any who reject a central tenet of the gospel. With the utmost sincerity the apostle warned, "For some have not the knowledge of God."

C. How Do the Dead Rise? (15:35-58)

1. The Resurrection of the Body (15:35). Objections concerning the Christian proclamation of the resurrection of the body had arisen from two different sources: Greeks and Jews.

Greeks rejected any notion of resurrection as a consequence of a main assumption of Greek philosophy: a dualism which drew a sharp distinction between the "physical body" and the "spiritual soul." From their perspective the dualistic nature of man was his dilemma and downfall. Greeks considered the physical body as only part of this life and felt the soul to be immortal, once it was released from the "prison" of the physical body. Therefore, to conceive of the soul "putting on" again that which was regarded as evil was both reprehensible and impossible. The Greeks viewed eternal existence as only being possible when the body and soul were separated. Paul, however, did not even discuss the possibility of an eternal existence apart from a body. He did not deny that the soul exists after death—he called this as being "unclothed" and viewed it as temporary (2 Corinthians 5:4-8). For Paul, as for Jesus (Matthew 22:29-32), the resurrection of the body is necessary because of the eternal nature of the soul. But an eternal existence without a resurrection is worse than annihilation, because it would be in sin. As he had just shown, if there is no resurrection, then Christ did not rise, and if that is true, we are still in our sins!

Pharisaic Judaism, such as the apostle Paul followed at one time, maintained a resurrection, but only to a life of the same essence and nature as present existence. The body that was raised was to be identical to the body that died. The Syriac Apocalypse of Baruch (50:2) reads that when the earth will restore the dead, "it shall make no change in their form, but as it has received, so shall it restore them." The Sadducees of the Gospels directed their disdain at such views. Moreover, Paul abandoned such a viewpoint, for it is far removed from the Christian belief in a resurrection in glory and incorruptability.

Paul denounced both the Jewish misunderstanding of resurrection and the Greek denial of it. He asked rhetorically two aggressive questions: "But some will say, 'How are the dead raised?' and 'with what body do they come?'" The questions show how impossible resurrection was thought to be by some skeptics. The questions of how the body will be raised are difficult enough if an individual has just died; but what of the person's body who has long been dead, how is a resurrection possible then?

Paul began by answering the last question about the kind of body with which the dead will be raised. He clarified the issue with a series of analogies (verses 36-41), and a series of antitheses (verses 42-44). Next he answered the question about how it is possible for the dead to be raised by referring to Christ as the "life-giving spirit" (verses 45-49). Then he spoke of the transformation that those living at the time of Christ's return will experience (verses 50-54). He concluded the most detailed teaching on resurrection in the New Testament by offering a hymn of praise (verses 55-57).

2. Analogies (15:36-41). Responding to possible objections his opponents might raise, Paul gave a series of analogies from nature. An analogy can illuminate an issue, but it does not necessarily prove it. Paul had previously offered historical proof of the resurrection of Christ. His resurrection was attested to and proclaimed by men who had nothing to gain in this life. On the contrary, because of their testimony they hourly risked their lives; they died daily (15:30f.). When the world responded to the challenge of the gospel with empty arguments, the apostle was less than tolerant. "Thou fool," he exclaimed. He thereby showed how he felt about his opponents' arguments.

To the opponent who maintained he believed only in the laws and principles of nature, Paul challenged: "But doesn't nature itself testify to the reality of the resurrection. Don't you throw seed on the ground, which, because it dies, is made alive again in a new plant?" God gives a body according to His will; it is different and yet at the same time similar. Creation does not merely reveal the power of God to create something from nothing, it also shows His ability to re-create from death to life. What is sown is not precisely what is raised; it comes not in its old, corruptible form, but in a new and glorious appearance. So too is the resurrection.

Paul employed other analogies to remind the Corinthians of other forms of life created by God. First, there is a great difference between men and animals, birds and fish. Likewise, the sun differs from the moon and other stars in its brilliance. If there is such variation within nature, shouldn't God be able to create spiritual bodies rather than earthly bodies in the resurrection? Some see in Paul's expression "heavenly bodies" (verse 40) an allusion to the celestial bodies in verse 41. However, he could also have been alluding to the "spiritual bodies" he spoke of in verse 44.

3. Four Antitheses (15:42-44). In order to show the difference between the body that dies and the body that is raised, Paul offered four antitheses. The statements have a poetical, rhythmical form, and are reminiscent of the kind of poetic message of the prophets. They also bring to mind the kind of sayings Jesus used to teach His disciples.

The body that dies is perishable, corruptible. It belongs to that part of the creation which falls under the dominion of sin's effects; it shares in the groaning of all creation (Romans 8:20-23). Still, it is not redeemed. It is like a house that is torn down (2 Corinthians 5:1).

But the resurrection body is imperishable, incorruptible. It is "eternal in the heavens." It should not be overlooked that the verse also suggests an analogy between physical and moral corruption (Morris, *Tyndale New Testament Commentaries*, 7:226). The strongest objections made by Greeks to the Christian message of resurrection were that the physical body, by nature, was corruptible, even evil. Their hope for the future was that the soul would be released from the confinement of the body, but Paul said that the resurrection body is incorruptible and imperishable.

The body that dies is subject to "dishonor." It lacks "glory" (Romans 3:23). Paul even called it "our lowly body" (Philippians 3:21, NIV), but there is no trace of the Greek contempt for the body as evil. Paul declared that it is precisely the lowly body that will be transformed into a glorious body like Christ's. That sown in dishonor will be raised in glory.

On the one hand, the body which dies is viewed as weak; it succumbs to sickness and death. It is only an inadequate instrument for the reborn spirit (cf. Mark 14:38). The resurrection body, on the other hand, will be characterized by power, might, and physical and mental vitality, empowered by the same power that raised Jesus from the dead (Romans 8:11; Ephesians 1:19f.).

The body that dies is a "natural" body. The expression points to the physical and mental qualities of the body. The same term, *psuchikos*, appears in 1 Corinthians 2:14 to describe the "natural" man. The emphasis is not that the body is *composed* of *psuché*, "life, breath," but that the fleshly body is *controlled* by the *psuché* (especially here the mental attitude). At the same time, the human soul (*psuché*) is influenced and tempted by sinful impulses and desires (cf. 1 Peter 2:11). The world influences the *psuché* through the "conduit" of the body. The "soul" is the rational principle of life; the body ruled by its "soul" is ruled by the "natural man," i.e., that part of the individual given to its natural inclinations.

In the eternal, spiritual realm all this will be different. The natural body—controlled by the *psuché*, "soul"—dies and is transformed into a "spiritual body" in the resurrection. This is not to say that the body is "spirit" or some other "spiritual substance," but it will be governed by the spirit of man instead of the present, natural man. The spiritual body will be a perfect expression of the individual's personality and spiritual being. This being "clothed with our heavenly dwelling" (2 Corinthians 5:2, NIV) means that finally the believer will become what God intended him or her to be.

4. The First and Last Adam (15:45-49). Having responded to the question about what kind of body the dead rise with, Paul returned to the answer to the first question, "How do the dead rise?" "What is the power at work in the resurrection?" In his preceding explanation, Paul employed the image of the seed of grain which becomes a mature plant by saying the body is "sown a natural body." But he also guarded against the misinterpretation that the body somehow reproduces itself. He stated explicitly in verse 38 that God gives a new body. It is further clarified when he says Christ is the Last Adam, "a life-giving spirit" (15:45).

The concept that Messiah would be the Second Adam appears in the teachings of Rabbi Abraham, of Catelonia (Godet, p.849; cf. Sadler, pp.289-292). In Romans 5:12-21 Paul presented the concept of the Second Adam. Jesus Christ is the new representative of the people of God; He restores what the first Adam lost. Undoubtedly this was included in Paul's oral preaching, and the Corinthians were probably familiar with it. Now Paul inserted the concept in this context. He demonstrated that Adam, not only because of the Fall but because he is "of the earth," had only an earthly inheritance to pass on to his descendants. Paul alluded to the Creation account, which says that man became a living soul. The earthly man was *psuchikos*; and as Adam was, so are his offspring. But the Last Adam, Christ, the "man from heaven" is a life-giving spirit. Through the redemption provided by Christ, the entire person is transformed. Not only is there a spiritual rebirth, the believer will also share in a new form of bodily existence, the same kind of existence that Jesus Christ has in His body of glory.

5. Resurrection and Transformation (15:50-58). No one will be able to participate in eternal life with God apart from the transformation of the body into a spiritual body. The physical body has some innate restrictions: "Flesh and blood cannot inherit the kingdom of God" (verse 50). However, this raises the question, "What about those who are alive at Christ's return? How will they be able to share in the Kingdom and its glory?" The Corinthians' problem was exactly opposite that of the Thessalonians, who wondered, "What about those who are asleep when the Lord returns?" (1 Thessalonians 4:13f.).

Paul may have been referring to two groups (verse 50). If that is true, "flesh and blood" would equal those who are alive at the coming of the Lord, while "that which is perishable" concerns the former "flesh and blood" which is dead and already decomposing (Godet, p.862). Some interpreters regard the two expressions as too synonymous to convey any strict division (Bruce, *New Century Bible*, 38:153f.), but the Semitic construction "flesh and blood" is used for persons alive, and this seems its usage in the New Testament. One thing is certain: no one, alive or dead, will share in the kingdom of God without experiencing a transformation. Having shown the possibility of such a transformation, Paul now showed its importance.

The Corinthians were invited to listen very carefully by Paul's use of the word "Behold." The term also emphasizes the significance of what is being said. Paul revealed something that was previously a "mystery," a "secret once hidden." Now, through a special revelation it has come to light. The mystery involves the great eschatological event for which the Church waits—the Parousia, the Second Coming of Christ and the consummation of all things. To some degree, all of God's plan of salvation might be termed a "mystery" (cf. Romans 16:25; Ephesians 3:3f.) that is known only through revelation by God. The apostle earlier spoke of the "hidden wisdom of God," the counsel of God which concerned what "God ordained before the world unto our glory" (2:7ff.). Paul reintroduced this thought toward the close of the letter. He explained that the glory destined for those who love the Lord also affects the redemption of the body at the return of Christ. Then the dead will rise imperishable; those alive at His coming will be "changed."

These are the two groups of believers. Resurrection awaits one group and transformation the other. In both instances the body is given a new form. Interestingly, as he did in a similar context in 1 Thessalonians 4:16ff., Paul utilized the "we-form" when he spoke of those alive at the coming of the Lord. Since he did not know precisely when the Lord would return, it is only natural that he would include himself among the living. As Jesus commanded, Paul lived in the expectation of Christ's imminent return (Luke 12:36). The apostle saw such expectation as normal for every believer (1 Thessalonians

1:10). Plainly Paul expected the return of Christ in his lifetime. If the first generation of Christians eagerly expected the Lord's return, how much more so should later generations look for their Lord's coming? There is no indication that Paul ever altered his position that the Lord's return could happen at any moment. Later, when he acknowledged his death was near (e.g., Acts 20:29; 2 Timothy 4:6ff.), he was not saying the Parousia was any less imminent.

The resurrection/transformation will occur "in a moment, in the twinkling of an eye, at the last trump." The Old Testament depicts the Day of the Lord as accompanied by a trumpet sound (Zephaniah 1:16), and trumpets are afforded a significant role in the apocalyptic portions of Scripture (e.g., Revelation). The coming of the Son of Man and the gathering of the elect will take place at the "sound of the trumpet." In the Book of Revelation a series of trumpet blasts are given. Paul explained in 1 Thessalonians 4:13-18 that the coming of the Lord, the resurrection of believers, and their transformation will be accompanied by the "trump of God."

Paul considered the resurrection/transformation as triumph over death. Those changed at the coming of Christ will never experience death; neither will those who died be conquered by death. Those who "sleep," as Paul put it, will be "awakened" from death. In principle, therefore, death has already been vanquished. It will be—and indeed has been— "swallowed up in victory" through Christ's death and resurrection. "O death where is thy sting? O grave, where is thy victory?" Like the scorpion without a sting, it has no poison. From Paul's perspective, all of this is in fulfillment of the promises of Scripture (cf. Isaiah 25:8; Hosea 13:14). Paul utilized both passages elsewhere.

Paul next offered praise to God who alone gives us the victory through Christ our Lord. In his second epistle to the Corinthians (2:14) he also offered thanksgiving to God for giving believers victory in all of life's circumstances. In this first epistle (15:57) he praised God for the final victory, salvation, and life in the eternal kingdom of God.

Moving abruptly from this climactic hymn of triumph, Paul suddenly warned: "Therefore, my beloved brethren, be ye stedfast, unmoveable, always abounding in the work of the Lord, forasmuch as ye know that your labour is not in vain in the Lord" (15:58). This shift is typical for Paul, and it often occurs in 1 Corinthians. Paul taught the deepest spiritual truths in conjunction with practical guidance. He joined the truths of the resurrection (chapter 15) with a discussion on assistance for the believers in Judea (chapter 16). The epistle concludes with greetings and a closing.

Overview–2 Corinthians

The entire Second Epistle to the Corinthians deals with the need for Paul to reestablish his apostolic authority in the church at Corinth. The epistle can be outlined as follows:

I. PAUL'S APOSTOLIC MINISTRY (1:1–7:16)
   A. Comfort in Christ (1:3-11)
      1. Comfort in Tribulation (1:3-7)
      2. Comfort in Tribulation Recently Endured (1:8-11)
   B. Changed Traveling Plans (1:12–2:17)
      1. Accused of Instability (1:12-22)
      2. The Cause of the Change (1:23–2:2)
      3. "The Epistle of Tears" (2:3-11)
      4. Paul in Troas and Macedonia (2:12-17)
   C. Ministers of a New Covenant (3:1-18)
      1. The Epistle of Christ (3:1-3)
      2. The Letter and the Spirit (3:4-6)
      3. The Veil and the Glory (3:7-18)
   D. Honesty in the Ministry (4:1–5:15)
      1. The Motive of Faith (4:1-15)
      2. The Motive of Hope (4:16–5:10)
      3. The Motive of Love (5:14,15)
   E. The Ministry of Reconciliation (5:16-21)
   F. The Ministry of Admonition (6:1–7:3)
      1. Exhortations by Paul (6:1,2)
      2. Without Offence (6:3-10)
      3. Fellowship and Separation (6:11–7:1)
   G. Comforted by the Corinthians (7:4-16)
II. HELP FOR JERUSALEM (8:1–9:15)
   A. The Motive of the Gift (8:1-15)
      1. The Example of the Macedonians (8:1-5)
      2. The Spiritual Abundance of the Corinthians (8:6-8)
      3. The Example of Christ (8:9)
      4. Similarity Between Believers (8:10-15)
   B. The Task of Titus (8:16–9:5)
      1. Supervision of the Distribution (8:16-24)
      2. The Collection Resumed (9:1-5)
   C. The Blessing of the Gift (9:6-15)
      1. Reaping Blessing (9:6-11)
      2. Causing Thanksgiving to God (9:12,13)
      3. Creating Spiritual Fellowship (9:13-15)
III. PAUL'S APOSTOLIC AUTHORITY (10:1–13:14)
   A. False Apostles (10:1–11:21)
      1. Who They Are
      2. The Tolerance of Heresy
      3. The Accusations of Paul's Opponents
   B. Forced Self-Praise (11:22–12:19)
      1. Jewish Background (11:22)
      2. Paul's Suffering (11:23-33)
        a. Christian activity (11:23)
        b. Persecution (11:23-25)
        c. Perils and danger (11:25,26)
        d. False brethren (11:26)
        e. A life filled with trouble (11:27)
        f. Church work (11:28,29)
        g. Damascus (11:32,33)
      3. Revelations (12:1-6)
      4. The Thorn in the Flesh (12:7-10)
      5. The Signs of an Apostle (12:11,12)
   C. Final Admonition (12:13–13:14)
      1. Paul's Readiness (12:13-19)
      2. Paul's Fear (12:20–13:5)
      3. Paul's Trust (13:6-10)
      4. Greeting and Blessing (13:11-14)

I. PAUL'S APOSTOLIC MINISTRY (1:1–7:16)

Initially, Paul does not engage in an open confrontation with the false apostles who have entered the church. He does that in the last division of the epistle. In the first division he states his apostolic authority positively, explaining to the Corinthians the ministry with which God has entrusted him. One might get a glimpse of Paul's opponents in the background all the time, but he only hints at their presence in the church and in a few passages defends himself openly against the suspicion and accusations of these people. This approach creates a rather different tone in the first and last divisions of the epistle. While the last division is strongly polemic, the first division is richly edifying. The same concern for the church characterizes the entire epistle. It is probably the most personal of all Paul's letters, and both the first and last divisions show the same warm concern.

It is not easy to subdivide the first division of the epistle. The whole presentation is connected like links in a chain, and it is not always easy to see where a new section starts. Of course, many subdivisions are possible.

Some characteristic features can help us get an overview of the material. As mentioned, this first division is concerned with Paul's apostolic ministry, and it is possible to identify four sections which directly relate to various aspects of his work. We note that two sections refer to the comfort Paul received during his tribulations. These two sections form the beginning and end of the first division of the epistle. Finally, there is a section where Paul explains changes in his traveling plans which forced him to postpone the visit he had intended to make to Corinth. From this point the first division of the epistle falls into seven subsections. First there is a short opening greeting where Paul introduces himself as Christ's apostle, a truth which confirms his authority from the very beginning.

A. Comfort in Christ (1:3-11)

Paul wrote of the need of comfort. He penned this epistle just after one of the most severe periods of trial in his life, and the crisis was not totally past. His continuing anxiety is evident from remarks throughout the epistle. In addition to outward opposition and persecution, great problems had arisen in many of the new churches Paul had founded. The Galatians had been influenced by agitators from Judaism and were on the verge of backsliding from the true Christian faith. In Corinth false apostles had entered the picture. They had undermined Paul's authority and were destroying the great work of God which had been accomplished there. Yet with all of this pressure on him, the apostle exclaimed, "Blessed be God, the God of all comfort!" (1:3).

1. Comfort in Tribulation (1:3-7). The apostle had a share in Christ's suffering (Romans 8:17; Philippians 3:10; 1 Peter 4:13). Therefore he could say, "So our consolation also aboundeth by Christ" (1:5). As always, Paul related his experiences to the great spiritual principles, the spiritual laws of life. Here was a man who had gone through the most severe tribulations and now was giving his views on the mystery of suffering. The reason God had allowed these heavy trials was that he could comfort others who were distressed. He could do this because of the comfort he had received from the Lord. His trials had not been just for his own experience but in order to enable him to give the comfort of Christ to others. In his own deep distress Paul felt the assurance that the Corinthians also would be delivered from their difficulties. "As ye are partakers of the sufferings, so shall ye be also of the consolation" (1:7).

2. Comfort in Tribulation Recently Endured (1:8-11). Paul did not write about old experiences. His severe period of tribulation was one he had just passed through, and he wanted the

Corinthians to know this. They had added to his burden which was heavy enough before. Now that he was telling them, he hoped they would be "helping together by prayer" (1:11). The Corinthians probably had a knowledge of Paul's tribulations in Asia Minor, but they did not know how serious they had been. Now he wrote that he and his coworkers had even doubted at times whether they would continue to stay alive. Yes, they had the sentence of death in themselves so they would know that only God's intervention could save them. They had trusted the God who raises the dead and Paul could testify: "Who delivered us from so great a death, and doth deliver" (1:10).

B. Changed Traveling Plans (1:12–2:17)

1. Accused of Instability (1:12-22). After this opening, Paul found it necessary to discuss immediately a matter about which his opponents in Corinth seemed to have made the most. He related that in the beginning he had planned twice to come to Corinth—first on his way to Macedonia and later on his way back from Macedonia (1:15,16). He had informed the church in Corinth of these plans. However, he had changed his original intention and had gone to Macedonia directly without visiting Corinth. Now there were some who cited this as evidence of Paul's being inconsistent and fickle, that he said yes when he meant no. They seem to have implied that the apostle was not led by God in his traveling plans but made his own plans "according to the flesh" (1:17).

Paul spoke out strongly against these accusations that he was a person one could not rely on. He declared that he had lived a holy and consistent life among them (1:12). The Son of God, Christ Jesus, whom Paul preached to them "was not yea and nay" and neither was Paul. In Christ all the promises of God have their yea and amen (1:20). Paul also had kept his promises. He was faithful as his Lord is faithful.

2. Cause of the Change (1:23–2:2). There was an actual reason for Paul's changing his route (Jesus himself had once changed His travel plans: John 7:8). Paul had received information from Corinth which gave him two reasons for waiting before making his visit. First, it would spare the church the punishment he would have to inflict against people who had sinned (1:23). "I determined this with myself, that I would not come again to you in heaviness" (2:1). It seems Paul had made a previous short visit to Corinth, and it had not been a joyful one. He would rather avoid such an experience again. He did not want to be made sorry by those who ought to make him glad or to make sorry those whom he wanted to make glad (2:2,3). Therefore, Paul postponed the visit so the church would have time to correct the bad situation before he arrived.

3. "The Epistle of Tears" (2:3-11). Instead of coming personally to Corinth, Paul had chosen to write an epistle. Now he tells the people he had written under great emotion: "Out of much affliction and anguish of heart I wrote unto you with many tears" (2:4). The traditional interpretation is that the epistle Paul spoke of here is the First Epistle to the Corinthians. However, during the last century opinions about this have differed. Some believe that in the period between the first two epistles Paul had paid a visit to Corinth as well as writing an epistle which has been lost. One of the arguments for this view is that the first epistle is not sharp enough to have made the church as sorry as Paul speaks of here and would not have caused him so much grief in writing it. In the first epistle he did not mention another visit to Corinth which should have caused grief, so the visit probably took place after the epistle was written, i.e., shortly before Paul wrote the second epistle.

On the other hand, some object to this more recent theory on the grounds that there would not be time for such a visit by Paul in the period between the two epistles. The change in travel plans which Paul explained in the second epistle had already taken place when he wrote the first epistle. In that message he said the same thing as he now says in the second, i.e., that he would not come to Corinth before he had been in Macedonia (1 Corinthians 16:5).

Although some object that Paul could not have felt such great distress when he wrote the first epistle, it must be admitted it is difficult for anyone to know how deeply concerned and sad Paul was when he wrote certain parts of this epistle (Odeberg). H.L. Goudge says it was probably easier for Paul to shed tears than it is for his modern interpreters (cf. Philippians 3:18) (*Westminster Commentaries, Second Corinthians*, p.13). If we look at the sections in question it seems it is indeed "an epistle of tears" for the one who wrote it as well as for those who received it (1 Corinthians 1:10-13; 3:1-3; 5:1-6; 6:8-10; 8:10-12; cf. 15:12,33,34). From these sections it appears that there were divisions in the church (1 Corinthians 1:10). The Corinthians were carnal (1 Corinthians 3:3).

Fornication was reported among them and they did not mourn over this sin (1 Corinthians 5:1,2). They mistreated other believers, and Paul declared that those who did this would not inherit the kingdom of God (1 Corinthians 6:8,9). Some of the Corinthians were eating meat in the temple where idols were worshiped (1 Corinthians 8:10). Some denied the resurrection (1 Corinthians 15:12) and Paul had to write to them: "Awake to righteousness, and sin not; for some have not the knowledge of God: I speak this to your shame" (1 Corinthians 15:34).

Thus Paul wrote in 2 Corinthians 2:4 that he penned his last letter with anguish and tears. He continued by saying that since the man who had fallen into sin had repented he should be restored to fellowship instead of being expelled (2:6,7). It is generally believed that this was the same individual Paul wrote about in 1 Corinthians 5:1. However, if the theory about a lost "epistle of tears" is accepted, he must have been referring to another person who had fallen into sin. Some have thought this referred to a sin against Paul personally or he would not have reacted so strongly. If this is true, then the man in 1 Corinthians 5:1 had committed an ethical sin, while the one referred to in 2 Corinthians 2:5 was simply a "trouble maker." Different arguments have been presented for this point of view, but no proof has been found.

4. Paul in Troas and Macedonia (2:12-17). We meet here a peculiarity in the composition of the first division of the epistle. Paul wrote of his traveling plan and his journey from Ephesus to Macedonia in three different sections: 1:15,16; 2:12,13; and 7:5. In the middle section he also referred back to the first section concerning a plan which was changed to the one mentioned in 1 Corinthians 16:5. Paul continued speaking of the unrest he felt in his spirit over the Corinthian church when he came to Troas and did not meet Titus there in accordance with their previous plans. Then Paul traveled to Macedonia in order to meet Titus. But he ended the story abruptly and said nothing about this meeting or the news he received about Corinth. Instead, he took up again the train of thought he began in 7:4. After the brief interruption to tell of his visit with Titus, he added what was the main content of the first division of the epistle, i.e., the statement of his ministry as an apostle.

Paul wrote that when he came to Troas there was an open door for preaching the gospel.

However, his knowledge of conditions in Corinth burdened him heavily. In addition to his personal feelings and his love for the church there, Paul had considered Corinth strategic to his missionary activity. Corinth was an important junction, a link between the eastern and western worlds. He had planned to travel farther west to Rome and all the way to Spain, but this would be very difficult if conditions in Corinth did not improve. If believers there were influenced by Judaizers, Gnostics, and teachers of so-called wisdom, it would mean that this strategic church had become a stronghold of the enemy. No matter what could be accomplished in Troas, it would not compensate for what was lost in Corinth (J.B. Meyer). Filled with deep unrest, Paul therefore left Troas and went to Macedonia to meet Titus as soon as possible. He wanted information about developments in Corinth.

Paul interrupted the description of his travels to thank God who always causes believers to triumph in Christ. He did not surrender to defeat. Even if preaching the gospel has sharply contrasting results, (life and death, salvation and judgment), the work of God still moves on to victory. In the section composed of 2:14-17 Paul referred back to what he had already written. At the same time this passage is a transition that opens the great section about the glory of the apostles' ministry (chapters 3 to 6).

C. Ministers of a New Covenant (3:1-18)

1. The Epistle of Christ (3:1-3). Paul had just finished telling of those who corrupt the Word of God for their own benefit (2:17). Now the apostle continued by hinting at "some others" who needed "commendation." They were infiltrating the church. They were false apostles, and for the first time he referred to them directly. These individuals had recommendations from certain people, and they made the most of the fact that Paul did not appear to have any. They used this to sow doubt about his relationship with the original apostles in Jerusalem (cf. Part III.A.3). Paul replied that he did not need any commendation from men (cf. Galatians 1:15-17). He was called to be an apostle by the Lord himself (1:1), and the Lord had written Paul's letter of recommendation. The Corinthians themselves were part of his recommendation. They were the work of God, brought into the kingdom of God through Paul's ministry. His letter of recommendation was not written on stone tablets but on "tables

of flesh," i.e., the hearts of believers. Paul's recommendation had not been written with ink but by the Spirit of the living God.

2. The Letter and the Spirit (3:4-6). Verse 3 refers to God's covenant between himself and Israel in the Old Testament. This covenant had as its basis the Law which Moses received, written on stone tablets (Exodus 34:1). The prophecies of Jeremiah 31:33 and Ezekiel 11:19 and 36:26 foretold a day when God would make a new covenant where He would write His law in the minds and hearts of men. The covenant into which Paul's ministry had brought the Corinthians was this new covenant, not the old covenant associated with tablets of stone.

Paul hinted here at some who had letters of recommendation but falsified the Word of God. It seems clear that Paul was engaging in a thinly veiled attack on these heretics in his continuing discussion. The Judaizers clung to the old covenant that emphasized the letter of the Law. Paul was a minister of the new covenant based not on the letter of the Law but the spirit it was intended to convey (3:6). It was the Spirit of God who breathed life into the new covenant.

In making a transition to the new theme, Paul changed his use of the illustration he had been employing. First he contrasted ink with the Holy Spirit, then stone tablets and tablets of flesh. Ink and stone tablets do not, of course, belong together (Kvalbein), but it served Paul's intention to use this double picture of contrast.

The two different covenants are referred to by "Spirit" and "letter." This was Paul's way of showing the contrast between Law and grace. This does not mean the old covenant was worthless, for it served God's purpose for its time. Its weakness was that it only showed what God expected of men but gave them no power to keep His commandments. Under the new covenant we do not merely read the "letter" of the Word and try our best in our own strength to keep it. Through grace we have received power by the indwelling Spirit to obey the law God has written in our innermost being.

We must not misunderstand Paul's teaching by imagining he was saying that Scripture is the letter that brings death and that under the new covenant we are "free" from the Scriptures. The apostle's point is that the Judaizers were sticking to the letter of the Scripture but rejecting the Christ through whom we receive the Spirit who has inspired the Scripture. The Spirit inspired the Old Testament as well as the New, and the Old Testament testified of Christ (John

5:39,40). In their apparent loyalty to the "letter," the Judaizers were ignoring what the Spirit had taught through the Scriptures. Thus they were destroying themselves by the Scripture they professed to believe. The testimony of Jesus is the spirit of the prophetic word (Revelation 19:10). The one who rejects the Spirit by rejecting Jesus has nothing left but the dead letter. This is the condition of the one who, in this age of grace, continues to "serve in the oldness of the letter" (Romans 7:6).

3. The Veil and the Glory (3:7-18). The apostles were ministers of a new covenant and the differences between the new and old were great. The old covenant did in fact have its glory, but it was a glory which disappeared just as the glory on Moses' face disappeared. Paul presented a series of contrasts. The difference between the old and new covenants is the difference between letter and Spirit (3:6), death and life (3:6), and condemnation and righteousness (3:9).

As an illustration, Paul mentioned the veil Moses put over his face when he had finished speaking to the people (Exodus 34:29,30). That veil hid from the people the glory of the Lord which was reflected in Moses' face. The glory was hidden so the people would not see it fade away. Paul said a veil also covers the old covenant, the Old Testament (3:14). This veil of unbelief kept the Jews from seeing that the old covenant was fulfilled in Christ and that its glory had passed away. This is totally different from the experience of those who follow Christ: "We all, with open face beholding as in a glass the glory of the Lord, are changed into the same image from glory to glory, even as by the Spirit of the Lord" (3:18).

D. Honesty in the Ministry: (4:1–5:15)

As one who had received such a ministry, Paul spoke openly and frankly and did not lose courage. He was constantly impelled by strong motives. First, he had received his ministry through grace. He owed it to God's mercy (4:1), and his faith in that mercy kept him fearless. Second, Paul had the hope of eternal life and eternal glory (5:1). Third, the love of Christ constrained him (5:14).

1. The Motive of Faith (4:1-15). "We faint not!" Paul declared. He expressed the honesty of his faith. He had received his ministry by grace, for he had not been deserving of it nor suited for it. Faith gave Paul the ability to speak honestly, and he was influenced by the indwelling Spirit who constantly quickened his faith (4:13). Paul wrote he had "renounced the hidden things of dishonesty, not walking in craftiness" (4:2). Those words imply a defense against the baseless accusations leveled at Paul. He assured the Corinthians that he acted openly in everything. He who stands before the Lord with an unveiled face (3:18) does not have to hide his face from men. Satan blinds the minds of unbelievers (4:3,4), but some will be won to Christ anyway, and the gospel will be preached to more and more people (4:15). Paul had his spiritual treasure in a human container, and his tribulations and temptations kept him reminded of this. It is as though he was constantly delivered to death, yet the life of Christ continued to be active through him (4:10-12).

2. The Motive of Hope (4:16-5:10). The other reason Paul did not lose his courage was that he possessed a hope. That hope assured him that if our physical house (the human body) falls into ruins, yet the true man—the inward man—is being continually renewed. If the earthly tent we live in is finally taken down, "we have a building of God, a house not made with hands, eternal in the heavens" (5:1). Paul longed to move into that house. "Therefore we are always confident," he said, that when we are absent from the body we will be present with the Lord (5:6,8). This hope impelled him in his work: "Wherefore we labor, that, whether present or absent, we may be accepted of him" (5:9). In this great hope there was also a holy fear: "We must all appear before the judgment seat of Christ" (5:10). "Knowing therefore the terror of the Lord, we persuade men" (5:11). This hope makes the believer invincible. It transforms all his suffering and humiliation into glory and exaltation.

3. The Motive of Love (5:14,15). The third motive Paul referred to was: "The love of Christ constraineth us." In this verse, Paul was probably referring to love in its fullest extent, i.e., Christ's love for all men as well as His love poured out into believers' hearts by the Spirit of God (Romans 5:5). Paul was thinking here of Christ's love for us and our love for Him. He loved us first. It was that love which led Him to die as our sacrifice. His love for us is the foundation of all Christian love. Christ revealed His love for all by dying for all. Because He died for all, those who live must not live any longer for themselves alone but for Him who died for them and rose again.

E. The Ministry of Reconciliation (5:16-21)

The ministry Paul had received was a ministry of reconciliation. It was based on the truth that God in Christ reconciled the world to himself. Paul became a participant in that reconciliation and prayed in Christ's stead, "Be ye reconciled to God" (5:20).

Paul's ministry was not based on knowing Christ "after the flesh" (5:16). Again we get a glimpse of Paul's opponents who appealed to a natural, human knowledge of Jesus. If we once knew Christ in such a way, Paul says, we do not know Him that way now. Paul's knowledge of Christ was a new spiritual knowledge obtained from the Spirit of God. That is why Paul did not know anyone "after the flesh" (5:16). He looked at his fellowmen in an entirely different way, i.e., as men for whom Christ died. And he who is in Christ is a new creature; the old is passed away, all things are become new.

Paul wrote that God had committed to him and his fellow apostles the "word of reconciliation" (5:19). That word of reconciliation is based on this truth: "He hath made him to be sin for us, who knew no sin; that we might be made the righteousness of God in him" (5:21). The message of the redemption provided in Christ was the central theme of Paul's preaching. Shortly after he wrote this epistle he came to Corinth, where he wrote the Epistle to the Romans, that mighty document of evangelical truth. We note here and in 2 Corinthians 5:15-21 how the message of the Cross penetrated and dominated all of Paul's preaching.

F. The Ministry of Admonition (6:1-7:3)

1. Exhortations by Paul (6:1,2). Paul's apostolic ministry was also a ministry of admonition (6:1). We meet this in all his writings. His epistles are often divided distinctly into sections of teaching and sections of admonition. The admonition is directed basically toward believers and is a vital part of the gospel. The intent of admonition is to "present every man perfect in Christ Jesus" (Colossians 1:28). All admonition is "by the Lord Jesus Christ" (1 Thessalonians 4:1,2; 2 Thessalonians 3:12), "by the name of our Lord Jesus Christ" (1 Corinthians 1:10), "for the Lord Jesus Christ's sake, and for the love of the Spirit" (Romans 15:30), "by the meekness and gentleness of Christ" (2 Corinthians 10:1), "by the mercies of God" (Romans 12:1). "Receive not the grace of God in vain"

is a challenge to bring forth fruit which demonstrates that our conversion is genuine.

2. Without Offense (6:3-10). Paul was determined that his ministry should not be blamed. For this reason he strove diligently to avoid giving offense in any way (6:3). Through the false accusations of his enemies he might have had a bad reputation with some and might have been considered by them as being in disgrace rather than honor. But he always determined to live a blameless life so these accusations would be seen as false.

3. Fellowship and Separation (6:11-7:1). This section concludes with a double admonition. First there is a plea to the Corinthians to enlarge their hearts and give Paul the room in their affections which he ought to have. He wanted their confidence and love, reminding them that he had never treated anyone unfairly nor wronged any of them. Then Paul gave a strong warning for believers not to be unequally yoked together with unbelievers.

G. Comforted by the Corinthians (7:4-16)

Here Paul resumed the train of thought from 2:13. In that verse he wrote of leaving Troas to go to Macedonia. Yet in 7:5 he said that when he came to Macedonia, "our flesh had no rest." In Troas Paul had a peaceful time, but in Macedonia he faced difficulties and different kinds of opposition: "We were troubled on every side; without were fightings, within were fears."

Then he recounted the comfort he received when he finally met Titus, who came from Corinth with good news. Much in the church had already been made right. Paul's epistle to them had had its effect. Most of the Corinthians had come to their senses and turned away from the false apostles. Now they had renewed their interest in Paul and his coworkers and loved him (7:12). Titus had received so much encouragement from the church that his joy was shared by Paul (7:13). The first division of the epistle concludes with Paul's strong expression of his confidence in the church.

II. HELP FOR JERUSALEM (8:1-9:15)

The second division of this epistle concerns money. Since Paul had been informed by Titus that the situation had improved in the church at Corinth, he could discuss again the matter about which he wrote them the previous year (1 Corinthians 16:1-4).

This concerned the assistance many churches had begun for the Christians suffering in Judea. No doubt Paul himself had taken the initiative. When Paul and the original apostles met in Jerusalem, one thing on which they agreed was to remember the poor (Galatians 2:6-10). At that time Paul and Barnabas had already brought a gift from the Gentile church in Antioch (Acts 11:27-30).

The part of the Second Epistle to the Corinthians which concerns financial help for the Jerusalem believers covers two chapters and can be divided into three sections: (1) Motive of the gift: 8:1-15. (2) The task of Titus: 8:16 to 9:15. (3) The blessing of the gift: 9:6-15.

A. The Motive of the Gift (8:1-15)

1. The Example of the Macedonians (8:1-5). As an encouragement to the Corinthians to give, Paul referred first to the example of the Macedonians. The apostle knew that it is often easier for people to make a sacrifice when they know others have already done so. The churches in Macedonia were very poor, yet they wanted a part in the financial ministry to their fellow believers in Jerusalem. Paul said their attitude came from God himself, that it was the "grace of God bestowed on the churches of Macedonia" (8:1).

2. The Spiritual Abundance of the Corinthians (8:6-8). It is interesting to note how often Paul spoke of spiritual abundance in the church at Corinth, especially when he rebuked them at the same time because so much was wrong. Paul was not blind to their good side! He challenged them by saying that since they were rich in so many spiritual ways, they must also become rich in this performance of financial help. They must give in a way that was proportionate to the spiritual abundance with which they had been blessed. A church's spiritual background often determines the people's financial sacrifices more than their economic situation.

3. The Example of Christ (8:9). The example of Christ himself is the third motive Paul presented for their giving. This verse says in essence that Christ became poor in order to make us rich. Thus the Corinthians' financial giving would express the mind of Christ. It would follow His great example.

4. Similarity Between Believers (8:10-15). The Bible teaches a reasonable distribution of material benefits. Paul referred to the manna God gave the Israelites, pointing out that he who gathered much had none left over, while the one who gathered less had no shortage. To avoid allowing a small number of people to

possess most of the property, God instituted the year of sabbath and the year of jubilee in Israel. At that time, property was returned to the original owner or his family. The New Testament makes frequent references to the care of those who need assistance. In fact, Christianity is not compatible with indifference to those in need (1 John 3:17)). Paul only expected the Corinthians to give according to their ability (8:11), although he praised the Macedonians for giving beyond their means (8:3). There must be the balance of justice in the matter. Nobody can expect to live off the gifts of others when the givers are poor themselves. However, the poverty in the church in Jerusalem was well known. At the beginning the members of that church who had property sold it and contributed to the common treasury (Acts 4:32). But now they were in financial straits. Possibly persecution had something to do with this.

B. The Task of Titus (8:16–9:5)

1. Supervision of the Distribution (8:16-24). It is evident from 12:16 that suspicion had been thrown on Paul. Apparently some were saying he had used some of the contributions for personal gain. Of course it was wicked of them to try to hurt Paul's reputation this way, but it is interesting how he responded to the accusation. He ordered the churches to choose their own representatives to collect the money and take it to Jerusalem, where they were to deliver it to the church. Paul would not receive the money himself and he was not willing that his close friend and co-worker Titus should bear all the responsibility. "Avoiding this, that no man should blame us in this abundance which is administered by us: providing for honest things, not only in the sight of the Lord, but also in the sight of men" (8:20,21).

2. The Collection Resumed (9:1-5). When Paul sent Titus and others to Corinth, it was to resume the work of collecting financial aid for Jerusalem. When the false apostles were in power, there was probably little to give others! But now their influence had been reduced and circumstances were becoming more normal, so the interrupted work of love could be continued. Paul reminded the Corinthians of their promise. He told them he had commended them to the church in Macedonia when they agreed the year before to make the collection. If this was just an empty promise, both Paul and the Corinthians would be embarrassed by having this known among other churches. This must not happen!

C. The Blessing of the Gift (9:6-15)

1. Reaping Blessing (9:6-11). Paul knew this church that was filled with newly converted people needed teaching about the blessing of giving. He used the illustration of sowing seed corn. The sower does not consider the seed lost; neither is a gift lost if it is made in love. It is seed which gives hope for a harvest because God makes it grow. But the stingy person who sows little cannot expect a bountiful harvest. To the one who gives, blessing shall be given. God himself gives willingly and richly, and He loves the one who gives with the same attitude (cf. Isaiah 55:10; Hosea 10:12; James 1:5,17).

2. Causing Thanksgiving to God (9:12,13). Paul considered it the highest joy and reward for others to thank God for the testimony of a believer's life (Ephesians 1:16; Philippians 1:3; Colossians 1:3; 1 Thessalonians 1:2; Philemon 4). The Corinthians' gift would cause many to thank God for them. They would be praised not only for their financial contribution but for their obedience to the gospel of Christ.

3. Creating Spiritual Fellowship (9:13-15). Those who received the gift would thank God for the fellowship they had with Gentile believers (9:13). This was one of Paul's chief motives for being so eager to arrange the gift. It would have great meaning for the unity of the Church. It would demonstrate that "the middle wall of partition" had been torn down (Ephesians 2:14). It would prompt the Jewish believers to pray for their Gentile brethren with a new sense of love for them (9:14). The whole matter opens up an eternal perspective. Many times Christians do not meet their benefactors personally on earth, but one day they will meet. Paul ended his "collection sermon" with praise: "Thanks be unto God for his unspeakable gift!"

III. PAUL'S APOSTOLIC AUTHORITY (10:1–13:14)

As we have seen, the Second Epistle to the Corinthians carries strong emphasis by Paul concerning his calling to be an apostle. In the first part of the epistle he referred to the glory of the new covenant of which he had become a minister. He built his defense by positive statements without paying any particular attention to his accusers and their accusations. Yet we do get glimpses of these opponents in the background. In 2:17 Paul said bluntly that these

people falsify the Word of God. In 3:1 he referred to them as "some others" who need letters of recommendation.

In the third division of the epistle Paul attacked his opponents openly. First he unveiled them as heretics and false apostles and rebuked the Corinthians for being attracted toward such people. Then in forced self-praise, Paul compared himself with the pseudo-apostles.

A. False Apostles (10:1–11:21)

1. Who They Are. Just who were these opponents of Paul and what was their doctrine? This was no mystery to the Corinthians who received this epistle. They knew very well who Paul meant by "certain others" (3:1; 10:12). He did not have to give details about the doctrine and activity of these opponents.

However, Paul did give information about them. They were not from Corinth, but came from the outside (11:4). They were Jews (11:22), and they had a letter of recommendation from some source (3:1). From 10:10 and 11:6 it is evident that they considered themselves superior to Paul in speaking ability (1 Corinthians 2:1). These false teachers had not founded any churches. Instead, they had invaded territory where others had done the work and exploited their labors for their own benefit (10:15). They also used the church for their financial benefit (11:12,20). Their behavior was very arrogant, even offending members of the church (11:20).

Paul characterized these opponents as "false apostles, deceitful workers, transforming themselves into the apostles of Christ" (11:13), while in reality they were Satan's servants transformed into supposedly ministers of righteousness (11:15). They preached "another Jesus" and "another gospel." They had "another spirit" completely opposed to the Spirit of Christ (11:4).

We do not need to know more than this about these who were causing such division by their heresy. However, it is possible to some extent to find a more detailed picture of what their teaching consisted. The doctrine of these false apostles was probably not unique to Corinth. It is unlikely that they were merely an isolated group. The error had not arisen in Corinth but was imported from without. Therefore, there must have been traces of similar error in other early churches.

From the writings of the New Testament and especially from the epistles it is clear that the early churches fought on two fronts. The false doctrine that threatened to penetrate the congregations was partly Gentile philosophy and partly Jewish legalism based on the Law. In the Epistle to the Galatians Paul opposed the infiltration of Judaism. He spoke against the Greek "wisdom" also, especially in the First Epistle to the Corinthians. From Paul's writing it is evident that the "wisdom" in Colosse did not have the same intellectual form as the wisdom and philosophy being proclaimed in Corinth. The Gnosticism in Colossae had a more esoteric character, being a "wisdom" reserved for the initiated ones and consisting of a mixture of Greek philosophy and Oriental myths.

However, of greater interest to us is that in Colosse the Greek wisdom had evidently become mixed with Judaism. False teachers there were following Jewish food laws, observing the Sabbath and the feasts (Colossians 2:16). What is then more natural than the development of similar error in Corinth? The "wisdom" in Corinth was just as susceptible to Judaistic influence as the "wisdom" in Colosse. The different tendencies and teachings did not exist in isolation but had influenced each other mutually. As in other Gentile churches there were groups of Jews in Corinth along with Jewish proselytes. Because of their synagogue background they were particularly vulnerable to Judaistic preaching. These may have formed the "Cephas party" (1 Corinthians 1:12).

It is worth noting that among the dispersed Jews a Jewish/Hellenistic religion had developed at this time. It was propagated by wandering Jewish preachers and originated with Philo of Alexandria, the Jewish philosopher. His central theme was that the Old Testament contained the highest philosophy which he would interpret for the "enlightened" and well-bred world in the vocabulary of Greek philosophy. In certain circles the division between Jewish theology and Greek philosophy was thus about to be torn down. It is just as reasonable that such a Greek-Jewish popular philosophy would appeal to certain groups in the new Gentile churches. It is also obvious that such a syncretism represented a deadly danger to the purity of the Christian message.

This period of early Christianity was a time of unusual doctrinal conflict. Within paganism as well as the Jewish religion there were many ideologies that contended with each other and influenced each other. The Judaism which penetrated the Christian churches was probably no united movement. In fact, the Jewish agitators sometimes acted differently from others in different areas, just as other false teachers did.

This may explain why Paul in the Second Epistle to the Corinthians did not attack the doctrine of the false apostles point by point. He could write to the Colossians: "Let no man therefore judge you in meat, or in drink, or in respect of a holyday, or of the new moon, or of the sabbath days" (Colossians 2:16). In Colosse a Jewish-Gnostic party had begun to agitate for celebrating the Sabbath and observing Jewish food laws. He could write to the Galatians: "Behold, I Paul say unto you, that if ye be circumcised, Christ shall profit you nothing" (Galatians 5:2), because in Galatia the Judaizers preached circumcision. But nothing seems to indicate that the false teachers in Corinth demanded such things of their audience—at least not yet. Up to this time they were being very cunning (cf. 11:3) as heretics always are. Their teaching was still in the early stages and was not as clearly exposed as error was in other places. If Paul referred to what the Judaizers were doing elsewhere, the false apostles in Corinth could claim no connection with them.

Another point to consider is that doctrinal questions in themselves had been secondary with the false apostles in Corinth. Their first goal was to seize power in the church and enrich themselves financially at the believers' expense.

The motive of false teachers was to make the gospel as widely acceptable as possible. To Paul the real message of Christianity was "the word of the cross," the deity of Christ, His atoning death, and His resurrection. To the false apostles, however, these teachings were obstacles. Their "gospel" was an ethical view of life. Their "Jesus" was no more than the promoter of this view. Their doctrine was a kind of popularized and "christened" Pharisaism. In Judaistic circles there had evidently been a tendency to adapt Christianity so it could be accepted as a part of the Jewish religion.

But at least in Corinth the Jewish teachers of error were concerned first of all with a practical goal: to make a financial profit for themselves. Thus there was probably no unified theme among them and they did not appear to be advocating any particular philosophy. They wanted to distort the gospel so it could pass for a "reasonable" view of life and not seem too different from other doctrinal systems of that time. When they tried to penetrate the church in Corinth they presented their teaching so carefully that it would provoke as little resistance as possible (Odeberg). Thus their error became an even greater threat to this church which consisted mostly of the recently converted.

Undoubtedly there were distinct proofs of heresy in Corinth or Paul could not have attacked his opponents so strongly. But it seems in fact that at first the false apostles were most concerned with undermining his influence. They attacked him personally. The conflict was over Paul's apostolic authority.

Therefore, Paul had to meet his opponents at their point of attack even though this must have been unpleasant to him personally. Unlike the epistles to the Galatians and Colossians, the Second Epistle to the Corinthians is not a confrontation with specific errors but a message about true and false apostles.

The false apostles rejected Paul's position as a preacher and apostle, "a teacher of the Gentiles in faith and verity" (1 Timothy 2:7). Thus they did raise the issue of doctrinal contrasts. Their teaching was a contrast to Paul's gospel (Romans 1:16; 16:25; 2 Corinthians 4:3; 2 Timothy 2:8), whose central theme was salvation by grace, not works, salvation by faith, not "wisdom." Therefore, the message of the false apostles was "another gospel" (11:4). They added to the gospel, subtracted from it, changed it, so their teaching ceased to be a real gospel.

2. The Tolerance of Heresy. The situation in Corinth was made all the more critical by the church's tolerance of the heretics. Paul had led these people to Christ and would have expected them to come to his defense when the false teachers began to slander him. Yet they listened readily to these individuals and did not object to the preaching of "another gospel" among them. Afflicted in his spirit and in deep earnest, Paul wrote to them: "If he that cometh preacheth another Jesus, whom we have not preached, or if ye receive another spirit, which ye have not received, or another gospel, which ye have not accepted, ye might well bear with him" (11:4).

Paul's subject here is the actual situation in Corinth. He was not dealing with possibilities or suppositions. He wrote about things which had already taken place. The Corinthians were tolerating the behavior of the intruders as well as their false doctrine. Thus they were partners in others' sins (1 Timothy 5:22) and accomplices in the evil works of the heretics (cf. 2

John 11). That is why Paul's warnings were so sharp—the souls of the Corinthian believers were in danger.

Paul's strong reaction sprang from his deep concern for these, his converts. He was appalled at the thought of their being unfaithful to Christ. He used John the Baptist's illustration, picturing himself as "the friend of the bridegroom" who has won a bride for Christ: "I have espoused you to one husband, that I may present you as a chaste virgin to Christ. But I fear, lest by any means, as the serpent beguiled Eve through his subtilty, so your minds should be corrupted from the simplicity that is in Christ" (11:2,3). The Christians at Corinth did not belong to Paul and were not baptized in his name (1 Corinthians 1:13). He had brought them into fellowship with Christ. Paul's picture was a well-known Old Testament illustration of God's people being called His wife. The Jews interpreted the Song of Solomon as an allegory about the Lord and the elect nation. Paul employed the same figure concerning Christ and the Church (cf. Ephesians 5:31,32), but with the variation that the Church is compared to a betrothed young lady who must maintain her purity until the wedding day. The wedding will take place at Jesus' coming back to earth (cf. Revelation 19:7). This admonition keeps recurring in Paul's epistles, i.e., that believers must be diligent about keeping their purity until the day of Christ's return (Ephesians 5:25; Philippians 1:10; 1 Thessalonians 5:23). The believers in Corinth and all others Paul had won for God would be his praise when Christ comes back (1:14—cf. Philippians 2:16).

But now Paul was full of fear for the church in Corinth. He was afraid believers there would be deceived and seduced even as Satan through the serpent beguiled Eve through his subtilty. The loyalty of the people to Christ was in danger because the false apostles were destroying the simplicity of the gospel. The Jesus they preached was "another Jesus," not the Jesus Paul had preached. Their spirit was "another spirit," not the Spirit of God the Corinthians had received. The intruders' gospel was another gospel.

Paul used two different words for "another." When he said these individuals preach another Jesus he used the Greek word *allon*, which can refer to the same person but in a distorted sense. The false apostles preached about Jesus of Nazareth, not another Jesus from a different place, but they gave a completely false picture of Him.

When Paul continued by saying the heretics had another spirit, he used the word *heteron*, which means another individual, one who is a different kind. False preaching about Christ was connected with a totally strange spirit. The Holy Spirit glorifies the true Christ and only the true Christ (John 16:14). When one confesses Jesus Christ as Lord it is a testimony to the activity of the Spirit of God (1 Corinthians 12:3). The spirit that confesses Jesus is the Christ who has come in the flesh is of God, but the spirit of antichrist proclaims a false christ (1 John 4:2,3).

Also, when Paul said the false apostles preached another gospel he used the term *heteron*, signifying that the "gospel" they proclaimed was something quite different from the true gospel. In Galatians 1:6,7 Paul used the difference of meaning in the two words and said the Galatians had turned away to a different gospel which was not another gospel of the same kind as the true gospel. In reality there is no other gospel than the one preached about the One who died for our sins and rose for our justification (Romans 4:25).

The heretics preached a false gospel, and it was alarming that the Corinthians were tolerating such a distortion of the truth. They were also enduring the bragging and self-exaltation of these men. With considerable irony Paul said the Corinthians were so wise that they endured fools. In other words, they showed their high intelligence by enjoying all the foolish bragging. Even more humiliating was the fact that the Corinthians tolerated the arrogant behavior of the "apostles." In one verse (11:20) Paul characterized this behavior in five indignant expressions, trying to bring the Corinthians to their senses so they could see how outrageous it was for them to be treated this way.

(1) They were being brought into bondage: The tyrannical heretics would enjoy having the Corinthians as their personal slaves. But even worse was the spiritual bondage into which they had brought their victims. The word Paul used for making slaves, *katadouloi*, is used in just one other New Testament verse. It is Galatians 2:4 where Paul writes about the Judaizers who had brought the Galatians under the bondage of the Law.

(2) They were being devoured: These men were using the Corinthians for their own financial gain and they were doing it shamelessly, just like the Pharisees who devoured widows' houses (Luke 20:47).

(3) They were being preyed upon: The false apostles were treating them like a bird caught in a snare or a fish in a net. They did not only take their money and property, they were taking the people themselves and making them slaves of men (cf. 1 Corinthians 7:23).

(4) They were being treated with contempt: The intruders were lording it over the believers and they were enduring it.

(5) They were being slapped in the face: The false apostles showed total disrespect for the church. It was similar to the treatment Micaiah the prophet received from the false prophet (1 Kings 22:24). Jesus endured similar humiliation from His enemies, although it was much more severe (Luke 22:64). Paul received the same kind of treatment (Acts 23:2; cf. Matthew 5:39), but this was not the situation at Corinth. It is clear that Paul considered the Corinthians' submission to the slaps in the face as a sign of their weakness. Their cowardice showed how completely they had been intimidated by these intruders. Paul had tried to appeal to the Corinthians' sense of spiritual responsibility in telling them to resist the false apostles. Now he appealed to their sense of honor and self-respect—the lack of which was evident by their meek submission to their mistreatment. Paul also reminded them that neither he nor his coworkers ever treated them in such a way. With friendly irony he wrote something like this: "I have to admit with shame that we have been weak compared with these domineering 'apostles' you now serve!" Some scholars think it is to be interpreted literally that the false apostles often struck their most obedient followers in the face. Such action expresses the most humiliating treatment.

By appealing to both their spiritual responsibility and their self-respect, Paul sought to urge the Corinthians to rid themselves of the authority of error under which they had allowed themselves to fall. Their weakness toward the intruders was inexcusable and could lead to the actual destruction of the church.

3. The Accusations of Paul's Opponents. Paul said bluntly that the false apostles were Satan's servants who were performing his work. They had been taught their sly methods of seduction by the great deceiver himself who transforms himself into an angel of light (11:14,15). They showed themselves to be false apostles by preaching another gospel. They also showed it by their attempts to divide and destroy the church. The fact that they opposed true servants of God emphasized their true character further. (Cf. Galatians 4:29 where it is said, "As then he that was born after the flesh persecuted him that was born after the Spirit, even so it is now.") Significantly Paul's discussion of the false apostle's attack on his apostolic authority developed into some of the strongest language in the entire epistle (11:5-15). Paul knew he belonged to Christ (10:7) and that he was called by God to his apostolic ministry (1:1). Thus he knew also that these individuals who were trying to undermine his position and hinder his work were carrying out Satan's strategy.

The accusations of Paul's opponents can be traced throughout the epistle. They become a long list if we try to sum them up: (1) Accusation of inconsistency and unreliability for changing his travel plans and postponing his visit to Corinth (1:15-24). This is discussed under point 2 in the division of the epistle. (2) Suggestions that he did not have good relations with the original apostles because he had no letter of recommendation from them (3:1). This is discussed under point 3 in the first division. (3) Suspicion thrown on Paul in connection with his part in gathering money for the church in Jerusalem (8:18-21; 12:16-18). This is discussed under point 2 in the second division. (4) Criticism of Paul's lack of eloquence (10:10; 11:6). (5) Criticism for his strong and frank epistles when he was absent (10:10). (6) Criticism for his weak and insignificant physical appearance when he was personally present (10:10,11; cf. 12:12). (7) Devaluating his ministry because he did not receive money from the church as salary for his work (11:7-13). The last four accusations will be discussed below.

Regarding Paul's lack of eloquence, he would not agree that he was inferior to his opponents except in one point. He admitted he was not a good speaker. He was not a professional orator as some of them claimed to be. Compared to Paul, his opponents did not really have much to boast about, so they had to make a great fuss over what they had. It seemed important to them that Paul lacked technical and professional education as a speaker. Paul himself, however, dismissed the entire matter as being unworthy of much attention. In the first epistle he discussed the situation and said he had arrived at a firm decision to conduct himself just as he did (1 Corinthians 2:1-5). As one who knew his call had come from God he had purposely desisted from the "wisdom of words" in his preaching of the gospel (1:17).

When Paul said he was "rude in speech" (11:6) he used a Greek term meaning "unlearned." Originally the word referred to one who was not interested in politics and public service. Such a person had little respect among the Greeks so the word gradually developed bad connotations. When the New Testament was written, the word was sometimes used in connection with being unskilled in a matter. Paul employed the term this way in 1 Corinthians 14:23,24. It could apply to one who lacked instruction in a trade and therefore only dabbled in it. In Acts 4:13 the word is used of Peter and John because they were lay people who were not educated in the rabbinical schools.

The opening speech of the orator Tertullus before Felix (Acts 24:1) is a good example of the type of rhetoric which Paul had not been taught and which he refused to use. One of the distinctive features of this speech was shameless flattery. Paul refused to use flattering words when he preached the gospel (1 Thessalonians 2:5), for he had renounced the hidden things of dishonesty (2 Corinthians 4:2). But it was characteristic of false teachers trying to gain access to the churches that "their mouth speaketh great swelling words, having men's persons in admiration because of advantage" (Jude 16).

What gave strength to Paul's preaching was his unfailing love of the truth. His speech was characterized by unaffected sincerity and marked by an appeal to his listeners' consciences (4:2). The progress of the gospel was not dependent on bombastic rhetoric. Paul's opponents might say "his speech is contemptible" (10:10), but none believed his preaching was powerless or insignificant. His activity as portrayed throughout the New Testament shows he was anything but powerless. In the churches he preached the deep spiritual truths "which the Holy Ghost teacheth" (1 Corinthians 2:13). Paul was actually one of the most effective missionaries in the Church's history. Throughout his journeys he established strong churches that grew and flourished spiritually. When we study Paul's speeches in the Book of Acts we see they are masterpieces. He may not have had the eloquence of Apollos nor the ability to be a popular speaker like Peter, but he could adapt to different situations as no one else could. He spoke in Jewish synagogues (Acts 19:8), in Christian assemblies (19:9,10), in Gentile marketplaces (17:22). He spoke to a gathering of excited Jews (22:1) and to a crowd of Gentiles (14:12ff.). He could speak before the high court of the Jews (23:1) and before kings and rulers (26:1). He spoke of the judgment to come in such a way that his examining judge was terrified (24:25). His testimony to the Christian faith caused King Agrippa to exclaim, "Almost thou persuadest me to be a Christian" (26:28). What argument could the so-called "apostles" in Corinth advance to counteract these facts, even with all their oratorical skill?

Regarding the strong nature of his epistles, Paul's opponents criticized him because they felt his epistles were too authoritative and bold. They accused him of being one who shoots best from a distance! They said the Paul who wrote letters was different from the one who visited Corinth. There was probably no more effective way to undermine his personal reputation and influence (10:10).

Even these opponents had to admit that Paul's letters were effective. The influence his epistles had on the church was demonstrated before their very eyes. Through one of his letters he had caused a sinning member of the church to "sorrow to repentance" (7:9). These apostolic epistles were considered as the Word of God by the churches and were read along with "the other epistles" with which they were compared (2 Peter 3:15,16). It is interesting that Scripture has preserved this testimony of opponents from the apostolic era in which the epistles were written.

Admission by Paul's opponents that his epistles were authoritative and courageous does not imply their recognition of Paul as a genuine apostle. They denied his apostolic authority in spite of the nature of his epistles. In their opinion his epistles were simply a collection of empty words. They said the authority present in Paul's writings was totally absent in his personal appearance. Paul rejected these accusations: "Such as we are in word by letters when we are absent, such will we be also in deed when we are present" (10:11). The Lord himself had given Paul his authority and the power of the Lord was effective through him. This power, however, was used to build up the church, not tear it down as the false apostles were doing (10:8). Paul had used his apostolic authority for the church's edification. Believers at Corinth had been saved through his preaching. Why then should they be frightened by his authoritative epistle? Certainly Paul never intended that they should be (10:9).

Regarding his unimpressive physical appear-

ance, Paul's opponents insisted he was so weak and unsure of himself that he dared to be brave only in writing from a distance. He did not show such authority and strength when he was personally present—as one would expect a real apostle to do! (10:10).

The false apostles and their followers had taken Paul's modesty and humility as a sign of weakness. Since they were strangers to the mind of Christ they could not understand or appreciate the spirit of a true Christian. This was Paul's natural behavior toward others. His tone and style in speaking were the same as in writing. This spirit is evident even now when Paul must openly confront the deceivers and their followers. Some modern commentators think Paul was unnecessarily severe in the third division of the epistle, but it should be noted that he soon pointed to the meekness and gentleness of Christ as his example (10:1).

Probably one reason for Paul's seeming severity was that he knew his opponents were receiving some support from members of the church concerning his being more outspoken in his epistles than when personally present. Paul often wrote his epistles because of some circumstance in a church which needed to be corrected. In this case he would have to admonish the offenders, who naturally thought he was too strict. It was different when he visited a church and lived among the people for a longer period. At those times situations could be prevented by dealing with a matter before it grew to larger proportions. Odeberg writes: "Thus it came to pass that his personal presence in a church left the memory of a modest, friendly, and humble man, but that his epistles did more show the strict corrector and warner," English translation.

But one thing emerges clearly: Paul was anything but a weak, passive man. The thought is absurd when we remember the kind of life he lived and the tribulations he endured. When we follow Paul's career in Acts and in his epistles we see an individual with a powerful personality. Depending on the kind of situation he was confronting, he could show tender care and compassion or the most determined inflexibility. The man who was put into stocks in the Philippian prison and filled the place with praise in the middle of the night was no weakling. His strength was probably shown even more by his refusal to leave the prison until high officials came to release him (Acts 16:37).

He pronounced a curse on Elymas the sorcerer (Acts 13:8-11). He called the high priest "thou whited wall" when that man behaved unjustly in court, and he was big enough to apologize for his words (Acts 23:2-5). Not for one moment did Paul retreat in cowardice from false brethren who would bring believers into bondage (Galatians 2:4,5). When his fellow apostle Peter "walked not uprightly according to the truth of the gospel," Paul rebuked him to his face (Galatians 2:11-14). He would also dare to speak just as bluntly to the false apostles in Corinth when he arrived there!

Such is the picture the Scriptures draw of Paul, the apostle to the Gentiles. It is not the picture of a weak or fearful man. It is the picture of a prince of God.

Finally, one of the strongest complaints against Paul seems to have been that he did not receive financial compensation from the church in Corinth for his work (11:7-12). This "accusation" has been linked to the one that he got money from congregations by underhanded means. So here are two accusations that are actually opposite to each other. The intention of the false apostles was to pile up as many accusations against Paul as possible.

We would not think it was a serious charge against a preacher of the gospel that he did his work without receiving pay (cf. Matthew 10:8). However, Paul's behavior in this matter caused great problems for his opponents. Their main motive in pretending to be religious workers was to receive a good living from it. Thus they felt uncomfortable over Paul's demonstrating openly that his motives were quite different. To the false apostles, preaching was simply a "job" and the church was the place where they worked. As a modern illustration, we can imagine the irritation of workers in a factory against a man who worked there without pay and thus reflected badly on them.

To Paul it was a usual practice to preach without pay. He practiced this in many places (Acts 20:33-35; 1 Corinthians 4:12; 9:7-12; 1 Thessalonians 2:9; 2 Thessalonians 3:6-10). He did this for several reasons. No doubt it was a necessity in many of the new territories where he preached to earn his living by manual labor. He also did this to show by example that a Christian should never shun work or shirk his duties. Sometimes it was to make things easier for his listeners to receive the gospel. Wandering Greek philosophers received money from those who listened to them and Paul did not want to be considered one of them. His work

as an unpaid preacher underscored the message that the salvation offered through Christ was by God's free grace and not something that could be earned.

In Corinth there was a special reason to follow this practice. It made it less convenient for the false apostles to receive pay from the church. Even apart from their erroneous theology and ideology, Paul considered these men traveling agitators who used the gospel only as a way of livelihood (1 Timothy 6:5; Titus 1:11; cf. 1 Peter 5:2; 2 Peter 2:3). They probably had heard how believers in the first church at Jerusalem gave their property to the apostles for the welfare of the whole congregation (Acts 4:34,35). This may have prompted them to pass themselves off as apostles—thinking they also could obtain the property of believers by underhanded means. They saw the great power which Christianity had over the people and wanted to utilize the new religion for their own profit. To achieve their aim, they had to break the believers' trust in the apostles so they could take apostolic authority themselves. Of course, this was not easy in Jerusalem where the original apostles lived. They considered Paul's apostleship easier to attack, so it was natural that they concentrated their activity in the new Gentile churches he had founded.

However, the false apostles met obstacles in their attempts to gain an economic advantage in the church where Paul had carefully refrained from doing so. Their selfishness and love of money soon began to be seen. Partly in self-defense and partly to undermine Paul, they began their attacks on his authority by pointing to his practice of not receiving pay. They insinuated this actually showed that Paul himself realized he was not a real apostle and therefore could not claim the support to which an apostle was entitled. Paul had worked as a tentmaker with Aquila and Priscilla when he was in Corinth (Acts 18:1-3). Was this consistent with the calling and authority of an apostle? This would arouse suspicion especially among the Greeks, who looked down on manual laborers.

If Paul answered the charge by saying he had received financial help from other churches to support his work in Corinth (11:8,9), this could also be used against him. His opponents could say this was because Paul did not really care for the church in Corinth, so he did not want to feel any debt of gratitude toward them. Paul had to assure the Corinthians solemnly and call on God as his witness that he had no ulterior motives for not receiving pay from their church (11:11). False rumors and unjust accusations surrounded Paul. Behind them all stood the false apostles who were systematically trying to throw suspicion on him and destroy his influence.

In 1 Corinthians 9:4-18 Paul had already discussed the matter thoroughly. It should not be necessary for anyone to require further explanation. Paul declared the Lord had ordained that those who preach the gospel should live by the gospel. He emphasized that he had this privilege but did not always use it. There were times when he voluntarily chose to labor without pay from the church. The purity of Paul's motives shines through these words: "It were better for me to die, than that any man should make my glorying void" (1 Corinthians 9:15). We might wonder what made Paul use such strong language. In 2 Corinthians 11:10 he repeated the same thing in the form of an oath: "As the truth of Christ is in me, no man shall stop me of this boasting in the regions of Achaia." Here he continued giving the reasons for maintaining this practice: "But what I do, that I will do, that I may cut off occasion from them which desire occasion; that wherein they glory, they may be found even as we. For such are false apostles, deceitful workers, transforming themselves into the apostles of Christ" (11:12,13).

Paul thus declared emphatically that he would not receive any salary from the church for his work and this made it impossible for the false apostles to use him as an example when they used the church for their financial benefit. Of course, the matter of money was not Paul's sole reason for discussing this matter. The economic side of the controversy was secondary to the real issue, which was the religious activity of the false apostles. Paul focused on the subject of money because it was what enabled these men to continue destroying the church spiritually. The church was paying them for destroying the church! Paul would not consent to any arrangement which could contribute to a continuation of these conditions. He would not touch the Corinthians' money with one finger if it gave the heretics more advantage in squeezing money from the church for their evil purposes.

Two things are evident concerning these accusations and Paul's reaction to them.

First: The real character of the false apostles was revealed by their list of false accusations against an apostle and servant of the Lord. These men had not merely strayed from the truth; they were vicious and evil.

Second: The temper and spiritual quality of Paul's life never appeared more clearly than when he answered these accusations. One must possess much grace to react correctly to injustice, and Paul was able to do so. He did not assume an injured air nor refuse to give any reply or explanation—as a guilty person often does when he is called to account. On the contrary, Paul wrote a long letter—a small book in fact—in order to deal with the matter and assert his right to the Corinthians' respect for his apostolic ministry and authority. It must have been extremely painful to be forsaken by his friends as he was, but courageously and without sentimental complaints, Paul responded to the problem. He argued forcefully and with unquestioned honesty. He explained everything patiently and diligently. In fact, he used every kind of approach: He spoke sharply, he used sarcasm, he employed friendly persuasion. What else could he do? Just one thing remained and he would make use of that too. Now he proceeded to meet his opponents on their own ground.

B. Forced Self-Praise (11:22–12:19)

The false apostles in Corinth not only brought another gospel, they brought another spirit (11:4). Those who followed them were infected with the same spirit and became very confused. One of the most certain signs of this infection of spirit was their refusal to be persuaded by any kind of argument. Paul had addressed them intelligently and with careful instruction. But how can you speak sense to one who is overcome by folly? The Corinthians had debased themselves by following these intruders. They had been carried away by foolishness. This reflected on their own level of spirituality and intelligence.

Paul replied soberly and intelligently to the outrageous behavior of the false apostles. He followed the advice, "Answer not a fool according to his folly, lest thou also be like unto him." But this passage also says, "Answer a fool according to his folly, lest he be wise in his own conceit" (Proverbs 26:4,5). Both aspects of this counsel have their time and place. In the very difficult situation prevailing at Corinth, Paul tried both approaches. He had previously tried to convince the Corinthians with sensible talk; now he would try with folly!

The false apostles had deceived the Corinthians by their folly and boasting. Paul would not be a fool who enjoys boasting, which is the greatest folly of all (11:16). Paul's nature rebelled against such a spirit. Seven times in these two chapters he declared how foolish boasting is. It is not "after the Lord" nor according to the mind, example, and will of Christ (11:17). In fact, boasting is totally incompatible with the One who was of a gentle spirit and humble heart and who humbled himself in order to provide salvation to the lost. Paul was willing to try any approach to rescue the Corinthians from those who had taken them captive. If false apostles had been able to gain entrance to the Corinthian church by false boasting, why should Paul not be able to win them back by truthful boasting?

Of course it should have been totally unnecessary for Paul to praise himself to the Corinthians because they knew him so well. On the contrary, they ought to be praising him! Yet none of his old friends in the church seemed to be willing to say a kind word for him to counteract the criticism and gossip, so they had forced him to commend himself (12:11). Paul did this very thoroughly, and the Holy Spirit inspired the inclusion of this teaching in the Scriptures. This is because it applied not only to the Corinthians at that time but to believers at all times when they are in danger of being seduced by boasting teachers of error.

The forced self-praise of Paul falls into four sections with their sub-sections. He boasted of his Jewish background, his sufferings as a servant of Christ, his revelations of truth, and finally of his weakness—his *real* self-praise.

1. Jewish background (11:22). Paul's opponents had capitalized on their Jewish ancestry. It might seem strange that this had such great appeal in a Gentile church like Corinth where Jewish members were in the minority. However, a traveling preacher's Jewish background gave him some advantages. Jesus was a Jew according to the flesh and the gospel had come from the Jews. The first disciples of Jesus were Jews. The Church's Bible at that time was the Old Testament, a Jewish book, and the great events of salvation history had taken place in the land of the Jews.

Paul used three expressions for the intruders' claim to authority because of their Jewish descent:

(1) "Are they Hebrews?" he asked and replied immediately, "So am I." Usually the word *Hebrew* is used to distinguish Jews from Gentiles. In this sense Paul was "an Hebrew of the Hebrews" (Philippians 3:5). He was born in Tarsus but had been brought up in Jerusalem and was educated at the feet of Gamaliel (Acts 22:3), so he could not be called a Jew of the diaspora in the real sense of the word. In race and religion Paul was a Hebrew. If someone could "have confidence in the flesh," he could have even more confidence (Philippians 3:4-6). In Acts 6:1 the term *Hebrew* is used to identify the Jews of Palestine who spoke Aramaic in contrast to the Greek-speaking Jews of the diaspora. It is evident from Acts 22:2 that Paul understood and spoke Aramaic. Hugo Odeberg maintains that the word *Hebrew* in 11:22 refers to being able to understand and speak the Hebrew language rather than the popular Aramaic. To master the basic language of the Old Testament was a mark of education and theological skill. Paul could study the Hebrew Old Testament and he could also preach a sermon in the Aramaic language which was spoken in Jerusalem. In no way was he inferior to the false apostles in Corinth, even though they acted as Jewish scribes.

(2) "Are they Israelites?" This is a term for the people of the covenant, "to whom pertaineth the adoption, and the glory, and the covenants, and the giving of the law, and the service of God, and the promises; whose are the fathers, and of whom as concerning the flesh Christ came" (Romans 9:4,5). Paul belonged to God's covenant people and not merely in the outward meaning of the expression. He was an Israelite in the true sense of the word. He did not lose his rights as an Israelite by becoming a Christian. On the contrary, "They are not all Israel, which are of Israel" (Romans 9:6).

(3) "Are they the seed of Abraham?" This identifies Israel as the people of the promise who participate in the blessing which God gave to Abraham and his descendants. In reply to the intruders' claims that they were Abraham's children, Paul replied, "So am I." However, he had just called these false apostles the servants of Satan (11:14,15). This passage is somewhat of a parallel to Jesus' discussion with the Pharisees in John 8:33. The Pharisees insisted they were Abraham's children, but Jesus said their father was the devil. The assertion of these false apostles that they were the children of Abraham was in fact a fraud. Abraham's children are those who have his faith (Romans 4:12; Galatians 3:7). Paul was not inferior to his op-

ponents in any manner. He was of Abraham's race, not just after the flesh but one of Abraham's spiritual children, an heir of the promises given to him (Galatians 3:9,29).

2. Paul's Suffering (11:23-33). The false apostles called themselves Christ's servants, but Paul had just called them the servants of Satan (11:13-15). He gave reasons why he was much more entitled than they to be called a servant of Christ. He had not only labored more than these men, he had endured more suffering and persecutions, and this more than anything else marks a true servant of Christ: "The servant is not greater than his lord. If they have persecuted me, they will also persecute you" (John 15:20). Actually Paul was completely wiping out the claims of these deceivers to apostleship. In short, concise sentences without sentimentality or extra elaboration, Paul showed that God had a plan for his life from the very beginning: "I will show him how great things he must suffer for my name's sake" (Acts 9:16).

a. Christian activity (11:23). When Paul said he had worked more, this must be understood in the proper context. He was not comparing his labors to the insignificant efforts of his opponents, which Paul easily surpassed. The very nature of his work was great and worthy of comparison with the efforts of anyone else. He had worked more than any of the original apostles, but he quickly added that it was the grace of God, not his natural ability, which accomplished so much. He had written about this to the Corinthians earlier (1 Corinthians 15:10).

b. Persecution (11:23-25). Paul then listed his sufferings. He had alluded earlier in this epistle to what he had undergone (4:8-10; 6:4-10), but now he gave details.

(1) Many times he had been imprisoned. From Acts 16 we have knowledge of one imprisonment before this epistle was written. This was in Philippi, but there were more imprisonments, including one at Ephesus, where there are ruins of a tower which from ancient times has been called "the prison of Paul." Later on there were times of imprisonment in Caesarea and Rome. Clement of Rome wrote that Paul was in prison seven times.

(2) Paul suffered corporal punishment from Jewish and Roman authorities several times. Five times he was punished by the Jewish lash, "forty stripes save one." That means in the most severe form possible. The Law stipulated that 40 stripes were the most which could be given (Deuteronomy 25:1-3). To be certain they did not exceed the limit of the Law, the Jews stopped with the 39th stripe. Paul was beaten three times by Roman authorities. He says concerning his punishment that it was *huperballontōs*, i.e., "immensely" or "beyond every reasonable limit."

(3) Once he had been stoned. According to Acts 14:19,20 this took place in Lystra during Paul's first missionary journey. The people who stoned Paul thought he was dead and dragged him outside the city, but while the disciples crowded around him, he stood up.

(4) He was often in deadly danger. In 1 Corinthians 15:30 Paul said he stood in jeopardy each day; in fact, he "died daily." In Romans 8:36,37 he quoted the Psalmist's words: "For thy sake we are killed all the day long; we are accounted as sheep for the slaughter." But he testified, "In all these things we are more than conquerors through him that loved us."

c. Perils and danger (11:25,26). Paul said he suffered shipwreck three times. Later he experienced the same thing on his voyage to Rome. During one of the shipwrecks it seems he floated around on the wreckage for 24 hours. When he remembered what he had experienced on his journeys it was too much to be described in detail, so he wrote: "In perils of waters, in perils of robbers, in perils by mine own countrymen, in perils by the heathen, in perils in the city, in perils in the wilderness, in perils in the sea, in perils among false brethren . . . ."

d. False brethren (11:26). Besides all these difficulties and conflict with enemies outside the Church, Paul also had perils from false brethren. The first church had its traitors, counterfeit believers who spied on the others and could thus become their accusers (cf. Matthew 24:10). The Judaizing heretics followed Paul's steps like a shadow, and they bore a deadly hatred toward him. False brethren had now found their way to Corinth. From what Paul wrote, it seems he considered them a danger to himself personally. However, he had decided to visit the church at Corinth anyway. He was the great missionary to the Gentiles who founded new churches everywhere. It seems strange to read that so much of his time had to be diverted from soul-winning work to fighting against these false brethren who spied on the churches and constantly looked for reasons to attack Paul.

e. A life filled with trouble (11:27). "In weariness and painfulness." This is how Paul characterized his life. He was not one who took his heavenly rest in advance! Wakeful nights often followed busy days. He knew hunger and thirst, cold and nakedness. Besides spiritual duties, he often had to work for his living, not only for personal necessities but also to have something to give those in need (Acts 20:34).

f. Church work (11:28,29). In addition to everything else, Paul had the daily supervision of members of the church and the care of the other churches. Concerning his stay in Ephesus he said, "Remember, that by the space of three years I ceased not to warn every one night and day with tears" (Acts 20:31). "Who is weak, and I am not weak? who is offended and I burn not?" (11:29). From his co-workers Paul received constant reports from the churches and kept in touch with them through his epistles. These epistles, as we know, form a large part of the New Testament. They were written originally to meet some urgent need in the Church or to answer spiritual questions, yet for nearly 2,000 years they have been the source of blessing to all Christians.

The man who wrote these epistles stood head and shoulders above his critics. Daily he carried the load of responsibility for the churches. Must he be considered suspect because of his opponents' accusations? Surely such questions must have arisen among the Corinthians when they read his words of forced self-praise.

g. Damascus (11:32,33). At first it seems Paul has ended his list of sufferings with the solemn assurance that he spoke the truth (11:31). But in 11:32,33 he continued by telling how in Damascus during the early days of his ministry, he avoided the guards of King Aretas who, with the Jews, kept watch at the city gate in order to seize him. Aretas was an Arab who ruled the area between the Red Sea and Euphrates River. Perhaps Paul had incurred Aretas' wrath after his stay in Arabia (cf. Galatians 1:17). When we compare Paul's statement in that verse with Acts 9:23-25, it seems that both the Jews and the people of King Aretas had combined their efforts in order to capture Paul. He avoided them because one night he was lowered in a basket outside the city wall. We can be certain that Paul could never forget that experience, which was the beginning of a long series of persecutions he met later. Now he added this at the end of his list, even though it should have been at the front. He mentioned all these situations to remind his friends in Corinth that through-

out his entire life as a Christian, he had endured persecution for preaching Jesus Christ.

3. Revelations (12:1-6). "I will come to visions and revelations," Paul wrote as he continued his forced self-praise. One should be careful about telling others of experiences the Lord has given him for his personal spiritual benefit. Paul's visions and revelations were not given in order to glorify him. On the contrary, they marked the beginning of humiliation that lasted the rest of his life in the form of a painful "thorn in the flesh." He said this happened so he would not boast of what he had experienced. Paul now laid bare what was the most personal aspect of his life, his most intimate feelings, as he discussed experiences which brought him both pain and blessing.

Why did Paul reveal these spiritual secrets? Why did he allow the accusations of his enemies to force from him what he had carried inside himself for so long? It was because of the concern he had for his spiritual children in Corinth. They would naturally expect an apostle to tell of his visions and revelations. They could not understand why he did not answer his antagonists by revealing these special experiences. No doubt the false apostles had claimed special religious experiences of their own and thus were of the number who were "intruding into those things which he hath not seen" (cf. Colossians 2:18), thus building up their own reputation and deceiving unsuspecting believers. It was in "competition" with these pseudo-prophets that Paul now told how the Lord had spoken directly to him in special revelations.

Of course it was known that Paul had visions, although he was slow to tell of them. His opponents had possibly said the "vision" on which he based his call to apostleship was only a delusion. Paul had many visions, some of which are referred to in Acts: The vision of Ananias in Damascus (9:12), the vision in the temple (22:17-21), the vision in Troas (16:9), the vision in Corinth (18:9), the vision during his last visit in Jerusalem (23:11), the vision during the voyage to Rome (27:23). In most of these visions the Lord himself appeared to Paul. There were two revelations which Paul placed in a particular class. One was "the heavenly vision" (26:19) on the way to Damascus. Paul did not consider this an experience of ecstasy like his vision in the temple (22:17), but an actual experience of Christ like His revelations to the disciples after the Resurrection (1 Corinthians 15:7). This vision of the risen Christ on the Damascus Road was the basis of Paul's apostleship.

The other revelation which Paul placed in a particular class is the one he now recounts to the Corinthians. This was not an experience of ecstasy like the vision in the temple. On this occasion he was "caught up," *harpagenta*. The same word is used in Acts 8:39 concerning Philip when he was caught away and found in Azotus. It is used also in 1 Thessalonians 4:17 concerning those who are caught up at the return of the Lord, and in Revelation 12:5 to describe the male child's being caught up to the throne of God. What Paul experienced seems similar to the vision on the Damascus Road, except that on that occasion the Lord descended and revealed himself to Paul, while in this experience Paul was caught up into the heavenly world where he heard words he could not repeat. To Paul it was easy to believe he was caught away bodily but he was not certain: "Whether in the body, I cannot tell; or whether out of the body, I cannot tell" (12:2).

Paul said he was caught up into the third heaven. The Jews had formed concepts of many "heavens," and this idea carried over to the New Testament (cf. Ephesians 4:10). From 1 Kings 8:27 some have concluded there are three heavens. Later Jewish and apocalyptic writings speak of seven heavens. We cannot be sure whether Paul thought the third heaven was the highest one. Scholars differ in their opinions (cf. Tasker, *Tyndale New Testament Commentaries*, 8:169-172; and Bruce, *New Century Bible*, 38:245-247). One might judge Paul's experience from rare ones which seem to resemble his. In this case, being caught up may indicate passing through several spheres (Odeberg).

Paul also spoke of being caught up into paradise, so it seems he used this word synonymously with the third heaven. *Paradise* is originally a Persian word which means "park," and the word was taken into both Hebrew and Greek. In the Septuagint—the Greek translation of the Old Testament—"paradise" is used for the Garden of Eden. In the New Testament the word is used to describe the dwelling place of believers after death (Luke 23:43) and for the new Garden of Eden (Revelation 2:7). The Jews believed that after the Fall, paradise was removed from earth to be protected in heaven by God. This belief may form the background of the final visions in the Book of Revelation where the New Jerusalem comes down from heaven, from God, and conditions of paradise are established (Revelation 21). What Paul experienced was thus a real foretaste of life in eternity.

Paul said nothing of what he saw in paradise, but he did hear "unspeakable words." They were unspeakable because they could not be expressed in human words. They were too holy for a human to try to repeat them. In the Greek word *exon*, translated "not lawful," both meanings are implied. In Daniel 12:4-10 and Revelation 10:2-4 we have other instances where a prophet was not permitted to make known what he had seen. The knowledge Paul received through this revelation was meant only for him.

He did not mention this experience until 14 years later and he did it then with hesitation and restraint. He did not rush to make it known the same day it happened! He was called to preach the gospel of Christ, not his visions. This vision, however, must have meant a great deal to Paul personally. If Second Corinthians was written in A.D. 56, Paul had this great experience during the quiet years in Tarsus, perhaps not long before Barnabas visited him. Before Paul began his first missionary journey and his ministry as the apostle to the Gentiles, he may have seen the throne of God like Isaiah and other special messengers of God.

"Of such an one will I glory!" Paul said. He had not deserved such revelations; they were only manifestations of God's grace to him. It is apparently for this reason that he used the third person and called himself "a man in Christ," as though to distance this "man" from himself. Not all Christians receive such visions and revelations, but each "man in Christ" shall one day participate by undeserved grace in the heavenly glory of which Paul received a foretaste.

4. The Thorn in the Flesh (12:7-10). Probably Paul could have related many visions and revelations, but he stopped with just one. "Now I forbear," he wrote (12:6). He did not want the Corinthians to think too highly of him because of these unusual experiences. And he had received something which kept *him* humble—a thorn in the flesh. Whatever it was, Paul called it Satan's messenger who kept striking him so he did not become too exalted because of his revelations. A great deal of speculation has centered around the identity of this thorn, but no real answer has been found.

The Greek words Paul used are not easy to interpret. *Skolops* (translated "thorn") in classical Greek meant a pole or stake. It is close to *stauros,* translated "cross" in 1 Corinthians 1:18 and many other passages. In time, *skolops* came to mean frequently a thorn like the term used mainly in the Septuagint (Numbers 33:55; Ezekiel 28:24; Hosea 2:6).

Sarx is the Greek word translated "flesh" in this verse. If "in the flesh" is the correct translation, this seems to refer to the physical body and this has influenced the interpretation that the thorn was some kind of bodily weakness. If it should be translated "for the flesh," it would be more natural to understand "flesh" as the fallen human nature—an expression Paul used often in his writing. If this is the correct interpretation, the thorn could be anything that hinders the tendency of the human nature to exalt itself. These different views of the correct translation have divided the interpreters into two main groups and both have had their spokesmen from ancient times to the present.

Tertullian is the first who supported the view of the thorn's being a sickness. Some scholars have thought he was building on tradition. In more recent theology this view has probably become predominant. Several kinds of "diagnosis" have been made: (1) Tertullian and Hieronymus: headache and earache. (2) J.T. Brown (1858): inflammation of the eyes. (3) M. Krengel and J. Klausner: epilepsy. (4) M. Dibelius: convulsive attacks. (5) W.M. Ramsay and E.B. Allo: malaria. (6) H. Clavier: depression. Some have also thought the verse meant Paul was physically disfigured.

From these views, one would think Satan had been allowed to strike Paul with some kind of painful sickness or bodily weakness as he did Job. Some quote Galatians 4:12-15 to support this view, pointing out that Paul reminds the readers it was because of a sickness that he first came to Galatia. Adherents to this interpretation understand "infirmity of the flesh" as synonymous with "a thorn in the flesh."

The second main division of interpretations is just as varied. Church fathers like Augustine, Chrysostom, and others thought the thorn referred to persecutions by Jews who stirred up opposition to Paul everywhere he went. Roman Catholic scholars of early times thought Paul was struggling with the sexual temptations that attacked monks and hermits. The reformers would not accept such an opinion. Calvin thought the thorn included all kinds of temptation to which the fallen nature is prone (*Calvin's Commentaries, Corinthians,* p.273). Luther limited the temptations to the internal

spiritual kind, i.e., doubts and blasphemous thoughts inspired by Satan, but he also thought outward persecutions had to be included (*Luther's Works,* 26:420f.).

Among modern commentators, Tasker belongs to the group who find it most reasonable that the thorn refers to attacks from opponents (*Tyndale New Testament Commentaries,* 8:177) (cf. Numbers 33:55 where the Scripture says the Canaanites would be troublesome to Israel like "thorns in your sides"). Beasley-Murray believes the thorn stands for Satan's accusations against Paul because of his earlier persecution of the Church. As support, he uses 1 Corinthians 15:9,10 and 2 Corinthians 12:7-9—two passages which contrast Paul's guilt to the grace of God. This thought can perhaps be developed further. If the thorn or stake in Paul's flesh was inner guilt over his persecution of the Church, this may throw light on the Lord's words to him on the Damascus Road: "Saul, Saul, why persecutest thou me? it is hard for thee to kick against the pricks" (Acts 26:14). Nothing indicates that Paul kicked against any "pricks" before his conversion. Neither is there any indication that the Lord used a "prick" to force him to be saved. When Jesus revealed himself to Paul and spoke to him, he asked immediately, "What shall I do, Lord?" (Acts 22:10). But it is evident from 1 Timothy 1:12-16 that the memory of that persecution period had been tormenting Paul throughout his later life. With this in mind he even went so far as to say (like his opponents) that he was not worthy to be called an apostle. It is only the grace of God which had made him what he is.

In Gethsemane Jesus prayed three times that the cup of agony should pass from Him. Three times Paul prayed to be delivered from his thorn. Disciples learn obedience through suffering just as their Master did. They learn to pray the greatest of all prayers: "Thy will be done!" As Jesus through His suffering and death in weakness (1 Corinthians 1:25) revealed the power of God for salvation, His apostle found that in his weakness the power of God was revealed. The climax of this passage is in the Lord's word of comfort for His servant: "My grace is sufficient for thee; for my strength is made perfect in weakness" (12:9). Then Paul declared his satisfaction was not in his own ability or strength, but his incapability (3:5) and weakness. "Most gladly therefore will I rather glory in my infirmities, that the power of Christ may rest upon me" (12:9).

5. The Signs of an Apostle (12:11,12). As Paul reached the climax of his praise, he boasted of his infirmities. He was at least greater in weakness than the false apostles! And because of this weakness the power of Christ worked through him.

The Corinthians had forced Paul to this folly of comparing himself to his opponents. Now he continued by asserting that he was not behind "the very chiefest apostles" in anything.

Just one point remains. Some would probably say it is the most important one, but Paul finished it with only a few lines. It concerns the question of a real apostle's characteristics. "The signs of an apostle" include the entire supernatural equipment which God gives an apostle. This includes what Paul mentioned in his summary: signs and wonders and powerful works. These signs had followed Paul during his entire service as an apostle (Acts 13:8-12; 14:3; 15:12; 19:11,12; Romans 15:18,19). But Paul did not list here all the signs which had followed his ministry. He referred to what should be the plainest evidence of all—the supernatural works the Corinthians themselves have seen. However, they must not think more highly of Paul than they ought to just because of these mighty works (12:6). False apostles and imposters might use signs and wonders as advertisements, but not a true servant of the Lord.

Signs, wonders, and miracles or powerful works are not meant as three different manifestations of supernatural power. Paul was simply discussing miraculous works from three different points of view. The same expression is used of Jesus (Acts 2:22) and of God's confirmation of the salvation message (Hebrews 2:3,4). However, it is not God's will that believers should follow every wonderworker. In the last days the Antichrist will use signs and wonders to deceive people (2 Thessalonians 2:9). Jesus said that on the Day of Judgment many will point to mighty works they have performed in His name, yet they will be rejected (Matthew 7:22,23). It appears that the false apostles in Corinth belonged to this group.

Signs and wonders are an indication of God's stamp of approval on a ministry only when they appear in the right context. They must be part of a total picture where sound doctrine and the fear of God are also given their rightful place. This had always been Paul's position. During trials and opposition of all kinds he had performed these works of power patiently and per-

sistently. Those wonders did indeed belong to "the signs of an apostle."

C. Final Admonition (12:13–13:14)

Paul had explained to his readers what his apostolic service consisted of and he had defended his apostolic authority. The controversy with opponents is ended. The epistle is almost finished. Paul concludes with some final and personal admonitions which should bless the church.

1. Paul's Readiness (12:13-19). In a way, Paul was back at the starting point. In the beginning of the epistle he had to defend himself against those who accused him of unreliability because of postponing his visit to Corinth. Some had probably indicated he did not dare come at all. Now he assured the church, "The third time I am ready to come to you" (12:14).

Thinking of the visit which now was drawing near, Paul mentioned once more that he did not receive financial support from the church. With friendly irony he said this was the only injustice he had committed against the Corinthians and asked them to forgive the "injustice." However, he did not promise any change of methods. He would not receive their gifts this time either because he wanted much more than money, i.e., themselves. He was their spiritual father and it was a parent's duty to gather for his children, the apostle says. He willingly offered all to them even though the result might be that the more he loved them, the less they loved him (13:15). Here we notice some of Paul's inner pain at their attitude, and it reminds us of his words to the Galatians: "Am I therefore become your enemy, because I tell you the truth?" (Galatians 4:16).

2. Paul's Fear (12:20–13:5). In deep earnest Paul then turned toward the church and uttered his fear that something was wrong with many of them. He mentioned especially two kinds of sin. First he wrote in 12:20 of a series of sins against the commandment to love, which was destroying the unity and solidarity of the church. In 12:21 he spoke of sins against the commandments of purity.

Paul said that to him it would be a great humiliation if it should turn out that the Corinthians did not stand the test. He had called this church his "praise" (1:14), his epistle of commendation (3:1), "the seal" of his apostleship (1 Corinthians 9:2). And what then if all his work should be a failure!

Hitherto Paul had been mild and restrained

among them, but this time he would not show leniency toward the unrepentant. So he asked them all to examine their own hearts to see if they were in the faith.

3. Paul's Trust (13:6-10). In spite of his fears, Paul hoped for better things. He trusted the Corinthians were aware that he would not be restrained this time. He may have implied that the judging and punishing of sin was one way that apostolic authority can be demonstrated. However, he was not limiting the purpose of his visit to such judgment and punishment. Actually, he considered this a humiliating defeat because it meant passing sentence on his own work (Meyer). What he hoped was that the church itself would examine itself carefully and be ready to pass the test when he saw them. Paul, too, would pass the test when his work stands (13:6,7). Therefore he wrote so they could have the opportunity to correct what was wrong. Then during his visit he could use the power the Lord had given him to build up, not break down. This was the real purpose for which he had received the power.

4. Greeting and Blessing (13:11-14). The conclusion of the epistle is very short, but the words are warm and filled with love. There are no personal greetings to or from certain persons. Perhaps he did not want to name them in an epistle to a church that had such serious problems. Yet in spite of all his stern words, Paul greeted the readers as Christian brethren.

The final words have been called the apostolic blessing, different from Aaron's blessing (Numbers 6:24-26). The apostolic blessing is trinitarian. The epistles to the Corinthians are among the earliest in the New Testament. So we have here one of the earliest testimonies in the New Testament to the faith of the Early Church in a triune God: "The grace of the Lord Jesus Christ, and the love of God, and the communion of the Holy Ghost, be with you all" (13:14).

Manuscripts

Egyptian Papyri

Note: (a) designates the section of the New Testament on which the manuscript is based; (b) designates the century in which it is believed the manuscript was written (using the Roman numerals); (c) provides information on the present location of the manuscript.

p1 (a) Gospels; (b) III; (c) Philadelphia, University of Pennsylvania Museum, no. E2746.

p2 (a) Gospels; (b) VI; (c) Florence, Museo Archeologico, Inv. no. 7134.

p3 (a) Gospels; (b) VI, VII; (c) Vienna, Österreichische Nationalbibliothek, Sammlung Papyrus Erzherzog Rainer, no. G2323.

p4 (a) Gospels; (b) III; (c) Paris, Bibliothèque Nationale, no. Gr. 1120, suppl. 2⁰.

p5 (a) Gospels; (b) III; (c) London, British Museum, P. 782 and P. 2484.

p6 (a) Gospels; (b) IV; (c) Strasbourg, Bibliothèque de la Université, 351ʳ, 335ᵛ, 379, 381, 383, 384 copt.

p7 (a) Gospels; (b) V; (c) now lost, was in Kiev, library of the Ukrainian Academy of Sciences.

p8 (a) Acts; (b) IV; (c) now lost; was in Berlin, Staatliche Museen, P. 8683.

p9 (a) General Epistles; (b) III; (c) Cambridge, Massachusetts, Harvard University, Semitic Museum, no. 3736.

p10 (a) Paul's Epistles; (b) IV; (c) Cambridge, Massachusetts, Harvard University, Semitic Museum, no. 2218.

p11 (a) Paul's Epistles; (b) VII; (c) Leningrad, State Public Library.

p12 (a) General Epistles; (b) late III; (c) New York, Pierpont Morgan Library, no. G. 3.

p13 (a) General Epistles; (b) III, IV; (c) London, British Museum, P. 1532 (verso), and Florence, Biblioteca Medicea Laurenziana.

p14 (a) Paul's Epistles; (b) V (?); (c) Mount Sinai, St. Catharine's Monastery, no. 14.

p15 (a) Paul's Epistles; (b) III; (c) Cairo, Museum of Antiquities, no. 47423.

p16 (a) Paul's Epistles; (b) III, IV; (c) Cairo, Museum of Antiquities, no. 47424.

p17 (a) General Epistles; (b) IV; (c) Cambridge, England, University Library, gr. theol. f. 13 (P), Add. 5893.

p18 (a) Revelation; (b) III, IV; (c) London, British Museum, P. 2053 (verso).

p19 (a) Gospels; (b) IV, V; (c) Oxford, Bodleian Library, MS. Gr. bibl. d. 6 (P.).

p20 (a) General Epistles; (b) III; (c) Princeton, New Jersey, University Library, Classical Seminary AM 4117 (15).

p21 (a) Gospels; (b) IV, V; (c) Allentown, Pennsylvania, Library of Muhlenberg College, Theol. Pap. 3.

p22 (a) Gospels; (b) III; (c) Glasgow, University Library, MS. 2-x. 1.

p23 (a) General Epistles; (b) early III; (c) Urbana, Illinois, University of Illinois, Classical Archaeological and Art Museum, G. P. 1229.

p24 (a) Revelation; (b) IV; (c) Newton Center, Massachusetts, Library of Andover Newton Theological School.

p25 (a) Gospels; (b) late IV; (c) now lost, was in Berlin, Staatliche Museen, P. 16388.

p26 (a) Paul's Epistles; (b) c. 600; (c) Dallas, Texas, Southern Methodist University, Lane Museum.

p27 (a) Paul's Epistles; (b) III; (c) Cambridge, England, University Library, Add. MS. 7211.

p28 (a) Gospels; (b) III; (c) Berkeley, California, Library of Pacific School of Religion, Pap. 2.

p29 (a) Acts; (b) III; (c) Oxford, Bodleian Library, MS. Gr. bibl. g. 4 (P.).

p30 (a) Paul's Epistles; (b) III; (c) Ghent, University Library, U. Lib. P. 61.

p31 (a) Paul's Epistles; (b) VII; (c) Manchester, England, John Rylands Library, P. Ryl. 4.

p32 (a) Paul's Epistles; (b) c. 200; (c) Manchester England, John Rylands Library, P. Ryl. 5.

p33 (a) Acts; (b) VI; (c) Vienna, Österreichische Nationalbibliothek, no. 190.

p34 (a) Paul's Epistles; (b) VII; (c) Vienna, Österreichische Nationalbibliothek, no. 191.

p35 (a) Gospels; (b) IV (?); (c) Florence, Biblioteca Medicea Laurenziana.

p36 (a) Gospels; (b) VI; (c) Florence, Biblioteca Medicea Laurenziana.

p37 (a) Gospels; (b) III, IV; (c) Ann Arbor, Michigan, University of Michigan Library, Invent. no. 1570.

p38 (a) Acts; (b) c. 300; (c) Ann Arbor, Michigan, University of Michigan Library, Invent. no. 1571.

p39 (a) Gospels; (b) III; (c) Chester, Pennsylvania, Crozer Theological Seminary Library, no. 8864.

p40 (a) Paul's Epistles; (b) III; (c) Heidelberg, Universitätsbibliothek, Inv. Pap. graec. 45.

p41 (a) Acts; (b) VIII; (c) Vienna, Österreichische Nationalbibliothek, Pap. K.7541-8.

p42 (a) Gospels; (b)VII, VIII; (c) Vienna, Österreichische Nationalbibliothek, KG 8706.

p43 (a) Revelation; (b) VI, VII; (c) London, British Museum, Pap. 2241.

p44 (a) Gospels; (b) VI, VII; (c) New York, Metropolitan Museum of Art, Inv. 14-1-527.

p45 (a) Gospels, Acts; (b) III; (c) Dublin, Chester Beatty Museum; and Vienna, Österreichische Nationalbibliothek, P. Gr. Vind. 31974.

p46 (a) Paul's Epistles; (b) c. 200; (c) Dublin, Chester Beatty Museum, and Ann Arbor, Michigan, University of Michigan Library, Invent. no. 6238.

p47 (a) Revelation; (b) late III; (c) Dublin, Chester Beatty Museum.

p48 (a) Acts; (b) late III; (c) Florence, Museo Medicea Laurenziana.

p49 (a) Paul's Epistles; (b) late III; (c) New Haven, Connecticut, Yale University Library, P. 415.

p50 (a) Acts; (b) IV, V; (c) New Haven, Connecticut, Yale University Library, P. 1543.

p51 (a) Paul's Epistles; (b) c. 400; (c) London British Museum.

p52 (a) Gospels; (b) early II; (c) Manchester, John Rylands Library, P. Ryl. Gr. 457.

p53 (a) Gospels, Acts; (b) III; (c) Ann Arbor, Michigan, University of Michigan Library, Invent. no. 6652.

p54 (a) General Epistles; (b) V, VI; (c) Princeton, New Jersey, Princeton University Library, Garrett Depos. 7742.

p55 (a) Gospels; (b) VI, VII; (c) Vienna, Österreichische Nationalbibliothek, P. Gr. Vind. 26214.

p56 (a) Acts; (b) V, VI; (c) Vienna, Österreichische Nationalbibliothek, P. Gr. Vind. 19918.

p57 (a) Acts; (b) IV, V; (c) Vienna, Österreichische Nationalbibliothek, P. Gr. Vind. 26020.

p58 (a) Acts; (b) VI; (c) Vienna, Österreichische Nationalbibliothek, P. Gr. Vind. 17973, 36133⁵⁴, and 35831.

p59 (a) Gospels; (b) VII; (c) New York, New York University, Washington Square College of Arts and Sciences, Department of Classics, P. Colt. 3.

p60 (a) Gospels; (b) VII; (c) New York, New York University, Washington Square College of Arts and Sciences, Department of Classics, P. Colt. 4.

p61 (a) Paul's Epistles; (b) c. 700; (c) New York, New York University, Washington Square College of Arts and Sciences, Department of Classics, P. Colt. 5.

p62 (a) Gospels; (b) IV; (c) Oslo, University Library.

p63 (a) Gospels; (b) c. 500; (c) Berlin, Staatliche Museen.

p64 (a) Gospels; (b) c. 200; (c) Oxford, Magdalen College Library.

p65 (a) Paul's Epistles; (b) III; (c) Florence, Biblioteca Medicea Laurenziana.

p66 (a) Gospels; (b) c. 200; (c) Cologny/ Genève, Bibliothèque Bodmer.

p67 (a) Gospels; (b) c. 200; (c) Barcelona, Fundación San Lucas Evangelista, P. Barc. 1.

p68 (a) Paul's Epistles; (b) VII (?); (c) Leningrad, State Public Library, Gr. 258.

p69 (a) Gospels; (b) III; (c) place (?)

p70 (a) Gospels; (b) III; (c) place (?)

p71 (a) Gospels; (b) IV; (c) place (?)

p72 (a) General Epistles; (b) III, IV; (c) Cologny/Genève, Bibliothèque Bodmer.

p73 (a) Gospels; (b)—; (c) Cologny/Genève, Bibliothèque Bodmer.

p74 (a) Acts, General Epistles; (b) VII; (c) Cologny/Genève, Bibliothèque Bodmer.

p75 (a) Gospels; (b) early III; (c) Cologny/ Genève, Bibliothèque Bodmer.

p76 (a) Gospels; (b) VI; (c) Vienna, Österreichische Nationalbibliothek, P. Gr. Vind. 36102.

Major Codices

01, aleph:	Sinaiticus
02, A:	Alexandrinus
03, B:	Vaticanus
04, C:	Ephraemi Rescriptus
05, D:	Bezae Cantabrigiensis
06, E:	Claromontanus

Majuscules

No.		Contents	Century
01,	*aleph*	Total New Testament	4th
02,	A	Total New Testament	5th
03,	B	New Testament, Revelation	4th
04,	C	Total New Testament	5th
05,	D	Gospels, Acts	6th
06,	D	Paul's Epistles	6th
07,	E	Gospels	8th
08,	E	Acts	6th
09,	F	Gospels	9th
010,	F	Paul's Epistles	9th
011,	G	Gospels	9th
012,	G	Paul's Epistles	9th
013,	H	Gospels	9th
015,	H	Paul's Epistles	6th
016,	I	Paul's Epistles	5th
017,	K	Gospels	9th
018,	K	Acts, Paul's Epistles	9th
019,	L	Gospels	8th
020,	L	Acts, Paul's Epistles	9th
021,	M	Gospels	9th
022,	N	Gospels	6th
023,	O	Gospels	6th
024,	P	Gospels	6th
025,	P	Acts, Paul's Epistles, Revelation	9th
026,	Q	Gospels	5th
028,	S	Gospels	10th
029,	T	Gospels	9th
030,	U	Gospels	9th
031,	V	Gospels	9th
032,	W	Gospels	5th
033,	X	Gospels	10th
034,	Y	Gospels	9th
036,		Gospels	10th
037,		Gospels	9th
038,		Gospels	9th
039,		Gospels	9th
040,		Gospels	6th-8th
041,		Gospels	9th
042,		Gospels	6th
043,		Gospels	6th
044,		Gospels, Acts, Paul's Epistles	8th-9th

In addition to these manuscripts identified by a letter (letter uncials), there are 200 other numbered majuscule manuscripts. Even though most of these manuscripts are very valuable, there is not enough room to list them all. Our apparatus gives the official numbers, 046, 047 etc.

Minuscules

There are about 2800 of these. A total classification of these is only possible in specialized literature dealing with textual criticism.

Early Versions

it	Itala, early Latin	II-IV
vul	Vulgate	IV-V
old syr	Old Syrian	II-III
syr pesh	"peshitta"	V
got	Gothic	IV
arm	Armenian	IV-V
geo	Georgian	V
cop	Coptic	VI
nub	Nubian	VI
eth	Ethiopian	VI

Early Church Fathers

Ambrosius, deacon of Alexandria, and intimate friend of Origen, died 250.

Athanasius, was bishop of Alexandria, 326; died in 373.

Athenagoras, a Christian philosopher of Athens, flourished in 178.

Augustine, 354-430.

Basil the Great, bishop of Caesarea, born in Cappadocia, 329; died 379.

Bede, the Venerable, born 673.

Chrysostom, bishop of Constantinople, born 344; died 407.

Clemens Alexandrinus, Clement of Alexandria, the preceptor of Origen, died 212.

Clemens Romanus, Clement of Rome, *supposed* to have been fellow laborer with Peter and Paul, and bishop of Rome, 91.

Cyprian, bishop of Carthage, in 248; was martyred, 258.

Cyrillus Alexandrinus, this Cyril was patriarch of Alexandria 412; died 444.

Cyrillus Hierosolymitanus, Cyril, bishop of Jerusalem, was born 315; died 386.

Ephraim Syrus, Ephraim the Syrian, was deacon of Edessa; and died 373.

Eusebius of Caesarea, c.260-340.

Gregory the Great, bishop of Rome, flourished in 590.

Gregory Thaumaturgus, was a disciple of Origen, and bishop of Neocaesarea in 240.

Hippolytus, a Christian bishop, flourished 230; died 235.

Ignatius, bishop of Antioch, was martyred about 110.

Irenaeus, disciple of Polycarp; born in Greece about 140; martyred 202.

Jerome, also called Hieronymus, one of the most eminent of the Latin fathers; author of the translation of the Scriptures called the Vulgate; born about 342, died in 420.

Justin Martyr, a Christian philosopher, martyred 165.

Origen, one of the most eminent of the Greek fathers, 185-254.

Tertullian, a most eminent Latin father, died about 220.

Books of the New and Old Testament and the Apocrypha

New Testament Books

Matthew
Mark
Luke
John
Acts
Romans
1 Corinthians
2 Corinthians
Galatians
Ephesians
Philippians
Colossians
1 Thessalonians
2 Thessalonians
1 Timothy
2 Timothy
Titus
Philemon
Hebrews
James
1 Peter
2 Peter
1 John
2 John
3 John
Jude
Revelation

Old Testament Books

Genesis
Exodus
Leviticus
Numbers
Deuteronomy
Joshua
Judges
Ruth
1 Samuel
2 Samuel
1 Kings
2 Kings
1 Chronicles
2 Chronicles
Ezra
Nehemiah
Esther
Job
Psalms
Proverbs
Ecclesiates
Song of Solomon
Isaiah
Jeremiah
Lamentations
Ezekiel
Daniel

Hosea
Joel
Amos
Obadiah
Jonah
Micah
Nahum
Habakkuk
Zephaniah
Haggai
Zechariah
Malachi

Books of the Apocrypha

1 & 2 Esdras
Tobit
Judith
Additions to Esther
Wisdom of Solomon
Ecclesiasticus or the
    Wisdom of Jesus
    Son of Sirach
Baruch
Prayer of Azariah and
    the Song of the Three
    Holy Children
Susanna
Bel and the Dragon
The Prayer of Manasses
1–4 Maccabees

Bibliography

Modern Greek Texts

Aland, K. et al. in cooperation with the Institute for New Testament Textual Research. *The Greek New Testament.* 2nd ed. London: United Bible Societies. 1968.

Aland, K. et al. in cooperation with the Institute for New Testament Textual Research. *The Greek New Testament.* 3rd ed. New York: United Bible Societies. 1975.

Nestle, E. and K. Aland. *Novum Testamentum Graece.* 25th ed. Stuttgart: Deutsche Bibelstiftung. 1963.

Nestle, E. and K. Aland. et al. *Novum Testamentum Graece.* 26th ed. Stuttgart: Deutsche Bibelstiftung. 1979.

General Reference Sources with Abbreviations

BAGD
Bauer, W., W.F. Arndt and F.W. Gingrich. *A Greek-English Lexicon of the New Testament and Other Early Christian Literature.* 2nd ed. Revised and augmented by F.W. Gingrich and F.W. Danker. Chicago: University of Chicago Press. 1958.

NIDNTT
Brown, Colin. ed. *The New International Dictionary of New Testament Theology.* 4 vols. Grand Rapids: Zondervan. 1975.

TDNT
Kittel, G. and G. Friedrich. *Theological Dictionary of the New Testament.* Trans. by G.W. Bromiley. 10 vols. Grand Rapids: Wm.B. Eerdmans. 1964-72.

LSJ
Liddell, H.G. and R. Scott. *A Greek-English Lexicon.* 9th ed., Ed. by H. Stuart Jones and R. McKenzie. Oxford: Clarendon. 1940.

M-M
Moulton, J.H. and G. Milligan. *The Vocabulary of the Greek Testament Illustrated from the Papyri and Other Non-Literary Sources.* London: Hodder and Stoughton. 1914-30. Reprint. Grand Rapids: Wm. B. Eerdmans. 1985.

General Bibliography

Achtemeier, Paul J. *Romans*. Atlanta: John Knox. 1985.

Barclay, William. *The Letter to the Romans*. *The Daily Study Bible*. Philadelphia: The Westminster Press. 1957.

Barclay, William. *The Letters to the Corinthians*. *The Daily Study Bible*. Philadelphia: The Westminster Press. 1956.

Barclay, William. *The Mind of St. Paul*. New York: Harper & Row. 1975.

Barrett, C. K. *A Commentary on the Epistle to the Romans*. *Harper's New Testament Commentaries*. Ed. by Henry Chadwick. New York: Harper & Row. 1957.

Barrett, C. K. *A Commentary on the First Epistle to the Corinthians*. *Harper's New Testament Commentaries*. Ed. by Henry Chadwick. New York: Harper & Row. 1968.

Barrett, C. K. *From First to Last Adam: A Study in Pauline Theology*. London: Adam & Charles Black. 1962.

Barth, Karl. *The Epistle to the Romans*. 6th. ed. Ed. by Edwyn C. Hoskyns. Grand Rapids: William B. Eerdmans Publishing Co. 1972.

Black, Matthew. *Romans*. Vol. 37 of *New Century Bible*. Ed. by Ronald E. Clements and Matthew Black. London: Oliphants. 1973.

Blass, F., and A. Debrunner. *A Greek Grammar of the New Testament and Other Early Christian Literature*. Trans. by Robert W. Funk. Chicago: The University of Chicago Press. 1961.

Brown, Francis, S. R. Driver, and Charles A. Briggs. *A Hebrew and English Lexicon of the Old Testament*. Oxford: The Clarendon Press. 1972.

Bruce, F. F. *1 and 2 Corinthians*. Vol. 38 of *New Century Bible*. Ed. by Ronald E. Clements and Matthew Black. London: Oliphants. 1976.

Bruce, F. F. *The Epistle of Paul to the Romans*. Vol. 6 of *Tyndale New Testament Commentaries*. Ed. by R. V. G. Tasker. Grand Rapids: William B. Eerdmans Publishing Co. 1963.

Calvin, John. *Commentary on the Epistles of Paul the Apostle to the Corinthians*. Trans. by John Pringle. *Calvin's Commentaries*. Grand Rapids: William B. Eerdmans Publishing Co. 1948.

Calvin, John. *Commentaries on the Epistle of Paul the Apostle to the Romans*. Trans. by John Owen. *Calvin's Commentaries*. Grand Rapids: William B. Eerdmans Publishing Co. 1947.

Calvin, John. *Institutes of the Christian Religion*. 2 vols. Trans. by Henry Beveridge. Grand Rapids: William B. Eerdmans Publishing Co. 1949.

Carver, Frank G. *2 Corinthians*. In *Romans, 1 and 2 Corinthians*. Vol. 8 of *Beacon Bible Commentary*. Ed. by Ralph Earle. Kansas City: Beacon Hill Press of Kansas City. 1968.

Clarke, Adam. *Romans to the Revelations*. Vol. 6 of *Clarke's Commentary*. Nashville: Abingdon Press. N.d.

Conybeare, W. J. and J. S. Howson. *The Life and Epistles of St. Paul*. Grand Rapids: William B. Eerdmans Publishing Co. 1978.

Cranfield, C. E. B. *A Critical and Exegetical Commentary on the Epistle to the Romans*. Rev. ed. 2 vols. *International Critical Commentary*. Ed. by J. A. Emerton and C. E. B. Cranfield. Edinburgh: T. & T. Clark. 1977.

Davies, W. D. *Paul and Rabbinic Judaism*. Philadelphia: Fortress Press. 1980.

Denney, James. *St. Paul's Epistle to the Romans*. In *Acts, Romans, First Corinthians*. Vol. 2 of *The Expositor's Greek Testament*. Ed. by W. Robertson Nicoll. Grand Rapids: William B. Eerdmans Publishing Co. 1951.

The Didache. Trans. by Maxwell Staniforth. In *Early Christian Writings: The Apostolic Fathers*. New York: Penguin Books. 1978.

Dieter, Melvin E., et al. *Five Views on Sanctification*. Grand Rapids: Zondervan Publishing House. 1987.

Dodd, C. H. *The Epistle of Paul to the Romans*. The Moffatt New Testament Commentary. London: Hodder & Stoughton Limited. 1960.

Dodd, C. H. *The Meaning of Paul for Today*. New York: World Publishing. 1957.

Drummond, Henry. *Essays and Addresses*. New York: James Pott and Company. 1904.

Edersheim, Alfred. *The Life and Times of Jesus the Messiah*. 2 vols. Grand Rapids: William B. Eerdmans Publishing Co. 1959.

Fee, Gordon D. *The First Epistle to the Corinthians*. The New International Commentary on the New Testament. Ed. by F. F. Bruce. Grand Rapids: William B. Eerdmans Publishing Co. 1987.

Godet, Frederic Louis. *Commentary on First Corinthians*. Edinburgh: T. & T. Clark. 1889. Reprint. Grand Rapids: Kregel Publications. 1977.

Goudge, H. L. *The Second Epistle to the Corinthians*. Westminster Commentaries. Ed. by Walter Lock and D. C. Simpson. London: Methuen & Co. Ltd. 1928.

Grosheide, F. W. *Commentary on the First Epistle to the Corinthians*. The New International Commentary on the New Testament. Ed. by F. F. Bruce. Grand Rapids: William B. Eerdmans Publishing Co. 1974.

Guthrie, Donald. *New Testament Introduction*. Downers Grove, Illinois: Inter-Varsity Press. 1970.

Guthrie, Donald. *The Apostles*. Grand Rapids: Zondervan Publishing House. 1980.

Harris, Murray J. *2 Corinthians*. In *Romans—Galatians*. Vol. 10 of *The Expositor's Bible Commentary*. Ed. by Frank E. Gaebelein. Grand Rapids: Zondervan Publishing House. 1976.

Hendriksen, William. *Exposition of the Epistle of Paul to the Romans*. New Testament Commentary. Grand Rapids: Baker Book House. 1975.

Henry, Matthew. *Matthew Henry's Commentary on the Whole Bible*. 6 vols. New York: Flemming H. Revell Company. N.d.

Hodge, Charles. *Commentary on the Epistle to the Romans*. Philadelphia: H. B. Garner. 1886. Reprint. Grand Rapids: William B. Eerdmans Publishing Co. 1972.

Horton, Stanley. *What the Bible Says about the Holy Spirit*. Springfield, MO: Gospel Publishing House. 1976.

Hughes, Philip Edgcumbe. *Paul's Second Epistle to the Corinthians*. The New London Commentary. London: Marshall, Morgan, and Scott. 1962.

Hughes, Robert R. *Second Corinthians*. Everyman's Bible Commentary. Chicago: Moody Press. 1985.

Ironside, H. A. *Addresses on the Second Epistle to the Corinthians*. New York: Loizeaux Brothers, Inc. N.d.

Jewett, Robert. *Paul's Anthropological Terms*. Leiden: E. J. Brill. 1971.

Kent, Homer A., Jr. *A Heart Opened Wide*. Grand Rapids: Baker Book House. 1982.

Lenski, R. C. H. *The Interpretation of St. Paul's First and Second Epistles to the Corinthians*. Minneapolis: Augsburg Publishing House. 1963.

Lightfoot, J. B. *The Apostolic Fathers*. London: MacMillan and Company. 1890.

Luther, Martin. *Lectures on Galatians, Chapters 1-4*. Vol. 26 of *Luther's Works*. Ed. and trans. by Jaroslav Pelikan. St. Louis: Concordia Publishing House. 1963.

Luther, Martin. *Lectures on Romans*. Trans. by Walter G. Tillmanns and Jacob A. O. Preus. Vol. 25 of *Luther's Works*. Ed. by Hilton C. Oswald. St. Louis: Concordia Publishing House. 1972.

Martin, Ralph P. *Reconciliation: A Study of Paul's Theology*. New Foundations Theological Library. Atlanta: John Knox. 1981.

Manson, T. W. *Romans*. *Peake's Commentary on the Bible*. Ed. by Matthew Black. London: T. Nelson. 1962.

Mayor, Joseph B. *The Epistle of St. James*. Reprint. Minneapolis: Klock and Klock Christian Publishers. 1977.

Meyer, Heinrich August Wilhelm. *Critical and Exegetical Handbook to the Epistles to the Corinthians*. Vol. 6 of *Meyer's Commentary on the New Testament*. Funk & Wagnalls. 1884. Reprint. Winona Lake, Indiana: Alpha Publications. 1979.

Meyer, Joh. P. *Ministers of Christ*. Milwaukee: Northwestern Publishing House. 1963.

Miller, Patrick D., Jr. "The Most Important Word: The Yoke of the Kingdom." *The Iliff Review* 41 (1984): 17-30.

Moody, Dale. *Romans*. In *Acts—1 Corinthians*. Vol. 8 of *The Broadman's Bible Commentary*. Ed. by Clifton J. Allen, et al. Nashville: Broadman Press. 1970.

Morris, Leon. *The First Epistle of Paul to the Corinthians*. Vol. 7 of *Tyndale New Testament Commentaries*. Ed. by R. V. G. Tasker. Grand Rapids: William B. Eerdmans Publishing Co. 1975.

Moule, C. G. Handley. *The Epistle of Paul to the Romans*. *The Expositor's Bible*. Ed. by W. Robertson Nicoll. London: Hodder & Stoughton Limited. 1894.

Murray, John. *The Epistle to the Romans*. *The New International Commentary on the New Testament*. Ed. by F. F. Bruce. Grand Rapids: William B. Eerdmans Publishing Co. 1982.

Nicoll, W. Robertson, ed. *The Expositor's Greek Testament*. Vol. 2, *Apostles, Romans, First Corinthians*. Grand Rapids: William B. Eerdmans Publishing Co. 1951.

Nygren, Anders. *Commentary on Romans*. Philadelphia: Fortress Press. 1949.

Packer, J. I. "Justification." *Evangelical Dictionary of Theology*. Ed. by Walter A. Elwell. Grand Rapids: Baker Book House. 1984.

Pearlman, Myer. *Knowing the Doctrines of the Bible*. Springfield, MO: Gospel Publishing House. 1937.

Proctor, W. C. G. *Second Corinthians*. *The New Bible Commentary*. Ed. by Francis Davidson. Grand Rapids: William B. Eerdmans Publishing Co. 1958.

Prohl, Russell. *Women in the Church*. Grand Rapids: William B. Eerdmans Publishing Co. 1957.

Bibliography Continued

Ramsay, William. *Pictures of the Apostolic Church.* London: 1910. Reprint. Grand Rapids: Baker Book House. 1959.

Robertson, Archibald, and Alfred Plummer. *A Critical and Exegetical Commentary on the First Epistle of Paul to the Corinthians. The International Critical Commentary.* 2nd. ed. Ed. by S. R. Driver, A. Plummer, and C. A. Briggs. Edinburgh: T. & T. Clark. 1975.

Rosenius, C. O. *The Believer Free from the Law.* Trans. by Adolf Hult. Rock Island, Illinois: Augustana Book Concern. 1923.

Sadler, M. F. *The First and Second Epistles to the Corinthians.* London: George Bell and Sons. 1889.

Sanday, William and Arthur C. Headlam. *A Critical and Exegetical Commentary on the Epistle to the Romans. International Critical Commentary.* 5th. ed. Ed. by S. R. Driver, A. Plummer, and C. A. Briggs. Edinburgh: T. & T. Clark. 1902.

Sanders, E. P. *Paul and Palestinian Judaism.* London: SCM Press Ltd. 1977.

Tasker, R. V. G. *The Second Epistle of Paul to the Corinthians.* Vol. 8 of *Tyndale New Testament Commentaries.* Ed. by R. V. G. Tasker. Grand Rapids: William B. Eerdmans Publishing Co. 1983.

Thayer, Joseph Henry. *Greek-English Lexicon of the New Testament.* Grand Rapids: Zondervan Publishing House. 1972.

The Syriac Apocalypse of Baruch. In *The Apocrypha and Pseudepigrapha of the Old Testament in English.* 2 vols. Ed. by R. H. Charles. Oxford: Clarendon Press. 1973.

Tozer, A. W. *The Knowledge of the Holy.* New York: Harper & Row. 1961.

Turner, Nigel. *Grammatical Insights into the New Testament.* Edinburgh: T. & T. Clark. 1965.

Vincent, Marvin R. *Word Studies in the New Testament.* 4 vols. Reprint. Grand Rapids: William B. Eerdmans Publishing Co. 1973.

Zahniser, Clarence H. *2 Corinthians.* In *Romans—Philemon.* Vol. 5 of *The Wesleyan Bible Commentary.* Ed. by Ralph Earle. Grand Rapids: William B. Eerdmans Publishing Co. 1971.

Various Versions Acknowledgments

Scripture quotations found in Various Versions were taken from the following sources with special permssion as indicated. The sources listed may be found in one or all of the volumes of THE COMPLETE BIBLICAL LIBRARY.

AB
Fitzmyer, Joseph A., S.J., trans. *The Gospel According to Luke I- IX; (Anchor Bible).* New York: Doubleday & Company, Inc. 1985. Reprinted with permission. ©1981, 1985.

ADAMS
Adams, Jay E. *The Christian Counselor's New Testament: a New Translation in Everyday English with Notations, Marginal References, and Supplemental Helps.* Grand Rapids, MI: Baker Book House. 1977. Reprinted with permission. ©1977.

ALBA
Condon, Kevin. *The Alba House New Testament.* Staten Island, NY: Alba House, Society of St. Paul copublished with The Mercier Press Ltd. 1972. Reprinted with permission. *The Mercier New Testament.* 4 Bridge Street. Cork, Ireland: The Mercier Press Ltd. ©1970.

ALFORD
Alford, Henry. *The New Testament of Our Lord and Saviour Jesus Christ: After the Authorized Version.* Newly compared with the original Greek, and revised. London: Daldy, Isbister. 1875.

AMPB
The Amplified Bible. Grand Rapids, MI: Zondervan Publishing House. 1958. Reprinted with permission from the *Amplified New Testament.* © The Lockman Foundation. 1954, 1958.

ASV
(American Standard Version) The Holy Bible Containing the Old and New Testaments: Translated out of the original tongues; being the version set forth A.D. 1611, compared with the most ancient authorities and rev. A.D. 1881-1885. New York: Thomas Nelson Inc., Publishers. 1901, 1929.

BARCLAY
Barclay, William. *The New Testament: A New Translation.* Vol. 1, *The Gospels and the Acts of the Apostles.* London: William Collins Sons & Co. Ltd. 1968. Reprinted with permission. ©1968.

BB
The Basic Bible: Containing the Old and New Testaments in Basic English. New York: Dutton. 1950. Reprinted with permission. *The Bible In Basic English.* © Cambridge University Press. 1982.

BECK
Beck, William F. *The New Testament in the Language of Today.* St. Louis, MO: Concordia Publishing House. 1963. Reprinted with permission. © Mrs. William Beck, *An American Translation.* Leader Publishing Company: New Haven, MO.

BERKELEY
The Holy Bible: the Berkeley Version in Modern English Containing the Old and New Testaments. Grand Rapids: Zondervan Publishing House. 1959. Used by permission. ©1945, 1959, 1969.

BEZA
Iesv Christi, D.N. Novum Testamentum. Geneva: Henricus Stephanus. 1565.

BLACKWELDER
Blackwelder, Boyce W. *The Four Gospels: An Exegetical Translation.* Anderson, IN: Warner Press, Inc. 1980.

BLACKWELL
Blackwell, Boyce W. *Letters from Paul: An Exegetical Translation.* Anderson, IN: Warner Press, 1971.

BRUCE

Bruce, F.F. *The Letters of Paul: An Expanded Paraphrase Printed in Parallel with the RV*. Grand Rapids: William B. Eerdmans Publishing Co. 1965. Reprinted with permission. F.F. Bruce. *An Expanded Paraphrase of the Epistles of Paul*. The Paternoster Press: Exeter, England. ©1965, 1981.

CAMPBELL

Campbell, Alexander. *The Sacred Writings of the Apostles and Evangelists of Jesus Christ commonly styled the New Testament:* Translated from the original Greek by Drs. G. Campbell, J. Macknight & P. Doddridge with prefaces, various emendations and an appendix by A. Campbell. Grand Rapids: Baker Book House. 1951 reprint of the 1826 edition.

CKJB

The Children's 'King James' Bible: New Testament. Translated by Jay Green. Evansville, IN: Modern Bible Translations, Inc. 1960.

CLEMENTSON

Clementson, Edgar Lewis. *The New Testament: a Translation*. Pittsburg, PA: Evangelization Society of Pittsburgh Bible Institute. 1938.

CONCORDANT

Concordant Version: The Sacred Scriptures: Designed to put the Englished reader in possession of all the vital facts of divine revelation without a former knowledge of Greek by means of a restored Greek text. Los Angeles: Concordant Publishing Concern. 1931. Reprinted with permission. *Concordant Literal New Testament*. Concordant Publishing Concern. 15570 Knochaven Road, Canyon Country, CA 91351. ©1931.

CONFRATERNITY

The New Testament of Our Lord and Savior Jesus Christ: Translated from the Latin Vulgate, a revision of the Challoner-Rheims Version edited by Catholic scholars under the patronage of the Episcopal Committee of the Confraternity Christian Doctrine. Paterson, NJ: St. Anthony Guild Press. 1941. Reprinted with permission by the Confraternity of Christian Doctrine, Washington, DC. ©1941.

CONYBEARE

Conybeare, W.J. and Rev. J.S. Howson D.D. *The Life and Epistles of St. Paul*. Rev. ed. 2 vols. London: Longman, Green, Longman, and Roberts. 1862.

COVERDALE

The New Testament: The Coverdale Version. N.p. 1535(?), 1557.

CRANMER

Cranmer or Great Bible. *The Byble in Englyshe, . . .* translated after the veryte of the Hebrue and Greke text, by ye dilygent studye of dyverse excellent learned men, expert in the forsayde tonges. Prynted by Richard Grafton & Edward Whitchurch. Cum privilegio ad Imprimendum solum. 1539.

DARBY

Darby, J.N. *The Holy Scriptures A New Translation from the Original Languages*. Lansing, Sussex, England: Kingston Bible Trust. 1975 reprint of the 1890 edition.

DOUAY

The Holy Bible containing the Old and New Testaments: Translated from the Latin Vulgate . . . and with the other translations diligently compared, with annotations, references and an historical and chronological index. New York: Kennedy & Sons. N.d.

ET

Editor's Translation. Gerard J. Flokstra, Jr., D.Min.

EVERYDAY

The Everyday Bible: New Century Version. Fort Worth: Worthy Publishing. 1987. Reprinted with permission. World Wide Publications. *The Everyday Study Bible: Special New Testament Study Edition*. Minneapolis: World Wide Publications. 1988.

FENTON

Fenton, Farrar. *The Holy Bible in Modern English.* London: A. & C. Black. 1944 reprint of the 1910 edition.

GENEVA

The Geneva Bible: a facsimile of the 1560 edition. Madison, WI: University of Wisconsin Press. 1969.

GENEVA (1557)

The Nevve Testament of Ovr Lord Iesus Christ. Printed by Conrad Badius. 1557.

GOODSPEED

The Bible: An American Translation. Translated by Edgar J. Goodspeed. Chicago: The University of Chicago Press. 1935.

HANSEN

Hansen, J.W. *The New Covenant.* 2nd. ed. 2 vols. Boston: Universalist Publishing House. 1888.

HBIE

The Holy Bible containing the Old and New Testaments: an improved edition (based in part on the Bible Union Version). Philadelphia: American Baptist Publication Society 1913.

HISTNT

The Historical New Testament: Being the literature of the New Testament arranged in the order of its literary growth and according to the dates of the documents: a new translation by James Moffatt. Edinburgh: T & T Clark. 1901.

HOERBER

Hoerber, Robert G. *Saint Paul's Shorter Letters.* Fulton, MO: Robert G. Hoerber. 1954.

JB

The Jerusalem Bible. Garden City, NY: Darton, Longman & Todd, Ltd. and Doubleday and Co, Inc. 1966. Reprinted by permission of the publisher. ©1966.

KJII

King James II New Testament. Grand Rapids: Associated Publishers and Authors, Inc. ©Jay P. Green. 1970.

KLEIST

The New Testament Rendered from the Original Greek with Explanatory Notes. Translated by James A. Kleist and Joseph L. Lilly. Milwaukee: The Bruce Publishing Company. 1954.

KLINGENSMITH

Klingensmith, Don J. *Today's English New Testament.* New York: Vantage Press. 1972. Reprinted by permission of author. ©Don J. Klingensmith, 1972.

KNOX

Knox, R.A. *The New Testament of our Lord and Saviour Jesus Christ: A New Translation.* New York: Sheen and Ward. 1946. Reprinted by permission of The Liturgy Commission.

LAMSA

Lamsa, George M. *The Holy Bible From Ancient Eastern Text.* Translated from original Aramaic sources. Philadelphia: Holman. 1957. From *The Holy Bible From Ancient Eastern Text* by George Lamsa. ©1933 by Nina Shabaz; renewed 1961 by Nina Shabaz. ©1939 by Nina Shabaz; renewed 1967 by Nina Shabaz. ©1940 by Nina Shabaz; renewed 1968 by Nina Shabaz. ©1957 by Nina Shabaz. Reprinted by permission of Harper & Row, Publishers, Inc.

LATTIMORE

Lattimore, Richmond. *Four Gospels and The Revelation:* Newly translated from the Greek. New York: Farrar, Straus, Giroux, Inc. 1979. Reprinted by permission of the publisher. © Richard Lattimore, 1962, 1979.

LAUBACH

Laubach, Frank C. *The Inspired Letters in Clearest English.* Nashville: Thomas Nelson Publishers. 1956.

LIVB

The Living Bible: Paraphrased. Wheaton, IL: Tyndale House Publishers. 1973. Used by permission of the publisher. © Tyndale House Publishers. 1971.

LOCKE

Locke, John. *A Paraphrase and Notes on the Epistles of St. Paul to the Galatians, First and Second Corinthians, Romans, and Ephesians:* To which is prefixed an essay for the understanding of St. Paul's Epistles. Campbridge, England: Brown, Shattuck; Boston: Hilliard, Gray, and Co. 1832.

MACKNIGHT

Macknight, James. *New Literal Translation:* From the original Greek, of all the Apostolical Epistles, with a commentary, and notes, philological, critical, explanatory, and practical. Philadelphia: Wardkem. 1841.

MACKNIGHT

Macknight, James. *Harmony of the Four Gospels:* 2 vols. in which the natural order of each is preserved, with a paraphrase and notes. London: Longman, Hurst, Rees, Orme and Brown. 1819.

MJV

English Messianic Jewish Version. May Your Name Be Inscribed in the Book of Life. Introduction and footnotes by The Messianic Vision. Washington, D.C.: ©1981. Bible text by Thomas Nelson, Inc. Nashville: Thomas Nelson Publishing Company. ©1979.

MOFFATT

The New Testament: A New Translation. New York: Harper and Row Publishers, Inc.; Kent, England: Hodder and Stoughton Ltd. c.1912. Reprinted with permission.

MONTGOMERY

Montgomery, Helen Barrett. *The Centenary Translation of the New Testament:* Published to signalize the completion of the first hundred years of work of the American Baptist Publication Society. Philadelphia: American Baptist Publishing Society. 1924. Used by permission of Judson Press. *The New Testament in Modern English* by Helen Barrett Montgomery. Valley Forge: Judson Press. 1924, 1952.

MURDOCK

Murdock, James. *The New Testament: The Book of the Holy Gospel of our Lord and Our God, Jesus the Messiah:* A literal translation from the Syriac Peshito version. New York: Stanford and Swords. 1851.

NAB

The New American Bible. Translated from the original languages with critical use for all the ancient sources by members of the Catholic Biblical Association of America. Encino, California: Benzinger. 1970.

NASB

The New American Standard Bible. Anaheim, CA: Lockman Foundation. 1960. Reprinted with permission. © The Lockman Foundation 1960, 1962, 1963, 1968, 1971, 1972, 1973, 1975, 1977.

NCV

The Word: New Century Version New Testament. Fort Worth, TX: Sweet Publishing. 1984.

NEB
The New English Bible: New Testament. Cambridge, England: Cambridge University Press. 1970. Reprinted by permission. ©The Delegates of the Oxford University Press and The Syndics of the Cambridge University Press 1961, 1970.

NIV
The Holy Bible: New International Version. Grand Rapids: Zondervan Publishing House. 1978. Used by permission of Zondervan Bible Publishers. ©1973, 1978, International Bible Society.

NKJB
The New King James Bible, New Testament. Nashville, TN: Royal Pub. 1979. Reprinted from *The New King James Bible-New Testament.* ©1979, 1982, Thomas Nelson, Inc., Publishers.

NLT
The New Life Testament. Translated by Gleason H. Ledyard. Canby, Oregon: Christian Literature Foundation. 1969.

NOLI
Noli, S. *The New Testament of Our Lord and Savior Jesus Christ: Translated into English from the Approved Greek Text of the Church of Constantinople and the Church of Greece.* Boston: Albanian Orthodox Church in America. 1961.

NORLIE
Norlie, Olaf M. *Simplified New Testament: In plain English for today's reader: A new translation from the Greek.* Grand Rapids: Zondervan Publishing House. 1961. Used by permission. ©1961.

NORTON
Norton, Andrews. *A Translation of the Gospels with Notes.* Boston: Little, Brown. 1856.

NOYES
Noyes, George R. *The New Testament:* Translated from the Greek text of Tischendorf. Boston: American Unitarian Association. 1873.

NTPE
The New Testament: A New Translation in Plain English. Translated by Charles Kingsley Williams. Grand Rapids: Wm. B. Eerdmans Publishing Company. 1963.

PANIN
Panin, Ivan., ed. *The New Testament from the Greek Text as Established by Bible Numerics.* Toronto, Canada: Clarke, Irwin. 1935.

PHILLIPS
Phillips, J.B., trans. *The New Testament in Modern English.* Rev. ed. New York: Macmillan Publishing Company, Inc. 1958. Reprinted with permission. ©J.B. Phillips 1958, 1960, 1972.

PNT
A Plain Translation of the New Testament by a Student. Melbourne, Australia: McCarron, Bird. 1921.

RHEIMS
The Nevv Testament of Iesus Christ. Translated faithfully into English, out of the authentical Latin, . . . In the English College of Rhemes. Printed at Rhemes by Iohn Fogny. Cum privilegio. 1582.

RIEU
Rieu, E.V. *The Four Gospels.* London: Penguin Books Ltd. 1952. Reprinted with permission. ©E.V. Rieu, 1952.

ROTHERHAM
Rotherham, Joseph B. *The New Testament:* Newly translated (from the Greek text of Tregelles) and critically emphasized, with an introduction and occasional notes. London: Samual Bagster. 1890.

RPNT
Johnson, Ben Cambell. *The Heart of Paul: A Relational Paraphrase of the New Testament*. Vol. 1. Waco: Word Books. 1976.

RSV
Revised Standard Version; The New Covenant commonly called the New Testament of our Lord and Saviour Jesus Christ: Translated from the Greek being the version set forth A.D. 1611, revised A.D. 1881, A.D. 1901. New York: Thomas Nelson Inc. Publishers. 1953. Used by permission. ©1946, 1952, 1971, 1973 by the Division of Christian Education of the National Council of the Churches of Christ in the U.S.A.

RV
The New Testament of our Lord and Savior Jesus Christ: Translated out of the Greek . . . being the new version revised 1881. St. Louis, MO: Scammell. 1881.

SAWYER
Sawyer, Leicester Ambrose. *The New Testament: Translated from the original Greek,* with chronological arrangement of the sacred books, and improved divisions of chapters and verses. Boston: Walker, Wise. 1861.

SCARLETT
Scarlett, Nathaniel. *A translation of the New Testament from the original Greek:* humbly attempted. London: T. Gillett. 1798.

SEB
The Simple English® Bible, New Testament: American edition. New York: International Bible Translators, Inc. 1981. Used by permission from International Bible Translators, Inc.

SWANN
Swann, George. *New Testament of our Lord and Saviour Jesus Christ.* 4th. ed. Robards, KY: George Swann Company. 1947.

TCNT
The Twentieth Century New Testament: a Translation into Modern English Made from the Original Greek: (Westcott & Hort's text). New York: Revell. 1900.

TEV
The Good News Bible, Today's English Version. New York: American Bible Society. 1976. Used by permission. © American Bible Society, 1966, 1971, 1976.

TNT
The Translator's New Testament. London: The British and Foreign Bible Society. 1973.

TORREY
Torrey, Charles Cutler. *The Four Gospels: A New Translation.* New York: Harper and Row Publishers Inc. 1933. Reprinted by permission. ©1933.

TYNDALE
Tyndale, William. *The Newe Testament dylygently corrected and compared with the Greke.* and fynesshed in the yere of oure Lorde God anno M.D. and XXXIIII in the month of Nouember. London: Reeves and Turner. 1888.

TYNDALE (1526)
The First New Testament in the English Language (1525 or 1526). Reprint. Bristol. 1862. Or Clevland: Barton. N.d.

WADE
Wade, G. W. *The Documents of the New Testament: Translated & Historically Arranged with Critical Introductions.* N.p., n.d.

WAY

Way, Arthur S., trans. *Letters of St. Paul: To seven churches and three friends with the letter to the Hebrews.* 8th ed. Chicago: Moody. 1950 reprint of the 1901 edition.

WESLEY

Wesley, John. *Explanatory notes upon the New Testament.* London: Wesleyan-Methodist Book-room. N.d.

WEYMOUTH

Weymouth, Richard Francis. *The New Testament in Modern Speech:* An idiomatic translation into everyday English from the text of the "Resultant Greek Testament." Revised by J. A. Robertson. London: James Clarke and Co. Ltd. and Harper and Row Publishers Inc. 1908. Reprinted by permission.

WILLIAMS

Williams, Charles B. *The New Testament: A Translation in the Language of the People.* Chicago: Moody Bible Institute of Chicago. 1957. Used by permission of Moody Press. Moody Bible Institute of Chicago. ©1937, 1966 by Mrs. Edith S. Williams.

WILLIAMS C. K.

Williams, Charles Kingsley. *The New Testament: A New Translation in Plain English.* Grand Rapids: William B. Eerdmans Publishing Co. 1963.

WILSON

Wilson, Benjamin. *The Emphatic Diaglott containing the original Greek Text of what is commonly styled the New Testament* (according to the recension of Dr. F.F. Griesback) with interlineary word for word English translation. New York: Fowler & Wells. 1902 reprint edition of the 1864 edition.

WORRELL

Worrell, A.S. *The New Testament: Revised and Translated:* With notes and instructions; designed to aid the earnest reader in obtaining a clear understanding of the doctrines, ordinances, and primitive assemblies as revealed. Louisville, KY: A.S. Worrell. 1904.

WUEST

Wuest, Kenneth S. *The New Testament: An Expanded Translation.* Grand Rapids: Wm. B. Eerdmans Publishing Company. 1961. Used by permission of the publisher. ©1961.

WYCLIF

Wyclif(fe), John. *The Holy Bible containing the Old and New Testaments with the Apocryphal Books:* in the earliest English version made from the Latin Vulgate by John Wycliffe and his followers. London: Reeves and Turner. 1888.

YOUNG

Young, Robert. *Young's Literal Translation of the Holy Bible.* Grand Rapids: Baker Book House.1953 reprint of the 1898 3rd edition.